BIBLIOGRAPHY OF AMERICAN LITERATURE

VOLUME 4

BIBLIOGRAPHY OF

American Literature

COMPILED BY JACOB BLANCK

for the Bibliographical Society of America

VOLUME FOUR

NATHANIEL HAWTHORNE TO JOSEPH HOLT INGRAHAM

NEW HAVEN AND LONDON: *Yale University Press*

1963

The compilation of the manuscript of *Bibliography of American Literature* was made possible by a grant from the Lilly Endowment, Inc., of Indianapolis, Indiana, to the Bibliographical Society of America.

This fourth volume of

Bibliography of American Literature

is dedicated to the memory of

MILDRED ROSENBERG FRIEDMAN BLANK

London 1874–Boston 1937

and

SELIG BLANK

Lomza, Poland 1867–Boston 1936

They found the lifted lamp beside the golden door.

Contents

Authors in Volume Four

Illustrations

Acknowledgments

*"No bibliography is the product of a single worker
and the present compilation is no exception."*

It is pleasant to record that in addition to the collaborators named in the preceding volumes of *Bibliography of American Literature* the following persons assisted in bringing the work thus far forward:

Matthew J. Bruccoli, who for a period was associated with the project as assistant to the editor.

Christina Carlow, who supplied (and continues to supply) much of the information relating to the publications printed at The Riverside Press.

Achilles Fang and P. D. Perkins, both of whom assisted in the compilation of the Lafcadio Hearn list; and particularly Dr. Fang, who supplied translations of the Japanese colophons which occur in certain of Hearn's books.

Donald C. Gallup, Curator of the Collection of American Literature at Yale University Library, whose talents have been liberally contributed to this work.

William M. Gibson and George Arms, compilers of the authoritative bibliography of William Dean Howells, who gave the *Bibliography* the benefit of their notes.

Robert V. Gross and Donald W. Krummel, who supplied many copyright deposit dates.

Rudolf Hirsch and Neda Westlake, of Pennsylvania University Library, whose aid enabled us to present a reasonably complete list of Joseph Holt Ingraham's books.

Richard Colles Johnson of The Yale Collection of American Literature, who cooperated mightily during his term as acting chief of that collection.

Mrs. Norma Matarese Kacen, of the John Hay Library, whose efforts were tireless and productive.

Norman Kane, an inveterate discoverer of obscure and unrecorded publications.

Dan H. Laurence, who called attention to five copyright printings of William Dean Howells.

Simon Nowell-Smith, who supplied (and continues to supply) much information relating to British publication of BAL authors.

Perry O'Neil, an unfailing source of information relating to books in The New York Public Library.

Norman Holmes Pearson who contributed much publication information to the Nathaniel Hawthorne list.

William H. Runge of The Alderman Library, whose talents (both bibliographic and culinary) have been contributed without stint to, respectively, BAL and its staff.

Eleanor M. Tilton and Parkman D. Howe, without whose ready and constant cooperation the list of Oliver Wendell Holmes's books herein would be woefully incomplete.

Edwin Wolf II, whose shrewd eye uncovered many of the gems described in these lists.

And finally, Jane Fulton Smith, the editor's tireless and invaluable assistant; the many libraries, librarians, antiquarian booksellers, and collectors whose continuing patient cooperation cannot be measured (these institutions and persons are named in the list of Location Symbols); and the staff of The Houghton Library, not excluding those indefatigable aides: Kenneth E. Carpenter, Thomas Matthews, Joseph P. McCarthy, Cynthia Naylor, Barbara Bolster, and Joseph R. Sullivan.

General References

The following references are mentioned in the lists under the designations given.

Allibone   A Critical Dictionary of English Literature, and British and American Authors . . . , by S. Austin Allibone, 3 Vols.; two supplementary volumes compiled by John Foster Kirk. 1858–1891.

Am Cat   The American Catalogue . . . , 1880–1911.

Appleton   Appletons' Cyclopaedia of American Biography . . . , 1887–1901.

B A L   Bibliography of American Literature Compiled by Jacob Blanck for the Bibliographical Society of America, 1955–   .

BMu Cat   The British Museum Catalogue of Printed Books, 1881–1905. And, British Museum General Catalogue of Printed Books . . . , 1931–   .

C H A L   The Cambridge History of American Literature . . . , 1917–1921.

D A B   Dictionary of American Biography . . . , 1928–   .

D N B   The Dictionary of National Biography . . . , 1885–   .

English Cat   The English Catalogue of Books . . . Issued in the United Kingdom . . . , 1864–   .

Evans   American Bibliography . . . 1639 . . . to . . . 1820, by Charles Evans, 1903–1934. Continued by Clifford K. Shipton, 1955–.

Foley   American Authors 1795–1895 a Bibliography of First and Notable Editions . . . , by P. K. Foley, 1897.

Griffin   American Historical Association. Bibliography of American Historical Societies . . . , by Appleton Prentiss Griffin, 1896.

Johannsen   The House of Beadle and Adams and Its Dime and Nickel Novels . . . , by Albert Johannsen, 1950.

Johnson   American First Editions . . . , by Merle Johnson, 1929, 1932. And, editions of 1936, 1942, revised by Jacob Blanck.

Kelly   See below under *Roorbach*.

L C Printed Cat   . . . A Catalog of Books Represented by Library of Congress Printed Cards . . . , 1942–   .

Leon Brothers   Catalogue of First Editions of American Authors, Poets, Philosophers, Historians . . . Compiled . . . and for Sale by Leon & Brother, New York, 1885.

Roorbach   Bibliotheca Americana. Catalogue of American Publications,
                Including Reprints and Original Works ... Compiled and
                Arranged by O. A. Roorbach, 1852–1861. Continued by
                James Kelly, 1866–1871.

Sabin   A Dictionary of Books Relating to America, from its Discovery
                to the Present Time, by Joseph Sabin; concluded by Wilber-
                force Eames and R. W. G. Vail, 1868–1936.

Stone   First Editions of American Authors a Manual for Book-Lovers
                ... , by Herbert Stuart Stone, 1893.

Thompson   American Literary Annuals & Gift Books 1825–1865, by Ralph
                Thompson, 1936.

U S Cat   The United States Catalog <of> Books in Print ... , 1900– .

Wegelin   The bibliographical studies of Oscar Wegelin, pioneer worker
                in the field of American literature, are cited by title within
                the lists.

Wright   American Fiction 1774–1850 a Contribution toward a Bibliog-
                raphy, by Lyle H. Wright, 1939, 1948. Or: American Fiction
                1851–1875 a Contribution toward a Bibliography, by Lyle H.
                Wright, 1957.

Principal Periodicals Consulted

A L B	Appleton's Literary Bulletin: A Monthly Record of New Books, English, French, German, and American (New York)
A L G	American Literary Gazette and Publishers' Circular (New York)
A M	Analectic Magazine (Philadelphia)
A Me	American Mercury (Hartford)
A Mi	American Minerva (New York)
A M M	American Monthly Magazine (New York)
A M R	American Monthly Review (Cambridge, Boston)
A P C	American Publishers' Circular and Literary Gazette (New York)
A Q R	American Quarterly Review (Philadelphia)
A R	Analytical Review; or, History of Literature, Domestic and Foreign (London)
Arc	Arcturus, a Journal of Books and Opinion (New York)
A R L J	The American Review and Literary Journal (New York)
Ath	Athenaeum; a Journal of Literature, Science, the Fine Arts, Music and the Drama (London)
A W R	American Review: A Whig Journal of Politics, Literature, Art and Science (New York)
B C	British Critic, and Quarterly Theological Review (London)
B J	Brother Jonathan (New York)
B Jl	Broadway Journal (New York)
Bkr	Bookseller (London)
B M	Bookseller's Medium and Publisher's Advertiser (New York)
B M L A	Bent's Monthly Literary Advertiser (London)
C	Critic; a Record of Literature, Art, Music, Science and the Drama (London)
C M	Canadian Monthly and National Review (Toronto)
C R	Critical Review; or, Annals of Literature (London)
C R N	Criterion, Literary and Critical Journal (New York)
E R	Eclectic Review (London)
G R R	General Repository and Review (Cambridge, Mass.)
H	The Harbinger (New York and Boston)
K	Knickerbocker, or New York Monthly Magazine (New York)
L A	Literary American (New York)
L G	Literary Gazette. A Weekly Journal of Literature, Science and the Fine Arts (London)
L G A A	Literary Gazette and American Athenaeum (New York)
L M	Literary Magazine and British Review (London)

L M A R	Literary Magazine, and American Register (Philadelphia)
L S R	Literary and Scientific Repository, and Critical Review (New York)
L W	Literary World (New York)
M A	Monthly Anthology, and Boston Review (Boston)
M M	The Monthly Magazine and American Review (New York)
M R	Monthly Review (London)
N & A	Nation and Athenaeum (London)
N A R	North American Review (Boston, New York)
N E	New Englander (New Haven, Conn.)
N E M	New-England Magazine (Boston)
N L A	Norton's Literary Advertiser (New York)
N L G	Norton's Literary Gazette and Publishers' Circular (New York)
N L R	New London Review (London)
N W	New World. A Weekly Family Journal of Popular Literature, Science, Art and News (New York)
N Y L G	New York Literary Gazette (New York), Sept. 1825–March, 1826. New York Literary Gazette and Journal of Belles Lettres, Arts, Sciences, &c., (New York), Sept. 1834–March, 1835. New York Literary Gazette (New York), Feb.–July, 1839.
N Y M	New-York Mirror: a Weekly Gazette of Literature and The Fine Arts (New York)
N Y R	New York Review (New York)
P	The Panoplist (Boston)
P C	Publishers' Circular and Booksellers' Record (London)
P F	Port Folio (Philadelphia)
P W	Publishers' Weekly (New York)
S L M	Southern Literary Messenger (Richmond, Va.)
S R	Southern Review (Charleston, S. C.)
S W M	Simm's Monthly Magazine, Southern and Western Monthly Magazine and Review (Charleston, S. C.)
T L S	Times Literary Supplement (London)
U A	Universal Asylum and Columbian Magazine (Philadelphia)
U S D R	United States Democratic Review (Washington, D. C.)
U S L A	United States Literary Advertiser, Publishers' Circular, and Monthly Register of Literature and Art (New York)
U S L G	United States Literary Gazette (Boston); United States Review and Literary Gazette (Boston, New York)
U S M D R	United States Magazine and Democratic Review (Washington, D. C., 1837–1840; New York, 1841–1851)
W M R	Western Monthly Review (Cincinnati, Ohio)
W P L N L	Wiley & Putnam's Literary News-Letter, and Monthly Register of New Books, Foreign and American (New York)
W T C	The Publishers' and Stationers' Weekly Trade Circular (New York)

Location Symbols

A A S	American Antiquarian Society, Worcester, Mass.
A H	Mr. Arthur Amory Houghton, Jr., Queenstown, Maryland.
A L	Mr. Arthur Lovell, Chicago, Illinois.
A M	The Adirondack Museum, Blue Mountain Lake, N. Y.
A N C	Academy of the New Church Library, Bryn Athyn, Pa.
A W	Mr. Ames W. Williams, Alexandria, Va.
B	Brown University Library, Providence, R. I.
B A	Boston Athenaeum, Boston, Mass.
B M L	Boston Medical Library, Boston, Mass.
B Mu	The British Museum, London.
B P L	Boston Public Library, Boston, Mass.
C	Cornell University Library, Ithaca, N. Y.
C A W	The late Carroll A. Wilson, New York, N. Y.
C C	The Century Association Library, New York, N. Y.
C F	Concord Free Public Library, Concord, Mass.
C H	Craigie-Longfellow House, Cambridge, Mass.
Ch H S	Chicago Historical Society, Chicago, Illinois.
C Ho	Mr. Charles Honce, New York, N. Y.
C H S	Connecticut Historical Society, Hartford, Conn.
C P	Cleveland Public Library, Cleveland, Ohio.
C P L	Cambridge Public Library, Cambridge, Mass.
C S S	Charles Scribner's Sons, New York, N. Y.
C U	Columbia University Libraries, New York, N. Y.
C U A	Catholic University of America Libraries, Washington, D. C.
C W B	Mr. Clifton Waller Barrett, New York, N. Y.
D	Dartmouth College Library, Hanover, N. H.
De V	Mr. Thomas De Valcourt, Cambridge, Mass.
D P L	Detroit Public Library, Detroit, Mich.
D U	Duke University Libraries, Durham, N. C.
E M	Edward Morrill & Son, Boston, Mass.
E M O R Y	Emory University Library, Atlanta, Ga.
F C W	The late Frank C. Willson, Melrose, Mass.
F H B	Mr. Francis Hyde Bangs, Ogunquit, Maine.
F L P	The Free Library of Philadelphia, Philadelphia, Pa.
F M	Rev. Frederick M. Meek, Chestnut Hill, Mass.
G	The Grosvenor Library, Buffalo, N. Y.
Gd	Goodspeed's Book Shop, Boston, Mass.
G E	The late Gabriel Engel, New York, N. Y.

Gi	Girard College Library, Philadelphia, Pa.
G M A	Mr. George Matthew Adams, New York, N. Y.
G O	Gilman's Old Books, Crompond, N. Y.
H	Harvard University Library, Cambridge, Mass.
H C	Hamilton College Library, Clinton, N. Y.
H Cr	College of the Holy Cross, Dinand Memorial Library, Worcester, Mass.
H E H	Henry E. Huntington Library & Art Gallery, San Marino, Cal.
H M	Mr. Howard S. Mott, Sheffield, Mass.
H M L	Howard-Tilton Memorial Library, Tulane University, New Orleans, La.
H S P	The Historical Society of Pennsylvania, Philadelphia, Pa.
H U	Howard University Library, Washington, D. C.
H U C	Hebrew Union College Library, Cincinnati, Ohio.
I H S	Indiana State Historical Society, Indianapolis, Indiana.
I S L	Indiana State Library, Indianapolis, Indiana.
I U	Indiana University Library, Bloomington, Indiana.
J B	Mr. Jacob Blanck, Chestnut Hill, Mass.
J C	John Crerar Public Library, Chicago, Illinois.
J D G	Mr. John D. Gordan, New York, N. Y.
J F D	James F. Drake, Inc., New York, N. Y.
J K L	Mr. J. K. Lilly, Indianapolis, Indiana.
J N	Mr. Jack Neiburg, Boston, Mass.
J N B	Mr. Jack N. Bartfield, New York, N. Y.
J S K	Mr. John S. Kebabian, New York, N. Y.
J T S	Jewish Theological Seminary of America Library, New York, N. Y.
J T W	Mr. John T. Winterich, Brayton Park, Ossining, N. Y.
J Z	Mr. Jacob Zeitlin, Los Angeles, Cal.
L B	Lever Brothers, Ltd., Port Sunlight, Cheshire, England.
L C	Library of Congress, Washington, D. C.
L C P	Library Company of Philadelphia, Philadelphia, Pa.
L S	Stanford University Libraries, Palo Alto, Cal.
M F	Mr. Mason Foley, Hingham, Mass.
M H	Mr. Maxwell Hunley, Beverly Hills, Cal.
M H S	Massachusetts Historical Society Library, Boston, Mass.
M I C	Midwest Inter-Library Center, Chicago, Illinois.
Mi H S	Minnesota Historical Society, St. Paul, Minn.
M L	The Pierpont Morgan Library, New York, N. Y.
M S L	Massachusetts State Library, Boston, Mass.
N	Newberry Library, Chicago, Ill.
N H S L	New Hampshire State Library, Concord, N. H.
N J H	The New Jersey Historical Society, Newark, N. J.
N L M	The National Library of Medicine, Washington, D. C.
N Y H S	The New-York Historical Society Library, New York, N. Y.
N Y P L	The New York Public Library, New York, N. Y.
N Y S	New York State Library, Albany, N. Y.

N Y S L	New York Society Library, New York, N. Y.
N Y U	New York University Libraries, New York, N. Y.
O	Oberlin College Library, Oberlin, Ohio.
O H S	The Ohio Historical Society, Columbus, Ohio.
O S	Ohio State University Libraries, Columbus, Ohio.
P	Princeton University Library, Princeton, N. J.
P D H	Mr. Parkman D. Howe, Needham, Mass.
P H S L	Presbyterian Historical Society, Philadelphia, Pa.
P L	Portland Public Library, Portland, Me.
P P L	Providence Public Library, Providence, R. I.
P S U	Pennsylvania State University Library, University Park, Pa.
R	Rutgers University Library, New Brunswick, N. J.
R B	Mr. Robert K. Black, Upper Montclair, N. J.
R E S	Mr. Roger E. Stoddard, Providence, R. I.
R G	The late Rodman Gilder, New York, N. Y.
R I H	Rhode Island Historical Society Library, Providence, R. I.
R L	Redwood Library & Athenaeum, Newport, R. I.
R L W	Prof. Robert Lee Wolff, Cambridge, Mass.
S	Swarthmore College Library, Swarthmore, Pa.
S G	Seven Gables Bookshop, New York, N. Y.
S M	Smithsonian Institution Libraries, Washington, D. C.
S R L	Sondley Reference Library, Pack Memorial Public Library, Asheville, N. C.
S U I	State University of Iowa Libraries, Iowa City, Iowa.
S W J	The late Stuart W. Jackson, Gloucester, Va.
U C	University of Chicago Library, Chicago, Ill.
U C B	University of California, General Library, Berkeley, Cal.
U C L A	University of California at Los Angeles, University Library, Los Angeles, Cal.
U G	The University of Georgia Libraries, Athens, Ga.
U I	University of Illinois Library, Urbana, Illinois.
U K	University of Kentucky Libraries, Lexington, Ky.
U Mi	University of Michigan Library, Ann Arbor, Mich.
U Mn	University of Minnesota Library, Minneapolis, Minn.
U N B	University of New Brunswick Library, Fredericton, New Brunswick, Canada.
U N C	University of North Carolina Library, Chapel Hill, N. C.
U P	University of Pennsylvania Library, Philadelphia, Pa.
U R	University of Rochester Library, Rochester, N. Y.
U S C	University of Southern California Library, Los Angeles, Cal.
U S D A	United States Department of Agriculture Library, Washington, D. C.
U T	The University of Texas, Austin, Texas.
U Tn	University of Tennessee, James D. Hoskins Library, Knoxville, Tenn.
U V	University of Virginia, Alderman Library, Charlottesville, Va.
U W	University of Wisconsin, General Library, Madison, Wis.

V	Vassar College Library, Poughkeepsie, N. Y.
V P	The late Nathan Van Patten, Palo Alto, Cal.
V S L	Virginia State Library, Richmond, Va.
W	Wellesley College Library, Wellesley, Mass.
W C	Williams College Library, Williamstown, Mass.
W C L	Washington Cathedral Library, Washington, D. C.
W F P L	Worcester Free Public Library, Worcester, Mass.
W H C	Mr. Warder H. Cadbury, Cambridge, Mass.
W L P	Mr. Walter L. Pforzheimer, Washington, D. C.
W M G	Mr. William M. Gibson, Upper Montclair, N. J.
W R	Western Reserve University Libraries, Cleveland, Ohio.
W S L	Washington University Libraries, St. Louis, Mo.
W U L	Wesleyan University, Olin Memorial Library, Middletown, Conn.
Y	Yale University Library, New Haven, Conn.

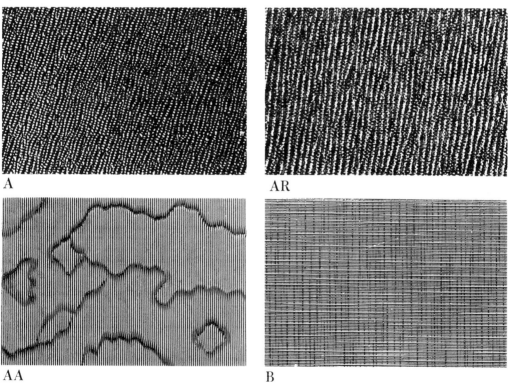

A

AR

AA

B

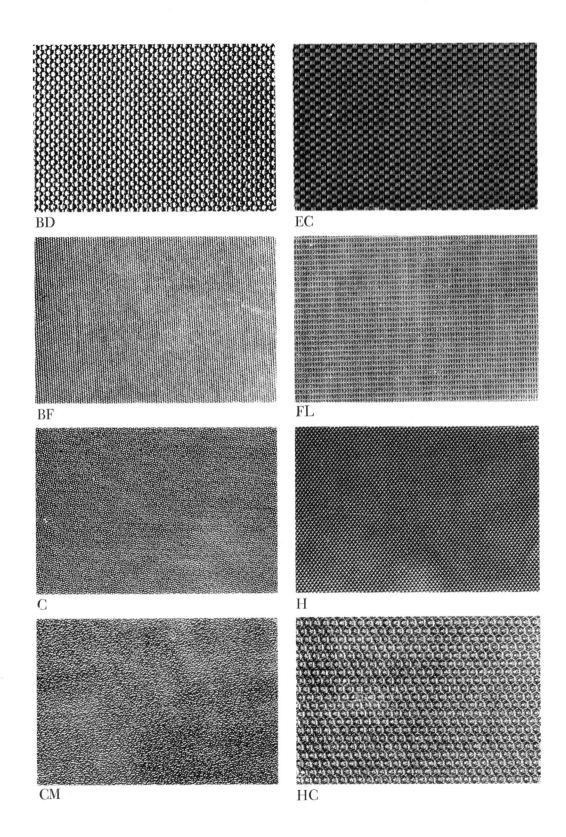

BD

EC

BF

FL

C

H

CM

HC

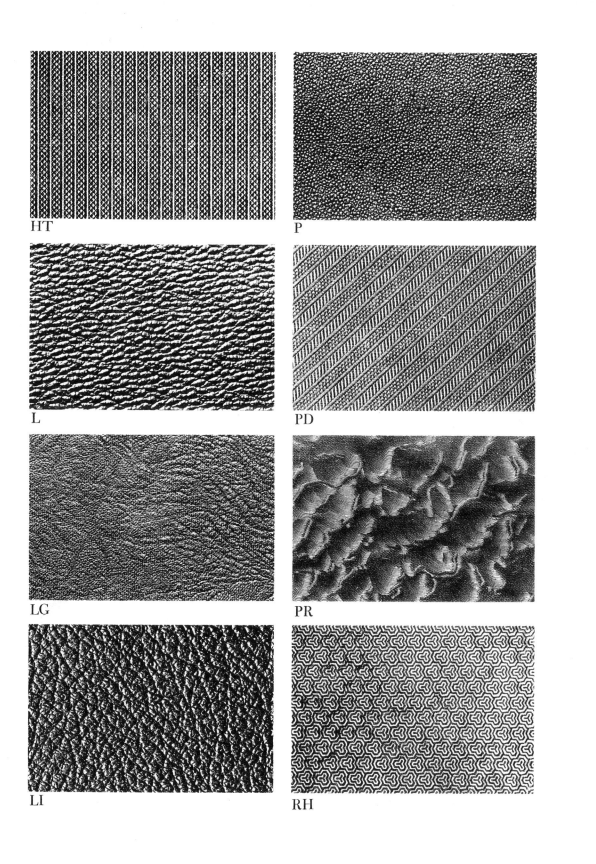

HT

P

L

PD

LG

PR

LI

RH

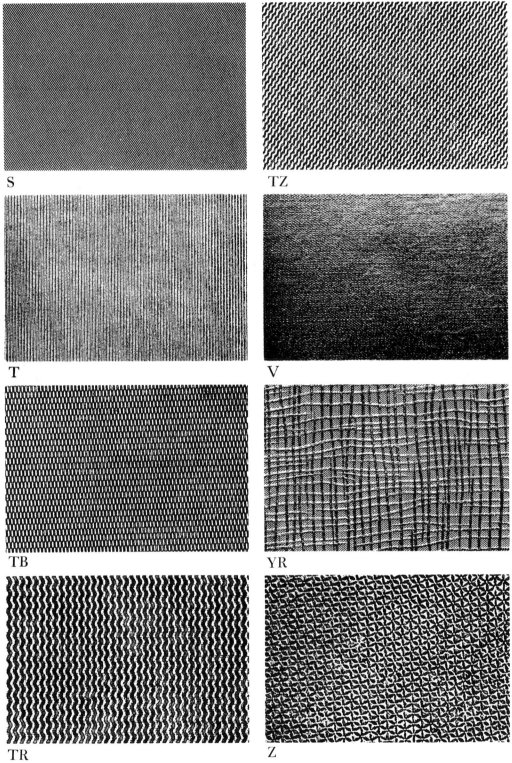

S

TZ

T

V

TB

YR

TR

Z

NATHANIEL HAWTHORNE

1 8 0 4 - 1 8 6 4

IT HAS BEEN thought useful to present this list in three sections as follows: *Section One:* Primary books; and, books by authors other than Hawthorne but containing first edition material by him. *Section Two:* Collections of reprinted material issued under Hawthorne's name; separate editions (*i.e.,* pieces reprinted from Hawthorne's books and issued in separate form); and, undated reprints. *Section Three:* Books by authors other than Hawthorne which contain material by him reprinted from earlier books.

7570. FANSHAWE, A TALE ...

BOSTON: MARSH & CAPEN, 362 WASHINGTON STREET. PRESS OF PUTNAM AND HUNT. 1828.

Anonymous.

⟨1⟩-141; blank, pp. ⟨142-144⟩. 7½" x 4⅝".

⟨1⟩-12⁶.

Brown paper boards, purple muslin shelfback, buff-coated paper label on spine. Flyleaves.

Reviewed by *Critic* (N.Y.), Nov. 22, 1828. For another publication of this story see under 1876.

BA H NYPL

7571. The Token; a Christmas and New Year's Present. Edited by S. G. Goodrich ...

Boston: Published by Carter and Hendee. MDCCCXXX.

"The Young Provincial," pp. ⟨127⟩-145. Presumably by Hawthorne. Collected in *The Complete Writings, Autograph Edition,* Vol. 16; see below under 1900.

"... attributed to Hawthorne by F. B. Sanborn on internal evidence, and accepted by M. D. Conway (see his article in the New York *Times Saturday Review,* June 8, 1901, on the *Tokens*)."—Cathcart, p. 4.

For coment see entry No. 3102.

7572. The Token; a Christmas and New Year's Present. Edited by S. G. Goodrich ...

Boston: Published by Gray and Bowen. MDCCCXXXI.

"Sights from a Steeple," pp. ⟨41⟩-51. Collected in *Twice-Told Tales,* 1837.

"The Fated Family," pp. ⟨57⟩-82. Authorship in doubt. Cathcart expresses doubt; listed by Browne as Hawthorne's.

"The Haunted Quack. A Tale of a Canal Boat," pp. ⟨117⟩-137. Here attributed to *Joseph Nicholson,* which may be one of Hawthorne's pseudonyms. Cathcart appears to accept this as by Hawthorne. Browne, p. 142, lists this as Hawthorne's without comment; but on p. 5 the cautionary word *attributed is* used. Cantwell, p. 163, states: "attributed to Hawthorne, though he never claimed it. He probably wrote it ..." F. B. Sanborn, in "A New Twice-Told Tale ..," (NEM Aug. 1898) asserts Hawthorne's authorship. Collected in *The Complete Writings, Autograph Edition,* Vol. 16, 1900.

"The New England Village," pp. ⟨155⟩-176. Cathcart describes this as *doubtful;* Browne appears to accept as Hawthorne's; Cantwell (p. 135) uses the cautionary statement: *attributed.* Collected in *The Complete Writings, Autograph Edition,* Vol. 16, 1900.

"The Adventurer," pp. ⟨189⟩-212. Almost certainly by John Neal. Cathcart states: "... attributed to Hawthorne by M. D. Conway, but not recognized by any other writer, nor is it included in any collected edition." Thompson, p. 68, almost categorically denies Hawthorne's authorship and says: "there seems to be no reason for disregarding the hint concerning ⟨John⟩ Neal's authorship printed in the annual ..." Browne lists the piece as though by Hawthorne. N. P. Willis(?) in AMM, Oct. 1830: "I do not think very well of the *Token* this year. *Lord Vapourcourt* is a good story, and the *Adventurer,* by Mr. Neal, is well told ..."

For comment see entry No. 6790.

7573. The Token; a Christmas and New Year's Present. Edited by S. G. Goodrich ...

Boston. Published by Gray and Bowen. MDCCCXXXII.

"The Wives of the Dead," by F———, pp.

⟨74⟩-82. Collected in *The Snow-Image*, 1852, as "The Two Widows."

"My Kinsman, Major Molineux," pp. ⟨89⟩-116. Collected in *The Snow-Image*, 1852.

"Roger Malvin's Burial," p. ⟨161⟩-188. Collected in *Mosses from an Old Manse*, 1846.

"The Gentle Boy," pp. ⟨193⟩-240. Collected in *Twice-Told Tales*, 1837.

"My Wife's Novel," pp. ⟨281⟩-315. Cathcart: "... incorrectly attributed by F. B. Sanborn to Hawthorne, but it was written by Edward Everett. It is also erroneously included in the *Autograph Edition*." Thompson, p. 70, is in agreement with Cathcart's statement. Listed by Browne as though by Hawthorne. George E. Woodberry (in *The Nation*, Oct. 9, 1902) also attributes the authorship to Everett.

For comment see entry No. 3256.

7574. The Token and Atlantic Souvenir. A Christmas and New Year's Present. Edited by S. G. Goodrich.

Boston. Published by Gray and Bowen. MDCCCXXXIII.

"The Seven Vagabonds," pp. ⟨49⟩-71. Collected in *Twice-Told Tales*, 1842.

"Sir William Pepperell," by H—————, pp. ⟨124⟩-134. Collected in *Fanshawe*, 1876.

"The Canterbury Pilgrims," pp. ⟨153⟩-166. Collected in *The Snow-Image*, 1852.

"The Bald Eagle," pp. ⟨74⟩-89. Not by Hawthorne although sometimes erroneously credited to him; the author was Henry Wadsworth Longfellow. "F. B. Sanborn thinks that this was written by Hawthorne, and it is included in volume 16 of the *Old Manse Edition*. It was, however, written by Longfellow, as is shown in his *Life*, v. 1, p. 292 ... ⟨*i.e., Life of Henry Wadsworth Longfellow ...*, edited by Samuel Longfellow, 1886, Vol. 1, p. 192 (*sic*)⟩."—Browne, p. 27. "... attributed to Hawthorne by F. B. Sanborn, M. D. Conway, and quoted by G. E. Woodberry, and ... included in the *Autograph Edition*, is found, from a letter of H. W. Longfellow which has recently come to light, to have been contributed by Longfellow, not by Hawthorne."—Cathcart, p. 6. For further comment see *Young Longfellow (1807-1843)*, by Lawrance Thompson, New York, 1938, pp. 133-135, 169, 375, 387.

For comment see entry No. 6126.

7575. The Mariner's Library or Voyager's Companion ...

Boston: Lilly, Wait, Colman and Holden. 1833.

"The Ocean," p. 34. For publication as sheet music see below under 1836.

For comment see entry No. 8724.

7576. The Token and Atlantic Souvenir. A Christmas and New Year's Present. Edited by S. G. Goodrich.

Boston. Published by Charles Bowen. MDCCCXXXV.

"The Haunted Mind," pp. ⟨76⟩-82. Collected in *Twice-Told Tales*, 1842.

"Alice Doane's Appeal," pp. ⟨84⟩-101. Collected in *Tales, Sketches ...*, 1883, *i.e.*, entry No. 7643, Vol. 12.

"The Mermaid: a Reverie," pp. ⟨106⟩-121. Collected in *Twice-Told Tales*, 1842, as "The Village Uncle."

For comment see entry No. 6799.

7577. Youth's Keepsake. A Christmas and New Year's Gift for Young People ...

Boston: Published by E. R. Broaders. 1835.

"Little Annie's Ramble," pp. ⟨147⟩-159. Collected in *Twice-Told Tales*, 1837.

For comment see entry No. 981.

7578. The Token and Atlantic Souvenir. A Christmas and New Year's Present. Edited by S. G. Goodrich.

Boston. Published by Charles Bowen. MDCCCXXXVI.

"The Wedding Knell," pp. ⟨113⟩-124. "The May-Pole of Merry Mount," pp. ⟨283⟩-297. "The Minister's Black Veil," pp. ⟨302⟩-320. All three collected in *Twice-Told Tales*, 1837.

For comment see entry No. 6804.

7579. The Ocean, the Words from the Boston Spectator. The Music Composed by Edward L. White.

Philadelphia, George Willig 171 Chesnut St. ⟨1836⟩

Sheet music. Title at head of p. ⟨2⟩. Anonymous.

Deposited Jan. 4, 1837. For earlier publication of the poem see *The Mariner's Library ...*, 1833, above.

H

7580. The Token and Atlantic Souvenir A Christmas and New Year's Present Edited by S. G. Goodrich.

Boston. Published by Charles Bowen. MDCCCXXXVII.

Leather.

"Monsieur du Miroir," pp. ⟨49⟩-64. "Mrs. Bull-frog," pp. ⟨66⟩-75. Collected in *Mosses from an Old Manse*, 1846.

"Sunday at Home," pp. ⟨88⟩-96. "David Swan," pp. ⟨147⟩-155. "The Great Carbuncle," pp. ⟨156⟩-175. "Fancy's Show Box," pp. ⟨177⟩-184.

"The Man of Adamant," pp. ⟨119⟩-128. Collected in *The Snow-Image*, 1852.

"The Prophetic Pictures," pp. ⟨289⟩-307. Collected in *Twice-Told Tales*, 1837.

Reviewed by κ Oct. 1836; by AMM Oct. 1836; Ath Nov. 5, 1836.

Y

7581. TWICE-TOLD TALES . . .

     BOSTON: AMERICAN STATIONERS CO. JOHN B. RUSSELL. 1837.

⟨1⟩-334; blank leaf. 7¾" x 4¾".

a⁴, ⟨A⟩-I, K-U, W-Z, 2A-2C⁶, 2D².

Noted in black, purple, brown cloth embossed with an all-over pattern of quatrefoil ornaments. Also noted in faded old-rose, green, black, brown AR-like cloth. Inserted at back: Publisher's catalog of 12 pp.; also noted with 16-page catalog inserted at back. Sequence, if any, not established.

Note: All examined copies have the error *78* for *76*, fifth entry, table of contents.

Noted as *in press* κ Feb. 1837. Published March 7, 1837, according to advertisements in *Boston Daily Advertiser,* March 7, 1837. Reviewed by κ April, 1837. Advertised PC March 1, 1838, as a *new American Publication.* Also see under 1842, 1851, 1865.

H NYPL

7582. Peter Parley's Universal History, on the Basis of Geography. For the Use of Families. Illustrated by Maps and Engravings . . .

     Boston: American Stationers' ⟨Stationers⟩ Company. John B. Russell. 1837.

2 Vols.

1: ⟨i⟩-viii, ⟨i⟩-⟨viii⟩, ⟨9⟩-380, 2 blank leaves. 2: ⟨i⟩-xii, ⟨13⟩-374, blank leaf. 6¹¹⁄₁₆" x 5¹⁄₁₆". Illustrated. Edges plain; or, gilded.

Noted in a variety of cloths with no known sequence if any. The following have been noted; the order is purely arbitrary; the designations are for identification only:

A: Black H cloth.

B: Brown S-like cloth damasked with a floral pattern.

C: Blue AR-like cloth.

D: Faded old rose T cloth embossed with a floral pattern.

E: Salmon S cloth embossed with an oak leaf pattern.

Very probably issued in other types of cloth as well.

The side stamping noted in the following styles; no sequence, if any, has been determined, and the designations are for identification only:

A: Sides blindstamped with a rococo frame. At inner top and inner bottom is a flourish resembling a cupid's-bow. At center: a gold-stamped lyre.

B: Sides blindstamped with a frame, the sides composed of pillar-like units, the corners floriated. No lyre stamped on the sides.

C: Sides blindstamped with a floral frame. At the center of the sides is a goldstamped lyre.

D: Sides blindstamped with a frame composed of six-rule units, ornamented at the inner corners. At the center of the sides is a goldstamped lyre.

Title-pages for the book in *two volumes* deposited for copyright on July 17, 1837. The *two-volume* book deposited for copyright July 29, 1837. A title-page for the work in *one volume* was deposited for copyright Nov. 22, 1837. The work in *one volume* was deposited for copyright Dec. 14, 1837. For a comment on the *one-volume* edition see below: *Peter Parley's Common School History,* 1838.

A NOTE ON THE BRITISH EDITIONS

Kennett. The two-volume edition was advertised as an importation in PC Oct. 2, 1837; BMLA Oct. 1837; Ath Oct. 7, 1837. Listed BMLA Oct. 1837, as published during the period Sept. 8–Oct. 7, 1837.

Parker. Listed LG and Ath Oct. 21, 1837. "This work, an entirely new production of its highly popular author, is reprinted from an unpublished copy, specially forwarded . . . for the purpose. In adapting it for the English public, great pains have been taken to avoid those national peculiarities by which . . . earlier works ⟨in the series⟩ have been disfigured . . . This genuine English edition will, therefore, it is confidently believed, be found an invaluable addition . . ." —PC Oct. 2, 1837.

Tegg. A presumed Tegg edition was listed by Ath Jan. 13, 1838; BMLA Feb. 1838. Reviewed by Ath Feb. 17, 1838.

NOTE

This work was compiled by Hawthorne and his sister Elizabeth. ". . . the Hawthornes contributed little of their own to the compilation . . . it seems conclusive that the *Universal History* was tailor-made, that very little in it can be safely labelled as Hawthorne's work or thought. It has been placed in the Hawthorne canon only because he and his sister were associated with it, but it represents nothing more than a piece of hack work accomplished by extracting materials from Parley books and other works easily available. Like most such chores, the book, despite its popularity, brought only slight monetary recompense to its compilers . . . the *Universal History* bears practically no trace of Hawthorne's own stamp and . . . it should be read out of the Hawthorne canon."—"Hawthorne and Parley's Universal History," by B. Bernard Cohen, in *The Papers of the Bibliographical Society of America*, Vol. 48, 1954, pp. 77-90.

Peter Parley was the pseudonym-eponym used by Samuel Griswold Goodrich, 1793–1860.

H LC NYPL

7583. The Token and Atlantic Souvenir, a Christmas and New Year's Present. Edited by S. G. Goodrich.

Boston: American Stationers' Company, M DCCC XXXVIII.

"Sylph Etherege," pp. ⟨22⟩-32. Collected in *The Snow-Image*, 1852.

"Peter Goldthwait's Treasure," pp. ⟨37⟩-65; "Endicott and the Red Cross," pp. ⟨69⟩-78; "Night Sketches, beneath an Umbrella," pp. ⟨81⟩-89; "The Shaker Bridal," pp. ⟨117⟩-125. This group of stories collected in *Twice-Told Tales*, 1842.

For comment see entry No. 6816.

7584. Peter Parley's Common School History
. . .

Boston: American Stationers' Company. J. B. Russell. 1838.

Cloth, leather shelfback. *Issued as a single volume.*

A very slightly revised edition of *Peter Parley's Universal History*, 1837.

Deposited for copyright Dec. 14, 1837, over four months after deposit of the two-volume work described above; see under 1837.

Note: On the copyright page of this revised edition appears the following statement: "A few copies of this work, with considerable additions, will be published in 2 vols. under the title of *Peter Parley's Universal History*. It will be executed in very beautiful style." The wording of the statement surely suggests that the one-volume, 1838, edition was published prior to the two-volume, 1837, edition. However, the reverse is correct; see above under the 1837 publication for a fuller statement of publication dates. The statement here quoted as appearing on the copyright page of the one-volume edition appears in printings as late as the *Eighth Edition* (so-called) which was issued under date of 1840.

H

7585. TIME'S PORTRAITURE. BEING THE CARRIER'S ADDRESS TO THE PATRONS OF THE SALEM GAZETTE FOR THE FIRST OF JANUARY, 1838 . . .

⟨Salem, Mass., Jan. 1, 1838⟩

At head of title: Vignette of an eagle and the word: INDEPENDENCE

Single sheet. 21¼" x 16⅜". Printed on one side of sheet only.

Anonymous.

Reissued, 1853, as an 8-page pamphlet. Collected in *The Dolliver Romance*, 1876.

NYPL

7586. THE SISTER YEARS; BEING THE CARRIER'S ADDRESS, TO THE PATRONS OF THE SALEM GAZETTE, FOR THE FIRST OF JANUARY, 1839.

SALEM. 1839.

Cover-title.

⟨1⟩-8. 9⅝" x 5⅞" scant.

⟨-⟩⁴.

Printed self-wrapper.

Anonymous.

Collected in *Twice-Told Tales*, 1842.

H NYHS NYPL Y

7587. The Gentle Boy: A Thrice Told Tale
. . .

Boston: Weeks, Jordan & Co. 121 Washington Street, New York & London: Wiley & Putnam. 1839.

Printed paper wrapper.

Reprint save for a one-page "Preface," p. ⟨4⟩. The story had prior publication in *The Token*, 1832; and, *Twice-Told Tales*, 1837.

Note: In all examined copies the error *recommendation* for *commendation* is present on p. ⟨4⟩, line 4 from bottom of page.

Note: Rumor persists that the frontispiece occurs in two states. All copies examined by BAL appear to be identical. It may be that the report had origin in the following advertisement in the *Daily Evening Transcript,* Boston, Feb. 25, 1839: "*Gentle Boy Illustrated,* with a beautiful etching. The etching to this beautiful story having been retouched and much improved by the artist, a new edition is this day issued." Cathcart comments: "in some copies the verso of the illustration faces title-page"; this may be nothing more than a binder's variant and of small significance; however, the possibility may not be overlooked that the position of the plate may hold the clue to the question.

Noted by *Boston Daily Advertiser,* Dec. 21, 1838, as *in press.* Listed *Boston Daily Advertiser,* Feb. 9, 1839. Advertised *Daily Evening Transcript,* Boston, Feb. 25, 1839: "a new edition is this day issued"; see note on the frontispiece above. Distributed in London by Wiley & Putnam; advertised Ath May 4, 1839; reviewed LG June 22, 1839.

H NYPL Y

7588. The Picturesque Pocket Companion, and Visitor's Guide, through Mount Auburn: Illustrated ...

Boston: Otis, Broaders and Company. MDCCCXXXIX.

Pictorial paper boards, leather shelfback.

"The Lily's Quest," pp. ⟨230⟩-239. Collected in *Twice-Told Tales,* 1842.

H Y

7589. The Boston Book. Being Specimens of Metropolitan Literature.

Boston: George W. Light, 1 Cornhill. 1841.

"Howe's Masquerade," pp. ⟨168⟩-189. Collected in *Twice-Told Tales,* 1842.

For comment see entry No. 631.

7590. GRANDFATHER'S CHAIR: A HISTORY FOR YOUTH ...

BOSTON: E. P. PEABODY. NEW YORK:—WILEY & PUTNAM. 1841.

⟨i⟩-⟨viii⟩, ⟨9⟩-140. 4$\frac{15}{16}$" x 3$\frac{1}{4}$".

⟨-⟩⁴, 1-8⁸, 9².

T cloth: plum. Also in a basket-weave grained cloth, bluish-plum; and, slate noted. Black paper label on front. Flyleaves.

Noted as *this day published* in *Boston Daily Advertiser,* Dec. 3, 1840. Deposited Dec. 28, 1840. Listed NYR Jan. 1841. Reviewed by both

NAR and by Arc Jan. 1841. Also see below under 1842.

H NYPL

7591. FAMOUS OLD PEOPLE: BEING THE SECOND EPOCH OF GRANDFATHER'S CHAIR ...

BOSTON: E. P. PEABODY, 13 WEST STREET. 1841.

⟨i⟩-⟨viii⟩, ⟨9⟩-158, blank leaf. 4$\frac{13}{16}$" x 3$\frac{3}{16}$".

⟨-⟩⁴, 1-9⁸, 10⁴.

C cloth: purple. P cloth: purple. S-like cloth, purple, embossed with a net-like pattern. Slate cloth embossed with a basket-weave grain. Flyleaves. Black paper label on front.

Noted as *in the press* by *Boston Daily Advertiser,* Jan. 13, 1841. Advertised as published *Boston Daily Advertiser* and *Boston Courier,* Jan. 18, 1841. Listed NAR April, 1841.

H NYPL Y

7592. LIBERTY TREE: WITH THE LAST WORDS OF GRANDFATHER'S CHAIR ...

BOSTON. E. P. PEABODY, 13 WEST STREET. 1841.

⟨i⟩-⟨viii⟩, ⟨9⟩-160. 4$\frac{7}{8}$" x 3$\frac{1}{8}$".

⟨-⟩⁴, 1-9⁸, 10⁴.

P cloth: blue; green. S-like cloth: green, embossed with coral branches and flowers. S-like cloth: mauve, embossed with flowers. T cloth (coarse ribbed): blue. T-like cloth: black, embossed with a virtually indescribable pattern of decorated lozenge-shaped links which form a chain of sorts, quatrefoils, etc. Black paper label on front. Tan end papers.

Two printings have been noted. The order of presentation is that generally accepted and is in all likelihood correct.

Printing A	*Printing B*
p. 24, line 2	
... meet in a Con-/	... meet in Con-/
p. 30, line 13	
... half burned out,/	... half burnt out,/
p. 34, line 5	
... be a governor ...	... be governor ...
p. 41, line 19	
... downfal ...	... downfall ...
p. 55 (extensive resetting)	
page ends: ... town/	page ends: ... and /
p. 67, line 1	
... and vic-/	... the vic-/

p. 75 (extensive resetting)
Last line of first paragraph

from Grandfather. /   father. /

Preface dated February 27, 1841. H copy (Printing A) inscribed by early owner March 18, 1841. Listed NYR April, 1841. The earliest British notice seen is an advertisement in Ath April 9, 1842. Listed LG April 9, 1842. Sheets of *Printing B* were issued with the original title-leaf excised, and another title-leaf inserted, imprinted: *Boston . . . 1851.*

H (A, 1851)   NYPL (A, B)

7593. Grandfather's Chair: A History for Youth . . . Second Edition, Revised and Enlarged.

Boston: Tappan and Dennet, 114 Washington Street. 1842.

For first edition see above under 1841.

Three styles of binding noted. Sequence, if any, not known. The following order is purely arbitrary.

A: Front stamped in blind with a leafy frame. Lettered in gold: GRANDFATHER'S CHAIR.

B: Front stamped in blind with an ornamental frame having a grill ornament at each corner. A throne-like chair goldstamped at center.

C: Front stamped in blind with a leafy frame. Stamped in gold at the center is an ornate throne-like chair.

Listed NAR Jan. 1842.

LC   NYPL   Y

7594. TWICE-TOLD TALES . . .

BOSTON: JAMES MUNROE AND COMPANY. MDCCCXLII.

2 Vols.

1: ⟨i-iv⟩, ⟨1⟩-331. 7″ x 4⅜″.
2: ⟨i⟩-iv, ⟨1⟩-356.

1: ⟨-⟩², 1-20⁸, 21⁶.
2: ⟨-⟩², 1-22⁸, 23².

T cloth: black; brown. Three styles of binding noted. No sequence, if any, known. The designations are for identification only.

A: Front cover unlettered. Spine lettered: TWICE-TOLD / TALES. / VOL. I. ⟨II.⟩ Cream-coated on white end papers.

B: Front cover lettered: HAWTHORNE. Spine lettered: TWICE-TOLD / TALES / FIRST ⟨SECOND⟩ SERIES / J. MUNROE & CO. Yellow end papers. Probably issued with flyleaves.

C: Front cover unlettered. Spine lettered: TWICE-TOLD / TALES. / FIRST ⟨SECOND⟩ SERIES Yellow end papers. Flyleaves.

Note: For an earlier collection issued under this same title see under 1837. This 1842 edition contains much material here first collected. Also see under 1851, 1865.

Noted as *just received* by *Boston Daily Advertiser,* Jan. 14, 1842. Noted as *in preparation* USDR Jan. 1842; as *recently issued* K March, 1842; as *just published* Arc April, 1842. Reviewed by Ath Aug. 23, 1845; no listing found in PC through 1845.

BPL (C)   CAW (B)   H (C)   NYPL (A)

7595. BIOGRAPHICAL STORIES FOR CHILDREN . . .

BOSTON: TAPPAN AND DENNET, 114 WASHINGTON STREET. 1842.

⟨i⟩-⟨vi⟩, ⟨7⟩-161. 6¹/₁₆″ x 3¹¹/₁₆″.

⟨1⟩-12⁶, 13⁸, ⟨14⟩¹.

T cloth: gray-brown; black; brown. Yellow end papers. Flyleaves.

Deposited April 12, 1842. Noted as *just published* in *Boston Daily Advertiser,* April 12, 1842.

NYPL Y

7596. THE CELESTIAL RAIL-ROAD . . .

BOSTON: PUBLISHED BY WILDER & CO., NO. 46 WASHINGTON STREET. 1843.

⟨1⟩-32. 5″ x 3¼″.

⟨1⟩-2*⁸.

Printed buff paper wrapper.

Note: Also occurs with the imprint: BOSTON: PUBLISHED BY JAMES F. FISH, NO. 52 WASHINGTON STREET. 1843.

The Wilder edition listed in NAR Jan. 1844.

H (*Wilder*) NYPL (*Wilder*) WSL (*Fish;* not seen)

7597. Journal of an African Cruiser . . . by an Officer of the U. S. Navy ⟨Horatio Bridge⟩. Edited by Nathaniel Hawthorne.

New-York & London. Wiley and Putnam. 1845.

Three printings noted; the order of presentation is all but arbitrary.

PRINTING A

Signature ⟨1⟩ comprises the following pages:

⟨i-ii⟩: Excised

⟨i⟩: Fly-title page

⟨ii⟩: Blank

⟨iii⟩: Title-page; *printed on a cancel*

⟨iv⟩: Copyright notice in *four* lines. The following imprints present: *R. Craighead's Power Press;* and, *Stereotyped by T. B. Smith.*

⟨v⟩: *Contents . . .*

vi-viii: Table of contents concluded

⟨v⟩: *Preface . . .*

vi: Preface concluded

At the head of each page of the body of the book: Running head and chapter number.

Issued as *Wiley and Putnam's Library of American Books,* No. 1.

Noted in printed paper wrapper only. Two states of the wrapper have been seen or reported:

Wrapper 1

On outer back wrapper three titles only listed under *Wiley and Putnam's Library of American Books.*

Wrapper 2

On outer back wrapper eight titles listed under *Wiley and Putnam's Library of American Books.* Reported; not seen by BAL.

Note: Unsold sheets were issued with a cancel title-leaf imprinted: *New York: John Wiley . . . 1848.* Copy in H.

Also note: A surviving copyright deposit copy (now rebound and hence not fully collatable) appears to be an example of *Printing A.* Also in LC is a copy in what appears to be an original leather binding bearing a presentation inscription, Bridge to "Mrs. Polk", July 16, 1845, which also appears to be an example of *Printing A.* It will be noted that in the Polk copy the binder has rearranged certain leaves in the front matter.

PRINTING B

Signature ⟨1⟩ comprises the following pages; all leaves properly conjugate; no cancelled leaves:

⟨i⟩: Blank

⟨ii⟩: Blank

⟨i⟩: Fly-title page

⟨ii⟩: Blank

⟨iii⟩: Title-page

⟨iv⟩: Copyright notice in *three* lines. Imprints of stereotyper and printer not present.

⟨v⟩: *Preface . . .*

vi: Preface concluded

⟨v⟩: *Contents . . .*

vi-viii: Table of contents concluded

At the head of each page of the body of the book: Running head and chapter number.

Noted in cloth only.

Also noted in cloth bound together with J. T. Headley's *Letters from Italy,* 1845.

Also noted in cloth bound together with George Henry Calvert's *Scenes and Thoughts in Europe . . . ,* 1846.

Also: Sheets of *Printing B* have been seen with cancel title-leaf imprinted: *London: Wiley and Putnam . . . 1845 . . .* Verso of title-leaf blank. Copy in H.

PRINTING C

Date of printing and publication not known. Located only with cancel title-leaf dated 1853. Copy in H.

In this printing the book is essentially in 12's; Printings A and B are essentially in 8's. The chapter numbers are not present in the running heads.

NOTE

In Printing B the copyright notice is not wholly correct in that it omits *of the United States.* The full name of the court, including *of the United States,* is present in Printing A. Sheets reissued with a cancel title-leaf dated 1848 have no copyright notice present; and, sheets issued with cancel title-leaf dated 1853 have the copyright notice in the shorter form; *i.e.,* without *of the United States.*

Deposited (apparently Printing A) June 20, 1845. Advertised as *just published* in *New-York Daily Tribune,* June 20, 1845. Listed ALB July, 1845. Listed WPLNL July, 1845. The London (Wiley & Putnam) edition advertised as *now ready* Ath July 12, 1845; PC July 15, 1845; listed PC July 15, 1845; Ath July 19, 1845; reviewed LG Aug. 2, 1845; Ath Sept. 6, 13, 1845.

AAS (Printing B bound with *Letters from Italy*) H (Printing B; also, Printing B bound with *Letters from Italy;* also, Printing A in Wrapper 1) NYPL (Printing B bound with *Scenes and Thoughts in Europe;* also, Printing A in Wrapper 1) Y (Printing B bound with *Letters from Italy;* also, Printing A in Wrapper 1)

7598. MOSSES FROM AN OLD MANSE . . .

NEW YORK: WILEY AND PUTNAM. 1846.

2 Vols.

1: ⟨i-vi⟩, ⟨1⟩-207. 7⁹⁄₁₆″ x 5⅛″.
2: ⟨i-vi⟩, ⟨1⟩-211.

1: $\langle 1 \rangle^2$, $\langle - \rangle^1$, $2\text{-}9^{12}$, 10^6, $\langle 11 \rangle^2$.

2: $\langle 1 \rangle^2$, $\langle - \rangle^1$, $2\text{-}9^{12}$, 10^6, $\langle 11\text{-}12 \rangle^2$.

Printed pale buff paper wrapper.

Issued as Nos. XVII-XVIII of *Wiley and Putnam's Library of American Books.*

Note: The wrapper has been noted in three states:

A: Back wrapper lists 18 volumes in the series.

B: Back wrapper lists 20 volumes in the series.

C: Back wrapper lists 22 volumes in the series.

Deposited June 5, 1846. Noted as *just ready* WPLNL June, 1846. Issued in June according to a notice in WPLNL July, 1846. All early publication notices refer to the book as in two paper-covered parts. Advertised as a single cloth-bound volume WPLNL Oct. 1846. Also see under 1854.

General Comment

Study indicates that the book was reprinted at least twice with the date 1846 in the imprint. Study also indicates that when issuing the book in cloth (as a single volume) the publishers used whatever sheets they had in stock, and copies in cloth, therefore, frequently are of intermediate status. It is certain that the earliest printings have both of the following imprints present on the copyright pages: *T. B. Smith, Stereotyper;* and, *R. Craighead's Power Press.* In later printings one or the other is absent; both may be absent; or, the imprint of *William Osborn, Printer,* may be present instead of the imprint of *R. Craighead's Power Press.* In the earliest printings p. $\langle 212 \rangle$, Vol. 2, is wholly blank; in known reprints this page is used as the title-page, dated 1846, for a publisher's catalog.

Note: Restored copies of this book have been seen with the back of the wrapper supplied from other publications in the series. Caution should be exercised in attempting to relate such copies to this collation.

British Editions

The first London edition was made up of American sheets and issued with cancel title-leaf bearing the London imprint of Wiley & Putnam. Advertised as *new* in LG July 11, 1846. Listed PC July 15, 1846; Ath July 18, 1846; LG July 25, 1846.

Routledge: Listed Ath Sept. 13, 1851. Another printing, issued in paper, listed PC Dec. 8, 1873.

Paterson (Edinburgh); and *Simpkin* (London): Advertised as though a new publication Bkr July, 1883.

Warne: Listed PC Nov. 1, 1884.

Note: Under the title *The New Adam and Eve* editions were issued by Paterson (Edinburgh) and Simpkin (London) in 1883; see PC Sept. 1, 1883. A Walter Scott (London) edition advertised for Sept. 25, 1894, in Bkr Sept. 1894.

The above entry was made on the basis of copies in AAS, BPL, H, LC, MHS, NYPL, Y.

7599. Æsthetic Papers. Edited by Elizabeth P. Peabody ...

Boston: The Editor, 13, West Street. New York: G. P. Putnam, 155, Broadway. 1849.

"Main-Street," pp. 145-174. Collected in *The Snow-Image,* 1852. Issued as a separate in 1901.

For comment see entry No. 5217.

7600. THE SCARLET LETTER, A ROMANCE ...

BOSTON: TICKNOR, REED, AND FIELDS. M DCCC L.

Title-page in black and red-orange.

$\langle i \rangle$-iv, $\langle 1 \rangle$-322, blank leaf. $7\frac{1}{8}''$ x $4\frac{1}{2}''$.

$\langle - \rangle^2$, $1\text{-}20^8$, 21^2.

T cloth: brown. Yellow end papers; cream end papers. Flyleaves. Publisher's list, 4 pp., dated *March 1, 1850,* inserted at front.

Note: Much has been made of the revisions and corrections done for the second edition (see next entry); the claim being that these changes occurred during the run of the first edition and that, therefore, there are two states of the first edition. The assertion is incorrect. All examined copies of the first edition are textually identical.

Advertised as in both cloth; and, printed paper wrapper * for March 16 in LW March 2, 1850. Published March 16, 1850, according to the publisher's records. Issued during the period March 16-23, according to LW March 30, 1850.

British Editions

Delf (i.e., Putnam), importation. Listed PC April 15, 1850. Reviewed Ath June 15, 1850.

Chapman importation. Advertised Ath June 28, 1851.

J. Walker, and others, London; Johnstone & Hunter, Edinburgh; James M'Glashan, Dublin. Listed Ath May 17, 1851; PC June 2, 1851.

Routledge, London. Listed Ath May 24, 1851; another printing PC Sept. 16, 1873.

Bohn, London. Listed Ath Nov. 15, 1851; PC Dec. 1, 1851.

* No copy of the first edition has been found in printed paper wrapper. The only located example of the wrapper is on a set of sheets of the second edition; sheets dated 1851; wrapper dated 1850.

Milner & Sowerby, Halifax. Advertised in PC Dec. 1, 1856.

Clarke, London. Listed Ath and LG Nov. 5, 1859; PC Nov. 15, 1859.

Dicks, London. Listed PC May 1, 1888.

H   NYPL

7601. The Scarlet Letter, a Romance ... ⟨Second Edition⟩

Boston: Ticknor, Reed, and Fields. M DCCC L.

Extended by the addition of a "Preface to the Second Edition," dated March 30, 1850, pp. ⟨iii⟩-iv. For first edition see preceding entry.

Two printings noted:

1: ⟨i-ii⟩, ⟨i⟩-vi, ⟨1⟩-322, blank leaf. *Metcalf and Company* imprint on the copyright page. Inserted catalog, when present, dated Oct. 1, 1849; or, May, 1850.

2: ⟨i-ii⟩, ⟨i⟩-vi, ⟨1⟩-307. *Hobart & Robbins* imprint on the copyright page. Inserted catalog, when present, dated Nov. 1850.

In this second edition certain errors present in the first edition are corrected.

A Boston letter dated April 11, 1850, in LW April 20, 1850, reported "a new edition has just been published." The publisher's records are not entirely clear but the first printing of the second edition appears to have been manufactured in April, 1850; published April 22, 1850. And, still according to the same uncertain source, the second printing of the second edition was manufactured in Sept. 1850.

BA (1st)   H (1st, 2nd)   NYPL (1st, 2nd)   Y (2nd)

7602. The Memorial: Written by Friends of the Late Mrs. Osgood and Edited by Mary E. Hewitt ...

New-York: George P. Putnam, 155 Broadway. 1851.

"The Snow-Image. A Childish Miracle," pp. 41-58. Collected in *The Snow-Image,* 1851 (London, Dec.); 1852 (Boston, Dec. 1851). Also issued as a separate, 1864.

For comment see entry No. 1187.

7603. Twice-Told Tales ... in Two Volumes ... a New Edition.

Boston: Ticknor, Reed, and Fields. MDCCCLI.

Reprint save for the "Preface," Vol. 1, pp. ⟨5⟩-12.

Listed LW March 22, 1851, as though published during the period March 8–22, 1851. The Lon-don (Chapman importation) advertised in Ath April 5, 1851; listed Ath April 19, 1851. For other editions see under 1837, 1842, 1865.

British Editions

Bohn, London. Listed Ath Nov. 29, 1851.

Routledge, London. Listed PC Dec. 15, 1851.

Milner & Sowerby, Halifax. Earliest issue of this publisher listed, as in the *Cottage Library,* PC Dec. 1, 1856.

Bell & Daldy, London. Listed PC April 1, 1871.

Warne, London. Listed Ath July 19, 1873.

H   NYPL

7604. THE HOUSE OF THE SEVEN GABLES, A ROMANCE ...

BOSTON: TICKNOR, REED, AND FIELDS. M DCCC LI.

⟨i⟩-⟨viii⟩, ⟨9⟩-344. 7⅛" x 4½".

⟨1⟩-21⁸, 22⁴.

T cloth: brown. Yellow end papers. Flyleaves.

NOTE

According to the publisher's records there were four printings in 1851:

First: March, 1851. 1690 copies. Published April, 1851.

Second: March, 1851. 1969 copies. Published April, 1851.

Third: April, 1851. 2051 copies. Published May, 1851.

Fourth: Aug. 1851. 1000 copies. Published September, 1852 ⟨sic⟩.

BAL has been unable to discover any variations in the sheets sufficiently sharp to clearly distinguish one printing from another. It is obvious that different weights of paper were used in the printings. BAL recognizes the danger in offering binding variations as evidence of printing sequence, particularly since sophisticated copies of this book are of fair frequency, but nevertheless suggests that the following binding sequence, based on contemporary inscriptions, inserted catalogs, type wear and type battering, is significant. All bindings are of brown T cloth; no attempt has been made to describe variations of shade or tone. The sequence for A and B is presumed correct; the sequence for C-E is not certain.

Binding A

Spine imprint: TICKNOR & CO. The ampersand is roman, not italic. The O in CO. is a capital letter. The line stamped from a face ⅛" high. The line is set 1¼" wide. Noted with inserted catalog dated March, 1851; both A and B printings of the catalog noted. See note below regarding the catalog.

Binding B

Spine imprint: TICKNOR & CO. The ampersand is roman, not italic. The O in CO. is a capital letter. The line stamped from a face $\frac{3}{32}$" high. The line is set $1\frac{1}{16}$" wide. Noted with inserted catalog dated March, 1851; printing A of the catalog noted. Also noted with inserted catalog dated May, 1851. See note below regarding the catalog.

Binding C

Spine imprint: TICKNOR & Co. The ampersand is italic, not roman. The o in Co. is lower case. The line stamped from a face $\frac{3}{32}$" high. The line is set $1\frac{1}{8}$" wide. Noted with inserted publisher's catalog dated July, 1853.

Binding D

Spine imprint: TICKNOR & CO. The ampersand is italic, not roman. The O in CO. is a capital letter. The line is stamped from a face $\frac{3}{32}$" high. The line is set $1\frac{3}{16}$" wide. Noted with publisher's catalog dated September, 1853.

Binding E

Spine imprint: TICKNOR & CO. The ampersand is roman, not italic. The O in CO. is a capital letter. The line stamped from a face $\frac{1}{8}$" scant high. The line is set $1\frac{1}{16}$" wide. No catalog present in the copy examined.

Note on the Catalog

The inserted catalog of *March, 1851,* occurs in two printings of unknown sequence:

A: Last entry, p. 3: ... POEMS OF /

B: Last entry, p. 3: ... POEMS OF MANY /

For a comment on the unreliable nature of inserted catalogs as evidence see BAL, Vol. 1, p. xxxiii.

For printing record see above. Title-page deposited March 1, 1851. Advertised as *in preparation* LW issues of March 22–April 12, 1851. Advertised as *in a few days* LW April 5, 1851. Published during the period March 23–April 5, 1851, LW April 5, 1851. Issued in April, 1851, according to the publisher's records. A single copy was deposited for copyright May 7, 1851; another, Dec. 22, 1851.

British Publication

The Boston edition, imported by Chapman, listed Ath May 3, 1851; PC May 16, 1851.

Bohn, London: Listed Ath May 31, 1851.

Routledge, London: Advertised as *just ready* Ath May 31, 1851; listed Ath June 7, 1851.

Milner & Sowerby, Halifax: Advertised in PC Dec. 1, 1856.

Paterson, Edinburgh; and, Simpkin, London: Advertised PC April 16, 1883.

White, Manchester; and, Simpkin, London: Listed PC Jan. 16, 1892.

The present entry based on examination of many copies in H and in NYPL.

7605. The Snow-Image, and Other Tales ...

London: Henry G. Bohn, York Street, Covent Garden. 1851.

Issued simultaneously with the Boston, 1852, edition? See entry No. 7607.

⟨i⟩-⟨viii⟩, ⟨1⟩-176. $7\frac{3}{16}$" x $4\frac{1}{2}$".

Noted in cloth. According to PC listing of Jan. 1, 1852, also issued in paper boards.

Advertised for December publication Ath Dec. 27, 1851. Listed Ath Dec. 27, 1851; LG Dec. 27, 1851; PC Jan. 1, 1852. Again listed Ath Jan. 3, 1852; LG Jan. 3, 1852.

H NYPL

7606. A WONDER-BOOK FOR GIRLS AND BOYS ...

BOSTON: TICKNOR, REED, AND FIELDS. MDCCCLII.

⟨i⟩-vi, ⟨7⟩-256. Frontispiece and 6 plates inserted. $6\frac{5}{8}$" x $4\frac{3}{8}$".

⟨1⟩-16⁸.

H cloth: purple. T cloth: black; blue; blue-green; lavender; red. Yellow end papers. Flyleaves. Issued in gilt binding (*i.e.,* edges plain; sides stamped in blind); and, in extra-gilt binding (*i.e.,* edges gilded, sides stamped in blind and gold).

Note: On the spine, separating the title from the author's name, is an ornament. On all examined copies save one the ornament is a three-unit device, the central unit being an upright ovoid. On a variant (NYPL) the ornament separating the title from the author's name is a simple rule in the centre of which is a crescent-like ornament. Status of the variant not determined.

Published Nov. 8, 1851 (publisher's records). Advertised for Nov. 15, 1851, in LW Nov. 15, 1851. Listed NLA Nov. 15, 1851. Listed LW Nov. 22, 1851. Deposited Dec. 22, 1851. The London (Bohn) edition listed Ath Dec. 27, 1851; PC Jan. 1, 1852.

H NYPL

7607. THE SNOW-IMAGE, AND OTHER TWICE-TOLD TALES ...

BOSTON: TICKNOR, REED, AND FIELDS. M DCCC LII.

Issued simultaneously with the London, 1851, edition? See entry No. 7605.

⟨3⟩-273. 7¹⁄₁₆″ x 4⁷⁄₁₆″.

⟨1⟩-17⁸.

T cloth: brown. Yellow end papers. Flyleaves. Publisher's catalog, pp. ⟨1⟩-4, dated *January, 1852,* inserted at front. Also noted with inserted catalog dated *July, 1852.*

The publisher's records are vague but the book appears to have been printed and bound in December, 1851. Advertised as *just published* LW Dec. 20, 1851. A copy in H inscribed by early owner Dec. 25, 1851. Listed LW Dec. 27, 1851, as published during the period Dec. 13-27, 1851. Listed NLG Jan. 15, 1852.

H NYPL

7608. *Entry cancelled.*

7609. Memorial of James Fenimore Cooper

New York G P Putnam 1852

Letter, dated Feb. 20, 1852, p. 33.

For comment see entry No. 1650.

7610. THE BLITHEDALE ROMANCE ...

LONDON: CHAPMAN AND HALL, 193, PICCADILLY. 1852.

2 Vols. For first American edition see next entry.

1: ⟨i⟩-iv, ⟨1⟩-259. 7¹³⁄₁₆″ x 4¹³⁄₁₆″.
2: ⟨i⟩-iv, ⟨1⟩-287. In all examined copies p. 64 is mispaged 46.

1: ⟨A⟩², B-I, K-R⁸, S².
2: ⟨A⟩², B-I, K-T⁸.

Coarse A-like cloth: blackish-brown; green. Unprinted yellow-coated on white paper end papers. There is reason to believe that some copies of each volume were issued with a leaf of advertisements tipped in at the front. Inserted at the back of some copies of Vol. 1 is a publisher's catalog, pp. ⟨i-ii⟩, ⟨1⟩-⟨34⟩, dated 1852. Also occurs with advertisements printed on the end papers. Spine lettered: THE / BLITHEDALE / ROMANCE / VOL. I. ⟨II.⟩ / BY / NATHANIEL / HAWTHORNE / LONDON. / CHAPMAN & HALL

Note: A variant binding has been seen (in NYPL) which may have been put on the sheets merely as protection and not intended to represent a finished binding. In this variant the author's signature is present on the front end

paper of each volume and so, presumably, is the author's own copy; perhaps an advance copy prepared for his personal use. The spine is crudely lettered: THE / BLITHEDALE / ROMANCE / VOL. I. ⟨II.⟩ / LONDON / CHAPMAN & HALL Yellow-coated on white end papers imprinted with advertisements.

Advertised in Ath June 26, 1852, as *in a few days.* PC July 1, 1852, noted that the book had been *published here ... in advance of its appearance in Boston.* Advertised as *now ready* Ath July 3, 1852. Listed Ath July 3, 1852; LG July 3, 1852. Reviewed LG July 3, 1852. Listed PC July 16, 1852.

BPL H NYPL

7611. THE BLITHEDALE ROMANCE ...

BOSTON: TICKNOR, REED, AND FIELDS. M DCCC LII.

First American edition. For prior publication see preceding entry.

⟨i⟩-viii, ⟨9⟩-288. 7⅛″ x 4⁷⁄₁₆″ (edges plain). 6⅞″ full x 4⅜″ (edges gilded).

⟨1⟩-18⁸.

T cloth: brown. Edges plain. Yellow end papers. Flyleaves. Sides blindstamped. Occurs with and without inserted catalog. The following inserted catalogs have been noted: undated (at back); *April, 1852* (at front); *July, 1852* (at front); *Sept. 1853* (at back); *Jan. 1854* (at back).

Also issued in extra-gilt binding. Noted in red T cloth but quite probably issued in other colors also. Edges gilded. Yellow-coated end papers. Flyleaves. Sides stamped in gold and blind. No inserted catalog.

Note: The spine imprint on the *cloth, gilt* (not gilt-extra) binding occurs in two states of unknown sequence. The following designations are for convenience only:

A: The *O* in *CO* is a capital letter.

B: The *o* in *Co* is a lower case letter.

A record of nineteen copies shows the following:

Binding A: No catalog. Four copies examined, three having author's undated presentation inscription.

Binding A: April, 1852, catalog. Six copies examined.

Binding A: July, 1852, catalog. Five copies examined.

Binding A: Sept. 1853, catalog. One copy examined.

Binding A: Jan. 1854, catalog. One copy examined.

Binding B: Undated catalog. Two copies examined.

Published July 14, 1852 (publisher's records). Listed NLG July 15, 1852, as a June publication. Copy in NYPL inscribed by early owner July 15, 1852 (*Binding A,* July, 1852, catalog). Issued during the period July 1-12, 1852, according to LW July 17, 1852. According to an advertisement in LW July 31, 1852, 4,000 copies were sold within six days of publication.

B   H   NYPL   UV   Y

7612. LIFE OF FRANKLIN PIERCE . . .

BOSTON: TICKNOR, REED, AND FIELDS. M DCCC LII.

‹1›-144. Engraved portrait frontispiece inserted. *Cloth:* 7⅛" x 4⁷⁄₁₆". *Wrapper:* 7⁷⁄₁₆" x 4½".

‹A›-I⁸. *Also signed:* ‹1›-12⁶.

Note: This book was issued as an election document and occurs in variant forms. It is entirely possible that all varieties were simultaneously issued; equally possible that both styles of the cloth binding; and, both forms of the wrapper, were simultaneously produced. Evidence is wanting, however, to support these suppositions.

Cloth

T cloth: brown; marbled red and black. Also issued in fine-grained TR-like cloth: black; green. Yellow end papers. Flyleaves.

Note: The spine imprint occurs in two forms. Sequence, if any, not known; the designations are for identification only:

A: Spine imprint is 2 mm. high. The surviving copyright deposit copy thus.

B: Spine imprint is 3 mm. high.

Copies were issued with; and, without, inserted catalogs. The following forms noted; sequence not known; designations are for identification only:

A: Issued without inserted catalog. A copy thus received from the publishers by BA on Sept. 11, 1852.

B: Inserted catalog dated *July, 1852.* Una Hawthorne's copy (in NYPL) thus.

C: Inserted catalog dated *September, 1852.* On p. ‹1› *The Golden Legend* is described as *Just Published;* note the capital initial *P.*

D: Inserted catalog dated *September, 1852.* On p. ‹1› *The Golden Legend* is described as *Just published;* note the lower case initial *p.* Two presentation copies with undated inscriptions by the author have been noted in this form. Also in this form is the surviving copyright

deposit copy. Another copy in this form was in the possession of JSK inscribed by the publishers Sept. 21, 1852.

Wrapper

Also issued in printed buff paper wrapper. Two printings of the wrapper as follows:

1: With the statement *Price 37½ cents* at the upper right corner of the front.

2: Without the statement of price. For a comment on this printing of the wrapper see note below.

Note

Under date of Oct. 2, 1852, Hawthorne wrote to his publisher, William D. Ticknor, regarding a Mr. Augustus Schell, who wished to "print an edition of the book for gratuitous circulation in the city of New York." Hawthorne was "in favor of granting the largest liberty" in the matter and approved the request. (See *Letters of Hawthorne to William D. Ticknor,* 1910, Vol. 1, pp. 5-6.) Prof. Norman Holmes Pearson informs BAL that Schell was chairman of the Tammany Hall General Committee in 1852, and head of the Democratic state committee from 1853–1856. Prof. Pearson further reports that on Sept. 29, 1852, Schell wrote as follows to candidate Franklin Pierce: "I have sent to Messrs. Ticknor & Co., of Boston to make arrangements for a large number of Hawthorne's work for distribution in this City. It will have the effect of counteracting the slanderous charges which are so frequently made by the whigs, and strengthen us with the masses." On Oct. 20, 1852, Jonathan Choulet reported to Pierce: "The 5000 copies of Hawthorne bought by Mr. Schell are well distributed." The letters quoted are in The New Hampshire Historical Society.

"The largest single sale was to the Democratic Committee in New York to whom ‹the publisher› . . . sold 5000 copies, in paper, at a discount of 62½ per cent."—*The Cost Books of Ticknor and Fields,* by Warren S. Tryon and William Charvat, 1949, p. 225.

Noted as *in press . . . will shortly publish* LW Aug. 14, 1852. Noted by *Boston Daily Advertiser,* Sept. 11, 1852, as *published this day.* BA copy received from the publisher Sept. 11, 1852. Noted as *now ready* LW Sept. 18, 1852. Advertised as in both cloth; and, in paper wrapper, LW Sept. 18, 1852. Issued during the period Sept. 4-25, 1852, LW Sept. 25, 1852. Deposited Nov. 9, 1852.

London Publication

The Trübner importation advertised in Ath Oct. 2, 1852. The Low importation listed PC Oct. 15, 1852. Advertised as though *en route*

from Boston to London Ath Nov. 13, 1852; PC
Nov. 15, 1852. Noted as *just imported* Ath Dec.
18, 1852; as *just issued* Ath Dec. 25, 1852. Listed
Ath and LG Feb. 12, 1853. What appears to be a
Routledge edition was listed in Ath Dec. 11,
1852; PC Jan. 1, 1853.

BA BPL H LC NYPL Y

7613. TANGLEWOOD TALES, FOR GIRLS
AND BOYS: BEING A SECOND WONDER-
BOOK ...

    LONDON: CHAPMAN AND HALL, 193, PICCADILLY.
1853.

For first American edition see next entry.

⟨i-vi⟩, ⟨1⟩-251. 6¾″ x 4¼″ scant. Frontispiece,
vignette title-page, and five plates inserted.

⟨A⟩³, B-I, K-Q⁸, R⁶. Leaf ⟨A⟩₂ (the title-leaf)
is printed on plate paper and is an insert.

TR-like cloth: green. Yellow-coated end papers.

"Mr. Hawthorne, who arrived in Liverpool last
week ... will publish his ... *Tanglewood Papers* ⟨sic⟩ first in this country, through Chapman & Hall."—PC Aug. 1, 1853. Noted as *in
press* PC Aug. 1, 1853. Advertised for Aug. 18,
1853, Ath Aug. 13; PC Aug. 15, 1853. Advertised for *this day* Ath Aug. 20, 1853. Listed Ath
and LG Aug. 20, 1853; PC Sept. 1, 1853. Advertised as *ready* Ath Sept. 10, 1853. Reviewed LG
Sept. 24, 1853.

Other London Editions

Knight & Son: Listed Ath July 7, 1855.
Routledge: Listed PC Nov. 1, 1867.
Warne: Advertised Ath Nov. 11, 1882.
Blackwood: Listed PC May 1, 1884.
Simpkin: Listed PC April 1, 1885.
Chatto & Windus: Listed Ath Dec. 10, 1887

H Y

7614. TANGLEWOOD TALES, FOR GIRLS
AND BOYS; BEING A SECOND WONDER-
BOOK ...

    BOSTON: TICKNOR, REED, AND FIELDS. M DCCC LIII.

For first London edition see preceding entry.

⟨1⟩-336. Vignette title-page and six plates inserted. 6⅝″ x 4⅜″.

⟨1⟩-21⁸.

Two printings noted:

1: Imprint of *Boston Stereotype Foundry* on
the copyright page. Imprint of *Geo. C. Rand* not
present on copyright page.

2: Imprints of both *Boston Stereotype Foundry*
and *Geo. C. Rand* on the copyright page.

T cloth: blue; brown; green; red; purple. Yellow end papers. Flyleaves.

Note: The spine is goldstamped: TANGLEWOOD
/ TALES / ⟨rule⟩ / Hawthorne / ⟨all the preceding in a leaf decorated oval⟩ / ILLUSTRATED
⟨in a leaf-decorated oval⟩ / TICKNOR & C? A
variant has been noted which has an arrangement of mythological characters stamped on the
spine; status not known.

Inserted at the front is a publisher's catalog,
pp. ⟨1⟩-8, which has been noted in the following four printings:

A: Dated *July, 1853*. At p. 2 *Tanglewood Tales*
is described as *In press* and is listed without
price.

B: Dated *August, 1853*. At p. 2 *Tanglewood
Tales* is described as *Just out* and is listed without price.

C: Dated *September, 1853*. At p. 2 *Tanglewood
Tales* is priced at *88 cents*.

D: Dated *October, 1853*. At p. 2 *Tanglewood
Tales* is priced at *88 cents*.

NYPL copy inscribed by Duyckinck Aug. 24, 1853;
presumably presented to Duyckinck in advance
of publication. Advertised for Sept. 3, 1853, in
LW Aug. 27, 1853. Reviewed by LW Sept. 10,
1853. According to the publisher's records the
book was published Sept. 20, 1853.

NYPL (1st) Y (2nd)

7615. Mosses from an Old Manse ... in Two
Volumes ... New Edition, Carefully Revised
by the Author.

    Boston: Ticknor and Fields. M DCCC LIV.

For first edition see under 1846. Contains the
following not present in the earlier edition:
"Feathertop: A Moralized Legend," "Passages
from a Relinquished Work," "Sketches from
Memory."

Noticed NLG April 1, 1854, as among the copyrights sold at Putnam's trade sale to Ticknor,
Reed & Fields. Announced by Ticknor, Reed &
Fields in NLG April 15, May 1, 1854. Announced
by Ticknor & Fields in NLG Aug. 15, 1854. Advertised for Sept. 9, 1854, in NLG Sept. 15, 1854.

BPL NYPL Y

7616. The Philosophy of the Plays of Shakspere
Unfolded. By Delia Bacon. With a Preface
by Nathaniel Hawthorne ...

    London: Groombridge and Sons, Paternoster
Row. 1857.

Preface, pp. ⟨vii⟩-xv. For first American edition
see next entry. For fuller comment see entry

No. 558. Also, see below, *Bacon-Shakespeare Controversy, 1856–1857*. Hawthorne's preface collected in *The Complete Writings, Autograph Edition*, Vol. 17, 1900.

7617. The Philosophy of the Plays of Shakspere Unfolded. By Delia Bacon. With a Preface by Nathaniel Hawthorne . . .

Boston: Ticknor and Fields. 1857.

Preface, pp. ⟨vii⟩-xv. For first London edition see preceding entry. For fuller comment see entry No. 559. Also, see below, *Bacon-Shakespeare Controversy, 1856–1857*. Hawthorne's preface collected in *The Complete Writings, Autograph Edition*, Vol. 17, 1900.

7618. *The Bacon-Shakespeare Controversy, 1856–1857*

Hawthorne was persuaded to write a preface for Delia Bacon's *The Philosophy of the Plays of Shakspere Unfolded* (see preceding two entries) and almost immediately found himself embroiled in the Bacon-Shakespeare debate. In his preface Hawthorne accused William Henry Smith, a confirmed Baconian, of having stolen Delia Bacon's theory of the authorship of Shakespeare's plays. The accusation was promptly answered by Smith and Hawthorne, convinced that he had unjustly accused Smith, immediately and publicly apologized. It seems desirable to present as a unit the several publications relating to the affair.

A

[For Private Circulation.] Was Lord Bacon the Author of Shakespeare's Plays? A Letter to Lord Ellesmere. By William Henry Smith.

London: Printed for the Author, by Woodfall and Kinder, Angel Court, Skinner Street. 1856.

Cover-title. Printed self-wrapper. Pp. ⟨1⟩-15. Contains nothing by Hawthorne. Copy in BPL.

B

Was Lord Bacon the Author of Shakespeare's Plays? A Letter to Lord Ellesmere. By William Henry Smith.

London: William Skeffington, 163, Piccadilly. 1856.

Cover-title. Printed self-wrapper. Pp. ⟨1⟩-15. Contains nothing by Hawthorne. Trade edition of the preceding. Copy in BPL.

C

Bacon and Shakespeare. An Inquiry Touching Players, Playhouses, and Play-Writers in the Days of Elizabeth. By William Henry Smith . . .

London: John Russell Smith, 36, Soho Square. M.DCCC.LVII.

Contains nothing by Hawthorne. Printed on laid paper. Pp. ⟨i⟩-viii, ⟨1⟩-162. Copy in BPL.

D

A reissue of the preceding. Extended by the insertion of a preface comprising two letters: one written by Smith to Hawthorne ⟨June 2, 1857⟩; the other Hawthorne to Smith, dated *Liverpool, June 5th, 1857*. The added material comprises a cut sheet folded to make four pages and inserted between the unsigned preliminary gathering and gathering 1. Pagination: ⟨i⟩-viii; ⟨1⟩-4 (being the inserted material); ⟨1⟩-162. Printed on laid paper. Copies in BPL Y.

"If it were necessary I could show, that for upwards of twenty years I have held the opinion that Bacon was the author of the Shakespeare Plays, but I trust that what I have written will be sufficient to induce you to withdraw the offensive imputation."—*Smith to Hawthorne.*
". . . I beg leave to say that I entirely accept your statement . . . my imputation of unfairness or discourtesy on your part falls at once to the ground, and I regret that it was ever made . . . my remarks did you great injustice, and I trust that you will receive this acknowledgment as the only reparation in my power."—*Hawthorne to Smith.*

E

Thick paper printing of the preceding. Printed on wove paper save for the inserted material which is printed on laid paper. The BPL copy is inscribed by the publisher: "A copy on thick paper only 6 so printed . . . July 2/58."

BPL also has two proofs of the inserted material, the second of which shows revisions.

The inserted four-page addition appears to have been available as a separate. BPL has a clipping from (almost certainly) an issue of *Smith's Old Book Circular* which reads in part: "This reissue ⟨of Smith's *Bacon and Shakespeare*, London, 1857⟩ has the correspondence between the author and Nathaniel Hawthorne . . . which may be had by former purchasers *gratis.*"

A comment in Ath Aug. 15, 1857, p. 1036, suggests that a copy of the four-page addition had been received by that periodical.

Comparison of the text as published, and as it appears in the proof copies (in BPL) indicates that Hawthorne probably had a direct hand in the publication of the correspondence. The two texts vary textually as follows:

Proof   *Published*

P. 3, line 1 of letter

... of 2nd inst. ...   *... of 2d instant ...*

P. 3, line 5 of letter

... and also ...   *... and likewise ...*

P. 4, line 2 of letter

... early advantage ...   *... easy advantage ...*

The punctuation in the published version also shows improvement.

7619. The Keepsake 1857. Edited by Miss Power ...

London: David Bogue, 86 Fleet Street; Bangs, Brother, and Co., New York; H. Mandeville, 15 Rue Dauphine, Paris. 1857.

"Uttoxeter," pp. ⟨108⟩-113. Collected in *Our Old Home*, 1863.

Advertised for Nov. 14, 1856, in Ath Nov. 8, 1856. Advertised as *now ready* Ath Nov. 15, 1856. Listed Ath Nov. 15, 1856; PC Dec. 1, 1856.

H

7620. TRANSFORMATION: OR, THE RO-MANCE OF MONTE BENI ... IN THREE VOLUMES ...

LONDON: SMITH, ELDER AND ⟨& in Vol. 2⟩ CO., 65, CORNHILL. M.DCCC.LX.

Issued simultaneously with the Boston edition? See note under entry No. 7621. Also see *Transformation*, second edition, London, 1860; and, *The Marble Faun*, second edition, Boston, 1860.

1: ⟨i⟩-⟨xvi⟩, ⟨1⟩-273; blank, p. ⟨274⟩; printer's imprint, p. ⟨275⟩. 7¾″ x 4¾″.
2: ⟨i-iv⟩, ⟨1⟩-294; printer's imprint, p. ⟨295⟩.
3: ⟨i-iv⟩, ⟨1⟩-285; printer's imprint, p. ⟨286⟩; advertisements, pp. ⟨1⟩-2; plus: Publisher's catalog, pp. ⟨1⟩-32, dated *February, 1860*.

1: ⟨-⟩⁸, 1-17⁸, 18².
2: ⟨-⟩², 19-36⁸, 37⁴.
3: ⟨-⟩², 38-55⁸; plus: A-B⁸.

TZ cloth: old rose.

Note: Folio 176, Vol. 1, occurs as *76*. The full folio, *176*, is present in the second and third printings.

Advertised as *just ready* PC Feb. 15, 1860. Advertised as *this day* PC March 1, 1860. Advertised as *now ready* Ath March 3, 1860. Listed Ath and LG March 3, 1860.

H NYPL

7621. THE MARBLE FAUN: OR, THE RO-MANCE OF MONTE BENI ... IN TWO VOLUMES ...

BOSTON: TICKNOR AND FIELDS. M DCCC LX.

For first London edition see preceding entry. Also see *Transformation*, second edition, London, 1860; *The Marble Faun*, second edition, Boston, 1860.

Note: The Boston and the London publishers attempted to publish simultaneously, Ticknor & Fields setting their edition from advance sheets of the London edition; see *Hawthorne and His Publisher*, by Caroline Ticknor, Boston, 1913; and, *Hawthorne*, by James T. Fields, Boston, 1876. Contemporary notices indicate that the London edition was issued prior to the Boston edition but simultaneous publication may have occurred.

1: ⟨i⟩-⟨xiv⟩, ⟨15⟩-283; blank, pp. ⟨284-288⟩. 7⅛″ x 4½″.
2: ⟨1⟩-284; blank, pp. ⟨285-288⟩.
1: ⟨1-18⟩⁸. *Signed:* ⟨1⟩-12¹².
2: ⟨1-18⟩⁸. *Signed:* ⟨1⟩-12¹².

T cloth: brown. Brown-coated on white end papers. Flyleaves. Publisher's catalog inserted at back of Vol. 1; see below.

Three printings noted:

1

As collated above.

2

1: ⟨i-ii⟩, ⟨i⟩-⟨xii⟩, ⟨15⟩-283; blank, pp. ⟨284-288⟩.
2: ⟨1⟩-284; blank, pp. ⟨285-288⟩.
1: ⟨1⟩-12¹².
2: ⟨1⟩-12¹².

3

1: ⟨i⟩-⟨xiv⟩, ⟨15⟩-283; blank, pp. ⟨284-288⟩.
2: ⟨1⟩-284; blank, pp. ⟨285-288⟩.
1: ⟨1⟩-12¹².
2: ⟨1⟩-12¹².

It will be observed that thus far no variation has been discovered that may distinguish the second printing from the third printing of Vol. 2.

Note: Issued in brown T cloth, with the spine lettered: THE / MARBLE / FAUN / ⟨rule⟩ / HAW-THORNE / VOL. I. ⟨II.⟩ / TICKNOR & CO. A secondary binding has been noted as follows: Black BD cloth. Spine lettered: ROMANCE / OF / MONTE-BENI / ⟨rule⟩ / HAWTHORNE / ⟨rule⟩ / VOL. I. ⟨II.⟩ Bound in at back of Vol. 2: Four pages of advertisements of books offered for sale by T. O. H. P. Burnham, Boston. On the basis of the books so offered this secondary binding was prepared either late in 1860 or early in 1861. A copy of the secondary binding is in CWB.

Title entered Feb. 27, 1860, Published Feb. 28, 1860, according to the publisher's records. Noted as *nearly ready* BM March 1, 1860. Issued during the period March 1-15, 1860, BM March 15, 1860. Deposited for copyright April 10, 1860.

The Inserted Catalog

The following is a record of the occurrence of the inserted catalog; fifteen copies examined.

Catalog dated *February, 1860:* Noted in 4 copies of first printing.

Catalog dated *March, 1860:* Noted in 1 copy of first printing; 5 copies of second printing; 5 copies of third printing.

H (1st, 2d, 3d)   NYPL (1st, 2d, 3d)   Y (1st, 2d)

7622. Transformation: Or, the Romance of Monte Beni ... in Three Volumes ... Second Edition.

  London: Smith, Elder and ⟨& in Vol. 2⟩ Co., 65, Cornhill. M.DCCC.LX.

Extended by the addition of a "Postscript," Vol. 3, pp. 286-294.

For first edition see above under 1860. See also entry No. 7624.

Advertised PC April 2, 1860. A "third edition" advertised as *in a few days*, PC April 16, 1860. An illustrated edition (illustrations by Walter Crane) announced PC May 1, 1865. A one-volume edition listed Bkr Dec. 1872; another (?) listed PC June 16, 1876.

NYPL   Y

7623. The Weal-Reaf. A Record of the Essex Institute Fair, Held at Salem, Sept. 4, 5, 6, 7, 8, with Two Supplementary Numbers, Sept. 10, 11, 1860.

An occasional newspaper consisting of 7 numbers, title-page and index, and an *Extra*.

"A Letter from Hawthorne," Aug. 28, 1860, in No. 2, p. 14; No. 3, p. 24. Collected in *The Dolliver Romance*, 1876, as "Browne's Folly."

H   NYPL

7624. The Marble Faun: Or, the Romance of Monte Beni. ⟨Second Edition⟩ ... in Two Volumes ...

  Boston: Ticknor and Fields. M DCCC LX.

For first edition see above under 1860. For London publication of this extended edition see entry No. 7622.

Extended by the addition of a "Conclusion," Vol. 2, pp. 284-288.

Note: The publication record of this second edition is not clear. It probably is the one recorded in the publisher's files as printed in April, 1860. Further, the publisher's records indicate there were four printings during the period April–Sept. 1860; BAL has been unable to discover any variations that might distinguish one from another. BAL presumes, but presumes only, that the London printing of this edition preceded the Boston printing in time of publication.

NYPL   Y

7625. Entry cancelled.

7626. OUR OLD HOME: A SERIES OF ENGLISH SKETCHES ...

  BOSTON: TICKNOR AND FIELDS. 1863.

⟨i⟩-⟨xii⟩, ⟨9⟩-398; advertisement, p. ⟨399⟩. 7³⁄₁₆" x 4⁹⁄₁₆".

⟨1², 2⁴, 3⁸, 4-18¹², 19⁸⟩. *Signed:* ⟨-⟩², ⟨1⟩-25⁸.

T cloth: brown. Brown-coated on white end papers. Flyleaves.

Two states (printings?) noted:

1: P. ⟨399⟩ imprinted with an advertisement.

2: P. ⟨399⟩ blank.

Announced as *just issued* APC Sept. 15, 1863. Listed APC Oct. 1, 1863. ALG Oct. 15, 1863, reported that the book had been "republished in London, on the 19th of September, by special arrangement with the author." A copy of the second state deposited for copyright Nov. 13, 1863.

Note: The work appears to have been issued simultaneously in London by Smith, Elder and Company; two volumes. PC Sept. 1, 1863, reported that Smith, Elder "made an arrangement with" Hawthorne for simultaneous publication. Advertised in Ath Sept. 12, 1863, for publication on Sept. 19, 1863. Advertised for *this day* Ath Sept. 19, 1863. Listed Ath Sept. 19, 1863.

Further note regarding the London edition:

The spine stamping of the London edition occurs in two forms. Sequence, if any, not determined. The following designations are for identification only.

A: The statement VOL. I. ⟨II.⟩ stamped from a face in which the component parts are thick and thin.

B: The statement VOL. I. ⟨II.⟩ stamped from a

face in which the component parts are of equal thickness.

H (1st, 2nd)　NYPL (1st, 2nd)　Y (2nd)

7627. PANSIE: A FRAGMENT. THE LAST LITERARY EFFORT OF NATHANIEL HAWTHORNE.

　　LONDON: JOHN CAMDEN HOTTEN, PICCADILLY. ⟨n.d., 1864⟩

⟨1⟩-48; plus: 16 pp. advertisements. $6^{11}/_{16}$″ scant x 4¼″.

⟨A⟩-C⁸, plus: ⟨D⟩⁸.

Printed yellow-coated paper wrapper.

First published *Atlantic Monthly*, July, 1864. Advertised for *this day* (almost surely prematurely) Bkr July 30, 1864. Reviewed Ath Sept. 10, 1864. Listed PC Sept. 15, 1864; Bkr Sept. 30, 1864. For first American book publication see *Good Company*, 1866. Collected in *Dolliver Romance*, 1876, under the title "A Scene from the Dolliver Romance."

H　NYPL　Y

7628. The High Tide, by Jean Ingelow, with Notices of Her Poems.

　　Boston: Roberts Brothers, Publishers, 143 Washington Street. 1864.

Printed paper wrapper.

Two-line comment, p. 3.

EM

7629. Twice-Told Tales ... a New Edition ...

　　Boston: Ticknor and Fields. 1865.

2 Vols. *Blue and Gold* edition.

Reprint save for a note, Vol. 1, p. 264, dated at end *September, 1860*, in which Hawthorne refers to an English review in which it was suggested he had based his "Dr. Heidegger's Experiment" on a story by Alexandre Dumas. Hawthorne, on the basis of irrefutable evidence, dismisses the suggestion. The original note (in H) was sent to James T. Fields under date Sept. 23, 1860, with the request that it be added to future printings of *Twice-Told Tales*. Fields appears not to have acceded to the request until publication of this 1865, *Blue and Gold,* edition.

For earlier editions of *Twice-Told Tales* see above under 1837, 1842, 1851.

LC　Y

7630. Good Company for Every Day in the Year ...

　　Boston: Ticknor and Fields. 1866.

"Little Pansie," pp. ⟨288⟩-304. For earlier publication see *Pansie: A Fragment*, n.d., 1864.

For comment see entry No. 5950.

7631. The Atlantic Almanac 1868 Edited by Oliver Wendell Holmes and Donald G. Mitchell ...

　　Boston: Ticknor and Fields, Office of the Atlantic Monthly ... 1867 ...

Pictorial wrapper.

"Visit to an Old English Abbey," pp. 44-45. Collected in *Passages from the English Note-Books*, 1870, Vol. 1, pp. 186-191, as "Furness Abbey."

For comment see entry No. 266.

7632. PASSAGES FROM THE AMERICAN NOTE-BOOKS OF NATHANIEL HAWTHORNE ...

　　BOSTON: TICKNOR AND FIELDS. 1868.

2 Vols. *See next entry.* Edited by Sophia Hawthorne.

1: ⟨i-ii⟩, ⟨1⟩-222. Laid paper. 7″ full x 4⁷⁄₁₆″.
2: ⟨i-iv⟩, ⟨1⟩-228.

1: ⟨1-9¹², 10⁴⟩. Signed: ⟨-⟩¹, 1-9¹², 10³. *Also signed:* ⟨-⟩¹, A-M⁸, N⁷.
2: ⟨-⟩², 1-9¹², 10⁶. *Also signed:* ⟨-⟩², A-N⁸, O².

Two printings of Vol. 2 have been noted:

1: As above.
2: ⟨i-ii⟩, ⟨1⟩-228, blank leaf. ⟨1-9¹², 10⁸⟩.

The publisher's records show that both volumes were reprinted during Oct. 1868, (the third printing was done in Oct. 1869), but thus far BAL has been unable to note any feature that may distinguish the first from the second printing.

C cloth: green. Brown-coated on white end papers. Flyleaves.

Two bindings noted:

1: With spine imprint: TICKNOR & CO.

2: With spine imprint: FIELDS, OSGOOD & CO

Note: The letter of April 14, 1844 (Vol. 2, pp. 145-147) is out of correct order but no bibliographical significance may be attached to this error which persists through the printing of 1874. The correct order first noted in the *Riverside Edition*, 1883.

Deposited Nov. 10, 1868. The H copy received Nov. 10, 1868. Listed ALG Dec. 1, 1868; PW Jan.

16, 1869. A two-volumes in one format listed ALG Nov. 1, 1871. The London (Smith, Elder) edition, in spite of early notices which suggest publication prior to publication in Boston, was not issued until Nov. 16-21, 1868. The following notes are pertinent: Advertised under *new and recent* PC Oct. 15, 1868. Advertised as *nearly ready* Ath Oct. 31, 1868; as *in a few days* PC Nov. 2, 1868; as *nearly ready* Ath Nov. 7, 1868; as *in a few days* Ath Nov. 14, 1868. Advertised as though ready PC Nov. 16, 1868. Advertised for *this day* Ath Nov. 21, 1868. Listed Ath Nov. 21, 1868; *Spectator* (London), Nov. 21, 1868; PC Dec. 10, 1868.

For a more recent publication of the material see *The American Notebooks . . .* , edited by Randall Stewart, New Haven, 1932.

H (1st)   NYPL (1st)   Y (1st, 2nd)

7633. Passages from the ⟨American⟩ Note-Books of the Late Nathaniel Hawthorne. With an Introduction by Moncure D. Conway . . .

London: John Camden Hotten, Piccadilly. 1869.

Cloth; and, printed paper wrapper. *See preceding entry.*

With the exception of the material on pp. ⟨27⟩-41, reprinted from *Passages from the American Note-Books,* 1868, *above.* The material on pp. ⟨27⟩-41 is here first published in book form; reprinted from *Atlantic Monthly,* July, 1867; collected in *Passages from the English Note-Books,* Boston, 1870, Vol. 1, pp. 201-216.

Advertised as *new,* in cloth, and in printed paper wrapper, Ath Dec. 5, 1868. Listed, paper only, Ath Dec. 5, 1868, with the title given as *Passages from the American Note-Books.* Listed (paper only) PC Dec. 10, 1868. Advertised as *new,* in both cloth, and in printed paper wrapper, PC Dec. 10, 1868; Bkr (paper only) Dec. 12, 1868. Noted PC Jan. 16, 1869, as *just published.* Received BMU March 9, 1869.

CAW (cloth)   Y (paper)

7634. PASSAGES FROM THE ENGLISH NOTE-BOOKS OF NATHANIEL HAW-THORNE . . .

BOSTON: FIELDS, OSGOOD, & CO. 1870.

2 Vols. Edited by Sophia Hawthorne.

1: ⟨i⟩-viii, ⟨1⟩-410, blank leaf. Laid paper. 7″ x 4½″.
2: ⟨i-ii⟩, ⟨1⟩-393.

1: ⟨-⟩⁴, 1-17¹², 18². *Also signed:* ⟨-⟩⁴, A-Y⁸, Z⁶.
2: ⟨1⟩-16¹², 17⁶. *Also signed:* A-X⁸, Y⁶. *Note:* All signature marks in Vol. 2 occur on the second leaf, recto, of the gatherings.

C cloth: green. Brown-coated on white end papers. Laid paper flyleaves.

Advertised for June 4, 1870, ALG May 16, 1870. Deposited June 3, 1870. BA copy received June 6, 1870. Listed ALG June 15, 1870. A one-volume format noted in ALG Oct. 2, 1871. *Note:* Quite probably issued simultaneously in London by Strahan & Company, in two volumes. The following is a record of the London publication: Advertised as *in preparation* Ath March 26, 1870; PC April 1, 1870. Advertised as *in the press* PC May 2, 1870. Advertised for June 4, 1870, Ath May 28, 1870. Advertised as *new* Ath June 11, 1870. Listed Ath June 11, 1870. Noted as a publication of the preceding fortnight PC June 15, 1870. Advertised as *new* PC June 15, 1870. Listed PC July 1, 1870. Reviewed Ath July 2, 1870.

For a more recent (and fuller) publication of the material see *The English Notebooks . . .* , edited by Randall Stewart, New York, 1941.

H   NYPL

7635. PASSAGES FROM THE FRENCH AND ITALIAN NOTE-BOOKS OF NATHANIEL HAWTHORNE . . .

STRAHAN & CO., PUBLISHERS 56 LUDGATE HILL, LONDON 1871

2 Vols. Edited by Una Hawthorne. For Boston edition see next entry.

1: ⟨i-iv⟩, ⟨1⟩-371; plus: Advertisements, pp. ⟨1⟩-4. 7¹³⁄₁₆″ x 5⅛″.
2: ⟨i-iv⟩, ⟨1⟩-368.

1: ⟨A⟩², B-I, K-U, X-Z, AA⁸, BB²; plus: ⟨CC⟩².
2: ⟨A⟩², B-I, K-U, X-Z, AA⁸.

C cloth: blue. Brown-coated on white end papers. Front covers stamped in gold and black. Publisher's device on spine of each volume: Anchor and initials AS. Advertisements at back of Vol. 1.

Note: The binding has been seen in the following forms. The first binding almost surely is the one described above. Sequence for the variant bindings has not been determined.

Binding Variant A

Front covers stamped in blind only. Advertisements bound in at back of Vol. 2. No publisher's device on spine. Copy in Y.

Binding Variant B

Front covers stamped in blind only. Advertisements bound in at back of Vol. 2. Anchor and initials AS on spine. Copy in BPL.

Binding Variant C

Front covers stamped in gold and black. Advertisements bound in at back of Vol. 2. Spine imprint of *Daldy, Isbister & Co.,* a firm not established until 1874. Copy in AAS.

Binding Variant D

Front covers stamped in gold and black. Advertisements bound in at back of Vol. 2. No device, no publisher's imprint on spine. Copy in LC.

Advertised with the title *First Impressions of France,* PC Oct. 1, 1871; Bkr Oct. 3, 1871. Advertised as *nearly ready* Ath Oct. 28, 1871; PC Nov. 1, 1871; Ath Nov. 4, 1871; Bkr Nov. 4, 1871. Advertised as *new* and as though published Ath Nov. 11, 1871; PC Nov. 16, 1871. Received BMU Nov. 17, 1871. Listed Ath Nov. 18, 1871; Bkr Dec. 2, 1871; PC Dec. 8, 1871.

Y

7636. PASSAGES FROM THE FRENCH AND ITALIAN NOTE-BOOKS OF NATHANIEL HAWTHORNE . . .

BOSTON: JAMES R. OSGOOD AND COMPANY, LATE TICKNOR & FIELDS, AND FIELDS, OSGOOD, & CO. 1872.

2 Vols. Edited by Una Hawthorne. For London edition see preceding entry.

1: ⟨i-iv⟩, ⟨1⟩-307. Laid paper. 7″ x 4⅐₁₆″.
2: ⟨i-iv⟩, ⟨1⟩-306, blank leaf.

1: ⟨-⟩², 1-12¹², 13¹⁰. *Also signed:* ⟨-⟩², A-S⁸, T².
2: ⟨-⟩², 1-12¹², 13¹⁰. *Also signed:* ⟨-⟩², A-S⁸, T².

C cloth: green. Brown-coated on white end papers. Flyleaves.

Note: Three states of the stamping have been noted. *State A* is presumed the earliest but no definite sequence has been established.

Binding A

Sides blindstamped with a rules frame, the rule twisted at each inner corner in a grolieresque design to enclose a quatrefoil ornament. The sides are not stamped with a classical male nude figure. Covers not bevelled. Spine goldstamped: NATHANIEL / HAWTHORNE'S / WORKS / FRENCH / AND / ITALIAN / JOURNALS / ⟨rule⟩ / VOL I. ⟨II.⟩ / ⟨all the preceding in a leafy ornament⟩ / ⟨publisher's monogram⟩

Copies thus at H, one being presented by the publisher to H Feb. 27, 1872; another inscribed by Herman Melville, March 23, 1872.

Binding B

Same as *Binding A* but with some slight variations in the stamping on the spine, the most notable variation being the absence of the rule. Noted on Vol. 2 only. Copy in NYPL.

Binding C

Sides blindstamped with a rules frame, the rules intersecting at the corners to form a box enclosing an ivy leaf. Stamped at the center of each side is a nude classical male figure. Spine goldstamped as on *Binding A* but with the following statement present: VOL. 19 ⟨20⟩ Covers bevelled. Copy in H.

Note: The H copy (presented by the publisher) has the following errors marked for correction. The errors occur in all examined copies; the corrections appear for the first time, so far as BAL has been able to determine, in the *Riverside Edition* of 1883.

Vol. 1

P. 106, line 8 up: *ower* for *over*
P. 151, line 3 up: *Laddeback* for *Saddleback*
P. 169, line 10 up: *crowded* for *corroded*
P. 171, line 10 up: *Vinioli* for *Vincoli*
P. 177, line 9: *Hillyard's* for *Hillard's*

Vol. 2

P. 18, line 10: *Bololi* for *Boboli*

Announced for Feb. 24, 1872, in WTC Feb. 15, 1872. Listed WTC March 7, 1872.

H (A,C)   NYPL (A,B)

7637. SEPTIMIUS: A ROMANCE . . .

LONDON: HENRY S. KING & CO., 65 CORNHILL. 1872.

Edited by Una Hawthorne and Robert Browning. For first Boston edition see next entry.

⟨i-iv⟩, ⟨1⟩-298, blank leaf. 7¾″ x 5″ full.

⟨A⟩², B-I, K-T⁸, U⁶.

P cloth: red. Green-coated on white end papers. On p. ⟨4⟩ of the front end paper is an advertisement for *The Life and Unpublished Stories of the Late Nathaniel Hawthorne* which is described as *shortly.* Inserted at back: Publisher's catalog, pp. ⟨1⟩-⟨24⟩, dated *May, 1872.* Top edges gilded. Covers bevelled.

Note: Two issues have been noted:

1: As above. Leaves ⟨A⟩1-2 are conjugate. P. ⟨iii⟩ undated.

2: As above but leaf ⟨A⟩₂ is a cancel. P. ⟨iii⟩ dated at end: *Notting Hill, London: / May 28, 1872.*

Advertised as *in the press* PC May 1, 1872; Ath May 4, 1872. Noted as *in a few days* PC May 16, 1872; as *next week* Ath May 18, 1872, May 25, 1872; as *this day* Ath June 1, 1872. Listed Ath June 8, 1872. Reviewed Ath June 22, 1872; PC July 1, 1872. Listed PC July 1, 1872.

H (1st, 2nd)   NYPL (2nd)

7638. SEPTIMIUS FELTON; OR THE
ELIXIR OF LIFE ...

BOSTON: JAMES R. OSGOOD AND COMPANY. 1872.

Edited by Una Hawthorne and Robert Browning. For first London edition see preceding entry.

⟨i-vi⟩, ⟨1⟩-229; blank, p. ⟨230⟩; plus: 1 page advertisements, blank leaf. 7″ x 4½″.

⟨1², 2-10¹², 11⁸; plus: 12²⟩. Signed: ⟨-⟩³, ⟨1⟩-9¹², 10⁷, ⟨11⟩². Also signed: ⟨-⟩³, ⟨A⟩-N⁸, O³, ⟨P⟩².

C cloth: green; terra-cotta. T cloth (moiréd): blue. V cloth: green; terra-cotta. Brown-coated on white end papers. Flyleaves.

Note: Not before 1880 unsold sheets were issued in S cloth. These occur in two states; sequence, if any, not determined:

A: With the spine imprint of Houghton, Mifflin & Co.

B: Publisher's spine imprint not present.

A copy in H received from the publisher July 23, 1872. Listed WTC July 25, 1872. A copy in H inscribed by early owner Aug. 1, 1872.

H (1st)   NYPL (1st; secondary bindings A, B)

7639. Memoir of Nathaniel Hawthorne with Stories Now First Published in This Country by H. A. Page ⟨i.e., Alexander Hay Japp⟩

London   Henry S. King & Co., 65 Cornhill 1872

Reprint save for:

"The Duston Family," pp. 225-237. Collected in Complete Writings, Vol. 17, (entry No. 7645). "April Fools," pp. 238-242. Uncollected.

"A Prize from the Sea," pp. 282-301. A version of "The Sunken Treasure," Grandfather's Chair, 1841. Wilson (Thirteen Author Collections of the Nineteenth Century ..., Vol. 1, p. 151) errs in identifying "A Prize from the Sea" with "Sir William Phips."

Announced in PC Oct. 1, 1872. Noted as shortly Ath Oct. 12, 1872; as just ready Ath Nov. 9, 1872. Listed Ath Nov. 16, 1872.

BA   NYPL   Y

7640. THE DOLLIVER ROMANCE AND OTHER PIECES ...

BOSTON: JAMES R. OSGOOD AND COMPANY. 1876.

Edited by Sophia Hawthorne.

⟨1⟩-213, blank leaf. 7″ x 4½″.

⟨1-9⟩¹². Signed: ⟨1⟩-2, ⟨3-7⟩, 8-18⁶. Signature mark 17 on p. 191.

C cloth: green. Covers bevelled; or, plain; sequence (if any) not known but a surviving copyright deposit copy has bevelled covers. Brown-coated on white end papers. Flyleaves.

Noted for June 24 PW June 17, 1876. Noted for this week PW June 24, 1876. Listed PW June 24, 1876.

H   NYPL

7641. FANSHAWE AND OTHER PIECES ...

BOSTON: JAMES R. OSGOOD AND COMPANY. 1876.

For first publication of "Fanshawe" see above under 1828.

⟨1⟩-243. 7″ x 4½″.

⟨1-10¹², 11²⟩. Signed: ⟨1-8⟩, 9, ⟨10-11⟩, 12-15, ⟨16⟩, 17-19, ⟨20⟩⁶, 21².

C cloth: green. Covers bevelled; or, plain; sequence (if any) not known but a surviving copyright deposit copy has bevelled covers. Brown-coated on white end papers. Flyleaves.

Noted for June 24 PW June 17, 1876. Noted for this week PW June 24, 1876. Listed PW June 24, 1876.

H   NYPL

7642. DOCTOR GRIMSHAWE'S SECRET A ROMANCE ... EDITED, WITH PREFACE AND NOTES BY JULIAN HAWTHORNE

BOSTON   JAMES R. OSGOOD AND COMPANY   1883

Trade Edition

⟨i-ii⟩, ⟨i⟩-⟨xiv⟩, ⟨1⟩-368. 4-page facsimile manuscript inserted. 7½″ x 4¹³⁄₁₆″ (trimmed). 7¹⁵⁄₁₆″ x 5⅛″ (untrimmed). A note in an untrimmed copy in NYPL suggests that but thirteen copies were prepared in untrimmed condition; further information wanting.

⟨1⁸, 2-16¹², 17⁴⟩. Signed: ⟨-⟩⁸, 1-23⁸.

V cloth: gray; gray-green. White laid paper end papers.

Note: According to the publisher's records the first printing (Dec. 1882) comprised 5022 copies; and, a second printing (March, 1883) comprised 516 copies. BAL has discovered no variations that may be useful in identifying the two printings.

Large Paper Edition

⟨i-ii⟩, ⟨i⟩-⟨xiv⟩, ⟨1⟩-368. Printed on handmade laid paper watermarked: John Dickinson & Co. Inserted: Frontispiece, vignette title-page, 4-page facsimile manuscript. 9¾″ scant x 6″ full.

⟨1-2², 3-49⁴⟩. Signed: ⟨-⟩⁸, 1-23⁸.

Gray-white paper boards, printed paper label on spine: Hawthorne's Works / Large Paper / Illustrated with Etchings / ⟨rule⟩ / DOCTOR

GRIMSHAWE'S / SECRET/ White laid paper end papers.

"Two Hundred and Fifty Copies Printed. No. . . ."—Certificate of issue.

Note: According to the publisher's records the *Large Paper Edition* was not printed until Oct. 1883, about ten months after printing of the first trade edition; 273 copies printed.

Noted for *this week* PW Dec. 16, 1882. A copy received by BA Dec. 20, 1882. Listed PW Dec. 23, 1882. The London (Longmans) edition may have been published simultaneously with the Boston edition; or, issued a few days prior; it was advertised as *now ready* Ath Dec. 16, 1882; listed Ath Dec. 16, 1882.

CAW (trade; large paper) NYPL (trade; untrimmed)

7643. ⟨Writings of Nathaniel Hawthorne. Riverside Edition⟩

Boston   Houghton, Mifflin and Company   New York: 11 East Seventeenth Street   The Riverside Press, Cambridge 1883

12 Vols. Edited by George Parsons Lathrop. Issued in a variety of bindings.

1: *Twice-Told Tales.*
Reprint. Advertised for Jan. 20 PW Jan. 13, 1883. Deposited Jan. 19, 1883. Listed PW Jan. 20, 1883.

2: *Mosses from an Old Manse.*
Reprint. Advertised for Jan. 20 PW Jan. 13, 1883. Listed PW Jan. 20, 1883. Deposited April 16, 1883.

3: *The House of the Seven Gables . . . The Snow Image and Other Twice-Told Tales.*
Reprint. Deposited Feb. 16, 1883. Advertised for Feb. 17 PW Feb. 10, 1883. Listed PW Feb. 17, 1883.

4: *A Wonder-Book   Tanglewood Tales . . . Grandfather's Chair.*
Reprint. Deposited Feb. 17, 1883. Advertised for Feb. 17 PW Feb. 10, 1883. Listed PW Feb. 17, 1883.

5: *The Scarlet Letter . . . The Blithedale Romance.*
Reprint. Deposited March 18, 1883. Advertised for March 21 PW March 10, 1883. Listed PW March 24, 1883.

6: *The Marble Faun.*
Reprint. Deposited March 18, 1883. Advertised for March 21 PW March 10, 1883. Listed PW March 24, 1883.

7-8: *Our Old Home . . . English Note-Books.*
Reprint. Advertised for April 14 PW April 7, 1883. Deposited April 16, 1883. Listed PW April 21, 1883.

9: *Passages from the American Note-Books.*
Reprint. Deposited May 19, 1883. Noted for *next week* PW May 19, 1883. Listed PW May 26, 1883.

10: *Passages from the French and Italian Note-Books.*
Reprint. Deposited May 21, 1883. Noted for *next week* PW May 19, 1883. Listed PW May 26, 1883.

11: *The Dolliver Romance   Fanshawe . . . Septimius Felton . . . Ancestral Footstep.*
Reprint save for "The Ancestral Footstep." Advertised for June 16 PW June 9, 1883. Deposited June 18, 1883. Listed PW June 23, 1883.

12: *Tales, Sketches, and Other Papers.*
Reprint save for the first collected appearance of "Alice Doane's Appeal," which had prior book publication in *The Token*, 1835; and, earliest located book publication of "Chiefly About War Matters." Advertised for June 16 PW June 9, 1883. Deposited June 18, 1883. Listed PW June 23, 1883.

Note: A large paper edition, limited to 250 copies, has been reported but not seen.

NYPL

7644. THE GHOST OF DOCTOR HARRIS . . .

⟨New York: The Tucker Publishing Co., 1900⟩

⟨1⟩-13, blank leaf. 7⅞″ x 5½″.

⟨-⟩⁸.

Printed olive-drab paper wrapper.

Issued as *The Balzac Library*, No. 1, under date of Feb. 19, 1900.

H   NYPL

7645. ⟨The Complete Writings. Autograph Edition⟩

Boston and New York   Houghton, Mifflin and Company   The Riverside Press, Cambridge MDCCCC

22 Vols. Cloth, printed paper label on spine. 500 numbered copies only, signed by Rose Hawthorne Lathrop and the publishers.

Note: Although deposited for copyright during the years 1900 and 1901 (see individual entries for dates) each volume is dated MDCCCC.

1: *Twice-Told Tales. Vol. 1.*
Deposited Dec. 20, 1900. Reprint.

2: *Twice-Told Tales. Vol. 2.*
Deposited Dec. 20, 1900. Reprint.

3: *The Snow Image and Other Twice-Told Tales.*
Deposited Dec. 20, 1900. Reprint.

4: *Mosses from an Old Manse. Vol. 1.*
Deposited Dec. 20, 1900. Reprint.

5: *Mosses from an Old Manse. Vol. 2.*
Deposited Dec. 20, 1900. Reprint.

6: *The Scarlet Letter.*
Deposited Dec. 20, 1900. Reprint.

7: *The House of the Seven Gables.*
Deposited Dec. 20, 1900. Reprint.

8: *The Blithedale Romance.*
Deposited Dec. 20, 1900. Reprint.

9: *The Marble Faun. Vol. 1.*
Deposited March 5, 1901. Reprint.

10: *The Marble Faun. Vol. 2.*
Deposited March 5, 1901. Reprint.

11: *Our Old Home.*
Deposited March 5, 1901. Reprint.

12: *The Whole History of Grandfather's Chair and Biographical Stories.*
Deposited Dec. 20, 1900. Reprint.

13: *A Wonder Book for Girls and Boys and Tanglewood Tales.*
Deposited Dec. 20, 1900. Reprint.

14: *The Dolliver Romance and Kindred Tales.*
Deposited Dec. 20, 1900. Reprint.

15: *Doctor Grimshawe's Secret.*
Deposited March 5, 1901. Reprint.

16: *Tales and Sketches.*
Deposited March 5, 1901. Reprint save for: "The Young Provincial," which had prior publication in *The Token*, 1830, *q.v.*

"The Haunted Quack," which had prior publication in *The Token*, 1831, *q.v.*

"The New England Village," which had prior publication in *The Token*, 1831, *q.v.*

Also contains "The Bald Eagle"; sometimes attributed to Hawthorne. See note regarding this under entry No. 7574.

17: *Miscellanies Biographical and Other Sketches and Letters.*
Deposited March 5, 1901. Reprint save for: First collected appearance of Hawthorne's preface to Delia Bacon's *Philosophy of the Plays of Shakspere Unfolded;* see above under 1857.

First book publication of:

"An Ontario Steamboat"

"Nature of Sleep"

"Bells"

"Hints to Young Ambition"

A group of letters gathered from various sources and printed at pp. 421-439.

And: "The Duston Family," which is here in its earliest located American book appearance. For an earlier book appearance see *Memoir of Nathaniel Hawthorne with Stories . . .* , London, 1872.

18: *Passages from the American Note-Books.*
Deposited March 5, 1901. Reprint.*

19: *Notes of Travel. Vol. 1.*
Deposited March 5, 1901. Reprint.*

20: *Notes of Travel. Vol. 2.*
Deposited March 5, 1901. Reprint.*

21: *Notes of Travel. Vol. 3.*
Deposited March 5, 1901. Reprint.*

22: *Notes of Travel. Vol. 4.*
Deposited March 5, 1901. Reprint.*

LC

7646. TWENTY DAYS WITH JULIAN AND LITTLE BUNNY A DIARY BY NATHANIEL HAWTHORNE NOW FIRST PRINTED FROM THE ORIGINAL MANUSCRIPT

NEW YORK   PRIVATELY PRINTED   1904

⟨i-viii⟩, ⟨1⟩-85; leaf excised. Frontispiece mounted to p. ⟨2⟩. Facsimile (2 leaves) of a Longfellow letter inserted. Van Gelder laid paper. 9¼" x 6⅛". See immediately below for comment on first and final leaves.

⟨1⁴, 2-3², 4-13⁴⟩. Leaves ⟨1⟩₁ and ⟨13⟩₄ excised or pasted under the end paper.

Gray laid paper boards sides, buff V cloth shelfback. Printed paper label on front. Leaf ⟨1⟩₂ used as front pastedown. True end paper at back of Van Gelder.

Thirty Copies Only Printed.—Certificate of issue. *Note:* Actually thirty-one copies were produced. The book was privately printed for Stephen H. Wakeman and according to a note laid into his own copy (now NYPL) thirty copies were printed on Van Gelder and one copy on vellum. The copy on vellum now in NYPL. Still according to Wakeman's note, all but six of the Van Gelder copies were presented to libraries or to individuals; the six copies not thus distributed were sold at $40.00 each by Dodd, Mead & Company, New York.

". . . a small portion . . . already . . . printed in the form of extracts in *Nathaniel Hawthorne and His Wife . . .*"—p. ⟨5⟩.

* These are the travel note-books. BAL has not compared the texts and merely assumes that the statement *reprint* is correct.

Deposited Dec. 12, 1904.

H NYPL

7647. LOVE LETTERS OF NATHANIEL
HAWTHORNE . . .

PRIVATELY PRINTED   THE SOCIETY OF THE
DOFOBS CHICAGO 1907

2 Vols. Title-pages in black and blue.

1: ⟨i⟩-⟨xii⟩, ⟨1⟩-248; DeVinne Press device, p.
⟨249⟩; 3 blank leaves. Laid paper. Frontispiece
inserted. Also inserted is a 4-page facsimile letter. 9⅛″ x 6¹⁄₁₆″.
2: ⟨i-viii⟩, ⟨1⟩-285; DeVinne Press device, p.
⟨286⟩; blank leaf. Four-page facsimile letter
inserted.

1: ⟨1⁶, 2-17⁸⟩.
2: ⟨1⁴, 2-19⁸⟩.

Gray cartridge paper sides, vellum shelfback and
corners. Vol. 1: At front, end papers of book
stock, single flyleaf of book stock; at back:
Leaf ⟨17⟩₈ used as pastedown. Vol. 2: At both
front and at back, end papers of book stock,
single flyleaf of book stock.

". . . Sixty-Two Copies . . . Printed . . . April,
Nineteen Hundred And Seven."—Certificate of
issue.

Deposited July 5, 1907.

H NYPL

7648. LETTERS OF HAWTHORNE TO
WILLIAM D. TICKNOR . . .

NEWARK NEW JERSEY THE CARTERET BOOK
CLUB 1910

2 Vols.

1: ⟨i-vi⟩, ⟨i⟩-⟨xii⟩, ⟨1⟩-123; blank leaf; leaf excised or pasted under the end paper. Facsimile
in text. Laid paper. 7″ x 4½″.
2: ⟨i-xvi⟩, ⟨1⟩-130; printer's imprint, p. ⟨131⟩;
blank leaf; leaf excised or pasted under the end
paper. Facsimile in text.

1: ⟨1⁸, 2², 3-10⁸⟩. Leaves ⟨1⟩₁ and ⟨10⟩₈ excised or pasted under the end paper.
2: ⟨1-9⁸, 10⁴⟩. Leaves ⟨1⟩₁ and ⟨10⟩₄ excised
or pasted under the end paper.

Three-quarters buff T cloth, olive-green laid
paper boards sides, engraved paper label on
spine. End papers of book stock.

"The Marion Press certifies that only one hun-
dred copies . . . have been printed . . . begun in
August, 1909, and completed in April, 1910.
This copy is number . . ."—Certificate of issue.
Note: The certificate of issue is printed on leaf
⟨1⟩₄, Vol. I, and is a cancel.

Deposited July 18, 1910.

H NYPL

7649. The Yarn of a Yankee Privateer Edited
by Nathaniel Hawthorne Introduction by
Clifford Smyth

Funk & Wagnalls Company New York and
London 1926

⟨i⟩-⟨xviii⟩, ⟨1⟩-308, blank leaf. Frontispiece
and 9 single plates inserted; 2 2-page facsimiles
inserted. 7⅜″ x 5″.

On copyright page: *Published, April, 1926.*
Listed PW May 8, 1926.

Reprinted from USDR Jan.–Sept. 1846. Presumed
author: Benjamin Frederick Browne, 1793–1873.
For a discussion of the authorship, and of Hawthorne's part in the publication, see *Essex Institute Historical Collections*, Vol. 13, Part II,
April, 1875.

H NYPL Y

7650. THE HEART OF HAWTHORNE'S
JOURNALS EDITED BY NEWTON
ARVIN

BOSTON AND NEW YORK HOUGHTON MIFFLIN
COMPANY THE RIVERSIDE PRESS CAMBRIDGE
1929

⟨i⟩-⟨xvi⟩, ⟨1⟩-345, blank leaf. Frontispiece inserted. 7⅞″ scant x 5⅜″.

⟨1-22⁸, 23⁶⟩.

T cloth: black-green. Top edges stained green.

Note: In addition to the trade edition some
copies were issued untrimmed. Leaf: 8¼″ x 5½″.
Bound in red V cloth, printed paper label on
spine. Edges plain.

Listed PW April 20, 1929. NYPL copy received
April 22, 1929. Deposited April 24, 1929.

AAS (red V) B NYPL

7651. HAWTHORNE AS EDITOR SELEC-
TIONS FROM HIS WRITINGS IN THE
AMERICAN MAGAZINE OF USEFUL AND
ENTERTAINING KNOWLEDGE BY AR-
LIN TURNER

LOUISIANA STATE UNIVERSITY PRESS UNIVERSITY,
LOUISIANA 1941

⟨i⟩-⟨viii⟩, 1-290, blank leaf. 9″ x 6″.

⟨1-17⁸, 18⁶, 19⁸⟩.

Blue balloon cloth.

Issued as *Louisiana State University Studies,
Number 42.*

H copy received April 22, 1941. Deposited May
12, 1941.

B H

IN THIS SECTION the following classifications are listed: *Collections* of reprinted material issued under the author's name; *separate* editions; and *undated* reprints. See *Section Three* for a list of books by others containing material by Hawthorne reprinted from earlier books.

7651A. The ⟨*sic*⟩ Rill from the Town Pump.

London, 1841?

Not located. Entry on the basis of the following note in Arc May, 1841: "*The Rill from the Town Pump*, the best known of Hawthorne's sketches, was stolen by a cunning London bookseller, the author's name omitted, and circulated as a temperance tract."

The sketch was first collected in *Twice-Told Tales*, 1837; issued as a separate in 1857. See entry No. 7657.

7651B. Famous Old People: Being the Second Epoch of Grandfather's Chair . . .

Boston: Tappan & Dennet, 114 Washington Street. 1842.

Deposited Dec. 23, 1841.

7652. Hawthorne's Historical Tales for Youth.

⟨Boston: Tappan & Dennet, 1842?⟩

Binder's title. A 2-volume set made up of the sheets of *Grandfather's Chair*, 1842; *Famous Old People*, 1842; *Liberty Tree*, 1842; *Biographical Stories*, 1842. A copy of Vol. 1 in Y inscribed by early owner Dec. 25, 1843.

7653. Mosses from an Old Manse . . . New Edition.

New York: George P. Putnam, 155 Broadway. 1850.

Noted as *in press* LW July 20, 1850. Advertised for *this week* LW Aug. 3, 1850.

7654. Twice Told Tales . . .

London: William Tegg and Co., 85, Queen Street, Cheapside. 1850.

7655. True Stories from History and Biography . . .

Boston: Ticknor, Reed, and Fields. M DCCC LI.

Three impressions noted:

1

Pp. 335.

Copyright notice dated 1850.

Bolles and Houghton imprint on copyright page.

P. ⟨iii⟩, line 3 from bottom: . . . *in the way with* . . .

P. ⟨iv⟩, line 8 from bottom: . . . *but which he* . . .

Signature mark *a**, p. ⟨iii⟩, set immediately below . . . *for a* . . .

2

Pp. 335.

Copyright notice dated 1850.

Bolles and Houghton imprint on copyright page.

P. ⟨iii⟩, line 3 from bottom: . . . *in the way, with* . . .

P. ⟨iv⟩, line 8 from bottom: . . . *but which, he* . . .

Signature mark *a**, p. ⟨iii⟩, set immediately below . . . *seat.*

3

Pp. 343.

Copyright notice dated 1851.

Thurston, Torry, and Emerson imprint on copyright page.

P. ⟨iii⟩, line 3 from bottom: . . . *in the way with* . . .

P. ⟨iv⟩, line 7 from bottom: . . . *but which, he* . . .

No signature mark on p. ⟨iii⟩.

Note: This third printing is completely reset.

Advertised for Nov. 16, 1850, LW Nov. 16, 1850. Deposited Nov. 22, 1850. Listed LW Nov. 30,

1850. The London (Low) edition listed Ath Dec. 25, 1852.

7655A. A Visit to the Celestial City. Revised by the Committee of Publication of the American Sunday-School Union.

> Philadelphia: American Sunday-School Union, No. 146 Chestnut Street. ⟨n.d., 1852⟩

Anonymous. A revised reprint ("revised by the Committee of Publication of the American Sunday-School Union") of Hawthorne's *The Celestial Rail-Road*, 1843.

Cloth; also, marbled boards, leather shelfback.

Note: There were several, perhaps many, printings of this publication. No attempt has been made to establish a sequence and the following designations are for identification only.

A: Illustrations in lithograph. Imprint of King & Baird on reverse of title-page.

B: Illustrations in lithograph. Reverse of title-page blank. 10 pp. advertisements at back.

C: Illustrations in lithograph. Reverse of title-page blank. No advertisements at back.

D: Illustrations printed from wood.

Also note: Copies issued with the publisher's address *1122 Chestnut Street* were published not before 1857.

Listed LW March 27, 1852.

7656. The Canterbury Pilgrims, and Other Twice-Told Tales ...

> London: Published by Knight & Son, 11, Clerkenwell Close. ⟨n.d., 1852?⟩

Reprint with the quite doubtful exception of "Little Daffydowndilly" which also appears in *The Snow-Image and Other Tales*, 1851; see entries 7605 and 7607.

BAL has been unable to establish a positive publication date for this Knight publication but it is presumed to be a reprint. Though proof is wanting there is inferential evidence that Knight & Son was not in existence before December, 1851, during which month *The Snow-Image and Other Tales* was issued in both London and in Boston, entries 7605 and 7607.

7656A. Little Annie's Ramble, and Other Tales ...

> Halifax: Milner and Sowerby. 1853.

7657. A Rill from the Town Pump ... with Remarks by Telba.

> Published for the Albion Society, by W. and F. G. Cash, 5, Bishopsgate Without. 1857. Price Twopence.

Cover-title. Printed paper wrapper. See entry No. 7651A.

7658. *Entry cancelled.*

7659. The Celestial Railroad ... with Additions and Alterations.

> Boston: Published by J. V. Himes, 99 Springfield Street. 1860.

Cover-title. Printed self-wrapper. The "alterations" presumably not by Hawthorne.

7660. The Snow-Image: A Childish Miracle ...

> New York: James G. Gregory, 540, Broadway. M DCCC LXIV.

A London (Low) edition was advertised for *next week* Ath Nov. 26, 1865; listed Ath Nov. 26, 1865.

7661. Nathaniel Hawthorne's Tales. In Two Volumes ...

> London: Bell & Daldy, 6, York Street, Covent Garden, and 186, Fleet Street. 1866.

Not seen. Vol. 1 listed PC Aug. 1, 1866. Vol. 2 advertised as *ready* Bkr Aug. 31, 1866. Deposited BMU Sept. 10, 1866.

7662. ... Celestial Railroad; or, Modern Pilgrim's Progress. After the Manner of Bunyan ... with Additions and Alterations.

> Buchanan, Michigan: Published by the W.A.C.P. Association. 1867.

Printed paper wrapper. An adaptation of *The Celestial Rail-Road*, 1843. At head of title: *Advent Tracts (Western Series)—No. 16*.

7663. Nathaniel Hawthorne's Tales ... ⟨erasure⟩ Twice Told Tales, First and Second Series; Snow Image, and Other Tales.

> London: Bell & Daldy, 6, York Street, Covent Garden, and 186, Fleet Street. 1866. ⟨i.e., ca. 1868⟩

An omnibus volume made up of the sheets of *Twice-Told Tales*, first and second series, London (Bohn), 1851; and *The Snow-Image, and Other Tales*, London (Bell & Daldy), 1868.

The only located copy has been rebound and BAL is therefore unable to state whether or not the three volumes here presented as a single unit were issued thus. It will be observed, and perhaps wondered at, that while the general title-page is dated 1866 there is also present a separate title-page for *The Snow-Image ...*, which is dated 1868.

This volume must be viewed with suspicion. It could be that it is part of a two-volume publication and that the erasure removed the statement *Vol. 1* ⟨2⟩.

7664. The Scarlet Letter . . .

Boston: James R. Osgood and Company, Late Ticknor & Fields, and Fields, Osgood, & Co. 1875.

Little Classic Edition, Vol. 6. 5⅞″ x 4⅛″. Deposited Oct. 22, 1874.

7665. Fanshawe, and Other Pieces . . .

Boston: James R. Osgood and Company, Late Ticknor & Fields, and Fields, Osgood, & Co. 1876.

Little Classic Edition, Vol. 22. 5⅞″ x 4⅛″. Listed PW Sept. 23, 1876.

7666. The Dolliver Romance, and Other Pieces . . .

Boston: James R. Osgood and Company, Late Ticknor & Fields, and Fields, Osgood, & Co. 1876.

Little Classic Edition, Vol. 23. 5⅞″ x 4⅛″. Listed PW Oct. 7, 1876.

7667. The Blithedale Romance . . .

Boston: James R. Osgood and Company, Late Ticknor & Fields, and Fields, Osgood, & Co. 1876.

Little Classic Edition, Vol. 8. 5⅞″ x 4⅛″.

7668. The House of the Seven Gables . . .

Boston: James R. Osgood and Company, Late Ticknor & Fields, and Fields, Osgood, & Co. 1876.

Little Classic Edition, Vol. 7. 5⅞″ x 4⅛″.

7669. The Marble Faun . . .

Boston: James R. Osgood and Company, Late Ticknor & Fields, and Fields, Osgood, & Co. 1876.

Little Classic Edition, Vols. 9-10. 5⅞″ x 4⅛″.

7670. Mosses from an Old Manse . . .

Boston: James R. Osgood and Company, Late Ticknor & Fields, and Fields, Osgood, & Co. 1876.

Little Classic Edition, Vols. 4-5. 5⅞″ x 4⅛″.

7671. Our Old Home . . .

Boston: James R. Osgood and Company, Late Ticknor & Fields, and Fields, Osgood, & Co. 1876.

Little Classic Edition, Vol. 11. 5⅞″ x 4⅛″.

7672. Passages from the American Note-Books . . .

Boston: James R. Osgood and Company, Late Ticknor & Fields, and Fields, Osgood, & Co. 1876.

Little Classic Edition, Vols. 15-16. 5⅞″ x 4⅛″.

7673. Passages from the English Note-Books . . .

Boston: James R. Osgood and Company, Late Ticknor & Fields, and Fields, Osgood, & Co. 1876.

Little Classic Edition, Vols. 17-18. 5⅞″ x 4⅛″.

7674. Passages from the French and Italian Note-Books . . .

Boston: James R. Osgood and Company, Late Ticknor & Fields, and Fields, Osgood, & Co. 1876.

Little Classic Edition, Vols. 19-20. 5⅞″ x 4⅛″.

7675. Septimius Felton . . .

Boston: James R. Osgood and Company, Late Ticknor & Fields, and Fields, Osgood, & Co. 1876.

Little Classic Edition, Vol. 21. 5⅞″ x 4⅛″.

7676. The Snow-Image . . .

Boston: James R. Osgood and Company, Late Ticknor & Fields, and Fields, Osgood, & Co. 1876.

Little Classic Edition, Vol. 3. 5⅞″ x 4⅛″.

7677. Tanglewood Tales . . .

Boston: James R. Osgood and Company, Late Ticknor & Fields, and Fields, Osgood, & Co. 1876.

Little Classic Edition, Vol. 14. 5⅞″ x 4⅛″.

7678. True Stories from History and Biography . . .

Boston: James R. Osgood and Company, Late Ticknor & Fields, and Fields, Osgood, & Co. 1876.

Little Classic Edition, Vol. 12. 5⅞″ x 4⅛″.

7679. Twice-Told Tales . . .

Boston: James R. Osgood and Company, Late Ticknor & Fields, and Fields, Osgood, & Co. 1876.

Little Classic Edition, Vols. 1-2. 5⅞" x 4⅛".

7680. A Wonder-Book . . .

Boston: James R. Osgood and Company, Late Ticknor & Fields, and Fields, Osgood, & Co. 1876.

Little Classic Edition, Vol. 13. 5⅞" x 4⅛".

7681. Legends of the Province House . . .

Boston: James R. Osgood and Company, Late Ticknor and Fields, and Fields, Oogood ⟨sic⟩, & Co. 1877.

Listed PW June 16, 1877. The London (Scott) edition issued Nov. 1894.

7682. Tales of the White Hills . . .

Boston: James R. Osgood and Company, Late Ticknor and Fields, and Fields, Osgood, & Co. 1877.

Listed PW June 23, 1877.

7683. Legends of New England . . .

Boston: James R. Osgood and Company, Late Ticknor and Fields, and Fields, Osgood, & Co. 1877.

Listed PW June 30, 1877.

7684. A Virtuoso's Collection, and Other Tales . . .

Boston: James R. Osgood and Company, Late Ticknor & Fields, and Fields, Osgood, & Co. 1877.

Listed PW July 14, 1877.

7685. Famous Stories by de Quincy ⟨sic⟩, Hawthorne . . . and Others . . . in Two Vols. . . .

New York: R. Worthington, 750 Broadway. 1878.

BA copy received June 26, 1878.

7686. . . . Hawthorne. By James T. Fields. Tales of the White Hills, Legends of New England, by Nathaniel Hawthorne . . .

Boston: Houghton, Mifflin and Company. The Riverside Press, Cambridge. ⟨1879; *i.e.*, not before 1880⟩

At head of title: *Modern Classics*. An omnibus volume printed from the plates of James T.

Fields's *Hawthorne*, 1876; and Hawthorne's *Tales of the White Hills*, 1877; and, *Legends of New England*, 1877.

7687. Works of Nathaniel Hawthorne. Globe Edition . . .

Boston: Houghton, Mifflin and Company. The Riverside Press, Cambridge. 1881.

6 Vols.

7688. American Classics for Schools ⟨Selections from⟩ Hawthorne

Boston Houghton, Mifflin and Company New York: 11 East Seventeenth Street The Riverside Press, Cambridge 1882

Advertised for April 18, 1882, PW April 15, 1882. Listed PW April 29, 1882. Deposited May 11, 1882.

7689. The New Adam and Eve . . . Being Second Series of Mosses from an Old Manse . . .

Edinburgh: William Paterson. 1883.

7690. . . . True Stories from New England History 1620–1692 . . . Grandfather's Chair Part I . . .

Houghton, Mifflin and Company Boston: 4 Park Street; New York: 11 East Seventeenth Street The Riverside Press, Cambridge 1883

At head of title: *The Riverside Literature Series* Printed paper wrapper. Issued as No. 7 of the series. Deposited May 21, 1883. Listed PW June 2, 1883.

7691. . . . True Stories from New England History 1692–1763 . . . Grandfather's Chair Part II . . .

Houghton, Mifflin and Company Boston: 4 Park Street; New York: 11 East Seventeenth Street The Riverside Press, Cambridge 1883

At head of title: *The Riverside Literature Series* Printed paper wrapper. Issued as No. 8 of the series. Deposited June 11, 1883. Listed PW June 23, 1883.

7692. . . . True Stories from New England History 1763–1803 . . . Grandfather's Chair Part III . . .

Houghton, Mifflin and Company Boston: 4 Park Street; New York: 11 East Seventeenth Street The Riverside Press, Cambridge 1883

At head of title: *The Riverside Literature Series* Printed paper wrapper. Issued as No. 9 of the series. Deposited June 11, 1883. Listed PW June 23, 1883.

7693. . . . Biographical Stories . . .

Houghton, Mifflin and Company Boston: 4 Park Street; New York: 11 East Seventeenth Street The Riverside Press, Cambridge 1883

At head of title: *The Riverside Literature Series* Printed paper wrapper. Issued as No. 10 of the series. Advertised for June 16, 1883, PW June 9, 1883. Listed PW June 23, 1883. Deposited Dec. 3, 1883. The London (Sonnenschein) edition listed PC Oct. 15, 1883.

7694. Sketches and Studies . . .

Boston: Houghton, Mifflin and Company. The Riverside Press, Cambridge. ⟨1883⟩

Little Classic Edition, Vol. 24. 5¾″ x 4¼″. Deposited Oct. 13, 1883. Listed PW Nov. 24, 1883.

7695. The Scarlet Letter, a Romance . . .

Edinburgh: William Paterson. ⟨n.d., 1883⟩

Listed PC May 15, 1883.

7696. . . . Little Daffydowndilly and Other Stories . . .

Houghton, Mifflin and Company Boston . . . New York . . . The Riverside Press, Cambridge 1887

At head of title: *The Riverside Literature Series* Printed paper wrapper. Issued as No. 29 of the series. Deposited Oct. 19, 1887.

7697. . . . Tales of the White Hills and Sketches . . .

Houghton, Mifflin and Company Boston . . . New York . . . The Riverside Press, Cambridge 1889

At head of title: *The Riverside Literature Series* Printed paper wrapper. Issued as No. 40 of the series. Deposited Feb. 23, 1889. Noted as *ready* PW Feb. 23, 1889. Listed PW May 4, 1889.

7698. . . . The Gray Champion and Other Stories and Sketches . . .

Boston and New York Houghton, Mifflin and Company The Riverside Press, Cambridge 1889

At head of title: *The Riverside Aldine Series.* Cloth, printed paper label on spine. Listed PW Oct. 12, 1889.

7699. Footprints on the Seashore . . .

Boston Samuel E Cassino MDCCCXCII

Imitation vellum binding. Deposited Dec. 19, 1891.

7700. . . . The Old Manse and a Few Mosses . . .

Houghton, Mifflin and Company Boston: 4 Park Street; New York: 11 East Seventeenth Street Chicago: 28 Lakeside Building The Riverside Press, Cambridge ⟨1894⟩

At head of title: *The Riverside Literature Series* Printed paper wrapper. Issued as No. 69 of the series. Issued under date Dec. 5, 1894. Deposited Jan. 14, 1895.

7701. . . . The Whole History of Grandfather's Chair or True Stories from New England History, 1620–1803 . . .

Houghton, Mifflin and Company Boston: 4 Park Street; New York: 11 East Seventeenth Street Chicago: 158 Adams Street The Riverside Press, Cambridge ⟨1896⟩

At head of title: *The Riverside Literature Series* Deposited Aug. 31, 1896. Reprint of entries 7690, 7691, 7692.

7702. Colonial Stories . . .

Boston Joseph Knight 1897

Deposited Nov. 13, 1896. The London (Sands) edition listed PC Nov. 12, 1898.

7703. Little Masterpieces Edited by Bliss Perry . . . Dr. Heidegger's Experiment . . .

New York Doubleday & McClure Co. 1897

7704. The New Adam and Eve . . . June 19, 1899 . . .

F. Tennyson Neely, Publisher, London. New York. Chicago.

Printed paper wrapper. Issued as *Neely's Booklet Library,* No. 25.

7705. . . . The Custom House and Main Street . . .

Houghton, Mifflin and Company Boston: 4 Park Street; New York: 11 East Seventeenth Street Chicago: 378-388 Wabash Avenue The Riverside Press, Cambridge ⟨1899⟩

At head of title: *The Riverside Literature Series* Printed paper wrapper. Issued under date Dec. 6, 1899, as No. 138 of the series. Deposited Feb. 6, 1900.

7706. Ethan Brand by Nathaniel Hawthorne The Chambered Nautilus by Oliver Wendell Holmes

The Riverside Press Houghton, Mifflin & Co.
4 Park Street, Boston; 11 East 17th Street,
New York; 378-388 Wabash Avenue, Chicago
⟨1900⟩

Cover-title. Printed paper wrapper. Deposited
June 27, 1900.

7707. ... The Gentle Boy and Other Tales ...

Houghton, Mifflin and Company Boston: 4
Park Street; New York: 11 East Seventeenth
Street Chicago: 378-388 Wabash Avenue
The Riverside Press, Cambridge ⟨1900⟩

At head of title: *The Riverside Literature Series*
Printed paper wrapper. Deposited Nov. 6, 1900.
Issued under date of December, 1900, as No. 145
of the series.

7708. Ethan Brand; or, the Unpardonable Sin
... and Other Stories ...

New York: The Arundel Print. ⟨n.d., *ca.*
1900⟩

7709. Main-Street ... with a Preface by Julian
Hawthorne

The Kirgate Press Lewis Buddy 3rd at 'Hillside,' in Canton Pennsylvania MCM&I

Boards, imitation vellum shelfback. Printed paper label on front. "... 950 copies ... printed
including 75 ... on Japan vellum."—P. ⟨viii⟩.
Deposited Dec. 20, 1901. Listed PW March 1,
1902.

7710. The Old Manse ...

⟨Cambridge, Mass.⟩ The Riverside Press 1904

Boards, cloth shelfback. 530 numbered copies
only. Deposited Feb. 20, 1904.

7711. ... Allegories of the Heart

Philadelphia Henry Altemus Company ⟨n.d.,
1905?⟩

At head of title: *Nathaniel Hawthorne* Color-
print pasted to front cover.

7712. In Colonial Days ...

L. C. Page & Company Boston MCMVI

Cloth; and, half leather. Deposited Aug. 23,
1906. Listed PW Sept. 8, 1906. A second printing
noted in PW Nov. 10, 1906.

7713. The Ghost of Doctor Harris ...

Printed for Gratuitous Distribution by the
Goerck Art Press Lewis W. Goerck, Prop.
925 Sixth Avenue, N. Y. ⟨n.d., 1910⟩

7714. The Golden Touch ...

Boston & New York: Houghton Mifflin Compy
⟨n.d., 1912?⟩

Pictorial boards. On reverse of title: *Printed at
the Arden Press, Letchworth, England*

7715. Little Annie's Ramble ...

Privately Printed for Jean and Josephine
Fisher and Their Friends Cedar Rapids
Iowa Christmas Nineteen Thirteen

Boards, printed paper label on front cover.
"Twenty Copies Printed"—*Certificate of issue.*

7716. *Entry cancelled.*

7717. ... The Golden Touch ...

F. A. Owen Publishing Co., Dansville, N. Y.
⟨n.d., *ca.* 1915⟩

Printed paper wrapper. Cover-title.

7718. The Seven Vagabonds ...

Boston & New York Houghton Mifflin Company The Riverside Press MDCCCCXVI

Printed paper boards, with printed paper label;
and, printed paper wrapper. Deposited Sept. 27,
1916.

7719. Leamington Spa, Warwick, Stratford-on-
Avon ...

Warwick: Printed by Henry H. Lacy, 8, High
Street. ⟨n.d., *ca.* 1920⟩

Printed paper wrapper.

7720. The Golden Touch ...

⟨San Francisco⟩ The Grabhorn Press MCM-
XXVII

Boards, imitation vellum shelfback. 240 copies
only.

7721. Mr. Higginbotham's Catastrophe ...

The Berkeley Printers Boston, Masstts
⟨1931⟩

Boards, cloth shelfback, printed paper label on
spine. Edited by Harry Lyman Koopman. Deposited Sept. 4, 1931. "The text ... is taken

from the first printing of the story in the *New England Magazine* for December, 1834 ... Printed ... July, 1931. Five hundred and forty ⟨numbered⟩ copies have been printed ..."— *Certificate of issue.*

7722. Hawthorne's Short Stories Edited and with an Introduction by Newton Arvin

New York: Alfred A. Knopf 1946

On copyright page: *First Borzoi Edition* Deposited April 26, 1946.

7723. The Maypole of Merrymount

⟨Boston⟩ With Greetings for the Year MDCCCCXLVII to the Friends of the Merrymount Press

Printed paper wrapper.

7724. The Portable Hawthorne Edited, with an Introduction and Notes, by Malcolm Cowley

New York The Viking Press 1948

On copyright page: *Published in July 1948*

IN THIS SECTION are listed books by authors other than Hawthorne which contain material by him reprinted from other books. See *Section Two* for a list of reprints issued under Hawthorne's name.

Autumn Leaves ...

New-York ... 1837.

For fuller entry see BAL, Vol. 1, p. 273.

Moral Tales ...

Boston: E. Littlefield. M DCCC XL.

2 Vols.

Moral Tales: Or a Selection of Interesting Stories. By the Author of Peter Parley.

New York: Published by Nafis & Cornish, 278 Pearl Street. ⟨1840⟩

Cloth; and, leather. Reprinted and reissued not before *ca.* 1850 imprinted: *New York: Published by Cornish, Lamport & Co.* ... ⟨1840⟩.

Tales for the Times: Being a Selection of Interesting Stories. By the Author of Peter Parley.

New York: Published by Nafis & Cornish, 278 Pearl Street. ⟨1840⟩

Tales of Humor ...

Boston: E. Littlefield. M DCCC XL.

2 Vols.

The Flower Basket: Or a Selection of Interesting Stories. By the Author of Peter Parley.

New York: Published by Nafis & Cornish, 278 Pearl Street. ⟨1840; *i.e.,* not before 1841⟩

Also issued under date ⟨1841⟩.

The Sunday School Society's Gift.

⟨Boston: The Sunday School Society, 1842⟩

Caption-title. The above at head of p. ⟨1⟩; imprint on p. 2. 16 pp. Printed self-wrapper. Issued after Sept. 1, 1842.

... The Temperance Almanac, of the Massachusetts Temperance Union ... 1843 ...

Boston: Printed by William S. Damrell, 11 Cornhill ... ⟨1842?⟩

Cover-title. At head of title: Vol. I.] [No. 5. Printed paper wrapper.

Voices of the True-Hearted ...

Philadelphia ... 1846.

For comment see entry No. 1024.

The Moss Rose ... Edited by S. G. Goodrich.

New York ... 1847.

For comment see entry No. 4855.

The Boston Book ...

Boston ... MDCCCL.

For comment see entry No. 5929.

... The (Old) Farmer's Almanack ... for the Year of Our Lord 1852 ... by Robert B. Thomas ...

Boston: Published by Jenks, Hickling & Swan ... 1851 ...

Printed wrapper. At head of title: Number Sixty. "The Breakfast-Table," p. 40, is a slightly altered extract from *The House of the Seven Gables,* 1851, p. 110.

Household Scenes for the Home Circle: A Gift for a Friend ...

Auburn and Buffalo: Miller, Orton & Mulligan. 1854.

Laurel Leaves ... Edited by Mary E. Hewitt ...

New York ... 1854.

For comment see BAL, Vol. 2, p. 496.

The Josephine Gallery. Edited by Alice and Phoebe Cary.

New York ... MDCCCLIX.

For fuller entry see No. 254.

Favorite Authors. A Companion-Book of Prose and Poetry ...

Boston ... M DCCC LXI.

For comment see entry No. 5943.

Autograph Leaves of Our Country's Authors.

Baltimore ... 1864.

For comment see entry No. 2418.

Good Stories. Part I . . .

> Boston: Ticknor and Fields. 1867.
>
> Printed paper wrapper.

Good Stories. Part III . . .

> Boston: Ticknor and Fields. 1868.
>
> Printed paper wrapper.

Child Life in Prose. Edited by John Greenleaf Whittier . . .

> Boston . . . 1874.
>
> For comment see BAL, Vol. 1, p. 73.

. . . Harper's Fifth Reader   American Authors New York . . . 1889

> For comment see entry No. 7917.

. . . Little Classics. Edited by Rossiter Johnson. Mystery . . .

> Boston: James R. Osgood and Company, Late Ticknor & Fields, and Fields, Osgood, & Co. 1875.
>
> At head of title: Eighth Volume.
>
> Advertised for March 27, PW March 13, 1875. Listed PW March 20, 1875.

Half-Hours with the Best Humorous Authors. Selected . . . by Charles Morris . . . American.

> Philadelphia . . . 1889.
>
> For comment see entry No. 3813.

Werner's Readings and Recitations. No. 2. Compiled . . . by Elsie M. Wilbor.

> New York . . . 1890.
>
> "The Elf-Child and the Minister," pp. ⟨1⟩-5, is extracted from *The Scarlet Letter*, 1850. For further comment see BAL, Vol. 1, p. 249.

Werner's Readings and Recitations. No. 5. . . . Compiled . . . by Sara Sigourney Rice.

> New York . . . 1891.
>
> "A Frolic of the Carnival," pp. 121-123, is extracted from *The Marble Faun*, 1860. For further comment see entry No. 3433.

Literary Anecdotes of the Nineteenth Century . . . Edited by W. Robertson Nicoll . . . and Thomas J. Wise

> London: Hodder & Stoughton   Paternoster Row MDCCCXCV
>
> Also issued with the imprint: *London   Hodder & Stoughton   New York   Dodd Mead & Company   1895*

The Young Folks' Library . . .

> . . . Boston ⟨1901–1902⟩
>
> For comment see entry No. 391.

REFERENCES AND ANA

The Token, a Christmas and New Year's Present.

> . . . Boston . . . MDCCCXXVIII.

For fuller description see entry No. 3094.

"The Adventures of a Rain Drop," pp. 78-83, sometimes erroneously attributed to Hawthorne; the author was Lydia Maria Child.

A Practical System of Rhetoric: Or the Principles & Rules of Style, Inferred from Examples of Writing. By Samuel P. Newman, Professor of Rhetoric in Bowdoin College. Second Edition.

> Published by Shirley & Hyde, Portland; and Mark Newman, Andover. 1829.
>
> Boards, leather shelfback.

"The First and Last Dinner," pp. 218-221; anonymous. *Note:* This story does not appear in the first edition of the book, Portland, 1827.

". . . a close comparison of ⟨*The First and Last Dinner*⟩ . . . with *Dr. Heidegger's Experiment* has shown me the plausibility of its being Hawthorne's own."—Louise Hastings: "An Origin for *Dr. Heidegger's Experiment*," in *American Literature*, Jan. 1938.

If by Hawthorne, why did he not refer to it when (as he did in the *Blue and Gold* edition of *Twice-Told Tales*, 1865) defending himself against the charge of having plagiarized the idea of "Dr. Heidegger's Experiment" from Alexandre Dumas? See entry No. 7629.

New-England Historical Sketches.

The above title listed in *Common School Journal* (Boston), April, 1840, as a book by "N. Hawthorne" to be included in *The Massachusetts Common School Library* series. Further information wanting. Possibly a tentative title for *Grandfather's Chair*, 1841; *Liberty Tree*, 1841; or, *Famous Old People*, 1841.

The Child's Friend . . . Edited by Eliza L. Follen . . .

> Boston: Leonard C. Bowles, and William Crosby, 1844.
>
> Contains Hawthorne's "A Good Man's Miracle," pp. 151-156.
>
> Not a book but a periodical although sometimes cataloged as a book.

Scenes in the Life of the Saviour: By the Poets and Painters. Edited by Rufus W. Griswold . . .

> Philadelphia . . . 1846.

For fuller description see entry No. 6672.

"Walking on the Sea," pp. 95-96; "The Star of Calvary," pp. 164-167. Herein credited to *Hawthorne*. Thompson (p. 154) fails to find reason for crediting these contributions to Nathaniel Hawthorne. Cathcart (p. 74) makes comment, and lists the publication in his section of attributions.

"... conclusive evidence that ‹Nathaniel Hawthorne› ... wrote them is lacking. A Walter Hawthorne, who contributed poetry to *Graham's* during Griswold's editorship of the magazine, seems to have a more logical claim than does the Salem prose writer."—*Rufus Wilmot Griswold ...*, by Joy Bayless, 1943, p. 83.

The Romance of a Dull Life. By the Author of Morning Clouds ‹*i.e.*, Mrs. A. J. Penny›

London: Longman, 1861

Not seen. Not located. Entry on the basis of contemporary notices. Listed PC Oct. 1, 1861.

On the title-page is a quotation from Hawthorne as follows: "The book, if you would see anything in it, requires to be read in the clear, brown, twilight atmosphere in which it was written; if opened in the sunshine, it is apt to look exceedingly like a volume of blank pages." The quotation is extracted from Hawthorne's preface to the 1851 edition of *Twice-Told Tales*.

Here included only because the book, as a result of ambiguity in contemporary listings and advertising, is sometimes attributed in part to Hawthorne.

‹Printed letter urging defeat of House of Representatives "A Bill to amend the Act respecting Copyrights."›

New York, ‹etc.› April 25, 1862.

4 pp. An open letter, signed by Hawthorne and many others. "Your attention is respectfully requested to the provisions of a bill (House File No. 343) introduced by Mr. Noble, March 6, 1862, and entitled *A Bill to amend the Act respecting Copyrights ...* It is therefore to be hoped that you will not lend your influence to support a measure apparently designed exclusively for private benefit at the expense of a portion of the public whose connection with literature and art should at least have protection from the evils of such special legislation."

Christ and the Twelve ... Edited by J. G. Holland ...

Springfield ... 1867.

For comment see entry No. 8604. For comment on the poems herein credited to Hawthorne see *Scenes in the Life of the Saviour ...*, 1846, above.

Hawthorne. By James T. Fields ...

Boston ... 1876.

For comment see entry No. 5965.

A Study of Hawthorne. By George Parsons Lathrop.

Boston: James R. Osgood and Company, Late Ticknor & Fields, and Fields, Osgood, & Co. 1876

Nathaniel Hawthorne. An Oration Delivered before the Alumni of Bowdoin College, Brunswick, Maine, July 10, 1878, by Joseph W. Symonds.

Portland: Published by the Alumni 1878.

Printed paper wrapper.

Hawthorne by Henry James ...

London   Macmillan and Co   1879 ...

Nathaniel Hawthorne by Richard Henry Stoddard

New York Charles Scribner's Sons 1879

Printed paper wrapper.

Hawthorne by Henry James ...

New York   Harper & Brothers, Publishers Franklin Square   1880

An Analytical Index to the Works of Nathaniel Hawthorne with a Sketch of His Life. ‹By Mrs. Evangeline Maria Johnson O'Connor›

Boston: Houghton, Mifflin and Company. New York: 11 East Seventeenth Street. The Riverside Press, Cambridge. 1882.

Little Classic Edition, Vol. 25.   Deposited Jan. 16, 1882.

Nathaniel Hawthorne and His Wife   A Biography by Julian Hawthorne ...

Cambridge   Printed at the University Press 1884

2 Vols. Boards, printed paper label on spine. Limited to 350 numbered copies. Limited edition deposited Nov. 1, 1884. Also issued in a trade edition: *Boston   James R. Osgood and Company, 1885*. The trade edition has been reported with imprint dated 1884; no copy so dated located by BAL.

Delia Bacon a Biographical Sketch ... ⟨by Theodore Bacon⟩

Boston and New York ... 1888

For comment see BAL, Vol. 1, p. 112. Contains many letters by Hawthorne.

Life of Nathaniel Hawthorne by Moncure D. Conway

London: Walter Scott, 24 Warwick Lane New York: 3 East 14th Street, and Melbourne. ⟨n.d., 1890⟩

Small paper edition: 6⅞" x 4¾". Large paper edition: 8³⁄₁₆" x 5½".

Personal Recollections of Nathaniel Hawthorne by Horatio Bridge ...

New York Harper & Brothers 1893

Deposited April 15, 1893. The London (Osgood, McIlvaine) edition advertised as though published Ath May 13, 1893; listed Ath April 29, 1893.

... Hawthorne by George William Curtis

... 1896 New York ...

For comment see entry No. 4407.

Memories of Hawthorne by Rose Hawthorne Lathrop

Boston and New York Houghton, Mifflin and Company The Riverside Press, Cambridge 1897

Deposited March 18, 1897. Listed PW March 27, 1897. The London (Kegan Paul) edition listed PC April 17, 1897.

Hawthorne's First Diary with an Account of Its Discovery and Loss by Samuel T. Pickard ...

Boston and New York Houghton, Mifflin and Company The Riverside Press, Cambridge 1897

Listed PW Oct. 16, 1897. The London (Kegan Paul) edition listed Ath Oct. 16, 1897.

Note: "The diary has proved a forgery."— Johnson. For Pickard's comments see *The Dial* (Chicago), Sept. 16, 1902, p. 155. "... Pickard became doubtful of the genuineness of this diary and withdrew the book from further sale."—DAB, Vol. XIV, p. 558. "The authenticity of this volume has never been proven, and the questions that have arisen concerning it have caused the editor to withdraw it from the market."—Cathcart, p. 79. "Julian Hawthorne calls this 'a clumsy and leaky fabrication'."—Browne, p. 103.

Nathaniel Hawthorne by Annie Fields

Boston Small, Maynard & Company MDCCC-XCIX

Listed PW Nov. 18, 1899.

... Nathaniel Hawthorne by George E. Woodberry

Boston and New York Houghton, Mifflin and Company The Riverside Press, Cambridge 1902

At head of title: American Men of Letters

Trade edition in maroon S cloth. Also a limited edition, 600 numbered copies, in cloth, printed paper label on spine.

Deposited Sept. 10, 1902. Noted for Sept. 20, 1902, PW Sept. 13, 1902. Advertised (trade edition only) for *to-day* PW Sept. 20, 1902. A copy of the limited edition, in H, inscribed by early owner Sept. 24, 1902. H copy of trade edition received from the author Sept. 27, 1902. Listed (trade edition only) PW Oct. 4, 1902. The London (Gay & Bird) edition listed Ath Dec. 13, 1902.

Hawthorne and His Circle by Julian Hawthorne ...

New York and London Harper & Brothers Publishers 1903

On copyright page: *Published October, 1903.* Deposited Oct. 8, 1903.

First Editions of the Works of Nathaniel Hawthorne together with Some Manuscripts, Letters and Portraits Exhibited at the Grolier Club from December 8 to December 24, 1904

New York The Grolier Club 1904

Printed paper wrapper. Leaf: 6¹⁵⁄₁₆" x 4¼". Also 40 numbered copies on large paper, 9⅛" x 6", "with ... additions ..."; bound in paper-covered boards; imprint dated 1905. Compiled by Jacob Chester Chamberlain.

The Proceedings in Commemoration of the One Hundredth Anniversary of the Birth of Nathaniel Hawthorne Held at Salem ... June 23, 1904

Salem, Mass. The Essex Institute 1904

Boards, cloth shelfback, printed paper label on spine. 250 numbered copies only.

A Bibliography of Nathaniel Hawthorne Compiled by Nina E. Browne

Boston and New York Houghton, Mifflin and Company MDCCCCV

Cloth, printed paper label on spine. 550 copies only.

Bibliography of the Works of Nathaniel Hawthorne by Wallace Hugh Cathcart

 Cleveland The Rowfant Club MCMV

 Boards, vellum shelfback, printed paper label on spine. 91 copies only.

The Life and Genius of Nathaniel Hawthorne by Frank Preston Stearns ...

 Philadelphia & London J. B. Lippincott Company 1906

Hawthorne and His Friends Reminiscence and Tribute by F. B. Sanborn

 The Torch Press Cedar Rapids, Iowa Nineteen Eight

 Boards, leather label on spine.

Hawthorne and His Publisher by Caroline Ticknor ...

 Boston and New York Houghton Mifflin Company MDCCCCXIII

 On copyright page: *Published November 1913*

A Pilgrimage to Salem in 1838 By a Southern Admirer of Nathaniel Hawthorne Reprinted from *"The Southern Rose"* (Charleston, S. C.) of March 2 and 16, 1839, with a *Foreword* by Victor Hugo Paltsits, *Another View* by John Robinson, and *A Rejoinder* by Mr. Paltsits.

 Salem: Newcomb & Gauss, Printers 1916

 Printed paper wrapper. Sometimes attributed to William Gilmore Simms. "The article was actually written by Dr. Samuel Gilman ... He reprinted it under the title *A Day of Disappointment in Salem* in his *Contributions to Literature* (Boston, 1856), pp. 474-496."—Jay B. Hubbell, in *The South in Literature*, 1954, p. 960.

Hawthorne A Study in Solitude by Herbert Gorman

 George H. Doran Company ... New York ⟨1927⟩

 First printing has publisher's device on the copyright page. Listed PW July 16, 1927.

The Rebellious Puritan: Portrait of Mr. Hawthorne by Lloyd Morris ...

 New York Harcourt, Brace and Company 1927

Hawthorne by Newton Arvin ...

 Boston 1929 Little, Brown, and Company

 Deposited Sept. 25, 1929. On copyright page: *Published September, 1929*

Hawthorne's Spectator Edited by Elizabeth L. Chandler [Reprint from the New England Quarterly, Volume IV, Number 2, 1931]

 Copyright 1931 by the Southworth Press ⟨Portland, Maine⟩

 Printed paper wrapper.

Hawthorne and Politics Unpublished Letters to William B. Pike Edited by Randall Stewart [Reprint from the New England Quarterly, Volume V, Number 2, 1932]

 Copyright 1932 by the Southworth Press Portland, Maine⟩

 Printed paper wrapper.

The American Notebooks by Nathaniel Hawthorne Based upon the Original Manuscripts in the Pierpont Morgan Library and Edited by Randall Stewart ...

 New Haven Yale University Press London. Humphrey Milford. Oxford University Press 1932

 See entry No. 7632. Deposited Dec. 2, 1932.

Nathaniel Hawthorne Representative Selections, with Introduction, Bibliography, and Notes by Austin Warren ...

 American Book Company New York ... ⟨1934⟩

 On copyright page of first printing: *W.P.I.*

The English Notebooks ... Based upon the Original Manuscripts in the Pierpont Morgan Library and Edited by Randall Stewart ...

 New York: Modern Language Association of America London: Oxford University Press 1941

 "Since readers ... heretofore have been seriously misled by Mrs. Hawthorne's extremely bowdlerized texts ... it has seemed desirable that the true texts ... be made available."—P. ⟨v⟩. For first printing (expurgated) see entry No. 7634. Deposited Oct. 6, 1941.

Hawthorne, the Artist Fine-Art Devices in Fiction ⟨by⟩ Leland Schubert

 Chapel Hill The University of North Carolina Press 1944

Maine Sources in the House of the Seven Gables by Thomas Morgan Griffiths ...

Waterville, Maine 1945

Boards, cloth shelfback. 600 copies only. Deposited July 29, 1945.

Nathaniel Hawthorne   A Biography by Randall Stewart

New Haven   Yale University Press ... 1948

Nathaniel Hawthorne   The American Years by Robert Cantwell

Rinehart & Company, Inc. New York Toronto ⟨1948⟩

Deposited Sept. 2, 1948.

Hawthorne's Last Phase by Edward Hutchins Davidson

New Haven   Yale University Press ... 1949

Published March 9, 1949, according to publisher's records.

JOHN MILTON HAY

1 8 3 8 - 1 9 0 5

THIS LIST is presented in three sections as follows: *Section I,* Primary books; and, books by authors other than Hay but containing first edition material by him. *Section II,* Collections of reprinted material issued under Hay's name; separate editions (*i.e.,* pieces reprinted from Hay's books and issued in separate form); and, undated reprints. *Section III,* Books by authors other than Hay which contain material by him reprinted from earlier books.

Much of Hay's output lies buried in the archives of the State Department of the United States. No attempt has been made to locate and describe these government publications.

7725. The Brown Paper. Vol. I. Brown University, November, 1857. No. I ...

⟨Providence, R. I., 1857⟩

An annual newspaper. 4 pp. Co-edited by Hay. Contains his "Sa! Sa!," p. ⟨3⟩; anonymous.

See entry No. 7804.

B

7726. ... An Oration and a Poem Delivered in the Chapel of Brown University; on Class Day, June 10, 1858. Printed for Private Distribution.

Providence: Knowles, Anthony & Co., Printers. 1858.

Printed paper wrapper. At head of title: Class of 1858.

"Erato; a Poem," pp. ⟨31⟩-43.

B BA LC NYPL Y

7727. .... Through the Long Days. Ballad ... Music by Francis Korbay.

New York Wm. A. Pond & Co. 547 Broadway. & 39 Union Square ... ⟨n.d., *ca.* 1860)

Sheet music. Cover-title. At head of title: To Mme Anne C. L. Botta. Plate number 8479. Collected in *Pike County Ballads,* 1871.

Two printings noted. No sequence has been established and the following designations are for identification only.

A: Back cover blank.

B: Back cover imprinted with an advertisement: ... *Everything in the Music Line ... Wm. A. Pond & Co. ...*

Other and later settings:

Boston: Oliver Ditson & Co. Setting by Francis Boott. 1878.

Boston: Arthur P. Schmidt. Setting by Arthur Foote. 1898.

B (A, B)

7728. CARRIER'S ADDRESS TO THE PATRONS OF THE DAILY ILLINOIS STATE JOURNAL.

SPRINGFIELD, ⟨ILLINOIS⟩ JANUARY 1, 1861.

Caption-title. The above at head of text. Text in three columns.

Anonymous.

Single sheet. 13¹⁄₁₆" x 11". Printed on recto only.

For a discussion of this publication and a note on the authorship, see *The Poetry of John Hay ...,* by Sister Saint Ignatius Ward, 1930.

B

7729. 1861. A NEW YEAR'S POEM, TO THE PATRONS OF THE MISSOURI DEMOCRAT ...

⟨n.p., *Daily Missouri Democrat,* St. Louis, Mo., Jan. 1, 1861.⟩

Caption-title. The above at head of p. ⟨1⟩. Printed in blue and red.

Carrier's address. Single cut sheet folded to make four pages. Pp. ⟨1⟩-4. Page: 8⅜" x 5¼".

By Hay? Found in his personal scrapbook (at B) and so presumed to be by him. The poem begins: *Toll for the dead year—/ Solemnly toll! / Let the dirge for the dead year / Prayerfully roll! /* Text otherwise unlocated.

B

7730. Celebration of the One Hundredth Anniversary of the Founding of Brown University, September 6th, 1864.

Providence: Sidney S. Rider & Bro. 1865.

Printed paper wrapper.

Eighteen 4-line stanzas, *A hundred times the bells of Brown*, pp. 156-159. Collected in *Pike County Ballads*, 1871, as "Centennial." For a separate printing see entry No. 7839.

B NYPL Y

7731. The American Thanksgiving Celebration in Paris ... December 7, 1865 ...

Paris. Printed by E. Brière Rue Saint-Honoré, 257. 1865.

Remarks, pp. 26-28.

For comment see entry No. 1422.

7732. The Farewell Banquet to Mr John Bigelow ... Grand Hotel December 19th 1866 by the American Residents of Paris

Paris Typographie de Henri Plon, Imprimeur de l'Empereur, 8, Rue Garancière. 1867

Printed paper wrapper.

"Speech," pp. 45-50.

AAS B NYPL Y

7733. ... Violet ...

Boston, G. D. Russell & Company 126 Tremont, opp. Park St ... 1870 ...

Sheet music. Cover-title. At head of title: Three Songs Composed by F. Boott ... Plate No. 1825.

Hark, the trumpet's snarling blast ... ; not elsewhere located.

Deposited Feb. 18, 1870.

LC

7734. "LITTLE BREECHES"

This popular poem appeared in a variety of forms. The following is a suggested publication sequence but the cautious will note that a definite sequence has not been established.

A

First published in *The New-York ⟨Weekly⟩ Tribune*, Nov. 30, 1870.

B

In: *Jim Bludso of the Prairie Belle, and Little Breeches*, Boston: Osgood, 1871.

Printed orange paper wrapper. Deposited May 15, 1871. Noted as *recently issued* ALG May 15, 1871. Listed ALG June 1, 1871. For a fuller description see entry No. 7739.

C

In: *Pike County Ballads and Other Pieces*, Boston: Osgood, 1871.

Deposited May 17, 1871. Noted as *just ready* ALG May 15, 1871. Listed ALG June 1, 1871. For a fuller description see entry No. 7740.

D

Issued as a separate: *Little-Breeches*, New York: Redfield, 1871.

Printed paper wrapper. On copyright page: *From "Poems by John Hay." In Press by J. R. Osgood & Co., Boston.* Deposited May 22, 1871. Listed ALG June 1, 1871. For a fuller description see entry No. 7741.

E

In: *How Common Sense Looks at It.* Boston: Whipple ⟨n.d., 1871?⟩

For fuller description see entry No. 7744.

F

In: ... *Extracts from Hay* ⟨n.p., n.d.⟩

For fuller description see entry No. 7815.

7735. Gettysburg. Description of the Painting of the Repulse of Longstreet's Assault Painted by James Walker ...

New York: Published by John B. Bachelder, 59 Beekman Street. 1870.

Printed paper wrapper.

Testimonial, p. ⟨47⟩.

H NYPL

7736. GOLYER ...

⟨n.p., n.d., *ca.* 1870⟩

Caption-title. The above preceding text. Single leaf. 10⅛" x 4⅝". Printed on recto only. Collected in *Poems*, 1890.

Presumably a galley proof and not issued in this form. Anonymous.

B

7737. "JIM BLUDSO OF THE PRAIRIE BELLE"

This popular poem appeared in a variety of forms. The following is a suggested publication sequence but the cautious will note that a definite sequence has not been established.

A

First published in *The New-York Semi-Weekly Tribune*, Jan. 6, 1871, p. 6.

B

In: *Jim Bludso of the Prairie Belle, and Little Breeches*, Boston: Osgood, 1871.

Printed orange paper wrapper. Deposited May 15, 1871. Noted as *recently issued* ALG May 15, 1871. Listed ALG June 1, 1871. For a fuller description see entry No. 7739.

C

In: *Pike County Ballads and Other Pieces*, Boston: Osgood, 1871.

Deposited May 17, 1871. Noted as *just ready* ALG May 15, 1871. Listed ALG June 1, 1871. For fuller description see entry No. 7740.

D

Broadside printing. Copy in H.

JIM BLUDSO. / [OF THE PRAIRIE BELLE.] / ⟨text⟩ / J. H. / ⟨n.p., n.d., before Aug. 5, 1871⟩

Single cut sheet of unwatermarked, white, wove paper. 11⅛″ x 4¹⁵⁄₁₆″. Printed on recto only. H copy received from Charles Sumner on Aug. 5, 1871.

E

Single leaf. Copies in B and in Y.

Jim Bludso / ⟨text⟩ / Actinic Eng. Co. 113 Liberty St. facimile ⟨sic⟩ from Ill. by H. Balling 835 Broadway N. Y. / ⟨n.d., ca. 1871–1873⟩

All of the above, save for the imprint, within a frame decorated at left and at bottom by heavenly figures, vignette of the *Prairie Belle* in flames, etc., etc. Text concluded on reverse of leaf.

At end of text: JOHN HAY.

Single leaf. White wove paper, unwatermarked. 10⁵⁄₁₆″ x 7″.

Note: Actinic Engraving Company was at the address given during the period 1871–1873. H. Balling, the illustrator, was at the address given during the period 1869–1870, 1871–1873.

F

Single leaf. Copy in B.

JIM BLUDSO / (OF THE PRAIRIE BELLE.) / ⟨text⟩ / SIXTEEN. / ⟨text⟩ / J. H. / ⟨double rule⟩ / ⟨n.p., n.d.⟩

Obviously a galley proof. Single leaf. Printed on recto only. 7¼″ x 4½″ scant. White wove paper, unwatermarked.

Note: The word SIXTEEN (in the lined-off matter above) almost surely refers to a galley number; it has no relation whatever to the text.

G

In: ... *Extracts from Hay* ⟨n.p., n.d⟩

For fuller description see entry No. 7815.

(For another treatment of the 'Jim Bludso' episode see Horatio Alger, Jr.'s poem, "John Maynard: A Ballad of Lake Erie.")

7738. Balloon Post ...

Boston, Mass., April ... 1871 ...

An occasional newspaper. 6 numbers. For fuller comment see entry No. 4038.

"Good and Bad Luck," No. III, p. ⟨1⟩. Collected in *Pike County Ballads*, 1871 (May).

Issued under date April 13, 1871.

7739. JIM BLUDSO OF THE PRAIRIE BELLE, AND LITTLE BREECHES ... WITH ILLUSTRATIONS BY S. EYTINGE, JR.

BOSTON: JAMES R. OSGOOD AND COMPANY, LATE TICKNOR & FIELDS, AND FIELDS, OSGOOD, & CO. 1871.

For other printings of these poems see entry Nos. 7734, 7737, 7815.

⟨1⟩-23. Illustrated. 7″ x 4⁹⁄₁₆″.

⟨-⟩¹².

Printed orange paper wrapper.

Note: Unsold sheets were reissued *ca.* 1876 in gray paper wrapper; the back wrapper imprinted with an advertisement for *John Greenleaf Whittier's Works*. Copy in B.

Deposited May 15, 1871. Noted as *recently issued* ALG May 15, 1871. Listed ALG June 1, 1871. Advertised by Trübner as an importation Bkr July, 1871.

B   H   NYPL

7740. PIKE COUNTY BALLADS AND OTHER PIECES ...

BOSTON: JAMES R. OSGOOD AND COMPANY, LATE TICKNOR & FIELDS, AND FIELDS, OSGOOD, & CO. 1871.

⟨i⟩-⟨xii⟩, ⟨13⟩-167. 6¾″ full x 4½″.

⟨1⟩-7¹². *Also signed:* ⟨A⟩-H, ⟨I⟩, J⁸, K⁴.

C cloth: brown; green; star-sprinkled purple; terra-cotta. FL cloth: purple; terra-cotta. P cloth: purple. Covers bevelled. Brown-coated on white end papers. Single flyleaves of either wove paper; or, laid paper. Johnson (1941) calls for copies in paper wrapper but no copies so bound have been otherwise reported or located; Johnson presumed to be in error.

Note: The publisher's monogram at foot of spine occurs in two states of unknown sequence. The designations are for identification only:

A: ⅞″ high.

B: ¾″ high.

Noted as *just ready* ALG May 15, 1871. Deposited May 17, 1871. Listed ALG June 1, 1871. Listed Bkr July, 1871, as a Trübner importation. A Maxwell (London) edition listed PC Feb. 15, 1886; a Routledge (London) edition listed PC Aug. 8, 1891.

B   H   NYPL   Y

7741. LITTLE-BREECHES   A PIKE COUNTY VIEW OF SPECIAL PROVIDENCE ... ILLUSTRATED BY J. F. ENGEL

NEW YORK   J. S. REDFIELD, PUBLISHER   140 FULTON STREET   1871

⟨1⟩-⟨16⟩. Illustrated. 9¼″ x 6″.

⟨-⟩⁸.

Printed self-wrapper.

Noted in the following forms:

First Printing

As described. Publisher's address: *140 Fulton Street.*

Second Printing

Publisher's address: *140 Fulton Street.*

Pagination: ⟨3⟩-⟨14⟩.

Collation: ⟨-⟩⁶.

Issued in a printed wrapper of glazed white paper.

Second Printing, Second State

Same as *Second Printing* but publisher's address altered to: *170 Fulton Street.*

On copyright page: *From "Poems by John Hay." In Press by J. R. Osgood & Co., Boston.* The book referred to is John Hay's *Pike County Ballads,* 1871.

Deposited May 22, 1871. Listed ALG June 1, 1871.

See entries 7734 and 7815.

B (1st; 2nd printing 2nd state)   BA (2nd printing)   BPL (2nd printing 2nd state)   NYPL (1st; 2nd printing 2nd state)

7742. CASTILIAN DAYS ...

BOSTON: JAMES R. OSGOOD AND COMPANY, LATE TICKNOR & FIELDS, AND FIELDS, OSGOOD, & CO. 1871.

⟨i-viii⟩, ⟨1⟩-414, blank leaf. 7″ x 4½″.

⟨-⟩⁴, 1-6, ⟨7⟩, 8-17¹², 18⁴. *Also signed:* ⟨-⟩⁴, A-I, ⟨J⟩, K-Z⁸.

Note: Two issues noted:

First

An error in imposition causes p. 411 to repeat the text of p. 408. Pagination and running heads unaffected by the error. Text on both pp. 408 and 411 begins: *tors, disarmed ...*

Second

The error corrected by means of a cancel. Pp. 411-412 on a stub.

C cloth: green; star-sprinkled purple; terra-cotta. FL cloth: terra-cotta. Covers bevelled. Brown-coated on white end papers. Flyleaves. *Note:* The publisher's monogram at foot of spine occurs in two states of unknown sequence. The designations are for identification only:

A: ⅞″ scant high.

B: ⅞″ full high.

A rebound copy in NYPL inscribed by Hay *September, 1871.* Listed ALG Oct. 2, 1871; Bkr Nov. 1871. The Trübner importation advertised Bkr Nov. 1871. For revised editions see entries 7770 and 7793.

B (1st)   BA (2nd)   H (1st)   NYPL (1st)

7743. Th: Nast's Illustrated Almanac for 1872 ...

... 1871 ... Harper & Brothers ... ⟨New York⟩

"Ye Gambolier," p. 25. This is an extensively revised version of a poem written by Hay and first published (presumably in a periodical) in 1863 under the title "Ye Armie Gambolier." For a comment see Ward, p. 69.

For fuller entry see No. 3332.

7744. How Common Sense Looks at It.

⟨Boston: Charles K. Whipple, n.d., not after 1871⟩

Single leaf folded to four pages. Title at head of p. ⟨1⟩. P. 4: ... *Thirteen Tracts, Intended to Teach Religion Without Superstition ... Charles K. Whipple, 43 Bowdoin Street, Boston ...*

According to Boston city directories Whipple was at the above address during the period 1869–1871.

"Little Breeches," pp. 2-3. Here reprinted? See entry No. 7734.

As here published the poem is prefaced by an editorial note which suggests publication soon after first appearance of the poem in *The New-York ⟨Weekly⟩ Tribune,* Nov. 30, 1870: "... a rough and coarse California ⟨sic⟩ poem, which I copy from the *New York Tribune* ..."

B NYPL

7745. The Similibus A Paper Published by the Managers of the Fair for the Benefit of the Homoeopathic Surgical Hospital ...

New-York ... 1872 ...

An occasional newspaper. 10 numbers, issued April 13-24, 1872. And, a two-page supplement issued under date April 24, 1872. "Complete sets ... ⟨in printed paper wrapper, cloth shelf-back⟩ ... may be obtained after the Fair closes ..."—Notice in the *Supplement,* p. ⟨1⟩.

"Christine," No. 4, p. 4. Collected in *Poems,* 1890.

B

7746. Not Pretty, But Precious, and Other Short Stories. By John Hay ... Harriet Prescott Spofford ...

Philadelphia   J. B. Lippincott & Co. 1872.

"The Blood Seedling," pp. 57-69.

For comment see entry No. 4608.

7747. Report of the Proceedings of the Society of the Army of the James, at the Second Triennial Reunion ... July 19th, 1871 ...

New York: G. W. Carleton & Co. Publishers, London: S. Low, Son & Co. M DCCC LXXII.

Printed paper wrapper. Notice from the treasurer regarding publication tipped in at front.

"Colonel John Hay's Remarks," pp. 41-42.

"The Advance Guard," pp. 42-43. Collected in *Poems,* 1890.

AAS   B

7748. One Hundred Choice Selections No. 7 ... Compiled ... by Phineas Garrett ...

Published by P. Garrett & Co., 702 Chestnut Street, Philadelphia, Pa., and 116 E. Randolph Street, Chicago, Ill. 1873.

Cloth; and, printed paper wrapper.

"A Triumph of Order," p. 86. Collected in *Poems,* 1890.

BPL   Y

7749. ... Oration, Poem, and History, Delivered before the Theta Delta Chi Society, at the Convention Dinner ... Metropolitan Hotel, New York City ... February 21st, 1873.

Privately Printed, under the Auspices of the Chi Charge, University of Rochester, N. Y. ⟨1873?⟩

Printed paper wrapper. At head of title: *Spahn Brougham Burdge*

"Fill up Your Blushing Goblets," p. 41. "Zeta Shouts Her Chorus," p. 45. Both collected in *Ward,* 1930.

B   H   Y

7750. Lotos Leaves ... Edited by John Brougham and John Elderkin ...

Boston: William F. Gill and Company, Late Shepard and Gill, 151 Washington Street. 1875.

"Liberty," pp. ⟨229⟩-230. Collected in *Poems.* 1890.

For comment see entry No. 3363.

7751. ... The Quarterly Elocutionist ... Edited ... by Mrs. Anna Randall-Diehl ... July, 1875 ...

... Anna Randall-Diehl, 27 Union Square, New York ... 1875.

Printed wrapper. Cover-title. At head of title: Vol. I, No. 3.

"Religion and Doctrine," pp. 202-203. Collected in *Poems,* 1890.

Deposited April 29, 1875. Reprinted and reissued with the publisher's later address: *35 Union Square.*

Y

7752. Dick's Recitations and Readings No. 1 ... Edited by Wm. B. Dick ...

New York: Dick & Fitzgerald, Publishers, No. 18 Ann Street. ⟨1876⟩

Cloth; and, printed paper wrapper.

"The Pledge at Spunky Point. A Tale of Virtuous Effort and Human Perfidy," pp. 12-14. Collected in *Poems*, 1890.

Deposited Oct. 7, 1876.

LC NYPL

7753. Dick's Recitations and Readings No. 2 ... Edited by Wm. B. Dick ...

New York: Dick & Fitzgerald, Publishers, No. 18 Ann Street. ‹1876›

Cloth; and, printed paper wrapper.

"The Law of Death," pp. 64-65. Collected in *Poems*, 1890.

Title entered Nov. 18, 1876. Listed PW Dec. 16, 1876. Deposited for copyright April 8, 1878 ‹sic›.

LC NYPL

7754. THE PIONEERS OF OHIO. AN ADDRESS DELIVERED BEFORE THE PIONEERS' ASSOCIATION OF THE WESTERN RESERVE, AT BURGESS' GROVE, CUYAHOGA COUNTY, OHIO, AUGUST 27th, 1879 ...

CLEVELAND, O.: LEADER PRINTING COMPANY, 146 SUPERIOR ST. 1879.

‹1›-20. 6¾" x 5½" scant.

‹1-2⁴, 3²›.

Printed blue paper wrapper.

A copy in B inscribed by early owner Sept. 14, 1879.

B MHS NYPL

7755. The Atlantic Monthly Supplement. The Holmes Breakfast ...

‹n.p., n.d., Boston, February, 1880›

Self-wrapper. Caption-title. Letter, dated December 1, 1879, p. 23.

H NYPL

7756. Rodman the Keeper: Southern Sketches. By Constance Fenimore Woolson ...

New York: D. Appleton and Company, 1, 3, & 5 Bond Street. 1880.

"Sister St. Luke," p. ‹42›. Collected in *Poems*, 1890.

Noted for *this day* PW March 20, 1880. Listed PW March 27, 1880. H copy received April 23, 1880. Noted by Ath July 17, 1880.

H

7757. Tales of the Chesapeake by Geo. Alfred Townsend ...

New York: American News Company, 39 and 41 Chambers Street. 1880.

Inserted leaf of testimonials: *A Literary Revelation. Tales of the Chesapeake ... Third Edition. Views of Writing Men.*

Contains a testimonial by Hay.

Listed PW May 15, 1880. Y copy inscribed by Townsend Aug. 17, 1880.

NYPL Y

7758. THE BALANCE SHEET OF THE TWO PARTIES. A SPEECH DELIVERED ... AT CLEVELAND, OHIO, JULY 31, 1880.

CLEVELAND: LEADER PRINTING COMPANY, 146 SUPERIOR STTEET. ‹sic› 1880.

‹1›-38, blank leaf. 7⅛" full x 4⅞".

‹1-2⁸, 3⁴›.

Printed gray paper wrapper.

Note: The speech was also published in *Supplement to the Cleveland Herald*, Aug. 2, 1880, pp. 4. Copy in B.

AAS B NYPL Y

7759. ‹Letter based upon the murderous attack upon the President›

New York September 16. 1881.

Single leaf folded to make four pages. 11¼" x 8⅝". Text on pp. ‹2-3› only.

Signed at foot of p. ‹2› by Hay and others.

H NYPL

7759A. ‹Advertisement for› Mr. ‹John James› Piatt's Poems ... Extracts from Letters ...

‹n.p., n.d., after Sept. 19, 1881›

Four-page leaflet. Issued as an advertisement for Piatt's poems. The above at head of p. ‹1›.

Brief comment, p. ‹1›.

WMG

7760. ... CHAPTERS I. TO XI., INCLUSIVE, OF THE BREAD-WINNERS, BEING THE FIRST HALF OF THE ANONYMOUS SERIAL STORY REPRINTED FROM THE AUGUST, SEPTEMBER, AND OCTOBER (1883) NUMBERS OF THE CENTURY MAGAZINE. TO BE COMPLETED IN THE NOVEMBER AND DECEMBER (1883) AND JANUARY (1884) NUMBERS ...

THE CENTURY CO. NEW-YORK. COPYRIGHT, 1883, BY THE CENTURY CO.

Cover-title. At head of title: PRICE, 10 CENTS.

Anonymous.

For complete publication see entry No. 7762. Also see entry No. 7783.

⟨i-ii⟩, ⟨567⟩-586; ⟨737⟩-752; ⟨889⟩-906. 9⅝″ x 6¹³⁄₁₆″.

⟨1⁴, 2-4⁸⟩.

Printed self-wrapper.

Deposited Oct. 24, 1883.

B LC

7761. *Entry cancelled.*

The Bread-Winners ...

London Frederick Warne & Co. Bedford Street, Strand 1883 ...

See note under next entry.

7762. THE BREAD-WINNERS A SOCIAL STUDY

NEW YORK HARPER & BROTHERS, FRANKLIN SQUARE 1884

Anonymous. See entry No. 7760. Also see entry No. 7783.

⟨1⟩-319. 6⅝″ x 4⅝″.

⟨1-2⟩, 3-20⁸.

C cloth: bronze-brown. S cloth: olive. V cloth: tan. Brown-coated on white end papers. Fly-leaves.

Note: Occurs with, and without, the statement THE END on p. 319; no sequence, if any, has been established. However, a surviving copyright deposit copy does not have the statement; and, the statement is present in undoubted reprints of the book.

Deposited Dec. 28, 1883. BPL copy inscribed by Hay Jan. 1, 1884. Listed PW Jan. 5, 1884.

Note: Not to be confused with *Bread-Winners*, by a Lady of Boston, ⟨*i.e.*, Susan D. Nickerson⟩, Boston, 1871.

B BPL H NYPL

Note on London Publication

Issued simultaneously with the New York edition? The publishers are unable to give precise date of publication. However, manuscript material in the John Hay archive (at B) records the concern of Harper & Brothers regarding unauthorized Canadian publication; and, that on Dec. 6, 1883, Harper instructed Warne to "publish ⟨a⟩ limited edition ... immediately

to assure copyright." No record of such copyright printing has been found.

The Bread-Winners A Novel

London Frederick Warne & Co. Bedford Street, Strand 1883 (All Rights Reserved.)

Anonymous.

⟨i⟩-⟨viii⟩, ⟨1⟩-310, blank leaf. 7½″ full x 5″ scant.

40 4to gatherings signed: ⟨-⟩, A, A2, B, B2, etc., etc., to T, T2, U.

V cloth: green; tan. Yellow-coated on white end papers.

Note: Two states noted; the order of presentation is presumed correct:

1: As described above. The title-leaf is an integral part of its gathering, not a cancel. Verso of title-leaf blank. The statement *A Novel* on title-page.

2: As described but with the following variations: The title-leaf is a cancel. The letter-press of the title-page has been reset and the statement *A Novel* is not present. On the verso of the title-leaf is the statement: *Entered at Stationers' Hall. / Copyright 1883. / 552.—29/11/83.—553.*

Noted as *in the press* Ath Nov. 24, 1883. Advertised for Dec. 1883, Ath Dec. 1, 1883. Noted as *at all libraries* Ath Dec. 22, 1883. The publishers inform BAL that publication occurred in January, 1884. Listed Ath Jan. 5, 1884; PC Jan. 18, 1884; Bkr Feb. 1884. A cheap edition (2/–, boards) listed PC Nov. 15, 1884.

AAS (1st London) B (1st London, 2nd London)

7763. An Old Scrap-Book. With Additions. Printed, but Not Published ... ⟨Edited by J. M. Forbes⟩

⟨Cambridge: The University Press⟩ February 8, 1884.

Errata slip inserted at copyright page.

"On A.B.," pp. 218-219.

Deposited Feb. 8, 1884.

B

7764. Dr. Charles Hay Born February 7, 1801. Died September 18, 1884.

⟨New York: The DeVinne Press, 1884?⟩

Printed paper wrapper.

"Attributed in part to John Hay"—Catalog, The John Hay Library, Brown University.

B LC

7765. Representative Poems of Living Poets American and English Selected by the Poets Themselves with an Introduction by George Parsons Lathrop

Cassell & Company, Limited   739 & 741 Broadway, New York 1886

Reprint save for "The Stirrup-Cup," p. 310. Collected in *Poems*, 1890.

For comment see entry No. 436.

7766. Amasa Stone. Born April 27, 1818. Died May 11, 1883.

⟨New York: The DeVinne Press, n.d., 1886?⟩

"Amasa Stone," pp. ⟨3⟩-12; anonymous. Reprinted from *Magazine of Western History* (Cleveland, Ohio), Dec. 1885, where it is signed at end: *J.H.*

Paul Leicester Ford in *Annual Report of the American Historical Association for the year 1889*, Washington, 1890, p. 275, states that the above publication was issued in 1883 in a printing of one hundred copies; and that a "second edition" was issued in 1884. BAL has been unable to find evidence to support the 1883 date, nor has a second edition, of any date, been located. Ford appears to be wholly incorrect since on pp. 19-21, is printed a letter dated *February 1, 1886*, which appears sufficient evidence for dismissing Ford's dates.

B

7767. Appletons' Cyclopaedia of American Biography Edited by James Grant Wilson and John Fiske ...

New York   D. Appleton and Company   1, 3 and 5 Bond Street   1887⟨–1889⟩

"Abraham Lincoln," Vol. 3, pp. 715-727. See *The Presidents of the United States ...* , 1894.

"Whitelaw Reid," Vol. 5, p. 217.

"Amasa Stone," Vol. 5, p. 699. Not the same as the sketch published in 1886, *supra*.

For comment see entry No. 6020.

7768. Camden's Compliment to Walt Whitman May 31, 1889 Notes, Addresses, Letters, Telegrams Edited by Horace L. Traubel

Philadelphia   David McKay, Publisher   23 South Ninth Street 1889

Five-line statement, p. 54.

NYPL

7769. POEMS ...

BOSTON AND NEW YORK   HOUGHTON, MIFFLIN AND COMPANY   THE RIVERSIDE PRESS, CAMBRIDGE   1890

Trade Edition

⟨i-ii⟩, ⟨i⟩-⟨viii⟩, ⟨9⟩-272. 7″ x 4⅝″.

⟨1¹, 2-18⁸⟩.

V cloth: green, green-coated on white end papers. V cloth: maroon, gray-coated on white end papers. Flyleaves. Top edges gilt. Sides not lettered. Spine goldstamped: POEMS / ⟨*rule*⟩ / ⟨*leaf and berry*⟩ / JOHN HAY / HOUGHTON / MIFFLIN & CO.

Trade Edition, Variant

A variant of unknown status has been noted:

S cloth: mustard; maroon. Front stamped in gold: POEMS / BY JOHN HAY Spine stamped in gold: ⟨*double rule*⟩ / ⟨*wavy dotted rule*⟩ / POEMS / BY / JOHN HAY / ⟨*double rule*⟩ / ⟨*wavy dotted rule*⟩ / ⟨*rule*⟩ Marbled end papers. Top edges gilt. Leaf: 7″ x 4¾″ scant.

De Luxe Edition

An unknown number of copies printed on laid paper watermarked *John Dickinson & Co.* Pp. ⟨i⟩-⟨viii⟩, ⟨9⟩-272. Page: 7⅝″ x 4¾″. Collation: ⟨1-22⁶, 23⁴⟩.

The only copies of this printing examined are bound in three-quarters brown morocco, marbled boards sides, top edges gilt. One of these was received at B on June 9, 1890, presented to the library by the author.

Note: In all examined copies of 1890 date the following errors are present: *Distiches* for *Distichs*, pp. v and ⟨221⟩. The error corrected, p. v, in the printing of 1891; both errors removed in the printings of 1899 and ⟨1899⟩.

Deposited May 1, 1890. Noted as *just issued* PW May 3, 1890. Listed PW May 10, 1890. A de luxe printing presented to B by the author June 9, 1890. British trade periodical notices suggest that the Boston printing was distributed in London by Brentano's; see, *e.g.*, PC Oct. 1, 1890.

AAS (trade)   B (trade; de luxe; variant)   NYPL (trade)   Y (trade)

7770. Castilian Days ... Revised Edition

Boston and New York   Houghton, Mifflin and Company   The Riverside Press, Cambridge   1890

"Preface to the Revised Edition," pp. ⟨iii⟩-v.

"I have ... nothing to add to this little book ... I have confined myself to the correction of the most obvious and flagrant errors ..." p. iv.

For first edition see entry No. 7742. For another revised edition see entry No. 7793.

Listed PW May 10, 1890.

B Y

7771. A Library of American Literature ... Edited by Edmund Clarence Stedman and Ellen Mackay Hutchinson ...

New-York ... 1888–1890.

11 Vols. For comment see entry No. 1350.

Reprint save for "The Death of Lincoln," Vol. 11, pp. 403-410. Written in collaboration with John G. Nicolay. Collected in *Abraham Lincoln: A History* ..., 1890, Vol. 10, pp. 282-302; see entry No. 7772.

Deposited July 29, 1890.

H

7772. ABRAHAM LINCOLN A HISTORY BY JOHN G. NICOLAY AND JOHN HAY ...

NEW YORK   THE CENTURY CO. 1890

10 Vols.

Note: Issued by subscription in several styles of binding. No sequence, if any, has been established and the following designations are for identification only. In each certain variations occur as to flyleaves, blank leaves, end papers.

A: Green H cloth. Top edges gilt, other edges untrimmed. Leaf: 9″ x 6″. Green-coated on white end papers.

B: Brown P cloth. Top edges plain. All edges trimmed. Leaf: 8$\frac{11}{16}$″ x 5$\frac{13}{16}$″. White end papers.

C: Brown P cloth. Top edges gilt, other edges untrimmed. Leaf: 9″ x 6″. White end papers.

D: In leather. Noted in sheep; half morocco. Possibly other leather bindings were available.

1

⟨i⟩-⟨xxiv⟩, ⟨1⟩-456. Frontispiece and 23 plates inserted; other illustrations and maps in text.

⟨a⟩^{4}, ⟨b⟩^{8}, 1-28^8, 29^4.

2

⟨i⟩-⟨xvi⟩, ⟨1⟩-447. Frontispiece and 24 plates inserted; 1 facsimile in text.

⟨a⟩^{8}, 1-28^8.

3

⟨i⟩-⟨xvi⟩, ⟨1⟩-449; 3 blank leaves. Frontispiece and 27 plates inserted; 1 facsimile in text.

⟨-⟩^{8}, 1-28^8, 29^4. *Note:* In a presumed later printing the collation is: ⟨-⟩^{8}, 1-28^8, 29^2.

4

⟨iii⟩-⟨xviii⟩, ⟨1⟩-470; blank leaf. Frontispiece and 30 plates inserted; 2 maps in text.

⟨-⟩^{8}, 1-29^8, 30^4.

5

⟨iii⟩-⟨xviii⟩, ⟨1⟩-460; 2 blank leaves. Frontispiece and 29 plates inserted; 2 2-page maps inserted; 1 map in text.

⟨-⟩^{8}, 1-29^8.

6

⟨iii⟩-xviii, ⟨1⟩-488. Frontispiece and 27 plates inserted; 6 2-page plates inserted; other illustrations in text.

⟨-⟩^{8}, 1-30^8, 31^4.

7

⟨iii⟩-⟨xviii⟩, ⟨1⟩-472. Frontispiece and 22 plates inserted; maps in text.

⟨-⟩^{8}, 1-29^8, 30^4.

8

⟨iii⟩-xviii, ⟨1⟩-486; blank leaf. Frontispiece and 26 plates inserted; other illustrations in text.

⟨-⟩^{8}, 1-30^8, 31^4.

9

⟨iii⟩-xviii, ⟨1⟩-496. Frontispiece and 27 plates inserted; maps in text.

⟨-⟩^{8}, 1-31^8.

10

⟨iii⟩-⟨xviii⟩, ⟨1⟩-482. Frontispiece and 21 plates inserted; other maps and illustrations in text.

⟨-⟩^{8}, 1-30^8, 31^1.

Vols. 1-9 deposited Sept. 23, 1890; Vol. 10 Dec. 1, 1890. Distributed in London by Unwin who advertised the work as *shortly* Ath Oct. 25, 1890; reviewed by Bkr (Christmas issue, Dec. 1890); and by Ath April 11, 1891.

B H

7773. The First Book of the Authors Club Liber Scriptorum ...

New York   Published by the Authors Club
M DCCC XCIII

"Euthanasia," p. ⟨276⟩. Collected *Complete Poetical Works*, 1916.

For comment see entry No. 1283.

7774. Abraham Lincoln Complete Works . . . Edited by John G. Nicolay and John Hay . . .

New York The Century Co. 1894

2 Vols.

"Preface," Vol. 1, p. ⟨v⟩.

The above edition deposited for copyright April 14, 1894. Commented on in Ath July 14, 1894, as *about to issue,* as though with the T. Fisher Unwin imprint. T. Fisher Unwin edition announced Ath Oct. 6, 1894. No copy with the Unwin imprint located and the presumption is that the book was distributed in Great Britain by Unwin but not issued with that imprint.

Various later printings by various publishers, including subscription houses. Sometimes occurs as Vols. 11-12 of a set embracing the ten volumes of *Abraham Lincoln A History,* 1890. The following reprints have been seen:

⟨Cumberland Gap, Tenn.⟩ Lincoln Memorial University ⟨1894; *i.e.,* issued not before 1924⟩

New York The Lamb Publishing Company ⟨1905⟩

New York Francis D. Tandy Company ⟨1905⟩ Reprinted and reissued by Tandy-Thomas Company.

LC NYPL

7775. The Presidents of the United States 1789–1894 by John Fiske . . . George Bancroft, John Hay, and Others Edited by James Grant Wilson . . .

New York D. Appleton and Company 1894

"Abraham Lincoln," pp. ⟨300⟩-333. A very slightly revised printing of the sketch in *Appletons' Cyclopaedia,* 1887.

Extended editions were published ⟨1898⟩ and 1914. Presumably neither contains new material by Hay although in each of the later editions the sketch is somewhat altered.

". . . The . . . writers of these model biographies . . . are not responsible for the brief notices of the ladies of the White House, for the sketches of other persons connected with the families of the Presidents . . . These have been added by the editor . . ."—Preface, editions of 1894 and ⟨1898⟩.

Deposited Dec. 5, 1894. Listed PW Dec. 22, 1894. The London (Gay & Bird) edition listed PC July 13, 1895.

H Y

7776. . . . A Prayer in Thessaly Sonnet . . . Music by Dorothea Hollins . . .

London & New York Novello, Ewer & Co. Author's Property. ⟨n.d., 1895⟩

Sheet music. Cover-title. At head of title: To W. Alison Phillips, Esqre. Plate number 9883

Originally in *Century Magazine* (N. Y.), Nov. 1893. Deposited BMU Jan. 14, 1895. Collected in *Complete Poetical Works,* 1916.

Not seen. Entry on the basis of a photostatic copy (in B) of the BMU original.

7777. Notable Single Poems American Authors Edited by Ina Russelle Warren

Buffalo Charles Wells Moulton Publisher ⟨n.d., 1895⟩

"On Landing in England," p. 49. Originally in *Pall Mall Magazine* (London), Dec. 1894.

For comment see entry No. 5672.

7778. THE PLATFORM OF ANARCHY. AN ADDRESS TO THE STUDENTS OF WESTERN RESERVE UNIVERSITY, CLEVELAND, O. OCTOBER 6th, 1896 . . .

⟨n.p., probably Cleveland, Ohio, 1896⟩

Cover-title.

⟨1⟩-27, 2 blank leaves. 9″ x 6″.

⟨-⟩¹⁶.

Printed salmon paper wrapper.

The BPL copy inscribed by William Winter Oct. 16, 1896.

B BPL MHS Y

7779. SPEECH . . . AT THE UNVEILING OF THE BUST OF SIR WALTER SCOTT IN WESTMINSTER ABBEY MAY 21, 1897

JOHN LANE, THE BODLEY HEAD LONDON & NEW YORK 1897

For first American edition see entry No. 7788.

⟨1⟩-14; printer's imprint, p. ⟨15⟩. Frontispiece of Scott inserted. Laid paper. 6⁹⁄₁₆″ x 5¹⁄₁₆″. Paper watermarked W.K.⟨?⟩.

⟨-⟩⁸.

Printed blue-gray laid paper boards. White laid paper end papers.

Noted as though published, PC July 10, 1897. Listed PC July 10, 1897. PW July 24, 1897, reported: *will publish shortly.* B copy received Aug. 12, 1897.

B NYPL

7780. . . . A Library of the World's Best Literature Ancient and Modern ⟨Edited by⟩ Charles Dudley Warner . . .

New York   The International Society MDCCCXCVII

Reprint save for:

"When Phyllis Laughs," Vol. 12, p. 7106.

"Night in Venice," Vol. 12, p. 7106. For publication as sheet music see below under 1902; collected in *Complete Poetical Works*, 1916.

For comment see entry No. 2165.

7781. IN PRAISE OF OMAR

Hay's address on Omar Khayyam, delivered at a dinner of the Omar Khayyam Club, London, December 8, 1897, appeared in the United States in a variety of forms. Earliest located publication is in *The Critic* (New York), Dec. 25, 1897. The following is a chronological list of the American appearances (1898–1899) thus far noted save for the 1898, 1899 reprints (which are so marked) published by Thomas B. Mosher, Portland, Me.

A

Rubaiyat of Omar Khayyam Rendered into English Verse by Edward Fitzgerald ⟨5th Mosher edition⟩

Portland, Maine   Thomas B. Mosher Mdcccxcviij

Printed flexible boards. 925 copies on Van Gelder paper. Mosher, in his bibliography of the *Rubaiyat*, p. 101, of this publication, records a printing of 100 copies on Japanese vellum. This last has not been located by BAL. Further according to Mosher's bibliography this *Fifth Edition* was published ⟨printed?⟩ February, 1898, in Mosher's *The Old World Series*.

At p. ⟨2⟩ is printed a short extract from the address.

B

The Hon. John Hay ⟨red⟩ / on / FitzGerald's Rubaiyat ⟨red⟩ / of / Omar Khayyam ⟨red⟩ / Critic Leaflet No. 2 / New York: The Critic Co. / 1898

Note: The first five lines of the above title printed in roman.

Cover-title. Single leaf, folded to make four pages. Page: 7¹⁵⁄₁₆" x 5⅛". Printed on Ruisdael laid paper. Unpaged. Text of address on pp. ⟨2-4⟩. Facsimile autograph, in red, at end of text.

Announced in *The Critic*, March 5, 1898. Noted as *just issued* PW March 19, 1898. Listed and advertised in *The Critic*, March 12, 1898. Listed PW March 26, 1898.

Note: There were at least two printings in this format. The sequence has not been determined and the designations are for identification only.

Ba

The Hon. John Hay ⟨red⟩ / on / FitzGerald's Rubaiyat / of / Omar Khayyam / ⟨preceding five lines printed in black letter⟩ / Critic Leaflet No. 2 / New York: The Critic Co. / 1898

Otherwise the same as *Printing B.*

c

In Praise of Omar   An Address before the Omar Khayyám Club by the Hon. John Hay

Printed for Thomas B. Mosher and Published by Him at XLV Exchange Street   Portland Maine   M DCCC XCVIII

Printed paper wrapper folded over flexible boards. 925 copies on Van Gelder paper; 50 numbered copies on Japanese vellum; and, 4 (?) copies on vellum.

Noted as *just issued* PW April 16, 1898. Advertised in PW April 23, 1898. A copy in H inscribed by Thomas Bailey Aldrich *May, 1898.* Another copy in H received June 6, 1898.

D

The Rubaiyat of Omar Khayyam, Rendered into English Verse by Edward FitzGerald; with the Address of John Hay at the Omar Khayyam Club, London

⟨Elbert Hubbard: East Aurora, New York, 1898⟩

Flexible suède binding. According to the certificate of issue the printing of this edition was completed on June 10, 1898. Reprints have been noted with certificate of issue reading *tenth day of September MDCCCXCVIII;* and, *March the ninth MDCCCXCIX.*

E

Rubaiyat of Omar Khayyam Translated by Edward Fitzgerald (Fourth Edition, 1879) Introduction by the Hon. John Hay   Critic Pamphlet, No. 3

1898   New York   The Critic Co.

Printed paper wrapper. The text of the address, with the *Rubaiyat*, published in *The Critic* (New York), Dec. 1898. Listed as a Critic publication in *The Critic*, Jan. 1899.

F

Rubáiyát of Omar Khayyám Translated into English Verse by Edward Fitzgerald with Address by the Hon. John Hay

> Published by Brentano's at 31 Union Square New York ⟨n.d., 1899⟩

> Advertised in PW April 8, 1899. No listing in PW found.

> This Brentano's edition noted in two printings. No sequence has been established and the order of presentation is completely arbitrary.

Fa

⟨1⟩-89; Little imprint, p. ⟨90⟩, 2 blank leaves. ⟨1⁹, 2-5⁸, 6⁶⟩. Leaf ⟨1⟩₂ inserted. *Signed:* ⟨1⟩-5⁸, 6⁷. P. ⟨4⟩ blank. *A Complete List of ⟨4⟩ Volumes in This Series*, p. ⟨2⟩. Publisher's device above imprint on the title-page.

Fb

⟨1⟩-89, blank, p. ⟨90⟩. ⟨1⁹, 2-5⁸, 6⁴⟩. Leaf ⟨1⟩₂ inserted. *Signed:* ⟨1⟩-5⁸, 6⁶. Little imprint on p. ⟨4⟩. P. ⟨90⟩ blank. Publisher's device not on title-page. *Complete List* not present.

B (B, Ba, C, D, Fa) BA (B) H (A, B, C, Fa, Fb) NYPL (E) Y (Ba, C, D)

7782. (2) LETTER FROM HON. JOHN HAY, SECRETARY OF STATE, TO COL. CHARLES DICK, CHAIRMAN OHIO REPUBLICAN STATE EXECUTIVE COMMITTEE. NEWBURY, N. H., SEPT. 11, 1899 ...

⟨AKRON, OHIO, 1899⟩

Caption-title. The above at head of p. ⟨1⟩.

Two states of undetermined sequence have been noted. The following designations are for identification only:

A: With the symbol (2) at the head of title.

B: Without the symbol (2) at head of title.

Single cut sheet folded to 4 pp. Page: 9⅜″ x 6³⁄₁₆″.

Issued as campaign material. *"I am sorry that my engagements are such as to render it impossible for me to accept your kind invitation to be present at the opening of the Ohio Republican State Campaign at Akron ..."*

B (B) MHS (A) Y (B)

7783. The Bread-Winners   Biographical Edition

> New York and London   Harper & Brothers, Publishers 1899

Anonymous. For earlier editions see entries 7760, 7762.

"A Prefatory Sketch," pp. ⟨iii⟩-ix, written for this edition.

Deposited Oct. 24, 1899.

B   H   NYPL

7784. The Hesperian Tree   An Annual of the Ohio Valley 1900   Edited by John James Piatt ...

> Published by George C. Shaw   Cincinnati, O., for the Editor ⟨1900⟩

"To One Absent," p. 436. Collected in *Complete Poetical Works*, 1916.

For comment see entry No. 2973.

7785. The Lawyer's Alcove   Poems by the Lawyer ... and about the Lawyer Edited by Ina Russelle Warren ...

> New York   Doubleday, Page & Company 1900

"A Client to His Lawyer," p. 123; translated from Martial.

Listed PW Dec. 8, 1900.

H

7786. SPEECH ... AT A DINNER GIVEN BY THE BOARD OF DIRECTORS OF THE PAN-AMERICAN EXPOSITION TO THE NATIONAL EDITORIAL ASSOCIATION, BUFFALO, JUNE 13, 1901

WASHINGTON 1901

Cover-title.

⟨1⟩-4. 9½″ x 6″.

⟨-⟩².

Printed white paper wrapper.

B   Y

7787. REMARKS ... IN REPLY TO THE TOAST OF "OUR RECENT DIPLOMACY" AT THE DINNER OF THE NEW YORK CHAMBER OF COMMERCE, NOVEMBER 19, 1901.

⟨n.p., n.d., probably New York, 1901⟩

Cover-title.

⟨1⟩-11. 9¼″ x 5⅞″.

⟨-⟩⁶.

Printed white paper wrapper.

Note: Also appears in *CXXXIII. Annual Banquet of the Chamber of Commerce of the State of New-York ... Speeches Made on the Occasion*, New York, 1901. Copy in H.

B   BPL   NYPL   Y

7788. SPEECH . . . AT THE UNVEILING OF THE BUST OF SIR WALTER SCOTT IN WESTMINSTER ABBEY MAY 21, 1897

HARPER & BROTHERS   NEW YORK AND LONDON ⟨n.d., 1901?⟩

Cover-title; printed in red and black.

For an earlier printing see entry No. 7779.

⟨1⟩-12; advertisements, pp. ⟨13-15⟩; blank, p. ⟨16⟩. 5⅜" x 3".

⟨-⟩⁸.

Printed self-wrapper.

Issued as an advertisement for Scott's *Waverley Novels*. A Harper edition of *Waverley Novels* listed PW April 13, 1901.

AAS   B   LC

7789. McKINLEY MEMORIAL ADDRESS

Two versions as follows:

Original Text

First published 1902. Begins: *For the third time the Congress of the United States . . .*

Revised Text

First published 1903. Begins: *Once more, and for the third time, the Congress of the United States . . .*

The following is a record of separate printings of this address. No precise sequence has been established and the following designations are for identification only.

Original Text, Printing A

WILLIAM McKINLEY MEMORIAL ADDRESS . . . DELIVERED IN THE CAPITOL FEBRUARY 27, 1902, BY INVITATION OF THE CONGRESS

⟨n.p., n.d., probably The Associated Press, 1902⟩

1-21, blank leaf. 9⅜" x 5⅞".

⟨-⟩¹².

Printed white glazed paper wrapper.

A copy in H received March 4, 1902.

Locations: H

Original Text, Printing A, Advance Issue

In addition to the regularly issued printing described above there was also an advance issue from the same setting prepared for the use of newspapers. Printed on one side of leaf only. Paged ⟨1⟩-22, 2 blank leaves. Printed self-wrapper. Leaf: 8⅞" x 5¹⁵⁄₁₆". ⟨1-3⟩⁸. At head of

p. 2 is a notice to editors and agents signed by Melville E. Stone, General Manager, Associated Press: "The following Memorial Address . . . is supplied . . . upon our pledge that it shall be held in strict confidence, and shall be published only upon a telegraphic release . . ." This notice is not present in the formal printing described above and designated *Original Text, Printing A*.

Locations: B   H

Original Text, Printing B

WILLIAM McKINLEY. MEMORIAL ADDRESS . . . HALL OF THE HOUSE OF REPRESENTATIVES FEBRUARY 27th, 1902. WITH THE EDITORIAL COMMENTS OF W. C. P. BRECKENRIDGE, EDITOR MORNING HERALD.

⟨Lexington, Ky.,⟩ TRANSYLVANIA PRESS. ⟨n.d., 1902⟩

Cover-title.

⟨1-20⟩. 8¾" scant x 6⅛" full.

⟨-⟩¹⁰.

Printed self-wrapper.

"This pamphlet is printed from type furnished by the *Morning Herald* and is presented with the compliments of Transylvania Company, 10 East Main Street, Lexington, Ky. . . ."—p. ⟨20⟩.

Surely printed after production of the Associated Press advance issue but not necessarily published after *Original Text, Printing A*.

Location: LC

Original Text, Printing C

WILLIAM McKINLEY. MEMORIAL ADDRESS . . . DELIVERED IN THE CAPITOL FEBRUARY 27, 1902, BY INVITATION OF THE CONGRESS.

WASHINGTON. ⟨Government Printing Office⟩ 1902.

⟨1⟩-15. 9" x 5¾".

⟨-⟩⁸.

Printed blue paper wrapper.

Locations: B   LC

Original Text, Printing D

William McKinley Memorial Address . . .

New York   Thomas Y. Crowell & Co. Publishers ⟨1902⟩

Printed boards.

Reprint. Deposited April 30, 1902. BA copy received May 13, 1902. Listed PW May 17, 1902.

Locations: B H LC

Revised Text, Printing A

Memorial Address on the Life and Character of William McKinley . . .

Washington   Government   Printing   Office
1903

Pp. 70. Printed paper wrapper; and, cloth. A copy in B (printed paper wrapper) has inserted a letter from Hay to Edmund Clarence Stedman, Jan. 2, 1904, in which Hay writes: "... I send you a copy ... which Congress, with its usual stately leisure, has just printed ..."

Locations: B LC Y

Revised Text, Printing B

Same as *Revised Text, Printing A* (above), but with the following statement at head of title: *57th Congress, 2d Session. House of Representatives. Document No. 453.* Issued in printed paper wrapper; cloth; three-quarters leather.

Locations: B H NYPL

Revised Text, Printing C

Same as *Revised Text, Printing A* (above), but with the following statement at head of title: *Senate Document, No. 219, 57th Congress.*

Location: LC

Revised Text, Printing D

Memorial Addresses Delivered before the Two Houses of Congress on the Life and Character of Abraham Lincoln ⟨by George Bancroft⟩ James A. Garfield ⟨by James G. Blaine⟩ William McKinley ⟨by John Hay⟩ Prepared ... by Charles Rowley Cushman . . .

Washington   Government   Printing   Office
1903

Locations: B LC Y

7790. Night in Venice ... Music ... by Rupert Hughes.

Edward Schuberth & Co. ... New York ... London ... Leipzig ... ⟨1902⟩

Sheet music. Cover-title. Plate number 3811. Deposited March 3, 1902.

The text had prior publication in *A Library of the World's Best Literature* ... , 1897, above. Collected in *Complete Poetical Works*, 1916.

LC

7791. ... REMARKS OF THE SECRETARY OF STATE WHITE LOT, WASHINGTON, OCTOBER 6, 1902

⟨n.p., n.d., Grand Army of the Republic, 1902?⟩

Cover-title. At head of title: Thirty-Sixth National Encampment, G.A.R.

⟨1⟩-4. 9⅜″ x 6″.

⟨-⟩².

Printed white paper wrapper.

Note: All examined copies omit the name *Harrison,* p. ⟨1⟩, line 11. All examined copies have the error *enternal* for *eternal* p. ⟨1⟩, line 15.

B H MHS Y

Memorial Address ... William McKinley ...

Washington ... 1903

See entry No. 7789.

7792. The Hesperian Tree An Annual of the Ohio Valley 1903 Edited by John James Piatt . . .

Columbus, Ohio S. F. Harriman 1903

"The Sewers of Paris and Their Origin," pp. 392-401.

For comment see entry No. 3013.

7793. Castilian Days ... with Illustrations by Joseph Pennell

Cambridge Printed at the Riverside Press MCMIII

For first edition see entry No. 7742. For another revised edition see entry No. 7770.

An abridgement, revised, omitting much political criticism and some comments on the Roman Catholic Church.

Boards, cloth shelfback and corners, printed paper label on spine. Limited to 350 numbered copies.

Also issued in a trade edition with the imprint: *Boston and New York Houghton, Mifflin and Company The Riverside Press, Cambridge MCMIII*

On copyright page of the trade edition: *Published November 1903*

Deposited (limited edition) Nov. 13, 1903. Advertised (trade edition) PW Nov. 14, 1903. Listed (trade edition) PW Nov. 21, 1903. Both trade and limited editions advertised PW Nov. 28, 1903. The London (Heinemann) edition listed PC Nov. 14, 1903.

B (trade) H (trade, limited) NYPL (limited) Y (limited)

7794. . . . Diplomatic Banquet of the Ohio So-
ciety of New York at the Waldorf-Astoria
Saturday, January 17th, 1903 to Hon. John
Hay . . . Annual Dinner of the Society . . .
November 29th, 1902 . . .

New York ⟨The Ohio Society of New York⟩
1903

At head of title: No. 1 Annual Publications
Ohio Society of New York 1902–1903

Cover-title. Printed paper wrapper.

"Response of John Hay," at the banquet, Jan.
17, 1903, pp. 12-15.

H LC

7795. Clarence King Memoirs The Helmet of
Mambrino

Published for the King Memorial Committee
of the Century Association by G. P. Putnam's
Sons New York and London 1904

"Clarence King," pp. 117-132.

For comment see entry No. 30.

7796. . . . ADDRESS OF THE SECRETARY
OF STATE AT THE OPENING OF THE
PRESS PARLIAMENT OF THE WORLD,
AT ST. LOUIS, ON MAY 19, 1904

⟨n.p., n.d., probably Washington, 1904⟩

Cover-title. At head of title: Press Parliament
of the World Louisiana Purchase Exposition

⟨1⟩-13, blank leaf. 9⅜″ x 5¹⁵⁄₁₆″.

⟨-⟩⁸.

Printed glazed white paper wrapper.

Note: A British printing was issued with the
following imprint: *London: "North-Eastern
Daily Gazette," 67, Fleet Street, E.C. 1904.*
Presumably a reprint. Copies in B LC NYPL.

The address also appears in: *Proceedings of the
World's Press Parliament Held at the Universal
Exposition Saint Louis, U.S.A. May 19, 20, 21,
1904,* Columbia, Missouri, U.S.A. . . . E. W.
Stephens 1904. Copy in LC.

B LC

7797. . . . FIFTY YEARS OF THE REPUBLI-
CAN PARTY . . .

⟨n.p., n.d., 1904⟩

Cover-title. At head of title: AN ADDRESS DE-
LIVERED AT JACKSON, MICH., JULY 6, 1904

⟨1⟩-29, blank leaf. 9⅜″ scant x 5⅞″.

⟨-⟩¹⁶.

Printed white paper wrapper.

Locations: B H NYPL Y

Note: The above printing is presumed to be the
first. Also issued as follows, without imprint, but
probably issued as campaign material by the
National Republican Committee. Sequence not
known and the designations below are for identification only.

Campaign Edition A

The Republican Party / "A party fit to gov-
ern" / An Address by / John Hay / Delivered
at Jackson, Mich., July 6, 1904 / and / The
Address of / Elihu Root / As Temporary
Chairman of the National Republican Convention / at Chicago, Ill., Tuesday, June 21, 1904 /
⟨New York, n.d., 1904⟩

Cover-title. Place of printing from union label,
p. 48.

⟨1⟩-48, 8⅛″ x 5½″. Wove paper.

Printed self-wrapper.

Locations: AAS B H NYPL

Campaign Edition B

The Republican Party / "A party fit to gov-
ern" / An Address by / John Hay / Secretary
of State of the United States / Delivered at
Jackson, Mich., July 6, 1904 / and / The Address of / Elihu Root / Former ⟨*sic*⟩ Secretary
of War of the United States / As Temporary
Chairman of the National Republican Convention / at Chicago, Ill., Tuesday, June 21,
1904 / ⟨New York, n.d., 1904⟩

Cover-title. Place of printing taken from union
label, p. 32.

⟨1⟩-32.

Printed self-wrapper.

Locations: H

Campaign Edition C

Apparently the same as *Campaign Edition B*
but issued in mottled gray paper wrapper imprinted on front: *Afro-American Souvenir* . . .

Location: B

Campaign Edition D

The Republican Party / "A party fit to gov-
ern" / By / John Hay / Secretary of State of
the United States / and / Elihu Root / For-
merly ⟨*sic*⟩ Secretary of War of the United
States / ⟨*rule*⟩ / Privately Printed / New York /
1904

Note: In this form the sheets occur in printed
self-wrapper; and, in printed wrapper.

⟨i-ii⟩, 1-57. Laid paper.

⟨1-3⁸, 4⁴, 5²⟩.

Locations: AAS B H Y

Campaign Edition E

Same as *Campaign Edition D* save for the collation which is: ⟨1-3⁸, 4⁶⟩.

Locations: B H MHS NYPL Y

Campaign Edition F

History of the Republican Party Reviewed / by Secretary Hay. / ⟨rule⟩ / ⟨text of speech⟩ / ⟨Chicago, n.d., 1904⟩

Caption title. The above on p. ⟨1⟩. Place of printing taken from union label, p. 8.

⟨1⟩-8.

Printed self-wrapper.

Locations: AAS B

Campaign Edition G

JOHN HAY / ON / THEODORE ROOSEVELT / ⟨*double rule*⟩ / EXTRACT OF AN ADDRESS / DELIVERED BY THE / Hon. John Hay / Secretary of State / of the United States, / AT JACKSON, MICH. / JULY 6th, 1904. / ⟨rule⟩ / PRIVATELY PRINTED BY / DR. ADOLPHE DANZIGER. / ⟨rule⟩ / NEW YORK, / 3082 Metropolitan Building. / ⟨*all the preceding in a double rule frame*⟩ / ⟨1904⟩

Cover-title.

⟨1⟩-13; halftone engraving of Roosevelt, p. ⟨14⟩; halftone engraving of Fairbanks, p. ⟨15⟩; *Vote Under This Emblem* . . . , p. ⟨16⟩. 8⅞″ x 6⅛″.

Printed self-wrapper.

Extracted from the full speech.

Locations: B NYPL

History of the Republican Party Reviewed . . .

⟨Chicago, n.d., 1904⟩

See entry No. 7797, *Campaign Edition F.*

John Hay on Theodore Roosevelt . . .

Privately Printed . . . New York . . . ⟨1904⟩

See entry No. 7797, *Campaign Edition G.*

7798. CONGRESS OF PEACE ADDRESS

This address has been noted in separate form as follows. Sequence unknown. The following designations are for identification only.

Printing A

The Congress of Peace / ⟨rule⟩ / Address by /

The Honorable John Hay / Secretary of State / ⟨n.p., 1904?⟩

⟨1⟩-12. Laid paper. 10″ full x 7⁹⁄₁₆″.

⟨-⟩⁶.

Printed paper wrapper. Two types of paper wrapper noted: yellow-green watermarked *Strathmore USA;* and, unwatermarked ecru. Tied with silk cord.

Note: There is in B a proof copy of the above setting; 9 leaves.

Location: B Y

Printing B

ADDRESS OF HON. JOHN HAY. / [After the formal opening of the Thirteenth / Peace Congress, Secretary John Hay was intro- / duced. He represented the Government of the / United States officially in welcoming the Con- / gress to America. Mr. Hay then made the / following address ⟨etc., etc., etc.⟩ / ⟨n.p., n.d., printed from the types of the *Lend a Hand Record,* Boston, Nov. 1904⟩

Caption-title. The above at head of column 1. Printed in 4 columns on recto only. Single sheet. 18⅞″ x 12″.

Location: LC

Note: The address appears also in:

Official Report of the Thirteenth Universal Peace Congress Held at Boston, Massachusetts, U.S.A., October Third to Eighth, 1904 . . . , Boston: The Peace Congress Committee, 1904.

Locations: H NYPL

7799. SPEECH . . . DELIVERED AT CARNEGIE HALL, NEW YORK, OCTOBER 26, 1904

⟨n.p., n.d., 1904⟩

Cover-title.

⟨1⟩-19. 9⅜″ x 6″ scant.

⟨-⟩¹⁰.

Printed white glazed paper wrapper.

B H NYPL Y

7800. Defend Us, O Lord! . . . Music by John W. Metcalf . . .

Arthur P. Schmidt, Boston . . . Leipzig . . . New York . . . London . . . 1906 . . .

Sheet music. Cover-title. Plate number: A.P.S. 7006-4.

Deposited Jan. 19, 1906. Reprinted and reissued not before 1916 with the imprint of The Arthur P. Schmidt Company.

B LC

7801. History of the Ohio Society of New York 1885–1905 ... by James H. Kennedy ...

The Grafton Press New York MCMVI

Note, Jan. 22, 1902, p. 354. The "remarks," pp. 403-405, reprinted from a speech delivered in 1903; see entry No. 7794.

Deposited July 27, 1906.

H NYPL

7802. ADDRESSES ...

NEW YORK THE CENTURY CO. 1906

⟨i-ii⟩, ⟨i⟩-vi, ⟨1⟩-353, blank leaf. Frontispiece portrait inserted. Laid paper. 8¼″ x 5½″.

⟨-⟩⁴, ⟨1⟩-5, ⟨6-7⟩, 8-11, ⟨12⟩, 13-15, ⟨16⟩, 17-21⁸, 22², ⟨23⟩⁸.

FL cloth: blue. White laid paper end papers. Laid paper flyleaves. Top edges gilt.

Note: A variant has been seen in blue S cloth. There may be some significance in the fact that the 1907 reprint occurs in blue S cloth also; but, the 1907 reprint has also been seen in blue FL and in blue T cloths. The copyright deposit copies are in blue FL cloth.

Deposited Sept. 1, 1906. On copyright page: *Published October, 1906* Listed PW Oct. 6, 1906.

H NYPL Y

7803. LETTERS OF JOHN HAY AND EX-TRACTS FROM DIARY ...

WASHINGTON 1908 PRINTED BUT NOT PUBLISHED

3 Vols.

1: ⟨i-iv⟩, i-xxii, 1-393, blank leaf. Laid paper watermarked *Alexandra*. 9½″ x 6¼″.
2: ⟨i-iv⟩, 1-368.
3: ⟨i-iv⟩, 1-350, blank leaf.

1: ⟨a⟩², ⟨b⟩⁸, ⟨c⟩¹, ⟨d⟩², ⟨1⟩-24⁸, 25⁴, ⟨26⟩².
2: ⟨a⟩², 1-23⁸.
3: ⟨a⟩², 1-⟨22⟩⁸.

Note: The signature marks indicate both the signature and the volume. Vol. 1: simple signatures; Vol. 2: the volume is indicated by the superior numeral 2; Vol. 3: the volume is indicated by the superior numeral 3.

V cloth: tan. Blue buckram. Printed paper label on spine. End papers of book stock. Flyleaves.

Edited by Henry Adams. See entry No. 33.

Note: In all examined copies leaf 44 (pp. 55-56), Vol. 2, is a cancel.

Dr. David A. Jonah, librarian of The John Hay Library, Brown University, informs BAL: "The best information that I can give you regarding the size of the edition of *Letters* ... was obtained ... from Frederick V. Furst, President of J. H. Furst Company, Baltimore, Maryland, the printers of this work. Mr. Furst wrote ... : *We printed about 200 copies for Mrs. Hay's private use and shipped them to her in Washington.*"

Deposited Dec. 29, 1908.

B H NYPL

7804. Memories of Brown Traditions and Recollections Gathered from Many Sources ⟨Edited by⟩ ... Robert Perkins Brown ... Henry Robinson Palmer ... Harry Lyman Koopman ... Clarence Saunders Brigham ...

Providence, Rhode Island Brown Alumni Magazine Company 1909

Contained in "John Hay As a Parodist of Emerson," by S. W. Abbott, pp. 135-136, is an undergraduate poem, "Sa! Sa!," which had original publication in *The Brown Paper*, 1857, entry No. 7725.

"The Angell Cradle," p. 167.

B

7805. A POET IN EXILE EARLY LETTERS OF JOHN HAY EDITED BY CAROLINE TICKNOR

BOSTON AND NEW YORK HOUGHTON MIFFLIN COMPANY MDCCCCX

Title-page in black and brown.

⟨i-xii⟩, ⟨1⟩-48; blank, p. ⟨49⟩; colophon, p. ⟨50⟩; blank leaf. Paper watermarked *British Hand Made*. Portrait frontispiece mounted on p. ⟨viii⟩. 1-page facsimile manuscript inserted. 8½″ x 5⅞″.

⟨1⁴, 2², 3-8⁴, 9²⟩.

Brown laid paper boards. Printed paper label on spine. End papers of book stock. Extra label tipped in at back.

440 copies printed.

H copy received May 14, 1910. Deposited May 16, 1910. Listed PW June 18, 1910.

H NYPL

7806. THE LIFE AND LETTERS OF JOHN HAY BY WILLIAM ROSCOE THAYER ...

BOSTON AND NEW YORK HOUGHTON MIFFLIN COMPANY MDCCCCXV

2 Vols.

1: ⟨i-ii⟩, ⟨i⟩-⟨xiv⟩, ⟨1⟩-456. Frontispiece and 8 plates inserted. 8⁹⁄₁₆″ x 5¹³⁄₁₆″.
2: ⟨i-viii⟩, ⟨1⟩-448; printer's imprint, p. ⟨450⟩; blank leaf. Frontispiece and 8 plates inserted.

1: ⟨1-29⁸, 30⁴⟩.
2: ⟨1⁴, 2-28⁸, 29¹⁰⟩.

V cloth: greenish black. Top edges gilt. Spine lettered in gold.

Note: Also issued in a so-called large paper edition. This is not a true large paper edition but sheets of the normal trade printing, wholly untrimmed. Leaf: 9″ x 6″. Issued in greenish black V cloth, printed paper label on spine. On copyright page is the following statement: *Of This First Edition Three Hundred Copies Have Been Bound Wholly Uncut, With Paper Label.*

A copy in B inscribed by Thayer Oct. 9, 1915. Deposited Oct. 20, 1915. Listed PW Oct. 23, 1915. On copyright page: *Published October 1915* The *Seventeenth Impression, August, 1916* (so marked) was extended by the addition of material to the "Appendix". The London (Constable) edition was made up of American sheets with cancelled title-leaf; deposited BMU Nov. 26, 1915; listed Bkr Nov. 5, 1915, and Dec. 3, 1915; PC Dec. 4, 1915.

AAS   B   H

7807. Walt Whitman, As Man, Poet and Friend ... Being Autograph Pages from Many Pens, Collected by Charles N. Elliot

Boston: Richard G. Badger   The Gorham Press ⟨1915⟩

Note, p. 113.

For comment see entry No. 6635.

7808. THE COMPLETE POETICAL WORKS ... INCLUDING MANY POEMS NOW FIRST COLLECTED ... INTRODUCTION BY CLARENCE L. HAY

BOSTON AND NEW YORK   HOUGHTON MIFFLIN COMPANY   MDCCCCXVI

Title-page printed in black and brown.

⟨i⟩-⟨xiv⟩, ⟨1⟩-⟨272⟩. 8⅝″ x 5¾″. Portrait frontispiece inserted.

⟨1², 2⁴, 3¹, 4-20⁸⟩.

White paper boards printed with a pattern in yellow; white linen shelfback; leather label on spine. Flyleaves.

1,000 numbered copies only.

BA copy received Oct. 28, 1916. Deposited Nov. 6, 1916. NYPL copy received Nov. 16, 1916. Listed PW Dec. 16, 1916.

H   LC   NYPL

7809. St. Nicholas Book of Verse Edited by Mary Budd Skinner and Joseph Osmun Skinner

. . .

Published by the Century Co.   New York and London   MCMXXIII

"Look Ahead," pp. 346-347.

For comment see entry No. 818.

7810. "1601" or Conversation at the Social Fireside As It Was in the Time of the Tudors ⟨by Samuel L. Clemens. Edited by Charles Erskine Scott Wood⟩

Privately Printed at ⟨the Grabhorn Press⟩ San Francisco MCMXXV

Boards, printed paper label on spine. Also leather. 100 copies only.

Letters to Alexander Gunn, pp. ⟨31-32⟩.

Note: This *sub rosa* production by Mark Twain went into an unknown number of printings prior to publication of the above. For a comment on the earliest printings (which do not contain the Hay letters) see BAL entries 3388, 3407. The nature of the publication being what it is there can be no certainty as to which of the many printings was the first to contain the John Hay letters. The present edition, because of its auspices, is included in this list as a matter of record but it may not be the earliest printing to include the Hay letters.

NYPL

7811. A COLLEGE FRIENDSHIP   A SERIES OF LETTERS FROM JOHN HAY TO HANNAH ANGELL

BOSTON   PRIVATELY PRINTED 1938

⟨i-ii⟩, ⟨i⟩-x, ⟨1⟩-65; colophon, p. ⟨67⟩. Laid paper watermarked *Glaslan France.* Photogravure portrait of Hannah Angell inserted. 8⅜″ x 6⅛″.

⟨1-5⟩⁸.

T cloth: gray-green. White laid paper end papers. Top edges gilt. Flyleaves.

350 copies only.

Deposited May 25, 1938.

B   LC

7812. Abraham Lincoln / by / John Hay

⟨n.p., n.d., New York: M. Harzof, *ca.* 1938–1939⟩

Title as shown above printed on front of the wrapper.

⟨1-17⟩, blank leaf. Illustrated. 8" x 5¼".

⟨-⟩¹⁰.

Printed light blue paper wrapper.

P. ⟨13⟩: *Reproduced from the Original ⟨letter dated Paris, Sept. 5, 1866.⟩ In the Collection of Lincolniana Formed by Wm. H. Herndon Now in the Possession of Gabriel Wells.*

Note: This pamphlet was issued as part of a sales promotion. During the run of the wrapper Messrs. John T. Winterich and Jacob Blanck happened into the Harzof establishment, where the wrapper was being printed on a small proof-press, and in a spirit of bibliophilic puckish-ness requested the printer to rearrange the types and produce a deliberate "error." The printer agreed and three or four copies were so produced. Hence the publication exists in the following three issues:

1: With the front wrapper reading: *Abraham Lincoln / by / John Hay*

2: With some rearrangement of the types which produced an "error." Both Messrs. Winterich and Blanck express regret that they cannot be more specific since neither has a precise recol-lection of the alteration; and each further re-grets that his personal copy of the pamphlet has long since disappeared.

3: With the front wrapper reading: *Abraham Lincoln / by / John Hay* It will be noted that there is no way of distinguishing the first issue from the third.

B   H   Y

7813. LINCOLN AND THE CIVIL WAR IN THE DIARIES AND LETTERS OF JOHN HAY SELECTED AND WITH AN INTRO-DUCTION BY TYLER DENNETT . . .

DODD, MEAD & COMPANY   NEW YORK   1939

⟨i⟩-⟨xiv⟩, 1-348, blank leaf. Frontispiece in-serted. 9¼" x 6¼".

⟨1-22⁸, 23⁶⟩.

T cloth: red.

Deposited Feb. 10, 1939. H copy received Feb. 24, 1939.

H   NYPL

COLLECTIONS of reprinted material issued under Hay's name; separate editions (*i.e.*, pieces reprinted from Hay's books and issued in separate form); and undated reprints. For a list of books by authors other than Hay containing reprinted Hay material see *Section III*.

7814. Little Breeches and Other Pieces . . .

London: John Camden Hotten, 74 & 75, Piccadilly . . . ⟨n.d., 1871⟩

Printed paper wrapper; and, cloth. Advertised for *July* Ath July 1, 1871. Listed Ath Sept. 23, 1871. Listed PC Oct. 2, 1871.

Two printings noted:

1: Printer's imprint on verso of title-leaf set 2⅜″ wide.

2: Printer's imprint on verso of title-leaf set 2¾″ wide.

7815. . . . Extracts from Hay. When You Partake of This Concoction, Be Tender-Hearted, and Cry If You Want To.

⟨n.p., n.d., 1871?⟩

At head of title: 15 Copies Printed for Private Use. Cover-title. Printed self-wrapper. Pp. ⟨1⟩-8. Laid paper. 8½″ x 5⁵⁄₁₆″.

Contains "Banty Tim," "Jim Bludso," and "Little Breeches." Presumably reprinted from *Pike County Ballads*, 1871, but definite information is wanting. See entries 7734, 7737, 7739, 7740, 7741, 7744.

7816. Short Stories for Spare Moments. By Harriet Prescott Spofford . . . John Hay . . . etc.

Philadelphia: J. B. Lippincott Company ⟨not before August, 1872⟩.

For comment see BAL, Vol. 1, p. 109.

7817. Entertaining Stories

⟨Philadelphia: J. B. Lippincott & Co., 1874⟩

Binder's title. An omnibus volume containing the following three separate publications brought together as a single book: *Not Pretty, but Precious, and Other Short Stories*, 1874, (see entry No. 7746 for first printing); *Rougegorge*

and Other Short Stories, 1870; and, *Rookstone*, 1871.

7818. . . . On the Bluff . . . Music by J. R. Thomas.

New York, Wm. A. Pond & Co. 547 Broadway. & 39 Union Sq. . . . 1874 . . .

Sheet music. Cover-title. At head of title: To Clarence Livingston, Esq. Plate number 8519. Reprinted from *Pike County Ballads*, 1871.

7819. Castilian Days . . .

Boston: Houghton, Mifflin and Company. The Riverside Press, Cambridge. 1880.

7820. Castilian Days . . .

Boston: Houghton, Mifflin and Company. The Riverside Press, Cambridge. 1882.

7821. Pike County Ballads and Other Poems . . .

London: John & Robert Maxwell, Milton House, St. Bride Street, Ludgate Circus, and Shoe Lane, Fleet Street, E.C. (All Rights Reserved.) ⟨n.d., 1886⟩

Printed paper wrapper. Also issued in cloth according to contemporary trade notices. Advertised as a *new book* Ath Jan. 30, 1886. Listed PC Feb. 15, 1886; Bkr March, 1886.

7822. Castilian Days . . . Seventh Edition.

Boston: Houghton, Mifflin and Company. The Riverside Press, Cambridge. 1887.

7823. The Enchanted Shirt . . .

Fleming H. Revell   New York . . . Chicago . . . ⟨1889⟩

Pictorial paper wrapper. Reprinted from *Pike County Ballads*, 1871. Deposited Aug. 15, 1889. Listed PW Nov. 2, 1889.

7824. . . . Pike County Ballads and Other Poems . . . The Vision of Don Roderick and the Field of Waterloo by Sir Walter Scott Edited . . . by Henry Morley . . .

London   George Routledge & Sons, Limited Broadway, Ludgate Hill . . . 1891

At head of title: Companion Poets Listed PC Aug. 8, 1891.

7825. ... Banty Tim ...

Robinson Press, 91 Oliver Street, Boston. ⟨n.d., *ca.* 1896–1898⟩

Caption-title. The above on p. ⟨2⟩. At upper left: Robinson Press ... Single cut sheet folded to make four pages. Text of "Banty Tim" on pp. ⟨2-3⟩. On p. ⟨1⟩: Vignette captioned: *Hon. Jay L. Torrey* ... On p. ⟨4⟩: *Robinson Press* ... Reprinted from *Pike County Ballads,* 1871.

7826. Pike County Ballads and Other Poems ... Edited ... by Henry Morley ...

London George Routledge & Sons, Limited Broadway, Ludgate Hill Manchester and New York 1897

Noted as *about to be issued* PC March 13, 1897.

7827. Castilian Days ...

London John Lane: The Bodley Head Houghton, Mifflin & Co. Boston 1897

Listed Ath May 22, 1897; PC July 10, 1897.

7828. Poems ...

London John Lane: The Bodley Head Houghton, Mifflin & Co. Boston 1897

Listed Ath May 22, 1897; PC July 10, 1897. Advertised as *now ready* Ath July 10, 1897. Noted by Ath July 17, 1897, where it is described as a "reprint."

7828A. ... American Humorous Poetry ... ⟨by⟩ John Hay ... James Russell Lowell ... Bret Harte ... Oliver Wendell Holmes ...

⟨London⟩ "Review of Reviews" Office. Entered at Stationers' Hall. ⟨n.d., 1897?⟩

At head of title: The Masterpiece Library. Printed paper wrapper. Issued as *The Penny Poets,* No. LVII.

7829. ... The White Flag ... Music ... by F. Korbay ...

Boosey & Co 295, Regent Street, London, W. and 9, East Seventeenth Street, New York ... 1898 ...

Sheet music. Cover-title. At head of title: Sung by Miss Susan Strong. Plate number H.2107. Reprinted from *Poems,* 1890. Deposited Feb. 7, 1898.

7830. The Presidents of the United States 1789–1898 By John Fiske ... George Bancroft, John Hay, and Others Edited by James Grant Wilson ...

New York D. Appleton and Company ⟨1898⟩

See entry No. 7775.

7831. Poems ...

Boston and New York Houghton, Mifflin and Company The Riverside Press, Cambridge 1899

Deposited May 18, 1899.

7832. Castilian Days ...

Boston and New York Houghton, Mifflin and Company The Riverside Press, Cambridge ⟨1899⟩

7833. Poems ...

London John Lane: The Bodley Head Houghton, Mifflin & Co. Boston 1901

Listed Ath Nov. 2, 1901.

7834. ... My Dearest Wish ...

Boston Oliver Ditson Company New York Chicago Philadelphia ... ⟨1902⟩

Sheet music. Cover-title. At head of title: Alfred E. Little ... Deposited Jan. 27, 1902. Otherwise "Love's Prayer," *Poems,* 1890.

7835. A Short Life of Abraham Lincoln Condensed from Nicolay & Hay's Abraham Lincoln ... by John G. Nicolay

New York The Century Co. 1902

Deposited Sept. 6, 1902. On copyright page: *Published October, 1902.*

7836. The Life of Sir Walter Scott Abridged from Lockhart's Life of Scott by Richard H. Hutton ... with an Introductory Appreciation by the Late Secretary of State John Hay

Philadelphia John D. Morris & Company ⟨n.d., 1905⟩

A subscription book and as such issued with varying imprints; and, in several styles of binding. "An Appreciation," pp. v-xi, is a reprint of Hay's address at the unveiling of the bust of Scott in Westminster Abbey, May 21, 1897. See entry numbers 7779, 7788. Listed PW April 28, 1906.

7837. ⟨The Stirrup Cup⟩

⟨n.p., n.d., 1905?⟩

Single leaf folded to four pages. Text on pp. ⟨2-3⟩. Page: 9⁷⁄₁₆″ x 5¾″. On p. ⟨3⟩: "The Stirrup Cup" by Hay; and, a 4-stanza continuation by E. P. Alexander. Pp. ⟨1⟩ and ⟨4⟩ blank. "The Stirrup Cup" reprinted from *Poems*, 1890.

7838. .... I Sent My Love Two Roses ... Music by Harold Fraser Simson ...

Boosey & Co. ... New York ... London ... 1907 ...

Sheet music. Cover-title. At head of title: Sung by Mr. John McCormack. Deposited Aug. 1, 1907. Otherwise "The White Flag." See entry No. 7829.

7839. Brown University 1764–1864 Centennial Poem by John Hay of the Class of 1858 ...

⟨n.p., n.d., probably Providence, R. I., *ca.* 1910⟩

Single sheet. 14¾″ x 10″. Printed on recto only. Three types of paper noted; sequence, if any, not determined. The following designations are for identification only: A: Watermarked with a tower ⟨crown?⟩ device and *Umbria Italia;* B: Watermarked with an oval device and the monogram *PCo;* C: Watermarked *Warren's Olde Style.*

Note: This same poem was also issued in a 4-page printing by H. C. Bumpus. See entry No. 7849.

For earlier printings of this poem see above under *Celebration* ... , 1865; and "Centennial" in *Pike County Ballads*, 1871.

7840. Expectation ... Music by Alexander Russell

The John Church Company Cinciinnati ⟨*sic*⟩ New York Chicago London Leipsic ⟨1911⟩

Sheet music. Cover-title. Plate number 16531-3. Deposited Sept. 18, 1911. Reprinted from *Poems*, 1890. What is presumed to be a reprint has the following reading on the front: *Songs for Men by American Composers* ...

7841. The Pike County Ballads ...

Houghton Mifflin Company Boston and New York ⟨1912⟩

Cloth, picture pasted to front cover. The spine imprint occurs in two states of unknown se-

quence, if sequence there is. The designations are for identification only. A: HOUGHTON / MIFFLIN / CO. B: HOUGHTON / MIFFLIN CO. On copyright page: *Published October 1912*

7842. .... Poems by John Hay   Brown 1858

Cambridge The Riverside Press 1913

At head of title: Ratcliffe Hicks Prize Brown University Leather. 150 copies only. *Note:* This is not the same selection as that similarly issued in 1935.

7843. Poems ...

Boston and New York   Houghton Mifflin Company The Riverside Press Cambridge ⟨1913⟩

7844. The Presidents of the United States 1789–1914 by John Fiske ... George Bancroft, John Hay, and Many Others Edited by James Grant Wilson ...

New York Charles Scribner's Sons 1914

See entry No. 7775. 2 Vols.

7845. When the Boys Come Home ... Music by Oley Speaks ...

G. Schirmer New York: 3 East 43d St. London, W.: 18, Berners St. Boston: The Boston Music Co. ⟨1915⟩

Sheet music. Cover-title. Plate number 28951. Deposited Oct. 9, 1915. Reprinted from *Pike County Ballads*, 1871. Reprinted and reissued with the imprint: G. Schirmer ... ⟨*1917*⟩. Other and later settings: Music by W. T. Porter; issued by The Willis Music Company, Cincinnati, 1918. Music by Frances Allitsen; issued by Boosey & Company, 1918.

7846. .... The Complete Poetical Works ... with an Introduction by Clarence L. Hay

Boston and New York   Houghton Mifflin Company The Riverside Press Cambridge 1917

Reprint of the 1916 edition but with added index of first lines and titles. At head of title: Household Edition Listed PW Sept. 22, 1917.

7847. .... Poems by John Hay   Brown 1858

Cambridge The Riverside Press 1935

At head of title: Ratcliffe Hicks Prize Brown University Three-quarters leather. 500 copies only. *Note:* This is not the same selection as that similarly issued in 1913.

7848. ... Twelve American Ballads

Periwinkle Press   Norton, Massachusetts 1940

At head of title: John Hay ...   60 copies only.

7849. The Enclosed Centennial Poem ... by John Hay ... May Not Have Come to Your Attention ...

⟨n.p., n.d., 1954?⟩ H. C. Bumpus

Single cut sheet folded to four pages. Gray paper. 7¾″ x 5³⁄₁₆″. For an earlier separate printing of this poem see entry No. 7839.

THE FOLLOWING publications contain material by Hay reprinted from earlier books. For a list of reprints issued under Hay's name see *Section II.*

Humorous Poems ... Edited by William Michael Rossetti ...

London ... ⟨n.d., 1872⟩

For comment see BAL, Vol. 1, p. 207.

The Poets and Poetry of America. By Rufus Wilmot Griswold. With Additions by R. H. Stoddard ... Carefully Revised, Much Enlarged, and Continued to the Present Time ...

New York: James Miller, Publisher, 647 Broadway. 1873.

According to an advertisement in WTC Nov. 28, 1872, issued in the following styles: Cloth, bevelled; cloth, gilt extra; half calf; morocco extra; morocco antique. Listed WTC Oct. 31, 1872; PW Oct. 3, 1874 ⟨sic⟩. Listed as an American book PC April 1, 1873.

Note: The printing imprinted: *New York: James Miller ... 779 Broadway.* ⟨*1872*⟩ was issued not before May 1, 1877.

The Echo. A Journal of the Fair ...

New York ... 1875 ...

For comment see entry No. 1744.

The Comic Poets of the Nineteenth Century ... by W. Davenport Adams ...

London ... ⟨n.d., 1875⟩

For comment see BAL, Vol. 3, p. 471.

Songs of Three Centuries. Edited by John Greenleaf Whittier.

Boston ... 1876.

For comment see entry No. 2857.

One Hundred Choice Selections No. 13 ...

... Philadelphia ... Chicago ... 1877.

For comment see entry No. 3372.

Dick's Recitations and Readings No. 6 ...

New York ... ⟨1877⟩

For comment see entry No. 3375.

Dick's Recitations and Readings No. 8 ...

New York ... ⟨1878⟩

For comment see BAL, Vol. 1, p. 378.

Poetry of America Selections from One Hundred American Poets from 1776 to 1876 ... by W. J. Linton.

London: George Bell & Sons, York Street, Covent Garden. 1878.

Poems of Places Edited by Henry W. Longfellow ... Western States.

Boston ... 1879.

For fuller entry see BAL, Vol. 1, p. 296.

Ceremonies at the Dedication of the Monument Erected by the City of Manchester, N. H., to the Men who Periled Their Lives to Save the Union in the Late Civil War, September 11, 1879.

Manchester, N. H.: Mirror Steam Printing Press. 1880.

The Cambridge Book of Poetry and Song ... by Charlotte Fiske Bates ...

New York ... ⟨1882⟩

For comment see entry No. 7887.

One Hundred Choice Selections No. 23 ...

... Philadelphia ... Chicago ... 1884.

For comment see entry No. 2490.

No. 4. Standard Recitations by Best Authors ... Compiled ... by ... Frances P. Sullivan ... June, 1884 ...

M. J. Ivers & Co., Publishers, 86 Nassau Street, N. Y. ... ⟨1884⟩

Printed paper wrapper. Deposited June 24, 1884. Reprinted and reissued with the publisher's later address: *379 Pearl Street.*

January Edited by Oscar Fay Adams ...

Boston ... ⟨1885⟩

For comment see entry No. 58.

Mark Twain's Library of Humor ...

New York ... 1888

For comment see entry No. 9636.

... Gems from an Old Drummer's Grip. Compiled by N. R. Streeter

Published by the Compiler. ⟨Groton, N. Y.⟩ 1889.

At head of title: "When trade is dull, collections bad ... Deposited for copyright Dec. 7, 1889.

Half-Hours with the Best Humorous Authors. Selected ... by Charles Morris ... American.

Philadelphia ... 1889.

For comment see entry No. 3813.

Best Selections for Readings and Recitations Number 18 Compiled by Silas S. Neff ...

Philadelphia   The Penn Publishing Company 1890

Cloth; and, printed paper wrapper. Deposited July 28, 1890.

The Poets' Year ... Edited by Oscar Fay Adams ...

Boston ... ⟨1890⟩

For comment see entry No. 80.

Local and National Poets of America ... Edited ... ⟨by⟩ Thos. W. Herringshaw ...

Chicago ... 1890.

For fuller entry see BAL, Vol. 2, p. 391.

Representative Sonnets by American Poets ... by Charles H. Crandall

Boston ... 1890

"In the Dim Chamber," p. 183; otherwise "The Haunted Room," in *Poems*, 1890. For fuller comment see BAL, Vol. 2, p. 275.

An Old Scrap-Book. With Additions. Printed, but Not Published ... Second Edition. ⟨Edited by J. M. Forbes⟩

⟨Cambridge, Mass., University Press⟩ February 8, 1891.

Younger American Poets 1830–1890 Edited by Douglas Sladen ...

... London ... 1891

For comment see entry No. 6557.

Younger American Poets 1830–1890 Edited by Douglas Sladen ...

... New York 1891

For comment see entry No. 6558.

The Lover's Year-Book of Poetry   A Collection of Love Poems for Every Day in the Year ⟨Compiled⟩ by Horace Parker Chandler Vol. II. July to December

Boston   Roberts Brothers   1892

Vol. 1, *January to June,* issued under date 1891.

The World of Wit and Humour ... ⟨New and Enlarged Edition⟩

... London ... 1895 ⟨–1896⟩ ...

For comment see BAL, Vol. 3, p. 400.

The Literature of America and Our Favorite Authors ...

... Philadelphia ... ⟨1897⟩

For comment see BAL, Vol. 1, p. 77.

Elements and Science of English Versification by William C. Jones

Buffalo: The Peter Paul Book Company. 1897.

Werner's Readings and Recitations No. 21 ...

New York ... 1899 ...

For comment see entry No. 4929.

An American Anthology ... Edited by Edmund Clarence Stedman ...

Boston ... M DCCCC

For comment see entry No. 3082.

Poets and Poetry of Indiana ... Compiled ... by Benjamin S. Parker and Enos B. Heiney ...

... New York ... ⟨1900⟩

For comment see entry No. 2974.

Modern Eloquence   Editor Thomas B Reed ...

John D. Morris and Company   Philadelphia ⟨1900; *i.e.,* 1903⟩

See below under 1903.

Edward Fitzgerald: An Aftermath by Francis Hindes Groome ...

... Thomas B. Mosher ... XLV Exchange Street, Portland   Maine MDCCCCII

Modern Eloquence   Editor Thomas B Reed ...

John D. Morris and Company   Philadelphia ⟨1900; *i.e.,* 1903⟩

The 1900 date is false. Vol. 12, which reprints Hay's McKinley address, could not have been published prior to McKinley's death on Sept. 14, 1901. Further, Hay's address was first delivered Feb. 27, 1902; and, Vol. 12 of the set was deposited Jan. 27, 1903, and not in 1900 as the printed copyright notice asserts.

... Masterpieces of Wit and Humor ... Introduction by Robert J. Burdette ...

Copyright, 1902 ...

For comment see entry No. 2013.

... Gems of Modern Wit and Humor with ... Introduction by Robert J. Burdette ...

⟨n.p., n.d., 1903⟩

Reprint of the preceding under revised title.

Widows Grave and Otherwise Compiled by Cora D. Willmarth ...

... 1903 ... Paul Elder and Company Publishers, San Francisco

Printed boards, cloth shelfback. Unpaged. A selection of quotations for each day of the year. Under the date *August Fourth* appears, unidentified, Hay's "Distich," No. V, *Pike County Ballads,* 1871.

A Book of American Humorous Verse ...

Chicago ... 1904

For comment see BAL, Vol. 1, p. 411.

Poems by E. H. Winans

⟨n.p., n.d., after June, 1907⟩

Leather.

Stories of Humor In Two Parts By Oliver Wendell Holmes ... and Others

New York Doubleday, Page & Company Publishers ⟨1908⟩

Deposited Oct. 13, 1908. Apparently printed from the plates of a two-volume work. Pagination: ⟨i-xvi⟩, 1-186, ⟨i-ii⟩, 1-184.

The World War   Utterances Concerning Its Issues ...

... New York 1919

For comment see entry No. 2198.

Roosevelt as the Poets Saw Him ... Edited by Charles Hanson Towne ...

New York ... 1923

For comment see entry No. 816.

Rhode Island in Verse Compiled by Mary Louise Brown

⟨Providence, R. I.⟩ 1936

REFERENCES AND ANA

Grand Pow-Wow of the Brunensian Model Artists ...

⟨n.p., n.d., almost certainly Providence, R. I., ca. 1858⟩

A four-page burlesque order of exercises. At end: *N.B.B. The publishers would announce that they were not responsible for any objectionable passages, or the puns contained in the above, as everything of this class was inserted by Hary.* The r in *Hary* struck out by hand with pen and ink, thus altering the name to *Hay.* Possibly Hay had a hand in this schoolboy production.

New-York Tribune.—Lecture Sheet No. 4.

⟨New York, 1873⟩

4 pp. According to an advance notice in PW March 8, 1873, this publication was to contain two pieces by Hay: "Daybreak in Spain" and "Heroic Life in Washington." Neither piece appears in the publication.

Drafted in A Sequel to the Bread-Winners A Social Study. By Faith Templeton ⟨*i.e.,* Harriet Boomer Barber⟩.

New York: Bliss Publishing Co., 235 Greenwich St. ⟨1888⟩

A Gross Miscarriage of Justice: Seven Years Penal Servitude; or, the Value of a Royal Pardon. Being the Remarkable Case of John Hay.

London: Literary Revision Society, 1895.

Not seen. Not located. Entry from *The English Catalogue;* and, PC Jan. 19, 1895. Pamphlet. Presumably not about the subject of this list.

Pike County Herald Published Once in a Great While by the Thanhouser Company. Extra! All about "Jim Bludso" by Hon. John Hay, Secretary of State ... Jim Bludso ... Banty Tim ... Little Breeches ...

⟨Milwaukee, Wis.⟩ The Schueppert-Zoeller Printing Co., 144 Reed St. ⟨n.d., *ca* 1900⟩

Single leaf. Printed on recto only. 11⅞" x 7⅞". Issued as an advertisement for "the first production of this stirring melodrama *Jim Bludso.*"

Handwriting Test Proves Hay Wrote "The Breadwinners."

From the New York Times August 20, 1905 ⟨New York, 1905⟩

Printed wrapper.

Memorial Address from the Jews of America and Great Britain to Mrs. Clara Hay in Honor of Her Deceased Husband John Hay ...

⟨New York, October 2, 1905⟩

Caption-title. The above at head of p. ⟨1⟩. Printed self-wrapper.

John Hay ... an Address Delivered before the Alumni Association of Brown University June 19, 1906 by Joseph Bucklin Bishop

Providence, Rhode Island 1906

Printed paper wrapper.

... Unveiling and Consecration of the John Hay Memorial Window at the Temple of the Reform Congregation of Keneseth Israel

Philadelphia   Sunday, December Second   Nineteen Six

At head of title: Series XX Number Five Printed paper wrapper.

John Hay Author and Statesman by Lorenzo Sears

New York   Dodd, Mead and Company   1914

Deposited Oct. 14, 1914.

... The Poetry of John Hay a Dissertation ... by Sister Saint Ignatius Ward ...

The Catholic University of America   Washington, D.C. 1930

At head of title: The Catholic University of America   Printed paper wrapper.

John Hay   From Poetry to Politics by Tyler Dennett ...

Dodd, Mead & Company   New York 1933

Deposited Oct. 17, 1933.

Abraham Lincoln & the Widow Bixby by F. Lauriston Bullard

New Brunswick   Rutgers University Press 1946

A discussion of the authorship of the so-called "Bixby Letter."

The Life and Works of John Hay ... A Commemorative Catalogue of the Exhibition Shown at the John Hay Library of Brown University in Honor of the Centennial of His Graduation at the Commencement of 1858

Brown   University   Library   Providence Rhode Island ‹1961›

Printed boards. Edited by John R. T. Ettlinger.

Discovery of a Genius   William Dean Howells and Henry James   Compiled and Edited by Albert Mordell ...

Twayne Publishers   New York   ‹1961›

Contains two pieces that may have been written by Hay. For comment see "William Dean Howells: Two Mistaken Attributions," by George Monteiro, in *The Papers of the Bibliographical Society of America*, Vol. 56, second quarter, 1962, pp. 254-257. For a fuller description of *Discovery of a Genius* see entry No. 9882B.

PAUL HAMILTON HAYNE

1 8 3 0 – 1 8 8 6

7850. POEMS ...

    BOSTON: TICKNOR AND FIELDS. M DCCC LV

⟨i⟩-viii, ⟨9⟩-108. 7³⁄₁₆″ x 4⁹⁄₁₆″.

⟨-⟩⁴, 1-6⁸, 7².

T cloth: brown. Yellow end papers. Flyleaves. Catalog dated *November, 1854,* inserted at back.

A copy in AAS inscribed by early owner Nov. 27, 1854. Noticed as though issued since Dec. 1, 1854, NLG Dec. 15, 1854. Deposited Dec. 18, 1854. Listed as an importation PC Jan. 16, 1855.

H NYPL

7851. SONNETS, AND OTHER POEMS ...

    CHARLESTON: HARPER AND CALVO, PUBLISHERS. 1857.

⟨i⟩-⟨xvi⟩, 1-72. 7⅛″ full x 5³⁄₁₆″.

⟨1⟩-2⁴, ⟨A⟩-I⁴.

T cloth: plum; slate. Moiréd T cloth: green. Buff end papers. Flyleaves.

H has two presentation copies (to Lowell and to Longfellow) each inscribed by the author Oct. 24, 1857.

H NYPL

7852. Address and Poem Delivered at Hibernian Hall, on the First Anniversary of the Carolina Art Association.

    Charleston: Steam Power Press of Walker, Evans & Co., 1859.

Probably issued in printed paper wrapper.

"Ode Delivered on the First Anniversary of the Carolina Art Association, February 10th, 1859," pp. ⟨19⟩-28. Collected in *Avolio,* 1860.

H

7853. AVOLIO; A LEGEND OF THE ISLAND OF COS. WITH POEMS, LYRICAL, MIS-CELLANEOUS, AND DRAMATIC ...

    BOSTON: TICKNOR AND FIELDS. M DCCC LX.

⟨i⟩-⟨xii⟩, ⟨1⟩-244. 7¹⁄₁₆″ x 4½″.

⟨A⟩⁶, 1-15⁸, 16².

T cloth: brown. Brown-coated on white end papers. Flyleaves. Inserted at back: Publisher's catalog dated *November, 1859.*

Deposited Nov. 14, 1859. BPL copy inscribed by early owner Dec. 2, 1859. Listed BM Dec. 1, 1859; PC Dec. 31, 1859.

H NYPL

7854. Confederate Monitor and Patriot's Friend. Containing Sketches of Numerous Important and Thrilling Events of the Present Revolution ... by H. W. R. Jackson ...

    Atlanta, Georgia: Franklin Steam Printing House, J. J. Toon & Co. 1862.

Printed paper wrapper.

"Butler's Proclamation," pp. 79-80.

B

7855. Rebel Rhymes and Rhapsodies Collected and Edited by Frank Moore

    New York George P. Putnam 1864

Cloth, leather shelfback.

"Beyond the Potomac," pp. 215-218. Collected in *Poems,* 1882.

Advertised as though just published ALG May 16, 1864. Noticed in ALG June 1; July 1, 1864.

H Y

7856. Lays of the South: Verses Relative to the War between the Two Sections of the American States.

    Printed for the Liverpool Bazaar, in Aid of the Southern Prisoners' Relief Fund. 1864.

"Vicksburg," pp. 31-33. Earliest located book appearance. For earliest located American book publication see *War Poetry of the South,* 1866, below.

"This little work is prepared and printed as a contribution to The Bazaar, to be opened at Liverpool, in October, for the benefit of sick, wounded, and destitute Confederates . . ."— From the "Preface," dated at end *August 22, 1864.*

H

7857. M.M.S. OF VOLUME FIRST OF THE WORK ENTITLED "POLITICS OF SOUTH CAROLINA, --- F. W. PICKENS' SPEECHES, REPORTS, &c." BY PAUL H. HAYNE . . .

⟨n.p., n.d., ca. 1865⟩

Caption-title. The above at head of p. ⟨1⟩.

⟨1⟩-104. 9^{11}/$_{16}$″ x 6¼″. *Note:* The measurement is approximate.

⟨1-13⟩⁴.

Folded sheets as above. Presumably prepared as manuscript and not published in this form. Incomplete. Several copies examined are in the same state; no complete copy known; and almost surely never completed.

BA   CWB   H

7858. Anecdotes, Poetry and Incidents of the War: North and South. 1860–1865. Collected and Arranged by Frank Moore . . .

New York: Printed for the Subscribers. 1866.

Reprint save for "The Kentucky Partisan," p. 403.

For comment see entry No. 3202.

7859. War Poetry of the South. Edited by William Gilmore Simms . . .

New York: Richardson & Company, 540 Broadway. 1866.

Contains the following poems collected in *Poems,* 1882:

"Charleston," pp. 84-86.

"My Mother-Land," pp. 117-123.

"Vicksburg—A Ballad," pp. 156-158. See *Lays of the South,* 1864, for a prior publication.

"Our Martyrs," pp. 277-279.

"The Battle of Charleston Harbor," pp. 319-322.

Also contains "Sonnet," (*Rise from your gory ashes stern and pale* . . .), p. 217; otherwise not located.

For comment see entry No. 3723.

7860. South Songs: From the Lays of Later Days. Collected and Edited by T. C. de Leon.

New-York: Blelock & Co., No. 19 Beekman Street. 1866.

"The River," pp. 40-43. Otherwise "Beyond the Potomac" which had prior publication in *Rebel Rhymes,* 1864, above.

"Beauregard's Appeal," pp. 90-91. Collected in *Poems,* 1882.

"Lines after Defeat," p. 116.

Y

7861. The Book of the Sonnet Edited by Leigh Hunt and S. Adams Lee . . .

Boston   Roberts Brothers   1867

2 Vols. For fuller comment see entry No. 1218.

Reprint save for:

"O Faithful Heart! On Balmy Nights Like This," p. 234.

"An Hour Agone!—And Prostrate Nature Lay," p. 235.

"Spirits There Are Inwrought with Vilest Clay," p. 237.

7862. The Southern Poems of the War. Collected and Arranged by Miss Emily V. Mason.

Baltimore: John Murphy & Co., Publishers, 182 Baltimore Street, 1867.

Reprint save for: "Away with the Dastards Who Whine of Defeat," pp. 136-137.

H

7862A. The Sunny Land; or, Prison Prose and Poetry, Containing the Productions of the Ablest Writers in the South, and Prison Lays of Distinguished Confederate Officers, By Col. Buehring H. Jones . . . Edited . . . by J. A. Houston . . .

Baltimore: 1868.

Reprint save for "The Substitute," pp. 377-383. Collected in *Poems,* 1882.

BA   NYPL

7863. The Southern Amaranth. Edited by Miss Sallie A. Brock.

New York: Wilcox & Rockwell, Successors to Blelock & Co., 49 Mercer St. 1869.

Reprint save for the following poems:

"Prize Poem," pp. 16-26. Collected in *Poems,* 1882, as "Ode . . . ," pp. 67-71.

"The Little White Glove," pp. 154-156.*

"Scenes," pp. 139-140.

"Stuart," pp. 213-216.*

"Scene in a Country Hospital," pp. 246-247.*

"The Southern Lyre," pp. 434-441.

"Stonewall Jackson," pp. 495-499.*

"Sonnet on the Present Condition of the South," pp. 573-574.

* Collected in *Poems*, 1882.

For comment see entry No. 5524.

7864. Appletons' Illustrated Almanac for 1871
. . .

New York: D. Appleton and Company, 90, 92 & 94 Grand Street . . . 1870 . . .

Pictorial paper wrapper.

"Strawberries and Strawberry Weather," pp. 24-25.

"October," p. 40. Collected in *Poems,* 1882.

Listed ALG Nov. 1, 1870.

NYPL

7865. LEGENDS AND LYRICS . . .

PHILADELPHIA: J. B. LIPPINCOTT & CO. 1872.

⟨i⟩-xii, 13-183. 6$\frac{15}{16}$″ x 4½″.

⟨1⟩-14^6, 15^8.

C cloth: green; terra-cotta. Covers bevelled. Brown-coated on white end papers. Flyleaves. A circular ornament is goldstamped on the front cover. Also noted in a variant binding of unknown status: Purple S cloth with sides unstamped save for a blindstamped rule frame.

BPL copy received Jan. 17, 1872. Advertised as *just published* WTC Jan. 25, 1872. Listed WTC Feb. 1, 1872.

AAS (variant)   B

7866. ADDRESS . . . BEFORE THE LADIES OF THE MEMORIAL ASSOCIATION OF ALABAMA, WEDNESDAY EVENING, MAY 1st, 1872.

MONTGOMERY, ALA.: BARRETT & BROWN, STEAM PRINTERS AND BOOK BINDERS. 1872.

Cover-title.

⟨1⟩-19. 8$\frac{7}{16}$″ x 5$\frac{5}{8}$″.

⟨1⟩^{8}, 2^2. *Note:* So signed.

Printed lavender paper wrapper.

DU

7867. The Poems of Henry Timrod. Edited, with a Sketch of the Poet's Life, by Paul H. Hayne.

New York: E. J. Hale & Son, Publishers, Murray Street. 1873.

"Memoir of Henry Timrod," pp. ⟨7⟩-69.

Cloth; and, cloth, gilt, listed PW Jan. 16, 1873.

Note: Text ends on p. 205. A "new revised edition" was issued with the same imprint, 1873, pp. 232; noted in PW April 19, 1873.

B (1st)   H (1st, 2nd)

7868. THE MOUNTAIN OF THE LOVERS; WITH POEMS OF NATURE AND TRADITION . . .

NEW YORK: E. J. HALE & SON, PUBLISHERS, MURRAY STREET. 1875.

⟨i-iv⟩, ⟨1⟩-153; leaf excised or pasted under the end paper. 7$\frac{3}{16}$″ x 4$\frac{13}{16}$″. Pp. ⟨i-ii⟩ excised or pasted under the end paper.

⟨1-10⟩^{8}. Leaves ⟨1⟩$_1$ and ⟨10⟩$_8$ excised or pasted under the end paper.

S cloth: green; mauve; terra-cotta. Covers bevelled. Brown-coated on white end papers. Blue-coated on white end papers. Edges gilt.

BPL copy received June 1, 1875. A copy in NYPL inscribed by Hayne June 9, 1875.

H NYPL

7869. Edgar Allan Poe   A Memorial Volume by Sara Sigourney Rice.

Baltimore: Turnbull Brothers. 1877.

"Poe," pp. 94-95.

For comment see entry No. 1757.

7870. W. GILMORE SIMMS. A POEM DELIVERED ON THE NIGHT OF THE 13th OF DECEMBER, 1877, AT "THE CHARLESTON ACADEMY OF MUSIC," AS PROLOGUE TO THE "DRAMATIC ENTERTAINMENT" IN AID OF THE "SIMMS MEMORIAL FUND." . . .

⟨n.p., n.d., Charleston, 1877⟩

Caption-title. The above at head of p. ⟨1⟩.

⟨1⟩-8. 8$\frac{15}{16}$″ x 5$\frac{7}{8}$″ scant.

⟨-⟩^{4}.

Self-wrapper.

Collected in *Poems,* 1882.

BPL NYPL

7871. LIVES OF ROBERT YOUNG HAYNE AND HUGH SWINTON LEGARÉ ...

CHARLESTON, S. C. WALKER, EVANS & COGSWELL, PUBLISHERS, NOS. 3 BROAD AND 109 EAST BAY STREETS. 1878.

⟨i⟩-iv, ⟨5⟩-158; blank leaf. 6½" x 5⁷⁄₁₆".

⟨1⟩-6¹², 7⁶, 8².

Flexible C cloth: brown; green. Flexible S cloth: green.

A copy in B inscribed by Hayne Nov. 17, 1878.

B H

7872. Poetry of America Selections from One Hundred American Poets from 1776 to 1876 ... by W. J. Linton.

London: George Bell & Sons, York Street, Covent Garden. 1878.

Reprint save for "The Why of a Blush," p. 282.

B H

7873. The Poems of Frank O. Ticknor, M. D. Edited by K.M.R. with an Introductory Notice of the Author by Paul H. Hayne.

Philadelphia: J. B. Lippincott & Co. 1879.

"Introductory Notice," pp. 9-17.

Listed PW Oct. 25, 1879.

B

7874. Christmas Snowflakes. Illustrated Poems by Favorite American Authors. ⟨Edited by Ella Farman Pratt⟩

Boston: D. Lothrop & Co., Publishers, 30 & 32 Franklin Street. ⟨1879⟩

Contains the following poems by Hayne:

"Motes." This poem appears also in *Wide Awake Pleasure Book* ⟨Vol. 7⟩, Boston ⟨1878⟩. For a comment on *Wide Awake Pleasure Books* see BAL, Vol. 1, p. 73. Collected in *Poems*, 1882.

"Kiss Me, Katie!" Collected in *Poems*, 1882.

Unpaged. For fuller comment see entry No. 433.

7875. At the Beautiful Gate, and Other Religious Poems. Compiled by the Editor of "The Changed Cross;" ⟨Anson D. F. Randolph⟩ ...

New York Anson D. F. Randolph & Company, 900 Broadway, Cor. 20th Street. 1880.

"Denial," p. 124. Collected in *Poems*, 1882.

For comment see BAL, Vol. 2, pp. 104-105.

7876. The Palace of the King, and Other Religious Poems. Compiled by the Editor of "The Changed Cross;" ⟨Anson D. F. Randolph⟩ ...

New York: Anson D. F. Randolph & Company, 900 Broadway, Cor. 20th Street. 1880.

"The Later ⟨sic⟩ Peace," p. 157. Collected in *Poems*, 1882, as "The Latter Peace."

For comment see BAL, Vol. 2, p. 105.

7877. Papyrus Leaves ... Edited by William Fearing Gill ...

New York: R. Worthington. 1880.

"Muscadines," pp. 347-352. Collected in *Poems*, 1882.

Deposited Dec. 26, 1879. For fuller comment see entry No. 2477.

7878. One Hundred Choice Selections No. 18 ...

Published by P. Garrett & Co., 708 Chestnut Street, Philadelphia, Pa., and 116 E. Randolph Street, Chicago, Ill. 1880.

Reprint save for "Macdonald's Raid.—A.D. 1780," pp. 119-121. Collected in *Poems*, 1882.

For comment see entry No. 2478.

7879. On the Tree Top by Clara Doty Bates and Others ...

Boston: D. Lothrop & Company Franklin Street, Cor. Hawley. ⟨n.d., 1880⟩

Unpaged. Pictorial boards, cloth shelfback.

"The Ground Squirrel." Appears also in *Wide Awake Pleasure Book* ⟨Vol. 9⟩, Boston ⟨1879⟩. For a comment on *The Wide Awake Pleasure Books* see BAL, Vol. 1, p. 73. Collected in *Poems*, 1882.

Advertised in PW Sept. 11, 1880, as one of the "new books for the holiday season of 1880–1881." Deposited Nov. 13, 1880.

B LC

7880. Official Programme of the Yorktown Centennial Celebration, October 18, 19, 20, 21, 1881. Under the Joint Resolution of Congress of June 7, 1880.

Published by Authority of the Yorktown Centennial Commission, by F. T. Wilson. Washington, D. C., 1881.

Printed (in either green or in red) white paper wrapper.

"Centennial Ode," pp. ⟨9-11⟩ or ⟨25-27⟩, depending on how one chooses to read the pagination which is erroneous. Collected in *Poems, 1882,* as "Yorktown Centennial Lyric."

Deposited Oct. 14, 1881.

B H LC

7881. Christmas Carols and Midsummer Songs. By American Poets . . .

Boston: D. Lothrop & Company, Franklin Street. ⟨1881⟩

"The Silken Shoe," pp. ⟨18⟩-19. Appears also in *Wide Awake Pleasure Book* ⟨Vol. 12⟩, Boston ⟨1881⟩. For a comment on the *Wide Awake Pleasure Books* see BAL, Vol. 1, p. 73. Collected in *Poems, 1882.*

For comment see entry No. 6297.

7882. In Memoriam. Gems of Poetry and Song on James A. Garfield. With Portrait and Eulogy . . .

Columbus, O⟨hio⟩. J. C. McClenahan & Company. 1881.

"On the Death of President Garfield," pp. 42-44. Collected in *Poems, 1882. Note:* This poem is not to be confused with Hayne's poem "Assassination," another poem on the death of Garfield.

For comment see entry No. 122.

7883. One Hundred Choice Selections No. 20 . . .

Published by P. Garrett & Co., 708 Chestnut Street, Philadelphia, Pa., and 116 E. Randolph Street, Chicago, Ill. 1881.

"Little Nellie in the Prison," pp. 76-78. Collected in *Poems, 1882.*

For comment see entry No. 5120.

7884. The Poets' Tributes to Garfield A Collection of Many Memorial Poems . . . ⟨Second Edition⟩

Cambridge, Mass. Published by Moses King Harvard Square 1882

"Assassination," p. 87. Not to be confused with Hayne's "On the Death of President Garfield." Collected in *Poems, 1882.*

For comment see entry No. 1248.

7885. . . . The Reading Club and Handy Speaker . . . Edited by George M. Baker. No. 10.

Boston: Lee and Shepard, Publishers. New York: Charles T. Dillingham. ⟨1882⟩

"Union of Blue and Gray," pp. 35-36. Collected in *Poems, 1882.*

Deposited March 20, 1882.

For comment see entry No. 3790.

7886. Henry W. Longfellow Biography Anecdote, Letters, Criticism by W. Sloane Kennedy . . .

Cambridge, Mass. Moses King, Publisher Harvard Square 1882

Eight lines of verse, p. 312, beginning *Some souls are vernal . . . ;* otherwise unlocated save for an anonymous appearance in LW Feb. 26, 1881, p. 84. Here credited to Hayne on the basis of Kennedy's attribution.

"Longfellow Dead!," pp. 332-333. Collected in *Poems, 1882.*

H copy received May 23, 1882. Listed PW May 27, 1882. Deposited for copyright June 2, 1882.

NYPL

7887. The Cambridge Book of Poetry and Song . . . by Charlotte Fiske Bates . . .

New York: Thomas Y. Crowell & Co., No. 13 Astor Place. ⟨1882⟩

Reprint save for "Lyric of Action," p. 827. Collected in *Poems, 1882.*

According to contemporary notices issued in cloth; half morocco; full morocco; tree calf.

Two printings have been noted:

1: Each page decorated with a frame printed in dull red. Imprint as given above.

2: The text is not printed within the decorative frames present in the first printing as described above. Imprint: *New York: Thomas Y. Crowell & Co., ⟨sic⟩ ⟨1882⟩* Issued not before Aug. 10, 1890, the date of John Boyle O'Reilly's death added to the text, p. li; nor issued after Nov. 25, 1891, on which date a copy was received by H.

Deposited Sept. 30, 1882. Listed PW Oct. 21, 1882.

B (1st)   H (2nd)

7888. The Poet and the Children Carefully Selected Poems . . . Edited by Matthew Henry Lothrop . . .

Boston D. Lothrop and Company Franklin Street ⟨1882⟩

Reprint save for: "The New Sister," pp. 209-210. Also appears in *Wide Awake Pleasure Book* ⟨Vol. 11⟩, Boston ⟨1880⟩. For a comment on *Wide Awake Pleasure Book* see BAL, Vol. 1, p. 73. Collected in *Poems*, 1882.

For comment see entry No. 3788.

7889. Poems . . . Complete Edition . . .

　　Boston　D. Lothrop and Company　32 Franklin Street, Corner of Hawley　1882

Contemporary notices indicate that this book was issued in several styles: Cloth; cloth, gilt; half calf; half morocco; full turkey morocco.

Deposited Dec. 9, 1882. Noted as *ready* PW Dec. 9, 1882. Listed PW Feb. 10, 1883.

"The friends and admirers of Paul H. Hayne will celebrate his fiftieth birthday, January 1, 1880, by an elegantly illustrated edition of his complete poetical works . . . together with the work done by him since the publication of his last volume. The poet is now engaged in arranging and revising . . . The work will be sold to subscribers only, and the profits go to the poet. Subscription cards will be supplied by Colonel John J. James, Superintendent Texas Military Institute, Austin, Texas."—PW May 31, 1879, p. 603.

"Between November 28 and December 8, 1882, James ⟨the dedicatee⟩ received a copy . . . which Hayne had asked the publisher to send and three dozen copies which he had ordered himself."—*A Collection of Hayne Letters*, 1944, p. 498.

H　Y

7890. In Memory. The Last Sickness, Death, and Funeral Obsequies, of Alexander H. Stephens, Governor of Georgia. By I. W. Avery.

　　Atlanta, Ga.　V. P. Sisson, Publisher. 1883

Printed paper wrapper.

"Poem . . . ," p. 77. Begins: *Past midnight now; the chill March moon is nigh* . . . Not elsewhere located. Not to be confused with Hayne's "To Alexander H. Stephens," *Poems*, 1882, p. 293.

H　NYPL

7891. A POEM WRITTEN FOR THE GRADUATING CLASS OF 1883, SMITH COLLEGE . . .

　　⟨n.p., Northampton, Mass., 1883⟩

Cover-title.

⟨1-8⟩. 9⅜″ x 6″.

⟨-⟩⁴.

Printed self-wrapper.

AAS　H

7892. Illustrated Stories from Wide Awake with Episodes from Serials

　　Boston　D. Lothrop and Company　Franklin Street ⟨1884⟩

Contains "Old Geoffrey's Relic."

For comment see entry No. 6307.

7893. THE BROKEN BATTALIONS . . .

　　⟨Baltimore, Maryland, 1885⟩

Title-page in black and red.

9 leaves. Printed on recto only. Paged ⟨1⟩-9. Laid paper watermarked *Crown Leghorn*⟨?⟩ *Linen*. 5⅛″ x 4¾.

Stiff off-white printed paper wrapper. Tied with blue braid.

Issued during a fair, Baltimore, Maryland, April 7-11, 1885, conducted by the Society of the Army and Navy of the Confederate States in the State of Maryland.

Deposited May 2, 1885.

LC

7894. . . . The Reading Club and Handy Speaker . . . Edited by George M. Baker. No. 15.

　　Boston. Lee and Shepard, Publishers. New York: Charles T. Dillingham. ⟨1885⟩

At head of title: No. 15 . . .

Printed paper wrapper.

"Praying for Shoes. A True Incident," pp. 40-42.

Deposited Nov. 5, 1885.

LC

7895. June Edited by Oscar Fay Adams . . .

　　Boston　D. Lothrop and Company　Franklin and Hawley Streets ⟨1886⟩

Reprint save for "June," p. ⟨xxviii⟩.

For comment see entry No. 64.

7896. No. 12. Standard Recitations by Best Authors . . . Compiled . . . by Frances P. Sullivan . . . June, 1886 . . .

　　M. J. Ivers & Co., Publishers, 86 Nassau Street, N. Y. . . . ⟨1886⟩

Printed paper wrapper.

"Face to Face," p. 47.

Deposited June 21, 1886.

LC NYPL

7897. August Edited by Oscar Fay Adams ...

Boston D. Lothrop and Company Franklin and Hawley Streets ⟨1886⟩

"August," p. 106.

For comment see entry No. 66.

7898. November Edited by Oscar Fay Adams ...

Boston D. Lothrop and Company Franklin and Hawley Streets ⟨1886⟩

Reprint save for "A November Picture," p. 141.

"Autumn Peace," pp. 45-46, is a reprinting of "The Two Summers," *Avolio,* 1860.

For comment see entry No. 69.

7899. Wayside Flowers Original and Contributed Poems Arranged by Ellen E. Dickinson ...

New York White, Stokes, and Allen 1886

Query: Should be dated 1884? 1885?

"The Wild Fleur de Lis," p. 23.

Advertised PW Sept. 27, 1884, for *immediate issue;* "poems ... contributed by the authors for this volume ... With covers in olive green bronze, and design of very large pansies ... with four colored designs ... fringed, each copy in envelope, $1."

PW Sept. 26, 1885 (classified list of fall publications): "... the following volumes have been made uniform and put into *Flower-Songs Series* as a part of it, at a lower price and in reduced size: ... *Wayside Flowers* ... French sateen, $1; or fringed, $1."

NYPL (rebound)

7899A. Golden Lays for Youthful Days. Selected Poems from the Best Poets. Together with Original Poems by ... Elizabeth Stuart Phelps ... Paul H. Hayne, Celia Thaxter, and Other English and American Authors ...

L. P. Miller & Co. Chicago ... Philadelphia ... Stockton, Cal. 1889.

Reprint.

Copyright notice in the name of L. P. Miller & Co. BAL suspects that this book was printed from the plates of a series of books issued by D. Lothrop Company, Boston.

EM

7900. Southern War Songs ... Collected and Arranged by W. L. Fagan ...

New York: M. T. Richardson & Co. 1890.

Issued in large paper format (9½" x 6¹¹⁄₁₆"); and, small paper format (8¾" x 6¹⁄₁₆").

"The Black Flag," pp. 163-164.

Listed PW Oct. 11, 1890.

H NYPL

7901. Werner's Readings and Recitations. No. 5. American Classics. Compiled and Arranged by Sara Sigourney Rice.

New York: Edgar S. Werner. 1891.

"The Story of an Ambuscade," pp. 124-127.

For comment see entry No. 3433.

7902. Autumn Leaves: A Pictorial Library of Prose, Poetry and Art, by ... Eminent Authors ... Celia Thaxter ... Paul Hamilton Hayne ... and Many Others ... Edited by Daphne Dale.

⟨n.p.,⟩ 1893. National Book Mart

Reprint.

EM

7903. Songs of the South Choice Selections from Southern Poets ... Edited by Jennie Thornley Clarke ...

Philadelphia J. B. Lippincott Company 1896

Reprint save for:

"In the Wheat-Field," pp. 144-145.

Untitled poem, facing title-page: *But stay! What subtle notes are these ...*

For comment see entry No. 7139.

7904. Letters of Sidney Lanier ... 1866–1881 ...

New York Charles Scribner's Sons 1899

"A Poet's Letters to a Friend," pp. ⟨217⟩-245. A group of letters, Lanier to Hayne, with editorial comment by Hayne.

Listed PW Oct. 21, 1899.

H

7905. Library of Southern Literature ... Edwin Anderson Alderman ⟨and⟩ Joel Chandler Harris Editors in Chief ...

The Martin & Hoyt Company New Orleans Atlanta Dallas ⟨1909–1913⟩

Reprint save for "Ante-Bellum Charleston," Vol. 5, pp. 2272-2285. Reprinted from *Southern Bivouac* (Louisville, Ky.), Sept.–Nov., 1885.

For comment see entry No. 7164.

7906. Poems of Country Life   A Modern Anthology by George S. Bryan . . .

New York   Sturgis & Walton Company   1912

"The Farmer's Wife," pp. 48-51.

On copyright page: *Published September, 1912* Listed PW Sept. 14, 1912.

H   NYPL

7907. A COLLECTION OF HAYNE LETTERS EDITED BY DANIEL MORLEY McKEITHAN

AUSTIN   THE UNIVERSITY OF TEXAS PRESS   1944

⟨i-iv⟩, ⟨i⟩-⟨xx⟩, ⟨1⟩-499; 2 blank leaves. 8⅞" x 5⅞".

⟨1-15¹⁶, 16⁸, 17¹⁶⟩.

Printed pale buff paper wrapper. Leaves ⟨1⟩₁ and ⟨17⟩₁₆ used as pastedowns.

Deposited May 19, 1944.

Y

7908. THE CORRESPONDENCE OF BAYARD TAYLOR AND PAUL HAMILTON HAYNE EDITED WITH AN INTRODUCTION AND NOTES BY CHARLES DUFFY

PUBLISHED BY THE LOUISIANA STATE UNIVERSITY PRESS   BATON ROUGE: 1945

⟨i-ii⟩, ⟨i⟩-⟨xii⟩, ⟨1⟩-111, blank leaf. 8⁹⁄₁₆" x 5½". Watermarked *Warren's Olde Style.*

⟨1-8⟩⁸.

V cloth: red. Top edges stained maroon.

"The twenty-seven letters by Hayne to Taylor are here printed for the first time. Of the nineteen letters by Taylor to Hayne, five have hitherto been unpublished; six have appeared in their entirety; and eight have appeared in fragments."—P. vii.

Published Nov. 15, 1945, according to date stamped in PW review copy. Deposited Jan. 17, 1946.

B   NYPL

7909. THE SOUTHERN DILEMMA: TWO UNPUBLISHED LETTERS OF PAUL HAMILTON HAYNE EDITED BY RICHARD BEALE DAVIS

REPRINTED FROM THE JOURNAL OF SOUTHERN HISTORY VOL. XVII, NO. 1 FEBRUARY, 1951

Cover-title.

⟨63⟩-70. Paper watermarked *Warren's Olde Style.* 10" x 6¾".

⟨-⟩⁴.

Printed stiff tan paper wrapper.

UV

REPRINTS

The following publications contain material by Hayne reprinted from earlier books.

The Book of Rubies . . .

New York . . . 1866.

For comment see entry No. 5522.

Poetry Lyrical, Narrative, and Satirical of the Civil War . . . Edited by Richard Grant White

New York . . . 1866

For comment see entry No. 4604.

The Grayjackets . . .

Jones Brothers & Co., Richmond . . . ⟨1867⟩

For comment see entry No. 562.

The Living Writers of the South. By James Wood Davidson . . .

New York . . . MDCCCLXIX.

For comment see entry No. 7097.

The Poets and Poetry of America. By Rufus Wilmot Griswold . . .

New York . . . 1873.

For comment see in list of John Hay reprints.

Florida: Its Scenery, Climate, and History . . . by Sidney Lanier . . .

Philadelphia: J. B. Lippincott & Co. 1876.

"The Mocking-Bird," p. 255. Reprint of "Sonnet," p. 55, *Legends and Lyrics,* 1872. Not to be confused with "The Mocking-Bird," in *Poems,* 1882.

Songs of Three Centuries. Edited by John Greenleaf Whittier.

Boston . . . 1876.

For comment see entry No. 2857.

Poems of Places Edited by Henry W. Longfellow . . . Southern States.

Boston . . . 1879.

For comment see BAL, Vol. 1, p. 74.

"South Carolina," pp. 9-10, is extracted from *W. Gilmore Simms* . . . ⟨1877⟩.

Poems of Places Edited by Henry W. Longfellow ... Oceanica ...

Boston ... 1879.

For comment see BAL, Vol. 1, p. 74.

Home Life in Song with the Poets of To-Day ...

New York ... ⟨1879⟩

For comment see entry No. 432.

Wide Awake Pleasure Book ⟨Vol. 8⟩.

Boston: D. Lothrop & Co., Publishers, 30 and 32 Franklin Street. ⟨1879⟩

Deposited Dec. 10, 1879. For a comment on *Wide Awake Pleasure Book* series see BAL, Vol. 1, p. 73.

In Memory of Amelie and Melanie DeGrasse ... the Restoration of Their Tomb ... St. Mary's Church Yard, October 19th, 1881.

⟨Printed for Mayor Courtenay, and for the Society of the Cincinnati of the State of South Carolina, by Walker, Evans & Cogswell, Charleston, S. C., 1881?⟩

Printed paper wrapper. "50 copies privately printed for Mayor Courtenay, and 50 copies for the Society of the Cincinnati of the State of South Carolina ..."—P. ⟨8⟩.

One Hundred Choice Selections No. 21 ...

... Philadelphia ... Chicago ... 1882.

For comment see entry No. 2486.

Christmas Snowflakes. Illustrated Poems by Favorite American Authors.

Boston: D. Lothrop & Co., Publishers, 30 & 32 Franklin Street. ⟨1883⟩

Unpaged.

Surf and Wave: The Sea as Sung by the Poets. Edited by Anna L. Ward ...

New York: Thomas Y. Crowell & Co. 13 Astor Place. ⟨1883⟩

My Curiosity Shop ...

Boston ... ⟨1884⟩

For comment see entry No. 6306.

January Edited by Oscar Fay Adams ...

Boston ... ⟨1885⟩

For comment see entry No. 58.

February Edited by Oscar Fay Adams ...

Boston ... ⟨1886⟩

For comment see entry No. 59.

Bugle-Echoes ... Edited by Francis F. Browne

New York ... MDCCCLXXXVI

For comment see BAL, Vol. 1, p. 75.

Songs and Ballads of the Southern People ... Edited by Frank Moore.

New York ... 1886.

For fuller entry see BAL, Vol. 2, p. 265.

Representative Poems of Living Poets ...

... New York 1886

For comment see entry No. 436.

May Edited by Oscar Fay Adams ...

Boston ... ⟨1886⟩

For comment see entry No. 63.

July Edited by Oscar Fay Adams ...

Boston ... ⟨1886⟩

For comment see entry No. 65.

October Edited by Oscar Fay Adams ...

Boston ... ⟨1886⟩

For comment see entry No. 68.

One Hundred Choice Selections No. 26 ...

... Philadelphia ... Chicago ... 1886.

For comment see entry No. 5551.

The Elocutionist's Annual Number 16 ... Compiled by Mrs. J. W. Shoemaker

Publication Department The National School of Elocution and Oratory Philadelphia 1888

Cloth; and, printed paper wrapper. Deposited Oct. 1, 1888.

Smith College Commencement Poems '79–'86 ...

⟨North Brookfield ... 1888⟩

For comment see BAL, Vol. 2, p. 274.

American Sonnets. Selected ... by William Sharp.

London ... ⟨n.d., 1889⟩

For comment see BAL, Vol. 3, p. 101.

... Harper's Fifth Reader   American Authors

New York ... 1889

For comment see entry No. 7917.

The Elocutionist's Annual Number 17 ... Compiled by Mrs. J. W. Shoemaker

Philadelphia ... 1889

For comment see entry No. 1270.

Boys' and Girls' New Pictorial Library ... Introduction by ... Rev. W. H. Milburn ...

Chicago ... 1889.

For comment see entry No. 6319.

No. 26. Standard Recitations by Best Authors ... Compiled ... by Frances P. Sullivan ... December, 1889 ...

    ... N. Y. ... ⟨1890⟩

For comment see entry No. 134.

No. 29. Standard Recitations by Best Authors ... Compiled ... by Frances P. Sullivan ... September, 1890 ...

    ... N. Y. ... ⟨1890⟩

For fuller entry see BAL, Vol. 3, p. 138.

The Poets' Year ... Edited by Oscar Fay Adams ...

    Boston ... ⟨1890⟩

For comment see entry No. 80.

American Sonnets Selected ... by T. W. Higginson and E. H. Bigelow

    Boston ... 1890

For comment see entry No. 8373.

Representative Sonnets by American Poets ... by Charles H. Crandall

    Boston ... 1890

For comment see BAL, Vol. 2, p. 275.

No. 30. Standard Recitations ... Compiled ... by Frances P. Sullivan ... December 1890 ...

    ... N. Y. ... ⟨1890⟩

For comment see entry No. 5561.

Songs from the Southland Selected by S. F. Price

    Boston D. Lothrop Company Washington Street Opposite Bromfield ⟨1890⟩

The Speakers' Library ... Edited by Daphne Dale.

    1890 ... Chicago Philadelphia.

For comment see entry No. 6324.

Young Folks' Story Book for 1891 by American Authors ...

    Syndicate Trading Company New York ⟨1890⟩

    Pictorial boards. Unpaged.

Younger American Poets 1830–1890 Edited by Douglas Sladen ...

    ... London ... 1891

For comment see entry No. 6557.

Younger American Poets 1830–1890 Edited by Douglas Sladen ...

    ... New York 1891

For comment see entry No. 6558.

The Lover's Year-Book of Poetry A Collection of Love Poems for Every Day in the Year ⟨Compiled⟩ by Horace Parker Chandler Vol. II. July to December

    Boston Roberts Brothers 1892

    Vol. 1, *January to June*, issued under date 1891.

No. 33. Standard Recitations by Best Authors ... Compiled ... by Frances P. Sullivan ... September 1891 ...

    ... N. Y. ... ⟨1891⟩

For comment see BAL, Vol. 2, p. 96.

Shoemaker's Best Selections ... Number 22

    Philadelphia ... 1894

For comment see BAL, Vol. 1, p. 260.

Young Folks' Story Book ...

    Boston ... ⟨1895⟩

For comment see BAL, Vol. 3, p. 101.

The Juvenile Temperance Reciter No. 5 ... Edited by Miss L. Penney ...

    New York: The National Temperance Society and Publication House. ⟨1896⟩

    Issued 1898? 1896? The only examined copy (NYPL) is in printed wrapper dated 1898.

War Poets of the South and Confederate Camp-Fire Songs ... ⟨Edited by Charles W. Hubners' ⟨n.p., n.d., Atlanta: U. P. Byrd, 1896⟩

Young Folks' Story Book ...

    Boston ... ⟨1897⟩

For comment see BAL, Vol. 3, p. 102.

Home and School Stories by George C. Eggleston ...

    Akron ... 1904 ...

For comment see entry No. 6373.

Little Lads by George Cary Eggleston ...

    Akron ... 1904 ...

For comment see entry No. 6375.

Our Girls Poems in Praise of the American Girl ...

    New York ... 1907

For comment see entry No. 1945.

Three Centuries of Southern Poetry ... ⟨by⟩ Carl Holliday ...

    Nashville ... ⟨1908⟩

For fuller entry see BAL, Vol. 1, p. 101.

Masterpieces of the Southern Poets by Walter Neale ...

    New York The Neale Publishing Company 1912

REFERENCES AND ANA

The Southern First Class Book ... Selected ... by M. M. Mason ...

> Macon ... 1839.
>
> Contains material sometimes erroneously credited to Paul Hamilton Hayne. For fuller entry see BAL, Vol. 1, p. 371.

Christmas-Tide Stories and Poems. By Hezekiah Butterworth and Others.

> Boston: D. Lothrop Company ⟨1888⟩
>
> *Not located.* Entry from an advertisement, PW Sept. 1, 1888. According to the advertisement contains a poem by Hayne.

Appletons' Cyclopaedia of American Biography ...

> New York ... 1887 ⟨–1889⟩
>
> Hayne listed as a contributor to Vols. 5-6. His contribution, or contributions, not identified. For fuller description see entry No. 6020.

... Check List of the Paul Hamilton Hayne Library

> Durham, North Carolina 1930
>
> Printed paper wrapper. At head of title:

Duke University Library Bulletin No. 2 July 1930

The Last Years of Henry Timrod ... Including Letters of Timrod to Paul Hamilton Hayne ... Drawn Chiefly from the Paul Hamilton Hayne Collection in the Duke University Library. Edited by Jay B. Hubbell

> 1941 Duke University Press Durham North Carolina
>
> Deposited Aug. 15, 1941.

Selected Letters John Garland James to Paul Hamilton Hayne and Mary Middleton Michel Hayne Edited by Daniel Morley McKeithan

> Austin The University of Texas Press 1946
>
> Printed paper wrapper.

Paul Hamilton Hayne: Life and Letters by Kate Harbes Becker ...

> Published by the Outline Company Belmont, N. C. 1951
>
> "... compiled from *A Collection of Hayne Letters,* and *Selected Letters of John Garland James to Paul Hamilton Hayne and Mary Middleton Michel Hayne* ... and *The Correspondence of Bayard Taylor and Paul Hamilton Hayne* ..."—P. x. See entry immediately preceding; and, entries 7907-7908.

LAFCADIO HEARN

1 8 5 0 – 1 9 0 4

Study of the complex problem of identifying the earliest printing of each of the five translations contributed by Hearn to *The Japanese Fairy Tale Series* inescapably leads to the conclusion that the problem is insoluble.

The bibliographer is presented with the extraordinary anomaly of seemingly explicit colophons that are but half truths. As a specific example see *The Old Woman Who Lost Her Dumpling.*

It is possible the varieties noted were simultaneously issued but the possibility is remote. To further complicate the problem the books were printed either wholly or in part from woodblocks which were replaced as needed; the blocks did not wear out simultaneously; and the colophons fail to mention such replacements.

Mr. P. D. Perkins, co-author of the bibliography of Hearn (1934), in a letter to BAL comments:

"... I think it is a mistake to regard them ⟨*i.e.,* the fairy tales⟩ as printed books. They are ... printed by woodblock and, being in color, many different blocks must be used. These blocks do not wear out uniformly but new blocks are continually being cut as needed. The pages for one complete book were not always printed at one time but at various times and in various quantities. Added to all this was the crepeing process which took weeks and sometimes in this crepeing process some leaves were damaged ... The 1923 earthquake destroyed Hasegawa's office-workshop and when they resumed work at their home in Kami Negishi they must have had to cut many new blocks. Much work both before and after the earthquake was done at their home and unfinished and partly finished work was kept at the house which when I saw it was a cluttered-up mess. They would discover some pages in a forgotten corner. Copies with the pre-earthquake colophon would be more likely to

be complete or part first or early printings. A woodblock print expert could probably come very close to deciphering what copies had all or nearly all early printed pages. The paper used might also have varied slightly ..."

BAL presents descriptions of certain features noted in the earliest printings; and, descriptions of certain features that occur in undoubted later printings. The production methods being what they were (and are) the errors of imposition noted in some copies of *Chin Chin Kobakama* cannot be considered indications of priority.

It is to be emphasized that the descriptions may not necessarily be of the earliest printing although every effort has been made to present a description of the first printing of each of the five fairy tales. Intermediates made up of mixed sheets of early and of late printings have been seen and are here described as such.

The fairy tales were issued on crepe paper. The creping process (applied to the sheets after printing) reduces the size of the leaf by a considerable degree. Hence, copies found on silky, uncreped, paper are not true large paper examples but unfinished copies; true large paper copies are on creped paper. Examples therefore may be found in the following three forms: *small paper* (creped); *large paper* (creped); and, as *unfinished examples* on uncreped paper. BAL is unable to state categorically that first printings of all five fairy tales were issued in both small paper and large paper formats.

BAL has photographically reproduced the earliest located colophons but it must be noted that the crepeing process frequently distorts the letterpress and makes it virtually impossible (unless one chooses to soak the leaf in question) to be certain of exact meanings; and, due to the nature of the crepe paper further distortion may be caused by the camera. *Therefore, these photographic copies may not be precise.* The later colophons have not been reproduced and users of these reproductions are urged to have translated *all* colophons that come into their ken; there may be colophons earlier than those located by BAL.

———

Certain of the Hearn publications, issued in both Japan and in the United States, are made up of lecture notes kept by Hearn's students. In this list such publications have been relegated to secondary position. As an example see entry No. 7957.

Japanese publications which contain no first book appearances of Hearn are merely listed with no attempt to present a publication record. No statement is given regarding later printings of such reprints.

Acknowledgments are made with thanks for the assistance of Dr. Achilles Fang who translated the colophons, converted the oriental dates to occidental, and who also made many useful and practical suggestions herein embodied. BAL also acknowledges the aid given by Mr. P. D. Perkins, Hearn's "official" bibliographer; BAL is particularly grateful for Mr. Perkins's long letters regarding the fairy tales.

7910. La Nouvelle Atala ou la Fille de l'Esprit Légende Indienne par Chahta-Ima ⟨pseudonym of Adrien Emmanuel Rouquette⟩ . . .

Nouvelle-Orléans 1879 Imprimerie du Propagatetr⟨sic⟩ Catholique 204, Rue de Chartres, 204

Printed paper wrapper.

"A Louisiana Idyl," pp. 126-129.

B H LC UT

7911. One of Cleopatra's Nights and Other Fantastic Romances. By Théophile Gautier. Faithfully Translated by Lafcadio Hearn . . .

New York: R. Worthington, 770 Broadway. 1882.

⟨i-iv⟩, ⟨1⟩-⟨4⟩, v-⟨x⟩, ⟨1⟩-321. Pp. ⟨i-ii⟩ excised or pasted under the end paper. Frontispiece inserted. 8⅛" x 5⁵⁄₁₆".

Note: Both Perkins and Johnson (see below) report that the spine imprint occurs in three forms; BAL has located the spine imprint in two forms only. The sequence has not been determined and the designations are for identification only.

A: Spine imprint is stamped in capitals and lower case.

B: Spine imprint is stamped in capitals (⅛" high) only. A reprint of 1888 also noted thus.

Both Perkins and Johnson state that the imprint occurs stamped from upper and lower

case letters; from "large" capital letters; and from "small" capital letters. BAL has located the book only as described above.

Deposited March 9, 1882.

H (B)   LC (B)   NYPL (A, B)   UT (B)   UV (A, B)
Y (B)

7912. STRAY LEAVES FROM STRANGE LITERATURE STORIES RECONSTRUCTED FROM THE ANVARI-SOHEÏLI, BAITÁL PACHÍSÍ, MAHABHARATA, PANTCHATANTRA, GULISTAN, TALMUD, KALEWALA, ETC. . . .

BOSTON   JAMES R. OSGOOD AND COMPANY 1884

⟨1⟩-225, blank leaf. 6⁹⁄₁₆" x 4¹⁵⁄₁₆".

⟨1-2⟩, 3-14⁸, ⟨15⟩².

V cloth: blue (robin's egg, blue-green, dark blue noted); gray; green (olive-green, yellow-green noted); terra-cotta. Pink end papers.

Note: An ambiguous entry in Johnson has caused some confusion regarding the stamping on this book. The correct spine imprint is *JR.O.&.CO* and not *Osgood* as the Johnson entry suggests.

Noted as *just ready* PW June 28, 1884. Deposited June 30, 1884. The British edition imprinted *London Kegan Paul, Trench, Trübner & Co. Limited ⟨1884⟩* was issued not prior to 1889, in which year the firm was founded.

H   LC   NYPL   UT

7913. La Cuisine Creole. A Collection of Culinary Recipes from Leading Chefs and Noted Creole Housewives, Who Have Made New Orleans Famous for Its Cuisine.

New York: Will H. Coleman, No. 70 Business Quarter, Astor House. ⟨1885⟩

Anonymous. Compiled by Hearn.

Three states noted. The sequence has not been determined and the designations are for identification only:

A

⟨i⟩-iv, ⟨1⟩-268. 7⅜" x 5¹¹⁄₁₆".

"Introduction" printed on two pages.

Line 9 of introduction: *Brùlot* . . .

B

⟨i-ii⟩, ⟨i⟩-ii, ⟨1⟩-268.

"Introduction" printed on two pages.

Line 9 of introduction: *Brùlot* . . .

C

⟨i-iv⟩, ⟨1⟩-268.

"Introduction" printed on one page.

Line 9 of introduction: *Brülot . . .*

Note: It has been asserted that a sequence may be established on the basis of the form of the word *brûlot;* that (or so the assertion) the correct form is *brûlot* and that, therefore, copies with *brûlot* are the earlier. The correct form is *brûlot,* hence the argument is invalid.

Deposited March 4, 1885. Listed PW July 4, 1885.

Note: The printings issued with the imprint of F. F. Hansell & Bro., Ltd., New Orleans ⟨1885⟩ were printed and published *ca.* 1922.

AAS (A, C)   BPL (A)   H (A)   LC (A, being a deposit copy)   NYPL (A)   UT (A, C)   UV (A, B)   Y (A)

7914. "Gombo Zhèbes." Little Dictionary of Creole Proverbs, Selected from Six Creole Dialects. Translated into French and Into English, with Notes, Complete Index to Subjects and Some Brief Remarks upon the Creole Idioms of Louisiana . . .

New York: Will H. Coleman, Publisher, No. 70, Business Quarter, Astor House. 1885.

⟨i-ii⟩, ⟨1⟩-⟨8⟩, ⟨7⟩(*sic*)-42, blank leaf; plus: 2 pp. publisher's advertisements printed on two leaves. Laid paper. 8⁷⁄₁₆" scant x 6⁹⁄₁₆".

A copy in H inscribed by Hearn Feb. 18, 1885; another copy in H inscribed by publisher Feb. 1885. Deposited April 9, 1885. Listed PW July 4, 1885. Distributed in Great Britain by Trübner; advertised Bkr Sept. 1886.

H   NYPL   UT

7915. . . . Historical Sketch Book and Guide to New Orleans and Environs. With Map . . . Edited and Compiled by Several Leading Writers of the New Orleans Press.

New York: Will H. Coleman, No. 70 Business Quarter, Astor House 1885.

"Père Antoine's Date Palm," p. 114. See entry No. 8044.

"The Scenes of Cable's Romances," pp. 293-299. Collected in *An American Miscellany,* 1924.

For fuller description see entry No. 2340.

7916. SOME CHINESE GHOSTS . . .

BOSTON: ROBERTS BROTHERS. 1887.

⟨i-iv⟩, ⟨i⟩-⟨viii⟩, ⟨9⟩-185; blank leaf. 7⅛" x 4⅞".

⟨1-12⟩⁸. *Signed:* ⟨-⟩², ⟨1⟩-11⁸, 12⁶.

Issued in a variety of cloths; the following noted by BAL; no probable sequence: S cloth: mustard. V cloth: maroon; mustard; red; red-orange; salmon. A single copy has been noted in white, floral brocaded, sateen. Front stamped in black; or, in brown. Top edges stained red. Flyleaves. The following types of end paper have been noted: Printed in green, also greenish-brown, with an all-over pattern of maple-like leaves and flowers; printed in slate with an all-over pattern of oak leaves and flowers; printed in brown with an all-over pattern of twig-like units; printed in brown with an all-over pattern of ivy leaves; printed in brown with a marble-vein effect.

Deposited March 11, 1887. Noted for March 12 in PW March 12, 1887. Listed Ath July 2, 1887.

H   NYPL   UT

7917. . . . Harper's Fifth Reader   American Authors ⟨Edited by James Baldwin⟩

New York   Harper & Brothers, Franklin Square 1889

At head of title: Harper's Educational Series

Cloth, leather shelfback.

"The Coming of the Hurricane," pp. 393-400. Collected in *Chita,* 1889, below.

Deposited Sept. 26, 1889.

H   LC

7918. CHITA: A MEMORY OF LAST ISLAND . . .

NEW YORK   HARPER & BROTHERS, FRANKLIN SQUARE 1889

⟨i-viii⟩, ⟨1⟩-204, 4 pp. advertisements. Laid paper. 7³⁄₁₆" full x 4⅞".

⟨-⟩⁴, ⟨1⟩-13⁸.

S cloth: salmon. End papers of book stock. Flyleaves in some copies.

Deposited Sept. 28, 1889. BPL copy received Oct. 4, 1889. Listed PW Oct. 5, 1889; PC Oct. 15, 1889; Ath Nov. 16, 1889.

H   NYPL   UT

7919. The Crime of Sylvestre Bonnard . . . by Anatole France   The Translation and Introduction by Lafcadio Hearn

New York   Harper & Brothers, Franklin Square 1890

⟨i-ii⟩, ⟨i⟩-⟨x⟩, ⟨1⟩-281; blank, p. ⟨282⟩; advertisements, pp. ⟨283-288⟩. *Paper:* 8" x 5⅝". *Cloth:* 8⁵⁄₁₆" x 5¹³⁄₁₆".

Four states (probably printings) noted:

1

P. ⟨283⟩: *Two Years in the French West Indies* described as *in press.*

P. ⟨286⟩: The two-volume, cloth-bound, format of *A Hazard of New Fortunes* listed without price and described as *in press. The Shadow of a Dream* not listed.

2

P. ⟨283⟩: The *in press* statement not present in the entry for *Two Years in the French West Indies.*

P. ⟨286⟩: The two-volume, cloth-bound, format of *A Hazard of New Fortunes* is listed without price and without the comment *in press. The Shadow of a Dream* not listed.

3

P. ⟨283⟩: The *in press* statement not present in the entry for *Two Years in the French West Indies.*

P. ⟨286⟩: The two-volume, cloth-bound, format of *A Hazard of New Fortunes* priced at $2.00; the *in press* statement not present. *The Shadow of a Dream* not listed.

4

P. ⟨283⟩: The *in press* statement not present in the entry for *Two Years in the French West Indies.*

P. ⟨286⟩: The two-volume, cloth-bound, format of *A Hazard of New Fortunes* priced at $2.00; the *in press* statement not present. *The Shadow of a Dream* listed.

Issued in printed blue paper wrapper. Also: S cloth, both maroon-brown; and, olive noted; printed paper label on spine.

Printed Paper Wrapper

The printed paper wrapper has been noted in the following forms. All issued under date of Jan. 1890, as No. 665 in *Harper's Franklin Square Library.* The order of presentation is presumed correct. Reference is to the inner front wrapper.

A: First number listed: *665.* Noted on 1st state sheets only.

B: First number listed: *668.* Noted on 3rd state sheets only.

C: First number listed: *671.* Noted on 3rd state sheets only.

D: First number listed: *675.* The only example thus far located (in H) is incomplete; the sheets are of one of the later states but which of these cannot be determined.

E: First number listed: *682.* Noted on 4th state sheets only.

A Note on the Cloth Binding

The UV copy, first state sheets, bound in cloth, inscribed by J. Henry Harper, Feb. 18, 1890 (at least two weeks after first publication): *One of eight copies printed.* BAL has been unable to find evidence to support the assertion. A copy in UT, first state sheets, bound in cloth, inscribed by one W. H. Patten, reportedly a member of the Harper establishment: *One of eight copies printed on heavy ⟨sic⟩ paper, before the appearance of the library ⟨i.e., wrappered⟩ edition.* All examined copies, including the Patten-UT copy, bulk 11⁄16″ to 3⁄4″. Untrimmed, cloth-bound copies, are sometimes erroneously referred to as large paper copies. The cloth binding has been seen on first and second state sheets. BAL has found no copy of the second state in printed paper wrapper which suggests that perhaps the whole of the second state was issued in cloth only.

Deposited Jan. 22, 1890. Listed, paper only, PW Feb. 1, 1890.

H (2nd in cloth; 3rd in wrapper B; 3rd in wrapper C; 4th in wrapper E; later printing, see note above, in wrapper D) LC (1st in wrapper A, being a deposit copy; 3rd in wrapper C) UT (1st in cloth) UV (1st in cloth; 1st in wrapper A; 2nd in cloth; 4th in wrapper E)

7920. TWO YEARS IN THE FRENCH WEST INDIES ...

NEW YORK HARPER & BROTHERS, FRANKLIN SQUARE 1890

⟨i-ii⟩, ⟨1⟩-431; blank, p. ⟨432⟩; 6 pp. advertisements. 36 full-page plates, integral parts of their respective gatherings, not reckoned in the printed pagination. 7¼″ x 4¹³⁄₁₆″.

⟨1⟩-5, ⟨6-7⟩, 8-9, ⟨10⟩, 11-12, ⟨13⟩, 14, ⟨15⟩, 16, ⟨17⟩, 18-24, ⟨25⟩, 26-31, ⟨32⟩⁸.

S cloth: olive. Flyleaves.

Deposited March 12, 1890. BPL copy received March 13, 1890. Listed PW March 15, 1890.

H LC NYPL UT

7921. YOUMA THE STORY OF A WEST-INDIAN SLAVE ...

NEW YORK HARPER & BROTHERS, FRANKLIN SQUARE 1890

⟨i-iv⟩, ⟨1⟩-193; blank, p. ⟨194⟩; 2 pp. advertisements. Laid paper. Frontispiece inserted. 7½″ x 5″.

⟨-⟩², 1-12⁸, 13².

The binding occurs as follows with the sequence not firmly established and based on little more than convention. However, Perkins (p. 20) makes the following categorical statement that may not be disregarded: *From the word of the binder, it is certain that the first issue was bound in white cloth with blue designs.* It is BAL's considered judgment that the statement is correct but BAL nevertheless suggests that any binding bearing the printed labels has a claim to primacy. Some copies were issued with flyleaves. All examined copies save one have top edges plain; the exception, status not known, has the top edges stained yellow.

Binding Aa

White cloth printed in blue with an all-over pattern. At least nine different patterns have been seen. Printed paper label on front and on spine. White laid paper end papers.

Binding Ab

White chintz-like cloth printed in blue and purple-brown to produce a pattern not unlike what one might hope to achieve by cross-breeding a dalmatian with a leopard. Printed paper label on front and on spine. White laid paper end papers.

Binding Ac

Blue sateen damasked with willow leaves. Printed paper label on front and on spine. White laid paper end papers. Laid paper flyleaves.

Binding Ad

Semi-polished V cloth printed in dark purple-brown with a marbled pattern. Printed paper label on front and on spine. White laid paper end papers.

Binding B

Red T cloth. Spine stamped in gold. No printed paper labels. White laid paper end papers. Laid paper flyleaves.

Note: The sheets occur in two states of unknown sequence, *if any.* The variations were surely produced in the bindery and the states are presumed simultaneous.

Binder's Variant A

⟨-⟩ is so folded as to produce:

⟨i⟩: Title-page

⟨ii⟩: Copyright page

⟨iii⟩: Dedication

⟨iv⟩: blank

Binder's Variant B

⟨-⟩ is so folded as to produce:

⟨i⟩: Dedication

⟨ii⟩: Blank

⟨iii⟩: Title-page

⟨iv⟩: Copyright page

Deposited May 14, 1890. BPL copy received May 14, 1890. Listed PW May 17, 1890; PC Aug. 1, 1890; Bkr Aug. 7, 1890.

H LC NYPL UT UV

7922. A Sappho of Green Springs. By Bret Harte . . .

Philadelphia: J. B. Lippincott Company ⟨1890⟩.

"Karma," pp. 667-682. Collected in *Karma*, 1918.

For comment see entry No. 7352.

7923. A Midsummer Trip to the West Indies . . . Reprinted from Harper's Monthly Magazine

Trinidad ⟨British West Indies⟩: The Caxton Press ⟨1891⟩

Cover-title. Printed paper wrapper.

Not seen. Description from a photostatic copy (in H) of the original in BMU.

First separate edition. Previously in *Two Years in the French West Indies*, 1890.

BMU copy received Nov. 7, 1891.

7924. Things Japanese . . . by Basil Hall Chamberlain . . . Second Edition Revised and Enlarged

London: Kegan Paul, Trench, Trübner & Co., Ltd. Yokohama . . . Kelly & Walsh, Limited. 1891 . . .

Extracts from letters, p. 235. "Pipes," pp. 342-344.

Reportedly issued in both small paper and large paper formats. BAL strongly suspects that these descriptives are incorrect and that the terms are misnomers for the *Japanese* and the *London* formats.

Japanese Format

Leaf: 7¾″ x 5⅜″ scant.

S cloth: blue-gray; terra-cotta; also (reported, not seen) green. Spine stamped in gold: ⟨double rule⟩ / THINGS / JAPANESE. / ⟨rule⟩ / CHAMBERLAIN. / ⟨double rule⟩

London Format

Leaf: 8¼″ x 5½″.

V cloth: black. Two states of undertermined sequence noted:

A: Spine stamped in gold: THINGS / JAPANESE / B. H./CHAMBERLAIN / KEGAN PAUL, / TRENCH, TRÜBNER & C? Inserted at back: London publisher's catalog dated *February 26, 1892.*

B: Spine stamped in gold: THINGS / JAPANESE / B. H. / CHAMBERLAIN / PAUL, TRENCH, TRÜBNER & C? No catalog at back.

Note: The Hearn material does not appear in the first edition of this book. The *Third Edition Revised* (London, etc., 1898) contains an added footnote, pp. 393-394, a letter from Hearn to Chamberlain regarding O-Kuni, one of "the founders of the modern Japanese stage." The *Third Edition* was published in Tokyo April 3, 1898, according to the colophon; listed PC Sept. 3, 1898; Bkr Sept. 7, 1898.

According to the colophon published in Tokyo Nov. 7, 1891.

H (all three forms)

7925. A Handbook for Travellers in Japan Third Edition Revised and for the Most Part Re-Written by Basil Hall Chamberlain ... and W. B. Mason ...

London: John Murray, Albemarle Street ... 1891 ...

"Route 48," pp. 347-352.

Distributed in United States with the cancel title-leaf of: *New York Charles Scribner's Sons ... 1893 ...*

In revised form Hearn's contribution appears in the *Fourth Edition* of the *Handbook*, London, 1894.

Perkins, pp. 21-22, quotes from a personal letter received from Basil Hall Chamberlain which confirms Hearn's authorship of the contribution.

Advertised Bkr Nov. 7, 1891, as *just out;* PC Nov. 28, 1891, as *next week;* PC Dec. 5, 1891, as *this week.*

NYPL

7926. GLIMPSES OF UNFAMILIAR JAPAN ...

BOSTON AND NEW YORK   HOUGHTON, MIFFLIN AND COMPANY   THE RIVERSIDE PRESS, CAMBRIDGE 1894

2 Vols.

1: ⟨i-ii⟩, ⟨i⟩-⟨xii⟩, ⟨1⟩-342. 8¹⁄₁₆″ x 5³⁄₁₆″.
2: ⟨i-iv⟩, ⟨343⟩-699; blank, p. ⟨700⟩; 2 pp. advertisements. Four full-page illustrations, each an integral part of its gathering, not reckoned in the printed pagination.

1: ⟨1-21⁸, 22¹⁰⟩.
2: ⟨1-23⁸, 24²⟩.

Two printings of Vol. 1 have been identified. Presumably Vol. 2 was also reprinted but thus far no distinguishing features have been noted.

First printing, Vol. 1: ⟨1-21⁸, 22¹⁰⟩.

Second printing, Vol. 1: ⟨1-22⁸, 23²⟩.

V cloth: black; olive. Slate-coated on white end papers. Flyleaves. Top edges gilt.

Note: The spine imprint stamped from two varying tools. *Simultaneous?* The designations are for identification only:

A: The name HOUGHTON measures 23⁄32″ wide.

B: The name HOUGHTON measures 5⁄8″ wide.

Deposited Sept. 20, 1894. BPL copy received Oct. 3, 1894. Listed PW Oct. 6, 1894. The London (Osgood, McIlvaine) edition noted for Sept. 29 in Ath Sept. 22, 1894; as *just ready* Ath Sept. 29, 1894; as *at once* PC Sept. 29, 1894. Listed Ath Oct. 6, 1894. Noted as *now ready* Ath Oct. 27, 1894.

H (1st, 2nd)   NYPL (1st, 2nd)   UT (1st)

7927. "OUT OF THE EAST" REVERIES AND STUDIES IN NEW JAPAN ...

BOSTON AND NEW YORK   HOUGHTON, MIFFLIN AND COMPANY   THE RIVERSIDE PRESS, CAMBRIDGE 1895

⟨i-viii⟩, ⟨1⟩-341; blank, p. ⟨342⟩; plus: 2 pp. advertisements, blank leaf. Laid paper. 7″ x 4¹¹⁄₁₆″.

⟨1¹, 2-22⁸, 23⁶, plus: 24²⟩.

Yellow linen. White laid paper end papers. Flyleaf at front. Top edges stained yellow.

Three printings noted:

1

As above.

Sheets bulk 1⅛″.

P. ⟨ii⟩: Out of the East is described as: *16mo, gilt top, $1.25.*

P. ⟨343⟩: Out of the East is described as: *1 vol. crown 8vo.*

Noted only in fairly coarse yellow linen, stamped in silver, top edges stained yellow.

Locations: BA (received March 12, 1895)   H LC (being a deposit copy)   NYPL

2

⟨i-viii⟩, ⟨1⟩-341; blank, p. ⟨342⟩; 2 pp. advertisements. Sheets bulk ⅞".

⟨1-22⟩⁸.

P. ⟨ii⟩: *Out of the East* described as: *16mo, $1.25.*

P. ⟨343⟩: *Out of the East* is described as: *1 vol. 16mo, gilt top, $1.25.*

Noted only in fairly coarse yellow linen, stamped in silver, top edges stained yellow.

Locations: H

3

⟨i-viii⟩, ⟨1⟩-341; blank, p. ⟨342⟩; 2 pp. advertisements. Sheets bulk 1" scant.

⟨1-22⟩⁸.

P. ⟨ii⟩: *Out of the East* described as: *16mo, $1.25.*

P. ⟨343⟩: *Out of the East* described as: *1 vol. 16mo, gilt top, $1.25.*

Noted only in V cloth: brown; green. Top edges gilded. Binding stamped in gold.

Locations: H

Deposited March 7, 1895. Advertised for *this week,* noted as *just ready,* PW March 9, 1895. Listed PW March 16, 1895. The London (Osgood, McIlvaine) edition advertised as *immediately* Ath May 25, 1895; listed Ath June 1, 1895.

The Dream of a Summer Day ...

    Boston ... ⟨1895; *i.e.,* 1922⟩

See entry No. 7978.

7928. KOKORO HINTS AND ECHOES OF JAPANESE INNER LIFE ...

BOSTON AND NEW YORK   HOUGHTON, MIFFLIN AND COMPANY   THE RIVERSIDE PRESS, CAMBRIDGE 1896

Title-page in black and red.

⟨i-x⟩, ⟨1⟩-388. Laid paper. 7" x 4¹¹⁄₁₆".

⟨1⁹, 2-24⁸, 25⁶⟩. Leaf ⟨1⟩2 inserted.

Green sateen. White laid paper end papers. Laid paper flyleaves. Top edges gilt.

Note: The spine imprint occurs in two states. *Simultaneous?* The designations are for identification only:

A: HOUGHTON / MIFFLIN & CO. / ⟨the whole set ¼" scant deep⟩ A deposit copy thus.

B: HOUGHTON / MIFFLIN & CO / ⟨the whole set ¼" deep⟩

Deposited March 10, 1896. BA copy received March 17, 1896. Listed PW March 21, 1896. Noted as *just ready* PW March 21, 1896. The London (Osgood, McIlvaine) edition listed Ath March 21, 1896; advertised as *just published* PC April 11, 1896. The Gay & Bird edition (London) was issued without date in 1903; and, again, with 1905 date. For another edition see entry No. 7968.

H   LC   NYPL   UT

7929. GLEANINGS IN BUDDHA-FIELDS STUDIES OF HAND AND SOUL IN THE FAR EAST ...

BOSTON AND NEW YORK   HOUGHTON, MIFFLIN AND COMPANY   THE RIVERSIDE PRESS, CAMBRIDGE 1897

Title-page in black and orange.

⟨i-vi⟩, ⟨1⟩-296; printer's imprint, p. ⟨297⟩; blank, pp. ⟨298-300⟩. Laid paper. 7" full x 4⅝" full.

⟨1⁹, 2-19⁸⟩. Leaf ⟨1⟩2 inserted.

V cloth: blue; green-blue. White laid paper end papers. Flyleaf at front. Top edges gilt.

Note: The spine imprint occurs in two states. *Simultaneous?* The designations are for identification only:

A: HOUGHTON / MIFFLIN & CO / A copyright deposit copy thus.

B: HOUGHTON / MIFFLIN & CO. / Note presence of period.

Deposited Sept. 1, 1897. Listed PW Oct. 2, 1897. PW Oct. 2, 1897, noted that the book was *published last week.* The London (Harper) edition listed Ath Oct. 2, 1897. Noted for *this day* PC Oct. 2, 1897. Listed PC Oct. 9, 1897.

H   LC   UT

7930. ... The Boy Who Drew Cats Rendered into English by Lafcadio Hearn

    ⟨Tokyo: T. Hasegawa, 1898⟩

At head of title: Japanese Fairy Tale Series No 23 *See note at head of list regarding this series.*

Cover-title.

⟨i-ii⟩, ⟨1⟩-18; tailpiece, p. ⟨19⟩; list of 22 numbered titles in the series, p. ⟨20⟩; tailpiece, p. ⟨21⟩; colophon, p. ⟨22⟩. 6¹³⁄₁₆" x 5" (small paper format). 7½" x 5⅜" (large paper format). Printed on crepe paper. Illustrated. Self-wrapper.

The following designations are for identification only and are not intended to suggest a sequence. *See note at head of list regarding this series.*

First Printings

A

On front of wrapper: *Japanese Fairy Tale Series No 23*

Publisher's address on inner front of wrapper: *10 Hiyoshicho* ...

Last line of text, p. ⟨1⟩: *father; and the little girls* /

P. ⟨21⟩: Imprinted with vase and branch decoration and the statement: *List of Books on Crêpe Paper ... 10 Hiyoshicho* ...

Locations: H (small paper; large paper) Y (large paper)

B

On front of wrapper: *Japanese Fairy Tale Series No 23*

Publisher's address on inner front of wrapper: *10 Hiyoshicho* ...

Last line of text, p. ⟨1⟩: *father; and the little girls* /

P. ⟨21⟩: Imprinted with vase and branch decoration only; not imprinted with letterpress.

Noted in large paper format only.

Locations: BA H LC NYPL UT UV

C

On front of wrapper: *Japanese Fairy Tale Series No 23*

Publisher's address on inner front of wrapper: *17 Kami Negishi* ...

Last line of text, p. ⟨1⟩: *father; and the little girls* /

P. ⟨21⟩: Imprinted with vase and branch decoration and the statement: *List of Books on Crêpe Paper ... 17 Kami-Negishi* ...

Noted in large paper format only.

Locations: UV

Intermediate Printing A

On front of wrapper: *Japanese Fairy Tale Series No 23*

Publisher's address on inner front of wrapper: *10 Hiyoshicho* ...

Last line of text, p. ⟨1⟩: *father; and the little girls* /

P. ⟨21⟩: Imprinted with vase and branch decoration and the statement: *List of Books on Crêpe Paper ... 17 Kami-Negishi* ...

Noted in large paper format (creped): 7½" x 5⅜". And, uncreped paper: 9⁵⁄₁₆" x 6¹⁵⁄₁₆".

Locations: UT (both creped; and, uncreped)

Intermediate Printing B

On front of wrapper: The statement *Japanese Fairy Tale Series No 23* is not present.

Publisher's address on inner front of wrapper: *17 Kami-Negishi* ...

Last line of text, p. ⟨1⟩: *father; and the little girls* /

P. ⟨21⟩: (Lacking in only located copy).

Noted in large paper format only.

Locations: NYPL

REPRINTS

On front of wrapper: The statement *Japanese Fairy Tale Series No 23* is not present.

Publisher's address on inner front of wrapper: *17 Kami-Negishi* ...

Last line of text, p. ⟨1⟩: *the little girls* /

P. ⟨21⟩: Imprinted with vase and branch decoration and the statement: *List of Books on Crepe Paper ... 17, Kami-Negishi* ...

Noted only in large paper format.

Locations: H

Published Aug. 10, 1898 (colophon). *See reproduction of colophon. Note:* All examined copies, all printings, contain the same colophon. UT has a letter from Hearn to Hasegawa, letter dated Sept. 27, 1898, acknowledging receipt of copies of the "plain paper" ⟨*i.e.,* uncreped paper⟩ printing on Sept. 26, 1898.

7931. EXOTICS AND RETROSPECTIVES

. . .

BOSTON   LITTLE,   BROWN,   AND   COMPANY
M DCCC XCVIII

Title-page in black and orange.

⟨i-xii⟩, 1-299. 4 plates inserted; other illustrations in text. 7⅜" x 4⅞" scant.

⟨-⟩², ⟨*⟩⁴, ⟨1⟩-18⁸, 19⁴, ⟨20⟩².

V cloth: olive. Flyleaves. Top edges gilt.

Deposited Dec. 12, 1898. Listed PW Dec. 24, 1898. The London (Low) edition listed PC Jan. 14, 1899.

H NYPL

7932. ... The Goblin Spider ⟨Translated⟩ by Lafcadio Hearn

T. Hasegawa, Publisher, Tokyo. ⟨1899⟩

Cover-title. At head of title: Japanese Fairy Tales. Second Series, No. 1

See note at head of list regarding this series.

⟨1-20⟩; list, p. ⟨21⟩; outer back wrapper, p. ⟨22⟩. Illustrated. 5¹⁵⁄₁₆″ x 4¹⁄₁₆″. Creped paper.

Published April 10, 1899 (colophon). *See reproduction of colophon.*

In what is presumed to be the earliest printing the colophon is printed in both Japanese and English; publication date (in Japanese) is given as April 10, 1899; present (in English) is the statement: ALL RIGHTS RESERVED. In those copies which are presumed to be reprints the colophon is printed wholly in Japanese and publication date (in Japanese) is given as July 10, 1899.

NYPL   UT

7933. Clarimonde   Translated by Lafcadio Hearn from the French of Theophile Gautier

Published by Brentano's at 31 Union Square New York ⟨1899⟩

Reprinted from *One of Cleopatra's Nights* . . . , 1882.

Note: In all examined copies, including a copyright deposit copy, p. ⟨83⟩ is devoted to *A Complete List of Volumes in This Series.* The *List* is printed on the recto of a single inserted leaf. Perkins, p. 38, reports copies with the list, plus a blank conjugate, in the front matter; no copy so distinguished has been located by BAL. BAL theorizes that the book may have been printed with the *List* as an integral part of the first gathering and the book may therefore exist in two binding variants of unknown sequence:

A: With the *List* and a conjugate blank as integral parts of the first gathering. *Not seen by BAL. Reported by Perkins, p. 38.*

B: With the list extracted from the first gathering, its blank conjugate discarded, and the list inserted at the back of the book.

Note: The book normally occurs in cloth. A single copy (in UV) is in what is presumed to be publisher's flexible black leather; in this copy the singleton leaf *List* is inserted in the front matter.

Deposited Sept. 13, 1899.

AAS   H   LC   NYPL   UV   Y

7934. IN GHOSTLY JAPAN . . .

BOSTON   LITTLE,   BROWN,   AND   COMPANY M DCCC XCIX

Title-page in black and orange.

⟨i-xii⟩, ⟨1⟩-241; blank, p. ⟨242⟩; 2 pp. advertisements. Frontispiece and 3 plates inserted, other illustrations in text. 7½″ x 4⅞″.

⟨-⟩², ⟨*⟩⁴, ⟨1-2⟩, 3-7, ⟨8⟩-15⁸, 16².

V cloth: blue. Flyleaves. Top edges gilt.

Deposited Oct. 28, 1899. Advertised as *ready* PW Nov. 4, 1899. H copy received Nov. 13, 1899. Listed PW Dec. 16, 1899. The London (Low) edition listed Ath Nov. 25, 1899.

H   LC   NYPL   UT

7935. SHADOWINGS . . .

BOSTON   LITTLE,   BROWN,   AND   COMPANY 1900

Title-page in black and orange.

⟨i-xii⟩, ⟨1⟩-268; publisher's device, p. ⟨269⟩; blank, p. ⟨270⟩; 4 pp. advertisements; blank leaf. 5 plates inserted. 7½″ x 4⅞″.

⟨-⟩⁶, ⟨1⟩-16⁸, 17¹⁰. The following leaves in ⟨-⟩ are conjugates: 1-6, 2-3, 4-5. The following are inserted conjugates: 17₈-9.

V cloth: blue. Top edges gilt.

Deposited Aug. 25, 1900. Noted as *in press* PW Sept. 22, 1900. BA copy received Oct. 2, 1900. Listed PW Oct. 13, 1900. American sheets, with cancel title-leaf, issued in London by Low; listed PC Oct. 13, 1900.

H   NYPL   UT

7936. A JAPANESE MISCELLANY . . .

BOSTON   LITTLE,   BROWN,   AND   COMPANY MDCCCCI.

Title-page in black and orange.

⟨i-xii⟩, ⟨1⟩-305; blank, p. ⟨306⟩; 2 pp. advertisements. Frontispiece and 1 plate inserted. Also inserted: 6 illustrations printed on 3 leaves. Other illustrations in text. 7½″ x 5″.

⟨-⟩⁶, ⟨1⟩-15, ⟨16⟩, 17-19⁸, 20². The following leaves in ⟨-⟩ are conjugates: 1-6, 2-3, 4-5.

V cloth: green. Flyleaf at back. Top edges gilt.

Two states of the copyright page have been noted. Sequence not determined. The designations are for identification only.

A: Without the statement *October 1901* A surviving copyright deposit copy thus.

B: With the statement *October 1901*

Note: There is a possibility that the two states were printed simultaneously from a multiple setting.

Deposited (state A) Oct. 17, 1901. NYPL copy (state A) received Oct. 19, 1901. Listed PW Nov. 23, 1901. American sheets with cancel title-leaf were distributed in London by Low; described as *ready* Bkr Nov. 1901; Ath Nov. 16, 1901. Listed Ath Nov. 16, 1901.

H (A, B) LC (A, being a deposit copy) NYPL
(A, B) UT (A)

7937. . . . The Old Woman Who Lost Her
Dumpling. Rendered into English by Lafcadio Hearn.

⟨Tokyo: T. Hasegawa, 1902⟩

At head of title: Japanese Fairy Tale Series
Nº 24. *See note at head of list regarding this
series.*

Cover-title.

Five "first printings" have been noted. The following designations are for identification only
and no sequence is suggested.

A

⟨1-21⟩; tailpiece (outer back wrapper), p. ⟨22⟩.
Crepe paper. 7⁹⁄₁₆″ x 5⅝″. Illustrated.

Colophon at foot of p. ⟨21⟩.

At foot of inner front wrapper (p. ⟨2⟩), printed
in blue only: ALL RIGHTS RESERVED. / T. HA-
SEGAWA, PUBLISHER & ART-PRINTER, / 17 Kami
Negishi, TOKYO /

According to the colophon (*see reproduction*)
printed May 15, 1902; published June 1, 1902;
illustrations printed by Y. Nishinomiya; text
printed by The Nakao Press; publisher's address
17 Kami Negishi.

Locations: NYPL

B

⟨1-21⟩; advertisements, pp. ⟨22-23⟩; tailpiece
(outer back wrapper), p. ⟨24⟩. Crepe paper.
7½″ full x 5⁷⁄₁₆″. Illustrated.

Colophon at foot of p. ⟨23⟩.

At foot of inner front wrapper (p. ⟨2⟩), printed
in brown and blue: ALL RIGHTS RESERVED. /
PUBLISHED BY / T. HASEGAWA, PUBLISHER &
ART-PRINTER, / TOKYO, JAPAN.

According to the colophon (*see reproduction*)
printed May 15, 1902; published June 1, 1902;
illustrations printed by T. Kaneko; text printed
by Y. Sahashi; publisher's address: 38 Hommura.

Locations: H NYPL

C

⟨1-21⟩; advertisements, pp. ⟨22-23⟩; tailpiece
(outer back wrapper), p. ⟨24⟩. Crepe paper.
7½″ x 5⅝″. Illustrated.

Colophon at foot of p. ⟨23⟩.

At foot of inner front wrapper (p. ⟨2⟩), printed
in brown and blue: ALL RIGHTS RESERVED. /
PUBLISHED BY / T. HASEGAWA, PUBLISHER & ART-
PRINTER, / TOKYO, JAPAN. /

According to the colophon (*see reproduction*)
printed May 15, 1902; published June 1, 1902.
Printing credited to K. Shibata, but whether
text or illustrations or both is not stated. Publisher's address: 17 Kami Negishi.

Locations: H

D

⟨1-21⟩; advertisements, pp. ⟨22-23⟩; tailpiece
(outer back wrapper), p. ⟨24⟩. Crepe paper.
7⁷⁄₁₆″ x 5⅝″. Illustrated.

Colophon at foot of p. ⟨23⟩.

At foot of inner front wrapper (p. ⟨2⟩), printed
in brown only: ALL RIGHTS RESERVED. / BREN-
TANO'S / 31 UNION SQUARE, NEW YORK. / T.
HASEGAWA / 38 YOTSUYA HOMMURA, TOKYO. /

According to the colophon (*see reproduction*)
printed May 15, 1902; published June 1, 1902;
illustrations printed by T. Kaneko; text printed
by Y. Sahashi; publisher's address: 20 2-Chōme,
Honzaimoku.

Locations: H

E

⟨1-21⟩; advertisements, pp. ⟨22-23⟩; tailpiece
(outer back wrapper), p. ⟨24⟩. Crepe paper.
7½″ x 5⅝″. Illustrated.

Colophon at foot of p. ⟨23⟩.

At foot of inner front wrapper (p. ⟨2⟩), printed
in brown only: ALL RIGHTS RESERVED. / PUB-
LISHED BY / T. HASEGAWA, TOKYO, JAPAN. /
SIMPKIN, MARSHALL, HAMILTON, KENT & CO., /
SOLE AGENTS IN LONDON. /

According to the colophon (*see reproduction*)
printed May 15, 1902; published June 1, 1902;
illustrations printed by T. Kaneko; text printed
by Y. Sahashi; publisher's address: 20 2-Chōme,
Honzaimoku.

Locations: H

General Note

In the first and early printings the following
features are present:

On front (p. ⟨1⟩): The publication is identified
as *Nº 24* of the series. In late reprints the
statement *Nº 24* is not present.

At head of first page of text the early printings have in the caption-title: . . . *Dumplings.*
In late reprints the reading, corrected, is:
. . . *Dumpling.* This alteration was made quite
late.

In the early printings the last line of text is:
rich. / In the late reprints the line reads: *and
in quite a short time she became rich.*

In the early printings the date of printing given
in the colophon is *May 15, 1902.* In late re-

prints the date is erroneously given: *May 5, 1902;* see reproduction of colophon F, entry No. 7937.

7938. KOTTŌ BEING JAPANESE CURIOS, WITH SUNDRY COBWEBS . . .

NEW YORK THE MACMILLAN COMPANY LONDON: MACMILLAN & CO., LTD. 1902 . . .

Title-page printed in orange and black.

⟨i⟩-⟨x⟩, ⟨1⟩-246, ⟨xi-xii⟩, 247-251; blank, p. ⟨252⟩; plus: 2 pp. advertisements. Frontispiece and 2 plates inserted; other illustrations in text. Laid paper. 7⅞″ full x 5⅜″.

⟨1-16⁸, 17⁴; plus: 18¹⟩. *Signed:* ⟨A⟩⁵, ⟨B⟩-E, ⟨F⟩-I, K-M, ⟨N⟩-P, ⟨Q-R⟩⁸.

T cloth: olive. White laid paper end papers. Top edges gilt.

Note: The title-page (black on a pictorial orange background) has been noted in the following forms. The sequence is presumed correct but not to be overlooked is the possibility that the title-pages were printed from multiple plates.

1

Background printed upside down, causing the artist's device to appear in the upper right corner. The leaf is an integral part of its gathering.

2

Background correctly printed. The artist's device appears at the lower left. The leaf is a cancel.

3

Background correctly printed. The artist's device appears at the lower left. The leaf is an integral part of its gathering, not a cancel. Both deposit copies are in this state.

On copyright page: *Set up and electrotyped October, 1902.* Noted as *in preparation* PW Sept. 13, 1902. Deposited Oct. 21, 1902. Listed PW Nov. 1, 1902; Ath Nov. 29, 1902.

BPL (1)   LC (3, being the deposit copies)   UT (1)   UV (1, 2)   Y (1)

7939. . . . Chin Chin Kobakama Rendered into English by Lafcadio Hearn

⟨Tokyo: T. Hasegawa, 1903⟩

At head of title: Japanese Fairy Tale Series No 25 *See note at head of list regarding this series.*

Cover-title.

⟨1-22⟩; copyright notice and colophon, p. ⟨23⟩; outer back wrapper, p. ⟨24⟩. Illustrated. 7⁹⁄₁₆″ x

5⁷⁄₁₆″ (creped paper). 9⅜″ scant x 7¼″ scant (uncreped paper).

The following designations are for identification only and are not intended to suggest a sequence. *See note at head of list regarding this series.*

A

P. ⟨23⟩: *T. Hasegawa, 38 Yotsuya Hommura, Tokyo,* named as publisher. The names of no other publishers or distributors present. In the Japanese colophon *T. Kaneko* is named as printer. *See reproduction.* Noted only on creped paper 7⁹⁄₁₆″ x 5⁷⁄₁₆″.

Locations: BA   BPL   H   LC   UV   Y

B

P. ⟨23⟩: *T. Hasegawa, 38 Yotsuya Hommura, Tokyo,* named as publisher. In addition the name *Simpkin Marshall, Hamilton, Kent & Co.,* appears as "sole agents in London". In the Japanese colophon *T. Kaneko* is named as printer. Noted on creped paper 7⁹⁄₁₆″ x 5⁷⁄₁₆″; and, on uncreped paper, 9⅜″ scant x 7¼″ scant. *See reproduction.*

Locations: H (creped)   UT (uncreped)

C

P. ⟨23⟩: *T. Hasegawa, 17 Kami Negishi, Tokyo,* named as publisher. The names of no other distributors or publishers present. In the Japanese colophon *K. Shibata* is named as printer. *See reproduction.*

Locations: H   NYPL   UT

Note: Quite late printings were issued by Y. Nishinomiya, successor to T. Hasegawa. *Also note:* Certain of Hasegawa's late printings have the colophon printed on the inner front of the wrapper; not on p. ⟨23⟩ as in the early printings; and, the designation *No 25* is not present on the front of the wrapper.

Published March 15, 1903 (colophon); *see reproductions.*

7940. KWAIDAN: STORIES AND STUDIES OF STRANGE THINGS . . .

BOSTON AND NEW YORK HOUGHTON, MIFFLIN AND COMPANY MDCCCCIV

Title-page in black and red-orange.

Three issues noted. No sequence has been established and simultaneous publication is quite possible.

A

⟨i-ii⟩, ⟨i⟩-⟨viii⟩, ⟨1⟩-240; blank, p. ⟨241⟩; printer's imprint, p. ⟨242⟩; blank leaf. 7⁷⁄₁₆″ x 5″. Frontispiece and 1 plate inserted.

⟨1⁹, 2-15⁸, 16⁶⟩. Leaf ⟨1⟩₅ ("Note on the Illustrations") is an insert.

Does not contain a publisher's "Introduction." The title-leaf is conjugate with ⟨1⟩₈.

B

⟨i-vi⟩, ⟨i⟩-⟨viii⟩, ⟨1⟩-240; blank, p. ⟨241⟩; printer's imprint, p. ⟨242⟩; blank leaf. 7⁷⁄₁₆″ x 5″. Frontispiece and 1 plate inserted.

⟨1¹¹, 2-15⁸, 16⁶⟩. Leaf ⟨1⟩₇ ("Note on the Illustrations") is an insert. Also inserted are conjugate leaves ⟨1⟩₃₋₄ which are imprinted with a publisher's "Introduction" dated at end *March, 1904*. The title-leaf is cancel.

C

⟨i-vi⟩, ⟨i⟩-⟨viii⟩, ⟨1⟩-240; blank, p. ⟨241⟩; printer's imprint, p. ⟨242⟩; blank leaf. 7⁷⁄₁₆″ x 5″. Frontispiece and 1 plate inserted.

⟨1¹¹, 2-15⁸, 16⁶⟩. Leaf ⟨1⟩₇ ("Note on the Illustrations") is an insert. Also inserted are conjugate leaves ⟨1⟩₃₋₄ which are imprinted with a publisher's "Introduction" dated at end *March, 1904*. The title-leaf is not a cancel but is conjugate with ⟨1⟩₁₀.

Note: The publisher's "Introduction" appears to be an afterthought inspired by the outbreak of the Russo-Japanese War in February, 1904. The publisher's "Introduction," dated March, 1904, is not present in the first London issue (made up of American sheets); it is present in the second London issue. The publisher's "Introduction" is also present in both copyright deposit copies; it is not present in an advance copy in UV. These facts suggest priority for those copies without the publisher's "Introduction" but nevertheless, and with equal force, suggest simultaneous publication both with and without the inserted publisher's "Introduction." The publisher's "Introduction" is present in the *Second Impression* (Boston & New York) where it appears as an integral part of the first gathering, not as an insert. (For a comment on the two London printings see below under publication notes.)

Common to all issues: On the copyright page is the statement *Published April 1904* On leaf ⟨1⟩₁ᵥ is a boxed advertisement headed *Books by Lafcadio Hearn* with six titles listed.

Noted in the following types of cloth; presumably all were used simultaneously: V cloth: greenish-black. Sateen-like cloth: pale blue damasked with willow leaves; beige: damasked with willow leaves; beige: damasked with flowers. Top edges gilt. Flyleaf at front.

Deposited March 17, 1904. Advertised for spring publication PW March 19, 1904. Published April 2, 1904 (date from publisher's stamped note on advance copy in UV). Noted for *to-day* PW April 2, 1904. Listed PW April 9, 1904. The London (Kegan Paul) issue, made up of American sheets, listed Ath April 30, 1904. *Note:* There were at least two London issues, both dated MDCCCIV, as follows:

First London

Sig. ⟨1⟩ is in 9; leaf 5 ("Note on the Illustrations") being a singleton; publisher's "Introduction" not present. Leaf 1 excised.

Second London

Sig. ⟨1⟩ is in 8. Leaf 1 excised. "Note on the Illustrations" and publisher's "Introduction" are not inserts but are integral parts of the gathering.

H (A, C. 1st and 2nd London) LC (B, being a deposit copy; the other deposit copy has been extensively repaired and rebound hence status not known; C) UV (A, being an advance copy in paper wrapper; C)

7941. JAPAN AN ATTEMPT AT INTERPRETATION . . .

NEW YORK THE MACMILLAN COMPANY LONDON: MACMILLAN & CO., LTD. 1904 . . .

⟨i⟩-⟨vi⟩, ⟨1⟩-541; blank, p. ⟨542⟩; 2 pp. advertisements; blank leaf. 7¾″ x 5¼″. Frontispiece inserted.

⟨1-34⁸, 35⁴⟩. *Signed:* ⟨A⟩³, ⟨B⟩, C-I, K-U, X-Z, 2A-2I, 2K-2M⁸, ⟨2N⟩¹.

T cloth: tan. White laid paper end papers. Top edges gilt.

On copyright page: *Published September, 1904*. Noted for *next month* PW March 19, 1904; Aug. 13, 1904. Deposited Oct. 4, 1904. Noted as *at once* PW Oct. 8, 1904. Listed PW Oct. 15, 1904. Advertised as *just ready* PW Oct. 29, 1904. The London edition advertised for *Tuesday* ⟨i.e., Nov. 1⟩ in Ath Oct. 1904. Listed Ath Nov. 5, 1904. See next entry.

H   LC   UT

7942. Japan An Attempt at Interpretation . . . ⟨4th Printing⟩

New York The Macmillan Company London: Macmillan & Co., Ltd. 1904 . . .

Contains an "Appendix," pp. 529-534, here first published. For first edition see preceding entry.

On copyright page: *. . . December, 1904*.

UT   UV   Y

7943. THE ROMANCE OF THE MILKY WAY AND OTHER STUDIES & STORIES . . .

HOUGHTON MIFFLIN AND COMPANY BOSTON AND NEW YORK 1905

Title-page in black and red.

⟨i-ii⟩, ⟨i⟩-⟨xiv⟩, ⟨1⟩-209; printer's imprint, p. ⟨210⟩, blank leaf. 7½″ x 5″.

⟨1¹², 2-13⁸, 14⁶⟩.

V cloth: gray. Flyleaf at front. Top edges stained yellow.

On copyright page: *Published October 1905* Advertised for fall publication PW Sept. 30, 1905. Deposited Oct. 9, 1905. Noted for Oct. 18 PW Oct. 14, 1905. Published Oct. 18, 1905 (publisher's records). BPL copy received Oct. 20, 1905. Advertised as *just published* PW Oct. 21, 1905. Listed PW Nov. 4, 1905. The London (Constable) edition advertised for *next week* Ath Oct. 28, 1905; listed Ath Nov. 18, 1905.

H NYPL UV

7944. THE LIFE AND LETTERS OF LAFCADIO HEARN BY ELIZABETH BISLAND . . .

BOSTON AND NEW YORK HOUGHTON, MIFFLIN AND COMPANY THE RIVERSIDE PRESS, CAMBRIDGE 1906

2 Vols.

Limited Edition

1: ⟨i-ii⟩, ⟨i⟩-⟨xii⟩, ⟨1⟩-475; printer's imprint, p. ⟨476⟩. Frontispiece, 1 page of manuscript, and 5 plates inserted. 9″ scant x 6″.
2: ⟨i-viii⟩, ⟨1⟩-554; blank, p. ⟨555⟩; printer's imprint, p. ⟨556⟩. Frontispiece and 9 plates inserted.

1: ⟨1⁷, 2-30⁸, 31⁶⟩. Leaf ⟨1⟩₆ inserted.
2: ⟨1⁴, 2-35⁸, 36⁶⟩.

V cloth: black-green. Printed paper label on spine. White laid paper end papers. Flyleaf at end of Vol. 1.

"*. . . Two Hundred Copies . . . Printed And Bound Entirely Uncut . . . Containing A Page Of Mr. Hearn's Manuscript*"—Certificate of issue, Vol. 1.

Trade Edition

1: ⟨i-ii⟩, ⟨i⟩-⟨xii⟩, ⟨1⟩-475; printer's imprint, p. ⟨476⟩. Frontispiece and 5 plates inserted. 8¹¹⁄₁₆″ x 5⅞″.
2: ⟨i-viii⟩, ⟨1⟩-554; blank, p. ⟨555⟩; printer's imprint, p. ⟨556⟩. Frontispiece and 9 plates inserted.

1: ⟨1⁷, 2-30⁸, 31⁶⟩. Leaf ⟨1⟩₆ inserted.
2: ⟨1⁴, 2-35⁸, 36⁶⟩.

T cloth: black-green. White laid paper end papers. Flyleaves in Vol. 1. Top edges gilt.

On copyright page: *Published December 1906* Noted for *the last of August* PW Aug. 18, 1906. Noted for fall publication PW Sept. 1, 1906. Deposited Nov. 30, 1906. Noted as *just ready* PW Dec. 1, 1906. Trade edition only listed PW Dec. 22, 1906. The London (Constable) edition was advertised, with reviews, Ath Jan. 19, 1907.

H (limited, trade) NYPL (limited, trade) UT (limited)

7945. LETTERS FROM THE RAVEN BEING THE CORRESPONDENCE OF LAFCADIO HEARN WITH HENRY WATKIN WITH INTRODUCTION AND CRITICAL COMMENT BY THE EDITOR MILTON BRONNER

NEW YORK BRENTANO'S 1907

⟨i-iv⟩, ⟨1⟩-201; blank leaf. Illustrated. 7½″ x 5″. *Note:* The full-page plates opposite pp. 36, 40, 70, 72, are integral parts of their respective gatherings but are not reckoned in the printed pagination.

⟨1-13⁸, 14⁴⟩.

Gray-brown paper boards, black V cloth shelfback. End papers of book stock. Top edges gilt.

Advertised for fall publication PW Sept. 28, 1907. Deposited Oct. 21, 1907. Listed PW Dec. 21, 1907. The London (Constable) edition announced Bkr Sept. 1907; advertised as though ready in Bkr's Christmas issue, 1907; *but* described as *next week* Ath Feb. 29, 1908; and, listed Ath March 21, 1908.

Note: The PW for Dec. 23, 1905, lists an edition of this book with the imprint of the Mintjie Press, Covington, Ky. No such edition has been found.

H NYPL UT

7946. . . . Clarimonde and Other Stories by Théophile Gautier Translated by Lafcadio Hearn

London & Edinburgh T. C. & E. C. Jack ⟨n.d., 1908⟩

At head of title: The World's Story Tellers Edited by Arthur Ransome

Reprint.

Listed Ath May 9, 1908.

UV

7947. ... Stories by Théophile Gautier Translated by Lafcadio Hearn

New York: E. P. Dutton and Company 1908

At head of title: The World's Story Tellers Edited by Arthur Ransome

Reprint.

Listed PW Aug. 15, 1908.

UV

7948. Tales from Théophile Gautier Translated by Lafcadio Hearn and Myndart Verelst ⟨i.e., Edgar Saltus⟩

New York   Brentano's   1909

Leather.

Reprint.

Listed PW Dec. 4, 1909.

H   NYPL

7949. The Temptation of St. Anthony by Gustave Flaubert Translated by Lafcadio Hearn

The Alice Harriman Company   New York and Seattle   1910

⟨i-xl⟩, 1-262, blank leaf. 7⅜″ scant x 4¹⁵⁄₁₆″.

On copyright page: *Published October, 1910* Noted for fall publication PW Sept. 24, 1910. Deposited Nov. 7, 1910. Listed PW Dec. 17, 1910. See under 1911 for an extended edition.

NYPL   UT

7950. THE JAPANESE LETTERS OF LAFCADIO HEARN EDITED WITH AN INTRODUCTION BY ELIZABETH BISLAND ...

BOSTON AND NEW YORK   HOUGHTON MIFFLIN COMPANY   THE RIVERSIDE PRESS   CAMBRIDGE 1910

Limited Edition

⟨i-ii⟩, ⟨i⟩-lx, ⟨1⟩-468; blank, p. ⟨469⟩; printer's imprint, p. ⟨470⟩. Frontispiece and 5 plates inserted. 8⅞″ x 5⅞″.

⟨1-33⁸, 34²⟩.

V cloth: green-black. Printed paper label on spine.

"Of This First Edition Two Hundred Copies Have Been Printed And Bound Entirely Uncut ..." —Certificate of issue.

Trade Edition

⟨i-ii⟩, ⟨i⟩-lx, ⟨1⟩-468; blank, p. ⟨469⟩; printer's imprint, p. ⟨470⟩. Frontispiece and 5 plates inserted. 8¹¹⁄₁₆″ x 5⅞″.

⟨1-33⁸, 34²⟩. In some copies leaf ⟨34⟩₂ is excised.

T cloth: green-black. Top edges gilt.

Note: The spine imprint occurs in two states of undetermined sequence, if sequence there is. The designations are for identification only:

A: Spine imprint set 1³⁄₁₆″ wide. A copyright deposit copy thus.

B: Spine imprint set 1⁵⁄₁₆″ wide.

Also note: All examined copies of the trade edition are bound in T cloth. The surviving copyright deposit copy is bound in V cloth.

On copyright page: *Published November 1910* Trade edition only advertised for Nov. 26 in PW Nov. 19, 1910. Trade edition only advertised PW Nov. 26, 1910. Deposited Dec. 9, 1910 (trade edition). Trade edition only listed PW Dec. 17, 1910. The London (Constable) edition announced Ath Aug. 1910; listed Bkr Jan. 20, 1911; Ath Jan. 28, 1911.

AAS (trade, B imprint) H (trade, A and B imprints) NYPL (limited; trade, A imprint) UT (limited)

7951. "Heart's Flower-of-Cherry" ... Music by Florence Newell Barbour ...

New York. The William Maxwell Music Co. 8 East 16th Street. ⟨1910⟩

Sheet music. Cover-title. Plate No. 1224-4.

Reprinted from *Gleanings in Buddha-Fields,* 1897, p. 197.

H

7952. The Temptation of St. Anthony by Gustave Flaubert Translated by Lafcadio Hearn ⟨Second Edition⟩

The Alice Harriman Company   New York 1911

Extended by the addition of "Addenda," pp. 262-265. For first edition see under 1910.

Deposited Oct. 2, 1911. The London (Richards) edition listed Bkr Nov. 3, 1911.

UT   UV

7953. LEAVES FROM THE DIARY OF AN IMPRESSIONIST EARLY WRITINGS BY LAFCADIO HEARN WITH AN INTRODUCTION BY FERRIS GREENSLET

BOSTON AND NEW YORK   HOUGHTON MIFFLIN COMPANY 1911

Title-page in black and blue.

⟨i-viii⟩, ⟨1⟩-179; colophon, p. ⟨180⟩. Laid paper watermarked *British Hand Made.* Inserts: 1-page facsimile; 2-page facsimile. 7″ x 4⅜″.

⟨1-23⁴, 24²⟩.

Blue laid paper boards sides, tan T cloth shelf-back. Blue paper label on spine printed in gold. End papers of book stock. Double flyleaves.

"Five Hundred And Seventy-Five Numbered Copies Printed . . . September, 1911 . . ."— Colophon.

Noted for Oct. 21, PW Oct. 21, 1911. Deposited Oct. 26, 1911. BA copy received Nov. 8, 1911. Listed PW Feb. 24, 1912.

BA NYPL

7954. EDITORIALS FROM THE KOBE CHRONICLE

⟨n.p., n.d., New York 1913⟩

Cover-title.

⟨i-viii⟩, 1-20, 20a-20b, 21-96. Wove paper watermarked *Gothic.* 9¾″ x 6⁵⁄₁₆″.

⟨1⁴, 2⁸, 3⁹, 4-7⁸⟩. Leaf ⟨3⟩₃ inserted.

Printed stiff white paper wrapper. Inserted at pp. ⟨vi-vii⟩ is a slip headed ADDENDA.

Edited and published by Merle Johnson although this information is nowhere stated in the publication.

Not to be confused with *Editorials,* 1926, below.

According to the certificate of issue, in Merle Johnson's hand, p. ⟨i⟩, the printing was limited to 100 copies. An incomplete set of galley proofs is in Lehigh University, Bethlehem, Penna.

NYPL UT

7955. FANTASTICS AND OTHER FANCIES . . . EDITED BY CHARLES WOODWARD HUTSON

BOSTON AND NEW YORK   HOUGHTON MIFFLIN COMPANY   1914

Title-page in black and blue.

⟨i-ii⟩, ⟨i⟩-⟨x⟩, ⟨1⟩-⟨242⟩; blank, p. ⟨243⟩; colophon, p. ⟨244⟩. Laid paper watermarked *British Hand Made.* 7¹⁄₁₆″ x 4⅜″.

⟨1², 2-16⁸, 17⁶⟩.

Blue laid paper boards sides, tan T cloth shelf-back, blue paper label on spine printed in gold. White laid paper end papers.

"Five Hundred And Fifty Numbered Copies Printed . . . October, 1914 . . ."—Colophon.

Deposited Jan. 2, 1915. A trade edition issued 1919.

H

7956. Japanese Lyrics Translated by Lafcadio Hearn

Boston and New York   Houghton Mifflin Company   The Riverside Press   Cambridge 1915

Printed paper wrapper over flexible boards.

Reprint. "Scattered through the pages of Lafcadio Hearn's writings are many Japanese lyrics . . . it has seemed worth while to bring them together . . ."—P. vii.

Two printings noted. The order is presumed correct.

A

⟨i⟩-⟨x⟩, ⟨1⟩-⟨86⟩; blank, p. ⟨87⟩; printer's imprint, p. ⟨88⟩; blank leaf. Leaf ⟨1⟩₁ᵥ blank. Leaf ⟨1⟩₂ (the title-leaf) is a cancel. No preliminary advertisements. A deposit copy thus.

B

⟨i-ii⟩, ⟨i⟩-⟨x⟩, ⟨1⟩-⟨86⟩; blank, p. ⟨87⟩; printer's imprint, p. ⟨88⟩. Boxed advertisement on leaf ⟨1⟩₁ᵥ. The title-leaf is not a cancel.

On copyright page: *Published April 1915* Deposited April 19, 1915. Listed PW May 1, 1915. The London (Constable) edition listed Bkr June 11, 1915.

BA (B)   LC (A, being a deposit copy)   UV (A,B) Y (A)

7957. Interpretations of Literature . . . Selected and Edited . . . by John Erskine . . .

New York   Dodd, Mead and Company   1915

2 Vols. 1: ⟨i⟩-⟨xvi⟩, 1-406, blank leaf. Frontispiece inserted. 2: ⟨i-viii⟩, 1-379, 2 blank leaves. 9″ x 6⅛″. Cloth, printed paper label on spine.

The text is based on lecture notes kept by Hearn's students. "In lecturing, Lafcadio Hearn used no notes, but for the convenience of his class, who were listening to a foreign language, he dictated slowly, and certain of his abler students managed to take down long passages, whole lectures, even a series of lectures, word for word . . . After Lafcadio Hearn's death these students . . . placed their notes at the disposal of Pay Director Mitchell McDonald, U.S.N., Hearn's friend and literary executor . . ."— Vol. 1, p. v.

Listed PW Nov. 6, 1915. Deposited Nov. 11, 1915. Issued in London, 1916, by Heinemann.

H UT

7958. Appreciations of Poetry . . . Selected and Edited . . . by John Erskine . . .

New York   Dodd, Mead and Company   1916

⟨i⟩-⟨xvi⟩, 1-408. 9¹⁄₁₆″ x 6⅛″. Cloth, printed paper label on spine.

The text is based on lecture notes kept by Hearn's students. For fuller comment see note under entry No. 7957.

Deposited Dec. 12, 1916. Listed PW Dec. 16, 1916. Issued in London, 1919, by Heinemann.

H   UT

7959. Life and Literature . . . Selected and Edited . . . by John Erskine . . .

New York   Dodd, Mead and Company   1917

⟨i⟩-⟨xii⟩, 1-393, blank leaf. 9¹⁄₁₆″ x 6⅛″. Cloth, printed paper label on spine.

The text is based on lecture notes kept by Hearn's students. For fuller comment see note under entry No. 7957.

Deposited Nov. 27, 1917. Listed PW Dec. 1, 1917. American sheets distributed in London with the cancel title-leaf of William Heinemann ⟨1917⟩. The date notwithstanding the book appears to have issued in London not before 1920. Earliest located announcement is in Bkr, Oct. 1920; advertised as though published Ath (Christmas supplement) Dec. 3, 1920; listed Ath Dec. 3, 1920. Reviewed as a new work Ath Jan. 28, 1921.

H   UT

. . . On Composition . . .

The Atlantic Monthly Press, Inc. Boston ⟨1917⟩

See below under 1920.

. . . On Reading in Relation to Literature . . .

The Atlantic Monthly Press, Inc. Boston ⟨1917⟩

See below under 1921.

7960. Japanese Fairy Tales ⟨Translated⟩ by Lafcadio Hearn and Others

New York   Boni and Liveright   1918

Boards, cloth shelfback.

First American book printing of Hearn's "Chin Chin Kobakama," "The Goblin Spider," "The Old Woman Who Lost Her Dumpling," "The Boy Who Drew Cats." For first publication of these translations see above under 1898, 1899, 1902, 1903.

Listed PW Dec. 7, 1918. Deposited Jan. 3, 1919.

H   Y

7961. KARMA . . .

NEW YORK   BONI AND LIVERIGHT   1918

Edited by Albert Mordell.

⟨1⟩-6, 11-163. 7⁵⁄₁₆″ x 4⁹⁄₁₆″.

⟨1-10⟩⁸.

Printed blue paper boards sides, white V cloth shelfback.

Listed PW Dec. 7, 1918. Deposited Jan. 3, 1919. Listed Ath Aug. 22, 1919. A Harrap (London) printing listed Bkr Sept. 1921.

H   UT

7962. . . . Diaries & Letters Translated and Annotated by Prof. R. Tanabe

1920   Hokuseido   Tokyo

At head of title: Lafcadio Hearn

Reprint except for four letters:

To Ochiai, Feb. 1896.

To Basil Hall Chamberlain, Feb. 25, 1894; March 9, 1894; June 1896.

Published Feb. 11, 1920 (colophon); *see reproduction*.

H   UT   UV

7963. . . . On Composition . . .

The Atlantic Monthly Press, Inc. Boston ⟨1917; *i.e.,* 1920⟩

At head of title: Atlantic Readings Number 13

Cover-title. Printed paper wrapper.

Reprinted from *Life and Literature,* 1917, *q.v.*

Publication date according to Perkins.

H

7964. Talks to Writers . . . Selected and Edited . . . by John Erskine . . .

New York   Dodd, Mead and Company   1920

Reprint. Cloth, printed paper label on spine.

The text is based on lecture notes kept by Hearn's students. For fuller comment see note under entry No. 7957.

Listed PW Oct. 20, 1920. Deposited Oct. 27, 1920. No London edition located. The only reference found to publication in Great Britain is an announcement in Ath (supplement) Oct. 8, 1920, crediting Eveleigh Nash with publication plans. No further British reference found.

AAS   NYPL   UT

7965. ... Impressions of Japan Translated and Annotated by T. Ochiai ...

1920 Hokuseido No. 7, Nishikicho 3-chome, Kanda, Tokyo

At head of title: Lafcadio Hearn

Hearn Memorial Translations, Vol. 2.

Reprint.

H UT

7966. ... Letters from Tokyo Translated and Annotated by M. Ōtani ...

1920 Hokuseido No. 7, Nishikicho 3-chome, Kanda, Tokyo

At head of title: Lafcadio Hearn

Hearn Memorial Translations, Vol. 3.

Reprint.

H UT

7967. ... Insect Literature Translated and Annotated by M. Ōtani ...

1921 Hokuseido No. 7, Nishikicho 3-chome, Kanda, Tokyo

At head of title: Lafcadio Hearn

Hearn Memorial Translations, Vol. 5.

Reprint.

H UT

7968. ... Kokoro Translated and Annotated by R. Tanabe ...

1921 Hokuseido No. 7, Nishikicho 3-chome, Kanda, Tokyo

At head of title: Lafcadio Hearn

Reprint save for "Obahsan-No-Hanashi," pp. ⟨322⟩-334.

Published April 25, 1921 (colophon); *see reproduction.* For another edition see entry No. 7928.

H UT UV

7969. ... Sea Literature Translated and Annotated by M. Ōtani ...

1921 Hokuseido No. 7, Nishikicho 3-chome, Kanda, Tokyo

At head of title: Lafcadio Hearn

Hearn Memorial Translations, Vol. 6.

Reprint.

H UT

7970. ... On Reading in Relation to Literature ...

The Atlantic Monthly Press, Inc. Boston ⟨1917, *i.e.,* 1921⟩

At head of title: Atlantic Readings Number 17

Cover-title. Printed paper wrapper.

Reprinted from *Life and Literature,* 1917, *q.v.*

Publication date according to Perkins.

AAS H UT

7971. Books and Habits from the Lectures of Lafcadio Hearn ... Edited ... by John Erskine ...

New York Dodd, Mead and Company 1921

Cloth, printed paper label on spine.

Reprint save for: "The Ideal Woman in English Poetry," "The New Ethics," "Note on the Influence of Finnish Poetry in English Literature".

The text is based on lecture notes kept by Hearn's students. For fuller comment see note under entry No. 7957.

Two issued noted. The following order is likely:

1: The statement *Printed In The U.S.A.* is not on the copyright page.

2: The statement *Printed In The U.S.A.* on copyright page.

Deposited Oct. 11, 1921. Listed PW Oct. 22, 1921. The London (Heinemann) edition first announced as *Lectures on Literature* N&A March 18, 1922; as *Books and Habits* advertised as though published Bkr May, 1922. Listed N&A May 20, 1922.

AAS (1)   BA (1)   LC (1, being a deposit copy) UV (1, 2)

7972. ... On Literature Translated and Annotated by T. Ochiai ...

1922 Hokuseido 7, Nishikicho 3-chome, Kanda, Tokyo

At head of title: Lafcadio Hearn

Hearn Memorial Translations, Vol. 7.

Reprint.

H UT

7973. ... Island Voyages Translated and Annotated by M. Otani ...

1922 Hokuseido No. 7, Nishikicho 3-chome, Kanda, Tokyo

At head of title: Lafcadio Hearn

Hearn Memorial Translations, Vol. 8.

Reprint.

H   UT

7974. Pre-Raphaelite and Other Poets ... Edited ... by John Erskine ...

New York   Dodd, Mead and Company 1922

Cloth, printed paper label on spine.

Reprint.

The text is based on lecture notes kept by Hearn's students. For fuller comment see note under entry No. 7957.

Deposited Oct. 17, 1922. Listed PW Oct. 28, 1922. The London (Heinemann) edition listed N&A April 21, 1923.

H   NYPL

7975. ... The Fountain of Youth   Rendered into English by Lafcadio Hearn

⟨Tokyo: T. Hasegawa, 1922⟩

At head of title: Japanese Fairy Tale   *See note at head of list regarding this series.*

Cover-title.

⟨1-16⟩; advertisement, p. ⟨17⟩; tailpiece, p. ⟨18⟩. Illustrated. 9⁹⁄₁₆″ x 7″ full (uncreped paper). 7½″ x 5⅜″ (creped paper).

Published Dec. 10, 1922 (colophon); *see reproduction.*

Note: The first printing, described above, save for a few copies was destroyed by fire. Two survivors (one being creped, the other uncreped), not seen by BAL, are in Tenri Central Library, Tenri University, Tenri, Nara, Japan. Examples of the uncreped state are in NYPL, UT, UV. The first printing has the colophon on the inner front wrapper and gives 1922 as year of printing and publication. The illustration on the front wrapper is a mountain scene as seen through an overhanging branch; not as seen through tree trunks.

The *Second Printing* was done in 1925 according to the colophon. The illustration on the front wrapper is of a mountain as seen through a group of trees. This 1925 printing has been noted in two forms; the designations are for identification only:

A

Inner back of wrapper imprinted: *Japanese Fairy Tale Series. English Edition* ...

Text printed from a roman face.

Location: H

B

Inner back of wrapper imprinted: *Japanese Fairy Tales Rendered into English* ...

Text printed from a semi-script face.

Locations: H   UT

Second printing (so identified in the colophon) published Dec. 10, 1925.

7976. LEAVES FROM THE DIARY OF AN IMPRESSIONIST   CREOLE SKETCHES AND SOME CHINESE GHOSTS ...

BOSTON AND NEW YORK   HOUGHTON MIFFLIN COMPANY   MDCCCCXXII

Title-page in black and red. Issued as *The Writings of Lafcadio Hearn,* Vol. 1. See next entry.

⟨i⟩-⟨xxx⟩, ⟨1⟩-⟨299⟩; blank leaf. Frontispiece and 3 plates, each with printed tissue, inserted. Also inserted: A leaf of Hearn manuscript; and, a leaf bearing Mrs. Hearn's autograph. 9″ x 6″.

⟨1-2¹, 3-22⁸, 23⁴⟩.

Reprint save for "Creole Sketches," pp. 107-⟨208⟩.

Issued in a variety of bindings. The following noted: brown paper boards sides, cloth shelfback, brown paper label printed in gold on spine; various styles of leather; green brocade with vellum shelfback.

"The Large-Paper Edition Is Limited To Seven Hundred And Fifty Copies ... Number ..." —Certificate of issue.

Deposited April 7, 1923.

NYPL   UT

7977. The Writings of Lafcadio Hearn   Large-Paper Edition in Sixteen Volumes ⟨fly-title⟩

Boston and New York   Houghton Mifflin Company   MDCCCCXXII

Limited to 750 numbered sets. Issued in a variety of bindings. The following bindings noted: brown paper boards sides, cloth shelfback, brown paper label printed in gold on spine; various styles of leather; green brocade with vellum shelfback. See preceding entry for a detailed description of Vol. 1. The individual volumes were deposited on April 7; or, 9, 1923. All reprint save for Vol. 1.

1: *Leaves from the Diary of an Impressionist* ... See preceding **entry.**

2: *Stray Leaves from Strange Literature; Fantastics and Other Fancies.*

3: *Two Years in the French West Indies,* Vol. 1.

4: *Two Years in the French West Indies,* Vol. 2. *Chita. Youma.*

5-6: *Glimpses of Unfamiliar Japan.*

7: *Out of the East. Kokoro.*

8: *Gleanings in Buddha-Fields. Romance of the Milky Way.*

9: *Exotics and Retrospectives. In Ghostly Japan.*

10: *Shadowings. A Japanese Miscellany.*

11: *Kottō. Kwaidan.*

12: *Japan: An Attempt at Interpretation.*

13-14: *Life and Letters.* Vols. 1-2.

15: *Life and Letters,* Vol. 3. *Japanese Letters,* Part 1.

16: *Japanese Letters,* concluded.

NYPL

7978. The Dream of a Summer Day . . .

Boston and New York   Houghton Mifflin Company   The Riverside Press   Cambridge 1922

Printed paper wrapper. Reprinted from *Out of the East,* 1895.

Note: Copies issued under date ⟨1895⟩ are reprints of the 1922 printing.

H   UT

7979. ESSAYS IN EUROPEAN AND ORIENTAL LITERATURE . . . EDITED BY ALBERT MORDELL

NEW YORK   DODD, MEAD AND COMPANY 1923

Title-page in black and red.

⟨i⟩-⟨xviii⟩, ⟨1⟩-339; blank leaf. 7⅜″ x 5⅛″.

⟨1⁴, 2-23⁸⟩.

Red buckram, printed paper label on spine. Top edges stained green.

BPL copy received Oct. 3, 1923. Deposited Oct. 4, 1923. Listed PW Oct. 6, 1923. The London (Heinemann) edition listed N&A Nov. 3, 1923; Bkr Nov. 1923.

LC   UT   UV

7980. . . . Kimiko and Other Japanese Sketches . . .

Boston and New York   Houghton Mifflin Company   The Riverside Press   Cambridge 1923

At head of title: The Evergreen Series

Printed paper boards.

Reprinted from *Kokoro,* 1896.

AAS   H   UT

7981. Koizumi Edition   The Writings of Lafcadio Hearn in Sixteen Volumes ⟨fly-title⟩

Boston and New York   Houghton Mifflin Company   The Riverside Press   Cambridge 1923

Boards, cloth shelf back. 16 Vols.

Reprint.

H

7982. CREOLE SKETCHES . . . EDITED BY CHARLES WOODWARD HUTSON . . .

BOSTON AND NEW YORK   HOUGHTON MIFFLIN COMPANY   THE RIVERSIDE PRESS   CAMBRIDGE 1924

⟨i⟩-⟨xxvi⟩, ⟨1⟩-201. Illustrated. 7½″ x 5¹⁄₁₆″.

⟨1-13⁸, 14¹⁰⟩.

V cloth: red.

Note: Much of the material herein had prior book publication in *The Writings,* Vol. 1, 1922, above.

BPL copy received April 12, 1924. Deposited April 14, 1924. Listed PW April 26, 1924.

LC   NYPL   UT

7983. Et Cetera   A Collector's Scrap-Book ⟨Edited by Vincent Starrett⟩

Chicago   Pascal Covici Publisher 1924

"The Chemise of Margarita Pareja," pp. 115-120. Translated by Hearn.

For comment see entry No. 4100A.

7984. AN AMERICAN MISCELLANY . . . ARTICLES AND STORIES NOW FIRST COLLECTED BY ALBERT MORDELL . . .

NEW YORK   DODD, MEAD AND COMPANY 1924

2 Vols. Title-page in black and red.

1: ⟨i⟩-⟨lxxxiv⟩, 1-227. 8⅝″ x 5¾″.
2: ⟨i-ii⟩, ⟨i⟩-⟨x⟩, 1-265; blank leaf.

1: ⟨1-19⁸, 20⁴⟩.
2: ⟨1-17⁸, 18⁴⟩.

Maroon buckram. Printed paper label on spine. Top edges stained green.

Note: In some copies leaf ⟨18⟩4, Vol. 2, is used as the terminal pastedown.

Listed PW Oct. 4, 1924. NYPL copy received Oct. 6, 1924. Deposited Oct. 7, 1924. *See next entry.*

NYPL   UT

7985. Miscellanies ... Articles and Stories Now First Collected by Albert Mordell ...

London   William Heinemann Ltd. 1924

2 Vols.

The sheets of *An American Miscellany*, (see preceding entry), with cancel title-leaves.

Announced for *next Thursday* ⟨*i.e.,* Nov. 6⟩ TLS Oct. 30, 1924; for Nov. 13 PC Nov. 8, 1924. Listed PC Nov. 22, 1924. Reissued, 1925, under the title *An American Miscellany*.

LC

7986. Kusa-Hibari ...

Montreal   Privately Printed   December 1924

Boards, printed paper label on front.

Reprinted from *Kottō*, 1902. Limited to 350 copies.

H   NYPL

7987. Saint Anthony and Other Stories by Guy de Maupassant ... Translated by Lafcadio Hearn Edited ... by Albert Mordell

Albert & Charles Boni   New York   1924

⟨i-ii⟩, ⟨i⟩-xviii, ⟨1⟩-293; blank leaf. 7⅜" x 5".

Noted for *this month* PW Oct. 4, 1924. Deposited Jan. 10, 1925. The London (Jarrolds) edition announced PC March 7, 1925; listed PC May 9, 1925.

H   LC

7988. Stories and Sketches ... Compiled ... by R. Tanabé ...

Hokuseido   Nishikicho   3-chome, Kanda, Tokyo ⟨1925⟩

Cloth, printed paper label on front.

Reprint save for "My Guardian Angel," pp. ⟨236⟩-246; "Idolatry," pp. ⟨247⟩-253.

Published March 13, 1925 (colophon).

Note: Not located; not seen. Entry on the basis of known reprints.

H   UT   Y

7989. Lands and Seas ... Compiled ... by T. Ochiai ...

Hokuseido   Nishikicho   3-chome, Kanda, Tokyo ⟨1925⟩

Cloth, printed paper label on front cover.

Reprint. *Note:* The first printings are pp. 293; later printings pp. 311.

AAS   H   LC   NYPL   UT

7990. OCCIDENTAL GLEANINGS ... SKETCHES AND ESSAYS NOW FIRST COLLECTED BY ALBERT MORDELL ...

NEW YORK   DODD, MEAD AND COMPANY 1925

2 Vols. Title-page in black and red.

1: ⟨i⟩-⟨xliv⟩, 1-275. 8⁹⁄₁₆" x 5¾".
2: ⟨i⟩-⟨xii⟩, 1-289; blank leaf.

1: ⟨1-20⟩⁸.
2: ⟨1-19⟩⁸.

V cloth: tan. Maroon buckram. Printed paper label on spine. Top edges stained green.

NYPL copy received Sept. 16, 1925. Deposited Sept. 24, 1925. Listed PW Oct. 10, 1925. The London (Heinemann) edition advertised TLS Oct. 15, 1925, as though published; reviewed TLS Oct. 22, 1925; listed PC Oct. 24, 1925.

NYPL   UT

7991. Life and Literature ... Compiled ... by R. Tanabé ...

Hokuseido   Nishikicho   3-chome, Kanda, Tokyo ⟨1925⟩

Cloth, printed paper label on front cover.

Reprint.

The text is based on lecture notes kept by Hearn's students. For fuller comment see note under entry No. 7957.

H   NYPL   UT

7992. SOME NEW LETTERS AND WRITINGS OF LAFCADIO HEARN COLLECTED AND EDITED BY SANKI ICHIKAWA ...

TOKYO   KENKYUSHA   1925

⟨i⟩-⟨xviii⟩, ⟨1⟩-430; colophon, p. ⟨431⟩; *see reproduction.* Frontispiece and 4 plates inserted. 7¹³⁄₁₆" x 5⁵⁄₁₆".

⟨1-28⁸, 29¹⟩.

V cloth: black. Printed paper label on spine. Cream-yellow end papers. Errata slip inserted in some copies.

Published Dec. 25, 1925 (colophon); *see reproduction.* According to PW Nov. 13, 1926, 2000 (*error for* 200?) sets of sheets were imported into the United States by Greenberg, New York. Reviewed by TLS Nov. 11, 1926.

H   LC   NYPL   UT   UV

7993. Poets and Poems ... Compiled ... by R. Tanabé ...

Hokuseido   Nishikicho   3-chome, Kanda, Tokyo ⟨1926⟩

Not located. Entry tentative.

Reprint save for "Poems about Children," pp. ⟨10⟩-43; and, "On Rossetti's *Sea Limits*," pp. ⟨236⟩-242.

The present entry is on the basis of the sixth printing (copies in H, LC, UT, UV). It is all but certain that the colophon of the first printing has but two lines of type at the very top; and that all reprints have three or more lines at the same place.

The first printing was issued Feb. 1, 1926; the sixth printing issued April 25, 1928.

7994. EDITORIALS ... EDITED BY CHARLES WOODWARD HUTSON

BOSTON AND NEW YORK   HOUGHTON MIFFLIN COMPANY   THE RIVERSIDE PRESS   CAMBRIDGE 1926

⟨i⟩-⟨xxii⟩, ⟨1⟩-356; blank leaf. 8³⁄₁₆″ x 5⁷⁄₁₆″, trimmed.

⟨1-23⁸, 24⁶⟩.

B cloth: olive.

Note: In addition to the above trade edition there was also issued a limited edition with certificate of issue reading: *Two Hundred And Fifty Copies Of This First Edition Have Been Bound With Uncut Edges.* Leaf: 8½″ x 5½″.

Also note: Not to be confused with *Editorials from the Kobe Chronicle*, 1913, above.

Deposited May 10, 1926. BPL copy received June 1, 1926. Listed PW June 5, 1926.

H   NYPL   UT

7995. INSECTS AND GREEK POETRY ...

NEW YORK   WILLIAM EDWIN RUDGE   1926

⟨1-21⟩; blank, p. ⟨22⟩; colophon, p. ⟨23⟩. 7″ x 4⁵⁄₁₆″.

⟨-⟩¹².

Printed blue paper boards.

Printed from the original *ms* according to *Atlantic Monthly*, May, 1913, where the text was first published. "This lecture was delivered ... before Japanese students ... and is here reprinted for the first time in book form."—P. ⟨5⟩. *Was the* ms *Hearn's original? or, that of a student?* For a comment on the problem of students' *mss* see note at head of this list.

Limited to 550 copies.

AAS   NYPL   UT

7996. Life and Books   Some of Lafcadio Hearn's Lectures Selected and Edited by Tseu Yih Zan

The Commercial Press, Limited   Shanghai, China ⟨1926⟩

Printed paper wrapper.

Reprint.

Note: Entry on the basis of a 1933 reprint. The first printing of 1926 may vary somewhat as to the title and imprint.

H

7997. Sanseido's New Selections from Lafcadio Hearn

The Sanseido Co., Ltd. Tokyo ⟨n.d., 1926⟩

Printed paper wrapper.

Reprint.

H

7998. A History of English Literature in a Series of Lectures ...

The Hokuseido Press   Kanda, Tokyo, Japan 1927 ...

2 Vols.

1: ⟨i-vi⟩, ⟨i⟩-⟨iv⟩, ⟨1⟩-478; blank, pp. ⟨479-480⟩; ⟨i⟩-xii, 2 blank leaves; frontispiece inserted. 2: ⟨i-vi⟩, ⟨i⟩-iv, ⟨479⟩-914; inserted blank leaf; ⟨i⟩-xii, 2 blank leaves; frontispiece inserted. 9¹³⁄₁₆″ x 6½″ full. Tipped to ⟨63⟩3, Vol. 1, is a note regarding Hearn's seal. Colophon tipped to ⟨63⟩4, Vol. 1; *see reproduction.* Colophon tipped to ⟨59⟩4, Vol. 2; *see reproduction.*

"Supplement" not listed, Vol. 1, p. iii. See under 1928 (May) for extended edition. For description of the "Supplement" see entry No. 8000.

Vol. 1 published May 25, 1927; Vol. 2 published Nov. 10, 1927 (colophons); *see reproductions.* Revised or extended editions issued 1928 (see under May, 1928, below); 1930; 1934; 1938; 1941.

"... the reader must remember that these lectures are word for word as they were taken down by ⟨Hearn's⟩ students at the time of their delivery, and appear here without any revision by Hearn himself, who indeed never dreamed of their publication."—Editorial note, Vol. 1.

"... taken solely from notes of Japanese students ... Hearn never saw the material, far less corrected it."—TLS Aug. 18, 1927, in reviewing Vol. 1. For further like comment see entry No. 7957.

H   UT   UV

7999. Some Strange English Literary Figures of the Eighteenth and Nineteenth Centuries in a series of Lectures . . . Edited by R. Tanabé

The Hokuseido Press Kanda, Tokyo, Japan . . . ⟨1927⟩

⟨i-viii⟩, ⟨1⟩-140. Frontispiece and 10 plates inserted. 7¼″ full x 4¹⁵⁄₁₆″. Colophon (see reproduction) tipped to a terminal flyleaf.

Published Nov. 25, 1927 (colophon); see reproduction. Also see comment under No. 7957.

H LC NYPL UT UV

8000. Supplement to a History of English Literature . . . Vol. I (From Ben Jonson to Restoration Drama)

⟨n.p., Tokyo⟩ The Hokuseido Press ⟨n.d., 1927⟩

Cover-title. ⟨1⟩-60. 10″ full x 6⁹⁄₁₆″. Printed gray paper wrapper. Pasted to inner front of wrapper: A printed slip, gray paper, 3⅜″ x 3⅞″, referring to the text. Reprinted in History of English Literature, Vol. 1, 1927; i.e., May, 1928.

The text is based on lecture notes kept by Hearn's students. For fuller comment see note under entry No. 7957.

H copy received Dec. 14, 1927; BPL Dec. 15, 1927.

BPL H NYPL UV Y

8001. The Fountain of Gold . . .

⟨Metropolitan Press, San Francisco, 1927⟩

Printed boards, cloth shelfback and corners.

Reprinted from Leaves from the Diary of an Impressionist, 1911, where this piece appears as "A Tropical Intermezzo."

150 numbered copies.

CU UCB

8002. . . . One of Cleopatra's Nights and Other Fantastic Romances Translated . . . by Lafcadio Hearn . . .

Brentano's Publishers New York ⟨1927⟩

Reprint.

At head of title: Theophile Gautier

Deposited Jan. 11, 1928.

LC

8003. Entry cancelled.

A History of English Literature in a Series of Lectures . . . Vol. 1. ⟨Second Edition⟩

. . . Tokyo . . . 1927 ⟨i.e., May, 1928⟩ . . .

See below under May, 1928.

8004. Japan and the Japanese . . . Compiled . . . by T. Ochiai . . .

Hokuseido Nishikicho 3-chome, Kanda, Tokyo ⟨1928⟩

Cloth, printed paper label on front.

Reprint.

H LC UT

8005. A History of English Literature in a Series of Lectures . . . Vol. 1. ⟨Second Edition⟩

The Hokuseido Press Kanda, Tokyo, Japan 1927 ⟨i.e., May, 1928⟩ . . .

See under 1927 for first edition.

Reprint. A reprinting of the first edition of 1927 with a supplement. The supplement had prior separate publication in 1927; see entry 8000.

Published May 25, 1928 (colophon).

H UV

8006. Lectures on Shakespeare . . . Edited by Iwao Inagaki . . .

The Hokuseido Press Kanda, Tokyo, Japan . . . ⟨1928⟩

⟨i-viii⟩, 1-120. Inserted frontispiece. 7⁷⁄₁₆″ x 5″. Colophon tipped to terminal flyleaf; see reproduction. Also see comment under No. 7957.

Published Aug. 30, 1928 (colophon); see reproduction.

H LC UT UV Y

8007. Romance and Reason . . . Compiled . . . by R. Tanabé . . .

Hokuseido Nishikicho 3-chome, Kanda, Tokyo ⟨1928⟩

Cloth, printed paper label on front.

Reprint save for "A King's Romance," pp. 68-85.

Published Aug. 31, 1928 (colophon); see reproduction.

H LC UT UV

8008. The Tale of a Fan . . .

1928 Targ's Book Store 808 N. Clark.⟨sic⟩ St. Chicago

Single cut sheet of laid paper, watermarked Georgian, french-folded to 4 leaves. 500 copies only. Printed in blue throughout.

LAFCADIO HEARN

Certain of the following colophons occur on creped paper, the texture of which distorts some of the ideographs. However, while distortion is present the effect is not sufficient to alter the text. No attempt has been made to reproduce the colophons in actual size.

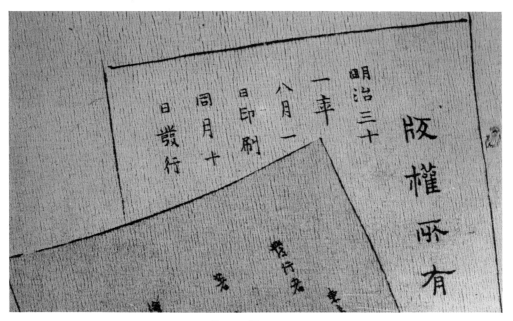

Entry No. 7930

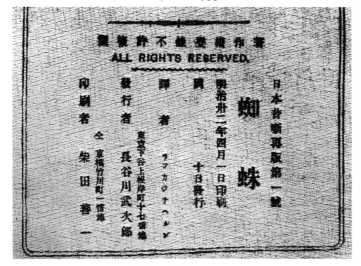

Entry No. 7932

and in quite a short time she became
rich.

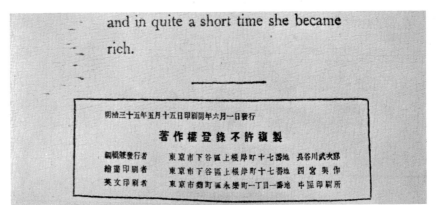

Entry No. 7937, Colophon A

JAPANISCHE DRAMEN: "Terakoya" und "Asagao," Übertragen
von Prof. Dr. Karl Florenz.

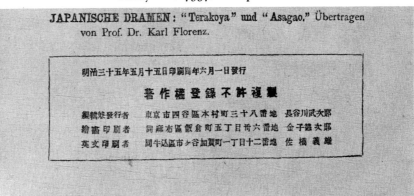

Entry No. 7937, Colophon B

JAPANISCHE DRAMEN: "Terakoya" und "Asagao," Übertragen
von Prof. Dr. Karl Florenz.

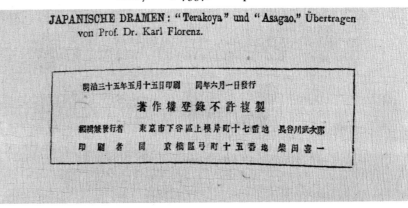

Entry No. 7937, Colophon C

JAPANISCHE DRAMEN: "Terakoya" und "Asagao," Übertragen
von Prof. Dr. Karl Florenz.

Entry No. 7937, Colophon D–E

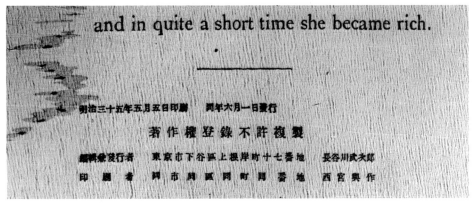

and in quite a short time she became rich.

明治三十五年五月五日印刷　同年六月一日發行

著作權登錄不許復製

編輯兼發行者　東京市下谷區上根岸町十七番地　長谷川武次郎

印　刷　者　同市同區同町同番地　西宮與作

Entry No. 7937, Colophon F

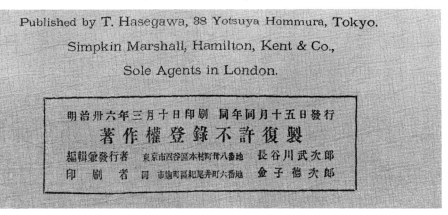

Published by T. Hasegawa, 88 Yotsuya Hommura, Tokyo.

明治卅六年三月十日印刷　同年同月十五日發行

著作權登錄不許復製

編輯兼發行者　東京市四谷區本村町卅八番地　長谷川武次郎

印　刷　者　同市麴町區紀尾井町六番地　金子德次郎

Entry No. 7939, Colophon A

Published by T. Hasegawa, 88 Yotsuya Hommura, Tokyo.

Simpkin Marshall, Hamilton, Kent & Co.,

Sole Agents in London.

明治卅六年三月十日印刷　同年同月十五日發行

著作權登錄不許復製

編輯兼發行者　東京市四谷區本村町卅八番地　長谷川武次郎

印　刷　者　同市麴町區紀尾井町六番地　金子德次郎

Entry No. 7939, Colophon B

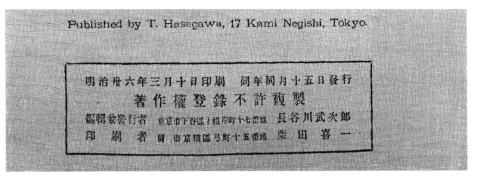

Published by T. Hasegawa, 17 Kami Negishi, Tokyo.

明治卅六年三月十日印刷　同年同月十五日發行

著作權登錄不許復製

編輯兼發行者　東京市下谷區上根岸町十七番地　長谷川武次郎

印　刷　者　同市京橋區弓町十五番地　柴田喜一

Entry No. 7939, Colophon C

大正九年二月　七　日印　刷

大正九年二月十一日發　行

Entry No. 7962

大正十年四月廿一日印　　刷

大正十年四月廿五日發　　行

Entry No. 7968

著作權所有

大正十一年十一月三十日印刷
同年十二月十日發行

英譯者
故　ラフカヂオ．ヘルン

編輯兼発行者
東京市下谷区上根岸町十七番地
長谷川武次郎

印刷者
右同所
西宮與作

Entry No. 7975

Entry No. 7992

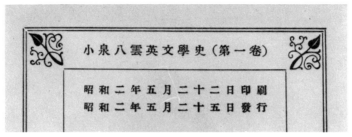

Entry No. 7998, Vol. 1

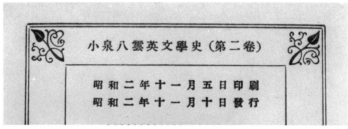

Entry No. 7998, Vol. 2

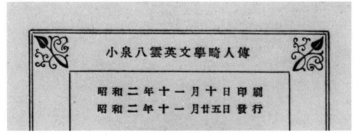

Entry No. 7999

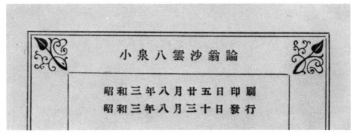

Entry No. 8006

昭和三年八月二十八日印　刷
昭和三年八月三十一日發　行

Entry No. 8007

和和四年一月十五日印　刷
昭和四年一月二十日發　行―

Entry No. 8010

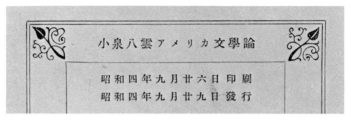

小泉八雲アメリカ文學論

昭和四年九月廿六日印刷
昭和四年九月廿九日發行

Entry No. 8011

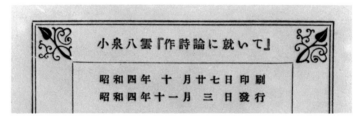

小泉八雲『作詩論に就いて』

昭和四年　十　月廿七日印刷
昭和四年十一月　三　日發行

Entry No. 8012

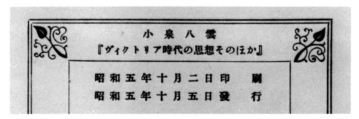

小泉八雲
『ヴィクトリア時代の思想そのほか』

昭和五年十月二日印　刷
昭和五年十月五日發　行

Entry No. 8018

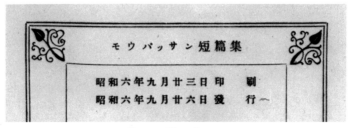

モウパッサン短篇集

昭和六年九月廿三日印　刷
昭和六年九月廿六日發　行―

Entry No. 8022

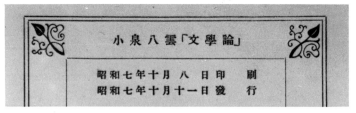

小泉八雲「文學論」

昭和七年十月 八 日印　刷
昭和七年十月十一日發　行

Entry No. 8024

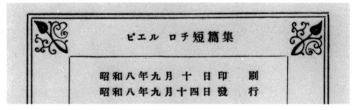

ピエル ロチ短篇集

昭和八年九月 十 日印　刷
昭和八年九月十四日發　行

Entry No. 8025

ON POETS

小泉八雲「詩人論」

昭和九年九月廿二日印　刷
昭和九年九月廿六日發　行

Entry No. 8028

ON POETRY

小泉八雲「詩論」

昭和九年九月廿二日印　刷
昭和九年九月廿六日發　行

Entry No. 8029

佛蘭西文學名篇集

昭和十年 九 月 五 日印刷
昭和十年 九 月 十 日發行

Entry No. 8032

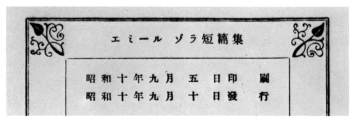

エミール ゾラ短篇集

昭和十年九月 五 日印　刷
昭和十年九月 十 日發　行

Entry No. 8033

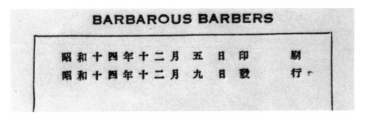

BARBAROUS BARBERS

昭和十四年十二月五日印　　刷
昭和十四年十二月九日發　　行

Entry No. 8039

BUYING CHRISTMAS TOYS

昭和十四年十二月五日印　　刷
昭和十四年十二月九日發　　行

Entry No. 8040

LITERARY ESSAYS

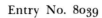

昭和十四年十二月五日印　　刷
昭和十四年十二月九日發　　行

Entry No. 8041

THE NEW RADIANCE

昭和十四年十二月五日印　　刷
昭和十四年十二月九日發　　行

Entry No. 8042

ORIENTAL ARTICLES

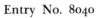

昭和十四年十二月五日印　　刷
昭和十四年十二月九日發　　行

Entry No. 8043

昭和十六年三月五日印　　刷
昭和十六年三月九日發　　行

HEARN : LECTURES ON TENNYSON

Entry No. 8045

Reprinted from *Fantastics and Other Fancies,*
1914.

H　UT

8009. Insect-Musicians & Other Stories &
Sketches ... Compiled ... by Prof. Jun Tanaka

The Kairyu-Do Press　Tokyo　MCMXXVIII

Reprint.

Not seen. Entry on the basis of a 1931 reprint.

Note: According to the colophon the book was
first issued, the date on the title-page notwithstanding, in Jan. 1929.

IU　UT

8010. Facts and Fancies ... Edited ... by R.
Tanabé

⟨Tokyo⟩ The Hokuseido Press ⟨1929⟩

Cloth, printed paper label on front cover.

First book appearance of "The Nun Ryōnen:
Fragments of a Japanese Biography," pp. 145-
164; previously in *Transactions of the Japan
Society,* Vol. 6, 1904.

Published Jan. 20, 1929 (colophon); *see reproduction.*

H　UV

8011. ESSAYS ON AMERICAN LITERA-
TURE ... WITH AN INTRODUCTION
BY ALBERT MORDELL EDITED BY
SANKI ICHIKAWA ...

THE HOKUSEIDO PRESS　KANDA, TOKYO, JAPAN
1929

Title-page in black and red.

⟨i⟩-xxxviii, ⟨1⟩-250. 9$\frac{13}{16}$″ x 6½″.

⟨1-36⁴⟩.

Maroon leather-grained cloth. Double flyleaf at
back. Top edges gilt. Colophon tipped in at
back; *see reproduction.*

Published Sept. 29, 1929 (colophon); *see reproduction.*

LC　NYPL　UT　Y

8012. Lectures on Prosody ...

⟨Tokyo⟩ The Hokuseido Press ⟨1929⟩

⟨i-viii⟩, 1-90, blank leaf. 7$\frac{5}{16}$″ x 4$\frac{15}{16}$″. Colophon tipped to terminal flyleaf; *see reproduc-
tion.*

Published Nov. 3, 1929 (colophon); *see reproduction.* Also see comment under No. 7957.

H　LC　NYPL　UT　UV　Y

8013. By the Japanese Sea. With Notes by Jun
Tanaka.

Tokyo: The Kairyu-Do Press. 1930.

Not located. Entry from Perkins, p. 170.

Reprinted from *Glimpses of Unfamiliar Japan,*
1894.

8014. Essays on English Poetry ... Compiled by
U. Miyagi ...

The Kairyu-Do Press　Tokyo　1930

Reprint.

UT

8015. Hearn and His Biographers　The Record
of a Literary Controversy by Oscar Lewis
Together with a Group of Letters from Lafcadio Hearn to Joseph Tunison Now First
Published

1930　The Westgate Press　San Francisco

Boards, cloth shelfback, printed paper label on
spine.

*Three Hundred and Fifty Copies printed in
May, 1930, by The Grabhorn Press*—Colophon.

BPL　NYPL　UT

8016. Reconciliation and Other Stories ... Selected by Kyohei Hagiwara

⟨Tokyo⟩ Kairyudo ⟨*sic*⟩ ⟨1930⟩

Printed paper wrapper.

Reprint.

UT

8017. In the Cave of the Children's Ghosts ...
Edited ... by Prof. Jun Tanaka

The Kairyu-Do Press　Tokyo　1930

Printed paper wrapper.

Reprint.

UT

8018. Victorian Philosophy ...

⟨Tokyo⟩ The Hokuseido Press ⟨1930⟩

⟨i-viii⟩, 1-97. 7$\frac{7}{16}$″ x 4$\frac{15}{16}$″. Colophon (*see reproduction*) tipped to a terminal flyleaf.

Published October 5, 1930 (colophon); *see reproduction*. See comment under No. 7957.

H   UT   UV   Y

8019. Select Readings ... First Series

⟨Tokyo⟩ The Hokuseido Press ⟨1930⟩

Printed paper wrapper.

Reprint.

H

8020. Select Readings ... Second Series

⟨Tokyo⟩ The Hokuseido Press ⟨1930⟩

Printed paper wrapper.

Reprint.

H

8021. William Collins ⟨by⟩ Ueda Bin ...

⟨Tokyo, 1930⟩

Cover-title. Printed paper wrapper. Facsimile of an article by Ueda Bin showing, in facsimile, Hearn's manuscript comments.

300 copies only.

UV

8022. The Adventures of Walter Schnaffs and Other Stories by Guy de Maupassant Translated by Lafcadio Hearn with an Introduction by Albert Mordell

⟨Tokyo⟩ The Hokuseido Press ⟨1931⟩

⟨1⟩-277. 7¼" x 5". Colophon tipped to terminal flyleaf; *see reproduction*.

Published Sept. 26, 1931 (colophon); *see reproduction*.

H

8023. A Passional Karma, the Dream of a Summer Day ... with Translation and Notes by K. Yamamoto

1931 Nihonbashi Tokyo Shunyodo

Reprint.

H

8024. Complete Lectures on Art, Literature and Philosophy ... Edited by Ryuji Tanabé ... Teisaburo Ochiai ... and Ichiro Nishizaki ...

The Hokuseido Press Kanda, Tokyo ⟨1932⟩

Complete Lectures series, Vol. 1. For Vols. 2-3 see under 1934.

Reprint save for "Great Translators," pp. 510-527. Based on lecture notes kept by Hearn's students. For comment see note under entry No. 7957.

Published Oct. 11, 1932 (colophon); *see reproduction*. A revised edition published Tokyo, 1941.

BA   H   NYPL   UT   UV   Y

8025. Stories from Pierre Loti Translated by Lafcadio Hearn with an Introduction by Albert Mordell

⟨Tokyo⟩ The Hokuseido Press ⟨1933⟩

⟨i⟩-⟨xii⟩, ⟨i⟩-ii, ⟨15⟩-241. 7³⁄₁₆" x 5" scant. Colophon (*see reproduction*) tipped to a terminal flyleaf.

Published Sept. 14, 1933 (colophon); *see reproduction*.

H   LC   NYPL   UT   UV

8026. GIBBETED: EXECUTION OF A YOUTHFUL MURDERER SHOCKING TRAGEDY AT DAYTON A BROKEN ROPE AND A DOUBLE HANGING SICKENING SCENES BEHIND THE SCAFFOLD-SCREEN ...

JOHN MURRAY   LOS ANGELES   1933

Title-page in black and orange. Edited by P. D. Perkins.

⟨1⟩-31; colophon, p. ⟨32⟩. Laid paper watermarked *Rye Mill England*. 7⅞" x 5".

⟨1-4⟩⁴.

Black buckram. Printed paper label on spine. End papers of book stock.

200 numbered copies only.

Deposited Nov. 20, 1933.

NYPL   Y

8027. SPIRIT PHOTOGRAPHY: HOW INTELLIGENT PEOPLE MAY BE HUMBUGGED THE METHOD WHEREIN A CINCINNATI ARTIST CARRIES ON BUSINESS

JOHN MURRAY   LOS ANGELES   1933

Title-page in black and brown. Edited by P. D. Perkins.

⟨1⟩-31; colophon, p. ⟨32⟩. Laid paper watermarked *Rye Mill England*. 7¾" x 5" full.

⟨1-4⟩⁴.

Brown buckram. Printed paper label on spine. End papers of book stock.

250 numbered copies only.

H UT

8028. Complete Lectures on Poets ... Edited
by Ryuji Tanabé ... Teisaburo Ochiai ...
and Ichiro Nishizaki ...

Tokyo The Hokuseido Press 1934

Complete Lectures series, Vol. 2. For Vol. 1 see
under 1932; Vol. 3 see under 1934.

Based on lecture notes kept by Hearn's students.
For comment see note under entry No. 7957.

⟨i-ii⟩, ⟨i⟩-viii, ⟨i⟩-ii, 1-841; blank, p. ⟨842⟩;
⟨i⟩-x. 8¾″ x 5¾″. Colophon inserted at back.

Published Sept. 26, 1934 (colophon); *see reproduction.* A *Popular Edition,* which appears to
be a straight reprint of the 1934 edition, issued
Tokyo, 1938. A *Third Revised Edition* issued
Tokyo, 1941.

NYPL UT UV Y

8029. Complete Lectures on Poetry ... Edited
by Ryuji Tanabé ... Teisaburo Ochiai ...
and Ichiro Nishizaki ...

Tokyo The Hokuseido Press 1934

Complete Lectures series, Vol. 3. For Vol. 1 see
under 1932; Vol. 2 see under 1934.

Based on lecture notes kept by Hearn's students. For comment see note under entry No.
7957.

⟨i-ii⟩, ⟨i⟩-viii, ⟨i⟩-ii, 1-750, ⟨i⟩-ix. 8¾″ scant x
5¾″. Colophon inserted at back.

Published Sept. 26, 1934 (colophon); *see reproduction.* A *Popular Edition,* which appears to
be a straight reprint of the 1934 edition, issued
Tokyo, 1938. A *Third Revised Edition* issued
Tokyo, 1941.

H UT UV Y

8030. ... Japanese Goblin Poetry Rendered into
English by Lafcadio Hearn and Illustrated by
His Own Drawings Compiled by ... Kazuo
Koizumi

1934 Published by Oyama Tokyo, Japan

At head of title: Lafcadio Hearn

⟨i-iv⟩, ⟨1⟩-⟨52⟩. 23 facsimile reproductions inserted by mounting. 16¾″ x 12¼″. Cloth, printed
paper label on front and on back. Colophon in
English and in Japanese inserted.

500 numbered copies only.

A somewhat variant text of "Goblin Poetry" in
The Romance of the Milky Way, 1905.

Published Sept. 26, 1934 (colophon).

H NYPL

8031. LETTERS FROM SHIMANE AND
KYŪSHŪ ...

KYOTO THE SUNWARD PRESS MCMXXXIV

⟨1⟩-71; colophon, p. ⟨72⟩. Laid paper watermarked with flower device. 10⅛″ x 7⅜″.

⟨1-4⁸, 5⁴⟩.

Brown shantung. Printed paper label on spine.
End papers of book stock.

100 numbered copies only.

UT UV

8032. Sketches and Tales from the French
Translated by Lafcadio Hearn Edited ... by
Albert Mordell

⟨Tokyo⟩ The Hokuseido Press ⟨1935⟩

⟨i⟩-xii, ⟨1⟩-196. 7³⁄₁₆″ x 4⅞″. Colophon tipped
to a terminal flyleaf; *see reproduction.*

Published Sept. 10, 1935 (colophon); *see reproduction.*

H NYPL UT UV

8033. Stories from Emile Zola Translated by
Lafcadio Hearn Edited ... by Albert Mordell

⟨Tokyo⟩ The Hokuseido Press ⟨1935⟩

⟨i⟩-⟨x⟩, ⟨1⟩-96; excised leaf. 7³⁄₁₆″ x 4⅞″. Colophon (*see reproduction*) tipped to a terminal
flyleaf.

Published Sept. 10, 1935 (colophon); *see reproduction.*

H LC UT UV

8034. ... My Japanese Garden An Excerpt
from Glimpses of Unfamiliar Japan

1935 Privately Printed New York

At head of title: By Lafcadio Hearn

Boards, printed paper label, cloth shelfback.

*Ten copies hand-set and printed at the New
School for Social Research by Eugenia Porter—*
Certificate of issue.

NYPL

8035. When I Was a Flower ...

Roblar Press 1935

Printed paper wrapper. Reprinted from *Fantastics*, 1914.

20 copies only.

Other separate printings noted: *North East, Penna., Bunny Press, Christmas, 1941*, 100 copies only; *Tempe, Arizona, Edwin B. Hill, 1948*, 40 copies only.

S

8036. Japanese Fairy Tales ... with a Prologue by Edward Larocque Tinker ...

Mount Vernon: The Peter Pauper Press MCMXXXVI.

950 copies in printed boards; and, 50 copies in leather.

Reprint save for "The Woodcutter and His Wife," pp. 61-64. Source of text not known; by Hearn?

Deposited Aug. 22, 1936.

BPL H LC

8037. The Soul of the Great Bell ...

San Francisco MCMXXXIX

Boards, cloth shelfback, printed paper label on spine.

"Fifteen copies printed ... January nineteen ⟨sic⟩ hundred and thirty nine ..."

Reprinted from *Some Chinese Ghosts*, 1887.

H

8038. Stories of Mystery ... Edited by Ichiro Nishizaki ...

Tokyo The Hokuseido Press 1939

Note: Not located; not seen. Entry on the basis of a known reprint.

Cloth, printed paper labels.

Reprint save for "The Accursed Fig Tree," pp. 131-134; "Wonders of Assassination," pp. 135-141.

Published April 15, 1939 (colophon).

UI

8039. BARBAROUS BARBERS AND OTHER STORIES ... EDITED BY ICHIRO NISHIZAKI ...

⟨Tokyo⟩ THE HOKUSEIDO PRESS ⟨1939⟩

⟨i⟩-viii, 1-319. 7½″ x 5¹⁄₁₆″.

⟨1-20⁸, 21⁴⟩. Leaf ⟨1⟩₂ (the title-leaf) is a cancel in all examined copies.

T cloth: green. Yellow end papers. Flyleaf at back. Top edges stained black. Colophon tipped to flyleaf; *see reproduction*.

Published Dec. 9, 1939 (colophon); *see reproduction*.

H NYPL UT UV

8040. BUYING CHRISTMAS TOYS AND OTHER ESSAYS ... EDITED BY ICHIRO NISHIZAKI ...

⟨Tokyo⟩ THE HOKUSEIDO PRESS ⟨1939⟩

⟨i⟩-⟨x⟩, 1-166. 7½″ x 5¹⁄₁₆″.

⟨1-11⁸⟩.

T cloth: green. Flyleaf at back. Cream paper end papers. Top edges stained black. Colophon tipped to flyleaf; *see reproduction*.

Published Dec. 9, 1939 (colophon); *see reproduction*.

NYPL UT UV Y

8041. LITERARY ESSAYS ... EDITED BY ICHIRO NISHIZAKI ...

⟨Tokyo⟩ THE HOKUSEIDO PRESS ⟨1939⟩

⟨i⟩-⟨x⟩, 1-209. 7½″ x 5¹⁄₁₆″.

⟨1-13⁸, 14², 15⁴⟩.

T cloth: green. Yellow end papers. Flyleaf at back. Colophon tipped to terminal flyleaf; *see reproduction*. Top edges stained black.

Published Dec. 9, 1939 (colophon); *see reproduction*.

NYPL UT UV Y

8042. THE NEW RADIANCE AND OTHER SCIENTIFIC SKETCHES ... EDITED BY ICHIRO NISHIZAKI ...

⟨Tokyo⟩ THE HOKUSEIDO PRESS ⟨1939⟩

⟨i⟩-viii, 1-238, blank leaf. 7½″ x 5¹⁄₁₆″.

⟨1-15⁸, 16⁴⟩.

T cloth: green. Yellow end papers. Colophon tipped to p. ⟨239⟩; *see reproduction*. Top edges stained black.

Published Dec. 9, 1939 (colophon); *see reproduction*.

H NYPL UT UV Y

8043. ORIENTAL ARTICLES ... EDITED BY ICHIRO NISHIZAKI ...

⟨Tokyo⟩ THE HOKUSEIDO PRESS ⟨1939⟩

⟨i⟩-viii, 1-260. 7½″ x 5¹⁄₁₆″.

⟨1-16⁸, 17², 18⁴⟩.

T cloth: green. Yellow end papers. Flyleaf at
back. Colophon (*see reproduction*) tipped to the
terminal flyleaf. Top edges stained black.

Published Dec. 9, 1939 (colophon); *see reproduction.*

H   UT   UV   Y

8044. PERE ANTOINE'S DATE PALM . . .

⟨Ysleta, Texas, 1940⟩

Single cut sheet, stiff yellow paper, folded to 4
pp. Title on p. ⟨1⟩.

⟨1-4⟩. 8½″ full x 5½″.

50 copies only, printed by Edwin B. Hill, March,
1940, according to the colophon, p. ⟨4⟩.

For an earlier appearance see entry No. 7915.

H   NYPL   UT

8045. Lafcadio Hearn's Lectures on Tennyson
Compiled by Shigetsugu Kishi . . .

The Hokuseido Press   Tokyo   ⟨1941⟩

⟨i-viii⟩, 1-181, blank leaf. 7³⁄₁₆″ scant x 5″. Colophon tipped to p. ⟨183⟩; *see reproduction.*
Cloth, printed paper labels. Also (for distribution in Japan?) paper boards, printed paper
labels. See comment under No. 7957.

According to the colophon (*see reproduction*)
issued on March 9, 1941, in a limited edition of
500 copies.

BPL   H   NYPL   UT   UV   Y

8046. AN ORANGE CHRISTMAS . . .

NEW ORLEANS, LOUISIANA   PRIVATELY PRINTED
CHRISTMAS, 1941

⟨1⟩-13; blank, pp. ⟨14-15⟩; printer's imprint,
p. ⟨16⟩. Linen weave paper. 8⅞″ x 5⅞″.

⟨-⟩⁸.

Printed paper wrapper.

150 copies only issued by Paul F. Veith.

BPL   H   UT

8047. Old Creole Days by George Washington
Cable together with the Scenes of Cable's Ro-
mances by Lafcadio Hearn . . . ⟨Edited by
Edward Larocque Tinker⟩

The Limited Editions Club   New York   1943

Leather. Issued in a limited edition, each copy
numbered, but the certificate of issue fails to
state the number of copies printed.

The Hearn material had prior publication in
The Historical Sketch Book . . . , 1885.

Deposited Sept. 16, 1943. Reprinted and reissued by The Heritage Press, New York ⟨1943⟩.

BPL   NYPL

8048. Japanese Fairy Tales by Lafcadio Hearn
and Others . . .

The Peter Pauper Press   Mount Vernon, New
York ⟨1948⟩

Printed paper boards.

Reprint with the exception of "Urashima," pp.
53-59; not elsewhere located; by Hearn? According to the editor, p. ⟨2⟩, "Urashima" was
written by Hearn.

Deposited Oct. 13, 1948.

LC

8049. The Selected Writings of Lafcadio Hearn
Edited by Henry Goodman with an Introduction by Malcolm Cowley

The Citadel Press   New York ⟨1949⟩

Reprint.

Deposited Nov. 14, 1949.

LC

8050. A Drop of Dew . . .

⟨Tokyo: The Hokuseido Press, 1950⟩

Printed paper boards. Facsimile of the original
manuscript, together with an editorial note by
Kazuo Koizumi. The text varies somewhat from
the appearance in *Kottô,* 1902.

350 numbered copies only.

H

8051. Tales Out of the East . . .

Story Classics   Emmaus, Pennsylvania ⟨1952⟩

Edited by Edward J. Fluck and J. I. Rodale.

Reprint.

Deposited June 2, 1952.

LC

8052. NEWLY DISCOVERED LETTERS
FROM LAFCADIO HEARN TO DR. RU-
DOLPH MATAS. ⟨Edited⟩ BY NISHIZAKI,
ICHIRO . . .

⟨Offprint from *Ochanomizu University Studies in Arts and Culture,* Tokyo, March, 1956⟩

Cover-title.

⟨85⟩-118. 10⅛" x 7³⁄₁₆". Illustrated.

⟨1-5⟩⁴. Leaves ⟨1⟩1-2 and ⟨5⟩4 excised. *Note:* Made up of sheets extracted from the periodical and issued in printed white paper wrapper.

H

8053. ... Tales and Essays from Old Japan Introduction by Edwin McClellan

Gateway Editions, Inc. Distributed by Henry Regnery Company Los Angeles Chicago New York ⟨1956⟩

At head of title: Lafcadio Hearn

Printed paper wrapper. Reprint.

Deposited Oct. 8, 1956.

LC

8054. ... Children of the Levee Edited by O. W. Frost ...

The University of Kentucky Press ⟨1957⟩

At head of title: Lafcadio Hearn

⟨i⟩-⟨viii⟩, ⟨1⟩-111; colophon, p. ⟨112⟩. Illustrated. Wove paper watermarked *Beckett.* 8⅞" x 5⁷⁄₁₆". Printed white paper boards, orange V cloth shelfback.

Reprint save for: "Jot," "Butler's," "Auntie Porter," "The Rising of the Waters," "Genius Loci."

Deposited April 5, 1957.

H LC

8055. Japanese Fairy Tales by Lafcadio Hearn and Others ...

The Peter Pauper Press Mount Vernon New York ⟨1958⟩

Printed paper boards.

Reprint.

Deposited Aug. 18, 1958.

LC

8056. NEW HEARN LETTERS FROM THE FRENCH WEST INDIES ⟨Edited⟩ BY ICHIRO NISHIZAKI ...

REPRINTED FROM OCHANOMIZU UNIVERSITY STUDIES IN ARTS AND CULTURE VOL. 12 JUNE 1959 TOKYO

Cover-title.

59-110. 8¼" x 5⅞".

⟨1-4⟩⁸. Leaves ⟨1⟩1-3 and ⟨4⟩6-8 excised. *Note:* Made up of sheets extracted from the periodical and issued in printed white paper wrapper. Conjugate leaves imprinted with material unrelated to the Hearn text usually excised.

H UV

REPRINTS

The following publications contain material by Hearn reprinted from earlier books.

The Zodiac by S.G.P. Coryn ...

London: Theosophical Publishing Society 7, Duke Street, Adelphi, W. C. 1893.

Printed paper wrapper. Cover-title.

The Louisiana Book: Selections from the Literature of the State. Edited ... by Thomas M'Caleb ...

New Orleans: R. F. Straughan, Publisher. 1894.

Short Story Classics ... Edited by William Patten ...

... New York ⟨1905⟩

5 Vols. For comment see entry No. 6378.

The South in Prose and Poetry Compiled ... by Henry M. Gill ...

New Orleans F. F. Hansell & Bro., Ltd. ⟨1916⟩

"Lost Kites," pp. ⟨282⟩-284; otherwise "A Dream of Kites" in *Fantastics,* 1914.

Modern Short Stories ... by Frederick Houk Law ...

New York ... 1918

For comment see BAL, Vol. 2, p. 427.

The Windmill: Stories, Essays, Poems & Pictures ... Edited by L. Callender

London: William Heinemann Ltd. MCMXXIII

Boards, cloth shelfback.

Twelve Best Short Stories from British and American Writers Selected by K. Kumano ... Revised Edition

⟨Tokyo⟩ The Hokuseido Press ⟨ca. 1925⟩

Tales from Gautier with a Preface by George Saintsbury

London Eveleigh Nash & Grayson Limited 1927

Listed Bkr Nov. 11, 1927.

Model English Prose Compiled by Tadashige Matsumoto Vol. I.

Maruzen Company, Ltd. Tokyo ⟨n.d., 1930⟩

Printed paper wrapper. All published?

Atlantic Harvest Memoirs of *The Atlantic* . . . Compiled by Ellery Sedgwick . . .

Little, Brown and Company Boston 1947

Published Sept. 24, 1947.

REFERENCES AND ANA

Ye Giglampz A Weekly Illustrated Journal Devoted to Art, Literature and Satire.

Cincinnati, June 21, 1874–Aug. 16, 1874.

A short-lived periodical edited by Hearn. Complete in 9 numbers. For an account of this publication see "Lafcadio Hearn and H. F. Farny in *Ye Giglampz,*" by Ichiro Nishizaki, in *Ochanomizu University Studies in Art and Culture,* Tokyo, Dec., 1957.

Tales before Supper from Théophile Gautier and Prosper Mérimée Told in English by Myndart Verelst and Delayed with a Proem by Edgar Saltus . . .

Brentanos 5 Union Square New York 101 State Street Chicago 1887

Jacob Blanck in PW June 19, 26, 1937, raised the question of the identity of the translator of Gautier's "Avatar" and suggested that either Hearn or Edgar Saltus translated the story as published in this 1887 publication. It may now be stated with certainty that the translation as herein published was not done by Hearn and almost surely was done by Saltus.

Mr. Whitman Bennett of New York City has in his possession (June, 1959) the manuscript of Hearn's translation of "Avatar" and it most definitely is not the translation published in *Tales before Supper,* 1887; 1890; ⟨1887; *i.e., ca.* 1903⟩; in *Gems from the French, Tales before Supper,* New York ⟨1887; *i.e., ca.* 1893⟩; in: *Tales from Theophile Gautier,* New York, 1909.

BAL has discovered no publication containing Hearn's translation of "Avatar" and it is presumed to be unpublished.

Transactions and Proceedings of the Japan Society, London. Volume VI. Twelfth Session, 1902–1903 . . .

London, 1904. Published for the Society by Kegan Paul, Trench, Trübner and Co., Limited, Dryden House, 43, Gerrard Street, Soho, W. . . .

Printed paper wrapper. Cover-title. "A Woman's Tragedy . . . ," pp. 125-149, had previous publication in *Kottō,* 1902, as "A Woman's Diary."

The Life and Letters of Lafcadio Hearn by Elizabeth Bisland . . .

Boston and New York Houghton, Mifflin and Company The Riverside Press, Cambridge 1906

2 Vols. For fuller description see entry No. 7944.

Concerning Lafcadio Hearn by George M. Gould . . . with a Bibliography by Laura Stedman

Philadelphia George W. Jacobs & Company Publishers ⟨1908⟩

Boards, cloth shelfback. Deposited May 4, 1908. Listed PW May 9, 1908. The London (Unwin) edition listed Ath Aug. 29, 1908.

Lafcadio Hearn in Japan by Yone Noguchi . . . with Mrs. Lafcadio Hearn's Reminiscences . . . with Sketches by . . . Mr. Hearn . . .

Vigo Street Elkin Mathews London Yokohama Kelly & Walsh Japan 1910

Printed boards. Issued in United States with the imprint: *2 East 29th Street Mitchell Kennerley New York . . . London . . . Yokohama . . . 1911*

Lafcadio Hearn by Nina H. Kennard Containing Some Letters from Lafcadio Hearn to His Half-Sister, Mrs. Atkinson

London Eveleigh Nash 1911

Issued in United States with the imprint: *New York D. Appleton and Company MCMXII;* deposited Feb. 14, 1912.

Lafcadio Hearn by Edward Thomas

London: Constable and Company Ltd. Boston & New York: Houghton Mifflin Company 1912

Issued in United States with the imprint: *Boston and New York Houghton Mifflin Company 1912*

Three Japanese Sketches ⟨Music⟩ by Fay Foster . . . The Cruel Mother-in-Law . . .

J. Fischer & Bro. New York 7, 8, 10 & 11, Bible House (Astor Place) ⟨1917⟩

Sheet music. Cover-title. Plate number *J.F. &B. 4329-7* (low voice). Adapted from the translation in *Shadowings,* 1900, pp. 171-173. Deposited May 19, 1917. Also issued for high voice. Reprinted and reissued with the imprint: *J. Fischer & Brother New York Fourth Avenue* . . .

Three Japanese Sketches ⟨Music⟩ by Fay Foster . . . The Honorable Chop-Sticks . . .

J. Fischer & Bro. New York 7, 8, 10 & 11, Bible House (Astor Place) ⟨1917⟩

Sheet music. Cover-title. Plate number *J.F. &B. 4326-4* (high voice). Plate number *J.F.&B. 4325-4* (low voice). Adapted from the translation in *A Japanese Miscellany*, 1901, pp. 224-225. Deposited May 19, 1917. Two reprints have been seen: *J. Fisher & Brother New York Fourth Avenue and Eighth Street (Astor Place)*; and, *J. Fischer & Bro. 119 West 40th Street New York*.

Three Japanese Sketches ⟨Music⟩ by Fay Foster . . . The Shadow of the Bamboo Fence . . .

J. Fischer & Bro. New York 7, 8, 10 & 11, Bible House (Astor Place) ⟨1917⟩

Sheet music. Cover-title. Plate number *J.F.&B. 4328-3* (high voice). Plate number *J.F.&B. 4327-3* (low voice). Adapted from the translations in *A Japanese Miscellany*, 1901, pp. 100-106. Deposited May 19, 1917. A reprint has been noted with the imprint: *J. Fischer & Brother New York Fourth Avenue and Eighth Street.*

. . . Art Songs of Japan . . . Traditional Japanese Themes and Poems ⟨Music⟩ by Gertrude Ross . . .

White-Smith Music Publishing Company Boston New York Chicago ⟨1917⟩

Sheet music. Cover-title. At head of title: *Low Voice* ⟨or:⟩ *High Voice* Plate number *15047-19* (low voice). Plate number *15048-19* (high voice). "Fireflies," pp. 12-13, "adapted from translations by Lafcadio Hearn."

Shadowings Five Poems from the Japanese by Lafcadio Hearn . . . Music by Harold Vincent Milligan . . .

New York G. Schirmer . . . ⟨1918⟩

Sheet music. Cover-title. Plate numbers *28058c* and *28058*. *Note:* These numbers for medium voice; possibly issued for low and high voices also. Deposited Sept. 21, 1918. The text adapted from Hearn's translations in *In Ghostly Japan*, 1899, pp. 158, 159, 164.

Reminiscences of Lafcadio Hearn by Setsuko Koizumi (Mrs. Hearn) Translated from the Japanese by Paul Kiyoshi Hisada and Frederick Johnson

Boston and New York Houghton Mifflin Company The Riverside Press Cambridge MCMXVIII

Deposited Oct. 2, 1918. Listed PW Oct. 12, 1918. BPL copy received Oct. 3, 1918.

Lafcadio Hearn's American Days by Edward Larocque Tinker . . .

New York Dodd, Mead and Company 1924

In addition to the trade edition there was also issued a de luxe edition limited to 150 copies, signed by the author. The trade edition listed PW Nov. 22, 1924; de luxe edition noted in PW Dec. 13, 1924. Deposited (trade edition) Nov. 13, 1924. Listed PC June 27, 1925, as though published by John Lane.

Studies by Members of the English Club Imperial University of Tokyo Vol. V (1923) . . .

⟨Tokyo, 1924⟩

Printed wrapper.

Contains "The Value of the Imaginative Faculty," pp. 7-43, in Japanese and in English; delivered as a lecture in 1890. Japanese text appeared in *Journal of the Educational Association of Shimane Prefecture*, 1891; the English text is a translation by an unknown. Also contains "Talks on West India," pp. 55-61, in Japanese.

Lafcadio Hearn an Appreciation. Being a Lecture Delivered . . . 11th May, 1926 by Chas. E. Ball . . .

Caxton Book Shop, 28 (Basement) Victoria Street, Westminster, S. W. 1. ⟨1926⟩

Paper wrapper, printed paper label on front.

Lafcadio Hearn by Elwood Hendrick

New York The New York Public Library 1929

Printed paper wrapper. 350 copies printed.

Hearn and His Biographers . . . by Oscar Lewis . . .

1930 The Westgate Press San Francisco

For a fuller description see entry No. 8015.

Blue Ghost A Study of Lafcadio Hearn ⟨by⟩ Jean Temple

New York Jonathan Cape Harrison Smith ⟨1931⟩

On copyright page: *First Published, January, 1931* Deposited Jan. 27, 1931.

...A Catalog of First Editions of Lafcadio Hearn with an Autobiographical Sketch Now Published in English for the First Time

Penguin Book Shop 9675 Wilshire Blvd. Beverly Hills, California

Cover-title. At head of title: *October 1933 Number Six* Printed paper wrapper.

Letters to a Pagan by Lafcadio Hearn ...

Robert Bruna Powers Detroit 1933

Paper boards sides, cloth shelfback. 550 numbered copies only according to the certificate of issue. Deposited Nov. 20, 1933. Not by Hearn. For a discussion of this spurious production see Albert Mordell's "*Letters to a Pagan* Not by Hearn," in *Today's Japan* (Tokyo), Nov.–Dec., 1959.

The Idyl: My Personal Reminiscences of Lafcadio Hearn by Leona Queyrouze Barel ...

The Hokuseido Press Kanda, Tokyo, Japan 1933

Printed paper label on front. 250 numbered copies only.

Japanese Stories from Lafcadio Hearn Put Into Basic ⟨English⟩ by T. Takata

London: Kegan Paul, Trench, Trubner & Co., Ltd Broadway House, Carter Lane, E. C. 1933

Printed paper boards, cloth shelfback, printed paper label on spine.

... Lafcadio Hearn a Bibliography Compiled by Martha Howard Sisson ...

Boston The F. W. Faxon Company 83-91 Francis Street 1933

Cover-title. Printed self-wrapper. At head of title: Bulletin of Bibliography Pamphlets, No. 29

Lafcadio Hearn a Bibliography ... by P. D. and Ione Perkins with an Introduction by Sanki Ichikawa ...

Boston and New York Houghton Mifflin Company 1934

Cloth, paper labels. Also: 200 numbered copies in leather-grained cloth imprinted: *Published for the Lafcadio Hearn Memorial Committee by the Hokuseido Press, Tokyo, 1934*

Father and I Memories of Lafcadio Hearn by Kazuo Koizumi

Boston and New York Houghton Mifflin Company The Riverside Press Cambridge 1935

Deposited June 13, 1935.

Lafcadio Hearn: First Editions and Values A Checklist for Collectors by William Targ ...

1935 The Black Archer Press Chicago

Printed paper label on front. 550 copies, of which 50 were printed on Inomachi Vellum paper.

Letters from Basil Hall Chamberlain to Lafcadio Hearn Compiled by Kazuo Koizumi

Tokyo The Hokuseido Press 1936

Unfamiliar Lafcadio Hearn by Kenneth P. Kirkwood

Tokyo The Hokuseido Press 1936

Cloth, paper labels.

More Letters from Basil Hall Chamberlain to Lafcadio Hearn And Letters from M. Toyama Y. Tsubouchi and Others Compiled by Kazuo Koizumi ...

Tokyo The Hokuseido Press 1937

Lafcadio Hearn's Ancestry by Kenneth P. Kirkwood

Nippon Bunka Chuo Renmei (Central Federation of Nippon Culture) Tokyo, Japan ⟨1938⟩

Printed paper wrapper.

The Dedication of the Lafcadio Hearn Room of the Howard-Tilton Memorial Library ... March 7, 1941

The Lafcadio Hearn Society of New Orleans Japan Institute, Inc. of New York ⟨1941⟩

Printed paper wrapper.

... Lafcadio Hearn

1946 The Riverside Press Cambridge Houghton Mifflin Co. Boston

At head of title: Vera McWilliams Deposited March 23, 1946.

The Selected Writings ... Edited by Henry Goodman ... Introduction by Malcolm Cowley

The Citadel Press New York ⟨1949⟩

Deposited Nov. 14, 1949.

Re-Echo by Kazuo Hearn Koizumi Edited by Nancy Jane Fellers Illustrated with Photographs and with Original, Hitherto Unpublished Pen and Watercolor Sketches by Lafcadio Hearn

The Caxton Printers, Ltd. Caldwell, Idaho 1957

1000 numbered copies only. Deposited March 11, 1957.

Young Hearn by O. W. Frost

Tokyo The Hokuseido Press 1958

HENRY WILLIAM HERBERT

(Frank Forester)

1 8 0 7 – 1 8 5 8

8057. THE BROTHERS. A TALE OF THE FRONDE . . .

NEW-YORK: PUBLISHED BY HARPER & BROTHERS, NO. 82 CLIFF-STREET. 1835.

2 Vols. Anonymous.

1: ⟨1⟩-220. 7⁷⁄₁₆″ x 4½″.

2: ⟨1⟩-239; blank, p. ⟨240⟩; 8 pp. advertisements.

1: A-I, K-S⁶, T².

2: ⟨A⟩⁴, B-I, K-U, X⁶.

A-like cloth: brown, damasked with a pattern of snake-like branches and leaves. Coarse-grained H: blue; purple; white. Purple muslin embossed with a maze-like pattern. Flyleaves. A copy of Vol. 2 has been noted with flyleaf at back only. Printed paper label on spine.

Two states of Vol. 2 noted. The sequence has not been established and the following designations are for identification only.

A

P. ⟨241⟩ is paged 25.

B

P. ⟨241⟩ is paged 17.

Other variations are present in the advertisements but the above notes are sufficient for identification.

Noted as *in press* AMM June, 1835. A copy in Y inscribed by early owner July 29, 1835. Noted as *in press* K July, 1835. Reviewed by K Aug. 1835.

H (B)   Y (A, B)

8058. The Magnolia. 1836. Edited by Henry W. Herbert.

New-York: Monson Bancroft, 389 Broadway. B. & S. Collins, Pearl-Street; and Wiley & Long, Broadway. Boston, Russell, Ordiorne ⟨sic⟩ & Co. Philadelphia, T. T. Ash. New-Orleans, Charles H. Bancroft. Wm. Van Norden, Print. ⟨1835⟩

Leather.

Two states noted:

1: With *Ordiorne* for *Odiorne* in the imprint.

2: With *Odiorne* so spelled.

In addition to editing this anthology Herbert contributed the following material:

"The Magnolia," pp. ⟨9⟩-10.

"The Death of Soto," pp. ⟨14⟩-23.

"The Conqueror. A Dream," pp. ⟨24⟩-27.

"The Rescue," pp. ⟨95⟩-97.

"Innocenza," pp. ⟨259⟩-260. Collected in *Poems,* 1888.

"The Fate of Pompey," pp. ⟨279⟩-296.

"Virginia," p. ⟨297⟩.

Briefly reviewed K Sept. 1835. Deposited Oct. 9, 1835. Fully reviewed K Oct. 1835. Noted NEM Oct. 1835. Reviewed NEM Dec. 1835. Listed NAR Jan. 1836.

BPL (2nd)   H (1st, 2nd)   LC (2nd)   NYPL (2nd) Y (2nd)

8059. The Magnolia for 1837. Edited by Henry William Herbert.

New-York: Bancroft & Holley . . . ⟨1836⟩

In addition to editing this anthology Herbert contributed the following:

"The Magnolia," pp. ⟨9⟩-10.

"To Esperanza," pp. ⟨11⟩-12.

"Three Days from the Life of Cavendish, the Rover," pp. ⟨13⟩-54.

"The Summer Storm," pp. ⟨145⟩-148.

"The Birth of Mary Stuart," pp. ⟨331⟩-345.

"Sunset on the Hudson," pp. ⟨92⟩-93.

Leather. For comment see entry No. 986.

8060. The Jewel, or Token of Friendship. 1837.

New-York: ... Bancroft and Holley ... M.DCCC.XXXVII.

"The Mother's Jewel," pp. ⟨9⟩-13; and, "Sonnet. On a Sleeping Infant," p. 172. These may have had prior publication in another anthological work of unknown title (*The Mother's Pearl?*); further information wanting.

"May Morning," pp. 174-175.

Leather? For comment see entry No. 988.

8061. CROMWELL. AN HISTORICAL NOVEL. BY THE AUTHOR OF "THE BROTHERS," ...

NEW-YORK: HARPER & BROTHERS, 82 CLIFF-ST. 1838.

2 Vols.

1: ⟨1⟩-267. Frontispiece inserted. 7$\frac{7}{16}$" x 4$\frac{7}{16}$".
2: ⟨1⟩-275; plus: publisher's catalog, pp. ⟨1⟩-2, 15-24.

1: ⟨1-21⁶, 22⁸⟩. *Signed:* ⟨A⟩-I, K-U, X-Y⁶, Z².
2: ⟨A⟩-I, K-Q, ⟨R⟩, S-U, X-Z⁶; plus: ⟨-⟩⁶.

A-like cloth: slate, embossed with snake-like branches. Coarse H: brown. Fine-grained P-like cloth: pale salmon. T-like cloth: green, damasked with a leafy pattern. Printed paper label on spine. Flyleaves.

Noted as *in press* K Feb. 1838. Listed AMM June, 1838, as a publication of the period March 15–May 26, 1838. Noted for *the present month* K March, 1838. Deposited May 3, 1838. The London (Wiley) edition advertised as though ready PC Aug. 15, 1838; listed BLMA Sept. 1838. *See next entry.* Also see *Oliver Cromwell ...* , 1856, for a revised edition.

H NYPL

8062. Oliver Cromwell: An Historical Romance. Edited by Horace Smith ... in Three Volumes ...

London: Henry Colburn, Publisher, Great Marlborough Street. 1840.

3 Vols. Boards, cloth shelfback, printed paper label on spine.

A reprint of the preceding entry with revisions by Horace Smith.

Advertised as *just ready* Ath July 18, 1840.

Y

8063. The History of Rome. By Dr. Goldsmith. Edited for the School District Library, by H. W. Herbert ...

New-York: Harper & Brothers, 82 Cliff-Street. 1840.

Goldstamped black P cloth; printed tan muslin. Reported in cloth, leather shelfback; not seen by BAL.

"... the present edition ... has been thoroughly revised throughout, and numerous valuable notes added by the distinguished author of *Cromwell.*"—P. ⟨vii⟩.

Issued as No. 87 in the *School District Library.*

Y

8064. The Magnolia. 1841. Edited by Henry W. Herbert.

New-York: Published by A. & C. B. Edwards, No. 3 Park Row. Aaron Guest, Print. ⟨1835; i.e., 1840⟩

Leather.

Reprint of entry No. 8058.

Listed NYR Jan. 1841.

B Y

8065. Quadruple Boston Notion ... Extra Number ...

Boston ... June 10, 1841 ...

A special issue of the *Boston Notion.*

"The Fortunes of the Maid of Arc," pp. 7-9. Collected in *Chevaliers of France,* 1853.

CU

8066. Quadruple Boston Notion ... Extra Quadruple Number.

Boston ... July 15, 1841 ...

A special issue of the *Boston Notion.*

"The Eve of St. Bartholomew," p. ⟨1⟩. "Written for the *Notion.*" The statement, "written for the *Notion,*" is false. "The Eve of St. Bartholomew" had prior publication in AMM Jan.–Feb. 1834. Collected in *The Brothers,* London, 1844; and, *Chevaliers of France,* N. Y., 1853.

"Spanish Captive's Story. The Death of Soto," p. 8. "Written for the *Notion.*" The statement "written for the *Notion*" is wholly false; the piece had prior publication in *The Magnolia. 1836,* N. Y. ⟨1835⟩.

EM

8067. The Magnolia. 1842. Edited by Henry W. Herbert.

New-York: Published by S. E. S. Brown, 76 Fulton-Street. ⟨1835; i.e., 1841⟩

Leather.

Reprint of entry No. 8058.

AAS B

8068. Sporting Scenes and Sundry Sketches; Being the Miscellaneous Writings of J. Cypress, Jr. ⟨William Post Hawes⟩ Edited by Frank Forester . . .

New York: Published by Gould, Banks & Co. No. 144 Nassau Street. 1842.

2 Vols.

"Advertisement," Vol. 1, pp. ⟨iii⟩-iv. "Memoir of the Late William P. Hawes," Vol. 1, pp. ⟨3⟩-14.

Issued all edges trimmed. Size of page 7¼" x 4½". Unsold sheeets, folded, untrimmed, measuring 7⅞" x 4¾", remained unbound for years and copies were offered during the later years of the 19th century as "large paper copies." Unbound, untrimmed sheets, are even today occasionally found in the hands of rare book dealers.

Issued in cloth, spine stamped in gold. Two states of binding noted; the sequence, if any, has not been firmly established although Van Winkle-Randall express a preference for the following order:

A

Spine stamped: SPORTING / SCENES / AND / SKETCHES / ⟨rule⟩ / VOL I ⟨2⟩ /

B

Spine stamped: SPORTING / SCENES / AND / SKETCHES / ⟨rule⟩ / F. FORESTER. / VOL. I. ⟨II.⟩ /

Deposited Sept. 19, 1842. Reviewed by BJ Oct. 1, 1842. "We have looked over the sheets . . . will be published early in the present month" —K Dec. 1842.

AAS (B)   BPL (A)   H (A)   Y (A)

8069. The Gift: A Christmas and New Year's Present. MDCCCXLIII.

Philadelphia: Carey and Hart. ⟨1842⟩

Leather.

"The Lover's Leap. A Tale of the Bay Province in the Olden Time," pp. 104-130.

Deposited Sept. 24, 1842. Reviewed BJ Oct. 15, 1842; LG Nov. 19, 1842. Listed NAR Jan. 1843.

H

8070. The Sporting Sketch Book: A Series of Characteristic Papers, by the Most Distinguished Sporting Writers of the Day . . . Edited by John William Carleton, Esq.

London: How and Parsons, Fleet Street. MDCCCXLII.

"The Last Bear: A Scrap from the Sketch Book of a Rhode Islander," pp. 189-200. Anonymous.

H

8071. The Magnolia. 1843. Edited by Henry W. Herbert.

New York: Robert P. Bixby & Co., 3, Park Row, opposite Astor House. ⟨n.d., 1842⟩

Leather.

Reprint of entry No. 8059.

B

8071A. MARMADUKE WYVIL; OR, THE MAID'S REVENGE. AN HISTORICAL ROMANCE . . .

LONDON: HENRY COLBURN, PUBLISHER, GREAT MARLBOROUGH-STREET. 1843.

3 Vols. For first American edition see next entry.

Note: The three title-pages vary from one another in the punctuation.

1: ⟨i⟩-⟨viii⟩, ⟨1⟩-319. 7¹³⁄₁₆" x 4⅞".
2: ⟨i-ii⟩, ⟨1⟩-343.
3: ⟨i-iv⟩, ⟨1⟩-333; blank, p. ⟨334⟩; advertisements, pp. ⟨335-336⟩.
1: ⟨A⟩⁴, B-I, K-U, X⁸.
2: ⟨A⟩¹, B-I, K-U, X-Y⁸, Z⁴.
3: ⟨A⟩², B-I, K-U, X-Y⁸.

Drab paper boards. Printed paper label on spine.

Errata notice, Vol. 1, p. ⟨vii⟩.

The book was reported *in press* LG Sept. 17, 1842. Advertised as *just ready* Ath June 3, 1843; LG June 3, 1843; Ath June 10, 1843; LG June 10, 1843. Advertised as *now ready* Ath June 17, 1843; LG June 17, 1843. Listed Ath June 17, 1843; LG June 24, 1843. Reviewed Ath June 24, 1843. Listed PC July 1, 1843. A Darton & Company printing issued in London, 1859. See under 1853 for revised edition.

LG   Y

8072. MARMADUKE WYVIL; OR, THE MAID'S REVENGE. A HISTORICAL ROMANCE . . .

NEW-YORK: J. WINCHESTER, NEW WORLD PRESS, 30 ANN-STREET ⟨1843⟩

Note: The period following the J in the imprint is either present; absent; or, present as a vestige.

See preceding entry.

⟨i-iv⟩, ⟨1⟩-218; 2 pp. advertisements. 8⅜" x 5⅝".

⟨-⟩², 1-9¹², 10².

According to Van Winkle-Randall issued in printed paper wrapper.

Three thousand copies printed according to Herbert's statement in the preface to the revised edition of 1853.

Prematurely announced USDR Dec. 1841. Title-page deposited March 28, 1843. Book deposited June 30, 1843. See under 1853 for revised edition.

AAS BPL H LC Y

8073. THE VILLAGE INN; OR THE ADVENTURE OF BELLECHASSAIGNE. A ROMANCE ...

NEW-YORK: J. WINCHESTER, NEW WORLD PRESS, 30 ANN-STREET. 1843.

⟨1⟩-41; blank, p. ⟨42⟩; *Caution* ... , pp. ⟨43-44⟩. 7⁹⁄₁₆″ x 5″.

⟨1¹⁸, 2⁴⟩. *Irregularly signed:* 2 on p. ⟨3⟩; 3 on p. 5; 4 on p. 7; 5 on p. 19.

Printed off-white paper wrapper.

Noticed by BJ Oct. 14, 1843.

UV Y

8074. Matilda: Or the Memoirs of a Young Woman A Novel. By Eugene Sue ... Translated from the French by Henry William Herbert ...

New York: J. Winchester New World Press, 30 Ann Street. 1843.

Issued in three paper-covered parts in *The New World Library of Fiction*.

1: ⟨i⟩-iv, ⟨3⟩-142. 8⅞″ full x 5½″.

2:

3:

Noted only (save for *Part 1*) stripped of original wrapper and rebound (not by the publisher) as a single volume. Pagination of the whole: ⟨i⟩-iv, ⟨3⟩-418; blank leaf; advertisements, pp. ⟨421-430⟩.

Advertised BJ Dec. 2, 1843: *Parts I & II now ready.* BJ Dec. 16, 1843, reported: "the third and last part" has been issued. Listed NAR Jan. 1844. Distributed in Great Britain by Wiley & Putnam and advertised PC March 15, 1844, Ath March 16, 1844. The London (Daly) edition listed Ath May 17, 1845.

AAS H N NYPL UK (*Part 1* in original state)

8075. RINGWOOD THE ROVER, A TALE OF FLORIDA. BY W. H. HERBERT ⟨sic⟩ ...

PHILADELPHIA: WILLIAM H. GRAHAM, 98 CHESTNUT STREET. 1843.

⟨1⟩-55. 9½″ x 6¼″.

⟨-⟩², ⟨1⟩-3⁸, 4².

Printed paper wrapper?

Note: In the *Second Edition* (copy in B) the author's name is correctly given on the title-page.

AAS CU H UC UP Y

My Shooting Box. By Frank Forester ...

Philadelphia: T. B. Peterson, 102 Chestnut Street. ⟨1843; *i.e.,* not before 1854⟩

Reprint. See under 1846.

The Deerstalkers: A Sporting Tale of the South-Western Counties. By Frank Forester ...

Philadelphia: T. B. Peterson, 102 Chestnut Street. ⟨1843; *i.e.,* not before 1854⟩

Reprint. For first edition see under 1849. Printed paper wrapper.

Other printings noted:

Philadelphia: T. B. Peterson & Brothers, 306 Chestnut Street. ⟨1843; *i.e.,* not before 1858⟩

Philadelphia: T. B. Peterson & Brothers; 306 Chestnut Street. ⟨1846; *i.e.,* not before 1858⟩

8076. The Opal: A Pure Gift for the Holy Days. Edited by N. P. Willis ...

New-York: John C. Riker 15 Ann Street. 1844.

"The Triumph of Christianity," pp. ⟨121⟩-145.

"The Daughter of Jairus," pp. ⟨173⟩-176.

For comment see entry No. 6648.

8077. The Brothers: A Tale of the Fronde. And Other Stories. By the Author of "Oliver Cromwell," ...

London: Henry Colburn, Publisher, Great Marlborough Street. 1844.

3 Vols. Almost surely issued in paper boards. Reprint save for the following material in Vol. 3:

"Haco, the Sea King," pp. ⟨19⟩-76.

"The Eve of St. Bartholomew," pp. ⟨77⟩-132. See entry No. 8066.

"The Sacrifice of Marcus Curtius," pp. ⟨133⟩-162.

"The Conspiracy: Or, the Oath of Catiline," pp. ⟨314⟩-338.

Possibly also first book publication of "The Lord of the Manor," pp. ⟨250⟩-313, which was published as a separate, Philadelphia, 1844, *q.v.*

Advertised as *just ready* LG Nov. 25, 1843; Ath Nov. 25, 1843. Advertised as *just published* PC Dec. 1, 1843; as *now ready* LG Dec. 2, 1843. Described as *new* Ath Dec. 2, 1843. Listed Ath Dec. 2, 1843; LG Dec. 2, 1843. Described as *new* LG Dec. 9, 1843. Listed PC Dec. 15, 1843. Reviewed Ath Dec. 30, 1843.

H

8078. GUARICA, THE CHARIB BRIDE. A LEGEND OF HISPANIOLA ...

PHILADELPHIA: A. J. ROCKAFELLAR, 98 CHESNUT STREET. 1844.

Note: All examined copies have the errors *Mistake* for *Mislike; burning* for *burnish'd* in the quotation from *The Merchant of Venice* on the title-page.

⟨1⟩-66, blank leaf. 9½″ x 6³⁄₁₆″.

⟨-⟩², ⟨1⟩-4⁸.

Printed brown paper wrapper.

Listed as a March publication in WPLNL April, 1844. The London (Ridgeway) edition received by BMU April 26, 1844. No British trade references located.

H

8079. THE LORD OF THE MANOR; OR ROSE CASTLETON'S TEMPTATION. AN OLD ENGLISH STORY ...

PHILADELPHIA: A. J. ROCKAFELLAR, 98 CHESNUT STREET. 1844.

⟨1⟩-64. 9⅝″ x 6″.

⟨-⟩², ⟨1⟩-3⁸, 4⁶.

Printed yellow paper wrapper.

No copyright entry found. Precise date of publication not known. See entry No. 8077.

Y

8080. The Magnolia. Edited by Henry W. Herbert.

New York: Robert P. Bixby & Co., 3, Park Row, opposite Astor House. ⟨n.d., 1844⟩

Reprint of entry No. 8058.

B

8081. The Salamander. A Naval Romance, by Eugene Sue ... Translated from the French by Henry William Herbert ...

New-York: J. Winchester, New World Press, 30 Ann Street. ⟨1844⟩

⟨i⟩-⟨xii⟩, ⟨13⟩-115; blank, p. ⟨116⟩; 4 pp. advertisements. 8⅝″ x 5⅜″. Printed drab paper wrapper.

LC Y

8082. The Wandering Jew. By Eugene Sue ... Translated from the French, by Henry W. Herbert ...

New-York: J. Winchester, New World Press. xxx Ann Street. ⟨1844⟩

Title-page as above occurs in *Part 1.*

Note: Inability to locate a complete set of this work in the original parts as issued prevents presentation of a full and detailed description. The present entry should be considered nothing more than a contribution toward a full collation.

The following sequence of imprints will be found useful in any attempt to assemble a complete set of first printings.

J. Winchester, New World Press

James W. Judd & Co., Successor to J. Winchester

E. Winchester, Successor to J. Winchester, New World Press.

The printed paper wrappers are of either white or of tan papers.

Note: On the basis of parts examined, and known reprints, it appears safe to state that sheets of the first printing (printings?) are not decorated with wavy rule frames enclosing the text. This feature seems to occur in the reprints only.

Part 1

⟨i⟩-vi, ⟨7⟩-48. Frontispiece portrait of Sue inserted. 9½″ x 5⅞″.

Noted in three variant wrappers. Sequence not known. The following designations are for identification only.

A

Last line of front wrapper: *See last page of Cover.*

Inner front wrapper: *Splendid Book For The Ladies ...*

B

Last line of front wrapper: *See last page of Cover.*

Inner front wrapper: *Unrivalled Family Paper ...*

C

Last line of front wrapper: *To be completed in from 16 to 20 weekly or semi-monthly parts.*

Note: "A portion of the first edition of No. 1 was printed on inferior paper . . ."—Advertisement, back wrapper of Part 2.

Part 2

49-96. Published by J. Winchester.

Part 3

97-144. Published by J. Winchester.

Noted in two variant wrappers. Sequence not known. The following designations are for identification only.

A

Outer back: *To The Public* . . .

B

Outer back: *Number One Now Ready* . . .

Part 4

145-192. Published by J. Winchester.

The following note appears on the inner front wrapper of Part 5: TO THE READER. A slight mistake occurred in the Fourth number . . . The Parisian copyist omitted two chapters in transcribing the manuscript . . . To rectify this, we reprint the last four pages of Part IV.; so that in binding the work, the reader will please to cut out these pages . . . *Query:* Were Parts 4-5 reprinted with altered pagination?

Part 5

189-212. Published by J. Winchester. See note under Part 4.

Part 6

213-236. Published by J. Winchester.

Noted in two variant wrappers. Sequence not known. The following designations are for identification only.

A

Inner back wrapper: *Part V Now Ready* . . . *Wandering Jew* . . .

B

Inner back wrapper: *New Whig Songs* . . .

Part 7

237-260. Published by J. Winchester.

Noted in two variant wrappers. Sequence not known. The following designations are for identification only.

A

Inner front wrapper: *Books For The People* . . .

B

Inner front wrapper: *The Repository* . . .

Part 8

261-284. Published by J. Winchester.

Noted in two variant wrappers. Sequence not known. The following designations are for identification only.

A

Inner front wrapper: *Books For The People* . . .

B

Inner front wrapper: *For Only 12½ Cents! Arrah Neil* . . .

Part 9

285-308. Published by James W. Judd & Co.

Part 10

309-332. Published by James W. Judd & Co.

Part 11

333-364. Published by E. Winchester.

Part 12

365-396. Published by E. Winchester.

Part 13

397-428. Published by E. Winchester.

Parts 14-26

Unlocated. Noted only in the so-called *Cheap Edition.* First issued thus?

K Aug. 1844, reported that Winchester had "begun publication." *Part 13* listed as a January, 1845, publication WPLNL Feb. 1845. *Part 19* listed as a May, 1845, publication WPLNL June, 1845. The Richards & Co., New York, 1845, edition, reviewed USDR Dec. 1845. The Harper edition is not the Herbert translation.

Parts 1-2 were reissued as a single part, probably not before 1845, by E. Winchester. Reissued by E. Winchester, N. Y., 2 volumes in 1, ‹1844; *i.e.,* 1845›; and, 1845.

All located examples of Parts 14-26 are marked *New and Cheap Edition.* All issued thus? Including the first printings?

The above entry made on the basis of incomplete sets in B H IU NYPL.

8083. RUTH WHALLEY. OR, THE FAIR PURITAN. A ROMANCE OF THE BAY PROVINCE . . .

BOSTON: HENRY L. WILLIAMS. 1844.

Not seen. Not located. Entry from Van Winkle-Randall, pp. 11-12. Ghost?

Pp. ‹1›-72. 7½" x 4¾".

Copies dated 1845 are in BPL, H, LC, Y. *See next entry.*

8084. RUTH WHALLEY; OR, THE FAIR
PURITAN. A ROMANCE OF THE BAY
PROVINCE ...

BOSTON: PUBLISHED BY H. L. WILLIAMS, NO. 22
CONGRESS STREET. 1845.

Cover-title.

See preceding entry for an 1844 printing reported by Van Winkle-Randall.

⟨1⟩-72. 8¼″ x 5½″.

⟨1-2⟩¹⁸.

Two states of the wrapper, pinkish-tan paper,
noted. The following sequence is *presumed* correct:

A

With the author's name given as WM. HENRY
HERBERT

B

With the author's name given as HENRY WIL-
LIAM HERBERT

The LC copy inscribed by an unknown person
(copyright clerk?) Jan. 22, 1845.

BPL (B wrapper, back wrapper supplied)   H (A
wrapper)   LC (B wrapper)   Y (both)

8085. THE WARWICK WOODLANDS, OR
THINGS AS THEY WERE THERE, TEN
YEARS AGO ...

PHILADELPHIA: G. B. ZIEBER & CO. 1845.

⟨i⟩-iv, ⟨5⟩-168. 7¼″ x 4⁷⁄₁₆″.

⟨1⟩-7¹².

Printed tan-yellow paper wrapper.

Issued April, 1845, according to ALB May, 1845.
See under 1851 for revised edition.

NYPL

8086. THE INNOCENT WITCH. A CON-
TINUATION OF RUTH WHALLEY. OR,
THE FAIR PURITAN. A ROMANCE OF
THE BAY PROVINCE ...

BOSTON: HENRY L. WILLIAMS. 1845.

⟨3⟩-50. 8¹¹⁄₁₆″ x 5³⁄₁₆″.

⟨1-2⟩¹².

Printed pink paper wrapper.

BPL

8087. THE REVOLT OF BOSTON. A CON-
TINUATION OF RUTH WHALLEY. OR,
THE FAIR PURITAN. A ROMANCE OF
THE BAY PROVINCE ...

BOSTON: HENRY L. WILLIAMS. 1845.

⟨1⟩-48. 9⅛″ x 6″.

⟨1-2⟩¹².

Printed pink paper wrapper.

BPL

8088. History of the Consulate and Empire

The present entry is based almost wholly on
examination of a single, incomplete, example
in Harvard University Library. The entry is
tentative only and should be used with caution.
The parts ⟨all?⟩ appear to have been reprinted
but whether such reprints are marked is not
known. On the inner front wrapper of *Part 2*
appears the following significant statement under date of April 1, 1845: *A New Edition of
No. 1 ... is now ready.*

The translation of the work is frequently
credited to Herbert. In large part this misat-
tribution is the result of inexact statements by
Carey & Hart, the publishers, regarding the
translator; see transcriptions of the title-pages
below. The translator was D. Forbes Campbell.
"The English translation is by Mr. Campbell
of London, and Messrs. C. & H. are not only
to publish it in advance, but with notes and
additions by Henry Wm. Herbert, Esq., one of
the most accomplished writers and ripest scholars in the country."—*Spirit of the Times* (N.Y.),
as quoted by Carey & Hart in an advertisement
in the terminal matter of the *History, Part 1.*

FORMAT

Issued in twelve paper-covered parts; buff,
tan, faun papers noted. Parts 1-7 carry the following statement on the front of the wrapper:
To be Completed in 10 Parts. On Parts 8-12
the statement reads: *To be Completed in Parts;*
note that the number of parts is not specified.

Cheap Edition

With publication of *Part 6* the statement
Cheap Edition appears at the head of the front
of the wrapper. This statement is not to be
interpreted as meaning a reprint at a reduced
price but was, almost certainly, intended to
emphasize the price (12½¢); and, to distinguish the *Cheap Edition* from the *Fine Edition*
offered at 25¢ a part. *See below.*

Fine Edition

On the front of the wrapper of *Part 1* is the
following notice: *Carey & Hart also publish an
Edition of this work on fine white paper, with
Steel Engravings, at 25 Cents a Part.* Like announcements appear on the back of the *Part 2*
wrapper and elsewhere. Presumably this *Fine
Paper* edition was issued but thus far no example has been seen or reported.

The Parts

It appears wise to repeat the cautionary note which introduces this entry: *The present entry is based almost wholly on examination of a single, incomplete, example in Harvard University Library. The entry is tentative only and should be used with caution.*

Part 1

Thiers' Life of Napoleon. Part 1 . . . The History of the Consulate and Empire under Napoleon. By M. A. Thiers . . . Translated from the French, by D. F. Campbell & H. W. Herbert . . .

Philadelphia: Carey and Hart . . . 1845 . . .

Cover-title. Pp. 17-152; advertisements, pp. 1-32. Frontispiece inserted. 9⅝" x 6".

Part 2

Thiers' Life of Napoleon. Part 2 . . . The History of the Consulate and Empire under Napoleon. By M. A. Thiers . . . Translated from the French, by D. F. Campbell, with Notes and Additions, by Henry W. Herbert . . .

Boston: Redding & Co. . . . 1845 . . .

Cover-title. Pp. 153-229; blank, p. ⟨230⟩; advertisements, pp. ⟨1⟩-2, ⟨1⟩-32.

According to Van Winkle-Randall also issued with the Carey & Hart imprint. The late Frank C. Willson owned a copy imprinted: *New York: Burgess, Stringer & Co. . . . 1845*. Occurrence of the variant imprints suggests strongly that the work was distributed throughout the United States with local imprints.

Part 3, No. 1

Part 3—No. 1 . . . The History of the Consulate and Empire under Napoleon. By M. A. Thiers . . . Translated from the French, with Notes and Additions, by Henry W. Herbert . . .

Philadelphia: Carey and Hart. Boston: Redding & Co. . . . 1845 . . .

Cover-title. Pp. 229-308; advertisements, pp. ⟨1⟩-8. *Note:* In *Part 2* p. 229 comprises approximately a half page of text. In *Part 3* p. 229 reprints the text as it appears in *Part 2* but with additional text to fill out the page. The late Frank C. Willson owned a copy imprinted: *Philadelphia: Carey and Hart. New York: Burgess, Stringer & Co. . . . 1845.*

Part 3, No. 2

Part 3—No. 2 . . . The History of the Consulate and Empire under Napoleon. By M. A. Thiers . . . Translated from the French, with Notes and Additions, by Henry W. Herbert . . .

Philadelphia: Carey and Hart. Boston: Redding & Co. . . . 1845 . . .

Cover-title. Pp. 309-415; blank, p. ⟨416⟩; advertisements, pp. ⟨1⟩-4. The late Frank C. Willson owned a copy imprinted *Philadelphia: Carey and Hart. New York: Burgess, Stringer & Co. . . . 1845.*

Part 4

Thiers' Life of Napoleon. Part 4 . . . The History of the Consulate and Empire under Napoleon. By M. A. Thiers . . . Translated from the French, with Notes and Additions, by Henry W. Herbert . . .

Philadelphia: Carey and Hart. Boston: Redding & Co. . . . 1845.

Cover-title. Pp. 415-568; advertisements, pp. ⟨1⟩-5. *Note:* P. 415 reprints the text of p. 415 as it appears in the preceding part but with additional text to fill out the page. The late Frank C. Willson owned a copy imprinted: *Philadelphia: Carey and Hart. New York: Burgess, Stringer & Co. . . . 1845.*

Part 5

Thiers' Life of Napoleon. Part 5 . . . The History of the Consulate and Empire under Napoleon. By M. A. Thiers . . . Translated from the French, with Notes and Additions, by Henry W. Herbert . . .

Philadelphia: Carey and Hart. Boston: Redding & Co. . . . 1845 . . .

Cover-title. Pp. 569-688.

Part 6

The Cheap Edition . . . Part 6 . . . The History of the Consulate and Empire under Napoleon. By M. A. Thiers . . . Translated from the French, by D. F. Campbell, with Notes and Additions, by Henry W. Herbert . . .

Boston: Redding & Co. . . . 1847 . . .

Cover-title. Pp. 9-155; blank, p. ⟨156⟩; advertisements, pp. ⟨1⟩-4. For a comment on the imprint see under *Part 2* above. According to Van Winkle-Randall also issued with the Carey & Hart imprint.

Part 7

The Cheap Edition . . . Part 7 . . . The History of the Consulate and Empire under Napoleon. By M. A. Thiers . . . Translated from the French, by D. F. Campbell, with Notes and Additions, by Henry W. Herbert . . .

Philadelphia: Carey and Hart. Boston: Redding & Co. . . . 1847 . . .

Cover-title. Pp. 153-332; advertisements, pp. ⟨1⟩-4. It will be observed that pp. 153-155 appear in both this part and in *Part 6.*

Part 8

The Cheap Edition . . . Part 8 . . . The History of the Consulate and Empire under Napoleon . . . by M. A. Thiers . . . Translated from the French by D. F. Campbell. With Notes and Additions, by Henry W. Herbert . . .

Philadelphia: Carey and Hart . . . 1849.

Cover-title. Pp. 333-424.

Part 9

The Cheap Edition . . . Part 9 . . . The History of the Consulate and Empire under Napoleon . . . by M. A. Thiers . . . Translated from the French by D. F. Campbell. With Notes and Additions, by Henry W. Herbert . . .

Philadelphia: Carey and Hart . . . 1849.

Cover-title. Pp. 425-506; advertisements, pp. ⟨1⟩-2.

Part 10

Not located. Entry from Van Winkle-Randall. Pp. 505-655. Issued under date 1850. Presumably issued by A. Hart, Philadelphia.

Part 11

Not located. Entry from Van Winkle-Randall. Pp. 655-764. Issued under date 1852. Presumably issued by A. Hart, Philadelphia.

Part 12

Not located. Entry from Van Winkle-Randall. Pp. 761-845. Issued under date 1852. Presumably issued by A. Hart, Philadelphia.

Reviewed, apparently as a single volume (Parts 1-5), by both AWR and SWM March 1845; no parts mentioned by either periodical. Under date of April 1, 1845, Carey & Hart advertised a "new edition of No. 1." See introductory paragraph above.

FCW (incomplete)   H (incomplete)

8089. The May Flower, for M DCCC XLVI. Edited by Robert Hamilton.

Boston: Published by Saxton & Kelt. 1846.

Leather.

"The Heart's Dirge," pp. ⟨53⟩-56.

"The Smuggler," pp. ⟨193⟩-216. Attributed to Herbert.

Deposited Aug. 19, 1845. Advertised as *just ready* ALB Oct. 1845.

H   NYPL

8090. Scenes in the Life of the Saviour: By the Poets and Painters. Edited by Rufus W. Griswold . . .

Philadelphia: Lindsay and Blakiston. 1846.

"The Woman Taken in Adultery," pp. 101-105.

For comment see entry No. 6672.

8091. MY SHOOTING BOX . . .

PHILADELPHIA: CAREY AND HART. 1846.

⟨i⟩-viii, 9-179; advertisements, p. ⟨180⟩. Frontispiece, vignette title-page, 2 plates inserted. 7¼" scant x 4³⁄₁₆".

⟨A⟩-I, K-P⁶.

Contemporary notices indicate that the book was issued in printed paper wrapper but no copy so bound has been located. Y has a copy bound in what appears to be original publisher's cloth but Van Winkle-Randall, p. 15, hesitate to accept it as original.

Two states noted:

1: Folio *iii* present. P. ⟨180⟩ devoted to advertisements: *Philadelphia, May, 1845. Carey & Hart's Cheap Publications* . . .

2: Folio *iii* not present. P. ⟨180⟩ blank.

Deposited April 29, 1846. Advertised as *just published* NYM May 2, 1846. Listed as an April publication WPLNL May, 1846.

Reprints

Reprinted and reissued not before 1854 imprinted: *Philadelphia: T. B. Peterson, 102 Chestnut Street* ⟨1843⟩. Folio *iii* not present.

Reprinted and reissued not before 1858 imprinted: *Philadelphia T. B. Peterson & Brothers; 306 Chestnut Street* ⟨1846⟩. Folio *iii* not present.

AAS (1st)   SG (1st, 2nd)   Y (1st)

8092. THE ROMAN TRAITOR; A TRUE TALE OF THE REPUBLIC . . .

LONDON: HENRY COLBURN, PUBLISHER, GREAT MARLBOROUGH STREET. 1846.

3 Vols. For first American edition see entry No. 8099.

1: ⟨i⟩-⟨viii⟩, ⟨1⟩-339; blank, p. ⟨340⟩; 4 pp. advertisements. 8" x 4⅞".

2: ⟨i-iv⟩, ⟨1⟩-312.

3: ⟨i-iv⟩, ⟨1⟩-333; leaf excised.

1: ⟨A⟩⁴, B-I, K-P¹², Q⁴.

2: ⟨A⟩², B-I, K-O¹².

3: ⟨A⟩², B-I, K-P¹². Leaf P₁₂ excised.

Drab paper boards sides, purple T-like cloth shelfback, printed paper label on spine.

Announced by Colburn in both Ath and LG July 20, 1844, as *just ready.* Listed LG Oct. 26,

1844, in its *Prospective View of the Publishing Season.* The preceding notices were wholly premature. No further word seen until Sept. 1846 when Colburn again announces the book: Advertised under *New Publications* (Ath and LG Sept. 26, 1846). Ath and LG Oct. 3, 10, note the book as *now ready.* Noted as *just published* Ath and LG Oct. 17, 1846. Listed Ath and LG Oct. 3, 1846, as in boards; PC Oct. 15, 1846, as in *cloth.* Reviewed LG Oct. 10, 1846; Ath Oct. 17, 1846.

Y

8093. Atar Gull, or the Slave's Revenge. Translated from the French of Eugene Sue, by Wm. Henry Herbert ⟨*sic*⟩ . . .

Published by Henry L. Williams: 1¾ Ann St., New York, and 22 Congress St., Boston. 1846

Printed paper wrapper. ⟨i⟩-⟨x⟩, ⟨11⟩-94; advertisements, pp. ⟨95-96⟩. 8¹⁵⁄₁₆″ x 5¹¹⁄₁₆″.

Note: Pagination postulated and on the basis of incomplete copies (AAS, Y) and the following:

Note: GD (catalog No. 401, entry 15, June, 1946) offered a copy of this publication with the following comment: "The first edition of Frank Forester's translation. According to Van Winkle-Randall, pages ix-x are wanting in all copies. This leaf is present in this copy. It consists of a half-title with blank reverse. Also, according to Van Winkle-Randall, pp. 95-96 are believed to be blank. They are here present and consist of two pages of advertisements of books published by H. L. Williams."

AAS   Y

8094. Diana of Meridor: Or, the Lady of Monsoreau. By Alexander Dumas. Translated by Henry Wm. Herbert . . .

New York: Williams & Co., 24 Ann Street. 1846.

2 Vols. Printed paper wrapper. 1: ⟨1⟩-237, blank leaf. 2 illustrations inserted. 2: ⟨i-ii⟩, ⟨241⟩-488; advertisements, pp. ⟨489-493⟩. 2 illustrations inserted. 8¾″ x 5¾″.

Reissued by T. B. Peterson, 102 Chestnut Street, Philadelphia, not before 1854.

Y

8095. The Fair Isabel; or, the Fanatics of the Cevennes. A Tale of the Huguenot War. By Eugene Sue . . . Translated from the French, by Henry Wm. Herbert . . . with Original Illustrations by the Translator.

New-York: Richards and Company, 30 Ann-Street. 1846.

⟨3⟩-231. 8½″ x 5³⁄₁₆″. 2 inserted illustrations; other illustrations in text. Almost certainly issued in printed paper wrapper.

Reprinted and reissued *ca.* 1850 with the imprint: *New York: Burgess & Garrett, 22 Ann Street* ⟨*1846*⟩.

Y

8096. Genevieve; or, the Chevalier of Maison Rouge. An Episode of 1793. By Alexander Dumas. Translated by Henry Wm. Herbert . . .

New York: Williams & Co., 1¾ Ann Street. 1846.

⟨1⟩-217; blank, p. ⟨218⟩; advertisements, pp. ⟨219-220⟩. Illustrated. 8¾″ x 5¹¹⁄₁₆″. Probably issued in printed paper wrapper.

Note: Pagination postulated. Entry on the basis of a rebound copy and Van Winkle-Randall. Van Winkle-Randall also record reprints issued by Peterson (Phila.); and, Burgess, Stringer (N. Y.).

Y

8097. Instructions to Young Sportsmen, in All That Relates to Guns and Shooting. By Lieut. Col. P. Hawker. First American, from the Ninth London Edition. To Which is Added the Hunting and Shooting of North America, with Descriptions of the Animals and Birds . . . by Wm. T. Porter, Esq. . . .

Philadelphia: Lea and Blanchard. 1846.

"The Game of North America," pp. ⟨181⟩-183. "The Woodcock . . . ," pp. ⟨184⟩-186; "The Quail . . . ," pp. ⟨187⟩-189; "Quail Shooting . . . ," pp. ⟨190⟩-198; "English and American Game," pp. 439-456.

NYPL

8098. The Magnolia. Edited by Henry W. Herbert.

New York: Published by Nafis and Cornish, 278 Pearl Street. 1846.

Leather.

Reprint of entry No. 8058.

B

8099. THE ROMAN TRAITOR: A TRUE TALE OF THE REPUBLIC. A HISTORICAL ROMANCE . . .

NEW YORK: WILLIAM TAYLOR & CO., NO. 2 ASTOR HOUSE. BALTIMORE: WM. TAYLOR & CO., JARVIS BUILDINGS, NORTH STREET. 1846.

2 Vols. For first London edition see entry No. 8092.

1: ⟨v⟩-xii, ⟨1⟩-242; blank leaf. 7⅝″ x 4⁹⁄₁₆″.
2: ⟨i-iv⟩, ⟨1⟩-245; blank leaf.

1: ⟨1⁴, 2-21⁶, 22²⟩. *Signed:* ⟨A⟩⁴, ⟨B⟩⁶, C¹², D⁶, E¹², ⟨F-H⟩⁶, ⟨K⟩⁶, L-M⁶, ⟨N⟩ (*sic*)¹⁵, N (*sic*)³, Q⁶, R (*sic*)⁶, R (*sic*)⁶, ⟨T⟩⁶, U⁸.
2: ⟨A⟩², B (*sic*)⁶, B (*sic*)⁶, C-E⁶, ⟨F⟩⁶, G-H⁶, ⟨J⟩⁶, K-L⁶, ⟨M⟩⁶, N-S⁶, R (*sic*)⁶, U⁶, ⟨V⟩⁴.

Printed faun paper wrapper. *Note:* Copies of first printing sheets have been noted in wrappers dated 1846; and, 1847.

Title-page for Vol. 1 only deposited July 7, 1846. The *Third edition (sic)* listed LW March 13, 1847, as having issued during Jan. or Feb. 1847. Reviewed AWR Oct. 1847. Reviewed NAR Oct. 1847. A Peterson (Philadelphia) edition noted as received NAR Oct. 1853; listed NLG Sept. 15, 1853.

Y

8100. THE MILLER OF MARTIGNÈ. A RO-MANCE . . .

NEW-YORK: PUBLISHED BY RICHARDS & COMPANY, 30 ANN STREET. ⟨1847⟩

⟨1⟩-124. 7⁹⁄₁₆″ x 4⁹⁄₁₆″.

⟨1-5¹², 6²⟩.

Printed paper wrapper.

Note: The final gathering occurs in two settings of unknown sequence. The designations are for identification only:

Setting A

P. 121, lines 5-6: . . . *level- / ling* . . .

P. 122, last line: *ers, rescue* . . .

P. 123, last line: *gates open* . . .

P. 124, last line of penultimate paragraph: *her hand* . . .

Setting B

P. 121, lines 5-6: . . . *level- / ing* . . .

P. 122, last line: *rescue* . . .

P. 123, last line: *the gates open* . . .

P. 124, last line of penultimate paragraph: *hand* . . .

Listed LW April 10, 1847.

AAS (A)   B (B)   Y (A,B)

8101. INGLEBOROUGH HALL, AND LORD OF THE MANOR . . .

NEW YORK: BURGESS, STRINGER, & CO., 222 BROADWAY, CORNER OF ANN STREET. 1847.

⟨1⟩-96. 8¹⁵⁄₁₆″ x 5⅝″.

Signed: ⟨1⟩-6⁸.

Printed paper wrapper. Noted in two states of wrapper; sequence, if any, not known. The following designations are for identification only:

A

Gray paper.

Inner front: . . . History of St. Giles & St. James . . .

Inner back: George . . .

Back: . . . Martin the Foundling . . .

B

Tan Paper.

Inner front: . . . Martin the Foundling . . .

Inner back: . . . George . . .

Back: . . . The Shakspeare Novels . . .

Listed LW Aug. 14, 1847.

BPL (B)   NYPL (A)

8102. Tales of the Spanish Seas . . .

New York: Burgess, Stringer, & Co., 222 Broadway, Corner of Ann Street. 1847.

Printed paper wrapper.

Reprint. Contains *Ringwood the Rover,* 1843; and, *Guarica . . . ,* 1844.

Listed LW Aug. 21, 1847.

LC   Y

8103. The Countess of Morion: Or, the Triumph of Woman. Translated from the French of Frederick Soulié, by Henry William Herbert.

New York: Williams Brothers, 24 Ann Street, 1847.

⟨1⟩-250. 9″ x 5½″. Printed paper wrapper.

Listed LW Sept. 25, 1847.

AAS   Y

8104. The Complete Angler; or, the Contemplative Man's Recreation. By Isaac Walton. And . . . Charles Cotton . . .

New York and London: Wiley & Putnam, 161 Broadway. 1847.

Edited by George W. Bethune.

Title-page for *Part One* as above. Title-page for *Part Two* as follows: *The Complete Angler . . . , New York: Wiley & Putnam, 161 Broadway. 1847.*

"Trout-Fishing on Long Island," *Part 2,* pp. 139-149.

Issued in the following formats:

Printed paper wrapper. 2 Vols. Nos. 101-102 of *Wiley & Putnam's Library of Choice Reading.* Leaf: 7⁹⁄₁₆″ x 4¹⁵⁄₁₆″.

Cloth. 2 volumes bound in one. Leaf: 7½″ x 4¹⁵⁄₁₆″. According to LW Nov. 20, 1847, issued in cloth, gilt; and, cloth extra gilt.

Large paper edition. Cloth? Limited to 50 copies according to publisher's advertisement LW Nov. 20, 1847. The H copy (trimmed) measures 10½″ x 6⅞″. Van Winkle-Randall report a copy measuring, untrimmed, 11¹⁄₁₆″ x 7¼″.

H (all three formats)

8105. Acté of Corinth: Or, the Convert of Saint Paul. A Tale of Greece and Rome. By Alexandre Dumas. Translated by Henry William Herbert, Esq.

New-York: E. P. Williams & Co., 24 Ann-Street. 1847.

⟨1⟩-121; blank, p. ⟨122⟩; advertisements, pp. ⟨123-128⟩. Frontispiece and 3 plates inserted. 8⅞″ x 5½″. Printed paper wrapper.

"This has also been noted with the plates printed as part of the last signature, in place of the advertisements on pages ⟨123-128⟩. Priority undetermined."—Van Winkle-Randall, p. 105. Not located by BAL.

The following note based on Van Winkle-Randall, p. 105:

Two states of wrapper noted. Sequence, if any, not determined. The designations are for identification only.

A

Pale blue paper wrapper.

Inner front: Advertisement for *The Monk's Revenge* and *Edward Manning.*

Inner back: Advertisement for *Isabel of Bavaria.*

Back: List of works for sale by Williams Brothers.

B

Slate paper wrapper.

Inner front: Advertisement for *Sin of Monsieur Antoine.*

Inner back: Advertisement for *Atar Gull.*

Back: Blank.

Y

Pierre, the Partisan . . .

New York . . . ⟨1847⟩

See below under 1848.

8106. ISABEL GRAHAM, OR, CHARITY'S REWARD . . .

NEW YORK: WILLIAMS, BROTHERS, 24 ANN-STREET. 1848.

⟨1⟩-108; 4 pp. advertisements. 9⁷⁄₁₆″ x 5⅞″.

⟨1⟩-7⁸.

Printed green paper wrapper. Two states noted. Sequence, if any, not determined. The designations are for identification only.

A

Inner front wrapper blank. Copy thus in LC.

B

Inner front wrapper imprinted with a Williams Brothers advertisement. Reported by Van Winkle-Randall, p. 23. Not seen by BAL.

Listed LW Dec. 25, 1847.

LC

8107. PIERRE, THE PARTISAN; A TALE OF THE MEXICAN MARCHES . . .

NEW-YORK: PUBLISHED BY WILLIAMS BROTHERS. 24 ANN-STREET. 1848.

⟨1⟩-99. 10⅜″ x 7″.

⟨1-2⟩, 3, ⟨4-5⟩, 6⁸, 7².

Printed tan paper wrapper.

Listed LW April 15, 1848.

Note: Reprinted and reissued, 1859, with the imprint: *New York: F. A. Brady, Publisher, 24 Ann Street ⟨1847⟩.* Listed BM Jan. 15, 1859.

LC

FIELD SPORTS

Note: This work was reprinted many times with certain of the reprintings containing added material or revisions. A brief summary of the several printings and editions is given here. Fuller entries are given in proper chronological position.

Field Sports . . .

London: Richard Bentley, 1848.

The first edition. BAL No. 8108.

Field Sports . . . Sixth Edition . . .

New-York: Stringer & Townsend ⟨1848; *i.e.,* 1856⟩

Reprint. BAL No. 8151.

Frank Forester's Field Sports ... New Edition ... ⟨Eighth Edition⟩

New York ... ⟨1848; *i.e., ca.* 1870⟩

Reprint. BAL No. 8172.

Frank Forester's Field Sports ...

New-York: Stringer & Townsend, 1849.

The first American edition, first printing. BAL No. 8112.

Frank Forester's Field Sports ...

New-York: Stringer & Townsend, 1849.

The first American edition, second printing. See BAL No. 8112.

Reprint.

Frank Forester's Field Sports ... Third Edition ...

New-York: Stringer & Townsend, 1851.

Not located. Reported by Van Winkle-Randall, p. 26.

Frank Forester's Field Sports ... Fourth Edition ...

New-York: Stringer & Townsend, 1852.

Revised. See BAL No. 8129.

Frank Forester's Field Sports ... Fifth Edition ...

No printing identified as *Fifth Edition* located.

Field Sports ... Sixth Edition ...

New-York: Stringer & Townsend ⟨1848; *i.e.,* 1856⟩

Reprint. BAL No. 8151.

Field Sports ... Seventh Edition ...

No printing identified as *Seventh Edition* located.

Frank Forester's Field Sports ... Eighth Edition ...

New York: W. A. Townsend, 377 Broadway, 1858.

Reprint. BAL No. 8161.

Frank Forester's Field Sports ... New Edition ...

New York: W. A. Townsend & Company, 1860.

Reprint. BAL No. 8167. Reprinted by Townsend under the dates 1864, 1868. Van Winkle-Randall report a reprint issued with the imprint: New York: Townsend & Adams, 1868.

Frank Forester's Field Sports ... New Edition ...

New York: Geo. E. Woodward ⟨1848; *i.e., ca.* 1870⟩

Reprint. BAL No. 8172.

Van Winkle-Randall report the following reprints, not located by BAL:

New York: George E. Woodward & Co., Orange Judd Company ⟨1873⟩

New York: The American News Company ⟨n.d.⟩

New York: The Excelsior Publishing House ⟨n.d., *ca.* 1880⟩.

8108. FIELD SPORTS IN THE UNITED STATES, AND THE BRITISH PROVINCES OF AMERICA. BY FRANK FORESTER ...

LONDON: RICHARD BENTLEY, NEW BURLINGTON STREET. PUBLISHER IN ORDINARY TO HER MAJESTY. 1848.

2 Vols. For first American edition see entry No. 8112.

1: ⟨i⟩-viii, ⟨1⟩-344. 7⅞″ x 4⅞″.
2: ⟨i⟩-⟨viii⟩, ⟨1⟩-343; printer's imprint, p. ⟨344⟩.
1: ⟨A⟩⁴, B-I, K-P¹², Q⁴.
2: ⟨A⟩⁴, B-I, K-P¹², Q̆⁴.

Noted in the following bindings. Sequence not known. The designations are for identification only.

A

T-like cloth: green. Sides blindstamped with a rule frame; at each inner corner a scroll ornament; at center: a scroll medallion. Spine lettered: FIELD / SPORTS / BY / FRANK / FORESTER / VOL. I. ⟨II.⟩ / LONDON/ BENTLEY Yellow-coated end papers.

B

TR-like cloth: green. Sides blindstamped with a filigree at each corner, the whole bordered by a triple rule. Spine lettered: FIELD / SPORTS / FRANK / FORESTER / VOL. I. ⟨II.⟩ Cream-coated end papers.

c

Not seen. For illustration see Van Winkle-Randall, opp. p. 25. Sides blindstamped with a rules frame enclosing an oval frame which is virtually the height of the cover.

d

T cloth: green. Sides blindstamped with a double rule frame, a triangular filigree at each inner corner; at center, a cartouche about four inches high with blank, upright, oval center. Spine lettered: FIELD / SPORTS / BY / FRANK / FORESTER / VOL. I. ⟨II.⟩ / LONDON / BENTLEY. Yellow-coated end papers imprinted with publisher's lists. *Issued not before 1849,* the date of publication of certain of the books offered for sale in the lists.

Ath and LG, Sept. 2, 1848, note publication for *the present month.* Listed PC Sept. 15, 1848; Ath Sept. 16, 1848; LG Sept. 16, 1848. Reviewed LG Sept. 23, 1848.

H (A)   Y (B,D)

8109. Lays of the Western World, Illuminated by T W Gwilt Mapleson Esq.

New York: Putnam ⟨n.d., 1848⟩

Unpaged. Contains Herbert's "The Tournament at Acre."

For comment see entry No. 1639.

8110. THE APPLE STAND; OR, HOW "THE PRESIDENT" MIGHT HAVE DONE IT. A HARMLESS FICTION RELATIVE TO RECENT FACTS. BY A STOCKHOLDER WHO DON'T MEAN TO BE DONE.

NEWARK, N. J.: SOLD AT THE PERIODICAL DEPOTS. 1848.

⟨1⟩-11. 7$\frac{5}{16}$" x 4$\frac{5}{16}$".

⟨-⟩^{6}.

Printed yellow paper wrapper.

Authorship attributed to Herbert on the authority of Van Winkle-Randall, pp. 21-22; and, *Books Pamphlets and Newspapers Printed at Newark New Jersey 1776–1900,* by Frank Pierce Hill and Varnum Lansing Collins, 1902, p. 61.

R

8111. Mark Manly: Or, the Skipper's Lad. By J. H. Ingraham . . .

New York: Published by Williams Brothers, Office of the "Morning Star," Corner of Ann and Nassau Streets. 1848.

Printed paper wrapper.

"Frederick St. Clair: Or the Young Man About Town," pp. ⟨76⟩-80.

Note: The Herbert story is not present in the first printing of 1843.

LC

Frank Forester's Field Sports of the United States . . . Sixth Edition . . .

New-York . . . ⟨1848; *i.e.,* 1856⟩

See entry No. 8151.

Frank Forester's Field Sports of the United States . . . New Edition . . . ⟨Eighth Edition⟩

New York . . . ⟨1848; *i. e., ca.* 1870⟩

Reprint. See BAL No. 8172.

8112. FRANK FORESTER'S FIELD SPORTS OF THE UNITED STATES, AND BRITISH PROVINCES, OF NORTH AMERICA . . .

NEW-YORK: STRINGER & TOWNSEND. (LATE BURGESS, STRINGER & CO) 222 BROADWAY. 1849.

2 Vols. For first London edition see entry No. 8108.

1: ⟨i-ii⟩, ⟨i⟩-x, ⟨11⟩-360; 3 blank leaves; leaf excised. Frontispiece and 5 plates inserted. 8$\frac{9}{16}$" x 5$\frac{7}{16}$".
2: ⟨i⟩-vi, ⟨7⟩-367; *Note,* p. ⟨368⟩. Frontispiece and 5 plates inserted.

1: ⟨-⟩^{2}, ⟨1⟩-7, 7, 9-21, ⟨22⟩-23^8. Leaves ⟨1⟩$_1$ and 23$_8$ excised. Superfluous signature marks present: 19 on p. 311; 20 on p. 341. Note that signature 8 is erroneously signed 7.
2: ⟨1⟩-12, 14, 14-23^8. Leaf ⟨1⟩$_1$ a cancel. Signature 13 erroneously signed 14. Superfluous signature mark 15 on p. 267.

Note: ⟨-⟩ (Vol. 1) and ⟨1⟩$_1$ (Vol. 2) are printed on paper unlike that used in the body of the book. Leaves ⟨-⟩$_2$ and ⟨1⟩$_1$ are the title-leaves. BAL suggests that the book was first printed with the imprint of *Burgess, Stringer & Co.,* and that the original title-pages were cancelled; and, the book was issued with altered title-pages bearing the imprint of the successor firm, Stringer & Townsend. Stringer & Townsend succeeded to Burgess, Stringer in Oct. 1848; see LW advertisements for Oct. 1848. BAL has not seen copies with the Burgess, Stringer imprint.

Fine-grained TR cloth: green. Sides blindstamped with a triple rule border, a strapwork filigree at each inner corner. At center: Vignette of game; goldstamped on front; blindstamped on back. Single flyleaf at front of Vol. 1; flyleaves in Vol. 2. Cream-white end papers.

The following imprints present on title-leaf verso:

Vol. 1

JOHN R. WINSER, Stereotyper, / 138 Fulton-Street.

Vol. 2

JOHN R. WINSER, Printer and Stereotyper, / 138 Fulton-Street.

Note: Van Winkle-Randall report existence of a copy with the spine imprint of *Burgess, Stringer & Co.* All early copies located by BAL have the spine imprint of *Stringer & Townsend*.

There were at least two printings issued with the 1849 imprint.

Postulated First Issue

Not located. Not reported. Postulated only. With each title-leaf an integral part of its respective gathering and in some feature varying from the *Stringer & Townsend* title-pages examined. Possibly with the imprint of *Burgess, Stringer & Company*.

Earliest Located Issue

As collated. Signing as above. The signatures are simple statements; *i.e.*, they occur without identification of the volume number.

Second Printing

The following features may, in fact, indicate not a single printing but may be the marks of two printings. However, the following features are present in the second and later printings:

The title-leaves are not cancels.

The signature marks are corrected and occur with identification of volume number. For example, the signature mark on p. 17, Vol. 1, reads: *Vol. I. 2*

Superfluous signature marks noted are not present.

Signature mark 22, Vol. 1, present.

In both volumes the printer's imprint on verso title-leaf is: JOHN R. WINSER, Stereotyper. ‹,› / 138 Fulton-Street.

Note: The second printing has been noted only in red A and purple-black TB cloths. Further, the stamping on the second printing occurs in two forms. No sequence known and the order of presentation is arbitrary.

Second Printing, Binding A

On the sides there is a strapwork ornament at each inner corner of the frame.

Second Printing, Binding B

The strapwork ornament is not present.

Advertised for Oct. 1 publication LW Sept. 16,

1848. Title-page deposited by Stringer & Townsend Oct. 9, 1848. Book deposited by Stringer & Townsend Oct. 17, 1848. Y copy (earliest located issue) inscribed by early owner Oct. 20, 1848. Noted for *this week* LW Oct. 21, 1848. Listed LW Oct. 21, 1848.

Note: Copies of the book dated ‹1848› were issued years after first publication of the first edition.

Y (all three forms described above)

8113. FRANK FORESTER AND HIS FRIENDS; OR, WOODLAND ADVENTURES IN THE MIDDLE STATES OF NORTH AMERICA . . .

LONDON: RICHARD BENTLEY, NEW BURLINGTON STREET. 1849.

3 Vols. Reprint, with some alterations, of *The Warwick Woodlands*, 1845; and, *My Shooting Box*, 1846. First book publication of *The Deerstalkers*, 1849; see next entry.

1: ‹i›-iv, ‹1›-299. 7¾″ x 4⅞″ full.
2: ‹i-ii›, ‹1›-315.
3: ‹i-ii›, ‹1›-312.

1: ‹A›², B-I, K-N¹², O⁶.
2: ‹A›¹, B-I, K-O¹², P².
3: ‹A›¹, B-I, K-O¹².

TR-like cloth: salmon. White end papers printed in blue with a pattern of small circular units; and, publisher's advertisements.

Advertised for *the present month* Ath March 3, 1849; *Immediately* Ath March 10, 1849. Announced for March 23, 1849, Ath March 17, 1849. Advertised for *this day* Ath March 24, 1849; as *now ready* Ath March 31, 1849; *this day* (again) Ath April 14, 1849.

Y

8114. THE DEERSTALKERS; OR, CIRCUMSTANTIAL EVIDENCE: A TALE OF THE SOUTH-WESTERN COUNTIES. BY FRANK FORESTER . . . ILLUSTRATED BY THE AUTHOR.

PHILADELPHIA: CAREY AND HART. 1849.

See preceding entry.

‹1›-‹6›, 13-198; plus: publisher's catalog, pp. 1-12. Vignette title-page and frontispiece inserted. 7⁹⁄₁₆″ x 4½″ full.

‹1›-16⁶; plus: ‹17›⁶.

Printed paper wrapper.

Note: Van Winkle-Randall report a copy with a 24-page catalog.

Note: A copy has been seen (SG, Feb. 1962) stripped of the original printed paper wrapper, terminal catalog not present, in the printed paper wrapper of Getz, Buck & Co., Philadelphia.

Title-page deposited April 18, 1849. Listed LW May 26, 1849. Advertised as *in press* LW May 26, 1849, with title given as *Woodland Adventures of Frank Forester and His Friends. Comprising the Deer-Stalkers.* Reviewed LA June 23, 1849. Reissued *ca.* 1860 with the imprint *T. B. Peterson & Brothers, Philadelphia* ⟨1843⟩.

CU Y

8115. DERMOT O'BRIEN: OR THE TAKING OF TREDAGH. A TALE OF 1649 ...

NEW-YORK: STRINGER & TOWNSEND, 222 BROADWAY. 1849.

⟨1⟩-166; blank leaf. 7¾″ x 5″. Double frontispiece inserted.

⟨1⟩-10⁸, 11⁴.

Printed off-white paper wrapper. Van Winkle-Randall report a copy in yellow paper wrapper.

Note

In all copies save one, see below, the title-page has the following features:

The line *A Tale of 1649.* is set 1½″ wide. The numeral *4* (in the date *1649*) is inverted. Title-leaf is an integral part of its gathering, not an insert or cancel. HENRY WILLIAM HERBERT, set 2⁵⁄₁₆″ wide.

In another copy, status not known, but quite probably sophisticated, the title-leaf is printed on a type of paper unlike that in the rest of the book and is clearly an insert. The types used for the title-page are not the normal types and several variations exist. The line *A Tale of 1649.* is set 1¹¹⁄₁₆″ wide. The numeral *4* (in the date *1649*) is not inverted. HENRY WILLIAM HERBERT, is set 2½″ wide.

Listed LW June 9, 1849.

H Y (variant)

8116. The Prometheus and Agamemnon of Æschylus. Translated into English Verse, by Henry William Herbert.

Cambridge: Published by John Bartlett. Bookseller to the University. 1849.

⟨i⟩-xii, ⟨1⟩-156. 7½″ x 4¹¹⁄₁₆″.

Noted in the following bindings. No sequence has been established and the designations are for identification only.

A

T cloth: black; brown; purple.

Lettered on spine only. The lettering placed,

virtually, at the very top of spine: THE / PROMETHEUS / AND / AGAMEMNON / OF / ÆSCHYLUS / ⟨rule⟩ / HERBERT

Spine decorated in blind with an arrangement of rules and fillets.

Sides stamped in blind only with a rules frame with, at each inner corner, a leafy-floral ornament, set off from the central portion of the sides by arched rules.

Locations: H (undated presentation inscription, Herbert to Charles Sumner) LC (being a deposit copy) Y

B

T cloth: black.

Lettered on spine only. The lettering placed about 1¼″ from top of spine: THE / PROMETHEUS / AND / AGAMEMNON / OF / ÆSCHYLUS / ⟨rule⟩ / HERBERT

Spine decorated in blind with an arrangement of rules.

Sides stamped in blind only with a rules frame with, at each inner corner, a leafy-floral ornament, set off from the central portion of the sides by arched rules.

Locations: H

C

T cloth: black. Also a black cloth embossed with a herringbone pattern.

Lettered on spine only. The lettering placed about 1⅜″ from top of spine: PROMETHEUS / AND / AGAMEMNON / ⟨rule⟩ / HERBERT

Spine decorated in blind with an arrangement of rules.

Sides stamped in blind only with a rule frame with, at each inner corner, a fruit, wheat-heads, and leaf ornament, set off from the central portion of the sides by curved rules twisted in gordian-knots.

Locations: H

D

T cloth: black.

Spine lettered up: PROMETHEUS.

Front lettered: THE / PROMETHEUS AND AGAMEMNON OF ÆSCHYLUS. / BY HENRY W. HERBERT.

Sides stamped in blind with a rule frame with, at each inner corner, a fruit, wheat-heads and leaf ornament, set off from the central portion of the sides by curved rules twisted in gordian knots.

Spine decorated in blind with an arrangement of rules.

Locations: H

E

T cloth: blackish brown.

Lettered on spine only, the lettering placed about ¼″ from the top: THE / PROMETHEUS / AND / AGAMEMNON / OF / ÆSCHYLUS / ⟨rule⟩ / HERBERT

Sides blindstamped with a rules frame, a leafy floral spray at each inner corner. The inner corners are not set off from the central portion of the cover by rules.

Spine decorated in blind with an arrangement of rules and filigrees.

Locations: H

F

T cloth: black.

Lettered on spine only, the lettering placed about 1⅝″ from top of spine: PROMETHEUS / AND / AGAMEMNON / ⟨rule⟩ / HERBERT

Sides stamped in blind with an ornate frame measuring about ⅝″ in thickness, a fan-like ornament at each corner, the whole within a rules frame.

Spine decorated in blind with an arrangement of rules and rococo ornaments.

Locations: H

Deposited Aug. 23, 1849. Listed LW Sept. 1, 1849. Distributed in London by Chapman; listed PC Oct. 1, 1849.

FRANK FORESTER'S FISH AND FISHING

Note: The following publication sequence of this work, together with the *Supplement,* may be useful. It is possible that the London and the New York editions were issued simultaneously; precise information is wanting.

Frank Forester's Fish and Fishing ... , New York: Stringer & Townsend, 1850.

First American edition. BAL No. 8117. Issued simultaneously with the London edition?

Frank Forester's Fish and Fishing ... , London: Richard Bentley, 1849.

First London edition. BAL No. 8118. Issued simultaneously with the New York edition?

Supplement ... Fish and Fishing ... , New York: Stringer & Townsend, 1850.

First edition. BAL No. 8119.

Frank Forester's Fish and Fishing ... , New York: Stringer & Townsend, 1850.

The so-called *Second Edition.* BAL No. 8120. The sheets of BAL Nos. 8117, 8119, bound together and issued as a single volume. *Not located.*

Frank Forester's Fish and Fishing ... Third Edition ... , New York: Stringer & Townsend, 1851.

Revised. BAL No. 8125.

Frank Forester's Fish and Fishing ... Revised ... , New York: W. A. Townsend & Co., 1859.

Herbert's final revision. BAL No. 8166.

The following reprints have been noted:

New York: W. A. Townsend Publisher. 1864.

New York: Geo. E. Woodward, 191 Broadway. ⟨1859; *i.e., ca.* 1870⟩

New York: The American News Company, 39 and 41 Chambers Street. ⟨1859; *i.e., ca.* 1880⟩

New York: Excelsior Publishing House ⟨n.d., *ca.* 1880⟩ *Not seen.* Entry from Van Winkle-Randall, p. 36.

Publication Synopsis, Fish and Fishing.

London: Advertised Ath May 12, 1849. Obviously premature.

London: Advertised Ath July 7, 1849. Obviously premature.

New York: Noted as *immediately* LW Aug. 18, 1849.

New York: Advertised for *early September* LW Aug. 25, 1849.

New York: Noted as *nearly ready* LW Aug. 25, 1849.

London: Advertised for *this day* ⟨in error?⟩ Ath Sept. 15, 1849.

London: Advertised (erroneously as in two volumes) Ath Sept. 22, 1849.

London: Advertised LG Sept. 22, 1849.

New York: Listed LW Sept. 29, 1849.

London: Listed PC Oct. 1, 1849.

London: Listed BMLA Oct. 10, 1849.

New York: Listed PC Nov. 1, 1849.

8117. FRANK FORESTER'S FISH AND FISH-ING OF THE UNITED STATES AND BRITISH PROVINCES OF NORTH AMER-ICA. ILLUSTRATED FROM NATURE BY THE AUTHOR. ...

NEW-YORK: STRINGER & TOWNSEND. 222 BROAD-WAY. 1850. ⟨*i.e.,* 1849⟩

First American edition. See next entry for first London edition. *See publication synopsis above.*

⟨i-ii⟩, ⟨i⟩-xvi, ⟨17⟩-359; plus: advertisements, pp. 1-16. Frontispiece and 11 plates inserted; other illustrations in text. 8¼″ full x 5¹⁵⁄₁₆″.

Note: No copy has been located in state fit for close examination of the folding. The book is not, however, in 8's as stated by Van Winkle-Randall.

A cloth: blue. Cream end papers. Triple fly-leaves.

All examined copies have *Jonh* for *John* in the stereotyper's imprint on the copyright page.

Noted as *immediately* LW Aug. 18, 1849. Advertised for early September LW Aug. 25, 1849. Noted as *nearly ready* LW Aug. 25, 1849. Listed LW Sept. 29, 1849; PC Nov. 1, 1849. For *Supplement* see entry No. 8119.

NYPL

8118. FRANK FORESTER'S FISH AND FISH-ING OF THE UNITED STATES, AND BRITISH PROVINCES OF NORTH AMER-ICA . . .

LONDON: RICHARD BENTLEY, PUBLISHER IN OR-DINARY TO HER MAJESTY. 1849.

First London edition. For first New York edition see preceding entry. *Also see publication synopsis preceding entry No. 8117.*

⟨i⟩-xvi, ⟨1⟩-455. 4 plates inserted; other illustrations in text. $8\frac{11}{16}$″ x $5\frac{1}{2}$″.

⟨A⟩-I, K-U, X-Z, AA-FF⁸, GG⁴.

Four variant bindings have been seen or reported. The sequence has not been determined and the designations are for identification only.

A

A cloth: blue. Sides blindstamped with a frame of stylized chains. Front goldstamped at center within a leafy frame: FRANK / FORESTER'S / FISH / AND / FISHING Spine lettered: FRANK / FOR-ESTER'S / FISH / AND / FISHING Yellow-white end papers.

B

TZ cloth: blue-green. Sides blindstamped with a border of leafy scrolls, a squared strapwork ornament at each corner. Spine lettered: FOR-ESTER'S / FISH & / FISHING / 16/- / ILLUSTRATED Yellow-coated end papers. Leaf ⟨A⟩1 excised.

C

Spine lettered: FISH / AND / FISHING. / H. W. HERBERT. / LONDON / BENTLEY. *Not seen.* Entry from Van Winkle-Randall, p. 33.

D

Spine lettered: FRANK / FORESTER'S / FISH AND FISHING. *Not seen.* Entry from Van Winkle-Ran-dall, p. 33.

Advertised Ath May 12, 1849; and, July 7, 1849, under the title *Excursions of an Angler in the*

U.S. and British Provinces of North America, 2 vols., unpriced. The preceding obviously well in advance of publication. Under the title *Fish and Fishing in the New World* advertised in Ath Sept. 15, 1849, for *this day* ⟨in error?⟩. As *Fish and Fishing . . .* , advertised Ath Sept. 22, 1849, erroneously as in *two volumes,* at 21/-. As *Fish and Fishing . . .* , advertised in LG Sept. 22, 1849, at 16/- (correctly priced). Listed PC Oct. 1, 1849; BMLA Oct. 10, 1849. The New York edition listed PC Nov. 1, 1849.

NYPL (A) Y (B)

FRANK FORESTER'S FISH AND FISHING OF THE UNITED STATES AND BRITISH PROVINCES OF NORTH AMERICA. IL-LUSTRATED FROM NATURE BY THE AUTHOR . . .

NEW-YORK: STRINGER & TOWNSEND. 222 BROAD-WAY. 1850. ⟨*i.e.,* 1849⟩

See entry No. 8117.

8119. SUPPLEMENT TO FRANK FORES-TER'S FISH AND FISHING OF THE UNITED STATES AND BRITISH PROV-INCES OF NORTH AMERICA . . .

NEW-YORK, STRINGER & TOWNSEND, 222 BROAD-WAY. 1850.

See entry No. 8117.

⟨i-ii⟩, ⟨i⟩-⟨viii⟩, ⟨9⟩-86. Frontispiece inserted. $8\frac{3}{8}$″ x $6\frac{1}{8}$″.

⟨1-5⁸, 6⁴⟩.

A cloth: red. TB cloth: blue. Yellow end pa-pers. Triple flyleaves.

In all examined copies: *Jonh* for *John* in stereo-typer's imprint on copyright page.

Noted for *early June* LW May 4, 1850. Listed, reviewed, advertised as *now ready* LW June 22, 1850. Distributed in Great Britain by Chapman; listed PC Aug. 1, 1850.

AAS NYPL Y

8120. Frank Forester's Fish and Fishing of the United States and British Provinces of North America . . .

New-York: Stringer & Townsend 222 Broad-way. 1850.

Not located. Entry from Van Winkle-Randall, p. 35.

The so-called *second edition.* According to Van Winkle-Randall made up of the sheets of BAL Nos. 8117, 8119 and issued as a single volume. This (?) edition advertised as *lately issued* LW June 22, 1850.

8121. A STATEMENT OF A RECENT AF-
FAIR IN PHILADELPHIA ...

COLUMBIA HOUSE, PHILADELPHIA, JUNE 19,
1850 ...

Caption-title. The above at head of p. 1.

1-8. 9⅛″ x 5⅞″ scant.

⟨-⟩⁴.

Self-wrapper.

An exchange of letters between Herbert, George
W. Barton, J. A. Dallas, Leon B. Hirst, regarding an affair of honor, so-called.

BPL   Y

8122. The Sportsman's Vade Mecum; by
"Dinks," ⟨i.e., Jonathan Peel⟩ Edited by
Frank Forester ...

New York: Stringer & Townsend, 222 Broadway. 1850.

Binder's title: Dinks on Dogs.

"Preface," p. ⟨3⟩.

Advertised as just published LW Nov. 9, 1850.
Listed LW Nov. 16, 1850. For revised editions
see under 1856; and, The Dog ... , 1857.

H   NYPL   Y

8123. The Coral, a Gift for All Seasons ...
Edited by Henry W. Herbert.

New York: Published by Cornish, Lamport
& Co. ⟨n.d., ca. 1850⟩

A reprint of BAL No. 8058.

NYPL

The Quorndon Hounds ...

Philadelphia ... ⟨1850; i.e., not before 1854⟩

Reprint. See entry No. 8132.

The Warwick Woodlands ...

Philadelphia ... ⟨1850⟩

Reprint. See next entry.

8124. The Warwick Woodlands; or, Things
As They Were There Twenty Years Ago. By
Frank Forester. New Edition, Revised and
Corrected with Illustrations by the Author.

New York: Stringer & Townsend, 222 Broadway. 1851.

Cloth; and, printed paper wrapper.

For first edition see entry No. 8085.

Advertised as just ready LW March 15, 1851.
Listed LW March 22, 1851. Deposited April 3,
1851.

Note: Van Winkle-Randall report two states of
the binding. Sequence not determined and the
designations are for identification only:

A: Spine lettering starts 3/16″ from top of spine.

B: Spine lettering starts 1¼″ from top of spine.

Reprinted from the same plates and reissued:

Philadelphia: T. B. Peterson, 102 Chestnut
Street. ⟨1850; i.e., ca. 1855⟩

Philadelphia: T. B. Peterson & Brothers, 306
Chestnut Street. ⟨1850; i.e., not before 1858⟩

NYPL   Y

8125. Frank Forester's Fish and Fishing of the
United States and British Provinces of North
America ... Third Edition, Revised and Cor-
rected ...

New York: Stringer & Townsend, 222 Broadway. 1851.

Revised. For first edition see entry No. 8117.

Advertised for the first week in April LW March
29, April 5, 1851. Advertised as now ready, just
published, LW April 26, 1851.

CU   H   NYPL

8126. The Sea-King: A Nautical Romance. By
the Author of the "Scourge of the Ocean."
Edited and Completed by the Editor of "Valerie." ...

Philadelphia: A. Hart, Late Carey and Hart.
126 Chestnut Street. 1851.

⟨1⟩-⟨4⟩, 11-203; blank leaf(?). 8¹³⁄₁₆″ x 5⁹⁄₁₆″.
Printed paper wrapper.

"The Author of The Scourge of the Ocean
⟨Robert Burts⟩ died before completing his
present work; and it has been finished, at the
request of the Publisher, by the same able hand
who completed ⟨Marryat's⟩ Valerie, which completion was adopted by the London Publisher,
Capt. Marryat having also died leaving his work
unfinished."—P. 3.

Listed LW June 7, 1851; NLA June, 1851. Reviewed USDR June, 1851. Reissued not before
1855; as: The Sea King. A Tale of the Sea ... ,
Philadelphia, T. B. Peterson, 102 Chestnut
Street, n.d., misattributed to Marryat.

AAS

8127. THE CAPTAINS OF THE OLD WORLD; AS COMPARED WITH THE GREAT MODERN STRATEGISTS, THEIR CAMPAIGNS, CHARACTERS AND CONDUCT, FROM THE PERSIAN, TO THE PUNIC WARS . . .

NEW YORK: CHARLES SCRIBNER, 145 NASSAU STREET. 1851.

⟨i⟩-⟨xx⟩, ⟨13⟩-364. Frontispiece, vignette title-page and 3 plates inserted. 7⅜″ scant x 4¹⁵⁄₁₆″.

⟨-⟩⁴, ⟨1⟩¹², 2*¹², 3-14¹², ⟨15⟩¹², 16².

Note: The third gathering noted in two states:

A: *Signed:* 2*.

B: *Signed:* 2. An 1852 reprint also occurs in this form.

Also note: The following superfluous signature marks are present in all examined copies of the 1851 printing: 4 on p. 65; 5 on p. 89; 6 on p. 113.

A cloth: green; purple; slate. Yellow end papers. Flyleaves.

Advertised as *in press* and *immediately* NLA Sept. 15, 1851. Deposited Oct. 29, 1851. Listed NLA Nov. 15, 1851. Reviewed LW Nov. 22, 1851. Listed LW Nov. 22, 1851. A reprinting advertised NLG Feb. 15, 1852. Reprinted by American News Company, New York, n.d.

AAS (B)   H (A)   LC (B, being a deposit copy) NYPL (B)

8128. The Morning Glory, a Gift, for All Seasons. By H. W. Herbert

New York: Cornish, Lamport & Co., Publishers, No. 8 Park Place. ⟨n.d., after 1851⟩

Reprint of No. 8058.

BPL

8129. Frank Forester's Field Sports of the United States, and British Provinces, of North America . . . by Henry William Herbert . . . Fourth Edition, Revised and Corrected . . .

New-York: Stringer & Townsend, 222 Broadway. 1852.

2 Vols. For first edition see No. 8112.

"Advertisement to the Fourth Edition," Vol. 1, pp. ⟨v⟩-vi. Dated at end *November 1, 1851.*

"I have little to say in the Preface to the fourth edition . . . Since issuing my first edition, many criticisms . . . have led me to review some of my opinions; and those which are found incorrect, will be found entirely altered and rewritten . . ." —Pp. ⟨v⟩-vi.

Listed NLG April 15, 1852. Advertised by Chapman as an importation Ath July 24, 1852.

AAS   BPL   Y

8130. THE CAVALIERS OF ENGLAND, OR THE TIMES OF THE REVOLUTIONS OF 1642 AND 1688 . . .

REDFIELD, CLINTON HALL, NEW YORK. 1852.

⟨1⟩-428; advertisements, pp. ⟨1⟩-4. P. 427 *mispaged* 327. 7⅜″ x 4⅞″.

⟨1-18⟩¹². *Signed:* ⟨1⟩-36⁶.

A cloth: green; purple; slate. T cloth: blue. TB cloth: purple. Yellow end papers. Flyleaves.

Note: All examined copies, including a copyright deposit copy, have the terminal advertisements paged ⟨1⟩, 2, 3, 4. Van Winkle-Randall report a copy with the terminal advertisements totally unpaged; not located.

Advertised as *in press* LW Jan. 3, 1852. Advertised as *just ready* LW May 8, 1852. Listed LW May 15, 1852; NLG May 15, 1852. Deposited May 26, 1852. Advertised by Chapman as an importation Ath July 3, 1852. A Low edition (importation?) advertised as *just issued* Ath Dec. 25, 1852. Issued in the Clarke, Beeton (London) *Readable Books* series; listed Ath March 5, 1853; PC March 15, 1853.

BPL   H   NYPL

8131. THE KNIGHTS OF ENGLAND, FRANCE, AND SCOTLAND . . .

REDFIELD, CLINTON HALL, NEW YORK. 1852.

⟨1⟩-426; 6 pp. advertisements. 7¼″ full x 4⅞″. ⟨1⟩-18¹².

A cloth: slate. Pale buff end papers. Flyleaves.

Under the title *The Knights of the Olden Time; or, the Chivalry of England, France and Spain,* advertised as *in press* LW Jan. 3, 1852. Advertised for *next week* LW June 19, 26, 1852. Advertised as *ready* LW July 10, 1852. Listed NLG July 15, 1852; LW July 17, 1852. Reviewed LW July 17, 1852. Distributed in London by Low; advertised as *just issued* Ath Dec. 25, 1852.

Y

8132. THE QUORNDON HOUNDS; OR, A VIRGINIAN AT MELTON MOWBRAY . . . WITH ILLUSTRATIONS BY THE AUTHOR.

PHILADELPHIA: GETZ, BUCK & CO. 1852.

⟨1⟩-173; blank, p. ⟨174⟩; 4 pp. advertisements; blank leaf. Frontispiece and 3 plates inserted. 7⅜″ x 4⅜″.

⟨1-6¹², 7-9⁶⟩. *Signed:* ⟨1⟩-15⁶.

A cloth: blue; red. T cloth: green. Yellow end papers. Triple flyleaf at front and at back. In some copies: Seven flyleaves at back. Reported (not seen) in printed paper wrapper.

Advertised as *just published* LW Aug. 28, 1852. Listed LW Sept. 4, 1852; NLG Sept. 13, 1852. The Philadelphia, Peterson printing, dated ⟨1850⟩, was issued not before 1854.

H   LC

8133. Commonwealth—Extra. Sermon of Rev. Theodore Parker, on the Death of ⟨Daniel⟩ Webster . . .

⟨Boston, November(?), 1852⟩

Single sheet. Caption-title.

"Hymn to the Sun," p. ⟨2⟩. Collected in *Poems,* 1888.

H

8134. . . . Morrell's Pocket Miscellany of Choice, Entertaining, and Useful Reading for Travelers and the Fireside . . .

New York: Arthur Morrell, 25 Park Row; Printed at Morrell's Steam Blank-Book Manufacturing and Printing Establishment, 196 Fulton-St. 1852.

At head of title: Economical Library for the People.

Note: Vols. 2-3 are titled: *Morrell's Miscellany for Travelers and the Fireside.* Caption-title, p. ⟨5⟩: *Morrell's Pocket Miscellany.*

3 Vols. All published? Printed paper wrapper.

"Adventures in the Northwest . . . the Wigwam and the Wilderness," Vol. 3, pp. ⟨101⟩-127.

Y

8135. THE CHEVALIERS OF FRANCE FROM THE CRUSADERS TO THE MARECHALS OF LOUIS XIV . . .

REDFIELD, 110 AND 112 NASSAU STREET, NEW YORK. 1853.

⟨1⟩-399; blank, p. ⟨400⟩; 8 pp. advertisements. 7³⁄₁₆″ x 4¹⁵⁄₁₆″.

⟨1⟩-17¹².

A cloth: green; purple. Cream end papers. Flyleaves.

Advertised for August in LW July 24, 1852. Deposited Dec. 6, 1852. Listed NLG Dec. 15, 1852. Reviewed LW Dec. 18, 1852. Listed LW Dec. 25,

1852; PC Jan. 17, 1853; Ath Feb. 12, 1853; LG Feb. 19, 1853.

LC   NYPL

8136. The Old Forest Ranger; or, Wild Sports of India . . . by Major Walter Campbell. Edited by Frank Forester . . .

New-York: Stringer & Townsend, 222 Broadway. M.DCCC.LIII.

"Introductory Preface," pp. ⟨7⟩-13.

Noted as *in preparation,* advertised, LW Feb. 12, 1853. Listed NLG May 15, 1853.

AAS   NYPL   Y

8137. Marmaduke Wyvil . . . Fourteenth Edition.—Revised and Corrected.

Redfield, 110 and 112 Nassau Street, New York. 1853.

For first edition see entry No. 8072.

"Preface," dated March 31, 1853, p. ⟨3⟩.

". . . thoroughly revised and corrected by the author . . ."—P. ⟨3⟩.

Advertised as *ready* NLG May 15, 1853. Listed LW June 11, 1853; NLG June 15, 1853.

BPL   Y

8138. AMERICAN GAME IN ITS SEASONS . . . ILLUSTRATED . . . BY THE AUTHOR.

NEW YORK: CHARLES SCRIBNER, 145 NASSAU STREET. 1853.

⟨i⟩-⟨xvi⟩, ⟨17⟩-343; blank, p. ⟨344⟩; 4 pp. advertisements. Illustrations; *see note below.* 7½″ x 5″ scant.

⟨1⟩-14¹², ⟨15⟩⁶.

A cloth: blue; red. Yellow end papers. Flyleaves.

Note: The illustrations occur in two forms. Priority, if any, not determined. The following designations are for identification only.

A

8(?) double-faced plates, inserted.

B

Frontispiece and 19 single-faced plates inserted. A surviving copyright deposit copy is in this form. Also in this form: the *Second Edition,* 1854; the *Revised Edition,* 1873.

Deposited June 2, 1853. Listed NLG June 15, 1853. Listed as an American book PC July 16, 1853.

NYPL (A, incomplete(?) rebound)   Y (B)

8139. The Life of Jane McCrea ... by D. Wilson. ⟨*i.e.*, David Wilson, 1818–1887⟩

New York: Baker, Godwin & Co., Printers, Corner Nassau and Spruce Streets. 1853.

"Jane McCrea," pp. 146-152; and, an extract on p. ⟨iv⟩. Collected in *Poems*, 1888.

H NYPL

8140. History of the French Protestant Refugees, from the Revocation of the Edict of Nantes to Our Own Days. By M. Charles Weiss ... Translated from the French by Henry William Herbert ⟨and Philip Anthon⟩ ...

New-York: Stringer & Townsend, 222 Broadway. 1854.

2 Vols. 1: ⟨1⟩-382; blank leaf; plus: 4 pp. advertisements. Frontispiece inserted. 2: ⟨i-iv⟩, ⟨1⟩-419. 7¾6″ x 4¾″. Pagination and size of leaf postulated.

Two printings noted:

1: With the imprint of John F. Trow on both copyright pages.

2: With the imprint of R. Craighead on both copyright pages.

Advertised as *just published* NLG April 15, 1854. Listed NLG April 15, 1854; PC May 15, 1854. Advertised by Low (PC June 1, 1854) as *in preparation* but no further word of a Low printing found.

BPL (1st)   LC (1st)   NYPL (2nd)

8141. PERSONS AND PICTURES FROM THE HISTORIES OF FRANCE AND ENGLAND FROM THE NORMAN CONQUEST TO THE FALL OF THE STUARTS ...

NEW YORK: RIKER, THORNE & CO., 129 FULTON STREET. 1854.

⟨1⟩-440. 7¾6″ x 4⅞″.

⟨1⟩⁴, ⟨2⟩-19¹².

A cloth: red. T cloth: purple; green. Yellow-coated end papers. Ecru end papers. Flyleaves.

Listed NLG June 1, 1854; PC, Aug. 16, 1854.

H LC NYPL

8142. THE CAPTAINS OF THE ROMAN REPUBLIC, AS COMPARED WITH THE GREAT MODERN STRATEGISTS; THEIR CAMPAIGNS, CHARACTER, AND CONDUCT FROM THE PUNIC WARS TO THE DEATH OF CAESAR. BY HENRY WILLAM ⟨sic⟩ HERBERT.

NEW YORK: CHARLES SCRIBNER, 145 NASSAU STREET. 1854.

All examined copies have the error WILLAM for WILLIAM on the title-page.

⟨i⟩-⟨xxii⟩, ⟨23⟩-511; 2 blank leaves. In some copies the final blank is excised. 7⁷⁄₁₆″ x 4¹⁵⁄₁₆″. Frontispiece inserted.

⟨1⟩-3, ⟨4⟩-18, ⟨19⟩-21¹², 22⁶. Leaf 22₆ excised in some copies.

Two states of the binding have been noted. Sequence, if any, not determined. The designations are for identification only.

A

A cloth: brown; purple. Sides blindstamped: at center with an arrangement of weapons; border has at each corner a decoration of willow-like (olive-like?) leaves. Yellow end papers. Flyleaf at front. A deposit copy thus.

B

C-like cloth: olive-green. As above save for decorations at the corners. In this state the decorations are rococo filigrees.

Quite prematurely advertised as *in press* and *immediately* NLG April 15, 1852. Advertised as *in press* NLG June 15; July 1, 15, 1854. Noted for Aug. 19 in NLG Aug. 1, 1854. According to the publisher deposited Sept. 9, 1854; but, Copyright Office reports deposited Feb. 16, 1855. Noted as though published NLG Sept. 15, 1854. Listed NLG Oct. 2, 1854; PC Nov. 15, 1854.

BPL (B)   LC (A, being a deposit copy)   Y (A)

8143. The Aloe, a Gift for All Seasons. Edited by Henry W. Herbert.

New York: Lamport, Blakeman & Law. 1854.

Leather.

Reprint of No. 8058.

B H

8144. ANNUAL ADDRESS OF THE CARRIERS OF THE NEWARK DAILY ADVERTISER, TO ITS PATRONS, JANUARY 1st, 1855.

NEWARK, NEW JERSEY: PRINTED AT THE DAILY ADVERTISER OFFICE. 1855.

Not seen. Entry on the basis of Van Winkle-Randall, p. 51; and, Mr. Gerald McDonald's unpublished (1962) bibliography of carrier's addresses. (The two copies located in NJHS were reported "lost", June 1, 1961.)

Pp. 8. Self-wrapper. Cover-title. 8⅛″ x 5½″. Text begins: *The dirge has been sung* ...

Authorship attributed to Herbert on the basis of Van Winkle-Randall; and, *Books Pamphlets and Newspapers Printed at Newark New Jersey*

1776–1900, by Frank Pierce Hill and Varnum Lansing Collins, 1902, p. 75.

BAL has been unable to find any evidence to support Van Winkle-Randall's conjecture (p. 51) that the address was issued also in broadside form.

8145. Lilies and Violets; or, Thoughts in Prose and Verse, on the True Graces of Maidenhood. By Rosalie Bell . . .

New York: J. C. Derby, 119 Nassau Street. Boston: Phillips, Sampson & Co. Cincinnati: H. W. Derby. 1855.

"Records," pp. 223-228. Collected in *Poems*, 1888.

For comment see entry No. 1658.

8146. MEMOIRS OF HENRY THE EIGHTH OF ENGLAND: WITH THE FORTUNES, FATES, AND CHARACTERS OF HIS SIX WIVES. AFTER THE BEST AUTHORITIES . . .

NEW YORK AND AUBURN: MILLER, ORTON & MULLIGAN. NEW YORK: 25 PARK ROW.—AUBURN: 107 GENESEE-ST. 1855.

⟨i⟩-xii, ⟨13⟩-441; blank, p. ⟨442⟩; 6 pp. advertisements. Frontispiece and 6 plates inserted. 7⁷⁄₁₆″ x 4¹⁵⁄₁₆″.

⟨1⟩-16, ⟨17⟩, 18-27, ⟨28⟩⁸. *Also signed:* ⟨A⟩-R¹², ⟨S⟩⁸.

A cloth: black. T cloth: brown. Yellow end papers. Flyleaves.

Three states (almost surely printings; see publication notes below) noted. The sequence has not been established and the designations are for identification only.

A: P. ⟨442⟩ blank. P. ⟨443⟩: *The Life of Napoleon Bonaparte* . . .

B: P. ⟨442⟩ blank. P. ⟨443⟩: *The Life of Gen. William H. Harrison* . . .

C: P. ⟨442⟩: *Popular Biographies* . . . *Note:* Noted only in rebound condition. Presumably pagination and signature collation as shown above. A copy thus received by Smithsonian Institution Nov. 24, 1855.

NLG July 15, 1854, noted that J. C. Derby was "shortly" to publish *The Queens of Henry VIII;* presumably a tentative title for *Memoirs of Henry the Eighth.* Under the title *Memoirs of Henry the Eighth* . . . announced APC Sept. 1, 1855. Listed APC Sept. 15, 1855. A second printing advertised as *ready* APC Oct. 13, 1855. A third printing advertised APC Oct. 20, 1855. Listed PC Dec. 17, 1855.

B (A)   NYPL (B)   SM (C, rebound)   Y (A)

8147. WAGER OF BATTLE; A TALE OF SAXON SLAVERY IN SHERWOOD FOREST . . .

NEW YORK: PUBLISHED BY MASON BROTHERS, 23 PARK ROW. 1855.

⟨i⟩-x, ⟨11⟩-336. 7³⁄₁₆″ x 4⅞″ full.

⟨1⟩-14¹².

A cloth: blue; purple; red; slate. Blue-coated end papers; gray-coated end papers; brown-coated end papers. Flyleaves.

Advertised as *in press* APC Sept. 1, 1855. Advertised for *next week* APC Oct. 13, 1855. Deposited Oct. 27, 1855. Listed APC Oct. 27, 1855. Advertised as *today* APC Oct. 27, 1855. Listed PC Nov. 15, 1855.

BA   H

8148. Organization and Dedicatory Services of the Fairmount Cemetery . . .

Newark, N. J. Printed for the Cemetery. 1855.

Printed paper wrapper.

Untitled poem, pp. 13-15, beginning: *This is God's Acre—meted years ago* . . .

Issued after Sept. 5, 1855.

NJH   P

8149. The Sportsman's Vade Mecum. By "Dinks," ⟨*i.e.,* Jonathan Peel⟩ . . . New Revised Edition. And Dogs: Their Management . . . by Edward Mayhew . . . Edited by Frank Forester . . .

New York: Stringer & Townsend, 222 Broadway. 1856.

For first edition see entry No. 8122.

Noted as *just ready,* CRN March 15, 1856. Listed CRN May 3, 1856.

AAS   NYPL

8150. Mr. Sponge's Sporting Tour. Edited by Frank Forester . . .

New York: Stringer & Townsend, 222 Broadway. 1856.

By Robert Smith Surtees.

"Editor's Preface," pp. ⟨5⟩-7.

Advertised as *nearly ready* CRN March 15, 1856. Listed CRN May 24, 1856.

AAS   H

8151. Frank Forester's Field Sports of the United States ... Sixth Edition, Revised and Corrected, with Additions ...

New-York: Stringer & Townsend, 222 Broadway. ⟨1848; *i.e.*, 1856⟩

2 Vols.

Reprint of the fourth edition, 1852. The preface altered merely by the substitution of the word *sixth* for the word *fourth*.

BPL copy inscribed by early owner June 21, 1856. BA copy received Oct. 22, 1856.

BPL NYPL

8152. Oliver Cromwell; or, England's Great Protector ...

New York and Auburn: Miller, Orton & Mulligan. New York: 25 Park Row—Auburn: 107 Genesee-St. 1856.

Revision of *Cromwell* ... , 1838. " ... thoroughly revised and corrected, and in some passages re-written ... "—P. ⟨v⟩.

"Preface," pp. ⟨v⟩-vi.

Deposited Sept. 13, 1856. Listed Ath Nov. 8, 1856; PC Nov. 15, 1858.

BPL MHS NYPL

8153. THE COMPLETE MANUAL FOR YOUNG SPORTSMEN: WITH DIRECTIONS FOR HANDLING THE GUN, THE RIFLE, AND THE ROD; THE ART OF SHOOTING ON THE WING; THE BREAKING, MANAGEMENT, AND HUNTING OF THE DOG; THE VARIETIES AND HABITS OF GAME; RIVER, LAKE, AND SEA FISHING ... PREPARED FOR THE INSTRUCTION AND USE OF THE YOUTH OF AMERICA. BY FRANK FORESTER ...

NEW YORK: STRINGER & TOWNSEND, 222 BROADWAY. 1856.

⟨i⟩-xvi, ⟨17⟩-480. Frontispiece, vignette title-page and 1 plate inserted. Other illustrations in text. 7⅜″ full x 4⅞″.

⟨1⟩-15, ⟨16⟩, 17-20¹².

Gilt Binding

T cloth: green. Yellow end papers. Flyleaves. Edges plain. Stamped in blind and in gold.

Extra-Gilt Binding

A cloth: blue; red. Yellow end papers. Flyleaves. Edges gilded. Stamped in gold; not in gold and blind.

Note: The reprint of 1863 contains an added appendix, "Appendix D," pp. ⟨481⟩-482, which almost certainly was not written by Herbert.

Advertised as *in preparation* CRN March 8, 15, 1856.

Y

8154. Aspen Court: A Story of Our Own Time. By Shirley Brooks ...

New York: Stringer & Townsend. 1856.

Letter, Jan. 1856, recommending the book, p. ⟨5⟩.

H

8155. Dog and Gun; a Few Loose Chapters on Shooting ... by Johnson J. Hooper ...

New York: C. M. Saxton & Company, Agricultural Book Publishers, 140 Fulton Street. 1856.

"My First Day's Partridge Shooting," pp. 76-79.

"The Yorkshire Moors," pp. 79-89.

Note: Reissued *ca.* 1870, with the imprint: *New York: Orange Judd & Company ... ⟨1856⟩.*

H

8156. Old Noll; or, the Days of the Ironsides. A Tale of Oliver Cromwell's Times.

New York: Robert M. DeWitt, 160 & 162 Nassau Street. ⟨n.d., *ca.* 1856⟩

Anonymous. Probably issued in printed paper wrapper.

A reprint of *Marmaduke Wyvil* ⟨1843⟩. Reprinted *ca.* 1860-1870 with the publisher's later address: 13 Frankfort Street.

BPL

8157. Frank Forester's Sporting Scenes and Characters ...

Philadelphia: T. B. Peterson, No. 102 Chestnut Street. ⟨1857⟩

2 Vols. An omnibus reprint of *My Shooting Box, The Deerstalkers, The Warwick Woodlands, The Quorndon Hounds.*

Vignette title-page, Vol. 1: *Frank Forester's Complete Book of Sporting Scenes and Characters.*

Reprinted and reissued by T. B. Peterson & Brothers, 306 Chestnut Street, Philadelphia ⟨1857; *i.e.*, not before 1858⟩.

Y copy inscribed by early owner Jan. 1857.

Y

8158. The Dog. By Dinks ⟨Jonathan Peel⟩, ⟨Edward⟩ Mayhew, and ⟨William Nelson⟩ Hutchinson. Compiled, Abridged, Edited, and Illustrated by Frank Forester ... Complete and Revised Edition.

New York: Stringer & Townsend, 222 Broadway. 1857.

"Editor's Preface," pp. ⟨iii⟩-vi.

A reissue of *The Sportsman's Vade Mecum*, 1856, with the following added material:

"Dog Breaking ... ," by Hutchinson, pp. ⟨455⟩-653.

"Editor's ⟨i.e., Herbert's⟩ Note" to the preceding, pp. ⟨654⟩-655.

The following printings contain no new material:

New York: W. A. Townsend, Publisher. 1863.

———————. 1864.

———————. 1866.

New York: W. A. Townsend & Adams, 1868.

New York: Geo. E. Woodward ⟨1873⟩.

New York: Excelsior Publishing House, 29 and 31 Beekman Street. ⟨1873; i.e., after 1873⟩.

H   LC   NYPL

8159. FRANK FORESTER'S HORSE AND HORSEMANSHIP OF THE UNITED STATES AND BRITISH PROVINCES OF NORTH AMERICA ...

NEW YORK: STRINGER & TOWNSEND, 222 BROADWAY. LONDON: TRÜBNER & CO. 1857.

2 Vols.

Note: The imprint in Vol. 2 varies from the above as follows: After NEW YORK a dot, not a colon; After BROADWAY a fragment of the period; or, no stop whatever.

1: ⟨1⟩-552. Vignette title-page, 8 plates, and 10 printed pedigrees inserted. Other illustrations in text. 10¹¹⁄₁₆" x 7⁹⁄₁₆".
2: ⟨1⟩-576. Vignette title-page and 6 plates inserted. Other illustrations in text.

1: ⟨1-69⟩⁴. *Signed:* ⟨1-2⟩, 3-34⁸, 35⁴.
2: ⟨1-72⟩⁴. *Signed:* ⟨1⟩-36⁸.

TZ cloth: slate. Blue-coated end papers. Flyleaves. Errata slip for both volumes inserted in Vol. 1. Also noted in brown morocco, edges gilded. *Note:* An advertisement in APC Oct. 24, 1857, offers the work in cloth; and, in seven styles of leather.

Listed APC Oct. 3, 1857. Listed as an importation Ath Nov. 7, 1857. Advertised as an importation PC Nov. 16, 1857. Listed as an American book PC Nov. 16, 1857. Advertised by Trübner Ath Nov. 22, 1856, as *in preparation;* again, Ath April 4, 1857. Advertised as in a variety of bindings BM May 1, 1859. An edition revised by S. D. & B. G. Bruce issued with the imprint: *New York: Geo. E. Woodward, Publisher, 191 Broadway, 1871.*

H

8160. Tales and Sketches for the Fire-Side, by the Best American Authors. Selected from Putnam's Magazine.

New York: A. Dowling, 36 Beekman Street 1857.

Contains Herbert's "A Few Words on the Day Owls of North America" in the issue of Sept. 1853.

Irregular pagination. For comment see entry No. 8239.

8161. Frank Forester's Field Sports of the United States ... Eighth Edition, Containing Numerous Corrections and Additions ...

New York: W. A. Townsend, 377 Broadway. 1858.

2 Vols. Reprint.

Advertised as *published this morning* BM Oct. 1, 1858.

NYPL

8162. FISHING WITH HOOK AND LINE; A MANUAL FOR AMATEUR ANGLERS. CONTAINING ALSO DESCRIPTIONS OF POPULAR FISHES, AND THEIR HABITS, PREPARATION OF BAITS, &c. &c. BY FRANK FORRESTER ⟨sic⟩.

NEW YORK: PUBLISHED AT THE BROTHER JONATHAN OFFICE. ⟨1858⟩

⟨1⟩-64. 8 plates inserted; other illustrations in text. 6⁷⁄₁₆" x 4⅛".

⟨1⟩-4⁸.

Printed off-white paper wrapper.

The following reprints have been noted:

New York: Peck & Snyder, 124 Nassau Street. ⟨n.d.⟩

New York: Hurst & Co., Publishers, 122 Nassau Street. ⟨n.d⟩

New York: Thomas O'Kane, Publisher. ⟨n.d.⟩

Also reprinted and reissued under the title *Frank Forrester's ⟨sic⟩ Fishermens' Guide ... ,* New York: Advance Publishing Company ⟨n.d.⟩.

H

8163. TRICKS AND TRAPS OF HORSE DEALERS

Two printings of this work have been noted. The sequence has not been determined but internal evidence favors priority of *Printing A*. The designations are for identification only.

PRINTING A

THE TRICKS AND TRAPS OF HORSE DEALERS. BY FRANK FORESTER ... PART I.

NEW YORK: DINSMORE AND COMPANY. 1858.

Presumably all published.

⟨i⟩-⟨viii⟩, ⟨7⟩-70. 5¾" x 3¾" full. Frontispiece portrait of Herbert, p. ⟨ii⟩; 1 folded plate inserted; other illustrations in text.

⟨1-6⟩⁶.

Presumably issued in printed paper wrapper.

Location: LC

PRINTING B

NUMBER 5. ⟨of the *Tricks and Traps of New York City* series⟩ 10 CENTS. TRICKS & TRAPS OF HORSE DEALERS.

NEW YORK: DINSMORE & CO. NO. 9 SPRUCE ST. MAILED FREE TO ANY PART OF THE UNITED STATES ON RECEIPT OF PRICE. ⟨1858⟩

Cover-title. Date on basis of Van Winkle-Randall; and, date on p. 67.

⟨iii⟩-⟨viii⟩, ⟨7⟩-70. Illustrated. 5⅞" x 3⅞".

Collation:

Printed gray paper wrapper.

Query: Was the above issued with a title-leaf? The only located copy may be incomplete.

Location: BPL

8164. The New American Cyclopaedia: A Popular Dictionary of General Knowledge. Edited by George Ripley and Charles A. Dana ...

New York: D. Appleton and Company, 346 & 348 Broadway. London: 16 Little Britain. M.DCCC.LVIII. ⟨—M.DCCC.LXIII.⟩

"Archery," Vol. 2, pp. 26-30.

"Armor," Vol. 2, pp. 115-119.

"Arms," Vol. 2, pp. 119-121.

"Austerlitz," Vol. 2, pp. 370-371.

"Balaklava," Vol. 2, pp. 506-507.

"The Saint Bartholomew Massacre," Vol. 2, pp. 684-687.

"Carthage," Vol. 4, pp. 493-498.

"Charles I," Vol. 4, pp. 723-728.

"Charles II," Vol. 4, pp. 728-730.

"Charles XII," Vol. 4, pp. 747-751.

Note: According to the list of contributors in Vol. 16, Herbert may have contributed certain other anonymous articles to this publication.

For comment see entry No. 3715.

8165. HINTS TO HORSE-KEEPERS, A COMPLETE MANUAL FOR HORSEMEN; EMBRACING HOW TO BREED A HORSE. HOW TO PHYSIC A HORSE. HOW TO BUY A HORSE ... HOW TO BREAK A HORSE. HOW TO GROOM A HORSE. HOW TO USE A HORSE. HOW TO DRIVE A HORSE. HOW TO FEED A HORSE. HOW TO RIDE A HORSE. AND CHAPTERS ON MULES AND PONIES ... WITH ADDITIONS ...

NEW YORK: A. O. MOORE & COMPANY, NO. 140 FULTON STREET. 1859.

⟨1⟩-425; blank, p. ⟨426⟩; advertisements, pp. ⟨1⟩-6. Frontispiece and 23 plates inserted; other illustrations in text. 7⅜" x 4¹⁵⁄₁₆".

⟨1⟩-18¹².

A cloth: brown; red. White end papers. Yellow end papers. Flyleaves (in some copies).

"The basis of the present work is the valuable matter written by Mr. Herbert shortly before his death, comprised within the first thirteen chapters. An extension of the work was undertaken by the author, and the outline of the remaining ⟨eleven⟩ chapters was being filled out by him, when that strange and fatal mood overshadowed his life, and terminated his earthly labors.

"In committing the unfinished task to other hands, we have been particularly fortunate in procuring ... competent ... aid ..."—P. 5.

Listed BM June 15, 1859.

H   Y

8166. Frank Forester's Fish and Fishing of the United States and British Provinces of North America ... New Edition, Revised and Corrected ...

New York: W. A. Townsend & Company. 1859.

Fourth edition. For first edition see entry No. 8117.

Author's "Announcement," p. ⟨v⟩.

"I am very happy to have it in my power to add to the new edition ... the ... treatise on ... the science of tying and ... using the artificial fly, by ... 'Dinks,' ... prepared for this edition ..."—P. ⟨v⟩.

Reprints noted:

New York: W. A. Townsend, 1864.

New York: Geo. E. Woodward ⟨1859; *i.e., ca.* 1868⟩.

New York: American News Company ⟨1859; *i.e., ca.* 1877⟩.

Advertised for publication *in a few weeks* BM May 1, 1859. Advertised as *recently published* BM Sept. 1, 1859.

BA

Frank Forester's Fish and Fishing ...

New York: The American News Company, 39 and 41 Chambers Street. ⟨1859; *i.e., ca.* 1880⟩

Reprint. See entry No. 8117.

Frank Forester's Fish and Fishing ...

New York: Geo. E. Woodward, 191 Broadway. ⟨1859; *i.e., ca.* 1870⟩

Reprint. See entry No. 8117.

8167. Frank Forester's Field Sports of the United States and British Provinces of North America ... New Edition ...

New York: W. A. Townsend & Company. 1860.

2 Vols. Reprint. Other printings:

New York: W. A. Townsend, Publisher, 1864; and, *1866.*

BPL

8168. The Convert of St. Paul; or, Acté of Corinth. A Tale of Greece and Rome. By Alexandre Dumas. Translated by Henry William Herbert, Esq.

Cincinnati: Published by U. P. James, No. 167 Walnut Street. ⟨n.d., *ca.* 1860; but certainly not before 1854⟩

Printed paper wrapper.

Reprint of *Acté of Corinth,* 1847.

Y

8169. History of the Consulate and the Empire of France Under Napoleon. By M. Adolphe Thiers ... Translated by D. Forbes Campbell and H. W. Herbert. With Notes and Additions ...

Philadelphia: J. B. Lippincott & Co. 1861.

4 Vols.

"... Herbert ... had no hand in ... the translating other than the work he did on the" first edition of 1845.—Van Winkle-Randall, p. 101.

See entry No. 8088.

LC

8170. The Dog. By Dinks, Mayhew, and Hutchinson ... Complete and Revised Edition.

New York: W. A. Townsend, Publisher. 1863.

Reprint. See entry No. 8158.

Reprinted and reissued: *New York: W. A. Townsend & Adams, 1868.*

Noted as *now ready* APC Sept. 15, 1863.

NYPL

8171. The Silent Rifleman. A Tale of the Texan Prairies ...

New York: Beadle and Company, Publishers, 98 William Street. ⟨1870⟩

Printed paper wrapper.

American Tales, Second Series, No. 18; *Complete Series,* No. 62.

Reprint of *Pierre, the Partisan,* 1848. Reprinted and reissued, 1880, under the title *The Silent Rifleman, a Tale of the Texan Plains;* as *Beadle's New York Dime Library,* Vol. 9, No. 110.

LC

8172. Frank Forester's Field Sports of the United States ... New Edition ... ⟨Eighth Edition⟩

New York: Geo. E. Woodward, Publisher. ⟨1848; *i.e., ca.* 1870⟩

2 Vols.

Reprint of the *Fourth Edition,* 1852, with the word *fourth* changed to *eighth* where required in the front matter, Vol. 1.

BPL

8173. Frank Forrester's⟨sic⟩ Fishermens' Guide. A Manual for Professional and Amateuer ⟨sic⟩ Anglers ...

New York: Advance Publishing Company, Nos. 3, 4 & 5 Mission Place, & 152 Worth Street. ⟨n.d., *ca.* 1870⟩

Printed paper wrapper.

Reprint of *Fishing with Hook and Line ...* ⟨1858⟩.

H Y

8174. American Game in Its Seasons ... Revised ...

New York: George E. Woodward. Orange Judd & Co., 245 Broadway. 1873.

A cursory examination indicates that this, in spite of the statement "revised," is a reprint. Printed from the plates of the 1853 edition.

Also noted with the imprint: *New York: The American News Company* ⟨*1873*⟩.

BPL LC Y

8175. The Fair Puritan. An Historical Romance of the Days of Witchcraft ...

Philadelphia: J. B. Lippincott & Co. 1875.

Reprint of *Ruth Whalley*, 1844; *The Innocent Witch*, 1845; *The Revolt of Boston*, 1845.

BA BPL H NYPL

8175A. The Newark Herbert Association to "Frank Forester." In Memoriam, May 19, 1876 ...

Newark, N. J.: Printed by Ward & Tichenor, 832 & 834 Broad St. 1876.

"To the Press of the United States of America," pp. 22-23. Collected in entry No. 8177.

LC NYPL

8176. FRANK FORESTER'S FUGITIVE SPORTING SKETCHES; BEING THE MISCELLANEOUS ARTICLES UPON SPORT AND SPORTING, ORIGINALLY PUBLISHED IN THE EARLY AMERICAN MAGAZINES AND PERIODICALS ... EDITED, WITH A MEMOIR ... BY WILL WILDWOOD ⟨*i.e.*, Frederick Eugene Pond⟩ ...

WESTFIELD, WISCONSIN. 1879.

⟨1⟩-147; blank, p. ⟨148⟩; advertisements, pp. i-iv; plus: advertisements, pp. v-viii. $7\frac{11}{16}$" x $5\frac{1}{4}$" (in paper wrapper). $7\frac{9}{16}$" x $5\frac{3}{16}$" (in cloth).

⟨1⟩⁴, 2-10⁸; plus: ⟨11⟩².

C cloth: brownish-black. S cloth: red; terracotta. Covers bevelled. Brown-coated end papers. Flyleaves. Also: Printed gray paper wrapper.

H NYPL

8177. Frank Forester's Sporting Scenes and Characters ... a New, Revised, and Enlarged Edition. ...

Philadelphia: T. B. Peterson & Brothers; 306 Chestnut Street. ⟨1881⟩

2 Vols.

Reprint save for some material by Herbert embodied in Will Wildwood's ⟨*i.e.*, Frederick E. Pond's⟩ introductory material, Vol. 1, pp. 9-52.

H LC

8178. Life and Writings of Frank Forester ... Edited by David W. Judd ...

New York: Orange Judd Company, 751 Broadway. 1882.

2 Vols. The "third volume" referred to in the "Publisher's Preface," Vol. 1, was not issued. Contains some material here first collected.

Deposited April 29, 1882. BA copy received May 9, 1882. The London (Warne) edition was made up of American sheets and issued in two styles: In one volume with a cancel titleleaf, preliminary matter of Vol. 2 excised; and, in two volumes, each with a cancel title-leaf. Listed PC Oct. 2, 1882.

BA H

8179. POEMS OF "FRANK FORESTER" ... COLLECTED AND EDITED BY MORGAN HERBERT ⟨*i.e.*, Margaret Morgan Herbert Mather⟩

NEW YORK   JOHN WILEY & SONS   15 ASTOR PLACE 1888

⟨i⟩-⟨xxviii⟩, ⟨1⟩-251. Frontispiece and 9 plates inserted. $12\frac{1}{8}$" x $9\frac{5}{8}$".

⟨1-3⁴, 4², 5-35⁴, 36²⟩.

Loose sheets issued in a portfolio; printed cream-white paper boards sides, green V cloth shelfback, printed paper label on spine. White tape ties.

Deposited March 10, 1888. Listed PW June 30, 1888.

According to the prospectus (a copy in B) "only two hundred and fifty copies ... will be issued."

Y

8180. Tom Draw ... from the Middletown (N.Y.) Whig Press, 1846 ...

⟨n.p., n.d., *ca.* 1925⟩

Caption-title. The above at head of p. ⟨1⟩. Single cut sheet folded to four pages. Wove paper watermarked *Warren's Olde Style*.

Reprinted from entry No. 8177, Vol. 1, pp. 40-43.

Probably privately printed for T. Harry Ward.

UV Y

8181. Trouting along the Catasauqua by Frank Forester with a Foreword by Harry Worcester Smith ...

Privately Printed by Eugene V. Connett for the Anglers' Club of New York MCMXXVII

Boards, cloth shelfback, printed paper labels. 423 numbered copies only.

Reprinted from *The Life and Writings* ... , 1882.

H NYPL

8182. The Hitchcock Edition of Frank Forester

⟨New York: The Derrydale Press, 1930⟩

4 Vols. Each imprinted: MCMXXX New York The Derrydale Press

1: The Warwick Woodlands

2: My Shooting Box

3: The Quorndon Hounds

4: The Deerstalkers

750 numbered sets only.

LC NYPL

8183. Frank Forester on Upland Shooting Edited, and with Supplementary Chapters, by A. R. Beverley-Giddings ...

William Morrow and Company New York, 1951

"... chapters from two of ... ⟨Herbert's⟩ best-known works, *Field Sports* and *Complete Manual for Young Sportsmen* ..."—P. 12.

Deposited Sept. 5, 1951.

LC

UNCOLLECTED AND APOCRYPHAL WORKS

Complete Manual for Young Sportsmen. 1852. and
Young Sportsman's Complete Manual of Fowling, Fishing, and Field Sports in General, 1852.

The above titles listed by DNB. Apparently each is a garbled entry for Herbert's *The Complete Manual for Young Sportsmen* ... , 1856.

———

The following entries, alphabetically arranged, are on the basis of Van Winkle-Randall and independent research.

The Falls of Wyalusing.
Pond * (p. 17): "... produced ... *The Falls of Wyalusing* ... in 1855 ..." Pond fails to make clear whether the reference is to a periodical appearance or separate publica-

tion. Van Winkle-Randall (p. 189): "... unable to trace ... in Herbert's magazine work nor ... locate any book by that title."

Nell Gwynne. By William Harrison Ainsworth.
Van Winkle-Randall (pp. 117-118): "either re-wrote, or enlarged, or wrote a continuation, or a conclusion" of this novel "for Carey and Hart, the Philadelphia publishers ... 1850."

The Puritans of New England.
Pond * (p. 17): "... the year 1853 ... witnessed the publication of another work from H. W. Herbert's pen, *The Puritans of New England: A Historical Romance of the Days of Witchcraft* ..." Also listed by DNB as an 1853 publication with the added comment that the book was reissued under the title *The Puritan's Daughter.* Under the title *The Puritans of New England* it was advertised as *nearly ready* by Redfield in NLG during the period Aug. 15–Dec. 15, 1853; no further notices or advertisements located. Van Winkle-Randall (pp. 72-73) surmise that *The Puritans of New England* (which they report as unlocated) "is identical with" *The Fair Puritan,* 1875, which is an omnibus reprint of three of Herbert's novels issued 1844–1845; see entry No. 8175. For a fuller discussion of this problem, including contemporary references, see Van Winkle-Randall, pp. 72-73.

The Royal Maries of Medieval History.
Pond * (p. 18): "... *Royal Maries of Medieval History* was ... published after the demise of the author ..." Van Winkle-Randall (p. 189): "... left unfinished by Herbert's death, but apparently was never published, and the manuscript has disappeared." Under the title *The Marys of History* advertised by J. C. Derby as *nearly ready* NLG Aug. 1, 1855; as *shortly* APC Sept. 1, 8, 1855; and noted under "announcements" in APC from Sept. 15–Nov. 17, 1855.

Valerie: An Autobiography. By Capt. Frederick Marryat.
Van Winkle-Randall (pp. 116-117) present evidence indicating that this work, left unfinished by Marryat, was completed by Herbert. No copy found. See entry No. 8126.

———

"His most profitable literary work was the translation of French romances. Of the novels of Eugène Sue he brought out *Matilda, The Wandering Jew, The Mysteries of Paris, John Cava-*

———
* *Frank Forester's Fugitive Sporting Sketches* ... , 1879.

lier, Atar-Gull, and *The Salamander ...*"—
DNB. BAL has been unable to associate Herbert
with two of these titles: *The Mysteries of Paris*
and *John Cavalier.* The latter appears to have
been translated by William J. Snelling; see *The
New World,* Dec. 30, 1843. As for *The Mysteries
of Paris,* at least two translations were done:
One by C. H. Town (which was imported into
Great Britain in 1843 by Wiley & Putnam);
and another translation by H. C. Deming. Regarding these see advertisements in Ath Dec.
16, 1843; March 16, 1844. For further on this
problem see Van Winkle-Randall, pp. 109, 185-
189.

REPRINTS

The following publications contain material
by Herbert reprinted from earlier books.

The Juvenile Forget Me Not; a Christmas,
New Year's and Birth Day Present, for 1839.

> Philadelphia: Thomas T. Ash & Henry F.
> Anners. ⟨1838⟩
>
> Leather.

The Magnolia. 1839. With Thirteen Fine Engravings, from Original Drawings by the First
Artists.

> New York: Monson Bancroft, Broadway.
> ⟨1839⟩
>
> Reprint of entry No. 8058.
>
> Two printings noted; the order of presenta-
> tion is presumed correct:
>
> 1: Dated ⟨1839⟩
>
> 2: Issued without date.

Friendship's Token ...

> New York: Published by Leavitt & Allen, No.
> 27 Dey Street. ⟨n.d., not before 1853⟩
>
> Reissue of entry No. 8058.

Memory ...

> New York: Leavitt & Allen, 27 Dey Street.
> ⟨1854⟩
>
> Reissue of entry No. 8058.

The Snow Flake: A Christmas, New Year, and
Birthday Gift.

> New York: Leavitt and Allen, 379 Broadway.
> ⟨n.d., ca. 1856⟩
>
> Leather. A partial reprint of entry No. 8058.

Christ and the Twelve ... Edited by J. G. Holland ...

Springfield ... 1867.

> For comment see entry No. 8604.

The Spider and the Fly; or, Tricks, Traps, and
Pitfalls of City Life. By One Who Knows ...

> New York: C. Miller & Co., Publishers. 1873.
>
> Reprints Herbert's *Tricks and Traps of Horse
> Dealers,* 1858.

No. 27. Standard Recitations by Best Authors
... March, 1890 ...

> ... N. Y. ... ⟨1890⟩
>
> For comment see entry No. 4161.

An American Anthology ... Edited by Edmund
Clarence Stedman ...

> Boston ... M DCCCC
>
> For comment see entry No. 3082.

REFERENCES AND ANA

In addition to his writing Herbert was also an
illustrator and engraver. No attempt has been
made here to list the books to which he contributed illustrations. His first known appearance in any book is in an edition of Gilbert
White's *Natural History of Selborne* ⟨1833⟩
which is here included for that reason alone.

The Natural History and Antiquities of Selborne. By the Late Rev. Gilbert White. A New
Edition ...

> London: ⟨Chiswick Press, C. Whittingham,
> College House⟩ Printed for J. and A. Arch
> ... ⟨1833⟩
>
> Preface signed at p. xii: *J. R. Lee, Kent, 16th
> June, 1832.*
>
> Fly-title dated 1833.
>
> "... additional information ... has been
> contributed by the Hon. and Rev. W. H. Her-
> bert ... a number of cuts have been en-
> graved ... some ... from drawings taken on
> the spot, by a gentleman who has taken
> great interest in the publication ..."—P. xii.
> The unnamed "gentleman" was Henry Wil-
> liam Herbert. Rev. W. H. Herbert was Her-
> bert's father.
>
> Contains at least two illustrations by Her-
> bert: pp. 58 and 126.

Albert Simmons: Or, the Midshipman's Revenge. A Tale of Land & Sea. By Frank Forester ...

> Boston: Published by F. Gleason, 1 1-2 Tre-
> mont Row. 1845.

Printed paper wrapper. Not by Herbert but almost certainly by Murray Maturin Ballou.

The Godolphin Arabian; or, the History of a Thorough-Bred. By Eugene Sue . . .

New-York: E. Winchester, New World Press, XXIV Ann-Street. 1845.

Printed paper wrapper. Sometimes attributed to Herbert. Identity of translator not known.

The Hotel Lambert; or, the Engraver's Daughter. A Tale of Love and Intrigue. By Eugene Sue . . . Translated from the French by a Lady of Boston.

New-York: E. Winchester, New World Press, XXIV Ann-Street. 1845.

Almost certainly issued in printed paper wrapper. The translation sometimes attributed to Herbert; identity of translator not known. In 1851 reprinted under the title *The Princess of Hansfeld.*

The Protege of the Grand Duke. A Tale of Italy. By Frank Forester . . .

Boston: Published by F. Gleason, 1 1-2 Tremont Row. 1845 . . .

Printed paper wrapper. Not by Herbert. Almost certainly by Murray Maturin Ballou.

The Temptation; or, the Watch-Tower of Koat-Vën. A Romantic Tale. By Eugene Sue . . .

New-York: E. Winchester, New World Press, XXIV Ann-Street. 1845.

Printed paper wrapper. Sometimes attributed to Herbert. Identity of translator not known.

The Sin of Monsieur Antoine. By George Sand . . .

Published by H. L. Williams and Company. 24 Ann-St., New-York, and 22 Congress-St., Boston. 1846.

Printed paper wrapper. Sometimes attributed to Herbert. Identity of translator not known.

The Seven Capital Sins. Envy: Or, Frederick Bastien. By M. Eugene Sue . . .

New-York: Burgess, Stringer & Co., 222 Broadway. 1848.

Printed paper wrapper. Sometimes attributed to Herbert. Identity of translator not known.

The Princess of Hansfeld. A Story of Love and Intrigue. Translated from the French of Eugene Sue . . .

Published by Lorenzo Stratton, No. 131 Main Street, Cincinnati. 1851.

Printed paper wrapper. The translation sometimes attributed to Herbert. A reprint of *The Hotel Lambert* . . . , 1845, above.

The Newark Herbert Association to "Frank Forester." In Memoriam, May 19, 1876 . . .

Newark, N. J.: Printed by Ward & Tichenor, 832 & 834 Broad St. 1876.

See entry 8175A.

. . . Vox Populi Leak in the Treasury or, Fraud in the Tammany Ring! An Itemized Story in Three Acts by Henry William Herbert.

Littleton, N. H.: Courier Publishing Company, Printers, 1893.

At head of title: Vol. I. No. 1. Printed paper wrapper. Not by the subject of this list.

Under Old Rooftrees ⟨by⟩ Mrs. E. B. Hornby

Jersey City, N. J. 137 Grant Avenue MCMVIII

Three-quarters suède, cloth sides. Recollections of Herbert, pp. ⟨227⟩-238. Deposited Aug. 21, 1908.

. . . Popularity of Frank Forester's Writings . . . ⟨by⟩ Charles Sheldon.

⟨New York, 1916⟩

Single leaf. Printed on recto only. At head of title: Reprinted from Forest and Stream, April, 1916

Life and Adventures of "Ned Buntline" with Ned Buntline's Anecdote of "Frank Forester" and Chapter of Angling Sketches by Fred E. Pond . . .

New York The Cadmus Book Shop 1919

Boards, cloth shelfback, printed paper labels. 250 copies only.

Hardly worth inclusion in a list of references since it contains but a slight contribution to our knowledge of Herbert; and that by a doubtful source: E. Z. C. Judson.

The First Editions of Henry William Herbert "Frank Forester" 1807–1858 A Checklist Compiled by Paul S. Seybolt

Privately Printed Boston 1932

Printed paper wrapper. Cover-title. 60 numbered copies only.

Frank Forester [Henry William Herbert] A Tragedy in Exile by William Southworth Hunt

Newark, New Jersey The Carteret Book Club 1933

200 copies only. Deposited May 13, 1933.

Henry William Herbert [Frank Forester] A
Bibliography of His Writings 1832–1858 Com
piled by William Mitchell Van Winkle with the
Bibliographical Assistance of David A. Randall

Portland, Maine   The Southworth-Anthoen-
sen Press   1936

Deposited June 30, 1936.

Henry William Herbert & the American Publishing Scene 1831–1858 by Luke White, Jr.

Newark, New Jersey   The Carteret Book
Club   1943

200 numbered copies only. Deposited July 2.
1943.

THOMAS WENTWORTH STORROW HIGGINSON

1 8 2 3 – 1 9 1 1

Higginson was an active member of many civic, religious and other groups to whose publications he contributed letters and other like material. The present list does not pretend to record all such appearances.

8184. Our Book. A Call from Salem's Watch-Towers, in Behalf of Destitute Churches of the Unitarian Faith. September 5, 1844.

Salem: Printed at the Gazette Office. 1844.

Boards, printed paper label on spine.

"La Madonna di San Sisto," anonymous, pp. 35-36. Collected in *Afternoon Landscape*, 1889.

H   NYPL

8185. The Liberty Bell. By Friends of Freedom . . .

Boston: Massachusetts Anti-Slavery Fair. MDCCCXLVI.

"Sonnet to William Lloyd Garrison," miscredited to J. W. Higginson, pp. 19-20.

For comment see entry No. 6495.

8186. Hymns, for the Rural Anti-Slavery Celebration, at Dedham, July 4, 1846 . . .

⟨n.p., n.d., Dedham, Mass., July 4, 1846⟩

Single cut sheet. Printed on recto only.

Prints *inter alia* Higginson's "National Anti-Slavery Hymn. 4th July, 1846. Written for the occasion . . ." *See next entry.*

B

8187. A Book of Hymns for Public and Private Devotion.

Cambridge: Metcalf and Company, Printers to the University. 1846.

Contains the following hymns by Higginson, each published here anonymously. Higginson's

copy (at H) has the authorship identified in a series of pencilled notes. The number given is that of the hymn, not the page.

"Prayer for Guidance," No. 34. Collected in *Afternoon Landscape*, 1889, as "I Will Arise and Go unto My Father."

"God Known through Love," No. 76. Collected in *Afternoon Landscape*, 1889, as "Pantheism and Theism."

"The Hope of Man," No. 187. Collected in *Afternoon Landscape*, 1889.

"American Slavery," No. 436. Presumably reprinted from the preceding entry where the hymn appears under the title "National Anti-Slavery Hymn."

For comment see entry No. 1630.

8188. University of Cambridge. Order of Exercises at the Thirty-First Annual Visitation of the Divinity School, Friday, July 16, 1847.

Cambridge: Metcalf and Company, Printers to the University. 1847.

Cover-title. Single leaf folded to four pages.

"Hymn," *To veil thy truth by darkening or by hiding*, p. 4.

H

8189. The Gospel of To-day. A Discourse Delivered at the Ordination of T. W. Higginson, as Minister of the First Religious Society in Newburyport, Mass., Sept. 15, 1847. By William Henry Channing . . .

Boston: Wm. Crosby and H. P. Nichols, 111 Washington Street. Newburyport: A. A. Call. 1847.

Printed paper wrapper.

"To the Committee of the First Religious Society in Newburyport," a letter dated Aug. 11, 1847, pp. 60-63.

Listed NAR Jan. 1848.

BA H LC NYPL

8190. The Liberty Bell. By Friends of Freedom . . .

Boston: National Anti-Slavery Bazaar.
MDCCCXLVIII.

"The Fugitives' Hymn," pp. 94-96.

H NYPL

8191. A SERMON: PREACHED AT THE
PLEASANT STREET CHURCH, NEW-
BURYPORT, THANKSGIVING DAY,
(NOV. 30, 1848.) . . . "MAN SHALL NOT
LIVE BY BREAD ALONE." . . .

NEWBURYPORT: HUSE & BRAGDON, ADVERTISER
PRESS. 1848.

All examined copies have the error *Mathew* for
Matthew on the title-page.

Cover-title.

⟨i-ii⟩, ⟨1⟩-4, blank leaf. 10½″ x 7⁹⁄₁₆″.

⟨-⟩⁴.

Printed self-wrapper.

"To the Editors of the Newburyport Advertiser:
Dear Sirs:— Your Friday's paper stated correctly my reasons for finally accepting your offer
to print my sermon. In view of the incorrect
verbal and printed reports which have gone
abroad, I regard this as simple justice to myself
and others . . ."—P. ⟨ii⟩. This notice suggests
that the sermon may have had prior separate
publication but no such possible printing has
been located. See next entry for a revised
edition.

BPL H

8192. "Man Shall Not Live by Bread Alone."
A Thanksgiving Sermon: Preached in Newburyport, Nov. 30, 1848 . . . Second Edition.

Newburyport: Charles Whipple. Boston:
Crosby & Nichols. 1848.

A somewhat revised version of the preceding
entry.

Pp. ⟨1⟩-12. Printed paper wrapper.

H Y

8193. Æsthetic Papers. Edited by Elizabeth P.
Peabody . . .

Boston: The Editor, 13, West Street. New
York: G. P. Putnam, 155, Broadway. 1849.

"The Twofold Being," pp. 245-246.

For comment see entry No. 5217.

8194. THE TONGUE: TWO PRACTICAL
SERMONS . . .

NEWBURYPORT: PUBLISHED BY A. AUGUSTUS CALL.
1850.

⟨1⟩-18. 8⅝″ x 5⁷⁄₁₆″.

⟨1-2⁴, 3¹⟩.

Printed paper wrapper: green; tan.

H copy inscribed by early owner Feb. 1850.

AAS H LC

8195. ADDRESS TO THE CITIZENS, IN BE-
HALF OF THE PUBLIC LIBRARY . . .
⟨by⟩ L. F. DIMMICK, CALEB CUSHING,
T. W. HIGGINSON . . .

NEWBURYPORT, SEPT. 19, 1850.

Single cut sheet. Printed on recto only. 19⅝″ x
13½″.

H copy inscribed by Higginson: *T. W. Higginson "Author of the address, with a few words
changed by other members of committee."*

H

8196. MR. HIGGINSON'S ADDRESS TO
THE VOTERS OF THE THIRD CON-
GRESSIONAL DISTRICT OF MASSACHU-
SETTS.

LOWELL: C. L. KNAPP, PRINTER, APPLETON BLOCK.
1850.

Cover-title.

⟨1⟩-7. 9⅛″ x 6³⁄₁₆″.

⟨-⟩⁴.

Printed self-wrapper.

Dated at end: Oct. 23, 1850.

BPL H LC NYPL

8197. THE BIRTHDAY IN FAIRY-LAND: A
STORY FOR CHILDREN . . .

BOSTON: WM. CROSBY AND H. P. NICHOLS, 111,
WASHINGTON STREET. 1850.

⟨1⟩-23. 6¹⁄₁₆″ x 3¾″.

⟨-⟩¹².

Printed peach paper wrapper.

H Y

8198. The Liberty Bell. By Friends of Freedom . . .

Boston: National Anti-Slavery Bazaar.
MDCCCLI.

"To a Young Convert," pp. 239-240. Collected in *Afternoon Landscape,* 1889.

A copy in H inscribed by original owner 1850.

H

8199. MERCHANTS: A SUNDAY EVENING LECTURE ...

NEWBURYPORT: A. A. CALL, PUBLISHER, HUSE AND BRAGDON, PRINTERS. 1851.

‹1›-31. 8⅞" x 5⁷⁄₁₆".

‹1›-2⁶, 3⁴.

Printed paper wrapper: blue; faun; green.

"... published by request. January 29, 1851."
—P. ‹2›.

BPL   H   Y

8200. Report of the Free Evening School ...

‹n.p., n.d., Newburyport, Mass., 1851›

Single cut sheet. Printed on both sides.

Issued after March 1, 1851.

CPL   H

8201. Senate ... No. 89. Commonwealth of Massachusetts. In Senate, April 9, 1851 ...

‹n.p., n.d., Boston: The Commonwealth of Massachusetts, 1851›

Cover-title?

One paragraph of testimony before the committee on personal liberty, p. 27.

Y

8202. The Annual Report of the School Committee of the Town of Newbury, for ... 1850–51.

Newburyport: Huse & Bragdon, Daily Union Press. 1851.

Cover-title. Printed paper wrapper.

Signed by Higginson and others.

H

8203. ‹Letter on Temperance›

Newburyport, Mass., Sept. 13, 1851 ...

Single cut sheet. Printed on recto only. Blue-gray wove paper.

"At a Temperance Convention recently held in this city, the undersigned were appointed a committee ..."

Signed at end by Higginson and others.

H

8204. All about the Maine Liquor Law. New-England Temperance Journal,—Extra. Published Simultaneously in Boston and in Worcester, by Goodrich, Brown & Co. (of Worcester,) for the Massachusetts "Central Executive Board." Orders Supplied at $5 per 1000 Copies ...

‹Boston and Worcester, October, 1851›

Caption-title. The above at head of p. ‹37›. Paged: ‹37›-40.

Resolutions as reported by Higginson, p. 40.

H

8205. To Every Temperance Man in Massachusetts. Additional Petitions!

Boston, Jan. 28, 1852 ...

Single cut sheet. Printed on recto only.

Letter, with *Petition to the Legislature.* *"The State Temperance Committee beg leave to call your attention to the importance of immediately circulating Petitions in aid of the previous Petitions for the Maine Law ..."*

H

8206. The Liberty Bell. By Friends of Freedom ...

Boston: National Anti-Slavery Bazaar. MDCCCLII.

"Forward!," p. 303; translated from von Fallersleben. Collected in *Such as They Are,* 1893.

Higginson's copy (in H) inscribed by the editor Jan. 1852.

Erratum, p. ‹304›.

H   NYPL

8207. The Ministry at Large on the Liquor Law. From the Massachusetts Life Boat ...

‹n.p., Boston (?), 1852›

Single cut sheet. Letter to Higginson from William H. Hadley, dated *Portland, March 10, 1852,* preceded by a fifteen-line introductory note signed *T.W.H.*

H

8208. Circular ... ‹Letter addressed to *Dear Sir,* dated at end:›

Boston, Sept. 18, 1852.

Single cut sheet. Printed on recto only. Signed at end by Higginson and others for the *State Temperance Committee*.

H

8209. THINGS NEW AND OLD: AN IN-STALLATION SERMON ...

WORCESTER: PRINTED FOR THE ⟨WORCESTER FREE CHURCH⟩ SOCIETY, BY EARLE & DREW, 212 MAIN STREET. 1852.

⟨1⟩-30, blank leaf. 9³⁄₁₆″ x 5¾″.

⟨1⟩-4⁴.

Printed paper wrapper: green, pink, tan, white.

The sermon was delivered Sept. 5, 1852. The printed publication listed NLG Oct. 15, 1852.

H NYPL

8210. ELEGY WITHOUT FICTION. A SERMON, PREACHED OCTOBER 31st, 1852 ...

⟨n.p., n.d., Worcester, Mass., 1852⟩

Caption-title. The above at head of first column. Single cut sheet. Printed on recto only. 20½″ x 13″. Text in 4 columns.

Printed from the types of *The Daily Spy* (Worcester, Mass). At the foot of the final column is a wholly irrelevant space-filler.

AAS BPL CPL H Y

8211. ⟨LETTER ON TEMPERANCE⟩

WORCESTER, DEC. 31, 1852 ...

Single cut sheet. Blue-gray laid paper. Printed on recto only. 10″ x 7¹¹⁄₁₆″.

"I take the liberty to address you as a friend of good morals, and of the Temperance cause ..."

H

8212. ... The Unitarian Congregational Register, for the Year 1853. Printed for the American Unitarian Association.

Boston: Crosby, Nichols, and Company, 111 Washington Street. Price 5 Cents. ⟨n.d., 1852⟩

Printed paper wrapper. At head of title: Annual Series. No. 3.

"The Past and the Future," pp. 69-70.

NYPL

8213. Address to the Citizens of Worcester ... Young Men's Library Association ...

⟨n.p., n.d., Worcester, Mass., 1852⟩

Single cut sheet. Printed on recto only.

An appeal for contributions. Signed at end by Higginson and others.

CPL H

8214. TO THE YOUNG MEN OF WORCESTER COUNTY. FELLOW CITIZENS: ⟨letter appealing for the formation of Freedom Clubs⟩

... FREEDOM CLUB OF WORCESTER. GEO. F. THOMPSON, PRESIDENT. WM. DAME, SECRETARY, ⟨sic⟩ ⟨n.d., 1852⟩

Single cut sheet. Printed on recto only. Blue paper. 9¹⁵⁄₁₆″ x 7⅞″. Anonymous.

The copy in H inscribed by Higginson: *Written by T. W. Higginson.*

CPL H

8215. The Liberty Bell. By Friends of Freedom ...

Boston: National Anti-Slavery Bazaar. MD-CCCLIII.

In all examined copies: P. *135* mispaged *185*.

"The Morning Mist," pp. 102-103. Collected in *Afternoon Landscape*, 1889.

"Am I My Brother's Keeper," pp. 145-160.

Higginson's copy (in H) inscribed by the editor Dec. 23, 1852.

H

8216. Address of the State Temperance Committee to the Citizens of Massachusetts on the Operation of the Anti-Liquor Law ...

⟨Boston, January 21, 1853⟩

Caption-title. Printed self-wrapper. Signed at end by Higginson and others.

AAS NYPL

8217. Thalatta: A Book for the Sea-Side ...

Boston: Ticknor, Reed, and Fields. MDCCC-LIII.

Edited anonymously by Higginson and Samuel Longfellow.

"The Morning Mist," p. 204, here reprinted. Previously in *The Liberty Bell*, 1853 (Dec. 1852).

For comment see entry No. 1380.

8218. WOMAN AND HER WISHES; AN ESSAY: INSCRIBED TO THE MASSACHUSETTS CONSTITUTIONAL CONVENTION ...

BOSTON: ROBERT F. WALLCUT, 21 CORNHILL. 1853.

⟨1⟩-26, blank leaf. 9⁷⁄₁₆″ x 5¹¹⁄₁₆″.

⟨1⟩-3⁴, 4².

Printed self-wrapper.

Cover-title.

This essay has been noted as follows:

First Edition

As described above. Does not contain Higginson's "Remarks" of June 3, 1853.

Second Edition

Extended by the addition of Higginson's "Remarks" of June 3, 1853. Of this second edition there were printings from two different settings. No sequence has been established and the following designations are for identification only:

A: Issued with the imprint: *New York: Fowlers and Wells ... Boston ... 1853 ... London ...* Cover-title. Printed self-wrapper. Copies in BPL H LC.

B: Issued as *Woman's Rights Tracts No. 4.* Issued without date not after 1854. Printed self-wrapper. Title at head of p. 1. Copies in BPL and H.

Second Edition, Second Issue

Copies of *Second Edition, Printing B,* brought together with Nos. 1, 2, 3, 5, of the series and issued in printed paper wrapper. On front of wrapper: ⟨double rule⟩ / Woman's Rights Tracts. / ⟨double rule⟩ Possibly issued *ca.* 1860. Copy in H.

Second Edition, Third Issue

Copies of *Second Edition, Printing B,* brought together with Nos. 1, 2, 3, 5, of the series and issued as a single volume. Two formats issued, in all likelihood simultaneously:

A: Cloth. Inserted title-page; and, inserted "Preface" by Lucy Stone. Title-page reads: *Woman's Rights Tracts ... Wendell Phillips ... Theodore Parker ... Mrs. John Stuart Mills* ⟨sic⟩ *... T. W. Higginson ... Mrs. C. I. H. Nichols.* ⟨n.p., n.d., 1893?⟩

B: Printed paper wrapper. Inserted "Preface" by Lucy Stone. Front of wrapper imprinted: *Woman's Rights Tracts ... Wendell Phillips ... Theodore Parker ... Mrs. John Stuart Mills* ⟨sic⟩ *... T. W. Higginson ... Mrs. C. I. H. Nichols.* ⟨n.p., n.d., 1893?⟩

On the basis of inscribed copies in BA, BPL, H, MHS and Y, this issue appears to have been prepared for distribution in Oct. 1893.

Also noted in an omnibus publication dated 1854. See entry No. 8226.

A copy of the first edition (described above) in AAS inscribed by early owner May 21, 1853. Listed as a May publication NLG June 15, 1853. The London (Chapman) edition advertised as *this day* Ath Jan. 7, 1854.

AAS   H   MHS   NYPL   Y

8219. REMARKS OF REV. T. W. HIGGINSON BEFORE THE COMMITTEE OF THE CONSTITUTIONAL CONVENTION ON THE QUALIFICATION OF VOTERS, JUNE 3d, 1853 ...

⟨n.p., 1853⟩

Note: The comma after *Voters* is absent in some copies.

Single cut sheet. 17″ full x 7¹⁵⁄₁₆. Printed on recto only.

H   Y

8220. The Whole World's Temperance Convention Held at Metropolitan Hall in the City of New York on Thursday and Friday, Sept. 1st and 2d, 1853 ...

New York: Fowlers and Wells, Publishers, Clinton Hall, 131 Nassau Street. 1853.

Printed paper wrapper.

Edited by Higginson; and, remarks, pp. 4, 5; and, address, pp. 12-14.

AAS   NYPL

8221. THE UNITARIAN AUTUMNAL CONVENTION, A SERMON ...

BOSTON: BENJAMIN B. MUSSEY & CO. 1853.

⟨1⟩-14, blank leaf. 9⅛″ scant x 5⅝″.

⟨-⟩⁸.

Printed tan paper wrapper.

AAS   H   NYPL

8222. To the Friends of the Cause of Woman ... January 15, 1854 ...

⟨n.p., probably Worcester, Mass., 1854⟩

Single cut sheet, blue laid paper, folded to make four pages. Printed on p. ⟨1⟩ only.

An appeal for information to be used in "the preparation of two essays, one on the *Educational Opportunities* of American Women, and one other on their *Business Opportunities."* Signed at end by Higginson and others.

BPL H NYPL

8223. MASSACHUSETTS IN MOURNING. A SERMON, PREACHED IN WORCESTER, ON SUNDAY, JUNE 4, 1854 ... REPRINTED ... FROM THE WORCESTER DAILY SPY.

BOSTON: JAMES MUNROE AND COMPANY. 1854.

⟨1⟩-15. 9⅚₆″ x 5¹³⁄₁₆″.

⟨-⟩⁸.

Printed tan paper wrapper.

AAS BA H NYPL

8224. THE WORCESTER CARSON LEAGUE ...

WORCESTER, OCT. 2, 1854 ...

Single cut sheet. Printed on recto only. 13″ x 6⅞″.

H

8225. SCRIPTURE IDOLATRY. A DISCOURSE ...

WORCESTER: JOHN KEITH AND COMPANY, 1854. PRICE 5 CENTS SINGLE; 37½ CENTS PER DOZEN.

Cover-title.

⟨1⟩-16. 7″ x 4⁷⁄₁₆″.

⟨-⟩⁸.

Printed self-wrapper.

Issued in London by Holyoake & Company, n.d., not after 1857.

AAS BA H MHS

8226. Woman's Rights Tracts. ⟨By⟩ Wendell Phillips ... T. W. Higginson ... Stereotype Edition.

Boston: Robert F. Wallcut, 21 Cornhill. 1854.

Reprint. See *Woman and Her Wishes,* 1853, above.

BPL

8227. Report of the School Committee of the City of Worcester, for the Year Ending December 31, 1854.

Worcester: Printed by Henry J. Howland, 199 Main Street, rear of Union Block. ⟨n.d., 1855⟩

⟨59⟩-106, blank leaf. 8¹³⁄₁₆″ x 5½″ full. Printed paper wrapper.

Prepared by Higginson and others.

NYPL

8228. ... DOES SLAVERY CHRISTIANIZE THE NEGRO? ...

⟨NEW YORK: AMERICAN ANTI-SLAVERY SOCIETY, n.d., 1854? 1855?⟩

Caption-title. Preceding at head of p. 1. At head of title: ANTI-SLAVERY TRACTS. NO. 4.

1-8. 7¹¹⁄₁₆″ x 4¾″.

1⁴.

Printed self-wrapper.

"Published for gratuitous distribution, at the Office of the American Anti-Slavery Society ... New York ... Boston ... Philadelphia."—P. 8.

Higginson, p. 406, dates this 1854. The BA copy inscribed by early owner March 10, 1855. Dated 1855 by LC.

"... we have set on foot a system of *Tract* publication ... The *Tracts* are intended for gratuitous distribution ... Fifteen *Tracts* have been issued and stereotyped, and great numbers distributed over the Country. Other *Tracts* will follow ..."—*Annual Report* ⟨22nd⟩, *Presented to the American Anti-Slavery Society* ... , N. Y., 1855, p. 111; issued after May 7, 1855. The report covers the period May 1, 1854–May 1, 1855.

"The enterprise of a wide ... distribution of ... Tracts ... was first undertaken ... in the autumn of 1854."—*Annual Reports* ⟨24th, 25th⟩ *of the American Anti-Slavery Society,* N. Y., 1859, p. 189.

AAS BA H NYPL

8229. ... Proceedings of the Anti-Slavery Meeting Held in Stacy Hall, Boston, on the Twentieth Anniversary of the Mob of October 21, 1835. Phonographic Report by J. M. W. Yerrinton.

Boston: Published by R. F. Wallcut. 1855.

Printed paper wrapper. At head of title: The Boston Mob of "Gentlemen of Property and Standing."

Speech, pp. 53-58.

H NYPL

8230. Proceedings of the Seventh ⟨i.e., *Sixth*⟩ National Woman's Rights Convention, Held in New York City, at the Broadway Tabernacle, on Tuesday and Wednesday, Nov. 25th and 26th, 1856 ...

New York: Edward O. Jenkins, Printer, Nos. 26 and 28 Frankfort Street. 1856.

Printed paper wrapper.

Remarks summarized, pp. 9-10, 28-34, 36-37, 39-41. Address, pp. 59-66. For a separate printing of the address see entry No. 8286. Also see entry No. 8243.

H NYPL

8231. ... A RIDE THROUGH KANZAS ...

⟨New York, n.d., 1856–1858⟩

Caption-title. The preceding at head of p. ⟨1⟩. At head of title: ANTI-SLAVERY TRACTS. NO. 20.; *but see note below.*

⟨1⟩-24. 7⁹⁄₁₆″ x 4¾″.

⟨1⟩-2⁶.

Printed self-wrapper.

At foot of p. 24: *Published ... at the Office of the American Anti-Slavery Society ... New York ... Boston ... Philadelphia ... Salem, Columbiana Co., Ohio.* See note below.

Note: Two printings have been noted. Sequence (if any) not determined. The designations are for identification only.

A: With the statement at head of title: *Anti-Slavery Tracts. No. 20.;* and, publication note at foot of p. 24.

B: Without the two features noted in *Printing A* above.

The text comprises a series of letters written, and so dated, during the period Sept. 12, 1856–Oct. 20, 1856. According to the several published reports of the American Anti-Slavery Society this series of tracts was started in the autumn of 1854. In the report for the year ending May 1, 1855, the Society reported publication of Tracts 1-15; in the report for 1855–1856, it reported publication of Tracts 16-17; in the report for the years ending May 1, 1857, May 1, 1858, the Society reported publication of Tracts 18-20.

AAS (A, B)   H (B)   NYPL (A)

8232. SPEECH ... AT THE WORCESTER DISUNION CONVENTION, JANUARY 15th, 1857. (PHONOGRAPHIC REPORT BY J. M. W. YERRINGTON ⟨sic⟩.) ...

⟨n.p., n.d., 1857⟩

Single cut sheet. Printed on recto only. 16¼″ x 9¾″.

Note: Appears also in: *Proceedings of the State Disunion Convention, Held at Worcester ... January 15, 1857. Phonographically Reported by J.M.W. Yerrinton,* Boston: Printed for the

Committee, 1857. In this publication the address appears at pp. 25-31; and, also contains resolutions by Higginson, pp. 11-12, 58.

AAS (separate)   H (both)   NYPL (pamphlet)

8233. Speech at the Twenty-Fifth Anniversary of the Massachusetts Anti-Slavery Society.

1857.

Not located. Broadside. Entry on the basis of Higginson, p. 407. The address has been seen in *The Liberator* (Boston), Jan. 16, 1857. The anniversary was celebrated at Faneuil Hall, Boston, Jan. 2, 1857. Otherwise unlocated.

8234. Statement on Spiritual Manifestations, April 15, 1857.

1857.

Not located. Broadside. Entry on the basis of Higginson, p. 407.

8235. THE NEW REVOLUTION: A SPEECH BEFORE THE AMERICAN ANTI-SLAVERY SOCIETY, AT THEIR ANNUAL MEETING IN NEW YORK, MAY 12, 1857 ...

BOSTON: R. F. WALLCUT, 21 CORNHILL. 1857.

Cover-title.

⟨1⟩-16. 9¹⁄₁₆″ x 5½″.

⟨1⟩-2⁴.

Printed self-wrapper.

AAS   BA   H   NYPL   Y

8236. Call for a Northern Convention. Whereas it must be obvious to all, that the American Union is constantly becoming more and more divided, by Slavery ... The undersigned respectfully invite their fellow citizens of the the Free States to meet in Convention, at ———————— in October, 1857 ...

⟨Worcester, July 8, 1857⟩

Single cut sheet, folded to make four pages. The above at head of p. ⟨1⟩.

P. ⟨1⟩: As above.

P. ⟨2⟩: Blank.

Pp. ⟨3-4⟩: Text of a letter, Worcester, July 8, 1857, signed at end by Higginson and others, beginning: *The State Disunion Convention ... recommended a National Convention ...*

Note: The *Call* was reprinted on a single cut sheet, 12⅜″ x 7¾″, printed on recto only. In this later printing are added the names of certain of the signers to the *Call* and the place and date of proposed convention: *Cleveland, Ohio, Oct. 28-29, 1857*. The explanatory letter which appears in the first printing of the *Call*, pp. ⟨3-4⟩, is not present.

H (both) Y (1st)

8237. . . . SONGS FOR CHRISTMAS FESTI-VAL, 1857 . . . THE CHRISTMAS TREE . . . GOOD BYE! THE OLD YEAR . . .

⟨WORCESTER, MASS.: WORCESTER FREE CHURCH, 1857⟩

Single cut sheet. At head of title: WORCESTER FREE CHURCH. Printed on recto only. 9⅝″ x 5¾″.

Anonymous. The copy in H is marked by Higginson indicating his authorship of the songs.

B H

8238. The Psalms of Life: A Compilation of Psalms, Hymns, Chants, Anthems, &c. . . . ⟨Compiled⟩ by John S. Adams . . .

Boston: Published by Oliver Ditson & Co. New York . . . Philadelphia . . . Cincinnati . . . ⟨1857⟩

"Strength of the Erring," p. 172.

H

8239. Tales and Sketches for the Fire-Side, by the Best American Authors. Selected from Putnam's Magazine.

New York: A. Dowling, 36 Beekman Street 1857.

An omnibus volume made up of the sheets of *Putnam's Monthly Magazine* for Aug.–Sept., 1853; Oct.–Dec., 1854; July, 1855, issued with inserted title-page as above. Irregular pagination.

"The Lovers," in issue of Sept. 1853.

"African Proverbial Philosophy," in issue of Oct. 1854.

HSM

8240. The Woman's Rights Almanac for 1858. Containing Facts, Statistics, Arguments, Records of Progress, and Proofs of the Need of It.

Worcester, Mass: ⟨sic⟩ Z. Baker & Co., 184 Main Street. Boston: R. F. Walcutt ⟨sic⟩, 21 Cornhill. ⟨n.d., 1857? 1858?⟩

Cover-title.

Anonymously edited by Higginson and Lucy Stone according to Higginson, p. 407.

Printed self-wrapper.

H LC NYPL

8241. The Liberty Bell. By Friends of Freedom . . .

Boston: National Anti-Slavery Bazaar, MD-CCCLVIII.

"The Romance of History in 1850," pp. 47-53.

H NYPL

8242. The Religious Aspects of the Age, with a Glance at the Church of the Present and the Church of the Future . . . Addresses Delivered at the Anniversary of the Young Men's Christian Union of New York, on the 13th and 14th Days of May, 1858 . . .

New York: Thatcher & Hutchinson, 523 (St. Nicholas Hotel) Broadway. 1858.

"Woman in Christian Civilization," pp. 79-88.

Printed paper wrapper.

H

8243. Consistent Democracy. The Elective Franchise for Women. Twenty-Five Testimonies of Prominent Men, *viz:* Ex-Gov. Anthony . . . Rev. T. W. Higginson . . . ⟨and others⟩

Worcester . . . Boston . . . New York . . . Salem, O. . . . Rochester, N. Y. . . . 1858.

Single cut sheet folded to four pages. The above on p. ⟨1⟩.

Higginson's statement, p. ⟨2⟩, is a condensed and somewhat altered extract from his address in entry No. 8230. Also see entry No. 8286.

LC

8244. THE RATIONALE OF SPIRITUAL-ISM. BEING TWO EXTEMPORANEOUS LECTURES DELIVERED AT DOD-WORTH'S HALL, DECEMBER 5, 1858 . . . REPORTED, PHONOGRAPHICALLY, BY T. J. ELLINWOOD.

NEW YORK: T. J. ELLINWOOD, PUBLISHER, 5 TYRON ROW. 1859.

⟨1⟩-32. 9⁹⁄₁₆″ x 5¾″.

⟨1⟩-2⁸.

Printed tan paper wrapper.

AAS H NYPL

8245. THE RESULTS OF SPIRITUALISM, A DISCOURSE, DELIVERED AT DOD-WORTH'S HALL, SUNDAY, MARCH 6, 1859 ... PHONOGRAPHICALLY REPORTED.

NEW YORK: S. T. MUNSON, 5 GREAT JONES ST. ‹n.d., 1859›

Cover-title.

‹1›-21, blank leaf. 7⅛" x 4¹⁵⁄₁₆".

‹-›¹².

Printed self-wrapper.

AAS   H   NYPL   Y

8246. Circular. Boston, Nov. 2, 1859. Dear Sir: —You are invited and urged to contribute and obtain contributions to aid in the defence of Capt. ‹John› Brown and his companions, on trial for their lives in Virginia ...

‹Boston, 1859›

Single cut sheet. Printed on recto only. Signed at end by Higginson and others.

BPL

8247. The Public Life of Capt. John Brown, by James Redpath ...

Boston: Thayer and Eldridge, 114 and 116 Washington St. 1860.

"The Route to North Elba," pp. 60-72. Collected in *Contemporaries*, 1899, as "A Visit to John Brown's House in 1859."

JB copy inscribed by early owner Dec. 1859.

AAS   H

8248. Second Annual Report of the Directors of the Free Public Library, Worcester.

Worcester: Printed by Order of the Directors. 1862.

‹1›-15. 9⅛" x 5¼". Printed gray paper wrapper.

On p. 14 is the statement: *For the Board, W. W. Rice* ... However, a copy in H is inscribed by Higginson indicating that he, and not Rice, was the sole author of the report.

H

8249. OUT-DOOR PAPERS ...

BOSTON   TICKNOR AND FIELDS   1863

‹i-iv›, ‹1›-370, blank leaf. Laid paper. 7¹⁄₁₆" x 4⁹⁄₁₆".

‹-›², ‹A›-W⁸, ‹X›². *Also signed:* ‹-›², 1-15¹², 16⁶.

HC cloth: brown; purple. TR cloth: brown. Z cloth: purple-brown. Brown-coated on white end papers. Laid paper flyleaves (usual). Wove paper flyleaves noted only in *Binding B;* see below.

Note: Two styles of stamping noted. The sequence has not been determined and the designations are for identification only:

Stamping A

Sides blindstamped with a rules border, a leaf ornament at each corner.

At center of sides: A blindstamped wreath.

A leaf-like pendant on the publisher's device at foot of spine.

Laid paper flyleaves.

Stamping B

Sides blindstamped with a rules border, twisted at each corner to form a quatrefoil ornament.

Center of sides unstamped.

A lozenge-shaped pendant on publisher's device at foot of spine.

Wove paper flyleaves.

Prematurely advertised in *Boston Daily Evening Transcript,* July 2, 1862, as *in press,* with title given as *Out-Door Life.* Announced APC May 1, 1863; LG May 1, 1863. Deposited June 12, 1863. Listed APC June 15, 1863; PC March 1, 1864.

BPL (A)   H (A)   LC (A, being a deposit copy) Y (A, B)

8250. First Anniversary of the Proclamation of Freedom in South Carolina, Held at Beaufort, S. C., January 1, 1864.

Free South Print, Wilkes & Thompson, Proprietors, Beaufort, S. C. 1864.

"Reply of Colonel Higginson," p. 17.

Printed paper wrapper.

H

8251. Memorial RGS ‹Robert Gould Shaw›

Cambridge University Press 1864

Letter, Aug. 30, 1863, pp. 150-151.

For comment see entry No. 3197.

8252. The Works of Epictetus ... a Translation from the Greek Based on That of Elizabeth Carter, by Thomas Wentworth Higginson.

Boston: Little, Brown, and Company. 1865.

⟨i-ii⟩, ⟨i⟩-⟨xviii⟩, ⟨1⟩-437, blank leaf. Laid paper. 7¹³⁄₁₆″ x 5″. Also a large paper edition, limited to 75 copies, imprint dated 1866, 8⅞″ x 5⅞″. Both formats simultaneously issued?

Advertised ALG Sept. 1, 1865, for Sept. 9, 1865. Advertised ALG Sept. 15, 1865, as *new*. Listed ALG Oct. 2, 1865. Noticed ALG Oct. 2, 1865. Listed PC Nov. 1, 1865. See under 1890 for another edition.

H (1865, 1866)   Y (1865)

8253. Harvard Memorial Biographies . . .

Cambridge: Sever and Francis. 1866.

2 Vols. Errata slip inserted between pp. ⟨ii-iii⟩, Vol. 2.

Edited by Higginson.

"Preface," pp. ⟨iii⟩-vi, Vol. 1.

Also contains the following sketches by Higginson:

Vol. 1

"James Richardson," pp. 41-53.

"Charles Francis Simmons," pp. 54-63.

"William Logan Rodman," pp. 64-78.

"Arthur Buckminster Fuller," pp. 79-94.

"John Franklin Goodrich," pp. 136-141.

"Lucius Manlius Sargent," pp. 142-146.

"Daniel Hack," pp. 371-372. A revision by Charles H. Brigham appears in the edition of 1867.

"Stephen George Perkins," pp. 373-381.

"Samuel Henry Eells," pp. 415-421.

Vol. 2

"Thomas Joseph Leavitt," pp. 259-260. A revision by a Miss C. Leavitt appears in the edition of 1867.

"James Ingersoll Grafton," pp. 283-288.

"Henry French Brown," pp. 391-392.

"Samuel Storrow," pp. 462-474.

BPL copy received Oct. 2, 1866. Listed PC Sept. 2, 1867. See under 1867 for revised edition.

H   Y

8254. Free Religion. Report of Addresses at a Meeting Held in Boston, May 30, 1867, to Consider the Conditions, Wants, and Prospects of Free Religion in America . . .

Boston: Published by Adams & Co. No. 25 Bromfield Street. ⟨n.d., 1867⟩

Printed wrapper.

"Remarks . . . ," pp. 48-52.

BA   H   NYPL

8255. Harvard Memorial Biographies . . .

Cambridge: Sever and Francis. 1867.

2 Vols. Cloth; and, half leather.

Edited by Higginson.

Revised edition. For first edition see above under 1866.

Listed ALG Aug. 1, 1867.

H   NYPL

8256. Slave Songs of the United States. ⟨Edited by William Francis Allen, Charles Pickard Ware, and Lucy McKim Garrison⟩

New York: A. Simpson & Co., 1867.

Part of Higginson's article, "Negro Spirituals," *The Atlantic Monthly*, June, 1867, pp. ix-x, xvii-xviii.

Noted as *in press* ALG Sept. 16, 1867. Listed ALG Dec. 2, 1867. Deposited Dec. 4, 1867.

H

8257. Annual Report of the School Committee of the City of Newport, R. I. . . . 1866-67.

Newport, R. I: ⟨*sic*⟩ Daily News Steam Printing Press. 1867.

Printed wrapper.

Report, pp. ⟨1⟩-3.

H

8258. Newport Free Public Library . . .

⟨n.p., n.d., Newport, 1867?⟩

Single cut sheet folded to make four pages. Caption-title. Signed by Higginson and others.

An appeal for "contributions in books and money"; and a statement of the history, organization, operation and needs of the library.

"The Directors of this institution take this method of respectfully calling the attention of the community to its history, plan, operation and needs."—P. ⟨1⟩.

H

8259. THE NONSENSE OF IT

Issued as an argument in favor of woman suffrage. BAL has noted four separate printings (undoubtedly there were others) as follows. The sequence of the first two has not been established.

A (B?)

THE NONSENSE OF IT. / ⟨rule⟩ / ⟨text⟩

⟨n.p., n.d., Boston?; Newport? 1867?⟩

Single cut sheet. Printed on both sides. 8⅛″ x 4⅞″. Anonymous.

B (A?)

THE NONSENSE OF IT. SHORT ANSWERS TO COMMON OBJECTIONS AGAINST WOMAN SUFFRAGE . . .

⟨n.p., n.d., Boston, 1867?⟩

Single cut sheet. Printed on both sides. 9⅝″ x 6¾″. Author's name present.

C (D?)

THE FRANCHISE FOR WOMEN. THE NONSENSE OF IT . . .

⟨Sydney: The Womanhood Suffrage League of New South Wales, n.d.⟩

Single cut sheet folded to make four pages. Author's name present.

D (C?)

THE NONSENSE OF IT. SHORT ANSWERS TO COMMON OBJECTIONS AGAINST WOMAN SUFFRAGE . . .

⟨Boston: Woman's Journal Office, 5 Park St. American Woman Suffrage Association, n.d., not before 1881⟩

Single cut sheet. Printed on both sides. 8⅞″ x 6¼″. Author's name present.

AAS (D) B (B) BPL (C) H (A, B) NYPL (B)

8260. Child-Pictures from Dickens . . .

Boston: Ticknor and Fields. 1868.

Edited anonymously by Higginson.

"These chapters . . . have been selected from my various books . . . Although they necessarily lose interest and purpose when detached from their context . . . this compilation is made for American children with my free consent. Charles Dickens. Boston, November, 1867."— Prefatory note.

Deposited Dec. 26, 1867. H copy received Dec. 26, 1867.

BPL Y

8261. Newport Free Library. Directors' Report. 1867–'68 . . .

⟨Newport⟩ Daily News Steam Press. ⟨1868⟩

Single cut sheet folded to four pages. Caption-title.

Statement by Higginson, March 31, 1868, p. ⟨1⟩.

H

8262. . . . Proceedings at the First Annual Meeting of the Free Religious Association, Held in Boston, May 28th and 29th, 1868.

Boston: Published by Adams & Co., No. 25 Bromfield Street. ⟨n.d., 1868⟩

Printed paper wrapper. At head of title: Free Religious Association.

"Remarks . . . ," pp. 67-68.

"Address," pp. 84-89.

H NYPL

8263. Eminent Women of the Age; Being Narratives of the Lives and Deeds of the Most Prominent Women of the Present Generation. By James Parton . . . T. W. Higginson . . . William Winter . . .

Hartford, Conn.: S. M. Betts & Company. 1868.

A subscription book and as such issued with variant imprints and in several styles of binding.

"Lydia Maria Child," pp. 38-65.

"Margaret Fuller Ossoli," pp. 173-201.

H Y

8264. MALBONE: AN OLDPORT ROMANCE . . .

BOSTON. FIELDS, OSGOOD, & CO., SUCCESSORS TO TICKNOR AND FIELDS. 1869.

⟨i-iv⟩, ⟨i⟩-iv, ⟨1⟩-244. 7″ x 4⁷⁄₁₆″.

⟨-⟩⁴, 1-10¹², 11². Also signed: ⟨-⟩⁴, A-O⁸, P².

C cloth: brown; green; purple. Brown-coated on white end papers. Flyleaves.

Advertised for May 15, 1869, in ALG March 1, 1869. Two copies in H inscribed May 28, 1869. Deposited May 31, 1869. Reviewed ALG June 1, 1869. Listed ALG June 15, 1869; PC Aug. 2, 1869.

BPL H NYPL

8265. . . . Proceedings at the Second Annual Meeting of the Free Religious Association, Held in Boston, May 27 and 28, 1869.

Boston: Roberts Brothers. 1869.

Printed wrapper. At head of title: Free Religious Association.

"Remarks . . . ," pp. 57-63.

BA H NYPL

8266. The Atlantic Almanac 1870 . . .

Boston: Fields, Osgood, & Co., Office of the Atlantic Monthly . . . 1869 . . .

"Swimming," pp. 19-21.

For comment see entry No. 1708.

8267. Address Delivered on the Centennial Anniversary of the Birth of Alexander von Humboldt . . . by Louis Agassiz . . .

Boston: Boston Society of Natural History. 1869.

Printed paper wrapper.

Response, pp. 65-67.

H NYPL

8268. Madame Thérèse; or, the Volunteers of '92. By MM. Erckmann-Chatrian. Translated from the Thirteenth Edition . . .

New York: Charles Scribner and Company. 1869

"Preface," pp. ⟨7⟩-12.

AAS H NYPL

8269. MEMOIR OF THADDEUS WILLIAM HARRIS . . .

BOSTON: ⟨BOSTON SOCIETY OF NATURAL HISTORY,⟩ 1869.

⟨ix⟩-xlvii. 9¼" x 5¹⁵⁄₁₆".

⟨1-2⁸, 3⁴⟩. Signed: ⟨A⟩⁴, B¹⁶.

Printed tan paper wrapper.

"From the Occasional Papers of the Boston Society of Natural History . . ."

Note: The list of Harris's writings appended to the Memoir was not compiled by Higginson but by Samuel H. Scudder. See Scudder's statement in Occasional Papers of the Boston Society of Natural History, Vol. 1, 1869, p. vii.

Also note: Higginson's Memoir appears also in Entomological Correspondence of Thaddeus William Harris . . . , edited by Samuel H. Scudder, Boston: Boston Society of Natural History, 1869.

H NYPL

8270. . . . OUGHT WOMEN TO LEARN THE ALPHABET? . . .

BOSTON: FOR SALE BY C. K. WHIPPLE, 43 BOWDOIN STREET. 1869.

Cover-title. At head of title: WOMAN'S SUFFRAGE TRACTS. NO. 4.

⟨1⟩-20; pp. ⟨21-22⟩: The New England Woman's Suffrage Association. Constitution; p. ⟨23⟩: Officers . . . ; p. ⟨24⟩: Woman's Suffrage Tracts . . . ⟨Nos. 1-5⟩. 7⅜" x 4¾".

⟨-⟩¹². Signed: ⟨1⟩-2⁶.

Printed self-wrapper.

Reprints noted:

Dated 1870.

Dated 1871.

Undated, but ca. 1871; date on the basis of an advertisement, p. ⟨24⟩.

Originally in Atlantic Monthly, Feb. 1859. Collected in Atlantic Essays, 1871.

AAS MHS

8271. ARMY LIFE IN A BLACK REGIMENT . . .

BOSTON: FIELDS, OSGOOD, & CO. 1870.

⟨i-iv⟩, ⟨i⟩-iv, ⟨1⟩-296. 7" x 4½".

⟨-⟩⁴, 1*¹², 2-12¹², 13*⁴. Also signed: ⟨-⟩⁴, A-R⁸, S⁴.

C cloth: blue; brown. Brown-coated end papers. Flyleaves.

Two binding issues noted:

1: Monogram of Fields, Osgood & Company at foot of spine.

2: Monogram of James R. Osgood & Company at foot of spine.

Deposited Sept. 21, 1869. BA copy received Sept. 27, 1869. Listed ALG Oct. 1, 1869; PC Nov. 1, 1869. See entry No. 8440 for extended edition.

H

8272. DECORATION DAY ADDRESS AT MOUNT AUBURN CEMETERY, MAY 30th, 1870 . . .

⟨n.p., n.d., 1870?⟩

Single cut sheet. Printed on recto only. 9⅞" x 7⅝". For a somewhat revised version see entry No. 8463.

AAS BPL H

8273. . . . . Proceedings at the Third Annual Meeting of the Free Religious Association, Held in Boston, May 26 and 27, 1870.

Boston: Press of John Wilson and Son. 1870

Printed wrapper. At head of title: Free Religious Association.

"Address ... a Glance at Mohammedanism," pp. 90-94.

BA H Y

8274. To-Day: A Paper Printed during the Fair of the Essex Institute and Oratorio Society, at Salem, Mass., from October 31st to November 4th, 1870.

⟨Salem, Mass., 1870⟩

An occasional newspaper. For comment see entry No. 1437.

"Sonnet from Petrarch," p. ⟨9⟩. Collected in *Afternoon Landscape*, 1889.

Short note, Oct. 24, 1870, p. ⟨9⟩.

8275. THE SYMPATHY OF RELIGIONS. AN ADDRESS, DELIVERED AT HORTICULTURAL HALL, BOSTON, FEBRUARY 6, 1870 ...

BOSTON: REPRINTED FROM THE RADICAL. OFFICE, 25 BROMFIELD STREET. 1871.

Cover-title.

⟨1⟩-23. 9⁹⁄₁₆″ x 5⅞″.

⟨1⟩⁸, 2⁴.

Printed paper wrapper: blue, lavender.

Originally in *The Radical*, Boston, Feb. 1871. For new edition see entry No. 8297.

AAS H NYPL

8276. ... Proceedings at the Fourth Annual Meeting of the Free Religious Association, Held in Boston, June 1 and 2, 1871.

Boston: Press of John Wilson and Son. 1871.

Printed paper wrapper. At head of title: Free Religious Association.

Remarks, pp. 47-50.

H NYPL

8277. ATLANTIC ESSAYS ...

BOSTON: JAMES R. OSGOOD AND COMPANY, LATE TICKNOR & FIELDS, AND FIELDS, OSGOOD, & CO. 1871.

⟨i-viii⟩, ⟨1⟩-341, blank leaf. 7″ x 4½″

⟨-⟩⁴, 1-14¹², 15⁴. *Also signed:* ⟨-⟩⁴, A-U⁸, V⁴.

C cloth: green; purple; terra-cotta. Covers bevelled. Brown-coated on white end papers. Flyleaves.

H copy received Sept. 16, 1871. Listed ALG Oct. 2, 1871. Noted by Ath Oct. 21, 1871. Advertised by Trübner in Bkr Nov. 1, 1871. Listed Bkr

Nov. 1, 1871; PC Nov. 1, 1871. Advertised by Low PC Sept. 17, 1872; Low edition listed Ath Oct. 19, 1872; PC Nov. 1, 1872.

H BPL

8278. ... "ARE YOU A CHRISTIAN?" ... [FROM THE INDEX OF JANUARY 25, 1873.] ...

⟨TOLEDO, OHIO, 1873⟩

Caption-title. At head of title: THE INDEX TRACTS.

⟨1⟩-3; advertisement, p. ⟨4⟩. 6¹⁵⁄₁₆″ x 4⅜″.

Single cut sheet folded to four pages.

H Y

8279. ... HIGHER EDUCATION OF WOMAN. A PAPER READ ... BEFORE THE SOCIAL SCIENCE CONVENTION, BOSTON, MAY 14, 1873.

BOSTON: WOMAN'S JOURNAL OFFICE, 3 TREMONT PLACE. 1873.

Cover-title. At head of title: WOMAN SUFFRAGE TRACTS. NO. 9.

⟨1⟩-16. 6⅛″ x 4″.

⟨-⟩⁸.

Printed self-wrapper.

Appears also in the following entry.

AAS BPL H

8280. The Liberal Education of Women: The Demand and the Method ... Edited by James Orton ...

A. S. Barnes & Company, New York and Chicago, 1873.

"On the Way to College," pp. ⟨183⟩-186. Reprinted from *The Woman's Journal*, Boston, Feb. 1871.

"The Higher Education of Woman," pp. ⟨309⟩-317. "From a paper read before the Social Science Convention, May 14, 1873." *See preceding entry.*

B

8281. ... Proceedings at the Sixth Annual Meeting of the Free Religious Association, Held in Boston, May 29 and 30, 1873.

Boston: Cochrane & Sampson, Printers, 9 Bromfield Street. 1873.

Printed paper wrapper. At head of title: Free Religious Association.

"Address," pp. 58-62.

H NYPL

8282. OLDPORT DAYS . . .

BOSTON: JAMES R. OSGOOD AND COMPANY, LATE
TICKNOR & FIELDS AND FIELDS, OSGOOD, & CO.
1873.

⟨1⟩-268, 2 blank leaves. Frontispiece and 9
plates inserted. 7½″ scant x 4⅞″.

⟨A⟩-Q⁸. *Also signed:* ⟨1⟩-11¹², 12⁴. *Note:* In
some copies leaf Q₈ is excised or pasted under
the terminal end paper.

C cloth: green. FL cloth: purple; terra-cotta.
Covers bevelled. Brown-coated on white end
papers. Flyleaves; or, flyleaf at front only.

BA copy received Sept. 18, 1873. Listed PW Sept.
20, 1873. H copy received Sept. 30, 1873.

BPL   H   LC

8283. Sex and Education. A Reply to Dr. E. H.
Clarke's "Sex in Education." Edited . . . by
Mrs. Julia Ward Howe.

Boston: Roberts Brothers. 1874.

Comment, pp. 32-51. Originally in *The Woman's
Journal,* Boston, Nov. 8, 15, 1873.

For comment see entry No. 9442.

8284. . . . Proceedings at the Seventh Annual
Meeting of the Free Religious Association,
Held in Boston, May 28 and 29, 1874.

Boston: Cochrane & Sampson, Printers, No. 9
Bromfield Street. 1874.

Printed paper wrapper. At head of title: Free
Religious Association.

"Address . . . ," pp. 49-58.

H   NYPL

8285. New-York Tribune. Extra No. 21. Scientific Series . . .

New-York, September 3, 1874 . . .

"The Word 'Philanthropy'," p. 3. See entry
No. 8295 for separate publication.

12 pp.

Y

8286. . . . SHOULD WOMEN VOTE? IMPOR-
TANT AFFIRMATIVE TESTIMONY . . .

⟨GRAND HAVEN, MICHIGAN: HERALD PRINT, n.d.,
1874⟩

Single cut sheet folded to 4 pp. Caption-title.
At head of title: READ AND CIRCULATE. Imprint at
foot of p. ⟨4⟩.

Date on the basis of Susan B. Anthony's copy
in LC which is inscribed: *Circulated in the
Michigan campaign . . . 1874.*

Note: This is the earliest located separate
printing of Higginson's address at the National
Woman's Rights Convention, Nov. 1856; see
entry No. 8230.

Also note: Higginson, p. 411, under the year
1869, lists as a Higginson production "Ought
⟨*sic*⟩ Women to Vote?". Presumably issued as
a separate in 1869 but BAL has failed to locate
any separate appearance prior to this 1874
production. Same as *Should Women Vote?* ?

LC

8287. YOUNG FOLKS' HISTORY OF THE
UNITED STATES . . .

BOSTON: LEE AND SHEPARD, PUBLISHERS. NEW
YORK: LEE, SHEPARD, AND DILLINGHAM. 1875.

Note: Possibly issued also with the single imprint: BOSTON: LEE AND SHEPARD, PUBLISHERS.
1875. No copy so imprinted located.

⟨i-ii⟩, ⟨i⟩-vi, 1-370, blank leaf. Double-page
map inserted. Illustrated. 6¾″ x 4⅞″.

⟨-⟩⁴, 1-23⁸, 24². Leaf 24₂ either present; or, excised, or pasted under the terminal end paper.

P cloth: terra-cotta. Blue-coated on white end
papers. Brown-coated on white end papers. In
some copies: Flyleaves.

Advertised in PW Jan. 16, 1875, as *about January 25th.* Listed PW Feb. 6, 1875; Ath Aug. 21,
1875; Bkr Sept. 1, 1875; PC Sept. 1, 1875. The
London edition appears to have been made up
of American sheets with Low's inserted title-
page; advertised for *this day* Ath Aug. 21, 1875;
advertised as *now ready* Ath Sept. 4, PC Sept. 16,
1875.

Note: There were many reprintings, some containing added material or revisions. The following have been noted; the list is undoubtedly
incomplete:

*Boston: Lee and Shepard, Publishers. New
York: Charles T. Dillingham. ⟨1875; i.e., not
before 1876⟩*

Pp. 382. Contains some minor revisions. Copy
in LC.

*Boston: Lee and Shepard, Publishers. New
York: Charles T. Dillingham. 1882.*

A cursory examination indicates that this is a
reprint of the preceding entry. Copies in LC
and O.

*Boston: Lee and Shepard, Publishers. New
York: Charles T. Dillingham. 1883.*

Pp. 394. Text extended. Listed PW Sept. 2, 1882. Copies in H and LC.

New York Longmans, Green, and Co. London and Bombay 1896

Pp. vi, 400, 33. Text extended. Contains a series of "Questions." For an earlier printing of the "Questions" see entry No. 8288. Copy in NYPL.

BPL   H

8288. Questions on Higginson's Young Folks' History of the United States. For the Use of Teachers . . .

⟨Boston, 1875⟩

Cover-title. Printed self-wrapper.

Compiled by Higginson as made clear by his "Prefatory Note," p. ⟨3⟩.

Not to be confused with *Topics for the Use of Teachers. To Accompany Higginson's Young Folks' History of the United States* ⟨1877⟩, described in the section of *References and Ana,* below.

Three printings noted:

1

Copyright notice dated 1875.

On copyright page the imprint reads: *Boston: / Electrotyped And Printed By / Rand, Avery, & Co.*

Questions end on p. 32.

"How to Study History," pp. 33-35.

P. ⟨36⟩ blank.

2

Copyright notice dated 1875.

On copyright page the imprint reads: *Franklin Press: / Rand, Avery, And Company, / 117 Franklin Street, / Boston.*

Questions end on p. 32.

"How to Study History," pp. 33-35.

Advertisement, p. ⟨36⟩.

3

Copyright notice undated.

No printer's imprint on copyright page.

Questions end on p. 33.

"How to Study History," pp. 34-36.

Issued not before 1878.

H (2nd)   LC (1st, being a deposit copy)   NYPL (3rd)

8289. . . . English Statesmen   Prepared by Thomas Wentworth Higginson

New York G. P. Putnam's Sons Fourth Ave. and 23d St. 1875.

At head of title: Brief Biographies

Edited by Higginson.

Brief Biographies of European Public Men, Vol. 1.

Listed PW April 10, 1875. Copies received by H and BPL April 21, 1875.

AAS   H   LC   Y

8290. The Harvard Book. A Series of Historical, Biographical, and Descriptive Sketches. By Various Authors . . . Collected and Published by F. O. Vaille and H. A. Clark, Class of 1874. Vol. II.

Cambridge: Welch, Bigelow, and Company, University Press. 1875.

"The Gymnasium, and Gymnastics in Harvard College," pp. ⟨186⟩-190.

For comment see entry No. 4045.

8291. . . . English Radical Leaders by R. J. Hinton.

New York G. P. Putnam's Sons Fourth Ave. and 23d St. 1875.

At head of title: Brief Biographies

Edited by Higginson.

Brief Biographies of European Public Men, Vol. 2.

Listed PW Dec. 18, 1875.

AAS   LC   Y

8292. FREE RELIGIOUS ASSOCIATION, 1875. INTRODUCTORY ADDRESS . . .

⟨n.p., 1875⟩

Caption-title.

⟨1⟩-6, blank leaf. 8⅜" full x 5¾".

⟨-⟩⁴.

Printed self-wrapper.

Appears also in: *Free Religious Association. Proceedings at the Eighth Annual Meeting of the Free Religious Association . . . Boston, May 27 and 28, 1875,* Boston, 1875; printed paper wrapper.

H   Y

8293. Johnson's New Universal Cyclopaedia . . .
Not to Exceed Four Volumes . . .

A. J. Johnson & Son, 11 Great Jones Street,
New York . . . MDCCCLXXV

Presumably issued in a variety of bindings.

"Emerson," Vol. 1, pp. 1541-1542.

NYPL

8294. Freedom and Fellowship in Religion. A
Collection of Essays and Addresses Edited by
a Committee of the Free Religious Association.

Boston: Roberts Brothers. 1875.

"The Word Philanthropy," pp. 323-337. See
next entry. Also see entry No. 8285.

"Radical Faith Affirmative," pp. 394-400. Reprinted from an unlocated annual report of the
Association.

BA copy received May 24, 1875. Listed PW May
29, 1875.

BA H NYPL

8295. THE WORD "PHILANTHROPY." . . .
REPRINTED FROM "FREEDOM AND
FELLOWSHIP IN RELIGION."

⟨n.p., n.d., 1875?⟩

⟨1⟩-17, blank leaf. Laid paper. 6⅞" x 4⅝".

⟨-⟩10.

Printed pale gray-green paper wrapper.

An offprint (preprint?) from the preceding entry. For earlier publication see entry No. 8285.

AAS H

8296. Laurel Leaves. Original Poems, Stories,
and Essays . . .

Boston: William F. Gill and Company, 309
Washington Street. 1876.

"A Moonglade," pp. 287-294. Collected in The
Procession . . . , 1897.

For comment see entry No. 4730.

8297. . . . The Sympathy of Religions . . . New
Edition, Revised and Enlarged.

Boston: Published by the Free Religious Association, No. 1 Tremont Place. 1876.

At head of title: Free Religious Tracts. No. 3.

For first edition see entry No. 8275.

"Preliminary Note," Jan. 1, 1876, p. ⟨3⟩.

Issued in both printed paper wrapper; and,
flexible cloth.

The printing issued with the imprint Unity
Mission Office: 175 Dearborn Street, Chicago
⟨1893⟩, was printed from the plates of the 1876
edition with one minor variation: The preliminary one-page note is altered; author of the
alterations not known.

BA copy received Feb. 10, 1876.

AAS   BA   H (both)   LC   NYPL

8298. . . . French Political Leaders by Edward
King.

New York   G. P. Putnam's Sons   Fourth Ave.
and 23d St. 1876.

At head of title: Brief Biographies

Edited by Higginson. "Editor's Preface," p. ⟨v⟩.

Brief Biographies of European Public Men,
Vol. 3.

Listed PW Feb. 26, 1876.

AAS   H

8299. . . . German Political Leaders by Herbert
Tuttle

New York   Geo. P. Putnam's Sons, 182 Fifth
Avenue. 1876.

At head of title: Brief Biographies

Edited by Higginson. "Editor's Preface," p. ⟨v⟩.

Brief Biographies of European Public Men,
Vol. 4.

Listed PW May 20, 1876. The London (Low)
edition listed PC Aug. 16, 1876.

AAS   H

8300. A History of Public Education in Rhode
Island, from 1636 to 1876 . . . Compiled by
Authority of the Board of Education, and
Edited by Thomas B. Stockwell . . .

Providence: Providence Press Company, Printers to the City and State. 1876.

"A History of the Public School System of
Rhode Island," pp. ⟨1⟩-128.

"A Sketch of the Public Schools in the City of
Newport," by Higginson in collaboration with
Thomas H. Clarke, pp. ⟨253⟩-266.

H copy received Nov. 8, 1876; BA copy received
Nov. 9, 1876.

BA   H

8301. Memoir of Dr. Samuel Gridley Howe. By
Julia Ward Howe: With Other Memorial
Tributes. Published by the Howe Memorial
Committee.

Boston: Printed by Albert J. Wright, 79 Milk Street (Corner of Federal). 1876.

Remarks, pp. 116-122.

For comment see entry No. 9448.

8302. Poems of Places Edited by Henry W. Longfellow ... Scotland. Denmark, Iceland, Norway, Sweden. Vol. III.

Boston: James R. Osgood and Company, Late Ticknor & Fields, and Fields, Osgood, & Co. 1876.

"Odensee," pp. 136-138.

Listed PW Dec. 23, 1876.

H NYPL

8303. The Reading Club and Handy Speaker ... Edited by George M. Baker. No. 4.

Boston: Lee & Shepard, Publishers. New York: Charles T. Dillingham. 1877.

Cloth; and, printed paper wrapper.

"Decoration. 'Manibus Date Lilia Plenis'," pp. 11-12. Collected in *Afternoon Landscape*, 1889.

Advertised PW Nov. 4, 1876. Listed PW Dec. 2, 1876.

H

8304. .... A Book of American Explorers by Thomas Wentworth Higginson ...

Boston Lee and Shepard New York Charles T. Dillingham 1877

At head of title: Young Folks' Series. Also issued with the imprint: *Boston Lee and Shepard 1877*

Edited by Higginson. "Preface," pp. v-vi.

"... a series of extracts ..." from "narratives of the early discoverers and explorers of the American coast ..."—P. v.

Noted as *on the eve of publication* PW March 31, 1877. BA copy received April 3, 1877. Listed PW April 14, 1877. In 1892 the work was reissued in eight paper-covered parts; incomplete set in H.

AAS LC Y

8305. The Cyclopaedia of Education ... Edited by Henry Kiddle ... and Alexander J. Schem ...

New York: E. Steiger. London: Trübner & Co. 1877.

"Rhode Island," pp. 734-739.

According to PW listing issued in cloth; library cloth; half Turkey morocco; half Russian morocco; morocco antique; full Russian morocco.

Listed PW April 21, 1877.

H NYPL

8306. .... Proceedings at the Tenth Annual Meeting of the Free Religious Association, Held in Boston, May 31 and June 1, 1877.

Boston: Published by the Free Religious Association, No. 231 Washington Street. 1877.

Printed paper wrapper. At head of title: Free Religious Association.

"Address," pp. 85-90.

H Y

8307. .... Forty-Fifth Annual Report of the Trustees of the Perkins Institution and Massachusetts Asylum for the Blind. October, 1876.

Boston: Albert J. Wright, State Printer, 79 Milk Street (Corner of Federal). 1877.

Printed paper wrapper. At head of title: Public Document No. 27.

"Remarks," pp. 162-165.

Issued after Oct. 19, 1876.

BPL

8308. Speech at a Conference of Liberal Thinkers, London, June 13, 1878.

London, 1878.

Not located. Entry from Higginson, p. 414, where the speech is described as a pamphlet.

8309. Hygiene of the Brain and Nerves and the Cure of Nervousness ... by M. L. Holbrook ...

New York: M. L. Holbrook & Company. 1878.

Letter, Nov. 11, 1877, pp. 182-183.

Two issues noted:

1: Copyright notice in the name of *C. P. Somerby* printed on reverse of the title-leaf.

2: Copyright notice in the name of *M. L. Holbrook* printed on a slip pasted over the original Somerby copyright notice.

Listed PW Oct. 19, 1878.

H (B) NYPL (A)

8310. Proceedings at a Reception in Honor of the Rev. O. B. Frothingham Given by the Independent Liberal Church at the Union League Theatre Tuesday Evening, April 22, 1879 . . .

New York   G. P. Putnam's Sons   182 Fifth Avenue   1879

Printed paper wrapper.

Address, pp. 36-43.

H NYPL

8311. THE INTER-COLLEGIATE LITER-ARY ASSOCIATION, ITS HISTORY, AIMS AND RESULTS . . .

⟨n.p., n.d., 1879?⟩

Caption-title.

⟨1⟩-8. 9³⁄₁₆″ x 5¾″.

⟨-⟩⁴.

Printed self-wrapper.

Note: Date according to Higginson, p. 414.

H

8312. SHORT STUDIES OF AMERICAN AU-THORS . . .

BOSTON: LEE AND SHEPARD, PUBLISHERS. NEW YORK: CHARLES T. DILLINGHAM. 1880.

⟨i-iv⟩, ⟨1⟩-60. 5⅞″ x 4⅛″.

⟨1-4⟩⁸.

S cloth: gray-blue; green; mustard. Stamped in gold and black. Brown-coated on white end papers; blue-gray end papers printed in gray with a leafy pattern. Flyleaves. *Note:* A variant binding, status not known, is in Y: Brown S cloth, stamped in black only; white end papers printed in pale tan with a leafy pattern.

Noted for Nov. 15, 1879, PW Nov. 8, 1879. BA copy received Dec. 18, 1879. Listed PW Dec. 27, 1879. Distributed in Great Britain by Trübner; noted by Ath Sept. 11, 1880. See under 1888 for an enlarged edition.

BA LC Y

8313. The Atlantic Monthly Supplement. The Holmes Breakfast . . .

⟨n.p., n.d., Boston, February, 1880⟩

Self-wrapper. Caption-title. "Colonel Higginson's Speech," p. 18.

H NYPL

8314. . . . Proceedings at the Dinner of the Early Members of the Union League Club of the City of New York. Thursday, May 20th, 1880.

New York: Koues & Toby, Printers and Stationers, 110 Broadway. 1880.

Printed paper wrapper. At head of title: Union League Club.

Statement on Negro troops, pp. 83-84.

NYPL

8315. The Two Hundred and Forty-Second Annual Record of the Ancient and Honorable Artillery Company, of Massachusetts. 1879–80. Sermon by Rev. Edward Everett Hale . . .

Boston: Alfred Mudge & Son, Printers, 34 School Street. 1880.

Printed paper wrapper.

"Response," pp. 60-61.

Issued not before July, 1880.

H

8316. The Memorial History of Boston . . . Edited by Justin Winsor . . . in Four Volumes . . .

Boston: James R. Osgood and Company. 1880–1881.

"From the Death of Winthrop to Philip's War," Vol. 1, pp. ⟨303⟩-310.

"French and Indian Wars," Vol. 2, pp. ⟨93⟩-130.

For comment see entry No. 2275.

8317. Sketches and Reminiscences of the Radical Club of Chestnut Street, Boston. Edited by Mrs. John T. Sargent.

Boston: James R. Osgood and Company. 1880.

"Sappho," pp. 109-114. This is an abbreviated and somewhat revised version of "Sappho" in *Atlantic Essays,* 1871.

Remarks elsewhere in the volume; and eighteen lines of verse, p. 400, which are otherwise unlocated.

Listed PW Dec. 25, 1880.

H

8318. The Fifth Half Century of the Arrival of John Winthrop at Salem, Massachusetts. Commemorative Exercises by the Essex Institute, June 22, 1880. [From the Historical Collections of the Essex Institute.]

Salem: Printed for the Essex Institute. 1880.

Printed paper wrapper.

"Response . . . ," pp. 33-36. Also appears in *Essex Institute Historical Collections,* Vol. 17, Salem, 1880.

H

8319. Benjamin Peirce . . . a Memorial Collection, by Moses King.

Cambridge, 1881. Massachusetts.

Printed paper wrapper.

Higginson's comments *"from The Woman's Journal, Oct. 23,"* 1880, pp. 30-32.

Listed PW March 12, 1881.

H NYPL

8320. ADDRESS . . . AT THE CELEBRATION OF THE BATTLE OF THE COWPENS AT SPARTANBURG, S. C., MAY 11, 1881. FROM THE CHARLESTON (S. C.) NEWS AND COURIER, MAY 12, 1881 . . .

⟨n.p., Charleston, S. C., 1881?⟩

Caption-title. Single cut sheet of white wove paper, folded to four pages. Some copies show all or part of the watermark: *Ravelstone.*

⟨1⟩-4. 8¼″ x 5⁷⁄₁₆″.

AAS BPL Y

8321. MEMORIAL ODE. BY THOMAS WENTWORTH HIGGINSON. READ BEFORE THE GRAND ARMY POSTS OF BOSTON, MASS., ON MEMORIAL DAY, MAY 30, 1881. BY MR. GEORGE RIDDLE . . .

⟨n.p., n.d., Boston, 1881⟩

Caption-title. Single cut sheet of laid paper folded to four pages. Watermarked: *Old Berkshire Mills*

⟨1-4⟩. 11″ x 8½″.

The ode appears also in: *Memorial Day. Oration by Gov. John D. Long: Ode by Col. Thomas W. Higginson, before the Grand Army Posts of Suffolk County, at Tremont Temple, Boston, May 30, 1881,* Boston, 1881; printed paper wrapper; listed PW July 30, 1881. Collected in *Afternoon Landscape,* 1889.

BPL CPL H Y

8322. Stories of Adventure Told by Adventurers. By Edward E. Hale.

Boston: Roberts Brothers. 1881.

Part of a review of Helen Hunt Jackson's *Bits of Travel,* p. ⟨7⟩ of the advertisements.

Note: Earliest located book appearance of Higginson's review; in all likelihood it had other, prior, book publication. *Bits of Travel* was first published in 1872 and so, presumably, the Higginson review had publication at about that time.

Deposited Sept. 12, 1881. Listed PW Oct. 15, 1881.

NYPL

8323. Memorial of the Dedication of the Public Latin and English High School-House. With a Description of the Building.

Boston: Rockwell and Churchill, City Printers, No. 39 Arch Street. 1881.

Printed paper wrapper.

"Address," pp. 65-66.

Note: The only examined copy of this publication has the following statements on p. ⟨2⟩: Under date of March 22, 1881, an order to print 1,000 copies; under date of June 14, 1881, an order to print "one thousand additional copies." Two printings? Does this publication occur without the notice of June 14, 1881?

H

8324. Exercises in Celebrating the Two Hundred and Fiftieth Anniversary of the Settlement of Cambridge Held December 28, 1880 . . .

Cambridge University Press: John Wilson and Son 1881

"Oration," pp. ⟨44⟩-65. "Response," pp. 111-114.

For comment see entry No. 8957.

8325. "The City and the Sea," with Other Cambridge Contributions, in Aid of the Hospital Fund . . .

Cambridge: John Wilson and Son, University Press. 1881.

Compiled by Helen Leah Reed.

"French Radical Eloquence," pp. ⟨55⟩-70.

Deposited Nov. 9, 1881.

H NYPL

8326. The Sword and the Pen . . .

Boston . . . 1881 . . .

An occasional newspaper. For comment see entry No. 123.

Reprint save for "A Short March with the Guards. From an English Diary," No. 10, p. 4.

8327. COMMON SENSE ABOUT WOMEN
. . .

BOSTON   LEE AND SHEPARD PUBLISHERS   NEW
YORK   CHARLES T. DILLINGHAM   1882

⟨i-vi⟩, 1-403; blank leaf. 6¾″ full x 4⁹⁄₁₆″.

⟨1-17¹², 18²⟩.

S cloth: brown. Pale yellow end papers.

Note: Copies dated ⟨1881⟩ and ⟨1882⟩ are reprints of the 1882 printing.

Deposited Dec. 12, 1881. BA copy received Dec.
14, 1881. Listed PW Dec. 24, 1881. The London
(Sonnenschein) edition listed Ath March 11,
1882.

AAS   BPL

8328. TESTIMONY, FEBRUARY 13, 1882

Higginson's testimony regarding a petition of
The Charles River Street Railway has been
noted in two publications. The sequence has
not been established and the designations are
for identification only.

A

Report of the Evidence and Arguments in Favor
of the Petition of the Charles River Street Railway Co. before the Committee on Street Rail-
ways, of the Massachusetts Legislature of 1882.

Printed for the Charles River Street Railway Co. ⟨n.d., 1882⟩

Printed paper wrapper. Cover-title. "Testimony . . . ," Feb. 13, 1882, pp. 49-70.

Received by Massachusetts State Library, June 1,
1882.

B

Charles River Railway V.S. ⟨*sic*⟩ Union &
Camb. Railroads   State House 1882 . . .

⟨n.p., n.d., probably Boston, 1882⟩

Cover-title. 2 Vols. Issued without title-pages.
"Testimony . . . ," Feb. 13, 1882, Vol. 1, pp. 44-
64.

MSL (both)

8329. Samuel Johnson ⟨1822–1882⟩. A Memorial . . .

Cambridge: Printed at the Riverside Press.
1882.

Edited by Augustus Mellen Haskell. Cloth;
and(?), printed paper wrapper.

"Remarks," pp. 23-26.

H copy received June 12, 1882.

H

8330. The Lincoln Memorial: Album-Immortelles . . . Edited by Osborn H. Oldroyd . . .

New York: G. W. Carleton & Co., Publishers.
London: S. Low, Son & Co. MDCCCLXXXII

Four-line comment, *Cambridge, 1880,* p. 325.
Appears also in the prospectus of the work issued
by Carleton. Otherwise unlocated save in somewhat revised form in *American Orators and
Oratory . . . ,* 1901, p. 91, entry No. 8444.

For comment see entry No. 1092.

8331. Proceedings of the Massachusetts Historical Society. Vol. XIX. 1881–1882 . . .

Boston: Published by the Society. M.DCCC.-
LXXXII.

Introductory remarks on a Calhoun letter, pp.
279-280. Presentation of a plan of Lebanon,
Conn., pp. 379-380.

H

8332. Wayside Gleanings for Leisure Moments.
Printed for Private Circulation.

⟨University Press: John Wilson and Son,
Cambridge⟩ 1882.

"Address at Cambridge Cemetery . . . May 30,
1879," pp. 82-83.

H

8333. A TIMELY PROTEST FROM MR.
HIGGINSON. FROM THE WOMAN'S
JOURNAL, OCT. 20th, 1883 . . .

⟨n.p., 1883?⟩

Single cut sheet. Printed on recto only. 8¹¹⁄₁₆″ x
6¼″.

H

8334. . . . Methods of Teaching History . . .

Boston: Published by Ginn, Heath, & Co.
1883.

At head of title: Pedagogical Library. Edited by
G. Stanley Hall. Vol. I.

"Why Do Children Dislike History?" pp. ⟨205⟩-
207.

Deposited Jan. 14, 1884. Listed PW Feb. 9, 1884.

B   LC   NYPL

8335. . . . Acceptance and Unveiling of the
Statue of John Bridge, the Puritan, Presented
to the City of Cambridge, Sept. 20, 1882, by
Samuel James Bridge . . . Unveiled November 28, 1882.

Cambridge: Tribune Publishing Company.
1883.

Printed paper wrapper. At head of title: City of Cambridge.

Address, pp. 15-18.

H

8336. ... Thirty-first Annual Report of the Trustees of the Public Library. 1883.

⟨Boston, 1883⟩

Printed wrapper. At head of title: [Document 103-1883.] City of Boston.

"Report of the Examining Committee ...," signed by Higginson and others, pp. 10-18.

"Report on the Parker Library," pp. 19-25.

H   NYPL

8337. WENDELL PHILLIPS ... RE-PRINTED FROM "THE NATION"

BOSTON   LEE AND SHEPARD, PUBLISHERS   NEW YORK   CHARLES T. DILLINGHAM   1884

⟨iii⟩-xxi. 8⅝₆″ x 5⅞″.

⟨-⟩¹⁰.

Printed paper wrapper. Two states of wrapper noted. Sequence, if any, not determined. The designations are for identification only.

Wrapper A

Peach paper. Front: WENDELL PHILLIPS. / BY / THOMAS WENTWORTH HIGGINSON. Wrapper otherwise blank.

Wrapper B

Faun paper. Front: WENDELL PHILLIPS, / BY / THOMAS WENTWORTH HIGGINSON. Inner front imprinted: *Thomas W. Higginson's Works ... ;* inner back imprinted: ... *The Complete Works of Charles Sumner ... ;* outer back imprinted: *Wendell Phillips's Writings ...*

Reprinted from *The Nation* of Feb. 7, 1884.

B (B)   H (B)   NYPL (A)

8338. ... MARGARET FULLER OSSOLI ...

BOSTON: HOUGHTON, MIFFLIN AND COMPANY. NEW YORK: 11 EAST SEVENTEENTH STREET. THE RIVERSIDE PRESS, CAMBRIDGE. 1884.

At head of title: AMERICAN MEN OF LETTERS.

⟨i-viii⟩, ⟨1⟩-323; plus: 4 pp. advertisements. Laid paper. Portrait frontispiece inserted. 6⅞″ x 4⅝″.

⟨1⁴, 2-14¹², 15⁶; plus: 16²⟩. Leaf ⟨1⟩₁ excised or pasted under the end paper. *Signed:* ⟨-⟩³, 1-3, ⟨4⟩-⟨6⟩, 7-20⁸, 21²; plus: ⟨22⟩².

S cloth: maroon. Gray-green coated on white end papers. Laid paper flyleaf at front; wove paper flyleaf at back. Top edges gilt.

Deposited May 9, 1884. Noted for May 10, PW May 3, 1884. BPL copy received May 12; BA May 13, 1884. Listed PW May 17, 1884.

MHS   NYPL

8339. THE YOUNG MEN'S PARTY ... RE-PRINTED FROM THE NEW YORK EVE-NING POST OF OCTOBER 4th, 1884.

⟨NEW YORK: NEW YORK EVENING POST, 1884⟩

Cover-title.

⟨1-16⟩. 5¹¹₆″ x 3½″. Noted on both laid; and, wove papers.

⟨-⟩⁸.

Printed self-wrapper.

AAS   CPL   H   Y

8340. Proceedings of the Massachusetts Historical Society. Vol. xx. 1882–1883 ...

Boston: Published by the Society. M.DCCC.-LXXXIV.

Discussion of the word *Ra'th*, pp. 227-229.

H   NYPL

8341. Memorial Services in the City of Cambridge, on the Day of the Funeral of General Grant, August 8, 1885.

Cambridge, Mass.: Press of H. E. Lombard. 1885.

Printed paper wrapper.

"Oration," pp. ⟨12⟩-17.

H

8342. December Edited by Oscar Fay Adams ...

Boston   D. Lothrop and Company   Franklin and Hawley Streets ⟨1885⟩

"December," pp. 13-14. Collected in *Afternoon Landscape*, 1889.

For comment see entry No. 57.

8343. A LARGER HISTORY OF THE UNITED STATES OF AMERICA TO THE CLOSE OF PRESIDENT JACKSON'S ADMINISTRATION ...

NEW YORK   HARPER & BROTHERS, FRANKLIN SQUARE   1886

⟨i⟩-xii, ⟨1⟩-470; advertisements, pp. ⟨1⟩-2; plus advertisements, pp. 3-6. Illustrated. 8⅞″ x 6⅑₆″.

‹-›⁶, 1-7, ‹8›, 9-21, ‹22›, 23-27⁸, 28-29⁴, 30⁸, 31⁴;
plus: ‹32›².

S cloth: gray-blue. Brown-coated on white end
papers; tan paper end papers. Flyleaves.

A rewriting of Higginson's *Young Folks' History of the United States*, 1875. "A wholly
fresh treatment" and not "a mere amplifica-
tion."—*From the "Preface."*

Deposited Oct. 12, 1885. Listed PW Oct. 17, 1885.
BA copy received Oct. 20, 1885. The London
(Low) edition listed Ath Oct. 17; PC Nov. 15,
1885. See *History of the United States . . .*,
1905, *below.*

H Y

8344. February Edited by Oscar Fay Adams . . .

Boston D. Lothrop and Company Franklin
and Hawley Streets ‹1886›

"The February Hush," p. 28. Collected in
Afternoon Landscape, 1889.

For comment see entry No. 59.

8345. November Edited by Oscar Fay Adams . . .

Boston D. Lothrop and Company Franklin
and Hawley Streets ‹1886›

"November," pp. 29-30.

For comment see entry No. 69.

8346. THE MONARCH OF DREAMS . . .

BOSTON LEE AND SHEPARD, PUBLISHERS 1887

‹i-vi›, ‹1›-52, 3 blank leaves. 5⅞" scant x 4³⁄₁₆".

‹1-4›⁸.

S cloth: golden-yellow; green; mauve; tan.
White paper end papers printed in green with
a four-pointed star-like pattern. Also: White
paper end papers printed in tan with a floral
pattern.

Deposited Nov. 24, 1886. BPL copy received Dec.
3, 1886. In H: A copy presented by Higginson
to Sarah Orne Jewett, Dec. 1886. Listed PW
Feb. 12, 1887. H copy received Feb. 12, 1887.
Advertised as *new* in Bkr April, 1887. Noticed
by Ath May 7, 1887.

H NYPL

8347. Appletons' Cyclopaedia of American Biography Edited by James Grant Wilson and
John Fiske . . . Volume I . . .

New York D. Appleton and Company 1, 3
and 5 Bond Street 1887

"John Brown of Osawatomie," pp. 404-407.

For comment see entry No. 6020.

8348. UNSOLVED PROBLEMS IN WOMAN
SUFFRAGE . . . REPRINTED FROM THE
NEW REVIEW, THE FORUM ‹of Jan.
1887›.

‹New York, n.d., 1887›

Cover-title.

‹439›-449. 8¹¹⁄₁₆" x 6⅛".

‹-›⁶.

Printed blue paper wrapper.

H MHS NYPL

8349. . . . HINTS ON WRITING AND
SPEECH-MAKING . . .

BOSTON   LEE AND SHEPARD PUBLISHERS   NEW
YORK   CHARLES T DILLINGHAM 1887

At head of title: HANDBOOK SERIES

‹1›-70; 2 pp. advertisements. 5⅞" x 4⅛".

‹1-4⁸, 5⁴›.

S cloth: brown. Unprinted pale tan paper end
papers. Also, white end papers imprinted with
publisher's advertisements. Flyleaves.

Deposited Feb. 24, 1887. BPL copy received
March 4, 1887. Listed PW March 19, 1887.

AAS H LC

8350. Around the World on a Bicycle . . . by
Thomas Stevens . . .

New York   Charles Scribner's Sons 1887–
1888

2 Vols. Vol. 1 dated 1887; Vol. 2 dated 1888.

"Preface," Vol. 1, pp. ‹vii›-viii.

Vol. 1 deposited May 26, 1887; listed PW June 11,
1887. Vol. 2 deposited Sept. 15, 1888; listed PW
Sept. 29, 1888.

H

8351. . . . Proceedings at the Twentieth Annual
Meeting of the Free Religious Association of
America, Held in Boston, May 26 and 27,
1887.

Boston: Published by the Free Religious Association. 1887.

Printed paper wrapper. At head of title: Free
Religious Association.

"Address," pp. 75-78; another "Address," pp.
132-136.

BPL H LC

8352. The College and the Church The "How I Was Educated" Papers and Denominational "Confessions" from the Forum Magazine

New York D. Appleton and Company 1887

"Second Paper," pp. ⟨18⟩-28. First published in *Forum*, April, 1886, under the title "How I Was Educated."

Note: According to Higginson, p. 417, this was issued as a separate. No separate publication located by BAL.

H copy received June 13, 1887. Deposited June 18, 1887. Listed PW June 18, 1887. Under the title *The How I Was Educated Papers*, dated 1888, listed PW Oct. 29, 1887.

H NYPL

8353. FOR SELF-RESPECT AND SELF-PRO-TECTION ... SPEECH AT THE ANNUAL MEETING OF THE AMERICAN WOMAN SUFFRAGE ASSOCIATION, HELD AT PHILADELPHIA, PA., NOV. 1, 1887 ...

⟨n.p., n.d.⟩

Caption-title. Single cut sheet folded to make four pages.

⟨1⟩-4. 12¾" x 6½".

Note: Higginson, p. 418, states that this address was issued in two formats: As a pamphlet; and, as a leaflet. Located only in the form described.

CPL H Y

8354. WOMEN AND MEN ...

NEW YORK HARPER & BROTHERS, FRANKLIN SQUARE 1888

⟨i-ii⟩, ⟨i⟩-vi, ⟨1⟩-326, 2 pp. advertisements. 6⅜" x 4⅜".

⟨-⟩⁴, 1-20⁸, 21⁴.

S cloth: olive-brown; tan. Covers bevelled. Brown-coated on white end papers. Flyleaves.

Deposited Nov. 30, 1887. BPL copy received Dec. 3, 1887. Listed PW Dec. 10, 1887.

BPL H NYPL

8355. What American Authors Think about International Copyright

New-York American Copyright League 1888

One-paragraph statement, p. 6.

For comment see entry No. 218.

8356. Short Studies of American Authors ... Enlarged Edition.

Boston: Lee and Shepard, Publishers. New York: Charles T. Dillingham. 1888.

See under 1880 for first edition.

"In the present enlarged edition two new chapters are added ... on Miss Alcott ... and ... on Mr. Whipple ..."—P. ⟨1⟩.

Listed PW May 19, 1888.

AAS H

8357. Reunion of the Free Soilers of 1848–1852 at the Parker House, Boston, Massachusetts, June 28, 1888.

Cambridge: John Wilson and Son. University Press. 1888.

Printed paper wrapper; and, cloth.

"Address ... ," pp. 24-27.

"Waiting for the Bugle," pp. 27-28.

H NYPL

8358. Col. Higginson's Letter of Acceptance. Cambridge, Mass., Oct. 4.⟨sic⟩ 1888 ...

⟨n.p., The Independent Committee of the Fifth Congressional District of Massachusetts, 1888⟩

The above on p. ⟨3⟩ of a four-page leaflet. Higginson's acceptance of the Committee's nomination as candidate for Congress.

CPL

8359. Proceedings of the American Antiquarian Society. New Series, Vol. IV. October, 1885–April, 1887.

Worcester: Published by the Society. 1888.

Printed paper wrapper.

Letter to S. S. Green, Jan. 28, 1886, pp. 72-73.

"English Sources of American Dialect," pp. 159-166.

BA H NYPL

8360. Proceedings of the Massachusetts Historical Society. Vol. III.—Second Series. 1886–1887 ...

Boston: Published by the Society. M.DCCC.-LXXXVIII.

Tribute to Charles C. Perkins, p. 61.

Remarks, pp. 319-320.

H NYPL

8361. The Protest against the Majority Report of the Joint Special Committee of the General Court of 1887, on the Employment and Schooling of Children ... and against Any Legislative Interference with Private Schools, Being a Digest of the Remarks of the Remonstrants, at the Hearings ... March, 1888.

⟨n.p., Boston, 1888⟩

Printed paper wrapper.

Comments, pp. 21-22.

H

8362. TRAVELLERS AND OUTLAWS EPISODES IN AMERICAN HISTORY ...

BOSTON 1889 LEE AND SHEPARD PUBLISHERS 10 MILK STREET NEXT "THE OLD SOUTH MEETING-HOUSE" NEW YORK CHARLES T. DILLINGHAM 718 AND 720 BROADWAY

⟨i-ii⟩, ⟨1⟩-⟨6⟩, 11-340; 6 pp. advertisements. $6^{13}/_{16}$" x $4^{13}/_{16}$".

⟨1-21⁸, 22⁴⟩.

S cloth: brown. Yellow end papers. Flyleaves.

Deposited Oct. 27, 1888. Listed PW Dec. 8, 1888. MHS copy received Dec. 12, 1888. Noted by Ath Feb. 16, 1889.

MHS NYPL

8363. THE AFTERNOON LANDSCAPE POEMS AND TRANSLATIONS ...

NEW YORK AND LONDON LONGMANS, GREEN, AND CO. 1889

⟨i⟩-⟨viii⟩, ⟨9⟩-106, blank leaf. Laid paper. $7^{1}/_{4}$" x $4^{7}/_{8}$".

⟨1-6⁸, 7⁶⟩.

Light brown V cloth sides, dark brown V cloth shelfback. Flyleaves, both wove paper and laid paper noted. Top edges gilt.

Deposited April 8, 1889. H copy received April 9, 1889. BA copy received May 7, 1889. Listed PW June 1, 1889. The London edition (Longmans) appears to be made up of the American sheets with altered title-leaf; listed Ath April 13, 1889; advertised PC May 15, 1889; reviewed Ath Aug. 10, 1889; listed Bkr Dec. 14, 1889.

BA H NYPL

8364. ... Proceedings at the Celebration of the 250th Anniversary of the Settlement of Guilford, Conn., September 8th, 9th, and 10th, 1889.

New Haven, Conn.: The Stafford Printing Co., 86-90 Crown Street. 1889.

Cloth; and, printed paper wrapper. At head of title: 1639.

Address, pp. ⟨211⟩-215.

H NYPL

8365. In a Fair Country Illustrated by Irene E. Jerome Essays from "Out-Door Papers" ...

Boston Lee and Shepard Publishers New York Charles T. Dillingham 1890

Reprint.

Deposited Sept. 14, 1889. BPL copy received Oct. 1, 1889. Listed PW Oct. 19, 1889.

According to the PW listing issued in cloth; English seal; Turkey morocco; tree calf.

B BPL H

8366. ... Plan Reported by Request to the Book Committee, for the Selection of Books Bought with the Citizens' Subscription Fund of 1889–1890 ...

⟨Cambridge, 1890⟩

Cover-title. At head of title: Cambridge Public Library.

⟨1⟩-6, blank leaf. $9^{1}/_{4}$" x $5^{3}/_{4}$". Printed self-wrapper.

Dated at end February 12, 1890.

H NYPL Y

8367. ... Memorial to Robert Browning ... King's Chapel, Tuesday, January 28, 1890 ...

Printed for the Society by the University Press, Cambridge. ⟨n.d., 1890⟩

"Opening Address," pp. ⟨14⟩-16.

For comment see entry No. 4062.

8368. The Art of Authorship ... Compiled ... by George Bainton.

London: James Clarke & Co., 13 & 14, Fleet Street. 1890.

Contribution, pp. 32-33.

For comment see entry No. 1271.

8369. The Art of Authorship ... Compiled ... by George Bainton

New York D. Appleton and Company 1890

Contribution, pp. 32-33.

For comment see entry No. 1272.

8370. Vestis Angelica Quartet for Mixed Voices ... Music by F. Boott ...

Boston . . . 1890 . . . Oliver Ditson Company ...

Sheet music. Cover-title. Plate number: 54343-2.

Reprinted from *Afternoon Landscape,* 1889. Deposited July 16, 1890.

LC

8371. Poems by Emily Dickinson Edited by Two of Her Friends Mabel Loomis Todd and T. W. Higginson

Boston Roberts Brothers 1890

"Preface," pp. <iii>-vi.

For comment see entry No. 4655.

8372. The Works of Epictetus ... Translated from the Greek by Thomas Wentworth Higginson. A New and Revised Edition ...

Boston: Little, Brown, and Company. 1890.

2 Vols.

"Preface to Revised Edition," Vol. 1, p. <iii>. For first edition see entry No. 8252.

Issued in cloth, half morocco, half leather according to listing in PW.

Deposited Nov. 10, 1890. H copy received Nov. 15, 1890. Advertised as *new* PW Nov. 22/29, 1890. Listed PW Dec. 20, 1890.

AAS H

8373. American Sonnets Selected and Edited by T. W. Higginson and E. H. Bigelow

Boston and New York Houghton, Mifflin and Company The Riverside Press, Cambridge 1890

"Preface," pp. <iii>-viii. Otherwise reprint.

Advertised for Nov. 26, 1890, in PW Nov. 15, 1890. Copy in BPL inscribed by Bigelow Nov. 26, 1890. BA copy received Dec. 2, 1890. Listed PW Dec. 6, 1890; PC Dec. 15, 1890.

BA BPL H

8374. Representative Sonnets by American Poets ... by Charles H. Crandall

Boston and New York Houghton, Mifflin and Company The Riverside Press, Cambridge 1890

Reprint save for "Mille fiate o dolce mia guerrera," translated from Petrarch, pp. 33-34.

Noted as *just ready* PW Dec. 6, 1890.

H

8375. History of Middlesex County, Massachusetts, with Biographical Sketches of Many of Its Pioneers and Prominent Men. Compiled under the Supervision of D. Hamilton Hurd. Vol. I ...

Philadelphia: J. W. Lewis & Co. 1890.

"Cambridge ... Literature," pp. 151-153.

Deposited Dec. 30, 1890.

NYPL

8376. ... Annual Report of the Trustees of the Public Library to the City Council for the Year Ending, Nov. 30, 1889.

Boston: Cashman, Keating & Co. 597 Washington Street, 1890.

Printed paper wrapper. At head of title: City of Cambridge.

"Report of the Trustees," pp. 3-11, signed at end by Higginson and others.

H NYPL

8377. ... Majority and Minority Reports of the Special Committee on Subject of Co-Education of the Sexes.

Boston: Rockwell and Churchill, City Printers. 1890.

Cover-title. At head of title: School Document No. 19—1890.

Printed paper wrapper.

Statement favoring co-education, May 29, 1890, pp. 20-21.

H

8378. ... Sixty and Six ... Music by F. Boott

Boston Published by Oliver Ditson Company 449-451 Wash'n St. ... <1890>

Sheet music. Cover-title. At head of title: To Miss M. W. H. Plate number 54328-3.

Reprinted from *Afternoon Landscape,* 1889.

H NYPL

8379. *Entry cancelled.*

8380. Life of John Boyle O'Reilly, by James Jeffrey Roche ...

New York: Cassell Publishing Company, 104 & 106 Fourth Avenue. <1891>

A subscription book and as such issued in a variety of bindings and probably with varying imprints. A known *reprint* was issued with the later address of the publisher in the imprint: *31 East 17th Street.*

Tribute to O'Reilly, pp. 367-368.

Noted for Jan. 1, 1891, PW Dec. 13, 1890. Listed Ath April 11, 1891.

H

8381. ... LIFE OF FRANCIS HIGGINSON FIRST MINISTER IN THE MASSACHU-SETTS BAY COLONY, AND AUTHOR OF "NEW ENGLAND'S PLANTATION" (1630) ...

NEW YORK DODD, MEAD, AND COMPANY PUB-LISHERS ‹1891›

At head of title: "MAKERS OF AMERICA"

‹i-iv›, ‹1›-158; advertisements, pp. ‹1›-2; plus: advertisements, p. 3; blank, p. ‹4›; blank leaf. Laid paper. 6⅞" x 4⁹⁄₁₆".

‹-›², 1-10⁸; plus: ‹11›². Note: Signature mark 10 lacking in some copies.

V cloth: red. White laid paper end papers.

See entry No. 8453.

Advertised for this week PW April 4, 1891. Deposited April 10, 1891. H copy received April 14, 1891. Listed PW April 18, 1891.

AAS BPL H LC

8382. ... ON THE STEPS OF THE HALL. (UNIVERSITY HALL, AUG. 28, 1837). IN-SCRIBED TO THE CLASS OF 1841, JUNE 23, 1891 ...

‹n.p., Cambridge(?), 1891›

At head of title: [PRIVATELY PRINTED.]

Single cut sheet folded to four pages. The above on p. ‹1›.

Text on pp. ‹1-3›; p. ‹4› blank. Leaf: 10⁹⁄₁₆" x 8". Wove paper watermarked: Kelso.

H Y

8383. Poems by Emily Dickinson Edited by Two of Her Friends T. W. Higginson and Mabel Loomis Todd   Second Series

Boston   Roberts Brothers   1891

For comment see entry No. 4656.

8384. Advice to Young Authors   To Write or Not to Write ... Edited by Alice R. Mylene ...

Boston, Mass.: Morning Star Publishing House, 1891.

Contribution, pp. 18-30.

For fuller entry see No. 6724A.

8385. ... Annual Report of the Trustees of the Cambridge Public Library, for the Year 1890.

Cambridge: Harvard Printing Company, 1891.

Printed paper wrapper. At head of title: City of Cambridge.

"Report ... ," signed by Higginson and others, pp. ‹3›-7.

NYPL

8386. List of Battles and Casualties of Massa-chusetts Troops during the War of the Re-bellion. By Col. T. W. Higginson and Flor-ence Wyman Jaques.

Boston: David Clapp & Son, Printers. 115 High Street. 1891.

Cover-title.

‹1›-16. Laid paper. 9¼" x 5¾". Printed self-wrapper. Note, dated Dec. 22, 1891, printed on wove paper watermarked Hypatia Mills Super-fine, inserted.

H

8387. Proceedings of the Massachusetts Histori-cal Society. Second Series. Vol. VI. 1890, 1891 ...

Boston: Published by the Society. M.DCCC.XCI.

Printed paper wrapper; and, cloth.

Address, Jan. 24, 1891, pp. 275-283.

H NYPL

8388. The Rindge Gifts to the City of Cam-bridge Massachusetts

Cambridge   Published by Order of the City Council   1891

Co-edited by Higginson and with the following by him: "Address," pp. 26-27; "Remarks," pp. 52-54; 59-61.

H

8389. The Abbess of Port Royal and Other French Studies by Maria Ellery Mackaye with an Introduction by Thomas Wentworth Hig-ginson

Boston   Lee and Shepard Publishers   10 Milk Street   1892

"Introduction," p. ‹v›.

Deposited Oct. 9, 1891. H copy received Oct. 10, 1891. Listed PW Oct. 24, 1891.

AAS H NYPL

8390. THE NEW WORLD AND THE NEW BOOK AN ADDRESS DELIVERED BEFORE THE NINETEENTH CENTURY CLUB OF NEW YORK CITY, JAN. 15, 1891 WITH KINDRED ESSAYS ...

BOSTON LEE AND SHEPARD PUBLISHERS 1892

⟨i⟩-viii, 1-239; blank, p. ⟨240⟩; 6 pp. advertisements; blank leaf. 7¼" full x 5".

⟨1-16⟩⁸.

H cloth: blue; brown; maroon; purple. Gray-coated on white end papers. Flyleaf at front. Top edges gilt.

Deposited Nov. 6, 1891. BA copy received Nov. 24, 1891. Listed PW Dec. 5, 1891. Reviewed PC Dec. 19, 1891. Noted as *on our table* Ath June 4, 1892.

H NYPL Y

8391. Lowell Memorial Number ... The Cambridge Tribune Vol. XIV No. 48.

Cambridge, Mass., Saturday, February 20, 1892 ...

Caption-title. The above at head of p. ⟨1⟩.

"Tribute to James Russell Lowell Read before the Massachusetts Commandery of the Loyal Legion of the United States," p. 2; prepared for this publication. See *Military Order of the Loyal Legion* ... ⟨1892⟩, below.

H

8392. CONCERNING ALL OF US ...

NEW YORK HARPER AND BROTHERS MDCCCXCII

Title-page in black, orange and buff.

⟨iii⟩-vi, ⟨1⟩-210; advertisements, pp. ⟨211-216⟩. Portrait frontispiece and printed tissue inserted. 6" x 3½". Laid paper.

⟨-⟩², 1-13⁸, 14⁴.

V cloth: green. White laid paper end papers. Top edges plain.

Three printings noted:

1

As described above.

Printed on laid paper.

P. 119, line 9 up: *American women* ...

On p. 191 the *i* in the word *in* (line 10) is directly below the *ce* in the word *glance* (line 9).

P. ⟨214⟩: *By George William Curtis. From the Easy Chair* ...

2

As described above but with the following variations:

Printed on wove paper.

P. 191 the *i* in the word *in* (line 10) is directly below the *e* in the word *glance* (line 9).

3

Printed on wove paper.

P. 119, line 9 up: *American woman* ...

On p. 191 the *i* in the word *in* (line 10) is directly below the *e* in the word *glance* (line 9).

P. ⟨214⟩: *By George William Curtis. James Russell Lowell: An Address* ...

Noted in white V cloth, top edges gilded; and, green V cloth, top edges plain.

Deposited April 9, 1892. BA copy (1st) received April 12, 1892. H copy (1st) presented by Higginson April 14, 1892. Listed PW April 16, 1892.

BA (1st) H (1st, 2nd) LC (1st, being deposit copies) NYPL (3rd) Y (1st, 3rd)

8393. A WORLD OUTSIDE OF SCIENCE ... [FROM THE NEW WORLD FOR DECEMBER, 1892]

⟨n.p., n.d.⟩

Cover-title.

⟨1⟩-8. 9⅛" x 5¾" full.

⟨-⟩⁴.

Printed self-wrapper.

Collected in *Book and Heart*, 1897.

H

8394. ... Annual Report of the Trustees of the Cambridge Public Library, for the Year 1891

Cambridge Harvard Printing Company 1892

Printed paper wrapper. At head of title: City of Cambridge

"Report ...," pp. ⟨3⟩-7, signed at end by Higginson and others.

NYPL

8395. Lectures to Young Men Delivered in the Church of the Divine Paternity ...

New York City 1892

Printed paper wrapper.

"Youth and Literary Life," pp. 32-44.

H Y

8396. Military Order of the Loyal Legion of the United States Commandery of the State of Massachusetts In Memoriam Companion James Russell Lowell

⟨Boston, 1892⟩

Cover-title. Printed paper wrapper.

A eulogy of James Russell Lowell, pp. ⟨4-8⟩. The eulogy also appears in the *Lowell Memorial Number* of the *Cambridge Tribune*, Feb. 20, 1892, *q.v.*.

Issued as *Circular No. 3, Series ⟨of⟩ 1892, Whole Number, 316,* under date of March 2, 1892.

NYPL Y

8397. ENGLISH HISTORY FOR AMERICAN READERS BY THOMAS WENTWORTH HIGGINSON ... AND EDWARD CHANNING ...

NEW YORK LONGMANS, GREEN, AND CO. 15 EAST SIXTEENTH STREET 1893

⟨i⟩-xxxii, ⟨1⟩-334; 2 pp. advertisements. Illustrated. Two folded maps inserted. 7½″ x 5⅛″.

⟨a⟩-b, 1-9, ⟨10-11⟩, 12-13, ⟨14⟩, 15-21⁸.

H cloth: red. White paper end papers printed in colors with maps.

Note: Several later printings, some revised. According to the bibliography in the 1914 edition the following editions were revised: March, 1896; July, 1897; August, 1902; September, 1914. Since Higginson died in 1911 it appears safe to exclude from this list any edition done after that year. The reprints and revised reissues were published under the title: *English History for Americans.* ...

Deposited Aug. 21, 1893. Listed PW Sept. 16, 1893; Ath Jan. 20, 1894.

AAS NYPL

8398. SUCH AS THEY ARE POEMS BY THOMAS WENTWORTH HIGGINSON AND MARY THACHER HIGGINSON

BOSTON ROBERTS BROTHERS 1893

⟨i-iv⟩, ⟨i⟩-⟨x⟩, 11-74, blank leaf. 6¾″ full x 5⅜″.

⟨1-10⟩⁴.

V cloth: green; white. Edges gilt.

Deposited Nov. 4, 1893. Advertised for Nov. 4 publication PW Nov. 4, 1893. Noted for *next week* PW Nov. 4, 1893. BPL copy received Nov. 6, 1893. BA copy received Nov. 9, 1893. NYPL

copy inscribed by the authors Nov. 15, 1893. Listed PW Dec. 2, 1893; PC Dec. 23, 1893.

BA H NYPL

8398A. ... Straight Lines or Oblique Lines? ...

⟨Boston, 1893⟩

Caption-title. At head of title: Woman Suffrage Leaflet. Published Bi-Monthly at the Office of The Woman's Journal, Boston, Mass. Vol. VI ... No. 6 ... November, 1893 ...

Single leaf. Front as above. 9¾″ x 5⅞″. See entry No. 8497.

H Y

8399. ... Reports of the Trustees and Librarian of the Public Library for the Year 1892.

Boston: Cashman, Keating & Co., Printers. 1893.

Printed paper wrapper. At head of title: City of Cambridge.

"Report ... ," pp. ⟨3⟩-7, signed at end by Higginson and others.

NYPL

8400. Speeches and Addresses of William E. Russell. Selected and Edited by Charles Theodore Russell, Jr. With an Introduction by Thomas Wentworth Higginson.

Boston: Little, Brown, and Company. 1894.

"Introduction," pp. ⟨xi⟩-xvi.

Deposited Dec. 19, 1893. Listed PW Dec. 30, 1893.

H MHS

8401. ... Proceedings at the Twenty-Sixth Annual Meeting of the Free Religious Association of America, Held in Chicago, Ill., September 20th, 1893 ...

Boston: Published by the Free Religious Association. 1894.

Printed paper wrapper. At head of title: Free Religious Association of America.

"Address," pp. 11-14. Also contains remarks, comments, etc., throughout.

BPL H LC Y

8402. Boston, Mass., July 1, 1894. Dear Friend, —In accordance with the amended constitution of the Free Religious Association, there has been appointed a committee of five ...

T. W. Higginson, for the Standing Committee. (Summer Address, Dublin, N. H.)

Single cut sheet. Printed on recto only. $7\frac{15}{16}$" x $5\frac{1}{4}$".

NYPL

8403. The Woman's Book   Dealing Practically with the Modern Conditions of Home-Life, Self-Support, Education, Opportunities, and Every-Day Problems ...

New York   Charles Scribner's Sons   1894

2 Vols. Cloth; and, half leather.

"Books and Reading," Vol. 1, pp. ⟨358⟩-368.

For comment see entry No. 7204.

8404. ... Annual Report of the Trustees of the Cambridge Public Library, for the Year 1893.

Cambridge: Harvard Printing Company, 1894.

Printed paper wrapper. At head of title: City of Cambridge.

"Report ... ," pp. ⟨3⟩-5.

H   NYPL

8405. ⟨Lights and Shadows. A Composite Poem⟩

⟨n.p., n.d., 1894⟩

The only located copy of this poem is printed in black, in facsimile autograph of the several authors, on a piece of beige satin, 12" x 10½". Presumably printed on recto only.

A poem written in collaboration with Julia Ward Howe, Louise Chandler Moulton, Louise Imogen Guiney, Richard Hovey, and others.

For a comment on the poem see *Boston Sunday Globe*, Jan. 14, 1894.

H

8406. *Entry cancelled.*

8407. ... Annual Report of the Trustees of the Public Library for the Year Ending November 30, 1894.

Boston: Cashman, O'Connor & Co., Printers. 1895.

Printed paper wrapper. At head of title: City of Cambridge.

"Report ... ," pp. ⟨3⟩-7.

H   NYPL

8408. The Free Religious Association   Proceedings at the Twenty-Eighth Annual Meeting Held in Parker Memorial Hall   Boston, Mass. ... May 30th and 31st 1895

Providence   Published by the Free Religious Association 1895

Printed paper wrapper.

"Opening Address ... ," pp. 6-9. Also contains remarks, comments, etc., throughout.

H

8409. Massachusetts in the Army and Navy during the War of 1861-65. Prepared under the Authority of the State by Thomas Wentworth Higginson ...

Boston: Wright & Potter Printing Co., State Printers, 18 Post Office Square. 1896. ⟨and⟩ 1895.

2 Vols. Vol. 1 dated 1896; Vol. 2 dated 1895.

"Preface," Vol. 1, pp. ⟨iii⟩-vi, signed at end: *T.W.H.*

"Introduction," Vol. 1, pp. ⟨vii⟩-xv; unsigned; presumably by Higginson.

"Note," Vol. 2, p. ⟨1⟩, signed at end: *T.W.H.*

BPL copy of Vol. 2 received Jan. 2, 1896. H copy (2 Vols.) received March 14, 1896. BA copy (2 Vols.) contains inserted letter of presentation dated March 20, 1896.

BA   BPL   H   Y

8410. Cambridge Sketches by Cambridge Authors, Edited by Estelle M. H. Merrill, "Jean Kincaid," with Preface by Dr. Alexander McKenzie.

Published by the Cambridge Young Women's Christian Association. ⟨1896⟩

"The Fairy Coursers," p. 180.

Deposited Feb. 24, 1896.

H   NYPL   Y

8411. The Cambridge of Eighteen Hundred and Ninety-Six   A Picture of the City and Its Industries Fifty Years after Its Incorporation Done by Divers Hands and Edited by Arthur Gilman ...

Cambridge   Printed at the Riverside Press 1896

"Life in Cambridge Town," pp. ⟨35⟩-42.

Deposited May 18, 1896.

H   NYPL

8412. A Souvenir and a Medley: Seven Poems and a Sketch by Stephen Crane ...

... The Roycroft Printing Shop ... East Aurora, N. Y.   Eighteen Hundred and Ninety-Six.

4-line statement, p. 13.

For comment see entry No. 4074.

8413. The Free Religious Association Proceedings at the Twenty-Ninth Annual Meeting Held in Parker Memorial Hall Boston, Mass. ... May 28th and 29th 1896

New Bedford Published by the Free Religious Association 1896

Printed paper wrapper.

"President's Address," pp. 11-14.

H LC

8414. Short Stories for Short People by Alicia Aspinwall ...

New York E. P. Dutton and Company 31 West Twenty-Third Street 1896

"Prefatory Note," pp. vii-viii.

BPL copy inscribed Aug. 1896. Listed PW Oct. 17, 1896.

BPL

8415. Essays from the Chap-Book ...

Chicago. Printed for Herbert S. Stone & Company ... 1896

"The School of Jingoes," pp. 141-145.

For comment see entry No. 1291.

8416. Young Folks' Book of American Explorers ...

New York Longmans, Green, and Co. 1896

A reprint of *A Book of American Explorers,* 1877.

LC

8417. BOOK AND HEART ESSAYS ON LITERATURE AND LIFE ...

NEW YORK HARPER & BROTHERS PUBLISHERS 1897

⟨i-iv⟩, ⟨i⟩-iv, ⟨1⟩-237; blank, p. ⟨238⟩; 2 pp. advertisements. 7½" x 5".

⟨-⟩⁴, ⟨1⟩-2, ⟨3⟩-4, ⟨5⟩-12, ⟨13⟩-15⁸.

S cloth: red. White laid paper end papers. Top edges gilt.

Deposited March 5, 1897. BA copy received March 9, 1897; H copy March 11, 1897. Listed PW March 13, 1897; PC March 27, 1897.

H NYPL

8418. The Authors Club Dinner to Richard Henry Stoddard. At the Savoy, New York, March 25, 1897 ... Reprinted from the Mail and Express, New York, Issue of March 26, 1897.

⟨n.p., n.d., New York, 1897⟩

Letter, p. 15.

For comment see entry No. 6581.

8419. The Procession of the Flowers and Kindred Papers ...

New York Longmans, Green, and Co. London and Bombay 1897

With the exception of "A Moonglade" reprinted from *Out-Door Papers,* 1863. "A Moonglade" had prior publication in *Laurel Leaves,* 1876, above.

Short prefatory note, dated Feb. 11, 1897, p. ⟨vii⟩.

Deposited April 1, 1897. BA copy received April 6, 1897. Listed PW April 10, 1897. The London (Longmans) edition advertised for *Monday next* Ath May 22, 1897.

BA H

8420. ... A Library of the World's Best Literature Ancient and Modern ⟨Edited by⟩ Charles Dudley Warner ...

New York The International Society MDCCCXCVII

Reprint save for:

"Joseph Joubert," Vol. 21, pp. 8385-8388. Vol. 21 deposited Dec. 20, 1897.

"Jeremy Taylor," Vol. 36, pp. 14551-14554.

For comment see entry No. 2165.

8421. The Boston Browning Society Papers Selected to Represent the Work of the Society from 1886–1897

New York The Macmillan Company London: Macmillan & Co., Ltd. 1897 ...

"The Biography of Browning's Fame," pp. ⟨1⟩-6.

Noted as *about to publish* PW May 22, 1897. Deposited Aug. 7, 1897.

H

8422. CHEERFUL YESTERDAYS ...

BOSTON AND NEW YORK HOUGHTON, MIFFLIN AND COMPANY THE RIVERSIDE PRESS, CAMBRIDGE MDCCC XCVIII

⟨i-xii⟩, ⟨1⟩-374; plus: printer's imprint, p. ⟨375⟩. Laid paper. 7⅜" x 5".

⟨1⁹, 2-24⁸; plus: 25¹⟩. Leaf ⟨1⟩₂ inserted.

Two printings noted:

1: As above.

2: Printed on wove (not laid) paper. Pp. ⟨i-x⟩, ⟨1⟩-374; printer's imprint, p. ⟨375⟩. ⟨1-24⁸, 25¹⟩.

T cloth: brown; green; maroon. White laid paper end papers. Flyleaf at back. Top edges gilt.

Deposited March 16, 1898. Noted for *today* PW March 19, 1898. Listed PW March 26, 1898. The London (Gay & Bird) edition noted as *just published* Ath May 28, 1898; listed Ath June 18, 1898.

BA (1st)   H (1st)   NYPL (1st, 2nd)

8423. The Free Religious Association Proceedings at the Thirty-First Annual Meeting Held in Boston, Mass. . . . May 26th and 27th 1898

Boston, Mass. Published by the Free Religious Association 1898

Printed paper wrapper.

"Address," pp. ⟨11⟩-14. Remarks, comments, etc., throughout.

BPL   H

8424. American Prose Selections with Critical Introductions by Various Writers and a General Introduction Edited by George Rice Carpenter . . .

New York   The Macmillan Company   London: Macmillan & Co., Ltd. 1898 . . .

"Charles Brockden Brown," pp. 84-88.

"James Fenimore Cooper," pp. 148-152.

"Henry David Thoreau," pp. 338-342.

Collected in *Carlyle's Laugh*, 1909.

"Leave has been obtained to reprint the papers on Brown, Cooper, and Thoreau, from Carpenter's *American Prose* . . . 1898 . . ."—From Higginson's prefatory note to *Carlyle's Laugh*, 1909.

Deposited Oct. 5, 1898. BA copy received Oct. 18, 1898. Listed PW Oct. 29, 1898.

H

8425. TALES OF THE ENCHANTED IS-LANDS OF THE ATLANTIC . . .

NEW YORK   THE MACMILLAN COMPANY   LON-DON: MACMILLAN & CO., LTD. 1898 ALL RIGHTS RESERVED

⟨i⟩-⟨xvi⟩, 1-259; blank, p. ⟨260⟩; 2 pp. advertisements; blank leaf. 7⁷⁄₁₆" x 5³⁄₁₆". Frontispiece and 5 plates inserted.

⟨A⟩-I, K-R⁸, S⁴.

V cloth: blue-black; green-blue.

Deposited Oct. 15, 1898. BA copy received Oct. 25, 1898. NYPL copy received Oct. 26, 1898. Listed PW Nov. 5, 1898. The London edition, made up of American sheets with cancel title-leaf, listed by both Ath and PC Jan. 21, 1899.

BA   NYPL

8426. . . . Historic Towns of New England Edited by Lyman P. Powell . . .

G. P. Putnam's Sons   New York & London   The Knickerbocker Press 1898

At head of title: American Historic Towns

"Boston the Trimountain City," pp. 167-185.

Deposited Nov. 17, 1898. BPL copy received Nov. 23, 1898. Listed PW Dec. 10, 1898.

H   LC

8427. Uncle Tom's Cabin or Life among the Lowly by Harriet Beecher Stowe with a Critical and Biographical Introduction by Thomas Wentworth Higginson . . .

New York   D. Appleton and Company 1898

Cloth?

"Harriet Beecher Stowe," pp. iii-xiv.

Deposited Feb. 4, 1899.

NYPL

8428. Address to the People of the United States. March 13, 1899 . . .

⟨n.p., 1899⟩

Single cut sheet. Printed on both sides. Signed at end by Higginson and others. Probably issued by the Anti-Imperialist League.

NYPL

8429. OLD CAMBRIDGE . . .

NEW YORK   THE MACMILLAN COMPANY   LON-DON: MACMILLAN & CO., LTD. 1899 ALL RIGHTS RESERVED

⟨i⟩-⟨vi⟩, ⟨1⟩-203; blank, p. ⟨204⟩; 2 pp. advertisements. Laid paper. 6¹⁵⁄₁₆" x 4¾".

⟨1-13⁸, 14²⟩. *Signed:* ⟨A⟩³, ⟨B⟩-I, K-⟨L⟩, M-N⁸, O⁷.

V cloth: maroon. White laid paper end papers. Top edges gilt.

Noted as *nearly ready* PW April 15, 1899. Deposited May 5, 1899. NYPL copy received May 13, 1899; BA May 16, 1899; H May 20, 1899. Listed PW June 3, 1899; Ath Aug. 12, 1899.

H   NYPL

8430. Cambridge Anti-Imperialist Broadside.

Published by Cambridge Anti-Imperialist League, May 17, 1899 . . .

Caption-title. The above at head of sheet. Single cut sheet. Printed on recto only.

Contains "Letter of Col. T. W. Higginson. In Boston Transcript)."

H

8431. The Free Religious Association Proceedings at the Thirty-Second Annual Meeting Held in Boston, Mass. . . . June 1st and 2d 1899

Boston, Mass. Published by the Free Religious Association 1899

Printed paper wrapper.

"Opening Remarks," pp. 57-58. Also contains remarks throughout.

BPL   H

8432. . . . "WHERE LIBERTY IS NOT, THERE IS MY COUNTRY." [FROM HARPER'S BAZAAR, AUG. 12, 1899.] . . .

⟨Washington, D. C., Anti-Imperialist League, 1899⟩

Single cut sheet. Caption-title. Printed in four columns on recto only. 10⅜″ x 10⁹⁄₁₆″. At head of title. SAVE THE REPUBLIC. ANTI-IMPERIALIST LEAFLET NO. 19. ANTI-IMPERIALIST LEAGUE, WASHINGTON, D. C.

Also contains material by others.

CPL   H   NYPL   Y

8433. CONTEMPORARIES . . .

BOSTON AND NEW YORK   HOUGHTON, MIFFLIN AND COMPANY   THE RIVERSIDE PRESS, CAMBRIDGE MDCCCXCIX

⟨i-viii⟩, ⟨1⟩-379; printer's imprint, p. ⟨380⟩. Laid paper. 7⁷⁄₁₆″ x 4¹⁵⁄₁₆″.

⟨1⁴, 2-32⁶, 33⁴⟩.

T cloth: blue; green; maroon. White laid paper end papers. Laid paper flyleaves. Top edges gilt.

Note: The spine imprint occurs in the following forms; sequence, if any, not determined:

A: With a period following the *CO* in the spine imprint. The deposit copies thus.

B: Without a period following the *CO* in the spine imprint.

Deposited Oct. 5, 1899. Listed PW Nov. 4, 1899. BPL copy received Nov. 13, 1899.

AAS (A)   LC (A)   NYPL (B)   Y (A)

8434. . . . Annual Report of the Trustees of the Cambridge Public Library for the Year Ending November 30, 1898 Published by Order of the City Council under the Direction of the City Clerk

⟨Cambridge, 1899⟩

Printed paper wrapper. At head of title: City of Cambridge

"Report . . . ," pp. ⟨5⟩-6.

H   NYPL

8435. Proceedings of the Massachusetts Historical Society. Second Series. Vol. XII . . .

Boston: Published by the Society. M.DCCC.XCIX.

Remarks, pp. 9-10.

AAS

8436. . . . Three Outdoor Papers . . .

Houghton, Mifflin and Company   Boston . . . New York . . . Chicago . . . The Riverside Press, Cambridge ⟨1900⟩

Printed paper wrapper. At head of title: The Riverside Literature Series

Issued as No. 141 of the series under date March 7, 1900.

Reprint.

Deposited April 14, 1900. Listed PW July 21, 1900. *Note:* Higginson, p. 419, describes this publication under the year 1889. No copy so dated located or elsewhere reported.

H   LC

8437. OCTAVIUS BROOKS FROTHINGHAM

This address has been located in the following two publications. The sequence has not been determined and the order of presentation is wholly arbitrary.

A

The Free Religious Association Proceedings at the Thirty-Third Annual Meeting Held in Boston, Mass. . . . May 31 and June 1 1900

Boston, Mass. Published by the Free Religious Association 1900

Printed paper wrapper. "Address . . . Octavius Brooks Frothingham," pp. 70-73.

B

Prophets of Liberalism Six Addresses before the Free Religious Association of America at Its Thirty-Third Annual Convention . . . Boston . . . June 1 1900 . . .

Boston The James H. West Company 1900

Printed paper wrapper. "Octavius Brooks Frothingham," pp. 67-70.

BPL (B)   H (A)   Y (B)

8438. THE ALLIANCE BETWEEN PILGRIM AND PURITAN IN MASSACHUSETTS AN ADDRESS DELIVERED BEFORE THE OLD PLANTERS SOCIETY . . . IN JACOB SLEEPER HALL, BOSTON UNIVERSITY JUNE 9th, 1900 TO WHICH IS ADDED AN ACCOUNT OF THE FORMATION OF THE SOCIETY . . .

SALEM, MASSACHUSETTS 1900

⟨1⟩-23. Laid paper. 9¹⁄₁₆″ x 5⅛″.

⟨1⁸, 2⁴⟩.

Printed green paper wrapper.

Higginson's address appears at pp. 3-10.

AAS   H   NYPL   Y

8439. REASONS FOR VOTING FOR BRYAN SUBMITTED TO THE REPUBLICANS BY COL HIGGINSON. [FROM THE SPRINGFIELD DAILY REPUBLICAN, SEPTEMBER 1, 1900.] . . .

DUBLIN, N. H., AUGUST 30, 1900.

Probably published at Springfield, Mass., 1900.

Single cut sheet. 8″ x 3⅛″. Printed on recto only.

CPL   H

8440. The Writings of Thomas Wentworth Higginson ⟨fly-title⟩

Boston and New York   Houghton, Mifflin and Company   The Riverside Press, Cambridge MDCCCC

Trade edition in cloth imprinted as above.

Large Paper Edition, boards, printed paper label on spine. Limited to 200 numbered sets. Vol. 1 signed by the author. Imprinted: *Cambridge Printed at the Riverside Press* MDCCCC

7 Vols.

1: *Cheerful Yesterdays*. Reprint.

2: *Contemporaries*. Reprint.

3: *Army Life in a Black Regiment.*
An extended edition of the 1870 printing with the following added material: A full-page dedication to Gen. Rufus Saxton, dated Dec. 22, 1899. And, "Fourteen Years After," pp. ⟨360⟩-387; originally in *Atlantic Monthly*, July, 1878, as "Some War Scenes Revisited"; no earlier book appearance located.

4: *Women and the Alphabet* . . .
A virtual reprint of *Common Sense about Women*, 1882. Contains a prefatory note written for this edition, pp. ⟨iii⟩-iv.

5: *Studies in Romance* . . .
Reprint save for the "Preface," pp. ⟨iii⟩-iv.

6: *Outdoor Studies Poems* . . .
Contains some material here first collected and a new "Prefatory Note," p. ⟨iii⟩.

7: *Studies in History and Letters* . . .
Contains some material here first collected.

Noted for *today* PW Sept. 22, 1900. Deposited (*Large Paper Edition* only) Sept. 24, 1900. Listed PW Oct. 13, 1900, on the basis of publisher's information; not seen by PW. Advertised for Oct. 31, 1900, in PW Oct. 27, 1900.

H   LC

8441. How Should a Colored Man Vote in 1900 by Thos. Wentworth Higgenson ⟨sic⟩. William Lloyd Garrison. George S. Boutwell.

⟨Chicago, 1900⟩

Single cut sheet folded to 4 pages. Page: 6¼″ x 3⅝″. Pp. ⟨1⟩-4.

Issued on behalf of the candidacy of William Jennings Bryan. Reprinted from *The Boston Herald*, Oct. 11, 1900.

CPL   H

8442. Civil War Papers Read before the Commandery of the State of Massachusetts, Military Order of the Loyal Legion of the United States . . .

Boston: Printed for the Commandery MCM

2 Vols.

"The Reoccupation of Jacksonville in 1863," Vol. 2, pp. 467-474.

Deposited Dec. 21, 1900.

BA   H   LC   NYPL

8443. . . . Annual Report of the Trustees of the Cambridge Public Library for the Year Ending November 30, 1899 Published by Order of the City Council under the Direction of the City Clerk.

⟨Cambridge, 1900⟩

Printed paper wrapper. At head of title: City of Cambridge

"Report of the Trustees . . . ," pp. ⟨5⟩-6, signed by Higginson and William Taggard Piper.

H   NYPL

8444. AMERICAN ORATORS AND ORA-TORY. BEING A REPORT OF LECTURES DELIVERED BY THOMAS WENT-WORTH HIGGINSON, AT WESTERN RESERVE UNIVERSITY, UNDER THE AUSPICES OF THE WESTERN RESERVE CHAPTER DAUGHTERS OF THE AMER-ICAN REVOLUTION

PRINTED BY THE IMPERIAL PRESS, CLEVELAND, OHIO, MARCH, 1901.

Title-page printed in black and red.

⟨i-ii⟩, ⟨1⟩-91, blank leaf. Laid paper water-marked *Ruisdael*. Double frontispiece inserted; other illustrations in text. 8¼″ x 5³⁄₁₆″.

⟨1-6⟩⁸.

T cloth: yellow. Printed paper label on spine. White laid paper end papers.

500 numbered copies only.

NYPL copy inscribed by early owner April 25, 1901. Listed PW May 11, 1901.

H   NYPL   Y

8445. The Old Planters Society. A field meeting will be held under the auspices of this society, on Saturday, June 7th, at 2.30 p.m., . . .

Salem, May 29, 1902.

Single cut sheet. Printed on recto only. Signed at end by Higginson (as president); and, Lucie M. Gardner (as secretary). 8⁷⁄₁₆″ x 5⁷⁄₁₆″.

JN

8446. The King Alfred Millenary . . . by Alfred Bowker . . .

London   Macmillan and Co., Limited   New York: The Macmillan Company   1902 . . .

Response to the toast, "Our Visitors," pp. 92-93.

Listed PW July 12, 1902.

H

8447. Nathaniel Higginson Royal Governor of Madras 1692–1698 Reprinted by Permission from "Two New England Rulers of Madras" by Bernard C. Steiner, in the "South Atlantic Quarterly," July 1902 . . .

1902   The Seeman Printery, Printing and Binding, Durham, N. C.

Printed paper wrapper.

A brief (12 lines) prefatory note by Higginson, p. ⟨3⟩.

BPL   H

8448. . . . HENRY WADSWORTH LONGFEL-LOW . . .

BOSTON AND NEW YORK   HOUGHTON, MIFFLIN AND COMPANY   THE RIVERSIDE PRESS, CAMBRIDGE 1902

Trade Edition

⟨i-ii⟩, ⟨i⟩-vi, ⟨1⟩-336; blank, p. ⟨337⟩; printer's imprint, p. ⟨338⟩, 2 pp. advertisements. Portrait frontispiece inserted. 6⅞″ full x 4⅝″.

At head of title: AMERICAN MEN OF LETTERS

⟨1⁴, 2-22⁸, 23²⟩.

S cloth: maroon. White laid paper end papers. Flyleaves. Top edges gilt.

Limited Edition

In addition to the trade edition there was also a limited edition. This was made up of the sheets of the first printing but issued wholly untrimmed. Pagination as above; page size: 7³⁄₁₆″ x 4¾″. Collation as above. Bound in red V cloth, printed paper label on spine. On copy-right page: . . . *Of this edition Three Hundred Copies have been printed and bound entirely uncut . . .*

Two printings noted; the following sequence is presumed correct:

1: As above.

2: Collation: ⟨1-21⁸, 22⁶⟩.

On copyright page: *Published October, 1902* Noted as forthcoming PW Sept. 13, 1902. Deposited Sept. 27, 1902. Noted for Oct. 4, PW Sept. 27, 1902. BA copy received Oct. 7, 1902. Listed PW Oct. 11, 1902. The London (Gay & Bird) edition listed Ath Dec. 13, 1902; a Constable edition listed Ath March 10, 1906.

B (1st)   BA (1st)   H (1st, 2nd, limited)   Y (limited)

8449. . . . JOHN GREENLEAF WHITTIER . . .

NEW YORK   THE MACMILLAN COMPANY   LONDON: MACMILLAN & CO., LTD. 1902 . . .

At head of title: ENGLISH MEN OF LETTERS   Title-page in black and red.

⟨i⟩-⟨x⟩, 1-196, 2 pp. advertisements. 7⁵⁄₁₆″ x 4⅞″.

⟨1-13⟩⁸. *Signed:* ⟨A⟩⁵, B-I, K-N⁸, O³.

H cloth: blue. Top edges gilt.

On copyright page: *Set up and electrotyped October, 1902.* Deposited Nov. 7, 1902. Listed PW Dec. 6, 1902.

BA H

8450. The Story without an End From the German of F. W. Carové ⟨by⟩ Sarah Austin With a Preface by Thomas Wentworth Higginson . . .

Boston, U.S.A. D. C. Heath & Co., Publishers 1902

"Preface," pp. v-vii.

Published Dec. 11, 1902, according to the publisher's records. Listed PW Jan. 31, 1903.

Location: Publisher's office.

8451. . . . Annual Report of the Trustees of the Cambridge Public Library for the Year Ending November 30, 1901 . . .

⟨Cambridge, 1902⟩

At head of title: City of Cambridge Massachusetts Printed paper wrapper.

"Report of the Trustees . . . ," pp. ⟨7⟩-8, signed at end by Higginson and William J. Rolfe.

H NYPL

8452. HORACE ELISHA SCUDDER. [FROM THE PROCEEDINGS OF THE AMERICAN ACADEMY OF ARTS AND SCIENCES, VOL. XXXVII.]

⟨n.p., n.d, Boston, 1902⟩

Cover-title.

23-⟨27⟩, blank leaf. 9⅝″ x 6¹⁄₁₆″.

⟨-⟩⁴.

Printed green paper wrapper.

Also appears in *Proceedings of the American Academy of Arts and Sciences, Vol. XXXVII, from May, 1901, to May, 1902,* Boston, 1902.

H Y

8453. In April, 1902, I addressed a letter to Colonel Thomas Wentworth Higginson calling his attention to the erroneous statement on the title-page of his memoir of the Rev. Francis Higginson in designating him as "the First Minister in the Massachusetts Bay Colony"; also to the mistake . . .

⟨n.p., 1902?⟩

Single cut sheet of laid paper folded to 4 pages. Page: 10″ x 6″. Text on pp. ⟨2-3⟩, otherwise unprinted.

Prefatory note (as above) preceding a letter from Higginson, April 11, 1902, to "Dear Mr. Rice" discussing the alleged errors. The reference is to Higginson's *Life of Francis Higginson,* New York ⟨1891⟩, *above; i.e.,* entry No. 8381.

AAS

8454. The New Volumes of the Encyclopaedia Britannica . . . The Tenth Edition . . . Vol. VII. Forming Vol. XXXI. of the Complete Work

Published by Adam and Charles Black London and Edinburgh The Encyclopaedia Britannica Company New York MCMII

Sketch of Wendell Phillips, pp. 672-673.

Y

8455. Proceedings of the Massachusetts Historical Society. Second Series. Vol. XV . . .

Boston: Published by the Society. MDCCCCII.

Tribute to Horace E. Scudder, pp. 494-496.

AAS

8456. The American Quarterly Livraisons

⟨Philadelphia and Boston, 1903⟩

Cover-title. Limp leather.

Printed from the plates of *The American Quarterly . . . Poet-Lore,* Jan.–March, 1903, with the following inserts: Certificate of issue stating: *This edition is limited to seventy-five Copies;* and, two translations from Petrarch which appear also in Higginson's *Fifteen Sonnets . . . ,* 1903. The two translations do not appear in the 1900 version (*Works,* Vol. 5) of Higginson's translations from Petrarch.

H

8457. . . . Mass Meetings of Protest against the Suppression of Truth about the Philippines Faneuil Hall Thursday, March 19, 3 and 8 P. M. . . .

Boston, March, 1903.

Printed self-wrapper. Cover-title. At head of title: *You are earnestly asked to hand this after reading to some other person* . . .

Remarks, p. ⟨3⟩.

Two editions noted:

1: Title set in capitals and lower case letters; printed from a serif'd face.

2: Title set in capital letters; printed from a *sans-serif* face.

H (1) NYPL (1, 2)

8458. The Centenary of the Birth of Ralph Waldo Emerson as Observed in Concord May 25 1903 under the Direction of the Social Circle in Concord . . .

Printed at the Riverside Press for the Social Circle in Concord June 1903

Address, pp. 58-66.

H

8459. The Emerson Centennial May 25, 1903 Extracts from a Few of the Many Tributes to Emerson Called Forth by the Centennial Observances from Some of the Leading Scholars of To-Day

⟨n.p., n.d., 1903?⟩

Printed paper wrapper. Cover-title.

An extract from Higginson's "The Personality of Emerson," pp. 5-7, reprinted from *The Outlook*, May 23, 1903.

Not to be confused with the preceding entry.

NYPL

8460. A READER'S HISTORY OF AMERICAN LITERATURE BY THOMAS WENTWORTH HIGGINSON AND HENRY WALCOTT BOYNTON

BOSTON, NEW YORK AND CHICAGO HOUGHTON, MIFFLIN AND COMPANY THE RIVERSIDE PRESS, CAMBRIDGE ⟨1903⟩

⟨i⟩-⟨viii⟩, ⟨1⟩-327; printer's imprint, p. ⟨328⟩. Inserted: frontispiece; 9 single plates; 2 four-page plates; 3 two-page plates. 7⁹⁄₁₆″ x 4⅞″.

⟨1⁴, 2-21⁸, 22⁴⟩

T cloth: maroon. White laid paper end papers. Flyleaves.

Noted for *to-day* PW Sept. 26, 1903. Deposited Oct. 1, 1903. BA copy received Oct. 13, 1903. Listed PW Dec. 26, 1903. Listed (again) PW Jan. 30, 1904.

BA LC NYPL

8461. Fifteen Sonnets of Petrarch Selected and Translated by Thomas Wentworth Higginson

Published by Houghton Mifflin & Company Boston and New York MDCCCCIII

⟨i-ii⟩, ⟨i⟩-xiv, ⟨1⟩-31; colophon, p. ⟨32⟩. Laid paper watermarked: *Unbleached Arnold*. 7⁷⁄₁₆″ x 4¼″ scant. Blue-green paper boards sides, white vellum shelfback.

Essentially a revised reprint of "Sunshine and Petrarch" in *Works*, Vol. 5, 1900.

430 numbered copies only.

Printed . . . September, MDCCCCIII. —Colophon. Deposited Oct. 12, 1903. Noted for Oct. 21 publication PW Oct. 17, 1903.

H NYPL

8462. The Heath Readers Sixth Reader . . .

D. C. Heath & Co. Publishers Boston New York Chicago London ⟨1903⟩

"James Russell Lowell," pp. 45-50. This had prior publication in somewhat varying form in *Old Cambridge*, 1899.

"Daniel Webster," pp. 237-242. A revision of a part of "Revolutionary Oratory . . . ," in *American Orators and Oratory*, 1901; *see above*.

"Ralph Waldo Emerson," pp. 304-307.

Deposited Jan. 27, 1904.

H

8463. Address on Decoration Day in Sanders Theatre, Harvard Memorial Hall, May 30, 1904 . . .

⟨n.p., Cambridge, 1904?⟩

Caption-title. The above at head of p. ⟨1⟩. Two leaves. 9⅛″ x 6″. Printed one side of leaf only.

A somewhat revised version of entry No. 8272.

H

8464. JAMES ELLIOT CABOT. [FROM THE PROCEEDINGS OF THE AMERICAN ACADEMY OF ARTS AND SCIENCES, VOL. XXXIX.]

⟨n.p., n.d., Boston, 1904?⟩

Cover-title.

⟨23⟩-29. 9⅝″ x 6¹⁄₁₆″.

⟨-⟩⁴.

Printed green paper wrapper.

Also appears in *Proceedings of the American Academy of Arts and Sciences, Vol. XXXIX, from June, 1903, to June, 1904*, Boston, 1904. Reprinted in *Proceedings of the Massachusetts Historical Society. Second Series, Vol. XX. 1906, 1907*, Boston, 1907.

H Y

8465. . . . Annual Report of the Trustees of the Cambridge Public Library for the Year Ending November 30, 1903 Printed for the Department

⟨Cambridge, 1904⟩

Printed paper wrapper. At head of title: City of Cambridge Massachusetts

"Report of the Trustees . . . ," pp. ⟨7⟩-9, signed at end by Higginson and others.

H NYPL

8466. The Hawthorne Centenary Celebration at the Wayside Concord, Massachusetts July 4-7, 1904

Boston and New York Houghton, Mifflin and Company The Riverside Press, Cambridge 1905

Edited by Higginson.

"Address . . . ," pp. ⟨3⟩-12; remarks, pp. 13, 15, 21, 23-26.

Deposited Jan. 10, 1905. On copyright page: *Published February, 1905* Advertised for *this day* PW Feb. 25, 1905. BPL copy received Feb. 27, 1905; BA Feb. 28, 1905. Listed PW March 11, 1905.

BA NYPL

8467. History of the United States from 986 to 1905 by Thomas Wentworth Higginson . . . and William Macdonald . . .

New York and London Harper & Brothers Publishers 1905

Contains no first edition material by Higginson.

"The original edition . . . ⟨of *A Larger History of the United States of America* . . . , 1886⟩ extended only to the close of President Jackson's administration . . . the publishers . . . have prepared this new edition, enlarged and revised to date."—P. ⟨iii⟩. See entry No. 8343.

Deposited March 16, 1905. BPL copy received March 21, 1905. Listed PW March 25, 1905. BA copy received March 28, 1905.

BA H

8468. Memorial Meeting George Sewall Boutwell . . . Faneuil Hall Boston April 18, 1905

⟨n.p., n.d., Boston, 1905⟩

Printed paper wrapper.

"Epitaph," p. 9.

H copy received May 27, 1905.

H

8469. GEORGE FRISBIE HOAR. [FROM THE PROCEEDINGS OF THE AMERICAN ACADEMY OF ARTS AND SCIENCES, VOL. XL.]

⟨n.p., n.d., Boston, 1905⟩

Cover-title.

⟨1⟩-8. 9⅝″ x 6¹⁄₁₆″.

⟨-⟩⁴.

Printed green paper wrapper.

AAS copy inscribed by early owner April 27, 1905.

Also appears in *Proceedings of the American Academy of Arts and Sciences, Vol. XL, from June, 1904, to May, 1905,* Boston, 1905.

AAS H Y

8470. The Aftermath of Slavery A Study of the Condition and Environment of the American Negro by William A. Sinclair . . . with an Introduction by Thomas Wentworth Higginson . . .

Boston Small, Maynard & Company MCMV

Introduction, pp. xi-xiii.

On copyright page: *Published April, 1905* Listed PW May 20, 1905.

H MHS NYPL

8471. Birthday Tributes to Mrs. Julia Ward Howe May 27, 1905

⟨Boston: Winthrop B. Jones, for The Authors Club, 1905⟩

"Eistedfodd," p. 8.

For comment see entry No. 96.

8472. PART OF A MAN'S LIFE . . .

BOSTON AND NEW YORK HOUGHTON, MIFFLIN AND COMPANY THE RIVERSIDE PRESS, CAMBRIDGE 1905

⟨i-ii⟩, ⟨i⟩-⟨x⟩, ⟨1⟩-311; printer's imprint, p. ⟨312⟩. Laid paper. Inserted: Portrait frontispiece; and, 39 leaves with facsimiles or other illustrations. 8¹¹⁄₁₆″ x 5⅞″.

⟨1⁶, 2-20⁸, 21⁴⟩.

T cloth: blue; green; greenish black; maroon. White laid paper end papers. Flyleaf at back. Top edges gilded.

On copyright page: *Published October 1905* Advertised for fall publication PW Sept. 30, 1905. Deposited Oct. 11, 1905. Noted for Oct. 18 in PW Oct. 14, 1905. NYPL copy received Oct. 18, 1905. Advertised as *just published* PW Oct. 21, 1905. Listed PW Nov. 4, 1905. The London (Constable) edition advertised for *next week* Ath Nov. 11, 1905; listed Ath Nov. 25, 1905.

H NYPL

8473. Football Grandma An Auto-Baby-Ogra-
phy as Told by Tony Edited by Carolyn S.
Channing Cabot with an Introduction by
Thomas Wentworth Higginson ...

Boston Small, Maynard & Company MCMV

"Introduction," p. ⟨vii⟩.

On copyright page: *Published, October, 1905*
Noted as *will issue* PW Oct. 21, 1905. Deposited
Oct. 25, 1905. Listed PW Dec. 9, 1905.

LC

8474. Country Homes of Famous Americans by
Oliver Bronson Capen with an Introduction
by Thomas Wentworth Higginson

New York Doubleday, Page & Company 1905

Introduction, pp. xxi-xxiii.

On copyright page: *Published, October, 1905*
Noted for Oct. 26 in PW Oct. 14, 21, 1905. Deposited Nov. 4, 1905. Listed PW Dec. 16, 1905.

NYPL

8475. A LETTER FROM THOMAS WENT-
WORTH HIGGINSON IN HARPER'S
WEEKLY. DUBLIN, N. H., JULY 14,
1905 ...

⟨Newark, N. J., Intercollegiate Socialist Society, 1905?⟩

Single cut sheet of blue paper. Page: 6¼" scant x
3⅜". Folded to 4 pp.

Higginson letter, p. ⟨1⟩.

At foot of p. ⟨4⟩: Union label, Newark, N. J.,
shop No. 2.

CPL H

8476. The Book of Elizabethan Verse ... Edited ... by William Stanley Braithwaite with
an Introduction by Thomas Wentworth Higginson

Boston Herbert B. Turner & Co. 1906

"Introduction," pp. ⟨ix-xi⟩.

Deposited Nov. 20, 1906. Listed PW Dec. 8, 1906.

BA Y

8477. ADDRESS AT THE CELEBRATION
OF THE TWO HUNDRED AND
SEVENTY-FIFTH ANNIVERSARY OF
THE FOUNDING OF CAMBRIDGE
SANDERS THEATRE, DEC. 21, 1905 ...
[REPRINTED FROM PROCEEDINGS OF
THE CAMBRIDGE HISTORICAL SOCI-
ETY, ⟨VOL.⟩ I]

⟨n.p., Cambridge, 1906⟩

Cover-title.

⟨48⟩-53. *Note:* Pp. ⟨47⟩ and ⟨54⟩ blank. Laid
paper. 9⅝" x 6½".

⟨-⟩⁴.

Printed tan laid paper wrapper.

H LC

8478. The Camp Conference Secretary's Report
1905-6

⟨n.p., Boston, 1906⟩

Cover-title. Printed paper wrapper.

"President's Address," pp. 13-16. Remarks, pp.
31-32 and elsewhere.

H

8479. REMINISCENCES OF JOHN BART-
LETT ... [REPRINTED FROM PRO-
CEEDINGS OF THE CAMBRIDGE HIS-
TORICAL SOCIETY, ⟨VOL.⟩ I]

⟨n.p., Cambridge, 1906⟩

Cover-title.

⟨78⟩-82, blank leaf. *Note:* p. ⟨77⟩ blank. Laid
paper. 9⅝" x 6¹¹⁄₁₆".

⟨-⟩⁴.

Printed tan laid paper wrapper.

H LC

8480. What's Next or Shall a Man Live Again?
... Compiled by Clara Spalding Ellis ...

Boston Richard G. Badger The Gorham
Press 1906

Statement, p. 24.

EM

8481. LIFE AND TIMES OF STEPHEN HIG-
GINSON MEMBER OF THE CONTI-
NENTAL CONGRESS (1783) AND AU-
THOR OF THE "LACO" LETTERS, RE-
LATING TO JOHN HANCOCK (1789) ...

BOSTON AND NEW YORK HOUGHTON, MIFFLIN
AND COMPANY THE RIVERSIDE PRESS, CAMBRIDGE
1907

⟨i-ii⟩, ⟨i⟩-⟨viii⟩, ⟨1⟩-⟨306⟩; blank, p. ⟨307⟩;
printer's imprint, p. ⟨308⟩; blank leaf. Laid paper. Portrait frontispiece and 16 plates inserted.
7¹¹⁄₁₆" x 5".

⟨1-20⟩⁸.

T cloth: olive-brown. White laid paper end papers. Laid paper flyleaf at front. Top edges
gilded.

On copyright page: *Published September, 1907*
Deposited Sept. 18, 1907. NYPL copy received
Sept. 28, 1907. BPL copy received Oct. 1, 1907.
Listed PW Oct. 5, 1907. Advertised as *just pub-
lished* PW Oct. 5, 1907.

H NYPL

8482. A Discourse of Matters Pertaining to Religion by Theodore Parker Edited with a
Preface by Thomas Wentworth Higginson ...

Boston   American Unitarian Association 25
Beacon Street ⟨1907⟩

"Editor's Preface," pp. v-vii.

Deposited Nov. 25, 1907.

H Y

8483. Addresses in Memory of Ernest Howard
Crosby (1856–1907) Cooper Union, New York
March 7, 1907

⟨New York⟩ Ernest Howard Crosby Memorial Committee ⟨1907⟩

Printed paper wrapper.

1-sentence statement, p. 26.

H NYPL

8484. The Cambridge Historical Society Publications ⟨Vol.⟩ II Proceedings October 23,
1906–October 22, 1907

Cambridge, Massachusetts Published by the
Society 1907

Printed paper wrapper.

"Cambridge Eighty Years Since," pp. 20-32.

"Address ... ," pp. 51-53.

"Address of the Chairman, Thomas Wentworth
Higginson," pp. 77-78.

AAS NYPL

8485. Dedication of the Massasoit Memorial at
Warren, Rhode Island, October Nineteenth
Nineteen Hundred and Seven

Published by the Massasoit Monument Association ⟨Warren, Rhode Island?⟩ Gazette
Press ⟨n.d., 1907?⟩

Printed paper wrapper.

"Massasoit," pp. 24-30.

H NYPL

8486. EDWARD ATKINSON. [FROM THE
PROCEEDINGS OF THE AMERICAN
ACADEMY OF ARTS AND SCIENCES,
VOL. XLII.]

⟨n.p., n.d., Boston, 1907?⟩

Cover-title.

⟨1⟩-9, blank leaf. 9⅝" x 6¼".

⟨-⟩⁶.

Printed gray paper wrapper.

H

8487. *Entry cancelled.*

8488. ... THINGS WORTH WHILE ...

NEW YORK   B. W. HUEBSCH 1908

At head of title: THE ART OF LIFE SERIES EDWARD
HOWARD GRIGGS, EDITOR

Title-page in black and orange.

⟨1⟩-73; blank, p. ⟨74⟩; 2 pp. advertisements; 2
blank leaves. 6¹⁵⁄₁₆" x 4⁹⁄₁₆".

⟨1-5⟩⁸.

V cloth: tan.

Deposited April 27, 1908. BA copy received May
5, 1908. Listed PW May 9, 1908. The London
(Gay & Hancock) edition listed Bkr Nov. 5, 1909.

AAS H NYPL

8489. ... History of the Cambridge Public Library ... Compiled ... by William James
Rolfe and Clarence Walter Ayer

Cambridge Printed for the Trustees 1908

At head of title: 1858–1908

"Address," pp. 57-63.

CPL H

8490. RELIGIOUS PROGRESS IN THE
LAST TWO GENERATIONS AN AD-
DRESS ...

UNITY PUBLISHING COMPANY CHICAGO, 1908

Cover-title.

⟨1-10⟩, blank leaf. 6¾" x 5" scant.

⟨-⟩⁶.

Printed self-wrapper.

"Reprinted from Unity of April 2, 1908."—P.
⟨10⟩.

H

8491. A Poem of the Olden Time Describing a Ball at Cambridge, Mass. in the Year 1840 Written by Miss Ann G. Storrow ...

⟨The Rosemary Press, Needham, Mass., 1909⟩

Caption-title. The above at head of p. ⟨3⟩.

Edited by Higginson and with a letter from him to the publisher, Charles D. Burrage, April 17, 1908, p. ⟨5⟩.

Printed paper boards, cloth shelfback.

"Read by Colonel Thomas Wentworth Higginson at the annual meeting of the Omar Khayyam Club of America, Saturday, March 28, 1908, at the Algonquin Club, Boston, Mass. ..."— P. ⟨3⟩.

100 copies only.

Deposited April 2, 1909. H copy inscribed by Higginson April 2, 1909. BPL copy inscribed by Higginson April 3, 1909.

BPL   H

8492. The Free Religious Association Proceedings at the Forty-Second Annual Meeting Held in Boston, Mass. ... May 27 and 28 1909

Boston, Mass. Published by the Free Religious Association 1909

Printed paper wrapper.

"Address," pp. 21-26.

BPL   H   Y

8493. A Mother's List of Books for Children Compiled by Gertrude Weld Arnold

Chicago   A. C. McClurg & Co. 1909

"A Mother's List," pp. xi-xv.

On copyright page: *Published October 9, 1909* Deposited Oct. 14, 1909. Listed PW Oct. 30, 1909.

LC

8494. Decisive Battles of America by Albert Bushnell Hart, Thomas Wentworth Higginson ⟨and Others⟩ ... Edited by Ripley Hitchcock ...

New York and London   Harper & Brothers Publishers MCMIX

"The Hundred Years' War between Early Colonists and the Indians," pp. 14-26.

On copyright page: *Published October, 1909.* NYPL copy received Oct. 28, 1909. Deposited Oct. 29, 1909. Listed PW Nov. 6, 1909.

H

8495. CARLYLE'S LAUGH AND OTHER SURPRISES ...

BOSTON AND NEW YORK   HOUGHTON MIFFLIN COMPANY   THE RIVERSIDE PRESS   CAMBRIDGE MDCCCCIX

⟨i-ii⟩, ⟨i⟩-viii, ⟨1⟩-388; blank, p. ⟨389⟩; printer's imprint, p. ⟨390⟩. Laid paper. 7⅜″ x 4¹⁵⁄₁₆″. Facsimile inserted between pp. 26-27.

⟨1-16¹², 17⁸⟩.

T cloth: blue; green; maroon. White laid paper end papers. Top edges gilt.

On copyright page: *Published October 1909* Noted for Oct. 30, 1909, PW Oct. 23, 1909. Advertised as *published to-day* PW Oct. 30, 1909. Deposited Nov. 8, 1909. BA copy received Nov. 10, 1909. Listed PW Nov. 13, 1909.

BA   H

8496. The Cambridge Historical Society Publications ⟨Vol.⟩ IV   Proceedings January 26– October 26, 1909

Cambridge, Massachusetts   Published by the Society   1909

Printed paper wrapper.

"A Dinner with Dr. Holmes," pp. 42-45.

AAS   NYPL

8497. DIRECT OR INDIRECT POWER OF WOMEN ...

⟨San Francisco: California Equal Suffrage Headquarters, n.d., 1909?⟩

Caption-title.

Single cut sheet of pale yellow laid paper folded to four pages.

⟨1-4⟩. 8⁹⁄₁₆″ x 5½″.

Note: Reprinted from *The Palo Alto Tribune,* Sept. 21, 1909. Under the title *Straight Lines or Oblique Lines?* another edition, varying somewhat textually, was issued as a single leaf: *Woman Suffrage Leaflet. Published Bi-Monthly at the Office of the Woman's Journal, Boston, Mass. Vol. VI ... No. 6 ... November, 1893 ...* See entry No. 8398A.

H (both)

8498. In After Days   Thoughts on the Future Life by W. D. Howells ... Thomas Wentworth Higginson ... ⟨and Others⟩

Harper & Brothers Publishers   New York and London   MCMX

"The Future Life," pp. 135-<152>. Reprinted from *Harper's Bazar*, May, 1909.

Note: The earliest binding is almost surely lavender S cloth. The PW listing (Feb. 19, 1910) describes the book as in cloth. Copies bound in tan boards with pinkish-brown V cloth shelf-back are presumed to be remainders; a copy thus in the collection of Mr. C. Bacon Colla-more, Nov. 1946. Messrs. Edel and Laurence (in *A Bibliography of Henry James*, 1957, pp. 231-232) report "two secondary bindings ... (a) issued in faded blue linen-grain cloth ... (b) issued in rust-brown half cloth, buff paper boards ..."

Deposited Feb. 11, 1910. BPL copy received Feb. 14, 1910; BA Feb. 16, 1910. Listed PW Feb. 19, 1910; Ath March 19, 1910.

BA   H

8499. Letters of Major Seth Rogers, M. D. Surgeon of the First South Carolina Volunteers ... 1862–1863 Communicated by Thomas Wentworth Higginson ...

Boston   John Wilson and Son   University Press   1910

Printed paper wrapper.

Contains a few comments by Higginson.

Offprint from *Massachusetts Historical Society Proceedings October, 1909–June, 1910*, Vol. 43, Boston, 1910, which also contains Higginson's comments on the Vassall tomb, pp. 192-193.

MHS

8500. Theodore Parker Commemoration The Free Religious Association Proceedings at the Forty-Third Annual Meeting Held in Boston, Mass. ... May 26 and 27 1910

Boston, Mass.   Published by the Free Religious Association   1910

Printed paper wrapper.

"Remarks," pp. 64-67.

BPL   H   Y

8500A. Proceedings of the American Academy of Arts and Letters and of the National Institute of Arts and Letters   Number I: 1909–1910

New York <June 10, 1910>

Printed paper wrapper.

"Ruskin and Norton ...," pp. 22-24.

H   Y

8501. DESCENDANTS OF THE REVEREND FRANCIS HIGGINSON   FIRST "TEACHER" IN THE MASSACHUSETTS BAY COLONY OF SALEM, MASSACHUSETTS AND AUTHOR OF "NEW-ENGLANDS PLANTATION" (1630) ...

PRIVATELY PRINTED 1910

<i>-xvi, 1-68. Laid paper. Watermarked *N.E.H.G.S. Standard*. Portrait frontispiece inserted. 9" x 5$\frac{15}{16}$".

<1², 2-6⁸>.

V cloth: brown. White laid paper end papers.

BPL   H   NYPL   Y

8502. The Cliff-Dwellers   An Account of Their Organization ...

Chicago   168 Michigan Avenue   MCMX

Printed paper wrapper.

Letter of greeting, p. 49.

H   NYPL

8503. Peter Rugg the Missing Man by William Austin   Introduction by Thomas Wentworth Higginson

John W. Luce & Co. Boston MCMX

"William Austin a Precursor of Hawthorne," pp. <9>-22.

PW May 16, 1908, reported the book "for early publication" with R. E. Lee Company, Boston, named as publisher. Noted by PW Sept. 26, 1908, as *forthcoming*; R. E. Lee Company, Boston, named as publisher. Listed PW Jan. 14, 1911, with John W. Luce & Co., named as publisher. Deposited July 31, 1911.

Note: All evidence points to R. E. Lee Company, Boston, as original projector of the book; abandonment by Lee; first publication by Luce. The AAS copy is inscribed by H.H.S. <i.e., Harrison Hale Schaff, co-founder with John W. Luce of John W. Luce & Company>: *The last published work of T.W.H. This volume was issued in Nov. 1910.* Schaff's inscription dated June 20, 1911.

AAS   H   NYPL

8504. Young Folks' Book of American Explorers ...

New York   Longmans, Green, and Co.   1910

Reprint of *A Book of American Explorers*, 1877.

NYPL

8505. Ruling at Second Hand

Not located.

Entry on the basis of a listing in the catalog of Cambridge Public Library. And, also listed in a checklist of Higginson's publications published in *Boston Evening Transcript,* May 17, 1911. Perhaps a bit of ephemera issued to promote woman suffrage.

8506. Days and Ways in Old Boston Edited by
    William S. Rossiter . . .

Boston   R. H. Stearns and Company 1915

Boards, printed paper labels.

"Other Days and Ways in Boston and Cambridge," pp. 27-38.

H

8507. Yesterdays in a Busy Life by Candace
    Wheeler . . .

Harper & Brothers Publishers   New York and London ‹1918›

"Ultra-Marine," p. 142.

On copyright page: *Published October, 1918;* and, code letters I-S, signifying: *Printed Sept. 1918.*

H NYPL

8508. LETTERS AND JOURNALS OF
    THOMAS WENTWORTH HIGGINSON
    1846–1906 EDITED BY MARY THACHER
    HIGGINSON

BOSTON AND NEW YORK   HOUGHTON MIFFLIN
COMPANY   THE RIVERSIDE PRESS   CAMBRIDGE
1921

‹i-viii›, ‹1›-358; blank, p. ‹359›; printer's imprint, p. ‹360›. Portrait frontispiece inserted. 8⅛" x 5½".

‹1-23›⁸.

Buckram: black; blue. Printed paper label on spine. Pale tan end papers.

BPL copy received Dec. 8, 1921. Deposited Dec. 12, 1921. BA copy received Dec. 13, 1921. Listed PW Jan. 14, 1921.

BPL H NYPL

8509. "An American Stonehenge" . . .

    ‹n.p., n.d., *ca.* 1925?›

Single cut sheet. Printed on recto only. 12" x 9⅛".

Previously in *Such as They Are,* 1893.

H

REPRINTS

The following publications contain material by Higginson reprinted from other books.

The Estray . . .

    Boston . . . 1847.

    For comment see BAL, Vol. 1, p. 100.

Selections from the Writings and Speeches of William Lloyd Garrison . . .

    Boston: R. F. Wallcut, 21 Cornhill. 1852.

The Harp and the Cross . . . Compiled by Stephen G. Bulfinch . . .

    Boston . . . 1857.

    For comment see entry No. 1388.

The Lady's Almanac, for the Year 1864.

    Boston, Published by George Coolidge, No. 3 Milk Street. New York: Sold by H. Dexter, Hamilton & Co. ‹1861; *i.e.,* 1863›

    The two paragraphs on spring, p. 25, reprinted from *Out-Door Papers,* 1863, pp. 320-321.

Lyra   Americana . . . Selected . . . by the Rev. George T. Rider . . .

    New York . . . 1865.

    For comment see entry No. 2827.

Lyra Americana: Hymns of Praise and Faith, from American Poets.

    London: The Religious Tract Society . . . 1865.

    Listed PC Oct. 2, 1865; Ath Oct. 7, 1865.

Lyra Sacra Americana: Or, Gems from American Sacred Poetry. Selected . . . by Charles Dexter Cleveland . . .

    New York: Charles Scribner and Company. London: Sampson Low, Son, and Marston. 1868.

    Reprints two of Higginson's hymns, here miscredited to *P. W. Higginson.*

Child Life in Prose. Edited by John Greenleaf Whittier . . .

    Boston . . . 1874.

    For comment see BAL, Vol. 1, p. 73.

The Reading Club and Handy Speaker . . . Edited by George M. Baker. No. 5.

    Boston . . . 1878.

    For comment see entry No. 7298.

The Cambridge Book of Poetry and Song ... by Charlotte Fiske Bates ...

New York ... ⟨1882⟩

For comment see entry No. 7887.

Study and Stimulants ... Edited by A. Arthur Reade.

Manchester ... 1883 ...

For comment see entry No. 3409.

... The Reading Club and Handy Speaker ... Edited by George M. Baker. No. 14.

Boston: Lee and Shepard, Publishers. New York: Charles T. Dillingham. ⟨1885⟩

"Oratory of Wendell Phillips," pp. 82-83; extracted from *Wendell Phillips*, 1884.

Sappho Memoir, Text, Selected Renderings and a Literal Translation by Henry Thornton Wharton ...

London   David Stott, 370, Oxford Street MDCCCLXXXV ...

Printed vellum binding.

Eminent Opinions on Woman Suffrage ...

Office "Woman's Journal," 5 Park Street, Boston ... American Woman Suffrage Association ⟨n.d., 1885?⟩.

Single leaf. Title at head of p. ⟨1⟩. Imprint at end. Note: *The Woman's Journal* was at the above address during the period 1881–1887. Contains an extract from *The Nonsense of It*, issued 1867(?); see entry No. 8259.

Issued as a political tract and therefore probably in a number of printings.

Representative Poems of Living Poets ...

... New York 1886

For comment see entry No. 436.

The "How I Was Educated" Papers from the Forum Magazine

New York D. Appleton and Company 1888

Printed paper wrapper. See entry No. 8352.

American Sonnets. Selected ... by William Sharp.

London ... ⟨n.d., 1889⟩

For comment see BAL, Vol. 3, p. 101.

The Poets' Year ... Edited by Oscar Fay Adams ...

Boston ... ⟨1890⟩

For comment see entry No. 80.

Local and National Poets of America ... Edited ⟨by⟩ Thos. W. Herringshaw ...

Chicago ... 1890.

For comment see BAL, Vol. 2, p. 391.

Readings and Recitations. No. 8 ... Edited by Miss L. Penney ...

New York: The National Temperance Society and Publication House, 58 Reade Street. 1891.

Printed paper wrapper. Deposited Jan. 26, 1891. "Roger Harlakenden's Christmas Eve," pp. 54-56, is an extract from "The Last Palatinate Light," in *Afternoon Landscape*, 1889.

Out of the Heart   Poems ... Selected by John White Chadwick ... and Annie Hathaway Chadwick ...

Troy, N. Y. ... 1891 ...

For comment see BAL, Vol. 2, p. 452.

Tributes to Shakespeare Collected ... by Mary R. Silsby

New York ... MDCCCXCII

For comment see entry No. 707A.

Sun Prints in Sky Tints ... by Irene E. Jerome

Boston ... 1893

For fuller entry see BAL, Vol. 2, p. 452.

The World's Parliament of Religions ... Edited by the Rev. John Henry Barrows ...

Chicago   The Parliament Publishing Company 1893

2 Vols. Continuous pagination.

Through Love to Light   A Selection ... by John White Chadwick and Annie Hathaway Chadwick

Boston ... 1896

For comment see entry No. 2633.

Poems of the Farm Selected ... by Alfred C. Eastman

Boston ... 1896

For comment see entry No. 6343.

Modern Eloquence ... ⟨Edited by⟩ Thomas B. Reed ...

... Philadelphia ⟨1900; *i.e.*, 1901⟩

For comment see entry No. 3467. "Literature in a Republic," Vol. V, pp. ⟨565⟩-578; otherwise "Youth and Literary Life" in *Lectures to Young Men* ... , 1892.

Colonial Stories Retold from St. Nicholas . . .

Published by the Century Co. New York . . .
MCMV

Listed PW Nov. 11, 1905. "Old Dutch Times in New York," pp. 101-121, extracted from *Young Folks' History of the United States*, Boston, 1875, pp. 88-98.

The Oxford Book of American Essays Chosen by Brander Matthews . . .

New York   Oxford University Press . . .
1914 . . .

For comment see in list of W. D. Howells reprints.

Papyrus Club   Forty-Fifth Anniversary Dinner Held at Young's Hotel   December First
MCMXVII

⟨n.p., Boston, 1917⟩

Printed paper wrapper, illustration pasted to front of wrapper.

Which? A Story by Elizabeth Tilton . . .

⟨Boston: Woman's National Committee for Law Enforcement, n.d., *ca.* 1925⟩

Printed paper wrapper. Cover-title. Higginson's poem," "The Trumpeter," (*Such as They Are*, 1893), reprinted on back of wrapper.

The Question of Henry James   A Collection of Critical Essays Edited by F. W. Dupee

New York: Henry Holt and Company ⟨1945⟩

On copyright page: *First Printing*   Listed PW Nov. 17, 1945.

REFERENCES AND ANA

References in the list to *Higginson* refer to *Thomas Wentworth Higginson . . . ,* by Mary Thacher Higginson, 1914.

Free Evening School. A Free Evening School Will be Kept on Four Evenings of Every Week, in the Hall over Wm. B. Morss's Store . . .

⟨Newburyport, Mass.⟩ Huse & Bragdon, Printers. ⟨n.d., 1851⟩

Handbill. Printed on recto only. 9⅞" x 7¼". The school was conducted "under the superintendence of Mr. T. W. Higginson." Copy in CPL.

Vindication of the Lord's Supper: A Sermon . . . First Universalist Church in Worcester, Sunday, November 27, 1853. By John G. Adams . . .

Worcester: Printed by Henry J. Howland No. 199 Main Street. ⟨1853?⟩

Printed paper wrapper. A reply to a portion of Higginson's sermon, *The Unitarian Autumnal Convention . . . ,* 1853; see entry No. 8221.

Read! Read! The State Temperance Committee of Massachusetts, respectfully ask their fellow citizens of this Commonwealth, to read carefully the following document. Rev. Mr. Hadley, its author, is a Clergyman, and his integrity and veracity is unimpeachable. As will be seen, this paper utterly refutes the statements of John Neal, and others, who are endeavoring to persuade the people of this State that the Maine Law is a failure in the State of its birth . . .

⟨Boston?, Massachusetts State Temperance Committee, 1853⟩

Broadside. Printed on recto only. Prints a letter from Rev. W. H. Hadley to T. W. Higginson, arguing for the Maine Law, etc., etc. See entry No. 8207.

Speech at the Legislative Temperance Society. 1853.

Entry from Higginson, p. 406. Search indicates that the *Life Boat* (to which publication the speech is credited) was a periodical and therefore not within the scope of BAL.

Italian Revolutionary Leaders. By W. J. Linton.

New York, *ca.* 1875–1880.

Apparently never published. A projected volume to have been included in the *Brief Biographies* series edited by Higginson. Noted as *in preparation* in the London, 1876, edition of Herbert Tuttle's *German Political Leaders*. Also so noted in the New York, 1880, edition.

Lectures by Thomas Wentworth Higginson, 1877 . . . "The Aristocracy of the Dollar." . . .

⟨New York: American Literary Bureau, Cooper Institute, 1877⟩

Handbill. Printed on recto only. Issued as an advertisement for Higginson's lectures "The Aristocracy of the Dollar," "Literature in a Republic" and "How to Study History."

Topics for the Use of Teachers. To Accompany Higginson's Young Folks' History of the United States.

Boston: Lee and Shepard, Publishers. New York: Charles T. Dillingham. ⟨1877⟩

Printed paper wrapper. Cover-title. No indication that this was compiled by Higginson.

Not to be confused with *Questions on Higginson's Young Folks' History of the United States* ... ‹1875›.

A German Translation.

"A German translation of one of ‹my books› ... was published three years since, I furnishing a special preface ..."—T. W. Higginson, in PW Jan. 31, 1880, p. 82. Further information wanting.

History of Woman Suffrage. Edited by Elizabeth Cady Stanton, Susan B. Anthony, and Matilda Joslyn Gage ... in Two Volumes ...

New York: Fowler & Wells, Publishers, 753 Broadway. 1881.

Note: As originally projected the work was to be complete in two volumes; it was completed in six. The title-pages and imprints of the several volumes vary:

1: As above.

2: ... *in Three Volumes* ...
New York: Fowler & Wells, Publishers, 753 Broadway. 1882.

3: ... *in Three Volumes* ...
Susan B. Anthony. Rochester, N. Y.: Charles Mann. London ... Paris ... 1887.

4: ... *Edited by Susan B. Anthony & Ida Husted Harper ... in Four Volumes* ...
Susan B. Anthony 17 Madison Street, Rochester, N. Y. ‹1902›

5-6: ... *Edited by Ida Husted Harper ... in Six Volumes* ...
National American Woman Suffrage Association ‹1922›

Contains speeches, letters and other material by Higginson.

Vol. 1 deposited June 9, 1881; Vol. 2 Sept. 5, 1882; Vol. 3 Oct. 22, 1886; Vol. 4 June 1, 1903.

To the Voters of the Fifth Congressional District: The undersigned, voters in this district, have endeavored, with others, to secure from the two parties the nomination of candidates satisfactory to Civil Service Reformers ... We have, however, found neither party prepared to make such a nomination as is here indicated ...

‹n.p., Boston?, 1882›

Single cut sheet. 11" x 8⁵⁄₁₆" full. Printed on recto only.

Prepared as proof only and presumably not published. Signed at end by Higginson and others. Copy in H.

Andrew Carnegie before the Nineteenth Century Club upon "The Aristocracy of the Dollar" an Address by Thomas Wentworth Higginson ...

‹n.p., n.d., 1884›

Not by Higginson. A rebuttal by Carnegie. Higginson's lecture was first delivered not later than 1877.

Thomas Wentworth Higginson. Author, Soldier and Statesman. Events in His Life ...

‹n.p., n.d., 1888›

4 pp. Issued as campaign material during the election of 1888.

The Defences of Norumbega and a Review of the Reconnaissances of Col. T. W. Higginson ... Dr. Francis Parkman ... ‹and Others› a Letter to Judge Daly ... by Eben Norton Horsford

Boston and New York   Houghton, Mifflin and Company   The Riverside Press, Cambridge 1891

... Proceedings of the Massachusetts Historical Society, March and April, 1893.

‹Boston: Massachusetts Historical Society, 1893›

At head of title: *III*. Printed paper wrapper. Cover-title.

Remarks, reported in "substance," pp. 174-182.

Thomas Wentworth Higginson by Edwin D. Mead ...

Reprinted from the Editor's Table of the New England Magazine for February 1900

Cover-title. Printed self-wrapper.

A Typical American Thomas Wentworth Higginson Translated from the French of Th. Bentzon ‹*pseud.* for Marie Thérèse Blanc› by E. M. Waller

London and New York   Howard Wilford Bell 1902

Boards, printed paper labels.

Reply to "T.W.H." in Boston Advertiser. ‹By Samuel C. Smith›

‹Lawrence, Kansas, 1903›

Printed paper wrapper. Cover-title. A review of Higginson's letter on Kansas history published over his initials in *Boston Daily Advertiser*, Sept. 15, 1879.

The Encyclopedia Americana ... in Sixteen
Volumes ...

> The Americana Company New York Chi-
> cago ⟨1903–1904⟩
>
> According to *Higginson*, p. 425, Higginson
> contributed to this publication but his name
> does not appear in the lists of contributors.

... A Bibliography of Thomas Wentworth Higginson

> Cambridge, Massachusetts December, 1906
>
> At head of title: Cambridge Public Library
>
> Cover-title. Printed self-wrapper.
>
> Compiled by Mrs. Winifred Mather with the
> assistance of Miss Eva G. Moore.

Thomas Wentworth Higginson. [From the Pro-
ceedings of the American Academy of Arts and
Sciences, Vol. XLVII.] ⟨By Andrew McFarland
Davis⟩

> ⟨n.p., n.d., Boston, 1911?⟩
>
> Printed paper wrapper. Cover-title.

The Cambridge Historical Society Publications
⟨Vol.⟩ VII Proceedings December 21, 1911–
October 22, 1912

> Cambridge, Massachusetts Published by the
> Society 1913
>
> Report of the Higginson memorial meeting.

Massachusetts Historical Society ... Proceedings
October, 1913–June, 1914 Volume XLVII ...

> Boston Published by the Society MDCCCCXIV
>
> "Memoir of Thomas Wentworth Higginson,"
> by Edward Channing, pp. 348-355.

Thomas Wentworth Higginson The Story of
His Life by Mary Thacher Higginson ...

> Boston and New York Houghton Mifflin
> Company The Riverside Press Cambridge
> 1914
>
> Bibliography, pp. ⟨403⟩-428. Deposited March
> 23, 1914.

Commemorative Tributes to Thomas Wentworth Higginson ... ⟨and others⟩ by Bliss
Perry Read at Public Session following Annual
Meeting of the American Academy of Arts and
Letters New York City December 13, 1912 Reprinted from Vol. VI Proceedings of the Academy

> American Academy of Arts and Letters 1922
>
> Printed paper wrapper.

Twenty-Seventh Annual Report of the Bibliophile Society 1901–1929

> ⟨Boston, 1929⟩
>
> "The Letters of ⟨William Dean⟩ Howells
> to Higginson," pp. 17-56.
>
> Boards, printed paper label on spine.

Thomas Wentworth Higginson: Disciple of
the Newness by Howard W. Hintz Abridgement of Thesis ... Accepted by the Graduate
School of New York University in Partial Fulfillment of the Requirements for the Degree of
Doctor of Philosophy at New York University,
1937

> Published under the Auspices of the Graduate
> School of New York University ⟨1939⟩
>
> Printed paper wrapper. Deposited Dec. 12,
> 1939.

Give Yourself Happiness Says Epictetus ...
from the Translation of Epictetus by Thomas
Wentworth Higginson Abridged and Rearranged by Clytie Sweet

> Kohnke Printing Company San Francisco
> 1940
>
> Printed boards. See entry No. 8372. Deposited
> May 22, 1940.

Epictetus Discourses and Enchiridion Based
on the Translation of Thomas Wentworth Higginson with an Introduction by Irwin Edman

> Published for the Classics Club by Walter J.
> Black New York ⟨1944⟩
>
> See entry No. 8372. Deposited Feb. 10, 1945.

JAMES ABRAHAM HILLHOUSE

1 7 8 9 – 1 8 4 1

8510. PERCY'S MASQUE: A DRAMA, IN FIVE ACTS.

LONDON: PRINTED FOR JOHN MILLER, BURLINGTON ARCADE, PICCADILLY. 1819.

Anonymous. For first American edition see next entry.

⟨i⟩-⟨viii⟩, ⟨1⟩-112. 7″ x 4¼″. Watermarked *Larking 1816*

⟨A⟩⁴, B-E¹², F⁸.

Tan paper boards. Printed paper label on spine.

Listed BC June, 1819; again, Oct. 1819.

B   Y

8511. PERCY'S MASQUE, A DRAMA, IN FIVE ACTS. FROM THE LONDON EDITION, WITH ALTERATIONS.

NEW-YORK: PRINTED BY C. S. VAN WINKLE, NO. 101 GREENWICH-STREET. 1820.

Anonymous. For first edition see preceding entry.

⟨i⟩-⟨viii⟩, ⟨9⟩-150, blank leaf. 7¹⁄₁₆″ x 4⅜″.

⟨1⟩-12⁶, 13⁴.

Tan paper boards. Printed paper label on spine. Flyleaves.

Title-page deposited June 3 or 7, 1820. Listed LSR June, 1820. "... now in the press, with alterations from the English edition."—*New York Literary Journal*, June 15, 1820.

AAS   BPL   H

8512. THE JUDGMENT, A VISION. BY THE AUTHOR OF PERCY'S MASQUE.

NEW-YORK: PUBLISHED BY JAMES EASTBURN, LITERARY ROOMS, BROADWAY. 1821.

⟨1⟩-46, blank leaf. 8½″ x 5¼″. Watermarked *RD*.

⟨1⟩-6⁴.

Tan paper boards. Printed paper label on spine. Flyleaves.

Title-page deposited April 24, 1821. Deposited May 3, 1821. Reviewed in *Literary Gazette* (Philadelphia), June 16, 1821.

Misdated 1812 by both Allibone and Appleton, the year the poem was delivered at Yale. Roorbach (1852) gives the title as *The Vision of Judgment*.

BPL   H   Y

8513. HADAD, A DRAMATIC POEM ...

NEW-YORK: PRINTED FOR E. BLISS & E. WHITE. MDCCCXXV.

Note: Also issued with the imprint: NEW-YORK: PRINTED FOR E. BLISS & E. WHITE. MDCCCXXV. LONDON: JOHN MILLER, 5, NEW BRIDGE STREET.

⟨i⟩-x, ⟨11⟩-208. 9⅜″ x 5⅞″.

⟨1⟩⁴, 2², 3-26⁴, 27².

Paper boards: brown; pink. Also: mottled salmon paper boards, green paper shelfback. Printed paper (green and orange noted) label on spine.

Note: All examined copies save one have p. 208 so paged; the exception, the author's own copy in Y, has p. 208 mispaged 207.

Also note: Sig. 2 presents a problem that requires further investigation. The gathering occurs (and the order of presentation is arbitrary):

A: As single inserted leaves.
B: As conjugates.

Comparison shows no textual variations in A *vs* B. In both the order is:

2₁ᵣ: P. ix

2₁ᵥ: P. x

2₂ᵣ: *Dramatis Personae* ...

2₂ᵥ: Blank

It may be theorized that an error in imposition produced a transposition in the front matter and copies may exist exhibiting such error.

PF March, 1825, commented on the text; from an advance copy? Title-page deposited March 17, 1825. Listed USLG April 1, 1825. Reviewed by NYR and by Ath June, 1825.

H (A, B)   LC (A, B)   NYPL (B)   Y (A)

8514. AN ORATION PRONOUNCED AT NEW-HAVEN, BEFORE THE SOCIETY OF PHI BETA KAPPA, SEPTEMBER 12, 1826. ON SOME OF THE CONSIDERATIONS WHICH SHOULD INFLUENCE AN EPIC OR A TRAGIC WRITER, IN THE CHOICE OF AN ERA . . .

NEW-HAVEN: PUBLISHED BY A. H. MALTBY AND CO. T. G. WOODWARD AND CO. PRINT. 1826.

⟨1⟩-32. 9⅜″ x 6⅛″.

⟨1⟩-4⁴.

Printed tan paper wrapper.

Noted by LGAA as *just issued,* Nov. 11, 1826. Reviewed by LGAA Nov. 18, 1826.

NYPL   Y

8515. The Memorial, a Christmas, New Year's and Easter Offering for 1828. Edited by Frederic S. Hill . . .

Boston: Published by True and Greene, and Richardson and Lord ⟨n.d., after Nov. 3, 1827⟩

"An Apologue," pp. ⟨391⟩-395. Anonymous. In table of contents listed as at p. 891.

Hillhouse named in the preface as a contributor. "An Apologue" republished in Kettell's *Specimens of American Poetry,* 1829, credited to Hillhouse.

For comment see entry No. 4586.

8516. The American Common-Place Book of Poetry, with Occasional Notes. By George B. Cheever.

Boston: Published by Carter, Hendee & ⟨sic⟩ Babcock. Baltimore: Charles Carter. 1831.

Reprint save for: "Extract from a Poem Written on Reading an Account of the Opinions of a Deaf and Dumb Child, before She Had Received Instruction. She Was Afraid of the Sun, Moon, and Stars," pp. 214-215.

Two states noted. For comment see entry No. 1330.

8517. AN ORATION, PRONOUNCED AT NEW HAVEN, BY REQUEST OF THE COMMON COUNCIL, AUGUST 19, 1834, IN COMMEMORATION OF THE LIFE AND SERVICES OF GENERAL LAFAYETTE . . .

NEW HAVEN: PUBLISHED BY H. HOWE & CO. 1834.

⟨1⟩-40. 9″ x 5¹¹⁄₁₆″.

⟨1⟩-5⁴.

Printed blue paper wrapper.

BA   H   NYPL   Y

8518. SACHEM'S-WOOD: A SHORT POEM, WITH NOTES.

NEW HAVEN: PUBLISHED BY B. & W. NOYES. HITCHCOCK & STAFFORD, PRINTERS. 1838.

Anonymous.

⟨1⟩-30, blank leaf. 9⅜″ x 5¾″.

⟨1⟩-4⁴.

Printed tan paper wrapper.

Note: Two states have been noted; sequence undetermined:

A: Signature mark 4 present.

B: Signature mark 4 absent.

Introductory note dated July 30, 1838. Y copy inscribed by Hillhouse Aug. 18, 1838. Listed NYR Oct. 1838. Reviewed NYR Oct. 1838.

AAS (B)   B (A)   BPL (A)   H (B)   MHS (A, B)   Y (A, B)

8519. DRAMAS, DISCOURSES, AND OTHER PIECES . . .

BOSTON: CHARLES C. LITTLE AND JAMES BROWN. 1839.

2 Vols.

1: ⟨i⟩-⟨xvi⟩, ⟨1⟩-296. 7⅛″ x 4⁷⁄₁₆″.
2: ⟨i-viii⟩, ⟨1⟩-⟨249⟩; blank, pp. ⟨250-251⟩; printer's imprint, p. ⟨252⟩; 2 blank leaves. In some copies the final leaf has been excised or pasted under the end paper.

1: ⟨-⟩⁸, 1-18⁸, 19⁴.
2: ⟨-⟩⁴, 1-16⁸.

Note: In some copies leaf 16₈, (Vol. 2), the final blank leaf, is excised or pasted under the end paper.

The following types of end papers noted: Cream-coated on white; peach-coated on white; cream-white; white; pale yellow. Usually found with single flyleaves at back and at front; but, copies also occur with a flyleaf at front only; flyleaf at back only; without flyleaves.

Thirteen styles of binding have been noted. The sequence has not been determined and the following designations are for identification only.

Binding A

T cloth: black. Sides blindstamped with a triple rule border, a floral ornament at each inner corner. Spine lettered in gold save as noted: HILLHOUSE'S / DRAMAS / DISCOURSES / &C / VOL. I. ⟨II.⟩ / ⟨the following in blind:⟩ BOSTON / C. C. LITTLE & Co.

Binding B

S-like cloth: blue; brown. Sides blindstamped with a grolieresque ornament. Spine lettered in gold save as noted: HILLHOUSE'S / DRAMAS / DISCOURSES / &C / VOL. I. ⟨II.⟩ / ⟨the following blindstamped:⟩ BOSTON / C. C. LITTLE & Co

Binding C

T cloth: black. Sides blindstamped with a triple rule border, a floral ornament at each inner corner. Spine lettered in gold: HILLHOUSE'S / DRAMAS / DISCOURSES / &C / VOL. I. ⟨II.⟩ / BOSTON / C. C. LITTLE & Co

Binding D

P cloth: blue. Sides blindstamped at center with a circular ornament. Spine lettered in gold: HILLHOUSE'S / DRAMAS / DISCOURSES / &C / VOL. I. ⟨II.⟩ / BOSTON / C. C. LITTLE & Co

Binding E

P cloth: brown; purple-brown. Sides blindstamped with a grolieresque ornament. Spine lettered in gold: HILLHOUSE'S / DRAMAS / DISCOURSES / &C / VOL. I. ⟨II.⟩ / BOS-TON / C. C. LITTLE & Co

Binding F

T cloth: black. Sides blindstamped with a triple-rule border, a floral ornament at each inner corner. Spine lettered in gold: HILLHOUSE'S / DRAMAS / &c / VOL. I. ⟨II.⟩ / BOSTON / C. C. LITTLE & Co

Binding G

T cloth: black. Sides blindstamped with a triple rule border, a floral ornament at each inner corner. Spine lettered in gold save as noted: HILLHOUSE'S / DRAMAS / &c / VOL. I. ⟨II.⟩ / ⟨the following in blind:⟩ BOSTON / C. C. LITTLE & CO.

Binding H

C cloth: brown. Sides blindstamped with a grolieresque ornament. Spine lettered in gold:

HILLHOUSE'S / DRAMAS / DISCOURSES / &C / VOL. I. ⟨II.⟩ /

Binding I

TB cloth: dull purple. Sides blindstamped with a triple-rule frame, a filigree at each inner corner; at center of sides: a cartouche. Spine lettered in gold: HILLHOUSE'S / DRAMAS / &c / VOL. I. ⟨II.⟩ /

Binding J

T cloth: black. Sides blindstamped with a heavy arabesque frame. Spine lettered in gold: HILL-HOUSE'S / DRAMAS / VOL. I. ⟨II.⟩ /

Binding K

Fine-grained H cloth: black. Sides blindstamped with a triple rule. Spine lettered in gold: HILL-HOUSE'S / DRAMAS / VOL. I. ⟨II.⟩

Binding L

T cloth: black. *Two volumes in one.* Spine lettered in gold: HILLHOUSE'S / WRITINGS / J. MUNROE & CO. Apparently a remainder issue.

Binding M

TR cloth: dull tan. *Two volumes in one.* Spine lettered in gold: HILLHOUSE'S / DRAMAS Apparently a remainder issue.

Deposited Oct. 15, 1839. Reviewed by NAR Jan. 1840. Advertised in Ath (by Green) Jan. 2, 1841.

AAS (K) B (D) BA (G) BPL (B, E, G, H) H (C) LC (A) NYPL (E, F) Y (B, E, I, J, K, L, M)

REPRINTS

The following publications contain material by Hillhouse reprinted from earlier books.

The Classical Reader; a Selection of Lessons in Prose and Verse . . . by Rev. F. W. P. Greenwood and G. B. Emerson . . .

Boston: Printed and Published by Lincoln & Edmands, No. 59 Washington-Street, (Cornhill.) 1826.

Leather. Title deposited Oct. 10, 1826.

The Class Book of American Literature . . . by John Frost.

Boston . . . 1826.

For comment see BAL, Vol. 1, p. 136.

Specimens of American Poetry . . . in Three Volumes. By Samuel Kettell . . .

Boston . . . MDCCCXXIX.

For comment see entry No. 3251.

Selections from the American Poets ...
Dublin ... 1834.
For comment see BAL, Vol. 2, p. 397.

The Young Lady's Book of Elegant Poetry ...
Philadelphia ... 1835.
For comment see BAL, Vol. 1, p. 206.

The Young Man's Book of Elegant Poetry ...
Philadelphia ... 1835.
For fuller entry see No. 1156.

Gems from American Poets.
London ... M DCCC XXXVI.
For comment see BAL, Vol. 2, p. 397.

Selections from the American Poets. By William Cullen Bryant.
New-York ... 1840.
For comment see entry No. 1617.

The Poets of America ... Edited by John Keese.
New York ... 1840.
For comment see BAL, Vol. 1, pp. 232-233.

American Melodies ... Compiled by George P. Morris ...
New-York ... 1841.
For comment see entry No. 997.

Gems from American Poets ...
New-York ... ⟨1842⟩
For comment see entry No. 5193.

The Poets and Poetry of America ... by Rufus W. Griswold ...
Philadelphia ... MDCCCXLII.
For comment see entry No. 6644.

The Poets of America ... Edited by John Keese. [Volume Second of the Series.]
New York ... 1842.
For comment see entry No. 3280.

Readings in American Poetry. By Rufus W. Griswold ...
New-York ... 1843.
For comment see entry No. 6647.

The Poets of Connecticut ... Edited by Rev. Charles W. Everest.

Hartford Case, Tiffany and Burnham. 1843.
Leather. Reviewed by BJ Sept. 30, 1843.

Gems from the American Poets ... by Rufus W. Griswold.
Philadelphia ... 1844.
For comment see entry No. 6657.

The Poetry of the Passions. Edited by Rufus W. Griswold ...
Philadelphia ... 1845.
For comment see entry No. 1021.

The Poetry of the Sentiments. Edited by R. W. Griswold.
Philadelphia ... 1845.
For comment see entry No. 6669.

The Poet's Gift ... Edited by John Keese.
Boston ... 1845.
For comment see BAL, Vol. 1, p. 206.

The Poetry of the Sentiments. Edited by R. W. Griswold.
Philadelphia ... 1846.
For comment see BAL, Vol. 1, p. 372.

The Lover's Gift; or Tributes to the Beautiful. American Series. Edited by Mrs. E. Oakes Smith ...
Hartford: Henry S. Parsons. 1848.
Contains an extract from "Demetria," Dramas ... , 1839, Vol. 1.

The Rosemary, a Collection of Sacred and Religious Poetry ...
Philadelphia: Lindsay and Blakiston. ⟨1849⟩

The Sacred Poets of England and America ... Edited by Rufus W. Griswold ...
New York ... M DCCC XLIX.
For comment see entry No. 6680.

Love's Whisper. A Token from the Heart.
New York: Leavitt & Company, 1851.
For comment see note under entry No. 1021.

Gift of Love. A Token of Friendship for 1853. Edited by Rufus W. Griswold ...
New-York: Leavitt & Allen, 27 Dey Street. M.DCCC.LIII.
Leather. For comment see note under entry No. 1021.

Gift of Love. A Token of Friendship for 1854. Edited by Rufus W. Griswold . . .

New-York: Leavitt & Allen, 27 Dey Street. M.DCCC.LIV.

Leather. For comment see note under entry No. 1021.

Lilies and Violets . . . By Rosalie Bell . . .

New York . . . 1855.

For comment see entry No. 1658.

Lyra Americana: Hymns of Praise and Faith, from American Poets.

London: The Religious Tract Society . . . 1865.

Listed PC Oct. 2, 1865; Ath Oct. 7, 1865.

Poems of Places Edited by Henry W. Longfellow . . . Asia. Syria.

Boston . . . 1878.

For comment see BAL, Vol. 1, p. 274.

An Old Scrap-Book. With Additions . . .

⟨Cambridge⟩ February 8, 1884.

For comment see entry No. 7763.

REFERENCES AND ANA

The Education of a Poet. An Oration Delivered at Yale University.

New Haven, 1811.

Entry from Foley. Not located and almost certainly a ghost. Delivered as an M.A. oration. Hazelrigg (p. 186) lists the title as "unpublished."

Scena Quarta del Quinto Atto di Adad . . . del . . . Giacomo A. Hillhouse. Tradotta in Verso Italiano da L. da Ponte . . .

New-York: Stampatori Gray e Bunce. 1825.

Unprinted paper wrapper. Pp. 17.

On the Relation ⟨sic⟩ of Literature to a Republican Government.

⟨n.p., 1836⟩

Not located and almost certainly a ghost. Entry from Sabin where the above appears as a note appended to entry No. 31886.

Hillhouse's oration, "On the Relations of Literature to a Republican Government" appears in his Dramas . . . , 1839.

". . . an ardent appeal for a greater emphasis on culture in America . . . Though Hillhouse must have known that this discourse contained his best prose, he delayed publishing it until 1839, when he brought out his collected works . . ."—Hazelrigg, pp. 149, 152.

An Epistle to James A. Hillhouse, Esq.

New Haven: Printed by B. L. Hamlen. 1838.

Printed paper wrapper. Pp. 11. Anonymous.

American Eloquence . . . with Biographical Sketches and Illustrative Notes, by Frank Moore . . . in Two Volumes . . .

New York: D. Appleton and Company, 346 & 348 Broadway. London: 16 Little Britain. 1857.

"Speech in the Case of John Smith," Vol. 2, pp. 147-154. Sometimes misattributed to the subject of this list. The author was James Hillhouse, 1754–1833.

Lyra Americana . . . Selected . . . by the Rev. George T. Rider . . .

New York . . . 1865.

For comment see entry No. 2827. "The Joy Unknown in Heaven," pp. 146-147, sometimes misattributed to the subject of this list. The author was Augustus Lucas Hillhouse, 1792–1859, brother of James Abraham Hillhouse. The poem, under the title "Forgiveness of Sins a Joy Unknown to Angels," correctly attributed, appears in Stedman (An American Anthology) and in Granger.

American Literary Pioneer: A Biographical Study of James A. Hillhouse by Charles Tabb Hazelrigg

New York: Bookman Associates, Publishers: 1953

CHARLES FENNO HOFFMAN

1 8 0 6 – 1 8 8 4

8520. "Sparkling and Bright"

ca. 1830.

This poem was first published in *The New York American,* May 8, 1830. It appears (earliest located book appearance) in *American Melodies,* 1841, described below; and, was collected in Hoffman's *The Echo . . . ,* 1844. Prior to book publication the poem was issued as sheet music; precise time of publication not known but each of the following three printings has a claim to primacy; the order of presentation is completely arbitrary.

Printing A

Sparkling & Bright . . . Music . . . by James B. Taylor.

New-York, Firth & Hall, 1 Franklin Sque. ⟨n.d., *ca.* 1832⟩

Printing B

Sparkling & Bright . . . Music . . . by James B. Taylor.

New York, Published by James L Hewitt. 239 Broadway. ⟨n.d., *ca.* 1832–1837⟩

Printing C

Sparkling and Bright . . . Music . . . by James B. Taylor.

New York: Thos. Birch. Music Engraver, Printer and Publisher, Wholesale and Retail. ⟨n.d.⟩

The following printings are unquestionably late:

New York. Atwill. Publisher. No. 201 Broadway. ⟨n.d., not before 1834⟩

N. York Published at Millets Music Saloon 329 Broadway W. D. Smith, Pittsburgh ⟨n.d., not before 1839⟩

AM

8521. A WINTER IN THE WEST. BY A NEW-YORKER . . .

NEW-YORK: PUBLISHED BY HARPER & BROTHERS, NO. 82 CLIFF-STREET. 1835.

2 Vols.

1: ⟨i-iv⟩, ⟨1⟩-337, blank leaf. 7⅜" x 4½".
2: ⟨i-iv⟩, ⟨1⟩-346, blank leaf.

1: ⟨-⟩², A-I, K-U, X-Z, Aa-Ee⁶, ⟨Ff⟩².
2: ⟨-⟩², A-I, K-U, X-Z, Aa-Ff⁶.

A-like cloth: rose-purple; slate. CM-like cloth: blue. Coarse H: purple. Wood-grained S: tan. Flyleaves.

A prepublication review appeared in AMM Jan. 1835: "By the kindness of the publishers we have ⟨seen⟩ this work, which will be given to the public, we presume, simultaneously with the appearance of ⟨this⟩ number." Title deposited Feb. 3, 1835. Reviewed NYLG Feb. 14, 1835. BA copy received March 2, 1835. Reviewed AQR March, 1835; K March, 1835. *See next entry.*

The London (Bentley) edition advertised in LG Feb. 14, 1835, as *just ready.* Described as *preparing for immediate publication* LG Feb. 21, 1835. Advertised as *just ready* LG Feb. 28, 1835. Announced as *just ready* Ath Feb. 28, 1835; March 7, 1835; LG March 7, 1835. Listed Ath March 14, 1835; LG March 14, 1835. Reviewed LG March 14, 1835. Advertised as *just published* LG March 14, 1835. Reviewed by Ath March 21, 1835, where the book is described as a "reprint of an American work." Listed BMLA April, 1835, as issued during the period March 9–April 9, 1835. Issued in 1848 as No. 6 of Bentley's *Cabinet Library.*

BA H UV

8522. A Winter in the West. By a New-Yorker . . . in Two Volumes . . . Second Edition.

New-York: Published by Harper & Brothers, No. 82 Cliff-Street. 1835.

Revised. For first edition see preceding entry.

BPL

8523. The Magnolia. 1836. Edited by Henry W. Herbert.

New-York . . . Boston . . . Philadelphia . . . New-Orleans . . . ⟨1835⟩

"A Night on the Enchanted Mountains," pp. ⟨261⟩-276. Collected in *Wild Scenes* ... , London, 1839, Vol. 2, p. 232 *et seq.*; *Wild Scenes* ... , New York, 1843, Vol. 2, p. ⟨75⟩ *et seq.*

For comment see entry No. 8058.

8524. The New-York Book of Poetry ...

New-York: George Dearborn, Publisher, No. 38 Gold Street. 1837.

Edited by Hoffman. Contains the following contributions by him:

"Advertisement," dated Dec. 24, 1836, p. ⟨iii⟩.

c "Moonlight on the Hudson," pp. 7-9.

e g "Song," pp. 17-18; *I know thou dost love me* ...

e "The Western Hunter to His Mistress," p. 36.

e "Chansonette," p. 50; *They are mockery all* ...

c "Indian Summer—1828," pp. 54-55.

e "Impromptu to a Lady Blushing," p. 58.

e "Song of Spring-Time," p. 63.

e "Love and Faith; a Ballad," pp. 66-67.

c "What is Solitude?," pp. 79-80.

e "Morning Hymn," p. 121; *Let there be light* ...

e g "Song—Rosalie Clare," p. 126.

e g "Anacreontic," pp. 172-173.

e "Epitaph upon a Dog," p. 182.

Note: See below: *Key to Other Appearances of the Individual Poems.*

Note: Barnes, p. 79, states: "A second issue of this book, identical in content with the first, appeared in the summer of 1837 ..." BAL assumes that Barnes here refers to the two states of the title-page; see entry No. 3272.

For comment see entry No. 3272.

8525. WILD SCENES IN THE FOREST AND PRAIRIE ...

LONDON: RICHARD BENTLEY, NEW BURLINGTON STREET, PUBLISHER IN ORDINARY TO HER MAJESTY. PRICE SIXTEEN SHILLINGS. 1839.

2 Vols. For first American edition see under 1843.

1: ⟨i⟩-⟨viii⟩, ⟨1⟩-292. 77⁄16″ x 4¾″.
2: ⟨i-iv⟩, ⟨1⟩-284.

1: ⟨A⟩⁴, B-I, K-T⁸, U².
2: ⟨A⟩², B-I, K-S⁸, T⁴, U².

Probably issued in paper boards, printed paper label on spine.

Noted as *just ready* LG Dec. 8, 1838; PC Dec. 15, 1838. Announced as *in a few days* LG Dec. 15, 1838. Announced as *now ready* LG Jan. 12, 1839. Listed LG Jan. 12, 1839; Ath Jan. 12, 1839; PC Jan. 15, 1839. Reviewed by Ath Jan. 19, 1839.

Note: Also issued two volumes in one, cloth, without date. Date of publication not known but presumed to be a reprint. A copy was received by BA Nov. 7, 1846.

AAS   Y

GREYSLAER

Absolute evidence is wanting but the London edition appears to have been published a few days prior to the New York edition. The following dates indicate the problem.

New York: Title-page deposited June 1, 1840.

London: Noted for the *present month* Ath June 6, 1840.

London: Noted for the *present month* Ath June 13, 1840.

London: Noted for the *present month* LG June 13, 1840.

London: Noted as *just ready* LG June 20, 1840.

London: Listed LG June 27, 1840.

London: Noted as *just published* Ath June 27, 1840.

London: Listed Ath June 27, 1840.

London: Advertised as though published PC July 1, 1840.

London: Advertised as though published LG July 4, 1840.

New York: Reviewed in *New Yorker*, July 4, 1840.

New York: *New Yorker*, July 11, 1840, reported: "now before us a copy of the second impression." Information wanting regarding a second printing.

London: Advertised, with extracts from reviews; described as *now ready*, LG July 11, 1840.

London: Reviewed LG July 11, 1840.

London: Reviewed Ath July 18, 1840.

New York: Reviewed by K Aug. 1840. The review implies that the book had gone into a fourth printing. BAL has found no evidence to suggest that this edition was reprinted during the year 1840.

8526. GREYSLAER: A ROMANCE OF THE MOHAWK . . .

LONDON: RICHARD BENTLEY, NEW BURLINGTON STREET. 1840.

3 Vols. For first American edition see next entry.

1: ⟨i⟩-⟨viii⟩, ⟨1⟩-303. 8″ x 4⅞″.
2: ⟨i-iv⟩, ⟨1⟩-315.
3: ⟨i-iv⟩, ⟨1⟩-326; advertisements, pp. ⟨327-328⟩.

1: ⟨A⟩⁴, B-I, K-N¹², O⁸.
2: ⟨A⟩², B-I, K-O¹², P².
3: ⟨A⟩², B-I, K-O¹², P⁸.

Brown paper boards sides, polished brown muslin shelfback. Printed paper label on spine.

See above for publication notes. See under 1841, 1849, for corrected editions.

UI

8527. GREYSLAER: A ROMANCE OF THE MOHAWK. BY THE AUTHOR OF "A WINTER IN THE WEST," . . .

NEW-YORK: HARPER & BROTHERS, 82 CLIFF-STREET. 1840.

2 Vols. For first London edition see preceding entry.

1: ⟨i-viii⟩, ⟨13⟩-243. 7⅝″ x 4½″.
2: ⟨1⟩-260.

1: ⟨A⟩⁴, B-I, K-U⁶, X².
2: ⟨A⟩⁴, B-I, K-U, X-Y⁶.

Blue C-like cloth embossed with an all-over pattern of tulip-like florets. Purple fine-grained T cloth embossed with an all-over pattern of leaves and flowers. Green TZ cloth. Blue-green V cloth embossed with an all-over pattern of small, flourish-like, ornaments. Blue and green C-like cloth embossed with an all-over pattern resembling the track of a crawling worm. Printed paper label on spine. Flyleaves.

See above for publication notes. See under 1841, 1849, for corrected editions.

NYPL UV Y

8528. American Melodies . . . Compiled by George P. Morris . . .

New-York: Published by Linen and Fennell, No. 229 Broadway. 1841.

"Sparkling and Bright," pp. 14-15. See entry No. 8520.

For comment see entry No. 997.

8529. Greyslaer: A Romance of the Mohawk. By the Author of "A Winter in the West," . . . A New Edition, Corrected by the Author.

Philadelphia: Lea & Blanchard. 1841.

2 Vols. For first edition see above under 1840.

Cloth, printed paper label on spine.

Note: PHILADELBHIA for PHILADELPHIA, imprint, Vol. 1. All examined copies thus.

"Preface to the New Edition," Vol. 1, pp. ⟨v⟩-vi, dated at end *November, 1840.*

Listed NYR Jan. 1841.

AAS NYPL

8530. Quadruple Boston Notion . . . Extra Number . . .

Boston . . . June 10, 1841 . . .

Contains a selection of Hoffman's poems. Reprint save for the following poems. See below: *Key to Other Appearances of the Individual Poems.*

e f "Thy Name"

e g "Song of the Drowned"

e f "I Do Not Love Thee"

e f "Withering—Withering"

e f g "Serenade" (*Sleeping! Why now sleeping . . .*)

e f "Ask Me Not Why I Should Love Her"

e "They Say That Thou Art Altered"

e f "Chansonette" (*She loves—but tis not me she loves*)

e f "Melody" (*When the flowers of friendship or love have decayed*) Also issued as sheet music, ca. 1853.

e f "I Will Love Her No More"

e f "Inscription for a Lady's Flora" Otherwise "The Wish."

d e f g "The Origin of Mint Juleps" Otherwise "The Mint Julep."

"I Lied in What I Writ" Collected in Barnes.

e "To a Waxen Rose"

"Tippecanoe" Otherwise unlocated.

For comment see entry No. 1000.

8531. Quadruple Boston Notion . . . Extra Number.

Boston . . . July 15, 1841 . . .

"The Poetry of Charles Fenno Hoffman. Second Collection," p. 4. Reprint save for the following pieces. See below: *Key to Other Appearances of the Individual Poems.*

e f "The Thaw-King's Visit to New-York"

e "Rhymes on West-Point"

c "The Bob-o'-Linkum" Also in *Poets of America,* 1842.

"Rhymes to His Muse, by a Briefless Barrister" (*'Tis dull to sit from nine till six o'clock*) Uncollected save for publication in Barnes.

e "Myne Heartte"

e f "A Portrait"

e g "The Ambuscade—In Imitation of Scott"

e f "To ――――" (*Think of me dearest, when day is breaking*)

e "On a Lady Weeping in Church"

"From the German. By an Austrian Officer on the Eve of a Duel" (*Let no shroud wrap my corse when in combat I fall . . .*) Otherwise unlocated.

d e f "Love and Politics—A Poet's Birth-Day Meditations"

e "The Declaration"

e "Holding a Rope for a Lady to Jump"

e "Birth-Day Thoughts"

e "To ―――――" (*Aye, there it is, that wizard smile*)

"To Lothario" (*Nay, look not coldly on me now*) Otherwise unlocated.

d e f "Dream"; otherwise: "Coming Out."

e "Closing Accounts—To My Cousin"

"To a Lady on Her Birth-Day" (*We'll quarrel not with time today*) Otherwise unlocated.

"Stanzas" (*I love thee, Nature! In every mood*) Otherwise unlocated.

e f Untitled poem beginning *Why seek her heart to understand.*

"To Miss N――― O'P――― Q" (*You bend on me that lovely brow*) Otherwise unlocated.

"Extracts from Reginald Wolfe, or Memoirs of a Partizan Officer,—An Unpublished Novel." Otherwise unlocated. P. 8.

EM

8532. The Token and Atlantic Souvenir, an Offering for Christmas and the New Year.

Boston: Published by David H. Williams . . . 1842.

"Enigma," pp. ⟨292⟩-293. Elsewhere unlocated.

For comment see entry No. 1005.

8533. The Poets of America . . . Edited by **John** Keese. [Volume Second of the Series.]

New York: Published by Samuel Colman . . . 1842.

"The Bob-O'Linkum," pp. 255-258. Also **in** *Quadruple Boston Notion . . . ,* Boston, July 15, 1841. Collected in *The Vigil . . . ,* 1842.

For comment see entry No. 3280.

8534. The Poets and Poetry of America. With an Historical Introduction. By Rufus W. Griswold . . .

Philadelphia: Carey and Hart, Chesnut Street. MDCCCXLII.

For comment see entry No. 6644. See below: *Key to Other Appearances of the Individual Poems.*

Contains a section of poems by Hoffman; reprint with the exception of the following:

a e "Ask Me Not Why I Should Love Her"

e "Boat-Song"

e "Byron"

b d e "Dream"; otherwise "Coming Out."

e "The Farewell" (*The conflict is over . . .*)

e g "Forest Musings"

e g "A Hunter's Matin"

a e "I Do Not Love Thee"

a e "I Will Love Her No More"

a e "Inscription for a Lady's Flora"; otherwise "The Wish."

c "Language of Flowers"

b d e "Love and Politics"; otherwise "A Birth-Day Meditation."

a e "Melody" (*When the flowers of friendship or love have decayed*) Also issued as sheet music, ca. 1853.

a d e g "The Origin of Mint Juleps"; otherwise "The Mint Julep."

b e "A Portrait"

b e "Seek Not To Understand Her"; otherwise, "Why Seek Her Heart to Understand."

a e g "Serenade" (*Sleeping! why now sleeping . . .*)

a e "She Loves, but 'tis Not Me"; otherwise "Chansonette."

e "The Student's Song" (*Thoughts—thoughts! why will ye wander . . .*)

b e "The Thaw-King's Visit to New York"

b e "Think of Me, Dearest"; otherwise "To ————."

a e "Thy Name"

d e "Thy Smiles" (*I know I share thy smiles with many*)

e "To ————" (*I knew not how I loved thee*)

c "Town Repinings"

e "Trust in Thee"

a e "Withering—Withering"

e "Written in a Lady's Prayer-Book"

e "Written in Springtime"

KEY TO OTHER APPEARANCES OF THE INDIVIDUAL POEMS

a: Previously in *Quadruple Boston Notion ... Extra Number ...* , June 10, 1841, entry No. 8530.

b: Previously in *Quadruple Boston Notion ... Extra Number ...* , July 15, 1841, entry No. 8531.

c: Collected in *The Vigil ...* , New York, 1842; entry No. 8535.

d: Collected in *The Vigil ...* , London, 1844 (Jan.); entry No. 8544.

e: Collected in *The Echo ...* , Philadelphia, 1844 (Oct.), entry No. 8546.

f: Also in *The Poets and Poetry of America,* 1842; entry No. 8534.

g: Also in *Wild Scenes ...* , N. Y., 1843; entry No. 8538.

8535. THE VIGIL OF FAITH, AND OTHER POEMS ...

NEW-YORK: PUBLISHED BY S. COLMAN: SOLD BY COLLINS, BROTHER & CO. PHILADELPHIA: THOMAS COWPERTHWAITE & CO. BOSTON: W. D. TICKNOR. M DCCC XLII.

⟨1⟩-84. 7³⁄₁₆" x 4¹¹⁄₁₆".

⟨-⟩², 1-6⁶, 7⁴.

White paper boards, printed paper label on spine. White-coated end papers; buff-coated end papers. Flyleaves.

Reviewed BJ March 12, 1842. Deposited April 20, 1842. Noted as *just published* USDR April, 1842. Also see entries 8544, 8556.

AAS UV

8536. The Lady's Book of Flowers and Poetry ... Edited by Lucy Hooper.

New York: J. C. Riker, 15 Ann Street. 1842.

Reprint? Publication date not known.

"To an Autumn Rose," p. 32. Also in (reprinted from?) *The Vigil of Faith,* 1842 (April) .

"Language of Flowers," p. ⟨47⟩. Also in (reprinted from?) *The Poets and Poetry of America,* 1842 (April); and, *The Vigil of Faith,* 1842, (April).

NYPL

8537. The Myrtle and Steel ... ⟨Music⟩ by F. J. Webster ...

New-York. Published by Firth & Hall, 1 Franklin Sq. & J. L. Hewitt, & Co. 239 Broadway. ⟨n.d., *ca.* 1842–1843⟩

Sheet music. Cover-title. Reprinted from *Greyslaer,* 1840.

Another setting, by Edward O. Eaton, was issued by Berry & Gordon, N.Y., 1854.

AM

8538. WILD SCENES IN THE FOREST AND PRAIRIE. WITH SKETCHES OF AMERICAN LIFE ...

NEW YORK: WILLIAM H. COLYER, NO. 5 HAGUE-STREET. 1843.

2 Vols. For first edition (London) see under 1839. *Note:* In this edition the preface is extended although the original date, *May, 1838,* (as present in the London edition) is retained.

1: ⟨i⟩-viii, ⟨13⟩-207. 7⅝" x 4½".
2: ⟨i-iv⟩, ⟨13⟩-211.

1: ⟨1⟩⁴, 2-17⁶, 18².
2: ⟨A⟩², B-I, K-R⁶, S⁴.

Binding: Paper boards?

Noted as *in press* USDR April, 1843. BPL copy (lacking S₄) inscribed by Hoffman May 21, 1843. Reviewed by BJ June 10, 1843. "Mr. ⟨John⟩ Keese has just looked in ... He tells me 2500 ⟨copies⟩ of *Wild Scenes* were published and 1500 have sold already. I hardly expected this for I have heard nothing of the book since it came out."—Letter, July 10, 1843, Hoffman to his sister Julia; letter in the possession of the Hoffman family; reported by Dr. Warder H. Cadbury.

BPL NYSL Y

8539. The Wintergreen, a Perennial Gift for 1844 ... Edited by John Keese ...

New York: Charles Wells & Co., No. 56 Gold-Street. ⟨1843⟩

"New Year's Visiting in Hades," pp. ⟨31⟩-43. Otherwise unlocated.

"The Last Man," pp. ⟨198⟩-208. Otherwise un-located; however, embodies "Town Repinings" previous published in *Vigil of Faith*, 1842.

"My Familiar," pp. ⟨227⟩-237. Otherwise un-located.

"The Sprig of Wintergreen," p. ⟨247⟩. Uncol-lected save for Barnes, pp. 310-311.

For comment see entry No. 4019.

8540. The Flower Vase; Containing the Lan-guage of Flowers and Their Poetic Senti-ments. By Miss S. C. Edgarton . . .

Lowell: Powers, Bagley and Company. Bos-ton: B. B. Mussey, Cornhill. 1843.

Reprint save for the following poems; all col-lected in *The Echo*, 1844:

"Cold-Hearted," p. 88.

"Purity," p. 90.

"Confidence," p. 118.

H

8541. Merrily, Merrily Sound the Bells, the Christmas Sleigh-Ride . . . Composed . . . by J. L. Hatton . . .

Boston . . . Oliver Ditson, 115 Washington St. . . . 1843 . . .

Sheet music. Cover-title. Plate number 1666. Collected in *The Echo*, 1844, as "The Sleigh Bells."

EM

8542. The Gift: A Christmas and New Year's Present. MDCCCXLIV.

Philadelphia: Carey and Hart. 1844.

"Heart-Augury. (Suggested by a Broken Apollo.)," pp. ⟨42⟩-43.

"Inman's Picture of Mumble-the-Peg, with the Story of Nick Ten Vlyck," pp. ⟨44⟩-61.

"The Fair Student," p. ⟨96⟩.

All three elsewhere unlocated.

For comment see entry No. 4021.

8543. The Opal: A Pure Gift for the Holy Days. Edited by N. P. Willis . . .

New-York: John C. Riker 15 Ann Street. 1844.

"Scenes on the Mississippi. Yellow Jack," pp. ⟨148⟩-172. Otherwise unlocated.

For comment see entry No. 6648.

8544. The Vigil of Faith, and Other Poems . . .

London: H. G. Clarke and Co., 66, Old Bailey. 1844.

According to contemporary notices issued in printed paper wrapper.

For first American edition see entry No. 8535. Also see entry No. 8556.

Reprint save for the following; all appear also in *The Echo* . . . , New York, 1844 (Oct.).

"The Origin of Mint Juleps." Previously in *Quadruple Boston Notion . . . Extra Number . . . June 10, 1841;* and, *Poets and Poetry of America,* 1842.

"The Student's Song." Collected in *The Echo* . . . , 1844, as Part XXII of "Songs—Eros and Anteros." Also in *Poets and Poetry of America,* 1842.

"Love and Politics. A Birth-Day Meditation." Collected in *The Echo* . . . , 1844, as "A Birth-Day Meditation." Also in *Quadruple Boston Notion . . . Extra Number . . . July 15, 1841.*

Listed Ath Jan. 6, 1844, as No. 2 in *American Series of Clarke's English Helicon.* Listed PC Jan. 15, 1844. Advertised in PC Feb. 15, 1844; and May 15, 1844, as No. 7 in *Clarke's Cabinet Series.*

BA

8545. Lives of John Sullivan, Jacob Leisler, Na-thaniel Bacon, and John Mason.

Boston: Charles C. Little and James Brown. 1844.

The Library of American Biography. Conducted by Jared Sparks. Second Series. Vol. III.

"The Administration of Jacob Leisler, a Chap-ter in American History," pp. ⟨179⟩-238.

Deposited Oct. 26, 1844. Reviewed NAR Jan. 1845.

H LC

8546. THE ECHO: OR, BORROWED NOTES FOR HOME CIRCULATION . . .

PHILADELPHIA: LINDSAY & BLAKISTON, CHESNUT STREET. 1844.

⟨i-ii⟩, 7-⟨8⟩, 3-iv, 7-48. 10⁷⁄₁₆″ x 6³⁄₁₆″.

⟨1⟩-⟨4⟩, 5-6⁴. *Also signed:* ⟨A⟩-D⁶. *Note:* Sig-nature mark B occurs on both p. 13 and on p. 19.

Printed cream paper wrapper.

Note: The wrapper imprint reads: *New York: Burgess & Stringer . . . Philadelphia, George B. Zieber & Co. . . . 1844.* These firms were unquestionably distributing agents of the publisher, Lindsay & Blakiston, which accounts for the suggestion in *Weekly Mirror*, N. Y., Dec. 14, 1844, that the book was published by Burgess & Stringer, New York.

Listed as an October publication by WPLNL, Nov. 1844.

AAS   BPL   H   NYPL

8547. Gems from the American Poets, with Brief Biographical Notices, by Rufus W. Griswold.

Philadelphia: H. Hooker, No. 178, Chestnut St. Opposite Masonic Hall. Stereotyped by C. W. Murray & Co. 1844.

"Le Faineant," pp. 88-89; also in (reprinted from?) *The Echo,* 1844 (Oct.).

BPL   Y

8548. The Mourner's Chaplet: An Offering of Sympathy for Bereaved Friends. Selected from American Poets, by John Keese ...

Boston: Gould, Kendall & Lincoln. 1844.

"Where Would I Rest?," pp. 117-118. Also in (reprinted from?) *The Echo,* 1844 (Oct.).

Preface dated Aug. 1844. Further publication information wanting. Reissued by Gould & Lincoln, Boston ⟨1844; *i.e.,* not before 1850⟩.

NYPL

8549. Proceedings of the New York Historical Society. For the Year 1843.

New York: Press of the Historical Society. 1844.

Paper on the distinctive character of the people of New York, pp. 95-106. Read at a meeting of the society Dec. 5, 1843.

Printed paper wrapper.

H

8550. An Address, Delivered before the New York Historical Society, at its Fortieth Anniversary, 20th November, 1844; by John Romeyn Brodhead, Esq., Historical Agent of the State of New York, to Holland, England, and France. With an Account of the Subsequent Proceedings at the Dinner Given in the Evening.

New York: Press of the New York Historical Society. 1844.

Issued in printed paper wrapper? Cover-title?

Response to a toast, "New York," pp. 99-105.

Reviewed by K March, 1845.

H

8551. ... Oneóta, or the Red Race of America: Their History, Traditions, Customs, Poetry, Picture-Writing, &c. In Extracts from Notes, Journals, and Other Unpublished Writings. By Henry R. Schoolcraft ...

New York: Published by Burgess, Stringer & Co., No. 222 Broadway, Corner of Ann Street American Museum Buildings. ⟨1844–1845⟩

Printed paper wrapper. Cover-title. At head of title: Price Twenty-Five Cents.

Note: Entry based on a single copy of *Part I* in original printed paper wrapper (in H); the Wiley & Putnam rebind of 1845 (see below); and on Sabin (see below).

"Originally issued in eight numbers of 64 pages each ... The first four numbers were published in 1844, beginning with Number I., in August; the other four appeared in 1845 ..."— Sabin, No. 77867.

Unsold parts were bound together as a single volume and issued with newly printed front matter including title-page: *Oneóta, or Characteristics of the Red Race of America ..., New York & London: Wiley & Putnam. 1845.* Copy in H.

For a discussion of this publication see "Pirated Editions of Schoolcraft's *Oneóta,*" by John Finley Freeman, in *Papers of the Bibliographical Society of America,* Vol. 53, 1959, pp. 252-261.

Hoffman contributed the following translations to this work:

⟨"Cradle Song"⟩, Part 4, p. 214. Collected in Barnes, pp. 311-312.

"Corn Song," Part 4, pp. 255-256. Collected in Barnes, pp. 312-314.

"⟨Algonquin⟩ War-Song," Part 6, pp. 348-349. Also in *The Vigil ...,* 1845, as "Indian War Song."

"⟨Algonquin⟩ Death-Song," Part 6, pp. 350-351. Also in *The Vigil ...,* 1845, as "Indian Death Song."

"The Loon upon the Lake," Part 7, p. 405, credited to E. F. Hoffman ⟨*sic*⟩. Also in *The Vigil ...,* 1845.

H

8552. The Gift: A Christmas, New Year, and Birthday Present. MDCCCXLV.

Philadelphia: Carey and Hart. 1845.

"A Prairie Jumbie," pp. ⟨134⟩-147.

For comment see entry No. 4024.

8553. American Wild Flowers in Their Native Haunts, by Emma C. Embury . . .

New York: D. Appleton & Company, 200 Broadway. Philadelphia: George S Appleton, 148 Chesnut Street. MDCCCXLV.

"The Wild Laurel," pp. ⟨115⟩-117. Collected in *The Vigil*, 1845, as "The Origin of the Laurel."

"Pollipell's Island," pp. ⟨152⟩-162. Otherwise unlocated.

"Stanzas," p. ⟨235⟩; *Oh! Tell not the stars, the free stars, of thy sadness* . . . Collected in *Songs*, 1846, as "Aimless Sentiment."

Deposited Oct. 18, 1844.

NYPL

8554. The Great Western Almanac for 1846

Published and Sold by Jos. McDowell, 37 Market Street, Philadelphia. ⟨n.d., 1845⟩

Cover-title. Printed paper wrapper.

"A Mouthful of Pickled Dog," pp. 4-5.

H

8555. Report of the Committee of the New York Historical Society, on a National Name, March 31, 1845.

⟨n.p., n.d., New York, 1845⟩

Caption-title. Preceding at head of p. ⟨1⟩. Pp. ⟨1⟩-8. Printed self-wrapper.

Signed at end by Hoffman, David Dudley Field and Henry R. Schoolcraft.

"The Committee, appointed by a resolution of the Society of the 4th instant, upon the subject of the irrelevant appellation, at present used for this country, with the view of enquiring whether a geographical name might not be suggested more distinctive and significant, and more likely to promote national associations, and prove efficient in History, Poetry, and Art; beg leave to Report . . .

"What we want is a sign of our identity. We want utterance for our nationality . . .

"That the name of *Allegania* be recommended as the best . . .

". . . it be proposed to the authors of school books and maps, to designate this country hereafter as the *Republic of Allegania* . . ."

NYHS   NYPL   Y

8556. The Vigil of Faith and Other Poems . . . Fourth Edition.

New York: Harper & Brothers. 1845.

For first edition see entry No. 8535; also see entry No. 8544.

Reprint with the exception of:

"Inscription," p. 7.

"The Loon upon the Lake," p. 81.*

"Indian War Song," pp. 85-86.*

"Indian Death Song," pp. 86-87.*

"The Origin of the Laurel," pp. 122-123. Previously in *American Wild Flowers* . . . , 1845, described above.

Note: Barnes (pp. 257-258) quotes a letter from Hoffman to Rufus Wilmot Griswold written in May(?), 1845, in which Hoffman writes in part: "I send you a copy of the *Vigil* to read proof by. I had one hundred copies struck off to send to my friends . . ." Further information wanting.

* Also in *Onéota*, 1844–1845, described above.

B   LC   Y

8557. The Opal: A Pure Gift for the Holy Days. MDCCCXLVI. Edited by John Keese . . .

New-York: J. C. Riker, 129 Fulton-Street. 1846.

Leather.

"The Ambush of Air," pp. ⟨91⟩-97.

Noted as *just ready* ALB Oct. 1845. Listed WPLNL Nov. 1845. Reviewed USDR Dec. 1845.

H

8558. A Morning Hymn.

London: Harvey and Darton, 1846.

Not seen. Entry on the basis of an advertisement in PC June 15, 1846, p. 181, where this title, credited to Hoffman, is offered as one of a series of poems by Hoffman and others. The series was advertised under the descriptive: *Select Poetical Pieces, by various Authors, adapted for sticking or hanging on the walls of Schools, Mechanics' Institutes, &c; with Notes and Illustrative Extracts. By H. G. Adams* . . .

Presumably a separate printing of Hoffman's poem which had been published in *New-York Book of Poetry*, 1837; and, *The Echo*, 1844.

8559. Songs and Other Poems . . . Fifth Edition, Complete.

New York: Harper & Brothers, 82 Cliff St. 1846.

Leather; and, printed paper wrapper.

Reprint with the exception of:

"The Streamlet," p. 40.

"Aimless Sentiment," p. 40. See entry No. 8553.

"Chansonette," p. 41. (*It haunts me yet! that early dream*)

Listed WPLNL Oct. 1846.

B Y

8560. The Opal: A Pure Gift for the Holydays. MDCCCXLVII. Edited by John Keese ...

New-York: J. C. Riker, 129 Fulton-Street. 1847.

"Concerning Dogs," pp. ⟨191⟩-194.

For comment see entry No. 6853.

8561. The Mayflower. For M DCCC XLVII ... Edited by Mrs. E. Oakes Smith ...

Boston: Published by Saxton & Kelt. 1847.

Leather.

"Knickerbocker *vs.* Pilgrim. A Retrospection," pp. ⟨17⟩-34.

"Le Temps Viendra," pp. 209-210. In table of contents: "La Temps Viendra."

Title deposited Aug. 25, 1846.

H

8562. "Rio Bravo" A Mexican Lament ... Music ... by Austin Phillips ...

New York ... Firth & Hall, 1 Franklin Sq. & Firth, Hall & Pond, 239 Broadway ... 1847 ...

Sheet music. Cover-title. Plate number 4149.

Collected in *Love's Calendar*, 1847 (Dec.)

Reviewed NYM July 24, 1847.

For a comment on this poem see *A Bibliography of John Greenleaf Whittier*, by Thomas Franklin Currier, Cambridge, 1937, pp. 318-320.

H

8563. The Mayflower. For M DCCC XLVIII ... Edited by Mrs. E. Oakes Smith ...

Boston: Published by Saxton and Kelt. 1848 ⟨*i.e.*, Oct. 1847⟩

Cloth?

"The Poetry of Trade, or Sunbeams from Cucumbers," pp. 52-74.

"Prophecy of the Flowers," p. 229.

"Impromptu," pp. 229-230.

"My Double; or, the Man Who Is Not Colonel Blank," pp. 290-299.

"The Forest Cemetery," pp. 300-304. Collected in *Love's Calendar*, 1847 (Dec.).

Reviewed LW Oct. 16, 1847.

NYPL

8564. Love's Calendar, Lays of the Hudson, and Other Poems ...

New-York: D. Appleton & Co., 200 Broadway. Philadelphia: Geo. S. Appleton, 148 Chesnut-St. 1847.

Reprint save for:

"The Forest Cemetery." Here first collected. Previously in *The Mayflower*, 1848 ⟨*i.e.*, Oct. 1847⟩; see preceding entry.

"Monterey."

"Rio Bravo." For prior publication in sheet music form see under 1847.

"The Men of Churubusco."

"Far Away."

"Afterthought."

"Buena Vista."

Note: Certain poems herein had prior publication in *The Echo*, 1844, under other titles; these changes are not here recorded.

Also note: The error *Yatcher* for *Yachter*, p. 5, sixth entry, occurs in all examined copies including the reprints of 1848 and 1851.

Advertised for *this week* LW Dec. 25, 1847. Listed LW Jan. 8, 1848, as a publication issued during the period Dec. 25, 1847–Jan. 8, 1848.

AAS H

The Mayflower. For M DCCC XLVIII ...

Boston ... 1848 ⟨*i.e.*, Oct. 1847⟩.

See above under 1847.

8565. THE PIONEERS OF NEW-YORK. AN ANNIVERSARY DISCOURSE DELIVERED BEFORE THE ST. NICHOLAS SOCIETY OF MANHATTAN, DECEMBER 6, 1847 ...

NEW-YORK: STANFORD AND SWORDS, 139, BROADWAY. 1848.

⟨1⟩-55. 8¹³⁄₁₆″ x 5¾″.

⟨1⟩-3⁸, 4⁴.

Printed tan paper wrapper.

Note: A type facsimile was issued by The Williams Printing Company, 1912, Collation: ⟨1-7⟩⁴. The seal on the front wrapper of the 1848 printing is (at its widest point) 1⅜"; in the reprint the measurement is 1⅛".

Listed LW Jan. 29, 1848, mistitled *St. Nicholas. An Address.* . . . Advertised LW Feb. 5, 1848, under the correct title, as *just published.*

H NYPL

8566. . . . International Copyright. Memorials of John Jay and of William C. Bryant and Others, in Favor of an International Copyright Law. March 22, 1848 . . .

⟨Washington, D. C.⟩ Tippin & Streeper, Printers. ⟨1848⟩

At pp. 32-33: "Memorial of W. C. Bryant and Others," signed at end by Hoffman and others.

For comment see entry No. 1637.

8567. Lays of the Western World, Illuminated by T W Gwilt Mapleson Esq.

New York: Putnam ⟨n.d., 1848⟩

Unpaged. Contains Hoffman's "Love's Requiem."

For comment see entry No. 1639.

8568. The Odd-Fellows' Offering, for 1848: Edited by James L. Ridgely and Paschal Donaldson.

New York: Published by Edward Walker, 114 Fulton Street. M DCCC XLVIII.

"Sonnet.—The Last of the Race," p. 236.

Title-page deposited April 22, 1847.

H

8568A. Gallery of the Old Masters . . .

⟨n.p., New York: George F. Nesbitt, n.d., 1848?⟩

Caption-title. The above at head of p. ⟨1⟩ of a single cut sheet of blue-gray paper folded to make four pages. A series of extracts from Hoffman and others, pp. ⟨1-3⟩; p. ⟨4⟩ blank.

Statement from Hoffmann ⟨*sic*⟩ on "the eminent advantages of New York as the centre of literatare ⟨*sic*⟩, science, and art," p. ⟨1⟩.

Probably issued as promotional material for an exhibition of art at The Lyceum Gallery, New York, 1848.

HSM

8569. Greyslaer; a Romance of the Mohawk . . . Fourth Edition

New York: Baker & Scribner, 145 Nassau Street, and 36 Park Row. 1849.

Revised and corrected. For first edition see under 1840.

"To the Reader," pp. ⟨v⟩-vi.

Advertised as *in a few days* LW Nov. 25, 1848. Listed LW Dec. 16, 1848.

H

8570. The Opal: A Pure Gift for All Seasons. Edited by Mrs. Sarah Josepha Hale.

New-York: J. C. Riker, 129 Fulton Street. 1849.

"The Marriage Ring," pp. ⟨13⟩-14.

For comment see entry No. 6866.

8571. The Ladies' Wreath: An Illustrated Annual. Edited by Mrs. S. T. Martyn.

New-York: J. M. Fletcher & Co. 143 Nassau-Street. 1851.

Vignette title-page imprinted Martyn & Miller.

A twilight book made up of the sheets of Vols. 5-6 of *The Ladies' Wreath* (N.Y.).

"Song of the Exile," Vol. 6, pp. ⟨297-299⟩.

NYPL

8572. Love's Calendar, Lays of the Hudson, and Other Poems . . .

New York: D. Appleton and Company, 200 Broadway. 1851.

Reprint.

WHC

8573. Select Poems . . .

London. W. Tweedie, 337, Strand. ⟨n.d., *ca.* 1852⟩

Reprint. Printed from the plates of *The Vigil of Faith* . . . , London, 1844.

H

8574. The Flowers of Friendship . . . Music . . . by H. Brinley Richards . . .

Published by Miller & Beacham Baltimore . . . ⟨n.d., 1853–1864⟩

Sheet music. Cover-title. Plate number 2436.

Reprinted from *The Echo*, 1844, where the poem appears under the title "Melody."

AAS

8575. The Poems of Charles Fenno Hoffman. Collected and Edited by His Nephew, Edward Fenno Hoffman.

Philadelphia: Porter & Coates. 1873.

Reprint with the exception of:

"Translation of an Indian Love Song," pp. 164-165.

"Tasso to Leonora," pp. 166-167.

Listed PW Oct. 11, 1873.

Note: Certain poems herein had prior publication under other titles; these changes are not here recorded.

BA   H

8576. ... Little Classics. Edited by Rossiter Johnson. Life ...

Boston: James R. Osgood and Company, Late Ticknor & Fields, and Fields, Osgood, & Co. 1875.

At head of title: Fourth Volume.

"The Man in the Reservoir," pp. ⟨189⟩-198.

BA copy received Nov. 19, 1874. Advertised as a *new book* PW Nov. 21, 1874. Listed PW Dec. 5, 1874.

NYPL

REPRINTS

The following publications contain material by Hoffman reprinted from earlier books.

The Southern First Class Book ... Selected ... by M. M. Mason ...

Macon ... 1839.

For comment see BAL, Vol. 1, p. 371.

The Magnolia. 1839 ...

New York ... ⟨1839⟩

For comment see in reprints section, Henry William Herbert list.

The Poets of America ... Edited by John Keese.

New York ... 1840.

For comment see BAL, Vol. 1, pp. 232-233.

Selections from the American Poets. By William Cullen Bryant.

New-York ... 1840.

For comment see entry No. 1617.

The Gems of American Poetry, by Distinguished Authors.

New-York: A. & C. B. Edwards. 1840.

Gems from American Poets ...

New-York ... ⟨1842⟩

For comment see entry No. 5193.

Readings in American Poetry. By Rufus W. Griswold ...

New-York ... 1843.

For comment see entry No. 6647.

The Cypress Wreath ... Edited by Rev. Rufus W. Griswold ...

Boston ... 1844.

For comment see entry No. 3281.

The Poetry of Love. Edited by Rufus W. Griswold ...

Boston ... 1844.

For comment see entry No. 1017.

The Forest Legendary, or Metrical Tales of the North American Woods. Edited by John Keese. No. 1 ...

New York: Published by Wm. van Norden, 39 William St. and Josiah Adams, Brick Church Chapel. 1845.

All published.

The Juvenile Gem, for 1846. Edited by Father Frank ...

New-York: Published by E. Kearny, Philadelphia: Thomas Cowperthwaite & Co. ⟨1845⟩

The Poetry of the Passions. Edited by Rufus W. Griswold ...

Philadelphia ... 1845.

For comment see entry No. 1021.

The Poetry of the Sentiments. Edited by R. W. Griswold.

Philadelphia ... 1845.

For comment see entry No. 6669.

The Poet's Gift ... Edited by John Keese.

Boston ... 1845.

For comment see BAL, Vol. 1, p. 206.

The Poetry of the Sentiments. Edited by R. W. Griswold.

Philadelphia ... 1846.

For comment see BAL, Vol. 1, p. 372.

The Ladies' Casket; Containing a Gem, together with its Sentiment, and a Poetical Description, for Each Day in the Week, and Each Month in the Year. By J. Wesley Hanson . . .

Lowell: Merrill and Heywood. Boston: B. B. Mussey. 1846.

Deposited Dec. 26, 1846. "Cinnamon Stone," p. 97; otherwise "Think of Me, Dearest," in *Poets and Poetry of America*, 1842; "Horn Stone," p. 98; otherwise "Thy Smiles," in *Poets and Poetry of America*, 1842.

The Estray . . .

Boston . . . 1847.

For comment see BAL, Vol. 1, p. 100.

The Prose Writers of America . . . by Rufus Wilmot Griswold . . .

Philadelphia . . . 1847.

For comment see entry Nos. 3158, 6676.

The Bouquet, for 1847 . . . Edited by Alfred A. Phillips.

New York: Nafis & Cornish. St. Louis, Nafis, Cornish & Co. 1847.

The Cottage Garland . . .

Williamsburgh . . . 1847.

For comment see BAL, Vol. 1, p. 206.

Pearls of American Poetry

. . . New York . . . ⟨n.d., 1847⟩

For comment see BAL, Vol. 3, p. 363.

The Golden Present, a Gift for All Seasons. Edited by Mrs. J. Thayer.

Nashua, N. H. Published by J. Buffum. 1849.

Also issued with the imprint: *Worcester: Published by S. A. Howland. 1849;* copyright notice in the name of J. Buffum. Reprinted and reissued with the imprint: *Boston: G. W. Cottrell and Company. New York: T. W. Strong* ⟨1848⟩.

The Lover's Gift; or Tributes to the Beautiful. American Series. Edited by Mrs. E. Oakes Smith . . .

Hartford: Henry S. Parsons. 1848.

Contains ten pieces by Hoffman, some under altered titles, here reprinted from earlier books. Included in the ten: Untitled eight lines beginning *And often bitter thoughts arise;* and, "To Alinda—Inglorious"; both these preceding extracted from "Love and Politics, a Birthday Meditation," in *Poets*

and Poetry of America, 1842. "Content," extracted from "Eros and Anteros," in *The Echo,* 1844. "Enshrined," extracted from "Platonics," in *The Echo,* 1844.

The Rosemary, a Collection of Sacred and Religious Poetry . . .

Philadelphia: Lindsay and Blakiston. ⟨1849⟩

Love's Whisper. A Token from the Heart.

New York . . . 1851.

For comment see note under entry No. 1021.

Scott and Graham Melodies; Being a Collection of Campaign Songs for 1852. As Sung by the Whig Clubs Throughout the United States.

Published by Huestis & Cozans, 104 & 106 Nassau-Street. New York. ⟨n.d., 1852⟩

Pictorial paper wrapper.

The Crystal Gem. Edited by J.S.A. . . .

Boston: J. Buffum, 11 Cornhill. ⟨1853⟩

The Gem: A Present for All Seasons. Edited by Father Frank . . .

Philadelphia: Henry F. Anners. 1853.

Gift of Love. A Token of Friendship for 1853. Edited by Rufus W. Griswold . . .

New-York: Leavitt & Allen, 27 Dey Street. M.DCCC.LIII.

For comment see note under entry No. 1021.

Gift of Love. A Token of Friendship for 1854. Edited by Rufus W. Griswold . . .

New-York: Leavitt & Allen, 27 Dey Street. M.DCCC.LIV.

For comment see note under entry No. 1021.

Ladies' Gems . . . from the Most Approved Authors.

New-York . . . 1855

For comment see BAL, Vol. 2, p. 399.

The Poets of the Nineteenth Century . . . Edited by . . . Robert Aris Willmott . . .

New York . . . 1858.

For comment see entry No. 1663.

The Poets of the West . . .

London . . . 1859.

For comment see BAL, Vol. 1, p. 101.

The Poets of the West . . .

London . . . New York . . . 1860.

For comment see BAL, Vol. 1, p. 374.

The Book of Rubies . . .

New York . . . 1866.

For comment see entry No. 5522.

The Book of the Sonnet Edited by Leigh Hunt
and S. Adams Lee . . .

Boston . . . 1867

Prepared for the press and partially edited
by George Henry Boker. For comment see
entry No. 1218.

Lyra Sacra Americana: Or, Gems from American Sacred Poetry. Selected . . . by Charles Dexter Cleveland . . .

New York: Charles Scribner and Company.
London: Sampson Low, Son, and Marston.
1868.

The Poets and Poetry of America. By Rufus
Wilmot Griswold . . .

New York . . . 1873.

For comment see in list of John Hay reprints.

. . . Little Classics. Edited by Rossiter Johnson.
Minor Poems . . .

Boston: James R. Osgood and Company. Late
Ticknor & Fields, and Fields, Osgood, & Co.
1875.

At head of title: Fifteenth Volume.

The Floral Kingdom, Its History, Sentiment
and Poetry . . . by Mrs. Cordelia Harris Turner
. . .

Chicago: Moses Warren, 103 State Street. 1877.

West Point Tic Tacs . . .

. . . New York. 1878.

For comment see entry No. 7299.

Poems of Places Edited by Henry W Longfellow
. . . British America . . .

Boston . . . 1879.

For comment see BAL, Vol. 1, p. 249.

Poems of Places Edited by Henry W. Longfellow . . . Middle States.

Boston . . . 1879.

For comment see BAL, Vol. 1, p. 74.

The Cambridge Book of Poetry and Song . . .
by Charlotte Fiske Bates . . .

New York . . . ⟨1882⟩

For comment see entry No. 7887.

Poems of American Patriotism Chosen by J.
Brander Matthews

New-York Charles Scribner's Sons 1882

Listed PW Dec. 2, 1882.

An Old Scrap-Book. With Additions . . .

⟨Cambridge⟩ February 8, 1884.

For comment see entry No. 7763.

The Life and Public Services of Ulysses Simpson
Grant . . . by James Grant Wilson . . . Revised
Edition.

New York: De Witt, Publisher . . . ⟨1885⟩

Deposited Sept. 18, 1885.

September Edited by Oscar Fay Adams . . .

Boston . . . ⟨1886⟩

For comment see entry No. 67.

November Edited by Oscar Fay Adams . . .

Boston . . . ⟨1886⟩

For comment see entry No. 69.

No. 15. Standard Recitations . . . Compiled . . .
by Frances P. Sullivan . . . March, 1887 . . .

. . . N. Y. . . . ⟨1887⟩

For comment see entry No. 5552.

The Lover's Year-Book of Poetry A Collection
of Love Poems for Every Day in the Year ⟨Com-
piled⟩ by Horace Parker Chandler Vol. II.
July to December

Boston Roberts Brothers 1892

Vol. 1, *January to June,* issued under date
1891.

Poets' Dogs . . . by Elizabeth Richardson . . .

. . . New York . . . 1895

For comment see BAL, Vol. 3, p. 288.

Poems of American Patriotism 1776–1898 Selected by R. L. Paget

Boston . . . MDCCCXCVIII

For comment see BAL, Vol. 1, p. 249.

A Book of American Humorous Verse . . .

Chicago . . . 1904

For comment see BAL, Vol. 1, p. 411.

Short Story Classics (American) . . . Edited by William Patten . . .

. . . New York ⟨1905⟩

5 Vols. For comment see entry No. 6378.

The Path on the Rainbow An Anthology of Songs and Chants from the Indians of North America Edited by George W. Cronyn . . .

Boni and Liveright New York 1918

REFERENCES AND ANA

The Thaw-King's Visit to New York

Possibly issued as a separate in 1831. See Barnes, footnote 19, p. 37; and, note 13, p. 333.

The poem has been located as follows: *Quadruple Boston Notion . . . Extra Number . . . July 15, 1841; Poets and Poetry of America,* 1842; collected in *The Echo . . . ,* Philadelphia, 1844.

The Red Spur of Ramapo

USDR Aug. 1841, reported that Hoffman was "busily engaged upon *The Red Spur of Ramapo*" and further reported that it was to be published in September, 1841.

The work remains unpublished. For an account of the destruction of the manuscript see Barnes, Chapter X.

Leisler, or the Man of the People.

According to USDR of Dec. 1843, the above was the title of a lecture given by Hoffman at a meeting of the New-York Historical Society in Feb. 1843. USDR suggests that publication was projected. NYHS reports (letter to BAL, June 3, 1959) that "the manuscript is not in our collection . . . and we never printed it." BAL has found no record of publication but one may not overlook the possibility that the lecture was published as Hoffman's contribution to Jared Sparks's *The Library of American Biography* (see entry No. 8545).

Lays of the Hudson

New York, 1846.

Entry from Johnson. Not found and presumed to be a ghost. Perhaps an erroneous entry for Hoffman's *Love's Calendar, Lays of the Hudson, and Other Poems . . . ,* 1847.

Catechising. A Tract for the People . . . by the Rev'd Chas. Fred'k Hoffman . . .

Philadelphia . . . New York . . . 1858 . . .

Printed paper wrapper. Sometimes erroneously credited to Charles Fenno Hoffman.

. . . A Winter in the West: Letters Descriptive of Chicago and Vicinity in 1833–4. By Charles Fenno Hoffman . . . Reprint, with the Original and New Notes.

Chicago: Fergus Printing Company. 1882.

At head of title: Fergus' Historical Series, No. 20.

Printed paper wrapper. Listed PW June 3, 1882.

Charles Fenno Hoffman by Homer F. Barnes

New York Columbia University Press 1930

On copyright page: *Published March, 1930* Deposited March 15, 1930. Bibliography, pp. 317-333; uncollected poems, pp. 289-316; correspondence, pp. 191-288.

JOSIAH GILBERT HOLLAND

1 8 1 9 – 1 8 8 1

8577. Cut-Flowers: A Collection of Poems. By Mrs. D. Ellen Goodman Shepard. Edited by J. G. Holland.

Springfield: Published by Bessey & Co. M DCCC LIV.

"In Memoriam," p. ⟨4⟩.

"Preface," p. ⟨6⟩.

"Obituary and Introductory," pp. ⟨9⟩-12.

Issued in two formats:

Cloth, gilt: Sides decorated in blind, edges plain.

Cloth, extra gilt: Sides decorated in blind and gold, edges gilded.

AAS copy inscribed by early owner Jan. 1, 1854.

AAS NYPL

8578. HISTORY OF WESTERN MASSACHU-SETTS. THE COUNTIES OF HAMPDEN, HAMPSHIRE, FRANKLIN, AND BERK-SHIRE. EMBRACING AN OUTLINE, OR GENERAL HISTORY, OF THE SECTION, AN ACCOUNT OF ITS SCIENTIFIC AS-PECTS AND LEADING INTERESTS, AND SEPARATE HISTORIES OF ITS ONE HUNDRED TOWNS ...

SPRINGFIELD: PUBLISHED BY SAMUEL BOWLES AND COMPANY. 1855.

2 Vols.

1: ⟨1⟩-520. Folded map inserted as frontispiece. 7⁹⁄₁₆" x 4¾".
2: ⟨1⟩-619, 2 blank leaves.

1: ⟨1⟩-42⁶, 43⁸.
2: ⟨1⟩-52⁶.

BD-like cloth: green; purple-brown. T cloth: black. Yellow end papers. Flyleaves. Also issued in half calf according to NLG June 15, 1855.

Note: Inserted in some copies (of both volumes) is a leaf of advertisements; both salmon and yellow papers noted.

Title deposited Feb. 8, 1855. BPL copy of Vol. 2 received May 14, 1855. Advertised as *now pub-lished and for sale* NLG May 15, 1855; reviewed NLG May 15, 1855. H copy received May 28, 1855. Advertised as in both muslin and in half calf NLG June 15, 1855.

H NYPL

8579. Exercises at the Dedication of the New City Hall, Springfield, Mass., Jan. 1st, 1856. Including the Address by Dr. J. G. Holland ...

Springfield: Samuel Bowles & Company, Printers. 1856.

Printed paper wrapper.

"Dr. Holland's Address," pp. ⟨5⟩-25.

H NYPL

8580. An Address Delivered at West Springfield, August 25, 1856. On Occasion of the One Hundredth Anniversary of the Ordination of the Rev. Joseph Lathrop, D. D. By William B. Sprague ... with an Appendix.

Springfield, Mass: Samuel Bowles & Company, Printers. 1856.

Printed paper wrapper?

Comments, pp. 75-76.

"Song," *Oh brightly hung the bending sky ...* , pp. 99-100.

Note: Not to be confused with the printing of Sprague's "Address" issued with the following imprint: *Albany: Van Benthuysen, Printer, 407 Broadway. 1856.* The Albany publication does not contain the material by Holland.

B

8581. THE BAY-PATH; A TALE OF NEW ENGLAND COLONIAL LIFE ...

NEW YORK: G. P. PUTNAM & CO., 321 BROADWAY. 1857.

⟨i⟩-⟨viii⟩, ⟨7⟩-418, blank leaf. 7¼" full x 4⅞".

⟨-⟩¹, ⟨1⟩-4, ⟨5⟩-⟨7⟩, 8-12, ⟨13⟩-17¹², 18⁶.

T cloth: black; blackish-brown; purple; slate-green. Green-coated end papers; yellow end papers. The flyleaves occur as follows: Flyleaf at front, double flyleaf at back; double flyleaves; single flyleaves. Edges stained red; and, edges plain.

H copy received Nov. 14, 1856. Deposited March 20, 1857. Listed; and, advertised as *now ready* PC April 15, 1857.

BPL H NYPL

8582. TITCOMB'S LETTERS TO YOUNG PEOPLE, SINGLE AND MARRIED. ⟨BY⟩ TIMOTHY TITCOMB, ESQUIRE.

NEW YORK: CHARLES SCRIBNER, NO. 124 GRAND STREET. 1858.

Title-page printed in black and salmon.

⟨i⟩-xii, ⟨13⟩-251. 7⁵⁄₁₆″ x 4⅞″.

⟨1⟩-10¹², 11⁶.

TZ cloth: brown; slate-purple. Yellow end papers. Flyleaves.

Advertised for July 20 in BM July 15, 1858. BA copy received July 29, 1858. Distributed in Great Britain by Low: listed Ath Aug. 28, 1858; PC Sept. 15, 1858. Reissued 1873 in Low's *American Series*. A Ward, Lock & Tyler edition, "rewritten by an English editor," listed Ath July 25, 1874; PC Aug. 1, 1874. Reissued in the *Friendly Counsel Series*; listed Bkr Jan. 1875. For another edition see entry No. 8637.

BPL H

8583. BITTER-SWEET A POEM ...

NEW YORK: CHARLES SCRIBNER, 124 GRAND STREET. MDCCCLIX.

⟨1⟩-220. 7³⁄₁₆″ x 4¾″. Pp. ⟨1-2⟩ excised or pasted under the end paper.

⟨1⟩-9¹², ⟨10⟩². Leaf ⟨1⟩₁ excised or pasted under the end paper.

A-like cloth: brown. TZ cloth: brown; slate. Yellow end papers. Flyleaf at back. Inserted at front is a 4-page catalog printed in red dated *November, 1858*. According to the catalog *Bitter-Sweet* was available with edges plain; and, edges gilded. Noted only with plain edges.

Two states of binding noted; sequence, if any, not determined. The following designations are for identification only:

Binding A

Sides blindstamped with a double-rule border, a leafy spray at each inner corner. Noted in A-like cloth only.

Binding B

Sides blindstamped with a double-rule border enclosing a frame made of small diamond-shaped units; an ornament at each corner of innermost frame. Noted on a copyright deposit copy; also noted on the 5th, 7th, 8th, 10th, 14th printings. Seen only in TZ cloth.

Deposited Nov. 20, 1858. Distributed in London by Low; listed Ath Dec. 4, 1858; advertised as *just received* Ath Dec. 11, 1858; listed PC Dec. 15, 1858; listed Bkr Dec. 1858. A cursory examination indicates that the following American printings are reprints of the first edition: 1863, 1881, 1886, 1892. See entry Nos. 8590, 8635.

H LC NYPL

8584. Celebration of the Two Hundredth Anniversary of the Settlement of Hadley, Massachusetts, at Hadley, June 8, 1859 ...

Northampton: Published by Bridgman & Childs. 1859.

Printed paper wrapper. Erratum slip inserted.

Letter, embodying a poem, pp. 73-74. The poem collected in *Marble Prophecy*, 1872, under the title "Verses Read at the Hadley Centennial."

H NYPL

8585. GOLD-FOIL, HAMMERED FROM POPULAR PROVERBS. BY TIMOTHY TITCOMB ...

NEW YORK: CHARLES SCRIBNER, 124 GRAND STREET. 1859.

⟨1⟩-358; 2 pp. advertisements. 7¼″ x 4¹⁵⁄₁₆″ (edges plain). 7³⁄₁₆″ x 4⅞″ (edges gilded).

⟨1⟩-15¹².

Cloth, Gilt

A cloth: slate-purple. BD cloth: blue; purple. Yellow end papers. Flyleaves. Sides stamped in blind. Edges plain.

Cloth, Gilt Extra

BD cloth: purple. Cream-coated end papers. Flyleaves. Sides stamped in blind and gold. Edges gilt.

Advertised for Oct. 10, 1859, BM Sept. 15, 1859; for Oct. 29, BM Oct. 15, 1859. Published during the period Oct. 15–Nov. 1, according to BM Nov. 1, 1859. A copy of the *Seventh Edition* deposited for copyright Nov. 26, 1859. Listed PC Dec. 1, 1859. Nimmo (London & Edinburgh) edition listed Ath Dec. 22, 1877; PC Dec. 31, 1877. See entry No. 8636.

BA H MHS Y

8586. MISS GILBERT'S CAREER: AN AMER-
ICAN STORY . . .

NEW YORK: CHARLES SCRIBNER, 124 GRAND
STREET. LONDON: SAMPSON LOW, SON & CO. 1860.

⟨i-ii⟩, ⟨i⟩-⟨vi⟩, ⟨i⟩-iv, ⟨1⟩-476; plus: advertisements (in some copies) paged: ⟨i⟩-iv, ⟨3⟩-14,
16-23. 7¾₆″ x 5″. See below for comment on first
leaf.

⟨a⟩⁴, ⟨b⟩², 1-19¹², 20¹⁰; plus (in some copies)
⟨21⟩¹². Leaf ⟨a⟩₁ excised or pasted under the
end paper.

BD cloth: brown. Yellow end papers. Flyleaf
at back.

Deposited Oct. 6, 1860. AAS copy inscribed by
early owner Oct. 12, 1860. Advertised for Oct.
15, 1860, BM Oct. 15, 1860. Issued during the
period Oct. 15–Nov. 1, 1860 according to BM
Nov. 1, 1860. The "eleventh thousand" advertised as *ready* BM Nov. 15, 1860. Listed PC Dec.
15, 1860. Reviewed Ath Feb. 2, 1861. A Ward,
Lock & Tyler edition, London, listed PC Sept.
16, 1876; Bkr Oct. 1876. A Goubaud & Son edition, London, listed PC Jan. 18, 1877. See *Heroes
of Crampton*, 1867.

AAS   NYPL

8587. Account of the Golden Wedding of James
and Mary Brewster, September 18, 1860 . . .

New Haven: Thomas J. Stafford, Printer.
1860.

" 'Golden Wedding' of James Brewster and
Mary Brewster, September 18, 1860," pp. ⟨27⟩-
28. Collected in *The Marble Prophecy*, 1872,
as "A Golden Wedding-Song."

B   H   Y

8588. Address at the Dedication of a Monument to Rev. W. B. O. Peabody, D. D. Delivered at Springfield, September 29, 1861,
by George Walker, Together with a Hymn
for the Occasion by J. G. Holland.

Springfield: Samuel Bowles & Company,
Printers. 1861.

Printed paper wrapper; also, printed paper
boards.

"Hymn . . . ," p. 22.

BPL   LC   NYPL

8589. LESSONS IN LIFE. A SERIES OF FA-
MILIAR ESSAYS. BY TIMOTHY TIT-
COMB . . .

NEW YORK: CHARLES SCRIBNER, 124 GRAND
STREET. 1861.

⟨1⟩-344. 7¼″ x 5″.

⟨1⟩-14¹², 15⁴.

BD cloth: purple-brown. White paper end papers; pale peach paper end papers. Flyleaves.
Note: According to a prepublication advertisement in APC Nov. 15, 1861, the book was to
be issued in cloth, gilt edges; half calf; turkey
morocco. Noted only in cloth, edges plain.

Advertised in APC Nov. 15, 1861, for *about the
20th November*. Deposited Nov. 19, 1861. *Fifth
Edition* listed APC Dec. 5, 1861. Listed PC Feb.
1, 1862. See under 1881 for revised edition.

BPL   NYPL

8590. Bitter-Sweet. A Poem . . . with Illustrations by E. J. Whitney.

New York: Charles Scribner, 124 Grand Street.
MDCCCLXII.

Reprint. First illustrated edition. For first edition see entry No. 8583; also see entry No.
8635.

According to an advertisement in *Boston Daily
Evening Transcript,* Dec. 3, 1862, the book was
available in "extra illuminated covers, full gilt
($4) ; Turkey morocco, extra, and antique ($6)."
Listed PC Jan. 17, 1863.

NYPL

8591. The Chapin Gathering. Proceedings at
the Meeting of the Chapin Family, in Springfield, Mass., September 17, 1862.

Springfield: Printed by Samuel Bowles and
Company. 1862.

Printed paper wrapper.

"Dr. Holland's Poem," pp. ⟨59⟩-64; "written
for the occasion."

B

8592. LETTERS TO THE JONESES. BY TIM-
OTHY TITCOMB . . .

NEW YORK: CHARLES SCRIBNER, 124 GRAND
STREET. 1863.

⟨1⟩-347. 7⁵₆″ x 4⅞″. Pp. ⟨1-2⟩ excised or pasted
under the end paper.

⟨1⟩-14¹², 15⁶. Leaf ⟨1⟩₁ excised or pasted under the end paper.

BD cloth: brownish-purple. HC cloth: slate. TR
cloth: black; purple. Yellow end papers. Flyleaves. *Note:* According to a prepublication advertisement in APC Oct. 1, 1863, the book was
to be available in cloth; cloth, full gilt; half
calf; Turkey extra. Noted only in cloth, edges
plain.

Advertised APC Oct. 1, 1863, as *ready about the 1st of November*. Advertised ALG Nov. 2, 1863, as *ready early in November*. Listed ALG Nov. 16, 1863. Deposited Nov. 19, 1863. BA copy received Nov. 24, 1863. The *Tenth Edition* advertised ALG Dec. 1, 1863. Listed PC Dec. 8, 1863. For revised edition see *Concerning the Jones Family*, 1881.

BA H

8593. The Laboring Man's Sabbath. To Benjamin Franklin Jones, Mechanic, Concerning His Habit of Staying away from Church. From "Letters to the Joneses." By Timothy Titcomb . . .

Springfield, Mass.: Published by G. & C. Merriam. (Price $1.50 per Hundred.) 1863.

⟨1⟩-12. 7½″ x 4⅝″. Printed paper wrapper, both blue and brown noted.

Also in (reprinted from?) *Letters to the Joneses*, 1863, above.

AAS H

8594. Household Friends for Every Season . . .

Boston   Ticknor and Fields   1864

"Daniel Gray," pp. ⟨295⟩-297. Collected in *The Marble Prophecy*, 1872.

For comment see entry No. 3773.

8595. Thoughts for the Christian Life. By Rev. James Drummond. With an Introduction by J. G. Holland.

New York: Charles Scribner, 124 Grand Street. 1864.

"Introduction," pp. ⟨vii⟩-xvi.

Listed ALG May 2, 1864. Deposited July 29, 1864. Distributed in England by Trübner: Advertised Bkr as *new* Oct. 31, 1864; listed Bkr Oct. 31, 1864; listed PC Dec. 8, 1864.

AAS

8596. The Boatswain's Whistle. Published at the National Sailors' Fair . . .

Boston, November 9-19, 1864.

"Salt and Fresh," No. 1, p. 3.

"Into Phillips," No. 1, p. 6.

For comment see entry No. 1416.

8597. Prospectus. It is proposed to establish on Mount Holyoke, near Mr. French's hotel at the summit, a suitable residence for invalids, devoted to their medical care . . .

Northampton ⟨Mass.⟩, August, 1865.

Single sheet of laid paper folded to make four pages. P. ⟨1⟩ as above. Leaf: 10″ x 8″.

Issued as a prospectus by one Dr. A. W. Thompson, of Northampton, Mass. On pp. ⟨2-3⟩ is a selection of "Opinions," the first being by Holland, dated Aug. 8, 1865.

H

8598. The Nation Weeping for Its Dead. Observances at Springfield, Massachusetts, on President Lincoln's Funeral Day, Wednesday, April 19, 1865, Including Dr. Holland's Eulogy . . .

Springfield, Mass.: Samuel Bowles & Co.: L. J. Powers. 1865.

Printed paper wrapper.

"Dr. Holland's Eulogy," pp. ⟨15⟩-30.

See next entry.

H NYPL

8599. EULOGY ON ABRAHAM LINCOLN

Two separate printings noted. The sequence has not been established and the designations are for identification only. Printed, with some rearrangement of the types, from the preceding entry.

Printing A

EULOGY ON ABRAHAM LINCOLN, LATE PRESIDENT OF THE UNITED STATES, PRONOUNCED AT THE CITY HALL, SPRINGFIELD, MASS., APRIL 19, 1865 . . .

SPRINGFIELD: PUBLISHED BY L. J. POWERS. 1865.

⟨1⟩-18, blank leaf. 9⅛″ x 5¾″.

⟨1⟩-2⁴, 3².

Printing B

EULOGY ON ABRAHAM LINCOLN, LATE PRESIDENT OF THE UNITED STATES, PRONOUNCED AT THE CITY HALL, SPRINGFIELD, MASS., APRIL 19, 1865 . . .

SPRINGFIELD: SAMUEL BOWLES & CO.: L. J. POWERS. 1865.

⟨1⟩-18, blank leaf. 9⅛″ scant x 5¾″ scant.

⟨1⟩², 2-3⁴.

Some significance may attach to the fact that the *Third Edition* (so marked) has the imprint as in *Printing B*.

Both printings issued in printed brown paper wrapper.

BA (B)   BPL (B)   H (A)   MHS (A)   Y (A, B)

8600. THE LIFE OF ABRAHAM LINCOLN
. . .

SPRINGFIELD, MASS.: PUBLISHED BY GURDON BILL.
1866.

⟨1⟩-544; plus, in some copies, 2 pp. advertisements. Frontispiece and 3 plates inserted. 8⅝6″ x
5½″.

⟨1⟩-348; plus, in some copies, ⟨35⟩1.

C cloth: brown. Brown-coated on white end
papers. Flyleaves. *Note:* This book was sold by
subscription, hence it was probably offered in a
variety of bindings.

Note: All examined copies have *conntry* for
country, p. 447, last line.

Title-page deposited Oct. 10, 1865. BA copy
received Jan. 17, 1866.

H   LC

8601. PLAIN TALKS ON FAMILIAR SUB-
JECTS. A SERIES OF POPULAR LEC-
TURES . . .

NEW YORK: CHARLES SCRIBNER & CO., 124 GRAND
STREET. 1866.

⟨1⟩-335; blank, p. ⟨336⟩; plus: 12 pp. advertisements. 7⅜6″ x 4¾″.

⟨1⟩-1412; plus: ⟨15⟩6. *Note:* In some copies
signature mark 13* is present on p. 335; sequence not determined.

Cloth, Gilt

C cloth: deep purple-brown. Sides blindstamped. Buff end papers. Flyleaves. Edges
plain.

Cloth, Gilt Extra

P cloth: blue. Sides goldstamped. Buff end papers. Flyleaves. Edges gilt.

Note: An advertisement in ALG Oct. 2, 1865,
offered the book in cloth; cloth, gilt; half calf;
morocco.

Advertised for *early in October* ALG Oct. 2, 1865.
Deposited Nov. 6, 1865. Listed ALG Nov. 15,
1865. BA copy received Nov. 15, 1865. Listed PC
Dec. 30, 1865. Reissued not before 1879 with
the imprint: *New York Charles Scribner's Sons
743 and 745 Broadway ⟨1865⟩.* See entry No.
8640.

Y

8602. The Flower of Liberty. Edited and Illustrated by Julia A. M. Furbish.

Boston: Ticknor and Fields. 1866.

"The Heart of the War," pp. 36-40. Collected
in *The Marble Prophecy,* 1872.

For comment see entry No. 1424.

8603. The Heroes of Crampton: A Novel . . .

London: Charles W. Wood, 13 Tavistock
Street, Strand. 1867.

An unauthorized version of *Miss Gilbert's Career,* 1860. *Not seen.*

"In altering the text and adapting the 18th
Edition of Mr. J. G. Holland's story to English
Readers, it is hoped that none of the intrinsic
merit of the work is lost . . ."—Preliminary
note, signed at end: *A.R. London, May 1867.*

"In 1867 C. W. Wood without authority published *Miss Gilbert's Career* under the name of
Heroes of Crampton, omitting the first chapter and substituting English for American names
throughout."—Letter, J. G. Holland, dated
March 18, 1874, in Ath April 4, 1874. Wood's
reply appeared in Ath April 18, 1874: "During
the short time I was . . . a publisher, a gentleman with whom I was acquainted came to me
. . . said he had printed the book *Heroes of
Crampton* on his own responsibility, and asked
if I would publish it for him. I consented . . .
The whole affair was his; the subsequent profit
or loss . . . was to be his; the alterations, if any,
were his, not mine. All I did was to issue the
book for him to the public. It turned out a failure."

Listed Ath May 4, 1867; PC June 1, 1867.

8604. Christ and the Twelve; or Scenes and
Events in the Life of Our Saviour and His
Apostles, As Painted by the Poets. Edited by
J. G. Holland . . .

Springfield, Mass.: Published by Gurdon Bill
& Company. 1867.

As a subscription book issued in a variety of
bindings and with varying imprints. The following variant imprint has been noted: *Published by Gurdon Bill & Company, Springfield,
Mass. Charles Bill, Chicago, Ill. H. C. Johnson,
Cincinnati, O. 1867.*

"Introduction," pp. ⟨iii⟩-vi.

Two states (printings?) noted. The order is presumed correct:

A

Last entry, p. xi: *The Mission of the Word* . . .

B

Last entry, p. xi: *The Better Land* . . .

Two bindings noted; the sequence has not been
determined:

Binding A

At each inner corner of the blindstamped frame on the sides is a filigree ornament measuring about 1¼″ high.

Binding B

At each inner corner of the blindstamped frame on the sides is a filigree ornament measuring about 2¼″ high.

Title-page deposited Jan. 10, 1867. No record of deposit of book found. A copy of State B (rebound) in BPL received June 26, 1867.

H (long imprint; B sheets; B binding) LC (not a deposit copy; long imprint; B sheets; A binding) Y (short imprint; A sheets; A binding. Also in Y: long imprint; B sheets; B binding)

8605. KATHRINA: HER LIFE AND MINE, IN A POEM . . .

> NEW YORK: PUBLISHED BY CHARLES SCRIBNER & CO. 1867.

⟨i-ii⟩, ⟨1⟩-287. 7⅜″ full x 5″.

⟨-⟩¹, ⟨1⟩-12¹².

C cloth: purple. Brown-coated on white end papers. Flyleaves. Inserted at back is a four-page catalog dated *Autumn of 1867*. According to an advertisement in ALG Sept. 2, 1867, the book was issued with edges plain; and, edges gilt. Noted only with plain edges.

Advertised for Sept. 21, 1867, ALG Sept. 2, 1867. Deposited Sept. 20, 1867. Published Sept. 21, 1867 (publisher's records). BA copy received Sept. 24, 1867. Listed ALG Oct. 1, 1867. ALG Oct. 15, 1867, noted that "the fourteenth thousand is already in press." Listed PC Nov. 1, 1867. See entries 8608, 8638.

BPL   H   LC   NYPL   Y (lacking ⟨-⟩)

8606. . . . TIMOTHY TITCOMB'S TESTIMONY AGAINST WINE . . .

> ⟨n.p., New York: National Temperance Society and Publication House, 172 William Street, n.d., 1867–1871⟩

Caption-title. The above at head of p. ⟨1⟩. At head of title: No. 54. Imprint at foot of p. 4.

Single leaf folded to make four pages.

⟨1⟩-4. 7″ x 4¾″.

Reissued *ca.* 1874 by the National Temperance Society and Publication House, 58 Reade Street, New York.

"Dr. Holland, who has recently visited Switzerland and other wine-producing countries, gives the results of his experience in the *Springfield*

Republican . . . There is no question that the people would be better, healthier, happier, and much more prosperous, if there were not a vineyard in the canton . . . there never was a greater mistake than the supposition that alcohol in any form is necessary as a daily beverage for any man or woman."

Gd (2nd)   SG (1st)

8607. International Copyright. Meeting . . . April 9, 1868 . . .

> New York: International Copyright Association. 661 Broadway. 1868.

Printed paper wrapper.

Two-paragraph statement, p. 10.

For fuller entry see No. 1703.

8608. Kathrina: Her Life and Mine, in a Poem . . . (Low's Copyright Cheap Editions of American Books.)

> London: Sampson Low, Son, & Marston, Crown Buildings, 188 Fleet Street. 1869.

Printed paper boards. See entries 8605, 8638.

"A Letter from the Author to the Publishers," pp. ⟨v⟩-vi, dated at end *Rome, February 1869*.

Advertised as *just ready* Ath May 22, 1869.

B

8609. The Sunday-School Speaker . . . Collected and Arranged by O. Augusta Cheney.

> Loring, Publisher, Corner Bromfield and Washington Streets, Boston. ⟨1869⟩

"Gradatim," pp. 76-77. Collected in *The Marble Prophecy*, 1872.

For comment see entry No. 1433A.

8610. . . . Where Shall the Baby's Dimple Be? Words by Dr. J. G. Holland Music by Albert W. Berg.

> New York. Published by Wm. A. Pond & Co. 547 Broadway . . . 1870 . . .

Sheet music. Cover-title. At head of title: **To Lilly.** Plate number 7788.

Deposited July 20, 1870. Collected in *The Marble Prophecy*, 1872.

The J.F.O. Smith setting, published by S. Brainard & Sons, Cleveland, Ohio, was deposited Sept. 12, 1870.

EM

8611. THE MARBLE PROPHECY, AND OTHER POEMS . . .

NEW YORK: SCRIBNER, ARMSTRONG & CO. 1872.

⟨i-viii⟩, ⟨i⟩-iv, ⟨1⟩-112; plus: 4 pp. advertisements. Frontispiece inserted. 7⁵⁄₁₆″ x 4¾″. The first leaf excised or pasted under the end paper.

Two printings noted. The sequence has not been established and the designations are for identification only.

Printing A

⟨1⁴, 2-3⁶, 4¹², 5-8⁶, 9¹⁰; plus: 10²⟩. Leaf ⟨1⟩1 excised or pasted under the end paper. *Signed:* ⟨-⟩⁵, 1-7⁸; plus: ⟨8⟩². Signature mark 6 absent in some copies.

Printing B

⟨1⁴, 2-9⁶, 10¹⁰; plus: 11²⟩. Leaf ⟨1⟩1 excised or pasted under the end paper. *Signed:* ⟨-⟩⁵, 1-7⁸; plus: ⟨8⟩². Signature mark 6 absent in some copies.

Note: The presence, or absence, of signature mark 6 in both printings was almost certainly caused by the use of mixed sheets. Printed from "duplicate" plates?

C cloth: green; purple; terra-cotta. FL cloth: blue; green; purple; terra-cotta. P cloth: blue; green. Covers bevelled. Brown-coated on white end papers. Flyleaf at back. According to the publisher's records issued with edges plain; and, edges gilt. Noted only with plain edges.

Listed PW Sept. 26, 1872. PW Sept. 26, 1872, reported that publication had been postponed until Oct. 2, 1872. Deposited Oct. 3, 1872. BPL copy received Oct. 8, 1872; BA copy received Oct. 10, 1872. Reviewed by Ath Feb. 15, 1873.

BA (A, received Oct. 10, 1872) BPL (A, received Oct. 8, 1872) H (A, B) LC (A, a copyright deposit copy) NYPL (A, B)

8612. Garnered Sheaves: The Complete Poetical Works of J. G. Holland.

New York: Scribner, Armstrong & Co. 1873.

An omnibus reprint of *Bitter-Sweet,* 1859; *Kathrina,* 1867; *The Marble Prophecy,* 1872.

Advertised as *ready this week* WTC Dec. 12, 1872. Listed WTC Dec. 12, 1872. Advertised in PC May 1, 1874, by Low, as an American book.

H NYPL

8613. THE REMARKS OF J. G. HOLLAND ON ASSUMING THE PRESIDENCY OF THE BOARD OF PUBLIC INSTRUCTION, JANUARY 15, 1873.

NEW YORK: N. Y. SCHOOL JOURNAL PRINT, 119 & 121 NASSAU STREET 1873.

⟨1⟩-10, blank leaf. 8¹³⁄₁₆″ x 5¾″ full.

⟨-⟩⁶.

Printed paper wrapper.

AAS NYPL Y

8614. ARTHUR BONNICASTLE, AN AMERICAN NOVEL . . .

LONDON: GEORGE ROUTLEDGE AND SONS, THE BROADWAY, LUDGATE. ⟨n.d., 1873⟩

Not seen. This London printing, *cloth-bound,* appears to have been published prior to the New York edition; see next entry.

⟨3⟩-401. Frontispiece and 11 plates inserted. 7⅛″ x 4¼″.

⟨B⟩-I, K-U, X-Z, AA-CC⁸.

C cloth: blue; brown. Yellow-coated end papers.

Advertised without comment Ath Aug. 16, 1873. Noted as "about to publish" Ath Aug. 23, 1873. Listed Ath Aug. 23, 1873. Noted as "about to publish" PC Sept. 1, 1873. Reviewed by Ath Sept. 6, 1873. Listed PC Sept. 16, 1873. Deposited BMU Sept. 17, 1873. Advertised as *new* Ath Sept. 30, 1873; PC Oct. 1, 1873; Bkr Oct. 2, 1873. Listed Bkr Oct. 2, 1873. A "new edition" *in printed paper boards* listed PC and Bkr April 1, 1874. Reissued in *Excelsior Series;* listed PC Dec. 15, 1884. A Ward, Lock & Tyler edition listed Ath March 7, 1874; PC March 16, 1874.

Extract from a letter, March 18, 1874, from Holland, in Ath April 4, 1874; "The novel was originally published in *Scribner's Monthly,* and I made, during its passage, an arrangement with Routledge to publish it. The closing chapters . . . were published in England first, and on these Routledge holds the copyright."

In a discussion of literary piracy (so-called) PC April 1, 1874, commented as follows: "Here is a case in point. Messrs. Ward & Lock have republished a Novel by Dr. J. G. Holland—*Arthur Bonnicastle*—but distinctly to avoid trenching on literary property, the concluding chapter is by another hand, and the story is so far spoilt. Mr. S. O. Beeton, in a preface since issued as a pamphlet, tells the public why this is done. The conclusion, 'an insignificant fragment' of the entire book, appeared in an edition published by Messrs. Routledge a day or two before the issue of the September number of *Scribner's Monthly,* wherein it was issued in America, and is thus looked upon, says Mr. Beeton, as carrying copyright . . ."

Copies of the Routledge printing, collated above, are in BMU and in Bodleian.

8615. ARTHUR BONNICASTLE, AN AMER-
ICAN NOVEL . . .

NEW YORK: SCRIBNER, ARMSTRONG & CO. 1873.

See preceding entry.

⟨1⟩-401; blank, p. ⟨402⟩; 6 pp. advertisements.
Frontispiece and 11 plates inserted. 7½″ x 5″.

⟨1⟩-15, ⟨16-17⟩¹². *Note:* Signature marks 4 (p.
73); and, 14 (p. 313) are present in the copies
first printed. In all examined copies, including
a reprint dated 1877, superfluous signature
mark 4 is present, p. ⟨77⟩.

Two states (printings?) noted. The following
feature is sufficient for identification:

1: P. ⟨2⟩: Eleven titles listed, the first being
Bitter-Sweet.

2: P. ⟨2⟩: Twelve titles listed, the first being
Arthur Bonnicastle.

C cloth: orange. FL cloth: green; purple; red;
terra-cotta. Yellow end papers. Flyleaves.

Title-page deposited July 23, 1873. Advertised
PW Aug. 30, 1873, for Sept. 6, 1873, "in ad-
vance of . . . completion in" *Scribner's Monthly
Magazine.*

Deposited Sept. 3, 1873. Listed PW Sept. 6, 1873.
Published Sept. 11, 1873 (publisher's records).

LC (1st, being a deposit copy)   NYPL (1st, 2nd)

8616. Illustrated Library of Favorite Song . . .
Edited by J. G. Holland . . . Sold Only by
Subscription.

New York: Scribner, Armstrong, and Company. Chicago: Hadley Brothers & Kane.
⟨1873⟩

Reprint save for Holland's "Introduction," pp.
⟨7⟩-10.

For comment see entry No. 2853.

8617. THE MISTRESS OF THE MANSE . . .

LONDON: SAMPSON LOW, MARSTON, LOW, &
SEARLE, CROWN BUILDINGS, 188 FLEET STREET.
1874.

Not seen. For first American edition see next entry; also see entries 8625, 8642, 8644.

⟨i-iv⟩, ⟨1⟩-188. 6⅛″ x 4⅛″ (cloth). 6¼″ x 4⅜″
(boards).

⟨-⟩², A-I, K-L⁸, M⁶.

S cloth: blue; green. Publisher's catalog, 48 pp.,
dated Oct. 1873, inserted at back. Also: Pictorial
paper boards.

Deposited (cloth) BMU Oct. 1, 1874. Advertised
as *now ready* in PC Oct. 2, 1874, and in Bkr

Oct. 5, 1874; described as No. 7 in the *Rose
Library* series, priced at 1/- (*i.e.*, boards); the
advertisement also states that the book "will
also be published . . . ⟨in⟩ cloth . . ." at either
2/6 or 3/6. The *Rose Library* binding is described as "enamelled" paper boards. Listed
(cloth) Ath Oct. 10, 1874. Advertised as in
boards and in cloth Ath Oct. 24, 1874; PC Nov.
2, 1874. Deposited (boards) BMU Nov. 3, 1874.
Listed at 2/6 (*i.e.*, cloth) Bkr Nov. 6, 1874.
Listed at 1/- (*i.e.*, boards) PC Nov. 16, 1874.

Copies in BMU and Bodleian.

8618. THE MISTRESS OF THE MANSE . . .

NEW YORK   SCRIBNER, ARMSTRONG & CO   1874

See preceding entry. Also see entries 8625, 8642,
8644.

⟨1⟩-245; blank, p. ⟨246⟩; 6 pp. advertisements.
7½″ x 4⅞″.

⟨1-4⟩, 5-10¹², 11⁶.

Two states (probably printings) noted:

1

P. ⟨249⟩: *An Important Historical Series.
Epochs of History . . . The Following Volumes
Are Now Ready . . . ⟨3 titles⟩*

2

P. ⟨249⟩: *Epochs of History . . . ⟨14 titles, the
first three described as (Now ready.)⟩*

C cloth: green; terra-cotta. S cloth: green; terra-
cotta. Yellow end papers. Flyleaves. *Note:* According to an advertisement in PW Oct. 17, 1874,
the book was issued with edges plain; and, edges
gilt. Noted only with plain edges.

Two states of binding noted. The following
order is presumed correct:

A: Spine imprint: SCRIBNER / ARMSTRONG & CO.

B: Spine imprint: SCRIBNER, / ARMSTRONG & C⁰

Advertised for Oct. 1, 1874, in PW Sept. 26,
1874. Deposited Oct. 10, 1874. Published Oct.
15, 1874 (publisher's records). BPL copy (1st) received Oct. 16, 1874. BA copy (1st) received Oct.
17, 1874. Listed PW Oct. 17, 1874. Advertised in
PW Oct. 17, 1874: *12,000 copies ordered in advance of publication.* Listed PC Nov. 1, 1874.

AAS (2d)   BA (1st)   BPL (1st)   H (1st)   LC (1st,
being a deposit copy)   NYPL (1st, 2d)   Y (2d)

8619. Report of the Proceedings of the Society
of the Army of the James, at the Third Triennial Reunion Held in New York City,
October 21st, 1874 . . .

New York: G. W. Carleton & Co., Publishers.
London: S. Low, Son & Co. MDCCCLXXIV.

Printed paper wrapper. Inserted is a slip dated Dec. 31, 1874, regarding payment for the publication.

"A Poem," (*Who, in this fair metropolis*), pp. 41-44. Letter, Oct. 14, 1874, p. 58.

AAS NYPL

8620. SEVENOAKS A STORY OF TO-DAY . . .

NEW YORK SCRIBNER, ARMSTRONG & CO. 1875.

⟨i-ii⟩, ⟨i⟩-⟨x⟩, 1-441; blank, p. ⟨442⟩; 2 pp. advertisements. Frontispiece and 11 plates inserted. 7⁵⁄₁₆″ x 4¾″.

⟨-⟩⁶, ⟨1⟩-3, ⟨4⟩-18¹², 19⁶.

FL cloth: green; purple; terra-cotta. Yellow end papers. Flyleaves.

Advertised for Oct. 15 PW Oct. 2, 1875. Published Oct. 16, 1875 (publisher's records). Listed PW Oct. 16, 1875. BA copy received Oct. 18, 1875. Listed PC Nov. 2, 1875. See entry No. 8632.

H NYPL

8621. . . . Rockaby, Lullaby. (Cradle Song.) . . . Music by James L. Gilbert . . .

New York . . . T. B. Harms & Co., 819 Broadway . . . 1875 . . .

Sheet music. Cover-title. At head of title: To Miss L. Florence Holmes.

Note: Entry on the basis of the Harms printing which is assuredly a reprint. In all likelihood the first printing was issued by Louis P. Goullaud, 1875. Harms was established in 1881.

Also in (reprinted from?) *The Mistress of the Manse*, 1874.

AAS

8622. Little Graves. Choice Selections of Poetry and Prose. With an Introduction by J. G. Holland . . .

New York: Nelson & Phillips. Cincinnati: Hitchcock & Walden. 1876.

Prefatory note by Holland, p. ⟨1⟩.

Listed PW Jan. 15, 1876.

AAS B

8623. EVERY-DAY TOPICS A BOOK OF BRIEFS . . .

NEW YORK SCRIBNER, ARMSTRONG AND COMPANY 1876.

⟨i-ii⟩, ⟨i⟩-⟨x⟩, ⟨1⟩-391; blank, p. ⟨392⟩; 4 pp. advertisements. 7¼″ x 4¹³⁄₁₆″.

⟨1⁶, 2-16¹², 17⁶⟩. *Signed:* ⟨-⟩⁶, ⟨1⟩-⟨7⟩, 8-16, ⟨17⟩-⟨21⟩, 22-24⁸, ⟨25⟩⁶.

S cloth: green; terra-cotta. Yellow end papers. Flyleaves.

Advertised for Sept. 14, 1876, PW Sept. 2, 1876. Listed PW Sept. 16, 1876. BPL copy received Sept. 18, 1876. See entry No. 8645.

AAS BPL Y

8624. NICHOLAS MINTURN. A STUDY IN A STORY . . .

NEW YORK: SCRIBNER, ARMSTRONG & CO. 1877 . . .

⟨i-iv⟩, ⟨i⟩-⟨viii⟩, ⟨13⟩-418; 2 pp. advertisements. Frontispiece and 10 plates inserted. 7¼″ x 4⅞″.

⟨1⟩-17¹², 18⁶.

Two states (probably printings) noted:

1: On the page preceding the frontispiece is a list of 15 titles, the first being *Everyday* ⟨sic⟩ *Topics.*

2: On the page preceding the frontispiece is a list of 18 titles, the first being *Nicholas Minturn.*

S cloth: green; terra-cotta. Yellow end papers. Flyleaves.

Advertised in PW Sept. 8, 1877, for Sept. 13, 1877 publication, in "an edition of about 15,000" copies. BPL copy (1st) received Sept. 14, 1877. Listed PW Sept. 15, 1877. The London edition (apparently a Low import) announced PC Oct. 2, 1877. Reviewed Ath Dec. 1, 1877.

AAS (1st, 2d) NYPL (2d)

8625. The Mistress of the Manse . . . Illustrations Drawn by Mary A. Hallock, Thomas Moran, Alfred Fredericks, Edwin A. Abbey and Helena DeKay.

New York Scribner, Armstrong & Company 1877

Pp. 251. A somewhat revised edition. For first edition see entry No. 8617; also see entry Nos. 8618, 8642, 8644.

LC

8626. Dick's Recitations and Readings No. 8 . . . Edited by Wm. B. Dick . . .

New York: Dick & Fitzgerald, Publishers, No. 18 Ann Street. ⟨1878⟩

Cloth; and, printed paper wrapper.

"The Palmer's Vision," pp. 102-104. Collected in *Complete Poetical Writings,* 1879.

Deposited Dec. 7, 1878.

LC

8627. . . . Bees in the Clover . . . ⟨Music by E.G.B. Holder⟩

New-York: Frederick Blume, 861 Broadway . . . 1878 . . .

Sheet music. Cover-title. At head of title: Respectfully Inscribed to Miss Clara Louise Kellogg.

Text reprinted from *The Mistress of the Manse,* 1874. For an earlier musical setting see *Rockaby, Lullaby,* 1875, above.

AAS

8628. The Complete Poetical Writings of J G Holland . . .

New York Charles Scribner's Sons 1879

Reprint with the exception of the following poems:

"Jacob Hurd's Child," "Selim and Nourmahal," "To Whittier on His 70th Birthday," "A Glimpse of Youth," "Old and Blind," "Her Argument," "A Legend of Leap Year," "False and True," "The Puritan's Guest." And, "The Palmer's Vision," which had prior book publication in *Dick's Recitations . . . No. 8 . . .* ⟨1878⟩, above.

Advertised for Nov. 13, 1879, in PW Nov. 8, 1879; offered in cloth; half calf; morocco. BA copy received Nov. 20, 1879. Listed PW Nov. 29, 1879.

AAS

8629. Forty-Sixth Annual Convention, Psi Upsilon. Public Exercises, Music Hall, New Haven, Wednesday, May 7th, 1879.

⟨n.p.⟩ Printed for the Fraternity. 1879.

Printed paper wrapper?

"The Learned Professions," pp. 23-33.

C Y

8630. The Knapsack A Daily Journal of the Seventh Regiment New Armory Fair . . .

New York . . . November 17, 1879 . . . ⟨to⟩ . . . December 6, 1879

An occasional newspaper. Complete in 18 numbers. No. 16 erroneously numbered 15.

"My Military Experience," No. 11, Nov. 28, 1879, p. ⟨1⟩.

H

8631. The Atlantic Monthly Supplement. The Holmes Breakfast . . .

⟨n.p., n.d., Boston, February, 1880⟩

Self-wrapper. Caption-title.

Letter, Nov. 20 ⟨1879⟩, p. 23.

H NYPL

8632. Paul Benedict; or, Written in Light . . .

London: Frederick Warne and Co., Bedford Street, Strand . . . ⟨n.d., 1880⟩

Reprint. Not seen. Printed boards. In *Warne's Companion Library* series.

"Notice. This work was originally published ⟨in New York⟩ under the title of *Sevenoaks;* but having been considered as referring to the town of Sevenoaks, in Kent, but to which it has no reference, it has been thought advisable to change the same."—Publisher's prefatory note. See entry No. 8620.

Listed PC April 1, 1880.

8633. The Art Autograph . . . ⟨May, 1880⟩

. . . The Art Interchange, 140 Nassau Street, New York . . . Copyright: 1880; by Wm. Whitlock.

Note, p. ⟨6⟩.

For comment see BAL, Vol. 3, p. 157.

NYPL

8634. The Poets' Tributes to Garfield The Collection of Poems Written for the Boston Daily Globe, and Many Selections . . . ⟨First Edition⟩

Cambridge, Mass. Published by Moses King Harvard Square 1881

Pp. ⟨1⟩-80. A second edition, pp. ⟨1⟩-168, was issued not before Jan. 16, 1882.

Printed paper wrapper; cloth; leather.

"The Dead President," pp. 52-53.

Deposited Oct. 5, 1881. H copy received Oct. 7, 1881. Listed PW Oct. 15, 1881.

H LC

8635. Bitter-Sweet . . .

New York Charles Scribner's Sons 743 and 745 Broadway 1881

"With the author's revision."—PW Nov. 5, 1881. BAL has been unable to discover any revisions. For first edition see under 1859.

Advertised PW Nov. 5, 1881, as published Nov. 1, 1881. Deposited Nov. 8, 1881. Listed PW Nov. 12, 1881.

H LC

8636. Gold-Foil Hammered from Popular Proverbs by Timothy Titcomb . . .

New York Charles Scribner's Sons 743 and 745 Broadway 1881

"Preface to the Revised Edition," pp. ⟨vii⟩-viii.

For first edition see entry No. 8585.

Advertised PW Nov. 5, 1881, as published Nov. 1, 1881. Deposited Nov. 8, 1881. Listed PW Nov. 12, 1881.

BA LC

8637. Titcomb's Letters to Young People Single and Married by Timothy Titcomb, Esquire Fiftieth Edition

New York Charles Scribner's Sons 743 and 745 Broadway 1881

For first edition see entry No. 8582.

"After twenty years of an exceptionally prosperous life, this book has been carefully revised, and is now issued in a new dress . . ."—From the "Preface."

Advertised PW Nov. 5, 1881, as published Nov. 1, 1881. Deposited Nov. 8, 1881. Listed PW Nov. 12, 1881.

LC Y

8638. Kathrina . . .

New York Charles Scribner's Sons 743 and 745 Broadway 1881

"With the author's revision."—PW Nov. 12, 1881; BAL has failed to discover any revisions. See entries 8605, 8608.

Advertised for Nov. 15, 1881, PW Nov. 12, 1881. Deposited Nov. 18, 1881. Listed PW Dec. 3, 1881.

H LC

8639. Lessons in Life A Series of Familiar Essays by Timothy Titcomb . . .

New York Charles Scribner's Sons 743 and 745 Broadway 1881

Revised. For first edition see entry No. 8589.

Advertised for Nov. 15, 1881, PW Nov. 12, 1881. Deposited Nov. 18, 1881. Listed PW Dec. 3, 1881.

LC

8640. Plain Talks on Familiar Subjects . . .

New York Charles Scribner's Sons 743 and 745 Broadway 1881

Extended edition. For first edition see entry No. 8601.

Reprint with the exception of: "Preface to the Revised Edition," "Hobby-Riding," "The Elements of Personal Power," "The Social Under-Tow."

Advertised for Nov. 15, 1881, PW Nov. 12, 1881. Deposited Nov. 18, 1881. Listed PW Dec. 3, 1881.

BA LC

8641. Concerning the Jones Family by Timothy Titcomb . . .

New York Charles Scribner's Sons 743 and 745 Broadway 1881

"The form in which this book was originally written has never satisfied me . . . So I have entirely rewritten the book."—From the author's preface. For first edition see *Letters to the Joneses,* 1863.

Advertised for Dec. 10, 1881, PW Dec. 10, 1881. Published Dec. 10, 1881 (publisher's records). Listed PW Dec. 17, 1881. Deposited Dec. 21, 1881.

AAS BA

8642. The Mistress of the Manse A Poem . . .

New York Charles Scribner's Sons 743 and 745 Broadway 1881

Pp. 187. Not illustrated. A very slightly revised version of No. 8625. Also see entry Nos. 8617, 8618, 8644.

Deposited Dec. 21, 1881.

B LC

8643. The Puritan's Guest and Other Poems . . .

New York Charles Scribner's Sons 743 and 745 Broadway 1881

Reprint.

Advertised for Dec. 10, 1881, PW Dec. 10, 1881. Listed PW Dec. 17, 1881. Deposited Dec. 21, 1881.

AAS H

8644. The Mistress of the Manse . . . Illustrations Drawn by Mary A. Hallock, Thomas Moran, Alfred Fredericks, Edwin A. Abbey and Helena DeKay.

New York Charles Scribner's Sons 1881

Copyright notice dated 1876. Pp. 251. For first edition see entry No. 8617.

Cursory comparison indicates that this is a re-issue of the sheets of the 1877 illustrated edition (entry No. 8625) with a cancel title-leaf.

B

8645. EVERY-DAY TOPICS   A BOOK OF BRIEFS ... SECOND SERIES

NEW YORK   CHARLES SCRIBNER'S SONS   743 AND 745 BROADWAY 1882

For first series see entry No. 8623.

⟨i⟩-⟨xii⟩, ⟨1⟩-370; blank leaf. 6¾″ x 4⁷⁄₁₆″.

⟨1⁶, 2-24⁸, 25²⟩. *Signed:* ⟨-⟩⁶, 1-15¹², 16⁶.

S cloth: blue; brown; green; maroon. White paper end papers imprinted in maroon with a floral pattern. Flyleaves.

Published Feb. 1, 1882 (publisher's records). Advertised for Feb. 1, 1882, PW Jan. 28, 1882. Listed PW Feb. 4, 1882. Deposited Feb. 9, 1882. BPL copy received Feb. 13, 1882.

BPL   NYPL

8646. The Lincoln Memorial: Album-Immortelles ... Edited by Osborn H. Oldroyd ...

New York: G. W. Carleton & Co., Publishers. London: S. Low, Son & Co. MDCCCLXXXII

Brief comment, p. 465.

For comment see entry No. 1092.

8647. The Complete Poetical Writings ...

New York   Charles Scribner's Sons   1891

Reprint.

LC

8648. The Complete Poetical Writings ...

New York   Charles Scribner's Sons   1900

Reprint.

LC   NYPL

REPRINTS

The following publications contain material by Holland reprinted from earlier books.

Folk Songs Selected and Edited by John Williamson Palmer ...

New York: Charles Scribner, 124 Grand Street. London: Sampson Low, Son and Company. M DCCC LXI.

Copy in CH inscribed by early owner Nov. 1, 1860.

Cloud Crystals; a Snow-Flake Album ... Edited by a Lady ...

New York ... 1864.

For fuller entry see BAL, Vol. 1, p. 295.

The School-Girl's Garland ... by Mrs. C. M. Kirkland. First Series ...

New York ... 1864.

For comment see entry No. 4837.

Songs of Home Selected from Many Sources ...

New York: Charles Scribner and Company. 1871.

Hymns for Mothers and Children. Second Series. Compiled by the Editor of "Hymns of the Ages." ⟨*i.e.,* Caroline Snowden Whitmarsh and Anne E. Guild⟩

Boston: Nichols and Hall. 1872.

Songs of Nature ...

New York ... 1873.

For comment see entry No. 4760.

One Hundred Choice Selections No. 6 ... Compiled ... by Phineas Garrett ...

... Philadelphia ... 1875.

For comment see entry No. 2463.

The Poets and Poetry of America. By Rufus Wilmot Griswold ...

New York ... 1873.

For comment see in list of John Hay reprints.

Little People of God and What the Poets Have Said of Them Edited by Mrs George L Austin

Boston   Shepard and Gill   1874

Listed PW Dec. 20, 1873.

The Elocutionist's Annual Number 2 ... Edited by J. W. Shoemaker ...

Philadelphia ... 1875.

For comment see BAL, Vol. 2, p. 247.

Poets and Poetry of Printerdom ... Edited by Oscar H. Harpel ...

Cincinnati ... 1875.

For comment see BAL, Vol. 3, p. 370.

One Hundred Choice Selections No. 11 ...

... Philadelphia ... 1875.

For comment see entry No. 4046.

... The Quarterly Elocutionist ... Edited ... by Mrs. Anna Randall-Diehl ... April, 1877 ...

... New York ...

For comment see entry No. 290.

Poems of Places Edited by Henry W. Longfellow ... Italy. Vol. II.

Boston ... 1877.

For comment see entry No. 4049.

Poems of Places Edited by Henry W. Longfellow ... Switzerland and Austria.

Boston ... 1877.

For comment see BAL, Vol. 1, p. 73.

One Hundred Choice Selections No. 14 ...

... Philadelphia ... 1877.

For comment see BAL, Vol. 2, p. 104.

The Elocutionist's Annual Number 5 ... Edited by J. W. Shoemaker ...

Philadelphia ... 1877.

For comment see BAL, Vol. 2, p. 463.

Dick's Recitations and Readings No. 6 ...

New York ... ⟨1877⟩

For comment see entry No. 3375.

Baby Days ... with an Introduction by the Editor of St. Nicholas ...

... New-York ⟨1877⟩.

For comment see entry No. 4770.

Poems of Places Edited by Henry W. Longfellow ... Germany. Vol. 1.

Boston ... 1877.

For comment see BAL, Vol. 1, p. 296.

Star Selections, 1876 ... ⟨Edited⟩ by Professor J. E. Goodrich.

New York ... 1877.

For comment see BAL, Vol. 3, p. 471.

The Elocutionist's Annual Number 6 ... Edited by J. W. Shoemaker ...

Philadelphia ... 1878.

For comment see BAL, Vol. 2, p. 248.

Garnered Treasures from the Poets ...

Philadelphia ... 1878.

For fuller entry see No. 4772.

Golden Thoughts ... Introduction by Rev. Theo. L. Cuyler ...

New-York ... ⟨1878⟩

For comment see BAL, Vol. 2, p. 104.

... The Reading Club and Handy Speaker ... Edited by George M. Baker. No. 6.

Boston ... 1879.

Deposited April 17, 1879. For fuller entry see BAL, Vol. 2, p. 249.

Warne's Illustrated International Annual ... Edited by Joseph Hatton

London Frederick Warne and Co. Bedford Street, Strand 1880 ...

In Memoriam. Gems of Poetry and Song on James A. Garfield ...

Columbus ... 1881.

For comment see entry No. 122.

In Memoriam. James A. Garfield ... Compiled by Henry J. Cookinham ...

Utica, N. Y. Curtiss & Childs, Publishers, 167 Genesee Street. MDCCCLXXXI.

Deposited Nov. 21, 1881.

The Poets' Tributes to Garfield ... ⟨Second Edition⟩

Cambridge ... 1882

For comment see entry No. 1248.

One Hundred Choice Selections No. 20 ...

... Philadelphia ... 1881.

For comment see entry No. 5120.

The Cambridge Book of Poetry and Song ... by Charlotte Fiske Bates ...

New York ... ⟨1882⟩

For comment see entry No. 7887.

... Selections for School Exhibitions and Private Reading ... Nos. 1, 2, 3 ...

Boston ... 1882.

For comment see BAL, Vol. 2, p. 472.

One Hundred Choice Selections No. 24 ...

Published by P. Garrett & Co., 708 Chestnut Street, Philadelphia, Pa., and 130 E. Adams Street, Chicago, Ill. 1885.

Cloth; and, printed paper wrapper. Deposited Feb. 25, 1885.

A LETTER

TO

DR. HENRY HALFORD JONES,

i.e. Josiah Gilbert Holland

(Editor of the Wintertown Democrat,)

Springfield Republican

CONCERNING

His Habit of Giving Advice to Everybody,

AND

HIS QUALIFICATIONS FOR THE TASK,

BY CARL BENSON.

Charles Astor Bristed

NEW YORK:

WM. C. BRYANT & CO., PRINTERS, 41 NASSAU ST., COR. LIBERTY.

1864.

JOSIAH GILBERT HOLLAND
A contemporary comment
Slightly reduced
(Harvard University Library)

St. Nicholas Songs . . .

   . . . New-York ‹1885›

For comment see entry No. 3800.

December Edited by Oscar Fay Adams . . .

   Boston . . . ‹1885›

For comment see entry No. 57.

Bugle-Echoes . . . Edited by Francis F. Browne

   New York . . . MDCCCLXXXVI

For comment see BAL, Vol. 1, p. 75.

The Elocutionist's Annual Number 14 . . . Compiled by Mrs. J. W. Shoemaker.

   . . . Philadelphia: 1886.

For comment see BAL, Vol. 1, p. 380.

One Hundred Choice Selections No. 26 . . .

   . . . Philadelphia . . . 1886.

   "Give Us Men," p. 30; otherwise "Wanted," in *The Marble Prophecy*, 1872. For comment see entry No. 5551.

Belford's Annual 1886–7. Edited by Thomas W. Handford . . .

   Chicago and New York: Belford Clarke & Co. ‹1886›

   Boards, printed in imitation of tree calf.

Prohibition Program for the Use of Juvenile Temperance Societies . . . Composed by Anna A. Gordon . . .

   Chicago: Woman's Temperance Publication Association. 161 La Salle Street. ‹n.d., 1886?›

   Printed paper wrapper.

No. 15. Standard Recitations . . . Compiled . . . by Frances P. Sullivan . . . March, 1887 . . .

   . . . N. Y. . . . ‹1887›

For comment see entry No. 5552.

The Pictorial Budget of Wonders and Fun . . .

   The Juvenile Publishing Company ‹1887›.

For comment see entry No. 3756.

   . . . Harper's Fifth Reader American Authors

   New York . . . 1889

For comment see entry No. 7917.

The Poets' Year . . . Edited by Oscar Fay Adams . . .

   Boston . . . ‹1890›

For comment see entry No. 80.

American Sonnets . . . by T. W. Higginson and E. H. Bigelow

   Boston . . . 1890

For comment see entry No. 8373.

Representative Sonnets by American Poets . . . by Charles H. Crandall

   Boston . . . 1890

For comment see BAL, Vol. 2, p. 275.

Werner's Readings and Recitations. No. 5 . . . Compiled . . . by Sara Sigourney Rice.

   New York . . . 1891.

For comment see entry No. 3433.

The Temperance Platform . . . Compiled by Miss L. Penney . . .

   New York: The National Temperance Society and Publication House, No. 58 Reade Street. 1892.

   Printed paper wrapper.

No. 40. Standard Recitations . . . Compiled . . . by Frances P. Sullivan . . . June 1893 . . .

   . . . N. Y. . . . 1893

   Deposited Oct. 20, 1893. For comment see BAL, Vol. 3, p. 370.

Poets' Dogs . . . by Elizabeth Richardson . . .

   . . . New York . . . 1895

For comment see BAL, Vol. 3, p. 288.

Childhood's Sunny Days . . . ‹by› Lucy Larcom . . . and Others . . .

   . . . 1895 . . . Chicago . . .

For comment see entry No. 4747.

Dew Drops and Diamonds A . . . Collection . . . for Boys and Girls . . .

   . . . 1898 . . . Chicago . . .

For comment see BAL, Vol. 1, p. 77.

Stickeen by John Muir

   Boston & New York Houghton Mifflin Company 1909

   On copyright page: *Published March 1909* Listed PW April 3, 1909.

The Dinnie-Dog Book Compiled for Dog Lovers by Dinnie-Dog

   Privately Printed by H. G. 1912

For comment see entry No. 6765A.

St. Nicholas Book of Verse Edited by Mary Budd Skinner and Joseph Osmun Skinner ...

... New York ... MCMXXIII

For comment see entry No. 818.

REFERENCES AND ANA

The Lady's Book of Flowers and Poetry ... Edited by Lucy Hooper.

New York: J. C. Riker, 15 Ann Street. 1842.

"Song of the Tulip," pp. 101-102. Sometimes attributed to the subject of this list. Authorship not known. Credited herein to *Holland*. Possibly by one of the following authors: John Holland, 1794–1872, an English poet; John Holland, an American, author of *Poems*, 1858, and *Star Streaks*, 1870; Henry Richard Vassall Fox, Lord Holland, 1773–1840; Edwin Clifford Holland, d. 1824, of Charleston, S. C., author of *Odes, Naval Songs* ..., 1813. By J. G. Holland?

Poems.

New York, 1858.

Not located. Not seen. Entry from Foley who gives the title thus: *Poems. 12mo. New York, 1858.* Presumably a ghost. The reference is probably to *Poems*, by John Holland, New York, 1858.

... Dearest O! Think of Me Written by J. C. ⟨sic⟩ Holland. Music by Francis Woolcott ...

St. Louis ... Balmer & Weber 56 Fourth St. ... ⟨1859⟩

Sheet music. Cover-title. Sometimes misattributed to the subject of this list. The author was one J. C. Holland (further information wanting), author of "Bell Brandon," "Birchen Canoe," "Pride of Daisy Dell."

Collected Works.

1863.

On the basis of a set (in leather), in MHS, presented to the society by Holland Jan. 5, 1864, no set in the accepted sense was issued. The "set" at MHS is made up of reprints of the separate works.

PW Dec. 1, 1863, carried an advertisement for a "new edition of Timothy Titcomb's Works" in six volumes, and each title listed is clearly identified as *40th edition, 20th edition*, etc., etc.

A set in seven volumes was advertised in PW Dec. 1, 1864, but in this advertisement no comment is made which suggests that the individual volumes were reprints.

It seems safe to conclude that no uniform set was attempted until 1881. See entry Nos. 8635–8645.

A Letter to Dr. Henry Halford Jones ⟨i.e., J. G. Holland⟩, (Editor of the Wintertown Democrat ⟨i.e., *Springfield Republican*⟩), Concerning His Habit of Giving Advice to Everybody, and His Qualifications for the Task, by Carl Benson ⟨i.e., Charles Astor Bristed⟩.

New York: Wm. C. Bryant & Co., Printers, 41 Nassau St., Cor. Liberty. 1864.

Printed paper wrapper.

The Psychology of Kathrina. By Thad. M. Stevens, M. D., of Indianapolis, Ind.

Reprint from Cincinnati Lancet & Observer, May, 1877.

Cover-title. Printed paper wrapper.

Josiah Gilbert Holland. A Memorial Address Delivered in His Native Town, Belchertown, Mass., Oct. 16, 1881, by Rev. P. W. Lyman.

⟨n.p., n.d., probably Belchertown, Mass., 1881⟩

Cover-title. Printed paper wrapper.

A Memorial of Josiah Gilbert Holland Discourses and Tributes Called forth by His Death, October 12, 1881

Printed, Not Published ⟨n.d., 1882?⟩

Printed paper wrapper. According to Princeton University Library edited by Richard Watson Gilder.

Josiah Gilbert Holland by Mrs. H. M. ⟨Harriette Merrick⟩ Plunkett ...

New York Charles Scribner's Sons 1894

Published March 28, 1894 (publisher's records). Deposited March 28, 1894.

Josiah Gilbert Holland in Relation to His Times by Harry Houston Peckham

Philadelphia University of Pennsylvania Press London: Humphrey Milford: Oxford University Press 1940

Emily Dickinson's Letters to Dr. and Mrs. Josiah Gilbert Holland Edited by Their Granddaughter Theodora van Wagenen Ward

Harvard University Press Cambridge, Massachusetts 1951

For comment see entry No. 4699.

MARY JANE HAWES HOLMES

1 8 2 5 – 1 9 0 7

Note: During the period 1899–1912 **Mrs. Holmes's** earlier books enjoyed a renewed popularity and were reissued by several publishers. Many of these are truncated versions, published under revised titles, and are presented in this list in their chronological position. Not all of these reprints have been located; see *Unlocated Titles* at end of this list. Also see at end of this list *Misattributions.*

8649. TEMPEST AND SUNSHINE; OR, LIFE IN KENTUCKY . . .

NEW-YORK: D. APPLETON & COMPANY, 346 AND 348 BROADWAY. MDCCCLIV.

⟨1⟩-381; blank, p. ⟨382⟩; 2 pp. advertisements. 7½″ scant x 4¹¹⁄₁₆″.

⟨1⟩-16¹².

Two states (probably printings) have been noted:

A

P. ⟨1⟩: *New Copyright Works* . . .

P. ⟨2⟩: *Sixth Edition . . . Knick-Knacks* . . .

B

P. ⟨1⟩: *D. Appleton & Company's Publications. Choice New English Works* . . .

P. ⟨2⟩: *New Light Reading Books* . . .

Note: The only located copy of the second state lacks the final leaf; hence, BAL cannot be certain that the leaf was imprinted with advertisements or otherwise.

Three bindings noted. The sequence, if any, has not been firmly established:

Binding A (B?)

TR-like cloth: purple. Sides blindstamped with a rules frame. Spine stamped in gold: ⟨*triple rule*⟩ / TEMPEST / AND ⟨*serif'd face*⟩ / SUNSHINE /OR / LIFE IN / KENTUCKY / ⟨*fillet composed of 7 small units*⟩ / MRS. M. J. HOLMES / ⟨*5 (6?) rules*⟩ / Pale buff end papers. Flyleaves. Noted on first state sheets.

Binding B (A?)

T cloth: gray. Sides blindstamped with a rules frame. Spine stamped in gold: ⟨*triple rule*⟩ / TEMPEST / AND ⟨*sans serif face*⟩ / SUNSHINE / OR / LIFE IN / KENTUCKY / ⟨*fillet composed of 5 small units*⟩ / MRS. M. J. HOLMES / ⟨*6 rules*⟩ Pale buff end papers. Flyleaves. Noted on first state sheets.

Binding C

T cloth: purple. Sides blindstamped with a rules frame. Spine stamped in gold: ⟨*rule*⟩ / TEMPEST / AND ⟨*sans serif face*⟩ / SUNSHINE / OR / LIFE IN / KENTUCKY / ⟨*fillet composed of 5 small units*⟩ / MRS. M. J. HOLMES / ⟨*2 rules*⟩ Pale buff end papers. Flyleaves. Noted on second state sheets.

Note: Noted NLG April 15, 1854, as in both paper; and, cloth. Otherwise unreported in printed paper wrapper.

Advertised as *nearly ready* NLG Feb. 1, 1854. Noted as *in press* NLG March 15, 1854; as *just ready* NLG April 1, 1854. Deposited April 14, 1854. Noted as *just ready* NLG April 15, 1854. Listed NLG May 1, 1854. Noted as *just ready* NLG May 15, 1854. Reviewed NLG May 15, 1854. Advertised by Trübner as an importation Ath June 17, 1854. The London (Blackwood) edition listed Ath Nov. 18, 1854; PC Dec. 6, 1854; (again) PC Dec. 16, 1854.

AAS (sheets A, binding A) H (sheets B, binding C) Y (sheets A, binding B)

8650. THE ENGLISH ORPHANS; OR, A HOME IN THE NEW WORLD . . .

NEW YORK: D. APPLETON & COMPANY, 346 & 348 BROADWAY. LONDON: 16 LITTLE BRITAIN. 1855.

⟨1⟩-331; blank, p. ⟨332⟩; 4 pp. advertisements. 7¼″ x 4¹¹⁄₁₆″.

⟨1⟩-14¹².

Two states (probably printings) have been noted:

A

P. <333>: *D. Appleton & Co.'s Publications* ...

B

P. <333>: *A List of New Works In General Literature* ...

T cloth: slate; tan. Blue-coated end papers. Flyleaves.

Note: According to an advertisement in APC Oct. 6, 1855, issued in both printed paper wrapper; and, in cloth. Noted only in cloth.

Deposited June 15, 1855. Listed NLG July 2, 1855. Reviewed NAR Oct. 1855. Listed PC (as an importation) Oct. 15, 1855.

AAS (A)   NYPL (B)   UV (A)

8651. THE HOMESTEAD ON THE HILL-SIDE, AND OTHER TALES ...

NEW YORK AND AUBURN: MILLER, ORTON & MULLIGAN. NEW YORK: 25 PARK ROW   AUBURN: 107 GENESEE-ST. 1856.

<i>-x, <11>-379; blank, p. <380>; advertisements, pp. <381-382>; blank leaf. 7⅜″ x 4⅞″.

<1>-7, <8>-24⁸. An incomplete set of lettered signatures for binding in 12's also present.

Moiréd T-like cloth: purple; tan. Yellow end papers. Flyleaf at front.

Note: Appleton dates (misdates?) this publication 1855.

Advertised for *early in December* APC Nov. 17, 1855. Title deposited Dec. 3, 1855. Advertised as *nearly ready* APC Dec. 8, 1855. Advertised for Dec. 20, 1855 APC Dec. 15, 1855. Listed APC Dec. 22, 1855; PC May 15, 1856. The Milner & Sowerby printing (Halifax and London) listed PC Aug. 15, 1867, as in the *Cottage Library*. As a title in the *Wide World Library* listed Bkr Nov. 2, 1868.

AAS   UV

8652. 'LENA RIVERS ...

NEW YORK AND AUBURN: MILLER, ORTON & MULLIGAN. NEW YORK: 25 PARK ROW   AUBURN: 107 GENESEE-ST. 1856.

<1>-416. 7⅜″ x 4⅞″.

<1>-26⁸. *Also signed:* <A>-P, O <sic>¹², <->⁴.

T cloth: red; slate. Yellow end papers. Flyleaves.

Title deposited Oct. 28, 1856. Advertised for Nov. 25, APC Nov. 8, 1856. Listed APC Nov. 29, 1856. Listed PC Jan. 16, 1857. The Milner &

Sowerby printing (Halifax and London) listed PC March 2, 1857.

UV

8653. MEADOW BROOK ...

NEW YORK: MILLER, ORTON & CO. 25 PARK ROW. 1857.

<i>-viii, 9-380; advertisements, pp. <381-384>. 7⁵⁄₁₆″ x 4¹³⁄₁₆″.

<1>-16¹².

T-like cloth: slate; tan. Yellow end papers. Flyleaves.

Deposited Nov. 19, 1857.

AAS

8654. DORA DEANE, OR THE EAST INDIA UNCLE; AND MAGGIE MILLER, OR OLD HAGAR'S SECRET ...

NEW YORK: C. M. SAXTON, 25 PARK ROW. 1859.

<i>-<viii>, 9-474; advertisements, pp. <475-480>. 7⁵⁄₁₆″ x 4¹³⁄₁₆″.

<1>-20¹².

T cloth: red. Yellow end papers. Flyleaves.

Note: Allibone lists *Maggie Miller; or, Hagar's Secret,* New York, 1858. Presumably an erroneous entry for the present title. Allibone dates *Dora Deane* ... , 1858; no copy so dated otherwise reported.

A title-page for *Dora Deane* ... was deposited by Moses S. Beach on Feb. 8, 1858. A title-page for *Maggie Miller; or, Old Hagar's Secret* was deposited by Moses S. Beach on Sept. 18, 1858. Moses S. Beach (according to DAB) was editor of the *New York Sun;* "fiction was one of his specialties and he bought liberally from the authors of the best-sellers of the time, Mary Jane Holmes, Horatio Alger, Jr. ...." Presumably the title-pages deposited in his name were preliminary to securing copyright for the novels as published in *The Sun.*

Advertised as *ready this day* BM Dec. 1, 1858.

AAS

8655. COUSIN MAUDE AND ROSAMOND ...

NEW YORK: C. M. SAXTON, BARKER & CO., 1860.

<i>-<x>, <11>-374. 6¹³⁄₁₆″ x 4¹¹⁄₁₆″.

<1>-15¹², 16⁷; *so signed.*

Binding:

Note: The present entry is tentative only.

Also note: Allibone's entry: *Rosamond, New York, 1860,* is presumed to be for this publication.

Announced BM March 15, 1860. Listed BM April 16, 1860.

H (rebound)

8656. MARIAN GREY; OR, THE HEIRESS OF REDSTONE HALL . . .

NEW YORK: CARLETON, PUBLISHER, 413 BROADWAY. M DCCC LXIII.

⟨1⟩-400; publisher's catalog, dated 1863, pp. ⟨1⟩-8. 7¼″ x 4⅞″.

Two states (almost certainly printings) noted.

1

⟨1⟩-17¹². Sheets bulk ¹⁵⁄₁₆″ scant.

A cloth: brown. Sides blindstamped with a frame composed principally of linked circles; at center of each side a blindstamped floret. Pale cream-coated end papers. Flyleaves.

P. ⟨2⟩: *Popular Tales* . . . ⟨6 numbered titles⟩

2

⟨1⟩-17¹². Sheets bulk ⅞″.

Binding as above; also: TR cloth: orange-brown; sides blindstamped with a frame composed principally of small triangular units; at center of each side is blindstamped: CARLETON ⟨in a circular device⟩ Gray-coated end papers. Flyleaves?

Listed APC June 1, 1863; PC June 15, 1863. The Milner & Sowerby printing (Halifax & London) advertised in PC Oct. 1, 1868. For revised edition see under 1899.

AAS (1)   H (2)   UV (2)

8657. DARKNESS AND DAYLIGHT. A NOVEL . . .

NEW YORK: CARLETON, PUBLISHER, 413 BROADWAY. M DCCC LXIV.

⟨i⟩-vi, ⟨7⟩-384. 7¼″ x 4⅞″.

⟨1⟩-16¹².

TR cloth: purple-brown; rusty black. Blue paper end papers. Flyleaves.

Advertised as *in press* ALG March 15, 1864. Advertised ALG May 16, 1864, as *this week;* also, June 1, 1864. Listed ALG June 15, 1864; Bkr Oct. 31, 1864. Under the title *Nina; or, Darkness and Daylight,* listed PC Dec. 31, 1883, as a Nicholson publication. A Putnam printing listed PC Jan. 15, 1887.

AAS   UV   Y

8658. HUGH WORTHINGTON. OF ⟨sic⟩ A NOVEL . . .

NEW YORK: CARLETON, PUBLISHER, 413 BROADWAY. M DCCC LXV.

⟨i⟩-vi, ⟨7⟩-370; 2 pp. advertisements, paged ⟨3⟩-4. 7¼″ x 4⅞″ full.

⟨1⟩-9, ⟨10⟩-15¹², 16⁶.

Two states (probably printings) noted:

A

As above.

Superfluous word OF on title-page.

P. 4 ⟨sic⟩ of terminal advertisements: Final entry is for Epes Sargent's *Peculiar.*

B

As above but with the following variations:

The superfluous word OF not present on title-page.

P. 4 ⟨sic⟩ of terminal advertisements: Final entry is for Richard B. Kimball's *In the Tropics.*

Coarse TR cloth: bluish slate. Blue end papers. Flyleaves.

Noted as *in press* ALG May 1, 1865. Advertised ALG May 15, 1865, as *ready this week.* Listed ALG June 1, 1865. Deposited June 8, 1865. The Milner & Sowerby printing (Halifax & London) listed PC Aug. 15, 1867.

AAS (B)   H (B)   LC (A)   Y (A)

8659. THE CAMERON PRIDE; OR, PURIFIED BY SUFFERING. A NOVEL . . .

NEW YORK: G. W. CARLETON & CO. PUBLISHERS. LONDON: S. LOW, SON & CO. MDCCCLXVII.

⟨i⟩-viii, ⟨9⟩-415; blank, p. ⟨416⟩; publisher's catalog, pp. ⟨3⟩-6. 7¼″ x 4¹³⁄₁₆″.

Note: In all examined copies the following folios are misplaced and appear at the wrong side of the page: viii, 336, 337, 338, 339.

⟨1⟩-17¹², ⟨18⟩⁶.

C cloth: green; terra-cotta. Blue end papers. Flyleaves.

Listed ALG June 15, 1867.

AAS   NYPL   Y

8660. ROSE MATHER: A TALE OF THE WAR . . .

NEW YORK: G. W. CARLETON & CO., PUBLISHERS, LONDON: S. LOW, SON & CO. MDCCCLXVIII.

⟨i⟩-viii, ⟨9⟩-407. 7¼″ x 4⅞″.

⟨1⟩-16, ⟨17⟩¹².

C cloth: green; purple; terra-cotta. Blue end papers. Flyleaves.

Y copy inscribed by early owner June 16, 1868. Listed ALG July 1, 1868.

AAS   H   OS   UP   Y

8661. THE CHRISTMAS FONT. A STORY FOR YOUNG FOLKS ...

NEW YORK: G. W. CARLETON, PUBLISHER. LONDON: S. LOW, SON, & CO. MDCCCLXVIII.

⟨5⟩-67. Frontispiece and 11 plates inserted. 5½″ x 4⅜″.

⟨1-4⟩⁸. *Signed:* ⟨1⁶, 2-3⁸⟩, 4⁸, 5².

C cloth: green; purple. Covers bevelled. White paper end papers decorated in gold and blue with an arrangement of arcs and dots; white paper end papers decorated in gold and red with a dot and rosette pattern; white paper end papers decorated in gold and blue with a pattern of dots and twig-like units. Flyleaves.

Listed ALG Dec. 15, 1868; PC Jan. 16, 1869.

AAS   LC

8662. ETHELYN'S MISTAKE; OR, THE HOME IN THE WEST. A NOVEL ...

NEW YORK: G. W. CARLETON, PUBLISHER. LONDON: S. LOW, SON & CO. M DCCC LXIX.

⟨i⟩-viii, ⟨9⟩-380; advertisements, paged: ⟨3⟩-6. 7³⁄₁₆″ scant x 4¹³⁄₁₆″.

⟨1⟩-16¹².

C cloth: brown; purple; terra-cotta. Blue end papers. Flyleaves.

Listed ALG June 1, 1869. The London (Milner) edition advertised as though just published PC Nov. 3, 1879.

H   NYPL   Y

8663. MILLBANK; OR, ROGER IRVING'S WARD. A NOVEL ...

NEW YORK: G. W. CARLETON & CO., PUBLISHERS. LONDON: S. LOW, SON & CO. M.DCCC.LXXI.

⟨i⟩-viii, ⟨9⟩-402; publisher's catalog, pp. ⟨3⟩-8. 7¼″ x 4⅞″.

⟨1⟩-17¹².

C cloth: green; purple. Lavender end papers. Flyleaves.

Listed ALG June 15, 1871. The British edition (Nicholson) listed Ath June 19, 1886.

H   NYPL   Y

8664. EDNA BROWNING; OR THE LEIGHTON HOMESTEAD. A NOVEL ...

NEW YORK: G. W. CARLETON & CO., PUBLISHERS. LONDON: S. LOW, SON & CO. M.DCCC.LXXII.

⟨i⟩-vi, ⟨7⟩-423; blank, pp. ⟨424⟩; publisher's catalog dated 1872, pp. ⟨1⟩-⟨8⟩. 7³⁄₁₆″ x 4⅞″.

⟨1⟩-18¹².

P cloth: green; purple. Lavender end papers. Flyleaves.

Listed WTC May 16, 1872. "... the publishers, have received advance orders for nearly 20,000 copies."—WTC May 16, 1872. The British edition (Wakefield & London: Nicholson, Simpkin Marshall) listed PC Oct. 16, 1878.

AAS   H   Y

8665. WEST LAWN AND THE RECTOR OF ST. MARK'S ...

NEW YORK: G. W. CARLETON & CO., PUBLISHERS. LONDON: S. LOW, SON & CO. M.DCCC.LXXIV.

⟨1⟩-413; blank, p. ⟨414⟩; publisher's catalog, pp. ⟨1⟩-⟨6⟩. 7³⁄₁₆″ x 4⅞″.

⟨1-2⟩, 3-8, ⟨9⟩-17¹², 18⁶.

Two styles of binding noted; sequence, if any, not determined. The designations are for identification only.

A

FL-like cloth: terra-cotta. Front stamped in black with a rules frame, the corners interlocked to form an arrangement of boxes. At center, also blackstamped: West / Lawn / ⟨dash⟩ / HOLMES   Back cover identically stamped in blind but without the lettering. Lavender end papers. Flyleaves.

B

FL-like cloth: green; purple. Sides identically stamped in blind with a greek key frame; publisher's circular device at center. Lavender end papers. Flyleaves.

Listed PW Oct. 10, 1874. The London (Milner) edition is dated 1878 by BMU. Under the title *Dora Freeman; or, West Lawn,* published in London by Nicholson; listed PC Oct. 1, 1884. Under the original title reissued by Nicholson in 1889.

H (A,B)   NYPL (B)   Y (B)

8666. EDITH LYLE. A NOVEL ...

NEW YORK: G. W. CARLETON & CO., PUBLISHERS. LONDON: S. LOW & CO. MDCCCLXXVI.

⟨i⟩-viii, ⟨9⟩-420. 7³⁄₁₆″ x 4⅞″.

⟨1⟩-17¹², 18⁶.

FL-like cloth: green. Blue paper end papers. Flyleaves.

"... ready next week ... for the first edition of which ⟨the publishers⟩ ... state they are printing 20,000 copies."—PW April 29, 1876. Listed PW May 6, 1876. H copy received May 18, 1876. "Messrs Belford & Co. published ⟨the book⟩ during the past month."—CM Aug. 1876. Reviewed CM Sept. 1876. The British edition (Wakefield & London: Nicholson, Simpkin Marshall) listed PC Oct. 16, 1878.

Note: During the period 1904–1912 several publishers issued an unlocated publication under the title *Edith Lyle's Secret.* This is presumed to be a version of *Edith Lyle, a Novel.*

AAS   Y

8667. MILDRED. A NOVEL ...

> NEW YORK: G. W. CARLETON & CO., PUBLISHERS. LONDON: S. LOW & CO. MDCCCLXXVII.

⟨1⟩-324. 7⅛″ x 4⅞″.

⟨1-2⟩, 3-7, ⟨8-9⟩, 10-13^{12}, ⟨14⟩^{6}.

FL-like cloth: green. Lavender end papers. Flyleaves.

Two states (possibly printings) noted:

1

No page reference numbers in the table of contents.

2

Page reference numbers present in the table of contents.

Common to both: Superfluous signature mark 6 on p. 81. This feature persists as late as the reprint of 1888.

AAS (2)   H (1)   Y (1)

8668. DAISY THORNTON AND JESSIE GRAHAM ...

> NEW YORK: COPYRIGHT, 1878, BY G. W. CARLETON & CO., PUBLISHERS. LONDON: S. LOW & CO. MDCCCLXXVIII.

Two printings noted:

1

⟨i⟩-viii, 9-377; blank, p. ⟨378⟩; 6 pp. advertisements paged: ⟨i-ii⟩, ⟨1⟩-4. 7⁷⁄₁₆″ x 4⅞″.

⟨1⟩-⟨7⟩, 8-16^{12}. Leaf ⟨1⟩₁ excised or pasted under the end paper.

P. ⟨1⟩ of terminal advertisements (*i.e.,* p. ⟨381⟩) dated at head: *1878.*

2

⟨i⟩-viii, 9-377; blank, p. ⟨378⟩; 6 pp. advertisements paged: ⟨1⟩-⟨6⟩. Collation as above.

P. ⟨1⟩ of terminal advertisements (*i.e.,* p. ⟨379⟩) dated at head: *1879.*

FL-like cloth: purple. Blue paper end papers. Flyleaf at back.

Listed PW Nov. 2, 1878. The British edition (Wakefield & London: Nicholson) listed Ath June 19, 1886.

AAS (1)   H (2)   LC (1)   UV (1)

8669. FORREST HOUSE. A NOVEL ...

> NEW YORK: G. W. CARLETON & CO., PUBLISHERS, MADISON SQUARE. MDCCCLXXIX.

⟨i⟩-vi, 7-394, 2 pp. advertisements. 7³⁄₁₆″ x 4¹¹⁄₁₆″.

⟨1⟩-16^{12}, 17^6.

FL-like cloth: green. Brown-coated on white end papers. Flyleaves.

Two states (probably printings) noted:

1

P. ⟨396⟩: *How to Save Your Doctor's Bills ... Every Man His Own Doctor ...*

2

P. ⟨396⟩: *A Valuable New Book ... Popular Quotations ...*

A copy of the second state in H inscribed by the author Nov. 1, 1879. Listed PW Jan. 3, 1880. The British edition (London: Nicholson) listed Ath Sept. 27, 1884; PC Jan. 16, 1892.

AAS (1)   H (2)

8670. CHATEAU D'OR. NORAH AND KITTY CRAIG ...

> NEW YORK: G. W. CARLETON & CO., PUBLISHERS, LONDON: S. LOW & CO. MDCCCLXXX.

⟨1⟩-389; blank, p. ⟨390⟩; advertisements, pp. ⟨1⟩-⟨6⟩. 7³⁄₁₆″ scant x 4⅞″.

⟨1⟩-⟨12⟩, 13-16^{12}, 17^6. Leaf ⟨1⟩₁ excised.

Two states (almost surely printings) noted. The sequence has not been determined and the order of presentation is arbitrary:

A

Sheets bulk 1⅛″.

P. ⟨5⟩ of terminal advertisements: *A Valuable New Book ... Popular Quotations ...*

B

Sheets bulk 1¹⁄₁₆″.

P. ⟨5⟩ of terminal advertisements: *Wonderful New Book ... Household Encyclopaedia ...*

Two states of binding noted. The sequence, if any, has not been determined and the order of presentation is arbitrary:

Binding A

The blindstamped border on the sides is a greek key pattern. Noted in FL-like cloth: green; purple. Tan end papers. Flyleaves.

Binding B

The blindstamped border on the sides is composed of a double-rule, twisted at the corners to form boxes. Noted in FL-like cloth: purple. Gray-blue end papers. Flyleaves.

Listed PW Dec. 4, 1880.

AAS (A sheets, A binding)   NYPL (B sheets, B binding)   UV (A sheets, A binding)   Y (B sheets, A binding)

8671. RED-BIRD. A BROWN COTTAGE STORY ...

NEW YORK: G. W. CARLETON & CO., PUBLISHERS, LONDON: S. LOW & CO. MDCCCLXXX.

⟨i⟩-viii, 9-107; 2 blank leaves. Pp. ⟨i-ii⟩ and final blank leaf excised or pasted under the end papers. Frontispiece and 7 plates inserted. $5\frac{11}{16}''$ x 4''.

⟨1⟩-7^8. Leaves ⟨1⟩$_1$ and 7_8 excised or pasted under the end papers.

S cloth: blue; mauve. Faun end papers.

Listed PW Dec. 4, 1880.

AAS   LC

8672. MADELINE. A NOVEL ...

NEW YORK: G. W. CARLETON & CO., PUBLISHERS. LONDON: S. LOW, SON & CO. MDCCCLXXXI.

⟨i⟩-vi, 7-374; publisher's catalog, pp. ⟨1⟩-⟨8⟩; blank leaf. $7\frac{3}{16}''$ x $4\frac{7}{8}''$. *See note below.*

⟨1⟩-16^{12}. *See note below.*

Note: In some copies leaf 16_{12} is excised; and in view of the following the absence of the leaf may be frustrating:

Two states (probably printings) noted:

A

Leaf 16_{12} (when present) is blank.

B

Leaf 16_{12} (when present) is imprinted on the recto: *Three Valuable Books ...*

FL-like cloth: green. Tan end papers. Flyleaves.

Listed PW Dec. 31, 1881.

AAS (16_{12} excised)   NYPL (A)   UV (A)   Y (B)

8673. QUEENIE HETHERTON. A NOVEL ...

NEW YORK: G. W. CARLETON & CO., PUBLISHERS. LONDON: S. LOW & CO. MDCCCLXXXIII.

⟨1⟩-454; advertisements, pp. ⟨1⟩-2. $7\frac{3}{16}''$ x $4\frac{13}{16}''$.

⟨1⟩-5, ⟨6⟩-16, ⟨17⟩-19^{12}.

FL-like cloth: green. Tan end papers. Flyleaves.

Deposited Oct. 4, 1883. Listed PW Nov. 24, 1883.

Y

8674. CHRISTMAS STORIES ...

NEW YORK: G. W. CARLETON & CO., PUBLISHERS. LONDON: S. LOW, SON & CO. MDCCCLXXXV.

⟨i-vi⟩, ⟨1⟩-372; 3 blank leaves. Pp. ⟨i-ii⟩ and the final blank leaf excised or pasted under the end papers. Portrait frontispiece inserted. $7\frac{1}{8}''$ full x $4\frac{7}{8}''$.

⟨1-16⟩^{12}. Leaves ⟨1⟩$_1$ and ⟨16⟩$_{12}$ excised or pasted under the end papers. *Signed:* ⟨-⟩^{3}, ⟨1⟩-⟨6⟩, 7, ⟨8-9⟩, 10-13, ⟨14⟩-15^{12}, 16^9.

FL-like cloth: green. Tan end papers.

Deposited Nov. 17, 1884. Listed PW Dec. 6, 1884.

AAS   H   Y

8675. BESSIE'S FORTUNE. A NOVEL ...

NEW YORK: G. W. CARLETON & CO., PUBLISHERS. LONDON: S. LOW, SON & CO. MDCCCLXXXVI.

⟨1⟩-453; blank, p. ⟨454⟩; publisher's catalog, pp. ⟨1⟩-2. $7\frac{3}{16}''$ x $4\frac{3}{4}''$.

⟨1⟩-16, ⟨17⟩-19^{12}.

FL cloth: green. Orange-tan paper end papers.

Listed PW Oct. 3, 1885.

NYPL

8676. GRETCHEN. A NOVEL ...

NEW YORK   G. W. DILLINGHAM, PUBLISHER, SUCCESSOR TO G. W. CARLETON & CO. LONDON: S. LOW, SON & CO. MDCCCLXXXVII.

⟨1⟩-452; publisher's catalog, pp. ⟨1⟩-4, dated 1887. Laid paper. $7\frac{1}{8}''$ x $4\frac{3}{4}''$.

⟨1⟩-19^{12}.

FL-like cloth: green. Sides blindstamped with a circular publisher's device and an ornate border. Terra-cotta end papers. Flyleaves of book stock.

Two printings noted:

1

As above.

On p. ⟨2⟩: *Gretchen* is described as *New.*

On the copyright page: Imprint of Samuel Stodder.

2

Pp. ⟨1⟩-452, 2 blank leaves.

On p. ⟨2⟩: *Gretchen* is listed without the statement *New.* Present is a listing (*inter alia*) for *Marguerite* which is described as *New.* (*Marguerite* was published in 1891.)

On the copyright page is the copyright notice only.

Noted only in brown C cloth, sides unstamped save for a blindstamped single rule frame. The plates are much worn; apparently reprinted without alteration of the date in the imprint.

Listed PW Oct. 19, 1887.

AAS (1st) H (1st) Y (2nd)

8677. MEN, DON'T BE SELFISH A TALK TO HUSBANDS BY THE LADIES' FAVORITE NOVELIST ... ON THE LITTLE ATTENTIONS THAT MAKE UP THE SUM OF WOMAN'S HAPPINESS—LATE MARRIAGES AND DOMESTIC CYCLONES—THE SPOILED BOY ...

BROCKPORT, N. Y., MARCH 2, 1888.

Single cut sheet. Printed on recto only. 27⅛″ x 5⅛″ full.

Possibly prepared for copyright purposes only; or, perhaps as a release issued to periodicals.

Deposited Feb. 28, 1888.

LC

8678. MARGUERITE. A NOVEL ...

NEW YORK: G. W. DILLINGHAM, PUBLISHER, SUCCESSOR TO G. W. CARLETON & CO. MDCCCXCI.

⟨i⟩-vi, ⟨7⟩-473; advertisements, pp. ⟨474-480⟩. Laid paper. 7³⁄₁₆″ x 4⅞″.

⟨1-30⟩⁸.

FL-like cloth: green. Yellow end papers.

Listed PW Aug. 1, 1891. Reprinted and reissued by G. W. Dillingham Company under date ⟨1890⟩.

AAS H

8679. The Boy: A Story of Easter. 1863.

⟨Rochester, N. Y., Democrat and Chronicle Print, 1891⟩

Contains "The Story," by Mrs. Holmes. Printed paper wrapper (?).

Not located. Entry on the basis of an entry in LC catalog. The publication appears to be no longer in LC.

Issued as an Easter souvenir by St. Luke's Church, Brockport, N. Y.

8680. Red-Bird's Christmas Story ...

New York ... G. W. Dillingham, Publisher, Successor to G. W. Carleton & Co. MDCCCXCII ...

Reprint of *Red-Bird* ... , 1880.

JN

8681. Mrs. Hallam's Companion ...

Philadelphia: J. B. Lippincott Company ⟨1894⟩.

The sheets of *Lippincott's Monthly Magazine,* Dec. 1894, with title-page as above. For formal book publication see below under 1896.

Deposited Nov. 20, 1894.

LC NYPL

8682. A Cunning Culprit or a "Novel" Novel A Composite Romance by Twenty Different Popular Writers

1895   The Hobart Publishing Company Chicago

Printed paper wrapper.

Chapter 18, "An American Abroad," pp. 269-280, by Mrs. Holmes.

Deposited June 17, 1895.

LC

8683. DOCTOR HATHERN'S DAUGHTERS. A STORY OF VIRGINIA, IN FOUR PARTS ...

NEW YORK. G. W. DILLINGHAM, PUBLISHER, SUCCESSOR TO G. W. CARLETON & CO. MDCCCXCV.

⟨i⟩-⟨viii⟩, ⟨9⟩-471; advertisements, pp. ⟨472-480⟩. 7¼″ x 4⅞″.

⟨1-30⟩⁸.

Two states (probably printings) noted:

A

As above.

Preface on p. ⟨vii⟩.

B

Pagination of front matter: ⟨i-ii⟩, ⟨i⟩-vi.

Preface on p. ⟨iii⟩.

C cloth: brown. Tan end papers.

Listed PW July 20, 1895. Issued in London Oct. 1895, according to *The English Catalogue of Books*.

H (B)   UV (A)   Y (B)

8684. MRS. HALLAM'S COMPANION. AND THE SPRING FARM, AND OTHER TALES ...

NEW YORK: G. W. DILLINGHAM, PUBLISHER, MD-CCCXCVI.

For prior publication of *Mrs. Hallam's Companion* see under 1894.

⟨1⟩-437; advertisements, pp. ⟨438-440⟩. 7¼″ x 4¾″.

⟨1-27⁸, 28⁴⟩.

C cloth: brown. Tan end papers.

Two states (probably printings) noted:

1: As above. On p. ⟨2⟩ is a list of twenty-eight titles, the final entry being for *Dr. Hathern's Daughters,* which is described as (*New*).

2: As above. The list on p. ⟨2⟩ extended by the addition of an entry for *Mrs. Hallam's Companion* which is described as (*New*).

Deposited Sept. 5, 1896. Listed PW Sept. 26, 1896. Issued in London Dec. 1896, according to *The English Catalogue of Books*. Reissued not before 1899 with the imprint: *G. W. Dillingham Company Publishers New York* ⟨1896⟩.

H (2nd)   NYPL (1st)

8685. Rose Mather and Annie Graham or, Women in War ...

The Mershon Company New York Rahway, N. J. ⟨n.d., 1896?⟩

Reprint of *Rose Mather ...* , 1868.

NYPL

8686. PAUL RALSTON. A NOVEL ...

NEW YORK: G. W. DILLINGHAM CO., PUBLISHERS. MDCCCXCVII.

⟨i⟩-vi, 7-393; blank, p. ⟨394⟩; advertisements, pp. ⟨1⟩-6. 7¼″ x 4¹³⁄₁₆″.

⟨1-25⟩⁸.

C cloth: brown. Brown paper end papers.

Two printings noted:

1

As above.

P. ⟨ii⟩: *Paul Ralston* not listed in the advertisement.

P. ⟨395⟩: Dated *1897.*

2

Issued not before 1902.

P. ⟨ii⟩: *Paul Ralston* listed. Final title listed is *The Cromptons* which was issued in Aug. 1902.

P. ⟨395⟩: *Mrs. Mary J. Holmes' Novels. Over Three Million Sold ...*

Deposited Oct. 25, 1897. Listed PW Nov. 6, 1897.

AAS (1st)   LC (1st)   NYPL (2nd)   Y (1st)

Paul Ralston's First Love ...

New York   Street & Smith, Publishers ⟨1897; *i.e., ca.* 1906⟩

See entry No. 8706.

Where Love's Shadows Lie Deep ...

New York   Street & Smith, Publishers ⟨1897; *i.e., ca.* 1906⟩

See entry No. 8707.

8687. Marian Grey; or, the Heiress of Redstone Hall ...

New York: G. W. Dillingham Co., Publishers. MDCCCXCIX.

Revised. For first edition see under 1863.

"When *Marian Grey* first appeared as a serial it added 50,000 new subscribers to the paper for which it was written. As a book it has been even more popular; 126,000 copies have been sold. The plates are now so worn as to render it almost unreadable, yet the sales keep on, and so great is the demand for it that this new edition, with the author's revisions and corrections, is presented ... Over two million copies of this author's novels have been sold ..."—"Publisher's Preface to the New Edition," p. 7.

Presumably issued in cloth.

Deposited Jan. 23, 1899.

LC

8688. THE TRACY DIAMONDS ...

NEW YORK   G. W. DILLINGHAM CO., PUBLISHERS MDCCCXCIX

⟨i-iv⟩, ⟨1⟩-390; 3 blank leaves. 7¼″ x 4⅞″ scant. ⟨1-25⟩⁸.

C cloth: brown. Tan end papers.

Listed PW Oct. 7, 1899. Reprinted and reissued by P. F. Collier & Son, New York ⟨1899⟩.

Y

8689. ... The Gable-Roofed House at Snowdon ...

⟨New York, 1901⟩

Not seen. Entry postulated. Entry on the basis of an entry in a catalog issued by Edward Morrill & Son, Boston.

Cover-title. At head of title: No. 224. Price, Five Cents. Copyright, 1901, by F. M. Lupton. The Leisure Hour Library. F. M. Lupton, Publisher, 23-27 City Hall Place, New York.

Printed self-wrapper.

Another printing issued *ca.* 1902 by Hurst & Company, New York; and another by The Prudential Book Company, N. Y., n.d., *ca.* 1915.

Reprinted from *The Homestead on the Hillside,* 1856.

8690. ... Ada Harcourt ...

⟨New York, 1901⟩

Cover-title. At head of title: No. 338. Price, Five Cents. Copyright, 1901, by F. M. Lupton. The Leisure Hour Library. F. M. Lupton, Publisher, 23-27 City Hall Place, New York.

Printed self-wrapper.

Reprinted from *The Homestead on the Hillside,* 1856.

EM

8691. ... The Old Red House among the Mountains ...

⟨New York, 1901⟩

Cover-title. At head of title: Price, Five Cents. The Leisure Hour Library. No. 350. F. M. Lupton, Publisher, 23-27 City Hall Place New York ... 1901 ...

Printed self-wrapper.

"The Old Red House among the Mountains," reprinted from *The Homestead on the Hillside,* pp. ⟨2⟩-15; material by authors other than Holmes pp. ⟨16⟩-32.

EM

8692. ... Rice Corner ...

⟨New York, n.d., 1901?⟩

Cover-title. At head of title: Price, Five Cents. The Leisure Hour Library. No. 383. F. M. Lupton, Publisher, 23-27 City Hall Place, New York.

Printed self-wrapper.

Reprinted from *The Homestead on the Hillside,* 1856.

JN

8693. THE CROMPTONS ...

G. W. DILLINGHAM COMPANY PUBLISHERS NEW YORK ⟨1902⟩

⟨1⟩-384. Laid paper. 7¼″ x 4¹³⁄₁₆″. Frontispiece inserted.

⟨1⟩-24⁸.

T cloth: green. White paper (both laid; and, wove noted) end papers.

Two printings noted:

1

As above.

Printed on laid paper.

The list opposite the title-page ends with *The Cromptons* which is described as (*New.*).

2

Printed on wove paper.

The list opposite the title-page ends with *Rena's Experiment* which was published in Aug. 1904.

On copyright page: *Issued August, 1902.* Listed PW Aug. 30, 1902.

AAS (1st)   LC (2nd)   Y (1st)

8694. THE MERIVALE BANKS ...

G. W. DILLINGHAM COMPANY PUBLISHERS NEW YORK ⟨1903⟩

⟨i-ii⟩, ⟨1⟩-318. Frontispiece inserted. 7¼″ x 4¹⁵⁄₁₆″. Laid paper.

⟨1-20⁸⟩. *Signed:* ⟨-⟩¹, ⟨1⟩-⟨8⟩, 9-⟨15⟩, 16-19⁸, 20⁷.

T cloth: green.

Two states (probably printings) noted:

1

33 titles listed on p. ⟨ii⟩. Noted only in green T cloth, stamped in gold and blind.

2

35 titles listed on p. ⟨ii⟩. Noted only in green V cloth, stamped in white and blind.

On copyright page: *Issued September, 1903*

Deposited Sept. 11, 1903. Listed PW Sept. 19, 1903.

LC (1st)   NYPL (2nd)   Y (1st)

8695. Cousin Maude or the Milkman's Heiress ...

New York The Federal Book Company Publishers ⟨n.d., *ca.* 1903⟩

Irregular pagination.

Reprint.

In addition to the title-story contains the following four stories: "Diamonds," "Bad Spelling," "Maggie Lee," and "The Answered Prayer." These four stories, with "Cousin Maude," published previously in *Cousin Maude* ... , 1860.

Copy in DU inscribed by early owner March 3, 1903.

DU

8696. RENA'S EXPERIMENT ...

G. W. DILLINGHAM COMPANY PUBLISHERS NEW YORK ⟨1904⟩

⟨1⟩-310; advertisements, pp. ⟨311-318⟩; blank leaf. Laid paper. Frontispiece inserted. 7³⁄₁₆" x 4¹³⁄₁₆".

⟨1⟩-20⁸.

T cloth: green.

On copyright page: *Issued August, 1904.* Deposited Aug. 4, 1904. Listed PW Aug. 20, 1904.

B   LC

8697. Bohemia Official Publication of the International League of Press Clubs for the Building and Endowment of the Journalists' Home ... Vol. I. Alexander K. McClure, Editor-in-Chief ...

... The International League of Press Clubs James S. McCartney Treasurer Journalists' Home Fund Philadelphia 1904.

All issued?

"Dunluce Castle," pp. 101-103.

Presumably issued in both a trade format and a de luxe format. Noted only in de luxe format, limited to 26 lettered copies.

EM

8698. Bad Hugh ...

Grosset & Dunlap Publishers New York ⟨n.d., *ca.* 1904⟩

A revision (by an unknown editor) of *Hugh Worthington*, 1865.

Note: There were several printings, by various publishers, of this title. The sequence is not known and the above may not be the first of the reprints. On the basis of contemporary records other printings were issued by Donohue; Hurst; Street & Smith. The first of the Street & Smith printings was issued as Nos. 340-341 of the *Eagle Series;* reissued as Nos. 340-341 of the *New Eagle Series.*

DU copy inscribed by an early owner Sept. 25, 1904.

DU

8699. Cousin Hugh ...

A. L. Burt Company, Publishers New York ⟨n.d., *ca.* 1904⟩

A revision (by an unknown editor) of *Hugh Worthington*, 1865.

HC

8700. THE ABANDONED FARM AND CONNIE'S MISTAKE ...

G. W. DILLINGHAM COMPANY PUBLISHERS NEW YORK ⟨1905⟩

⟨i-ii⟩, ⟨1⟩-319. Laid paper. Frontispiece inserted. 7¼" x 4⅞".

⟨1⟩⁹, 2-7, 7 ⟨*sic*⟩, ⟨9-10⟩, 11-12, ⟨13⟩-16, ⟨17-19⟩, 20⁸. Leaf ⟨1⟩3 inserted.

T cloth: green. White laid paper end papers.

Deposited Sept. 15, 1905. On copyright page: *Issued October, 1905.* Listed PW Oct. 7, 1905.

UV

8701. LUCY HARDING A ROMANCE OF RUSSIA ...

THE AMERICAN NEWS COMPANY PUBLISHERS' AGENTS NEW YORK ⟨1905⟩

⟨9⟩-266; advertisements, pp. ⟨267-272⟩. Frontispiece and 7 plates inserted. 7¼" x 4¹⁵⁄₁₆".

⟨1-16⁸, 17⁴⟩.

V cloth: green.

Listed PW Dec. 30, 1905, with American News Company given as publisher. Advertised by American News Company, PW Oct. 28, 1905.

Note: There were several later printings, some undated; some with date ⟨1905⟩. On the basis of contemporary records the following notes are offered for the purpose of identifying the reprints: Reissued *ca.* 1906 by Street & Smith as No. 489 in *Eagle Series; ca.* 1920 as No. 489 in *New Eagle Series.* Reissued *ca.* 1912 by Grosset & Dunlap. Reported, not seen, a reprint in the *People's Library* (American News Company).

Y

8702. Rector of St. Marks . . .

Chicago   M. A. Donohue & Company   407-429 Dearborn Street ‹n.d., *ca.* 1905›

Reprinted from *West Lawn,* 1874; and, *Cousin Maude,* 1860.

Note: There were several printings, by various publishers, of this title. The sequence is not known and the above may not be the first of the reprints. On the basis of contemporary records other printings were issued by: A. L. Burt Company; Hurst.

H

8703. Rosamond or, the Youthful Error . . .

New York   The Federal Book Company Publishers ‹n.d., *ca.* 1905›

Cloth, color print pasted to front.

An omnibus volume printed from the plates of several shorter volumes; or, from plates extracted from other books. Irregular pagination.

Reprint with the possible exception of "The Criminal Witness" which has not been found in any of Mrs. Holmes's books. It is wholly likely that the piece was not written by Mrs. Holmes.

Also contains several short stories by one Frances Henshaw Baden.

Y copy inscribed by early owner Nov. 29, 1905.

Y

8704. Rosamond by Mary J. Holmes . . .

Grosset & Dunlap   Publishers, New York ‹n.d., *ca.* 1905›

A reprint of the preceding entry. Pagination regularized.

CP

8705. Maggie Miller. The Story of Old Hagar's Secret . . .

A. L. Burt, Publisher, 52-58 Duane Street, New York ‹n.d., *ca.* 1906›.

Reprinted from *Dora Deane* . . . , 1859.

Note: There were several printings, by various publishers, of this title. The sequence is not known and the above may not be the first of the

reprints. On the basis of contemporary records other printings were issued by: American News Company; Conkey; Donohue; Federal Book Company; Grosset & Dunlap; Hurst; Ogilvie; Street & Smith; Log Cabin Press.

NYPL

8706. Paul Ralston's First Love; or, the Percys of Virginia . . .

New York   Street & Smith, Publishers ‹1897; *i.e., ca.* 1906›

Not located. Entry on the basis of publisher's records and a reprint of *ca.* 1920.

Eagle Library, No. 964. Printed paper wrapper. Reissued *ca.* 1920 by Street & Smith as No. 964, *New Eagle Library.*

Reprint of *Paul Ralston,* 1897, chapters 1-23. See next entry.

NYPL (*ca.* 1920)

8707. Where Love's Shadows Lie Deep . . .

New York   Street & Smith, Publishers ‹1897; *i.e., ca.* 1906›

Not located. Entry on the basis of publisher's records.

Printed paper wrapper. *Eagle Series,* No. 965. Reissued *ca.* 1920 by Street & Smith as No. 965 in *New Eagle Series.*

Reprint of the final half of *Paul Ralston,* 1897. See preceding entry.

8708. Aikenside . . .

Grosset & Dunlap Publishers   New York ‹n.d., *ca.* 1912›

Reprinted from *Madeline,* 1881.

Note: There were several printings, by various publishers, of this title. The sequence is not known and the above may not be the first of the reprints. On the basis of contemporary records other printings were issued by Hurst; Street & Smith; New York Book Company; Donohue; Burt.

H

8709. Family Pride . . .

A. L. Burt Company, Publishers   New York ‹n.d., *ca.* 1912›

Reprint of *The Cameron Pride,* 1867.

Note: There were several printings, by various publishers, of this title. The sequence is not known and the above may not be the first of the reprints. On the basis of contemporary records other printings were issued by: Donohue; Street & Smith; Hurst; Grosset & Dunlap.

B

8710. The Leighton Homestead ...

A. L. Burt Company, Publishers   New York ⟨n.d., *ca.* 1912⟩

Reprinted from *Edna Browning; or, the Leighton Homestead,* New York, 1872.

Color print pasted to front cover.

Note: There were several printings, by various publishers, of this title. The sequence is not known and the above may not be the first of the reprints. On the basis of contemporary records other printings were issued by: Donohue; Grosset & Dunlap; Hurst; Street & Smith.

Y

8711. Miss McDonald ...

M. A. Donohue & Co.   Chicago   New York ⟨n.d., *ca.* 1912⟩

Printed from the plates of other, earlier, publications. Irregular pagination.

"Miss McDonald" is a revised printing, editor unknown, of *Daisy Thornton,* 1878.

Also contains material by authors other than Mrs. Holmes.

Note: There were at least three printings of this book by as many publishers. The sequence is not known and the Donohue printing may not be the first of the reprints. The other known printings were published by Hurst; and, Street & Smith.

Y

8712. Old Hagar's Secret; or, Maggie Miller ...

Philadelphia, Pa.: Royal Publishing Co ⟨n.d., *ca.* 1912⟩

Printed paper wrapper. *The Royal Series,* No. 101.

Reprinted from *Dora Deane* ... , 1859.

P

8713. Georgie's Secret   A Sequel to "The Leighton Homestead" ...

Street & Smith Corporation   Publishers   79-89 Seventh Avenue, New York ⟨n.d., *ca.* 1915⟩

Printed paper wrapper. *Select Library,* No. 216.

A truncated version by an unknown editor of *Edna Browning,* 1872.

UT

8714. At Mather House.

New York: Street & Smith, *ca.* 1928.

Not seen. Entry from *The United States Catalog ... 1928.*

Presumably a reprint of *Rose Mather,* 1868.

REPRINTS

The following publications contain material by Mrs. Holmes reprinted from earlier books.

The Woman's Story as Told by Twenty American Women ... ⟨Edited⟩ by Laura C. Holloway ...

New York   John B. Alden, Publisher   1889

Deposited Jan. 21, 1889. Also issued with the cancel title-leaf of Nims & Knight, Troy, N. Y., 1889.

Treasure Island ... by Robert Louis Stevenson

New York   The New York Book Company 1910 ...

Printed paper wrapper. Cover-title. Material by Mrs. Holmes, pp. ⟨70⟩-90, reprinted from *Homestead on the Hillside,* 1856.

UNLOCATED TITLES

The following books remain unlocated and are here entered on the basis of entries in *The United States Catalog ... 1902,* and *The United States Catalog ... 1928.* Titles marked with an asterisk are from the 1902 issue; otherwise from the 1928. Presumably none of the following books is an original printing; presumably each is a reprint, with perhaps some revisions, of an earlier work issued under a revised title.

The Beauty That Faded. New York: Street & Smith.

The Colonel's Bride. New York: Street & Smith.

He Loved Her Once. New York: Street & Smith.

*The Heiress. Chicago: M. A. Donohue.

*The Hepburn Line. Philadelphia: Lippincott. Possibly reprinted from *Mrs. Hallam's Companion,* 1896.

Her Husband Was a Scamp. New York: Street & Smith.

Magda's Choice. New York: Street & Smith.

Mightier Than Pride. New York: Street & Smith.

She Loved Another. New York: Street & Smith.

*The Thanksgiving Party. New York: Hurst & Co.

The Unloved Husband. New York: Street & Smith.

When Love Spurs Onward. New York: Street & Smith.

MISATTRIBUTIONS

The subject of this list must not be confused with *Mary Johnson Holmes,* author of *The House of Five Gables, Ashes, Sins of the Fathers, A Fair Puritan.* In 1907 the Library of Congress believed Mary Jane Hawes Holmes and Mary Johnson Holmes to be one and the same. In 1960 the library was unable to support the identification or furnish birth and death dates for Mary Johnson Holmes. BAL theorizes that Hurst & Company originated the name Mary Johnson Holmes in a deliberate attempt to mislead purchasers into believing they were obtaining Mary Jane Holmes's writings. Mary Johnson Holmes was "not related to Mrs. Mary J. Holmes" according to *The Annual American Catalog 1891 . . . ,* New York, 1892, p. 92.

Like caution must be exercised lest books issued under the names *Mrs. M. E. Holmes* and *Mrs. M. A. Holmes* be included in the Mary Jane Holmes canon. Frequently books of these authors are credited to Mary Jane Holmes. BAL has been unable to discover any biographical material relating to either Mrs. M. E. Holmes or Mrs. M. A. Holmes and suspects that these names are pseudonyms created to mislead Mary Jane Holmes readers. The following titles were issued *ca.* 1885–1905 as books by either Mrs. M. E. Holmes or Mrs. M. A. Holmes:

A Desperate Woman
For a Woman's Sake
The Grass Widow
A Heartless Woman
Her Fatal Sin
The Midnight Marriage
That Fair False Woman
The Tragedy of Redmont
An Unwilling Bride
Who Will Save Her?
A Wife's Peril
A Wife's Secret
Woman against Woman
A Woman's Love
A Woman's Vengeance

————

What Would You Do, Love? A Novel by the Author of "What Will the World Say?"

Chicago: Belford Clarke & Co. St. Louis: Belford & Clarke Publishing Co. 1881.

Printed brown paper wrapper.

Not by Mary Jane Holmes. A reprint of a novel by Charles Gibbon (1843–1890), author

of *What Will the World Say?* and many other novels. Here included because of the following reprints:

What Would You Do, Love? A Novel. By the Author of "What Will the World Say?"

Chicago: Belford, Clarke & Co., 1883

Printed brown paper wrapper. Anonymous save for the single name HOLMES on the spine.

What Would You Do, Love? A Novel by Mrs. Holmes Author of "What Will the World Say?" etc.

Chicago W. B. Conkey Company ‹1903›

—

. . . What Will the World Say? A Novel. By Charles Gibbon . . .

New York: George Munro, Publisher, 17 to 27 Vandewater Street.

Caption-title. The above on first page. At head of title: The Seaside Library . . . Vol. LXXIV . . . No. 1495 . . . February 19, 1883.

The above was reprinted by Homewood Publishing Company, Chicago ‹1902› with the authorship erroneously credited to Mrs. Mary Jane Holmes.

Note: Not to be confused with another novel of the same title, *What Will the World Say?,* by Ojos Morenos ‹pseud. for Mrs. John M. Clay›, Philadelphia, 1873.

ANA

Tempest and Sunshine A Southern Comedy-Drama in Four Acts by Marie Doran . . . Based upon Incidents in a Story by Mary J. Holmes . . .

Entered . . . July, 1908 . . . Copyright, April, 1911 . . . Original Production, July, 1908 Copyright, 1913 . . . New York Samuel French Publisher 28-30 West 38th Street London . . .

Printed paper wrapper. Issued as No. 258 of *French's International Copyrighted Edition of the Works of the Best Authors.*

Lena Rivers A Comedy Drama in Four Acts by Marie Doran Based upon Incidents in a Story by Mary J. Holmes

Entered . . . 1907 Copyrighted, 1911 . . . 1918 . . . Fitzgerald Publishing Corporation 18 Vesey Street New York

Printed paper wrapper. Deposited May 17, 1918.

Lena Rivers A Modern Dramatization of Mary J. Holmes' Most Popular Novel in Three Acts by Ned Albert ⟨*i.e.,* Wilbur Braun⟩

Copyright, 1936, by Samuel French . . . 25 West 45th Street, New York . . . Los Angeles . . .

Printed paper wrapper. NYPL copy received Oct. 3, 1936. Deposited Dec. 23, 1936.

Tempest and Sunshine A Thoroughly Modern Dramatization of Mary J. Holmes' World Famous Novel in Three Acts by Ned Albert ⟨*i.e.,* Wilbur Braun⟩

Copyright, 1937, by Samuel French . . . 25 West 45th Street, New York . . . Los Angeles . . .

Printed paper wrapper. NYPL copy received Aug. 5, 1937. Deposited Aug. 11, 1937.

Dora Dean ⟨*sic*⟩ A Three-Act Comedy Drama by Virginia Mitchell Based on the Novel by Mary J. Holmes . . .

Copyright, 1940, by Samuel French . . . 25 West 45th Street . . . New York Los Angeles . . .

Printed paper wrapper. NYPL copy received Nov. 25, 1940⟨*sic*⟩. Deposited Feb. 20, 1941.

OLIVER WENDELL HOLMES

1809 – 1894

IT HAS BEEN thought useful to present this list in three sections as follows: *Section One:* Primary books; and, books by authors other than Holmes but containing first edition material by him. *Section Two:* Collections of reprinted material issued under Holmes's name; separate editions (*i.e.,* pieces reprinted from Holmes's books and issued in separate form); and, undated reprints. *Section Three:* Books by authors other than Holmes which contain material by him reprinted from earlier books.

8715. The Offering, for 1829.

Cambridge: Published by Hilliard and Brown. 1829.

"The Lover's Return," pp. ⟨193⟩-194. Signed *R. L.* Uncollected.

"Burial of a Maiden at Sea," p. ⟨195⟩. Anonymous. Uncollected.

For a discussion of Holmes's contributions to this publication see Eleanor M. Tilton's "Literary Bantlings: Addenda to the Holmes Bibliography," *Papers of the Bibliographical Society of America,* Vol. 51, first quarter, 1957.

For comment see entry No. 3099.

8716. Illustrations of the Athenæum Gallery of Paintings.

Boston: Published by Frederic S. Hill. M DCCC XXX.

Printed tan paper wrapper.

Contains the following poems by Holmes:

¶"The Monkeys," pp. ⟨5⟩-7.

*"To a Certain Portrait," pp. ⟨11⟩-13. Later titled "To the Portrait of a Gentleman." Not the same as "A Portrait."

†"The Dying Seneca," pp. ⟨21⟩-22.

¶"The Fish Pieces," pp. ⟨23⟩-24.

¶"The Gipsy," pp. ⟨27⟩-29.

†"The Departure," pp. ⟨30⟩-31.

¶"Lady Drinking," pp. ⟨34⟩-35.

*"Poultry," pp. ⟨36⟩-37. Later titled "A Noontide Lyric."

*"Landscape. [The September Gale.]," pp. ⟨38⟩-40.

¶Uncollected. *Poems,* 1836. †*The Harbinger,* 1833.

Noted as published by *New-England Galaxy,* Boston, Aug. 6, 1830.

B H

The Gleaner …

Boston … 1830

See entry No. 8719.

8717. The Token; a Christmas and New Year's Present. Edited by S. G. Goodrich …

Boston: Published by Gray and Bowen. MDCCCXXXI. ⟨*i.e.,* 1830⟩

"The Lost Boy," signed O.W.H., pp. ⟨27⟩-28. Uncollected.

For comment see entry No. 6790.

8718. Youth's Keepsake; a Christmas and New Year's Gift for Young People …

Boston: Published by Carter and Hendee, 1831. ⟨*i.e.,* 1830⟩

Boards, leather shelfback.

"Crossing the Ford," p. ⟨198⟩. Uncollected.

"The Fairy World," pp. ⟨207⟩-209. Uncollected.

Title deposited Sept. 25, 1830. Noted by AMM Oct. 1830. Reviewed by LG Jan. 1, 1831, with Obadiah Rich named as distributor.

H NYPL

8719. The Gleaner, or Selections in Prose and Poetry; from the Periodical Press.

Boston: Office of the New-England Galaxy. 1830.

Boards, cloth shelfback. Printed paper label on spine.

*"Banditti," pp. 33-35.

*"Evening," By a Tailor, pp. 111-112.

*"The Treadmill Song," pp. 125-126.

†"The Two Shadows," pp. 133-134.

¶"Infelix Senectus," pp. 161-162.

¶"The Flies," pp. 162-163.

¶"The Graduate's Song," p. 222.

Note: All of the above published anonymously.

¶Uncollected. *Poems, 1836. †*The Harbinger*, 1833.

Noted as though published by *New-England Galaxy*, Boston, Jan. 14, 1831. No record of copyright deposit found, Oct. 1830–Feb. 1831.

AAS H

8720. "THE BALLAD OF THE OYSTER-MAN"

First published in *The Amateur* (Boston), July 17, 1830. The poem achieved popularity and appeared in several separate forms, under varying titles, both as sheet music and in handbill form. The following list is presented in what is believed to be correct sequence. It must be noted that other printings may exist and that one of these could have been issued prior to BAL's earliest located separate printing.

A

Love and Oysters Parody on Hero and Leander as Sung with the Greatest Applause by Mr. G. Dixon Written and Arranged to the Celebrated Air Partant pour la Syrie by R. Stevenson Esqr.

New York Firth & Hall 358 Pearl St. ⟨n.d., not after 1831⟩

Sheet music. The above at head of p. ⟨1⟩. Anonymous. No record of copyright deposit found. Reprinted and reissued with the publisher's later address: *1 Franklin Sqr.*

B

In: *The Harbinger*, Boston, 1833. See entry No. 8723.

C

OLD KING COLE, / AND THE / BALLAD OF THE OYSTER-MAN. /

⟨n.d., Boston, not before 1834⟩

Caption-title. Single leaf. 8½″ x 8³⁄₁₆″. Printed on recto only.

Dividing the two columns of text, set between rules, is: *Sold wholesale and retail, with a variety of other articles, by J. G. & H. HUNT, at N. E. Corner of Quincy Market, Boston.*

D

TALL YOUNG / OYSTER MAN, / AND THE YOUNG / MUTINEER. /

⟨n.d., Boston, Mass., and Middlebury, Vt., *ca.* 1832–1838⟩

Caption-title. Single leaf. 8¾″ x 7⅝″. Printed on recto only.

Dividing the two columns of text, set between rules, is: *Sold wholesale and retail, by L. DEMING, No. 61, Hanover St. Boston, and at MIDDLEBURY, Vt.*

E

The Tall Young Oysterman ... Words by B. ⟨*sic*⟩ Holmes Esqr ... Music ... by Mr. Shaw.

Philadelphia, George Willig 171 Chesnut St. ... 1842 ...

Sheet music. The above at head of p. ⟨1⟩. Deposited Feb. 12, 1842.

F

Affecting Ballad of the Oysterman ... ⟨Music⟩ by J. L. Hatton ...

Boston ... Oliver Ditson 115 Washington St. ... 1849 ...

Sheet music. Cover-title. Plate number 1667. Deposited Feb. 1, 1849.

Three states (printings?) noted. The sequence is tentative:

1: Price on front cover: *38 cts. nett.*

2: Price on front cover: *35 cts nett.*

3: Price on front cover: Numeral 4 within a seven pointed star; indicating, 40¢.

Note

The following printings were issued without clue to time of publication. Both were issued *ca.* 1830–1840; either or both may have preceded the printings described above.

G

THE TALL YOUNG / OYSTERMAN / ⟨rule⟩ / ⟨text⟩ / A variety of popular songs, for sale wholesale and retail at / No. 42, North Main-street Providence, nearly / opposite the Museum. / ⟨n.d.⟩

Single leaf. 9³⁄₁₆″ x 6″. Printed on recto only.

H

THE TALL YOUNG / OYSTERMAN. / ⟨ornament⟩ / ⟨text⟩ / ⟨n.p., n.d.⟩

Single leaf. 10⅞″ x 7⅝″. Printed on recto only.

B (D,G) BA (F, No. 2) H (F, Nos. 1, 3; H) LC
(E; F, No. 1, being a deposit copy) PDH (A)
UV (C)

8721. Flora's Interpreter: Or, the American
Book of Flowers and Sentiments. ⟨Edited⟩ by
Mrs. S. J. Hale . . .

Boston: Marsh, Capen and Lyon. 1832.

*"Sentiment," p. 127. *Yes, dear departed cher-
ished days . . .*

¶"Sentiment," pp. 133-134. *Nor yet too brightly
strive to blaze . . .*

¶"Sentiment," p. 144. *Alas, that in our earliest
blush . . .*

†"Sentiment," p. 180. *What is a poet's love . . .*
Anonymous.

†"Sentiment," p. 181. *The bright black eye,
the melting blue . . .*

Poems, London, 1846; Boston, 1849. ¶Uncol-
lected. †*The Harbinger*, 1833.

For comment see entry No. 6792.

8722. The Token and Atlantic Souvenir. A
Christmas and New Year's Present. Edited by
S. G. Goodrich.

Boston. Published by Gray and Bowen.
MDCCCXXXIII.

"A Portrait," p. ⟨337⟩. Begins: *A still, sweet,
placid moonlight face . . .* Not the same as "To
a Certain Portrait."

"The Wasp and the Hornet," p. ⟨309⟩.

"The Philosopher to His Love," pp. ⟨310⟩-311.

The above collected in *Poems*, 1836.

For comment see entry No. 6126.

8723. THE HARBINGER; A MAY-GIFT.

BOSTON: CARTER, HENDEE AND CO. M DCCC
XXXIII.

Anonymous.

"Part II," pp. ⟨31⟩-61, 17 poems, by Holmes.

For comment see entry No. 977.

8724. The Mariner's Library or Voyager's Companion . . .

Boston: Lilly, Wait, Colman and Holden.
1833.

Cloth, printed paper label on spine.

"Old Ironsides," p. 425. Collected in *Poems*,
1836.

Two states (printings?) noted:

1: Copyright notice pasted to reverse of title-
leaf; and, printed on p. ⟨iii⟩.

2: Copyright notice printed on reverse of title-
leaf. P. ⟨iii⟩ blank.

Title-page deposited Jan. 1, 1833.

H (2) UV (1)

8725. . . . The Yankee, or Farmer's Almanac for
the Year . . . 1836 . . . by Thomas Spofford . . .

Boston: Published at Stationers' Hall, 82
State-st., by Lemuel Gulliver . . .

Printed wrapper. At head of title: Vol. 3. No.
4.] An Astronomical Diary for 1836. [Whole No.
20. Unpaged.

Reprint save for "The Comet." Collected in
Poems, 1836.

NYPL

8726. The Laurel: A Gift for All Seasons. Being
a Collection of Poems. By American Authors.

Boston: Edward R. Broaders. 1836.

Reprint save for the following; all collected in
Poems, 1836.

"To a Blank Sheet of Paper," pp. 23-25.

"The Last Prophecy of Cassandra," pp. 53-55.

"To My Companions," pp. 95-97.

"The Star and the Lily," pp. 139-141.

For comment see entry No. 984.

8727. The Token and Atlantic Souvenir A
Christmas and New Year's Present Edited by
S. G. Goodrich.

Boston. Published by Charles Bowen.
MDCCCXXXVII. ⟨*i.e.,* Oct. 1836⟩

"The Claudian Aqueduct," pp. ⟨337⟩-338. Collected in *Poems*, 1836 (Nov.), as "The Roman
Aqueduct."

For comment see entry No. 7580.

8728. Library of Practical Medicine. Published
by Order of the Massachusetts Medical Society
for the Use of Its Fellows. Volume VII. Containing Boylston Prize Dissertations for 1836,
by Oliver W. Holmes . . . ⟨and Others⟩

Boston: Printed by Perkins & Marvin. 1836.

"Dissertation," pp. ⟨191⟩-286. Collected in entry No. 8732.

BPL H LC Y

8729. POEMS . . .

> BOSTON: OTIS, BROADERS, AND COMPANY. M DCCC XXXVI.

Also issued with the imprint: BOSTON: OTIS, BROADERS, AND COMPANY. NEW YORK: GEORGE DEARBORN AND COMPANY. M DCCC XXXVI.

⟨i⟩-⟨xvi⟩, ⟨1⟩-163; printer's imprint, p. ⟨164⟩. 7⅞″ x 4¾″.

⟨a⟩⁶, b², 1-13⁶, 14⁴.

Issued in S-like cloth, embossed in the following patterns. Precedence, if any, not known. The designations are for identification only. Flyleaves. Printed paper label on spine.

Cloth A

Black; brown. Embossed with a floral pattern. The flowers measure about ⅛″ in diameter.

Cloth B

Brown; green. Embossed with a floral pattern. The flowers measure about ¼″ in diameter.

Cloth C

Black; brown; green; red-brown. Embossed with a zigzag pattern.

Copy in H inscribed by early owner Nov. 12, 1836. CAW copy inscribed Nov. 15, 1836. Deposited Nov. 23, 1836. BA copy received Nov. 29, 1836. Noted by K Dec. 1836.

AAS H NYPL

The Token and Atlantic Souvenir . . .

> Boston . . . MDCCCXXXVII. ⟨*i.e.*, Oct. 1836⟩

See entry No. 8727.

8730. The Boston Book. Being Specimens of Metropolitan Literature. Edited by B. B. Thatcher.

> Boston: Light & Stearns, 1 Cornhill. 1837 ⟨*i.e.*, 1836?⟩

Reprint with the possible exception of "Our Yankee Girls," pp. ⟨117⟩-118; also in (*reprinted from?*) *Poems*, 1836 (Nov.).

Title-page deposited Oct. 20, 1836. No record of deposit of book found in the records of 1836–1837. Listed NAR April, 1837.

BA H

8731. The Token and Atlantic Souvenir, a Christmas and New Year's Present. Edited by S. G. Goodrich.

> Boston: American Stationers' Company, M DCCC XXXVIII.

"The Only Daughter," pp. ⟨33⟩-36. Collected in *Poems*, London, 1846; and, entry No. 8753.

For comment see entry No. 6816.

8732. BOYLSTON PRIZE DISSERTATIONS FOR THE YEARS 1836 AND 1837 . . .

> BOSTON: CHARLES C. LITTLE AND JAMES BROWN. M.DCCC.XXXVIII.

For earlier publication of the 1836 dissertation see entry No. 8728.

⟨i⟩-⟨xvi⟩, ⟨1⟩-371. Folded map inserted. 9¼″ x 5¹¹⁄₁₆″.

⟨a⟩-b⁴, 1-46⁴, 47².

Issued in several types of cloth. Precedence, if any, not known. The designations are for identification only. Flyleaves.

Cloth A

Blue muslin embossed with a coral-branch pattern.

Cloth B

C-like cloth: black. Embossed with a curly maze pattern.

Cloth C

C-like cloth: green. Embossed with a zigzag pattern.

Cloth D

S-like cloth: purple. Embossed with a zigzag pattern.

Cloth E

S-like cloth: purple. Embossed with an oak leaf pattern.

Cloth F

S-like cloth: tan. Embossed with a pattern of wavy ribs producing the effect of wood grain.

Cloth G

T cloth: green; purple.

BA copy received from the author March 8, 1838. Listed NYR April, 1838.

AAS H Y

8733. Principles of the Theory and Practice of Medicine. By Marshall Hall . . . First American Edition. Revised and Much Enlarged, by Jacob Bigelow . . . and Oliver Wendell Holmes . . .

> Boston: Charles C. Little and James Brown. MDCCCXXXIX.

Leather.

Title deposited Sept. 12, 1839. Listed NAR Jan. 1840.

H　Y

8734. The Boston Book. Being Specimens of Metropolitan Literature.

Boston: George W. Light, 1 Cornhill. 1841.

Reprint save for "The Steamboat," pp. ⟨25⟩-27. Collected in *Poems,* London, 1846; Boston, 1849.

For comment see entry No. 631.

8735. "THE STARS THEIR EARLY VIGILS KEEP"

Written by Holmes and sung by him at a dinner in honor of Charles Dickens, Boston, Feb. 1, 1842. Collected in *Poems,* London, 1846; Boston, 1849.

Two principal editions of the song have been noted. BAL has been unable to establish a sequence although Currier-Tilton express a definite preference for the Oakes edition.

The Oakes edition was published Feb. 9, 1842, according to a notice in the *Daily Evening Transcript,* Boston, Feb. 9, 1842. An unspecified edition was noted as *new* in the *Boston Morning Post,* Feb. 17, 1842.

The following designations are for identification only and are not intended to suggest a sequence.

A

The Stars Their Early Vigils Keep. Ballad Written and Sung by Dr. Oliver W. Holmes, at the Dinner Given in Boston to Charles Dickens . . . Feby. 1, 1842 . . . ⟨Music⟩ by James C. Maeder.

Boston, Published by W. H. Oakes. New York: Firth & Hall . . .

The above at head of first page of text and music. Copyright notice dated 1842 in the name of W. H. Oakes. 2 leaves. Also noted, and presumed to be a reprint, with the New York imprint removed from the plate.

B

The Stars Their Early Vigils Keep, Song. As Sung at the Complimentary Dinner to Charles Dickens . . . Written by Dr. O. W. Holmes . . .

Boston. Published by Henry Prentiss 33 Court St. . . . 1842 . . .

Sheet music. Preceding at head of p. ⟨3⟩. Plate number 225.

Note

The poem appears also in:

Report of the Dinner Given to Charles Dickens,

in Boston, February 1, 1842. Reported by Thomas Gill and William English . . .

Boston: William Crosby and Company 1842.

Printed paper wrapper. The song is at p. 33. At p. 53 is a sentiment by Holmes. H copy received Feb. 21, 1842. Copies in H　NYPL　Y.

AAS (B)　H (A,B)

8736. HOMŒOPATHY, AND ITS KINDRED DELUSIONS; TWO LECTURES DELIVERED BEFORE THE BOSTON SOCIETY FOR THE DIFFUSION OF USEFUL KNOWLEDGE . . .

BOSTON: WILLIAM D. TICKNOR, M D CCC XLII.

⟨i⟩-⟨viii⟩, ⟨1⟩-72. 7⅖₁₆″ x 4⅝″.

⟨-⟩⁴, 1-6⁶.

Tan paper boards. Printed paper label on spine.

Advertised in *Boston Daily Advertiser,* April 4, 1842, as *this day published.*

H　NYPL

8737. [The Boston Society for Medical Improvement has recently been presented with the Library of its late respected associate, Dr. GEORGE B. DOANE. The following list of the works of which it consists has been prepared for the use of the members . . .

⟨n.p., n.d., Boston: Boston Society for Medical Improvement, 1842⟩

Single cut sheet folded to make four pages. The above at head of p. ⟨1⟩.

⟨1⟩-4. 9⅞″ x 7⅖₁₆″.

Compiled anonymously by Holmes. For comment see Currier-Tilton, pp. 31-32.

BML

8738. THE CONTAGIOUSNESS OF PUERPERAL FEVER. READ BEFORE THE BOSTON SOCIETY FOR MEDICAL IMPROVEMENT, AND PUBLISHED AT THE REQUEST OF THE SOCIETY.* . . .

⟨n.p., n.d., Boston, 1843? 1844?⟩

Note: The asterisk in the title refers to the following note: *From the New England Quarterly Journal of Medicine and Surgery.* ⟨April, 1843⟩

Caption-title. The above at head of p. ⟨1⟩.

⟨1⟩-28. 9⅖₁₆″ x 5⅝″.

1-3⁴, 4².

Printed buff paper wrapper.

First published in *New England Quarterly Journal of Medicine and Surgery*, April, 1843. "... the few copies I had struck off separately were soon lost sight of among the friends to whom they were sent ..."—Holmes, p. 6, *Puerperal Fever ...* , 1855. Listed WPLNL May, 1844, as an April, 1844, publication. Receipt of a copy noted by *New York Journal of Medicine*, May, 1844. For a revised edition see *Puerperal Fever ...* , 1855, below.

BA BPL H NYPL Y

8739. THE POSITION AND PROSPECTS OF THE MEDICAL STUDENT. AN ADDRESS DELIVERED BEFORE THE BOYLSTON MEDICAL SOCIETY OF HARVARD UNIVERSITY, JANUARY 12, 1844 ...

BOSTON: JOHN PUTNAM, PRINTER. 1844.

⟨1⟩-28. 8⅞″ x 5⅝″.

⟨1⟩-3⁴, 4².

Printed tan paper wrapper.

Issued in April, 1844, according to WPLNL May, 1844.

BA H NYPL

8740. The Berkshire Jubilee, Celebrated at Pittsfield, Mass. August 22 and 23, 1844.

Albany: Weare. C. Little. E. P. Little, Pittsfield. 1845.

Printed paper wrapper; and, cloth.

Address, pp. 161-163, including an untitled poem beginning *Come back to your Mother ...* Poem collected in *Poems*, London, 1846; Boston, 1849.

H Y

8741. The Memorial. Saturday Morning, December 27. ⟨1845⟩ ...

⟨Plymouth, Mass.: The Old Colony Memorial, 1845⟩

Caption-title. The above at head of first column.

Single sheet folded to make four pages. Pp. ⟨1⟩ and ⟨4⟩ blank. Text on pp. ⟨2-3⟩. Page: 25¾″ x 19″.

Untitled poem ("The Pilgrim's Vision"), p. ⟨2⟩. Collected in *Poems*, 1849. Also see entry No. 8744.

Note: Possibly not issued in this form; perhaps a stone proof of *The Old Colony Memorial*, a newspaper published in Plymouth, Mass. However, Currier-Tilton, p. 36, consider this an "offprint".

AAS

8742. The Bridal Wreath, a Wedding Souvenir. Edited by Percy Bryant.

Boston: William J. Reynolds, 1845.

Reprint save for "A Health," pp. 60-61. Collected in *Poems*, London, 1846, as "Song ... New York Mercantile Library Association"; *Poems*, Boston, 1849, as "Song for a Temperance Dinner ..."

BA Y

8743. Poems ...

London: O. Rich & Sons, 12, Red Lion Square. MDCCCXLVI.

Note: "Holmes himself said that this edition was printed, at Ticknor's suggestion, in London, and that the responsibility for it was the publisher's ⟨*i.e.*, Ticknor's⟩ ... The entry shows that Ticknor bought the printed sheets in England and had them bound in Boston, probably by Bradley."—*The Cost Books of Ticknor and Fields ...* , by Warren S. Tryon and William Charvat, N. Y., 1949, p. 82. That the binder of at least some copies was indeed Bradley is made clear by the presence of his ticket in some copies of the book. BAL suspects, but cannot prove, that some copies may have been bound in England; and, if this is true, then Rich shipped both bound volumes and unbound sheets to Ticknor; but of this there is no certain evidence. According to the publisher's records there were three styles of binding: paper boards; cloth gilt; cloth extra gilt. However, BAL has noted six styles or varieties of the binding; see below.

Reprint of *Poems*, Boston, 1836, with the following additions:

*"Departed Days." Previously in *Flora's Interpreter*, 1832, above.

*"Lines Recited at the Berkshire Festival." Previously in *The Berkshire Jubilee*, 1845, above.

†"The Only Daughter." Previously in *The Token*, 1838, above.

*"The Parting Word." Here first in book form.

*"Song, Written for the Anniversary Dinner of the New York Mercantile Library Association, Nov. 1842; to Which Ladies Were Invited." Previously in *The Bridal Wreath*, 1845, above.

*"Song, Written for the Dinner Given to Charles Dickens, by the Young Men of Boston, Feb. 1, 1842." Previously issued as sheet music; see above under 1842.

*"The Steamboat." Previously in *The Boston Book*, 1841.

*"Terpsichore." Here first in book form.

*"Lines Recited at the Cambridge Phi Beta Kappa Society's Dinner in 1844." Here first in book form.

*See *Poems . . . New and Enlarged Edition*, Boston (William D. Ticknor & Co.), 1849, for first collected American publication.

†See *Poems . . . New and Enlarged Edition*, Boston (Ticknor, Reed & Fields), 1849, for first collected American publication.

Six styles or varieties of the binding have been noted; see note above. The following designations are for identification only and are not intended to suggest a sequence:

Binding A

T cloth: brown.

Blindstamped wreath on the sides.

At foot of spine: LONDON

Edges plain.

No inserted catalog.

Locations: H

Binding B

T cloth: brown.

Blindstamped ovoid filigree on the sides.

At foot of spine: TICKNOR & CO.

Edges plain.

No inserted catalog.

Locations: AAS B Y

Binding C

T cloth: green; red.

Goldstamped wreath on the sides.

At foot of spine: *London*

Edges gilded.

No inserted catalog.

Locations: AAS

Binding D

T cloth: blue.

Goldstamped ovoid filigree on the sides.

At foot of spine: *London*

Edges gilded.

No inserted catalog.

Locations: CAW

Binding E

T cloth: brown.

Blindstamped wreath on the sides.

At foot of spine: *London*

Edges plain.

No inserted catalog.

Locations: LC

Binding F

Gray-brown paper boards, printed paper label on spine.

Edges plain.

Inserted in some copies is 4-page catalog of William D. Ticknor & Company, dated January 1, 1846.

Locations: BA BPL H Y

Reviewed NYM Dec. 13, 1845. EM (Jan. 1948) owned a copy (Ticknor spine imprint) inscribed by an early owner Dec. 25, 1845. Noted by K Dec. 1845. Listed WPLNL Dec. 1845; again, Jan. 1846. NYPL copy (Ticknor spine imprint) inscribed by an early owner Jan. 1, 1846.

8744. History of the Old Township of Dunstable . . . by Charles J. Fox.

Nashua: Charles T. Gill, Publisher. 1846.

Errata slip inserted at back.

"The Pilgrim's Vision," pp. 51-54. For another appearance of this poem see *The Memorial . . .* , 1845, above. The poem also appears in (reprinted) *Guide to Plymouth, and Recollections of the Pilgrims*, by William S. Russell, Boston, 1846; issued not before Oct. 1846; nor after Dec. 30, 1846. Collected in *Poems*, 1849.

H copy received July 6, 1846.

H

8745. URANIA: A RHYMED LESSON . . . PRONOUNCED BEFORE THE MERCANTILE LIBRARY ASSOCIATION, OCTOBER 14, 1846.

BOSTON: WILLIAM D. TICKNOR & COMPANY. MDCCCXLVI.

⟨1⟩-⟨32⟩. 9⅜" x 5⅛".

⟨1⟩-4⁴.

Printed blue paper wrapper. *Note:* Two copies have been noted in unprinted tan paper wrapper; status not known.

Deposited Oct. 30, 1846. Listed as a November publication WPLNL Dec. 1846; ALB Dec. 1846. Reviewed Ath Feb. 20, 1847.

H LC NYPL

8746. AN INTRODUCTORY LECTURE, DE-
LIVERED AT THE MASSACHUSETTS
MEDICAL COLLEGE, NOVEMBER 3,
1847 . . .

BOSTON: WILLIAM D. TICKNOR & COMPANY, COR-
NER OF WASHINGTON AND SCHOOL STREETS.
M DCCC XLVII.

⟨1⟩-38, blank leaf. 8¹⁵⁄₁₆″ x 5¹¹⁄₁₆″.

⟨1⟩-5⁴.

Printed peach paper wrapper.

Three states of the wrapper have been noted;
the order is presumed correct:

1: With the erroneous date, *November 13, 1847*,
on the front; advertisements on the back.

2 (3?): With the correct date on the front,
November 3, 1847; advertisements on the back.

3 (2?): With the correct date on the front,
November 3, 1847; back of wrapper blank.

Deposited Nov. 29, 1847. BA copy (wrapper 2) received Dec. 1, 1847.

AAS (2, 3)   BA (2)   BPL (2)   CAW (1)   H (2)   LC
(2)

8747. A Descriptive Catalogue of the Anatomical Museum of the Boston Society for Medical
Improvement. By J.B.S. Jackson . . .

Boston: William D. Ticknor and Company.
1847.

Notes by Holmes, pp. 4, 113, 185-186.

H

8748. Some Account of the Letheon; or, Who
Was the Discoverer? By Edward Warren. Second Edition.

Boston: Dutton and Wentworth, Printers, No.
37, Congress Street. 1847.

Cover-title. Printed paper wrapper.

Letter, Boston, Nov. 21, 1846, p. 79.

Note: In spite of the statement *Second Edition*
this is, in fact, a third edition. The first and
second editions do not contain this notable
Holmes letter.

Y

8749. Report of the Committee on Medical Literature. [Extracted from the Transactions of
the Am. Med. Ass., Vol. I.]

⟨n.p., n.d., Philadelphia, 1848.⟩

Caption-title. The above at head of p. ⟨1⟩.
Errata slip, p. ⟨1⟩. Unprinted brown paper
wrapper.

Signed at end by Holmes and others.

BPL   H

8750. Poems . . . New and Enlarged Edition.

Boston: William D. Ticknor & Company.
M DCCC XLIX.

Not to be confused with *Poems . . . New and Enlarged Edition,* Boston: Ticknor, Reed & Fields,
M DCCC XLIX; see entry No. 8753.

Note: All examined copies have the error PERP-
SICHORE for TERPSICHORE in the running head,
p. 187.

"From a Letter of the Author to the Publishers,"
pp. ⟨v⟩-vi.

Reprint save for the following poems. Unless
otherwise stated each is here in its earliest located book appearance.

"Departed Days." Previously in Nos. 8721, 8743.

"Extracts from a Medical Poem" comprising the
following three parts:

"The Stability of Science." Previously in No.
8739.

"A Portrait." *Simple in youth, but not austere
in age . . .*

"A Sentiment." *. . . life is but a song . . .*

"Lines Recited at the Berkshire Festival." Previously in Nos. 8740, 8743.

"A Modest Request."

"Nux Postcœnatica."

"On Lending a Punch-Bowl."

"The Parting Word." Previously in No. 8743.

"The Pilgrim's Vision." Previously in Nos. 8741,
8744.

"A Sentiment." *The pledge of friendship . . .*

"Song for a Temperance Dinner . . . ." Previously in Nos. 8742, 8743.

"A Song of Other Days."

"Song, Written for the Dinner Given to Charles
Dickens . . . ." See entry No. 8735.

"The Steamboat." Previously in Nos. 8734,
8743.

"The Stethoscope Song."

"Terpsichore." Previously in No. 8743.

"Verses for After-Dinner. P.B.K. Society, 1844."
Previously in No. 8743.

Binding

According to an advertisement in LW, Nov. 18,
1848, the book was available in three styles of
cloth: *cloth; cloth with gilt edges; cloth with gilt*

sides and gilt edges. BAL has seen the book in the following styles; presumably issued simultaneously. The designations are for identification only.

Binding A

Tan-gray paper boards, printed paper label on spine. Inserted at front: Publisher's catalog, pp. ⟨1⟩-4, dated *January 1, 1849.* Edges plain. The late Carroll A. Wilson owned a copy in this style with the error POMES for POEMS on the label. For a comment see BAL Vol. 1, p. xxxiv.

Cloth

T cloth: brown. Sides wholly blindstamped. Spine lettered in gold with an arrangement of blindstamped rules. Noted with inserted publisher's catalog, pp. ⟨1⟩-4, dated *May 1, 1848.* Edges plain.

Cloth, Gilt Edges

Not located by BAL. Currier-Tilton, p. 42, describe this format as with sides stamped in gold and in blind.

Cloth, Gilt Extra

T cloth: blue; purple; striped black and blue; striped black and white. Sides and spine highly decorated in gold; no blind stamping. All edges gilded.

Noted for Nov. 10, 1848, LW Oct. 28, 1848. NYPL copy inscribed by early owner Nov. 11, 1848. BA copy received from Holmes Nov. 14, 1848. Advertised LW Nov. 18, 1848. Listed LW Nov. 25, 1848. Reviewed LW Nov. 25, 1848. Listed PC as a Chapman importation July 16, 1849.

AAS   BPL   NYPL   Y

8751. American Medical Association. Annual Meeting, Boston, Tuesday, May 1, 1849.

Boston, 1849.

Not seen. Not located. Entry from Currier-Tilton, p. 425.

Leaflet, signed by Holmes and six others.

Although Currier-Tilton locate this in The Boston Medical Library that institution (Nov. 1960) reported inability to find the publication in its collections.

8752. A SCINTILLA. THE TASK . . .

⟨n.p., n.d., June 20, 1849⟩

Anonymous.

Two states (printings?) noted. No sequence has been established and the following designations are for identification only:

A

Blue-gray laid paper watermarked with a Britannia device. Note that since we are here dealing with a cut sheet not all the copies have the full watermark; some have but a portion present. 7$^{15}\!/_{16}$″ x 6$^{5}\!/_{16}$″. Printed on recto only.

B

Blue-gray wove paper. Unwatermarked. 7$^{13}\!/_{16}$″ x 4$^{15}\!/_{16}$″. Printed on recto only.

Also appears in *Addresses at the Inauguration of Jared Sparks . . . As President of Harvard College, Wednesday, June 20, 1849,* Cambridge, 1849.

AAS (B)   B (A)   BPL (A)   H (A, B)

8753. Poems . . . New and Enlarged Edition.

Boston: Ticknor, Reed & Fields. M DCCC XLIX.

Not to be confused with *Poems . . . New and Enlarged Edition,* Boston: William D. Ticknor & Company, M DCCC XLIX; see entry No. 8750.

Reprint save for:

"The Author to the Publishers," January 13th, 1849, pp. ⟨v⟩-vi. Not same as the prefatory note in the *Boston: William D. Ticknor & Company* edition.

*"The Island Hunting Song"

*"Lexington"

"The Only Daughter." Previously in *The Token,* 1838, above; and, *Poems,* London, 1846.

*"Questions and Answers"

*"A Song for the Centennial Celebration of Harvard College, 1836"

Earliest located book appearance.

Two printings noted:

1

Imprint of George A. Curtis on the copyright page.

P. ⟨241⟩: *Notes. / This Poem Was Delivered* . . .

2

Imprints of George A. Curtis; and, Thurston, Torry & Co., on the copyright page.

P. ⟨241⟩: *Notes. / ⟨rule⟩ / Note 1* . . .

Binding

Issued in several styles of binding. It is probable that first printings occur also in bindings other than those noted by BAL. The designations are for identification only and no sequence is here suggested:

Binding A

Drab paper boards. Printed paper label on spine. Inserted publisher's catalog, pp. ⟨1⟩-4, dated *January 1, 1849*. Noted on both first and second printings.

Binding B

T cloth: brown. Sides wholly blindstamped. Inserted publisher's catalog, pp. ⟨1⟩-4, dated *January 1, 1849*. Noted on both first and second printings.

Binding C

A cloth: blue; brown-black. Stamped in gold only. Edges gilded. No catalog. Noted on second printing sheets.

Binding D

A cloth: slate. Sides stamped in gold and blind. Edges gilded. No catalog. Noted on second printing sheets.

Listed (as a Chapman importation) PC Oct. 1, 1849. Advertised as *just ready* LW Oct. 6, 1849. Delf importation advertised PC April 15, 1851. Listed PC April 15, 1851; Ath April 19, 1851; LG April 19, 1851. Advertised as an American book by Delf & Trübner Ath April 27, 1852.

H (1, 2)   AAS (2)   Y (2)

8754. The Boston Book. Being Specimens of Metropolitan Literature.

Boston: Ticknor, Reed, and Fields. MDCCCL.

Reprint save for "The Morning Visit," pp. ⟨89⟩-92. Collected in *Before the Curfew*, 1888.

For comment see entry No. 5929.

8755. Practical Views on Medical Education. Submitted to the Members of the American Medical Association, by the Medical Faculty of Harvard University.

Boston: David Clapp, Printer 184 Washington Street. Medical and Surgical Journal Office. 1850.

Cover-title. Printed self-wrapper.

Signed by Holmes and others. *Note:* Currier-Tilton, pp. 451-452, suggest that this publication was the product of Dr. Henry Jacob Bigelow.

H

8756. A POEM ... DELIVERED AT THE DEDICATION OF THE PITTSFIELD CEMETERY, SEPTEMBER 9, 1850.

⟨n.p., n.d., Pittsfield, Mass.: Axtel, Bull & Marsh, Printers, 1850⟩

⟨1⟩-8. 9¼″ x 5¾″.

⟨-⟩⁴.

Unprinted drab paper wrapper.

Offprint from *An Address by Rev. Henry Neill . . .*, 1850; see below.

Note: The poem also appears in the following publications. Currier-Tilton, pp. 49-51, present evidence favoring the following sequence:

A

Memorials for the Dead. An Address by Rev. Henry Neill, and a Poem by Oliver Wendell Holmes, Delivered at the Dedication of the Pittsfield Rural Cemetery, September 9, 1850 . . .

Pittsfield: Axtel, Bull & Marsh Printers. 1850.

Printed paper wrapper.

B

An Address by Rev. Henry Neill, and a Poem by Oliver Wendell Holmes, Delivered at the Dedication of the Pittsfield (Rural) Cemetery, September 9th, 1850 . . .

Pittsfield, Mass: Axtel, Bull and Marsh Printers. 1850.

Printed paper wrapper; and, cloth.

A copy in LC has p. 56 mispaged 30; status not determined.

Collected in *Poetical Works*, London, 1852; *Songs in Many Keys*, Boston, 1862.

H (separate; B)   MHS (separate)   Y (A)

8757. ASTRÆA: THE BALANCE OF ILLUSIONS. A POEM DELIVERED BEFORE THE PHI BETA KAPPA SOCIETY OF YALE COLLEGE, AUGUST 14, 1850 . . .

BOSTON: TICKNOR, REED, AND FIELDS. MDCCCL.

⟨1⟩-39. 7¼″ x 4⅝″.

⟨1⟩-2⁸, 3⁴.

According to *The Cost Books of Ticknor & Fields . . .*, by Warren S. Tryon and William Charvat, N. Y., 1949, p. 170, there were two printings of this publication; the first (Sept. 1850) of 2500 copies; the second (Oct. 1850) of 2000 copies. It is almost certain that the sequence is as here presented. Slight variations of spacing are present on the title-page, the copyright page, and elsewhere. The following features are sufficient for identification:

First Printing, State A (B?)

Ampersand in the printer's imprint on the copyright page is set somewhat above the line.

Signature mark 3 (p. 33) is set under the *en* in the word *fragment*.

First Printing, State B (A?)

Ampersand in the printer's imprint on the copyright page is set somewhat above the line.

Signature mark 3 (p. 33) is set under the *ag* in the word *fragment*.

Second Printing, State A (B?)

The ampersand in the printer's imprint on the copyright page is properly set.

Signature mark 3 (p. 33) is set under the *r* in *fragment*.

Second Printing, State B (A?)

The ampersand in the printer's imprint on the copyright page is properly set.

Signature mark 3 (p. 33) is set under the *gm* in *fragment*.

Binding

Noted in several styles of binding. Undoubtedly the earliest binding is the one here designated *Binding A*. The sequence of the later bindings is tentative.

Binding A

Printed glazed cream-yellow paper boards. Yellow end papers. Flyleaves. Inserted at the front of some copies is a publisher's list, pp. <1>-4, dated *October, 1850.* Noted on *First Printing, A, B.*

Binding B

A cloth: brown, purple. Front lettered in gold: ASTRAEA Sides stamped in blind with a rococo cartouche having an oval center. Noted on *First Printing, B; Second Printing, A.*

Binding C

T cloth: brown. Sides blindstamped with a rules frame, a floret at each inner corner, a large filigree ornament at the center. Spine lettered in gold, reading up: *Astraea;* the lettering stamped from an Old English face. Noted on *Second Printing, A.*

Binding D

C cloth: green; terra-cotta. Sides blindstamped with a rules frame, a floret at each inner corner, a large filigree ornament at the center. Spine lettered in gold, reading down: ASTRAEA. Noted on *Second Printing, A, B.* (Perhaps not before *ca. 1875?*)

Deposited Oct. 5, 1850. BA copy (A sheets) received from Holmes Oct. 28, 1850. Listed LW Nov. 2, 1850, under the title *Illusions.*

AAS (1st printing A, binding A; 2nd printing A, binding B) H (1st printing A, binding A; 1st printing B, binding A; 2nd printing A, binding C; 2nd printing A, binding D) LC (1st printing B, binding B) MHS (2nd printing A, binding B) NYPL (1st printing A, binding A; 1st printing B, binding A; 2nd printing B, binding D) Y (1st printing B, binding A)

8758. THE BENEFACTORS OF THE MEDICAL SCHOOL OF HARVARD UNIVERSITY; WITH A BIOGRAPHICAL SKETCH OF THE LATE DR. GEORGE PARKMAN. AN INTRODUCTORY LECTURE, DELIVERED AT THE MASSACHUSETTS MEDICAL COLLEGE, NOVEMBER 7, 1850

. . .

BOSTON: TICKNOR, REED, AND FIELDS. MDCCCL.

<1>-37, blank leaf. 9 7/16" x 5¾" full.

<1>-5⁴.

Printed tan paper wrapper.

A copy was received by BA Dec. 18, 1850. Noted NAR Jan. 1851.

H   LC   NYPL

8759. Trial of Prof. Webster

Accounts of this trial, containing Holmes's testimony, varying in both accuracy and fullness, were issued by several Boston publishers. *Of those seen* by BAL the two following have claim to priority:

A

Trial of Professor John W. Webster, for the Murder of Dr. George Parkman in the Medical College, November 23, 1849 ... Stenographic Report, Carefully Revised and Corrected. Splendidly Illustrated.

John A. French, Boston Herald Steam Press, 1850.

Printed paper wrapper.

Holmes's testimony, pp. 27, 60.

"Just published and ready for delivery ... We shall this morning publish ..."—*Boston Herald,* April 1, 1850.

H   Y

B

The Parkman Murder. Trial of Prof. John W. Webster. For the Murder of Dr. George Parkman, November 23, 1849 ... with Numerous Accurate Illustrations.

Boston: Printed at the Daily Mail Office, 14 & 16 State Street. <n.d., 1850>

Cover-title. Printed self-wrapper.

Holmes's testimony, pp. 16, 42.

"... will be ready from the *Mail* office this day ... 50,000 copies ... will be ready for delivery this day at 12 o'clock ..."—*Boston Daily Mail,* April 1, 1850.

H

Other Editions

Fetridge & Co., Boston. *Not seen.*

Noted as though published, *Boston Daily Evening Transcript,* April 1, 1850. Noted as "this day published," *ibid.,* April 1 and 2, 1850.

Redding & Co., Boston. *Not seen.*

"Will be issued ... immediately upon the closing up of the trial."—*Boston Daily Evening Transcript,* March 31, April 1, 1850. Noted as though published, *ibid.,* April 1, 1850.

Stimson's News Letter Sheet Extra. *Not seen.*

"The publisher of the *News Letter Sheet* will issue today upon a large sheet of folio post writing paper a condensed report of the trial of Dr. Webster; also in a quarto form and covers."—*Boston Daily Evening Transcript,* April 2, 1850. "Letter sheet report of the trial ... Persons wishing to mail to their friends a beautiful edition of the recent great Trial will find the whole matter ... ⟨including⟩ Sentence—condensed in *Stimson's News Letter Sheet Extra,* printed on a Double Sheet of fine Letter Paper ..."—*ibid.,* April 2, 1850.

Report of the Trial of Prof. John W. Webster, Indicted for the Murder of Dr. George Parkman ... Phonographic Report, by Dr. James W. Stone.

Boston: Phillips, Sampson & Company, 110 Washington Street. 1850.

Printed paper wrapper. The sense of the preface, and inclusion of a letter (pp. 312-314) dated April 3, 1850, indicate that this edition could not have preceded any of the above in time of publication.

All of the above appear to have been published prior to Webster's execution, Aug. 30, 1850. Editions containing an account of the execution obviously could not have been issued prior to entry Nos. 8759A,B.

8760. A SONG OF '29 ...

⟨n.p., Jan. 2, 1851⟩

Anonymous. Caption-title. Preceding at head of p. ⟨1⟩.

Single cut sheet folded to make 4 pages.

⟨1-3⟩. 7¼″ x 4¾″.

Collected in *The Poetical Works. Household Edition,* 1877. Also appears in entry No. 8766.

H

8761. Report of a Committee of the Massachusetts Medical Society on Homoeopathy. Adopted by the Counsellors, Oct. 2, 1850, and Ordered to be Printed ...

⟨Boston, n.d., 1851⟩

4 pp. Caption-title. The above at head of p. ⟨1⟩. Signed on p. 4 by Holmes and two others.

Offprint, with some rearrangement of the types, from *The Boston Medical and Surgical Journal,* March 5, 1851.

Note: The report also appears in *Reports of the Massachusetts Medical Society, and the Massachusetts Homoeopathic Medical Society;* broadside, printed in four columns, printed on recto only. This broadside was issued after April 25, 1851, the date of a meeting here reported of The Massachusetts Homoeopathic Medical Society. Copies in H and Y.

BA   H

8762. The Poetical Works ... First English Edition.

London: G. Routledge & Co., Farringdon Street. MDCCCLII.

Reprint save for:

"To an English Friend," pp. ⟨xv⟩-xvi; and "The Ploughman," pp. 283-285. Both collected in *Songs in Many Keys,* 1862.

Two printings noted:

1: Imprint of *Savill and Edwards* on verso of the title-leaf.

2: Imprint of *Stewart and Murray* on verso of the title-leaf.

Copies of the first printing noted only in cloth; copies of the second printing noted in both cloth; and, printed paper boards.

Advertised as *now ready* Ath May 29, 1852. Listed Ath June 5, 1852; LG June 5, 1852; PC June 16, 1852. A cheap edition in boards listed PC Dec. 5, 1853; presumably the same edition listed Ath Nov. 5, 1853.

AAS (1st)   B (2nd)   BPL (1st, 2nd)   H (1st)   LC (1st)

8763. RESPONSE . . . TO THE FOLLOWING TOAST, PROPOSED AT THE ENTERTAINMENT GIVEN TO THE AMERICAN MEDICAL ASSOCIATION, BY THE PHYSICIANS OF THE CITY OF NEW YORK, AT METROPOLITAN HALL, ON THE 5th OF MAY, 1853. TOAST.—"THE UNION OF SCIENCE AND LITERATURE—A HAPPY MARRIAGE, THE FRUITS OF WHICH ARE NOWHERE SEEN TO BETTER ADVANTAGE THAN IN OUR AMERICAN HOLMES . . .

PUBLISHED BY THE COMMITTEE OF ARRANGEMENTS AND RECEPTION OF THE AMERICAN MEDICAL ASSOCIATION. BAKER, GODWIN & CO., PRINTERS, 1 SPRUCE ST., N. Y. ⟨1853⟩

Caption-title.

Single cut sheet. 12½″ x 7¾″. Printed on recto only. Collected in *Songs in Many Keys,* 1862.

H   MHS   Y

8764. Remonstrance to the Legislature of the Faculty of the Massachusetts Medical College against the Petition of the Boylston Medical School for Power to Confer Medical Degrees.

Boston, March 6, 1854 . . .

Caption-title.

Single cut sheet. Wove blue paper. Printed on both sides. 9¹¹⁄₁₆″ x 7⅝″.

Signed at end by Holmes, Jacob Bigelow and J.B.S. Jackson, as a committee.

MHS

8765. THE NEW EDEN. READ BEFORE THE BERKSHIRE HORTICULTURAL SOCIETY, AT STOCKBRIDGE, SEPT. 13, 1854 . . .

⟨n.p., Pittsfield, 1854⟩

Cover-title.

Single cut sheet folded to four pages.

⟨1-4⟩. 7½″ x 4¹¹⁄₁₆″.

Collected in *Songs in Many Keys,* 1862.

H

8766. SONGS OF THE CLASS OF MDCCCXXIX. [PRINTED FOR THE USE OF THE CLASS ONLY.]

BOSTON:—PRENTISS AND SAWYER, PRINTERS, 1854.

⟨1⟩-⟨12⟩. 7⁷⁄₁₆″ x 4¹¹⁄₁₆″.

⟨-⟩⁶.

Printed cream-yellow paper wrapper lined with white paper.

Contains the following poems by Holmes:

"A Song of '29 . . . for the Annual Meeting, 1851," pp. ⟨3⟩-6. For prior separate publication see entry No. 8760.

"For the Class Meeting, Nov. 29, 1853. An Impromptu—Not Premeditated," p. ⟨9⟩. Collected in *The Poetical Works. Household Edition,* 1877.

"Questions and Answers," pp. ⟨10⟩-11. Reprint.

Also see entry No. 8785.

AAS   BPL   Y

8767. The Knickerbocker Gallery: A Testimonial to the Editor of the Knickerbocker Magazine from Its Contributors . . .

New-York: Samuel Hueston, 348 Broadway. MDCCCLV.

"A Vision of the Housatonic. Epilogue to a Lecture on Wordsworth," pp. ⟨23⟩-26. A somewhat shorter version collected in *Songs in Many Keys,* 1862.

For comment see entry No. 1033.

8768. Puerperal Fever, As a Private Pestilence . . .

Boston: Ticknor and Fields. M DCCC LV.

Printed paper wrapper; and, cloth.

Reprint of the first edition of 1843–1844 (entry No. 8738) with a new introduction, pp. ⟨5⟩-24.

Deposited Jan. 23, 1855.

BPL   H   NYPL

8769. ⟨Untitled poem:⟩ A TRIPLE HEALTH TO FRIENDSHIP, SCIENCE, ART . . .

MAY 1st, 1855.

Anonymous.

Single cut sheet folded to make four pages.

P. ⟨1⟩ as above; pp. ⟨2-4⟩ blank. 7⁵⁄₁₆″ x 4¾″.

Collected in *Songs in Many Keys,* 1862.

MHS

8770. ⟨"THE HEART'S OWN SECRET"⟩ PRIVATE COPY . . .

⟨n.p., n.d., 1855⟩

Anonymous. *The curtain rose; in thunders long and loud . . .*

Caption-title.

36 unpaged leaves as follows: 5 blank leaves; 31 leaves printed on recto only. 10⅛″ x 8½″.

⟨1-18⟩².

Unprinted tan paper wrapper.

Privately printed for the author's use in a reading at Tremont Temple, Boston, Nov. 15, 1855. Collected in *Songs in Many Keys,* 1862.

H

8771. Cyclopaedia of American Literature ... by Evert A. Duyckinck and George L. Duyckinck ...

New York: Charles Scribner. 1855.

2 Vols.

"Abiel Holmes," Vol. 1, pp. 512-513.

Paragraph on Charles Chauncy Emerson, Vol. 2, p. 366.

Title deposited Dec. 11, 1855.

AAS H Y

8772. The Seventy-Fourth Anniversary of the Birth-Day of Daniel Webster ... Revere House Boston, January 18, 1856.

Boston: Published at the Office of the Daily Courier. 1856 ...

Printed paper wrapper. Cover-title.

Untitled poem, *When life hath run its largest round,* pp. 49-51. Collected in *Songs in Many Keys,* 1862.

H Y

8773. Celebration of the 124th Anniversary of the Birth-Day of Washington, by the Mercantile Library Association.

⟨n.p., Boston: Watson's Press, 25 Doane Street⟩ February 22, 1856.

Cover-title.

Single cut sheet folded to make four pages. Issued as a program.

"Ode. Written for the Occasion ... ," pp. ⟨2-3⟩. Collected in *Songs in Many Keys,* 1862.

AAS B H

8774. Speeches of Drs. Thompson ... O.W. Holmes ... at the Annual Dinner of the Mass. Medical Society, Boston, May, 1856.

Boston: Traveller Printing House, 31 State Street. 1856.

Printed paper wrapper.

Speech, pp. 9-11.

AAS H Y

8775. Sir, The Medical School of Harvard University finds itself in a position of restricted usefulness ...

⟨n.p., n.d., July, 1856⟩

Single cut sheet folded to make 4 pp. Printed on pp. ⟨1⟩-3; p. ⟨4⟩ blank. Page: 9¾″ x 7⅝″.

An appeal for $50,000 in support of the Harvard Medical School. Signed by Holmes and others.

H

8776. ORATION DELIVERED BEFORE THE NEW ENGLAND SOCIETY, IN THE CITY OF NEW YORK ... AT THEIR SEMI-CENTENNIAL ANNIVERSARY, DECEMBER 22, 1855.

⟨n.p., n.d., New York: Wm. C. Bryant & Co., Printers, 1856⟩

⟨3⟩-46. 9⅛″ x 5¹³⁄₁₆″.

⟨-⟩¹, ⟨1⟩-2⁸, 3⁵.

Printed tan paper wrapper. Flyleaves.

Note: Made up of sheets extracted from *Semi-Centennial Celebration of the New England Society ... December, 1855. Oration: By Oliver Wendell Holmes ... ,* New York, 1856. Sig. 3 was originally in 8; as it occurs in the separate the final three leaves are excised.

H copy received Dec. 27, 1856.

BPL H LC Y

8777. HARVARD COLLEGE. FESTIVAL OF THE ASSOCIATION OF THE ALUMNI, JULY 16, 1857. THE PARTING SONG ...

⟨n.p., n.d., Cambridge, 1857⟩

Single leaf. 8¹⁄₁₆″ x 4¹¹⁄₁₆″. Printed on recto only.

Anonymous. Collected in *Songs in Many Keys,* 1862.

H

8778. ⟨MEETING OF THE ALUMNI OF HARVARD COLLEGE, 1857⟩

JULY 16, 1857.

A single cut sheet, 23½″ x 7⅛″. Printed on recto only. Eighteen four-line stanzas beginning *I thank you, Mr. President, you've kindly broke the ice ...*

Prepared for Holmes's use in reading at the alumni dinner, July 16, 1857. Collected in *Songs in Many Keys*, 1862.

Anonymous.

H   MHS

8779. Report of the Twenty-Fourth National Anti-Slavery Festival.

Boston: Printed for the Managers 1858.

Cover-title. Printed paper wrapper.

"The Chambered Nautilus," on inner back wrapper. Collected in *The Autocrat ...* , 1858.

H   NYPL   Y

8780. VALEDICTORY ADDRESS, DELIV-ERED TO THE MEDICAL GRADUATES OF HARVARD UNIVERSITY, AT THE ANNUAL COMMENCEMENT, WEDNES-DAY, MARCH 10, 1858 ...

BOSTON: DAVID CLAPP   184 WASHINGTON STREET. MEDICAL AND SURGICAL JOURNAL OFFICE. 1858.

⟨1⟩-15. 9⁵⁄₁₆″ x 5¾″.

⟨1⟩-2⁴.

Printed salmon paper wrapper.

H   NYPL   Y

8781. THE AUTOCRAT OF THE BREAK-FAST-TABLE ...

BOSTON: PHILLIPS, SAMPSON AND COMPANY. M DCCC LVIII.

Title-page in black and red. Anonymous. Also see entries 8912, 8970, 8979, 9093.

⟨i-ii⟩, ⟨i⟩-viii, ⟨1⟩-373, blank leaf. Vignette title-page and 8 plates inserted. 7⅛″ x 4⁹⁄₁₆″.

⟨-⟩⁵, ⟨1⟩-15¹², 16⁸. Leaf ⟨-⟩₃ inserted. *Also signed:* ⟨-⟩⁵, ⟨1⟩-2, 2*, 3-⟨4⟩, 4*, 5-⟨6⟩, 6*, 7-⟨8⟩, 8*, 9-⟨10⟩, 10*, 11-⟨12⟩, 12*, 13-⟨14⟩, 14*, 15-⟨16⟩⁸, 24⁴ ⟨sic⟩.

Two printings noted:

1

As above. Note presence of the period after the word COMPANY in the imprint.

2†

As above but with the following variations:

Period not present after the word COMPANY in the imprint.

Vignette title-page not present.

† BAL suspects that the so-called *Second Printing* may in fact represent two or more printings; possibly produced from two sets of plates.

Pp. ⟨375-376⟩ imprinted with advertisements.

Note: An intermediate has been noted; possibly the result of mixed sheets:

Period present after the word COMPANY in the imprint.

Vignette title-page not present.

Pp. ⟨375-376⟩ imprinted with advertisements.

Note: Also issued with the following multiple imprints. Sequence, if any, not known. The designations are for identification only.

Multiple Imprint A

BOSTON: PHILLIPS, SAMPSON AND COMPANY. CIN-CINNATI: RICKEY, MALLORY & CO. M DCCC LVIII.

Multiple Imprint B

BOSTON: PHILLIPS, SAMPSON AND COMPANY. LON-DON: SAMPSON LOW, SON, AND COMANY. M DCCC LVIII.

Multiple Imprint C

LONDON: SAMPSON LOW, SON, & CO., 47, LUDGATE HILL. BOSTON:—PHILLIPS, SAMPSON, & COMPANY. MDCCCLVIII.

See entry No. 8781A.

BINDING

The binding occurs in the following styles. The sequence has not been firmly established and the order is all but tentative.

Binding A

A cloth: green; purple; red. BD cloth: blue; brown; tan; green. Sides identically stamped in blind with an ornate frame having *curved inner corners*; and, a circular device at the center. Spine goldstamped: ⟨double rule⟩ / Autocrat / of the / Breakfast / Table / ⟨rule⟩ / HOLMES / ⟨3 fleur-de-lis, each within a ring⟩ / ⟨publisher's monogram within a ring⟩ / ⟨double rule⟩

Pale buff paper end papers imprinted with advertisements as follows:

Front:
    ⟨ii⟩: Works Of Permanent Value.
    ⟨iii⟩: Works Of Permanent Value.

Back:
    ⟨ii⟩: Poetry And The Drama.
    ⟨iii⟩: School Books.

Flyleaves.

Binding Aa

As above but with the following variation: The spine is decorated with four, not three, ringed fleur-de-lis and the publisher's ringed monogram.

Binding Ab

Same as *Binding A* but the end papers are of unprinted blue paper.

Binding Ac

Same as *Binding A* but the end papers are of unprinted yellow paper.

Binding Ad

Same as *Binding A* but the terminal end papers vary and are headed: MISCELLANEOUS.

Binding B

The blindstamped frame on the sides is squared, not curved, at the inner corners. Does not have at each corner of the frame an eight-petalled floret. Spine lettered in gold: Autocrat / of the / Breakfast / Table / ⟨rule⟩ / HOLMES / BOSTON Unprinted blue paper end papers.

Binding C

The blindstamped frame on the sides is squared, not curved, at the inner corners. Present at each corner of the frame is an eight-petalled floret in a ring. Spine lettered in gold: Autocrat / of the / Breakfast / Table / ⟨rule⟩ / HOLMES / BOSTON Unprinted blue paper end papers. *Note:* This frame has been seen on the 1858 and 1859 reprints.

Announced as *this day published* in *Boston Evening Transcript,* Nov. 12, 1858. Deposited Nov. 22, 1858. Issued during the period Nov. 15–Dec. 1, 1858, according to BM Dec. 1, 1858.

LARGE PAPER EDITION

See entry No. 9093.

Locations

First Printing, Binding A: H LC Y
First Printing, Binding Aa: H
First Printing, Binding Ab: H
First Printing, Binding Ac: Y
Intermediate sheets, Binding A: H
Second Printing, Binding Ad: H Y
Second Printing, Binding B: H
Second Printing, Binding C: LC Y

8781A. The Autocrat of the Breakfast-Table . . .

London: Sampson Low, Son, & Co., 47, Ludgate Hill. Boston:—Phillips, Sampson, & Company. MDCCCLVIII.

Sheets of the Boston printing prepared for distribution in Great Britain. By BAL definition a reprint. For first edition see entry No. 8781.

Advertised as *just received* Ath Dec. 11, 1858. Listed as an importation Ath Dec. 11, 1858; LG Dec. 11, 1858; PC Dec. 15, 1858. Advertised as *just received* PC Dec. 15, 1858.

H

Other British Editions

Edinburgh: Strahan. London: Hamilton, Adams.
Advertised for Nov. 24, 1858, Ath Nov. 20, 1858. A copy in the collection of Rev. Dr. Frederick Meek, Boston, inscribed by the publisher Nov. 24, 1858. Listed Ath Nov. 27, 1858; LG Nov. 27, 1858; Bkr Nov. 29, 1858. Advertised as *now ready* PC Dec. 1, 1858; LG Dec. 11, 1858. Listed PC Dec. 15, 1858. Reviewed LG Dec. 25, 1858; Ath Jan. 15, 1859.

Edinburgh ⟨Strahan?⟩. London: Sampson Low.
Listed Ath March 30, 1861; PC April 15, 1861.

London: Strahan; London: Sampson Low.
Popular Edition (in paper) listed PC Nov. 1, 1865. In cloth listed Ath Nov. 18, 1865; PC Dec. 8, 1865. Both listed (as November publications) Bkr Dec. 30, 1865.

London: Ward, Lock, & Tyler.
Listed PC Nov. 15, 1865. Another edition, with introduction by G. A. Sala, listed Bkr March 1, 1870.

London: Beeton.
Listed PC Jan. 17, 1866; Bkr Jan. 31, 1866.

London: Hotten.
Listed Bkr Dec. 12, 1867. Another edition, with introduction by G. A. Sala, listed PC Jan. 18, 1871.

London: Routledge.
Listed PC and Bkr March 2, 1868. Various reprints listed during the period 1871–1874.

London: Strahan.
Listed PC Dec. 17, 1870; Bkr Jan. 4, 1871.

London: Chatto & Windus.
Advertised Bkr Oct. 1874.

Edinburgh: Paterson. London: Simpkin.
Listed PC and Bkr July 1, 1883.

London: Scott.
Listed PC Sept. 16, 1889; Bkr Oct. 1889.

8782. The New American Cyclopaedia: A Popular Dictionary of General Knowledge. Edited by George Ripley and Charles A. Dana . . .

New York: D. Appleton and Company, 346 & 348 Broadway. London: 16 Little Britain. M.DCCC.LVIII. ⟨–M.DCCC.LXIII.⟩

"Charles Jackson," Vol. 9, pp. 688-689. The contribution embodies sketches of Charles, James and Patrick Jackson.

For comment see entry No. 3715.

8783. Celebration of the Hundredth Anniversary of the Birth of Robert Burns, by the Boston Burns Club. January 25th, 1859.

Boston: Printed by H. W. Dutton and Son, Transcript Building. 1859.

Printed paper wrapper; and, cloth.

Contains the following material by Holmes:

An introductory poem, *I have come with the rest . . .* , pp. 19-20. Otherwise unlocated.

Untitled poem, *The mountains glitter in the snow*, pp. 20-21. Collected in *Songs in Many Keys*, 1862.

Note: Both of the above poems were written for the Burns centennial of 1856 but are here first located.

Untitled poem, *His birthday—nay, we need not speak*, pp. 44-45. Collected in *Songs in Many Keys*, 1862, under the title, "His Birthday."

Issued after Feb. 2, 1859. *Boston Daily Evening Transcript*, Jan. 26, 1859, reported that an account of the meeting would be published "at an early day" but no further mention has been found.

H NYPL

8784. THE PROMISE . . .

⟨n.p., Boston, March 20, 1859⟩

Single cut sheet folded to four pages. Laid paper. 8″ x 5″. Text on p. ⟨1⟩, otherwise blank. Stationer's device embossed at upper left, p. ⟨1⟩.

Written for the fair in aid of the Channing Home for Sick and Destitute Women, Boston, March, 1859. Collected in *Songs in Many Keys*, 1862.

H

8785. Songs and Poems of the Class of Eighteen Hundred and Twenty-Nine. Second Edition . . .

Boston: Prentiss, Sawyer, & Company, Printers, 19 Water Street. 1859.

Note: In some copies folio *19* occurs as *9*. *Also:* Occurs with and without inserted portrait frontispiece of Holmes.

Reprint with the exception of:

"The Boys," pp. 29-31. Collected in *Songs in Many Keys*, 1862.

"A Poem. Written for the Class Meeting, November, 1856," pp. 20-21. Collected in *Songs in Many Keys*, 1862.

"Song. Written for the Class Meeting, January 10, 1856," pp. 17-19. Collected in *Poetical Works, Household Edition*, 1877.

Noted in a variety of bindings: Boards, leather shelfback, leather label on front cover; flexible blue TZ cloth; leather; flexible green A cloth.

Note: The stamping on the front cover of the cloth copies occurs in two styles; the following sequence is presumed correct:

A: SONGS & POEMS /

B: SONGS AND POEMS /

Holmes correspondence in H indicates that the book was issued during the month of March, 1859. Copies were reissued in 1861 with inserted supplement paged 47-50. For first edition see entry No. 8766.

AAS BPL H Y

8786. . . . The Dime Speaker: Being Gems of Oratory for the School, the Exhibition-Room, the Home Circle, and the Study . . . ⟨Selected⟩ by Louis Legrand, M.D.

New York: Irwin P. Beadle, Publisher, No. 137 William Street. ⟨1859⟩

"The Professor on Phrenology," pp. 48-51. Reprinted from *Atlantic Monthly*, Aug. 1859. Collected in *Professor at the Breakfast-Table*, 1860.

Also contains, pp. 56-57, "The Weather," credited to Holmes. Not by Holmes; see Currier-Tilton, p. 416.

For comment see entry No. 1523A.

8787. BOSTON COMMON. THREE PICTURES . . .

⟨Boston: F. H. Underwood, 1859⟩

Title at head of p. ⟨2⟩.

Single cut sheet folded to make 4 pp. Laid paper. Watermarked JOYNSON 1857 Page: 8¾″ x 7³⁄₁₆″. Pp. ⟨1⟩ and ⟨4⟩ blank.

Text in facsimile autograph. At upper left corner of p. ⟨1⟩: The embossed stamp of De la Rue & Co., London.

Collected in *Songs in Many Keys*, 1862.

CAW

8788. Gifts of Genius: A Miscellany of Prose and Poetry, by American Authors . . .

New York: Printed for C. A. Davenport. ⟨1859⟩

"The Beni-Israel," pp. 260-263. A revised version collected in *Songs of Many Seasons*, 1875, under the title, "At the Pantomime."

Noted in BM Dec. 15, 1859.

H NYPL

8789. The Illustrated Pilgrim Almanac 1860 . . .

Hammatt Billings and George Coolidge, 289 Washington Street, Boston, Mass. Cambridge, Mass.: H. O. Houghton & Co., Printers. ⟨1859⟩

Printed paper wrapper. *Note:* Issued with varying imprints as required by the several distributors.

"Robinson of Leyden," p. 20. Collected in (reprinted from?) *The Professor at the Breakfast-Table,* 1860.

Precise publication date not known. A title-page for the *Almanac* was deposited for copyright May 16, 1859; further copyright information wanting. "Robinson of Leyden" was first published in *Atlantic Monthly,* July, 1859. At pp. 49-50 of the *Almanac* is an account of the "Laying of the Corner-Stone of the National Monument to the Forefathers," whence the following: *Since the preceding part of the Almanac was put to press, the corner-stone of the National Monument to the Forefathers has been laid. This event took place at Plymouth on the 2d of August, 1859 . . .* The same source (p. 50) reports that a copy of the *Almanac* was deposited within the corner stone; presumably an incomplete copy. On p. ⟨53⟩ of the *Almanac* is a letter dated Aug. 8, 1859. Publication, therefore, could not have been prior to Aug. 8, 1859.

H

8790. To the Literature of the Language What a Dictionary of Words is to the Language Itself. Allibone's Dictionary of Authors . . .

Childs & Peterson, 602 Arch Street, Philadelphia. ⟨1859⟩

Cover-title. Printed self-wrapper.

Letter, Feb. 7, 1859, p. 5.

NYPL

8791. THE PROFESSOR AT THE BREAKFAST-TABLE; WITH THE STORY OF IRIS . . .

BOSTON: TICKNOR AND FIELDS. M DCCC LX.

Trade Edition

⟨i-iv⟩, ⟨1⟩-410, blank leaf. 7⁹⁄₁₆″ full x 4⅞″. Sheets bulk ⅞″.

⟨-⟩², 1-17¹², 18².

BD cloth: brown. Brown-coated on white end papers. Flyleaves.

Note: Also issued with the imprint: BOSTON: TICKNOR AND FIELDS. PHILADELPHIA: J. B. LIPPINCOTT AND COMPANY. M DCCC LX.

Large Paper Edition

Leaf: 8⅝″ scant x 5¹¹⁄₁₆″. Sheets bulk 1¹⁄₁₆″.

BD cloth: brown. Covers bevelled. Brown-coated on white end papers. Flyleaves. Edges gilded.

Note: Some copies of the large paper edition were trimmed and issued as ordinary copies of the trade edition. These may be distinguished by the bulk of the sheets: 1¹⁄₁₆″ *vs.* the ⅞″ of the trade edition. A copy thus in CAW.

Also note: A copy of the trade edition has been seen in white linen, blue leather label on spine lettered in gold: ⟨*double rule*⟩ / THE / PROFESSOR / AT THE / BREAKFAST-TABLE / ⟨*rule*⟩ / HOLMES / ⟨*double rule*⟩ Boston-Philadelphia imprint. Status not known. Possibly a publisher's binding; perhaps a set of folded sheets put into binding by the buyer. Copies of Holmes's *Ralph Waldo Emerson,* 1885, have also been seen in a like binding.

Advertised as "rapidly passing through the press and will be ready in season for the Holiday Sales"—BM Dec. 1, 1859. Large paper edition deposited Dec. 10, 1859 (publisher's records). Trade edition deposited Dec. 20, 1859 (publisher's records). Deposited (format unknown) Dec. 21, 1859 (Copyright Office records). Trade edition noted as *ready to-day* by *Boston Evening Transcript,* Dec. 22, 1859. Trade edition (5000 copies) published Dec. 1859 (publisher's records). Trade edition listed BM Jan. 2, 1860. Large paper edition (500 copies) published Jan. 1860 (publisher's records). Listed PC June 1, 1860; again (with corrected price) June 15, 1860. Reviewed Ath June 30, 1860.

H (trade, large paper)   HSM (variant binding)

8792. The Life of John Collins Warren . . . by Edward Warren . . .

Boston: Ticknor and Fields. M.DCCC.LX.

2 Vols. "Dr. Holmes's Remarks," Vol. 2, pp. 296-302.

Deposited Jan. 3, 1860.

H

8793. Proceedings of the American Academy of Arts and Sciences. Vol. IV. From May, 1857, to May, 1860 . . .

Boston and Cambridge: Welch, Bigelow, and Company. 1860.

Contribution on reflex vision, pp. 373-375.

Cloth?

H NYPL

8794. CURRENTS AND COUNTER-CUR-
RENTS IN MEDICAL SCIENCE. AN AD-
DRESS DELIVERED BEFORE THE MAS-
SACHUSETTS MEDICAL SOCIETY, AT
THE ANNUAL MEETING, MAY 30, 1860
. . .

BOSTON: PUBLISHED BY TICKNOR AND FIELDS.
D. CLAPP, PRINTER MED. AND SURG. JOURNAL
OFFICE. MDCCCLX.

<1>-48. 9¾₆″ x 5¹¹⁄₁₆″.

<1>-6⁴.

Printed salmon paper wrapper.

A copy in CAW inscribed by early owner July 21,
1860. H copy received July 27, 1860. See next
entry for a second edition.

AAS H NYPL

8795. Currents and Counter-Currents in Medical Science. An Address Delivered before the
Massachusetts Medical Society . . . May 30,
1860 . . . <Second Edition>

Boston: Published by Ticknor and Fields.
D. Clapp, Printer Med. and Surg. Journal
Office. MDCCCLX.

Printed paper wrapper.

See preceding entry for first edition.

Extended by the addition of a series of obitu-
aries, pp. <49>-55, those of Drs. Marshall Sears
Perry and Joseph Roby being by Holmes.

H

8796. Proceedings of the Massachusetts Historical Society. 1858–1860 . . .

Boston: Printed for the Society. M.DCCC.LX.

"Dr. Holmes's Remarks <on the death of Washington Irving>," pp. 418-422.

H copy received April 28, 1860.

Note: Holmes's remarks appear also in:

Washington Irving. Mr. Bryant's Address on
His Life and Genius. Addresses by Everett, Bancroft, Longfellow, Felton, Aspinwall, King,
Francis, Greene. Mr. Allibone's Sketch of His
Life and Works. With Eight Photographs, New
York: G. P. Putnam, 1860. According to a prospectus for this work (in NYPL) 150 copies only
were to be prepared, available as a volume
bound in cloth; and, in folded sheets in a portfolio. However, no such suggestions occur in
the following contemporary trade references:
Advertisement in APC July 28, 1860; and, Sept.
1, 1860, where the publication is advertised for
Sept. 1 in cloth; and, in leather.

H (Boston, New York) MHS (Boston)

8797. Proceedings and Debates of the Fourth
National Quarantine and Sanitary Convention . . . Boston, June 14, 15 and 16, 1860 . . .

Boston: Geo. C. Rand & Avery, City Printers,
No. 3 Cornhill. 1860.

Brief introductory remarks and an untitled
poem, What makes the Healing Art divine, pp.
134-136. Poem collected in   Songs in Many
Keys, 1862, as "For the Meeting of the National
Sanitary Association."

Note: Sixteen lines of the poem, under the title
"Extract from a Poem on Sanitary Science," was
issued as a handbill advertisement by one Dr.
Beardsley, n.p., n.d., ca. 1860. Printed on recto
only. 8¼″ x 5⁷⁄₁₆″. Copy in B.

B H

8798. Order of Exercises at the Music Festival
in Honor of Lord Renfrew, to be Given by
the City of Boston, at the Music Hall, on
Thursday, October 18, 1860, Commencing at
Five O'Clock, P.M.

Geo. C. Rand and Avery, City Printers, Boston. <1860>

Single cut sheet folded to four pages.

"International Ode. Our Fathers' Land," p. <2>.
The poem appears also in a similar program
issued by the City of Boston for the festival held
Oct. 20, 1860. Collected in Songs in Many Keys,
1862.

H Y

8799. Addresses at the Inauguration of Cornelius Conway Felton . . . as President of Harvard College, and at the Festival of the
Alumni, Thursday, July 19, 1860.

Cambridge: Sever and Francis, Booksellers to
the University. 1860.

Cloth; and, printed paper wrapper.

Remarks, pp. <121>-124; 126-127; 132; 138; 141;
142; 144; 147.

Title deposited Oct. 26, 1860. H copy received
Nov. 13, 1860.

H NYPL Y

8800. Memorial of the Commemoration by the
Church of the Disciples, of the Fiftieth Birth-
Day of Their Pastor, James Freeman Clarke,
April 4, 1860 . . .

Boston: Prentiss & Deland, Printers. 1860.

Untitled poem, Who is the shepherd sent to
lead, pp. 19-20. Collected in Songs in Many

Keys, 1862, as "A Birthday Tribute to J. F. Clarke ..."

B Y

8801. ELSIE VENNER: A ROMANCE OF DESTINY ...

BOSTON: TICKNOR AND FIELDS. MDCCCLXI.

2 Vols. Also see entry No. 8976.

1: ⟨i⟩-xii, ⟨13⟩-288. 7³⁄₁₆″ x 4⅝″.
2: ⟨i⟩-iv, ⟨5⟩-312.

1: ⟨1-12⟩¹². *Signed:* ⟨1⟩-18⁸.
2: ⟨1-13⟩¹². *Signed:* ⟨1⟩-19⁸, 20⁴.

Note: According to the publisher's records there were four printings during the period Jan.–April, 1861. BAL recognizes the danger in basing a sequence on the evidence of type wear (alone) or of inserted dated catalogs; nevertheless these elements suggest the following sequence which is presented with some hesitation; it should be considered tentative and used with caution.

Probable First Printing, Vol. 1

P. ⟨ii⟩: *Currents* ... described as *nearly ready.*

P. ⟨ix⟩, line 3 up: ... *It was* ... unbattered.

P. ⟨13⟩, line 6 up: *richer* ... unbattered.

P. 23, line 8: ... *all* unbattered.

P. 23, line 9: ... *it's* unbattered.

Noted with inserted catalogs dated January, 1861; February, 1861.

Probable Second Printing, Vol. 1

P. ⟨ii⟩: *Currents* ... described as *nearly ready.*

P. ⟨ix⟩, line 3 up: The *s* in the word *was* is almost wholly gone; in some copies the merest trace is present.

P. ⟨13⟩, line 6 up: *richer* ... unbattered.

P. 23, line 8: ... *all* unbattered.

P. 23, line 9: ... *it's* unbattered.

Noted with inserted catalog dated February, 1861.

Probable Third Printing, Vol. 1

P. ⟨ii⟩: *Currents*... described as *just published.*

P. ⟨ix⟩, line 3 up: The *s* in the word *was* is almost wholly gone; in some copies the merest trace is present.

P. ⟨13⟩, line 6 up: The initial *r* in the word *richer* is absent.

P. 23, line 8: The final *l* in the word *all* absent.

P. 23, line 9: the *s* not present in the word *it's.*

The only located copies have no inserted catalog.

Probable Fourth Printing, Vol. 1

P. ⟨ii⟩: *Currents* ... described as *nearly ready.*

P. ⟨ix⟩, line 3 up: The *s* in the word *was* is almost wholly gone; in some copies the merest trace is present.

P. ⟨13⟩, line 6 up: The initial *r* in the word *richer* has been replaced.

P. 23, line 8: The final *l* in the word *all* has been replaced.

P. 23, line 9: The *s* in the word *it's* not present.

Noted with inserted catalogs dated February, 1861; March, 1861.

Note: Thus far no definite features have been discovered in Vol. 2 that are immediately useful in identifying the four printings.

T cloth: brown. Brown-coated on white end papers. Flyleaves.

Also note: The inserted catalog, when present, usually occurs in Vol. 1; it is sometimes found in Vol. 2.

Deposited Feb. 13, 1861. Advertised for Feb. 15 publication in APC Feb. 9, 1861. BA copy (first printing) received Feb. 19, 1861. Listed APC Feb. 23, 1861; BM March 1, 1861. For British editions see next entry.

H (1,3)   NYPL (1,2,3,4)   Y (2,3)

8802. Elsie Venner. A Romance of Destiny ...

Cambridge: Macmillan and Co. and 23, Henrietta Street, Covent Garden, London. ⟨n.d., 1861⟩

First British edition. For first edition see preceding entry.

Reprint save for the "Preface," pp. ⟨v⟩-vi, which is a very slightly extended version of that in the Boston edition.

Advertised for *next week* Ath Feb. 23, 1861. Listed PC March 1, 1861; Ath March 2, 1861. Reviewed *Spectator* (London) March 9, 1861.

WUL

Other British Editions

London: Routledge, Warne and Routledge. Listed Ath March 16, 1861.

London: Clarke. Listed Ath Sept. 28, 1861; PC Oct. 1, 1861. *Note:* in May, 1862, Darton & Hodge purchased the book from Clarke.

London: Ward, Lock & Co. Listed PC Aug. 16, 1886.

Edinburgh: Paterson. Listed PC May 1, 1887.

8803. CURRENTS AND COUNTER-CUR-RENTS IN MEDICAL SCIENCE. WITH OTHER ADDRESSES AND ESSAYS . . .

BOSTON: TICKNOR AND FIELDS. M DCCC LXI.

Note: With the exception of the "Preface," "Some More Recent Views on Homœopathy" and "Mechanism of Vital Actions," all the material in this book had prior separate publication.

⟨i-ii⟩, ⟨i⟩-⟨xii⟩, ⟨1⟩-406; advertisements, pp. ⟨407-408⟩. 7⅝" x 4¹⁵⁄₁₆".

⟨-⟩⁷, 1-17¹². Leaf ⟨-⟩₂ (the dedication leaf) inserted. *Also signed:* ⟨-⟩⁷, ⟨A⟩-X, ⟨Y⟩⁸, Z⁴.

Note: A single copy (PDH) has been noted with Sig. 2 printed from wrongly imposed plates which produced scrambled text. The pagination thus produced is: 25; 6-7; 28-29; blank; unpaged divisional title-page; 32-41; 22-23; 44-45; 18-19; 48. The publisher's records show that twenty-four pages were cancelled in production and undoubtedly the reference is to this faulty printing of Sig. 2. It therefore appears quite safe to state that all copies of the book, save for at least this one example, were issued with the corrected printing of Sig. 2. In the PDH copy the dedication leaf (normally inserted ⟨-⟩₂) occurs as inserted ⟨-⟩₆. Bound in black HC cloth; first stamping as described below.

Also note: A CAW copy (noted at p. 98, Currier-Tilton; p. 541, Wilson) has an abnormality: Sig. 1 is erroneously backed with the inner forme of Sig. 2, thus producing the following pagination: 1, 30-31, 4-5, 26-27, 8, 33, 10-11, 36-37, 14-15, 40, 17, ⟨46⟩-47, 20-21, 42-43, 24. This represents a fairly common type of pressman's error and no special bibliographical status may be claimed.

Also note: Wilson (pp. 540-541) describes a copy thus: "The last leaf, an integral part of the book, is blank, and there are no ads, clearly the first form." (This copy, now in UV, recorded by Currier-Tilton, p. 98.) The Wilson description is highly erroneous. The "last leaf" is not 17₁₂ but a flyleaf. Wilson was misled by not recognizing the fact that in his copy leaf 17₁₂ had been excised and then compounded the error by taking the flyleaf to be the conjugate of 17₁.

First Binding

A cloth: salmon. BD cloth: gray-green. TR cloth: purple. Sides blindstamped with a triple rule frame; at center a cartouche enclosing T&F. Spine goldstamped save as noted: ⟨*blindstamped triple rule*⟩ / Currents / AND / Counter-Currents / ⟨*rule*⟩ / O. W. HOLMES / TICKNOR & CO / ⟨*blindstamped triple rule*⟩

Note: The spine imprint is stamped from a

sans-serif face. Brown-coated on white end papers. Flyleaves. Usually (not always) found with inserted terminal catalog dated April, 1861.

Note: The book had a slow sale and not all the sheets were put into binding at the same time. The sheets occur also in the following variant bindings. A copy in the binding described above presented to Harvard by the publishers April 13, 1861.

Binding Variant A

Leaf 17₁₂ present. Sides blindstamped with a quadruple frame, a leaf at each corner; at center: A cartouche enclosing T&F. Spine goldstamped: Currents / AND / Counter-Currents / ⟨*rule*⟩ / O. W. HOLMES / TICKNOR & CO *Note:* Spine imprint stamped from a serif'd face.

Binding Variant B

Leaf 17₁₂ excised. The decoration on the sides is an ornate filigree, 3½" high, which does not embody the publisher's initials. The spine imprint stamped from a serif'd face.

Binding Variant C

Leaf 17₁₂ excised. Issued not before *ca.* 1870. Spine imprint of James R. Osgood & Co.

Deposited April 11, 1861. H copy (first binding) received from the publishers April 13, 1861. Advertised *this day published* APC April 13, 1861. Listed APC April 20, 1861.

Note: The bibliographical comment in Johnson (*Fourth Edition*) relating to this book is erroneous.

AAS (Variant A)   B (1st)   H (1st; Variant C)   UV (1st; Variant B)

8804. War Songs of the American Union . . .

Boston: William V. Spencer, 94 Washington Street. ⟨1861⟩

Printed paper wrapper.

Reprint with the exception of:

"Northern Fire," p. 8. This is a truncated version of "A Voice of the Loyal North" which appears in *Chimes of Freedom and Union*, Boston, 1861 (ca. Aug.). Collected in *Songs in Many Keys*, 1862 (*i.e.,* Nov. 1861).

"Brother Jonathan's Lament for Sister Caroline," pp. 70-71. This appears also in *Chimes of Freedom and Union*, Boston, 1861 (ca. Aug.). Collected in *Songs in Many Keys*, 1862 (*i.e.,* Nov. 1861).

Title-page entered April 19, 1861; no record of deposit of book. *This day published—Boston Daily Evening Transcript*, April 26, 1861.

H

8805. ARMY HYMN

This hymn (five stanzas) was first published in *The Atlantic Monthly*, June, 1861. For an extended version (six stanzas) see entry No. 8822. Collected in *Songs in Many Keys*, 1862. Almost certainly its first publication other than in a periodical was in:

A

Order of Exercises at the Prize Declamation of the Public Latin School, Saturday, May 25, 1861 ...

> Geo. C. Rand & Avery, Printers, 3 Cornhill. ⟨1861⟩
>
> Single cut sheet folded to make four pages. Cover-title.
>
> Hymn on p. ⟨4⟩.
>
> Locations: H

The hymn was also published in leaflet form by several publishers. The following have been noted; it is reasonable to suppose that the following list is incomplete. No attempt has been made to establish a sequence which, desirable though it may be, appears to be an utter impossibility. The designations are for identification only.

B

ARMY HYMN. / ⟨rule⟩ / BY OLIVER WENDELL HOLMES. / ⟨rule⟩ / ⟨text⟩ / ⟨n.p., n.d.⟩ / ⟨all the preceding in a double-rule box⟩

> Single leaf. Printed on recto only. $7\frac{13}{16}''$ x $4\frac{15}{16}''$. AAS has two copies, each printed on similar, but different, paper. In one the chain lines are $1\frac{1}{4}''$ apart; in the other the chain lines are $1''$ apart. On each, at the upper right corner, is an embossed stationer's device; the devices are not the same.
>
> Locations: AAS

C

ARMY HYMN. / [FROM THE ATLANTIC MONTHLY FOR JUNE.] / TUNE—"Old Hundred." / ⟨text⟩ / ⟨rule⟩ / S. CHISM,—Franklin Printing House, Hawley-st., Boston. / ⟨n.d.⟩ / ⟨all the preceding in a double rule box, a filigree at each inner corner⟩

> Single leaf. Printed on recto only. $8\frac{1}{16}''$ x $5\frac{1}{8}''$.
>
> Locations: PDH

D

ARMY HYMN. / BY OLIVER WENDELL HOLMES. / [As sung by the 2d Regiment, N.H.V.M., June 20th, 1861.] / ⟨text and music⟩ / ⟨rule⟩ / Balch, Printer, 34 School St, Boston. / ⟨n.d.⟩

> Single leaf. Printed on recto only. $5''$ x $6\frac{3}{8}''$ scant.
>
> Locations: B

E

No. 708. / ARMY HYMN. / BY OLIVER WENDELL HOLMES. / (Tune.—OLD HUNDRED). / ⟨wavy rule⟩ / ⟨text⟩ / ⟨rule⟩ / Published by / HORACE PARTRIDGE / WHOLESALE DEALER IN AND IMPORTER OF / ⟨3 lines beginning: Fancy Goods ...⟩ / No. 27 Hanover Street, Boston, / Nearly opposite AMERICAN HOUSE. / ⟨n.d.⟩ / ⟨all the preceding in an ornate frame⟩

> Single leaf. Printed on recto only. $9''$ x $5\frac{5}{8}''$.
>
> Locations: H

F

UNION WAR SONGS. / ⟨spreadeagle and flag printed in red and blue⟩ / ARMY HYMN. / BY OLIVER WENDELL HOLMES. / (Tune.—OLD HUNDRED.) / ⟨music⟩ / ⟨text⟩ / Atlantic Monthly / ⟨n.p., n.d.⟩ / ⟨all the preceding in an ovoid double rule frame printed in red⟩ / ⟨all the preceding printed in blue save as noted⟩

> Single leaf. Printed on recto only. $8''$ x $4\frac{7}{8}''$.
>
> *Note:* The same setting was used to imprint, in colors as indicated above, the reverse of a Civil War patriotic envelope; copy in B.
>
> Locations: BPL

G

THE / ARMY HYMN. / No 2. Air: Old Hundred. / ⟨ornamented rule⟩ / ⟨text⟩ / ⟨all of the preceding in a hand-colored frame: Arms of the United States at top; at sides elongated American flags, soldier, Negro, etc.; within bottom portion of frame:⟩ H. DE MARSAN, Publisher, / 54 Chatham Street, New-York. / ⟨n.d.⟩

> Single leaf. Printed on recto only. $9\frac{7}{8}''$ x $6\frac{1}{2}''$.
>
> Locations: B H HEH

H

No. 812. / THE / ARMY HYMN. / By Oliver Wendell Holmes. / AIR.—Old Hundred. / ⟨decorated rule⟩ / ⟨text⟩ / ⟨all the preceding in an ornate frame depicting a troubadour, lady, etc.⟩ / ⟨below the frame:⟩ J. WRIGLEY, Publisher, of Songs, Ballad's ⟨sic⟩ ⟨etc., etc., etc.⟩ NEW YORK. ⟨n.d.⟩

> Single leaf. Printed on recto only. $10''$ scant x $6\frac{1}{4}''$ full.
>
> Locations: B

Ha

Same as the preceding save for the frame. In this printing the frame, in blue and red, possibly stencilled, is composed of red stripes and white stars on a blue field. A trimmed example measures: 8⅛″ x 5¼″.

Locations: PDH

I

ARMY HYMN./ "OLD HUNDRED." / ⟨diamond rule⟩ / ⟨text⟩ / ⟨n.p., n.d.⟩

Single leaf. Printed on recto only. 7¾″ x 4⅛″ scant.

Locations: B

In addition to the above the hymn appeared also in many compilations and programs issued in 1861. BAL has noted the following; others are listed in Currier-Tilton, p. 564. No sequence has been established for these later printings and the order of presentation is alphabetical.

J

Army Melodies ... Adapted ... by Rev. J. W. Dadmun ... ⟨and⟩ Rev. Arthur B. Fuller ...

Boston ... New York ... 1861 ...

Printed paper wrapper. Deposited Sept. 18, 1861.

K

Beadle's Dime Union Song Book ...

New York and London ... ⟨1861⟩

Printed paper wrapper.

L

The Causes, Principles and Results of the Present Conflict. A Discourse Delivered before the Ancient and Honorable Artillery Company ... June 3, 1861. By S. K. Lothrop ...

Boston ... 1861.

Printed paper wrapper.

M

Chimes of Freedom and Union. A Collection of Poems for the Times, by Various Authors ...

Boston ... MDCCCLXI.

Printed paper wrapper.

N

City of Boston. Eighty-Fifth Anniversary of American Independence ... Order of Exercises before the City Council of Boston, in the Music Hall, Thursday July 4, 1861 ...

J. E. Farwell & Co. ... Boston.

Programme. 4 pp.

O

Hymns, Religious and Patriotic, for the Soldier and the Sailor.

Published by the American Tract Society, 28 Cornhill, Boston. ⟨1861⟩

Flexible cloth.

P

Leslie's Glee Book; a Collection of Choruses Glees, and Part-Songs; Original and Selected. By Ernest Leslie.

Boston: Published by Russell & Patee. ⟨1861⟩

Printed paper boards, leather shelfback.

Q

Order of Exercises ... 223d Anniversary of the Ancient and Honorable Artillery Company, June 3, 1861 ...

Wright & Potter ... Boston.

Single cut sheet.

R

Order of Exercises at the Raising of a Flag on the Andover Theological Seminary. Army Hymn ...

⟨n.p., n.d., Andover, Mass., June 4, 1861⟩

Single leaf. Printed on recto only. 9¹⁵⁄₁₆″ x 5½″. Date based on a report in *Andover Advertiser*, June 8, 1861.

S

Psalms of Freedom, for the American Christian Patriot. Selected, Arranged, and Composed, by George Leach ... No. 1.

New York ... 1861.

Cover-title. Printed paper wrapper. "Army Hymn" appears herein as "The Nation's Prayer."

T

The Soldier's Companion ...

Boston ... 1861.

Cover-title. Printed paper wrapper.

U

The Soldier's Manual of Devotion ... Prepared by J. G. Forman ...

Alton, Illinois ... 1861.

Flexible cloth.

V

Songs for the Fourth of July Celebration, 1861 ...

Boston ... 1861.

Cover-title. Printed paper wrapper. For a comment on this publication see notes of next entry.

8806. THE STAR-SPANGLED BANNER

Holmes wrote two supplementary stanzas to Key's "The Star-Spangled Banner." The present entry is probably not all-inclusive. It is nevertheless hoped that the following is a reasonably complete record of the earliest printings. For an exhaustive study of the many printings in sheet music form see Currier-Tilton, pp. 519-523. It will be noted that in their several appearances the texts vary. It is all but certain that D-G (and possibly H) were issued simultaneously.

A

Boston Evening Transcript, April 29, 1861, p. 2.

One stanza (8 lines) only, beginning:

When our land is illumined by liberty's smile,
  If a foe from within strike a blow at her glory,
Down, down with the traitor that dares to defile
    The flag of her stars and the page of her story! ...

The printing herein is preceded by an editorial note: "The following splendid verse ... having been inaccurately printed, we give a corrected copy." *Innacurately printed where?*

B

ADDITIONAL VERSE, / To The Star-Spangled Banner. / ⟨etc., etc., n.p., n.d., Boston, Mass., Abram E. Cutter, 1861⟩

Slip of white, wove, unwatermarked paper. 2⁹⁄₁₆″ x 4¼″. Printed on recto only. Anonymous.

One stanza (8 lines) only, beginning:

When our land is illumined with liberty's smile,
  If a foe from within strike a blow at her glory,
Down, down with the traitor that dares to defile
    The flag of her stars and the page of her glory!
By the millions unchain'd who our birthright
    have gain'd, ...

The only located copy of this printing (in BPL) is accompanied by contemporary correspondence which indicates that it was printed for Abram E. Cutter not after May 22, 1861.

C

The Star Spangled Banner. Song & Chorus. With an Additional Verse (5th.) by Dr. O. W. Holmes ...

  Boston ... Oliver Ditson & Co 277 Washington St. ... 1861 ...

Sheet music. The above, save for the imprint, at head of first page of text and music. Imprint on front cover.

The "additional verse", 8 lines, begins:

When our land is illum'd with liberty's smile,

If a foe from within strike a blow at her glory,
Down, down with the traitor that dares to defile
    The flag of her stars and the page of her story, ...

Deposited June 5, 1861.

Many printings. The earliest noted by BAL (not necessarily the earliest) has the following features:

Seven entries (not titles) listed on the front. Known later printings list eleven or more entries.

The price on the front is given in code: 2½ ⟨i.e., 25¢⟩. Known later printings have the price at 3 ⟨i.e., 30¢⟩; or, 3½ ⟨i.e., 35¢⟩.

Also, in the earliest printings the fifth line of Holmes's stanza reads: ... *who our birthright have gained.* This was later revised to: ... *when our birthright was gained.* Since the earlier reading has been noted in several of the early printings it is of small value in determining the earliest printing.

Publisher: *Oliver Ditson & Co.* Later: *Oliver Ditson Co.*

D

Songs for the Fourth of July Celebration, 1861. Charles Butler, Choir Director.

  Boston: J. E. Farwell & Co., City Printers, No. 32 Congress Street. 1861.

Cover-title. Printed self-wrapper.

Pp. ⟨1⟩-9. *Incomplete? Proof printing only?*

P. 5: Signature mark not present.

P. 6, line 6 from bottom: *Fly to battle, what if beaten? /*

P. 7, line 1: *Rise then patriots, name endearing; /*

P. 9: Two stanzas, each of eight lines, credited to *Oliver Wendel* ⟨sic⟩ *Holmes.* The stanzas begin:

There's a world-renowned banner that⟨'⟩s floating on high,
  Whose wide spreading folds are are ⟨sic⟩ illumined in story—
Whose stars, like the bright glittering gems of the sky,
  Gleam brightly, reflected unfading in glory,
    ...

***

When our land is illumined with Liberty's smile,
  If a foe from within, strikes a blow at her glory,

Down, down with the traitor who dares to defile
   The flag of her stars and the page of her
   glory! . . .

P. ⟨10⟩: Blank

Note: On p. ⟨3⟩ Holmes's "Army Hymn" is
reprinted; credited to *O. W. Holmes.* For earlier
publication see entry No. 8805.

E

Songs for the Fourth of July Celebration, 1861.
Charles Butler, Choir Director.

   Boston: J. E. Farwell & Co., City Printers,
   No. 32 Congress Street. 1861.

Cover-title. Printed self-wrapper.

Pp. ⟨1⟩-12.

P. 5: Signature mark 1* present.

P. 6, line 6 from bottom: *Fly to battle,—what
if beaten? /*

P. 7, line 1: *Rise then patriots; name endearing, /*

P. 9: Two stanzas, each of eight lines, credited
to *Oliver Wendell* ⟨sic⟩ *Holmes.* The stanzas
begin:

There's a world-renowned banner that's floating
   on high,
   Whose wide spreading folds are illumined in
   story—
Whose stars, like the bright glittering gems of
   the sky,
   Gleam brightly, reflected unfading in glory,
      . . .

***

When our land is illumined with Liberty's
   smile,
   If a foe from within strikes a blow at her
   glory,
Down, down with the traitor who dares to defile
   The flag of her stars and the page of her
   glory! . . .

P. 10: "Union War Song". Anonymous.

Note: On p. ⟨3⟩ Holmes's "Army Hymn" is reprinted; credited to *O. W. Holmes.* For earlier
publication see entry No. 8805.

F

Songs for the Fourth of July Celebration, under
the Direction of the Committee on Music, etc.
Charles Butler, Choir Director.

   Boston: J. E. Farwell & Co., City Printers,
   No. 32 Congress Street. 1861.

Cover-title. Printed self-wrapper. Note extended
title.

Pp. ⟨1⟩-12.

P. 5: Signature mark 1* present.

P. 6, line 6 from bottom: *Fly to battle,—what
if beaten? /*

P. 7, line 1: *Rise then patriots; name endearing, /*

P. 9: Three stanzas, each of eight lines, with
the statement: *Third Verse by O. W. Holmes.*
(The first and the second stanzas are Key's.)
Holmes's stanza begins:

When our land is illumined with Liberty's
   smile,
   If a foe from within strike a blow at her
   glory,
Down, down with the traitor who dares to defile
   The flag of her stars and the page of her
   story! . . .

P. 10: "Union War Song". Credited to W. T.
Adams.

Note: On p. ⟨3⟩ Holmes's "Army Hymn" is
reprinted; credited to *Oliver Wendell Holmes.*
For earlier publication see entry No. 8805.

G

City of Boston. Eighty-Fifth Anniversary of
American Independence . . . Order of Exercises
before the City Council of Boston, in the Music Hall, Thursday, July 4, 1861 . . .

   J. E. Farwell & Co., Printers, 32 Congress
   Street, Boston.

4 pp. Issued as a program. Holmes's "Army
Hymn" reprinted on p. ⟨3⟩; for an earlier printing see entry No. 8805. On p. ⟨2⟩ Holmes's additional stanza to "The Star-Spangled Banner,"
eight lines, beginning:

When our land is illumined with Liberty's smile,
   If a foe from within strike a blow at her glory,
Down, down with the traitor who dares to de-
file
   The flag of her stars and the page of her
   story! . . .

H

Songs for the Mayhew School.

   Boston: J. E. Farwell & Co., City Printers, No.
   32 Congress Street. 1861.

Printed paper wrapper. Cover-title. "Star-Spangled Banner," p. 5.

According to *Boston Evening Transcript,* July
5 and 11, 1861, a children's concert was given
as part of the July 4 celebrations; various public
schools participated. The performance was repeated July 11, 1861. It is possible, therefore,
that this booklet was issued for one or both of

the celebrations. If for the celebration on July 4 (likely) then this and entries D-G, were issued simultaneously. Unfortunately at the time (1947) the description of this pamphlet was made, BAL was unaware of the problem and is therefore unable to comment on the text. Inquiry has failed to locate a copy of the pamphlet which was seen only in CAW.

I

... Star Spangled Banner ...

Boston   Published by Russell & Tolman 291 Washington St. ⟨1861⟩

Sheet music. Cover-title. At head of title: National Melodies Plate number 3363.

Publication date unknown. The Copyright Office reports no record found of copyright deposit.

Note: All examined copies, including obvious reprints, have the error *Keys* for *Key* in the heading, p. 3.

Reprinted and reissued by S. T. Gordon, New York.

Holmes's additional stanza (8 lines) begins:

When our land is illumined with Liberty's smile
    If a foe from within strike a blow at her glory,
Down, down with the traitor that dares to defile
    The flag of her stars and the page of her story!
By the millions unchained, when our birthright was gained ...

J

Psalms of Freedom, for the American Christian Patriot. Selected, Arranged, and Composed, by George Leach ... No. 1.

New York: George Leach, 40 Fourth Avenue. S. T. Gordon, 706 Broadway. 1861.

Cover-title. Printed paper wrapper.

Holmes's stanza, p. 11:

When our land was illumined by Liberty's smile,
    If a foe from within strike a blow at her glory,
Down, down with the traitor that dares to defile
    The flag of her stars and the page of her story! ...

Date of publication not determined. The Copyright Office reports inability to find date of deposit. *Here reprinted?*

Reprints

Holmes's addition to "The Star-Spangled Banner" reprinted in the following 1861 publications:

Chimes of Freedom and Union ... by Various Authors ...

Boston ... Benjamin B. Russell ... MDCCCLXI.

Printed paper wrapper. Issued *ca.* Aug. 1861.

Army Melodies ... Adapted ... by Rev. J. W. Dadmun ... ⟨and⟩ Rev. Arthur B. Fuller ...

Boston: Benj. B. Russell ... New York ... 1861 ...

Printed paper wrapper. Deposited Sept. 18, 1861.

Sheet music comments based on examples in:
AAS BA H LC NYPL PDH

AAS (G)   BA (D)   BPL (B)   CAW (H)   H (A)
IU (E, F)   Y (J)

8807. The Union Memorial ...

Boston: Published by Abel Tompkins, 38 & 40 Cornhill. 1861.

Printed paper wrapper.

"Under the Washington Elm, Cambridge, April 27, 1861," p. 33. Collected in *Songs in Many Keys,* 1862 (*i.e.,* Nov. 1861).

Title-page deposited May 15, 1861. H copy received from the publisher July 13, 1861.

H

8808. Chimes of Freedom and Union. A Collection of Poems for the Times, by Various Authors ... ⟨Compiled by Mrs. J. H. Hanaford and Mrs. Mary T. Webber⟩

Boston: Published by Benjamin B. Russell, 515 Washington Street. MDCCCLXI.

Printed paper wrapper.

Reprint save for "A Voice of the Loyal North," pp. 44-45. A truncated version, under the title "Northern Fire," appeared in *War Songs of the American Union,* Boston ⟨1861⟩; see entry No. 8804. Collected in *Songs in Many Keys,* 1862.

H copy presented by the editors Aug. 22, 1861. Listed NAR Oct. 1861.

H NYPL

8809. The Address of Mr. Everett and the Poem of Dr. O. W. Holmes, at the Dinner Given to H.I.H. Monseigneur the Prince Napoleon, September 25th, 1861.

Cambridge: Privately Printed. 1861.

Printed flexible boards.

"Vive la France!," pp. ⟨19⟩-20. Collected in *Songs in Many Keys,* 1862.

Introductory note by the editor dated Oct. 4, 1861. Copy in MHS inscribed by Edward Everett Oct. 29, 1861.

Note: For separate printings of the poem in French translation see under 1861 in *References and Ana.*

BA   BPL   H   Y

8810. ASSOCIATE MEMBERS OF THE UNITED STATES SANITARY COMMISSION MEETING IN BOSTON. ADDRESS TO THE PUBLIC ...

⟨Boston, Dec. 2, 1861⟩

Caption-title. The above on p. ⟨1⟩; place and date on p. 4.

Single cut sheet folded to make four pages.

⟨1⟩-4. 9⅞″ x 7¾″.

An appeal for the United States Sanitary Commission.

"At a meeting of the Associate Members of the United States Sanitary Commission ... November 27th, 1861, the above address ... presented by Dr. Holmes from the Committee on Addresses, was accepted, and ordered to be printed. Boston, December 2, 1861."—P. 4.

H

8811. Proceedings in Behalf of the Morton Testimonial.

Boston: Printed by Geo. C. Rand & Avery, No. 3 Cornhill 1861.

Printed paper wrapper.

"The Boston Appeal," pp. ⟨33⟩-34, signed by Holmes and others. Letter to Dr. Willard Parker, p. 50.

H   NYPL

8812. ... HOLMES' PARTING HYMN ...

PUBLISHED BY HORACE PARTRIDGE, WHOLESALE DEALER ... AND IMPORTER ... NO. 27 HANOVER STREET, BOSTON. NEARLY OPPOSITE AMERICAN HOUSE. ⟨n.d., 1861?⟩

At head of title: NO. 709.

Single leaf. 9¹⁄₁₆″ x 5¹¹⁄₁₆″. Printed on recto only.

The poem had first publication in *The Atlantic Monthly,* Aug. 1861. Collected in (reprinted from?) *Songs in Many Keys,* 1862 (Nov. 1861).

H

8813. SONGS IN MANY KEYS ...

BOSTON: TICKNOR AND FIELDS. 1862.

⟨i-ii⟩ (excised or pasted under the end paper); ⟨i⟩-x, ⟨1⟩-308. 7¼″ x 4⅝″.

⟨-⟩⁶, 1-12¹², 13⁶, ⟨14⟩⁴. Leaf ⟨-⟩₁ excised or pasted under the end paper. *Also signed:* ⟨-⟩⁶, A-M, ⟨N⟩-R, ⟨S⟩⁸, ⟨T⟩².

Note: According to the publisher's records there were five printings of this book during the period Oct. 1861–Feb. 1862; all, presumably, were issued under date 1862. The same source indicates that all five printings were done on the same weight of paper. Nevertheless copies occur in which the sheets, not including the terminal catalog, bulk 1³⁄₁₆″; and other copies, not including the terminal catalog, bulk 1⁵⁄₁₆″. It is quite probable that the copies first printed have a period at the end of the third line from the bottom, p. 42; the period is lacking in late reprints.

A-like cloth: purple. BD cloth: green. TR cloth: green; plum; slate. TZ cloth: purple. Covers bevelled. Brown-coated on white end papers. Flyleaves. Top edges gilt. Inserted at back of some copies is a publisher's catalog, pp. ⟨1⟩-16, dated Nov. 1861.

Advertised for *Autumn* APC Oct. 14, 1861. Advertised for Nov. 30, 1861, APC Nov. 15, 1861. Deposited Nov. 21, 1861. H copy received from publisher Nov. 25, 1861. Listed APC Dec. 5, 1861. Listed as an importation PC Feb. 1, 1862. Advertised for *Wednesday (i.e.,* Feb. 5) in PC Feb. 1, 1862. Advertised as *ready* Ath Feb. 8, 1862. Reviewed Ath March 8, 1862.

H   NYPL   Y

8814. BORDER LINES OF KNOWLEDGE IN SOME PROVINCES OF MEDICAL SCIENCE. AN INTRODUCTORY LECTURE, DELIVERED BEFORE THE MEDICAL CLASS OF HARVARD UNIVERSITY, NOVEMBER 6TH, 1861 ...

BOSTON: TICKNOR AND FIELDS. 1862.

⟨i-iv⟩, ⟨1⟩-80. 7¹¹⁄₁₆″ scant x 4⅞″.

⟨-², 1-6⁶, 7⁴⟩. *Signed:* ⟨-⟩², 1-3¹², 4⁴. *Also signed:* ⟨-⟩², ⟨A⟩-E⁸.

BD cloth: brown; green; purple. TR cloth: black; brown. Brown-coated on white end papers. Flyleaves.

Two bindings noted:

1: With the spine imprint: TICKNOR & CO.

2: Issued not before 1878; with the spine monogram of Houghton, Osgood & Co.

Deposited Jan. 17, 1862. H copy received Jan. 21, 1862. Published Jan. 22, 1862 (publisher's records). Listed APC Feb. 1862. *Note:* The Wakeman copy (Wakeman sale catalog, entry No.

493) bears a forged inscription dated Dec. 26, 1861. The date is obviously incorrect since the book was not manufactured until Jan. 1862. The December, 1861, date should therefore be disregarded in establishing publication date of the book. The forgery, cataloged as such, is preserved in H.

H (1st) NYPL (1st) Y (1st; also, 2nd binding)

8815. A Sermon Preached in the Appleton Chapel, March 9, 1862, Being the Sunday after the Funeral of Cornelius Conway Felton ... President of Harvard University. By Andrew P. Peabody ...

Cambridge: Sever and Francis, Booksellers to the University. 1862.

Printed paper wrapper.

"Proceedings of the Faculty of the Museum of Comparative Zoölogy," pp. 22-23.

H NYPL

8816. List of the Publications of George W. Childs,

628 & 630, Chestnut Street, Philadelphia. July, 1862.

Caption-title. The above at head of p. ⟨1⟩ of a single cut sheet of blue-gray paper, printed on both sides. On p. ⟨2⟩ is a series of letters recommending Lossing's *Pictorial History of the Great Rebellion* including one from Holmes dated March 20, 1862.

Gd

8817. The Poems ...

Boston: Ticknor and Fields. 1862.

Blue and Gold edition.

Reprint save for:

"To My Readers," pp. ⟨iii⟩-v.

"Voyage of the Good Ship Union," pp. 398-401.

Advertised as *in press, Boston Daily Transcript* July 2, 1862. Deposited Aug. 22, 1862. H copy received Oct. 17, 1862. Published Oct. 18, 1862 (publisher's records). Advertised *Boston Daily Transcript,* Oct. 18, 1862, as *this day.* Listed PC Dec. 8, 1862.

AAS H

8818. War-Songs for Freemen. Dedicated to the Army of the United States ... ⟨Edited by Francis J. Child⟩

Boston: Ticknor and Fields. 1862 ...

Printed paper wrapper.

Reprint save for "Trumpet Song," pp. 32-33.

Deposited Jan. 12, 1863. Extended reissues published not before 1863 by *American News Company, N. Y.* ⟨1862⟩; and, *Oliver Ditson & Co.,* Boston, 1862.

H

8819. Medical Directions Written for Governor Winthrop by Ed: Stafford, of London, in 1643. With Notes, by O. W. Holmes, M. D. Reprinted from the Proceedings of the Massachusetts Historical Society.

Boston: Printed by John Wilson and Son, 22, School Street. 1862.

Printed paper wrapper.

Reprinted from *Proceedings of the Massachusetts Historical Society, 1860–1862,* Boston, 1862.

BA H

8820. NOW OR NEVER

This poem, read at a dinner of P.B.K., Harvard University, July 17, 1862, has been seen in a number of printings. No sequence has been established and the designations are for identification only. Collected in *Songs of Many Seasons,* 1875, as "Never or Now."

A

NOW OR NEVER. / BY DR. O. W. HOLMES. / ⟨text⟩ / ⟨n.p., n.d., *ca.* 1862⟩

Single leaf. 8″ x 4⁹⁄₁₆″. Printed on recto only.

Locations: BPL LCP NYPL

B

⟨Printed in red and blue on the back of a Civil War patriotic envelope; headed: Union War Songs.⟩

Locations: CAW

C

... Fill up the Ranks Boys ⟨Music⟩ by J. P. Webster.

Chicago ... H. M. Higgins 117 Randolph St. ... 1862 ...

Sheet music. Cover-title. At head of title: The Celebrated Rallying Song

Title entered Jan. 21, 1863. No record of deposit of finished publication.

Locations: H (photostat)

D

Now or Never ... Music by Richard Culver.

Boston ... Oliver Ditson & Co. 277 Washington St. ... ⟨n.d., *ca.* 1862⟩

Sheet music. Cover-title. Plate No. 21724. No record of copyright found.

Locations: H

8821. THUS SAITH THE LORD, I OFFER THEE THREE THINGS." ...

⟨n.p., n.d., Boston: Loyal Publication Society, 1862?⟩

Single leaf. Printed on recto only. 8¼″ x 4⅝″.

Also appears in *Songs of the War* ... , 1863; see entry No. 8825. First published in *Boston Evening Transcript,* Aug. 29, 1862. Collected in *Songs of Many Seasons,* 1875.

B   BPL   MHS   NYPL

8822. ARMY HYMN

Six four-line stanzas. For a five-stanza version see entry No. 8805.

Three appearances noted; the order here presented is probably correct:

A

Boston Music Hall. Grand Jubilee Concert, Thursday Afternoon, January 1, 1863, in Honor of the Day! The Proclamation! The Emancipation of the Slave! The Spirit of the Fathers and the Constitution! ...

⟨Boston⟩ S. Chism.—Franklin Printing House, 112 Congress Street.

Single cut sheet folded to four pages. Cover-title. Issued as a program. The added stanza was written for this occasion.

"Army Hymn," p. ⟨3⟩.

Noted on two types of paper; almost surely issued simultaneously: (a) thin, onion skin-like; and (b) appreciably thicker paper.

Locations: H   MHS

B

Army Hymn ... ⟨Music⟩ Composed by Otto Dresel ...

Boston. G. D. Russell & Company 126 Tremont, opposite Park St. ... 1863 ...

Sheet music. Cover-title.

Two printings noted:

1

On front cover the name *Otto Dresel* printed from a shaded face.

No plate number.

Issued with (?) inserted, unpaged, leaf, printed on recto only, with text of chorus and music for soprano, alto, tenor and bass.

2

On front cover the name *Otto Dresel* printed in black letter.

Plate No. 33 present.

Issued with an inserted, unpaged, leaf, printed on recto only, with text of chorus and music for soprano, alto, tenor and bass.

Reprinted and republished, not before 1877, by Oliver Ditson & Co., Boston, n.d.

Locations: H (2nd)   PDH (1st)

C

In:

Odes for the Union League.

Boston: Published by Samuel T. Cobb & Co., "Union League" Office, 22 School Street. 1863.

Printed paper wrapper. Cover-title. The hymn appears on p. 6.

Issued after Sept. 26, 1862, on which date "The Battle Cry of Freedom," herein contained, was deposited for copyright; but probably, if not surely, issued after the Jan. 1, 1863, program described above.

Locations: H

8823. THE HUMAN WHEEL, ITS SPOKES AND FELLOES, AN ARTICLE BY PROF. OLIVER WENDELL HOLMES, IN THE ATLANTIC MONTHLY, MAY, 1863 ...

REPUBLISHED BY PERMISSION OF THE AUTHOR, AND PUBLISHERS, BY B. FRANK. PALMER, SURGEON-ARTIST, PHILADELPHIA ... 1863 ...

⟨1⟩-15; advertisement, p. ⟨16⟩. Illustrated. 9⅛″ x 5⅞″.

⟨-⟩⁸.

Tan paper wrapper. Letterpress of the title-page repeated on both front and on outer back wrapper, in a double-rule frame.

Collected in *Soundings from the Atlantic,* 1864.

Note: Copies stripped of the original wrapper were reissued in 1870 bound together with other pamphlet publications relating to the same subject. The wrapper of the 1870 reissue is imprinted: *The Human Wheel ... Value of the Palmer Limbs ... Selections from 1860 to 1870* ...

MHS

8824. The Loyal National League. Opinions of Prominent Men Concerning the Great Questions of the Times Expressed in Their Letters to the Loyal National League ...

New York: C. S. Westcott & Co., Printers, No. 79 John Street. 1863.

Letter, Boston, April 4, 1863, pp. 55-56.

For fuller entry see No. 1198.

8825. Songs of the War ...

Albany: J. Munsell, 78 State Street. 1863.

Reprint save for:

"Thus Saith the Lord, I Offer Thee Three Things," pp. 31-32. *Here reprinted?* For a separate printing see entry No. 8821.

"To Canaan! A Song of the Six Hundred Thousand," pp. 81-83. Anonymous. Holmes claimed authorship of this in a letter (transcript in CAW) to an unknown correspondent, April 14, 1872. Currier-Tilton, p. 516, report four musical settings issued in 1862.

Both collected in *Songs of Many Seasons*, 1875.

For comment see entry No. 259.

8826. ORATION, JULY 4, 1863

PRINTED MANUSCRIPT

Printed as manuscript for the author's use. No front matter. Text only.

⟨1⟩-71. 11⅚⁄₁₆″ x 9⁹⁄₁₆″ (trimmed).

⟨1-18⟩² (?).

P. ⟨1⟩: [PRIVATE COPY.] / ORATION. / ⟨*decorated rule*⟩ / FELLOW-CITIZENS AND FRIENDS: / ⟨*text*⟩

P. 71, line 10: *Queen of the free nations* ...

Leather. Edges gilded.

Locations: H

There were several printings of this oration. The following is a record of the earliest separate printings. The order of presentation is arbitrary. BAL has been unable to find any evidence to support a publication sequence. It is wholly possible, perhaps likely, that the trade editions were printed and published before completion or distribution of the elaborate large paper printings.

SUPPLEMENT, BOSTON DAILY
ADVERTISER

Supplement—Monday, July 6, 1863. Daily Advertiser: Boston. Supplement ... The Fourth of July ... Oration by Oliver Wendell Holmes ...

Single cut sheet. Printed on both sides. 25″ x 18⅞″.

Prints the text of the oration, news notes, advertisements, etc.

Locations: H

PRIVATELY PRINTED EDITION

ORATION DELIVERED BEFORE THE CITY AUTHORITIES OF BOSTON, ON THE FOURTH OF JULY, 1863, BY OLIVER WENDELL HOLMES. PRIVATE COPY.

BOSTON: J. E. FARWELL AND COMPANY, PRINTERS, 37 CONGRESS STREET. 1863.

⟨i-viii⟩, ⟨1⟩-71. 11⁷⁄₁₆″ x 9¹⁄₁₆″.

⟨1-20⟩² (?).

P. ⟨1⟩: [PRIVATE COPY.] / ORATION. / ⟨*decorated rule*⟩ / FELLOW-CITIZENS AND FRIENDS: / ⟨*text*⟩

P. 71, line 10: *Queen of the broad continent* ...

Leather; and, cloth. Edges gilded.

"The reader has before him the first draft of the author's Address ... By the liberality of the City Authorities, twelve copies ... were printed ... No others were struck off, with the exception of those which the printers were allowed to preserve as typographical specimens."—P. ⟨iii⟩.

Holmes presented copies to BPL Aug. 18, 1863; H Sept. 8, 1863.

Locations: BA BPL H

PUBLISHED EDITION, LARGE PAPER

ORATION DELIVERED BEFORE THE CITY AUTHORITIES OF BOSTON, ON THE FOURTH OF JULY, 1863. BY OLIVER WENDELL HOLMES.

BOSTON: J. E. FARWELL AND COMPANY, PRINTERS TO THE CITY, 37 CONGRESS STREET. 1863.

⟨1⟩-75. 11¼″ x 9⁹⁄₁₆″.

⟨1-19⟩².

P. ⟨1⟩: PRINTED BY ORDER OF THE COMMON COUNCIL.

P. ⟨5⟩: ORATION. / ⟨*rule*⟩ / MR. MAYOR AND GENTLEMEN OF THE COMMON COUNCIL, / FELLOW-CITIZENS AND FRIENDS: / ⟨*text*⟩

Leather. Edges gilded.

Locations: H LC Y

PUBLISHED EDITION, SMALL PAPER

ORATION DELIVERED BEFORE THE CITY AUTHORITIES OF BOSTON, ON THE FOURTH OF JULY, 1863, BY OLIVER WENDELL HOLMES.

BOSTON: J. E. FARWELL & COMPANY, PRINTERS TO THE CITY, 37 CONGRESS STREET. 1863.

⟨1⟩-60. 9¹⁄₁₆″ x 5¾″ (cloth). 9⅜″ scant x 5⅝″ (printed paper wrapper).

⟨1⟩-7⁴, 8².

Printed paper wrapper: cream, green; pink noted. Also: HC cloth: slate, brown-coated on white end papers, flyleaves.

Issued after July 10, 1863.

Locations: AAS H MHS NYPL

TRADE EDITION

Printed from the same setting as *Published Edition, Small Paper.*

ORATION DELIVERED BEFORE THE CITY AUTHORITIES OF BOSTON, ON THE FOURTH OF JULY, 1863, BY OLIVER WENDELL HOLMES.

BOSTON: TICKNOR AND FIELDS. 1863.

⟨1⟩-60. 9⁷⁄₁₆″ x 5⅞″.

⟨1⟩-7⁴, 8².

Printed salmon paper wrapper.

Issued after July 10, 1863. H copy received July 31, 1863.

BA H NYPL

PHILADELPHIA EDITION

ORATION DELIVERED BEFORE THE CITY AUTHORITIES AT BOSTON, ON THE EIGHTY-SEVENTH ANNIVERSARY OF THE NATIONAL INDEPENDENCE OF AMERICA. BY OLIVER WENDELL HOLMES.

PHILADELPHIA: PRINTED FOR GRATUITOUS DISTRIBUTION. 1863.

⟨1⟩-30, blank leaf. 9″ x 5¹¹⁄₁₆″.

⟨1⟩-2⁸.

Printed paper wrapper: buff; yellow.

Note: The wrapper occurs in two states of undetermined sequence; the designations are for identification only.

A: No statement at head of front of wrapper.

B: At head of front of wrapper: *No. 13.*

Note: This is presumed to be the printing issued in August, 1863, by the Union League of Philadelphia. See: *List of Pamphlets Distributed by the Board of Publication of the Union League of Philadelphia* ⟨Philadelphia, 1866⟩.

B (A) H (A) LC (A) MHS (A, B)

8827. ⟨ADDRESS AT THE COMMENCEMENT DINNER OF THE HARVARD ALUMNI ASSOCIATION, HARVARD HALL, 1863⟩ BROTHERS OF THE ASSOCIATION OF THE ALUMNI: ...

⟨n.p., n.d., Boston, July 16, 1863.⟩

The above at head of p. ⟨1⟩. Anonymous.

⟨1⟩-8. 11″ x 8⅜″. Laid paper. Watermarked *J. E. Farwell & Co* Printed on rectos only.

8 separate leaves.

It is your misfortune and mine that you must accept my services as your presiding officer in the place of your honored President ...

Variously reported as printed in an edition of 6 and 8 copies.

H

8828. LECTURE.—1863. [PRIVATE COPY.]

⟨n.p., n.d., Boston, Nov. 3, 1863⟩

The above at head of p. ⟨1⟩. Anonymous.

⟨1⟩-81. 11¾″ x 9⁹⁄₁₆″.

⟨1⟩-20², 21¹.

Unprinted faun paper wrapper.

The separation of the young from its parent is a very gradual process in the higher animals ...

According to both Johnson and Currier-Tilton but six copies were printed.

H

8829. SOUNDINGS FROM THE ATLANTIC ...

BOSTON: TICKNOR AND FIELDS. 1864.

Title-page in black and red.

⟨i-viii⟩, ⟨1⟩-468. Illustrated. 7⅛″ x 4⁹⁄₁₆″.

⟨-⟩⁴, 1-19¹², 20⁶. *Also signed:* ⟨-⟩⁴, A-Z, AA-CC⁸, DD².

BD cloth: purple. C cloth: purple. HT cloth: green; purple. P cloth: purple. TR cloth: green; purple. Z cloth: green; purple; slate. Brown-coated on white end papers. Flyleaves. Inserted at back of some copies is a catalog, pp. ⟨1⟩-22, blank leaf, dated Nov. 1863.

Announced APC Sept. 15, 1863. Noted as *in press* APC Sept. 15, 1863. H copy received from publisher Nov. 21, 1863. BA copy received Nov. 24, 1863. Listed ALG Dec. 1, 1863. Deposited Dec. 28, 1863. Listed PC Dec. 31, 1863; Ath Jan. 9, 1864; Bkr Feb. 29, 1864.

H NYPL Y

8830. The Drum Beat

Published by the Brooklyn and Long Island Fair, for the Benefit of the U. S. Sanitary Commission ... Brooklyn ... 1864 ...

Letter, Jan. 28, 1864, No. IV, p. 3.

For fuller comment see entry No. 148.

8831. An Address to the Graduating Class of the Medical School in the University at Cambridge, on Wednesday, March 9, 1864. By John A. Andrew . . .

Boston: Ticknor and Fields. 1864.

Printed paper wrapper.

Letter, signed by Holmes and others, p. ⟨iii⟩.

H

8832. Musical Festival in Honor of Admiral Lessoffsky and the Officers of the Russian Fleet, by the Pupils of the Public Schools, of the City of Boston, at the Boston Music-Hall . . . June 8, 1864 . . .

J. E. Farwell & Co. Printers to the City, 37 Congress Street, Boston. ⟨1864⟩

Single cut sheet folded to four pages. Program. The festival was repeated, Boston, June 11, 1864. The program for the repetition also includes the song.

"Song of Welcome," p. ⟨2⟩. Anonymous.

Note: Copies occur on white laid paper watermarked *J. E. Farwell & Co.;* and, on pink laid paper.

The poem reprinted in:

Complimentary Banquet Given by the City Council of Boston to Rear-Admiral Lessoffsky and the Officers of the Russian Fleet . . . June 7, 1864.

Boston: J. E. Farwell and Company, Printers to the City, 37 Congress Street. 1864.

Printed paper wrapper. The wrapper occurs in two states of undetermined sequence: (a) front wrapper printed in colors with flags, seal, etc.; and, (b) front wrapper printed in black with the seal of the City of Boston. It is probable that *a* represents an attempt at a de luxe form; both the menu (printed on satin) and its protective envelope, issued at the banquet, have the flags, seal, etc., printed in colors.

Annual Report of the School Committee of the City of Boston. 1864.

Boston: J. E. Farwell and Company, Printers to the City, 37 Congress Street. 1864.

H

8833. HYMN FOR THE GREAT CENTRAL FAIR

Three printings noted. Sequence not established. The designations are for identification only.

A

⟨*Seal of the Great Central Fair*⟩ / HYMN BY OLIVER WENDELL HOLMES. / ⟨*rule*⟩ / Written expressly for the Great Central Fair. / ⟨*rule*⟩ / ⟨*text and music*⟩ / ⟨*rule*⟩ / Entered, according to Act of Congress, in the year 1864, by G. W. CHILDS. / ⟨*Philadelphia, 1864*⟩

A single leaf of cream-white paper. 12$\frac{1}{16}$" x 6$\frac{3}{4}$". Printed on recto only.

AAS   B   Y

B

⟨*Seal of the Great Central Fair*⟩ / HYMN. / ⟨*rule*⟩ / BY OLIVER WENDELL HOLMES. / ⟨*rule*⟩ / Written expressly for the Great Central Fair. / ⟨*rule*⟩ / ⟨*text, without music*⟩ / ⟨*rule*⟩ / Entered according to Act of Congress, in the year 1864, by / G. W. CHILDS. / ⟨*Philadelphia, 1864*⟩

Printed on the recto of a piece of silk; white, red, blue noted. 12$\frac{1}{8}$" x 5$\frac{1}{8}$". Edges scalloped.

H   PDH   Y

C

In:

Our Daily Fare . . .

Philadelphia . . . June 8. ⟨to⟩ June 21. 1864.

The hymn appears in No. 1, p. 7.

Letter, Dec. 14, 1863, No. 9, p. ⟨65⟩.

"The Poet's Reply," No. 2, p. 13.

For fuller comment see entry No. 1206.

8834. National Sailors' Fair.

Boston, (Mass.,) Sept. 1, 1864 . . .

Single leaf. 8" x 5". Printed on recto only.

A seventeen-line appeal for literary contributions to be published in a paper which was to be sold for the benefit of the National Sailors' Fair. Signed at end by Holmes and others.

"In November next a National Sailors' Fair is to be held in Boston, for the purpose of establishing a Home for Sailors and Marines . . . It is proposed, during the period for which the Fair shall be open, to publish . . . a daily paper . . ."

The paper was issued under the title *The Boatswain's Whistle;* see entry No. 8836.

H

8835. Pansie: A Fragment. The Last Literary Effort of Nathaniel Hawthorne.

London: John Camden Hotten, Piccadilly. ⟨n.d., 1864⟩

"Nathaniel Hawthorne," pp. ‹3›-14. Reprinted from *Atlantic Monthly,* July, 1864.

For comment see entry No. 7627.

8836. The Boatswain's Whistle. Published at the National Sailors' Fair ...

Boston, November 9-19, 1864.

Holmes served as a member of the editorial board.

"A Sea Dialogue," No. 4, p. 27.

"The Jubilee," No. 5, p. 37.

Both collected in *Humorous Poems,* 1865.

For comment see entry No. 4709. Also see entry No. 8834.

8837. ‹NEW ENGLAND'S MASTER-KEY›

‹n.p., n.d., Cambridge, Nov. 15, 1864›

‹1-61›. 11¾″ x 9½″.

1-15², ‹16›¹. *Note:* The leaves of 15 are not conjugates; one or the other may be a cancel.

Unprinted terra-cotta paper wrapper.

Privately printed (6 copies only?) for the author's use.

Anonymous.

Issued without title-page or title.

Text begins: *In cultivating the general intelligence of our people to an extent never equalled before in the world's history ...*

See next entry.

H

8838. NEW ENGLAND'S MASTER-KEY ...

‹n.p., n.d., Cambridge, 1864›

The above at head of p. ‹2›. P. ‹1› blank.

‹1-59›. 11¾″ x 9½″.

1², ‹2›¹, 3-15², ‹16›¹.

Unprinted terra-cotta paper wrapper.

Privately printed (6 copies only?) for the author's use.

Anonymous.

Note: This is a revision of the first edition (see preceding entry) and is made up of the sheets of the first edition, with certain cancellations and insertions. Text begins: *The dust of the political battle-field, harder to breathe than the smoke of conflict ...*

CAW   H (incomplete)

8839. Fifty-Eighth Anniversary Celebration of the New England Society, in the City of New York, at the Astor House, December 22, 1863 ...

New York: Wm. C. Bryant & Co., Printers, 41 Nassau St., Cor. of Liberty. 1864.

Printed paper wrapper.

Letter, Dec. 16, 1863, pp. 45-47.

H   NYPL   Y

8840. The High Tide, by Jean Ingelow, with Notices of Her Poems.

Boston: Roberts Brothers, Publishers, 143 Washington Street. 1864.

Printed paper wrapper.

Four-line comment, p. 3. A brief extract from the comment is also on the front of the wrapper.

EM

8841. ... The (Old) Farmer's Almanack ... for the Year ... 1865 ... by Robert B. Thomas ...

Boston: Published by Brewer & Tileston ... 1864 ...

Printed paper wrapper. At head of title: Number Seventy-Three.

"The Loved and Lost," p. 39; extract from "Our Classmate, F.W.C."; see *Songs and Poems of the Class of 1829,* 1868.

H   NYPL

8842. The Bugle Call. A Holiday Sheet for the Soldiers.

New Year's ‹Day›, 1865. Boston, Mass.

A four-page occasional newspaper edited by Edward P. Thwing.

"Great Moral Exhibition of Architectural Models," p. 4.

Note: This is an extended edition of a publication of the same name issued in Quincy, Mass., Christmas, 1864. The Holmes contribution does not appear in the Quincy edition.

Note: The Holmes contribution, embodied in a letter dated Dec. 15, 1864, appears in *Fifty-Ninth Anniversary Celebration of the New England Society, in the City of New York, at the Astor House, Dec. 22, 1864,* New York, 1865. The letter does not appear in *The Bugle Call.*

H

8843. The Bryant Festival at "The Century," November 5, M.DCCC.LXIV.

New York: D. Appleton and Company, 443 & 445 Broadway. M.DCCC.LXV.

"Bryant's Seventieth Birthday," pp. 43-46. Collected in *Songs of Many Seasons*, 1875.

For comment see entry No. 1692.

8844. HYMN. WRITTEN FOR THE OCCASION BY OLIVER WENDELL HOLMES. TUNE—"OLD HUNDRED." GIVER OF ALL THAT CROWNS OUR DAYS ...

⟨n.p., n.d., Boston, Feb. 4, 1865.⟩

Single leaf. Laid paper. 7⅞" x 4¹⁵⁄₁₆". Printed on recto only. It is quite possible that as originally issued the leaf had a blank conjugate.

The hymn also appears in:

Order of Exercises at the Boston Music Hall, on Saturday Evening, February 4th, 1865, to Celebrate the Progress of Freedom's Great Work in the United States of America ...

Single cut sheet, printed on recto only. Both the separate and *Order of Exercises* printing are from the same setting.

Collected in *Songs of Many Seasons*, 1875, under the title "Hymn after the Emancipation Proclamation."

B (*Order* ...)   H (separate)   LC (separate)

8845. "FOR THE SERVICES IN MEMORY OF ABRAHAM LINCOLN"

This poem has been noted in the following publications; the sequence is clear.

A

City of Worcester. Memorial Services in Honor of Abraham Lincoln, the Late President of the United States, at Mechanics Hall, Thursday, June 1, 1865, at 2½ o'Clock ...

Adams & Brown, Printers, Worcester. ⟨Mass.⟩

Cover-title. Single leaf folded to make four pages. The poem appears on p. ⟨4⟩.

B

City of Boston. Memorial Services in Honor of Abraham Lincoln ... at Music Hall, Thursday, June 1, 1865, at 3 o'Clock, ...

⟨Boston, 1865⟩

Cover-title. Single leaf folded to make four pages. The poem appears on p. ⟨3⟩.

C

A Memorial of Abraham Lincoln ...

Boston: Printed by Order of the City Council, 1865.

Issued after June 7, 1865.

Collected in *Songs of Many Seasons*, 1875.

AAS (A, B)   B (A, C)   H (B, C)   LC (B)   Y (B)

8846. No Time Like the Old Time ... Music by Ernest Leslie ...

Boston G. D. Russell & Company 126 Tremont, Opp. Park St. ... 1865 ...

Sheet music. Cover-title. Plate number 665.

Deposited Oct. 19, 1865. Collected in *Before the Curfew*, 1888.

H   Y

8847. Humorous Poems ...

Boston: Ticknor and Fields. 1865.

Printed paper wrapper; and, cloth.

Reprint save for:

"Our Oldest Friend," pp. 95-97.

"A Farewell to Agassiz," pp. 97-100.

"A Sea Dialogue," pp. 89-90. Previously in *The Boatswain's Whistle*, 1864, above.

"The Jubilee," pp. 91-92. Previously in *The Boatswain's Whistle*, 1864, above.

Advertised for Sept. 1, 1865, ALG June 15, 1865. Advertised for October, ALG Oct. 2, 1865. Deposited Nov. 17, 1865. Listed (as in paper wrapper) ALG Dec. 1, 1865. Listed Bkr Dec. 30, 1865; PC Dec. 30, 1865. Advertised (Trübner importation) as *this day* Bkr Dec. 30, 1865. Listed Bkr (again) Feb. 28, 1866.

BPL   H   Y

8848. Fifty-Ninth Anniversary Celebration of the New England Society, in the City of New York, at the Astor House, Dec. 22, 1864 ...

New York: John F. Trow, Printer, 50 Greene St. 1865.

Printed paper wrapper.

Letter, Boston, Dec. 15, 1864, p. 20.

H

8849. LECTURE. 1865. [PRIVATE COPY.]

⟨n.p., probably Boston, 1865⟩

Otherwise "The Poetry of the War." Anonymous.

Not seen. Entry on the basis of Currier-Tilton, pp. 127-128, where the piece is described as a privately printed production, 54 pp., designed for the author's personal use. "The only copy noted is in the Huntington Library, being the Wakeman copy, lot 511 of the sale catalogue ... It has never been included in any of Holmes's published books ..."

8850. "OUR FIRST CITIZEN"

Written on the death of Edward Everett. Noted in the following publications. Sequence, if any, undetermined. Collected in *Songs of Many Seasons,* 1875.

A

A Memorial of Edward Everett, from the City of Boston.

> Boston: Printed by Order of the City Council. MDCCCLXV.

> "Our First Citizen," pp. 189-191.

> Issued in three formats. For comment see entry No. 4463.

B

Tribute of the Massachusetts Historical Society, to the Memory of Edward Everett, January 30, 1865.

> Boston: Massachusetts Historical Society. 1865.

> "Our First Citizen," pp. 65-67.

> Printed from the types of *Printing A,* above.

> Currier-Tilton (p. 567) report both small and large paper formats. BAL has noted this printing in but one format, size varying from 10¹³⁄₁₆″ x 6⁹⁄₁₆″ to 10¹⁵⁄₁₆″ x 6½″. Cloth; and, printed paper wrapper.

H (A, B)   NYPL (A, B)

8851. Verses from the Island Book.

> Cambridge: Printed at the Riverside Press. 1865.

Reprint save for "Prelude," pp. ⟨iii⟩-iv.

Y

8852. OBITUARY NOTICES OF HON. ISAAC EDWARD MORSE ...

> ⟨n.p., n.d., 1866⟩

Caption-title. The above on p. ⟨1⟩.

Single cut sheet folded to make four pages. Unpaged. 11″ x 8⅜″ full. Text on pp. ⟨1⟩ and ⟨3⟩; otherwise unprinted.

On p. ⟨3⟩: *From the New Orleans Crescent. The Late Isaac E. Morse ... O.W.H.*

H

8853. ⟨ADDRESS AT THE DINNER OF THE HARVARD ALUMNI ASSOCIATION, 1866⟩ BROTHERS OF THE ASSOCIATION OF THE ALUMNI ...

> ⟨n.p., n.d., 1866⟩

Caption-title. The above on p. ⟨1⟩.

5 separate leaves. 11⅛″ x 5⅝″. Printed on rectos only. Unpaged.

Anonymous. Printed for the author's use in reading, July 19, 1866.

Before I can open my lips to speak the few brief words of welcome ...

H

8854. Proceedings of the Massachusetts Historical Society. 1864–1865.

> Boston: Published for the Society, by Wiggin and Lunt. M. DCCC. LXVI.

Reprint save for:

"Dr. Holmes's Remarks ⟨on Dante⟩," pp. 277-278.

"Dr. Holmes's Remarks ⟨on George Livermore⟩," pp. 456-458. *Here reprinted from the next entry?*

H

8855. Tribute of the Massachusetts Historical Society to the Memory of George Livermore.

> Boston: Massachusetts Historical Society. 1866.

Printed paper wrapper.

"Remarks," pp. 17-19. Also in (reprinted from?) the preceding entry.

H   Y

8856. THE GUARDIAN ANGEL ... IN TWO VOLUMES ...

> LONDON: SAMPSON LOW, SON, AND MARSTON, MILTON HOUSE, LUDGATE HILL. 1867 ...

2 Vols. For first American edition see next entry.

1: ⟨i⟩-xvi, ⟨1⟩-294, 2 pp. advertisements. 7⁷⁄₁₆″ x 4⅞″.
2: ⟨i⟩-⟨viii⟩, ⟨1⟩-302, 2 pp. advertisements.

1: ⟨-⟩⁸, 1-18⁸, 19⁴.
2: ⟨-⟩⁴, 1-19⁸. *Note:* Signature mark 3 lacking in some copies; significance not determined.

C cloth: plum. Cream end papers. Inserted at back of Vol. 2 is a publisher's catalog, pp. ⟨1⟩-24, dated Oct. 1867.

Advertised as *in preparation* Ath July 27, 1867. Advertised under *New Novels* Ath Aug. 31, 1867. Announced PC Sept. 2, 1867. Advertised under *New Novels* Ath Sept. 7, Sept. 14, 1867. "A very handsome sum has been paid to ... ⟨Holmes⟩ by an English publisher for advance sheets, and the novel will appear in London the same day it is issued complete in Boston." —ALG Sept. 16, 1867. Announced PC Sept. 16, Oct. 1, 1867. Noted as *forthcoming* Ath Oct. 5, PC Oct. 15, 1867. Published Oct. 25, 1867, according to Bkr Aug. 1868. Noted as *this day* Ath Oct. 26, 1867. Noted as *now ready* PC Nov. 1, 1867. Listed PC Nov. 1, 1867; Ath Nov. 2, 1867. Noted as *now ready* Ath Nov. 2, 1867. Advertised, with extracts from four English reviews, PC Nov. 15, 1867. Listed ALG Dec. 2, 1867.

CAW

8857. THE GUARDIAN ANGEL ...

BOSTON: TICKNOR AND FIELDS. 1867.

First American edition. See preceding entry.

⟨i⟩-xii, ⟨1⟩-420. 7 1/16″ x 4 1/2″.

⟨-⟩6, 1-1712, 186. *Also signed:* ⟨-⟩6, A-D, ⟨E⟩-W, ⟨X⟩-Z8, AA2.

C cloth: blue; green; purple; terra-cotta. Brown-coated on white end papers. Flyleaves.

Copy in H inscribed by Holmes Nov. 2, 1867; another, Nov. 3, 1867. Deposited Nov. 4, 1867. Advertised for Nov. 5, ALG Nov. 1, 1867. Listed ALG Nov. 15, 1867.

BA   H   NYPL

8858. The Atlantic Almanac 1868 Edited by Oliver Wendell Holmes and Donald G. Mitchell ...

Boston: Ticknor and Fields, Office of the Atlantic Monthly ... 1867 ...

"The Seasons," pp. 2-13. Collected in *Pages from an Old Volume of Life,* 1883.

For comment see entry No. 266.

8859. Russian Account of the Official Mission to Russia of Hon. G. V. Fox, in 1866. Translated by S. N. Buynitzky for the Department of State ...

Washington: Government Printing Office. 1867.

Printed paper wrapper.

"Poem," *Though watery deserts hold apart,* pp. 18-19. Collected in *Songs of Many Seasons,* 1875.

B   H   NYPL

8860. TEACHING FROM THE CHAIR AND AT THE BEDSIDE. AN INTRODUCTORY LECTURE DELIVERED BEFORE THE MEDICAL CLASS OF HARVARD UNIVERSITY, NOVEMBER 6, 1867 ...

BOSTON: DAVID CLAPP & SON 334 WASHINGTON STREET. 1867.

⟨1⟩-45, blank leaf. 9 1/4″ x 5 11/16″.

⟨1⟩-64.

Printed gray paper wrapper.

AAS   H   Y

8861. LINES READ AT A FAREWELL DINNER GIVEN TO LONGFELLOW, BEFORE HIS DEPARTURE FOR EUROPE, MAY 27, 1868.

⟨n.p., n.d., 1868⟩

Cover-title. Single cut sheet folded to make four pages.

⟨1⟩-3. 8 5/16″ full x 5 3/8″.

At end of text: *O.W.H.*

The lines were read at a dinner on May 23, 1868. Longfellow sailed on May 27, 1868.

Note: A galley-proof of the poem as published in the *Boston Daily Advertiser,* May 26, 1868, dated at end May 23, 1868, is in H.

B   H

8862. Reception and Entertainment of the Chinese Embassy, by the City of Boston. 1868.

Boston: Alfred Mudge & Son, City Printers, 34 School Street. 1868.

Printed paper wrapper; and, cloth.

"Poem," *Brothers, whom we may not reach,* pp. 41-42. Collected in *Songs of Many Seasons,* 1875.

AAS   H   NYPL

8863. Songs and Poems of the Class of Eighteen Hundred and Twenty-Nine. Third Edition ...

Boston: Prentiss & Deland, Book and Job Printers, No. 40, Congress Street. 1868.

Reprint save for:

*"All Here," pp. 90-92.

*"Choose You This Day Whom Ye Will Serve," pp. 69-71.

†"In Memory of J.D.R.," p. 63.

*"The Last Charge," pp. 77-78.

†"Lines. Written for the Class Meeting, 1860," pp. 41-42.

*"My Annual.—For the Boys of '29," pp. 84-86.

*"Once More," pp. 96-99.

*"Our Classmate. F.W.C.," pp. 73-75. A portion had prior publication in *The (Old) Farmer's Almanac ... for ... 1865 ...* , Boston, 1864, above.

*"Sherman's in Savannah!," p. 83.

•Collected in *Songs of Many Seasons*, 1875.

†Collected in *Poetical Works, Household Edition*, 1877.

AAS copy received Aug. 1868.

AAS   H   Y

8864. The Atlantic Almanac 1869 Edited by Donald G. Mitchell ...

Boston: Ticknor and Fields, Office of The Atlantic Monthly ... 1868 ...

"Talk Concerning the Human Body and Its Management," pp. 47-58. Collected in *Pages from an Old Volume of Life,* 1883.

For comment see entry No. 4037.

8865. Medical Jurisprudence. The Annual Address before the Massachusetts Medical Society, June 3, 1868. By Henry Grafton Clark ... ⟨Second Edition⟩

Boston: David Clapp & Son 334 Washington Street. 1868.

Printed paper wrapper.

Note: The first edition, which does not contain the Holmes material, is paged ⟨1⟩-27. The second edition is made up of the sheets of the first edition with an added gathering paged ⟨29⟩-36. The added matter may have had prior publication, or perhaps simultaneous publication, in another larger, unlocated, publication. The setting of the added matter is not from the setting of either the *Boston Medical and Surgical Journal;* or, *Proceedings of the Massachusetts Historical Society.*

Contains Holmes's appreciation of Dr. James Jackson, pp. 31-32; and, his address on J. Mason Warren, pp. 33-34.

All examined copies of both editions have the following features:

P. 9: A pasted-down erratum slip comprising four lines of verse.

P. 23, line 5 up: The error *he* for *one.*

BML

8866. TRIBUTES FROM THE UNITED STATES OF AMERICA TO CHRISTIAN GOTTFRIED EHRENBERG ON HIS FIFTIETH ANNIVERSARY AS DOCTOR OF MEDICINE NOVEMBER 5. 1868. (EXTRACT.)

⟨Berlin, n.d., 1868⟩

Caption-title. Preceding at head of p. ⟨1⟩. Single cut sheet folded to make four pages.

⟨1-4⟩. 9¹³⁄₁₆″ x 7¹³⁄₁₆″.

Text of Holmes's poem, pp. ⟨1-2⟩. German translation, pp. ⟨3-4⟩. Collected in *Songs of Many Seasons,* 1875.

Offprint from: *Tributes from the United States of America to Christian Gottfried Ehrenberg on His Fiftieth Anniversary as Doctor of Medicine November 5. 1868* ⟨Berlin, n.d., 1868⟩. Cover-title. Printed self-wrapper.

PDH

8867. ⟨Hymn for the 1869 reunion, Harvard University, Class of 1829⟩ THOU GRACIOUS POWER, WHOSE MERCY LENDS ...

⟨n.p., Cambridge, Mass.⟩ JAN. 6th, 1869.

Anonymous.

Single leaf. Printed on recto only. 7⅞″ x 5″. Collected in *Songs of Many Seasons,* 1875.

Two printings noted. Sequence, if any, not determined. Publication may have been simultaneous. The designations are almost purely arbitrary.

A

Printed on unwatermarked wove paper.

The letter *l* in *lends* (line 1) is set immediately over the *d* in *friends* (line 2).

B

Printed on laid paper. Some copies show the watermark, or a portion thereof: *Rand, Avery & Co. Boston*

The letter *l* in *lends* (line 1) is set immediately over the *s* in *friends* (line 2).

B (B)   H (A,B)   NYPL (A)

8868. THE MEDICAL PROFESSION IN MASSACHUSETTS. A LECTURE OF A COURSE BY MEMBERS OF THE MASSACHUSETTS HISTORICAL SOCIETY, DELIVERED BEFORE THE LOWELL INSTITUTE, JAN. 29, 1869 . . .

BOSTON: PRESS OF JOHN WILSON AND SON. 1869.

⟨1⟩-45, blank leaf. Laid paper. 9⅛" full x 5⅞". ⟨1-6⟩⁴. *Signed:* ⟨1⟩-3⁸.

Printed gray paper wrapper.

Offprint from: *Lectures Delivered in a Course before the Lowell Institute, in Boston, by Members of the Massachusetts Historical Society, on Subjects Relating to the Early History of Massachusetts,* Boston, 1869. Issued after Feb. 16, 1869; further publication information wanting; copies in MHS NYPL Y.

BPL copy received from Holmes May 20, 1869.

AAS   BPL   H   Y

8869. "A HYMN OF PEACE"

There were several near-simultaneous printings of this hymn. The sequence is uncertain save for the first three of the following entries. The other entries, save for the *History . . .* , 1871, are listed arbitrarily. Collected in *Songs of Many Seasons,* 1875.

A

The National Peace Jubilee, and Musical Reporter.

Boston . . . May 15, 1869 . . . ⟨to⟩ July 24, 1869 . . .

An occasional newspaper. Complete in ten numbers. Issued weekly save for the week of June 19, for which no number was issued.

"A Hymn of Peace," issue of June 5, p. ⟨1⟩.

Locations: B

B

. . . Music to be Performed at the Grand National Peace Jubilee! To be Held in Boston, June, 1869 . . .

Boston: Published by Oliver Ditson & Co. 277 Washington Street. New York: C. H. Ditson & Co., 711 Broadway. ⟨1869⟩

Cloth; and, printed paper wrapper. At head of title: "Let Us Have Peace."

"A Hymn of Peace," pp. 9-11, of the appendix.

Title deposited Feb. 20, 1869. Book deposited June 10, 1869. Reissued in 1872: *Music to be Performed at the World's Peace Jubilee and International Musical Festival, in Boston, June, 1872,* Boston, 1872.

Locations: H   Y

C

"Let Us Have Peace." Programme of the National Peace Jubilee Concert. First Day. Boston, Tuesday, June 15, 1869 . . .

A. M. Lunt, Printer, 112 Washington Street. ⟨Boston⟩

Single leaf folded to four pages. Cover-title.

"Hymn of Peace," p. ⟨3⟩.

Two states of undetermined sequence noted:

A: Period following the date 1869 on front.

B: Comma following the date 1869 on front.

Locations: B   H   NYPL   Y

D

Official Monthly Bulletin of the Great National Peace Jubilee and Musical Festival, to be Held in the City of Boston, on Tuesday, Wednesday, & Thursday, June 15, 16 & 17, 1869, in Honor of the Restoration of Peace and Union throughout the Land . . .

Published by George Coolidge, 3 Milk Street, Boston. ⟨1869⟩

An occasional publication. Complete in five numbers:

No. 1. February, 1869. The Copyright Office reports that a title-page for this publication was deposited Feb. 2, 1869; no further copyright action for this or for the succeeding parts found in the records.

No. 2. March and April, 1869.

No. 3. March and April, 1869 ⟨*sic*⟩.

No. 4. May and June, 1869. "A Hymn of Peace," p. 4. *Note:* Currier-Tilton, p. 326, report deposit date of June 9, 1869; the Copyright Office reports inability to support the statement.

No. 5. May and June, 1869 ⟨*sic*⟩. "A Hymn of Peace," p. 4.

Note: The title-pages and imprints vary from number to number.

Also note: No. 3 is printed, with some alterations, from the setting of No. 2; No. 5 is an altered reprint of No. 4.

Locations: H

E

A Hymn of Peace. Written for the National Peace Jubilee by Oliver Wendell Holmes, to the Music of Keller's "American Hymn." . . .

⟨n.p., n.d., 1869⟩

Almost certainly prepared as a proof and not designed for publication in this form. Single leaf. 3⅞" x 2½". Printed on recto only. The H copy inscribed in pencil: *June 15, 1869.*

Locations: H

F

... A Hymn of Peace ...

Boston   Oliver Ditson & Co ... 1869 ...

Sheet music. Cover-title. At head of title: Selections from Music Performed at the Peace Festival Jubilee Boston 1869 ...   Plate number 25358.

Two printings noted:

1: P. ⟨6⟩ blank.

2: P. ⟨6⟩ imprinted with advertisements.

Locations: H (1,2)

G

The Poems of Arlington . . . Published by M.A.C. Finch.

Washington, D. C.: Powell & Ginck, Prs., 409 F St. 1869.

Printed paper wrapper. "The Hymn of Peace," pp. ⟨17-18⟩.

Title entered June 11, 1869; no record of deposit of book.

Locations: AAS   NYPL

H

History of the National Peace Jubilee and Great Musical Festival ... by P. S. Gilmore ...

Published by the Author, and for Sale by Lee and Shepard, 149 Washington Street, Boston; Lee, Shepard, and Dillingham, 49 Greene Street, New York. 1871.

"A Hymn of Peace," p. 295. An account of the writing of the hymn, p. 290 *et. seq.*

Locations: H

8870. IN MEMORY OF FITZ-GREENE HALLECK. READ AT THE DEDICATION OF HIS MONUMENT, IN GUILFORD, CONNECTICUT, JULY 8, 1869.

⟨n.p., n.d., Boston, 1869⟩

Anonymous. Caption-title. Preceding at head of p. ⟨1⟩. Single cut sheet folded to make four pages. Text on pp. ⟨1-2⟩, otherwise blank.

⟨1-4⟩. 8⅛" scant x 5".

Currier-Tilton, p. 137, quote a letter from Holmes (in HEH) indicating that this leaflet was printed prior to the following, in which the poem also appears: *A Description of the Dedication of the Monument Erected at Guilford, Connecticut, in Honor of Fitz-Greene Hal-*

leck ... , New York, 1869; printed paper wrapper.

Collected in *Songs of Many Seasons,* 1875.

H   Y

8871. BONAPARTE, AUG. 15th, 1769.—HUMBOLDT, SEPT. 14th, 1769 ...

⟨Boston⟩ SEPTEMBER 14, 1869.

Caption-title. Anonymous.

Single leaf. 10¹³⁄₁₆" x 6¹⁄₁₆". Printed on recto only. Printed for the author, with some textual variations, from the setting used in *Atlantic Monthly,* Nov. 1869.

Issued October, 1869, according to a letter by Holmes quoted by Currier-Tilton, p. 137. Collected in *Songs of Many Seasons,* 1875. Reprinted in *Address Delivered on the Centennial Anniversary of the Birth of Alexander von Humboldt ...* , by Louis Agassiz, Boston, 1869; issued after Nov. 17, 1869.

CAW

8872. HISTORY OF THE AMERICAN STEREOSCOPE, JOSEPH L. BATES. BOSTON. PATENTED AUG 13th 1867. FROM THE PHILADELPHIA PHOTOGRAPHER, JANUARY, 1869.

⟨Boston, 1869⟩

Cover-title.

⟨1⟩-14; advertisements, pp. 15-16. 6½" x 4¼".

⟨-⟩⁸.

Printed self-wrapper.

Two states noted; the order is all but certain:

A

On p. 16, last two lines: JOSEPH L. BATES, / 129 WASHINGTON STREET, BOSTON. /

B

On p. 16, last two lines: JOSEPH L. BATES, / BOSTON. /

Note: Although the copyright notice is in the name of Benerman & Wilson the pamphlet was almost certainly issued by Joseph L. Bates, Boston, whose advertisement is on p. 16. The copyright notice, dated 1868, p. ⟨3⟩, relates to the copyright of the periodical in which the article first appeared; the periodical, issue of Jan. 1869, was deposited for copyright in 1868.

Pp. ⟨3⟩-9 are devoted to Holmes's text; pp. 10-14 devoted to an editorial on Holmes's article.

MHS (A,B)

8873. NEARING THE SNOW-LINE ...

⟨n.p., n.d., Boston, 1869⟩

Single leaf. Printed on recto only. 4⅞" x 5¹¹⁄₁₆" scant. Anonymous. Printed from the types of *The Atlantic Monthly*, Jan. 1870. *Proof only?* The text varies somewhat from the text in the periodical. Collected in *Songs of Many Seasons*, 1875.

CAW

8874. ... Services on the Laying of the Corner Stone of Memorial Hall, October 6, 1870.

⟨Cambridge: John Wilson and Son, 1870⟩

At head of title: Harvard College. Single cut sheet folded to four pages. The above on front.

"Hymn," *Not with the anguish of hearts*, pp. 3-4. Collected in *Songs of Many Seasons*, 1875.

AAS H Y

8875. ... A Descriptive Catalogue of the War-ren Anatomical Museum. By J.B.S. Jackson ...

Boston: A. Williams and Company. 1870.

At head of title: Harvard University.

Contains a series of descriptive notes by Holmes.

H copy received June 13, 1870.

H

8876. MECHANISM IN THOUGHT AND MORALS. AN ADDRESS DELIVERED BE-FORE THE PHI BETA KAPPA SOCIETY OF HARVARD UNIVERSITY, JUNE 29, 1870. WITH NOTES AND AFTER-THOUGHTS ...

BOSTON: JAMES R. OSGOOD & CO., LATE TICK-NOR & FIELDS, AND FIELDS, OSGOOD, & CO. 1871.

⟨1⟩-101, blank leaf. 6⅞" x 4⁷⁄₁₆".

⟨1⟩-6⁸, 7⁴.

C cloth: green; purple; terra-cotta. C cloth em-bossed with a sprinkling of small stars: purple. FL cloth: terra-cotta. Covers bevelled. Brown-coated on white end papers. Flyleaves.

Two printings noted:

1: As above.

2: ⟨1-3¹², 4-5⁶, 6⁴⟩. *Signed:* ⟨1⟩-6⁸, 7⁴.

Note: The following contemporary notices sug-gest that the Boston and the London (Low) edi-tions were simultaneously issued:

Boston: Published in January according to a note in ALG Feb. 1, 1871.
London: Advertised as *immediately* Ath Jan. 7, 14, 1871.

London: Advertised as *this day* Ath Jan. 28, 1871.
London: Listed Ath Jan. 28, 1871.
London: Advertised as *this day* PC Feb. 1, 1871.
Boston: BA copy received Feb. 1, 1871.
Boston: H copy received Feb. 4, 1871.
Boston: Listed ALG Feb. 15, 1871.
Boston: Deposited Feb. 17, 1871.
Boston: Listed as a Trübner importation Bkr April 3, 1871.

H (1st)   NYPL (1st, 2nd)   Y (1st)

8877. VALEDICTORY ADDRESS, DELIV-ERED TO THE GRADUATING CLASS OF THE BELLEVUE HOSPITAL COLLEGE, MARCH 2, 1871 ... [REPRINTED FROM THE N. Y. MEDICAL JOURNAL, APRIL, 1871.]

NEW YORK: D. APPLETON & COMPANY, 549 & 551 BROADWAY. 1871.

⟨1⟩-23. 9⅛" x 5¹³⁄₁₆" scant.

⟨1⟩⁸, 2⁴.

Printed yellow-coated on white paper wrapper.

Listed ALG May 15, 1871.

H

8878. Order of Exercises at the Musical Enter-tainment, in Honor of His Imperial High-ness, the Grand Duke Alexis, of Russia ... Boston Music Hall ... December 9, 1871 ...

Rockwell & Churchill, City Printers, 122 Washington Street, Boston. ⟨1871⟩

Single cut sheet folded to four pages. The above on front.

"Song," *Shadowed so long by the storm-cloud of danger*, p. ⟨2⟩. Collected in *Songs of Many Seasons*, 1875.

AAS

8879. The Buyers' Manual and Business Guide; Being a Description of the Leading Business Houses ... of the Pacific Coast ... Compiled by J. Price and C. S. Haley.

San Francisco: Francis & Valentine ... 1872.

"Aunt Tabitha," p. 142. Collected in *The Poet at the Breakfast-Table*, 1872.

For comment see entry No. 7261.

8880. One Hundred Choice Selections No. 5 ... Compiled ... by Phineas Garrett ...

... P. Garrett & Co., 702 Chestnut Street, Philadelphia ... Chicago ... 1872.

"Bill and Joe," pp. 46-48. Collected in *Songs of Many Seasons,* 1875.

For comment see entry No. 4759.

8881. THE POET AT THE BREAKFAST-TABLE. HIS TALKS WITH HIS FELLOW-BOARDERS AND THE READER.

BOSTON: JAMES R. OSGOOD AND COMPANY, LATE TICKNOR & FIELDS, AND FIELDS, OSGOOD, & CO. 1872.

Anonymous.

⟨i-iv⟩, ⟨1⟩-418, blank leaf. Frontispiece. 7⁷⁄₁₆″ x 4⅞″.

⟨a⟩², A-Z⁸, ⟨b⟩². *Also signed:* ⟨a⟩², 1-⟨8⟩, 9-17¹², 18⁶.

Two states noted:

1: P. 9, running head: TALLE for TABLE

2: P. 9, running head: TABLE correctly spelled.

C cloth: green; purple. FL cloth: purple; terracotta. P cloth: green. Covers bevelled. Brown-coated on white end papers. Flyleaves.

Noted for Oct. 7 WTC Oct. 3, 1872. Noted as *soon* WTC Oct. 10, 1872. H (2nd) received from publisher Oct. 16, 1872. BPL (2nd) received from publisher Oct. 18, 1872. Deposited (2nd) Oct. 19, 1872. Copies of both states received by BA Oct. 19, 1872. Copy of the 1st in H inscribed by Holmes Oct. 20, 1872. Listed WTC Oct. 24, 1872.

Note on the London Editions

The London (*Hotten*) edition comprises the first half of the book as published in Boston; reprinted from *Atlantic Monthly,* Jan.–June, 1872. Possibly preceded the Boston edition but the record is not clear; perhaps issued simultaneously with the Boston edition. The following publication notes indicate the problem: *Spectator,* Oct. 19, 1872, listed the Hotten edition as one of the "publications of the week." An unidentified edition (Hotten?) listed by Ath Oct. 19, 1872. Listed PC Nov. 16, 1872. The *Routledge* edition listed Ath Nov. 9; PC Nov. 16; Bkr Dec. 1872.

AAS (2nd)   H (1st, 2nd)   LC (1st; not a deposit copy)   NYPL (1st, 2nd)

8882. THE CLAIMS OF DENTISTRY. AN ADDRESS DELIVERED AT THE COMMENCEMENT EXERCISES OF THE DENTAL DEPARTMENT IN HARVARD UNIVERSITY, FEBRUARY 14, 1872 ...

BOSTON: PRINTED BY RAND, AVERY, & CO. 1872.

⟨1⟩-35. 9⅛″ x 6⅛″.

⟨1⟩-4⁴, 5².

Printed pinkish-tan paper wrapper. Two printings of the wrapper have been noted; sequence not established:

A: Outer back wrapper imprinted: *Harvard University. Dental Department* ...

B: Outer back wrapper blank.

H   NYPL   Y

8883. His Imperial Highness the Grand Duke Alexis in the United States of America during the Winter of 1871–72 ... for Private Distribution

Cambridge   Printed at the Riverside Press 1872

Leather. Also cloth?

Untitled poem, *One word more to the guest we have gathered to greet,* pp. 97-98. Collected in *Songs of Many Seasons,* 1875.

H   Y

8884. One Hundred Choice Selections No. 6 ... Compiled ... by Phineas Garrett ...

... P. Garrett & Co., 702 Chestnut Street, Philadelphia ... Chicago ... 1873.

"First Appearance in Type," pp. 175-176. Not located elsewhere. *By Holmes?*

For comment see entry No. 2463.

8885. The Tonic ...

⟨Portland, Maine, 1873⟩

An occasional newspaper issued for the benefit of the Maine General Hospital. Presumably complete in ten numbers, the first dated June 7, 1873; the tenth dated June 19, 1873.

"A Puzzle." In issue of June 19, 1873. For first book appearance see *Fair Play,* 1875, below.

PL

8886. AUTHOR'S PRIVATE COPY. NO. ...

⟨n.p., n.d., Cambridge, 1873⟩

Caption-title. The above at head of text, p. ⟨1⟩. Anonymous. Single cut sheet folded to make four pages.

⟨1⟩-4. 10⅞″ full x 6⅞″.

Untitled poem, *Hang out our banners on the stately tower,* written for the opening of The Fifth Avenue Theatre, New York, Dec. 3, 1873. Collected in *Songs of Many Seasons,* 1875.

Note: Privately printed in a small edition; each copy numbered; H has copies 1 and 18.

H

8887. Centennial of the Boston Pier, or the Long Wharf Corporation. 1873.

Cambridge: Press of John Wilson and Son. 1873.

Printed paper wrapper.

"Remarks"; and, poem, *Dear friends, we are strangers,* pp. 18-20. Poem collected in *Songs of Many Seasons,* 1875.

H NYPL Y

8888. . . . Memorial Services in Honor of Charles Sumner, at Music Hall, Wednesday, 29th April, 1874.

Rockwell & Churchill, City Printers, 122 Washington Street, Boston.

Single cut sheet folded to four pages. At head of title: City of Boston. The above on front. Issued as a program.

"Hymn," *Once more, ye sacred towers,* p. ⟨3⟩. Collected in *Songs of Many Seasons,* 1875.

The hymn was reprinted in *New-York Tribune. Extra No. 18, Sumner Eulogies,* May, 1874; and, *A Memorial of Charles Sumner, from the City of Boston . . . ,* Boston, 1874.

BA BPL H Y

8889. . . . Dedication Day. June 23, 1874.

⟨n.p., Cambridge, 1874⟩

Single cut sheet folded to four pages. At head of title: Harvard College. Issued as a program. The above on first page.

"Hymn," p. ⟨3⟩, *Where, girt around by savage foes . . .* Collected in *Songs of Many Seasons,* 1875.

Note: Occurs on at least two colors of paper: Pale green T-grained paper; pale blue T-grained paper.

AAS H Y

8890. . . . Proceedings of the Massachusetts Historical Society, from January to June, 1874 . . .

⟨Boston: Massachusetts Historical Society, 1874⟩

Printed paper wrapper. Cover-title. At head of title: IV.

"Remarks . . . ⟨on Joseph Scaliger⟩," pp. 315-317. Revised and reprinted in the Society's

Proceedings . . . 1873–1875, Boston, 1875. The following is sufficient to identify the two texts:

Original

P. 317, line 1: *prodigality which was prevalent, and of the singular activity in /*

Revised

prodigality which was prevalent. On the whole, after living /

Y

8891. REMARKS ON MEDICAL EDUCATION

Two printings noted. Sequence not known although some significance may attach to the fact that the broadside printing is (in part) from the setting of the *Boston Daily Advertiser,* Oct. 23, 1874.

A

THE HARVARD MEDICAL COLLEGE. / ⟨*rule*⟩ / Meeting to Promote the Erection of a New / Building. / ⟨*rule*⟩ / ⟨*text, set in three columns, divided by vertical rules*⟩ / ⟨*n.p., n.d., but almost certainly Boston, Oct. 1874*⟩

Single cut sheet. Printed on recto only. 20⅛″ x 9⅛″.

Contains Holmes's remarks, about 1¼ columns.

Locations: H

B

MEDICAL EDUCATION. / ⟨*decorated rule*⟩ / The Harvard Medical School, by its new system of medical instruction, now in / successful operation ⟨*etc., etc.*⟩ / [Extracts from addresses delivered at a public meeting held in Hor- / ticultural Hall, October 22, 1874.] / ⟨*etc., etc.*⟩ / REMARKS OF DR. OLIVER WENDELL HOLMES. / ⟨*etc., etc.*⟩ / ⟨*n.p., n.d., 1874?*⟩

Single cut sheet folded to four pages. Unpaged. Page: 10½″ x 8″. Holmes's remarks (abridged) pp. ⟨2-3⟩.

Locations: BA

8892. PROFESSOR JEFFRIES WYMAN. A MEMORIAL OUTLINE . . . REPRINTED FROM THE ATLANTIC MONTHLY FOR NOVEMBER, 1874.

⟨n.p., n.d., Boston, 1874⟩

Cover-title.

⟨1⟩-15. 9½″ x 6¹⁄₁₆″.

⟨-⟩⁸.

Printed self-wrapper.

H LC NYPL

8893. In Memoriam. Died at Newport, R. I., September 30, 1874, Gardner Brewer ...

Boston: Printed for Private Distribution. 1874.

Printed paper wrapper.

Tribute, pp. 8-12.

H Y

8894. Proceedings of a Special Meeting of the Massachusetts Historical Society, December 16, 1873 ...

Boston: Press of John Wilson and Son. 1874.

Printed paper wrapper.

"A Ballad of the Boston Tea Party," pp. 56-58. Collected in *Songs of Many Seasons, 1875.*

H NYPL Y

8895. SONGS OF MANY SEASONS. 1862–1874 ...

BOSTON: JAMES R. OSGOOD AND COMPANY, LATE TICKNOR & FIELDS, AND FIELDS, OSGOOD, & CO. 1875.

Three printings (Oct. 1874; Nov. 1874; Feb. 1875) have been identified:

1

⟨i⟩-xii, ⟨1⟩-216. $6^{11}/_{16}$" x $4^{11}/_{16}$". Wove paper.

⟨-⟩⁶, 1-9¹². *Also signed:* ⟨-⟩⁶, A-M⁸, N⁴.

2

⟨i⟩-xii, ⟨1⟩-216. Laid paper.

⟨-⟩⁶, 1-9¹². *Also signed:* ⟨-⟩⁶, A-M⁸, N⁴.

3

⟨i⟩-xii, ⟨1⟩-216. Laid paper.

⟨-⟩⁶, A-K, ⟨L⟩-M⁸, N-⟨O⟩². *Also signed:* ⟨-⟩⁶, 1-9¹².

S cloth: purple. C cloth: green; purple. FL cloth: terra-cotta. Covers bevelled. Brown-coated on white end papers. Flyleaves.

A copy of the first printing received by H Oct. 24, 1874. Listed PW Oct. 24, 1874. Deposited Oct. 27, 1874. Reviewed Ath Feb. 6, 1875.

AAS (3rd) H (1st, 2nd) LC (1st, being a deposit copy)

8896. The Ark ...

Boston ... 1875 ...

An occasional newspaper. For comment see entry No. 281.

"Suggestive Hints from Oliver Wendell Holmes," Vol. 1, No. 5, p. ⟨1⟩.

8897. CRIME AND AUTOMATISM. WITH A NOTICE OF M. PROSPER DESPINE'S PSYCHOLOGIE NATURELLE ...

⟨n.p., n.d., Boston, 1875⟩

Caption-title. The above on p. ⟨1⟩.

⟨1⟩-16. $9^{1}/_{2}$" x $6^{1}/_{16}$".

⟨-⟩⁸.

Printed self-wrapper.

Offprint from the *Atlantic Monthly,* April, 1875.

BML

8898. Memorial Bunker Hill ...

James R. Osgood & Co., Publishers, Boston. ⟨1875⟩

Printed paper wrapper. Cover-title.

"Grandmother's Story of Bunker-Hill Battle: As She Saw it from the Belfry," pp. ⟨1-4⟩. Collected in *Poetical Works, Household Edition,* 1877. For a privately printed separate edition see entry No. 8911.

Deposited June 8, 1875. Listed PW June 12, 1875.

Note: Review copies were issued with an inserted slip, 7 lines, headed: TO THE PRESS.

BA H NYPL

8899. The Harvard Book. A Series of Historical, Biographical, and Descriptive Sketches. By Various Authors ... Collected and Published by F. O. Vaille and H. A. Clark, Class of 1874 ...

Cambridge: Welch, Bigelow, and Company, University Press. 1875.

2 Vols. Cloth; and, leather.

Reprint save for:

"The Medical School," Vol. 1, pp. ⟨239⟩-251.

"The Holmes Estate," Vol. 2, pp. ⟨424⟩-426.

BA copy received Aug. 17, 1875.

H

8900. Order of Exercises at the Inauguration of the Statue of Gov. Andrew, at the "Old Meeting House," Hingham, Thursday, October 7th, 1875.

Journal Press, Hingham. ⟨1875⟩

Single cut sheet folded to four pages. The above on front. Issued as a program.

"Hymn," *Behold the shape our eyes have known!*, p. <2>. Collected in *Poetical Works, Household Edition*, 1877.

Y

8901. Fair Play ...

Waltham: Printed by Phinney & Barry. October, 1875.

Printed paper wrapper.

A rhymed enigma by Holmes, *My name declares my date to be*, p. <3>. Previously in *The Tonic*, June 19, 1873; see above.

BA   Y

8902. Proceedings of the Bunker Hill Monument Association ... June 23, 1875 ...

Boston: Bunker Hill Monument Association. M DCCC LXXV.

"Joseph Warren," p. 154. Collected in *Poetical Works, Household Edition*, 1877.

H copy received Dec. 22, 1875.

H

Cambridge in the "Centennial." ...

Cambridge ... M DCCC LXXV. <*i.e.*, 1876>

See entry No. 8904.

8903. Laurel Leaves. Original Poems, Stories, and Essays ...

Boston: William F. Gill and Company, 309 Washington Street. 1876.

Facsimile of a letter, p. <vii>.

" 'Old Cambridge',", pp. 169-175. Collected in *Poetical Works, Household Edition*, 1877.

For comment see entry No. 116.

8904. Cambridge in the "Centennial." Proceedings, July 3, 1875, in Celebration of the Centennial Anniversary of Washington's Taking Command of the Continental Army, on Cambridge Common.

Cambridge: Printed by Order of the City Council. M DCCC LXXV. <*i.e.*, 1876>

Printed paper wrapper; and, cloth.

Reprint save for Holmes's response, p. 88.

Contains a complete fiscal statement for the year 1875; hence, issued not before Jan. 1, 1876.

BA   H

8905. Fair Words ... Published in Aid of the St. Luke's Home for Convalescents ...

Boston, February 14, 1876 ...

An occasional newspaper.

"A Rhymed Riddle," p. 12; begins: *"I'm going to* blank," *with failing breath* ... For first book appearance see entry No. 8921.

BA

8906. ... International Exhibition 1876. The National Commemoration, July 4, 1876. Independence Square, Philadelphia ...

Single cut sheet folded to four pages. The above on p. <1>. At head of title: 1776 1876 Issued as a program.

"Welcome to All Nations," p. <1>. Collected in *Poetical Works, Household Edition*, 1877.

Locations: AAS

Note: The poem appears also in the following publications. Those with known publication dates are clearly reprints; those others of unknown date are listed for the record only since it appears obvious that none could have been issued prior to the program.

A

The Centennial Liberty Bell ... by Jos. S. Longshore ... and Benjamin L. Knowles ...

Philadelphia ... 1876.

Deposited Sept. 27, 1876.

B

His Royal Highness Prince Oscar at the National Celebration of the Centennial Anniversary of American Independence ... Philadelphia ... July 4, 1876.

Boston: Printed at the Riverside Press for Private Distribution. 1876.

No record of copyright deposit. H copy received Nov. 13, 1876.

C

Jubilee Collection of Standard Glees and Choruses ...

... Oliver Ditson & Company. New York ... Chicago ... <1876>

Printed paper wrapper. Cover-title. No record of copyright deposit found.

D

New-York Tribune. Extra, No. 33 ... Independence Day Orations and Poems July 4, 1876 ...

<New York, 1876>

Printed paper wrapper. Cover-title. According to an advertisement on the inner front wrapper the publication was available both as a pamphlet and in "sheet form."

E

Barnes' Centenary History. One Hundred Years of American Independence. By the Author of Barnes' Brief History of the United States for Schools ⟨*i.e.,* Joel Dorman Steele⟩.

A. S. Barnes & Company, New York ... 1876.

12(?) parts each in printed paper wrapper. On the basis of internal evidence the book was issued long after July 4, 1876.

8907. Parks for the People. Proceedings of a Public Meeting Held at Faneuil Hall, June 7, 1876.

Boston: Franklin Press: Rand, Avery, & Co. 1876.

Printed paper wrapper.

"Speech ... ," pp. 20-25.

H copy received Oct. 10, 1876.

BA H NYPL

8908. Memoir of Dr. Samuel Gridley Howe. By Julia Ward Howe: With Other Memorial Tributes. Published by the Howe Memorial Committee.

Boston: Printed by Albert J. Wright, 79 Milk Street (Corner of Federal). 1876.

"A Memorial Tribute," pp. 89-91. Collected in *Poetical Works. Household Edition,* 1877. Also in ... *Forty-Fifth Annual Report of the Trustees of the Perkins Institution ... October, 1876,* Boston, 1877; issued after Oct. 19, 1876; before Dec. 22, 1876; reprinted herein?

For comment see entry. No. 9448.

8909. The History of Pittsfield, (Berkshire County,) Massachusetts, from the Year 1800 to the Year 1876. Compiled and Written ... by J.E.A. Smith ...

Springfield: Published by C. W. Bryan & Co., 1876.

Preface to a report on a plowing-match, pp. 666-667. Collected in *The Complete Poetical Works ... Cambridge Edition ...* ⟨1895⟩.

Issued after July, 1876. H copy received Nov. 1, 1876.

H

8910. ⟨Prospectus of⟩ The Native Races of the Pacific States of North America. By Hubert Howe Bancroft.

New York: D. Appleton and Company, 549 & 551 Broadway. 1876.

Printed paper wrapper. Cover-title.

Letter, Jan. 3, 1875, p. 16.

H

8911. NO. ⟨*space for insertion of number*⟩ / [PRIVATE COPY.] / Grandmother's Story of Bunker-Hill Battle: / AS SHE SAW IT FROM THE BELFRY. / ⟨*double rule*⟩ / BY OLIVER WENDELL HOLMES. / ⟨*n.p., n.d., 1876?*⟩

Cover-title.

10 leaves, paged ⟨1⟩-10, printed on rectos only. 14" x 10½".

Printed blue-gray paper wrapper.

BPL copy, presented by Holmes March 2, 1877, inscribed by Holmes: *Six Printed.*

For an earlier appearance of this poem see *Memorial Bunker Hill ...* ⟨1875⟩. "There is no possibility that this printing antedates the *Memorial ...*"—Currier-Tilton, p. 152. Collected in *Poetical Works, Household Edition,* 1877.

BPL

8912. Der Tisch-Despot ... Deutsch von L. Abenheim.

Stuttgart. Verlag von Aug. Berth. Auerbach. ⟨n.d., 1876⟩

Printed paper wrapper. Issued as Vol. 1 of *Philosophen der Neuen Welt* series.

Inserted in the front matter is a facsimile, on a single folded leaf, of a letter from Holmes to the publisher, Boston, Sept. 16, 1876, regarding "your proposal to publish a German translation of the *Breakfast-Table Series.*"

H

8913. Edgar Allan Poe A Memorial Volume by Sara Sigourney Rice.

Baltimore: Turnbull Brothers. 1877.

Facsimile letter to the editor, Sept. 18, 1875, pp. ⟨79-80⟩

For comment see entry No. 1757.

8914. TURNER SARGENT ...

⟨n.p., Boston, 1877⟩

Title at head of text.

Single leaf of mourning stationery folded to make four pages. Laid paper. Watermarked *Original Turkey Mill*⟨?⟩. Page: 6¹³⁄₁₆″ x 4⅜″. Text on pp. ⟨1⟩ and ⟨3⟩ only. Fifty copies only according to Currier-Tilton, p. 166.

Mr. Turner Sargent died at his residence in Boston on Saturday, February 24, from an attack of pneumonia ... At end of text: H. / February 27, 1877.

BPL   H

8915. THE FIRST FAN.¹ READ AT A MEETING OF THE BOSTON BRIC-A-BRAC CLUB, FEBRUARY 21, 1877 ...¹REPRINTED FROM THE ATLANTIC MONTHLY FOR JUNE, 1877.

⟨n.p., n.d., Boston, 1877⟩

Single cut sheet folded to make four pages. The above on p. ⟨1⟩.

⟨1⟩-4. Laid paper. 7⅝″ x 5″.

The CAW copy inscribed by Holmes May 19, 1877.

Collected in *Poetical Works, Household Edition*, 1877.

B   H   MHS   Y

8916. AN ADDRESS DELIVERED AT THE ANNUAL MEETING OF THE BOSTON MICROSCOPICAL SOCIETY ... [REPRINTED FROM THE BOSTON MEDICAL AND SURGICAL JOURNAL, MAY 24, 1877.]

CAMBRIDGE: PRINTED AT THE RIVERSIDE PRESS. 1877.

Cover-title.

⟨1⟩-12. 9¾″ x 6⅛″.

⟨-⟩⁶.

Printed gray paper wrapper.

H   LC   NYPL   Y

8917. A FAMILY RECORD. WOODSTOCK, CONNECTICUT, JULY 4th, 1877.

⟨n.p., n.d., Cambridge, 1877⟩

Caption-title. The above at head of p. ⟨1⟩. Anonymous.

⟨1⟩-11. 10⅞″ x 8⅜″.

1-3².

Unprinted gray-blue paper wrapper. Flyleaves; or, flyleaf at front only.

Collected in *Poetical Works, Household Edition*, 1877.

H   MHS   Y

8918. Tribute of the Massachusetts Historical Society to the Memory of Edmund Quincy and John Lothrop Motley

Boston   Massachusetts   Historical   Society 1877

Printed paper wrapper.

Remarks on Motley, pp. 16-23.

Preprinted from *Proceedings of the Massachusetts Historical Society*. ⟨*Vol. 15*⟩*1876–1877* ... , Boston, 1878. Appears also in ... *Proceedings of the Massachusetts Historical Society, March to December, 1877* ... ⟨Boston, 1878⟩.

H

8919. The Poetical Works ... Household Edition.

Boston: James R. Osgood and Company, Late Ticknor & Fields, and Fields, Osgood, & Co. 1877.

Contains 26 poems here first collected.

All examined copies have the error *A Good Time Coming!* for *A Good Time Going!*, on p. viii, fourth entry.

Listed PW Sept. 15, 1877.

AAS   BPL   H   LC   Y

8920. Golden Songs of Great Poets ...

New York: Sarah H. Leggett, No. 1184 Broadway. 1877.

Contains "On the Threshold." Collected in *The Iron Gate*, 1880.

For comment see entry No. 1760.

8921. Queeries; a Collection of Charades and Conundrums Original and Selected. Printed for the Old South Fair, Waltham, December, 1877.

⟨n.p., Waltham, Mass.⟩ Free Press Job Printing Office. ⟨1877⟩

Printed paper wrapper.

Reprint save for conundrum No. XIV, p. 12. Anonymous. Begins: *Parted! Alas, it brings my first to mind* ...

Also contains a rhymed riddle which had prior publication in entry No. 8905.

Y

8922. ⟨The Golden Calendar⟩ Count not the years that hoarding time has told ... ⸱

⟨1877?⟩

Not located. Not seen. Entry from Currier-Tilton, p. 160.

Single leaf.

"This poem for Whittier's birthday ... reproduced in hectograph facsimile from Holmes's manuscript ... ⟨possibly⟩ trial reproductions; good copies may never have been made."

8923. HARVARD. "CHRISTO ET ECCLE-SIÆ." ... "VERITAS." ...

⟨n.p.,⟩ FEBRUARY 21, 1878.

Anonymous.

Single leaf. 8⁹⁄₁₆″ x 5½″. Printed on recto only. Prepared for distribution at a dinner, Harvard Club of New York, Feb. 21, 1878.

Two sonnets; both collected in *The Iron Gate,* 1880; reprinted in *Proceedings of the Harvard Club of New York City ... Delmonico's February 21st, 1878,* New York, 1878; also contains a letter, Feb. 19, 1878, not present in the leaflet printing.

H   MHS   NYPL   Y

8924. ⟨Appeal for funds, Boston Medical Library Association⟩ 5 Hamilton Place, Boston. Feb. 25, 1878. The time has come when the rooms thus far occupied by the Boston Medical Library Association no longer meet its requirements ...

Single cut sheet. 14″ x 8⁷⁄₁₆″.

Signed at end by Holmes and others.

H

8925. ⟨THE SCHOOL-BOY⟩ [PRIVATE COPY.] ⟨These hallowed precincts, long to memory dear ...⟩

⟨n.p., n.d., June 6, 1878⟩

Issued without title. The above at head of p. ⟨1⟩. Anonymous.

⟨1⟩-20. 11⅜″ x 9⅝″.

⟨1-5⟩².

Unprinted blue-gray paper wrapper.

Privately printed for the author's use. Read at Phillips Academy, Andover, Mass., June 6, 1878. See below under 1879 for trade edition.

H

8926. Visions: A Study of False Sight (Pseudopia.) By Edward H. Clarke, M. D. With an Introduction and Memorial Sketch by Oliver Wendell Holmes, M. D.

Boston: Houghton, Osgood and Company. The Riverside Press, Cambridge. 1878.

"Introduction," pp. ⟨vii⟩-xxii.

Listed PW May 25, 1878. Advertised as *nearly ready* PW June 1, 1878. Advertised in PW June 8, 1878, for June 15 publication. BPL copy received June 18, 1878.

AAS   BA   Y

8927. OFFICE OF MABIE, TODD & BARD, GOLD PEN MANUFACTURERS, NO. 180 BROADWAY. NEW YORK, OCTOBER, 1878. GENTLEMEN: WE TAKE PLEASURE IN HANDING YOU HEREWITH A FAC-SIMILE OF A LETTER RECEIVED FROM OLIVER WENDELL HOLMES ...

⟨New York, 1878⟩

Single cut sheet folded to four pages. The above on p. ⟨4⟩.

⟨1-4⟩. 9″ x 6″.

Letter from Holmes, p. ⟨1⟩, Boston, Sept. 17, 1878, addressed to Mabie, Todd & Co., recommending their pen. Inner pages blank.

Note: The letter appears also in the September, 1880, issue of the *Indiana Railway Guide,* Indianapolis ⟨1880⟩.

FM

8928. JOHN LOTHROP MOTLEY. A MEMOIR ... ENGLISH COPYRIGHT EDITION.

LONDON: TRÜBNER   &   CO.,   LUDGATE   HILL. 1878 ...

For first American edition see entry No. 8933.

⟨i⟩-⟨xii⟩, ⟨1⟩-275. 7½″ scant x 5″.

⟨A⟩⁶, B-I, K-S⁸, T².

S cloth: brown. Brown-coated on white end papers.

Note: The spine imprint occurs in two states; no sequence has been established and the designations are for identification only:

A

Below the *o* in *Co* is an ovoid horizontal dot.

B

Below the *o* in *Co* is a short hyphen-like dash.

Advertised as *nearly ready* Ath Nov. 30, 1878. Received BMU Dec. 3, 1878. Listed Ath Dec. 7,

1878. Advertised as *ready* Ath Dec. 7, 1878. Listed PC (under *Motley*) Dec. 18, 1878. Reviewed Ath Dec. 21, 1878. Advertised as *nearly ready* (but with two British reviews) Bkr Jan. 1879. Boston edition listed Bkr March, 1879.

H   Y

8929. Index to the North American Review. Volumes I.–CXXV. 1815–1877 . . . by William Cushing . . .

Cambridge: Press of John Wilson and Son. 1878.

Note, p. ⟨ii⟩.

Issued not before July, 1878.

H

8930. . . . Proceedings of the Massachusetts Historical Society, March to December, 1877 . . .

⟨Boston, 1878⟩

At head of title: III. Printed paper wrapper. Cover-title.

Reprint save for "Remarks by Dr. Holmes ⟨on George T. Davis⟩," pp. 310-311.

MHS   Y

8931. THE SCHOOL-BOY . . .

BOSTON: HOUGHTON, OSGOOD AND COMPANY. THE RIVERSIDE PRESS, CAMBRIDGE. 1879.

First published edition. For a privately printed edition see under 1878.

⟨i⟩-⟨xii⟩, 13-79. Illustrated. With the exception of the title-leaf, printed on one side of the leaf only; the blank pages are considered in the printed pagination. $8\frac{7}{16}''$ x $5\frac{15}{16}''$.

⟨1-10⟩^{4}.

S cloth: blue; chocolate; green; powder blue; purple black; tan; terra-cotta. Covers bevelled. White end papers printed in pale green and orange with a leaf and berry pattern; also, white end papers printed in silver and black with an arrangement of kites, butterflies, cricket bats, birds, etc., etc.; also, plain yellow end papers; also, blue-coated on white end papers. Edges gilded. Flyleaves. *Note:* The binding was stamped from a series of brasses; on all examined copies (save one) there is a bird at the top of the spine, a butterfly at the foot. In the exception (at Y) the butterfly is at the top, the bird at the bottom. This variation was caused by error in the stamping process and is merely a binder's fault.

Note: Advertised as in cloth, morocco, and tree calf in PW Nov. 23/30, 1878. Seen by BAL in cloth only.

Advertised for Nov. 13, in PW Nov. 9, 1878; for Nov. 20, in PW Nov. 16, 1878. Deposited Nov. 27, 1878. The London (Routledge) edition listed PC Oct. 16, 1879.

H   LC   NYPL   Y

8932. DEDICATORY ADDRESS AT THE OPENING OF THE NEW BUILDING AND HALL OF THE BOSTON MEDICAL LIBRARY ASSOCIATION . . . [REPRINTED FROM THE BOSTON MEDICAL AND SURGICAL JOURNAL, DECEMBER 12, 1878.]

CAMBRIDGE: PRINTED AT THE RIVERSIDE PRESS. 1879.

Cover-title.

⟨1⟩-14, blank leaf. $9\frac{9}{16}''$ x $6\frac{1}{16}''$.

⟨1⟩-2^4.

Printed gray paper wrapper.

AAS   H

8933. JOHN LOTHROP MOTLEY. A MEMOIR . . .

BOSTON: HOUGHTON, OSGOOD AND COMPANY. THE RIVERSIDE PRESS, CAMBRIDGE. 1879.

See entry No. 8928.

LARGE PAPER EDITION

⟨i⟩-⟨viii⟩, ⟨1⟩-278, blank leaf. Portrait frontispiece inserted. Wove paper. $8\frac{5}{16}''$ x $6\frac{5}{8}''$.

⟨1-14^8, 15-16^4, 17-18^8, 19-20^4⟩.

S cloth: brown; green; terra-cotta. Covers bevelled. Blue coated end papers. Single (sometimes double) flyleaf at front; flyleaf at back of some copies. Top edges gilded.

TRADE EDITION

⟨i⟩-⟨viii⟩, ⟨1⟩-278, blank leaf. Portrait frontispiece inserted. Laid paper. $7\frac{1}{16}''$ x $4\frac{5}{8}''$.

⟨1-18⟩^{8}.

S cloth: blue; brown; green; terra-cotta. V cloth: black; slate. Blue coated end papers. Flyleaves.

Both formats advertised in PW Nov. 23/30, 1878. A large paper copy, inscribed by Holmes, Dec. 13, 1878, in CAW. BPL copy (small paper) received Dec. 16, 1878. BA copy (small paper) received Dec. 19, 1878. Deposited Dec. 23, 1878. Listed (small paper only) PW Dec. 28, 1878. *See next entry.*

H (both)   NYPL (both)

8934. John Lothrop Motley. A Memoir ... Re-printed from the Proceedings of the Massachu-setts Historical Society, 1878.

Boston: Press of John Wilson and Son. 1879.

Printed paper wrapper.

A reprint, with slight revisions, of the preced-ing entry.

Issued after Jan. 16, 1879; date on the basis of letter (in CAW) from Holmes to the printer. Ap-pears also in *Proceedings of the Massachusetts Historical Society. 1878 ...* , Boston, 1879.

H

8935. ... Proceedings of the Massachusetts His-torical Society, January to April, 1879 ...

⟨Boston, 1879⟩

Printed paper wrapper. Cover-title. At head of title: I.

"Remarks ⟨on Jacob Bigelow and George S. Hillard⟩," pp. 38-44.

MHS   Y

8936. The Life, Travels, and Literary Career of Bayard Taylor ... by Russell H. Conwell ...

Boston: B. B. Russell & Co., No. 57 Cornhill ... 1879.

Cloth; and, half morocco.

Address, pp. 325-326.

Listed PW May 17, 1879.

H   NYPL

8937. Testimonials ⟨to the qualifications of F. E. Abbot⟩.

Privately Printed   Not Published. Boston: Press of George H. Ellis, 101 Milk Street. 1879.

Printed paper wrapper.

Letter, April 21, 1867, p. 33.

H copy received June 19, 1879.

H   NYPL

8938. ⟨Printed letter⟩ BOSTON, JUNE 1, 1879./ Dear Brother / On the approaching Com-mencement, June 25th, the / Class of 1829 will reach the FIFTIETH Anniversary of its / graduation. ⟨etc., etc., etc.⟩ / GEO. WM. PHILLIPS, / Of Class Committee. / SAMUEL MAY, / Class Secretary.

Presumably a single cut sheet folded to make four pages. Wove paper. Watermarked RAVEL

⟨*incomplete watermark*⟩. Page: 8½" scant x 5⁵⁄₁₆".

Embodies an extract from a letter written by Holmes.

H

8939. The Huguenots in the Nipmuck Country or Oxford Prior to 1713 by George F. Daniels with an Introduction by Oliver Wendell Holmes ...

Boston   Estes & Lauriat   1880

"Introductory," pp. ⟨x⟩-xiv.

Listed PW Nov. 29, 1879.

H   Y

8940. Papyrus Leaves ... Edited by William Fearing Gill ...

New York: R. Worthington. 1880.

"In Response," pp. ⟨39⟩-41.

"Enchanter of Erin," pp. 271-273.

Both collected in *The Iron Gate*, 1880.

Deposited Dec. 26, 1879. For fuller comment see entry No. 2477.

8941. Boston, February 14th, 1880. / MY DEAR SIR: / ⟨*letter of regret, inability to attend an-nual dinner of the Harvard Club, New York*⟩ / O. W. HOLMES. / ⟨*to*⟩ JOHN O. SARGENT, ESQ., / President of the Harvard Club. /

Single leaf. Printed on recto only. 9⁵⁄₁₆" x 7¹³⁄₁₆".

Printed as proof only?

H

8942. The Atlantic Monthly Supplement. The Holmes Breakfast ...

⟨n.p., n.d., Boston, February, 1880⟩

Self-wrapper. Caption-title.

"The Iron Gate," pp. 4-5. Collected in *The Iron Gate*, 1880.

"Dr. Holmes's Reminiscence," p. 5.

H   NYPL

8943. For Private Circulation only.] / TO THE HONORARY SECRETARIES OF THE RABELAIS CLUB. / ⟨ornament⟩ / BOSTON, / March 21st, 1880. / GENTLEMEN, / ⟨text of letter⟩ / ⟨London, 1880?⟩

The above on p. ⟨2⟩.

Single cut sheet of pink paper folded to make four pages. Page: 8⅝₁₆″ x 5⅛″. Pp. ⟨1⟩ and ⟨4⟩ blank.

Text of letter (accepting membership in the Rabelais Club) pp. ⟨2-3⟩.

H

8944. To James Freeman Clarke. / April 4th 1880.

⟨Boston, 1880?⟩

Single cut sheet of laid note paper folded to make four pages. The above on p. ⟨1⟩. Page: 8″ x 5″.

Text on pp. ⟨1⟩ and ⟨3⟩. Produced by hectograph. Presumably ⟨sic⟩ prepared for distribution at the seventieth birthday celebration of James Freeman Clarke. Also appears in *Seventieth Birthday of James Freeman Clarke. Memorial of the Celebration by the Church of the Disciples, Monday Evening, April 5, 1880,* Boston, 1880. Collected in *The Iron Gate,* 1880.

H

8945. Tales of the Chesapeake by Geo. Alfred Townsend ...

New York: American News Company, 39 and 41 Chambers Street. 1880.

Inserted leaf of testimonials: *A Literary Revolution. Tales of the Chesapeake ... Third Edition. Views of Writing Men.*

Contains a testimonial by Holmes.

Listed PW May 15, 1880. Y copy inscribed by Townsend Aug. 17, 1880.

NYPL Y

8946. ⟨*Address of welcome, Unitarian Festival, Boston, May 27, 1880*⟩ LADIES AND GENTLEMEN: / The pleasant duty of bidding a hearty/welcome to the clergy—to the wives and / daughters of the clergy—to the ministers, / ⟨etc., etc.⟩ /

⟨n.p., n.d., Boston, 1880⟩

Caption-title. The above on p. ⟨1⟩.

Five separate leaves. 11¾″ x 7¼″. Printed on rectos only. Unwatermarked wove paper. Tied with blue ribbon. Anonymous. Privately printed for the author's use.

H

8947. The Art Autograph ... ⟨May, 1880⟩

... The Art Interchange, 140 Nassau Street, New York ... Copyright: 1880; by Wm. Whitlock.

"The Album Fiend," p. ⟨11⟩.

For comment see BAL, Vol. 3, p. 157.

NYPL

8948. JONATHAN EDWARDS. AN ESSAY. (FROM THE INTERNATIONAL REVIEW.)

A. S. BARNES & COMPANY, NEW YORK AND CHICAGO. ⟨1880⟩

Cover-title.

⟨i-ii⟩, ⟨1⟩-28, blank leaf. 9⅛″ scant x 6¹³₁₆″.

⟨-⟩¹⁶.

Printed self-wrapper.

Save for the wrapper printed from the plates of the *International Review,* July, 1880.

H MHS Y

8949. THE IRON GATE, AND OTHER POEMS ...

BOSTON: HOUGHTON, MIFFLIN AND COMPANY. THE RIVERSIDE PRESS, CAMBRIDGE. 1880.

⟨1⟩-82. Frontispiece portrait inserted. Laid paper. 7½″ x 4¹⁵₁₆″.

⟨1⟩-5⁸, 6¹.

S cloth: blue; brown; green; olive; red-brown. V cloth: black. Covers bevelled. White laid paper end papers printed in lavender with a scattering of florets. Flyleaves. Top edges gilded.

BA copy received Sept. 16, 1880. Listed PW Sept. 18, 1880. Copy in H presented by Holmes to T. B. Aldrich Sept. 29, 1880. The London (Low) edition listed Ath Nov. 13, 1880.

H NYPL Y

8950. Sketches and Reminiscences of the Radical Club of Chestnut Street, Boston. Edited by Mrs. John T. Sargent.

Boston: James R. Osgood and Company. 1880.

Contains a truncated version of Holmes's "Jonathan Edwards," pp. 362-369; see above, *Jonathan Edwards,* 1880. In addition the book contains scattered "remarks" by Holmes.

BA copy received Dec. 15, 1880. Listed PW Dec. 25, 1880.

BA H

8951. .... BENJAMIN PEIRCE: ASTRONOMER, MATHEMATICIAN. 1809–1880 ...

⟨n.p., n.d., Boston, Dec. 1880⟩

Caption-title. The above at head of text. At head of title: From the Atlantic Monthly for December. (Private Copy.)

Single leaf. 10¼" x 6". Printed on recto only. Collected in *Poetical Works*, 1881 (Sept.). Earliest located book publication: *Benjamin Peirce ... a Memorial Collection*, by Moses King, Cambridge, 1881 (March); issued in cloth; and, printed paper wrapper.

Printed from the setting of the *Atlantic Monthly*, Dec. 1880.

B   H   Y

8952. ... THE PULPIT AND THE PEW ...

⟨n.p., n.d., New York, 1881⟩

Caption-title. At head of title: (FROM THE NORTH AMERICAN REVIEW.)

⟨117⟩-138. Laid paper. 9³⁄₁₆" x 5⅞".

⟨1³, 2⁸⟩. Originally ⟨1⁴, 2⁸⟩; a leaf of extraneous matter excised from ⟨1⟩.

Printed self-wrapper.

Printed from the slightly altered plates of NAR, Feb. 1881.

PDH

8953. Harvard University, Cambridge, Mass., 11 March, 1881. Dear Sir: The need of a Laboratory of Physics has long been seriously felt in the University ... A friend of the University has promised to give $100,000 for the erection of a Laboratory of Physics ... on condition that the further sum of $75,000 be obtained from other sources ...

⟨Cambridge, March 11, 1881⟩

Single cut sheet. Wove paper watermarked *Old Berkshire Mills*. 10¹⁵⁄₁₆" x 8⁷⁄₁₆". Printed on recto only.

Signed by Holmes and others.

H

8954. The Poetical Works of Oliver Wendell Holmes ...

Boston   Houghton, Mifflin and Company The Riverside Press, Cambridge   1881

2 Vols. Cloth; half calf; morocco; tree calf; and, seal.

Reprint save for:

"Boston to Florence."

"Post-Prandial."

"Our Home—Our Country." See *Exercises* ...

Two Hundred and Fiftieth Anniversary of the Settlement of Cambridge ..., 1881, below.

"Poem at the Centennial Anniversary Dinner of the Massachusetts Medical Society." Appears also in, month of publication not known, *Medical Communications of the Massachusetts Medical Society. Vol. XII—No. VII.—1881. Second Series. Vol. VIII.—Part VII ...*, Boston, 1881.

"Benjamin Peirce." Here first collected. For an earlier private printing see above under 1880.

"Rhymes of a Lifetime." Herein untitled; begins *From the first gleam of morning to the gray* ...

Listed PW Sept. 24, 1881. Deposited Nov. 18, 1881. The London (Low) edition described as *now ready* PC Oct. 1, 1881; noted as *at once* PC Nov. 1, 1881; listed PC Nov. 1, 1881.

BPL   LC

8955. The Poets' Tributes to Garfield   The Collection of Poems Written for the Boston Daily Globe, and Many Selections ... ⟨First Edition⟩

Cambridge, Mass. Published by Moses King Harvard Square   1881

Pp. ⟨1⟩-80. A second edition, pp. ⟨1⟩-168, was issued not before Jan. 16, 1882.

Printed paper wrapper; cloth; leather.

"After the Burial," pp. 28-30. Collected in *Before the Curfew*, 1888.

Deposited Oct. 5, 1881. H copy received Oct. 7, 1881. Listed PW Oct. 15, 1881.

Note: The poem was first published on the front page of *The Boston Daily Globe*, Vol. xx, No. 89, Sept. 27, 1881. The *Globe* also published, presumably within a day or so, a printing of the first page on satin, printed on recto only, with the statement in the heading: *Vol. IX, No. 39* ⟨*sic*⟩. A copy of the separate printing on satin is in Y.

H   LC   Y

8956. Leaflets from Standard Authors. Holmes. Poems and Prose Passages from the Works of Oliver Wendell Holmes ... Compiled by Josephine E. Hodgdon ...

Boston: Houghton, Mifflin and Company. The Riverside Press, Cambridge. 1881.

Reprint save for "The Poet to the Children. Dr. Holmes's Letter to the School Children of Cincinnati, Ohio, on Their Celebration of His Seventy-First Year," p. 11. The letter is dated *Boston, November 20, 1880.*

Two formats issued. Presumably issued simultaneously since a copy of each was deposited for copyright on the same day, Oct. 14, 1881.

Book Form

⟨i⟩-vi, 7-107; blank, p. ⟨108⟩; advertisements, pp. ⟨1⟩-12. Issued in printed gray paper wrapper.

Leaflet Form

A set of separate leaves paged as above. Issued in printed paper box.

Noted for Sept. 24, 1881, in PW Sept. 24, 1881. Y copy (book form) inscribed by F. B. Sanborn, Oct. 3, 1881. Listed PW (format unmentioned) Oct. 8, 1881. Deposited (both formats) Oct. 14, 1881.

LC (both)   Y (book)

8957. Exercises in Celebrating the Two Hundred and Fiftieth Anniversary of the Settlement of Cambridge Held December 28, 1880 . . .

Cambridge University Press: John Wilson and Son   1881

Edited by Robert P. Clapp.

Also issued with the imprint: *Cambridge Charles W. Sever   University Bookstore 1881*

"Home," a poem with a few prefatory remarks, pp. 32-35. The poem, without the remarks, had prior publication in *The Poetical Works of Oliver Wendell Holmes . . . ,* Boston, 1881 (Sept.) above.

Letter, Boston, Nov. 5, 1880, p. 126.

H copy (Wilson imprint) received Oct. 13, 1881. BA copy (Wilson imprint) inscribed by T. W. Higginson Oct. 15, 1881. Listed PW (Sever imprint) Dec. 24, 1881.

BA (Wilson)   H (Wilson)   Y (Sever)

8958. Boston Medical Library Association. 19 Boylston Place, Boston, Mass, ⟨sic⟩ October, 1881 . . .

⟨Boston, 1881⟩

Caption-title. Single cut sheet, 8⁷⁄₁₆″ x 5⁷⁄₁₆″. An appeal for funds for the Boston Medical Library Association. Signed at end by Holmes and others as an executive committee. Printed on recto only.

H

8959. The Memorial History of Boston . . . Edited by Justin Winsor . . . in Four Volumes . . .

Boston: James R. Osgood and Company. 1880–1881.

"Additional Memoranda" ⟨to "Medicine in Boston," by Samuel A. Green⟩, Vol. 4, pp. 549-570.

For comment see entry No. 2275.

8960. MEDICAL EDUCATION. (REPRINTED FROM THE ADVERTISER, JANUARY 16, 1882.) THE HARVARD MEDICAL SCHOOL . . .

⟨Boston, 1882⟩

Single cut sheet. Printed on recto only in three columns. 17¹⁄₁₆″ x 8¼″.

Contains Holmes's "Endowment of the Harvard Medical School."

H

8961. HARVARD CLUB, NEW YORK. FEBRUARY 21, 1882 . . .

⟨n.p., n.d., 1882⟩

Single leaf. Laid paper. 7¹³⁄₁₆″ x 5³⁄₁₆″. Printed on recto only.

Untitled sonnet; begins: *Yes, home is sweet . . .*

Prepared for distribution at a Harvard Club of New York dinner, Feb. 21, 1882.

H

8962. OUR DEAD SINGER . . .

⟨n.p., n.d., 1882?⟩

Single leaf. 10³⁄₁₆″ x 5⁹⁄₁₆″. Printed on recto only.

Three sonnets on the death of Longfellow. Collected in *Before the Curfew,* 1888.

H

8963. "Eulogy on Longfellow"

Holmes's eulogy on Longfellow, delivered before the Massachusetts Historical Society, has been noted in the following three publications. Publication date of the *Proceedings of the Massachusetts Historical Society* is not known hence the sequence here presented is all but arbitrary.

A

Henry W. Longfellow Biography Anecdote, Letters, Criticism by W. Sloane Kennedy . . .

Cambridge, Mass. Moses King, Publisher Harvard Square 1882

Extracts from the eulogy, pp. 292-297.

H copy received May 23, 1882. Listed PW May 27, 1882. Deposited June 2, 1882.

Locations: H

B

Tributes to Longfellow and Emerson by the
Massachusetts Historical Society . . .

> Boston: A. Williams and Co., Publishers, Old
> Corner Bookstore, 283 Washington St. 1882.

> Trade edition in cloth; and, in printed
> boards. Also a de luxe edition printed on
> Whatman paper, limited to 25 numbered
> copies, with certificate of issue.

> "Remarks ⟨*i.e.,* the Longfellow eulogy⟩," pp.
> 13-22.

> "Address ⟨on the death of Ralph Waldo
> Emerson⟩," pp. 39-50.

> A copy in H received June 25, 1882. Listed
> PW June 29, 1882.

> Locations: H

C

. . . Proceedings of the Massachusetts Historical
Society, from January to June, 1882 . . .

> ⟨Boston, 1882⟩

> Printed paper wrapper. Cover-title. At head
> of title: III.

> Eulogy on the death of R. H. Dana, Jr., pp.
> 197-199.

> Eulogy on the death of Longfellow, pp. 269-
> 275.

> Eulogy on the death of Ralph Waldo Emer-
> son, pp. 303-310.

> Locations: H   MHS   Y

8964. MEDICAL HIGHWAYS AND BY-WAYS.
A LECTURE DELIVERED BEFORE THE
STUDENTS OF THE MEDICAL DEPART-
MENT OF HARVARD UNIVERSITY, MAY
10, 1882 . . .

> CAMBRIDGE: PRINTED AT THE RIVERSIDE PRESS.
> 1882.

> ⟨1⟩-32. 7⁷⁄₁₆″ x 5″.

> ⟨1⟩-2⁸.

> Printed gray paper wrapper.

> H   Y

8965. Tributes to Longfellow and Emerson by
the Massachusetts Historical Society . . .

> Boston: A. Williams and Co., Publishers, Old
> Corner Bookstore, 283 Washington St. 1882.

See entry No. 8963.

8966. The Lincoln Memorial: Album-Immortelles . . . Edited by Osborn H. Oldroyd . . .

> New York: G. W. Carleton & Co., Publishers.
> London: S. Low, Son & Co. MDCCCLXXXII . . .

Five-line statement dated Boston, 1882, p. 243.
Not elsewhere found; presumably written for
this publication.

For comment see entry No. 1092.

8967. Mr. Lane's Chester Miracle. Verbatim
"Copye of a Letter Discribing the Wonder-
ful Worke of God in Deliveringe a Mayden
within the Cittie of Chest'r, from a Horrible
Kinde of Torment and Sicknes, the 10 of
Februarie, 1564." . . . To Which is Added a
Characteristic Letter from Dr. Oliver Wendell
Holmes . . . by Thomas Hughes . . .

> Chester: Printed at the "Courant" Office, for
> Private Circulation Only. 1882.

Printed paper wrapper.

Letter, June 3, 1881, pp. 10-11.

NLM

8968. The Atlantic Monthly Supplement. The
Birthday Garden Party to Harriet Beecher
Stowe.

> ⟨Boston, 1882⟩

Caption-title. Pp. ⟨1⟩-16.

Untitled poem, *If every tongue that speaks her
praise,* p. 6. Collected in *Before the Curfew,*
1888.

For comment see entry No. 4621.

8969. FAREWELL ADDRESS . . . TO THE
MEDICAL SCHOOL OF HARVARD UNI-
VERSITY, TUESDAY, NOVEMBER 28, 1882
. . .

> CAMBRIDGE: PRINTED AT THE RIVERSIDE PRESS.
> 1882.

> ⟨1⟩-24. 7½″ full x 5″.

> ⟨1⁸, 2-3²⟩.

> Printed gray-blue paper wrapper.

> H   MHS

8970. The Autocrat of the Breakfast-Table . . .
New and Revised Edition . . .

> Boston   Houghton, Mifflin and Company
> New York: 11 East Seventeenth Street   The
> Riverside Press, Cambridge   1883

For first edition see entry No. 8781. Also see
entries 8912, 8979, 9093.

"To the Readers of the Autocrat of the Breakfast-Table," pp. ⟨iii⟩-v.

Advertised for Nov. 25, 1882, in PW Nov. 25, 1882. Deposited Nov. 27, 1882. Noted as *just published* PW Dec. 2, 1882. Listed PW Dec. 23, 1882. A *Library Edition* was advertised by Douglas in PC March 15, 1883. A *Handy Volume* edition listed PC June 15, 1883. Listed PC July 2, 1883, as in *Paterson's Shilling Library*. An undated printing issued by Routledge (London) is presumed to be a quite late printing; no record found in PC for 1882–1883.

H NYPL

8971. The Poet at the Breakfast-Table ...

> Boston Houghton, Mifflin and Company New York: 11 East Seventeenth Street The Riverside Press, Cambridge 1883

For first edition see under 1872.

"Preface," pp. ⟨iii⟩-iv, written for this printing.

Listed PW Jan. 20, 1883; PC Feb. 15, 1883. A Routledge edition listed PC May 15, 1883. An *Author's Edition* (Edinburgh: Douglas) listed PC Dec. 6, 1883.

H

8972. The Professor at the Breakfast-Table with the Story of Iris

> Boston Houghton, Mifflin and Company New York: 11 East Seventeenth Street The Riverside Press, Cambridge 1883

For first edition see under 1860.

"Preface to Revised Edition," pp. ⟨iii⟩-vi.

Listed PW March 3, 1883; PC March 15, 1883. The Douglas (Edinburgh) edition listed PC June 15, 1883. As a part of *Paterson's Shilling Library* listed PC July 16, 1883. An *Author's Edition* (Edinburgh: Douglas) listed PC Nov. 1, 1883.

CAW

8973. The Guardian Angel ...

> Boston Houghton, Mifflin and Company New York: 11 East Seventeenth Street The Riverside Press, Cambridge, 1883

For first edition see under 1867.

"To My Readers," pp. ⟨v⟩-x.

Advertised for March 21, 1883, in PW March 10, 1883. Listed PW March 31, 1883.

CAW

8974. Proceedings at the Dinner Given by the Medical Profession of the City of New York April 12, 1883 to Oliver Wendell Holmes ... Edited by Wesley M. Carpenter ...

> New York G. P. Putnam's Sons 27 & 29 West 23d Street 1883

Cloth; and, leather.

"Poem ...," *Have I deserved your kindness?* ..., pp. 16-23. Collected in *The Complete Poetical Works ... Cambridge Edition ...* ⟨1895⟩.

Issued as a souvenir of the dinner was a burlesque telegram in printed envelope of the *American Rabid Telegraph Company* bearing Holmes's rhymed acceptance to the dinner. The rhyme had prior publication as part of "A Noontide Lyric" in *Poems*, 1836.

H NYPL Y

8975. Medical Essays 1842–1882 ...

> Boston Houghton, Mifflin and Company New York: 11 East Seventeenth Street The Riverside Press, Cambridge 1883

Reprint save for "Preface to the New Edition," pp. ⟨iii⟩-iv.

Advertised for April 14, 1883, in PW April 7, 1883. Deposited April 16, 1883. BPL copy received April 21, 1883. BA copy received April 26, 1883. Listed PW April 28, 1883.

BA H Y

8976. Elsie Venner. A Romance of Destiny ...

> Boston Houghton, Mifflin and Company New York: 11 East Seventeenth Street The Riverside Press, Cambridge 1883

For first edition see entry No. 8801.

"A Second Preface," pp. ⟨xi⟩-xiii.

Listed PW April 28, 1883.

CAW

8977. ⟨*Address, Unitarian Festival, Boston, May 31, 1883*⟩ BROTHERS, SISTERS AND FRIENDS: / My first, pleasant duty is to give ex- / pression to the cordial delight with which we / greet our guests and each other on this most / agreeable occasion. Faces which we have / ⟨*etc., etc., etc.*⟩ / ⟨*n.p., n.d., Boston, 1883*⟩

Caption-title. The above on p. ⟨1⟩.

Thirteen separate leaves. 12⅛″ x 7¾″. Printed on rectos only. Unwatermarked wove paper. Tied with blue ribbon. Anonymous. Privately printed for the author's use.

H

8978. PAGES FROM AN OLD VOLUME OF LIFE A COLLECTION OF ESSAYS 1857–1881 ...

> BOSTON HOUGHTON, MIFFLIN AND COMPANY NEW YORK: 11 EAST SEVENTEENTH STREET THE RIVERSIDE PRESS, CAMBRIDGE 1883

⟨i-iv⟩, ⟨1⟩-433; blank, p. ⟨434⟩; publisher's catalog, pp. ⟨1⟩-16; leaf, excised or pasted under the end paper. Laid paper. Illustrated. 7½″ full x 4¹⁵⁄₁₆″.

⟨1², 2-19¹², 20¹⁰⟩. Leaf ⟨20⟩₁₀ excised or pasted under the end paper. *Signed:* ⟨-⟩², 1-27⁸, 28⁹.

Two printings noted:

1: As above.

2: ⟨1-19⟩¹². Leaf ⟨19⟩₁₂ excised or pasted under the end paper.

S cloth: green. Covers bevelled. Blue-black coated end papers. Flyleaves. Top edges gilded.

Note: Contains much material reprinted from earlier books; and, some material here first in book form.

Deposited June 11, 1883. Advertised for June 16, 1883, in PW June 9, 1883. Listed PW June 23, 1883.

BPL (1st)   H (1st, 2nd)

8979. The Autocrat of the Breakfast Table . . .

Edinburgh   David Douglas, Castle Street 1883

2 Vols. Printed paper wrapper; and, cloth. For first edition see entry No. 8781. Also see entries 8912, 8970, 9093.

"An After-Breakfast Talk," Vol. 1, pp. ⟨ix⟩-xl. Originally in the *Atlantic Monthly,* Jan. 1883. Collected in *The Autocrat's Miscellanies* . . . , New York ⟨1959⟩.

Listed PC Sept. 15, 1883. Advertised PC Sept. 15, 1883, as *now ready.*

H

8980. The Professor at the Breakfast-Table; with the Story of Iris . . .

Leipzig   Bernhard Tauchnitz 1883

Printed paper wrapper. Issued as No. 2203 of the series. Back wrapper dated Nov. 1883.

For first edition see entry No. 8791.

Reprint save for a three-line note, p. ⟨5⟩, in which Holmes states that this printing is authorized.

H

8981. An Old Scrap-Book. With Additions. Printed, but Not Published . . . ⟨Edited by J. M. Forbes⟩

⟨Cambridge: The University Press⟩ February 8, 1884.

Errata slip inserted at copyright page.

Reprint with the exception of:

"Hunting-Song," *Not a buck was shot, nor a doe, nor a fawn* . . . , pp. 212-213.

"Hunting-Song for 1839," *Ye hunters of New England* . . . , pp. 206-207.

Deposited Feb. 8, 1884.

B

8982. Lyrics of the Law . . . by J. Greenbag Croke ⟨*pseud.* for Joseph Hasbrouck⟩ . . .

San Francisco: Sumner Whitney & Co., 1884

"A Response," read at the annual banquet of the Boston Bar Association, Jan. 1883, pp. 30-32.

A statement, reprinted from the *Boston Evening Transcript,* Jan. 31, 1883, p. 296.

Note: "A Response" was reprinted in E. E. Brown's *Life of Oliver Wendell Holmes,* Boston ⟨1884⟩ (deposited March 31, 1884).

Deposited Feb. 25, 1884. Listed PW May 17, 1884.

NYPL

8983. The New Century and the New Building of the Harvard Medical School. 1783–1883. Addresses and Exercises at the One Hundredth Anniversary of the Foundation of the Medical School of Harvard University, October 17, 1883.

Cambridge: John Wilson and Son. University Press. 1884.

Cloth; and, printed paper wrapper.

Reprint save for:

"The Address Delivered in Huntington Hall," pp. ⟨3⟩-35.

BA   BPL   H   NYPL   Y

8984. Seventh, Eighth, and Ninth Reports Made to the Boston Medical Library Association, October VII., M DCCC LXXXIV . . . Report of the Special Meeting Held on November xxv., M DCCC LXXXIV . . .

⟨n.p., n.d., Boston, 1884⟩

Printed paper wrapper. Cover-title.

Remarks on the bust of J. Marion Sims, pp. 10-11.

H   NYPL

8985. Illustrated Poems . . .

Boston   Houghton, Mifflin and Company New York: 11 East Seventeenth Street   The Riverside Press, Cambridge 1885

Reprint save for "Ave," pp. ⟨ix-x⟩.

Noted in cloth. Advertised as in morocco; and, tree calf, pw Nov. 22/29, 1884.

bpl copy received Nov. 11, 1884. Listed pw Nov. 15, 1884. The London (Macmillan) edition advertised as *nearly ready* Ath Nov. 15, 1884; listed Ath Dec. 6, 1884.

bpl   h   y

8986. ... RALPH WALDO EMERSON ...

BOSTON: HOUGHTON, MIFFLIN AND COMPANY. NEW YORK: 11 EAST SEVENTEENTH STREET. THE RIVERSIDE PRESS, CAMBRIDGE. 1885.

At head of title: AMERICAN MEN OF LETTERS.

⟨i-iv⟩, ⟨i⟩-viii, ⟨1⟩-441; leaf excised or pasted under the end paper; plus: 8 pp. advertisements. Frontispiece portrait of Emerson inserted. Laid paper. 6⅞" x 4⁹⁄₁₆".

⟨1⁶, 2-18¹², 19⁶, 20¹²; plus: 21⁴⟩. Leaf ⟨20⟩12 excised or pasted under the end paper. *Signed:* ⟨-⟩⁶, ⟨1⟩-24, ⟨25⟩-27⁸, 28⁵; plus: ⟨29⟩⁴.

S cloth: maroon. Olive-green-coated on white end papers. Flyleaves. Top edges gilt.

Note: Copies have been seen (caw, h) bound in white linen, goldstamped red leather label on spine; untrimmed; leaf: 7¼" x 4⅞." Status not determined. A set of untrimmed sheets (at y) is bound in pale violet paper boards with printed paper label on the spine. Definite information regarding this binding is wanting but it was almost surely produced by or for a private collector and not by the publisher.

Also note: Copies of the first printing (the second printing bears the statement *Fourth Thousand* on the title-page) occur stitched with thread; or, stitched with wire. No sequence has been established (if sequence there is) but all examined reprints are stitched with thread.

Deposited Dec. 10, 1884. Advertised for Dec. 10, 1884, in pw Dec. 6, 1884. Listed pw Dec. 20, 1884. The London (Kegan Paul, Trench) edition was advertised for *next week* in Ath Jan. 10, 1885; listed by Ath Jan. 17, 1885.

h   lc   nypl   y

8987. A WELCOME TO DR. BENJAMIN APTHORP GOULD.

⟨Boston, 1885⟩

Anonymous. Cover-title.

Single leaf of laid paper watermarked *Crane's Grecian Antique* folded to make four pages. Page: 8" full x 5³⁄₁₆" scant. Unpaged.

According to the printer's records (Riverside Press) but fifty copies were printed on May 26,

1885. The y copy inscribed by Holmes May 27, 1885. Also appears in (reprint?) *Addresses at the Complimentary Dinner to Dr. Benjamin Apthorp Gould. Hotel Vendôme, Boston, May 6, 1885,* Lynn, Mass., 1885; printed paper wrapper. Collected in *Before the Curfew,* 1888.

h   y

8988. A MORTAL ANTIPATHY FIRST OPENING OF THE NEW PORTFOLIO ...

LONDON   SAMPSON LOW, MARSTON, SEARLE, & RIVINGTON   CROWN BUILDINGS, 188, FLEET STREET 1885 ...

Cover-title.

8 leaves, printed in two columns. Text on pp. ⟨3⟩-14; final leaf blank. 9½" x 6".

Not seen. Presumably prepared for copyright purposes only. The text appears on pp. ⟨283⟩-307 of *A Mortal Antipathy,* Boston, 1885; see next entry.

Received by bmu Nov. 11, 1885.

bmu   h (photostat)

8989. A MORTAL ANTIPATHY FIRST OPENING OF THE NEW PORTFOLIO ...

BOSTON AND NEW YORK   HOUGHTON, MIFFLIN AND COMPANY   THE RIVERSIDE PRESS, CAMBRIDGE 1885

⟨i-viii⟩, ⟨1⟩-307; blank, p. ⟨308⟩; publisher's catalog, pp. ⟨1⟩-4; plus: pp. 5-13; leaf excised or pasted under the end paper. Pp. ⟨i-ii⟩ excised or pasted under the end paper. Laid paper. 7⁹⁄₁₆" x 4¹⁵⁄₁₆".

⟨1⁴, 2-14¹²; plus: 15⁶⟩. Leaves ⟨1⟩1 and ⟨15⟩6 excised or pasted under the end paper. *Signed:* ⟨-⟩³, 1-20⁸, ⟨21⟩¹.

Two printings noted:

1

As above.

In the advertisement opposite the title-page *Elsie Venner* is listed at $1.50; *The Breakfast-Table Series,* in 8 volumes, is offered at $14.00.

The final entry, p. 2 of the terminal advertisements, is: *Albert Gallatin. By John Austin Stevens.*

2

⟨i-vi⟩, ⟨1⟩-307; publisher's catalog, pp. ⟨1⟩-13. Laid paper.

⟨1-13¹², 14⁸⟩. *Signed:* ⟨-⟩³, 1-20⁸, ⟨21⟩¹.

In the advertisement opposite the title-page *Elsie Venner* is listed at $2.00; *The Breakfast-Table Series*, in 8 volumes, is offered at $13.50.

The final entry, p. 2 of the terminal advertisements, is: *James Madison. By Sydney Howard Gay.*

S cloth: green. Covers bevelled. Blue-black-coated end papers. Flyleaves. Top edges gilded.

See preceding entry. H has a presentation copy (first printing) inscribed by Holmes Nov. 26, 1885. BPL copy (first printing, rebound) received Nov. 27, 1885. Deposited (first printing) Nov. 27, 1885. Listed PW Dec. 5, 1885. Advertised as *just published* PW Dec. 5, 1885. The London (Low) edition advertised as *nearly ready* PC Dec. 7, 1885; listed Ath Dec. 12, 1885.

AAS (1st)   BPL (1st rebound; 2nd)   H (1st, 2nd)   LC (1st, being a deposit copy)   Y (1st, 2nd)

8990. Reception and Dinner Given to the Hon. John Lowell, by the Boston Merchants' Association, May 23, 1884.

    Boston: Press of Rockwell and Churchill, No. 39 Arch Street. 1885.

Printed paper wrapper.

Remarks on "Dorothy Q," pp. 29-32.

H   NYPL

8991. Recreations of the Rabelais Club. 1882-1885 . . .

    Printed for the Members . . . ⟨London, 1885?⟩

Vellum. 100 numbered copies only. Errata slip inserted between pp. x-⟨xi⟩.

"To the Rabelais Club," pp. ⟨1⟩-2, being a letter dated *Boston, January 21, 1882.*

H

8992. The Last Leaf . . . Illustrated by George Wharton Edwards & F. Hopkinson Smith

    Houghton Mifflin & Co   The Riverside Press Cambridge MDCCCLXXXVI.

"The Last Leaf" reprinted from *The Harbinger*, 1833; and, *Poems*, 1836. Contains (written for this edition) a three-page statement titled "The History of This Poem," dated July 9, 1885. See entry No. 9055.

Trade Edition

Cloth. Leaf: 12⅞16″ x 9¼″. Reported (not seen by BAL) in leather. Deposited Oct. 29, 1885. Published Oct. 31, 1885 (publisher's statement). Advertised for Oct. 31, 1885, in PW Oct. 17, 1885.

BA copy received Nov. 3, 1885. Listed PW Nov. 7, 1885.

Large Paper Edition

Printed boards, vellum shelfback. Leaf: 14⅞″ x 11½″. According to the publisher's records issued in Dec. 1885. The first notice seen is an advertisement in PW Jan. 30, 1886, where both the large paper and the trade editions are listed as 1885 publications.

British Edition

Distributed in Great Britain by Low. Advertised as *ready* Ath Dec. 5, 1885. Listed Ath Dec. 5, 1885. Advertised PC Dec. 7, 1885. Reviewed by Ath Dec. 26, 1885.

BA (trade)   CAW (large paper)   NYPL (trade)

8993. HYMN: THE WORD OF PROMISE

Lord, Thou hast led us as of old . . .

Prior to inclusion in *Before the Curfew*, 1888, this hymn was published in the following forms; periodical publication is here ignored:

A

⟨Hymn. The Word of Promise. Being (by Supposition) a Hymn Sung by the Great Assembly, Newtown, Dec. 1, 1636. Written by Oliver Wendell Holmes for the 250th Anniversary of the Organization of the First Church in Cambridge, Feb. 12, 1886⟩

    Single leaf. Laid paper. Watermarked *Crane's Grecian Antique.* 10⁹⁄16″ x 7″. Seven 4-line stanzas. Printed on recto only.

    Currier-Tilton, pp. 202-203, clearly establish that this is the earliest printing of the hymn and that but twelve copies were printed.

    Anonymous.

    Locations: H   Y

B

. . . Order of Services at the Two Hundred and Fiftieth Anniversary of the Organization of the First Church in Cambridge . . .

    ⟨Cambridge⟩ February 12, 1886.

    Cover-title. At head of title: 1636. 1886.

    Printed self-wrapper. The hymn appears on p. ⟨6⟩.

    Locations: H

C

HYMN: THE WORD OF PROMISE, / (BY SUPPOSITION), / An Hymn set forth to be sung by the Great Assembly at NEWTOWN, / MO. 12. 1. 1636. / WRITTEN BY / OLIVER WENDELL HOLMES, / Eldest Son of Rev. ABIEL HOLMES, Eighth Pastor of the First Church. / ⟨*diamond rule*⟩ / ⟨*text*⟩ / ⟨*all the preceding in a frame*⟩ / ⟨*n.p., n.d., Cambridge, 1886*⟩

Single leaf. Wove paper. 9⅝″ x 6¹³⁄₁₆″. Printed on recto only from the setting of *Order of Services* . . . , 1886, above.

Locations: H

D

Services at the Celebration of the Two Hundred and Fiftieth Anniversary of the Organization of the First Church in Cambridge, February 7-14, 1886.

Cambridge: John Wilson and Son. University Press. 1886.

Printed paper wrapper; and, cloth. The hymn appears herein, together with remarks here in their first book publication, on pp. 120-121.

Locations: BA   H   Y

8994. Life of Henry Wadsworth Longfellow with Extracts from His Journals and Correspondence Edited by Samuel Longfellow . . .

Boston   Ticknor and Company 1886

2 Vols.

Untitled poem, *In gentle bosoms tried and true,* Vol. 2, pp. 434-435. Written on the occasion of Longfellow's sixtieth birthday, 1867.

Also contains (here reprinted from *Songs of Many Seasons,* 1875,), Vol. 2, pp. 438-439, the poem written on the occasion of Longfellow's departure for Europe, 1868.

H copy received March 12, 1886. Listed PW (as in cloth; half cloth; half morocco; and, edition de luxe) March 20, 1886. The London (Kegan Paul) edition announced for *this day* Ath March 27, 1886; listed Ath March 27, 1886.

H   NYPL

8995. . . . DR. OLIVER WENDELL HOLMES VISITS THE JAPANESE VILLAGE, AND HIS IMPRESSIONS OF THE SAME: [FROM THE BOSTON SUNDAY HERALD, FEB. 21, 1886.] . . .

⟨n.p., 1886⟩

Single leaf. Printed on recto only. 14½″ x 10¼″. At head of title: BEECHER'S HALL, BIDDLE HOUSE BUILDING, JEFFERSON AVENUE.

Issued as an advertisement for The Japanese Village exhibition; written as a letter first published in *The Boston Sunday Herald,* Feb. 21, 1886.

The above was issued as advance publicity for a showing scheduled for May 17, 1886, opening.

The letter had prior publication in *Explanation of the Japanese Village and Its Inhabitants,* ⟨Boston: The Japanese Village Company, 1886⟩; printed paper wrapper; issued at the exhibition at Horticultural Hall, Boston, not before Feb. 21, 1886; nor, after March 20, 1886, on which date the Boston exhibition closed. The inner back wrapper of the pamphlet is imprinted with an advertisement for the Japanese Village, and has the following notice below text: *This Page For Sale for next Edition;* which suggests that the pamphlet may have been reprinted with an advertisement on the inner back wrapper other than that of the Japanese Village.

H (pamphlet)   NYPL (handbill)

8996. Memoir of Jonathan Mason Warren, M.D. By Howard Payson Arnold. Printed for Private Distribution.

Boston: 1886.

Tribute to Dr. Jackson, p. 119; prose.

Tribute to Dr. Jackson, p. 178; verse. Reprinted from "Poetry, a Metrical Essay," *Poems,* 1836.

Note to Dr. Warren, June 6, 1864, pp. 254-255.

Part of a tribute to Dr. Warren at a meeting of the Suffolk District Medical Society, p. 256.

H copy received Oct. 7, 1886.

H   NYPL

8997. ⟨POEM FOR THE 250th ANNIVERSARY OF THE FOUNDING OF HARVARD COLLEGE, NOV. 8, 1886⟩

⟨n.p., n.d., 1886⟩

18 printed leaves; and, 2 manuscript leaves. Each approximately 10″ x 9″. Printed on rectos only.

Begins: *Twice had the mellowing sun of autumn crowned* . . . Collected in *Before the Curfew,* 1888.

Privately printed for the author's use for reading in public. "There was not time to set up the rest and it had to be copied—which I did myself. OWH"—Note in Holmes's hand on the unique copy in H.

Location: H

Note: The poem appears also in the following:

The Atlantic Monthly Supplement. The Oration by James Russell Lowell, and the Poem by Oliver Wendell Holmes, Delivered in Sanders Theatre, Cambridge, November 8, 1886, on the Two Hundred and Fiftieth Anniversary of the Foundation of Harvard University. Oration.

⟨n.p., n.d., Boston, 1886⟩

Caption-title. The above at head of p. ⟨1⟩.

Issued as a supplement to *The Atlantic Monthly,* Dec. 1886.

⟨1⟩-28. 9¼″ full x 5⅞″.

⟨1⁸, 2⁶⟩.

Printed self-wrapper.

The poem appears on pp. 18-28.

Location: H

8998. . . . Commemorative Services King's Chapel, Boston, upon the Completion of Two Hundred Years, Wednesday, December 15, 1886 . . .

⟨Boston, 1886⟩

Printed self-wrapper. Cover-title. At head of title: 1686. 1886.

"Hymn," *O'ershadowed by the walls that climb . . . ,* p. ⟨9⟩. Collected in *Before the Curfew,* 1888.

B   H   NYPL   Y

8999. Response to the Toast "The President of the United States" together with the Response of the Guest of the Evening Dr. Oliver Wendell Holmes, at the Banquet to His Honour by the Liverpool Philomathic Society August 20th 1886

⟨Liverpool, for Private Circulation, 1886⟩

Cover-title. Printed self-wrapper.

Holmes's response, pp. ⟨13-15⟩.

AAS   H

9000. Speeches at the First Dinner of the Phillips Academy Alumni Association, Parker House, Boston, March 24, 1886 . . .

Boston: Printed by Nathan Sawyer & Son, No. 70 State Street. 1886.

Printed paper wrapper; and cloth.

"Speech," pp. 21-26. *Note:* The poem, "Bill and Joe," embodied in the speech, reprinted from *Songs of Many Seasons,* 1875.

H   Y

9001. The Commemoration by King's Chapel, Boston, of the Completion of Two Hundred Years . . .

Boston: Little, Brown, and Company. 1887.

Reprint save for the poem, *Is it a weanling's weakness for the past,* pp. 131-133. Collected in *Before the Curfew,* 1888.

H copy received May 4, 1887.

H   Y

9002. Beecher Memorial Contemporaneous Tributes to the Memory of Henry Ward Beecher Compiled and Edited by Edward W. Bok

Privately Printed   Brooklyn, New York   1887

Contribution, pp. ⟨1⟩-3.

For comment see entry No. 2148.

9003. . . . A Record of the Commemoration, November Fifth to Eighth, 1886, on the Two Hundred and Fiftieth Anniversary of the Founding of Harvard College.

Cambridge, N. E.: John Wilson and Son. University Press. 1887.

At head of title: 1636. Harvard University. 1886.

Reprint save for a speech, pp. 302-303.

Note: It is possible that this publication went into two printings but no wholly reliable evidence has been found to support the possibility. The following notes indicate the problem.

A

Received by H June 2, 1887. Printed throughout on laid paper. The two plates inserted between pp. 50-51 are printed on separate leaves.

B

A copy characterized as a "second edition" (so marked on the title-page by Justin Winsor, editor of the work and librarian of Harvard College Library) was received by H on June 27, 1887. This varies from the above in the following features: Printed on mixed papers, both laid paper and wove paper being used. The two plates inserted between pp. 50-51 are printed on a single folded cut sheet.

H (A,B)

9004. HAIL, COLUMBIA!

Two printings of this song have been noted. The sequence has not been determined and the order of presentation is arbitrary. For comment see Currier-Tilton, pp. 312-314. Collected in *Before the Curfew,* 1888.

A

HAIL, COLUMBIA! 1798–1887. JOSEPH HOPKINSON. OLIVER WENDELL HOLMES.

⟨n.p., probably Philadelphia, *1887*⟩

Single leaf folded to four pages. Page: 10⁹⁄₁₆″ x 6¾″. Cover-title. Paper watermarked *L. L. Brown Paper Company.*

Text of Hopkinson's "Hail, Columbia!," p. <2>; text of Holmes's additional three stanzas, p. <3>, dated at end Aug. 29, 1887.

Locations: H LC NYPL

B

NEW HAIL COLUMBIA! OLIVER WENDELL HOLMES . . .

A. W. AUNER'S CARD AND JOB PRINTING ROOMS, TENTH AND RACE STS., PHILADELPHIA, PA. <n.d., presumably 1887>

Single leaf. 7⅞" x 4⅝". Printed on recto only. Dated in heading Aug. 24, 1887.

Locations: B

9005. OUR HUNDRED DAYS IN EUROPE
. . .

LONDON   SAMPSON LOW, MARSTON, SEARLE, & RIVINGTON   ST. DUNSTAN'S HOUSE   FETTER LANE, FLEET STREET, E. C. 1887 . . .

For first American edition see next entry.

<i>–vi, <1>–308. 6⅞" x 4¾" full.

<A>², <->¹, B-I, K-U⁸, X².

V cloth: maroon. Covers bevelled. Black-coated on white end papers. Top edges gilded.

Noted for *the present month* PC Sept. 1, 1887. Reviewed PC Sept. 15, 1887. Advertised as *now ready* PC Sept. 15, 1887; Ath Sept. 17, 1887; *Saturday Review,* Sept. 17, 1887; *Spectator,* Sept. 17, 1887. Listed Ath Sept. 24, 1887; *Spectator,* Sept. 24, 1887. Advertised, with reviews, *Saturday Review,* Oct. 1, 1887. Reviewed by *Spectator* Oct. 15, 1887. A second edition was noted as *now ready* PC Oct. 15, 1887. A third edition deposited in BMU Nov. 11, 1887. A large paper edition was advertised as *ready shortly* PC Feb. 1, 1888; listed Ath Feb. 18, 1888.

NYPL Y

9006. OUR HUNDRED DAYS IN EUROPE
. . .

BOSTON AND NEW YORK   HOUGHTON, MIFFLIN AND COMPANY   THE RIVERSIDE PRESS, CAMBRIDGE 1887

See preceding entry.

<i-iv>, <i>-iv, <1>-329; blank, p. <330>; advertisements: pp. <1>-2; plus: 3-14. Laid paper. 7½" x 4¹⁵⁄₁₆".

<1⁴, 2-21⁸, 22⁶; plus: 23⁶>.

Three bindings noted; sequence, if any, not determined:

A

V cloth: gray-green; olive-green. Front stamped in green with lettering and vignette of water-side cathedral. Covers not bevelled. White laid paper end papers watermarked: *The Riverside Press.* Single flyleaves; also, double flyleaves. Top edges gilded. Copies thus in H: The author's personal copy, uninscribed; copy presented by Holmes to his wife, Oct. 13, 1887; to his son, Oct. 30, 1887.

B

S cloth: dark green. Covers bevelled. Gold-stamped urn on front cover; blindstamped urn on back cover. Blue-black coated paper end papers. Flyleaves. Top edges gilded. A copy thus in H presented by Holmes to Thomas Bailey Aldrich, Nov. 5, 1887.

C

S cloth: dark green. Covers bevelled. Gold-stamped urn on front cover; back cover unstamped. Blue-black coated end papers. Flyleaves. Top edges gilded.

Deposited Sept. 22, 1887. BPL copy (now rebound) received Sept. 26, 1887. Listed PW Oct. 8, 1887.

AAS (C) H (A,B) NYPL (B)

9007. POEM FOR THE DEDICATION OF THE FOUNTAIN AT STRATFORD-ON-AVON

Three separate printings of this poem have been located. Currier-Tilton, pp. 214-217, present sufficient evidence to indicate that the printing here designated *A* was the first separate printing. The sequence of printings *B* and *C* has not been established. Collected in *Before the Curfew,* 1888.

A

POEM/ for the / DEDICATION OF THE FOUNTAIN / AT STRATFORD-ON-AVON / Presented by / GEORGE W. CHILDS, ESQUIRE, / Of Philadelphia, U.S.A. / <rule> / By / OLIVER WENDELL HOLMES. / <n.p., 1887>

Cover-title.

<1-7>. Laid paper. 10" x 8".

<->⁴.

Printed self-wrapper. Sewn with red cord.

Locations: B H UV Y

B

POEM / BY / OLIVER WENDELL HOLMES / FOR THE / DEDICATION OF THE FOUNTAIN AT STRATFORD-ON-AVON / PRESENTED BY / GEORGE W. CHILDS, / OF PHILADELPHIA. / <n.p., 1887>

Preceding at head of p. <1>.

<1-3>. Laid paper. 8" full x 5" scant.

Single cut sheet folded to four pages.

Locations: B H LC NYPL UT UV Y

C

POEM / FOR THE / DEDICATION OF THE FOUNTAIN
AT STRATFORD-ON-AVON, / PRESENTED BY / George
W. Childs, Esquire, of Philadelphia, U.S.A. /
⟨rule⟩ / By Oliver Wendell Holmes. / ⟨double
rule⟩ / ⟨text⟩ / OLIVER WENDELL HOLMES. /
August 29th, 1887. / ⟨n.p., 1887⟩

The only located copy is in two pieces, mounted
in a scrapbook, and consequently one may not
be certain of the original format. The piece
appears to have been, originally, a single cut
sheet approximately 19½″ x 5¾″. Printed on
recto only.

Locations: BPL

9008. ⟨EYESIGHT LEAFLET⟩

BOSTON, NOVEMBER 1st, 1887.

Single cut sheet folded to make four pages.
Page: 5⅛″ x 4⅞″.

Printed on p. ⟨1⟩ is a 5-line note, dated as
above, reading: DR. HOLMES *regrets that im-
paired eyesight and the large demands ...
oblige him to contract his ... correspondence ...*

Note: Currier-Tilton, pp. 211-212, report four
printings of this leaflet during the period 1887–
1888. BAL has no information that may serve to
distinguish the printings. It is probable that
the fourth printing was dated 1888. See below
under 1889, 1893, for other, similar, leaflets.

MHS

9009. No. 17. Standard Recitations by Best Authors ... Compiled ... by Frances P. Sullivan ... September, 1887 ...

M. J. Ivers & Co., Publishers, 86 Nassau
Street, N. Y. ... ⟨1887⟩

Printed paper wrapper.

Reprint save for "Our Brother," p. 48. Collected in *Before the Curfew,* 1888.

The statement on the title-page, *September,
1887,* is false. The title-page for this issue was
deposited for copyright Nov. 8, 1887; no record of deposit of the completed book.

NYPL

9010. Patriotic Addresses in America and England, from 1850 to 1885 ... by Henry Ward
Beecher Edited ... by John R. Howard

New York Fords, Howard, & Hulbert 1887

"The Minister Plenipotentiary," pp. ⟨422⟩-434.

H

9011. What American Authors Think about International Copyright

New-York American Copyright League 1888

Letter, April 27, 1885 ⟨sic⟩, p. 11.

For comment see entry No. 218.

9012. BEFORE THE CURFEW AND OTHER
POEMS, CHIEFLY OCCASIONAL ...

BOSTON AND NEW YORK HOUGHTON, MIFFLIN
AND COMPANY THE RIVERSIDE PRESS, CAMBRIDGE
1888

⟨i-ii⟩, ⟨i⟩-vi, ⟨1⟩-⟨110⟩, blank leaf. Laid paper. Trimmed: 7″ x 4¹¹⁄₁₆″. Untrimmed: 7³⁄₁₆″ x
4¾″ full.

Two printings noted:

1

⟨1-7⁸, 8⁴⟩.

In the preliminary advertisement *Before the
Curfew* is priced $1.25.

2

⟨1⁴, 2-8⁸⟩.

In the preliminary advertisement *Before the
Curfew* is priced at $1.00.

Five bindings noted. The sequence has not been
determined but it is presumed that bindings A,
Aa and Ab were simultaneous.

Binding A

Gray cartridge paper sides, white V cloth shelfback and corners. Stamped in gold. On the
spine the name HOUGHTON is flanked by dots.
White laid paper end papers. Flyleaf at front.
Top edges gilt. Noted on first and second printing sheets.

Binding Aa

White V cloth sides, green V cloth shelfback.
Stamped in gold and green. White laid paper
end papers. Flyleaf at front. Top edges gilt.
Noted on sheets of the first and second printings.

Binding Ab

V cloth: blue. Unstamped. Printed paper label
on spine. Noted only on untrimmed sheets of
the first printing. White laid paper end papers.
Flyleaf at front.

Binding B

Three quarters brown morocco. Noted only on
a set of second printing sheets.

Binding C

Gray cartridge paper sides, white V cloth shelf-back and corners. Stamped in gold. The name HOUGHTON on the spine is not flanked by dots. White laid paper end papers. Flyleaf at front. Top edges gilt. Noted on second printing sheets only.

Noted for *next week* PW April 7, 1888. Advertised for April 14, 1888, PW April 7, 1888. Deposited (Aa binding) April 9, 1888. BA copy (Aa binding) received April 14, 1888. H copy (Aa binding) received April 14, 1888. A copy in H (A binding) inscribed by Holmes April 15, 1888. BPL copy (Ab binding) received April 17, 1888. Listed (cloth; and, *uncut*) PW April 21, 1888. The London (Low) edition listed Ath April 14, 1888.

BA (1st printing, Aa binding) BPL (1st printing, Ab binding) CAW (2nd printing, B binding) H (1st printing, A binding; 1st printing, Aa binding; 1st printing, Ab binding; 2nd printing, A binding) LC (1st printing, Aa binding, being a deposit copy) NYPL (1st printing, Aa binding; 1st printing, Ab binding; 2nd printing, A binding) Y (1st printing, Ab binding; 2nd printing, C binding)

9013. Appletons' Cyclopaedia of American Biography Edited by James Grant Wilson and John Fiske . . . Volume IV . . .

New York   D. Appleton and Company   1, 3 and 5 Bond Street   1888

"John Lothrop Motley," pp. 438-440.

For comment see entry No. 6020.

9014. Performing Seals . . .

⟨Boston, 1888?⟩

An advertising card, 4⅜″ x 2⅝″ scant.

A 9-line letter, March 24, 1888, addressed to Messrs. Batcheller and Kyle, regarding their trained seals; printed on the reverse of the card. On the recto of the card is a lithographed picture of a group of seals in various domestic attitudes.

CAW

9015. ⟨BOSTON PUBLIC LIBRARY⟩
       Proudly beneath her glittering dome . . .

⟨n.p., n.d., Boston, 1888⟩

Single cut sheet folded to four pages. Page: 11¹³⁄₁₆″ x 9¾″ full. Text on pp. ⟨1⟩ and ⟨3⟩, otherwise unprinted. Anonymous.

Privately printed for the author's use. Appears also in *Proceedings on the Occasion of Laying the Corner-Stone of the New Library Building of the City of Boston. November 28, 1888,* Boston, 1889; issued after Sept. 16, 1889. Collected in *The Poetical Works,* Vol. 3, 1891.

CAW

9016. ⟨EYESIGHT LEAFLET⟩

BOSTON, JANUARY 1st, 1889.

Single cut sheet folded to make four pages. Page: 5⅞″ x 4¾″ scant.

Printed on p. ⟨1⟩ is the earlier note of 1887, *q.v.,* and an added seven line note dated as above. Also see entry No. 9049.

CAW

9017. . . . Proceedings of the Massachusetts Historical Society, from June, 1888, to January, 1889 . . .

⟨Boston, 1889⟩

Printed paper wrapper. Cover-title. At head of title: III.

"Tribute to Dr. Clarke," pp. 144-147.

MHS   Y

9018. Banquet at the Metropolitan Opera House April 30th 1889, Given in Honor of the Centennial of the Inauguration of George Washington . . .

⟨New York, 1889⟩

Cover-title. Printed paper boards. A souvenir program issued (presumably) at the banquet.

On p. 6 is an untitled poem beginning: *Sceptres and thrones the morning realms have tried . . .* Appears also in *Library of Tribune Extras. Vol I. May, 1889. No. 5. The Washington Centenary . . . ;* for a comment on this publication see entry No. 685.

AAS   MHS

9019. Franklin Square Song Collection: Two Hundred Favorite Songs . . . No. 6. Selected by J. P. McCaskey . . .

New York. Harper & Brothers, Franklin Square. ⟨1889⟩

Printed paper boards, cloth shelfback; printed paper wrapper; cloth.

On p. ⟨2⟩ appears the final stanza of Holmes's "To Rev. S. F. Smith, Aet. 80, Oct. 21, 1888." For publication of the complete poem see entry No. 9057.

Deposited Sept. 7, 1889.

H

9020. EMERSON.

PHILADELPHIA: J. B. LIPPINCOTT COMPANY. 1889.

Anonymous.

⟨1⟩-15. 7⅝″ x 5⅛″.

⟨-⟩⁸.

Printed mottled gray paper wrapper.

Deposited Sept. 30, 1889. Almost surely prepared for copyright purposes only and not issued in this form. Formally published in *Chambers Encyclopedia*, Vol. 4, Philadelphia, 1889;
listed PW Dec. 28, 1889.

LC

9021. TO THE ELEVEN LADIES WHO PRE-
SENTED A LOVING CUP TO ME AU-
GUST 29 M DCCC LXXXIX.

⟨n.p., n.d., 1889⟩

Cover-title. The above on the first page of a
single cut sheet folded to four pages. Page:
8½″ x 5⁹⁄₁₆″. Japan paper.

Poem on pp. ⟨2-3⟩. On p. ⟨4⟩: *Twelve copies
printed. Number ⟨space for insertion of num-
ber⟩*

Loosely inserted is a leaf of Japan paper imprinted on the recto with the names of the
eleven ladies.

Collected in *Over the Teacups*, 1891.

H

9022. Proceedings of the Massachusetts Historical Society. Vol. IV. Second Series. 1887–
1889 . . .

Boston: Published by the Society. M.DCCC.
LXXXIX.

Reprint save for: "Memoir of William Amory,
A. M.," pp. 414-417.

BA   H

9023. The Art of Authorship . . . Compiled . . .
by George Bainton.

London: James Clarke & Co., 13 & 14, Fleet
Street. 1890.

Contribution, p. 207.

For comment see entry No. 1271.

9024. The Art of Authorship . . . Compiled . . .
by George Bainton

New York D. Appleton and Company 1890

Contribution, p. 207.

For comment see entry No. 1272.

9025. THE BROOM-STICK TRAIN: OR
THE RETURN OF THE WITCHES.

⟨Roxbury, Mass. South End Industrial School
Press, n.d., 1890?⟩

⟨1-8⟩; blank leaf embossed: *South End Industrial School Press, 45 Bartlett St., Roxbury.*
5⅜″ x 4⁷⁄₁₆″. Printed throughout in blue.

⟨1⁴, 2¹⟩.

Blue paper wrapper, the front slotted to ac-
commodate the insertion of a white paper label
imprinted: THE BROOM-STICK TRAIN

Originally in *Atlantic Monthly*, Aug. 1890. Collected in (reprinted from?) *Over the Teacups*,
1891, *i.e.*, Nov. 1890.

NYPL

9026. No. 29. Standard Recitations by Best Authors . . . Compiled . . . by Frances P. Sullivan . . . September, 1890 . . .

M. J. Ivers & Co., Publishers, 86 Nassau
Street, N. Y. . . . ⟨1890⟩

Printed paper wrapper.

"After the Curfew," pp. 24-25. The poem was
first published in *Atlantic Monthly*, Feb. 1890;
collected in *Over the Teacups*, 1891, *i.e.*, Nov.
1890.

Note: There is no certainty that this publication was issued prior to publication of *Over the
Teacups*. The Copyright Office reports that
copies were not deposited for copyright although a title-page for the publication was deposited Oct. 13, 1890.

NYPL

9027. OVER THE TEACUPS . . .

BOSTON AND NEW YORK HOUGHTON, MIFFLIN
AND COMPANY THE RIVERSIDE PRESS, CAMBRIDGE
1891 ⟨*i.e.*, Nov. 1890⟩

First Printing

⟨i-iv⟩, ⟨1⟩-319. *Note:* Pp. ⟨i-ii⟩ present in ex-
amples of *Binding A*; excised in examples of
Binding B. 7⁵⁄₁₆″ x 4⅛″ (Binding A). 7½″ x 4⅛″
(Binding B).

⟨1¹⁰, 2-20⁸⟩. Leaves ⟨1⟩₃,₄ inserted. *Note:* Leaf
⟨1⟩₁ present in examples of *Binding A*; excised
in examples of *Binding B*. For comment on
bindings see below.

Binding: See below for description of the four
known bindings.

Two states of the first printing have been noted;
in the following comments reference to *The
Breakfast-Table Series* is to the listing fifth from
the bottom of the boxed advertisement.

1

In the advertisement opposite the title-page *Over the Teacups* is listed without price; *The Breakfast-Table Series* is described as in *10 vols.* and is priced at $17.00.

2

In the advertisement opposite the title-page *Over the Teacups* is priced at $1.50; *The Breakfast-Table Series* is described as in *11 vols.* and is priced at $18.50.

Second Printing

⟨i-ii⟩, ⟨1⟩-319.

⟨1⁹, 2-20⁸⟩. Leaf ⟨1⟩2 inserted.

In the advertisement opposite the title-page *Over the Teacups* is priced at $1.50; *The Breakfast-Table Series* is described as in *11 vols.* and is priced at $18.50.

Variant Printing

The position of this variant has not been firmly established but it certainly is not the earliest printing.

⟨i-iv⟩, ⟨1⟩-319, blank leaf.

⟨1², 2¹, 3-22⁸⟩.

In the advertisement opposite the title-page *Over the Teacups* is priced at $1.50; *The Breakfast-Table Series* is described as in *11 vols.* and is priced at $18.50.

Binding

Four states of the binding have been noted. On the basis of occurrence and contemporary inscriptions *Binding A* and *Binding B* appear to be simultaneous. On the same type of evidence the sequence of *Binding C* and *Binding D* is presumed correct.

Binding A

V cloth: olive-green. Goldstamped save as noted. Covers not bevelled.

Front: OVER THE / TEA-CVPS / ⟨teapot⟩ / ⟨front cover bordered by a leafy frame.⟩

Spine: ⟨leafy fillet⟩ / OVER ⟨dot⟩ THE / TEA-CVPS / ⟨floret⟩ / O ⟨dot⟩ W ⟨dot⟩ HOLMES / HOUGHTON / MIFFLIN & CO. / ⟨leafy fillet⟩

Back: Blindstamped with a leafy frame.

End papers: Yellow manila; also, white laid paper. Flyleaf inserted between leaves ⟨1⟩1-2. Flyleaf at back. Edges stained yellow.

Noted on first printing, first state; and, first printing, second state.

Binding B

S cloth: dark green. Covers bevelled. Goldstamped save as noted.

Front: ⟨winged urn⟩

Spine: OVER THE / TEA CUPS / O. W. HOLMES / HOUGHTON MIFFLIN & CO.

Back: ⟨blindstamped winged urn⟩

End papers: Blue-black-coated on white. Flyleaves. Top edges gilded.

Noted on first printing, first state; first printing, second state; second printing.

Binding C

V cloth: olive-green. Goldstamped save as noted. Covers not bevelled.

Front: OVER THE / TEACVPS / ⟨teapot⟩ / ⟨front bordered by a leafy frame⟩

Spine: ⟨leafy fillet⟩ / OVER ⟨dot⟩ THE / TEACVPS / ⟨floret⟩ / O ⟨dot⟩ W ⟨dot⟩ HOLMES / HOUGHTON / MIFFLIN & CO. / ⟨leafy fillet⟩

Back: Blindstamped with a leafy frame.

End papers: White laid paper. Flyleaves. Top edges gilded.

Noted on the second printing; variant printing; *Thirteenth Thousand.*

Binding D

S cloth: dark green. Covers bevelled. Goldstamped save as noted.

Front: ⟨winged urn⟩

Spine: OVER THE / TEACUPS / O. W. HOLMES / HOUGHTON MIFFLIN & CO.

Back: ⟨blindstamped winged urn⟩

End papers: Blue-black-coated on white. Flyleaves. Top edges gilded.

Noted on copies of the second printing. Also noted on copies of the extended edition dated MDCCCXCI.

Deposited Nov. 5, 1890. A copy of the first printing, second state (in H), binding A, presented by Holmes to "Wendell and Fanny," Nov. 8, 1890. Noted for *today* PW Nov. 8, 1890. A copy of the first printing, second state (in H) binding A, presented by Holmes to Sarah Orne Jewett, Nov. 10, 1890. On Nov. 11, 1890, H received a copy of the first printing, second state, binding B. On Nov. 11, 1890, BA received a copy of the second printing, binding B. Listed PW Nov. 15, 1890. The variant printing (LC) inscribed by Holmes to W. H. Rideing Nov. 25, 1890. The London (Low) edition, dated 1890, was advertised for *next week* in Ath Nov. 29, 1890; listed Ath Dec. 13, 1890. *See* Writings, *Vol. 4, 1891, below.*

AAS (1st printing, 2nd state, binding B)   BA (2nd printing, binding B)   H (1st printing, 1st state, binding A; 1st printing, 1st state, binding B;

1st printing, second state, binding A; 1st printing, 2nd state, binding B; 2nd printing, binding C; 2nd printing, binding D) LC (1st printing, 1st state, binding B, being a deposit copy. *Note:* Simultaneously with deposit of the preceding the publishers also deposited a copy of the *second printing* which is now rebound. Variant printing, binding C) Y (2nd printing, binding C; 2nd printing, binding D)

9028. Henry J. Bigelow, M. D. Memorial Meeting.

⟨Boston, 1890?⟩

Issued in printed paper wrapper? Printed self-wrapper?

"Remarks," pp. 2-4.

H

9029. Typical Elms and Other Trees of Massachusetts. Introductory Chapter by Oliver Wendell Holmes. Descriptive Text by Lorin L. Dame. Plates by Henry Brooks …

Boston: Little, Brown, and Company. 1890

"Introduction," pp. ⟨7⟩-10.

Noted as *just ready* PW Jan. 3, 1891. Deposited Jan. 5, 1891. Listed PW April 4, 1891.

NYPL Y

OVER THE TEACUPS …

Boston … 1891 ⟨*i.e.,* Nov. 1890⟩

See entry No. 9027.

9030. A Fellow of Trinity by Alan St. Aubyn ⟨pseud. for Mrs. Frances Marshall⟩ … A New Edition with a Note by Oliver Wendell Holmes …

London Chatto & Windus, Piccadilly 1891

"A Note by the Author of The Autocrat of the Breakfast-Table," p. ⟨iii⟩, dated Nov. 26, 1890.

Not seen.

Note: The above is a one-volume reprint of a three-volume novel issued under date 1890. The 1890 printing does not contain the Holmes note.

Listed PC Feb. 14, 1891; Bkr March, 1891.

Bodleian

9031. MEMOIR OF HENRY JACOB BIGELOW … [REPRINTED FROM THE PROCEEDINGS OF THE AMERICAN ACADEMY OF ARTS AND SCIENCES, VOL. XXVI.]

CAMBRIDGE: JOHN WILSON AND SON. UNIVERSITY PRESS. 1891.

⟨1⟩-15. Laid paper. 10¹⁄₁₆″ x 6⅝″.

⟨-⟩⁸.

Printed terra-cotta laid paper wrapper.

BA H

9032. JAMES RUSSELL LOWELL. 1819–1891 … FROM THE ATLANTIC MONTHLY FOR OCTOBER.

⟨n.d., The Riverside Press, Cambridge, 1891⟩

Single leaf of laid paper. 10½″ x 6″. Printed on recto only. Watermarked *The Riverside Press.* It will be noted that since the production is done on a cut sheet not all copies will have the full watermark present.

Issued not after Sept. 28, 1891; the C. E. Norton copy (in H) is in an envelope so postmarked.

Currier-Tilton, p. 226, report a postcard reprinting of the poem. No copy located by BAL. Collected in *The Poetical Works,* 1891, Vol. 3.

H MHS Y

9033. THE WRITINGS OF OLIVER WENDELL HOLMES

Issued in two formats:

Large-Paper Edition. Limited to 275 numbered sets. Issued in a variety of bindings including boards, cloth shelfback, printed paper label on spine; cloth; various styles and types of custom leather binding. Imprint: *Cambridge Printed at the Riverside Press 1891–1892.* Vols. 1-13 dated 1891; Vol. 14 dated 1892.

Riverside Edition. Issued in cloth. Imprint: *Boston and New York: Houghton, Mifflin and Company The Riverside Press, Cambridge* M DCCC XCI The fourteenth volume appears to have been added not before 1898 or 1899.

Precise publication information is wanting. The records of the Copyright Office and of the publishers are somewhat contradictory.

Vols. 1-13 were distributed in London by Sampson Low; listed PC Dec. 5, 1891; Bkr Jan. 1892.

1

The Autocrat of the Breakfast-Table

Reprint save for "Preface to the New Edition."

Large-Paper Edition: Noted for Sept. 12, 1891, PW Sept. 5, 1891. Deposited Sept. 19, 1891. Published Sept. 19, 1891 (publisher's records). Listed PW Oct. 10, 1891.

Riverside Edition: Published Sept. 19, 1891 (publisher's records). Listed PW Oct. 10, 1891. No record of copyright deposit.

2

The Professor at the Breakfast-Table with the Story of Iris

Reprint save for "Preface to the New Edition."

Large-Paper Edition: Noted for Sept. 12, 1891, in PW Sept. 5, 1891. Deposited Sept. 19, 1891. Published Sept. 19, 1891 (publisher's records). Listed PW Oct. 10, 1891.

Riverside Edition: Published Sept. 19, 1891 (publisher's records). Listed PW Oct. 10, 1891. No record of copyright deposit.

3

The Poet at the Breakfast-Table

Reprint save for "Preface to the New Edition."

Large-Paper Edition: Published Sept. 26, 1891 (publisher's records). Deposited Sept. 28, 1891. Listed PW Oct. 10, 1891.

Riverside Edition: Published Sept. 26, 1891 (publisher's records). Listed PW Oct. 10, 1891. No record of copyright deposit.

4

Over the Teacups

Reprint save for a preface dated *August, 1891.*

Note: Also issued as a separate volume, being part of no set. The publication record is far from clear and no publication date for this trade format has been established.

Large-Paper Edition: Deposited Sept. 28, 1891. Listed PW Oct. 10, 1891.

Riverside Edition: Published Sept. 19, 1891 (publisher's records). Listed PW Oct. 10, 1891. No record of copyright deposit.

Note: The manufacturing and publication records for this title are both sparse and confusing.

5

Elsie Venner

Reprint save for "Preface to the New Edition."

Large-Paper Edition: Deposited Oct. 9, 1891. Noted for *today* PW Oct. 10, 1891. Published Oct. 10, 1891 (publisher's records). Listed PW Oct. 24, 1891.

Riverside Edition: Published Oct. 10, 1891 (publisher's records). Listed PW Oct. 24, 1891. No record of copyright deposit.

6

The Guardian Angel

Reprint save for "Preface to the New Edition."

Large-Paper Edition: Deposited Oct. 9, 1891. Noted for *today* PW Oct. 10, 1891. Published Oct. 19, 1891 (publisher's records). Listed PW Oct. 24, 1891.

Riverside Edition: Published Oct. 19, 1891 (publisher's records). Listed PW Oct. 24, 1891. No record of copyright deposit.

7

A Mortal Antipathy

Reprint save for a new preface.

Large-Paper Edition: Deposited Oct. 22, 1891. Published Oct. 28, 1891 (publisher's records). Listed PW Nov. 7, 1891.

Riverside Edition: Published Oct. 28, 1891 (publisher's records). Listed PW Nov. 7, 1891. No record of copyright deposit.

8

Pages from an Old Volume of Life

Reprint save for "Preface to the New Edition."

Large-Paper Edition: Deposited Oct. 22, 1891. Published Oct. 28, 1891 (publisher's records). Listed PW Nov. 7, 1891.

Riverside Edition: Published Oct. 28, 1891 (publisher's records). Listed PW Nov. 7, 1891. No record of copyright deposit.

9

Medical Essays

Reprint save for "Preface to the New Edition."

Large-Paper Edition: Deposited Jan. 2, 1892.

Riverside Edition: Advertised for *immediate publication* PW Dec. 5, 1891. Deposited Dec. 17, 1891.

Note: The publishers report that a copy of this volume, format not known, was sent to the Copyright Office on Sept. 28, 1891. Further information wanting. Special copyright printing?

10

Our Hundred Days in Europe

Reprint.

Large-Paper Edition: Published Dec. 15, 1891 (publisher's records). Deposited Jan. 2, 1892.

Riverside Edition: Advertised for *immediate publication* PW Dec. 5, 1891. Published Dec. 15, 1891 (publisher's records). Deposited Dec. 17, 1891.

11-13

The Poetical Works, Vol. I

Reprint. For publication note see under Vol. 13.

The Poetical Works, Vol. II

Reprint. For publication note see under Vol. 13. *Note:* In the first printings of this volume the dates for Benjamin Peirce, p. 89, are given as 1809–1890; in later printings the date is correctly given: 1809–1880. The error has been noted in printings as late as that of 1895.

The Poetical Works, Vol. III

Reprint save for:

"To James Russell Lowell," pp. 133-135. See above under 1891 for a privately printed issue of the poem.

"For the Window in St. Margaret's," p. 183.

"For the Dedication of the New City Library, Boston," pp. 181-183. See above under 1888 for a privately printed issue.

"To My Old Readers," pp. 200-203.

Large-Paper Edition: Published Nov. 21, 1891 (publisher's records). Deposited Nov. 27, 1891. Listed PW Dec. 5, 1891. *Note:* Some copies lack the first three lines of text, p. 227; these are presumed to be of the earliest issue.

Riverside Edition: Published Nov. 21, 1891 (publisher's records). Listed PW Dec. 5, 1891. No record of copyright deposit.

14

Ralph Waldo Emerson. John Lothrop Motley

Reprint.

Large-Paper Edition: Deposited May 13, 1892. Listed PW June 25, 1892.

Riverside Edition: Manufactured Oct. 1898 (publisher's records). No record of copyright deposit.

The above entry on the basis of sets in BA CAW H LC NYPL

The Poetical Works of Oliver Wendell Holmes Household Edition With Illustrations

Boston and New York Houghton, Mifflin and Company The Riverside Press, Cambridge ⟨1891; *i.e.,* not before 1894⟩

See entry No. 9054.

9034. The One Hoss Shay ... How the Old Horse Won the Bet & The Broomstick Train ...

Boston and New York Houghton, Mifflin and Company The Riverside Press, Cambridge MDCCCXCII

Suède. Reported (not seen) in cloth.

Reprint save for the "Preface," pp. 4-7.

Two printings noted:

1: ⟨1⁵, 2-10⁸, 11²⟩. Leaf ⟨1⟩₂ inserted.

2: ⟨1⁹, 2-9⁸, 10⁶⟩. Leaf ⟨1⟩₂ inserted.

Deposited Oct. 3, 1891. Noted as *just ready* PW Oct. 3, 1891. BA copy received Oct. 5, 1891. Listed (leather only) PW Oct. 17, 1891. The London (Gay & Bird) edition listed PC Nov. 21, 1891.

H (1st, 2nd)

9035. Lowell Memorial Number ... The Cambridge Tribune Vol. XIV No. 48.

Cambridge, Mass., Saturday, February 20, 1892 ...

Caption-title. The above at head of p. ⟨1⟩.

"Holmes on Lowell," p. 3. A prose appreciation written for this special issue of the *Cambridge Tribune.*

H

9036. Lines / by / Oliver Wendell Holmes / on the presentation / of his portrait to the / Philadelphia College of / Physicians / Saturday, April 30th / 1892

⟨n.p., 1892⟩

Single cut sheet folded to four pages. The above on p. ⟨1⟩. Laid paper watermarked: *Old Berkshire Mills 1890* Page: 9⁷⁄₁₆″ x 6″. Text on pp. ⟨2-4⟩. At end: *Boston, April 28, 1892.*

Note: Currier-Tilton, p. 236, describe an 1898(?) printing in which the title is: Lines by / Dr. Oliver Wendell Holmes, / ⟨etc., etc.⟩

H

9037. *Entry cancelled.*

9038. ⟨In Memoriam⟩ David Humphreys Storer

⟨Boston: S. J. Parkhill & Co., Printers, n.d., 1892⟩

Cover-title. Printed paper wrapper. Tribute, pp. 6-8.

H copy received July 25, 1892.

H

9039. The Poetical Works of Oliver Wendell Holmes ...

Edinburgh David Douglas, Castle Street 1892

4 Vols. Cloth; and, pictorial printed paper wrapper.

Reprint save for "Author's Preface to the Edinburgh Edition," Vol. 1, pp. ⟨v⟩-vi.

Advertised as though ready Ath Oct. 1, 1892. Listed Ath Oct. 15, 1892; PC Nov. 5, 1892; Bkr Nov. 1892. Noticed by Ath Nov. 5, 1892.

H

9040. LETTER FROM DR. HOLMES. AT THE WHITTIER COMMEMORATION LAST WEEK ⟨Oct. 16, 1892⟩ AT THE YOUNG MEN'S CHRISTIAN UNION, PRESIDENT BALDWIN READ THE FOLLOWING LETTER, WRITTEN AS HIS CONTRIBUTION TO THE SERVICE BY DR. OLIVER WENDELL HOLMES ...

⟨n.p., n.d., Boston, 1892⟩

Single cut sheet folded to make four pages. The above at head of p. ⟨2⟩. Text on pp. ⟨2-3⟩, otherwise unprinted. Page: 9¹³⁄₁₆″ x 6″. Laid paper.

BPL copy received from Pres. W. H. Baldwin Nov. 3, 1892.

BPL

9041. Fame's Tribute to Children ...

Chicago   A. C. McClurg and Company   1892

Reprints, pp. 97-99, "The Boys." Appended at the end, however, is a note (here in its earliest located book appearance) in which Holmes identifies the characters mentioned in the poem.

For fuller entry see BAL, Vol. 1, p. 76.

9042. Dorothy Q together with a Ballad of the Boston Tea Party & Grandmother's Story of Bunker Hill Battle ...

Boston and New York   Houghton, Mifflin and Company   The Riverside Press, Cambridge   M DCCC XCIII

Trade edition bound in cloth; also, 250 de luxe copies bound in vellum imprinted: *Cambridge Printed at the Riverside Press   M DCCC XCIII*

Reprint save for the "Preface," pp. 5-⟨7⟩.

Two issues noted:

1: P. 50, line 8: ... *flashed* ...

2: P. 50, line 8: ... *clashed* ...

Trade edition deposited Oct. 31, 1892. De luxe edition deposited Nov. 1, 1892. Listed (both formats) PW Nov. 5, 1892. The London (Gay & Bird) edition advertised for *next week* PC Nov. 12, 1892.

Note: BAL has noted no copies of the second issue in the de luxe format.

B (1st de luxe; 2nd trade)   BA (1st trade)   BPL (1st trade; 2nd trade)   H (1st de luxe; 1st trade; 2nd trade)   LC (1st de luxe; 1st trade; both being deposit copies)

9043. DR. HOLMES' POEM ... TEACHERS OF TEACHERS! YOURS THE TASK, ... FEB. 23, 1893.

⟨n.p., n.d., 1893?⟩

Caption title. The above on the recto of a single leaf, 8¹⁄₁₆″ x 5⅜″ scant.

Prepared as proof only?

See note regarding this poem under entry No. 9059.

CAW

9044. Quabbin   The Story of a Small Town With Outlooks upon Puritan Life by Francis H. Underwood ...

Lee and Shepard Publishers   Boston ...   ⟨n.d., 1893⟩

Single cut sheet. Wove paper. Folded to make four pages. Paged 1-4. Page: 7″ x 5⅝″. P. 1 as above.

Issued as an advertisement for the second printing of Underwood's *Quabbin*, Boston, 1893.

Letter of commendation, p. 2.

Note: The letter also appears (reprinted in?) in the terminal matter of *The Poet and the Man   Recollections and Appreciations of James Russell Lowell,* by Francis H. Underwood, Boston, 1893.

MHS

9045. Horatian Echoes   Translations of the Odes of Horace by John Osborne Sargent with an Introduction by Oliver Wendell Holmes

Boston and New York   Houghton, Mifflin and Company   The Riverside Press, Cambridge 1893

"Introduction," pp. vii-ix. Copies occur on both laid; and, on wove papers.

Two formats noted; sequence, if any, not determined:

A: All edges trimmed. Bound in white cloth stamped in gold.

B: Untrimmed. Bound in red cloth, printed paper label on spine.

Advertised for *this day*, no indication of two formats, PW April 15, 1893. Listed PW, "in white and gold," April 22, 1893. BPL copy (A format) received April 27, 1893. Listed PC May 13, 1893.

BPL (A)   H (A)   CAW (B)

9046. ... Proceedings of the Massachusetts Historical Society, March and April, 1893.

⟨Boston, 1893⟩

Printed wrapper. Cover-title. At head of title: III.

"Comments ⟨on an article relating to the history of Georgia⟩," p. 174.

MHS   Y

9047. Dinner. American Gynecological Society, Continental Hotel, Philadelphia, Tuesday, May 16th, 1893 ...

⟨Philadelphia: Wm. F. Fell & Co., Prs., 1893⟩

A four-page menu. Cover-title. Contains a facsimile letter by Holmes, May 8, 1893.

BML

9048. HYMN WRITTEN FOR THE RECEPTION IN HONOR OF THE TWENTY-FIFTH ANNIVERSARY OF THE REORGANIZATION OF THE BOSTON YOUNG MEN'S CHRISTIAN UNION ... WEDNESDAY EVENING, MAY 31, 1893 ... OLIVER WENDELL HOLMES. MAY 28, 1893.

⟨Boston, 1893⟩

Card. Printed on recto only. 6¼" x 3½".

Two issues (printings?) have been noted; the sequence has not been determined and the designations are for identification only:

A: There is a period present after the date *1893* at foot of card.

B: No period after the date *1893* at foot of card.

Collected in *Complete Poetical Works ... Cambridge Edition* ⟨1895⟩.

Note: An undated reprint of the poem, printed in brown on a card, 5⁵⁄₁₆" x 3⅜", was issued *ca.* 1925 by Walter M. Hatch, Inc., Boston. This reprint carries the text and name of author only; it does not reprint the preliminary matter.

Also note: The poem also appears in: *No. 39. Standard Recitations by Best Authors ... Compiled ... by Frances P. Sullivan ... March 1893 ...*, New York ⟨1893⟩; printed paper wrap-

per. This is a lovely example of the frequent use of spurious dates on serial publications such as this. The poem was written for the twenty-fifth anniversary of the reorganization of the Boston Young Men's Christian Union, May 31, 1893, and printed copies of the hymn, almost surely the first to be published in any form, were distributed at the reception. According to Holmes's own statement (at the end of the poem) the poem was completed on May 28, 1893. Yet, the recitation book is dated March, 1893. Significantly, the recitation book was not deposited for copyright until Aug. 16, 1893.

AAS (B)   H (A,B)   MHS (A)   Y (A)

9049. ⟨*Printed letter*⟩ BEVERLY FARMS, MASS. 1893. Dear ⟨*space for insertion of name*⟩ ... I can do little more than acknowledge the reception of the very numerous communications which come to me ...

⟨1893⟩

Card. 3½" x 4½". Printed on recto only. For similar printed notices see above under 1887, 1889.

Note: A presumed proof of the above (in PDH) is headed: *Boston, Mass. Beverly Farms ...*

PDH

9050. Quaker Poems A Collection of Verse Relating to the Society of Friends. Compiled by Charles Francis Jenkins.

Philadelphia: John C. Winston & Co. 1893.

"In Memory of John Greenleaf Whittier," pp. 132-134. Collected in *Complete Poetical Works ... Cambridge Edition* ⟨1895⟩.

H

9051. FRANCIS PARKMAN ...

⟨n.p., n.d., Boston, 1894⟩

Single cut sheet folded to four pages. Page: 8" x 5". Laid paper watermarked: *Rand, Avery & Co. Boston.* Text on pp. ⟨1⟩ and ⟨3⟩; otherwise blank.

Anonymous. Collected in *Complete Poetical Works ... Cambridge Edition* ⟨1895⟩. Reprinted in *Proceedings of the Massachusetts Historical Society, October and November, 1893.*

Note: The CAW collection had a galley proof of the above with an annotation in Holmes's hand asking for fifty copies. Currier-Tilton, p. 245, indicate that seventy-seven copies were printed.

H   MHS   Y

9052. Memorials of the Sixtieth Wedding Anniversary of Sarah Swain Hathaway and John Murray Forbes. Feb. 8, 1834–1894. Edited by Edith Forbes.

Boston: Printed for Private Distribution. 1894.

"Poem ... to J.M.F. on His Eightieth Birthday," pp. ⟨85⟩-86.

H

9053. AN UNPUBLISHED POEM ...

⟨n.p., n.d., 1894⟩

Cover-title.

⟨1⟩-8. 7⅝" scant x 4¹³⁄₁₆".

⟨-⟩⁴.

Printed gray-green laid paper wrapper.

BA   H   MHS

9053A. Proceedings of the Massachusetts Historical Society. Second Series. Vol. VIII. 1892–1894 ...

Boston: Published by the Society. M.DCCC.XCIV.

Reprint save for a letter, Nov. 7, 1892, pp. 21-22; and some remarks, p. 174.

H   MHS

9054. The Poetical Works of Oliver Wendell Holmes Household Edition With Illustrations

Boston and New York   Houghton, Mifflin and Company   The Riverside Press, Cambridge ⟨1891; i.e., not before 1894⟩

Pp. xvi, 426.

Contains a multi-dated copyright notice, the latest date being 1891. However, the book could not have been published prior to Jan. 1894 since it contains Holmes's poem on the death of Francis Parkman which was first printed in Jan. 1894. This book *may* be the first to contain the poems listed below; but note carefully that these poems appear also in *The Complete Poetical Works, Cambridge Edition*, Boston ⟨1895⟩. Until a positive publication date for this book can be determined its status remains doubtful; but until such date is established it challenges the primacy of *The Complete Poetical Works, Cambridge Edition*, Boston ⟨1895⟩ insofar as the following poems are concerned:

"But One Talent," pp. 403-404.

"An Impromptu at the Walcker Dinner upon the Completion of the Great Organ for Boston Music Hall," p. 395.

"To James Russell Lowell, at the Dinner ... February 22, 1889," pp. 400-402.

ANC

9055. The Last Leaf ... Illustrated by George Wharton Edwards & F. Hopkinson Smith

Houghton Mifflin & Co   The Riverside Press Cambridge MDCCCXCV.

Reprint save for the prefatory letter dated July 12th, 1894. For an earlier edition see entry No. 8992.

Deposited Sept. 27, 1894. Listed PW Nov. 3, 1894. The London (Low) edition advertised as *just ready* Ath Oct. 13, 1894; listed PC Nov. 3, 1894.

BA   H   NYPL

9056. A Brief History of the Lotos Club. By John Elderkin.

Club House, 556 and 558 Fifth Avenue, New York. ⟨1895⟩

Remarks extracted from Holmes's speech of April 14, 1883, (herein misdated April 15), pp. 61-64. For publication of the speech in its entirety see *Speeches ... , 1901*.

For comment see entry No. 3443.

9057. Poems of Home and Country. Also, Sacred and Miscellaneous Verse. By Rev. Samuel Francis Smith, D. D. Edited by Gen. Henry B. Carrington ...

Silver, Burdett and Company, Boston   New York   Chicago. 1895.

"To the Reverend S. F. Smith ... on his eightieth birthday, Oct. 21, 1888," p. ix. For a partial printing of this poem see entry No. 9019.

Trade edition: 8⁷⁄₁₆" x 5⁹⁄₁₆"; bound in maroon T cloth.

Edition de Luxe: 8¾" x 5¾"; red buckram sides, white V cloth shelfback. Limited to 250 copies signed by Smith.

Deposited June 24, 1895. Listed PW July 6, 1895.

EM (de luxe)   H (trade)

9058. The Poet among the Hills. Oliver Wendell Holmes in Berkshire ... by J.E.A. Smith ...

Pittsfield, Mass.: George Blatchford. 1895.

Reprint save for:

"A Vision of Life," with introductory remarks, pp. 110-113.

"Camilla," pp. 153-154.

"A Dollar's Worth," pp. 156-157.

Also contains letters, and extracts from letters, pp. 47-48, 90-94, 165.

Noted as *just ready* PW June 29, 1895. Listed PW Aug. 3, 1895.

H NYPL Y

9059. The Complete Poetical Works of Oliver Wendell Holmes   Cambridge Edition ⟨*vignette*⟩

Boston and New York   Houghton, Mifflin and Company   The Riverside Press, Cambridge ⟨1895⟩

Note: See entry No. 9054.

Also note: Currier-Tilton, p. 253, report twenty printings of this collection between publication of the first printing (Nov. 1895) and 1939. The first printings bear the imprint of Houghton, Mifflin & Company; later printings, the imprint of Houghton Mifflin Company. Thus far no feature that may distinguish the first from the later Houghton, Mifflin & Company printings has been discovered by BAL.

Contains several poems here first collected. Also contains the following in earliest (?) located book publication; *but see entry No. 9054.*

"An Impromptu at the Walcker Dinner upon the Completion of the Great Organ for Boston Music Hall in 1863," pp. 215-216.

"Harvard [Read at Commencement Dinner . . . 1880 . . .]," p. 268.

"Youth [Read at the Celebration of the thirty-first anniversary of the Boston Young Men's Christian Union, May 31, 1882]," p. 290.

"To James Russell Lowell at the Dinner in His Honor at the Tavern Club, on His Seventieth Birthday, February 22, 1889," pp. 293-295.

"But One Talent," pp. 295-296.

"To the Teachers of America," p. 298. For a separate (proof?) printing of this poem see entry No. 9043. The poem appears also in E. E. Brown's *Life of Oliver Wendell Holmes,* Boston ⟨1894⟩, which was deposited for copyright Nov. 30, 1894, about a week later than deposit date of *The Complete Poetical Works . . .* ⟨1895⟩.

Deposited Nov. 22, 1895. BPL copy received Nov. 27, 1895. Listed PW Dec. 7, 1895. The London (Low) edition listed Ath Jan. 18, 1896; PC Jan. 25, 1896; Bkr Feb. 1896.

BA H

9060. LIFE AND LETTERS

Issued in two formats.

Trade Edition

LIFE AND LETTERS OF OLIVER WENDELL HOLMES BY JOHN T. MORSE, JR.

. . .

BOSTON AND NEW YORK   HOUGHTON, MIFFLIN AND COMPANY   THE RIVERSIDE PRESS, CAMBRIDGE 1896

2 Vols. Title-pages printed in black.

1: ⟨i⟩-⟨viii⟩, ⟨1⟩-358, blank leaf. Laid paper. Frontispiece, 6 plates, 6 printed protective tissues, inserted. 7¾" x 5".
2: ⟨i-viii⟩, ⟨1⟩-335. Frontispiece, 2 plates, 3 printed protective tissues, and a 3-page facsimile of the *ms* of "The Last Leaf" inserted.

1: ⟨1⁴, 2-23⁸, 24⁴⟩.
2: ⟨1⁴, 2-22⁸⟩.

Four states of the trade edition binding have been noted. No sequence, if any, has been determined and the order of presentation is arbitrary.

A

T cloth: grass-green; light olive-green; maroon. White laid paper end papers. Top edges gilded. Flyleaf at front of Vol. 1; flyleaf at back of Vol. 2. LIFE AND / LETTERS (on the spine) is stamped from a plain roman face.

B

T cloth: maroon. Unstamped. Printed paper label on spine. White laid paper end papers. Top edges gilded. Flyleaf at front of Vol. 1; flyleaf at back of Vol. 2.

C

T cloth: maroon. White laid paper end papers. Top edges gilded. Flyleaf at front of Vol. 1; flyleaf at back of Vol. 2. LIFE AND / LETTERS (on the spine) is stamped from a decorated roman face; the A (for example) has an exaggerated horizontal serif at the top.

D

S cloth: red-orange. Brown leather label stamped in gold on spine. Flyleaf at front of Vol. 1; flyleaf at back of Vol. 2. Top edges gilded. Bound thus as Vols. 14-15 of the *Collected Works.*

According to an advertisement in PW May 2, 1896, the trade edition was also available in half calf; and, half morocco.

Limited Edition

LIFE AND LETTERS OF OLIVER WENDELL HOLMES BY JOHN T. MORSE, JR.

. . .

CAMBRIDGE   PRINTED AT THE RIVERSIDE PRESS 1896

2 Vols. Title-pages printed in black and red.

1: ⟨i-ii⟩, ⟨i⟩-⟨viii⟩, ⟨1⟩-358. Laid paper water-marked *The Riverside Press* Frontispiece, 6 plates, 6 printed protective tissues, inserted. 8⅞" x 5⅞".
2: ⟨i-viii⟩, ⟨1⟩-335. Frontispiece, 4 plates, 3 printed protective tissues inserted.

1: ⟨1², 2-23⁸, 24⁶⟩.
2: ⟨1², 2-22⁸, 23²⟩.

Gray laid paper boards sides, white V cloth shelfback. Printed paper label on spine. White laid paper end papers. Flyleaves.

Limited to 275 numbered copies.

Limited edition deposited April 30, 1896. Noted for *next week* PW May 2, 1896. Trade edition advertised for May 9 publication PW May 2, 1896. Both formats listed PW May 16, 1896. Contemporary British trade notices indicate that the London (Low) edition, made up of American sheets, was issued simultaneously with the American edition.

BPL (limited)   H (trade, bindings A, C, D)   NYPL (trade, binding B)

9061. ... Odes in Ohio, and Other Poems, by John James Piatt ...

The Robert Clarke Company, Publishers, 31 to 39 East Fourth Street, Cincinnati, O. ⟨n.d., 1897⟩

Single leaf. Printed on recto only. 8" x 5". At head of leaf: Quotation from Bayard Taylor.

Issued as an advertisement for Piatt's *Odes in Ohio ...* , 1897. Embodies a letter from Holmes to Piatt, June 11, 1878, acknowledging receipt of "The Ode which you so kindly sent me."

PDH

9062. A Quaker of the Olden Time, Being a Memoir of John Roberts, by His Son Daniel Roberts ... Edited by Edmund T. Lawrence, with Prefatory Letter by Oliver Wendell Holmes ...

London: Headley Brothers, 14, Bishopsgate Street without, E. C. 1898.

Cloth?

Prefatory letter, March 1, 1883, pp. 13-14.

Received by BMU June 30, 1898.

NYPL

9063. Speeches at the Lotos Club Arranged by John Elderkin Chester S. Lord Horatio N. Fraser

New York Privately Printed MCMI

"At an Informal Reunion, April 14, 1883," pp. 61-64. For a partial printing of this speech see *Brief History ...* , 1895, above.

For comment see entry No. 3469.

9064. A Memoir of Dr. James Jackson ... by James Jackson Putnam, M. D.

Boston and New York Houghton, Mifflin and Company The Riverside Press, Cambridge 1905

Letter, Nov. 4, 1834, pp. 314-316.

Untitled poem, four 4-line stanzas, dated Oct. 3, 1857, pp. 414-415; begins: *This shrine a precious gift enfolds ...*

Deposited Nov. 18, 1905. On copyright page: *Published November, 1905*

H

9065. THE AUTOCRAT'S THEOLOGY. UN-PUBLISHED LETTERS OF OLIVER WENDELL HOLMES. WITH NOTES BY EMORY S. TURNER.

⟨n.p., n.d., New York, 1909⟩

Cover-title.

⟨i-vi⟩, ⟨662⟩-⟨668⟩; 2 blank leaves. Illustrated. 9¾" x 6¾".

⟨-⟩⁹. Leaf ⟨-⟩₇ inserted.

Printed gray linen-weave paper wrapper.

Printed from the plates of *Putnam's Magazine*, Sept. 1909. In referring to this publication the Wakeman sale catalog (N. Y., 1924, entry No. 600) states: "Special issue printed for Mr. E. S. Turner, of which not more than 30 copies were printed ...". BAL has not attempted to verify the statement.

Y

9066. OUR BATTLE-LAUREATE ... RE-PRINTED FROM THE ATLANTIC MONTHLY, MAY, 1865 ...

⟨Boston and New York: Houghton Mifflin Company, n.d., 1912⟩

Caption-title. The above on p. ⟨1⟩.

Single cut sheet folded to make four pages. Page: 7¹³⁄₁₆" x 5⁵⁄₁₆".

Issued as an advertisement for Henry Howard Brownell's *Lines of Battle and Other Poems*, 1912.

Y

9067. Julia Ward Howe 1819–1910 by Laura E. Richards and Maud Howe Elliott Assisted by Florence Howe Hall . . .

Boston and New York　Houghton Mifflin Company 1915

2 Vols.

Untitled poem, Vol. 1, pp. 140-141, "never before printed," 10 four-line stanzas. Begins: *If I were one, O Minstrel wild* . . . Written on the occasion of the publication of Mrs. Howe's *Passion-Flowers*, 1854.

For comment see entry No. 9530.

9068. Anna Cabot Mills Lodge . . . ⟨Edited by Henry Cabot Lodge⟩

⟨Boston: The Merrymount Press⟩ Privately Printed MDCCCCXVIII

Unprinted paper boards, cloth shelfback.

". . . the following verses, which are not in his ⟨*i.e.*, Holmes's⟩ collected works, and which I do not think have ever been printed or published. ⟨32-line poem beginning:⟩ *The token of a nameless knight* . . ."—pp. 9-10.

H

9069. South County Studies of Some Eighteenth Century Persons Places & Conditions in That Portion of Rhode Island Called Narragansett by Esther Bernon Carpenter with an Introduction by Caroline Hazard Compiled Largely from Letters . . . by Oliver Wendell Holmes

Boston　Printed for the Subscribers 1924

Boards, cloth shelfback.

Six letters to Esther Bernon Carpenter, pp. ix-xv.

BA copy received July 24, 1924. Deposited Aug. 23, 1924.

BA　H　NYPL

9070. The History of Woodstock Connecticut by Clarence Winthrop Bowen . . .

Privately Printed by the Plimpton Press Norwood, Mass., U.S.A. 1926

Introduction, pp. 1-8; also a note dated March 5, 1891, p. 8.

450 numbered copies.

H

9071. LETTERS OF DR. OLIVER WENDELL HOLMES REPRINTED FROM THE HARVARD ALUMNI BULLETIN OF DECEMBER 22, 1927.

⟨n.p., n.d., 1927?⟩

Cover-title.

⟨1⟩-8. Illustrated. 9½″ x 6⅝″.

⟨-⟩⁴.

Printed self-wrapper.

NYPL

9072. A DISSERTATION ON ACUTE PERICARDITIS . . .

BOSTON　THE WELCH BIBLIOPHILIC SOCIETY MDCCCCXXXVII

Title-page in black and red.

⟨i-iv⟩, ⟨1⟩-39, 2 blank leaves. Laid paper watermarked *Canterbury Laid*⟨?⟩. 7½″ x 5³⁄₁₆″.

⟨1-3⁸⟩.

Printed cream white paper boards. Leaves ⟨1⟩1 and ⟨3⟩8 used as pastedowns.

On copyright page: *First Printing*

BA copy received Jan. 17, 1938; H Jan. 19, 1938. Deposited Dec. 19, 1938.

BA　H　NYPL

9073. AT DARTMOUTH　THE PHI BETA KAPPA POEM READ BY DR. OLIVER WENDELL HOLMES AT THE DARTMOUTH COMMENCEMENT EXERCISES JULY 24, 1839 PRIOR TO HIS APPOINTMENT ⟨*sic*⟩ TO THE CHAIR OF ANATOMY AND PHYSIOLOGY AT DARTMOUTH MEDICAL SCHOOL WITH AN INTRODUCTION BY MISS ELEANOR M. TILTON . . .

SCHUMAN'S　NEW YORK　1940

Title-page in black and brown.

⟨i-ii⟩, ⟨1⟩-44; colophon, p. ⟨45⟩. Watermark present in some copies: *Vidalon*. One facsimile in text. 10″ x 6⁹⁄₁₆″.

⟨1-3⟩⁸.

Green paper boards. Halftone portrait of Holmes pasted to front cover.

Present in some copies is an erratum slip correcting the error on the title page: *prior to his appointment to the chair* which should be: *prior to the assumption of his appointment* . . . The error is present in all examined copies.

100 numbered copies only.

Deposited May 28, 1940.

H　NYPL

9074. TWO OLIVER WENDELL HOLMES LETTERS ‹Edited› BY HENRY R. VIETS

  . . .

‹n.p., n.d., Cambridge, 1943›

Cover-title.

‹1-3›. 9⅜″ x 6¼″.

‹-›².

Printed gray laid paper wrapper watermarked: *Strathmore*.

AAS

9075. Captain Jolly on the Picturesque St. Croix by . . . William H. Dunne . . . with Notes . . . by Willis Harry Miller . . . and Five Letters of Oliver Wendell Holmes

Published by the St. Croix County Historical Society, Hudson, Wisconsin   August 1953 Star-Observer Print

Printed paper wrapper.

Contains six ‹sic› letters from Holmes to Dr. Irving D. Wiltrout, pp. 35-37.

AAS   Y

9076. THE AUTOCRAT'S MISCELLANIES BY OLIVER WENDELL HOLMES EDITED BY ALBERT MORDELL

TWAYNE PUBLISHERS   NEW YORK 3 ‹1959›

‹1›-356. 8⁷⁄₁₆″ x 5½″.

‹1-21⁸, 22¹⁰›.

V cloth: tan.

A gathering of hitherto uncollected material (selected from periodicals); occasional speeches and addresses (which had prior publication either as separates or in various published proceedings; etc., etc.).

Deposited Nov. 18, 1959.

LC

OLIVER WENDELL HOLMES
SECTION II

IN THIS SECTION the following classifications are listed: *Collections* of reprinted material issued under the author's name; separate editions. See *Section III* for a list of books by others containing material by Holmes reprinted from earlier books.

9077. Old King Cole, and the Ballad of the Oyster-Man ...

⟨Boston, n.d., *ca.* 1834⟩

For comment see entry No. 8720.

9078. The Tall Young Oysterman ... Words by B. Holmes Esqr ⟨*sic*⟩ ... Music ... by Mr. Shaw ...

Philadelphia ... 1842 ...

For comment see entry No. 8720.

9079. Affecting Ballad of the Oysterman ... ⟨Music⟩ by J. L. Hatton ...

Boston ... 1849 ...

For comment see entry No. 8720.

9080. Poems ... New and Enlarged Edition.

Boston: Ticknor, Reed & Fields. M DCCC L.

Boards, printed paper label on spine.

9081. Poems ... New and Enlarged Edition.

Boston: Ticknor, Reed, and Fields. M DCCC LI.

9082. Our Yankee Girls ... ⟨Music⟩ by Hermann Kotzschmar ...

Portland ... J. S. Paine 113 Middle St. ... 1852 ...

Sheet music. Cover-title. Also issued with the imprint: *New York Published by the Author* ...

9083. Poems ... New and Enlarged Edition.

Boston: Ticknor, Reed, and Fields. M DCCC LII

9084. Poems ... New and Enlarged Edition.

Boston: Ticknor, Reed, and Fields. M DCCC LIII.

9085. God Bless Our Yankee Girls ... ⟨Music⟩ by T. Comer.

Boston ... Oliver Ditson, 115 Washington St. ... 1854 ...

Sheet music. Cover-title. Plate No. 7202. Deposited July 10, 1854. For an earlier setting see entry No. 9082.

9086. Poems ... New and Enlarged Edition.

Boston: Ticknor, Reed, and Fields. M DCCC LIV.

9087. Poems ... New and Enlarged Edition.

Boston: Ticknor and Fields. M DCCC LIV.

9088. ... The Last of the Knickerbockers, (or the Last Leaf) ...

New-York ... G. B. Demarest 409 Broadway ... 1855 ...

At head of title: Songs and Ballads Composed and Sung by D. D. Griswold ... Sheet music. Cover-title.

9089. Poems ... New and Enlarged Edition.

Boston: Ticknor and Fields. M DCCC LV.

9090. Poems ... New and Enlarged Edition.

Boston: Ticknor and Fields. M DCCC LVI.

9091. Battle of Lexington ... Music by L. Heath ...

Boston ... Oliver Ditson & Co. 277 Washington St. ... 1858 ...

Sheet music. Cover-title. Plate number 18917.

9092. Poems ... New and Enlarged Edition.

Boston: Ticknor and Fields. M DCCC LVIII.

9093. The Autocrat of the Breakfast-Table ...

Boston: Phillips, Sampson and Company M DCCC LIX.

Anonymous. Large paper printing. Leaf: 8⁷⁄₁₆″ x 5½″. Illustrated.

Note: According to contemporary evidence (for citation of which see Currier-Tilton) Holmes was displeased with the illustrations and ordered them excised. Since the illustrations are unpaged the excisions do not affect the printed pagination. In this note copies with the illustrations present are designated *State A;* copies lacking the illustrations are designated *State B.*

Three states of the binding have been noted:

Binding A (B?)

Spine stamped in gold: AUTOCRAT / OF THE / BREAKFAST / TABLE / ⟨rule⟩ / HOLMES / BOSTON Edges gilded.

Binding B (A?)

Spine stamped in gold: AUTOCRAT / ⟨decorated rule⟩ / HOLMES / BOSTON Edges gilded.

Binding C

Spine stamped in gold: AUTOCRAT / OF THE / BREAKFAST / TABLE / ⟨rule⟩ / HOLMES / TICKNOR & CO Edges gilded.

LOCATIONS

A Sheets, Binding A (B?)

H: Inscribed by Holmes Christmas, 1858.

H: Inscribed by Holmes Dec. 13, 1859.

H: Inscribed by Holmes without date; two copies thus.

A Sheets, Binding B (A?)

CAW: Inscribed by early owner Jan. 1, 1859.

A Sheets, Binding C

H: Thomas Bailey Aldrich's copy. Inscribed by Aldrich Nov. 1858. The date is highly suspicious. See publication record, entry No. 8781. Aldrich was a collector of first editions and not invariably accurate in his bibliographic annotations.

B Sheets, Binding A (B?)

H: Presented by Holmes to his son; inscription dated Dec. 25, 1858.

H: Presented by Holmes to Emerson; inscription undated.

H: Presented by Holmes to his wife; inscription undated.

H: Presented by Holmes to Charles Eliot Norton; inscription undated.

H: Presented by Holmes to Longfellow; inscription undated.

9093A. Poems ... Seventeenth Edition.

Boston: Ticknor and Fields. M DCCC LIX.

9094. The Professor at the Breakfast-Table; with the Story of Iris ...

London: Sampson Low, Son & Co., 47 Ludgate Hill. 1860.

Advertised as *nearly ready* PC Nov. 1, 1860; as *just ready* Ath Nov. 3, 1860; as *nearly ready* Ath Nov. 10, 1860; *now ready* PC Nov. 15, 1860. Advertised as *new* Ath Nov. 17, 1860. Listed Ath Nov. 17, 1860; LG Nov. 17, 1860; PC Dec. 1, 1860. A new edition was advertised as *ready* PC April 1, 1862.

9095. Flag of the Heroes Union & Liberty ... Music by C. E. Kimball ...

Boston. Published by Oliver Ditson & Co. 277 Washington St. ... 1861 ...

Sheet music. Cover-title. Plate No. 21382. *Reprint?* The poem was first published in *Atlantic Monthly*, Dec. 1861; collected in *Songs in Many Keys*, 1862 (deposited Nov. 21, 1861). No copyright entry for the sheet music found. The Kimball setting listed *Dwight's Journal of Music*, Jan. 4, 1862; a setting by Gustave Blessner noted Jan. 18, 1862.

9096. Poems ... Twentieth Edition.

Boston: Ticknor and Fields. M DCCC LXI.

9097. The Poetical Works ... New Edition.

London: Routledge, Warne, and Routledge, Farringdon Street. 1861.

9098. Union and Liberty A National Song, Words by Oliver Wendell Holmes. Music by Edgar J. Day.

Published for the Benefit of the New-York Ladies Educational Union, (334 Sixth Avenue.) For the Children of Deceased and Disabled Soldiers ... ⟨1862⟩

Sheet music. Cover-title. Deposited June 20, 1862.

9099. ... The Flower of Liberty ... Music by O. B. Brown ...

Boston. Russell & Patee 108 Tremont St. ... 1862 ...

At head of title: 2 National Songs Sheet music.
Cover-title.

9100. The Poems . . .

Boston: Ticknor and Fields. 1863.

Blue and Gold edition. On copyright page:
Fourth Edition.

9101. Union and Liberty . . . Music by Chas. G.
Degenhard.

Toledo . . . Louis Doebele . . . ⟨1863⟩

Sheet music. Cover-title. Plate No. 1473-4. Another and later setting: Composer, F. Boott;
published by Oliver Ditson Co., Boston, 1894.

9102. The Poems . . .

Boston: Ticknor and Fields. 1864.

On copyright page: *Fifth Edition.*

9103. The Poems . . .

Boston: Ticknor and Fields. 1864.

Blue and Gold edition. On copyright page:
Sixth Edition.

9104. The Poems . . .

Boston: Ticknor and Fields. 1864.

Blue and Gold edition. On copyright page:
Seventh Edition.

9105. The Poems . . .

Boston: Ticknor and Fields. 1864.

On copyright page: *Eighth Edition.*

9106. The Autocrat of the Breakfast-Table . . .

Boston: Ticknor and Fields. 1865.

9107. The Poems . . .

Boston: Ticknor and Fields. 1866.

On copyright page: *Tenth Edition.*

9108. The Poems . . .

Boston: Ticknor and Fields. 1866.

Blue and Gold edition. On copyright page:
Eleventh Edition.

9109. The Poems . . .

Boston: Ticknor and Fields. 1866.

On copyright page: *Twelfth Edition.*

9110. There's No Time Like the Old Time . . .
Music by Asa, B, Hutchinson, . . .

Oliver Ditson Company. Boston . . . 1866 . . .

Sheet music. Cover-title. Plate No. 23350. For
an earlier setting of the poem see entry No.
8846.

9111. Wit & Humour Poems by the Autocrat
of the Breakfast-Table

London John Camden Hotten, Piccadilly,
W. 1867 . . .

Advertised (prematurely) Ath May 5, 1866. Advertised as *this day* Bkr Oct. 31, 1866. Listed
Ath Dec. 1, 1866. Advertised PC Dec. 8, 1866.
Listed PC Dec. 15, 1866; Bkr Dec. 31, 1866; ALG
Jan. 1, 1867. Received by BMU Nov. 5, 1867. A
"new edition" listed PC Dec. 31, 1869; presumably in printed paper wrapper. Reissued 1875
by Ward, Lock & Tyler.

9112. . . . There Is No Time Like the Old Time
. . . Music by R. E. Hennings . . .

Cincinnati . . . John Church, Jr . . . ⟨1867⟩

Sheet music. Cover-title. At head of title: To
J. M. Jolley, Esq. Mansfield Ohio. Plate No.
1036-4. For an earlier setting see entry No. 8846.

9113. The Guardian Angel . . .

London: Ward, Lock & Tyler, 1868.

Not seen. Title and imprint postulated. Listed
Ath May 2, 1868; PC May 15, 1868; Bkr June
2, 1868. Printed paper boards. Suppressed. Bkr
Aug. 1868 reported on the lawsuit successfully
brought by Low against Ward, Lock & Tyler to
restrain the latter from publishing *The Guardian Angel.* The report states that the novel com-
menced publication in the *Atlantic Monthly,*
Jan. 1867; that in March, 1867, Holmes jour-
neyed to Montreal to establish "residence" and
thus qualify for British copyright protection;
that on Oct. 25, 1867, by arrangement with
Holmes, Low published the book in London;
that in April, 1868, Ward, Lock & Tyler published a two shilling edition in one volume.

9114. The Guardian Angel . . . New Edition.

London: Sampson Low, Son, & Marston,
Crown Buildings, 188 Fleet Street. 1869 . . .

Printed flexible boards. The "new preface" appears also in the Boston, 1867, edition. Advertised for Dec. 1, 1868, PC Sept. 15, 1868; Ath
Sept. 19, 1868. Listed Ath Dec. 5, 1868; PC Dec.
10, 1868. As a title in Low's *Rose Library* listed
PC May 16, 1876.

9115. The Poems . . .

Boston: Fields, Osgood, & Co., Successors to Ticknor and Fields. 1869.

On copyright page: *Fourteenth Edition.*

9116. The Poems . . .

Boston: Fields, Osgood, & Co., Successors to Ticknor and Fields. 1869.

On copyright page: *Fifteenth Edition.*

9117. The Professor at the Breakfast Table; with the Story of Iris . . .

London: John Camden Hotten, 74 & 75 Piccadilly. ⟨n.d., 1870⟩

Not seen. Presumably issued in cloth; and, printed paper wrapper. Noted as *forthcoming* Ath Nov. 13, 1869. Listed PC May 2, 1870; Ath May 7, 1870. Received by BMU June 20, 1870.

Note: In the copies first printed the list on the title-page reads: *Author of "The Autocrat of the Breakfast-Table,"* . . . In a later printing (with inserted terminal catalog dated 1872) the statement reads *Author of "The Autocrat of the Breakfast Table,"* . . . ; note absence of the hyphen.

9118. Compliments to Homoeopathists . . .

⟨n.p., n.d., *ca.* 1870⟩

Single leaf. Yellow paper. 6⅛″ x 8⁷⁄₁₆″. Printed on recto only. Otherwise "The Stability of Science," *Poems,* 1849. Printed together with "A Return Compliment to Allopathists," by C. D., *i.e.,* Carroll Dunham.

9119. Companion Poets . . .

Boston: James R. Osgood and Company, Late Ticknor & Fields, and Fields, Osgood, & Co. 1871.

9120. The Song of a Clerk . . . Music by A. J. Goodrich . . .

New York. C. H. Ditson & Co. 711 Broadway . . . 1871 . . .

Sheet music. Cover-title. Plate number 26311. Otherwise "Lines by a Clerk," *Poems,* 1836.

9121. The Professor at the Breakfast-Table; with the Story of Iris . . .

London: George Routledge and Sons, The Broadway, Ludgate. ⟨n.d., 1872⟩

According to contemporary notices issued in both cloth; and, printed paper wrapper. Listed

PC June 17, 1872. Received by BMU Sept. 12, 1872.

9122. . . . An Evening Thought . . . Music by Yates van Antwerp.

Philadelphia Lee & Walker . . . W. H. Boner & Co. . . . O. Ditson & Co. Boston . . . 1872 . . .

Sheet music. Cover-title. At head of title: Respectfully Dedicated to Miss Mollie L. Waelder. Plate number 13165.5. Reprinted from *Poems,* 1836.

9123. The Poems . . .

Boston: James R. Osgood and Company, Late Ticknor & Fields, and Fields, Osgood, & Co. 1872.

On copyright page: *Seventeenth Edition.*

9124. . . . Wit and Humour: Poems by Oliver Wendell Holmes . . .

London: Ward, Lock and Tyler, Warwick House, Paternoster Row. ⟨n.d., 1875⟩

Not seen. At head of title: Beeton's Humorous Books. Listed PC Aug. 16, 1875; Bkr Sept. 1875.

9125. Funny Stories and Humorous Poems. By Mark Twain and Oliver Wendell Holmes.

London: Ward, Lock, & Tyler, Warwick House Paternoster Row, E. C. ⟨n.d., 1875⟩

Not seen. Received by BMU Nov. 20, 1875.

9126. The Autocrat of the Breakfast-Table . . . with an Introduction by George Augustus Sala.

London: Chatto and Windus, Piccadilly. 1875.

9127. The Poems . . .

Boston: James R. Osgood and Company, Late Ticknor & Fields, and Fields, Osgood, & Co. 1875.

Blue and Gold edition. On copyright page: *Twentieth Edition.*

9128. The Professor at the Breakfast Table . . .

London: Chatto & Windus, 74 & 75, Piccadilly ⟨n.d., 1875?⟩

9129. Thou Art Near . . . Music by A. Plumpton . . .

. . . John Church & Co. Cincinnati. Root & Sons Music Co. Chicago . . . 1875 . . .

Sheet music. Cover-title. Plate number 1861–3. Otherwise "Hymn of Trust," *Professor at the Breakfast-Table,* 1860.

9130. Silhouettes and Songs Illustrative of the Months. Twelve Designs by Helen Maria Hinds. Edited by Edward E. Hale . . . and Poems by John G. Whittier. Oliver Wendell Holmes . . . ⟨and Others⟩

Boston: Lockwood, Brooks, & Co. 1876.

Cloth; and, leather. Listed PW Nov. 20, 1875. Re-issued as *Childhood's Happy Days with Silhouettes Illustrative of the Months . . . ,* New York: The Arundel Publishing Co. ⟨n.d., *ca.* 1885⟩.

9131. The Poems . . .

Boston: James R. Osgood and Company, Late Ticknor & Fields, and Fields, Osgood, & Co. 1876.

Blue and Gold edition. On copyright page: *Twenty-Second Edition.*

9132. The Story of Iris . . .

Boston: James R. Osgood and Company, Late Ticknor & Fields, and Fields, Osgood, & Co. 1877.

Listed PW Aug. 25, 1877.

9133. Poems of the "Old South" by Henry Wadsworth Longfellow, Oliver Wendell Holmes . . . ⟨and Others⟩

Boston   William F. Gill & Co 1877

Listed PW Dec. 15, 1877.

9134. "While stands the Coliseum, Rome shall stand, / When falls the Coliseum, Rome shall fall; / ⟨rule⟩ / ⟨etc., etc., etc.⟩

Caption-title. The above at head of p. ⟨2⟩. Single leaf folded to four pages. Page: 7⅞″ x 5″. Pp. ⟨1⟩ and ⟨4⟩ blank. Text (facsimile of a fair copy of the poem in Holmes's autograph) on pp. ⟨2-3⟩. Otherwise "The Brave Old South." Reprinted from *The Poetical Works . . . Household Edition,* Boston, 1877 (Sept.). Currier-Tilton, pp. 160-161, reasonably place publication of this leaflet in Dec. 1877.

9135. Favorite Poems . . .

Boston: James R. Osgood and Company, Late Ticknor & Fields, and Fields, Osgood, & Co. 1877.

9136. What Flower Is This? . . . Music by H. P. Keens.

New York. Wm. A. Pond & Co. 547 Broadway. And 39 Union Square . . . 1877 . . .

Sheet music. Cover-title. Plate No. 9257. Otherwise "The Flower of Liberty," *Songs in Many Keys,* 1862.

9137. The One Hoss Shay . . . Illustrated by J. F. Goodridge.

The Heliotype Printing Co. 220 Devonshire St. Boston ⟨1878⟩

Printed paper wrapper. Cover-title.

9138. Poems . . . New Revised Edition. With Numerous Illustrations.

Boston: James R. Osgood and Company, Late Ticknor & Fields, and Fields, Osgood, & Co. 1878.

Title-page in black and red. Pp. 324.

9139. The Poetical Works . . . Household Edition.

Boston: Houghton, Osgood and Company. The Riverside Press, Cambridge. 1878.

9140. Nautilvs.

⟨n.p., n.d., 1879⟩

Cover-title. Two leaves of laid paper (personal stationery) folded to make eight pages. Page: 7¹⁄₁₆″ x 4½″. Watermarked: *Royal Irish Linen Marcus Ward & Co.* Wholly unsewn or otherwise bound. Unpaged. A reprinting of "The Chambered Nautilus," *Autocrat . . . ,* 1858; together with a translation into Latin by E.S.D., *i.e.,* Epes Sargent Dixwell.

9141. THE BRAVE OLD SOUTH. / OLIVER WENDELL HOLMES. / ⟨etc., etc., etc.⟩

⟨n.p., n.d., Boston, 1879⟩

Single leaf. 8⁷⁄₁₆″ x 5⅜″. Printed on recto only. For an earlier separate printing of this poem see entry No. 9134.

9142. . . . The Dear Old Times . . . Music by T. Brigham Bishop . . .

San Francisco: Bancroft, Knight & Co. 733 Market Street . . . 1879 . . .

Sheet music. Cover-title. At head of title: T. Brigham Bishop's Last and Best Song. Plate number 53-3. For an earlier setting see entry No. 8846.

9143. Poems of the "Old South" . . .

Boston Published by the Old South Fair Committee 1879

Note: In addition to the regular trade edition copies were offered with original autographs of the several contributors.

9144. The Poetical Works . . . Household Edition.

Boston: Houghton, Osgood and Company. The Riverside Press, Cambridge. 1879.

9145. The Poems . . .

Boston: Houghton, Osgood, and Company. The Riverside Press, Cambridge. 1880.

On copyright page: *Twenty-Fourth Edition.*

9146. Poems . . . New Revised Edition. With Numerous Illustrations.

Boston: Houghton, Mifflin and Company. The Riverside Press, Cambridge. 1880.

Pp. 324. Red-line edition. Noted only in leather but surely issued in a variety of cloth and leather bindings.

9147. The Poetical Works . . . Household Edition.

Boston: Houghton, Mifflin and Company. The Riverside Press, Cambridge. 1880.

Pp. 324. Noted in the following bindings of undetermined sequence, if any:

A: Front cover stamped in gold and intaglio: HOLMES'S POEMS / COMPLETE

B: Front cover stamped in gold with a bespectacled urn.

9148. . . . L'Inconnue . . .

New York, G. Schirmer, 35, Union Square . . . ⟨n.d., 1880–1892⟩

Sheet music. Cover-title. Plate number 8004. At head of title: To My Master and Friend F. E. Gladstone . . . Music by Charles Hoby.

Note: According to the list on the front cover a complete suite consisted of the following four songs, text by Holmes: "L'Inconnue," "Under the Violets," "Sweet Mary" and "The Parting Word." All four reprinted from earlier books.

9149. . . . Sweet Mary . . .

New York: G. Schirmer, 35, Union Square . . . ⟨n.d., 1880–1892⟩

Sheet music. Cover-title. Plate number 8004. At head of title: To My Master and Friend F. E. Gladstone . . . Music by Charles Hoby.

See note under preceding entry. Otherwise "From a Bachelor's Private Journal," in *The Harbinger*, 1833.

9150. Additional Songs and Poems of the Class of 1829. 1868–1881.

⟨Boston, n.d., 1881⟩

On cover: . . . *Part II* . . .

9151. Mirthful Medley . . . Edited by Henry L. Williams.

London . . . ⟨n.d., 1881⟩

Not seen. Not located. For comment see BAL, Vol. 3, p. 472.

9152. The Poetical Works . . . Household Edition.

Boston: Houghton, Mifflin and Company. The Riverside Press, Cambridge. 1881.

9153. Yankee Ticklers . . .

London: John and Robert Maxwell, Milton House, Shoe Lane, Fleet Street ⟨n.d., 1881⟩

Not seen. Not located. Title and imprint postulated. Presumably a 32-page pamphlet containing material by Holmes and others. Issued as No. 15 of the *Funny Folks Library*. Almost certainly contains no first edition material by Holmes.

9154. . . . The Story of Iris, and Favorite Poems. By Oliver Wendell Holmes. Health . . . by John Brown . . .

Boston: Houghton, Mifflin and Company. New York: 11 East Seventeenth Street. The Riverside Press, Cambridge. 1882.

At head of title: Modern Classics. Advertised for March 11, 1882, in PW March 4, 1882. Listed PW March 25, 1882.

9155. Fun Burst . . .

London: John and Robert Maxwell, Milton House, Shoe Lane, Fleet Street ⟨n.d., 1882⟩

Not seen. Not located. Title and imprint postulated. Presumably a 32-page pamphlet containing material by Holmes. Almost certainly contains no first edition material.

9156. Poems ... New Revised Edition. With Numerous Illustrations.

Boston: Houghton, Mifflin and Company. The Riverside Press, Cambridge. 1882

Pp. 324.

9157. The Poetical Works ...

Boston   Houghton, Mifflin and Company   The Riverside Press, Cambridge   1882

2 Vols.

9158. The Poetical Works ... Household Edition.

Boston: Houghton, Mifflin and Company. The Riverside Press, Cambridge. 1882.

9159. Queer Chaps and Odd Girls ...

London: John and Robert Maxwell, Milton House, Shoe Lane, Fleet Street ⟨n.d., 1882⟩

Not seen. Not located. Title and imprint postulated. Presumably a 32-page pamphlet containing material by Holmes and others. Issued as No. 28 of a series; *Illustrated Merry Folks Library?* Almost surely contains no first edition material.

9160. The Poetical Works ...

London   George Routledge and Sons   Broadway, Ludgate Hill   New York: 9 Lafayette Place   1883

Listed PC Aug. 15, 1882; Bkr Sept. 1882.

9161. ... Grandmother's Story and Other Poems ... with Notes and a Biographical Sketch

Boston   Houghton, Mifflin and Company   New York: 11 East Seventeenth Street   The Riverside Press, Cambridge   1883

At head of title: The Riverside Literature Series   *Not seen.* Entry on the basis of an 1884 reprint. Title and imprint postulated. Issued as No. 6 of the series. Printed paper wrapper. Advertised for June 16, 1883, PW June 9, 1883. Listed PW June 23, 1883.

9162. The Professor at the Breakfast-Table ...

Edinburgh: William Paterson. 1883.

Cloth; and, printed paper wrapper. Listed PC July 16; Bkr Aug. 1883.

9163. Grandmother's Story of Bunker Hill Battle ... Illustrated by H. W. McVickar ...

... New York ... Dodd, Mead & Company ... ⟨1883⟩

Deposited Aug. 31, 1883. Listed PW Oct. 20, 1883.

9164. ... Favorite Poems, and My Hunt after "The Captain." ...

Boston: Houghton, Mifflin and Company. New York: 11 East Seventeenth Street. The Riverside Press, Cambridge. ⟨1883⟩

At head of title: Modern Classics.

9165. Jovial Tars. By Saxe, Holmes, Thackeray, and Others.

London: John and Robert Maxwell, Milton House, Shoe Lane, Fleet Street ⟨n.d., 1883⟩

Not seen. Not located. Title and imprint postulated. Presumably a 32-page pamphlet containing material by Holmes and others. Issued as No. 41 of an unknown series. Almost surely contains no first edition material by Holmes.

9166. The Poetical Works ...

Boston   Houghton, Mifflin and Company   The Riverside Press, Cambridge   1883

2 Vols.

9167. ... Selections from the Breakfast-Table Series, and Pages from an Old Volume of Life ...

Boston: Houghton, Mifflin and Company. New York: 11 East Seventeenth Street. The Riverside Press, Cambridge. ⟨1883⟩

At head of title: Modern Classics   Two bindings noted; the following order is probable:

A: Front stamped: HOLMES ⟨*intaglio on gold*⟩ / ⟨*etc., etc., etc.*⟩

B: Front blindstamped: MODERN CLASSICS / ⟨*etc., etc., etc.*⟩

9168. ⟨*flowers, in color*⟩ / ⟨8 lines of verse beginning: *Some years ago, a dark-eyed girl*⟩ / Oliver Wendell Holmes / Boston Oct. 24th 1883. / From an early Poem / by special request, / O.W.H. / ⟨*flowers, in color, to the left of the text*⟩ / ⟨*a blue line to the right and the bottom of the text*⟩ / ⟨1883?⟩

Facsimile of an original manuscript, printed on recto of a single leaf, 8⅞″ x 7⁹⁄₁₆″. Issued in printed cream paper wrapper. Appears also, printed from the same stones, in *Roses and Forget-Me-Nots   A Valentine ...* , edited by Susie B. Skelding, New York, 1884. The poem is extracted from "Illustration of a Picture. A Spanish Girl in a Reverie," *Poems*, 1836.

9169. ... Thou Art Near (Hymn of Trust.) Sacred Song ... Music by Albert J. Holden ...

New-York. Wm. A. Pond & Co. 25 Union Sq. Chicago. The Chicago Music Co. 152 State St. ... 1883 ...

Sheet music. Cover-title. Plate number 10894. At head of title: To Miss Pauline Lyon ... For an earlier setting see entry No. 9129.

9170. "Dorothy Q. A Family Portrait"

First published in *Atlantic Monthly*, Jan. 1871. Collected in *Songs of Many Seasons*, 1875.

Four separate printings have been seen or reported. The sequence here presented is probable.

A

DOROTHY Q. / A FAMILY PORTRAIT. / ⟨*text, set in two columns, divided by a vertical rule*⟩ / ⟨n.p., n.d., 1884?⟩

Anonymous.

Single cut sheet. Laid paper. 14″ x 11″. Printed on recto only. Comma, not semi-colon, at end of fourth line.

The only copy seen by BAL (in PDH) signed at end by the author: *Oliver Wendell Holmes / May 22d 1884 /*

B

⟨*vignette of Holmes*⟩ / Oliver Wendell Holmes. ⟨*facsimile autograph*⟩ / DOROTHY Q. / A FAMILY PORTRAIT. / ⟨*text, set in two columns, divided by a vertical rule*⟩ / ⟨n.p., n.d., 1884?⟩

Single cut sheet of heavy, cream-colored, wove paper. 13¾″ x 9″. Printed on recto only. Comma, not semi-colon, at end of fourth line.

Possibly a proof printing.

UV

C

⟨*woodcut engraving of Dorothy Q.*⟩ / [From the Original Painting.] / DOROTHY Q. / A FAMILY PORTRAIT. / ⟨*text, set in two columns, divided by a vertical rule*⟩ / Oliver Wendell Holmes. ⟨*facsimile autograph*⟩ / ⟨n.p., n.d., 1884?⟩

Single cut sheet. Wove paper. Printed on recto only. 15½″ x 9⅛″. Semi-colon, not comma, at end of fourth line.

BPL

D

Not seen. Entry from Currier-Tilton. Issued without title. Anonymous. Printed "in great primer type (18 point) for use in public readings. The only copy reported is in the Huntington Library, being the Wakeman copy ... Four leaves, 14⅛ x 11⅛ inches ..." Dated *1887?* by Currier-Tilton.

This printing appears in the Wakeman catalog as entry No. 529 and is assigned the date ⟨1871⟩, apparently on no more substantial evidence than first publication of the poem in that year. The catalog further describes the piece as bearing an 1887 inscription by Holmes.

9171. The Holmes Calendar with Selections for Every Day in the Year ⟨1885⟩

Copyright 1884 by Houghton, Mifflin & Co. Boston.

Pictorial card, printed in colors, to which is mounted a calendar pad for the year 1885, one slip for each day of the year, each with an extract from Holmes. Card: 12⁵⁄₁₆″ x 8⅝″.

9172. The Poet at the Breakfast Table ... Author's Edition ...

Edinburgh   David Douglas, Castle Street 1884

2 Vols.

9173. The Poetical Works ... Fourth Edition.

Boston   Houghton, Mifflin and Company   The Riverside Press, Cambridge   1884

2 Vols.

9174. The Poetical Works ... Household Edition.

Boston: Houghton, Mifflin and Company. The Riverside Press, Cambridge. 1884.

9175. The Poet at the Breakfast-Table ...

William Paterson, 10 Lovell's Court, Paternoster Row, London. ⟨n.d., 1885⟩

Listed PC April 1, 1885, as in both cloth; and, in printed paper wrapper. At foot of spine: *Edinburgh*. Note: Another printing from the same plates was issued not before 1892 by Walter Scott, Ltd., London, n.d.

9176. ... Maidens Who Laughed thro' the Vines ... Music by Sebastian B. Schlesinger

New York, C. H. Ditson & Co. 867 Broadway ... 1885 ...

Sheet music. Cover-title. At head of title: To the Papyrus Club of Boston. Plate number 51289.5. Reprinted from *The Autocrat* ... , 1858, p. 53.

9177. The Poetical Works ... Sixth Edition

Boston   Houghton, Mifflin and Company   New York: 11 East Seventeenth Street. The Riverside Press, Cambridge   1885

2 Vols.

9178. The Professor at the Breakfast-Table . . .

London: Walter Scott, 24 Warwick Lane.
⟨n.d., 1885⟩

9179. Old Lines in New Black and White
Lines from Lowell Holmes Whittier With
Illustrations by F. Hopkinson Smith

Boston & New York Houghton Mifflin and
Co The Riverside Press Cambridge 1886

On front: Printed paper label, sealing-wax seal,
ribbon. Deposited Dec. 9, 1885. Listed PW Dec.
12, 1885. Currier-Tilton, p. 209, report a de
luxe edition on India paper issued in March,
1886; not located by BAL.

9180. Poems . . .

London George Routledge and Sons Broadway, Ludgate Hill New York: 9 Lafayette
Place 1886

Listed PC Jan. 15, 1886. Three formats noted;
sequence, if any, not determined:

A: Mottled paper boards, red V cloth shelfback. Edges trimmed.

B: Mottled paper boards, tan V cloth shelfback. Edges untrimmed.

C: Mottled paper boards, green V shelfback
and corners. Top edges gilded.

9181. Latin Elegiacs for the Jones Medal, 1886.
[The Exercises to be Sent in on Saturday,
June 12th.] From "The Autocrat of the Break-
fast Table." . . . The Two Armies . . .

⟨n.p., Cambridge, 1886⟩

Single leaf. Printed on both sides. 8¹³⁄₁₆″ x 5⅝″.

9182. The Autocrat of the Breakfast-Table . . .
Forty-Fourth Edition with Illustrative Notes

Boston   Houghton, Mifflin and Company
New York: 11 East Seventeenth Street The
Riverside Press, Cambridge 1886

Deposited July 31, 1886.

9183. . . . Holmes Calendar ⟨for 1887⟩

⟨At head of title:⟩ Copyright 1886 by Houghton Mifflin & Company Boston and New York

Pictorial card, printed in colors, calendar pad
mounted to card, each leaf with an extract from
Holmes. Card: 8⅞″ scant x 12⅜″.

9184. The Poetical Works . . . Household Edition . . .

Boston and New York Houghton, Mifflin and
Company The Riverside Press, Cambridge
1886

9185. The Poetical Works . . . Seventh Edition

Boston   Houghton, Mifflin and Company
New York: 11 East Seventeenth Street The
Riverside Press, Cambridge 1886

2 Vols. Cloth; and, flexible leather.

9186. . . . My Hunt after the Captain and Other
Papers . . .

Houghton, Mifflin and Company Boston: 4
Park Street; New York: 11 East Seventeenth
Street   The Riverside Press, Cambridge
⟨1887; i.e., 1888 or later⟩

At head of title: The Riverside Literature Series
Printed paper wrapper. A reprint of the printing dated 1888; see below.

9187. The Complete Poetical Works . . . with
Illustrations

Boston and New York Houghton, Mifflin and
Company The Riverside Press, Cambridge
1887

9188. Poems . . .

London George Routledge and Sons Broadway, Ludgate Hill 1887

Boards, cloth shelfback.

9189. The Poetical Works . . . Household Edition with Illustrations

Boston and New York Houghton, Mifflin
and Company The Riverside Press, Cambridge 1887

9190. The Poetical Works . . . Household Edition with Illustrations

Boston and New York Houghton, Mifflin
and Company The Riverside Press, Cambridge ⟨1887⟩

9191. . . . My Hunt after the Captain and Other
Papers . . .

Houghton, Mifflin and Company Boston:
4 Park Street; New York: 11 East Seventeenth
Street The Riverside Press, Cambridge 1888

At head of title: The Riverside Literature Series Printed paper wrapper. Issued as No. 31 of the series under date of Dec. 7, 1887. Deposited Jan. 19, 1888.

9192. Selections from the Writings of Oliver Wendell Holmes Arranged under the Days of the Year . . .

Boston and New York: Houghton, Mifflin & Co. The Riverside Press, Cambridge 1888

Flexible cloth. Deposited Aug. 2, 1888. Reprinted and reissued under date ⟨1887⟩.

9193. O Love Divine . . . Music by J. P. Vance.

New York. C. H. Ditson & Co. 867 Broadway . . . 1888 . . .

Sheet music. Cover-title. Plate number 52785-3. Otherwise "Hymn of Trust," *Professor at the Breakfast-Table*, 1860. Other and later settings noted:

Music by Geo. B. Nevin; published by the John Church Co., N. Y., 1896. Music by G. W. Marston; published by Arthur P. Schmidt, Boston, 1900. For an earlier setting see entry No. 9129.

9194. The Poetical Works . . . Ninth Edition

Boston   Houghton, Mifflin and Company New York: 11 East Seventeenth Street   The Riverside Press, Cambridge   1888

2 Vols.

9195. Medical Essays 1842–1882 . . .

Boston   Houghton, Mifflin and Company New York: 11 East Seventeenth Street   The Riverside Press, Cambridge   1889

Deposited Jan. 21, 1889.

9196. The Holmes Birthday Book . . .

Boston and New York   Houghton, Mifflin and Company   The Riverside Press, Cambridge ⟨1889⟩

Cloth; and, leather. Deposited March 27, 1889. Listed PW April 13, 1889. CAW copy inscribed by Holmes April 13, 1889.

9197. The Poetical Works . . . Household Edition with Illustrations

Boston and New York   Houghton, Mifflin and Company   The Riverside Press, Cambridge ⟨1889⟩

Deposited Nov. 7, 1889.

9198. The Autocrat of the Breakfast-Table . . .

⟨Boston⟩ Houghton Mifflin and Company MDCCCLXXXX

2 Vols. Cloth, spine stamped in gold; leaf 7″ x 4¹¹⁄₁₆″; top edges gilded; other edges rough-trimmed; copies thus deposited for copyright Oct. 10, 1889, Vol. 1; Nov. 25, 1889, Vol. 2. Also issued in unstamped cloth; printed paper label on spine with the misstatement *First Edition;* top edges unopened, other edges rough-trimmed; leaf: 7³⁄₁₆″ x 4¹¹⁄₁₆″.

9199. Selections from the Writings of Oliver Wendell Holmes . . .

Boston and New York: Houghton, Mifflin & Co. The Riverside Press, Cambridge 1890

Printed paper wrapper. Copyright notice dated 1887.

9200. Medical Essays 1842–1882 . . .

Boston   Houghton, Mifflin and Company New York: 11 East Seventeenth Street   The Riverside Press, Cambridge   1890

Deposited Jan. 9, 1890.

9201. The Poetical Works . . . Household Edition with Illustrations

Boston and New York   Houghton, Mifflin and Company   The Riverside Press, Cambridge ⟨1890⟩

Deposited July 2, 1890.

9202. The Golden Flower   Chrysanthemum Verses by ⟨Various Authors⟩ . . . Collected, Arranged and Embellished with Original Designs by F. Schuyler Mathews . . .

. . . 1890 . . . L. Prang & Co   Boston . . .

Listed PW Nov. 1, 1890.

9203. Over the Teacups . . .

London   Sampson Low, Marston, Searle & Rivington Limited   St. Dunstan's House   Fetter Lane, Fleet Street, E. C. 1890 . . .

Printed in England by William Clowes & Sons, Ltd., from a set of American plates. Advertised for *November* Ath Sept. 27, 1890; Bkr Oct. 1890. Advertised for *next week* Ath Nov. 29, 1890. Advertised as though published PC Dec. 1, 1890; Ath Dec. 6, 1890. Reviewed Bkr Dec. 13, 1890. Described as a *new Xmas book* Bkr Dec. 13, 1890. Listed Ath Dec. 13, 1890; PC Dec. 15, 1890.

9204. The Poetical Works … Eleventh Edition

Boston   Houghton, Mifflin and Company   New York: 11 East Seventeenth Street   The Riverside Press, Cambridge   1890

2 Vols.

9205. The Poetical Works of Oliver Wendell Holmes with Illustrations

Boston and New York   Houghton, Mifflin and Company   The Riverside Press, Cambridge ⟨1890⟩

Printed in two columns.

9206. The Poet at the Breakfast-Table …

⟨Boston⟩ Houghton Mifflin and Company MDCCCXCI

2 Vols. Deposited Oct. 16, 1890.

9207. The Carrier's Dream and the Broomstick Train. The Carrier Boys of the Salem Gazette and Essex County Mercury to Their Patrons.

January 1, 1891. Salem ⟨Mass.⟩: 1891.

Cover-title. Pp. 12. Printed self-wrapper. "The Broomstick Train," pp. ⟨9⟩-12, reprinted from *Over the Teacups*, 1891 (Nov. 1890).

9208. The Latest Poems of the Class of 1829. 1882–1889.

⟨n.p., n.d., 1891⟩

On front cover: … Part III …

9209. The Professor at the Breakfast-Table …

⟨Boston⟩ Houghton Mifflin and Company MDCCCXCI

2 Vols. Deposited Oct. 16, 1890.

9210. Pages from an Old Volume of Life …

Boston   Houghton, Mifflin and Company   New York: 11 East Seventeenth Street   The Riverside Press, Cambridge   1891

Deposited Aug. 15, 1891.

9211. Fifty-Two Further Stories for Boys by George A. Henty … Oliver Wendell Holmes … and Other Writers. Edited by Alfred H. Miles …

London: Hutchinson & Co. 25, Paternoster Square. ⟨1891⟩

Not seen. "Pigwacket Centre School," pp. 139-144; extracted from *Elsie Venner*, 1861. Listed

Ath Nov. 7, 1891; PC Nov. 21, 1891; received by BMU Dec. 3, 1891

9212. … Grandmother's Story and Other Poems …

Boston   Houghton, Mifflin and Company   New York: 11 East Seventeenth Street   The Riverside Press, Cambridge ⟨1891⟩

At head of title: The Riverside Literature Series Issued under date of April 21, 1886 ⟨*sic*⟩. Deposited Dec. 5, 1891.

9213. Standard Library Edition. The Works of Oliver Wendell Holmes.

Boston and New York   Houghton, Mifflin and Company   The Riverside Press, Cambridge ⟨1892⟩

Title from fly-title. Each volume imprinted as above. Deposited, all volumes, Nov. 19, 1892.

1: The Autocrat of the Breakfast-Table
2: The Professor at the Breakfast-Table with the Story of Iris
3: The Poet at the Breakfast-Table
4: Over the Teacups
5. Elsie Venner
6: The Guardian Angel
7: A Mortal Antipathy
8: Pages from an Old Volume of Life
9: Medical Essays
10: Our Hundred Days in Europe
11: Ralph Waldo Emerson   John Lothrop Motley   Two Memoirs
12: The Poetical Works … Volume 1
   Note: In the copies first printed the dates for Benjamin Peirce on p. 375 are erroneously: 1809–1890; a copyright deposit copy thus. In a copy in H the dates are stated correctly: 1809–1880.
13: The Poetical Works … Volume 2.

9214. Artists' Edition. The Works of Oliver Wendell Holmes.

Boston and New York   Houghton, Mifflin and Company   The Riverside Press, Cambridge ⟨1892⟩

Title from general title-page. Each volume imprinted as above. Deposited, all volumes, May 29, 1893. Limited to 750 numbered sets. Probably issued in a variety of custom bindings; a deposit copy is bound in red silk, white vellum shelfback.

1: The Autocrat of the Breakfast-Table
2: The Professor at the Breakfast-Table with the Story of Iris
3: The Poet at the Breakfast-Table
4: Over the Teacups

5: Elsie Venner
6: The Guardian Angel
7: A Mortal Antipathy
8: Pages from an Old Volume of Life
9: Medical Essays
10: Our Hundred Days in Europe
11: Ralph Waldo Emerson   John Lothrop Motley.   Two Memoirs
12: The Poetical Works ... Volume 1
13: The Poetical Works ... Volume 2

9215. The Autocrat of the Breakfast-Table ...

Cambridge   Printed at the Riverside Press
M DCCC XCIV

2 Vols. Vellum. Limited to 250 numbered copies. Deposited Nov. 4, 1893. Also issued in a trade edition imprinted: *Boston and New York Houghton, Mifflin and Company The Riverside Press, Cambridge   M DCCC XCIV* Trade edition deposited Oct. 26, 1893.

9216. The Oliver Wendell Holmes Year Book

Boston and New York   Houghton, Mifflin and Company, The Riverside Press, Cambridge ⟨1894⟩

Deposited Nov. 17, 1894. Advertised as *new* PW Dec. 1, 1894. Listed PW Dec. 8, 1894. The London (Gay & Bird) edition listed Bkr Dec. 7, 1895.

9217. Poems ...

New York: Hurst & Company, Publishers. 134 Grand St. ⟨n.d., 1894⟩

Advertised PW Nov. 17/24, 1894.

9218. ... Union and Liberty   National Anthem ... Music by F. Boott

Oliver Ditson Company. Boston   New York   Phila   London   Chicago, Lyon & Healy ...
MDCCCXCIV

Sheet music. Cover-title. Plate number 91-58096-3. At head of title: No. 8595. Oliver Ditson Company's Secular Selections ...

9219. Poems ...

Philadelphia   Henry Altemus   1895

Deposited July 26, 1895.

9220. *Entry cancelled.*

9221. *Entry cancelled.*

9222. One-Hoss-Shay and Other Poems ...

⟨New York: W. L. Allison Co., Publishers, 105 Chambers St., New York, n.d., 1895–1898⟩

Caption-title. Printed self-wrapper? Cover-title?

9223. ... O Love Divine ... Music by Geo. B. Nevin ...

The John Church Company, Cincinnati ... ⟨1896⟩

Sheet music. Cover-title. At head of title: To Miss Emma C. Wilson   Plate number 12014-5. Otherwise "Hymn of Trust," *Professor at the Breakfast-Table,* 1860. For an earlier setting see entry No. 9129.

9224. ... The Wonderful "One-Hoss-Shay" ... and Other Poems ...

New York   Frederick A. Stokes Company   Publishers ⟨1897⟩

Paper boards; paper boards, cloth shelfback; printed paper wrapper. At head of title: Collection of "Masterpieces" Oliver Wendell Holmes   Deposited Oct. 29, 1897.

9224A. ... American Humorous Poetry ... ⟨by⟩ John Hay ... James Russell Lowell ... Bret Harte ... Oliver Wendell Holmes ...

⟨London⟩ "Review of Reviews" Office. Entered at Stationers' Hall. ⟨n.d., 1897?⟩

For comment see entry No. 7828A.

9225. ... Selected Poems ... with Introduction and Notes by E. H. Turpin

New York   Maynard, Merrill, & Co. New Series, No. 44. March 23, 1898. Published Semi-Weekly ...

Printed paper wrapper. At head of title: Maynard's English Classic Series. No. 205   Deposited March 25, 1898.

9226. The Stereoscope and Stereoscopic Photographs ...

Underwood & Underwood   New York and London   Ottawa, Kans. ⟨sic⟩ Toronto, Can. ⟨1898⟩

Printed paper wrapper. Deposited April 15, 1898.

9227. ... The One-Hoss-Shay and Other Poems ...

W. L. Allison Company   105 Chambers St., New York. Entered at the P. O., New York, as Second-Class Matter.

Printed paper wrapper. Cover-title. At head of title: The Irving Library ... Vol. 5, No. 511, July 1, 1898 ... Deposited Aug. 2, 1898.

9228. ... The Toadstool ... Music by H. Chilver Wilson ...

   ... MDCCCXCVIII ... J. B. Cramer & Co. Ltd. 207 & 209, Regent Street, London, W. New York, Edward Schuberth & Co. ...

Sheet music. Cover-title. At head of title: Dedicated to the Countess of Rosslyn Plate number 11,015. Deposited Aug. 18, 1898.

9229. The Early Poems of Oliver Wendell Holmes with an Introduction by Nathan Haskell Dole

   T. Y. Crowell & Company New York ‹1899›

Printed boards, cloth shelfback. Deposited June 17, 1899.

9230. The Complete Poetical Works ... Cabinet Edition

   Boston and New York Houghton, Mifflin and Company The Riverside Press, Cambridge 1899

Noted in PW Sept. 30, 1899.

9231. Poems ...

   New York: Hurst & Company, Publishers. ‹n.d., ca. 1899›

H copy inscribed by early owner Christmas, 1899.

9232. ... Poems

   Philadelphia Henry Altemus ‹1895; i.e., 1899›

At head of title: Oliver W. Holmes Boards, cloth shelfback. Note: Copyright notice dated 1895; copyright notice on the frontispiece dated 1899.

9233. The One-Hoss Shay   The Chambered Nautilus and Other Poems, Gay and Grave ...

   Boston and New York Houghton, Mifflin and Company The Riverside Press, Cambridge 1900

Deposited May 28, 1900.

9234. The Early Poems of Oliver Wendell Holmes with a Biographical Sketch by Henry Ketcham

   New York A. L. Burt, Publisher ‹1900›

Deposited June 27, 1900.

9235. Ethan Brand by Nathaniel Hawthorne The Chambered Nautilus by Oliver Wendell Holmes

   The Riverside Press Houghton, Mifflin & Co. 4 Park Street, Boston; 11 East 17th Street, New York; 378-388 Wabash Avenue, Chicago ‹1900›

Printed paper wrapper. Cover-title. Deposited June 27, 1900.

9236. The Complete Poetical Works ... Library Edition ...

   Boston and New York Houghton, Mifflin and Company The Riverside Press, Cambridge MDCCCC

Deposited Nov. 9, 1900.

9237. The Deacon's Masterpiece or the Wonderful "One-Hoss Shay." ...

   Compliments of Columbus Buggy Company. Columbus, O. ‹n.d., ca. 1900›

Printed paper wrapper.

9238. Flowers of Friendship ...

   Raphael Tuck & Sons, Ltd. Publishers to Her Majesty the Queen, London, Paris, New York. ‹n.d., ca. 1900›

Pictorial paper wrapper.

9239. Holmes ‹sic› Poems ...

   ... The Henneberry Company Chicago ‹n.d., ca. 1900›

Flowered paper boards, cloth shelfback.

9240. In Friendship's Name. Selections from Oliver Wendell Holmes ...

   Raphael Tuck & Sons, Ltd. Publishers to Her Majesty the Queen, London, Paris, New York. ‹n.d., ca. 1900›

Pictorial paper wrapper.

9241. No Time Like the Old Time ... Music by R. Bruce Wilson ...

   New-York: Harding's Music Office, 229 Bowery ... ‹n.d., ca. 1900›

Sheet music. Cover-title. For earliest located setting see entry No. 8846.

9242. ... O Love Divine ...

   Arthur P. Schmidt. Boston, Leipzig, New York ... ‹1900›

Sheet music. Cover-title. At head of title: Sacred Songs and Duetts by G. W. Marston . . . Plate number 5113-5. Otherwise "Hymn of Trust." For an earlier setting see entry No. 9129.

9243. Opals from Holmes

Boston   De Wolfe, Fiske & Co. ⟨n.d., *ca.* 1900–1905⟩

Padded pictorial boards.

9244. Pearls from Holmes

Buffalo   New York   The Hayes Lithographing Co. ⟨n.d., *ca.* 1900–1905⟩

Pictorial paper boards.

9245. The Early Poems of Oliver Wendell Holmes with an Introduction by Nathan Haskell Dole

T. Y. Crowell & Company   New York ⟨1901⟩

9246. . . . "Freedom, Our Queen" . . . Music . . . by Frederick R. Burton . . .

New York. Luckhardt & Belder ⟨1901⟩

Printed paper wrapper. At head of title: Composed for the Inauguration Concert at Washington, D. C. March 4th 1901. Cover-title.

9247. . . . Hymn of Trust . . . Music by Mrs. H. H. A. Beach . . .

Arthur P. Schmidt, Boston, Leipzig, New York . . . 1901 . . .

Sheet music. Cover-title. At head of title: To H. Plate number 5521-5. For an earlier setting see entry No. 9129.

9248. Beautiful Thoughts from John Greenleaf Whittier and Oliver Wendell Holmes Arranged by F.W.H. ⟨F. W. Hallam⟩

New York   James Pott & Company   MCMII

Listed PW Oct. 2, 1902. Deposited Oct. 20, 1902.

9249. The Poetical Works . . . Household Edition . . .

Boston and New York   Houghton, Mifflin and Company   The Riverside Press, Cambridge ⟨1902⟩

Deposited Nov. 18, 1902.

9250. . . . Grandmother's Story of Bunker Hill Battle and Other Verse and Prose . . .

Boston, New York, and Chicago   Houghton, Mifflin & Company   The Riverside Press, Cambridge ⟨1903⟩

At head of title: The Riverside School Library   Cloth, leather shelfback. Deposited May 29, 1903.

9251. . . . Four Songs with Piano Accompaniment . . . The Last Leaf . . .

New York: G. Schirmer . . . 1903 . . .

Sheet music. Cover-title. At head of title: Sidney Homer   Also noted with the imprint: *G. Schirmer, Inc., New York . . . 1903.*

9252. . . . Hymn of Trust . . . Music by Frances Allitsen . . .

New York: Boosey & Co. . . . MCMIII . . .

Sheet music. Cover-title. Plate number 3035. At head of title: Sung by Madame Albani . . . For an earlier setting see entry No. 9129.

9253. The Anatomist's Hymn. [Extracted from the Eagle, Vol. xxv, No. 134, June 1904.]

⟨n.p., n.d.⟩

Cover-title? Issued in unprinted paper wrapper? Otherwise "The Living Temple," *Autocrat of the Breakfast-Table,* 1858. Contains Holmes's text together with a translation into German by Donald MacAlister.

9254. Gems from Holmes

Boston   De Wolfe, Fiske & Co. ⟨1904⟩

Padded paper boards. Deposited Sept. 15, 1904.

9255. . . . Grandmother's Story of Bunker Hill Battle with . . . Notes by Margaret Hill McCarter . . .

Crane & Company, Publishers   Topeka, Kansas   1904

At head of title: The Crane Classics   Deposited Dec. 7, 1904.

9256. The Silent Watchers. [Extracted from the Eagle, Vol. xxvi, No. 135, December 1904.]

⟨n.p., n.d., 1904⟩

Single cut sheet folded to make four pages. Otherwise "Album Verses," *Autocrat of the Breakfast-Table,* 1858. Contains Holmes's text together with a translation into German by Donald MacAlister. BML copy received Dec. 1904.

9257. The Poetical Works ... Household Edition ...

Boston and New York Houghton, Mifflin and Company The Riverside Press, Cambridge ‹1905›

Deposited Sept. 14, 1905.

9258. The One-Hoss Shay with Its Companion Poems ...

Boston and New York Houghton, Mifflin and Company The Riverside Press, Cambridge MDCCCCV

Deposited Oct. 16, 1905.

9259. The Poetical Works ... Household Edition ...

Boston and New York Houghton, Mifflin and Company The Riverside Press, Cambridge ‹1906›

Deposited Oct. 22, 1906. An edition (this?) listed PW Feb. 16, 1907.

9260. Selections from the Poems of Oliver Wendell Holmes Edited ... by J. H. Castleman ...

New York The Macmillan Company London: Macmillan & Co., Ltd. 1907 ...

Deposited May 29, 1907.

9261. ... The Chambered Nautilus Cantata for Women's Voices ... ‹Music› by Mrs. H.H.A. Beach ...

Arthur P. Schmidt, Boston, Leipzig, New York ... 1907 ...

At head of title: To the Saint Cecilia Club, New York ... Plate number 7699-25.

9262. The Complete Poetical Works ... Cabinet Edition

Boston and New York Houghton Mifflin Company The Riverside Press Cambridge ‹1908›

Deposited Aug. 8, 1908.

9263. Stories of Humor In Two Parts By Oliver Wendell Holmes ... and Others

New York Doubleday, Page & Company Publishers ‹1908›

Deposited Oct. 13, 1908. Apparently printed from the plates of a two-volume work. Pagination: ‹i-xvi›, 1-186, ‹i-ii›, 1-184.

9264. The Complete Poetical Works ... Cambridge Edition ...

Boston and New York Houghton Mifflin Company The Riverside Press, Cambridge ‹1908›

9265. ... The Inevitable Trial ...

‹Boston: The Old South Association, n.d., 1908›

Printed self-wrapper. The above at head of p. ‹1›. At head of title: Old South Leaflets. No. 192. Reprint of a portion of Holmes's oration, July 4, 1863. Reprinted with the imprint of The Directors of the Old South Work.

9266. ... Certain Writings of Oliver Wendell Holmes ...

‹Boston: The Directors of the Old South Work, 1909›

Printed self-wrapper. The above at head of p. ‹1›. At head of title: Old South Leaflets. No. 201. August, 1909. Possibly preceded by a printing with the imprint of The Old South Association.

9267. The Height of the Ridiculous ... Music by Charles Henry Hart ...

The John Church Company Cincinnati New York ... ‹1909›

Sheet music. Cover-title. Plate number 16114-4.

9268. ... The Complete Poetical Works ...

Boston and New York Houghton Mifflin Company The Riverside Press Cambridge 1910

At head of title: Autograph Poets

9269. From Day to Day with Holmes Compiled by Wallace and Frances Rice

New York Barse & Hopkins ... ‹1911›

Deposited July 13, 1911.

9270. Address Delivered at the Dedication of the Hall of the Boston Medical Library Association, on December III, MDCCCLXXVIII ... Reprinted with the Omission of a Few Paragraphs

Minneapolis The H. W. Wilson Company 1911

Printed tan paper wrapper.

9271. Old Ironsides ⟨Music⟩ by B. G. Wilder ...

Boston Oliver Ditson Company New York Chicago ... ⟨1912⟩

Sheet music. Cover-title. Plate number 5-92-69332-4.

9272. Too Young? ⟨by Oliver Wendell Holmes⟩ Too Old? ⟨by Elizabeth Akers Allen⟩

⟨n.p., n.d., Putnam, Conn., 1912?⟩

For comment see entry No. 450.

9273. ... The Chambered Nautilus ... Music by Deems Taylor ...

Boston Oliver Ditson Company New York Chicago ... ⟨1914⟩

Printed paper wrapper. At head of title: Cantata for Mixed Voices ...

9274. Union and Liberty ...

⟨San Francisco: Samuel Levinson, n.d., ca. 1915⟩

Postcard.

9275. ... Too Young for Love ...

Carl Fischer ... New York ... ⟨1917⟩

Sheet music. Cover-title. Music by Enrico Barraja. Plate number 19849-4.

9276. Freedom, Our Queen ... Music by R. L. Herman ...

The Arthur P. Schmidt Co. Boston New York ... 1918 ...

Sheet music. Cover-title. Plate number 11543-6.

9277. ... The Height of the Ridiculous ...

New York G. Schirmer Boston ⟨1920⟩

Sheet music. Cover-title. At head of title: Six Cheerful Songs ... by Sidney Homer ... Plate number 29818, high voice; 29817, low voice.

9278. On Lending a Punch-Bowl ...

New York Privately Printed Christmas 1920

Boards, printed paper label on spine. "... three hundred copies ... printed for Thomas Nast Fairbanks by The Marchbanks Press ..."

9279. Build Thee More Stately Mansions ... Song by Mark Andrews ...

G. Schirmer, Inc. New York ⟨1924⟩

Sheet music. Cover-title. Plate number 31873, low voice; 31872, high voice. Otherwise "The Chambered Nautilus," *Autocrat of the Breakfast-Table,* 1858.

9280. ... Diamond Dew ... ⟨Music by⟩ Daniel Protheroe ...

H. T. Fitzsimmons Music Publisher 509 S. Wabash Ave. Chicago, Ill. ⟨1925⟩

Sheet music. Cover-title. At head of title: Aeolian Series of Choral Music ... Plate number 3006-4. Deposited May 21, 1925. Otherwise "Fantasia," *Poet at the Breakfast-Table,* 1871.

9281. To a Katydid Cantata for Children's Chorus Words by Oliver Wendell Holmes Music by Carl Busch ...

Theodore Presser Co. 1712 Chestnut Street Philadelphia ... 1929 ...

Printed paper wrapper. Deposited March 28, 1929.

9282. ... Ode for Washington's Birthday ... ⟨Music by⟩ L. van Beethoven ...

Boston: Oliver Ditson Company, Inc. ... ⟨1931⟩

Sheet music. Cover-title. Plate number 77130-2. At head of title: Music Relating to George Washington ... Deposited Dec. 2, 1931.

9283. ... God Rest Our Glorious Land ... ⟨Music by Carl⟩ Engel ...

C. C. Birchard & Co. Boston ... ⟨1932⟩

Sheet music. Cover-title. At head of title: Laurel Octavo ... Plate number 1562. Deposited April 15, 1932. Otherwise "International Ode," *Songs in Many Keys,* 1862.

9284. Choral Song for a Reunion ... ⟨Music by⟩ Leslie Heward ...

Copyright, 1932, by Leslie Heward

Sheet music. Caption-title. Deposited Nov. 10, 1932. Otherwise "Hymn for the Class-Meeting, 1869," *Songs of Many Seasons,* 1875.

9285. ... Beauteous Morn ... Music by Edward German ...

London: Novello & Company, Limited; New York: The H. W. Gray Co. ... 1933 ...

Sheet music. Cover-title. For an earlier setting see entry No. 9280. Deposited Jan. 25, 1933. At head of title: No. 285 Novello's Octavo Edition ...

OLIVER WENDELL HOLMES

SECTION III

IN THIS SECTION are listed books by authors other than Holmes which contain material by him reprinted from earlier books. See *Section II* for a list of collections of reprinted material issued under Holmes's name and separate editions.

The American Common-Place Book of Poetry, with Occasional Notes. By George B. Cheever.

Boston . . . 1831.

For comment see entry No. 1330.

The Boston Book . . .

Boston . . . 1836.

For comment see entry No. 6805.

The Book of the Months, a Gift for the Young.

Boston: William Crosby and Company. 1839.

Printed paper boards.

The Poets of America . . . Edited by John Keese.

New York . . . 1840.

For comment see BAL, Vol. 1, pp. 232-233.

Selections from the American Poets. By William Cullen Bryant.

New-York . . . 1840.

For comment see entry No. 1617.

American Melodies . . . Compiled by George P. Morris . . .

New-York . . . 1841.

For comment see entry No. 997.

The Poets of America . . . Edited by John Keese. [Volume Second of the Series.]

New York . . . 1842.

For comment see entry No. 3280.

The Poets and Poetry of America . . . by Rufus W. Griswold . . .

Philadelphia . . . MDCCCXLII.

For comment see entry No. 6644.

Gems from American Poets . . .

New-York . . . ⟨1842⟩

For comment see entry No. 5193.

The Lady's Book of Flowers and Poetry . . . Edited by Lucy Hooper.

New York: J. C. Riker, 15 Ann Street. 1842.

"Lines to a Belle," pp. 23-25; otherwise "A Souvenir," *Poems*, 1836.

Songs, Odes, and Other Poems, on National Subjects; Compiled . . . by Wm. McCarty. Part Second—Naval . . .

Philadelphia: Published by Wm. McCarty . . . 1842.

Readings in American Poetry. By Rufus W. Griswold . . .

New-York . . . 1843.

For comment see entry No. 6647.

The Poetry of Love. Edited by Rufus W. Griswold . . .

Boston . . . 1844.

For comment see entry No. 1017.

The Poetry of Flowers . . . Edited by Rufus W. Griswold.

Philadelphia . . . 1844.

For comment see entry No. 4023.

The Poetry of the Passions. Edited by Rufus W. Griswold . . .

Philadelphia . . . 1845.

For comment see entry No. 1021.

The Poet's Gift . . . Edited by John Keese.

Boston . . . 1845.

For fuller entry see BAL, Vol. 1, p. 206.

The Young American's Magazine of Self-Improvement . . . Edited by George W. Light . . . First Volume.

Boston ... 1847.

"A Hint on Street Manners," p. 121; extracted from *Urania*, 1846. See entry No. 5922.

... The (Old) Farmer's Almanack ... for the Year of Our Lord 1848 ... by Robert B. Thomas ...

Boston: Published and Sold by Jenks, Palmer & Co. ... 1847 ...

Printed paper wrapper. At head of title: Number Fifty-Six.

The Fountain: A Temperance Gift. Edited by J. G. Adams and E. H. Chapin ...

Boston: George W. Briggs, 403 Washington-Street. 1847.

The Rosary of Illustrations of the Bible. Edited by Rev. Edward E. Hale ...

Boston: Phillips, Sampson and Company. 1848.

"A Sabbath in Boston," pp. <263>-269; extracted from *Urania*, 1846. Noted as *just published* LW Sept. 23, 1848. Deposited Sept. 27, 1848. Listed LW Dec. 16, 1848, as in cloth; and, morocco. Reissued, New York, n.d., as *The Scripture Gift Book*, with preface dated 1849.

The Present, or a Gift for the Times. Edited by F. A. Moore ...

Manchester, N. H.   Robert Moore. 1850.

Memory and Hope.

Boston: Ticknor, Reed, and Fields. MDCCCLI.

Cloth; and, leather. Noticed LW Jan. 18, 1851. "Woodlawn Cemetery," pp. 219-221; otherwise *A Poem ... Dedication of the Pittsfield Cemetery, September 9, 1850;* see entry No. 8756.

Love's Whisper. A Token from the Heart.

New York ... 1851.

For comment see note under entry No. 1021.

Garden Walks with the Poets. By Mrs. C. M. Kirkland.

New-York ... 1852.

For comment see entry No. 1379.

The String of Diamonds ... by a Gem Fancier.

Hartford ... 1852.

For fuller entry see No. 1190.

Thalatta: A Book for the Sea-Side ..

Boston ... MDCCCLIII.

For comment see entry No. 1380.

Gift of Love. A Token of Friendship for 1853. Edited by Rufus W. Griswold ...

New-York: Leavitt & Allen, 27 Dey Street. M.DCCC.LIII.

For comment see note under entry No. 1021.

The Humorous Speaker: Being a Choice Collection of Amusing Pieces, Both in Prose and Verse ... Selected ... by Oliver Oldham ...

New York: Newman & Ivison, 178 Fulton Street. Cincinnati: Moore, Anderson & Co. Chicago: S. C. Griggs & Co. Auburn: J. C. Ivison & Co. Detroit: A. M'Farren 1853.

Cloth, leather shelfback.

Gift of Love. A Token of Friendship for 1854. Edited by Rufus W. Griswold ...

New-York: Leavitt & Allen, 27 Dey Street. M.DCCC.LIV.

For comment see note under entry No. 1021.

Household Scenes for the Home Circle: A Gift for a Friend ...

Auburn and Buffalo: Miller, Orton & Mulligan. 1854.

The Young Lady's Cabinet of Gems: A Choice Collection of ... Poetry and Prose. <Edited> by Virginia de Forrest.

Boston: Kelley & Brother. 1854.

The Humorous Poetry of the English Language, from Chaucer to Saxe ... with Notes ... by J. Parton.

New York: Published by Mason Brothers, 108 and 110 Duane Street. 1856.

Advertised as *this day Criterion* (N. Y.), July 12, 1856.

... The (Old) Farmer's Almanack ... for the Year of Our Lord 1857 ... by Robert B. Thomas ...

Boston: Published by Hickling, Swan & Brown ... 1856 ...

Printed paper wrapper. At head of title: Number Sixty-Five.

The Harp and the Cross ... Compiled by Stephen G. Bulfinch ...

Boston ... 1857.

For comment see entry No. 1388.

The Poets of the Nineteenth Century ... Edited by ... Rev. Robert Aris Willmott ...

New York ... 1858.

For comment see entry No. 1663.

... The (Old) Farmer's Almanack ... for the Year of Our Lord 1860 ... by Robert B. Thomas ...

Boston: Published by Hickling, Swan & Brewer ... 1859.

Printed paper wrapper. At head of title: Number Sixty-Eight. Deposited Nov. 21, 1859.

A Budget of Humorous Poetry. Comprising Specimens of the Best and Most Humorous Productions of the Popular American and Foreign Poetical Writers of the Day. By the Author of the "Book of Anecdotes and Budget of Fun."

Philadelphia: G. G. Evans, Publisher, No. 439 Chestnut Street. 1859.

The Poets of the West ...

London ... 1859.

For comment see BAL, Vol. 1, p. 101.

The New England Tour of His Royal Highness the Prince of Wales ...

Boston: Bee Printing Company, 1860.

Printed paper wrapper.

The Centennial Birth-Day of Robert Burns as Celebrated by the ... Burns Club of the City of New York Tuesday, January, 25th 1859. Edited by J. Cunningham.

Published by Lang & Laing ... 117, Fulton Street, N. Y. 1860.

"His Birthday," pp. 124-126, here reprinted. However, this publication contains a letter from Holmes, Nov. 27, 1858, p. 50, which is here in its earliest located book appearance.

College Song Book. A Collection of American College Songs ... Compiled ... by C. Wistar Stevens.

Boston: Published by Russell & Tolman, 291 Washington Street. ⟨1860⟩

Contains three songs by Holmes, each reprinted here. "A Song for the Centennial Celebration of Harvard College, 1836," appears herein under the title "When the Puritans Came Over."

Reprinted and reissued by Henry Tolman & Company, Boston.

History, Theory, and Practice of the Electric Telegraph. By George B. Prescott ...

Boston: Ticknor and Fields. M DCCC LX.

"De Sauty ... ," pp. 353-355; reprinted from The Professor at the Breakfast-Table, 1860.

Lady's Almanac 1861.

Boston: Chase, Nichols, & Hill ... ⟨1854; i.e., 1860⟩

The Poets of the West ...

London ... New York ... 1860.

For fuller entry see BAL, Vol. 1, p. 374.

The Loves and Heroines of the Poets. Edited by Richard Henry Stoddard.

New York ... M D CCC LXI.

For fuller entry see BAL, Vol. 1, p. 72.

Hymns of the Ages. Second Series ...

Boston ... M DCCC LXI.

For comment see entry No. 1397.

Citizens Celebration Newport, R. I., July 4, 1861. Services at the North Baptist Church ...

⟨Newport, R. I.,⟩ F. A. Pratt & Co., Printers. ⟨1861⟩

Single cut sheet. Blue paper.

Army Melodies: A Collection of Hymns and Tunes, Religious and Patriotic, Original and Selected. Adapted to the Army and Navy. By Rev. J. W. Dadmun ... ⟨and⟩ Rev. Arthur B. Fuller ...

Boston: Benj. B. Russell, 515 Washington Street, J. P. Magee, 5 Cornhill New York: E. Goodenough, 122 Nassau Street ... 1861 ...

Printed paper wrapper. Deposited Sept. 18, 1861.

Dedication of the New School House for the Adams School. Dorchester ... Nov. 25th, 1861 ... Order of Exercises ...

⟨n.p., 1861⟩

Single cut sheet folded to four pages.

Favorite Authors. A Companion-Book of Prose and Poetry ...

Boston ... M DCCC LXI.

For comment see entry No. 5943.

Folk Songs Selected and Edited by John Williamson Palmer . . .

New York: Charles Scribner, 124 Grand Street. London: Sampson Low, Son and Company. M DCCC LXI.

Copy in CH inscribed by editor Nov. 1, 1860.

The Mosaic. Edited by J.H.B.

Buffalo: Breed, Butler & Co. 1861.

Extracts from *The Autocrat of the Breakfast-Table*, 1858, pp. 5, 37, 51-52, 77-78, 86-87.

Poems of Old Age . . .

Boston: George Coolidge, 13 Tremont Row. 1861.

Jewels from the Quarry of the Mind . . . Edited by James H. Head . . .

Boston . . . 1862.

For comment see entry No. 1036.

Army and Navy Melodies . . . Selected. By Rev. J. W. Dadmun, and Rev. Arthur B. Fuller . . .

Boston . . . 1862 . . .

For comment see entry No. 5945A.

. . . The (Old) Farmer's Almanack . . . for the Year of Our Lord 1863 . . . by Robert B. Thomas . . .

Boston: Swan, Brewer & Tileston . . . 1862 . . .

Printed paper wrapper. At head of title: Number Seventy-One. Reprinted and reissued with the imprint of Brewer & Tileston.

Songs for War Time. German Airs with English Words . . .

Boston . . . 1863.

For comment see entry No. 1680.

The Patriotic Glee Book . . .

. . . 1863 . . . H. M. Higgins . . . ⟨Chicago⟩

Printed paper boards. Deposited Jan. 11, 1864.

Poetical Pen-Pictures of the War: Selected . . . by J. Henry Hayward . . .

New York . . . 1863.

For comment see entry No. 1037.

Household Friends for Every Season . . .

Boston . . . 1864

For comment see entry No. 3773.

Lyrics of Loyalty . . . Edited by Frank Moore

New York . . . 1864

For comment see entry No. 1203. "An Appeal," pp. 241-242; otherwise "Never or Now."

The School-Girl's Garland . . . by Mrs. C. M. Kirkland. Second Series . . .

New York . . . 1864.

For comment see entry No. 6994.

Autograph Leaves of Our Country's Authors.

Baltimore . . . 1864.

For comment see entry No. 2418.

. . . Soldiers' and Sailors' Patriotic Songs. New York, May, 1864.

New York . . . 1864

For comment see BAL, Vol. 3, p. 156.

Pen-Pictures of the War. Lyrics, Incidents, and Sketches of the Rebellion . . . Compiled Ry ⟨sic⟩ Ledyard Bill.

New York. Sold Only by Subscription. 1864.

Deposited June 20, 1864. Contains reprinted material. Also contains, pp. 89-90, a poem by Julia Ward Howe here miscredited to Holmes.

Songs of the Soldiers . . . Edited by Frank Moore

New York . . . 1864

For comment see entry No. 261.

Personal and Political Ballads . . . Edited by Frank Moore

New York . . . 1864

For comment see entry No. 1208.

History of the Great Western Sanitary Fair.

. . . Cincinnati . . . ⟨1864⟩

For comment see entry No. 414. Reprints "The Promise," pp. 178-179. Contains two letters by Holmes, pp. 179-181, here in their earliest located book appearance.

Patriotism in Poetry and Prose . . . Selected . . . by James E. Murdoch . . .

Philadelphia . . . 1864.

For comment see BAL, Vol. 1, p. 248.

Declamation for the Million . . by R. G. Hibbard . . .

Chicago . . . 1864.

For fuller entry see No. 1041. "The Good Ship Union," pp. 13-15; otherwise "Voyage of the Good Ship Union."

... Lyrics of the War

Philadelphia: Barclay & Co., 602 Arch Street
... 1864 ...

Cover-title. Printed paper wrapper. At head
of title: Second Number ... "Never or Now"
appears herein under the title "The New Call
for Troops."

Looking Toward Sunset ... by L. Maria Child
...

Boston ... 1865.

For comment see entry No. 3198.

Hymns of the Ages. Third Series.

Boston ... 1865.

For comment see entry No. 415.

Lyra Americana ... Selected ... by the Rev.
George T. Rider ...

New York ... 1865.

For comment see entry No. 2827.

Home Ballads by Our Home Poets ...

New York ... 1865.

For comment see BAL, Vol. 1, p. 248.

Harvard College. Commemoration Day, July 21,
1865.

⟨Cambridge, 1865⟩

Single cut sheet folded to four pages.

Poetical Tributes to the Memory of Abraham
Lincoln.

Philadelphia ... 1865.

For comment see entry No. 2828.

Lyra Americana: Hymns of Praise and Faith,
from American Poets.

London: The Religious Tract Society ..
1865.

Listed PC Oct. 2, 1865; Ath Oct. 7, 1865.

The Great Organ in the Boston Music Hall ...

Boston: Ticknor and Fields. 1865.

Printed paper wrapper.

Rebel Brag and British Bluster; a Record of
Unfulfilled Prophecies, Baffled Schemes ... By
Owls-Glass.

New York: The American News Company.
119 & 121 Nassau St. ⟨1865⟩

The extract from Holmes, p. 12, taken from

The Autocrat of the Breakfast-Table, 1858,
p. 74.

The Book of Rubies ...

New York ... 1866.

For comment see entry No. 5522.

The Flower of Liberty. Edited ... by Julia A.
M. Furbish.

Boston ... 1866.

For comment see entry No. 1424.

Poetry Lyrical, Narrative, and Satirical of the
Civil War ... Edited by Richard Grant White

New York ... 1866

For comment see entry No. 4604.

Anecdotes, Poetry and Incidents of the War ...
Arranged by Frank Moore ...

New York ... 1866.

For comment see entry No. 3202.

Yankee Drolleries ...

London: Ward, Lock, and Tyler. 1866.

For comment see entry No. 1542.

A Collection of Songs of the American Press,
and Other Poems Relating to the Art of Printing. Compiled by Charles Munsell.

Albany, N. Y. 1868.

Faith and Freedom in America ... by Rev.
Samuel Osgood ...

New York ... 1868.

For fuller entry see BAL, Vol. 1, p. 376.

Lyra Sacra Americana: Or, Gems from American
Sacred Poetry. Selected ... by Charles Dexter
Cleveland ...

New York: Charles Scribner and Company.
London: Sampson Low, Son, and Marston.
1868.

Reprints "Army Hymn" and "Hymn of
Trust." Also reprints (pp. 131-132) "Parting
Hymn," under the title "Prayer during War";
and (pp. 132-133) "A Sun-Day Hymn," under
the title "The Lord of Life."

Tom Hood's Comic Readings in Prose and
Verse ...

London ... ⟨n.d., 1869⟩

For comment see entry No. 1546.

More Yankee Drolleries ...

London ... ⟨n.d., 1869⟩

For comment see entry No. 1547.

The Great September Gale of 1869, in Providence and Vicinity.

Providence: Tillinghast & Mason, 1869.

Printed paper wrapper.

One Hundred Choice Selections ... No. 2 ... Compiled ... by Phineas Garrett.

... Philadelphia ... 1869.

For comment see entry No. 2910.

Rock of Ages. Original and Selected Poems. ⟨Edited⟩ By Rev. S. F. Smith ...

Boston: D. Lothrop & Co., 38 and 40 Cornhill. Dover, N. H., G. T. Day & Co. ⟨n.d., 1870⟩

Listed ALG Jan. 1, 1870. Reissued ⟨1877⟩.

A 3rd Supply of Yankee Drolleries ...

London ... ⟨n.d., 1870⟩

For comment see BAL, Vol. 2, p. 246.

One Hundred Choice Selections No. 4 ... by Phineas Garrett ...

... Philadelphia ... 1871.

For comment see entry No. 2461.

Good Selections ... by W. M. Jelliffe ...

New York ... 1871.

For comment see entry No. 3330.

Songs of Home Selected from Many Sources ...

New York: Charles Scribner and Company. 1871.

Child Life: A Collection of Poems, Edited by John Greenleaf Whittier ...

Boston ... 1872.

For comment see entry No. 2913.

The World of Wit and Humour. Edited by George Manville Fenn.

... London ... ⟨n.d., 1871–1872⟩

For comment see BAL, Vol. 3, p. 470.

Humorous Poems ... Edited by William Michael Rossetti ...

London ... ⟨n.d., 1872⟩

For comment see BAL, Vol. 1, p. 207.

Hymns for Mothers and Children. Second Series. Compiled by the Editor of "Hymns of the Ages." ⟨i.e., Caroline Snowden Whitmarsh and Anne E. Guild⟩

Boston: Nichols and Hall. 1872.

The Elocutionist's Annual ... by J. W. Shoemaker ...

... Philadelphia. 1873.

For comment see entry No. 7268.

Illustrated Library of Favorite Song ... Edited by J. G. Holland ...

New York ... ⟨1873⟩

For comment see entry No. 2853.

The Poets and Poetry of America. By Rufus Wilmot Griswold ...

New York ... 1873.

For comment see in list of John Hay reprints.

Public and Parlor Readings: Prose and Poetry for the Use of Reading Clubs and for Public and Social Entertainment. Miscellaneous. Edited by Lewis B. Monroe.

Boston: Lee and Shepard, Publishers. New York: Lee, Shepard, and Dillingham. 1873.

"Hats," pp. 224-225; extracted from Autocrat of the Breakfast-Table, 1858.

Sea and Shore ...

Boston ... 1874.

For comment see entry No. 4043.

New-York Tribune. Extra No. 18. Sumner Eulogies ...

New-York, May, 1874 ...

4 pp.

The Muses of Mayfair ... by H. Cholmondeley-Pennell ...

London ... 1874

For comment see entry No. 279.

One Hundred Choice Selections No. 9 ... Compiled ... by Phineas Garrett ...

... Philadelphia ... 1874.

For comment see BAL, Vol. 2, p. 168.

Half Hours with the Poets ...

New York ... 1874.

For comment see entry No. 5529.

Vers de Société Selected . . . by Charles H. Jones . . .

New York . . . 1875

For comment see BAL, Vol. 1, p. 73.

. . . Little Classics. Edited by Rossiter Johnson. Laughter . . .

Boston: James R. Osgood and Company, Late Ticknor & Fields, and Fields, Osgood, & Co. 1875.

At head of title: Fifth Volume.

BA copy received Jan. 13, 1875. Advertised as *ready* and listed PW Jan. 16, 1875.

. . . Little Classics. Edited by Rossiter Johnson. Romance . . .

Boston: James R. Osgood and Company, Late Ticknor & Fields, and Fields, Osgood, & Co. 1875.

At head of title: Seventh Volume.

Listed PW March 13, 1875.

The New York Herald. Whole No. 14,119. New York, Monday, April 19, 1875 . . . Revolutionary Extra Edition . . .

8 pp. "The Battle of Lexington," p. ‹1›; otherwise, "Lexington."

One Hundred Choice Selections No. 10 . . . Compiled . . . by Phineas Garrett . . .

. . . Philadelphia . . . 1875.

For comment see BAL, Vol. 1, p. 248.

. . . Little Classics. Edited by Rossiter Johnson. Minor Poems . . .

Boston: James R. Osgood and Company, Late Ticknor & Fields, and Fields, Osgood, & Co. 1875.

At head of title: Fifteenth Volume.

More Yankee Drolleries: A Second Series of Celebrated Works by the Best American Humourists . . . with an Introduction by George Augustus Sala.

London: Chatto and Windus, Piccadilly. 1875.

. . . Proceedings of the Massachusetts Historical Society. From April to June, 1875 . . .

‹Boston, 1875›

Printed paper wrapper. Cover-title. At head of title: I.

Memorial of Jesse Lee and the Old Elm. Eighty-Fifth Anniversary of Jesse Lee's Sermon under the Old Elm, Boston Common, Held Sunday Evening, July 11, 1875 . . .

Boston: James P. Magee, 38 Bromfield Street. (New England Depository.) 1875.

Printed imitation leather wrapper. The paragraph on New England elms, p. ‹46›, reprinted from *Elsie Venner*, 1861, Vol. 1, pp. 77-78.

The Comic Poets of the Nineteenth Century . . . by W. Davenport Adams . . .

London . . . ‹n.d., 1875›

For comment see BAL, Vol. 3, p. 471.

Ballads of the War

‹n.p., Boston› Heliotype ‹n.d., *ca.* 1875›

Cover-title. 15 leaves, the final leaf being blank. Tied with ribbon. The whole production done in facsimile of the original *mss* of the several contributing authors. Unpaged.

Date on the basis of the Holmes contribution which is dated at end June 28, 1875.

The Heliotype process mentioned in the advertisements of James R. Osgood & Co., Boston, during the period 1873–1880. The Heliotype Printing Company, Boston, James R. Osgood, treasurer, was established in 1877.

Songs of Three Centuries. Edited by John Greenleaf Whittier.

Boston . . . 1876.

For comment see entry No. 2857.

Golden Treasures of Poetry, Romance, and Art . . .

Boston . . . 1876

For comment see entry No. 1749.

Theatrum Majorum. The Cambridge of 1776 . . . Edited . . . by A. G. . . .

Cambridge . . . M D CCC LXX VI.

For comment see entry No. 9570. "Old Cambridge," p. ‹110›, extracted from *Autocrat of the Breakfast-Table*, 1858.

Yankee Drolleries Second Series . . .

London . . . ‹n.d., 1876›

For comment see entry No. 1553.

Roadside Poems for Summer Travellers. Edited by Lucy Larcom.

Boston . . . 1876.

For comment see BAL, Vol. 1, p. 73.

Poems of Places Edited by Henry W. Longfellow ... England. Vol. I

> Boston ... 1876.

> For comment see BAL, Vol. I, p. 101.

The Mountains ...

> Boston ... 1876.

> For comment see entry No. 1239.

Poetic Localities of Cambridge. Edited by W. J. Stillman ...

> Boston: James R. Osgood and Company, Late Ticknor & Fields, and Fields, Osgood, & Co. 1876.

Proceedings of the Massachusetts Historical Society. 1875–1876 ...

> Boston: Published by the Society. M.DCCC.-LXXVI.

The Reading Club and Handy Speaker ... Edited by George M. Baker. No. 3.

> Boston: Lee and Shepard ... 1876.

> Cloth; and, probably printed paper wrapper.

Footsteps of the Master ... by Harriet Beecher Stowe

> New York   J. B. Ford & Company 1877

> Listed PW Dec. 2, 1876. The London (Low) edition listed Ath Dec. 30, 1876. The Toronto (Belford) edition listed *Canadian Monthly,* Jan. 1877.

> "The Love of Christ," p. 132; otherwise, "Hymn of Trust," *Professor at the Breakfast-Table,* 1860, p. 360.

Poems of Places Edited by Henry W. Longfellow ... France and Savoy. Vol. II.

> Boston: James R. Osgood and Company ... 1877.

> Listed PW Jan. 27, 1877.

First Annual Masquerade Party of the Light Fantastics, Monday Evening, Feb. 5th. 1877.

> ⟨n.p., probably Providence, R. I., 1877⟩

> Title as above on p. ⟨1⟩. Single cut sheet folded to make four pages. Issued as a dance program.

Poems of Places Edited by Henry W. Longfellow ... Italy. Vol. I.

> Boston: James R. Osgood and Company ... 1877.

Listed PW April 28, 1877. *Two binding issues noted:* 1: With spine imprint of James R. Osgood & Co.; 2: with spine imprint of Houghton, Osgood.

Poems of Places Edited by Henry W. Longfellow ... Italy. Vol. II.

> Boston ... 1877.

> For comment see entry No. 4049.

Hillside and Seaside in Poetry ... Edited by Lucy Larcom

> Boston ... 1877

> For comment see entry No. 1466.

Poems of Places Edited by Henry W. Longfellow ... Spain, Portugal, Belgium, Holland. Vol. II.

> Boston: James R. Osgood and Company, Late Ticknor & Fields, and Fields, Osgood, & Co. 1877.

> The Holmes material, pp. 107-109, extracted from "Agnes," *Songs in Many Keys,* 1862. Also reprints "Robinson of Leyden." Listed PW June 30, 1877.

The Life of Edgar Allan Poe by William F. Gill ...

> ... New York ... 1877

> For comment see BAL, Vol. I, p. 73.

One Hundred Choice Selections No. 14 ...

> ... Philadelphia ... 1877.

> For comment see BAL, Vol. 2, p. 104.

Companion Autographs.

> ⟨Boston⟩ Copyright, Perry Mason & Co. 1877.

A Memorial of Fitz-Greene Halleck ...

> ... New York. 1877.

> Reprint save for a three-line note, May 5, ⟨1877⟩, p. 40. For fuller entry see No. 2244.

Our National Centennial Jubilee. Orations, Addresses and Poems Delivered on the Fourth of July, 1876. In the Several States of the Union. Edited by Frederick Saunders ...

> New York: E. B. Treat, 805 Broadway ... Chicago ... Cincinnati ... San Francisco. 1877.

Star Selections, 1876 ... ⟨Edited⟩ by Professor J. E. Goodrich.

> New York ... 1877.

> For comment see BAL, Vol. 3, p. 471.

Poems of Places Edited by Henry W. Longfellow ... Russia.

Boston: Houghton, Osgood and Company ...
1878.

Listed PW April 27, 1878.

Song and Sense from "Uncle Sam." Collected
by Thomas Nicholson. First Series.

London: Charing Cross Publishing Company,
Limited, 5, Friar Street, Broadway, E. C. 1878.

Not seen. Noticed by Ath April 20, 1878. Reviewed Bkr April, 1878.

West Point Tic Tacs ...

... New York. 1878.

For comment see entry No. 7299.

Poems of Places Edited by Henry W. Longfellow ... Asia. Persia ...

Boston: Houghton, Osgood and Company ...
1878.

Listed PW Aug. 10, 1878.

Dick's Recitations and Readings No. 8 ...

New York ... ⟨1878⟩

For comment see entry No. 8626.

Garnered Treasures from the Poets ...

Philadelphia ... 1878.

For comment see entry No. 4772.

Golden Thoughts ... Introduction by Rev.
Theo. L. Cuyler ...

New-York ... ⟨1878⟩

For comment see BAL, Vol. 2, p. 104.

A Memorial Volume Containing the Exercises
at the Dedication of the Statue of John A. Andrew, at Hingham, October 8, 1875 ...

Boston: Published by the Association. MD-
CCCLXXVIII.

Printed paper wrapper.

Our Children's Songs. With Illustrations.

New York: Harper & Brothers, Publishers,
Franklin Square. 1878.

Pictorial paper boards, cloth shelfback.

Poetry of America Selections from One Hundred American Poets from 1776 to 1876 ... by
W. J. Linton.

London: George Bell & Sons, York Street,
Covent Garden. 1878.

Tunes with Hymns for Use in King's Chapel.

⟨Boston, 1878⟩

Printed paper wrapper.

Poems of Places Edited by Henry W. Longfellow ... New England. Vol. I.

Boston ... 1879.

For comment see BAL, Vol. 1, p. 86.

Contains several poems by Holmes here reprinted under their original titles. Also contains two selections under revised titles as
follows: "Church Bells," pp. 104-106, extracted from *Urania*, 1846; "The Frankland
Mansion," pp. 248-251, extracted from "Ag-
nes," *Songs in Many Keys*, 1862.

Poems of Places Edited by Henry W. Longfellow ... Middle States.

Boston ... 1879.

For comment see BAL, Vol. 1, p. 74.

Poems of Places Edited by Henry W. Longfellow ... Western States.

Boston ... 1879.

For comment see BAL, Vol. 1, p. 296.

Essays from the North American Review. Edited
by Allen Thorndike Rice.

New York ... 1879.

For comment see entry No. 679.

One Hundred Choice Selections No. 17 ...

... Philadelphia ... 1879.

For comment see BAL, Vol. 2, pp. 248-249.

Home Life in Song with the Poets of To-Day
...

New York ... ⟨1879⟩

For comment see entry No. 432.

Rhymes of Science: Wise and Otherwise ...

New York: Industrial Publication Company.
1879. Copyright Secured.

Cloth?

Birthplace Commemorative Services of the 100th
Anniversary of the Birth of William Ellery
Channing, Newport, R. I., April 7th, 1880.

⟨Newport: News Press, 1880⟩

Four-page program.

One Hundred Choice Selections No. 18 ...

... Philadelphia ... 1880.

For comment see entry No. 2478.

... The Reading Club and Handy Speaker ... Edited by George M. Baker. No. 8.

Boston ... 1880.

For comment see entry No. 7316.

One Hundred Choice Selections No. 19 ...

... Philadelphia ... 1881.

For comment see entry No. 3392.

In Memoriam. Gems of Poetry and Song on James A. Garfield ...

Columbus ... 1881.

For comment see entry No. 122.

In Memoriam. James A. Garfield ... Compiled by Henry J. Cookinham ...

Utica, N. Y. Curtiss & Childs, Publishers, 167 Genesee Street. MDCCCLXXXI.

Deposited Nov. 19, 1881.

One Hundred Choice Selections No. 20 ...

... Philadelphia ... 1881.

For comment see entry No. 5120.

Dedication of the New Building and Hall of the Boston Medical Library Association, 19 Boylston Place, December 3, 1878 ...

Cambridge: Printed at the Riverside Press. 1881.

Printed paper wrapper.

Franklin Square Song Collection ... by J. P. McCaskey ...

New York ... 1881

For comment see BAL, Vol. 1, p. 86.

"The Visions of Morning," p. 110; otherwise, "Questions and Answers," *Poems*, 1849.

The Poets' Tributes to Garfield ... ⟨Second Edition⟩

Cambridge ... 1882

For comment see entry No. 1248.

The Poet and the Children ... Edited by Matthew Henry Lothrop ...

Boston ... ⟨1882⟩

For comment see entry No. 3788.

Ralph Waldo Emerson ... by Alexander Ireland Second Edition ...

London ... 1882 ...

For comment see BAL, Vol. 3, p. 68.

The Cambridge Book of Poetry and Song ... by Charlotte Fiske Bates ...

New York ... ⟨1882⟩

For comment see entry No. 7887.

... Selections for School Exhibitions and Private Reading ... Nos. 1, 2, 3 ...

Boston ... 1882.

For comment see BAL, Vol. 2, p. 472.

Wayside Gleanings ...

⟨Cambridge⟩ 1882.

For comment see BAL, Vol. 1, p. 297.

Flowers from Hill and Dale Poems Arranged and Illustrated by Susie Barstow Skelding ...

New York White, Stokes, and Allen 1883

Listed PW Oct. 13, 1883.

Surf and Wave: The Sea As Sung by the Poets. Edited by Anna L. Ward ...

New York: Thomas Y. Crowell & Co. 13 Astor Place. ⟨1883⟩

Flowers from Glade and Garden Poems Arranged ... by Susie Barstow Skelding ...

New York ... 1884

For comment see BAL, Vol. 2, p. 39.

Graduating Exercises of the Class of '84, Amesbury High School Friday, June 27.

⟨Amesbury, 1884⟩

Four-page program. The "Class Song," p. 3, reprinted from *Songs in Many Keys*, 1862.

Excelsior Recitations and Readings No. 1 ... Edited by T. J. Carey.

New York: Excelsior Publishing House, 29 and 31 Beekman Street. ⟨1884⟩

Printed paper wrapper. Deposited Aug. 30, 1884.

Fifty Years among Authors, Books and Publishers. ⟨By⟩ J. C. Derby ...

New York ... MDCCCLXXXIV.

For comment see entry No. 4349. Issued Dec. 1884.

The poem on *Uncle Tom's Cabin*, p. 456, had prior publication in *The Atlantic Monthly Supplement* ‹1882›; *Life of Oliver Wendell Holmes,* by E. E. Brown ‹1884› (April).

Medical Rhymes ... Selected ... from a Variety of Sources, by Hugo Erichsen ...

J. H. Chambers & Co., St. Louis, Mo., Chicago, Ill. Atlanta, Ga. 1884.

Roses and Forget-Me-Nots A Valentine ... Arranged and Illustrated by Susie B. Skelding

New York White, Stokes, & Allen 1884

Pictorial paper wrapper.

... The Reading Club and Handy Speaker ... Edited by George M. Baker. No. 16.

Boston ... ‹1885›

For comment see BAL, Vol. 2, p. 95.

Childhood's Happy Days with Silhouettes Illustrative of the Months. Designs by Helen Maria Hinds. Poems by Eminent Authors. Edited by Edward Everett Hale.

New York: The Arundel Publishing Co. ‹n.d., ca. 1885›

Pictorial paper boards, cloth shelfback. Reprint, with revised title, of *Silhouettes and Songs ...* , 1876.

April Edited by Oscar Fay Adams ...

Boston ... ‹1886›

For comment see entry No. 61.

Bugle-Echoes ... Edited by Francis F. Browne

New York ... MDCCCLXXXVI

For comment see BAL, Vol. 1, p. 75.

Representative Poems of Living Poets ...

... New York 1886

For comment see entry No. 436.

July Edited by Oscar Fay Adams ...

Boston ... ‹1886›

For comment see entry No. 65.

The Elocutionist's Annual Number 14 ... Compiled by Mrs. J. W. Shoemaker.

... Philadelphia: 1886.

For comment see BAL, Vol. 1, p. 380.

November Edited by Oscar Fay Adams ...

Boston ... ‹1886›

For comment see entry No. 69.

Belford's Annual 1886–7. Edited by Thomas W. Handford ...

Chicago and New York: Belford Clarke & Co. ‹1886›

Boards, printed in imitation of tree calf.

"Spring," p. 97, is an extract from "At the Close of a Course of Lectures," *Songs in Many Keys,* 1862. "When to Strike," p. 110, extracted from *Urania,* 1846.

Report of the Class of '68. Phillips Exeter Academy. March 1, 1886. For Circulation among the Members of the Class.

Beacon Press: Thomas Todd Printer, 1 Somerset Street, Boston. ‹1886›

Printed paper wrapper.

Opening Addresses Edited by Laurence Hutton ...

New-York ... 1887

For comment see entry No. 1045.

... New Verses from the Harvard Advocate, 1876–1886, Reprinted for the Use of Later Undergraduates ...

‹New York: Privately Printed by Kilbourne Tompkins, 1887›

Cloth, printed paper label on spine. At head of title: "Dulce est Periculum."

H copy received May 23, 1887.

Franklin Square Song Collection ... No. 4. Selected by J. P. McCaskey ...

New York. Harper & Brothers ... ‹1887›

Printed boards, cloth shelfback; printed paper wrapper; cloth.

Mark Twain's Library of Humor ...

New York ... 1888

For comment see entry No. 9636.

Franklin Square Song Collection ... No. 5. Selected by J. P. McCaskey ...

New York. Harper & Brothers ... ‹1888›

Printed boards, cloth shelfback; printed paper wrapper; cloth.

Deposited Sept. 15, 1888.

The Elocutionist's Annual Number 16 ... Compiled by Mrs. J. W. Shoemaker

... Philadelphia 1888

For comment see in list of Hayne reprints.

Recreations of the Rabelais Club. 1885–1888 ...

Printed for the Members ... ⟨London, 1888?⟩

100 numbered copies only. On p. ⟨39⟩ appears an untitled 10-line extract from "The Old Player," *Songs in Many Keys*, 1862.

History of the Celebration of the One Hundredth Anniversary of the Promulgation of the Constitution of the United States. Edited by Hampton L. Carson ... in Two Volumes ...

Published under the Direction and by the Authority of the Commission, by J. B. Lippincott Company, Philadelphia. 1889.

American Sonnets. Selected ... by William Sharp.

London ... ⟨n.d., 1889⟩

For comment see BAL, Vol. 3, p. 101.

The Elocutionist's Annual Number 17 ... Compiled by Mrs. J. W. Shoemaker

Philadelphia ... 1889

For comment see entry No. 1270.

Beiträge von Literaten und Künstlern zum Deutschen Hospital Bazaar ...

⟨New York, 1889⟩

For comment see entry No. 4369. Unpaged. Untitled sonnet herein; otherwise "Rhymes of a Life-Time," *Poetical Works*, 1881.

Half-Hours with the Best Humorous Authors. Selected ... by Charles Morris ... American.

Philadelphia ... 1889.

For comment see entry No. 3813.

... Harper's Fifth Reader   American Authors

New York ... 1889

For comment see entry No. 7917.

The Life-Work of the Author of Uncle Tom's Cabin. By Florine Thayer McCray ...

Funk & Wagnalls   New York: London: 1889 ...

The material at p. 432 extracted from "The World's Homage," *Before the Curfew*, 1888. Listed PW Nov. 9, 1889.

Ballads of the Brave   Poems of Chivalry ... Selected ... by Frederick Langbridge ...

London   Methuen and Co., 18 Bury Street, W. C. 1890

Not seen. Reviewed PC Oct. 15, 1889. Advertised as *just ready* Bkr Nov. 1889. Listed Bkr Nov. 1889.

No. 27. Standard Recitations by Best Authors ... March, 1890 ...

... N. Y. ... ⟨1890⟩

For comment see entry No. 4161.

The Poets' Year ... Edited by Oscar Fay Adams ...

Boston ... ⟨1890⟩

For comment see entry No. 80.

American Sonnets Selected ... by T. W. Higginson and E. H. Bigelow

Boston ... 1890

For comment see entry No. 8373.

Representative Sonnets by American Poets ... by Charles H. Crandall

Boston ... 1890

For comment see BAL, Vol. 2, p. 275.

Local and National Poets of America ... Edited ... ⟨by⟩ Thos. W. Herringshaw ...

Chicago ... 1890.

For comment see BAL, Vol. 2, p. 391.

Occasional Addresses Edited by Laurence Hutton and William Carey

New-York ... 1890

For comment see entry No. 5655.

The Speakers' Library   The Latest and Most Popular Literary Gems for Public and Parlor Entertainment ... Edited by Daphne Dale.

1890. Elliott & Beezley, Chicago   Philadelphia.

The Star Safety Razor ...

⟨n.p., New York, after April 1, 1890⟩

Single cut sheet folded to make four pages. The above at head of p. ⟨1⟩. Issued as an advertisement by the Star Safety Razor.

"Glorious Tribute from the Pen of Dr. Oliver Wendell Holmes ... ," p. ⟨4⟩; reprinted from *Our Hundred Days in Europe*, 1887.

Out of the Heart   Poems ... Selected by John White Chadwick ... and Annie Hathaway Chadwick ...

Troy, N. Y. ... 1891

For comment see BAL, Vol. 2, p. 452.

Harvard College during the War. By Capt. Nathan Appleton. Harvard Memorial Poems ...

Reproduced from the New England Magazine. ⟨Boston, 1891?⟩

Printed paper wrapper. Cover-title.

Tributes to Shakespeare Collected . . . by Mary R. Silsby

New York . . . MDCCCXCII

For comment see entry No. 707A.

Fair Topics . . . Organ of the Actors' Fund Fair . . .

New York . . . 1892 . . .

"Life and the Stage," No. 6, p. 4; extracted from "The Old Player," *Songs in Many Keys,* 1862. For comment see entry No. 359.

The Lover's Year-Book of Poetry A Collection of Love Poems for Every Day in the Year ⟨Compiled⟩ by Horace Parker Chandler Vol. II. July to December

Boston   Roberts Brothers   1892

Vol. 1, *January to June,* issued under date 1891.

Book-Song An Anthology . . . Edited by Gleeson White . . .

London . . . 1893

For comment see entry No. 717.

"In a Copy of *Over the Teacups,*" p. 61, is an extract from "To My Readers," *Poems,* 1862.

Children's Souvenir Song Book Arranged by William L. Tomlins . . .

London and New York   Novello, Ewer & Company ⟨1893⟩

Printed paper wrapper.

Random Rhymes. ⟨Edited by Roland R. Conklin⟩

⟨n.p., Kansas City, Mo., 1893⟩

Scrap Book Recitations No. 10. By H. M. Soper . . .

Chicago . . . ⟨1894⟩

For comment see BAL, Vol. 2, p. 40.

Notable Single Poems American Authors Edited by Ina Russelle Warren

Buffalo . . . ⟨n.d., 1895⟩

For comment see entry No. 5672.

The World of Wit and Humour . . . ⟨New and Enlarged Edition⟩

. . . London . . . 1895 ⟨–1896⟩ . . .

For comment see BAL, Vol. 3, p. 400.

No. 43. Standard Recitations by Best Authors . . . March 1894 ⟨sic⟩ . . .

. . . N. Y. . . . 1896 . . .

For comment see entry No. 2520.

Through Love to Light A Selection . . . by John White Chadwick and Annie Hathaway Chadwick

Boston . . . 1896

For comment see entry No. 2633.

The Cambridge of Eighteen Hundred and Ninety-Six . . . Edited by Arthur Gilman . . .

Cambridge . . . 1896

For comment see entry No. 8411. "The Gambrel-Roofed House," pp. ⟨43⟩-46, extracted from *The Poet at the Breakfast-Table,* 1872.

Poems of the Farm Selected . . . by Alfred C. Eastman

Boston . . . 1896

For comment see entry No. 6343.

Werner's Readings and Recitations Number Sixteen Compiled . . . by Fowler Merritt . . .

New York   Edgar S. Werner Publishing & Supply Co. . . . 1896 . . .

Cloth; and, printed paper wrapper.

Voices of Doubt and Trust Selected by Volney Streamer

New York   Brentano's   1897

Deposited Sept. 2, 1897. "The Ancient Faith," p. 195, extracted from *Urania,* 1846.

The Doctor's Window . . . Edited by Ina Russelle Warren . . .

Buffalo . . . Eighteen-Hundred-Ninety-Eight

For comment see BAL, Vol. 2, p. 275.

Poems of American Patriotism 1776–1898 Selected by R. L. Paget

Boston . . . MDCCCXCVIII

For comment see BAL, Vol. 1, p. 249.

Spanish-American War Songs . . . Compiled . . . by Sidney A. Witherbee.

. . . Detroit . . . 1898.

For comment see entry No. 738.

Book Lovers' Verse ... Compiled ... by Howard S. Ruddy ...

Indianapolis ... ⟨1899⟩

For comment see entry No. 745.

The Lawyer's Alcove ... Edited by Ina Russelle Warren ...

New York ... 1900

For comment see entry No. 4933.

Modern Eloquence ... ⟨Edited by⟩ Thomas B. Reed ...

... Philadelphia ⟨1900; i.e., 1901⟩

For comment see entry No. 3467.

Songs of Nature Edited by John Burroughs

New York ... MCMI ...

For comment see entry No. 2169.

The New England Society Orations ... 1820–1885 ... Edited by Cephas Brainerd and Eveline Warner Brainerd ...

New York ... MCMI

For comment see entry No. 5308.

Love-Story Masterpieces ... Chosen by Ralph A. Lyon

William S. Lord   Evanston   1902

Deposited June 3, 1902. Cloth?

... Masterpieces of Wit and Humor ... Introduction by Robert J. Burdette ...

Copyright, 1902 ...

For comment see entry No. 2013.

... Gems of Modern Wit and Humor with ... Introduction by Robert J. Burdette ...

⟨n.p., n.d., 1903⟩

Reprint of the preceding under a revised title.

A Book of American Humorous Verse ...

Chicago ... 1904

For comment see BAL, Vol. 1, p. 411.

Consecration Service Preceding the Opening of the International Peace Congress   Symphony Hall, Boston   Sunday Evening, October 2, 1904

⟨Boston, 1904⟩

Cover-title. Printed self-wrapper.

Mark Twain's Library of Humor   Men and Things ...

... New York ... MCMVI

For comment see entry No. 3666.

Essays That Every Child Should Know ... Edited by Hamilton Wright Mabie

New York   Doubleday, Page & Company   1908

On copyright page: Published, March, 1908

The Little Book of Friendship ... Edited ... by Wallace and Frances Rice

... Chicago ⟨1910⟩

For comment see BAL, Vol. 3, p. 65.

The Oxford Book of American Essays Chosen by Brander Matthews ...

New York   Oxford University Press ... 1914 ...

For comment see in list of W. D. Howells reprints.

Songs of the New Day ... Music by Luthera E. Sibley ... One Breath of Song ...

Published by Luthera E. Sibley   64 Charlesgate East   Back Bay, Boston, Mass. ⟨1922⟩

Cover-title.

American Mystical Verse   An Anthology Selected by Irene Hunter ...

D. Appleton and Company   New York   MCMXXV

REFERENCES AND ANA

The Memorial, a Christmas, New Year's and Easter Offering for 1828. Edited by Frederic S. Hill ...

Boston: Published by True and Greene, and Richardson and Lord ⟨n.d., after Nov. 3, 1827⟩

For comment see entry No. 4586. Also see note under next entry.

The Token; a Christmas and New Year's Present. Edited by N. P. Willis.

Boston: S. G. Goodrich, 141 Washington Street. MDCCCXXIX.

For comment see entry No. 6781.

Note: This, and the entry preceding, were once considered possible entries for the Holmes canon. See catalog of the Carroll A. Wilson collection (Thirteen Author Collections ..., edited by J.C.S. Wilson and David A. Randall, N. Y., 1950, Vol. 2, pp. 455-456). More particularly see Eleanor M. Tilton's

"Literary Bantlings: Addenda to the Holmes Bibliography," in *Papers of the Bibliographical Society of America,* Vol. 51, first quarter, 1957.

Auld Lang Syne . . .

⟨n.p., n.d., Cambridge, Mass., 1836⟩

Single leaf. Printed on both sides. Begins: *Come youth and age, come grave and gay* . . .

Sometimes misattributed to Holmes. The author was Nathaniel Langdon Frothingham. For comment see Currier-Tilton, p. 278.

Original Charades . . .

Cambridge: Sold at the Ladies' Fair, Held on the 17th and 18th of July, 1839.

According to a catalog description, clipped from an unidentified American book auction catalog, this publication may contain an anonymous contribution by Holmes. Further information wanting.

Original Charades, Prepared for the Fair in Aid of the Bunker Hill Monument, Held in Boston, September, 1840 . . .

Boston, Printed by Samuel N. Dickinson, 52 Washington Street. ⟨1840⟩

According to a catalog description, clipped from an unidentified American book auction catalog, this publication may contain an anonymous contribution by Holmes. However, the Harvard copy of this book has the identities of the authors inserted in a contemporary hand and the name of Oliver Wendell Holmes is not present.

An Answer to the Homoeopathic Delusions, of Dr. Oliver Wendell Holmes . . . by Charles Neidhard, M. D. . . .

Philadelphia: J Dobson, 106 Chesnut Street. 1842.

Cover-title? Printed self-wrapper? Printed paper wrapper?

Homoeopathy: With Particular Reference to a Lecture by O. W. Holmes . . . by A. H. Okie . . .

Boston: Otis Clapp . . . New York . . . Philadelphia. 1842.

Printed paper wrapper. Listed NAR July, 1842.

Some Remarks on Dr. O. W. Holmes's Lectures on Homoeopathy and Its Kindred Delusions . . . by Robert Wesselhoeft . . .

Boston: Otis Clapp . . . New York . . . Philadelphia. 1842.

Printed paper wrapper.

A Report on the Trees and Shrubs Growing Naturally in the Forests of Massachusetts ⟨by George B. Emerson⟩ . . .

Boston: Dutton and Wentworth, State Printers, No. 37, Congress Street. 1846.

Statistical report on the measurement of elm trees, p. 295, by Holmes.

The Old Man Dreams.

⟨Boston, 1854⟩

Entry from Johnson. *Not located.* Quite probably issued as a single leaf but not located as such. A proof printing, n.p., n.d., is in PDH; at end of text: O.W.H.; printed without title; single leaf, 13¾" x 6¼", laid paper watermarked with a flying eagle. Eleven 4-line stanzas.

The poem was written by Holmes for the meeting of the Harvard Class of 1829, Nov. 23, 1854; published in *Atlantic Monthly,* Jan. 1858; collected in *Autocrat of the Breakfast-Table,* 1858.

Mare Rubrum.

⟨Boston, 1858⟩

Entry from Johnson. Not located as a separate save for a proof printing in PDH. The proof is of the appearance of the poem in entry No. 8785. At end of text: *January 14, 1858.* O.W.H. Printed without title; single leaf, 13¾" x 5⅞", laid paper watermarked SUPERFIN⟨E⟩ / 1857 Seven 8-line stanzas.

Written by Holmes for the meeting of the Harvard Class of 1829, Jan. 14, 1858; published (as part of *Autocrat of the Breakfast-Table*) in *Atlantic Monthly,* March, 1858. Collected in *Autocrat of the Breakfast-Table,* 1858.

. . . The Constellation

New York, 1859. George Roberts, Editor & Publisher . . .

Caption-title. At head of title: Illuminated Quadruple Sheet. A novelty newspaper. Page: 4'2" x 2'11". Pp. 8. ". . . 28,000 Copies . . . printed . . ."—p. 8.

Contains a digest, p. 2, of Holmes's lecture, "The Chief End of Man."

Songs of Williams . . .

New York: Baker & Godwin, Printing-House Square. 1859.

Printed paper wrapper. "The Summer Dawn Is Breaking," pp. 65-66, is a truncated version of Holmes's "A Song of '29."

Associate Members Of The United States Sanitary Commission Meeting In Boston. Address To The Public. The United States Sanitary Commission was appointed by the War Department to aid and co-operate with the Medical Bureau, in providing for the Sanitary interests of the new raised Volunteer forces ...

⟨Boston, December 2, 1861⟩

Single cut sheet folded to make four pages. Holmes named as a member of the *Committee on Addresses*, p. 2

Vive la France! Toast ...

1861

Translation into French of Holmes's toast at the dinner to Prince Napoleon, Revere House, Boston, Sept. 25, 1861. For publication of the original text see *The Address of Mr. Everett and the Poem of Dr. O. W. Holmes* ..., Cambridge, 1861.

Two versions noted. The sequence has not been established and the designations are for identification only.

A

VIVE LA FRANCE! / TOAST / PORTÉ AU DINER OFFERT A S.A.I. LE PRINCE NAPOLEON / A LA REVERE HOUSE DE BOSTON / LE 25 SEPTEMBRE 1861 / Par Olivier Wendell Holmes, / TRADUIT EN FRANÇAIS / PAR MAUNSELL B. FIELD, DE NEW-YORK, / ⟨etc., etc.⟩

⟨Imprimerie de H. de Mareil, 40, Howard Street, New-York. n.d., 1861?⟩

Single cut sheet folded to make four pages. Title as above at head of p. ⟨1⟩; imprint at foot of p. 3. Copy in B.

B

VIVE LA FRANCE! / ⟨decorated rule⟩ / Toast porté par OLIVER WENDELL HOLMES, au diner offert à / S.A.I. LE PRINCE NAPOLÉON à la Revere House, à Boston, / le 25 Septembre, 1861. Traduit en Français par MAUNSELL B. / FIELD, de New York, ⟨etc., etc.⟩

⟨n.p., n.d., 1861?⟩

Single leaf. Laid paper.

Printed on recto only. Copy in MHS.

⟨Printed letter urging defeat of House of Representatives "A Bill to amend the Act respecting Copyrights."⟩

New York, ⟨etc.⟩ April 25, 1862.

4 pp. An open letter signed by **Holmes and** many others. For fuller note see in Nathaniel Hawthorne, list of *References and Ana*.

Pen-Pictures of the War. Lyrics, Incidents, and Sketches of the Rebellion ... Compiled Ry ⟨*sic*⟩ Ledyard Bill.

New York. Sold Only by Subscription. 1864.

Deposited June 20, 1864. Contains reprinted material. Also contains, pp. 89-90, a poem by Julia Ward Howe here miscredited to Holmes.

Lyra Bicyclica: Forty Poets on the Wheel. By J. G. Dalton ...

Boston: Published for the Author. 1880.

Contains several adaptations of poems by Holmes; and, "The Youth and the Bicycle," pp. 20-21. This last may be by Holmes; or, possibly by Oliver Wendell Holmes, Jr.

American Humorists by ... H. R. Haweis ...

New York: Funk & Wagnalls, Publishers, 10 and 12 Dey Street. ⟨1883⟩

Printed paper wrapper.

Study and Stimulants ... Edited by A. Arthur Reade.

Manchester ... 1883 ...

For comment see entry No. 3409. Statement by the editor regarding Holmes's views, p. 69; *Autocrat of the Breakfast-Table*, 1858, p. 200, quoted, p. 116.

Oliver Wendell Holmes ... by William Sloane Kennedy ...

Boston S. E. Cassino and Company 1883

Deposited April 18, 1883.

Life of Oliver Wendell Holmes by E. E. Brown ...

Boston D. Lothrop and Company Franklin Street ⟨1884⟩

Deposited March 31, 1884. H copy received April 14, 1884. Listed PW May 17, 1884. *Two editions:* First edition, text ends on p. 304. Second edition: Issued with the imprint of *Lothrop Publishing Company* ⟨1894⟩; text (extended) ends on p. 336; deposited Nov. 30, 1894. The *Second Edition* was reprinted (with the "Bibliography," pp. 333-336 omitted) and published by The Werner Company ⟨1895⟩; deposited June 10, 1895.

Homes and Haunts of the Poets Original Etchings by W. B. Closson ... Holmes ...

... L. Prang & Co., Boston ... 1886 ...

Seven leaves, loosely laid into a folded paper wrapper, comprising: Printed title-page and six etchings.

The four lines of Holmes verse herein, dated at end April 27, 1886, reprinted from "Class of '29," *Songs in Many Keys,* 1862.

Oliver Wendell Holmes by Walter Jerrold . . .

London: Swan Sonnenschein and Co. New York: Macmillan and Co 1893.

A Bibliography of Oliver Wendell Holmes Compiled by George B. Ives

Boston and New York   Houghton, Mifflin and Company   MDCCCCVII

Cloth, printed paper label on spine. Limited to 530 copies. Noted for March 16, 1907, PW Mar. 9, 1907. Listed PW Mar. 23, 1907.

Address on Oliver Wendell Holmes April 27, 1909 by Edward Waldo Emerson

[Reprinted from Proceedings of the Cambridge Historical Society, IV] ⟨1909⟩

Cover-title. Printed paper wrapper.

Oliver Wendell Holmes   The Autocrat and His Fellow-Boarders by Samuel McChord Crothers with Selected Poems

Boston and New York   Houghton Mifflin Company   MDCCCCIX

Trade edition; and, a limited edition with certificate of issue: *Three Hundred ⟨numbered⟩ Copies Printed . . . August, 1909* . . .

Deposited Oct. 7, 1909.

Dr. Holmes's Boston Edited by Caroline Ticknor . . .

Boston and New York   Houghton Mifflin Company   MDCCCCXV

Deposited Oct. 11, 1915.

Selections from the Medical Writings and Sayings of Dr. Oliver Wendell Holmes ⟨by⟩ George H. Monks, M. D. Reprinted from the Boston Medical and Surgical Journal Vol. 197, No. 30, pp. 1385-1394, Jan. 26, 1928

⟨Boston, 1928⟩

Printed paper wrapper. Cover-title.

Holmes of the Breakfast-Table by M. A. De-Wolfe Howe

Oxford University Press   London   New York 1939

Deposited April 10, 1939.

Oliver Wendell Holmes   Representative Selections, with Introduction, Bibliography, and Notes by S. I. Hayakawa . . . and Howard Mumford Jones . . .

American Book Company   New York   Cincinnati   Chicago   Boston   Atlanta ⟨1939⟩

On copyright page of first printing: W.P.I

The Psychiatric Novels of Oliver Wendell Holmes   Abridgement, Introduction and Annotations by Clarence P. Oberndorf . . .

Columbia University Press   New York   1943

Deposited Oct. 11, 1943. A revised and enlarged edition was issued by Columbia University Press, 1946; deposited Aug. 23, 1946.

Amiable Autocrat   A Biography of Dr. Oliver Wendell Holmes by Eleanor M. Tilton

New York   Henry Schuman ⟨1947⟩

Trade edition (as above) deposited Oct. 30, 1947. Copies were prepared with a cancel title-leaf imprinted: *Amiable Autocrat   A Biography of Dr. Oliver Wendell Holmes by Eleanor Marguerite Tilton   Submitted in Partial Fulfillment of the Requirements for the Degree of Doctor of Philosophy, in the Faculty of Philosophy, Columbia University, New York   Henry Schuman   ⟨1947⟩*

A Bibliography of Oliver Wendell Holmes by Thomas Franklin Currier Edited by Eleanor M. Tilton for the Bibliographical Society of America

1953   New York University Press   Washington Square   New York   London: Geoffrey Cumberlege   Oxford University Press

The Wit and Wisdom of Oliver Wendell Holmes Father and Son Edited . . . by Lester E. Denonn

The Beacon Press   Boston   ⟨1953⟩

Deposited Nov. 12, 1953.

WILLIAM HOWE CUYLER HOSMER

1814 – 1877

9286. THE PIONEERS OF WESTERN NEW-YORK: A POEM, PRONOUNCED AT GENEVA, N. Y., BEFORE THE LITERARY SOCIETIES OF GENEVA COLLEGE, AUGUST 1st, 1838 . . .

GENEVA, N. Y. PRINTED BY IRA MERRELL. 1838.

⟨1⟩-24. 7⁹⁄₁₆″ x 4¹⁵⁄₁₆″.

⟨1⟩-2⁶.

Printed pink paper wrapper.

AAS H LC NYPL

9287. The Moss-Rose, a Parting Token. Edited by C. W. Everest . . .

Hartford: Gurdon Robins, Jr., 180 Main Street. 1840.

"Scene from a Manuscript Drama," pp. 50-52.

NYPL copy inscribed *June 28th, 1840.*

H NYPL

9288. American Melodies . . . Compiled by George P. Morris . . .

New-York: Published by Linen and Fennell, No. 229 Broadway. 1841.

"A Festal Song," pp. 238-239. Collected in *Poetical Works,* 1854.

For comment see entry No. 997.

9289. THE PROSPECTS OF THE AGE. A POEM, DELIVERED BEFORE THE LITERARY SOCIETIES OF THE UNIVERSITY OF VERMONT, AT BURLINGTON, AUGUST 3, 1841 . . .

BURLINGTON: CHAUNCEY GOODRICH. MDCCCXLI.

⟨1⟩-19. 9″ x 5½″.

⟨A⟩-B⁴, C².

Printed tan paper wrapper.

AAS H

9290. The Poets of America . . . Edited by John Keese. [Volume Second of the Series.]

New York: Published by Samuel Colman . . . 1842.

"Where Lives the Soul of Poetry," pp. 292-294. Collected in *Themes of Song,* 1842.

For fuller entry see No. 3280.

9291. The Poets and Poetry of America . . . by Rufus W. Griswold . . .

Philadelphia: Carey and Hart, Chesnut Street. MDCCCXLII.

Reprint save for "A Floridian Scene," p. 449. Collected in *Poetical Works,* 1854, as "Lay of a Wanderer."

For comment see entry No. 6644.

9292. THEMES OF SONG: A POEM, READ BEFORE THE AMPHICTYON ASSOCIATION, OF THE GENESEE WESLEYAN SEMINARY, AT THE ANNUAL EXHIBITION OF THAT INSTITUTION, SEPTEMBER 30th, 1842 . . .

ROCHESTER: PRINTED BY WILLIAM ALLING, 12 EXCHANGE-STREET. 1842

⟨1⟩-34, blank leaf. 9⁹⁄₁₆″ x 5¾″.

⟨1⟩-4⁴, 5².

Printed paper wrapper; both green; and, pinkish-tan noted.

H NYPL Y

9293. YONNONDIO, OR WARRIORS OF THE GENESEE: A TALE OF THE SEVENTEENTH CENTURY . . .

NEW-YORK: WILEY & PUTNAM. ROCHESTER: D. M. DEWEY, 2 ARCADE HALL. 1844.

⟨i⟩-vi, 7-239. 7⁵⁄₁₆″ x 4⅜″.

⟨A⟩-I, K-U⁶.

T cloth: blue; brown; green. Colored paper end papers pasted to white; the following colors noted: blue; pale peach; peach; yellow. Double flyleaves.

Title-page deposited Sept. 25, 1844. Reviewed USDR Dec. 1844; *Weekly Mirror* (New York), Jan. 11, 1845.

AAS H

9294. An Address Delivered before the Was-Ah Ho-De-No-Son-Ne or New Confederacy of the Iroquois, by Henry R. Schoolcraft ... at Its Third Annual Council, August 14, 1846 ⟨sic⟩. Also, Genundewah, a Poem, by W.H.C. Hosmer ...

Rochester: Printed by Jerome & Brother, Talman Block, Sign of the American Eagle, Buffalo-Street. 1846.

Printed paper wrapper.

"Genundewah, [A Legend of Canandaigua Lake.]," pp. ⟨37⟩-48. Collected in *Poetical Works,* 1854.

Note: The date on the title-page, *August 14, 1846,* is erroneous. In all examined copies the date is altered to *August 14, 1845,* by overprinting but with only partial (and confusing) success.

Noted by K July, 1846.

BPL H LC NYPL

9294A. The Ladies' Casket; Containing a Gem, together with its Sentiment, and a Poetical Description, for Each Day in the Week, and Each Month in the Year. By J. Wesley Hanson ...

Lowell: Merrill and Heywood. Boston: B. B. Mussey. 1846.

Contains the following poems by Hosmer; collected in *The Months,* 1847.

"November," pp. 106-108; "December," pp. 121-123; "January," pp. 133-135; "February," pp. 144-146.

Deposited Dec. 26, 1846.

B

9295. The Opal: A Pure Gift for the Holydays. MDCCCXLVII. Edited by John Keese ...

New-York: J. C. Riker, 129 Fulton-Street. 1847.

"Poet and Snow-Bird," pp. ⟨26⟩-27. Collected in *Poetical Works,* 1854.

For comment see entry No. 6853.

9296. The Fountain. A Gift: "To Stir up the Pure Mind by Way of Remembrance." ... Edited by H. Hastings Weld.

Philadelphia: William Sloanaker. 1847.

Leather.

"The Murdered Czar," pp. 165-168. Collected in *Poetical Works,* 1854.

The Daily Chronotype (Boston), Nov. 6, 1846, prints an extract from *The Fountain.* Reviewed NYM Nov. 21, 1846.

H NYPL

9297. THE MONTHS ...

BOSTON: WILLIAM D. TICKNOR & COMPANY. M DCCC XLVII.

⟨i-ii⟩, ⟨i⟩-vi, ⟨1⟩-71; *Notes,* p. ⟨72⟩. 7$\frac{5}{16}$" x 4$\frac{7}{8}$" scant.

⟨1⁴, 2-5⁸, 6⁴⟩. *Signed:* ⟨-⟩⁴, 1-6⁶.

Illuminated white paper wrapper. Inserted at front: Publisher's list dated Jan. 1, 1846; a copyright deposit copy thus. Also noted with inserted list dated July 1, 1847.

Deposited Aug. 5, 1847. Listed NYM Aug. 14, 1847. Reviewed USDR Oct. 1847.

AAS H LC

9298. A Memorial of Sa-Sa-Na, the Mohawk Maiden; Who Perished in the Rail Road Disaster at Deposit, N. Y., February, 18, 1852. Containing ... Obituary Notice by Hon. C. P. Avery ... Sermon ... by S. H. Norton ... Poem by W.H.C. Hosmer, Esq.

Hamilton: Waldron & Baker, Printers, 1852.

Printed paper wrapper.

"Lament for Sa-Sa-Na," pp. 25-28. Collected in *Poetical Works,* 1854.

LC

9299. ... Morrell's Pocket Miscellany of Choice, Entertaining, and Useful Reading for Travelers and the Fireside ...

New York: Arthur Morrell, 25 Park Row; Printed at Morrell's Steam Blank-Book Manufacturing and Printing Establishment, 196 Fulton-St. 1852.

3 parts. For comment see entry No. 8134.

"Flying Visits to Famous Places ... Cherry Valley," Part 2, pp. 24-30.

"Flying Visits to Famous Places ... Hyde Hall —Mount of Vision—Otsego Lake—J. Fennimore ⟨sic⟩ Cooper—The Hall—Rose Lawn," Part 3, pp. 127-133.

9300. THE POETICAL WORKS OF WIL-
LIAM H. C. HOSMER ...

REDFIELD 110 & 112 NASSAU-STREET, NEW YORK.
1854.

2 Vols.

Vol. 1: YONNONDIO. LEGENDS OF THE SENECAS.
INDIAN TRADITIONS AND SONGS. BIRD-NOTES. THE
MONTHS.

Vol. 2: OCCASIONAL POEMS. HISTORIC SCENES. MAR-
TIAL LYRICS. SONGS AND BALLADS. FUNERAL ECHOES.
SONNETS. MISCELLANEOUS POEMS.

1: ⟨i-ii⟩, ⟨i⟩-⟨x⟩, ⟨1⟩-374. Frontispiece inserted.
7³⁄₁₆″ full x 4¹⁵⁄₁₆″ full.
2: ⟨i⟩-⟨x⟩, ⟨11⟩-⟨377⟩; blank, p. ⟨378⟩; 2 pp.
advertisements.

1: ⟨-⟩⁶, 1-15¹², 16⁶, ⟨17⟩¹.
2: ⟨1⟩-15¹², 16¹⁰.

A cloth: purple. Cream end papers. Flyleaves.

Deposited March 30, 1854. Listed NLG April 1,
1854.

BA H

9301. The Knickerbocker Gallery: A Testimonial to the Editor of the Knickerbocker Magazine from Its Contributors ...

New-York: Samuel Hueston, 348 Broadway.
MDCCCLV.

"Dryden and Milton," pp. ⟨131⟩-133.

For comment see entry No. 1033.

9302. Services at the Funeral of the Rev. Jacob
Brodhead ... on Friday, the 8th of June,
1855 ...

New-York: Printed by John A. Gray, 95 & 97
Cliff St., Cor. Frankfort. 1855.

Printed paper wrapper.

"Tribute to the Memory of the Late Rev. Jacob
Brodhead, D. D., pp. ⟨25⟩-26. Collected in *Later
Lays*, 1873.

B NYPL

9303. "DIRGE FOR THE BRAVE"

First published in *Daily Union and Advertiser*
(Rochester, N. Y.) May 20, 1862. This poem has
been noted in the following separate publications. The sequence has not been established
and the order of presentation is arbitrary.

A

Excelsior Battle-Song ... Dirge for the Brave:
Suggested by the Fall of Captain Henry Brooks
O'Rielly, of the First Excelsior Regiment ...

⟨n.p., n.d., 1862?⟩

Single leaf. 10⅝″ x 8¼″. Printed on recto only.
Prints Hosmer's poem together with other material.

B

A Brief Memento of Captain Henry Brooks
O'Rielly ... Who Fell in the Battle of Williams-
burg ... May 5, 1862.

⟨n.p., n.d., 1862⟩

Printed self-wrapper. Cover-title. The poem appears on p. ⟨2⟩.

B (A, B)   H (B)   NYPL (B)

9304. DIRGE FOR LT. COL. McVICAR ...

AVON, N. Y., MAY 14, 1863.

Single leaf. 8″ x 4⅞″. Printed on recto only.

B

9305. Lyrics of Loyalty Arranged and Edited
by Frank Moore

New York   George P. Putnam   1864

"War Song," pp. 53-54.

For comment see entry No. 1203.

9306. Personal and Political Ballads Arranged
and Edited by Frank Moore

New York   George P Putnam   1864

"Answer to *My Maryland*," pp. 241-244.

For comment see entry No. 1208.

9307. AGRICULTURAL ODE: READ NO-
VEMBER 16th, 1864 ... AT THE COM-
MENCEMENT OF THE STATE AGRI-
CULTURAL COLLEGE, LANSING, MICH-
IGAN, AFTER THE BACCALAUREATE
AND ANNUAL ADDRESSES, PRO-
NOUNCED BY PRESIDENT T. C. ABBOT,
AND HON. C. P. AVERY.

⟨n.p., n.d., 1864? 1865?⟩

Cover-title. Collected in *Later Lays*, 1873.

⟨1-13⟩, blank leaf. 8″ full x 5³⁄₁₆″.

⟨-⟩⁸.

Printed self-wrapper.

The copy in LC (ex-Smithsonian Institution)
dated by Smithsonian on p. ⟨14⟩: Jan. 16, 1865.

LC

9308. Poetical Tributes to the Memory of Abraham Lincoln.

Philadelphia   J. B. Lippincott & Co.   1865.

Untitled poem beginning: *The muffled drum and tolling bell*, pp. 76-77.

For comment see entry No. 2828.

9309. A Collection of Songs of the American Press, and Other Poems Relating to the Art of Printing. Compiled by Charles Munsell.

Albany, N. Y. 1868

"Franklin's Birth-Day," pp. 127-128.

Cloth?

B   NYPL

9310. THE BABY'S WELCOME. INSCRIBED TO MR. AND MRS. ROBERT MORTON . . .

ROSE LAWN, NOV. 27, A.D. 1872.

Single cut sheet folded to make four pages. Imprinted on p. ⟨1⟩ only. Letter-press in gold. Leaf: 8″ x 5″.

B

9311. LATER LAYS AND LYRICS . . .

ROCHESTER, N. Y.   D. M. DEWEY, 1873.

⟨i-iv⟩, ⟨1⟩-168. 7″ x 4½″.

⟨-⟩², 1-7¹².

P cloth: blue; green; purple. Covers bevelled. Brown-coated on white end papers. Flyleaves.

H   NYPL   Y

9312. The Poets and Poetry of Buffalo Edited by James N. Johnston

Buffalo, New York MCMIV

"Funeral Ode," pp. 239-240; dated at end *Avon, April 23, 1867.*

NYPL

REPRINTS

The following publications contain material by Hosmer reprinted from earlier books.

The Poet's Gift . . . Edited by John Keese.

Boston . . . 1845.

For comment see BAL, Vol. 1, p. 206.

Leaflets of Memory: An Illuminated Annual for MDCCCLV.

Philadelphia: . . . E. H. Butler & Co. 1855.

Leather.

Songs of the Soldiers . . . Edited by Frank Moore

New York . . . 1864

For comment see entry No. 261. "Union Song," pp. 239-241, is a reprint of "Independence Ode," *Poetical Works*, 1854.

. . . Ballads of the War.

New York . . . ⟨1864⟩

For comment see BAL, Vol. 1, p. 248.

The Book of the Sonnet Edited by Leigh Hunt and S. Adams Lee . . .

Boston . . . 1867

Prepared for the press and partially edited by George Henry Boker. For fuller comment see entry No. 1218.

The Poets and Poetry of America. By Rufus Wilmot Griswold. With Additions by R. H. Stoddard . . .

New York . . . 1873.

For comment see *Section III*, John Hay list.

Poems of Places Edited by Henry W. Longfellow . . . Asia. Asia Minor, Mesopotamia . . .

Boston: Houghton, Osgood and Company . . . 1878.

Listed PW Aug. 10, 1878.

Poems of Places Edited by Henry W. Longfellow . . . New England. Vol. II.

Boston . . . 1879.

For comment see entry No. 1473.

Poems of Places Edited by Henry W. Longfellow . . . Middle States.

Boston . . . 1879.

For comment see BAL, Vol. 1, p. 74.

Poems of Places Edited by Henry W. Longfellow . . . Southern States.

Boston . . . 1879.

For comment see BAL, Vol. 1, p. 74.

Mountain, Lake, and River . . . by N. P. Willis . . .

Boston . . . 1884.

For comment see BAL, Vol. 3, p. 253.

ANA

The Fall of Tecumseh: A Drama.

Avon, 1830.

Not located and presumed to be a ghost. Entry from Appleton, Foley, and Wegelin's

Early American Plays . . . , 1905. In a letter to BAL, Sept. 19, 1961, Wegelin states: "I have never seen a copy."

Bird-Notes.
Indian Traditions and Songs.
Legend ⟨*sic*⟩ of the Senecas.

The above three titles from Appleton. Not located as separate publications as reported by Appleton and BAL presumes that Appleton errs in listing these as having been issued separately in 1850. Located only in *Poetical Works,* 1854.

Venal Authors.

Not located. Entry from K Aug. 1853 which reported that Hosmer "has in press a pungent poem" of this title. Presumably unpublished.

EMERSON HOUGH

1 8 5 7 – 1 9 2 3

9313. Shooting on Upland, Marsh, and Stream. A Series of Articles . . . Edited by William Bruce Leffingwell . . .

Chicago and New York: Rand, McNally & Company, Publishers. 1890 . . .

"Plover-Shooting," pp. 197-216.

Listed PW May 17, 1890, as in cloth; and, half morocco. Deposited May 8, 1890.

H

9314. THE SINGING MOUSE STORIES . . .

NEW YORK: FOREST AND STREAM PUB. CO. 1895.

⟨1⟩-⟨177⟩; blank, p. ⟨178⟩; tailpiece and quotation, p. ⟨179⟩; blank, p. ⟨180⟩; colophon, p. ⟨181⟩; tailpiece, p. ⟨182⟩; blank leaf. Vignettes and marginal illustrations. 6⅞" full x 3¹¹⁄₁₆".

⟨1-11⁸, 12⁴⟩.

Green buckram. Top edges gilt.

Listed PW Feb. 22, 1896. For an extended edition see under ⟨1910⟩.

NYPL   Y

9315. THE STORY OF THE COWBOY . . .

NEW YORK   D. APPLETON AND COMPANY   1897

⟨i⟩-xii, 1-349; blank, p. ⟨350⟩; 6 pp. advertisements. Frontispiece and 9 plates inserted. 7⁷⁄₁₆" x 5".

⟨1⟩-23⁸.

V cloth: brown-orange. Tan-coated end papers. Flyleaves.

Deposited Sept. 4, 1897. BA copy received Sept. 15, 1897. Noted as *just ready* and advertised as *new* PW Sept. 18, 1897. Listed PW Oct. 2, 1897. The London (Gay & Bird) edition advertised as *ready* Ath Nov. 13, 1897; listed Ath Nov. 13, 1897; PC Nov. 20, 1897; Bkr Dec. 1897.

BA   H   NYPL

. . . The Cowboy . . .

New York   America of the Americans Society Publishers ⟨1897; *i.e., ca.* 1920⟩

See entry No. 9356.

9316. THE GIRL AT THE HALFWAY HOUSE   A STORY OF THE PLAINS . . .

NEW YORK   D. APPLETON AND COMPANY   1900

Title-page in black and red.

⟨i⟩-viii, 1-371; blank, p. ⟨372⟩; 4 pp. advertisements. 7⅜" x 4¹⁵⁄₁₆" full.

⟨1⟩-24⁸.

Two states (probably printings) noted. The order of presentation is presumed correct.

A

P. ⟨373⟩: *Dr. Barton's New Novel. Pine Knot* . . .

B

P. ⟨373⟩: *"A Fresh and Charming Novel." The Last Lady of Mulberry* . . .

Two bindings noted. The order of presentation is presumed correct.

Binding A

T cloth: blue-black. Top of spine not decorated by vignette of covered wagon stamped in colors. Flyleaves.

Binding B

T cloth: blue-black. Top of spine decorated with a vignette, stamped in colors, of a covered wagon. Flyleaves.

BA copy (A sheets, A binding) received July 31, 1900. Listed PW Aug. 11, 1900. The London (Heinemann) edition advertised for *next week* Ath Feb. 23, 1901; listed Ath March 9, 1901.

AAS (A sheets, A binding; B sheets, A binding; B sheets, B binding)   BA (A sheets, A binding)   H (B sheets, A binding)   Y (A sheets, A binding)

9317. Comedy

McClure, Phillips & Co. New York MCMI

Stories from McClure's series.

"The Horse Thief. How the Live Stock Expert and His Partner Came to Leave Montana," pp. 155-174.

Deposited Oct. 2, 1901. Listed PW Oct. 26, 1901.

Y

9318. THE MISSISSIPPI BUBBLE HOW THE STAR OF GOOD FORTUNE ROSE AND SET AND ROSE AGAIN, BY A WOMAN'S GRACE, FOR ONE JOHN LAW OF LAURISTON A NOVEL ...

THE BOWEN-MERRILL COMPANY PUBLISHERS, INDIANAPOLIS ⟨1902⟩

Title-page in black and orange.

Note: The Bowen-Merrill Company reprinted *The Mississippi Bubble* an unknown number of times. Advertised April 19, 1902: "The first and second printings ... exhausted ... third printing ... in process ... publication day ... deferred ... until April 26th." Again advertised PW April 26, 1902: "First, second, and third printings were sold before publication day."

It is all but certain that the first printing is as here described. Not so certain is the sequence of the reprints; these fall into patterns and for the purpose of identification are here designated Printings B, C, D, E, although there is good reason to believe that each designation may represent not a single printing but several. Obvious reprints (*i.e.,* those issued by Bobbs-Merrill Company; Grosset & Dunlap; McKinlay, Stone & Mackenzie) are here disregarded.

The statement APRIL is on the copyright page. This feature is of no value in determining sequence since it is present in all known copies of the book including quite late reprints. Also present on the copyright page is the imprint of Braunworth & Co., a feature present in all examined copies of all printings issued by The Bowen-Merrill Company.

Similarly, and of no significance in establishment of a sequence for the Bowen-Merrill printings:

In all examined Bowen-Merrill printings, and in all examined Bobbs-Merrill printings, the last line of p. 132 reads: *... with no confidant ...* In all examined copies issued by Grosset & Dunlap and by McKinlay, Stone & Mackenzie the reading is: *... without confidant ...*

⟨i-x⟩, ⟨1⟩-452; *A List of Recent Fiction ...,* p. ⟨453⟩; publisher's advertisements, pp. ⟨454-456⟩; plus: publisher's advertisements, pp. ⟨457-472⟩. Frontispiece and five plates inserted. 7⁷⁄₁₆" x 5¹⁄₁₆".

⟨1⁹, 2-29⁸; plus: 30⁸⟩. Leaf ⟨1⟩₂ inserted.

P. ⟨453⟩: *A List of Recent Fiction ...*

P. ⟨456⟩: *... Hearts Courageous ...*

P. ⟨457⟩: *... The 13th District ...*

PRINTING B

⟨1⁹, 2-29⁸; plus: 30⁸⟩. Leaf ⟨1⟩₂ inserted.

Frontispiece and five plates inserted.

P. ⟨453⟩: Blank.

P. ⟨456⟩: *... The Strollers ...*

P. ⟨457⟩: *... The Fighting Bishop ...*

PRINTING C

⟨1⁹, 2-29⁸; plus: 30⁸⟩. Leaf ⟨1⟩₂ inserted.

Frontispiece and six plates inserted. *Note:* Advertisements in PW prior to Nov. 22, 1902, described the book as with six illustrations; *i.e.,* frontispiece and five other plates. With the PW issue of Nov. 22, 1902, the book is described as with seven illustrations; *i.e.,* frontispiece and six other plates.

P. ⟨453⟩: Blank.

P. ⟨456⟩: *... Hearts Courageous ...*

P. ⟨457⟩: *... The Strollers ...*

PRINTING D

⟨1⁹, 2⁸, 3-16¹⁶⟩. Leaf ⟨1⟩₂ inserted.

Frontispiece and six plates inserted.

P. ⟨453⟩: Blank.

P. ⟨456⟩: *... Hearts Courageous ...*

P. ⟨457⟩: *... The Mississippi Bubble ...*

In this printing the divisional title-page, *Book II America,* appears on p. ⟨160⟩. In all other printings the feature is (correctly) on p. ⟨159⟩.

PRINTING E

⟨1⁹, 2-29⁸; plus: 30⁸⟩. Leaf ⟨1⟩₂ inserted.

Frontispiece and six plates inserted.

P. ⟨453⟩: Blank.

P. ⟨456⟩: *... Hearts Courageous ...*

P. ⟨457⟩: *... Francezka ...*

THE BINDING

At least nine varieties of the binding have been seen. On the basis of occurrence on first printing sheets the following appears to be, almost without question, the earliest:

T cloth: olive green. Stamped in gold save as noted.

Front: THE / MISSISSIPPI / BUBBLE ⟨*the preceding three lines stamped on a white fleur-de-lis backed by a circular gold field*⟩ / EMERSON HOUGH

Spine: THE / MISSISSIPPI / ⟨*fleur-de-lis backed by a circular white field*⟩ / BUBBLE / ⟨*rule*⟩ / HOUGH / BOWEN / MERRILL

White end papers.

The later bindings vary considerably as to stamping and (in some) as to the type of cloth. One of the most apparent variations is the style in which the author's name appears on the spine. In the first binding it is given simply as: HOUGH In later bindings the name occurs: EMERSON / HOUGH The later bindings have been noted in the following types of cloth: *S cloth:* olive. *T cloth:* gray (several shades noted); gray-green; maroon (prepared for The Tabard Inn Library?); olive. *V cloth:* gray.

"The first and second printings . . . exhausted . . . third printing . . . in process . . . publication day . . . deferred . . . until April 26th."—Advertisement, PW April 19, 1902. "First, second, and third printings were sold before publication day."—Advertisement, PW April 26, 1902. Listed PW May 3, 1902. The London (Methuen) edition announced in Ath Aug. 1, 1903; advertised as *just published* Ath Aug. 22, 1903.

Copies of the first printing in Binding A located in JB, RES. Known reprints, in the several later bindings, in: H JB LC NYPL RES Y

9319. THE WAY TO THE WEST AND THE LIVES OF THREE EARLY AMERICANS BOONE—CROCKETT—CARSON . . .

INDIANAPOLIS   THE   BOBBS-MERRILL   COMPANY PUBLISHERS ⟨1903⟩

Title-page in black and red.

⟨i-x⟩, 1-446. Frontispiece and five plates inserted. 7⅜" x 5".

⟨1⁴, 2-29⁸⟩.

Gray buckram.

On copyright page: *October* Deposited Oct. 23, 1903. Listed PW Nov. 14, 1903. The London (Hodder & Stoughton) edition listed PC June 6, 1925.

AAS   H

9320. The Maid of Athens A Musical Comedy in Three Acts by L. Frank Baum and Emerson Hough

Copyright, 1903, by L. Frank Baum and Emerson Hough All Rights Reserved

Cover-title.

11 leaves. Printed on rectos only. Paged: ⟨1⟩-11. 10½" x 7". Stapled at top.

Prepared for copyright purposes. Does not contain the full text of the comedy; synopsis only.

Deposited Nov. 27, 1903.

LC

9321. MY LADY'S PLUMES. [REPRINTED FROM FOREST AND STREAM.] . . .

⟨Humane Education Committee, Providence, R. I., n.d., *ca.* 1903⟩

Caption-title. The above at head of p. 1. Imprint at foot of p. 4.

Single cut sheet folded to make four pages. Page: 9⁵⁄₁₆" x 5¹⁵⁄₁₆".

Paged: 1-4. Illustrated.

Two printings noted:

1: As above. P. 4 so paged. Publication note in three lines, p. 4.

2: P. 4 not paged. Publication note in nine lines, p. ⟨4⟩.

A copy of each received by B in 1903. Closer date not found.

B (1, 2)   NYPL (1)

9322. THE LAW OF THE LAND OF MISS LADY, WHOM IT INVOLVED IN MYSTERY . . . OF JOHN EDDRING . . . A NOVEL . . .

INDIANAPOLIS   THE   BOBBS-MERRILL   COMPANY PUBLISHERS ⟨1904⟩

Title-page in black and orange.

⟨i-x⟩, 1-416; blank leaf; publisher's catalog, pp. ⟨419-424⟩. Frontispiece and five plates inserted. 7⅜" scant x 4⅞".

⟨1⁹, 2-27⁸⟩. ⟨1⟩₂ inserted.

V cloth: tan.

On copyright page: *October* Listed PW Oct. 22, 1904.

H   Y

9323. HEART'S DESIRE THE STORY OF A CONTENTED TOWN CERTAIN PECULIAR CITIZENS AND TWO FORTUNATE LOVERS . . .

THE MACMILLAN COMPANY   NEW YORK MCMV LONDON: MACMILLAN & CO., LTD.

⟨i⟩-⟨xii⟩, 1-367; blank, p. ⟨368⟩; 4 pp. advertisements. Frontispiece and 7 plates inserted. Laid paper. 7½″ x 5⅛″.

⟨1-24⁸⟩. *Signed:* ⟨A⟩⁶, B-I, K-U, X-Z⁸, 2A⁸, ⟨2B⟩².

T cloth: mottled pale orange. Top edges gilded.

On copyright page: *Published October, 1905.* Advertised as *shortly* PW Sept. 16, 1905. Deposited Oct. 2, 1905. Noted for "about the middle of this month" PW Oct. 7, 1905. Listed PW Oct. 28, 1905. The London edition advertised as published Ath Dec. 2, 1905; listed Ath Dec. 9, 1905; reviewed Ath Dec. 30, 1905; listed Bkr Jan. 1906.

BA BPL H

9324. ... Heart Throbs in Prose and Verse Dear to the American People ...

The Chapple Publishing Company, Ltd. Boston, Mass. ⟨1905⟩

"My Stout Old Heart and I," pp. 390-391.

Deposited Dec. 11, 1905. For fuller comment see entry No. 2016.

9325. THE KING OF GEE-WHIZ ... WITH LYRICS BY WILBUR D. NESBIT ...

INDIANAPOLIS THE BOBBS-MERRILL COMPANY PUBLISHERS ⟨1906⟩

⟨i-viii⟩, 1-210. Frontispiece and 7 plates inserted; other illustrations in text including five full-page plates which are not reckoned in the printed pagination. 9⁵⁄₁₆″ x 7⅛″.

⟨1-14⁸, 15²⟩.

Three forms of the book have been noted:

First Printing, First Issue

Erroneous imposition of pp. ⟨26⟩ and ⟨140⟩ produces the following faulty reading:

P. ⟨26⟩ ends: ... *an Enchanted Banjo.* / ⟨tailpiece⟩

P. ⟨140⟩ ends: ... *DOWN!* / ⟨tailpiece⟩

Pp. ⟨26⟩ and ⟨140⟩ are cancels.

First Printing, Second Issue

The erroneous imposition corrected by means of cancels, the reading is:

P. ⟨26⟩ ends: ... *DOWN!* / ⟨tailpiece⟩

P. ⟨140⟩ ends: ... *an Enchanted Banjo.* / ⟨tailpiece⟩

Pp. ⟨26⟩ and ⟨140⟩ are not cancels.

Second Printing

The erroneous reading is not present, pp. ⟨26⟩ and ⟨140⟩, and the leaves cited are not cancels. Reading as in *First Printing, Second Issue.*

V cloth: green.

Advertised PW Aug. 18, 1906. Deposited Aug. 20, 1906. Listed PW Dec. 8, 1906.

AAS (2d issue) H (2d printing) LC (1st issue) Y (2d printing)

9326. THE STORY OF THE OUTLAW A STUDY OF THE WESTERN DESPERADO WITH HISTORICAL NARRATIVES OF FAMOUS OUTLAWS; THE STORIES OF NOTED BORDER WARS; VIGILANTE MOVEMENTS AND ARMED CONFLICTS ON THE FRONTIER ...

NEW YORK THE OUTING PUBLISHING COMPANY 1907

Title-page in black and orange.

⟨i⟩-xiv, 1-401. Laid paper. Frontispiece and 16 plates inserted. 7¼″ x 4¹⁵⁄₁₆″.

⟨1-26⁸⟩.

Wood veneer sides, brown T cloth shelfback.

"First state has rule at top of page v."—Johnson. Undoubtedly the first printing is as described by Johnson. In the first printing p. v is headed: ⟨rule⟩ / Preface v / ⟨double rule⟩ The rules are not present in the third printing; BAL has been unable to locate a copy of the second printing.

Deposited Jan. 30, 1907. Listed PW March 16, 1907. The earliest British edition noted was issued by Hodder & Stoughton, London; listed PC June 6, 1925.

BA NYPL

9327. THE WAY OF A MAN ...

NEW YORK THE OUTING PUBLISHING COMPANY MCMVII

Title-page in black and orange.

⟨i-ii⟩, ⟨i⟩-⟨x⟩, 1-345; blank, p. ⟨346⟩; printer's imprint, p. ⟨347⟩. Laid paper. Frontispiece and 4 plates inserted. 7⅞″ full x 5⁵⁄₁₆″.

⟨1⁶, 2-22⁸, 23⁶⟩.

T cloth: red.

Deposited Aug. 29, 1907. Advertised for Oct. 1, 1907, PW Sept. 28, 1907. Listed PW Oct. 12, 1907. The earliest British edition (Methuen) noted by BAL was listed Ath Jan. 28, 1911.

H NYPL

The Frontier Omnibus . . .

New York . . . ⟨1907; *i.e.,* 1936⟩

See entry No. 9366.

9328. THE YOUNG ALASKANS . . .

HARPER & BROTHERS PUBLISHERS   NEW YORK AND LONDON   MCMVIII

⟨i-x⟩, 1-⟨292⟩, blank leaf. Frontispiece and 3 plates inserted. 7⅜″ x 4¹⁵⁄₁₆″.

⟨1⟩-19⁸.

V cloth: tan-orange.

On copyright page: *Published October, 1908* Deposited Oct. 22, 1908. Listed PW Nov. 7, 1908.

AAS   Y

9329. . . . The Cowboy . . .

New York   The Brampton Society Publishers ⟨1908⟩

At head of title: National Edition   Complete in Twelve Volumes   Builders of the Nation . . .

2 Vols. Cloth, printed paper label on the spine.

Reprint of *The Story of the Cowboy,* 1897.

UP

9330. 54-40 OR FIGHT . . .

INDIANAPOLIS   THE BOBBS-MERRILL COMPANY PUBLISHERS ⟨1909⟩

⟨i-xii⟩, 1-402, blank leaf. Frontispiece and 3 plates inserted. 7⅜″ x 5″ scant.

⟨1-26⁸⟩.

T cloth: brown; maroon; olive.

Two states noted. The sequence has not been determined and the designations are for identification only:

A: No printer's imprint on copyright page.

B: With the *Braunworth* imprint on the copyright page.

Two states of the binding noted. The sequence has not been determined and the designations are for identification only:

A: The publisher's name is not present on the front cover.

B: With the publisher's name, THE BOBBS-MERRILL COMPANY, embossed at the bottom of the maze-like decoration on the front cover.

On copyright page: *January*   Listed PW Jan. 16, 1909. Noted for Jan. 20, 1909, PW Jan. 16, 1909. The earliest British edition (Hodder & Stoughton) noted by BAL was listed by PC Nov. 1, 1924.

H (A sheets, A binding)   NYPL (B sheets, B binding)   Y (A sheets, A binding; B sheets, B binding)

9331. THE SOWING   A "YANKEE'S" VIEW OF ENGLAND'S DUTY TO HERSELF AND TO CANADA . . .

CHICAGO, LONDON, TORONTO: VANDERHOOF-GUNN CO., LIMITED WINNIPEG   1909

⟨i-vi⟩, ⟨i⟩-⟨xviii⟩, 1-222; blank leaf. Frontispiece and 29 plates inserted. 7⁷⁄₁₆″ x 5³⁄₁₆″. *See signature collation.*

⟨1⁴, 2-16⁸⟩. Leaf ⟨1⟩₁ excised or pasted under the end paper.

C cloth: green. White paper end papers printed in green with a pattern of clover leaves and blossoms. Flyleaf at back. Issued with all edges plain; and, top and fore-edges gilded.

Copy in H inscribed by early owner Dec. 14, 1909. BPL copy inscribed by the publishers Dec. 30, 1909. Listed (this edition?) Ath Jan. 8, 1910. Copies received at the Copyright Office (but not deposited for copyright) June 7, 1910. Listed PW Oct. 1, 1910.

BPL   H   Y

9332. MY LADY'S HAT   THE BONNET OF WILHELMINA LOUISA, AND WHAT IT MEANS   MY LADY'S FURS WHAT THEY COST . . .

GREENWICH, CONN. 1909

Cover-title.

⟨1⟩-⟨35⟩. Illustrated. 7⅝″ x 4¹⁵⁄₁₆″.

⟨-⟩¹⁸.

Printed pinkish-white paper wrapper.

AAS

9333. THE PURCHASE PRICE OR THE CAUSE OF COMPROMISE . . .

INDIANAPOLIS   THE BOBBS-MERRILL COMPANY PUBLISHERS ⟨1910⟩

⟨i-xii⟩, 1-⟨415⟩; 2 blank leaves. *Note:* In some copies the final blank leaf is used as a pastedown; see binding note below. Frontispiece and 6 plates inserted; other illustrations in text. 7⅜″ x 4¹⁵⁄₁₆″.

⟨1-27⁸⟩.

S cloth: olive. T cloth: maroon; olive. In some copies: White paper end papers; in other copies: White paper end paper at front, leaf ⟨27⟩₈ used as terminal pastedown.

Note: Occurs on two weights of paper. Sequence, if any, not known and the designations are for identification only:

A: Sheets bulk 1¼″. Both copyright deposit copies thus.

B: Sheets bulk 1⅛″.

Listed PW Nov. 19, 1910. Deposited Nov. 29, 1910. The London (Hodder & Stoughton) edition, listed PC April 4, 1925, appears to be the first British edition.

H (A)   NYPL (A, B)   Y (A, B)

9334. The Singing Mouse Stories . . .

Indianapolis   The Bobbs-Merrill Company Publishers ⟨1910⟩

Revised and extended edition. Contains six stories not present in the edition of 1895.

Deposited Nov. 28, 1910. Listed PW Dec. 17, 1910.

AAS   H   NYPL   Y

9335. THE YOUNG ALASKANS ON THE TRAIL . . .

HARPER & BROTHERS PUBLISHERS   NEW YORK AND LONDON   MCMXI

⟨i-x⟩, 1-⟨322⟩, 2 blank leaves. Frontispiece and 7 plates inserted. 7⁵⁄₁₆″ x 4¹⁵⁄₁₆″.

⟨1⟩-21⁸.

V cloth: orange. White end paper at front; at back: leaf 21₈ used as a pastedown.

On copyright page: *Published October, 1911* Deposited Oct. 21, 1911. Listed PW Oct. 28, 1911.

AAS   H

9336. JOHN RAWN PROMINENT CITIZEN . . .

INDIANAPOLIS   THE BOBBS-MERRILL COMPANY PUBLISHERS ⟨1912⟩

⟨i-x⟩, 1-385, 2 blank leaves. Frontispiece and 5 plates inserted.

⟨1-25⁸⟩.

ADVANCE ISSUE

Leaf: 7⁹⁄₁₆″ x 5⅛″.

Gray and brown mottled paper boards sides, gray T cloth shelfback. Goldstamped. Front cover lettered: JOHN / RAWN / BY / EMERSON / HOUGH / ⟨*the preceding 5 lines in intaglio*⟩ / ADVANCE COPY

TRADE ISSUE

Leaf: 7⁵⁄₁₆″ full x 4⅞″.

T cloth: maroon. Stamped in white. Front let-

tered: JOHN / RAWN / BY / EMERSON / HOUGH / ⟨*the preceding five lines in intaglio*⟩ / ⟨*publisher's imprint embossed in blind*⟩ /

Advertised for March 2, 1912, PW Feb. 24; March 2, 1912. Listed PW March 2, 1912.

H (trade)   NYPL (both)   Y (advance)

9337. . . . GOD'S ACRE   WHERE IT IS AND WHY, WHAT IT IS, AND WHOSE IT IS . . .

⟨New York: The Illustrated Outdoor World, 1912⟩

Caption-title. The above at head of p. ⟨1⟩. At head of title: REPRINTED FROM THE ILLUSTRATED OUTDOOR WORLD VOL. XLVI, NO. 5 (NEW SERIES) APRIL, 1912 . . .

⟨1⟩-8. Illustrated. 13¼″ x 10⅛″.

⟨-⟩⁴.

Printed self-wrapper.

Y

9338. The Morris Book Shop   Impressions of Some Old Friends in Celebration of the xxvth Anniversary

Chicago ⟨The Morris Book Shop⟩ 1912

Contains Hough's "The Tavern in Our Town."

For comment see entry No. 5799.

9339. THE LADY AND THE PIRATE   BEING THE PLAIN TALE OF A DILIGENT PIRATE AND A FAIR CAPTIVE . . .

INDIANAPOLIS   THE BOBBS-MERRILL COMPANY PUBLISHERS ⟨1913⟩

⟨i-x⟩, 1-436, blank leaf. Frontispiece and 3 plates inserted. 7⅜″ x 4⅞″.

⟨1-28⁸⟩.

T cloth: red.

Listed PW Aug. 9, 1913.

H   NYPL   Y

9340. THE YOUNG ALASKANS IN THE ROCKIES . . .

HARPER & BROTHERS PUBLISHERS   NEW YORK AND LONDON   MCMXIII

⟨i-ii⟩, ⟨1⟩-⟨326⟩. Frontispiece and 7 plates inserted. 7⁵⁄₁₆″ x 4¹⁵⁄₁₆″.

⟨-⟩⁴, ⟨1⟩-20⁸.

V cloth: greenish-tan. White paper end papers printed in olive with bookplate and publisher's device at front; publisher's device at back.

On copyright page: *Published September, 1913*; and, code letters G-N (signifying *printed July, 1913*). Deposited Sept. 13, 1913. Listed PW Oct. 4, 1913; Bkr Oct. 3, 1913.

AAS H NYPL

9341. GETTING A WRONG START A TRUTHFUL AUTOBIOGRAPHY

NEW YORK THE MACMILLAN COMPANY 1915 …

Anonymous.

⟨i-viii⟩, 1-234; publisher's advertisements, pp. ⟨235-241⟩; blank, p. ⟨242⟩; blank leaf. 7⁹⁄₁₆″ x 5⅛″.

⟨1-15⁸, 16⁶⟩.

B cloth: terra-cotta.

On copyright page: *Published March, 1915* Deposited March 25, 1915. Advertised as though published Ath June 12, 1915.

LC

9342. OUT OF DOORS …

NEW YORK AND LONDON D. APPLETON AND COMPANY 1915

⟨i⟩-⟨viii⟩, ⟨1⟩-⟨301⟩; blank leaf. 7¼″ x 4¹⁵⁄₁₆″.

⟨1-19⁸, 20⁴⟩.

T cloth: green.

Symbol (1) below text, p. ⟨301⟩.

Deposited Oct. 19, 1915. Listed PW Nov. 6, 1915; Bkr July, 1916.

AAS Y

9343. LET US GO AFIELD …

NEW YORK AND LONDON D. APPLETON AND COMPANY 1916

⟨i-x⟩, ⟨1⟩-⟨319⟩; blank leaf. *Note:* In some copies the final blank leaf is excised or pasted under the end paper. Frontispiece and 7 plates inserted. 7⅜″ scant x 4¹⁵⁄₁₆″.

⟨1-20⁸, 21⁶⟩. Leaf ⟨21⟩₆ in some copies excised or pasted under the end paper.

T cloth: green.

Symbol (1) below text, p. ⟨319⟩.

BPL copy received May 10, 1916. Deposited May 17, 1916. Listed PW May 27, 1916.

BA H

9344. THE MAGNIFICENT ADVENTURE … BEING THE STORY OF THE WORLD'S GREATEST EXPLORATION, AND THE ROMANCE OF A VERY GALLANT GENTLEMAN …

D. APPLETON AND COMPANY NEW YORK LONDON 1916

⟨i-x⟩, ⟨1⟩-⟨356⟩, blank leaf. Frontispiece and 3 plates inserted. 7⁵⁄₁₆″ x 4¹⁵⁄₁₆″.

⟨1⟩-23⁸.

T cloth: blue. Printed silhouette pasted to front cover.

Symbol (1) below text, p. ⟨356⟩.

Deposited Aug. 30, 1916. Noted for *today* PW Sept. 2, 1916. Y copy inscribed by early owner Sept. 10, 1916. Listed PW Sept. 16, 1916. The earliest London edition (Hodder & Stoughton) noted listed PC March 6, 1926.

AAS H Y

9345. The Chicago Anthology A Collection of Verse from the Work of Chicago Poets Selected and Arranged by Charles G. Blanden and Minna Mathison …

Chicago The Roadside Press 1916

"A Song for a Man," pp. 29-31.

Deposited Feb. 21, 1917.

H NYPL

9346. THE FIREFLY'S LIGHT

⟨New York, 1916⟩

⟨i-x⟩, One - Twenty-three; blank leaf. Paper watermarked *Old Stratford.* 5 plates inserted. 7⁹⁄₁₆″ x 4⁵⁄₁₆″.

⟨1-3⁴, 4⁶⟩.

Blue B cloth sides, leather shelfback. End papers of book stock. Top edges gilded.

"Reprinted, by Permission, from the Saturday Evening Post The Trow Press New York"— p. ⟨viii⟩.

LC UMi Y

9347. THE MAN NEXT DOOR …

D. APPLETON AND COMPANY NEW YORK LONDON 1917

⟨i⟩-⟨x⟩, 1-⟨310⟩. Frontispiece and 3 plates inserted. 7⅜″ x 4⅞″.

⟨1-10¹⁶⟩.

T cloth: red.

Symbol (1) below text, p. ⟨310⟩.

Deposited Feb. 12, 1917. Listed PW Feb. 17, 1917; PC March 22, 1919.

AAS   Y

9348. THE BROKEN GATE . . .

D. APPLETON AND COMPANY   NEW YORK   LONDON   1917

⟨i-x⟩, 1-⟨349⟩. Frontispiece and 3 plates inserted. 7⅜" full x 4⅞".

⟨1-22⁸, 23⁴⟩.

T cloth: green.

Symbol (1) below text, p. ⟨349⟩.

Deposited Aug. 20, 1917. Listed PW Sept. 8, 1917. According to *The English Catalogue* issued in London, Dec. 1917.

AAS   H

9349. THE WAY OUT   A STORY OF THE CUMBERLANDS TO-DAY . . .

D. APPLETON AND COMPANY   NEW YORK   LONDON   1918

⟨i-x⟩, ⟨1⟩-⟨313⟩. Frontispiece and 3 plates inserted. 7⅜" x 4¹⁵⁄₁₆".

⟨1-20⁸, 21²⟩.

T cloth: green.

Symbol (1) below text, p. ⟨313⟩.

Advertised for May 24, 1918, PW May 4, 1918. Listed PW June 1, 1918. Deposited June 3, 1918.

AAS   Y

9350. THE PASSING OF THE FRONTIER   A CHRONICLE OF THE OLD WEST . . .

NEW HAVEN: YALE UNIVERSITY PRESS   TORONTO: GLASGOW, BROOK & CO.   LONDON: HUMPHREY MILFORD   OXFORD UNIVERSITY PRESS   1918

Title-page in black and blue.

⟨i-ii⟩, ⟨i⟩-x, 1-181, blank leaf. 8¹⁄₁₆" x 5¹⁄₁₆". Wove paper watermarked with the Yale device and *The Chronicles of America*. Frontispiece and 7 plates, each with printed protective tissue, inserted. Also inserted: 1 folded map.

⟨-⟩⁶, ⟨1⟩-11⁸, ⟨12⟩⁴.

V cloth: blue. Top edges gilded.

First issued as Vol. 26, *The Chronicles of America, Abraham Lincoln Edition*. Reissued 1921 in the *Extra Illustrated Edition;* 1922 in the *Roosevelt Edition;* 1922 in the *Textbook Edition;* 1924 in the *Benjamin Franklin Edition*. Reissued ⟨1918; i.e., 1924⟩ as *The Last Frontier*.

Deposited Aug. 23, 1918.

Y

9351. YOUNG ALASKANS IN THE FAR NORTH . . .

HARPER & BROTHERS PUBLISHERS   NEW YORK AND LONDON   ⟨1918⟩

⟨i-x⟩, 1-⟨251⟩; blank, p. ⟨252⟩; advertisement, p. ⟨253⟩; blank, p. ⟨254⟩. Frontispiece and 3 plates inserted. 7¼" x 4¹⁵⁄₁₆".

⟨1⟩-16⁸, 17⁴.

V cloth: green.

On copyright page: *Published September, 1918;* and, code letters G-S (signifying *printed July, 1918*). Deposited Aug. 27, 1918. Listed PW Sept. 7, 1918.

AAS   Y

9352. THE INDEFINITE AMERICAN ATTITUDE TOWARD THE WAR AND WHEN SHALL IT CHANGE? . . .

PUBLISHED BY AMERICAN DEFENSE SOCIETY, INC. NATIONAL HEADQUARTERS 44 EAST 23rd STREET, NEW YORK ⟨1918⟩

Cover-title.

⟨1-11⟩; list, p. ⟨12⟩. 9¼" x 3¾".

⟨-⟩⁶.

Printed self-wrapper.

Note: Two printings noted; the order of presentation is arbitrary. The nature of the text considered it is possible that more than two printings were issued.

A (B?)

The statement *No. 18* not present on p. ⟨1⟩.

On p. ⟨12⟩ five executive officers listed.

B (A?)

The statement *No. 18* at foot of p. ⟨1⟩.

On p. ⟨12⟩ four executive officers listed.

NYPL (B)   Y (A)

9352A. . . . WHAT THE WAR MEANS TO US (CONTRIBUTED BY EMERSON HOUGH TO THE NATIONAL SECURITY LEAGUE'S CAMPAIGN OF PATRIOTISM THROUGH EDUCATION.) . . .

⟨New York: The National Security League, n.d., ca. 1918.⟩

Single leaf. Printed on recto only. 11¹⁵⁄₁₆" x 6¹⁄₁₆".

At head of title: FROM THE NATIONAL SECURITY LEAGUE 19 WEST 44TH STREET, NEW YORK . . .

HM

The Last Frontier . . .

New Haven . . . ⟨1918; *i.e.,* 1924⟩

Reprint of entry No. 9350. See under 1924.

9353. THE SAGEBRUSHER A STORY OF THE WEST . . .

D. APPLETON AND COMPANY NEW YORK LONDON 1919

⟨i⟩-⟨viii⟩, 1-⟨319⟩. Frontispiece and 3 plates inserted. 7⅜″ scant x 4¹⁵⁄₁₆″.

⟨1-18⁸, 19⁴, 20-21⁸⟩.

T cloth: green.

Symbol (1) below text, p. ⟨319⟩.

Deposited April 2, 1919. Listed PW April 12, 1919; Bkr Jan. 1920.

AAS H

9354. . . . THE WEB . . .

THE REILLY & LEE CO. CHICAGO ⟨1919⟩

At head of title: THE AUTHORIZED HISTORY OF THE AMERICAN PROTECTIVE LEAGUE

⟨1⟩-511. 7¹¹⁄₁₆″ full x 5¼″. Folded chart inserted.

⟨1-32⁸⟩.

V cloth: tan. Inserted in some copies is a numbered certificate: *Special Member's Edition* . . .

Listed PW May 24, 1919. BA copy received June 10, 1919. Deposited Aug. 7, 1919.

BA H Y

9355. Yellowstone National Park Wyoming Montana Idaho

United States Railroad Administration National Park Series ⟨1919⟩

Cover-title. Printed paper wrapper.

"An Appreciation of Yellowstone National Park," pp. 3-4.

BPL

9356. . . . The Cowboy . . .

New York America of the Americans Society Publishers ⟨1897; *i.e.,* ca. 1920⟩

At head of title: Argonaut Edition . . .

2 Vols. Leather.

Reprint of *The Story of the Cowboy,* 1897.

A subscription book and as such probably issued in a variety of bindings and with varying imprints. The copy examined has a certificate of issue stating that the *Argonaut Edition* "is limited to seventy numbered copies . . ."

Y

9357. MAW'S VACATION THE STORY OF A HUMAN BEING IN THE YELLOWSTONE . . .

SAINT PAUL J. E. HAYNES, PUBLISHER 1921

⟨i-ii⟩, ⟨1⟩-61; *Standard Books on the Yellowstone,* p. ⟨62⟩. Frontispiece and 3 plates inserted. 7¾″ x 5³⁄₁₆″.

⟨1-4⁸⟩.

Printed cream paper wrapper. Flyleaves.

Deposited May 24, 1921. Listed PW Sept. 24, 1921.

AAS LC NYPL

9358. My Maiden Effort Being the Personal Confessions of Well-Known American Authors as to Their Literary Beginnings with an Introduction by Gelett Burgess

Published for the Authors' League of America by Doubleday, Page & Company Garden City, N. Y., and Toronto 1921

Contribution, pp. 107-110.

On copyright page: *First Edition* Advertised for Oct. 28, 1921, PW Sept. 24, 1921. Deposited Nov. 17, 1921.

H NYPL

9359. THE COVERED WAGON . . .

D. APPLETON AND COMPANY NEW YORK LONDON MCMXXII

⟨i-viii⟩, 1-⟨379⟩. Frontispiece inserted. 7⅜″ x 5″.

⟨1-23⁸, 24¹⁰⟩.

T cloth: red. White paper end papers; front end paper printed in black with a map of the United States showing the route west.

Note: In all examined copies, including the surviving copyright deposit copy, the table of contents (leaf ⟨1⟩3) is a cancel. *Regarding this the publishers state "when originally printing after coming off press we discovered there were two transposed lines in the Contents. We immediately had cancels printed for the entire edition and tipped in before any copies were sent out."*—Johnson.

Symbol (1) below text, p. ⟨379⟩.

Deposited May 29, 1922. Listed PW June 10, 1922; Bkr July, 1922.

LC NYPL

9360. THE YOUNG ALASKANS ON THE MISSOURI ...

HARPER & BROTHERS PUBLISHERS NEW YORK AND LONDON ⟨1922⟩

⟨i-vi⟩, 1-⟨378⟩. Frontispiece and 3 plates inserted. 7⅜″ x 4¹⁵⁄₁₆″.

⟨1⟩-24⁸.

V cloth: buff.

On copyright page: *First Edition*; and, code letters I-W (signifying *printed Sept. 1922*). Deposited Nov. 11, 1922. Listed PW Nov. 18, 1922.

LC NYPL

9361. A GOOD BOOK—BROTHERS A REVIEW BY EMERSON HOUGH IN "THE STEP LADDER," ...

⟨Indianapolis: The Bobbs-Merrill Company, n.d., 1922⟩

Caption-title. The above at head of p. ⟨1⟩.

Single cut sheet folded to make four pages. Leaf: 4¾″ x 3⅜″.

A review of *Vandemark's Folly*, by Herbert Quick, which was listed in PW Feb. 18, 1922. The review appeared in *The Step Ladder*, Chicago, May, 1922.

NYPL

9362. NORTH OF 36 ...

D. APPLETON AND COMPANY NEW YORK 1923 LONDON

⟨i⟩-⟨x⟩, 1-429; blank, p. ⟨430⟩; advertisements, pp. ⟨431-437⟩. Frontispiece and 3 plates inserted. 7⅜″ scant x 5″.

⟨1-28⁸⟩.

B cloth: green.

The symbol (1) below text, p. 429.

Deposited July 6, 1923. Listed PW July 21, 1923; Bkr Oct. 1923.

AAS NYPL Y

9363. MOTHER OF GOLD ...

D. APPLETON AND COMPANY NEW YORK 1924 LONDON

⟨i-vi⟩, 1-⟨327⟩; blank, p. ⟨328⟩; advertisements, pp. ⟨329-330⟩. Frontispiece inserted. 7⅜″ x 5″.

⟨1-21⁸⟩.

T cloth: orange.

Deposited Feb. 12, 1924. Listed PW Feb. 23, 1924; TLS April 10, 1924; PC April 12, 1924.

H NYPL

9364. The Last Frontier Part 1: The Forty-Niners by Stewart Edward White Part 2: The Passing of the Frontier by Emerson Hough

New Haven: Yale University Press Toronto: Glasgow, Brook & Co. London: Humphrey Milford Oxford University Press ⟨1918; *i.e.*, 1924⟩

Vol. 16, *The Chronicles of America, Benjamin Franklin Edition.*

Reprint. See *The Passing of the Frontier*, 1918.

NYPL

9365. THE SHIP OF SOULS ...

D. APPLETON AND COMPANY NEW YORK 1925 LONDON

⟨i⟩-⟨viii⟩, 1-⟨292⟩; blank, p. ⟨293⟩; advertisements, pp. ⟨294-296⟩. Frontispiece inserted. 7⅜″ x 5″.

⟨1-19⁸⟩.

T cloth: red.

Symbol (1) below text, p. ⟨292⟩.

Deposited Feb. 24, 1925. Listed PW March 7, 1925; PC April 4, 1925.

AAS LC

9366. The Frontier Omnibus ... Three Complete Novels by Emerson Hough ...

New York Grosset & Dunlap Publishers ⟨1903; 1907; *i.e.*, 1936⟩

Reprint.

LC Y

REFERENCES AND ANA

Note

The printed materials referred to in the following extracts have not been located.

"... every cross-lode gives an excellent occasion for a lawsuit—as the history of Mr. Heinze and the Amalgamated Copper Company can well testify.

"One enterprising citizen located across us in this fashion to the effect that the said citizen, all the counsel for our company, the deputy mineral surveyor, and others came near having an insurrection in comparison to which the Mexican revolution would have seemed mild. There was no shooting of consequence, however. The other fellow hired the only other lawyer … in town … and we went to the Supreme Court ⟨of New Mexico⟩ with our case. I sent a copy of our printed brief, with my name *Of Counsel,* on the cover, to my father back home …"—*Getting a Wrong Start,* 1915, pp. 52-53.

"… my young artist friend and I organized ourselves into the Blank and Blank Engraving Company, and we set out to illustrate Kansas towns in such boom fashion as had never been seen before.

"… We would go to the owner of the leading daily in our selected town … and … tell him that we proposed to furnish him … with a large, illustrated supplement showing his city … This … would mean a large sale for the paper …" *Ibid.,* pp. 106-108.

Madre d'Oro; a Four-Act Spectacular Drama, Illustrating Aztec Life and Tradition at the Time of the Spanish Conquest By E. Hough.

Published at 175 Monroe St., Chicago, Ill., by E. Hough, Author and Owner. ⟨n.d., 1889⟩

Title-page (printed), with typescript of play. Prepared for copyright purposes only. Deposited April 18, 1889. Copy in LC. Not to be confused with Hough's novel, *Mother of Gold,* 1924.

The Men Who Make Our Novels by George Gordon

New York Moffat, Yard & Company 1919

Emerson Hough His Place in American Letters A Tribute by Lee Alexander Stone …

⟨Chicago⟩ 1925

Paper wrapper, printed paper label on front.

RICHARD HOVEY

1 8 6 4 – 1 9 0 0

9367. POEMS . . .

WASHINGTON: N. B. SMITH, PRINTER, 615 7TH STREET, N.W., 1880.

⟨1⟩-59. 7″ full x 4⅞″ (paper wrapper); 8⅞″ x 5¾″ (cloth).

⟨1-5⁶⟩.

Printed mottled blue-gray paper wrapper. S cloth: green, bevelled covers, brown-coated on white endpapers, flyleaves.

BPL   H

9368. The American College Song Book. A Collection of the Songs of Fifty Representative American Colleges.

Chicago: Published by Orville Brewer & Co. Copyright. 1882, by Orville Brewer & Co.

"Dartmouth Hall," p. 72.

H

9369. HANOVER BY GASLIGHT OR WAYS THAT ARE DARK BEING AN EXPOSÉ OF THE SOPHOMORIC CAREER OF '85 . . .

IMPRINTED FOR THE CLASS OF '85 ⟨n.p., Hanover, N. H., n.d., 1883(?)⟩

⟨1⟩-44; blank, pp. ⟨45-46⟩; *History of Sophomore Year, C.S.D. '85 by Maurice L. Clark*, pp. ⟨1⟩-13. Laid paper. 9¼″ x 5¾″.

⟨1⟩-7⁴, 8².

Printed terra-cotta laid paper wrapper.

B   H

9370. Dartmouth Lyrics A Collection of Poems from the Undergraduate Publications of Dartmouth College Edited by Ozora Stearns Davis . . . and William Drummond Baker . . .

Cambridge   Printed at the Riverside Press 1888

*"Squab Flights," pp. 3-4.
*"Wedded," p. 57.

*"At the Club," p. 74.
*"Vita Nuova," p. 78.
†"Kronos," p. 80.

*Collected in *Dartmouth Lyrics,* 1924.
†Collected in *To the End of the Trail,* 1908.

H

9371. THE LAUREL; AN ODE. TO MARY DAY LANIER . . .

PUBLISHED BY THE AUTHOR, AT WASHINGTON, A.D. MDCCCLXXXIX.

18 leaves printed on rectos only (save for the title-leaf which carries an 1889 copyright notice on the verso) paged: ⟨1⟩-⟨17⟩, blank leaf. 7⁷⁄₁₆″ x 5³⁄₁₆″. Paper watermarked with a helmet device and: *Jos. Eichbaum and Co. Pittsburgh.*

Printed blue-white paper wrapper, grained in imitation of leather.

Deposited Jan. 3, 1890.

B   H   LC   Y

9372. HARMONICS.

⟨n.p., n.d., probably Washington, D. C., *ca.* 1890⟩

Title-page printed in silver, gold and pink.

Anonymous. The only located copy is inscribed: *Compliments of the writer, Richard Hovey.*

⟨1-8⟩.

⟨-⟩⁴. The leaves, respectively, measure 5¼″ x 3¾″; 5⁵⁄₁₆″ x 3¹³⁄₁₆″; 5⁵⁄₁₆″ x 4¾″ scant; 5⁵⁄₁₆″ x 4¾″ scant.

Unprinted yellow-green wrapper of felt-like paper, deckled, tied with white silk cord.

A *fin de siècle* production made up as follows: Leaves ⟨-⟩₁,₄, white wove paper embossed with a leather-like grain; leaves ⟨-⟩₂-₃, stiff white bristol. Text on pp. ⟨3, 5⟩. Tailpiece, p. ⟨8⟩, in silver, gold and pink.

CWB

HANOVER BY GASLIGHT

OR

Ways That Are Dark

BEING

AN EXPOSÉ OF THE SOPHOMORIC CAREER OF '85

BY

RICHARD HOVEY

"If there's a hole in a' your coats,
I rede you tent it :
A chield 's amang you takin notes
And faith he'll prent it."

IMPRINTED FOR
THE CLASS OF '85

9373. Younger American Poets 1830–1890 Edited by Douglas Sladen . . .

Griffith, Farran, Okeden & Welsh Newbery House, Charing Cross Road London and Sydney 1891

"Beethoven's Third Symphony," p. 356. Collected in *Along the Trail,* 1898.

For comment see entry No. 6557.

9374. Younger American Poets 1830–1890 Edited by Douglas Sladen . . .

The Cassell Publishing Company New York 1891

"Beethoven's Third Symphony," p. 356. Collected in *Along the Trail,* 1898.

For comment see entry No. 6558.

9375. LAUNCELOT AND GUENEVERE A POEM IN DRAMAS . . .

NEW YORK UNITED STATES BOOK COMPANY SUC-CESSORS TO JOHN W. LOVELL COMPANY 142 TO 150 WORTH STREET ⟨1891⟩

⟨1⟩-263. Laid paper. 7⅜″ x 4¹⁵⁄₁₆″.

⟨1⟩-16⁸, 17⁴.

V cloth: maroon. Top edges gilded.

NYPL copy presented by Hovey to Richard Watson Gilder, Oct. 28, 1891. Listed PW Dec. 12, 1891. Deposited Dec. 26, 1891. Reviewed Ath July 9, 1892. See *The Marriage of Guenevere,* 1895, below.

H NYPL

9376. SEAWARD AN ELEGY ON THE DEATH OF THOMAS WILLIAM PAR-SONS . . .

BOSTON D. LOTHROP COMPANY 1893

Title-page in black and orange.

⟨1-56⟩. Frontispiece portrait of Parsons inserted. Laid paper. 8⅛″ x 5⅞″.

⟨1-7⁴⟩.

V cloth: gray; green. White laid paper end papers. Top edges gilt.

Originally in *The Independent,* New York, Nov. 17, 1892. Noted for *early publication* PW Jan. 21, 1893. Deposited May 3, 1893. Listed PW May 6, 1893. Reviewed Ath March 3, 1894.

BA H NYPL

9377. Dartmouth Sketches. By Students of Dartmouth College. Second Edition, Revised and Enlarged. ⟨Edited by⟩ G. C. Selden . . . A. G. Bugbee . . .

Concord, N. H.: Republican Press Association. 1893.

Cloth, leather label on spine.

"The Genius of Tobacco," pp. ⟨12⟩-15.

H copy received June 10, 1893.

H

9378. . . . Oration and Poem at the Sixtieth Annual Convention of the Fraternity, with the Zeta Chapter, Dartmouth College, Hanover, N. H., May 17, 18 and 19, 1893.

Rochester, N. H.: Lougee & McDuffee, the Courier Press. 1893.

At head of title: Psi Upsilon Fraternity. Zeta Chapter.

Printed paper wrapper.

"Comrades," pp. ⟨14⟩-21. A truncated version collected in *Songs from Vagabondia,* 1894.

BPL copy presented by Hovey Nov. 29, 1893.

BPL

9379. Dartmouth Lyrics . . . New Edition ⟨Edited by⟩ Bertrand A. Smalley . . .

Hanover, N. H. Published by Charles C. Merrill . . . and Bertrand A. Smalley . . . 1893

Reprint save for:

" 'Sub Jove Frigido'," p. 24.

"Winter Beauty," p. 61. Collected in *Dartmouth Lyrics,* 1924.

"Song," *There's a song in my soul that is growing,* pp. 73-74.

"On the Hill," pp. 105-106. Collected in *Dartmouth Lyrics,* 1924.

H

9379A. ⟨Lights and Shadows. A Composite Poem⟩

⟨n.p., n.d., 1894⟩

A poem written in collaboration with Thomas Wentworth Higginson, Julia Ward Howe, Louise Imogen Guiney, and others.

For comment see entry No. 8405.

9380. SONGS FROM VAGABONDIA ⟨by⟩ BLISS CARMAN ⟨and⟩ RICHARD HOVEY ...

BOSTON COPELAND AND DAY LONDON ELKIN MATHEWS AND JOHN LANE M DCCC XCIV

For comment see entry No. 2622.

9381. The Plays of Maurice Maeterlinck Princess Maleine The Intruder The Blind The Seven Princesses Translated by Richard Hovey

Chicago Stone & Kimball MDCCCXCIV

⟨i-viii⟩, ⟨1⟩-369; blank, p. ⟨370⟩; colophon, p. ⟨371⟩. Laid paper watermarked *Stone & Kimball Chicago*. 6¾" x 4¼".

"This first edition on small paper is limited to six hundred copies ..."—p. ⟨v⟩. In spite of an implied large paper edition the small paper edition is the only format noted.

Printed Sept. 1894, according to the colophon. Deposited Dec. 10, 1894. Listed PW Feb. 23, 1895. Reissued, 1906, by Duffield & Co., N. Y.

AAS H

9382. The Marriage of Guenevere A Tragedy ...

Chicago Stone & Kimball MDCCCXCV

A somewhat revised version of the text as published in *Launcelot and Guenevere* ⟨1891⟩, and printed from the altered plates of that edition.

Deposited Sept. 5, 1895. Reprinted and reissued by Small, Maynard & Co., Boston, 1899; deposited Feb. 1, 1899.

AAS H Y

9383. Echoes from Dartmouth ... Edited by H. J. Hapgood ... and Craven Laycock ...

Hanover, N. H. MDCCCXCV.

Reprint save for:

"Men of Dartmouth," pp. ⟨11⟩-12. Collected in *Along the Trail,* 1898.

H

9384. The Plays of Maurice Maeterlinck Second Series Alladine and Palomides Pélléas and Mélisande Home The Death of Tintagiles Translated by Richard Hovey

Chicago Stone & Kimball MDCCCXCVI

⟨i⟩-⟨xvi⟩, ⟨1⟩-235; blank, p. ⟨236⟩; colophon, p. ⟨237⟩; blank leaf. Laid paper watermarked *Stone & Kimball Chicago.* 6¾" x 4¼".

Printed March, 1896, according to the colophon. Advertised as *now ready* in *The Chap-Book,* March 15, 1896. Deposited June 17, 1896. Noted as *just ready* PW July 14, 1896. Reissued, 1906, by Duffield & Co., N. Y.

AAS

9385. MORE SONGS FROM VAGABONDIA ⟨by⟩ BLISS CARMAN ⟨and⟩ RICHARD HOVEY ...

BOSTON COPELAND AND DAY LONDON ELKIN MATHEWS M DCCC XCVI

For comment see entry No. 2634.

9386. The Quest of Merlin ...

Boston Small Maynard and Company MDCCCXCVIII

Paper boards, vellum shelfback.

A somewhat revised version of the text as published in *Launcelot and Guenevere* ⟨1891⟩, and printed from the altered plates of that edition.

Deposited June 11, 1898. Listed PW Dec. 3, 1898. NYPL copy received Dec. 20, 1898.

BA BPL H NYPL Y

9387. THE BIRTH OF GALAHAD ...

BOSTON SMALL MAYNARD AND COMPANY MDCCCXCVIII

⟨i-vi⟩, ⟨1⟩-124. With the exception of pp. ⟨v-vi⟩, which are printed on wove paper, the book is printed on laid paper. *See under binding for size of leaf.*

⟨a⟩², ⟨b⟩¹, ⟨1⟩-7⁸, 8⁶.

Two bindings noted. The sequence presented is probable.

A

Sides: Rough-toothed gray-tan paper boards.

Edges: Plain; or, stained light brown.

The three preliminary leaves comprising ⟨a⟩ and ⟨b⟩ are sidestitched.

Leaf: 6¾" x 4⅜".

B

Sides: Smooth tan paper boards.

Edges: Stained light brown.

The three preliminary leaves comprising ⟨a⟩ and ⟨b⟩ are not sidestitched.

Leaf: 6¾" scant x 4¼".

Noted under *new and forthcoming* PW March 12, 1898. Three ⟨sic⟩ copies (Binding A) deposited June 13 and 14, 1898. BPL copy (Binding

A) received June 25, 1898. Listed PW Dec. 3, 1898. BA copy (Binding A) received Dec. 13, 1898. H copy (Binding B) received May 11, 1900.

B (A) BA (A) BPL (A) H (B) LC (A, being deposit copies) NYPL (A, B)

9388. ... A Stein Song ...

Boston Oliver Ditson Company New York ... Philadelphia ... Chicago ... ‹1898›

Sheet music. Cover-title. Plate number: 4-31-61037-4. A reprint noted has plate number: 4-31-61825-4.

At head of title: Songs by Frederic Field Bullard ...

Deposited June 16, 1898.

Reprinted from *More Songs from Vagabondia*, 1896.

LC

9389. ALONG THE TRAIL A BOOK OF LYRICS ...

BOSTON SMALL, MAYNARD AND COMPANY 1898

Title-page in black and brown.

‹i-ii›, ‹i›-x, ‹1›-115. Laid paper. 6¾″ full x 4⁵⁄₁₆″.

‹a›², ‹b›⁴, ‹1›-7⁸, 8².

T cloth: brown. White laid paper end papers.

Deposited Dec. 12, 1898. BA copy received Dec. 13, 1898. Listed PW Feb. 4, 1899.

AAS BA

9390. Dartmouth Songs A New Collection of College Songs Compiled by Edwin Osgood Grover ... and Musically Edited by Addison Fletcher Andrews ...

Published by Grover and Graham Hanover, New Hampshire 1898

Printed paper wrapper.

Reprint save for the following poems (*but note queries*):

"Our Liege Lady, Dartmouth," pp. 19-21. Also in (reprinted from?) *Along the Trail*, 1898.

"Here's a Health to Thee, Roberts!," pp. 46-51. Collected in *Dartmouth Lyrics*, 1924.

"Eleazar Wheelock," pp. 76-78. Collected in *Dartmouth Lyrics*, 1924.

"My Love's Waitin'," pp. 98-100. Collected in *Dartmouth Lyrics*, 1924.

"Hanover Winter Song," pp. 101-107. Also in (reprinted from?) *Along the Trail*, 1898.

Date of publication not known.

JN

9391. TALIESIN A MASQUE ...

BOSTON SMALL MAYNARD AND COMPANY MDCCCC

‹i-iv›, 1-58, 2 blank leaves. 6¾″ x 4¼″.

‹1⁵, 2-8⁴›. Leaf ‹1›₂ inserted. *Signed:* ‹1›¹⁰, ‹2›⁸, 3⁸, 4⁷.

Brown paper boards sides, white vellum shelf-back. End papers of white wove paper; and, white laid paper. Edges stained brown.

Two printings noted:

1

As above.

P. ‹ii›: Seven titles listed in the advertisement.

Date *1900* in publisher's spine imprint.

2

‹i-x›, 1-58; advertisements, pp. ‹59-67›; blank, p. ‹68›; 2 blank leaves.

‹1⁴, 2¹, 3-11⁴›. *Signed:* ‹-›⁵, ‹1-2›, 3-4⁸, ‹5›⁴. Leaves ‹1›₁ and ‹11›₄ used as pastedowns.

P. ‹viii›: Eight titles listed in the advertisement.

Date *1898* ‹sic› in publisher's spine imprint.

Advertised PW Sept. 30, 1899. Deposited Dec. 19, 1899. BA copy (first printing) received Dec. 27, 1899. Listed PW Feb. 10, 1900.

AAS (2nd) BA (1st) H (1st) LC (1st; being a deposit copy) NYPL (1st) Y (1st)

9392. LAST SONGS FROM VAGABONDIA ‹by› BLISS CARMAN ‹and› RICHARD HOVEY ...

BOSTON SMALL, MAYNARD AND COMPANY M DCCCC I

For comment see entry No. 2646.

9393. Songs of the Hill Winds ... Compiled and Edited by Kendall Banning and Moses Bradstreet Perkins

New York: Arranged and Printed for the Editors at the Cheltenham Press MCMI

500 numbered copies only.

Reprint save for:

"English Violets," pp. 5-6.

"Bohemia," pp. 43-45. Collected in *Dartmouth Lyrics*, 1924.

"Winter," pp. 49-50.

NYPL

9394. ... Summer Wind. From Richard Hovey's Launcelot and Guenevere. ⟨Music by⟩ Edward MacDowell ...

.... 1902 ... Arthur P. Schmidt, Boston & New York.

Sheet music. The above on p. 1. At head of title: Octavo Series (Women's Voices) No. 372. Price 10 Cents.

Plate number 5936-2.

NYPL

9395. THE HOLY GRAAL AND OTHER FRAGMENTS ... BEING THE UNCOMPLETED PARTS OF THE ARTHURIAN DRAMAS EDITED WITH INTRODUCTION AND NOTES BY MRS. RICHARD HOVEY AND A PREFACE BY BLISS CARMAN

NEW YORK DUFFIELD & COMPANY 1907

⟨1⟩-128; plus: 4 pp. advertisements. Laid paper. 6¹¹⁄₁₆" scant x 4⅛".

⟨1-8⁸, plus: 9²⟩.

S cloth: green.

On copyright page: *Published September, 1907* Deposited Oct. 3, 1907. Listed PW Oct. 19, 1907.

H NYPL

9396. Hunting Song "Tarantara" ... Words by Bliss Carman ⟨*sic*⟩ Music by Albert Nordheimer ...

The Nordheimer Piano & Music Co., Limited Toronto Montreal Hamilton London ... MCMVIII ...

Sheet music. Cover-title.

Note: Although the text is credited to Bliss Carman the author was Richard Hovey. It was first collected in *More Songs from Vagabondia*, 1896. Later incorporated in Hovey's *The Holy Graal*, 1907, pp. 97-98, edited by Mrs. Richard Hovey and Bliss Carman.

Deposited Jan. 18, 1908.

LC

9397. TO THE END OF THE TRAIL ... EDITED WITH NOTES BY MRS. RICHARD HOVEY

NEW YORK DUFFIELD & COMPANY 1908

⟨i-ii⟩, ⟨i⟩-⟨x⟩, ⟨1⟩-148; 4 pp. advertisements. Frontispiece portrait inserted. Laid paper. 6⅝" x 4¹⁄₁₆".

⟨1¹⁰, 2-10⁸⟩.

S cloth: green.

Advertised for *this month* PW Jan. 11, 1908; for Feb. 29, 1908, in PW Feb. 13, 1908. Deposited April 13, 1908. BA copy received April 14, 1908. Listed PW May 9, 1908.

H NYPL

9398. The Intruder The Blind The Seven Princesses The Death of Tintagiles by Maurice Maeterlinck Translated by Richard Hovey

New York Dodd, Mead and Company 1916

Reprinted from *The Plays of Maurice Maeterlinck ...* , 1894, 1896.

NYPL

9399. Barney McGee ...

San Francisco John Henry Nash 1917

Printed paper boards, paper vellum shelfback. 250 copies only.

Reprinted from *More Songs from Vagabondia*, 1896.

Y

9400. The Sea Gypsy ...

⟨New York: The Unbound Anthology. Published by the Poets' Guild, n.d., *ca.* 1922⟩

Single leaf. Printed on one side only.

Reprinted from *More Songs from Vagabondia*, 1896.

NYPL

9401. DARTMOUTH LYRICS BY RICHARD HOVEY EDITED BY EDWIN OSGOOD GROVER

BOSTON SMALL, MAYNARD & COMPANY PUBLISHERS ⟨1924⟩

⟨i⟩-xiv, ⟨1⟩-94. Laid paper. 7⅜" x 4¹⁵⁄₁₆".

⟨1-4⁸, 5⁶, 6-7⁸⟩.

T cloth: green. Top edges stained green.

Contains many poems here first collected.

Deposited April 4, 1924. Listed PW April 5, 1924.

AAS BPL

9402. . . . The Sea Gypsy ⟨Music by⟩ Geoffrey O'Hara . . .

Chappell-Harms, Inc. 62 W. 45th Street New York . . . ⟨1933⟩

Sheet music. Cover-title. At head of title: . . . Chappell's Vocal Library of Part Songs Arranged for Male Voices . . . Plate number C.-H. 8254-7.

Reprinted from *More Songs from Vagabondia*, 1896.

Deposited Feb. 3, 1933.

LC

9403. A POEM & THREE LETTERS . . .

BAKER LIBRARY PRESS ⟨Hanover, N. H.⟩ 1935

⟨1-12; blank, p. 13; colophon, p. 14⟩, blank leaf. Laid paper watermarked: *Worthy*. 8¹⁄₁₆" x 5¼".

⟨-⟩⁸.

Printed green laid paper wrapper.

". . . none of this material has heretofore appeared in print . . ."—p. ⟨3⟩.

125 numbered copies only.

Printed June 17, 1935, according to the colophon. Deposited July 3, 1935.

AAS   NYPL

9404. Songs from Vagabondia and More Songs from Vagabondia by Bliss Carman and Richard Hovey

Dodd, Mead & Company New York MCMXXXV

Reprint.

Cloth, printed paper labels.

B

9405. Dartmouth Lyrics by Richard Hovey Introduction by Francis Lane Childs

Dartmouth College Publications Hanover New Hampshire 1938

Reprint.

Deposited Aug. 6, 1938.

B   LC

9406. The Spirit of Dartmouth . . .

Christmas 1941

Printed paper wrapper.

Previously in *A Poem & Three Letters*, 1935.

"This is a copy of a very limited edition . . .

privately printed for Mr. Basil O'Connor . . . December, 1941."—Certificate of issue.

B

REPRINTS

The following publications contain material by Hovey reprinted from earlier books.

Cap and Gown Second Series Selected by Frederic Lawrence Knowles

Boston L. C. Page and Company . . . MDCCCXCVII

Dartmouth Musical Clubs Season of 1900–1901 Program

⟨Hanover, N. H.: Dartmouth Press, 1900⟩

Printed paper wrapper.

Papyrus Club Thirtieth Anniversary Dinner Held at the Revere House February Fourteenth Mcmiii

⟨n.p., n.d., Boston, 1903⟩

Printed wrapper.

Tech Songs The M.I.T. Kommers Book Edited by Frederic Field Bullard . . .

Boston Oliver Ditson Company New York Chicago Philadelphia . . . ⟨1903⟩

A Book of American Humorous Verse . . .

Chicago . . . 1904

For comment see BAL, Vol. 1, p. 411.

The Friendship of Art by Bliss Carman . . .

. . . Boston MCMIIII

For comment see entry No. 2665.

The Younger American Poets by Jessie B. Rittenhouse . . .

Boston Little, Brown, and Company 1904

Listed PW Nov. 12, 1904.

Our Girls Poems in Praise of the American Girl . . .

New York . . . 1907

For comment see entry No. 1945.

The Humbler Poets (Second Series) A Collection . . . by Wallace and Frances Rice

Chicago . . . 1911

For comment see BAL, Vol. 2, p. 505.

Chief Contemporary Dramatists ... Selected and Edited by Thomas H. Dickinson ...

Boston New York Chicago Houghton Mifflin Company The Riverside Press Cambridge ⟨1915⟩

Deposited March 6, 1915.

An American Woman's Plea for Germany by Helen Bartlett Bridgman Reprinted from the Standard Union, Brooklyn, N. Y.

The Fatherland New York 1915.

Printed paper wrapper.

The Soul of the City ... Compiled by Garland Greever and Joseph M. Bachelor

Boston ... 1923

For comment see BAL, Vol. 3, p. 288.

American Mystical Verse An Anthology Selected by Irene Hunter ...

D. Appleton and Company New York MCMXXV

Silver Linings Poems of Hope and Cheer Collected by Joseph Morris and St. Clair Adams ...

New York George Sully & Company ⟨1927⟩

REFERENCES

Press Notices of Songs from Vagabondia ... Seaward ... Plays of Maeterlinck ... Quest of Merlin . . . Marriage of Guenevere . . . Gandolfo.

⟨n.p., n.d., *ca.* 1895⟩

Cover-title. Printed paper wrapper.

"This play, *Gandolfo,* first called *Anselmo,* is the violent story of the moral breakdown of the once saintly Archbishop of Milan. ... ⟨Hovey⟩ put his faith in this play all his life, but it was dogged by bad luck. Though copyrighted at the end of 1892 and even printed in plates, it was never published because of the failure of the United States Book Company ..."—Macdonald, pp. 102-103. A titlepage for *Gandolfo* was deposited Sept. 28, 1892; no copyright record for text found.

Richard Hovey Man & Craftsman ⟨by⟩ Allan Houston Macdonald

⟨Durham, N. C.⟩ Duke University Press 1957

"A Bibliography of the First Editions of Books by Richard Hovey based on the Collection of Hovey's Works in the Dartmouth College Library," by Edward Connery Lathem, pp. ⟨229⟩-250.

Deposited Feb. 27, 1957.

JULIA WARD HOWE

1 8 1 9 – 1 9 1 0

9407. Lays of the Western World, Illuminated by T W Gwilt Mapleson Esq.

New York: Putnam ⟨n.d., 1848⟩

Unpaged. Contains Mrs. Howe's "Lees in the Cup of Life." Also in (reprinted from?) the next entry.

For comment see entry No. 1639.

9408. The Female Poets of America. By Rufus Wilmot Griswold . . .

Philadelphia: Carey and Hart, Chesnut Street. MDCCCXLIX.

Contains the following poems by Mrs. Howe, pp. 321-324:

"The Burial of Schlesinger"; "Wordsworth," collected in *At Sunset*, 1910; "Woman"; "To a Beautiful Statue"; "Waning"; "Lees from the Cup of Life," also in (reprinted from?) the preceding entry; "Speak, for Thy Servant Heareth"; "A Mother's Fears."

For comment see entry No. 6681.

9409. PASSION-FLOWERS.

BOSTON: TICKNOR, REED, AND FIELDS. MDCCCLIV.

Anonymous.

⟨i⟩-iv, ⟨1⟩-187. 7⅛″ x 4⁹⁄₁₆″.

⟨-⟩², 1-11⁸, 12⁴, 13².

Two bindings of undetermined sequence, if sequence there is, have been noted:

A

T cloth: brown; green; purple; purple-brown; red; tan. Sides stamped in blind with a border and, at center, an upright oval decoration about 2⅞″ tall. Yellow end papers. Flyleaves. Publisher's file copy thus. At back of some copies is an inserted catalog, the catalogs variously dated: Oct., Nov., and Dec. 1853.

B

T cloth: brown. Sides stamped in blind with a border and, at center, a filigree decoration about 3½″ tall. Yellow end papers. Flyleaves. At back of some copies is an inserted catalog, the catalogs variously dated: Oct., Nov., and Dec. 1853.

Copy presented by the author to H. W. Longfellow, binding A, Dec. 22, 1853; in H. Copy presented by the author to Charles Sumner, binding B, Dec. 23, 1853; in H. Published Dec. 24, 1853 (publisher's records). Noticed by LW Dec. 31, 1853. Deposited Feb. 21, 1854. Listed PC March 15, 1854.

BPL (A)   H (A, B)   NYSL (A)

9410. A Memorial of the Life and Character of John W. Francis, Jr. . . .

New-York. 1855.

Edited anonymously by H. T. Tuckerman.

"Traces of the Departed," pp. 83-84.

H   NYPL

9411. WORDS FOR THE HOUR. BY THE AUTHOR OF "PASSION-FLOWERS."

BOSTON: TICKNOR AND FIELDS. M DCCC LVII.

⟨i⟩-iv, ⟨5⟩-165; blank, p. ⟨166⟩; advertisement, p. ⟨167⟩. 7⅛″ x 4½″.

⟨1⟩-10⁸, 11⁴.

A cloth: red. T cloth: brown. TZ cloth: black; blue; green; purple. Yellow end papers. Flyleaves. Catalog dated Jan. 1857, inserted in some copies.

Deposited Dec. 27, 1856. Copies were presented, Dec. 27, 1856, by Mrs. Howe to: Theodore Parker (in BPL); Longfellow (in H); Charles Sumner (in H). NYPL has two presentation copies inscribed by Mrs. Howe Jan. 1, 1856 ⟨i.e., error for 1857⟩. Listed PC Feb. 16, 1857.

H   NYPL   NYSL

9412. THE WORLD'S OWN.

Two editions noted. The sequence is not known and the following designations are for identification only. The texts vary and one appears to be a revision of the other but BAL has been un-able to determine which of the texts is the earlier.

Edition A

THE WORLD'S OWN . . .

BOSTON: TICKNOR AND FIELDS. M DCCC LVII.

⟨i⟩-⟨vi⟩, 7-141, blank leaf. 7⅛″ full x 4⁹⁄₁₆″ full.

⟨1⟩-9⁸.

A cloth: blue; green. T cloth: slate-purple. Yellow end papers. Flyleaves. Publisher's catalog dated April, 1857, inserted at back.

Deposited Feb. 27, 1857. Listed APC April 11, 1857. BA received April 13, 1857. Listed Ath June 6, 1857.

Edition B

. . . LEONORE; OR, THE WORLD'S OWN, A TRAGEDY, IN FIVE ACTS . . .

NEW YORK: BAKER & GODWIN, BOOK AND JOB PRINTERS, CORNER OF NASSAU AND SPRUCE STREETS. 1857.

At head of title: STUART'S REPERTORY OF ORIGINAL AMERICAN PLAYS. NO. 1.

⟨1⟩-63. 8⅞″ x 5¹³⁄₁₆″.

⟨1⟩-4⁸.

Printed paper wrapper; both white paper and pale buff papers noted.

BPL (A, B)   H (A, B)   NYPL (A, B)   NYSL (A)

9413. Gifts of Genius: A Miscellany of Prose and Poetry, by American Authors.

New York: Printed for C. A. Davenport. ⟨1859⟩

"The Bee's Song," pp. 160-162.

"Limitations of Benevolence," pp. 162-163.

For comment see entry No. 3717.

9414. A TRIP TO CUBA . . .

BOSTON: TICKNOR AND FIELDS. M DCCC LX.

⟨i-iv⟩, ⟨1⟩-iv, ⟨1⟩-251, 2 blank leaves. 7³⁄₁₆″ full x 4⅝″.

⟨-⟩⁴, 1-10¹², 11⁸.

BD cloth: blue-green; brown; purple-brown. TZ cloth: blue. Brown-coated end papers. Flyleaves. Inserted at back: Publisher's catalog, pp. ⟨1⟩-16, dated Feb. 1860.

Note: Unsold sheets were issued *ca.* 1868 with the spine imprint of Fields, Osgood & Co.

Deposited Feb. 11, 1860. NYPL copy inscribed by Duyckinck Feb. 11, 1860. BA copy received

Feb. 14, 1860. Listed BM March 1, 1860; PC March 15, 1860.

BA BPL H NYPL

9415. Memorial of the Commemoration by the Church of the Disciples, of the Fiftieth Birth-Day of Their Pastor, James Freeman Clarke, April 4, 1860 . . .

Boston: Prentiss & Deland, Printers. 1860.

Untitled poem, *A weight I bear, and a task I share,* pp. 14-15. Collected in *At Sunset,* 1910, as "For the Fiftieth Birthday of James Freeman Clarke April 4, 1860."

H

9416. "THE BATTLE HYMN OF THE RE-PUBLIC"

The following is a record of significant appearances noted by BAL. The sequence is tentative. It is highly probable that other printings occurred.

A

In: *The Atlantic Monthly,* Feb. 1862.

B

Praising God in Troublous Times. A Thanksgiving Discourse, Delivered in Lynnfield Centre and Stoneham, November 21, 1861. By William C. Whitcomb . . .

Salem, Mass.: Printed at the Office of the Gazette and Mercury. 1861. ⟨i.e., 1862⟩

Printed paper wrapper. Prefatory note dated *January, 1862.*

The hymn printed on the inner back wrapper.

Locations: BA

C

Army and Navy Melodies: A Collection of Hymns and Tunes, Religious and Patriotic . . . Selected. By Rev. J. W. Dadmun, and Rev. Arthur B. Fuller . . .

Boston: J. P. Magee, 5 Cornhil⟨sic⟩, Benj. B. Russell, 515 Washington Street. New York: E. Goodenough, 122 Nassau Street . . . 1862 . . .

Printed paper wrapper.

The hymn appears on p. 26.

Note: This 1862 publication is a revision of *Army Melodies* . . . , 1861 (Sept.), which does not contain Mrs. Howe's hymn.

Issued not before late January, 1862.

Locations: AAS

D

Battle Hymn of the Republic Adapted to the Favorite Melody of "Glory, Hallelujah," Written by Mrs. Dr. S. G. Howe, for the Atlantic Monthly ⟨figure 2½; signifying: 25¢; in a star-like frame⟩

Boston . . . Oliver Ditson & Co. 277 Washington St. . . . 1862 . . .

Sheet music. Cover-title. Plate No. 21454.

Note: Copies, presumably reprints, occur with the figure *3* in the star-like frame on the front cover.

Advertised in *Dwight's Journal of Music,* Boston, March 1, 1862, as though published and offered at *25¢.* Listed, *ibid.,* April 5, 12, 19, 26, 1862, as *new,* at *25¢.* Deposited April 9, 1862.

Locations: BA (both varieties)

E

The Battle-Cry of Freedom . . . Battle Hymn of the Republic . . .

Published by T. C. Boyd, Montgomery Street, Corner of Pine, San Francisco . . . Boyd's Circulating Library . . . T. C. Boyd, Designer and Engraver on Wood . . . ⟨n.d., *ca.* Sept. 1862⟩

Single leaf. Printed on recto only. 8¾″ x 5⅛″.

Date of issue based on copyright deposit date of the title-page of "The Battle-Cry of Freedom," Sept. 26, 1862.

Locations: B   H   HEH   NYPL

F

. . . Battle-Hymn of the Republic . . .

⟨n.p., Philadelphia⟩ Johnson, Printer and Publisher, 7 North Tenth St. ⟨n.d., *ca.* Sept. 1862⟩

Single cut sheet. Printed on recto only. 7⅞″ x 12⅞″.

The only located copies have the hymn as the central panel of a triptych, each panel bearing the imprint as given. Printed together with other songs: "The Battle-Cry of Freedom," "God Save the State!," "Initiation Ode," and "Red, White & Blue!". In addition to the songs are stage directions which suggest that the printing was used as a song sheet at a function unknown to BAL.

Date of issue based on copyright deposit date of the title-page of "The Battle-Cry of Freedom," Sept. 26, 1862.

Locations: B   LCP

G

Battle Hymn of the Republic . . .

Published by the Supervisory Committee for Recruiting Colored Regiments ⟨n.p., n.d., *ca.* 1863⟩

Single leaf. Printed on recto only. 9⁹⁄₁₆″ x 5⅞″.

Issued after June 8, 1863, on which date a preliminary meeting was held for the purpose of establishing the Supervisory Committee for Recruiting Colored Regiments.

Locations: Y

H

Battle Hymn of the Republic. Sung by Our Prisoners in Libby Prison on Hearing of the Brilliant Victory Gained after the Hard Fought Battle of Gettysburg . . .

Sold by A. Anderson, No. 420 South Tenth Street, Philadelphia . . . ⟨n.d., *ca.* 1863⟩

Single leaf. Printed on recto only. 8¼″ x 5⅛″.

Issued after July 3, 1863.

Locations: H

I

Collected in Mrs. Howe's *Later Lyrics,* 1866, *q.v.*

9417. Order of Exercises at the Unitarian Festival,

⟨Boston⟩ Music Hall, Tuesday, May 27, 1862 . . .

Single cut sheet folded to four pages. Title as above on p. ⟨1⟩.

"Original Hymn," *In this glad time of Spring,* p. ⟨2⟩.

H

9418. War-Songs for Freemen. Dedicated to the Army of the United States . . . ⟨Edited by Francis J. Child⟩

Boston: Ticknor and Fields. 1862 ⟨Jan. 1863⟩ . . .

"Harvard-Students' Song," pp. 14-15. *See next entry.*

For comment see entry No. 8818.

9419. . . . Harvard Student's Song . . . Adapted to a German Melody

Boston. Published by Oliver Ditson & Co. 277 Washington St. . . . 1863 . . .

Sheet music. Cover-title. At head of title: War Songs for Freemen   Plate number: 21986. Deposited Aug. 8, 1863. *See preceding entry.*

LC

9420. The Spirit of the Fair . . .

New York, April 5-9, 11-16, 18-23, 1864.

"Victory," No. 9, p. 101. Collected as "Left Behind," *Later Lyrics*, 1866.

For comment see entry No. 413.

9421. Autograph Leaves of Our Country's Authors. ⟨Compiled by John Pendleton Kennedy and Alexander Bliss⟩

Baltimore, Cushings & Bailey 1864.

"Our Orders," pp. 158-159. Collected in *Later Lyrics*, 1866.

For comment see entry No. 2418.

9422. The Boatswain's Whistle. Published at the National Sailors' Fair . . .

Boston, November 9-19, 1864.

Edited by Mrs. Howe. For fuller comment see entry No. 1416.

Contains the following material by Mrs. Howe:

"Salutatory," No. 1, p. 4.

Editorial, No. 2, p. 12.

Editorial, No. 3, p. 20. Relates to the Century Association Bryant festival and includes "A Leaf from the Bryant Chaplet"; see next entry.

Editorial, No. 4, p. 28.

"The Next Stage," No. 6, p. 44.

Editorial, No. 8, p. 60.

Editorial, No. 10, p. 76.

"Journal of a Fancy Fair," No. 2, p. 14; No. 3, p. ⟨17⟩; No. 4, p. 30; No. 5, p. 38; No. 6, p. 42; No. 7, pp. ⟨49⟩, 53.

9423. The Bryant Festival at "The Century," November 5, M.DCCC.LXIV.

New York: D. Appleton and Company, 443 & 445 Broadway. M.DCCC.LXV.

"A Leaf from the Bryant Chaplet," pp. 36-38. See preceding entry. Collected in *Later Lyrics*, 1866.

For comment see entry No. 1692.

9424. . . . Eighty-Ninth Anniversary of American Independence, July 4, 1865. Order of Exercises before the City Council of Boston, in the Music Hall . . .

J. E. Farwell and Company, City Printers, 37 Congress Street.

The above on p. ⟨1⟩. At head of title: City of Boston. Single cut sheet folded to four pages.

"Original Hymn," *Our fathers built the house of God*, p. ⟨3⟩. Collected in *At Sunset*, 1910.

AAS   B

9425. Poetical Tributes to the Memory of Abraham Lincoln.

Philadelphia   J. B. Lippincott & Co. 1865.

Untitled poem, pp. 15-16, beginning *Crown his blood-stained pillow* . . .

Note: Mrs. Howe's poem also appears in *The Lincoln Memorial* ⟨Second Edition⟩, edited by John Gilmary Shea, 1865, p. ⟨224⟩. Date of publication not known. For comment see entry No. 5245.

For comment see entry No. 2828.

9426. The Barnstable Ball: A Lyric. Appointed to be Sung in All Social Meetings on the Cape

Barnstable, Mass., 1865.

Not located. Entry on the basis of *Julia Ward Howe 1819–1910*, by Laura E. Richards and Maud Howe Elliott, Vol. 1, pp. 231-233, where the text is given together with the comment: "Our mother went with Governor and Mrs. Andrew and a gay party to Barnstable for the annual festival and ball. The Ancient and Honorable Artillery Company acted as escort . . . The party broke up in disorder far from 'admired,' and our mother crystallized the general feeling in the following verses, which the Barnstableites promptly printed in a 'broadside,' and sang to the then popular tune of *Lanigan's Ball* . . . "

9427. LATER LYRICS . . .

BOSTON: J. E. TILTON & COMPANY. 1866.

⟨i⟩-vi, 7-326, blank leaf. 7⅛" scant x 4½".

⟨1-27⁶, 28²⟩. *Signed:* ⟨1⟩-20⁸, 21⁴.

C cloth: green; purple. Front stamped in gold; publisher's imprint at foot of spine. Brown-coated on white end papers. Flyleaves. Inserted between pp. 326-⟨327⟩: Publisher's catalog, 8 pp., printed in red and black.

Note: Sheets also occur in what appears to be a remainder binding of terra-cotta S cloth; front stamped in blind; publisher's imprint not present on spine. This same style of binding noted on the reprint of 1887. The BA copy inscribed by an early owner Christmas, 1882.

In H is the copy presented by Mrs. Howe to Longfellow Dec. 22, 1865. Reviewed ALG Jan. 15, 1866. Deposited Jan. 17, 1866.

B (remainder)   BA (remainder)   H   NYPL   NYSL

9428. Eulogy on John Albion Andrew, Delivered by Edwin P. Whipple ...

Boston: Alfred Mudge and Son, City Printers, 34 School Street 1867.

Printed paper wrapper.

"Poem ... ," *I stood before his silent grave*, pp. 35-36.

H NYPL

9429. FROM THE OAK TO THE OLIVE. A PLAIN RECORD OF A PLEASANT JOURNEY ...

BOSTON: LEE AND SHEPARD. 1868.

Binder's title on front: RECORDS OF A PLEASANT JOURNEY

⟨i-ii⟩, ⟨i⟩-vi, 1-304. 6¹³⁄₁₆" x 4⁹⁄₁₆".

⟨1⁴, 2-3⁶, 4¹², 5-24⁶, 25⁸⟩. *Signed:* ⟨-⟩⁴, ⟨1⟩-19⁸.

C cloth: green; purple. Covers bevelled. Brown-coated on white end papers. Flyleaves.

Deposited June 22, 1868. Listed ALG July 15, 1868; PC Oct. 1, 1868.

BPL   H   Y

9430. A Memorial of Mrs. Louisa C. McAllister. Privately Printed for the Family.

New York: 1869.

Printed paper wrapper.

"In Memoriam," pp. ⟨5⟩-7.

GD

9431. ... Proceedings at the Second Annual Meeting of the Free Religious Association, Held in Boston, May 27 and 28, 1869.

Boston: Roberts Brothers. 1869.

Printed paper wrapper. At head of title: Free Religious Association.

"Essay," pp. 45-57.

H NYPL

9432. Address Delivered on the Centennial Anniversary of the Birth of Alexander von Humboldt ... by Louis Agassiz ...

Boston: Boston Society of Natural History. 1869.

Printed paper wrapper.

Untitled poem, *Give me, O Nature, from thy summer teaching*, pp. 88-89.

B NYPL   Y

9433. APPEAL TO WOMANHOOD THROUGHOUT THE WORLD ...

BOSTON, SEPTEMBER, 1870.

"Again, in the sight of the Christian world, have the skill and power of two great nations exhausted themselves in mutual murder ... In the name of womanhood and of humanity, I earnestly ask that a general congress of women, without limit of nationality, may be appointed and held at some place deemed most convenient, and at the earliest period consistent with its objects, to promote the alliance of the different nationalities, the amicable settlement of international questions, the great and general interests of peace."

Single leaf. Laid paper. Printed on recto only. 8" x 4⅞" scant.

"I had felt a great opposition to Louis Napoleon from the period of the infamous act of treachery which made him emperor ... As I was revolving these matters in my mind, while the ⟨Franco-Prussian⟩ war was still in progress, I was visited by a sudden feeling of the cruel and unnecessary character of the contest ... I could think of no better way of expressing my sense ... than that of sending forth an appeal to womanhood throughout the world, which I then and there composed ... My first act was to have my appeal translated into various languages, to wit: French, Spanish, Italian, German, and Swedish, and to distribute copies of it as widely as possible ..."—*Reminiscences*, pp. ⟨327⟩-329.

LC

9434. World's Peace Congress. A Meeting for the purpose of considering and arranging the steps necessary to be taken for calling a World's Congress of Women in behalf of International Peace, will be held in Union League Hall ... New York, on Friday, December 23 ⟨1870⟩. Fully impressed with the evils of the present war between Prussia and France ...

⟨n.p., n.d., probably New York, 1870⟩

Single leaf. Laid paper. Printed on recto only. 8¹⁄₁₆" x 4⅞". Signed at end by Julia Ward Howe, William Cullen Bryant, Mary F. Davis.

H

9435. Baby's Shoes ... Music by F. Boott ...

Philadelphia Lee & Walker 922 Chestnut St. W. H. Boner & Co. 1102 Chestnut St. O. Ditson & Co. Boston   Chas. W. Harris, New York. ⟨1870⟩

Sheet music. Cover-title. Plate number 11429-5.

Reprinted from *Later Lyrics*, 1866.

Title deposited Oct. 24, 1870. Copies deposited Jan. 28, 1871.

LC

9436. Proceedings of a Peace Meeting Held at Union League Hall, New York, December 23d, 1870, for the Purpose of Free Consultation on the Subject of a Woman's Peace Congress for the World, as Proposed by Mrs. Julia Ward Howe of Boston.

Philadelphia: John Gillam & Co., Printers, No. 608 Arch Street. 1871.

Printed paper wrapper.

"Opening Address," pp. 4-6.

"Address to the Women of the World," pp. 6-10.

"Closing Remarks," p. 29.

"Putting down Murder," p. 30.

AAS   H

9437. A HYMN FOR THE CELEBRATION OF ITALIAN UNITY ... FOR THE MU-SIC-HALL MEETING, FEB. 23, 1871 ...

⟨n.p., n.d., Boston, 1871⟩

Single leaf. Printed on recto only. 8⅞6″ x 5½″.

Apparently prepared for distribution at the celebration. Appears also in *The Unity of Italy ...*, New York, 1871; see entry No. 1729.

JN

9438. Order of Exercises. Howe Family Gathering at Harmony Grove, South Framingham, August 31, 1871 ...

C. T. Evans & Son, Printers, 106 Washington St., Boston.

Single cut sheet folded to make four pages. P. ⟨1⟩ as above.

"Song of Welcome ...," *The year that flings her blossoms wide*, p. ⟨2⟩.

B

9439. The Howe Family Fathering, at Harmony Grove, South Framingham, Thursday, August 31, 1871. By Rev. Elias Nason ...

Published by Elias Howe, 103 Court Street, Boston. 1871. Price Fifty Cents.

Printed paper wrapper.

Reprint save for "I Sit and Look out of My Window," p. ⟨23⟩.

H

9440. Address of the Republican Women of Massachusetts. To the Women of America ...

Boston, Sept. 25, 1872.

Signed at end by Mrs. Howe and others.

For comment see entry No. 170.

9441. Historical Sketch of the First Universalist Church and Society in New Haven, Conn. By Rev. Phebe A. Hanaford, Pastor.

New Haven: Printed by Hoggson & Robinson. 1873.

Printed paper wrapper.

"Installation Hymn," *Thy temples, Lord, are Freedom's shrines*, p. 19.

Y

9442. Sex and Education. A Reply to Dr. E. H. Clarke's "Sex in Education." Edited ... by Mrs. Julia Ward Howe.

Boston: Roberts Brothers. 1874.

"Introduction," pp. ⟨5⟩-11. Comment, pp. ⟨13⟩-31.

BA copy received March 13, 1874. Advertised as *just ready* PW March 14, 1874. Listed PW March 21, 1874. Noted by Bkr May 1, 1874.

BPL   Y

9443. The Hospital Bazaar ...

Chicago ... 1874 ...

"The Physician," No. 2, p. ⟨19⟩.

"Days in Samana, Santo Domingo," No. 3, pp. 36-37.

For comment see entry No. 7274.

9444. Papers, Read at the Second Congress of Women, Chicago, October 15, 16, and 17, 1874 ... The Influence of Literature upon Crime, by Julia Ward Howe ...

Chicago: Fergus Printing Company. 1874.

Printed paper wrapper. Cover-title.

"The Influence of Literature upon Crime," pp. 11-17.

BPL

WORLD'S PEACE CONGRESS.

A Meeting for the purpose of considering and arranging the steps necessary to be taken for calling a World's Congress of Women in behalf of International Peace, will be held in Union League Hall, Madison avenue and Twenty-sixth street, New York, on Friday, December 23.

Fully impressed with the evils of the present war between Prussia and France, and with the desirableness of settling all international questions by the appeal to reason, not to arms; and conscious of the great need of effort to bring about in the present and for the future such a peaceable settlement of difficulties, we cordially invite from all parts of the country the attendance of persons interested in the objects of the proposed Congress.

There will be addresses by distinguished and eloquent speakers, European and other correspondence will be read, and arrangements will be made to secure in the Congress (probably to be held in London) an American representation.

There will be two sessions, commencing at 10.30 o'clock A. M. and 8 P. M.

JULIA WARD HOWE,
WILLIAM CULLEN BRYANT,
MARY F. DAVIS,

Committee.

JULIA WARD HOWE
Entry No. 9434
(Harvard University Library)

9445. One Hundredth Anniversary, April 19, 1875. Battle of Lexington.

⟨Boston, 1875⟩

Single cut sheet folded to make four pages. P. ⟨1⟩ as above. Issued as a program.

"April 19th, 1875," pp. ⟨3-4⟩. Collected in *At Sunset*, 1910, as "Lexington Centennial."

The poem also noted in the following later publications:

The New York Herald. Whole No. 14,119. New York, Monday, April 19, 1875 . . . Revolutionary Extra Edition.

Proceedings at the Centennial Celebration of the Battle of Lexington, April 19, 1875, Lexington, 1875.

Centennial Orations Commemorative of the Opening Events of the American Revolution . . . , Boston, 1875.

H   NYPL

9446. Papers Read at the Third Congress of Women, Syracuse, October 13, 14, and 15, 1875.

⟨Chicago: Fergus Printing Company, n.d., 1875?⟩

Cover-title. Printed paper wrapper.

"On the Formation of Art Groups," pp. 104-105.

Y

9447. Silhouettes and Songs Illustrative of the Months. Twelve Designs by Helen Maria Hinds. Edited by Edward E. Hale . . . and Poems by John G. Whittier . . . Julia Ward Howe . . . ⟨and Others⟩

Boston: Lockwood, Brooks, & Co. 1876.

Unpaged. Contains "June" by Mrs. Howe.

For comment see entry No. 9130.

9448. MEMOIR OF DR. SAMUEL GRIDLEY HOWE. BY JULIA WARD HOWE: WITH OTHER MEMORIAL TRIBUTES. PUBLISHED BY THE HOWE MEMORIAL COMMITTEE.

BOSTON: PRINTED BY ALBERT J. WRIGHT, 79 MILK STREET (CORNER OF FEDERAL). 1876.

⟨i⟩-⟨viii⟩, 1-127. 8" full x 5⅜" (cloth). 8½" x 5¾" scant (wrapper). Frontispiece inserted.

⟨-⟩⁴, ⟨1⟩-8⁸.

C cloth: black. Covers bevelled. Slate-coated end papers. Flyleaves. Also issued in printed gray paper wrapper; double flyleaves; inserted in

some copies of the wrappered format is a four-page notice regarding the publication.

Mrs. Howe's memoir appears at pp. ⟨1⟩-62. Also appears in (reprinted from?): *Forty-Fifth Annual Report of the Trustees of the Perkins Institution and Massachusetts Asylum for the Blind,* Boston, 1877.

BPL copy received Nov. 1, 1876. Listed PW Nov. 11, 1876.

BA   H   LC   NYPL

9449. Poems of the "Old South" by Henry Wadsworth Longfellow . . . Julia Ward Howe . . . ⟨and Others⟩

Boston   William F. Gill & Co   1877

"The Old South," pp. 12-15. Collected in *From Sunset Ridge,* 1898, under the title "Save the Old South!".

Listed PW Dec. 15, 1877.

H   NYPL

9450. Papers Read at the Fourth Congress of Women, Held at St. George's Hall, Philadelphia, October 4, 5, 6, 1876 . . .

Washington, D. C.: Todd Brothers, Book and Job Printers. 1877.

Printed paper wrapper.

"Paternity," pp. 74-79.

Y

9451. Poems of the Life beyond and within . . . Edited and Compiled by Giles B. Stebbins . . .

Boston: Colby and Rich, Publishers, 9 Montgomery Place. 1877.

"Better Glories," p. 226.

H   NYPL

9452. . . . . Seasons Have Passed Away. Song. Words by Mrs. Julia Ward Howe. Music by Richard Hoffman . . .

New-York. Wm. A. Pond & Co. 547 Broadway, & 39 Union Square . . . 1877 . . .

Sheet music. Cover-title. At head of title: To Mrs. Geo. M. Robeson. Plate number 9279.

Earliest located book appearance: *An Old Scrap-Book . . . ,* 1884; see entry No. 7763. Collected in *Original Poems and Other Verse,* 1908.

AAS

9453. Charlotte Cushman: Her Letters and Memories of Her Life. Edited by ... Emma Stebbins ...

Boston: Houghton, Osgood and Company. The Riverside Press, Cambridge. 1878.

Tribute, pp. 300-301.

Listed PW May 25, 1878.

H

9454. The Atlantic Monthly Supplement. The Holmes Breakfast ...

⟨n.p., n.d., Boston, February, 1880⟩

Self-wrapper. Caption-title. "Mrs. Howe's ⟨Remarks and⟩ Poem," pp. 7-8. Minus the remarks collected under the title "To Oliver Wendell Holmes," *At Sunset*, 1910.

H NYPL

9455. Seventieth Birthday of James Freeman Clarke. Memorial of the Celebration by the Church of the Disciples, Monday Evening, April 5, 1880.

Boston: By the Committee. 1880.

"James Freeman Clarke," pp. 14-16. Collected in *At Sunset*, 1910.

H

9456. Sketches and Reminiscences of the Radical Club of Chestnut Street, Boston. Edited by Mrs. John T. Sargent.

Boston: James R. Osgood and Company. 1880.

"Limitations," pp. 30-32. Also contains remarks elsewhere in the book.

Listed PW Dec. 25, 1880.

BA H

9457. Childhood's Appeal ...

⟨Boston, 1880–1881⟩

"Sunset on the Nile," No. 11, p. 2.

For comment see entry No. 3783.

9458. MODERN SOCIETY ...

BOSTON: ROBERTS BROTHERS. 1881.

⟨1⟩-88; 8 pp. advertisements. 6⁵⁄₁₆″ x 4⁵⁄₁₆″.

⟨1⟩-2, ⟨3⟩-6⁸.

S cloth: gray; mauve; red; terra-cotta. Mottled gray end papers printed in gray-tan with a floral pattern; also, pale tan end papers printed in tan with a floral pattern. Flyleaves.

Listed PW Dec. 18, 1880.

H LC Y

9459. The Poets' Tributes to Garfield The Collection of Poems Written for the Boston Daily Globe, and Many Selections ... ⟨First Edition⟩

Cambridge, Mass. Published by Moses King Harvard Square 1881

See entry No. 8955 for comment.

"J.A.G.," pp. 37-38. Collected in *At Sunset*, 1910. Appears also in *The Boston Daily Globe*, Sept. 27, 1881. For a comment on the *Globe* see entry No. 8955.

9460. The Lectures and Journal of Proceedings of the American Institute of Instruction, July 5–8, 1881, at St. Albans, Vt. ⟨Edited by⟩ E. Norris-Sullivan ...

Boston, Mass.: American Institute of Instruction. 1882.

"How Far Does American Education Satisfy the Needs of American Life?," pp. ⟨226⟩-246.

BA

9461. Essays from "The Critic" by John Burroughs ... and Others ...

Boston James R. Osgood and Company 1882

"English Society and 'Endymion'," pp. 153-162.

Deposited May 31, 1882. Listed PW June 3, 1882.

H Y

9462. ... MARGARET FULLER (MARCHESA OSSOLI) ...

BOSTON: ROBERTS BROTHERS. 1883.

At head of title: FAMOUS WOMEN

⟨i-ii⟩, ⟨i⟩-x, ⟨1⟩-298, 10 pp. advertisements. Laid paper. 6¹¹⁄₁₆″ x 4½″.

⟨-⟩⁶, 1-18⁸, 19¹⁰. *Note:* Sig. 19 is an 8vo plus inserted conjugates 6-7.

S cloth: brown; mustard. White paper end papers imprinted in green with a floral pattern. Flyleaves.

BPL copy received Oct. 15, 1883. Deposited Oct. 19, 1883. Listed PW Oct. 20, 1883. The London (Allen) edition listed Ath Oct. 20, 1883.

H LC

9463. Our Famous Women. An Authorized Record of the Lives and Deeds of Distinguished American Women of Our Times ... Sold Only by Subscription.

Hartford, Conn.: A. D. Worthington & Co., Publishers. A. G. Nettleton & Co., Chicago, Ills. 1884.

"Maria Mitchell," pp. 437-461.

Deposited Oct. 22, 1883. For fuller comment see entry No. 204.

9464. Re-Union of the Sons and Daughters of Newport, R. I., Friday, July 4, 1884. [Daily News Report.]

1884: Davis & Pitman, Printers, Newport, R. I.

Printed paper wrapper.

"A Song for Newport's Festival," p. 16.

B

9465. The Genius and Character of Emerson Lectures at the Concord School of Philosophy Edited by F. B. Sanborn

Boston   James R. Osgood and Company 1885

"Emerson's Relation to Society," pp. 286-309.

For comment see entry No. 131.

9466. Proceedings at the Presentation of a Portrait of John Greenleaf Whittier to Friends' School, Providence, R. I. Tenth Month, 24th, 1884

Cambridge   Printed at the Riverside Press 1885

Printed paper wrapper.

Remarks, pp. 45-47.

H NYPL

9467. Proceedings at the Unveiling of a Bust of Elizabeth Fry at Friends' School, Providence, R. I. Ninth Month, 29th, 1885

Providence Rhode Island Printing Company 1885

Printed paper wrapper.

"Elizabeth Fry," pp. 6-7.

NYPL

9468. ... Memorial Services in Honor of Ulysses S. Grant, at Tremont Temple, Thursday, October 22, 1885.

Rockwell & Churchill, Printers, 39 Arch St., Boston.

Single cut sheet folded to four pages. The above on first page. At head of title: City of Boston. Prepared as a program.

"Ode," *Great Freedom! Maid divinely born,* p. <2>. Reprinted in *A Memorial of Ulysses S. Grant from the City of Boston ...* , Boston, 1885.

B BA

9469. The Life and Genius of Goethe Lectures at the Concord School of Philosophy Edited by F. B. Sanborn

Boston Ticknor and Company 1886

"Goethe's Women," pp. 345-367.

BA copy received Feb. 10, 1886. Deposited Feb. 12, 1886.

BPL

9470. Memorial Meeting. Proceedings of the Metaphysical Club ... March 24, 1886, in Memory of Its Late President, Julia Romana Anagnos.

Boston: Press of Henry H. Clark & Co. 1886.

Printed paper wrapper.

"In Memoriam," pp. 13-15.

400 copies only.

H

9471. Wayside Flowers Original and Contributed Poems Arranged by Ellen E. Dickinson ...

New York White, Stokes, and Allen 1886

"Thy Neighbor's Flower-Bed," p. 24.

For comment see entry No. 7899.

9472. Beecher   Memorial   Contemporaneous Tributes to the Memory of Henry Ward Beecher Compiled and Edited by Edward W. Bok

Privately Printed Brooklyn, New York 1887

"Henry Ward Beecher, Preacher, Patriot, Philanthropist," pp. 23-24.

For comment see entry No. 2148.

9473. Appletons' Cyclopaedia of American Biography Edited by James Grant Wilson and John Fiske ...

New York D. Appleton and Company 1, 3 and 5 Bond Street 1887

"Thomas Crawford," Vol. 2, p. 5.

For comment see entry No. 6020.

9474. Later Lyrics . . .

Boston Lee and Shepard, Publishers No. 10 Milk Street 1887

Reprint. For first edition see under 1866.

B   Y

9475. . . . Papers Read before the Association for the Advancement of Women. 14th Women's Congress. Louisville, Kentucky, October, 1886 . . .

Atlantic Highlands, N. J. Leonard & Lingle, Printers. 1887.

Printed paper wrapper. At head of title: A.A.W. Truth, Justice and Honor.

"Opening Address," pp. ⟨7⟩-11.

"Marriage and Divorce," pp. ⟨89⟩-105.

B   H

9476. . . . Papers Read before the Association for the Advancement of Women. 15th Women's Congress. New York City, October, 1887 . . .

Fall River, Mass.: J. H. Franklin & Co., Publishers and Printers. 1888.

Printed paper wrapper. At head of title: A.A.W. Truth, Justice and Honor.

"Opening Address," pp. ⟨7⟩-10.

Note: Listed in the table of contents is "On Aristophanes," by Mrs. Howe, with the note: *Withdrawn from Publication.*

H

9477. The Julia Ward Howe Birthday Book Selections from Her Works . . . Edited by . . . Laura E. Richards

Boston, 1889 Lee and Shepard, Publishers 10 Milk Street, Next "Old South Meeting-House" New York: Charles T. Dillingham 718 and 720 Broadway ⟨1888⟩

Reprint save for "The Word," *Had I one of the words, my Master,* p. 3. Collected in *From Sunset Ridge,* 1898.

Noted as *just ready* PW Dec. 1, 1888. Deposited Dec. 22, 1888. Listed PW Jan. 5, 1889.

AAS   B   LC

9478. Jvlia Ward Howe President of the New England Women's Clvb . . . A Birth Day Anniversary May XXVII MDCCCXIX–MDCCCLXXXIX

⟨Boston: L. Prang & Co., 1889⟩

Single cut sheet. Paper vellum. Folded to make four pages. Front as above. Unpaged. Page: 12″ x 9″. Printed throughout in colors.

On p. ⟨2⟩ is an account by Mrs. Howe of the composition of "The Battle Hymn of the Republic."

H

9479. The Forum Extra . . . Vol. 1. No. 4 . . .

The Forum Publishing Company, 253 Fifth Avenue, New York . . . June, 1890 . . .

Printed self-wrapper. Caption-title.

"Men, Women, and Money," pp. ⟨13⟩-20.

NYPL

9480. Woman's Work in America Edited by Annie Nathan Meyer with an Introduction by Julia Ward Howe

New York Henry Holt and Company 1891

"Introduction," pp. 1-2.

Listed PW Feb. 28, 1891.

AAS

9481. Services and Addresses at the Semi-Centennial Celebration of the Church of the Disciples April 27, 1891

Boston Geo. H. Ellis, 141 Franklin Street 1891

Printed paper wrapper.

"The Ministry of James Freeman Clarke," pp. ⟨32⟩-41

H   NYPL   Y

9482. Fame's Tribute to Children . . . ⟨Edited by Martha S. Hill⟩

Chicago A. C. McClurg and Company 1892

Untitled poem, p. 113, *I have tended six pretty cradles.* Collected in *At Sunset,* 1910, as "Six Pretty Cradles."

For comment see BAL, Vol. 1, p. 76.

LC

9483. Bazaar Book of the Boston Teachers' Mutual Benefit Association. Bazaar Held at Music Hall, December 5th to 10th, 1892.

Alfred Mudge & Son, Printers, Boston. ⟨1892⟩

Printed paper wrapper.

"Extract from Address Delivered . . . Columbus Day, at the School-House in South Portsmouth, R. I.," pp. 57-59.

SG

9484. Society of American Friends of Russian Freedom. Protest against the Russian Extradition Treaty . . .

⟨Boston, 1893⟩

4 pp. The above at head of p. ⟨2⟩. At foot of p. ⟨3⟩: Boston, Feb. 25, 1893. Text on pp. ⟨2-3⟩, otherwise blank.

Signed at end by Mrs. Howe and others.

AAS   H

9485. The National Exposition Souvenir What America Owes to Women Edited by Lydia Hoyt Farmer with an Introduction by Julia Ward Howe

Buffalo Chicago New York Charles Wells Moulton 1893

"A Summing Up," pp. ⟨15⟩-16.

Listed PW Aug. 19, 1893.

H NYPL

9486. Children's Souvenir Song Book Arranged by William L. Tomlins . . .

London and New York Novello, Ewer & Company ⟨1893⟩

Printed paper wrapper.

"Child's American Hymn," p. 114.

Listed PW Aug. 26, 1893.

EM

9487. . . . Art and Handicraft in the Woman's Building of the World's Columbian Exposition Chicago, 1893 Edited by Maud Howe Elliott . . .

Goupil & Co. Boussod, Valadon & Co., Successors Paris and New York 1893

At head of title: Official Edition

"Associations of Women," pp. 147-156.

Listed PW Aug. 19, 1893, as in cloth; paper; leather.

BPL

9488. The World's Congress of Religions with an Introduction by Rev. Minot J. Savage

Boston Arena Publishing Company Copley Square 1893

"What is Religion?," pp. 113-116.

Issued as a subscription book and available in a variety of bindings.

Listed PW Jan. 20, 1894.

Note: Mrs. Howe's contribution appears also in *The World's Parliament of Religions . . . Edited by the Rev. John Henry Barrows . . . ,* Chicago, 1893, Vol. 2, pp. 1250-1251; listed PW Feb. 3, 1894. *Reprint?*

NYPL

9488A. ⟨Lights and Shadows. A Composite Poem⟩

⟨n.p., n.d., 1894⟩

A poem written in collaboration with Richard Hovey, Thomas Wentworth Higginson, Louise Chandler Moulton and others.

For comment see entry No. 8405.

9488B. Memoirs of Anne C. L. Botta Written by Her Friends . . .

New-York J. Selwin Tait & Sons Publishers 31 East 17th Street MDCCCXCIV

"A Laurel Wreath," pp. 58-59.

Listed PW Feb. 10, 1894.

H

9489. The American Tropics.

Boston: Perry Mason, 1894?

Selections from Youth's Companion, No. 3. Printed paper wrapper.

Not located. Entry based on examination of advertisements in other issues of this series. Title and imprint postulated.

Contains "A Trip to Santo Domingo," by Mrs. Howe. Perhaps a reprint of "Days in Samana, Santo Domingo," in *The Hospital Bazaar,* 1874, *q.v.?*

9490. Bryant Centennial Cummington August the Sixteenth 1894 November the Third 1794 November the Third 1894

⟨Springfield, Mass.: Clark W. Bryan Co., Printers, n.d., 1894?⟩

"Poem . . . ," pp. ⟨54⟩-55. Collected in *From Sunset Ridge,* 1898, under the title "The Centennial of William Cullen Bryant's Birth."

H NYPL Y

9491. The Congress of Women Held in the Women's Building, World's Columbian Exposition, Chicago ... 1893 ... Edited by Mary Kavanaugh Oldham Eagle ...

Western W. Wilson, New York, N. Y. 1894

"Women in the Greek Drama. Extract from Julia Ward Howe's Lecture," pp. 102-103.

Issued as a subscription book and probably available in a variety of bindings.

NYPL

9492. IS POLITE SOCIETY POLITE? AND OTHER ESSAYS ...

BOSTON & NEW YORK   LAMSON, WOLFFE, & COMPANY 1895

⟨i-viii⟩, ⟨1⟩-202; printer's imprint, p. ⟨203⟩; 2 blank leaves. Laid paper. Portrait frontispiece inserted. 7⅞″ x 5¾″ full.

⟨1⁴, 2-14⁸⟩.

Tan paper boards. Printed paper label on spine. White laid paper end papers.

Noted as *nearly ready* PW Nov. 16, 1895. Listed (as *not seen*) PW Dec. 21, 1895. BA copy received Dec. 24, 1895. Deposited Dec. 26, 1895. Listed PW Jan. 4, 1896.

Note: Unsold sheets were issued with the cancel title-leaf of Houghton, Mifflin & Co., 1899.

AAS   B

9493. ... Proceedings at the Twenty-Ninth Annual Meeting Held in Parker Memorial Hall Boston, Mass. ... May 28th and 29th 1896

New Bedford   Published by the Free Religious Association 1896

Printed paper wrapper. At head of title: The Free Religious Association

"Address," pp. 94-97.

H   LC

9494. The Story of Evangelina Cisneros (Evangelina Betancourt Cosio y Cisneros) Told by Herself   Her Rescue by Karl Decker   Introduction by Julian Hawthorne ...

MDCCCXCVIII   Continental Publishing Company   25 Park Place, New York

Letter "To His Holiness, Pope Leo XIII," pp. 39-40. An appeal addressed "To All Good Men and True Women," pp. 40-42.

H copy received May 25, 1898.

H

9495. ... Proceedings at the Thirty-First Annual Meeting Held in Boston, Mass. ... May 26th and 27th 1898

Boston, Mass. Published by the Free Religious Association 1898

Printed paper wrapper. At head of title: The Free Religious Association

Response, p. 120.

BPL   H

9496. FROM SUNSET RIDGE   POEMS OLD AND NEW ...

BOSTON AND NEW YORK   HOUGHTON, MIFFLIN AND COMPANY   THE RIVERSIDE PRESS, CAMBRIDGE 1898

⟨i⟩-viii, ⟨1⟩-190; printer's imprint, p. ⟨191⟩. Laid paper. 7⅞″ x 5″.

⟨1⁴, 2-13⁸⟩.

Slate-blue laid paper boards sides, blue T cloth shelfback; also: gray-blue laid paper boards sides, ecru T cloth shelfback. White laid paper end papers. Flyleaves. Top edges gilt.

Deposited Oct. 27, 1898. BA copy received Nov. 1, 1898. Listed PW Nov. 5, 1898.

BPL   H   NYPL   NYSL

9497. John Sullivan Dwight ... a Biography by George Willis Cooke

Boston   Small, Maynard & Company 1898

"To John S. Dwight," pp. 296-297.

Listed PW Feb. 4, 1899.

H   NYPL

9498. ... THE USES OF VICTORY ...

COPIES OF THIS TRACT MAY BE OBTAINED AT $1.50 PER HUNDRED OF THE PUBLISHERS, CHRISTIAN REGISTER ASSOCIATION, 141 FRANKLIN STREET, BOSTON. ⟨n.d., 1898?⟩

Cover-title. At head of title: REGISTER TRACT NEW SERIES NO. 1.

⟨1⟩-10, blank leaf. 6½″ x 4¾″.

⟨-⟩⁶.

Printed self-wrapper.

BA   H

9499. Souvenir Festival Hymns

Boston   Free Religious Association 1899

"Raphael's Saint Cecilia at Bologna," pp. 52-53. Collected in *At Sunset,* 1910. *See note under next entry.*

Published June 2, 1899.

EM

9500. . . . Proceedings at the Thirty-Second Annual Meeting Held in Boston, Mass. . . . June 1st and 2d 1899

Boston, Mass. Published by the Free Religious Association 1899

Printed paper wrapper. At head of title: The Free Religious Association

"Remarks," pp. 118-120.

Note: On pp. 120-121 appears Mrs. Howe's hymn, "Raphael's Saint Cecilia at Bologna," with an introductory remark by T. W. Higginson: "Now let us turn to the 52d page of our little book, and sing the hymn which Mrs. Howe has written for us." *See preceding entry.*

H

9501. REMINISCENCES 1819–1899 . . .

BOSTON AND NEW YORK   HOUGHTON, MIFFLIN AND COMPANY   THE RIVERSIDE PRESS, CAMBRIDGE 1899

⟨i-iv⟩, ⟨i⟩-vi, ⟨1⟩-465; printer's imprint, p. ⟨466⟩; blank leaf. Laid paper. 8¹⁄₁₆" x 5¼". Frontispiece, 23 plates, 1 folded facsimile (4 pp.) inserted.

⟨1⁴, 2¹, 3-31⁸, 32²⟩.

T cloth: blue; green; brown; maroon. White laid paper end papers. Top edges gilt.

Deposited Nov. 18, 1899. BPL copy received Dec. 4, 1899; BA Dec. 5, 1899. Listed PW Dec. 9, 1899. The London (Gay & Bird) edition advertised as *just published* Ath March 17, 1900.

H NYPL Y

9502. THE MESSAGE OF PEACE . . . REPRINTED BY PERMISSION OF THE SUNDAY SCHOOL TIMES . . .

⟨Philadelphia: The Sunday School Times, n.d., 1899?⟩

Single leaf folded to four pages. Page: 8¼" x 5¼". Text on p. ⟨1⟩. Pp. ⟨2-3⟩ blank.

"To the Editor: Please be free to reprint Mrs. Howe's new poem, with any of the accompanying matter you choose, crediting it to *The Sunday School Times* . . ."—p. ⟨4⟩.

B

9503. Masterpieces of American Eloquence [Christian Herald Selection] with Introduction by Julia Ward Howe

New York   The Christian Herald   Louis Klopsch, Proprietor   1900

"Introduction," pp. ⟨1⟩-4.

Deposited Dec. 10, 1900.

NYPL Y

9503A. . . . Proceedings at the Thirty-Third Annual Meeting Held in Boston, Mass. . . . May 31 and June 1 1900

Boston, Mass. Published by the Free Religious Association 1900

Printed paper wrapper. At head of title: The Free Religious Association

"Remarks," pp. 149-150.

H

9504. The 19th Century A Review of Progress during the Past One Hundred Years in the Chief Departments of Human Activity

G. P. Putnam's Sons   New York and London The Knickerbocker Press   1901

"Changes in the Legal and Political Status of Woman," pp. 179-190.

BA copy received March 5, 1901. Listed PW March 9, 1901.

BA

9505. . . . Proceedings at the Thirty-Fourth Annual Meeting Held in Boston, Mass. . . . May 30 and 31 1901

Boston, Mass. Published by the Free Religious Association   1901

Printed paper wrapper. At head of title: The Free Religious Association

"Remarks," pp. 133-135.

H Y

9506. Proceedings at the Celebration of the One Hundredth Anniversary of the Birth of Dr. Samuel Gridley Howe, November 11, 1901.

Boston: Wright & Potter Printing Company, 18 Post Office Square. 1902.

Printed paper wrapper.

"Remarks," pp. 37-38.

H NYPL

9507. ... Proceedings at the Thirty-Fifth Annual Meeting Held in Boston, Mass. ... May 29 and 31 1902

Boston, Mass. Published by the Free Religious Association 1902

Printed paper wrapper. At head of title: The Free Religious Association

"Remarks," pp. 111-113.

H Y

9508. Love-Letters of Margaret Fuller 1845–1846 with an Introduction by Julia Ward Howe ...

New York D. Appleton and Company 1903

"Introduction," pp. v-xii.

For comment see entry No. 6511.

9509. Bohemia Official Publication of the International League of Press Clubs for the Building and Endowment of the Journalists' Home ... Vol. I. Alexander K. McClure, Editor-in-Chief ...

... The International League of Press Clubs James S. McCartney Treasurer Journalists' Home Fund Philadelphia 1904.

All issued?

"What and Where is Bohemia?," pp. 394-395.

Noted only in a de luxe format, leather, limited to 26 lettered copies.

EM

9510. New England Library of Popular Biographies ... Representative Women of New England Compiled by Mary Elvira Elliot ... and Others under the Editorial Supervision of Julia Ward Howe, Assisted by Mary H. Graves ...

Boston New England Historical Publishing Company 1904

"Editor's Preface," p. ⟨3⟩.

Leather. Also issued in cloth?

Listed PW Aug. 5, 1905.

BPL

9511. Official Report of the Thirteenth Universal Peace Congress Held at Boston, Massachusetts ... October Third to Eighth, 1904 ...

Boston: The Peace Congress Committee. 1904

Printed paper wrapper.

Remarks, pp. 98-99. "Address," pp. 126-127.

H NYPL

9512. The Hawthorne Centenary Celebration at the Wayside Concord, Massachusetts July 4-7, 1904

Boston and New York Houghton, Mifflin and Company The Riverside Press, Cambridge 1905

"Address," pp. 30-40. Remarks, pp. ⟨79⟩-80, 104, 135.

For comment see entry No. 8466.

9513. Birthday Tributes to Mrs. Julia Ward Howe May 27, 1905

⟨Boston: Winthrop B. Jones, for the Authors Club, 1905⟩

"Mrs. Howe's Reply," pp. 17-18.

For comment see entry No. 96.

9514. The Value of Simplicity Edited by Mary Minerva Barrows Introduction by Julia Ward Howe

H. M. Caldwell Co. Boston MCMV

"Introduction," pp. v-xii.

AAS H Y

9515. ... Seventy-Fifth Annual Report of the Trustees 1906

Boston 1907 Wright and Potter Printing Co.

Printed paper wrapper. At head of title: Perkins Institution and Massachusetts School for the Blind

"Michael Anagnos," pp. 267-268. See next entry.

H

9516. Michael Anagnos 1837–1906

Boston 1907 Wright and Potter Printing Co.

Printed paper wrapper.

Reprint save for a tribute to Anagnos, April, 1907, pp. 144-145.

"... reprinted and revised from the 75th annual report of the Perkins Institution ..."—p. 6. See preceding entry.

EM

9517. ... Proceedings at the Fortieth Annual Meeting Held in Boston, Mass. ... May 30 and 31 1907

Boston, Mass. Published by the Free Religious Association 1907

Printed paper wrapper. At head of title: The Free Religious Association

"Remarks ... the Removal of Impediments," pp. 78-79.

BPL   H   Y

9518. WHITTIER ... (READ AT HAVERHILL, DEC. 17, 1907) ...

⟨n.p., n.d., 1907?⟩

Single leaf. Printed on recto only. 9⁷⁄₁₆″ x 4⅛″.

Prepared as proof? Collected in *At Sunset*, 1910.

H

9519. ORIGINAL POEMS AND OTHER VERSE

De Luxe Edition

ORIGINAL POEMS AND OTHER VERSE SET TO MUSIC AS SONGS BY JULIA WARD HOWE

THE BOSTON MUSIC COMPANY   COPYRIGHT, 1908, BY G. SCHIRMER.

Title-page printed in brown.

⟨i-vi⟩, ⟨1⟩-26. Vellum paper. 11½″ x 8⅞″. Portrait of Mrs. Howe tipped to p. ⟨iv⟩.

⟨1-4⟩⁴.

Printed vellum paper wrapper folded over the end papers. Edges gilt. Paper vellum end papers.

Certificate of issue tipped between pp. ⟨vi⟩-⟨1⟩: "Edition de luxe, 100 copies ... published for the eighty-ninth birthday anniversary of Julia Ward Howe, May 27, 1908."

Trade Edition

Original Poems and Other Verse Set to Music as Songs by Julia Ward Howe   Price $1.50   Edition de Luxe, $5.00

The Boston Music Company   G. Schirmer 26 & 28 West Street, Boston, Massachusetts ... London ... Melbourne ... Leipzig ... ⟨1908⟩

Title-page printed in black.

De luxe format published May 27, 1908 (certificate of issue). Both formats listed PW Sept. 19, 1908. Trade format deposited Oct. 16, 1908.

BPL (de luxe)   H (de luxe)   LC (trade)

9520. ... Proceedings at the Forty-First Annual Meeting Held in Boston, Mass. ... May 28 and 29 1908

Boston, Mass. Published by the Free Religious Association 1908

Printed paper wrapper. At head of title: The Free Religious Association

"Remarks," pp. 70-73.

H   BPL   Y

9521. MILLENNIUM SEEN IN DREAM VISION BY JULIA WARD HOWE. [FROM PROGRESSIVE THINKER, JULY 11, 1908.] ...

⟨n.p., n.d., 1908?⟩

Caption-title. The above at head of p. ⟨1⟩.

Single leaf folded to make four pages. Page: 5⅝″ x 3⅜″.

G

9522. REPLY TO MRS. HUMPHRY WARD

Two printings noted. The sequence has not been established and the order of presentation is wholly arbitrary. Mrs. Ward's letter appeared in *The Times,* London, Oct. 1, 1908.

A

MRS. JULIA WARD HOWE'S RE- / PLY TO MRS. HUMPHRY WARD. / ⟨rule⟩ / ⟨text⟩ / ⟨*Warren, Ohio, National American Woman Suffrage Association, n.d., 1908?*⟩

The above at head of p. 1.

1-8. 5¾″ scant x 3½″.

⟨-⟩⁴ (?).

Printed self-wrapper.

B

⟨*fillet*⟩ / Mrs. Julia Ward Howe's Reply to / Mrs. Humphry Ward / ⟨rule⟩ / ⟨text⟩ / ⟨*Warren, Ohio, National American Woman Suffrage Association, n.d., 1908?*⟩

The above at head of p. 1.

1-⟨8⟩. 6″ full x 3½″.

⟨-⟩⁴.

Printed self-wrapper.

LC (B)   NYPL (A)

9523. POEM WRITTEN BY MRS. JULIA WARD HOWE IN HER NINETIETH YEAR, AND READ BY HER AT THE ONE HUNDREDTH ANNIVERSARY OF THE BIRTH OF ABRAHAM LINCOLN SYMPHONY HALL, BOSTON, FEBRUARY 12, 1909 ...

⟨Boston, 1909⟩

Single cut sheet. Printed on recto only. 9" x 5¾". Noted on two types of paper of unknown sequence, if sequence there is: (a): Watermarked R. C. LEDGER; (b): Watermarked C⟨RANE'S?⟩ / LINEN

Collected in *At Sunset,* 1910.

H LC

9524. In After Days Thoughts on the Future Life by W. D. Howells ... Julia Ward Howe ... ⟨and Others⟩

Harper & Brothers Publishers New York and London MCMX

"Beyond the Veil," pp. 91-⟨103⟩. Collected in *The Walk With God* ⟨1919⟩.

For comment see entry No. 8498.

9525. Proceedings of the American Academy of Arts and Letters and of the National Institute of Arts and Letters Number 1: 1909–1910

New York ⟨June 10, 1910⟩

Printed paper wrapper.

"The Capitol," p. 35. Collected in *At Sunset,* 1910.

Y

9526. AT SUNSET ...

BOSTON AND NEW YORK HOUGHTON MIFFLIN COMPANY THE RIVERSIDE PRESS CAMBRIDGE 1910

Edited by Laura E. Richards.

⟨i-ii⟩, ⟨i⟩-xii, ⟨1⟩-150; printer's imprint, p. ⟨152⟩; blank leaf. Frontispiece inserted. Laid paper. 7⁷⁄₁₆" x 4¹⁵⁄₁₆".

⟨1-10⁸, 11⁴⟩.

T cloth: green. White laid paper end papers. Top edges gilt.

On copyright page: *Published December 1910* Advertised for *next week* PW Dec. 3, 1910. Noted as published on Dec. 10, 1910, PW Dec. 10, 1910. BPL copy received on Dec. 14, 1910; (another on Jan. 9, 1911). BA copy received Dec. 21 1910.

Listed PW Dec. 24, 1910. Noted as *just published* PW Dec. 24, 1910. Deposited Jan. 13, 1911.

H NYSL

9527. Theodore Parker Commemoration The Free Religious Association Proceedings at the Forty-Third Annual Meeting Held in Boston, Mass. ... May 26 and 27 1910

Boston, Mass. Published by the Free Religious Association 1910

Printed paper wrapper.

"Greetings from Mrs. Julia Ward Howe," p. 70.

BPL H Y

9528. JULIA WARD HOWE ON SUFFRAGE (ADDRESS AT MAY FESTIVAL OF NEW ENGLAND WOMAN SUFFRAGE ASSOCIATION.) ...

⟨New York, n.d., *ca.* 1910.⟩

Caption-title. The above on p. ⟨1⟩.

Single leaf folded to make four pages. Page: 6" scant x 3⁹⁄₁₆".

LC

9529. JULIA WARD HOWE AND THE WOMAN SUFFRAGE MOVEMENT A SELECTION FROM HER SPEECHES AND ESSAYS, WITH INTRODUCTION AND NOTES BY HER DAUGHTER, FLORENCE HOWE HALL ...

BOSTON DANA ESTES & COMPANY PUBLISHERS ⟨1913⟩

⟨i-ii⟩, ⟨1⟩-241, 6 blank leaves. Frontispiece portrait inserted. 7⅜" full x 5".

⟨1-16⟩⁸.

T cloth: maroon.

BPL copy received Dec. 5, 1913; NYPL copy Dec. 6, 1913. Listed PW Jan. 3, 1914.

H

9530. JULIA WARD HOWE 1819–1910 BY LAURA E. RICHARDS AND MAUD HOWE ELLIOTT ASSISTED BY FLORENCE HOWE HALL ...

BOSTON AND NEW YORK HOUGHTON MIFFLIN COMPANY 1915

2 Vols. Title-pages in black and red.

1: ⟨i-xii⟩, ⟨1⟩-392. 9⅛" scant x 6³⁄₁₆". Inserts: Frontispiece with printed tissue; 12 full-page plates; folded 4 pp. facsimile; 1 leaf of original Howe manuscript.

2: ⟨i-viii⟩, ⟨1⟩-434; blank, p. ⟨435⟩; certificate of issue, p. ⟨436⟩. Inserts: Frontispiece with printed tissue; 9 full-page plates.

1: ⟨1⁶, 2-25⁸, 26⁴⟩. Leaves ⟨1⟩1,6 are conjugates; ⟨1⟩2,3 are conjugates; ⟨1⟩4,5 are singletons. 2: ⟨1-2², 3-29⁸, 30²⟩.

Tan paper boards sides, tan buckram shelfback. Goldstamped leather label on spine. White laid paper end papers. Flyleaf at back of Vol. 1; flyleaves in Vol. 2.

On copyright page: *Published December 1915* Deposited Dec. 30, 1915.

Limited to 450 numbered copies.

Note: The present work contains so much material by Mrs. Howe here first published that it may properly be considered a primary production.

Also note: A trade edition imprinted *Boston and New York Houghton Mifflin Company The Riverside Press Cambridge 1916,* 2 Vols., cloth, was issued in 1916. On copyright page: *Published March 1916*

H

9531. THE WALK WITH GOD ... EXTRACTS FROM MRS HOWE'S PRIVATE JOURNALS, TOGETHER WITH SOME VERSES HITHERTO (WITH A FEW EXCEPTIONS) UNPUBLISHED; AND AN ESSAY ON IMMORTALITY ENTITLED "BEYOND THE VEIL" EDITED BY HER DAUGHTER LAURA E. RICHARDS

NEW YORK   E. P. DUTTON & COMPANY   681 FIFTH AVENUE ⟨1919⟩

⟨i-ii⟩, ⟨i⟩-x, ⟨1⟩-161; blank leaf. *Note:* The blank leaf is present; or, excised; or, pasted under the end paper. Frontispiece inserted. 7½″ x 5⅛″.

⟨1-11⟩⁸. *Note:* Leaf ⟨11⟩8 present; or, excised; or, pasted under the end paper.

B cloth: blue-gray; green.

Deposited April 14, 1919. Listed PW April 26, 1919. BPL copy received April 26, 1919.

BPL H NYPL

9532. A Troutbeck Letter-Book (1861–1867) Being Unpublished Letters ... with an Introduction by George Edward Woodberry ...

Amenia New York Privately Printed at the Troutbeck Press Christmas, MDCCCCXXV

Troutbeck Leaflets Number Nine.

Printed paper wrapper.

Letter, Nov. 8, 1867, pp. 17-18.

200 copies only.

H NYPL

9533. Mother Goose Songs and Dances for Children by Julia Ward Howe with Additional Words to Accompany "Little Madcap's Journey" a Play by Isabel Anderson ...

White-Smith Music Publishing Company Boston New York ... ⟨1931⟩

Cover-title. Printed paper wrapper.

"Hunting Song," pp. 14-15; "words and music by Julia Ward Howe."

Note: A companion piece to the above is *Little Madcap's Journey, a Fairy Extravaganza,* by Isabel Anderson, music by Julia Ward Howe, Boston: Walter H. Baker Company ⟨1931⟩; pp. 32; printed paper wrapper; deposited Dec. 12, 1931. Contains neither music nor text by Mrs. Howe.

BA

9534. Italian Recognition Addresses Acknowledging Courtesies from the Italian Government ...

⟨n.p., n.d., Boston?, ca. 1932–1934⟩

Cover-title. Printed paper wrapper.

"A Message from Mrs. Julia Ward Howe to the Italian Citizens of Boston upon the Conferring of the Honor of Knight of the Order of the Crown of Italy upon Professor ⟨James⟩ Geddes," pp. 8-9.

Note: The "message" was delivered in March, 1909.

B BA BPL H

9535. Monte Cristo by Charles Fechter as Played by James O'Neill & Other Plays ... Edited by J. B. Russak

Princeton New Jersey Princeton University Press 1941

America's Lost Plays, Vol. 16.

"Hippolytus," printed from the original manuscript, pp. ⟨71⟩-128.

BA copy received Sept. 15, 1941. Deposited Sept. 17, 1941.

BA H NYPL

REPRINTS

The following publications contain material by Mrs. Howe reprinted from earlier books.

Folk Songs . . . Edited by John Williamson Palmer ...

New York ... M DCCC LXI.

For comment see BAL, Vol. 1, p. 72.

Beadle's Dime Union Song Book No. 3 ... Patriotic Songs for the Times.

New York and London: Beadle and Company, 141 William St., N. Y. 44 Paternoster Row, London. <1862>

Printed paper wrapper. Published March 20, 1862 (Johannsen).

Our Soldier's Armor of Strength ... a Brief Course of Non-Sectarian Devotional Exercises ... by Pilgrim John ...

Brooklyn, E. D.: Published and Sold by D. S. Holmes, 67 Fourth-Street. 1862.

Printed paper wrapper. Cover-title: *The Soldier's Armor* ... Deposited June 28, 1862.

Musical String of Pearls: A Collection of Hymns and Tunes, Original and Selected ... <Compiled> by Rev. J. W. Dadmun ...

Boston: For Sale by J. P. Magee, 5 Cornhill ... New York ... Buffalo ... Pittsburgh ... Cincinnati ... Chicago ... 1862 ...

Printed paper wrapper. H copy received Sept. 27, 1862. Deposited Oct. 15, 1862.

War-Songs for Freemen. Dedicated to the Army of the United States ... Second Edition. <Edited by Francis J. Child>

Boston: Ticknor and Fields. 1863 ...

Printed paper wrapper. Reprints noted: *Third Edition,* Boston, 1863; *Fourth Edition,* Boston, 1863. The *Boston: Oliver Ditson & Co., 1862,* printing is a reprint of the *Fourth Edition* of 1863. *The American News Company edition, New York <1862>* is also a reprint of the *Fourth Edition* of 1863.

Students of Harvard College Who Have Died in the Country's Service from the Beginning of the Rebellion to July 15, 1863 ...

<n.p., n.d., probably Cambridge, Mass., 1863>

Single cut sheet. 14" x 8⅞6". The above at head of sheet.

John Brown, and "The Union Right or Wrong" Songster ...

San Francisco ... 1863.

For comment see BAL, Vol. 1, p. 329.

Lyrics of Loyalty ... Edited by Frank Moore

New York ... 1864

For comment see entry No. 1203.

... Soldiers' and Sailors' Patriotic Songs. New York, May, 1864.

New York ... 1864.

For comment see BAL, Vol. 3, p. 156.

Pen-Pictures of the War. Lyrics, Incidents, and Sketches of the Rebellion ... Compiled Ry <sic> Ledyard Bill.

New York. Sold Only by Subscription. 1864.

Deposited June 20, 1864. Contains three poems by Mrs. Howe here reprinted. "An Adjuration," pp. 89-90, miscredited to Oliver Wendell Holmes, had prior publication under the title "Our Orders" in *Autograph Leaves of Our Country's Authors,* 1864 (April or May).

... Lyrics of the War <Second Number>

Philadelphia ... 1864 ...

For fuller entry see No. 1213.

The Flower of Liberty. Edited ... by Julia A. M. Furbish.

Boston ... 1866.

For comment see entry No. 1424.

Poetry Lyrical, Narrative, and Satirical of the Civil War ... Edited by Richard Grant White

New York ... 1866

For comment see entry No. 4604.

Anecdotes, Poetry and Incidents of the War ... Arranged by Frank Moore ...

New York ... 1866.

For comment see entry No. 3202.

Illustrated Library of Favorite Song ... Edited by J. G. Holland ...

New York ... <1873>

For comment see entry No. 2853.

Sea and Shore ...

Boston ... 1874.

For comment see entry No. 4043.

Freedom and Fellowship in Religion ...

Boston ... 1875.

For comment see entry No. 115.

Ballads of the War

<n.p., Boston> Heliotype <n.d., *ca.* 1875>

For comment see in O. W. Holmes list, Sec. III.

Songs of Three Centuries. Edited by John Greenleaf Whittier.

> Boston ... 1876.

> For comment see entry No. 2857.

Poems of Places Edited by Henry W. Longfellow ... France and Savoy. Vol. II.

> Boston: James R. Osgood and Company ... 1877.

> Listed PW Jan. 27, 1877.

Poems of Places Edited by Henry W. Longfellow ... Italy. Vol. II.

> Boston: James R. Osgood and Company ... 1877.

> Listed PW April 28, 1877.

Poems of Places Edited by Henry W. Longfellow ... New England. Vol. I.

> Boston ... 1879.

> For comment see BAL, Vol. 1, p. 86.

Poems of Places Edited by Henry W Longfellow ... British America ...

> Boston ... 1879.

> For comment see BAL, Vol. 1, p. 249.

In Memoriam. Gems of Poetry and Song on James A. Garfield ...

> Columbus ... 1881.

> For comment see entry No. 122.

The Poets' Tributes to Garfield ... ⟨Second Edition⟩

> Cambridge ... 1882

> For comment see entry No. 1248.

The Cambridge Book of Poetry and Song ... by Charlotte Fiske Bates ...

> New York ... ⟨1882⟩

> For comment see entry No. 7887.

Poems of American Patriotism Chosen by J. Brander Matthews

> New-York   Charles Scribner's Sons   1882

> Listed PW Dec. 2, 1882.

An Old Scrap-Book. With Additions ...

> ⟨Cambridge⟩ February 8, 1884.

> For comment see entry No. 7763.

Childhood's Happy Days with Silhouettes Illustrative of the Months. Designs by Helen Maria

Hinds. Poems by Eminent Authors. Edited by Edward Everett Hale.

> New York: The Arundel Publishing Co. ⟨n.d., ca. 1885⟩

> Pictorial boards, cloth shelfback. Reprint, with revised title, of *Silhouettes and Songs* ... , 1876.

Representative Poems of Living Poets ...

> ... New York 1886

> For comment see entry No. 436.

August Edited by Oscar Fay Adams ...

> Boston ... ⟨1886⟩

> For comment see entry No. 66.

Local and National Poets of America ... Edited ... ⟨by⟩ Thos. W. Herringshaw ...

> Chicago ... 1890.

> For fuller entry see BAL, Vol. 2, 391.

The Lover's Year-Book of Poetry ... Vol. I. January to June

> Boston ... 1891

> For comment see entry No. 4015.

Tributes to Shakespeare Collected ... by Mary R. Silsby

> New York ... MDCCCXCII

> For comment see entry No. 707A.

Teaching Truth. By Mary Wood Allen ...

> ⟨Toledo, Ohio, 1892⟩

> Printed paper wrapper. Deposited July 25, 1892 (copyright notice). The untitled poem, pp. 23-24, had prior publication in *The Female Poets of America*, 1849, as "Woman."

The Story of Patriots' Day   Lexington and Concord   April 19, 1775 with Poems ... ⟨Compiled⟩ by Geo. J. Varney

> Boston   Lee and Shepard Publishers   10 Milk Street   ⟨1895⟩

The Literature of America and Our Favorite Authors ...

> ... Philadelphia ... ⟨1897⟩

> For comment see BAL, Vol. 1, p. 77.

Poems of American Patriotism 1776–1898 Selected by R. L. Paget

> Boston ... MDCCCXCVIII

> For comment see BAL, Vol. 1, p. 249.

... By Land and Sea

1900 Perry Mason & Company Boston, Mass.

At head of title: The Companion Series

Modern Eloquence ... ⟨Edited by⟩ Thomas B. Reed ...

... Philadelphia ⟨1900; *i.e.,* 1901⟩

For comment see entry No. 3467.

... Strange Lands Near Home

Boston, U.S.A. Ginn & Company, Publishers The Athenaeum Press 1902

At head of title: Youth's Companion Series

The World War Utterances Concerning Its Issues ...

... New York 1919

For comment see entry No. 2198.

St. Nicholas Book of Verse Edited by Mary Budd Skinner and Joseph Osmun Skinner ...

... New York ... MCMXXIII

For comment see entry No. 818.

REFERENCES AND ANA

Review of de Lamartine's Jocelyn. Jocelyn Episode. Journal Trouvé chez un Curé de Village. Par Alphonse de Lamartine.

⟨n.p., n.d., *ca.* 1840⟩

Caption-title. The above at head of p. ⟨1⟩. Anonymous. Pp. ⟨1⟩-14, blank leaf. 8¼″ x 5½″ scant. ⟨1⟩-2⁴. Issued in unprinted drab paper wrapper? Offprint from an unidentified periodical.

By Mrs. Howe? If so this is her first separate publication. The only copy examined (in MHS) inscribed in an unknown hand: *By Miss Julia Ward (Mrs. S. G. Howe).*

"When Julia published her first literary venture, a translation of Lamartine's *Jocelyne* ⟨*sic*⟩, Uncle John ⟨Ward⟩ showed her a favorable notice of it in a newspaper ..."— *Julia Ward Howe 1819–1910,* by Laura E. Richards, Maud Howe Elliott, Florence Howe Hall, 1916, Vol. 1, p. 65. The action described occurred about 1840.

"The Buffalo *Express,* in its report of the proceedings of the Women's Congress held there recently, inserts the following sketch of Julia Ward Howe:—... As a school-girl she knew the wealth of Goethe and Schiller, and even published a review of Lamartine's

Jocelyn, creditable to any years ..."—*Wayside Gleanings for Leisure Moments, Printed for Private Circulation* ⟨Cambridge, Mass.⟩ 1882, p. 110.

... The Golden Eagle: Or, the Privateer of '76. A National Drama, in Three Acts, and a Prologue. By J. Burdett Howe ...

New-York: Samuel French ... ⟨1857⟩

Printed paper wrapper. At head of title: French's Standard Drama. No. CLXXI.

Sometimes misattributed to Mrs. Howe.

The Modern Phoenix.

⟨n.p., probably Boston, Feb. 24, 1868⟩

Cover-title. Printed self-wrapper. Pp. 43. Anonymous. Author unknown. Sometimes attributed to Mrs. Howe.

Concord Lectures on Philosophy ...

Cambridge, Mass. Moses King, Publisher Harvard Square. ⟨1883⟩

Printed paper wrapper; and, cloth. Listed PW April 14, 1883.

Contains two abstracts "made from the Lectures delivered at the Concord Summer School of Philosophy during the Term of 1882 ... in a concise form ..."-P. ⟨3⟩.

How They Succeeded Life Stories of Successful Men Told by Themselves by Orison Swett Marden ...

Lothrop Publishing Company Boston ⟨1901⟩

"The Author of the Battle Hymn of the Republic Her Views of Education for Young Women," an interview, pp. 209-219.

For comment see this title in the William Dean Howells list, *References and Ana.*

Letters and Journals of Samuel Gridley Howe Edited by ... Laura E. Richards The Greek Revolution ...

Boston: Dana Estes & Company London: John Lane ⟨1906⟩

On copyright page: *Copyright, October 18, 1906*

Julia Ward Howe. ⟨By A. J. Bloor⟩

⟨n.p., n.d., 1908⟩

Caption-title. The above on p. ⟨1⟩. Printed self-wrapper.

Letters and Journals of Samuel Gridley Howe Edited by ... Laura E. Richards The Servant of Humanity ...

Boston: Dana Estes & Company   London: John Lane ⟨1909⟩

On copyright page: *Copyright, May 19, 1909*

Julia Ward Howe's Peace Crusade ⟨by Edwin D. Mead⟩

⟨Boston: World Peace Foundation, 1910⟩

Caption-title. The above on p. ⟨1⟩. Printed self-wrapper.

Commonwealth of Massachusetts   The General Court of Massachusetts. Suffolk SS. No. 380. *In Re* Petition of Julia Ward Howe et Ali. Brief for Petitioners. Statement of Case . . .

⟨Boston, n.d., 1910⟩

Caption-title. The above at head of p. 1. Printed self-wrapper.

Julia Ward Howe by Ellen M. Mitchell

⟨n.p., n.d., after 1910⟩

Cover-title. Printed self-wrapper.

Two Noble Lives   Samuel Gridley Howe   Julia Ward Howe   By Their Daughter Laura E. Richards

Boston   Dana Estes and Company Publishers ⟨1911⟩

Deposited Aug. 3, 1911. Halftone pasted to front cover.

The Eleventh Hour in the Life of Julia Ward Howe by Maud Howe

Boston   Little, Brown, and Company   1911

Paper boards, cloth shelfback. On copyright page: *Published, October, 1911*   Deposited Oct. 28, 1911.

Memorial Exercises in Honor of Julia Ward Howe Held in Symphony Hall, Boston . . . January 8, 1911 . . .

City of Boston   Printing Department   1911

Julia Ward Howe 1819–1910 by Laura E. Richards and Maud Howe Elliott Assisted by Florence Howe Hall . . .

Boston and New York   Houghton Mifflin Company   1915

See entry No. 9530.

The Story of the Battle Hymn of the Republic by Florence Howe Hall . . .

Harper & Brothers   New York and London ⟨1916⟩

Paper boards, cloth shelfback. On copyright page: *Published October, 1916*; and, code letters K-Q, signifying *printed Oct. 1916*. Deposited Nov. 7, 1916.

The Composer of the Battle Hymn of the Republic by John J. MacIntyre

William H. Conklin Publisher   195-197 Fulton Street New York City   ⟨1916⟩

Printed paper wrapper.

Commemorative Tributes to Thomas Wentworth Higginson   Julia Ward Howe . . . ⟨and Others⟩ by Bliss Perry Read at Public Session following Annual Meeting of the American Academy of Arts and Letters New York City December 13, 1912 Reprinted from Vol. VI Proceedings of the Academy

⟨New York⟩ American Academy of Arts and Letters 1922

Printed paper wrapper.

Three Saints and a Sinner   Julia Ward Howe, Louisa, Annie and Sam Ward by Louise Hall Tharp . . .

Little, Brown and Company   Boston   Toronto   ⟨1956⟩

On copyright page: *First Edition*   Deposited Sept. 6, 1956.

WILLIAM DEAN HOWELLS

1 8 3 7 – 1 9 2 0

9536. "OLD BROWN." . . .

⟨n.p., presumably Columbus, Ohio⟩ NOV. 25, 1859.

Single leaf. 8″ x 3¹⁵⁄₁₆″. Printed on recto only.

Proof only?

Also appears in *Echoes of Harper's Ferry* . . . , 1860; entry No. 143.

H

9537. POEMS OF TWO FRIENDS.

COLUMBUS: FOLLETT, FOSTER AND COMPANY. 1860.

Poems by John J. Piatt, pp. ⟨1⟩-79; by Howells, pp. ⟨83⟩-132.

⟨i⟩-⟨x⟩, ⟨1⟩-132. P. vi mispaged v. 7⁵⁄₁₆″ scant x 4⅝″.

⟨A⁴, B¹⟩, ⟨1⟩-5, ⟨6⟩-8⁸, 9². *Note:* In some copies ⟨B⟩, a divisional title-page, is printed on paper unlike that used in the body of the book.

BD cloth: brown; pink-brown. Cream-coated on white; and, yellow-coated on white, end papers. Top edges gilt. Flyleaves.

Title-page deposited Dec. 24, 1859. No record found for deposit of book. Reported as published BM Jan. 2, 1860.

AAS   BPL   H   NYPL   Y

9538. LIVES AND SPEECHES OF ABRAHAM LINCOLN AND HANNIBAL HAMLIN.

COLUMBUS, O: FOLLETT, FOSTER & CO. 1860.

⟨1⟩-⟨8⟩, ⟨ix⟩-⟨xvi⟩, 17-⟨154⟩, 157-170. 7⅝″ x 4¹¹⁄₁₆″.

⟨1⟩⁴, 2⁸, 3-14⁸·⁴. *Note:* Signature mark 14 appears on p. 161. Superfluous signature mark 15 occurs on p. 169.

Printed buff paper wrapper.

Howells's life of Lincoln, pp. 17-94. The life of Hamlin, pp. 157-170, is by J. L. Hayes.

Advertised by Rickey, Mallory & Company "in the *Cincinnati Daily Press* on June 25, 1860, for the first time, announcing that they had 'now on sale' a supply of Howells' life of Lincoln, in paper, at twenty-five cents."—*Campaign Lives of Abraham Lincoln, 1860,* by Ernest James Wessen, 1937, p. 18.

Two states noted in the following probable order:

A

p. 33: Footnote reads: **Near Petersburgh.*

p. 46, last line: ⟨i⟩*mportance* . . .

p. 75: Footnote not present.

PP. ⟨95-96⟩: Blank

B

Has the same features noted in *State A* save for p. ⟨96⟩ which is imprinted with an engraving of The Republican Wigwam, Chicago.

Common to both: On p. 5 is a list of three illustrations. (In fact *State A* contains no illustrations; *State B* contains but one, that of The Republican Wigwam, p. ⟨96⟩.)

Locations: B (*State A*, rebound) H (*State B*, lacking the wrapper) Miami University Library, Oxford, Ohio (*State B*, lacking back of wrapper and leaves ⟨1⟩2-3, 24-5, 94-5.)

EXTENDED EDITION, pp. 406

This work was issued as presidential campaign material and went into an unknown number of printings of which several variants exist. The variants were caused by printing from multiple plates(?), mixed sheets, corrections and changes in the text, a combination of all three factors. The result is a bibliographical morass. The text is heavy with errors most of which went uncorrected; in all examined copies, for example, on p. 19 Lincoln's mother is named as *Lucy Hanks*. Two corrections and certain other typographic features give a clue to sequence but BAL considers an absolute sequence a near-impossibility.

Add to the above the fact that the bindings vary, as do the imprints, and it becomes quite

"OLD BROWN."

BY W. D. HOWELLS.

Success goes royal crowned through time,
  Down all the loud applauding days,
  Purpled in history's silkenest phrase,
And brave with many a poet's rhyme;

While Unsuccess, his peer and mate,
  Born of the same heroic race,
  Begotten of the same embrace,
Dies at his brother's palace gate.

The insolent laugh, the blighting sneer,
  The pointing hand of vulgar scorn,
  The thorny path, the crown of thorn,
The many-headed's stupid jeer

Show where he fell   And by-and-by
  Comes history, in the waning light,
  Her pen nib-worn with lies, to write
The failure into infamy.

Ah, God! but here and there there stands
  Along the years, a man to see,
  Beneath the victor's bravery,
The spots upon his lilly hands—

To read the secret will of good,
  (Dead hope, and trodden into earth,)
  That beat the breast of strife for birth,
And died birth-choked in parent blood.

II.

Old Lion! tangled in the net,
  Baffled, and spent, and wounded sore,
  Bound, thou who ne'er knew bonds before,
A captive, but a lion yet:

Death kills not. In a later time,
  Oh, slow, but all-accomplishing,
  Thy shouted name abroad shall ring,
Wherever right makes war sublime.

When in the perfect scheme of God,
  It shall not be a crime for deeds
  To quicken liberating creeds,
And men shall rise where slaves have trod:

Then he, the fearless future man,
  Shall wash the guilt and stain away,
  We place upon thy name to-day,
Thou hero of the noblest plan.

Oh, patience! felon of the hour!
  Over thy ghastly gallows tree,
  Shall climb the vine of Liberty,
With ripened fruit and fragrant flower.
  Nov. 25, 1859.

clear that the number of variants is large. It is highly probable that not all of the variants are here listed. The designations are all but arbitrary and are for identification only.

Of but two features can we be reasonably certain: *One:* That the complete (406 pp.) edition was issued, and perhaps printed, after publication of the shorter (170 pp.) version. And, *Two:* We may assume that copies with the error on p. 33 *may* have been *issued* prior to copies with the corrected text. But such assumption must be treated cautiously; it is possible that both the corrected and the uncorrected texts were printed and issued simultaneously.

Note: Present in some copies is an erratum slip, inserted between pp. 74-75, relating to misstatements on pp. 74-75. The slip has been noted by BAL in some copies of Variants A and B but copies of Variants C and D may have been issued with the slip also. The misstatements noted by the slip are not present in Variant E.

Howells's life of Lincoln, pp. 17-94.

VARIANT A

No terminal advertisements.

p. 33: Footnote reads: **Near Petersburgh.*

p. 46: Last line: <i>mportance ...

p. 75: Footnote not present.

p. <96>: Illustration present.

Noted with the following imprints

a

COLUMBUS, O.: / FOLLETT, FOSTER & CO. / CHICAGO: S. C. GRIGGS & CO. PITTSBURGH: HUNT & MINER. / CLEVELAND: INGHAM & BRAGG. / 1860.

Locations: B LC

b

COLUMBUS, O: / FOLLETT, FOSTER & CO. / 1860.

Locations: B LC Y

c

COLUMBUS, O.: / FOLLETT, FOSTER & CO. / BOSTON: BROWN & TAGGARD. / 1860.

Locations: B H LC

d

COLUMBUS, O.: / FOLLETT, FOSTER & CO. / DETROIT: PUTNAM, SMITH & CO. / 1860.

Locations: H

e

COLUMBUS, O.: / FOLLETT, FOSTER & CO. / BOSTON: CROSBY, NICHOLS, LEE & CO. / 1860.

Locations: B

VARIANT B

No terminal advertisements.

p. 33: Footnote reads: **Near Petersburgh.*

p. 46, last line: *importance ...*

p. 75: Footnote not present.

p. <96>: Illustration present.

Noted with the following imprints

a

COLUMBUS, O: / FOLLETT, FOSTER & CO. / 1860.

Locations: AAS H LC

b

COLUMBUS, O.: / FOLLETT, FOSTER & CO. / BOSTON: BROWN & TAGGARD. / 1860.

Locations: H LC

VARIANT C

No terminal advertisements.

p. 33: Footnote reads: **Now Petersburgh.*

p. 46: last line: <i>mportance ...

p. 75: Footnote not present.

p. <96>: Illustration present.

Noted with the following imprints

a

COLUMBUS, O.: / FOLLETT, FOSTER & CO. / CINCINNATI: RICKEY, MALLORY & CO. / 1860.

Locations: LC

b

COLUMBUS, O.: / FOLLETT, FOSTER & CO. / CHICAGO: S. C. GRIGGS & CO. PITTSBURGH: HUNT & MINER. / CLEVELAND: INGHAM & BRAGG. / 1860.

Locations: LC

VARIANT D

No terminal advertisements.

p. 33: Footnote reads: **Now Petersburgh.*

p. 46, last line: *importance ...*

p. 75: Footnote not present.

p. <96>: Illustration present.

Noted with the following imprints

a

COLUMBUS, O: / FOLLETT, FOSTER & CO. / 1860.

Locations: LC

b

NEW YORK: / W. A. TOWNSEND & CO., / COLUMBUS: FOLLETT, FOSTER & CO. / 1860.

Locations: B H LC Y

VARIANT E

Note: Contains terminal advertisements printed as an integral part of the final gathering. This feature is not present in the other variants.

p. 33: Footnote reads: **Near Petersburgh.*

p. 46, last line: ⟨i⟩mportance . . .

p. 75: Footnote present.

p. ⟨95⟩ (*sic*): Illustration present.

Noted with the following imprints

a

COLUMBUS, O.: / FOLLETT, FOSTER & CO. / CHICAGO: S. C. GRIGGS & CO. PITTSBURGH: HUNT & MINER. / CLEVELAND: INGHAM & BRAGG. / 1860.

Locations: B LC

b

COLUMBUS, O.: / FOLLETT, FOSTER & CO. / BOSTON: BROWN & TAGGARD. / 1860.

Locations: B LC

BINDING

Four variant bindings have been noted. The sequence has not been established. The designations are for identification only. There is a real possibility that all four bindings were simultaneous.

BINDING VARIANT A

Sides blindstamped with a triple rule frame; a filigree ornament at center. At top of spine: Goldstamped simple rules. Spine imprint of Follett, Foster & Co. Types of cloth noted: A: purple. BD: gray; plum

Noted on: Aa Ba Cb Da

BINDING VARIANT B

Sides blindstamped with a rules frame, the rules enclosing a series of bull's-eye ornaments; a filigree ornament at center. At top of spine: A goldstamped ornate filigree. Spine imprint of Follett, Foster & Co. Types of cloth noted: BD: slate. T: red.

Noted on: Aa Ab

BINDING VARIANT C

Sides blindstamped with a rules frame, the rules enclosing a series of bull's-eye ornaments; a filigree ornament at center. At top of spine: Goldstamped simple rules. Spine imprint of Follett, Foster & Co. Types of cloth noted: A: brown; purple. BD: brown; green; purple; slate. T: black; purple; red.

Noted on: Aa Ab Ac Ad Ae Ba Bb Ca Ea Eb

BINDING VARIANT D

Sides blindstamped with a double rule border only. Filigree not present on sides. Spine imprint of W. A. Townsend & Co. Types of cloth noted: BD: brown. TZ: purple.

Noted on: Db

Note: Wessen, *op. cit.*, p. 20, reports an imprint not located by BAL: *Columbus: Follett, Foster & Company,* in combination with: *New York: M. Doolady.*

"Published on July 5, 1860, and reviewed the following day in the editorial columns of Howells' own paper, the *Ohio State Journal.*"—Wessen, *op. cit.*, p. 21.

9539. The Poets and Poetry of the West: With Biographical and Critical Notices. By William T. Coggeshall . . .

Columbus: Follett, Foster and Company. 1860.

Reprint save for:

"Helen Louisa Bostwick," p. 550.

"John Herbert A. Bone," p. 589.

"Gordon A. Stewart," p. 612.

"Mary R. Whittlesey," p. 640.

"The Poet's Friends," p. 680. Collected in *Poems,* 1873.

"The Bobolinks are Singing," p. 681. Collected in *Poems,* 1873.

"Summer Dead," p. 681. The final four stanzas of "Pleasure-Pain," *Atlantic Monthly,* April, 1860. Collected in *Poems,* 1873, as "In August."

For comment see entry No. 2819.

9540. Three Years in Chili. By a Lady of Ohio. ⟨Mrs. C. B. Merwin⟩

Columbus: Follett, Foster and Company. Boston: Brown & Taggard. New-York: Sheldon & Co. 1861.

Also issued with the imprint: Columbus: Follett, Foster and Company. Philadelphia: J. B. Lippincott & Co. Chicago: S. C. Griggs & Co. 1861.

"Howells edited and rewrote this volume . . ." —Gibson & Arms, p. 18.

Unsold sheets were issued with a cancel title-leaf imprinted: *New York: Follett, Foster and Company. J. Bradburn (Successor to M. Doolady), 49 Walker Street. 1863.* Copy in H. Other unsold sheets were issued with cancel title-leaf under the revised title: *Chili, through American Spectacles;* imprinted: *New York: John*

Bradburn, (Successor to M. Doolady,) 49 Walker Street. ⟨n.d.⟩. Copy in Y.

H   NYPL

9541. Executive Documents Printed by Order of the House of Representatives, During the Third Session of the Thirty-Seventh Congress. 1862–'63. In Twelve Volumes ...

Washington: Government Printing Office. 1863.

Consular report, Sept. 30, 1862, Vol. 12, pp. 376-380.

H

9542. The Battle in the Clouds ... Composed by M. Keller ...

Jefferson, Ohio ... J. A. Howells & Co. ... 1864 ...

Sheet music. Cover-title. Plate number 4895.

Deposited July 15, 1864. Reprinted and reissued with the imprint of Wm. Hall & Son, New York. Collected in *Poems,* 1873.

H

9543. Executive Documents Printed by Order of the House of Representatives, During the First Session of the Thirty-Eighth Congress, 1863–'64. In Sixteen Volumes ...

Washington: Government Printing Office. 1864.

Consular report, Oct. 5, 1863, Vol. 10, pp. 360-362.

H

9544. Venice. Her Art-Treasures and Historical Associations. A Guide to the City and the Neighbouring Islands. Translated from the Second German Edition of Adalbert Müller. With a Map of the City and Lagoons.

Venice. H. F. & M. Münster. 1864.

Flexible cloth. Map inserted in pocket in back cover. ⟨i⟩-xxiv, ⟨1⟩-344. 5¹³⁄₁₆″ x 4¼″. Marbled edges.

"In Venice, I translated this book from the German in the winter of 1862-3, Elinor writing great part of it from my dictation. The publisher paid me $75, or florins 150, and I bought with this my watch, the chromo. of St. Barbara, and Kugler's Italian Art. W. D. Howells, New York, Feb. 3, 1903."—Inscription in the H copy (*State A*). For further comment see *Life in Letters of William Dean Howells,* Vol. 2, p. 136.

Two states of binding noted; sequence, if any, not known. The designations are for identification only:

A

A cloth: red. On the front cover the space between the bottom of the lion device and the bottom of the lettering below is 1⁵⁄₁₆″.

B

C-like cloth: red. The space indicated is 1½″ scant.

H (A,B)

9545. Executive Documents Printed by Order of the House of Representatives During the Second Session of the Thirty-Eighth Congress, 1864–'65. In Fifteen Volumes ...

Washington: Government Printing Office. 1865.

Consular report, March 31, 1864, credited to W. D. Howell ⟨*sic*⟩, Vol. 11, pp. 462-467. Reprinted in (in extended form) *Venetian Life,* second edition, 1867.

H

9546. VENETIAN LIFE ...

LONDON: N. TRÜBNER & CO., 60, PATERNOSTER ROW. MDCCCLXVI. [RIGHT OF TRANSLATION AND REPRODUCTION RESERVED.]

See entry Nos. 9547, 9550, 9562, 9664, 9784.

Two binding variants noted; the sequence, if any, is not known. The designations are completely arbitrary.

A

⟨i-xiv⟩, ⟨1⟩-359; printer's imprint, p. ⟨360⟩. 7¹³⁄₁₆″ x 4⅞″. See note below regarding cancels. P. 208 mispaged 20.

⟨a⁴, b¹, c²⟩, 1-22⁸, 23⁴. See note below regarding cancels.

B

⟨i-x⟩, ⟨1⟩-359; printer's imprint, p. ⟨360⟩; *Errata,* pp. ⟨361-364⟩. 7¹³⁄₁₆″ x 4⅞″. See note below regarding cancels. P. 208 mispaged 20.

⟨a⁴, b¹⟩, 1-22⁸, 23⁴, ⟨24⟩².

Note: Gathering ⟨c⟩, binding *Variant A;* and, gathering ⟨24⟩, binding *Variant B,* are devoted to the errata; by insertion at front *Variant A* results; by insertion at back *Variant B* results.

CANCELS

Contains the following cancels: 3₄, 4₂, 4₅, 4₇, 6₆, 10₆, 13₄, 14₄, 16₇, 20₂, 21₄, 21₆.

C cloth: green; purple. Brown-coated on white end papers.

Advertised as *shortly* Ath Dec. 30, 1865, with title given as *Life in Venice*. Advertised as *shortly* Ath Feb. 3, 1866, with title given as *Venetian Life*. Advertised for *early next month* Ath May 19, 1866. Listed (prematurely?) Ath May 19, 1866. Advertised as *this day* Bkr May 31, 1866. Listed PC June 1, 1866. Reviewed Ath June 2, 1866. Advertised as *just published* Ath June 30, 1866.

LC (B)   Y (A)

9547. VENETIAN LIFE . . .

NEW YORK: HURD & HOUGHTON. MDCCCLXVI.

First American edition. Made up of the sheets of the London printing (see preceding entry) with certain additional cancels. For a comment on the cancels see note below. See entry Nos. 9550, 9562, 9664, 9784.

⟨i-viii⟩, ⟨1⟩-359. 7½″ x 4¾″. See note below regarding cancels. P. 208 mispaged 20.

⟨1⟩⁴, 1-22⁸, 23⁴. See note below regarding cancels.

CANCELS

"As for the American edition, I spent my whole percentage from it in replacing certain portions of the London sheets with corrected pages, where the errors seemed too gross. I had then gone to live in Cambridge, where errors, especially in foreign languages, were not tolerated; these were in Italian, and worse yet, they were my own blunders."—*Venetian Life*, 1907, pp. xx-xxi.

The book is printed on two types of wove paper: (a) the original sheets; and, the British-printed cancels; (b) the American-printed cancels. The British-printed cancels are single leaves, printed on book stock; the American cancels are each of two conjugate leaves and are printed on paper appreciably thinner than that used by the British printers. The American leaves are printed from a face similar to, but not the same as, that used by the British printers.

British-Printed Cancels

34, 42, 45, 47, 6₆, 106, 134, 144, 167, 202, 214, 216.

American-Printed Cancels

41.8, 91.8, 92.7, 122.7, 123.6, 142.7, 143.6, 191.8, 194.5, 201.8, 211.8, 212.7, 223-6, 224.5, 231.4.

A cloth: purple. P cloth: purple-brown. Yellow-coated on white end papers. Flyleaves.

Deposited Aug. 8, 1866. Listed ALG Aug. 15,

1866. Advertised for Aug. 25, 1866, ALG Sept. 1, 1866. Listed (again) ALG Sept. 1, 1866.

AAS H LC NYPL Y

9548. Executive Documents Printed by Order of the House of Representatives, During the First Session of the Thirty-Ninth Congress, 1865–'66. In Sixteen Volumes . . .

Washington: Government Printing Office. 1866.

Consular statement, Vol. 10, pp. 355-356.

H

9549. Poems of Religious Sorrow, Comfort, Counsel, and Aspiration Selected by F. J. Child . . .

New York Published by Hurd and Houghton Boston: E. P. Dutton and Company 1866

"A Thanksgiving," p. ⟨271⟩. Collected in *Poems*, 1873.

H

9550. Venetian Life . . . Second Edition.

New York: Published by Hurd and Houghton, 1867.

Extended edition. "In correcting this book for a second edition . . . I have given a new chapter sketching the history of Venetian Commerce . . ."—p. ⟨5⟩. For other editions see entry Nos. 9546, 9547, 9562, 9664, 9784.

First appearance for "Advertisement to the Second Edition," p. ⟨5⟩; and, "Commerce," pp. 237-257. A shorter version of "Commerce" had prior publication in *Executive Documents . . . 1864–'65*, Washington, 1865; see entry No. 9545.

Deposited Feb. 20, 1867. Listed ALG March 1, 1867; PC (Trübner) May 15, 1867.

CC H NYPL

9551. ITALIAN JOURNEYS . . .

NEW YORK: PUBLISHED BY HURD AND HOUGHTON, 459 BROOME STREET. 1867.

⟨1⟩-320. 7⅛″ x 4¹¹⁄₁₆″. *Note:* All examined copies are printed on mixed types of laid paper.

⟨1⟩-20⁸.

C cloth: green; purple; terra-cotta. Peach-coated on white end papers. Laid paper flyleaves.

Deposited Nov. 22, 1867. Listed ALG Dec. 2, 1867. Copies were received by BA and by BPL Dec. 3, 1867. The London (Low) edition listed

Ath Jan. 18, 1868. See entry Nos. 9560, 9742, 9743.

CC H NYPL

9552. NO LOVE LOST A ROMANCE OF TRAVEL ...

NEW YORK G. P. PUTNAM & SON 661 BROADWAY 1869

⟨i-ii⟩, ⟨1⟩-58; blank leaf; blank leaf, excised or pasted under the end paper. Pp. ⟨i-ii⟩ excised or pasted under the end paper. Frontispiece, vignette title-page, 1 plate inserted. 6¾″ x 5⁵⁄₁₆″.

⟨1-4⟩⁸. Leaves ⟨1⟩₁ and ⟨4⟩₈ excised or pasted under the end papers. Signed: ⟨-⟩¹, ⟨1⟩-⟨3⟩⁸, 4⁷.

C cloth: green; purple; terra-cotta. Covers bevelled. Brown-coated on white end papers. Edges gilt.

Deposited Nov. 27, 1868. Listed ALG Dec. 1, 1868; PC Jan. 16, 1869.

H NYPL

9553. The Atlantic Almanac 1870 ...

Boston: Fields, Osgood & Co., Office of the Atlantic Monthly ... 1869 ...

Printed paper wrapper.

"Bopeep: A Pastoral," pp. 12-16. Collected in *Poems*, 1873.

Deposited Oct. 12, 1869. Listed ALG Nov. 1, 1869.

H NYPL

9554. The Poets and Poetry of Europe. With Introductions and Biographical Notices. By Henry Wadsworth Longfellow. A New Edition, Revised and Enlarged ...

Philadelphia: Porter and Coates, 822 Chestnut Street. 1871.

Contains the following material by Howells, pp. 872-885; all, save for the final title listed, collected in *Modern Italian Poets*, 1887. The final title, "Willing or Loath," remains uncollected.

"On the Likeness of a Beautiful Woman Carven upon Her Tomb"; translated from Leopardi.

"To Sylvia"; translated from Leopardi.

"The Fair Prisoner to the Swallow"; translated from Grossi.

"The Duchess"; translated from Carrer.

"Sonnet," *I am a pilgrim swallow, and I roam;* translated from Carrer.

"The Midnight Ride"; translated from Prati.

"From an Hour of My Youth"; translated from Aleardi.

"From the Primal Histories"; translated from Aleardi.

"From Monte Circello"; translated from Aleardi.

"Nanna"; translated from Carcano.

"Saint Ambrose"; translated from Giusti.

The following ten translated from Dall' Ongaro: "Pio Nono," "The Woman of Leghorn," "The Sister," "The Lombard Woman," "The Decoration," "The Cardinals," "The Ring of the Last Doge," "The Imperial Egg," "To My Songs" and "Willing or Loath."

Two issues noted:

First Issue

Pagination: ⟨i⟩-⟨xxviii⟩, ⟨1⟩-916. Engraved portrait frontispiece of Goethe inserted. Also inserted: Engraved vignette title-page with the joint imprint of Porter & Coates; and, S. Low, Son, & Co., London.

Front matter: ⟨a⁸, b⁶⟩.

Final gathering, pp. 913-916: 115².

A copy thus presented to H by Longfellow Nov. 2, 1870.

Note: Also issued with the cancel title-leaf of James R. Osgood & Co., Boston, 1871. According to the Osgood records 250 sets of sheets were purchased March 7, 1871 and the first bound copies were received April 20, 1871, approximately six months after first publication of the Porter & Coates issue.

Also Note: Wilson, Vol. 1, p. 257, reports a copy of the first issue with engraved portrait frontispiece of Longfellow instead of engraved portrait frontispiece of Goethe.

Second Issue

Pagination: ⟨i⟩-⟨xxii⟩, ⟨1⟩-⟨922⟩. Engraved portrait frontispiece of Goethe inserted. Also inserted: Engraved vignette title-page with the joint imprint of Porter & Coates; and, S. Low, Son, & Co., London.

Front matter: ⟨a⟩¹, ⟨b⟩², ⟨c⟩⁸.

Final gatherings, pp. 897-⟨922⟩: ⟨-⟩⁸, ⟨*⟩⁴, ⟨#⟩¹.

Note: Also seen with engraved portrait frontispiece of Longfellow instead of the portrait frontispiece of Goethe.

Note: The differing pagination is the result of reprinting certain of the pages of the front and the terminal matter. The reprinting transposed to the back of the book the indices relating to the supplement. See Porter & Coates's letter, Nov. 1, 1870, quoted below.

Extracts from letters, Porter & Coates to Longfellow; originals in the Longfellow papers in H:

June 9, 1870: "We shall probably print one thousand (1000) copies, the first edition, during July."

July 18, 1870: "We shall go to press the latter part of this week with one thousand copies ... We enclose proof of old title, do you want to make any alteration ..."

Oct. 3, 1870: "Owing to the scarcity of water &c we have had great difficulty in getting the paper for your book. Although ordered in July it has only recently been received. As soon as the last sheet leaves the printer's you will hear from us."

Nov. 1, 1870: "We sent you ... yesterday eight copies of our new edition of your *Poets and Poetry of Europe* for distribution among your friends ... The arrangement of the contents of the body of the work and that of the supplement, and likewise the two indices of authors and lists of books referred to, all in the beginning of the book, is not satisfactory. We should have preferred to let the supplemental index, contents & list of authorities follow page 776, but Messrs Welch Bigelow & Co in paging the supplement made no allowance whatever for them and we were compelled to place them in their present position. It was a tight fit however, but it does not look badly. As soon ⟨as⟩ the copies in fine binding are ready, we will send you some. We printed one thousand copies, and, according to our agreement are to have seventy five copies free of copyright. This will include the two copies for the copyright office at Washington ..."

Some copies were shipped Oct. 31, 1870; see letter of Nov. 1, 1870 quoted above. H copy (first issue) presented by Longfellow Nov. 2, 1870. Title-page deposited Nov. 5, 1870. Deposited Nov. 7, 1870. Advertised ALG Dec. 1870, as in cloth; sheep; half calf; turkey antique. Listed ALG Jan. 2, 1871; PC Feb. 1, 1871; Ath March 4, 1871.

Note: Wilson, Vol. 1, p. 257, states that "there are two copyrights at Washington, June 27 and Nov. 5 ...". The Copyright Office reports inability to explain the June 27 date. BAL conjectures that a title-page of some sort, perhaps an experimental form, may have been deposited on that date as a preliminary to securing copyright; the records show that a title-page was deposited Nov. 5, 1870.

H (Porter & Coates, 1st; Osgood, 1st)   LC (Porter & Coates, 1st, not a deposit copy)   UV (Porter & Coates, 2nd)

9555. SUBURBAN SKETCHES ...

NEW YORK: PUBLISHED BY HURD AND HOUGHTON. CAMBRIDGE: RIVERSIDE PRESS. 1871.

⟨1⟩-234; 3 blank leaves. *Note:* In some copies the third blank is excised or pasted under the end paper. Laid paper. $7\frac{3}{8}$" x 5".

⟨1⟩-15⁸. In some copies leaf 15₈ is excised or pasted under the end paper.

C cloth: green; terra-cotta. Covers bevelled. Yellow-coated on white end papers. Top edges gilt.

Note: Two states have been noted. The sequence has not been determined and the following suggested sequence is tentative:

A

Sheets bulk $\frac{7}{8}$" scant. The title-leaf is an integral part of its gathering, not a cancel. The line *Published by Hurd and Houghton.* in the imprint is set $3\frac{1}{8}$" wide.

B

Sheets bulk $\frac{3}{4}$" scant. The title-leaf is a cancel. The line indicated is set $2\frac{7}{8}$" wide.

Deposited (State A) Dec. 19, 1870. H copy (State A) presented to T. B. Aldrich by Howells, Dec. 25, 1870. Listed ALG Jan. 2, 1871. The London (Low) edition advertised (prematurely) as *just ready* Ath Feb. 18, 1871; listed PC April 1, 1871; advertised as *just ready* PC April 1, 1871; listed Ath April 8, 1871. See entry No. 9561.

AAS (A)   H (both)   LC (A)   NYPL (A)

9556. Balloon Post ...

Boston, Mass., April ... 1871 ...

An occasional newspaper. For fuller comment see entry No. 4038.

"Some Traits of a Good, Brisk Day," No. 2, p. 3.

9557. The Unity of Italy. The American Celebration of the Unity of Italy, at the Academy of Music, New York, Jan. 12, 1871, with the Addresses, Letters, and Comments of the Press ...

New York: G. P. Putnam & Sons, Association Building. 1871.

Letter, Jan. 7, 1871, p. 76.

For comment see entry No. 1729.

9558. THEIR WEDDING JOURNEY ...

BOSTON: JAMES R. OSGOOD AND COMPANY. LATE TICKNOR & FIELDS, AND FIELDS, OSGOOD, & CO. 1872.

⟨i-iv⟩, ⟨1⟩-287. Illustrated. 7⅜" x 4⅞".

⟨-⟩², 1-18⁸.

Note: Copies occur as follows in the following probable sequence:

A

Period present after the *CO* in the imprint.

B

Period not present after the *CO* in the imprint.

C cloth: blue; green; orange. FL cloth: green; terra-cotta. Orange cloth embossed with alternating simple rules and dotted rules. Yellow-coated on white end papers. Flyleaves.

Note: There are two states of the binding. The following is presumed the correct sequence.

A

The figure of Cupid on the front cover is stamped in a vertical position; the left foot seems to be stepping upward.

B

The figure of Cupid on the front cover is stamped in a tilted position; Cupid appears to be walking forward.

H copy (A sheets, B binding) inscribed by early owner Dec. 25, 1871. CC copy (A sheets, A binding) inscribed by Howells Dec. 25, 1871. Deposited Dec. 27, 1871. Listed ALG Jan. 1, 1872; PC Feb. 1, 1872. A Toronto (Belford) edition advertised as *forthcoming* in Toronto *Evening Mail,* Oct. 6, 1876; described as a *Canadian reprint* by the *Canadian Monthly,* Toronto, Nov. 1876. See entry No. 9632.

AAS (B sheets, B binding) CC (A sheets, A binding) H (A sheets, A binding; A sheets, B binding; B sheets, B binding)

9559. The Pellet ...

Boston: Published by the Fair. 1872 ...

An occasional newspaper. For fuller comment see entry No. 169.

"Incident," No. 2, p. 4.

9560. Italian Journeys ... New and Enlarged Edition.

Boston: James R. Osgood and Company. Late Ticknor & Fields, and Fields, Osgood, & Co. 1872.

Printed from the plates of the first edition, 1867, with the addition of "Ducal Mantua," pp. ⟨321⟩-398. See under 1882 for a separate printing. Also see entry Nos. 9551, 9742, 9743.

Deposited May 18, 1872. Listed WTC May 23, 1872.

AAS   H   LC

9561. Suburban Sketches ... New and Enlarged Edition ...

Boston: James R. Osgood and Company. Late Ticknor & Fields, and Fields, Osgood, & Co. 1872.

Reprint save for "Some Lessons from the School of Morals," pp. ⟨220⟩-240.

For first edition see entry No. 9555.

Deposited May 18, 1872. Listed WTC May 23, 1872.

AAS   LC   NYPL

9562. Venetian Life ... New and Enlarged Edition.

Boston: James R. Osgood and Company. Late Ticknor & Fields, and Fields, Osgood, & Co. 1872.

Reprint save for "Our Last Year in Venice," pp. ⟨399⟩-434.

For other editions see entry Nos. 9546, 9547, 9550, 9664, 9784.

Deposited May 18, 1872. Listed WTC May 23, 1872.

BPL   H   Y

9563. Jubilee Days. An Illustrated Daily Record of the Humorous Features of the World's Peace Jubilee ...

Boston: James R. Osgood and Company, (Late Ticknor & Fields, and Fields, Osgood, & Co.) 1872.

An occasional newspaper. For comment see entry No. 275.

9564. ... The Song of the Sea ... Music by F. Boott.

New York. C. H. Ditson & Co. 711 Broadway. Boston, O. Ditson & Co. ... 1872 ...

Sheet music. Cover-title. At head of title: To Mrs. Richard Aulick ... Plate number 27187.

In somewhat revised form collected in *Poems,* 1873, under the title "By the Sea."

Deposited Sept. 26, 1872.

H   LC

9565. The Poets and Poetry of America. By Rufus Wilmot Griswold. With Additions by R. H. Stoddard ... Carefully Revised, Much Enlarged, and Continued to the Present Time ...

New York: James Miller, Publisher, 647 Broadway. 1873.

Reprint save for the following poems; all, save as noted, collected in *Poems*, 1873.

"Andenken," pp. ⟨655⟩-656; and, "Pleasure-Pain," pp. 656-657. These two poems, totalling fifty-two stanzas, were first published in *Atlantic Monthly*, Jan. and April, 1860. Stanzas 30-38, 1-8, 13-29, in the order here given, collected in *Poems*, 1873, with slight revisions, under the title "Pleasure-Pain." Stanzas 49-52 under the title "Summer Dead" published in *The Poets and Poetry of the West ...* , 1860; see above; and under the title "In August," collected in *Poems*, 1873. Stanzas 9-12, 39-48, uncollected.

"Before the Gate," p. 657.

"The First Cricket," p. 657. See entry No. 9573.

For a comment on the Griswold editions of this compilation see entry No. 6644.

Listed WTC Oct. 31, 1872. Advertised WTC Nov. 28, 1872, as in cloth, bevelled; cloth, gilt extra; half calf; morocco; morocco antique. Listed PC April 1, 1873; PW Oct. 3, 1874⟨sic⟩. Reissued not before May 1, 1877, imprinted: *New York: James Miller ... 779 Broadway ⟨1872⟩.*

H

9566: A CHANCE ACQUAINTANCE ...

BOSTON: JAMES R. OSGOOD AND COMPANY, LATE TICKNOR & FIELDS, AND FIELDS, OSGOOD, & CO. 1873.

Title-page in black and red.

⟨i-vi⟩, ⟨1⟩-279; printer's device, p. ⟨280⟩; 6 pp. advertisements. 5⅞" x 4⅛".

⟨1², 2-19⁸⟩. *Signed:* ⟨-⟩³, 1-11¹², 12¹¹. *Also signed:* ⟨-⟩³, A-Q⁸, R⁷.

S cloth: blue; brown; green; terra-cotta. T (moiréd): blue; green. V cloth: blue; green; terra-cotta. Blue-coated; green-coated, on white end papers. Flyleaves. Edges stained red.

Note: An advertisement in PW May 24, 1873, states: "First large edition exhausted before publication. Third large edition ready Saturday, May 24." BAL has been unable to discover any features that might distinguish the three printings.

Listed PW May 10, 1873. Deposited May 27, 1873. Noted by Ath June 28, 1873. An illustrated edition (illustrations by W. L. Shepard),

dated 1874, listed PW Nov. 15, 1873. The Canadian (Belford) edition advertised in *Weekly Mail*, Toronto, apparently as a new book, Oct. 6, 1876; listed *Canadian Monthly*, Toronto, Jan. 1877. See entry No. 9616.

CC   H   NYPL

9567. POEMS ...

BOSTON: JAMES R. OSGOOD AND COMPANY, LATE TICKNOR & FIELDS, AND FIELDS, OSGOOD, & CO. 1873.

Title-page in black and red.

⟨i-iv⟩, ⟨i⟩-ii, ⟨3⟩-172, 2 blank leaves. 5⅞" scant x 4⅛".

⟨-⟩², ⟨A⟩-K⁸. *Also signed:* ⟨-⟩², ⟨1⟩-7¹², 8⁴.

S cloth: blue; terra-cotta. T cloth (moiréd): green. V cloth: green; terra-cotta. Blue-black-coated on white; blue-coated on white end papers. Edges stained red-orange.

Note: The binding occurs in two states of undetermined sequence; the designations are for identification only:

A: With the word *Illustrated* on the spine.

B: The word *Illustrated* not present on spine.

BA copy received Sept. 26, 1873. Listed PW Sept. 27, 1873. Deposited Sept. 30, 1873. See entry No. 9622.

BPL (A)   H (A,B)   LC (B, being a deposit copy)

9568. A FOREGONE CONCLUSION ...

BOSTON: JAMES R. OSGOOD AND COMPANY. LATE TICKNOR & FIELDS, AND FIELDS, OSGOOD, & CO. 131 FRANKLIN STREET. 1875.

Two printings noted:

1

⟨i-ii⟩, ⟨1⟩-265. 7⅜" x 4¹³⁄₁₆".

⟨1¹, 2-12¹², 13¹⟩. *Signed:* ⟨-⟩¹, 1-16⁸, 17⁵.

P. 9, line 10: ... *Europeans,/*

P. 75, line 5: ... *the merchant of Venice* ...

2

⟨i-iv⟩, ⟨1⟩-265, blank leaf.

⟨1-11¹², 12⁴⟩. *Signed:* ⟨-⟩², 1-16⁸, 17⁶.

P. 9, line 10: ... *European /*

P. 75, line 5: ... *the Merchant of Venice* ...

Leaf ⟨1⟩₁ᵥ imprinted with an advertisement, a feature not present in the first printing.

FL cloth: green; terra-cotta. Brown-coated on white end papers. Flyleaves.

Copies of the first printing (in H) presented by Howells Nov. 27, Nov. 28, 1874, respectively, to Mrs. Howells and to Oliver Wendell Holmes. Deposited Dec. 3, 1874. Listed PW Dec. 5, 1874. Advertised by Low as a new American book PC Dec. 31, 1874. See entry No. 9750.

H (1st, 2nd)   NYPL (1st)

9569. ... ⟨Extracts from⟩ The Atlantic for July ...

H. O. Houghton and Company, Boston. Hurd and Houghton, New York. ⟨n.d., 1875⟩ ...

Contains "Education of an Italian Gentleman in the Last Century," "Italian Nobles in the Last Century." Both extracted from Howells's "An Obsolete Fine Gentleman," *Atlantic Monthly*, July, 1875; collected in *Modern Italian Poets*, 1887.

For comment see entry No. 282.

9570. ... The Cambridge of 1776 ... Edited for the Ladies Centennial Committee by A.G. ⟨i.e., Arthur Gilman⟩ ...

Cambridge: Printed on the Site of Fort Number One: Over against the Town of Brighton, on the River's Side. To be Sold in Boston by Lockwood, Brooks, and Company, on Washington and Bromfield Streets. M D CCC LXX VI.

At head of title: Theatrum Majorum.

"Dorothy Dudley," p. ⟨1⟩.

Three states of binding noted. The sequence, if any, has not been determined and the designations are for identification only. Reference is to the stamping on the front cover.

A: Lettering in gold. *In black:* Vignette of the Washington Elm; no background present. A copy thus in GD (March, 1960) presented Jan. 4, 1876, by Alice M. Longfellow, chairman of the publication committee, to Mary Williams Greely, the copyright claimant.

B: Lettering in gold. *In black:* Vignette of the Washington Elm; beneath the branches are seen smaller trees, houses, etc. In this form the vignette is much the same as the illustration on p. 13.

C: As the preceding but *all* stamping in gold. A copy thus in MHS inscribed by the editor Oct. 14, 1876.

Note: Also issued in printed paper wrapper according to PW listing and an advertisement, both PW Jan. 29, 1876.

Noted as *soon* PW Dec. 11, 1875. GD copy inscribed Jan. 4, 1876; see under *Binding A* above.

Listed PW Jan. 29 1876. Advertised PW Jan. 29, 1876. Deposited May 7, 1877.

H (A, B)   MHS (C)

9571. A Day's Pleasure ...

Boston: James R. Osgood and Company, Late Ticknor & Fields, and Fields, Osgood, & Co. 1876.

Reprinted from *Suburban Sketches*, 1871.

Two states of p. ⟨iii⟩ of the front end paper noted. Sequence, if any, not known and the designations are for identification only. Both forms may well have been issued simultaneously.

A

... *The first issues will be as follows:—Snow-Bound .. Evangeline ... Power, Wealth, Illusions ... Culture, Behavior, Beauty ...*

B

... *The first issues include:—Snow-Bound ... ⟨to⟩ A Day's Pleasure ...*

Listed PW Feb. 12, 1876. Deposited Feb. 18, 1876. See entry No. 9593.

BA (B)   H (B)   LC (B, being a deposit copy)   NYPL (A, B)   Y (B)

9572. SKETCH OF THE LIFE AND CHARACTER OF RUTHERFORD B. HAYES ... ALSO A BIOGRAPHICAL SKETCH OF WILLIAM A. WHEELER ...

NEW YORK: PUBLISHED BY HURD AND HOUGHTON. BOSTON: H. O. HOUGHTON AND COMPANY. CAMBRIDGE: THE RIVERSIDE PRESS. 1876.

⟨i-ii⟩, ⟨i⟩-vi, ⟨1⟩-195; blank, p. ⟨196⟩; ⟨1⟩-31; blank, p. ⟨32⟩; plus 4 pp. advertisements. Frontispiece and 1 plate inserted. $6^{13}\!/_{16}''$ x $4^{3}\!/_{8}''$.

⟨-⟩⁴, 1-2, ⟨3⟩-4, ⟨5-6⟩, 7-12⁸, 13², ⟨14-15⟩⁸; plus: ⟨16⟩².

S cloth: blue; green; mauve; red; terra-cotta. Yellow end papers. Flyleaves. Erratum slip inserted between pp. 96-97; the error noted, *seven hundred days*, p. 96, line 8 from the bottom, is present in all examined copies. *Note:* Advertised PW Sept. 2, 1876, as in both cloth and in printed paper wrapper; noted in cloth only.

It will be published immediately ... —PW Aug. 12, 1876. Advertised as *in a few days* PW Sept. 2, 1876. Deposited Sept. 15, 1876. Listed PW Sept. 16, 1876. BA copy received Sept. 16, 1876.

H   NYPL

9573. The First Cricket . . . Music by F. Boott
. . .

    Boston   Oliver Ditson & Co   451 Washington
St. . . . 1876 . . .

Sheet music. Cover-title. Plate number 45354.
Reprinted from *Poems*, 1873. Also in entry No.
9565.

Deposited Nov. 24, 1876.

H

9574. THE PARLOR CAR. FARCE . . .

    BOSTON: JAMES R. OSGOOD AND COMPANY, LATE
TICKNOR & FIELDS, AND FIELDS, OSGOOD, & CO.
1876.

⟨1⟩-74, blank leaf. 4¹¹⁄₁₆″ x 3⁵⁄₁₆″.

⟨1-4⁸, 5⁶⟩.

V cloth: green; terra-cotta. White end papers
printed in red with publisher's advertisements.

Deposited Dec. 4, 1876. Listed PW Dec. 23, 1876.
H copy inscribed by early owner Dec. 25, 1876.

BA   H

9575. OUT OF THE QUESTION. A COMEDY
. . .

    BOSTON: JAMES R. OSGOOD AND COMPANY. LATE
TICKNOR & FIELDS, AND FIELDS, OSGOOD, & CO.
1877.

Title-page in black and red.

⟨i-iv⟩, ⟨1⟩-183. 5¹³⁄₁₆″ x 4³⁄₁₆″.

⟨-⟩², ⟨1⟩-8, ⟨9⟩-11⁸, 12⁴.

S cloth: green; mauve; terra-cotta. Blue-coated;
green-coated end papers. Flyleaves. Edges
stained red.

CC copy received from Howells April 20, 1877.
Noted for *this week* PW April 21, 1877. BPL and
H copies received April 23, 1877. Deposited
April 25, 1877. Listed PW April 28, 1877. The
earliest located British printing appears to be
the Edinburgh (Douglas) edition; advertised in
Ath Sept. 23, 1882.

CC   H

9576. Poems of Places Edited by Henry W.
Longfellow . . . Italy. Vol. III.

    Boston: James R. Osgood and Company, Late
Ticknor & Fields, and Fields, Osgood, & Co.
1877.

Reprint save for:

"The White Flag on the Lagoon Bridge at
Venice," translated from the Italian of Fusinato,
pp. 195-197.

"Tortona," translated from the Italian of Nic-
colini, p. 253.

"Garibaldi," translated from the Italian of Ongaro, p. 255. Collected in *Modern Italian Poets*,
1887.

For comment see entry No. 4050.

9577. A COUNTERFEIT PRESENTMENT.
COMEDY . . .

    BOSTON: JAMES R. OSGOOD AND COMPANY. LATE
TICKNOR & FIELDS, AND FIELDS, OSGOOD, & CO.
1877.

Title-page in black and red.

⟨i-ii⟩, ⟨1⟩-155; 2 blank leaves. 5¹³⁄₁₆″ x 4³⁄₁₆″.

⟨1⟩⁹, 2-10⁸. *Note:* Sig. ⟨1⟩ is made up as follows:
Conjugates, 1 and 9, 3 and 7, 5 and 6; leaf 2
(the title-leaf) is tipped to the stub of excised
original (conjugate of leaf 8); leaf 4 (divisional
title-page) is an insert. *Also note:* Inserted in
some copies is a printed slip of green laid paper, 5″ x 3¼″: PUBLISHER'S NOTICE. *The right of
dramatic representation . . . has been purchased
by . . . Lawrence Barrett . . .*

S cloth: green; mauve; terra-cotta. Blue-coated;
black-coated end papers. Flyleaf at front. Edges
stained red.

Noted for *this week* PW Sept. 29, 1877. Deposited
Oct. 5, 1877. H copy inscribed by Howells Oct.
5, 1877. Listed PW Oct. 13, 1877.

H   LC   NYPL   Y

9578. Autobiography. Memoirs of Frederica
Sophia Wilhelmina, Princess Royal of Prussia
. . . with an Essay by William D. Howells . . .

    Boston: James R. Osgood and Company, Late
Ticknor & Fields, and Fields, Osgood, & Co.
1877.

2 Vols. *Choice Autobiographies*, Vols. 1-2.

Howells's essay, Vol. 1, pp. ⟨1⟩-28.

Issued successively with the imprints:

1: As above.

2: Ticknor & Company ⟨1877; *i.e.*, ca. 1885⟩.
Copy in H.

3: Houghton, Mifflin and Company ⟨1905⟩. In
this form probably prepared for copyright purposes only. Copy in LC.

Three issues of the binding noted:

1: JRO monogram on spine.

2: HO monogram on spine.

3: HM monogram on spine.

BPL copy received Oct. 8, 1877. Deposited Oct. 12, 1877. Listed PW Oct. 13, 1877.

AAS (1st binding) H (bindings 1, 2, 3) Y (1st binding)

9579. Autobiography. Lives of Lord Herbert of Cherbury and Thomas Ellwood. With Essays by William D. Howells.

Boston: James R. Osgood and Company, Late Ticknor & Fields, and Fields, Osgood, & Co. 1877.

Choice Autobiographies, Vol. 3.

"Edward Lord Herbert," pp. ⟨1⟩-14. "Thomas Ellwood," pp. ⟨169⟩-179.

Three issues of the binding noted:

1: JRO monogram on spine.

2: HO monogram on spine.

3: T&CO monogram on spine.

Deposited Oct. 15, 1877. Listed PW Oct. 20, 1877.

AAS (3rd binding) H (1st, 2nd, bindings) Y (1st binding)

9580. Autobiography. Life of Vittorio Alfieri. With an Essay by William D. Howells.

Boston: James R. Osgood and Company, Late Ticknor & Fields, and Fields, Osgood, & Co. 1877.

Choice Autobiographies, Vol. 5.

"Vittorio Alfieri," pp. ⟨5⟩-51.

Note: Unsold sheets were issued *ca.* 1890 with the cancel title-page of Houghton, Mifflin & Company ⟨1877⟩; HM monogram at foot of spine. Copy in Y.

BA copy received Oct. 30, 1877. Listed PW Nov. 3, 1877. Deposited Nov. 6, 1877.

BA Y

9581. Autobiography. Memoirs of Carlo Goldoni. Translated from the Original French, by John Black. With an Essay by William D. Howells.

Boston: James R. Osgood and Company, Late Ticknor & Fields, and Fields, Osgood, & Co. 1877.

Choice Autobiographies, Vol. 4

"Carlo Goldoni," pp. ⟨5⟩-29.

Two issues of the binding noted:

1: JRO monogram on spine.

2: HM monogram on spine.

Deposited Nov. 13, 1877. Listed PW Nov. 17, 1877.

AAS (2nd binding) H (1st binding) LC (1st binding) Y (2nd binding)

9582. Autobiography. Memoirs of Edward Gibbon, Esq. With an Essay by William D. Howells.

Boston: James R. Osgood and Company, Late Ticknor & Fields, and Fields, Osgood, & Co. 1877.

Choice Autobiographies, Vol. 6.

"Edward Gibbon," pp. ⟨5⟩-41.

Deposited Dec. 20, 1877. Listed PW Dec. 22, 1877.

BA BPL H Y

9583. Autobiography. Memoirs of Jean François Marmontel. With an Essay by William D. Howells . . .

Boston: Houghton, Osgood and Company. The Riverside Press, Cambridge. 1878.

2 Vols. *Choice Autobiographies*, Vols. 7-8.

"Jean François Marmontel," Vol. 1, pp. ⟨5⟩-27.

Two issues of the binding noted:

1: HO monogram on the spine.

2: HM monogram on the spine.

Deposited May 17, 1878. Listed PW May 25, 1878.

AAS (1st) H (1st, 2nd) Y (1st)

9584. THE LADY OF THE AROOSTOOK . . .

BOSTON: HOUGHTON, OSGOOD AND COMPANY. THE RIVERSIDE PRESS, CAMBRIDGE. 1879.

Three printings noted:

1

⟨i-iv⟩, ⟨1⟩-326, blank leaf. $7\frac{7}{16}''$ x $4\frac{3}{4}''$.

⟨1^2, $2\text{-}3^6$, 4^{12}, $5\text{-}26^6$, 27^8⟩. *Signed:* ⟨-⟩^{2}, $1\text{-}20^8$, 21^4.

Period present after ETC. on title-page.

P. ⟨ii⟩ (leaf ⟨1⟩$_1$^{v}) blank.

The statement *All rights reserved* not on copyright page.

2

⟨i-ii⟩, ⟨1⟩-326, blank leaf; blank leaf excised or pasted under the end paper.

⟨$1\text{-}27^6$, 28^4⟩. Leaf ⟨28⟩$_4$ excised or pasted under the end paper. *Signed:* ⟨-⟩^{1}, $1\text{-}20^8$, 21^5.

Period present after ETC. on title-page.

P. ⟨ii⟩ (leaf ⟨1⟩1ᵛ) is the copyright page.

The statement *All rights reserved* not on copyright page.

3

⟨i-iv⟩, ⟨1⟩-326, blank leaf.

⟨1-27⁶, 28⁴⟩. *Signed:* ⟨-⟩², 1-20⁸, 21⁴.

Period not present after ETC on title-page.

P. ⟨ii⟩ (leaf ⟨1⟩1ᵛ) imprinted with a list of books.

The statement *All rights reserved* present on copyright page.

S cloth: brown; green; terra-cotta. Green-coated, gray-coated, brown-coated, end papers; these being unprinted. *Note:* Copies of the second and third printings issued with coated end papers imprinted with an all-over leafy pattern. Flyleaves present in copies of the first printing; flyleaf at front only of second printing; flyleaves in copies of the third printing.

Advertised in PW Feb. 1, 1879, for *on or about February 20.* Copy (in H) presented by Howells to his wife Feb. 21, 1879. Deposited Feb. 27, 1879. CC copy inscribed by Howells Feb. 27, 1879. Listed PW March 1, 1879.

BPL (2nd) CC (1st) H (1st, 2nd, 3rd) NYPL (1st, 3rd) Y (1st, 2nd, 3rd)

9585. Editorial Right A Question of Honesty and Plain Speech W. J. Linton *v.* the Atlantic Monthly

⟨n.p., n.d., New Haven, 1879⟩

Caption-title. The above at head of p. ⟨1⟩. Pp. ⟨1⟩-8. 8⅝″ x 5¹¹⁄₁₆″. Printed self-wrapper.

Linton's account of his argument with *The Atlantic Monthly* regarding editorial liberties taken with his "Art in Engraving on Wood," *Atlantic,* June, 1879. Contains the correspondence between Linton and the *Atlantic,* including Howells's letter to Linton, May 14, 1879, p. 3.

NYPL

9586. Gould Memorial Home and Schools, Rome, Italy. Meeting of the Boston Ladies' Association, February 28, 1879.

⟨Beacon Press: Thomas Todd, 1 Somerset St., Boston, n.d., 1879?⟩

Printed paper wrapper.

"Address," pp. 17-⟨20⟩.

AAS H

9587. The Atlantic Monthly Supplement. The Holmes Breakfast ...

⟨n.p., n.d., Boston, February, 1880⟩

Self-wrapper. Caption-title. "Mr. Howells's Response," pp. 6-7. Howells served as toastmaster and his introductory remarks precede the several speeches and poems.

H NYPL

9588. The Art Autograph ... ⟨May, 1880⟩

... The Art Interchange, 140 Nassau Street, New York ... Copyright: 1880; by Wm. Whitlock.

Note, p. ⟨6⟩.

For comment see BAL, Vol. 3, p. 157.

NYPL

9589. THE UNDISCOVERED COUNTRY ...

BOSTON: HOUGHTON, MIFFLIN AND COMPANY. THE RIVERSIDE PRESS, CAMBRIDGE. 1880.

Two printings noted; the sequence presented is probable:

A

⟨i-iv⟩, ⟨1⟩-419. 7½″ x 4¾″.

⟨1², 2-18¹², 19⁶⟩. *Signed:* ⟨-⟩², 1-26⁸, 27².

B

⟨i-viii⟩, ⟨1⟩-419, 2 blank leaves. First and final leaves excised or pasted under the end paper. ⟨1⁴, 2-18¹², 19⁸⟩. Leaves ⟨1⟩1 and ⟨19⟩8 excised or pasted under the end papers. *Signed:* ⟨-⟩⁴, 1-26⁸, 27⁴.

Two bindings noted; the sequence presented is probable.

a

S cloth: blue; brown; green; dark olive drab; purple; terra-cotta. Front lettered. Slate-coated end papers. Flyleaves.

b

S cloth: blue; brown; terra-cotta. Front not lettered. Black-coated end papers.

Note: Other stamping variations are present; the above is sufficient for immediate identification.

Advertised for June 19, 1880, PW June 12, 1880. CC copy (Aa) inscribed by Howells June 16, 1880. Two copies (Aa) received by H June 21, 1880. A copy in H (Aa) presented by Howells to Thomas Bailey Aldrich June 21, 1880. Deposited June 24, 1880. Listed PW June 26, 1880. The London (Low) edition listed Ath Sept. 11, 1880. See entry No. 9788.

BA (Bb)　CC (Aa)　H (Aa, Ba)　LC (Ba)　NYPL (Aa, Ba)

9590. Childhood's Appeal . . .

⟨Boston, 1880–1881⟩

"A Perfect Success," No. 9, p. ⟨1⟩.

For comment see entry No. 3783.

9591. A FEARFUL RESPONSIBILITY AND OTHER STORIES . . .

BOSTON　JAMES R. OSGOOD AND COMPANY　1881

⟨i-iv⟩, ⟨1⟩-255. 7⅜" x 4¹³⁄₁₆".

⟨1⁸, 2-20⁶, 21⁸⟩. Leaves ⟨1⟩2-3 are inserted conjugates. *Signed:* ⟨-⟩², ⟨1⟩-13, ⟨14⟩-16⁸.

S cloth: blue; green; olive; terra-cotta. Gray-green coated end papers. Flyleaves.

BA copy received July 11, 1881. Deposited July 13, 1881. CC copy inscribed by Howells July 15, 1881. H copy inscribed by early owner July 17, 1881. Listed PW July 23, 1881. An Edinburgh edition listed Bkr Dec. 1882.

CC　H

9591A. DR. BREEN'S PRACTICE　A NOVEL . . .

LONDON　TRUBNER & CO. LUDGATE HILL 1881 . . .

Cover-title. *Not seen.*

Prepared for copyright purposes only. Text incomplete. For published edition see entry No. 9594.

⟨1⟩-61. 8" x 5".

Printed buff paper wrapper.

Received at BMU July 14, 1881.

BMU

9592. "The City and the Sea," with Other Cambridge Contributions, in Aid of the Hospital Fund . . .

Cambridge: John Wilson and Son, University Press. 1881.

"My First Friend in Cambridge," pp. ⟨73⟩-78.

For comment see entry No. 8325.

9593. . . . A Day's Pleasure, and Other Sketches . . .

Boston: Houghton, Mifflin and Company. The Riverside Press, Cambridge. 1881

At head of title: Modern Classics.

Reprint save for "Buying a Horse." See entry Nos. 9571, 9839.

Deposited Nov. 18, 1881.

LC

9594. DOCTOR BREEN'S PRACTICE　A NOVEL . . .

BOSTON　JAMES R. OSGOOD AND COMPANY　1881

⟨i-ii⟩, ⟨1⟩-272, blank leaf. 7⅜" full x 4¹³⁄₁₆".

⟨1-23⟩⁶. *Signed:* ⟨-⟩¹, ⟨1-4⟩, 5-17⁸, ⟨*⟩¹.

S cloth: blue; blue-green; grass-green; tan; terracotta. White paper end papers imprinted in green or pale orange with a floral pattern. Flyleaves.

Deposited Dec. 2, 1881. Listed PW Dec. 10, 1881. CC copy inscribed by Howells Dec. 27, 1881. The London (Trübner) edition listed Ath Dec. 31, 1881. For a copyright printing see entry No. 9591A.

CC　H　NYPL

9595. ⟨Advertisement for⟩ Mr. ⟨John James⟩ Piatt's Poems . . . Extracts from Letters . . .

⟨n.p., n.d., after Sept. 19, 1881⟩

Four-page leaflet. Issued as an advertisement for Piatt's poems. The above at head of p. ⟨1⟩.

Extract from an article by Howells, reprinted from *Atlantic Monthly*, pp. 3-4.

WMG

9596. Eighth Annual Dinner of the New York Press Club. January 6, 1881.

New York: Privately Printed. 1881.

Printed paper wrapper.

Letter, Jan. 5, 1881, p. 57.

Y

9597. A MODERN INSTANCE　A NOVEL . . .

LONDON　TRÜBNER AND CO. LUDGATE HILL ⟨n.d., 1882⟩

Prepared for copyright purposes only. For published editions see entry Nos. 9601, 9602.

Presumably the whole work was prepared in this copyright form but pp. ⟨1⟩-77 only, comprising four parts, each in unprinted blue paper wrapper, have been located; these are in The Bodleian Library. Part 6 was listed in Ath April 15, 1882.

Not seen.

9598. . . . Living Truths from the Writings of Charles Kingsley Selected by E. E. Brown Introduction by W. D. Howells

Boston   D. Lothrop and Company   32 Franklin Street   ⟨1882⟩

At head of title: Spare Minute Series.

"Introduction," pp. ⟨3⟩-4.

Listed PW July 1, 1882. Deposited July 20, 1882.

AAS   Y

9599. The Lincoln Memorial: Album-Immortelles . . . Edited by Osborn H. Oldroyd . . .

New York: G. W. Carleton & Co., Publishers. London: S. Low, Son & Co. MDCCCLXXXII

6-line comment, dated Belmont, 1880, p. 407.

For comment see entry No. 1092.

9600. Ducal Mantua . . .

⟨Bangor, Maine, 1882⟩

Caption-title. The above at head of p. ⟨1⟩.

Issued in printed paper wrapper as No. 39 in *The Monograph* series, "a serial collection of indexed essays, published monthly" by Q. P. Index, Bangor, Maine; and, J. W. Christopher, New York.

⟨1⟩-12. *Also paged:* 427-438. 8¾6″ x 5¾″.

Published 1st October, 1882.—P. 12.

Reprinted, with the author's permission, from The North-American Review.—P. 10. The statement is misleading. The text is a truncated, revised, version of the piece as published in NAR. Yet another version appears in *Italian Journeys*, 1872.

H

9601. A MODERN INSTANCE   A NOVEL . . .

EDINBURGH   DAVID DOUGLAS 1882 . . .

2 Vols.

For a copyright printing see entry No. 9597.

Study of contemporary trade notices indicates that this Edinburgh edition was issued a few days prior to the American printing, entry No. 9602.

1: ⟨i-iv⟩, ⟨1⟩-344. 7″ plus x 4¾″.
2: ⟨i-iv⟩, ⟨1⟩-336.

1: ⟨-⟩², A-I, K-U, X⁸, Y⁴.
2: ⟨-⟩², A-I, K-U, X⁸.

S cloth: mottled gray-blue. Printed paper label on spine. Brown-coated end papers. Inserted at back of some copies, Vol. 2: Publisher's list, 4 pp., dated Sept. 1882.

According to a note in Ath Sept. 2, 1882, the book was to be published in October. Advertised for Oct. 2, 1882, Ath Sept. 30, 1882. Reviewed by Ath Oct. 7, 1882. Listed PC, Nov. 1, 1882; Bkr, Nov. 6, 1882.

H   Y

9602. A MODERN INSTANCE   A NOVEL . . .

BOSTON   JAMES R. OSGOOD AND COMPANY   1882

First American edition. See preceding entry. Also see entry No. 9597.

Two printings noted:

1

⟨i-ii⟩, ⟨1⟩-514, blank leaf. 7⁷⁄₁₆″ x 4¹³⁄₁₆″.

⟨1¹, 2-22¹², 23⁶⟩. *Signed:* ⟨-⟩¹, ⟨1⟩-32⁸, 33².

2

⟨i-ii⟩, ⟨1⟩-514.

⟨1-21¹², 22⁶⟩. Signed: ⟨-⟩¹, ⟨1⟩-32⁸, 33¹. In some copies there is inserted at the back a publisher's catalog dated *Autumn, 1882.*

S cloth: blue; terra-cotta. Ecru end papers. Flyleaf at front.

Deposited Oct. 7, 1882. Noted for Oct. 7, 1882, PW Oct. 7, 1882. Listed PW Oct. 14, 1882.

BPL (2nd)   H (1st, 2nd)   NYPL (2nd)

9603. Out of the Question and at the Sign of the Savage . . .

Edinburgh   David Douglas, Castle Street 1882

Printed boards; and, printed paper wrapper.

Reprint.

Advertised Ath Sept. 23, 1882. Advertised as *in the press* PC Oct. 2, 1882. Received BMU Oct. 21, 1882. Listed PC Nov. 1, 1882.

H

9604. Harper's Christmas   Pictures & Papers . . . Done by the Tile Club & Its Literary Friends

Published by Harper & Brothers   Franklin Square, New York   ⟨1882⟩

"The Sleeping-Car. A Farce," pp. 6-7. For separate publication see entry No. 9609.

For comment see entry No. 316.

9605. A Fearful Responsibility and Tonelli's Marriage . . .

Edinburgh   David Douglas, Castle Street 1882

Reprint.

Probably issued in printed paper boards; and, printed paper wrapper.

Received BMU Dec. 6, 1882. Listed PC Dec. 6, 1882.

H

9606. Poems . . .

Boston: Houghton, Mifflin and Company, The Riverside Press, Cambridge. 1882.

Reprint. See entry No. 9567.

B

9607. Suburban Sketches . . . New and Enlarged Edition . . .

Boston: Houghton, Mifflin and Company. The Riverside Press, Cambridge. 1882.

Reprint.

B

9607A. A WOMAN'S REASON A NOVEL . . .

EDINBURGH   DAVID DOUGLAS 1883 . . .

Not seen. Prepared for copyright purposes only.

Text incomplete. For published edition see entry No. 9610.

Ten paper-covered parts. The dates are those of receipt by BMU.

1: ⟨i-iv⟩, ⟨1⟩-64. 7″ x 4½″. Jan. 12, 1883.
2: 65-128. Feb. 15, 1883.
3: 129-160. March 17, 1883.
4: 161-192. April 17, 1883.
5: 193-250. May 5, 1883.
6: ⟨1⟩-32. June 26, 1883.
7: 33-64. Aug. 10, 1883.
8: 65-96. Aug. 10, 1883.
9: 97-128. Sept. 20, 1883.
10: 129-160. Oct. 11, 1883.

BMU

9608. Study and Stimulants . . . Edited by A. Arthur Reade.

Manchester: Abel Heywood and Son, 56 and 58, Oldham Street. London: Simpkin, Marshall, and Co. 1883 . . .

Statement, dated March 2, 1882, p. 71.

For comment see entry No. 3409.

9609. THE SLEEPING-CAR A FARCE . . .

BOSTON   JAMES R. OSGOOD AND COMPANY   1883

⟨i-iv⟩, ⟨1⟩-74, blank leaf. 5¼″ x 3⁹/₁₆″.

⟨1-5⁸⟩. *Signed:* ⟨-⟩², ⟨1⟩-4⁸, 5⁶.

S cloth: green. End papers printed in red with publisher's advertisements. Edges stained red.

For prior publication see entry No. 9604. Advertised for March 25, 1883, PW March 24, 1883. BA copy received March 26, 1883. Deposited March 31, 1883. Listed PW April 28, 1883.

H NYPL

9610. A WOMAN'S REASON A NOVEL . . .

BOSTON   JAMES R. OSGOOD AND COMPANY   1883

⟨i-vi⟩, ⟨1⟩-466. 7⁷/₁₆″ x 4⅞″.

⟨1-19¹², 20⁸⟩. *Signed:* ⟨-⟩³, A-I, K-U, X-Z, 2A-2F⁸, 2G¹.

S cloth: grass-green; gray-blue; gray-green; tan; terra-cotta. Gray paper end papers. Flyleaves.

H copy received Sept. 22, 1883. Deposited Sept. 24, 1883. Listed PW Sept. 29, 1883. Noted as *just ready* PW Sept. 29, 1883. The British edition (Edinburgh: Douglas) advertised (prematurely?) as *now ready* Ath Oct. 20, 1883; PC Nov. 1, 1883; listed PC Nov. 15, 1883. For a copyright printing see entry No. 9607A.

CC H NYPL

9611. "The Story of a Country Town." By E. W. Howe . . .

⟨n.p., n.d., probably Atchison, Kansas, 1883–1884⟩

Single leaf. Printed on recto only. 7½″ x 4⅝″.

Letter from Howells to Howe. For a comment on this letter see *Mark Twain-Howells Letters* . . . , (entry No. 9881), Vol. 2, pp. 491-492.

H

9612. A LITTLE GIRL ⟨*i.e.,* Mildred Howells⟩ AMONG THE OLD MASTERS WITH INTRODUCTION AND COMMENT BY W. D. HOWELLS

BOSTON   JAMES R. OSGOOD AND COMPANY   1884

Title-page in black and orange.

Note: According to contemporary advertisements this book was to be issued in cloth ($2); and, parchment ($3). The book has been noted by BAL in cloth only although both Johnson, and Gibson and Arms, report a de luxe edition. BAL presumes that no de luxe edition was published. BAL *theorizes* that copies done on wove paper were intended for the cloth format; and copies on laid paper for the parchment, or de luxe, format; that the plan for issuing two formats was abandoned and that both laid paper sheets and wove paper sheets were simultaneously issued in cloth at the same price.

Also note: The title-leaf occurs in varying papers as noted below. No reason for the variations has been determined but it may be that the publishers used whatever paper was available.

Three forms noted. The sequence, if any, not known. The designations are for identification only.

A

Letterpress on *wove* paper.

The title-leaf is a singleton printed on paper heavier than that used for the letterpress. Title-leaf printed on both sides and reckoned as pp. ⟨1-2⟩; otherwise the leaves are printed on recto only.

65 leaves of *wove* paper: Title-leaf, pp. ⟨1-2⟩; 63 leaves printed on recto only and paged 3-65; blank leaf. 5¹³⁄₁₆″ x 8¹³⁄₁₆″.

54 inserted plates numbered 1-54.

⟨1¹, 2-33²⟩.

The deposit copies thus. Deposited Nov. 15, 1883.

H LC

B

Letterpress on *laid* paper save for the title-leaf.

The title-leaf is a singleton printed on *wove* paper; printed on both sides and reckoned as pp. ⟨1-2⟩; otherwise the leaves are printed on recto only.

65 leaves as follows: Title-leaf (*wove* paper), pp. ⟨1-2⟩; 63 leaves of *laid* paper printed on recto only and paged 3-65; blank leaf of *laid* paper. 5¹³⁄₁₆″ x 8⅞″.

54 inserted plates numbered 1-54.

⟨1¹, 2-33²⟩.

BA copy received Dec. 10, 1883. A copy in H inscribed by early owner *Christmas, 1883.*

BA H

C

Letterpress on *laid* paper throughout.

The title-leaf is conjugate with a preliminary blank leaf. Title-leaf printed on both sides and reckoned as pp. ⟨1-2⟩; otherwise the leaves are printed on recto only.

66 leaves of *laid* paper: Blank leaf; title-leaf, pp. ⟨1-2⟩; 63 leaves printed on recto only and paged 3-65; blank leaf. 5¹³⁄₁₆″ x 8⅞″

54 inserted plates numbered 1-54.

⟨1-33²⟩.

A copy in H inscribed by early owner *Dec. 25, 1883.*

H

Binding

V cloth: blue; gray; mustard; olive. Edges stained orange. End papers noted: white, printed in blue-green with a floral pattern; white, printed in ochre with a floral pattern; mottled, undecorated, blue-gray paper. Noted both with and without flyleaf at front.

Deposited Nov. 15, 1883. Listed PW Dec. 22, 1883. A copy received by BA (form B) Dec. 10, 1883. An edition in parchment (see preliminary notes above) advertised PW Jan. 26, 1884. A copy of the London (Trübner) edition, issued without date, in H inscribed by early owner Jan. 7, 1884; listed Ath Feb. 1884. The London edition presumably was printed from the original American setting and produced at the same time and place as the Boston edition although the book contains no indication of place of production; the Osgood imprint appears at the foot of the spine.

9613. THE REGISTER FARCE ...

BOSTON JAMES R. OSGOOD AND COMPANY 1884

⟨i-ii⟩, ⟨1⟩-91, blank leaf. 5⁵⁄₁₆″ x 3⅝″.

⟨1-6⁸⟩. *Signed:* ⟨-⟩¹, ⟨1⟩-5⁸, 6⁷.

S cloth: green. White end papers imprinted in red with publisher's advertisements. Edges stained red.

BPL copy received March 13, 1884. Deposited March 17, 1884. Listed PW March 22, 1884.

H Y

9614. THREE VILLAGES ...

BOSTON JAMES R. OSGOOD AND COMPANY 1884

Title-page in black and red.

⟨i-ii⟩, ⟨1⟩-198, blank leaf. 5¾″ x 4³⁄₁₆″.

⟨1⟩⁹, 2-12⁸, 13⁴. Leaf ⟨1⟩₄ inserted.

S cloth: blue-green; brown; olive-green; pale green. Dark blue-coated end papers. Edges stained orange. *Note:* Two binding issues noted:

1: Spine imprint of James R. Osgood & Co.

2: Spine imprint of Houghton, Mifflin & Co.

Noted as *just ready* PW May 17, 1884. BPL copy received May 17, 1884; BA copy May 20, 1884.

Deposited May 22, 1884. Listed PW May 24, 1884. Noted by Ath July 19, 1884.

BA (1st) H (1st) NYPL (1st) Y (2nd)

9614A. THE RISE OF SILAS LAPHAM ...

    EDINBURGH DAVID DOUGLAS 1885 ...

Title-page as above; presumably issued with the final part as leaf 2K4.

Prepared for copyright purposes only. The dates are those of receipt at BMU. 9 paper-covered parts. 6¹³⁄₁₆″ x 4½″ (trimmed).

Not seen. For formal publication see entry No. 9619.

1: ⟨1⟩-51. Oct. 8, 1884.
2: 52-98. Nov. 6, 1884.
3: 99-150. Dec. 8, 1884.
4: 151-191. Jan. 21, 1885.
5: 192-241. Feb. 9, 1885.
6: 242-293. March 7, 1885.
7: 294-340. April 16, 1885.
8: 341-394. May 16, 1885.
9: 395-515. July 11, 1885.

BMU

9615. NIAGARA REVISITED ...

    PUBLISHED BY D DALZIEL CHICAGO ⟨n.d., 1884?⟩

Title-page printed in colors.

This book exhibits such abnormalities that it is best to present a verbal description.

Leaf: 8⅞″ scant x 7¼₆″.

Title-leaf and conjugate leaf printed in colored lithograph; enveloping pp. 1-2 of text.

Two conjugate leaves of illustrations printed in colored lithograph; enveloping pp. 3-4 of text.

Two conjugate leaves of illustrations printed in colored lithograph; enveloping pp. 5-6 of text.

Leaf of illustrations printed in colored lithograph with blank conjugate leaf; enveloping the following:

Pp. 7-8 of text; being a singleton leaf.

Pp. 9-12 of text; being a cut sheet folded to two conjugate leaves.

16 pp. advertisements, printed on paper appreciably thinner than that used in the body of the book. The advertisements are for the Hoosac Tunnel Route; Erie Railway; etc., etc. The advertisements comprise a single 8vo gathering.

"This book was made by a Chicago firm for the Fitchburg Railroad Company, and the Chicago people were to pay Mr. Howells a certain sum for the privilege of using his sketch, which had already appeared in the *Atlantic Monthly* ⟨May, 1883⟩. But they failed to meet their obligations toward the author, and consequently Mr. Howells served a notice upon the railroad company, through his attorneys, which prevented the publication of the book."—Albert Lee in *The Book Buyer,* New York, March, 1897, p. ⟨143⟩.

Buff paper boards printed in colored lithograph. Pale tan paper end papers (oxidized white paper?) printed in brown with a floral pattern; also, printed in blue with a pattern of circular ornaments and leaf-like ornaments.

Note: The CU copy does not have the terminal advertisements nor is there any evidence that the copy was issued with that feature.

First published in *Atlantic Monthly,* May, 1883. The UV copy inscribed by early owner Nov. 11, 1885. For an account of the manufacture and suppression of this book see "*Niagara Revisited* ... the Story of Its Publication and Suppression," by Rudolf and Clara M. Kirk, in *Essays in Literary History* ... , edited by Rudolf Kirk and C. F. Main, Rutgers University Press ⟨1960⟩.

CU UV Y

A Sea-Change or Love's Stowaway A Comic Opera ... by W. D. Howells ⟨Music⟩ Composed by Georg Henschel

    Boston ... ⟨1884; *i.e.,* 1888⟩.

See entry No. 9638.

9616. Glimpses of Quebec, in Twelve Photographs, Illustrating *A Chance Acquaintance* ...

    Boston: Cupples, Upham & Co. Copyright, 1884, by E. L. Coleman.

Cover-title. See entry No. 9566.

A series of twelve photographs mounted on boards. Issued in printed brown paper wrapper. 13½″ full x 11⅝₆″.

Bound in as front matter is a cut sheet of laid paper, folded to make four pages, bearing a short statement by Howells relating to the photographs.

Deposited Jan. 3, 1885.

LC

9617. THE ELEVATOR FARCE ...

    BOSTON JAMES R. OSGOOD AND COMPANY 1885

⟨i-ii⟩, ⟨1⟩-84, blank leaf. 5¼″ x 3⁹⁄₁₆″.

⟨1-5⁸, 6⁴⟩.

S cloth: green. Edges stained red. End papers printed in red with advertisements.

Noted as *just ready* PW Jan. 17, 1885. Deposited Jan. 30, 1885. Listed PW Jan. 31, 1885.

H   LC   NYPL

9618. INDIAN SUMMER ...

EDINBURGH: DAVID DOUGLAS 1885 ...

Prepared for copyright purposes only. *Not seen.* For published edition see entry No. 9624.

Cover-title. Printed pink paper wrapper.

Pp. ⟨1⟩-395. Eight parts; received, respectively: June 9; July 11; Aug. 10; Sept. 12; Oct. 12; Nov; Dec. 11, 1885; Jan. 13, 1886.

Copies in BMU and Bodleian.

9619. THE RISE OF SILAS LAPHAM ...

BOSTON   TICKNOR AND COMPANY   1885

⟨i-viii⟩, ⟨1⟩-515, 2 blank leaves. The first and final leaves excised or pasted under the end papers. 7⅜″ x 4¾″.

⟨1⁴, 2-22¹², 23⁸⟩. Leaves ⟨1⟩1 and ⟨23⟩8 excised or pasted under the end papers. *Signed:* ⟨-⟩⁴, A-I, K-U, X-Z, 2A-2I⁸, 2K⁴.

Two states (almost certainly printings) noted:

1

On p. ⟨vi⟩ is a boxed advertisement headed MR. HOWELLS'S LATEST WORKS.

2

On p. ⟨vi⟩ is a boxed advertisement headed MR. HOWELLS'S LATEST NOVELS.

Note: The above sequence is based on a study of many copies of the book. The copies first printed have the word *sojourner,* p. 176, last line, printed from undamaged metal; all the known reprints from the original setting, not necessarily from the original plates, have the word printed from battered type. Quite possibly the damage occurred during the course of the first printing since copies with the earlier form of the advertisement, p. ⟨vi⟩, have been seen with the type either damaged or undamaged. According to PW Aug. 22, 1885, *more than 5000 copies ... were ordered in advance of publication, and the subsequent sale has been very large.* PW Sept. 5, 1885, reported *Ticknor & Co. have had a very great success with ... Silas Lapham ... Eight thousand copies have already been sold* ... Hence, one may presume that perhaps the first and the second printings were

simultaneously issued. One may not overlook the possibility that copies with the earlier form of the advertisement, and with the word *sojourner* printed from battered metal, may have been made up of mixed sheets; *i.e.,* sheets of the first and later printings. One such copy (*i.e.,* earlier form of the preliminary advertisement, battered metal on p. 176) is worth special mention; it was seen at GD (June 11, 1957) and inscribed by Howells: *First Copy. Susan W. Farwell, with the regard and gratitude of Winifred's papa ... Aug. 19, 1885.* Thus far BAL has not located a copy with the later form of the preliminary advertisement and unbattered type on p. 176.

S cloth: blue; green; green-gray; tan; terracotta. Gray paper end papers.

Noted for *this week* PW Aug. 15, 1885. GD copy (see note above) inscribed by Howells Aug. 19, 1885. Listed PW Aug. 22, 1885. H copy (earlier advertisement; battered type, p. 176) inscribed by early owner Aug. 22, 1885. Another copy in H (earlier advertisement; unbattered type, p. 176) inscribed by early owner Aug. 27, 1885. Deposited (see note below) Oct. 5, 1885. The Edinburgh (Douglas) edition advertised as *immediately* Ath Sept. 5, 1885; listed Ath Sept. 26, 1885; PC Oct. 1, 1885; Bkr Oct. 8, 1885. For a copyright printing see entry No. 9614A.

Note: The copyright records show that two copies were received on Aug. 21, 1885; and that two additional copies were received on Oct. 5, 1885. The copies deposited Aug. 21 are no longer in the Library of Congress; the copies deposited Oct. 5, have the later form of the advertisement and the battered metal, p. 176. No information found regarding the reason for depositing four copies on two different dates.

Also note: NYPL has a set of untrimmed sheets bound in unprinted yellow paper boards, printed paper label on spine reading: W. D. HOWELLS, 1st ED./⟨rule⟩   The status of this copy, with the later form of the advertisement and battered type on p. 176, is not known. However, the binding may have been put on for a private collector, William Augustus White. Certain other books have been seen in the same style of binding; to cite examples: Halleck's *Fanny,* second edition, 1821, in H; Holmes's *Ralph Waldo Emerson,* 1885, in Y; Irving's *Letters of Jonathan Oldstyle,* 1824, in BA.

H (earlier advertisement, unbattered *sojourner;* earlier advertisement, battered *sojourner*) LC (later advertisement, battered *sojourner*) NYPL (earlier advertisement, unbattered *sojourner*)

9620. TUSCAN CITIES ...

BOSTON TICKNOR AND COMPANY   1886

⟨i-ii⟩, ⟨i⟩-⟨vi⟩, ⟨1⟩-251; blank, p. ⟨252⟩; 2 pp. advertisements; blank leaf. Illustrated. 8¹³⁄₁₆″ x 6⅝″.

⟨1-33⁴⟩. *Signed:* ⟨-⟩⁴, ⟨1⟩-⟨3⟩, 4-⟨6⟩, 7-⟨13⟩, 14-16⁸.

V cloth: blue; olive; tan. Covers bevelled. Edges gilt. White paper end papers printed in brown; also printed in orange; with an all-over floral pattern. Flyleaves.

Two binding issues noted:

1: Ticknor & Co. spine imprint.

2: Houghton Mifflin Co. spine imprint.

Noted as *just published* PW Oct. 24, 1885. Deposited Oct. 26, 1885. BA copy received Oct. 27, 1885. Listed PW Nov. 7, 1885. The Edinburgh (Douglas) edition listed Ath Dec. 5, 1885. See entry No. 9688.

AAS (1st)   H (1st, 2nd)

9620A. Complimentary Banquet ⟨Jan. 12, 1885⟩ to Gen. Augustus P. Martin, by His Neighbors and Friends of the Shoe and Leather Trade, at the Expiration of His Term As Mayor of Boston.

⟨n.p., Boston⟩ Shoe and Leather Reporter Press. ⟨n.d., 1885⟩

Printed paper wrapper.

"Remarks," pp. 21-22.

BPL

9621. Col. Sellers as a Scientist. A Comedy. By S. L. Clemens and W. D. Howells ...

⟨n.p., n.d., *ca.* 1885⟩

Synopsis only; for comment see entry No. 3417. For first publication of the full text see entry No. 9882.

9622. Poems ...

Boston   Ticknor and Company   211 Tremont Street   MDCCCLXXXVI

Reprint save for: "The Song the Oriole Sings," "Pordenone" and "The Long Days."

Three binding issues noted:

1: Vellum over flexible boards. Stamped in black and red. *Ticknor & Co.* imprint on spine.

2: Vellum. Stamped in gold. *Houghton, Mifflin & Co.* imprint on spine.

3: Vellum. Stamped in gold. *Houghton Mifflin Co.* imprint on spine.

Deposited Nov. 14, 1885. BPL copy received Nov. 14, 1885; BA copy received Nov. 17, 1885. See entry No. 9567.

B (1st)   BA (1st)   BPL (1st)   H (1st, 3rd)   LC (1st)   NYPL (1st)   WMG (2nd)   Y (1st)

9623. THE GARROTERS   FARCE ...

NEW YORK   HARPER & BROTHERS   1886

⟨i-ii⟩, ⟨1⟩-90; plus: 8 pp. advertisements. Frontispiece and 2 plates inserted. 5¼″ x 3⅝″.

⟨1-5⁸, 6-7¹, 8⁴; plus: 9⁴⟩.

S cloth: green. Edges stained red.

Deposited Dec. 21, 1885. Noted for *this week* PW Dec. 26, 1885. BPL copy received Dec. 26, 1885. Listed PW Jan. 2, 1886. The Edinburgh (Douglas) edition listed PC July 31, 1897.

LC   NYPL   Y

9624. INDIAN SUMMER ...

BOSTON   TICKNOR AND COMPANY   1886

⟨i-viii⟩, ⟨1⟩-395; 2 blank leaves. *Note:* Pp. ⟨i-ii⟩ and final blank leaf excised or pasted under the end papers. 7⅜″ x 4¾″.

⟨1⁴, 2-17¹², 18⁸⟩. Leaves ⟨1⟩₁ and ⟨18⟩₈ excised or pasted under the end papers. *Signed:* ⟨-⟩⁴, A-I, K-U, X-Z, 2A-2B⁸.

S cloth: blue; brown; olive; terra-cotta. Gray paper end papers. *Note:* Also noted in a binding of unknown status: White S cloth, lettered leather label on spine; wholly untrimmed; leaf size 8″ scant x 5⅛″.

Noted for Feb. 17, 1886, PW Feb. 13, 1886. H copy received Feb. 17, 1886. Deposited Feb. 19, 1886. Listed PW Feb. 27, 1886. The Edinburgh (Douglas) edition was advertised as *nearly ready* Ath Feb. 13, 1886; as *now ready* Ath March 13, 1886; listed Ath March 13, 1886. The preceding British notes apply to the work in one volume; a two-volume edition advertised in Ath May 21, 1887. For a copyright printing see entry No. 9618.

H   NYPL   Y

9625. George Fuller His Life and Works ...

Boston and New York   Houghton, Mifflin and Company   The Riverside Press, Cambridge   MDCCCLXXXVI

Printed paper boards, vellum shelfback and corners.

"Sketch of George Fuller's Life," pp. ⟨1⟩-52.

Limited to 300 numbered copies.

Deposited April 19, 1886. Listed PW May 8, 1886.

Y

9626. THE MINISTER'S CHARGE OR THE APPRENTICESHIP OF LEMUEL BARKER
. . .

EDINBURGH DAVID DOUGLAS 1886 . . .

First British edition. For first American edition see next entry.

⟨i-iv⟩, ⟨1⟩-463. 7⅛″ scant x 4⅞″.

⟨-⟩², A-I, K-U, X-Z, 2A-2F⁸. Signature mark F present only as a vestige.

V cloth: red. Brown-coated on white end papers. Inserted at back: Publisher's catalog, pp. ⟨1⟩-20, dated *October 1886*.

Advertised as *nearly ready* Ath Sept. 11, 1886. Noted in PC Oct. 1, 1886, as *nearly ready*. Advertised as *nearly ready* Ath Oct. 30, 1886. Listed Ath Nov. 6, 1886; PC Dec. 6, 1886; Bkr Dec. 16, 1886. Reviewed Ath Dec. 18, 1886.

UV

9627. THE MINISTER'S CHARGE OR THE APPRENTICESHIP OF LEMUEL BARKER
. . .

BOSTON TICKNOR AND COMPANY 1887

First American edition. See preceding entry.

⟨i-iv⟩, ⟨1⟩-463; plus: publisher's catalog, pp. ⟨1⟩-24. 7⁷⁄₁₆″ x 4¾″.

⟨1-19¹², 20⁶; plus: 21¹²⟩. *Signed:* ⟨-⟩², A-I, K-U, X-Z, 2A-2F⁸; plus: ⟨*⟩¹².

S cloth: blue; tan; terra-cotta. Gray paper end papers. Flyleaves.

Two binding issues noted:

1: Spine imprint of Ticknor & Co.

2: Spine imprint of Houghton Mifflin & Co.

Various other variations are present but the above is sufficient for ready identification.

Published Dec. 9, 1886, according to note in publisher's file copy in BPL. H copy received from publisher Dec. 9, 1886. Deposited Dec. 11, 1886. Noted as *just ready* PW Dec. 11, 1886. Listed PW Dec. 18, 1886.

BA (2nd) BPL (1st) H (1st) NYPL (1st, 2nd) Y (2nd)

9628. Sebastopol by Count Leo Tolstoï Translated from the French by Frank D. Millet with Introduction by W. D. Howells . . .

New York Harper & Brothers, Franklin Square 1887

"Leo Tolstoï," pp. ⟨5⟩-12.

Deposited July 2, 1887. Noted as *just issued* PW July 2, 1887. Listed PW July 9, 1887.

H LC NYPL

9629. MODERN ITALIAN POETS ESSAYS AND VERSIONS . . .

NEW YORK HARPER & BROTHERS, FRANKLIN SQUARE 1887

⟨i-viii⟩, ⟨1⟩-⟨370⟩, blank leaf. 11 plates inserted. 7⅝″ scant x 5⅛″.

⟨-⟩⁴, 1-15¹², 16⁶.

Green-gray V cloth sides, imitation white vellum shelfback. Flyleaves. Top edges gilt. 12-line errata slip inserted between pp. ⟨370-371⟩.

Noted as *shortly* PW Sept. 10, 1887. Deposited Oct. 1, 1887. Listed PW Oct. 8, 1887. The Edinburgh (Douglas) edition announced for *October* Ath Oct. 1, 1887; advertised as though ready Ath Oct. 15, 1887; listed Ath Dec. 3, 1887.

H NYPL

9630. APRIL HOPES A NOVEL . . .

EDINBURGH DAVID DOUGLAS 1887 . . .

First British edition. For first American edition see entry No. 9634.

⟨i-iv⟩, ⟨1⟩-484. 7⁷⁄₁₆″ x 4⅞″.

⟨-⟩², A-I, K-U, X-Z, 2A-2G⁸, 2H².

V cloth: red. Brown-coated on white end papers. Inserted at back: Publisher's catalog, pp. ⟨1⟩-20, dated *Oct. 1887*.

Advertised for *October* Ath Oct. 1, 1887. Noted as *in a few days* Ath Oct. 15, 1887. Listed Ath Oct. 22, 1887; PC Nov. 1, 1887; Bkr Nov. 1, 1887. Noted as though published Ath Nov. 5, 1887. Reviewed Ath Nov. 19, 1887.

H

9631. The Elocutionist's Annual Number 15 . . . Compiled by Mrs. J. W. Shoemaker.

Publication Department, The National School of Elocution and Oratory. Philadelphia: 1887.

"The Mouse Trap," pp. 172-188. "Abridged from *Harper's Magazine* of December, 1886, by kind permission of the publishers."

For full publication see entry No. 9642.

H

9632. Their Wedding Journey ...

Boston: Houghton, Mifflin and Company. New York: 11 East Seventeenth Street. The Riverside Press, Cambridge. 1887.

Not seen. Entry from Johnson; and, Gibson & Arms.

Reprint; see entry No. 9558. Contains, however, the first collected appearance of "Niagara Revisited" which had prior separate publication; see entry No. 9615.

9633. CLEMENCY FOR THE ANARCHISTS. A LETTER FROM MR. W. D. HOWELLS. TO THE EDITOR OF THE ⟨New York⟩ TRIBUNE ... DANSVILLE, N. Y., NOV. 4, 1887.

⟨n.p., n.d., 1887?⟩

Caption-title. Single leaf. Printed in blue on recto only. 10" x 5¾" scant.

First published in the *New York Tribune,* Nov. 6, 1887, p. 5. Collected in *Life in Letters,* 1928.

H

9634. APRIL HOPES ...

NEW YORK HARPER & BROTHERS, FRANKLIN SQUARE 1888

First American edition. For prior publication see entry No. 9630.

⟨i-iv⟩, ⟨1⟩-484; 8 pp. advertisements. 7⅜" x 4¾" full.

⟨-⟩², 1-20¹², 21⁶.

V cloth: red. Flyleaves. Stamped in gold. *Note:* A presumed remainder binding (copy in AAS) is bound in dull red V cloth, stamped in black, leaf ⟨-⟩₁ excised or pasted under the end paper; no flyleaves.

Deposited Dec. 10, 1887. Noted as *ready* PW Dec. 10, 1887. H copy presented by Howells to C. E. Norton, Dec. 16, 1887. Listed PW Dec. 17, 1887.

H NYPL

9635. What American Authors Think about International Copyright

New-York American Copyright League 1888

One-paragraph statement, p. 6.

For comment see entry No. 218.

9636. Mark Twain's Library of Humor ...

New York Charles L. Webster & Company 1888

Two states noted:

1: Index of titles, pp. xvi-xix, arranged by order of appearance in the book. "Warm Hair," p. 8, credited to Mark Twain.

2: Titles, pp. xvi-xix, arranged alphabetically. Mark Twain not credited with authorship of "Warm Hair," p. 8.

According to Harold Blodgett (*American Literature,* March 1938) the introduction was written by Howells.

"Howells was editor of this volume."—Gibson & Arms, p. 35.

"... Mark Twain did not play a major part in the editing of *Mark Twain's Library of Humor.*"—Harold Blodgett, *op. cit.*

"Although the book was not published until 1888, work on it engaged his ⟨i.e., Clemens's⟩ attention for several years. Since Howells, Osgood, and a Hartford newspaperman, Charles Clark, helped with the collection, biographers have believed that Clemens had relatively little to do with it. But letters show clearly that he was quite active—that he made the initial selections, that by March, 1882, he had accumulated selections totaling more than 93,000 words, and that he planned to continue his reading of humorous works during the summer of 1882."—*Mark Twain and Huck Finn,* by Walter Blair, Berkeley and Los Angeles, 1960, p. 243.

For further comment see *Mark Twain-Howells Letters ...,* (entry No. 9881), Vol. 2, p. 945.

For publication notes see entry No. 1982.

9637. Library of Universal Adventure by Sea and Land ... Compiled and Edited by William Dean Howells and Thomas Sergeant Perry ...

New York Harper & Brothers, Franklin Square 1888

Also issued with the imprint: *New York Harper & Brothers, Franklin Square Springfield, Mass. Winter & Company 1888*

Issued in cloth; and, leather.

"Introduction," pp. ⟨v⟩-viii. If one may accept at face the sense of the introduction it was written jointly by Howells and Perry.

Deposited May 17, 1888. Listed PW June 30, 1888.

H LC Y

9637A. ANNIE KILBURN ...

EDINBURGH DAVID DOUGLAS 1888 ...

Cover-title. *Not seen.* Title-page issued with Part 6.

Prepared for copyright purposes only. For published editions see entry Nos. 9639, 9641.

Six paper-covered parts. The dates are those of receipt by BMU.

1: <1>-54. 7″ x 4⅝″. May 24, 1888.
2: 55-104. June 26, 1888.
3: 105-152. July 20, 1888.
4: 153-206. Aug. 21, 1888.
5: 207-266. Sept. 19, 1888.
6: 267-331; front matter for the whole, pp. <i-iv>. Oct. 20, 1888.

BMU

9638. A SEA-CHANGE OR LOVE'S STOW-AWAY A LYRICATED FARCE IN TWO ACTS AND AN EPILOGUE ...

BOSTON TICKNOR AND COMPANY 211, TREMONT STREET 1888

<1>-151. 5¾″ x 4⅛″.

<1-9⁸, 10⁴>.

S cloth: blue-green; brown; green; olive. Edges stained orange. Double flyleaves. Black-coated end papers; blue-coated end papers.

Two binding issues noted:

1: Front stamped in gold and blind. Ticknor & Co. imprint on spine.

2: Front stamped in black only. Houghton, Mifflin imprint on spine.

Noted as *ready today* PW Aug. 4, 1888. BA and H copies received Aug. 6, 1888. Deposited Aug. 8, 1888. Listed PW Aug. 11, 1888.

Also issued as a libretto:

A Sea-Change or Love's Stowaway A Comic Opera in Two Acts and an Epilogue Written by W. D. Howells Composed by Georg Henschel

Boston Arthur P. Schmidt and Company Nos. 13 and 15 West Street. <1884>

Printed paper wrapper. Pp. <1>-320. 11¹³⁄₁₆″ x 9⅜″.

The date of copyright, 1884, refers to the music and, possibly, ms copy of the text. *Boston Evening Transcript*, Nov. 3, 1888, refers to the libretto as though just issued. Libretto deposited Aug. 24, 1888. A printing from the same plates was issued in London by Trübner & Company and carries the following statement on the verso of the title-leaf: *J. Frank Giles, Music Printer, Boston.*

H (text, first binding. Libretto) LC (text, first binding. Libretto) NYPL (text, first binding; text, second binding) Y (libretto)

9639. ANNIE KILBURN A NOVEL ...

EDINBURGH DAVID DOUGLAS 1888 ...

For a copyright printing see entry No. 9637A. For American edition see entry No. 9641.

<i-iv>, <1>-331. 7¹⁄₁₆″ x 4¹³⁄₁₆″.

<->², A-I, K-U⁸, X⁶.

V cloth: red. Brown-coated end papers. Inserted at back: Publisher's catalog, pp. <1>-20, dated *October 1888.*

Advertised for *November* Ath Oct. 13; 27; Nov. 3, 1888. Listed Ath Nov. 24, 1888. Advertised as though published Ath Dec. 1, 1888. Listed PC Dec. 6, 1888. Reviewed Ath Dec. 22, 1888.

UV

9640. Italian Journeys ... New and Enlarged Edition. Twelfth Edition.

Boston: Houghton, Mifflin and Company New York: 11 East Seventeenth Street. The Riverside Press, Cambridge. 1888.

Reprint. See entry No. 9560.

LC

9641. ANNIE KILBURN A NOVEL ...

NEW YORK HARPER & BROTHERS, FRANKLIN SQUARE 1889

For a copyright printing see entry No. 9637A. For British edition see entry No. 9639.

<i-iv>, <1>-331; plus: 4 pp. advertisements. 7¼″ full x 4⅞″.

<->², <1>-13¹², 14¹⁰; plus: <15>².

V cloth: red. Flyleaves.

Deposited Dec. 15, 1888. CC copy inscribed by Howells Dec. 17, 1888. H copy inscribed by Howells Dec. 18, 1888. Listed PW Dec. 22, 1888.

CC H NYPL

9641A. A HAZARD OF NEW FORTUNES ...

EDINBURGH DAVID DOUGLAS 1889 ...

Cover-title. *Not seen.*

Prepared for copyright purposes only. For published edition see entry No. 9646. Also see entry No. 9809.

Eleven paper-covered parts. The dates are those of receipt by BMU.

1: <1>-47. 7″ x 4⅝″. April 10, 1889.
2: 48-132. May 9, 1889.
3: 133-171. June 8, 1889.

4: 172-212. July 6, 1889.
5: 213-280. Aug. 6, 1889.
6: 281-354. Aug. 16, 1889.
7: 355-404. Sept. 24, 1889.
8: 405-459. Sept. 24, 1889.
9: 460-523. Oct. 10, 1889.
10: 524-572. Oct. 23, 1889.
11: 273-664. Nov. 1, 1889.

BMU

9642. THE MOUSE-TRAP AND OTHER FARCES . . .

NEW YORK   HARPER & BROTHERS, FRANKLIN SQUARE   1889

⟨i-viii⟩, ⟨1⟩-184; plus: 2 pp. advertisements. Frontispiece inserted. Also inserted: 8 plates reckoned in the printed pagination. Laid paper. 7⁵⁄₁₆″ x 4¾″ full.

⟨-⟩⁴, ⟨1⟩-10⁸, 11⁴; plus: ⟨12⟩¹.

V cloth: red. White laid paper end papers.

Noted as *just ready* PW April 13, 1889. Deposited April 17, 1889. BPL copy received April 18, 1889. Listed PW April 20, 1889. The earliest London edition noted is the Edinburgh (Douglas) printing; listed PC June 5, 1897. See entry No. 9631.

H NYPL

9643. The Sleeping-Car and Other Farces . . .

Boston and New York   Houghton, Mifflin and Company   The Riverside Press, Cambridge 1889

Reprint.

Deposited May 13, 1889. Listed PW June 1, 1889.

AAS   H

9644. Character and Comment Selected from the Novels of W. D. Howells by Minnie Macoun

Boston and New York   Houghton, Mifflin and Company   The Riverside Press, Cambridge 1889

Reprint.

BPL copy received Sept. 30, 1889. Listed PW Oct. 12, 1889.

H NYPL Y

9645. Samson. A Tragedy in Five Acts, by Ippolito d'Aste. Translated by W. D. Howells. With the English and Italian Words, as Performed by Signor Salvini, during His Farewell American Tour, under the Direction of Mr. A. M. Palmer.

Charles D. Koppel, Publisher, 115 & 117 Nassau Street, New York . . . 1889 . . .

Printed faun paper wrapper.

Two printings noted. The sequence has not been determined and the order of presentation is tentative.

PRINTING A

⟨i-ii⟩, ⟨1⟩-51. 9½″ x 6¾″.

⟨1⁹, 2-3⁸, 4²⟩. Leaf ⟨1⟩₂ inserted.

PRINTING B

⟨i-ii⟩, ⟨1⟩-51, blank leaf. 9⁷⁄₁₆″ x 6¾″.

⟨1-3⁸, 4⁴⟩.

Note: Two states (printings?) of the wrapper have been noted. The sequence, if any, has not been determined and the following designations are for identification only:

WRAPPER A

Inner front imprinted with an advertisement for Ehrich Bros.

WRAPPER B

Inner front blank.

In a forthcoming bibliographical study by Mildred E. Nickerson (The Houghton Library) it is made clear that while Howells's translation of *Samson* was done in 1874 it was not published until 1889; that another translation by an unknown hand was published in 1873; and that the preliminary "Argument" which appears in the Howells version was lifted (with a few minor alterations) from the 1873 translation. Miss Nickerson produces evidence which indicates that the Howells translation may have been ready for distribution at the performance of *Samson* in New York on Oct. 10, 1889.

Deposited Oct. 19, 1889.

AAS (A sheets, wrapper B)   B (B sheets, wrapper B)   H (A sheets, wrapper B; B sheets, wrapper B)   NYPL (B sheets, wrapper A)   Y (B sheets, wrapper B)

9646. A HAZARD OF NEW FORTUNES   A NOVEL . . .

NEW YORK   HARPER & BROTHERS, FRANKLIN SQUARE   1890 ⟨i.e., 1889⟩

Issued under date Nov. 1889, as No. 661, *Harper's Franklin Square Library, New Series.*

⟨i-iv⟩, ⟨1⟩-171. Frontispiece and 15 plates inserted. 9⁷⁄₁₆″ x 6⁵⁄₁₆″.

⟨-⟩², 1-10⁸, 11⁶.

Printed pink-tan laid paper wrapper.

Two states (printings?) of the wrapper noted:

A

The first title listed on the inner front of the wrapper, *A Hazard of New Fortunes,* is described as in paper at 75¢; the cloth-bound printing, in two volumes, is described as *in press.*

B

As above but with the following exception: The cloth-bound printing, in two volumes, of *A Hazard of New Fortunes,* is priced at $2.00.

Note: Gibson & Arms, p. 37, state that the front of the wrapper occurs with "two paper labels, one printed *November, / 1889 / Extra / Harper's Franklin Square / Library / New Series /* and the other *661.*" No copy examined by BAL, including the surviving copyright deposit copy, bears such labels. Since Gibson & Arms do not describe the letterpress on the spine; and further, since the label lettering described by Gibson & Arms occurs on the spine, BAL conjectures that Gibson & Arms collated a copy in binding which had portions of the backstrip removed, preserved and pasted to the front of the wrapper.

Deposited Nov. 27, 1889. Listed PW Dec. 7, 1889.

Note: There is a possibility that the Edinburgh (Douglas) edition, 2 volumes, was issued simultaneously with the one-volume New York edition. The following is a publication record of the one-volume New York edition; the two-volume Edinburgh edition; and the two-volume New York edition. See entry No. 9641A for a copyright printing. Also see entry No. 9809.

Edinburgh: Advertised as *nearly ready* Ath Oct. 19, 1889.

Edinburgh: Listed (prematurely?) PC Nov. 15, 1889. Listing possibly based on the copyright printing (entry No. 9641A) and publisher's information.

Edinburgh: Advertised as *nearly ready* Ath Nov. 16, 1889; Nov. 23, 1889.

New York (1 Vol.): Deposited Nov. 27, 1889.

Edinburgh: Deposited BMU Dec. 2, 1889.

New York (1 Vol.): Listed PW Dec. 7, 1889.

Edinburgh: Advertised as though published, and listed, Ath Dec. 7, 1889.

New York (2 Vols.): Advertised as *in press* PW Jan. 4, 1890.

New York (2 Vols.): Deposited Jan. 27, 1890.

AAS (wrapper B) H (wrapper A; 2-Vol. New York) LC (wrapper A; Edinburgh; 2-Vol. New York) NYPL (wrapper A; 2-Vol. New York) Y (wrapper A)

9647. Camden's Compliment to Walt Whitman May 31, 1889 Notes, Addresses, Letters, Telegrams Edited by Horace L. Traubel

Philadelphia David McKay, Publisher 23 South Ninth Street 1889

Brief letter, p. 62

NYPL

A Hazard of New Fortunes ...

New York ... 1890 〈*i.e.,* 1889〉

See entry No. 9646.

9648. ... Pastels in Prose Translated by Stuart Merrill ... Introduction by William Dean Howells

New York Harper & Brothers, Franklin Square 1890

At head of title: From the French

"The Prose Poem," pp. 〈v〉-viii.

Deposited April 5, 1890. BPL copy received April 10, 1890. Listed PW April 12, 1890; PC May 15, 1890.

H NYPL Y

9649. The Art of Authorship ... Compiled ... by George Bainton.

London: James Clarke & Co., 13 & 14, Fleet Street. 1890.

Contribution, pp. 334-335.

For comment see entry No. 1271.

9650. THE SHADOW OF A DREAM A NOVEL ...

EDINBURGH DAVID DOUGLAS 1890 ...

For first American edition see next entry.

〈i-iv〉, 〈1〉-218; advertisements, p. 〈219〉. 7¹⁄₁₆" x 4⅞" scant.

〈-〉², A-I, K-N⁸, O⁶.

V cloth: red. Brown-coated end papers. Inserted at back: Publisher's catalog, pp. 〈1〉-20, dated *March 1890.*

Listed Ath May 24, 1890. Advertised as *now ready* Ath May 31, 1890. Listed PC June 16, 1890. Reviewed Ath June 28, 1890. Listed Bkr July, 1890. A *Cheap Edition,* in printed paper wrapper, advertised as though new Ath Dec. 6, 1890, in Douglas's series of *American Authors.*

LC

9651. THE SHADOW OF A DREAM A STORY ...

NEW YORK HARPER & BROTHERS, FRANKLIN SQUARE 1890

For first British edition see preceding entry.

Note: Issued in both cloth; and, in printed paper wrapper. It is probable that the book was available in both formats on the day of publication but no positive proof to support this supposition has been found by BAL.

WRAPPER FORMAT

⟨i-iv⟩, ⟨1⟩-218, 2 pp. advertisements. Trimmed: 7⁵⁄₁₆″ x 4¾″. Fore and bottom edges untrimmed: 7½″ scant x 5⅛″. Sheets bulk ⅝″.

⟨-⟩², A-I, K-N⁸, O⁶.

Pale buff paper wrapper printed in greenish-blue. Issued under date May, 1890, as No. 672 of *Harper's Franklin Square Library, New Series.*

Deposited May 31, 1890.

CLOTH FORMAT

⟨i-iv⟩, ⟨1⟩-218, 2 pp. advertisements. 7⁵⁄₁₆″ x 4¾″ full. Sheets bulk ¹³⁄₁₆″.

⟨-⟩², A-I, K-N⁸, O⁶.

V cloth: red. Stamped in gold. Flyleaves.

Deposited June 7, 1890.

Note: Copies, presumed to be of a remainder issue, occur in red V cloth, stamped in black only. Sheets bulk ⅝″. The definite status of such copies has not been determined but it is possible that the sheets may have been prepared for publication in printed paper wrapper format.

Deposited (wrapper format) May 31, 1890. Deposited (cloth format) June 7, 1890. Listed PW, wrapper only, June 7, 1890.

AAS (cloth; wrapper; variant) H (cloth; wrapper; variant) LC (cloth; wrapper) Y (cloth)

9652. The Art of Authorship ... Compiled ... by George Bainton

New York D. Appleton and Company 1890

Contribution, pp. 334-335.

For comment see entry No. 1272.

9653. ... The House by the Medlar-Tree ... Translation by Mary A. Craig ...

New York Harper & Brothers, Franklin Square 1890

At head of title: Giovanni Verga

"Introduction," pp. ⟨iii⟩-vii.

Deposited Aug. 13, 1890. Listed PC Feb. 20, 1892.

AAS H Y

9654. A BOY'S TOWN DESCRIBED FOR "HARPER'S YOUNG PEOPLE" ...

NEW YORK HARPER & BROTHERS, FRANKLIN SQUARE 1890

⟨i-ii⟩, ⟨i⟩-vi, ⟨1⟩-247. Frontispiece and 22 plates inserted. 7⁵⁄₁₆″ scant x 4⅞″.

⟨-⟩⁴, 1-15⁸, 16⁴.

Two states (probably printings) noted:

1

P. ⟨iv⟩: Vignette present

P. ⟨v⟩: The 11th caption reads: *"The boys began to celebrate the Fourth ...*

P. vi: Vignette present

P. 44: Vignette not present

P. 109: Vignette not present

2

P. ⟨iv⟩: Vignette not present

P. ⟨v⟩: The 11th caption reads: *"The boys began to celebrate it ...*

P. vi: Vignette not present

P. 44: Vignette present

P. 109: Vignette present

Note: The caption referred to above is on the plate inserted at p. ⟨110⟩; the plate depicts a winter scene, illustrating a Christmas celebration. In all copies examined issued prior to 1902 the error is present on the plate.

S cloth: blue-green; maroon. Flyleaves.

Deposited Oct. 11, 1890. H copy (1st) received Oct. 11, 1890. Listed PW Oct. 18, 1890.

BPL (2nd) CC (1st) H (1st) LC (1st, being a deposit copy) NYPL (1st) Y (1st, 2nd)

9655. WINIFRED HOWELLS.

⟨n.p., n.d., 1891⟩

Cover-title.

⟨3⟩-26. 8⅝″ x 5¹¹⁄₁₆″. 3 inserted illustrations.

⟨1-3⁴⟩.

White imitation vellum wrapper imprinted as above. At front and at back: A single cut sheet folded to make four pages.

At end of text: W.D.H.

"Only a hundred copies were printed ..."— Letter, Feb. 1, 1891, Howells to Louise Chandler

Moulton, in: *Life in Letters of William Dean Howells,* 1928, Vol. 2, p. 16.

BA BPL H

9656. CRITICISM AND FICTION ...

NEW YORK HARPER AND BROTHERS MDCCCXCI

Title-page in black, red, tan.

⟨i-iv⟩, ⟨1⟩-188; 4 pp. advertisements. Laid paper. 5¹⁵⁄₁₆″ x 3⅝″ full. Frontispiece and printed tissue inserted. Top edges trimmed and gilded, otherwise untrimmed. Pp. ⟨i-iv⟩ printed on paper somewhat heavier and whiter than that in the body of the book.

⟨-⟩², 1-12⁸.

V cloth: white. White laid paper end papers. Top edges gilt.

Note: Also occurs in green V cloth, top edges trimmed (not gilded), fore edges trimmed; bottom edges rough trimmed. Leaf: 5⅞″ full x 3½″. This appears to be the binding described by Gibson & Arms as a "second issue". However, a copyright deposit copy, received May 9, 1891, is in this format as are also the following copies: a copy presented in 1891 by Howells to Charles Eliot Norton (in H); and the BA copy which was received on May 13, 1891. The listings and advertisements noted by BAL make no mention of two formats and the book is offered at $1.00.

Deposited May 9, 1891. Noted as *immediately* PW May 9, 1891. BA copy received May 13, 1891. Listed PW May 16, 1891. The London (Osgood, McIlvaine) edition noted as *shortly* PC May 23, 1891; advertised as *in the press* PC and Ath July 11, 1891; noted for *this day* Ath July 18, 1891; listed Ath July 18, 1891; listed PC July 25, 1891; reviewed PC Aug. 1, 1891; reviewed Ath Aug. 15, 1891. See entry No. 9814.

BA BPL H LC

9657. THE ALBANY DEPOT. FARCE ...

⟨n.p., n.d., 1891?⟩

Caption-title. The above on p. ⟨1⟩.

26 leaves. Printed on recto only. Leaves numbered ⟨1⟩-26. 8¼″ x 5³⁄₁₆″.

⟨1-6⁴, 7²⟩.

Unprinted gray-blue mottled paper wrapper.

Printed for professional use; not published in this form. No record of copyright deposit. Presumably printed prior to trade publication; see next entry.

AAS

9658. THE ALBANY DEPOT ...

NEW YORK HARPER AND BROTHERS 1892

First published edition. See preceding entry.

Noted in the following forms. The sequence presented appears plausible but further investigation is indicated.

Presumed First Printing, State A (B?)

⟨1⟩-68; advertisements, pp. ⟨69-70⟩. Illustrated. 5³⁄₁₆″ x 3¹¹⁄₁₆″.

⟨1-4⟩, 5-7, ⟨8⟩⁴, ⟨9⟩³. Leaf ⟨9⟩₂ inserted.

P. ⟨69⟩: *From the Easy Chair* described as (*Nearly Ready.*).

Presumed First Printing, State B (A?)

⟨1⟩-68; advertisements, pp. ⟨69-70⟩. Illustrated. 5³⁄₁₆″ x 3¹¹⁄₁₆″.

⟨1-4⟩, 5-7, ⟨8⟩⁴, ⟨9⟩³. Leaf ⟨9⟩₂ inserted.

P. ⟨69⟩: The statement (*Nearly Ready.*) not present in the entry for *From the Easy Chair.*

Presumed Second Printing

⟨1⟩-68; advertisements, pp. ⟨69-72⟩. Illustrated. 5³⁄₁₆″ x 3¹¹⁄₁₆″.

⟨1-4⟩, 5-7, ⟨8-9⟩⁴.

P. ⟨69⟩: *By William Dean Howells* ...

P. ⟨71⟩: *From the Easy Chair* described as (*Nearly Ready.*).

Presumed Third Printing

⟨1⟩-68; advertisements, pp. ⟨69-72⟩. Illustrated. 5³⁄₁₆″ x 3¹¹⁄₁₆″.

⟨1-4⟩, 5-7, ⟨8-9⟩⁴.

P. ⟨69⟩: *By Constance F. Woolson* ...

P. ⟨71⟩: The statement (*Nearly Ready.*) not present in the entry for *From the Easy Chair.*

V cloth: White. White laid paper end papers.

Deposited Oct. 10, 1891. Listed PW Oct. 17, 1891. An Edinburgh (Douglas) edition listed PC Dec. 11, 1897.

Note: According to *The United States Catalog ... 1921–1924,* the Samuel French, N. Y., edition issued under copyright date 1891, was in fact issued in 1922.

AAS (B) H (A; 2nd; 3rd) LC (A, being a deposit copy) Y (A; 2nd)

9659. AN IMPERATIVE DUTY. A NOVEL ...

NEW YORK HARPER & BROTHERS, FRANKLIN SQUARE 1892 ⟨*i.e.*, 1891⟩

⟨i-ii⟩, ⟨1⟩-150, 6 pp. advertisements, blank leaf. 7¼″ scant x 4¹³⁄₁₆″.

⟨1⟩-10⁸.

Three states (printings?) noted:

1: P. ⟨151⟩: *W. D. Howells. Criticism and Fiction* . . .

2: P. ⟨151⟩: *W. D. Howells. An Imperative Duty* . . .

3: P. ⟨151⟩: *W. D. Howells. The Quality of Mercy* . . .

V cloth: red. White laid paper end papers.

Note: All examined copies, all states, have the error *Hc* for *He,* p. 12, line 2 from bottom.

Deposited Nov. 14, 1891. BA copy (rebound; p. ⟨151⟩ lacking) received Nov. 18, 1891. Listed PW Dec. 5, 1891. The Edinburgh (Douglas) edition listed PC Nov. 28, 1891.

AAS (2nd)   CC (1st)   H (1st)   NYPL (1st)   Y (3rd)

9660. Advice to Young Authors To Write or Not to Write . . . Edited by Alice R. Mylene . . .

Boston, Mass.: Morning Star Publishing House, 1891.

Contribution, pp. 40-41.

For fuller entry see No. 6724A.

9661. Doña Luz by Juan Valera . . . Translated by Mary J. Serrano

New York D. Appleton and Company 1891

"Valera and Doña Luz," pp. ⟨3⟩-4.

Y

9662. 50th Anniversary of the Founding of the Tribune, Celebrated April 10, 1891, at the Metropolitan Opera House, New York.

⟨New York: The Tribune, 1891⟩

Printed paper wrapper. Cover-title.

Note, p. 26.

LC

9663. A Genre Dramatic Production. Mr. and Mrs. Jas. A. Herne in Margaret Fleming "An American Play without a Soliloquy." At Chickering Hall, Boston, Week of May 4, 1891.

⟨n.p., 1891⟩

Single cut sheet folded to make four pages. Blue paper. Watermarked: U. S. TREASURY BOND

O & K. BOSTON   Page: 8¹³⁄₁₆″ x 5⅜″. Printed in blue.

Letter, p. ⟨4⟩.

BPL

An Imperative Duty . . .

New York   Harper & Brothers, Franklin Square 1892

See entry No. 9659.

9664. Venetian Life . . .

Limited Edition

Imprinted:

Cambridge   Printed at the Riverside Press M DCCC XCII

2 Vols. Printed on Japan vellum, bound in vellum, limited to 250 numbered sets.

"Preface," pp. ⟨v⟩-vi, Vol. 1.

Trade Edition

Imprinted:

Boston and New York   Houghton, Mifflin and Company   The Riverside Press, Cambridge M DCCC XCII

2 Vols.

"Preface," pp. ⟨v⟩-vi, Vol. 1.

Note: The publishers also prepared an album of the 18 color plates, each plate mounted. Issued without title-page or other identification save for title on front cover. Issued in leather.

Also note: Contemporary trade notices and listings suggest that the London (Longmans, Green) edition was issued simultaneously with the American edition. The London edition has the imprint of *The Riverside Press, Cambridge, Mass., U.S.A.,* on the verso of the title-leaves.

Trade edition advertised in PW Oct. 24, 1891, for Oct. 28, 1891. London edition listed Ath Oct. 31, 1891. Both the trade and the limited formats listed PW Nov. 7, 1891. London edition listed PC Nov. 7, 1891. Deposited (limited edition) Nov. 11, 1891. London edition deposited BMU Jan. 11, 1892. For other editions see entry Nos. 9546, 9547, 9550, 9562, 9784.

AAS (trade)   H (both)   Y (both)

9665. MERCY A NOVEL . . .

EDINBURGH   DAVID DOUGLAS   1892 . . .

For first American edition see next entry.

⟨i-iv⟩, ⟨1⟩-474; blank leaf. 7⅛″ x 4⅞″.

⟨-⟩², A-I, K-U, X-Z, 2A-2F⁸, 2G⁶.

V cloth: maroon. Brown-coated end papers.

Listed Ath Feb. 6, 1892; PC Feb. 6, 1892. Advertised (with extract from a review) Ath Feb. 13, 1892. Reviewed Ath March 12, 1892. Listed Bkr March, 1892.

H

9666. THE QUALITY OF MERCY A NOVEL ...

NEW YORK HARPER & BROTHERS, FRANKLIN SQUARE 1892

First American edition. See preceding entry for earlier publication.

⟨i-ii⟩, ⟨1⟩-474, 4 pp. advertisements. 7³⁄₁₆″ x 4³⁄₄″.

⟨1⟩-30⁸.

V cloth: red. White laid paper end papers.

Deposited March 26, 1892. H copy inscribed by Howells April 2, 1892. Listed PW April 9, 1892. Under date of Sept. 1892, reprinted and reissued in printed paper wrapper as No. 726 in *Harper's Franklin Square Library;* deposited Oct. 1, 1892.

H NYPL

9667. A LETTER OF INTRODUCTION FARCE ...

NEW YORK HARPER AND BROTHERS 1892

⟨1⟩-61; blank, p. ⟨62⟩; 2 pp. advertisements; plus: 6 pp. advertisements; blank leaf. Frontispiece and 3 plates inserted, all reckoned in the printed pagination. 5¼″ x 3³⁄₄″.

⟨1⟩-7⁴; plus: ⟨8⟩⁴.

V cloth: white. White laid paper end papers.

Deposited July 25, 1892. Listed PW Aug. 6, 1892. The Edinburgh (Douglas) edition listed PC Oct. 9, 1897.

Note: According to *The United States Catalog ... 1921–1924,* the Samuel French, N. Y., edition issued under copyright date 1892, was in fact issued in 1922.

H NYPL Y

9668. South-Sea Idyls by Charles Warren Stoddard

New York Charles Scribner's Sons 1892

"Introductory Letter," pp. ⟨v⟩-vi.

Deposited Sept. 10, 1892. Listed PW Sept. 24, 1892.

H NYPL

9669. A LITTLE SWISS SOJOURN ...

NEW YORK HARPER & BROTHERS, FRANKLIN SQUARE 1892

⟨i-viii⟩, ⟨1⟩-119. Illustrated. 5¼″ x 3¹¹⁄₁₆″.

⟨-⟩⁴, 1-6, ⟨7⟩⁸, 8⁴.

V cloth: white. White laid paper end papers.

Advertised as *just ready* PW Sept. 24, 1892. Deposited Sept. 28, 1892. BA copy received Oct. 4, 1892.

BA H NYPL

9670. The Poems of George Pellew Edited, with an Introduction, by W. D. Howells

Boston W. B. Clarke & Co. 340 Washington St. ⟨1892⟩

Printed paper boards.

"Introduction," pp. ⟨v⟩-xi.

BA copy received Dec. 7, 1892. NYPL copy presented to Paul Leicester Ford, Dec. 1892. Deposited July 1, 1893.

BA H NYPL Y

9671. CHRISTMAS EVERY DAY AND OTHER STORIES TOLD FOR CHILDREN ...

NEW YORK HARPER & BROTHERS PUBLISHERS 1893

Title-page in black and red.

⟨i-x⟩, ⟨1⟩-150, 2 pp. advertisements. Illustrated. 7³⁄₁₆″ x 4³⁄₄″.

⟨-⟩⁵, ⟨1⟩-3, ⟨4⟩-9⁸, 10⁴. Leaf ⟨-⟩3 inserted.

S cloth: brown-orange. White laid paper end papers.

Deposited Dec. 7, 1892. Noted as *just published* PW Dec. 10, 1892. BA copy received Dec. 13, 1892. Listed PW Dec. 17, 1892.

H NYPL

9672. THE WORLD OF CHANCE A NOVEL ...

EDINBURGH DAVID DOUGLAS 1893 ...

See next entry.

⟨i-iv⟩, ⟨1⟩-375. 7¹⁄₁₆″ x 4⅞″.

⟨-⟩², A-I, K-U, X-Z⁸, 2A⁴.

V cloth: maroon. Brown-coated on white end papers. In some copies there is inserted at the back a publisher's catalog, 8 pp., dated *May, 1892.*

Received by BMU March 14, 1893. Advertised as though ready Ath March 18, 1893. Listed Ath March 25, 1893; PC March 25, 1893.

WMG

9673. THE WORLD OF CHANCE A NOVEL ...

NEW YORK   HARPER & BROTHERS PUBLISHERS 1893

First American edition. See preceding entry.

⟨i-ii⟩, ⟨1⟩-375; blank, p. ⟨376⟩; 4 pp. advertisements; blank leaf. 7¼″ x 4⅞″.

⟨1⟩-24⁸.

Polished V cloth: red. Stamped in gold. White laid paper end papers. *Also* noted in the following (almost surely) later bindings: Rough-toothed red V cloth: and, green V cloth; stamped in black. *Also* issued as No. 736 of *Harper's Franklin Square Library, New Series;* printed paper wrapper; only located copy defective but probably the date *July, 1893,* imprinted at foot of spine.

All examined copies have the error *succeesive* for *successive,* p. 333, line 2.

Deposited March 29, 1893. Listed PW April 1, 1893.

H NYPL

9674. THE UNEXPECTED GUESTS   A FARCE ...

NEW YORK   HARPER & BROTHERS PUBLISHERS 1893

⟨i-iv⟩, ⟨1⟩-54; 2 pp. advertisements; plus: 2 pp. advertisements; blank leaf. Frontispiece and 5 plates inserted. 5⅛″ scant x 3¹¹⁄₁₆″.

⟨-⟩², 1-7⁴; plus: ⟨8⟩².

V cloth: white. White laid paper end papers.

Deposited May 17, 1893. Listed PW May 20, 1893. The Edinburgh (Douglas) edition listed PC Nov. 6, 1897.

Note: According to *The United States Catalog ... 1921–1924,* the Samuel French, N. Y., edition issued under copyright date 1893, was in fact issued in 1922. In this reprint the title is erroneously given as *The Unexpected Guest.*

H NYPL

9675. The Niagara Book   A Complete Souvenir of Niagara Falls Containing Sketches ... by W. D. Howells ... and Others ...

Buffalo   Underhill and Nichols   1893

"Niagara, First and Last," pp. ⟨1⟩-27.

For comment see entry No. 3437.

9676. MY YEAR IN A LOG CABIN ...

NEW YORK   HARPER & BROTHERS PUBLISHERS 1893

⟨i-ii⟩, ⟨1⟩-62. Frontispiece and 1 plate inserted. 5¼″ scant x 3¹¹⁄₁₆″.

⟨1⟩-8⁴.

V cloth: white. White laid paper end papers.

Deposited Oct. 10, 1893. H copy inscribed by Howells Oct. 13, 1893. Advertised as *just ready* PW Oct. 14, 1893. Listed PW Oct. 14, 1893.

H NYPL

9677. EVENING DRESS   FARCE ...

NEW YORK   HARPER & BROTHERS PUBLISHERS 1893

⟨i-iv⟩, ⟨1⟩-59; blank, p. ⟨60⟩; 2 pp. advertisements. Frontispiece and 2 plates inserted. 5¼″ x 3¾″.

⟨1⟩⁵, 2-8⁴. Leaf ⟨1⟩₂ inserted.

V cloth: white. White laid paper end papers.

Deposited Oct. 25, 1893. BA copy received Nov. 2, 1893. Listed PW Nov. 4, 1893. The Edinburgh (Douglas) edition listed Bkr July, 1897.

Note: According to *The United States Catalog ... 1921–1924,* the Samuel French, N.Y., edition issued under copyright date 1893, was in fact issued in 1922.

H NYPL

9678. JUDGMENT DAY ...

⟨n.p., n.d., New York, 1893⟩

Single leaf. Printed on recto only. 9¼″ x 6⁵⁄₁₆″. Printed on heavy laid paper watermarked in hollow-face capitals; the watermark unreadable.

Offprint (preprint?) from *The First Book of the Authors Club ...,* New York, 1893, (BAL No. 1283), wherein the poem appears on p. ⟨288⟩.

LC

9679. THE COAST OF BOHEMIA A NOVEL ...

NEW YORK   HARPER & BROTHERS PUBLISHERS 1893

⟨i-iv⟩, ⟨1⟩-340, 4 pp. advertisements. Frontispiece and 7 plates inserted. 7¼″ x 4¹³⁄₁₆″.

⟨-⟩², 1-21⁸, 22⁴.

V cloth: red. White laid paper end papers.

Deposited Nov. 3, 1893. Noted as *immediately* PW Nov. 4, 1893. BA copy received Nov. 9, 1893. Listed PW Nov. 11, 1893. See entry No. 9724.

H NYPL

9680. Main-Travelled Roads Being Six Stories of the Mississippi Valley by Hamlin Garland, with an Introduction by W. D. Howells . . .

Cambridge and Chicago Published by Stone and Kimball . . . MDCCCXCIII

"Introduction," pp. 1-6.

Trade edition: 6½″ x 4⅚″. Also a large paper edition limited to 110 numbered copies: 7¹¹⁄₁₆″ x 5⅞″.

Listed PW Dec. 2, 1893. Deposited Dec. 4, 1893. The London (Unwin) edition listed PC June 30, 1894.

B BPL (large paper) H

9681. . . . Eight Songs . . . Composed by E. A. Mac-Dowell . . .

Breitkopf & Härtel, Leipzig, Brussels, New York . . . 1893 . . .

Printed paper wrapper. At head of title: To Clara Kathleen Rogers.

Reprint.

H

9682. Fame's Tribute to Children . . . ⟨Second Edition. Edited by Mrs. George L. Dunlap and Martha S. Hill⟩

Chicago ⟨Hayes and Company⟩ 1893

"Except as Little Children," p. 24.

For comment see entry No. 1284A.

9683. FROM MR. WILLIAM D. HOWELLS. THE FOLLOWING INTERESTING LETTER FROM THIS DISTINGUISHED AUTHOR . . . IS HIS CONTRIBUTION TO THE CURRENT DISCUSSION CONCERNING OUR MOUNTAIN FORESTS. ⟨Reproduction of a typewritten letter headed: *40 West 59th St., New York. Dear Mr. Harrison* . . .⟩

⟨n.p., n.d., 1893?⟩

Single leaf. 10⅛″ x 5⅝″. Printed on recto only.

A somewhat revised printing of a letter first published in *Boston Evening Transcript*, Jan. 7, 1893.

NYPL

9684. A Likely Story . . .

New York Harper and Brothers 1894

Reprinted from *The Mouse-Trap and Other Farces*, 1889.

Deposited May 29, 1894. Listed PW June 2, 1894. The Edinburgh (Douglas) edition listed PC Dec. 24, 1897.

Note: According to *The United States Catalog . . . 1921–1924*, the Samuel French, N. Y., edition issued under copyright date 1894, was in fact issued in 1922.

BA H NYPL

9685. A TRAVELER FROM ALTRURIA ROMANCE . . .

NEW YORK HARPER & BROTHERS PUBLISHERS 1894

⟨i-ii⟩, ⟨1⟩-318. 7¼″ x 4⅞″.

⟨1⟩-20⁸.

V cloth: red. White laid paper end papers.

Deposited May 29, 1894. Listed PW and PC June 2, 1894, which suggests simultaneous publication in United States and Great Britain. The British edition was published by David Douglas, Edinburgh. See entry No. 9882A.

H NYPL

9686. The Mouse-Trap . . .

New York Harper and Brothers 1894

Reprinted from *The Mouse-Trap and Other Farces*, 1889.

Deposited June 8, 1894. Listed PW June 16, 1894.

H NYPL

9687. Five O'Clock Tea . . .

New York Harper and Brothers 1894

Reprinted from *The Mouse-Trap and Other Farces*, 1889.

Deposited June 19, 1894. Advertised as *just published* PW June 23, 1894. Listed PW June 23, 1894. The Edinburgh (Douglas) edition listed PC Sept. 4, 1897.

Note: According to *The United States Catalog . . . 1921–1924*, the Samuel French, N. Y., edition issued under copyright date 1894, was in fact issued in 1922.

H NYPL

9688. Tuscan Cities ...

Boston and New York   Houghton, Mifflin and Company   The Riverside Press, Cambridge   1894

Reprint save for a new "Preface," p. ⟨vii⟩. For first edition see entry No. 9620.

Listed PW Dec. 8, 1894.

H

9689. The Book-Lover's Almanac for 1895

Duprat & Co   New-York   ⟨1894⟩

Printed wrapper. Limited to 100 copies on Japan paper, 400 copies on Van Gelder paper.

A statement on woman suffrage, p. 47.

H   NYPL

9690. Venetian Life ... New and Enlarged Edition   Nineteenth Edition

Boston: Houghton, Mifflin and Company. The Riverside Press, Cambridge. 1895

Reprint. Possibly prepared for copyright renewal only.

Deposited Jan. 18, 1895.

LC

9691. Notable Single Poems   American Authors Edited by Ina Russelle Warren

Buffalo   Charles Wells Moulton Publisher ⟨n.d., 1895⟩

"Conscience," p. 40. Collected in *Stops of Various Quills*, 1895.

For comment see entry No. 5672.

9692. Recollections of Life in Ohio, from 1813 to 1840, by William Cooper Howells. With an Introduction by His Son, William Dean Howells.

Cincinnati: The Robert Clarke Company, 1895.

"Introduction," pp. iii-viii. "Conclusion," pp. 196-207.

"It was at my suggestion that my father began, ten or twelve years ago, to set down the facts of his early life ... He was never able to finish it, and the work of revision fell to me after his death."—From the "Introduction," p. iii.

Listed PC March 31, 1894, as a book which Sampson Low *can import in about three weeks.* Announced as from Robert Clarke & Co., Bkr April 6, 1894. Both of the preceding are obviously quite premature. Deposited Feb. 13,

1895. BA and H copies received Feb. 15, 1895. Listed PW Feb. 23, 1895. Received by BMU Oct. 3, 1896.

BPL   H

9693. Master and Man by Count Leo Tolstoy Translated by A. Hulme Beaman with an Introduction by W. D. Howells

New York   D. Appleton and Company   1895

"Introduction," pp. v-xv.

Advertised as *new* PW May 15, 1895. Deposited May 17, 1895. Listed PW June 1, 1895.

H   LC   Y

9694. MY LITERARY PASSIONS ...

NEW YORK   HARPER & BROTHERS PUBLISHERS 1895

⟨i⟩-iv, ⟨1⟩-261; blank, p. ⟨262⟩; 6 pp. advertisements. 7¼" x 4⅞".

⟨-⟩², A-B, ⟨C⟩-E, ⟨F⟩-⟨H⟩, I, K-Q⁸, R⁶.

V cloth: red. White laid paper end papers.

Deposited June 18, 1895. Listed PW June 22, 1895. BA copy received June 25, 1895. See entry Nos. 9807, 9814.

H   NYPL

9695. Don't Wake the Children ... Music by Clarence Wilber Bowers

Published by J. A. Howells & Co. Jefferson O. ... 1895 ...

Sheet music. Cover-title.

Not seen. Entry from Edwin H. Cady's "Howells Bibliography ... ," in *Studies in Bibliography   Papers of the Bibliographical Society of the University of Virginia,* edited by Fredson Bowers, Charlottesville, Virginia, 1959.

The "poem, not elsewhere printed."—Cady.

The title was deposited for copyright Aug. 19, 1895. No record of deposit of the completed work.

9696. Italian Journeys ... New and Enlarged Edition

Boston: Houghton, Mifflin and Company New York: 11 East Seventeenth Street. The Riverside Press, Cambridge. 1895

Reprint. Presumably prepared for copyright renewal only.

Deposited Aug. 21, 1895.

LC

9697. STOPS OF VARIOUS QVILLS ...

Trade Edition

Imprint: NEW YORK HARPER AND BROTHERS MD-CCCXCV

Title-page in black and red.

58 leaves. Printed on one side only, save for the title-leaf which carries a copyright notice on the verso. 8¼″ x 5¾″. Unpaged. Illustrated.

⟨1-2², 3-8⁸, 9⁶⟩.

V cloth: tan. White laid paper end papers. Top edges gilt. Ribbon marker bound in.

Limited Edition

Imprint: NEW YORK HARPER AND BROTHERS MD-CCCXCVI

Title-page in black and brown.

60 leaves. Printed on one side only, save for the title-leaf which carries a copyright notice on the verso. 10¼″ x 7⅝″. Unpaged. Frontispiece and two illustrations, all printed on tissue and tipped to leaves ⟨1⟩3, ⟨4⟩2, ⟨6⟩4, respectively.

⟨1⁴, 2-8⁸⟩.

Paper boards, cloth shelfback and corners, printed paper label on spine. Top edges gilt.

Limited to fifty numbered copies signed by Howells and the illustrator, Howard Pyle.

Note: BAL has been unable to find any evidence to support the assertion that the large paper edition was issued after publication of the trade edition. However, the imprint dates do suggest that the trade edition was issued prior to the limited. The PW listing (Nov. 2, 1895) gives both formats but the description given of the large paper format is quite faulty and suggests that PW did not receive the large paper edition and that the entry was not made on the basis of first-hand examination.

Both formats announced PW Sept. 21/28, 1895. Deposited (trade edition only) Oct. 25, 1895. BA copy (trade) received Oct. 29, 1895. H copy (trade) inscribed by Howells Oct. 31, 1895. Listed PW (both formats; but see note above) Nov. 2, 1895. Both formats advertised PW Nov. 23/30, 1895. Listed PC (trade) Dec. 28, 1895.

H (both)   NYPL (both)   Y (large paper)

9698. 'The Time Has Come', the Walrus Said ⟨• • •|⟩

⟨n.p., Elbert Hubbard: East Aurora, N. Y., December 19, 1895⟩

Short statement, p. ⟨5⟩.

For comment see entry No. 4072.

9699. Poems ...

Boston and New York   Houghton, Mifflin and Company   The Riverside Press, Cambridge   MDCCCXCV

Vellum.

Reprint.

B

9700. Report of the American Humane Association on Vivisection and Dissection in Schools

Chicago ⟨The American Humane Association⟩, 1895

Cover-title.

Extract from "Replies to the Second Circular," pp. 38-39.

NYPL

9701. From W: M. Griswold,

25 Craigie St., Cambridge, Mass. ... ⟨1895?⟩

Caption-title. The above at head of p. ⟨1⟩.

Single cut sheet of blue paper folded to make four pages. Apparently a bill head. On p. ⟨2⟩ is an extract from Howells's comments on Griswold's publications, reprinted from *Harper's Magazine,* Feb. 1892.

Note: Not located as a separate; found only as an insertion in Griswold's *A Descriptiv List of Books for the Young,* Cambridge, 1895.

H

My Literary Passions   Criticism & Fiction ...

... New York ... ⟨1895; *i.e. ca.* 1910⟩

Pp. 283.

See entry No. 9807.

9702. ... Doña Perfecta   Translation by Mary J. Serrano   Introduction by William Dean Howells

New York   Harper & Brothers Publishers 1896

At head of title: B. Perez Galdos

"Introduction," pp. ⟨v⟩-xiii.

Advertised as *today* PW Nov. 9, 1895. Listed PW Nov. 16, 1895. The London (Gay & Bird) edition listed PC July 4, 1896.

AAS   H   Y

9703. THE DAY OF THEIR WEDDING A NOVEL . . .

NEW YORK HARPER & BROTHERS PUBLISHERS 1896

⟨i-iv⟩, ⟨1⟩-158, 2 pp. advertisements. Frontispiece and 6 plates inserted. 7¼″ x 4¹³⁄₁₆″.

⟨-⟩², 1-10⁸.

V cloth: red. White laid paper end papers.

Deposited Feb. 14, 1896. BA copy received Feb. 18, 1896. Listed PW Feb. 22, 1896.

H NYPL

9704. A PARTING AND A MEETING STORY . . .

NEW YORK HARPER & BROTHERS PUBLISHERS 1896

Title-page in black and orange.

⟨i-iv⟩, ⟨1⟩-⟨99⟩; blank, p. ⟨100⟩; 4 pp. advertisements. Frontispiece and 2 plates inserted. 5¹³⁄₁₆″ x 4⁵⁄₁₆″.

⟨-⟩², 1-6⁸, 7⁴.

Unbleached linen. White laid paper end papers.

Deposited April 7, 1896. Listed PW April 11, 1896. BA copy received April 15, 1896.

H NYPL

9705. Maggie a Child of the Streets by Stephen Crane . . .

London William Heinemann 1896

"An Appreciation," pp. v-vii. For first located American book appearance see entry No. 9873.

Received BMU June 8, 1896. Listed Ath Sept. 12, 1896; PC Sept. 19, 1896.

H UV

9706. IMPRESSIONS AND EXPERIENCES . . .

NEW YORK HARPER & BROTHERS PUBLISHERS 1896

⟨i-iv⟩, ⟨1⟩-281; blank, p. ⟨282⟩; 2 pp. advertisements. 7⁷⁄₁₆″ x 5″.

⟨-⟩², A-K, ⟨L⟩-Q⁸, R⁶.

S cloth: red. White laid paper end papers. Top edges gilt.

Deposited Sept. 25, 1896. Noted as *just ready* PW Oct. 24, 1896. BPL copy received Oct. 26, 1896; BA copy Oct. 27, 1896. Listed PW Oct. 31, 1896. The Edinburgh (Douglas) edition listed Ath Oct. 10, 1896; PC Oct. 17, 1896; advertised as though published Ath Oct. 17, 1896; reviewed Ath Nov. 28, 1896; listed Bkr Nov. 1896. *First published in Edinburgh?*

H NYPL

9707. Lyrics of Lowly Life by Paul Laurence Dunbar with an Introduction by W. D. Howells . . .

New York Dodd, Mead and Company 1896

"Introduction," pp. xiii-xx.

For comment see entry No. 4918.

9708. Idyls in Drab . . .

Edinburgh David Douglas, Castle Street 1896

Printed paper wrapper.

Reprint of *The Day of Their Wedding*, 1896 (Feb.); and, *A Parting and a Meeting*, 1896 (April).

Listed PC Dec. 5, 1896; Bkr Dec. 11, 1896.

H NYPL Y

9709. Francis Parkman

Boston Little, Brown, and Company 1896

Cover-title. Printed paper wrapper.

Extract from a review, p. 10.

H

The Country Printer . . .

Privately Printed ⟨1896; *i.e.,* 1916⟩

See entry No. 9843.

9710. English Society Sketched by George du Maurier

New York Harper & Brothers, Publishers 1897

"George du Maurier," pp. 1-9.

Deposited Dec. 17, 1896. Noted as *just ready* PW Dec. 19, 1896. The London (Osgood, McIlvaine) edition listed PC Jan. 16, 1897.

H Y

9711. A PREVIOUS ENGAGEMENT COMEDY . . .

NEW YORK HARPER & BROTHERS PUBLISHERS 1897

⟨i-vi⟩, ⟨1⟩-65; tailpiece, p. ⟨66⟩; 2 pp. advertisements; blank leaf. Inserted frontispiece. Two illustrations in the text, not included in the printed pagination. 6″ x 4⁹⁄₁₆″.

⟨1⟩-5⁸.

Printed red paper wrapper.

Deposited Jan. 29, 1897. NYPL copy received Feb. 13, 1897. Listed PW Feb. 20, 1897.

Note: According to *The United States Catalog ... 1921–1924,* the Samuel French, N. Y., edition issued under copyright date 1897, was in fact issued in 1922.

LC NYPL

9712. The Authors Club Dinner to Richard Henry Stoddard. At the Savoy, New York, March 25, 1897 ... Reprinted from the Mail and Express, New York, Issue of March 26, 1897.

⟨n.p., n.d., New York, 1897⟩

Letter, p. 13.

For comment see entry No. 6581.

9713. THE LANDLORD AT LION'S HEAD ...

EDINBURGH DAVID DOUGLAS 1897 ...

For first American edition see next entry. Also see entry No. 9810.

⟨i-iv⟩, ⟨1⟩-460. 7¹⁄₁₆″ x 4⁷⁄₈″.

⟨-⟩², A-I, K-U, X-Z, 2A-2E⁸, 2F⁶.

V cloth: maroon. Brownish-black coated end papers.

Advertised as *this day* Ath March 20, 1897. Listed Ath March 27, 1897; PC March 27, 1897; Bkr April, 1897. Reviewed Ath May 22, 1897.

H

9714. THE LANDLORD AT LION'S HEAD A NOVEL ...

NEW YORK HARPER & BROTHERS PUBLISHERS 1897

See preceding entry. Also see entry No. 9810.

⟨i-ii⟩, ⟨i⟩-⟨vi⟩, ⟨1⟩-461; blank, p. ⟨462⟩; 2 pp. advertisements. Frontispiece and 22 plates inserted. 7³⁄₁₆″ full x 4⁷⁄₈″.

⟨-⟩⁴, A-E, ⟨F⟩-Z, AA-CC⁸.

Two states (printings?) noted:

A: P. ⟨463⟩: *By George Du Maurier English Society ...*

B: P. ⟨463⟩: *By George Du Maurier The Martian ...*

V cloth: red. White laid paper end papers. Flyleaf at front of some copies.

Noted for *next week* PW April 3, 1897. Deposited April 9, 1897. A copy in H (State A) presented to C. E. Norton by Howells, April 11, 1897. Listed PW April 17, 1897.

H (A) NYPL (B) Y(A)

9715. AN OPEN-EYED CONSPIRACY AN IDYL OF SARATOGA ...

NEW YORK AND LONDON HARPER & BROTHERS PUBLISHERS 1897

⟨i-iv⟩, ⟨1⟩-181; blank, p. ⟨182⟩; 4 pp. advertisements; blank leaf. 7¼″ x 4⁷⁄₈″ scant.

⟨-⟩², A-B, ⟨C⟩-J, ⟨K⟩⁸, L⁶.

V cloth: red. White laid paper end papers.

Noted for Sept. 3, PW Aug. 21, 1897. Deposited Sept. 3, 1897. Noted as *just ready* PW Sept. 11, 1897. Listed PW Sept. 11, 1897. The Edinburgh (Douglas) edition listed Ath March 12, 1898.

H NYPL

9716. STORIES OF OHIO ...

NEW YORK CINCINNATI CHICAGO AMERICAN BOOK COMPANY 1897

⟨1⟩-287. Illustrated. 7¼″ x 4¹⁵⁄₁₆″.

⟨1⟩-18⁸.

Note: On the copyright page of the first printing is the printing code symbol: *W.P.1.*

V cloth: gray. Flyleaves.

Deposited Dec. 15, 1897. Copy in NYPL inscribed by Howells Dec. 18, 1897. Listed PW Dec. 25, 1897.

H NYPL

9717. ... A Library of the World's Best Literature Ancient and Modern ⟨Edited by⟩ Charles Dudley Warner ...

New York The International Society MDCCCXCVII

"Lyof Tolstoy," Vol. 37, pp. 14985-14994.

For comment see entry No. 2165.

9718. Out of the Question and at the Sign of the Savage ...

Edinburgh David Douglas, Castle Street 1897

Reprint.

Printed paper wrapper.

H

9719. THE STORY OF A PLAY   A NOVEL
. . .

NEW YORK AND LONDON   HARPER & BROTHERS
PUBLISHERS   1898

⟨i-iv⟩, ⟨1⟩-312. 7¼″ x 4¹³⁄₁₆″.

⟨-⟩², A-S⁸, T⁴.

V cloth: red. White laid paper end papers.

Note: The New York and the London editions
may have been issued simultaneously. Issued in
London under the imprint: *London and New
York   Harper & Brothers Publishers   1898*
Publication record:

London: Advertised for *next week* PC June 11,
1898.
New York: Deposited June 15, 1898.
New York: H copy received June 16, 1898.
London: Deposited BMU June 16, 1898.
New York: Noted for *this week* PW June 18,
1898.
London: Listed in *Spectator* June 18, 1898.
London: Listed PC June 18, 1898.
London: Listed Ath June 18, 1898.
New York: BA copy received June 20, 1898.
New York: A copy in H inscribed by Howells
June 20, 1898.
New York: Listed PW June 25, 1898.
London: Again listed PC June 25, 1898.

BPL (London) H (New York) NYPL (New York)

9720. American Prose Selections   With Critical
Introductions by Various Writers . . . Edited
by George Rice Carpenter . . .

New York   The Macmillan Company   London: Macmillan & Co., Ltd. 1898 . . .

"George William Curtis," pp. 417-420.

Deposited Oct. 5, 1898. BA copy received Oct.
18, 1898. Listed PW Oct. 29, 1898.

H

9721. The Blindman's World and Other Stories
by Edward Bellamy with a Prefatory Sketch
by W. D. Howells

Boston and New York   Houghton, Mifflin
and Company   The Riverside Press, Cambridge   1898

"Edward Bellamy," pp. ⟨v⟩-xiii.

For fuller description see entry No. 968.

9722. Suburban Sketches . . .

Boston and New York   Houghton, Mifflin
and Company   The Riverside Press, Cambridge   1898

Reprint. Presumably prepared for copyright renewal only.

Deposited Nov. 12, 1898.

LC

9723. RAGGED LADY   A NOVEL . . .

NEW YORK AND LONDON   HARPER & BROTHERS
PUBLISHERS   1899

⟨i-iv⟩, ⟨1⟩-357; blank, p. ⟨358⟩; 6 pp. advertisements. Frontispiece and 9 plates inserted.
7¼″ x 4¹³⁄₁₆″.

⟨-⟩², A-B, ⟨C⟩-L, ⟨M-N⟩, O-V⁸, W⁶.

V cloth: red. White laid paper end papers.

Deposited Feb. 16, 1899. H copy received Feb.
21, 1899. Listed PW Feb. 25, 1899. The London
(Harper) edition listed Ath May 6, 1899.

H NYPL

9724. The Coast of Bohemia . . . Biographical
Edition

New York and London   Harper & Brothers,
Publishers   1899

"Introductory Sketch," pp. ⟨iii⟩-vii. See entry
No. 9679.

Deposited Nov. 2, 1899.

H LC NYPL

9725. Their Wedding Journey . . . with an Additional Chapter on Niagara Revisited . . .

Boston and New York   Houghton, Mifflin
and Company   The Riverside Press, Cambridge   1899

Reprint. Presumably prepared for copyright
renewal only.

Deposited Nov. 2, 1899.

LC

9726. THEIR SILVER WEDDING JOURNEY
. . .

NEW YORK AND LONDON   HARPER & BROTHERS
PUBLISHERS   MDCCCXCIX

2 Vols. Title-pages in black and orange.

1: ⟨i-iv⟩, ⟨i⟩-⟨vi⟩, 1-⟨401⟩, blank leaf. Illustrated. 7¹⁵⁄₁₆″ x 5¼″.
2: ⟨i-iv⟩, ⟨i⟩-vi, 1-⟨464⟩. Illustrated.

1: ⟨-⟩⁵, A-B, ⟨C⟩-E, ⟨F⟩-I, K, ⟨L-M⟩, N-Q,
⟨R-S⟩, T-U, X-⟨Y⟩, ⟨Z⟩, ⟨2A⟩-2B⁸, ⟨2C⟩². Leaf
⟨-⟩₃ inserted.
2: ⟨-⟩⁵, ⟨A⟩-C, ⟨D-E⟩, F-G, ⟨H⟩-I, ⟨K⟩-L, M-
P, ⟨Q⟩-U, X-Z, 2A-⟨2B⟩, 2C-2F⁸. Leaf ⟨-⟩₃ inserted. *Note:* Signature mark M absent in some

copies; it is absent in the surviving copyright deposit copy.

T cloth: gray. White laid paper end papers.

Deposited Dec. 8, 1899. BPL copy received Dec. 12, 1899. Listed PW Dec. 16, 1899. BA copy received Dec. 20, 1899. The London (Harper) edition advertised as *in the press* PC Sept. 30, 1899; *will be published* PC Jan. 27, 1900; advertised as *just ready* Ath March 3, 1900.

H NYPL Y

9727. Kiplingiana . . .

M. F. Mansfield & A. Wessels New York ⟨1899; *i.e.*, 1900⟩

"Most Famous Man in the World," pp. 139-141.

Note: This publication was first issued as a serial, *A Kipling Note Book*, New York, Feb. 1899–Jan. 1900, inclusive. The Howells piece was first published NAR May, 1899; reprinted in *A Kipling Note Book*, Oct. 1899.

H Y

9728. . . . Doorstep Acquaintance and Other Sketches . . .

Houghton, Mifflin and Company Boston . . . New York . . . Chicago . . . The Riverside Press, Cambridge ⟨1900⟩

At head of title: The Riverside Literature Series

Printed paper wrapper. Issued as No. 139 of the series under date Jan. 3, 1900.

Reprint.

Deposited March 1, 1900.

H LC

9729. The Joy of Captain Ribot Authorized Translation from the Original of A. Palacio Valdés by Minna Caroline Smith

New York Brentano's 1900

The "Introduction" contains much material by Howells extracted from his review, "A Charming Spanish Novel," in *Literature* (N. Y.), May 12, 1899.

Listed PW April 28, 1900.

WMG

9730. The Hesperian Tree An Annual of the Ohio Valley 1900 Edited by John James Piatt . . .

Published by George C. Shaw Cincinnati, O., for the Editor ⟨1900⟩

"Success and Unsuccess," p. 38, is an extract from "Old Brown"; see above under 1859.

"The Mulberries in Pay's Garden," pp. 431-436; see under 1906 for publication in separate form.

For comment see entry No. 2973.

9731. BRIDE ROSES A SCENE . . .

BOSTON AND NEW YORK HOUGHTON, MIFFLIN AND COMPANY MDCCCC

⟨1⟩-48; blank, p. ⟨49⟩; printer's imprint, p. ⟨50⟩; blank, p. ⟨51⟩; *Plays and Poems* . . . , p. ⟨52⟩; 2 blank leaves. Laid paper. 5⅞" x 3⁹⁄₁₆".

⟨1-7⁴⟩.

V cloth: blue. White laid paper end papers. Laid paper flyleaf at front. Top edges stained yellow.

Note: All examined copies save two collate as above. The copyright deposit copies vary in that leaves ⟨7⟩2-4 are excised and the flyleaf is of wove, not laid, paper. It is possible that the deposit copies were hurried into binding and do not represent a published form.

Deposited May 21, 1900. BPL copy received May 24, 1900; BA copy May 29, 1900. Listed PW June 2, 1900.

BA H NYPL

9732. ROOM FORTY-FIVE A FARCE . . .

BOSTON AND NEW YORK HOUGHTON, MIFFLIN AND COMPANY MDCCCC

⟨1⟩-61; printer's imprint, p. ⟨62⟩; advertisements, p. ⟨63⟩. Laid paper. 5⅞" x 3⁹⁄₁₆".

⟨1-8⁴⟩.

V cloth: blue. White laid paper end papers. Laid paper flyleaves. Top edges stained yellow.

Deposited May 21, 1900. BA copy received May 29, 1900. Listed PW June 2, 1900.

BA H NYPL

9733. AN INDIAN GIVER A COMEDY . . .

BOSTON AND NEW YORK HOUGHTON, MIFFLIN AND COMPANY MDCCCC

⟨i-ii⟩, ⟨1⟩-99; printer's imprint, p. ⟨100⟩; blank leaf. *See note below.* Laid paper. 5¹⁵⁄₁₆" x 3⅝".

⟨1-13⁴⟩.

Two printings noted; the order of presentation is presumed correct.

A

P. ⟨ii⟩: Advertisement present.

P. ⟨101⟩: Blank.

B

P. ⟨ii⟩: Blank.

P. ⟨101⟩: Advertisement present.

The copyright deposit copies have been repaired and may lack pp. ⟨i-ii⟩; it is therefore virtually impossible to state whether or not the leaf bore the advertisement or was blank. P. ⟨101⟩ is blank.

V cloth: blue. Stamped in silver and gold. Spine lettered up. White laid paper end papers. Top edges stained yellow. Flyleaf at back of some copies.

Note: A variant (remainder?) binding has been seen on B sheets: blue V cloth; stamped in silver only; title on spine lettered down; no fly-leaves; top edges plain.

Deposited Aug. 15, 1900. Listed PW Oct. 6, 1900.

AAS (B)   BPL (A)   H (B)   NYPL (B)   Y (B in variant binding)

9734. THE SMOKING CAR A FARCE . . .

BOSTON AND NEW YORK   HOUGHTON, MIFFLIN AND COMPANY   MDCCCC

⟨i-ii⟩, ⟨1⟩-70; blank, p. ⟨71⟩; printer's imprint, p. ⟨72⟩; advertisements, p. ⟨73⟩. Laid paper. 5⅞″ full x 3⅝″.

⟨1-9⁴, 10²⟩.

V cloth: blue. White laid paper end papers. Top edges stained yellow.

Note: The copyright deposit copies do not have present leaf ⟨10⟩2; it appears to have been excised before casing.

Deposited Aug. 15, 1900. BA copy received Sept. 24, 1900. Listed PW Oct. 6, 1900.

BA   H   LC   NYPL

9735. The Howells Story Book Edited by Mary E. Burt and Mildred Howells . . .

New York   Charles Scribner's Sons   1900

Reprint.

Noted for the *29th inst.* PW June 23, 1900. Published Sept. 1, 1900 (publisher's records). Deposited Sept. 1, 1900. Listed PW Dec. 15, 1900.

AAS   H   Y

9736. LITERARY FRIENDS AND AC-QUAINTANCE   A PERSONAL RETRO-SPECT OF AMERICAN AUTHORSHIP . . .

HARPER & BROTHERS PUBLISHERS   NEW YORK AND LONDON   1900

⟨i-ii⟩, ⟨i⟩-⟨x⟩, 1-⟨288⟩; plus: blank, p. ⟨289⟩; advertisements, pp. ⟨290-291⟩; blank, p. ⟨292⟩. Frontispiece and 71 plates inserted. 8¼″ x 5⅜″.

⟨-⟩⁶, A-D, ⟨E⟩-I, K-S⁸; plus: ⟨T⟩².

T cloth: sage. White laid paper end papers. Top edges gilt. Reported but not seen in red T cloth.

Note: In addition to the trade edition there was issued an *Autograph Edition* which was made of the sheets of the trade edition, Sig. ⟨T⟩ not present. Inserted at front a certificate of issue: *Autograph Edition Limited to 150 Copies . . . Number . . . ⟨signature of Howells⟩.* Bound in brown buckram, white laid paper end papers, top edges gilt.

Noted for *this month* PW Sept. 8, 1900. Advertised as *shortly* PW Oct. 6, 1900. Deposited Nov. 17, 1900. BA copy received Nov. 20, 1900. A copy in H presented by Howells to C. E. Norton Nov. 20, 1900. Listed PW Dec. 1, 1900. The London (Harper) edition advertised for March 19, Ath March 16, 1901. See entry No. 9811.

H (trade; *Autograph Edition*)   NYPL (trade)   Y (*Autograph Edition*)

9737. A Chance Acquaintance . . .

Boston and New York   Houghton, Mifflin and Company   The Riverside Press, Cambridge   1901

Reprint. Presumably prepared for copyright renewal only.

Deposited Dec. 22, 1900.

LC

9738. The Niagara Book by W. D. Howells, Mark Twain . . . and Others   New and Revised Edition . . .

New York   Doubleday, Page & Co. 1901

For first edition see entry No. 9675.

Advertised (PW March 9, 1901) as containing "new sketches, stories and essays." Contains no new material by Howells although some extremely minor revisions are present.

Deposited April 25, 1901. BA copy received April 30, 1901. Listed PW May 4, 1901.

BA   H   Y

9739. A PAIR OF PATIENT LOVERS . . .

NEW YORK AND LONDON   HARPER & BROTHERS PUBLISHERS   1901

Title-page in black and brown.

⟨i-iv⟩, ⟨1⟩-368. Portrait frontispiece inserted. Laid paper. 7¹¹⁄₁₆″ x 5⅛″.

Two printings noted; the following sequence is probable:

A: ⟨1², 2-11¹⁶, 12-14⁸⟩. *Signed:* ⟨-⟩², A-I, K-U, X-Z⁸.

B: ⟨-⟩², A-I, K-U, X-Z⁸.

Brown V cloth shelfback and corners, marbled paper boards sides. End papers printed in green and pink-brown and lettered: HARPER'S PORTRAIT COLLECTION OF SHORT STORIES VOLUME I. Top edges gilt.

Deposited May 23, 1901. H (printing A) copy inscribed by Howells May 26, 1901. Listed PW June 1, 1901. The London (Harper) edition advertised for June 19, Ath June 15, 1901.

H (A)   BPL (A)   LC (A, 2 copies, both being deposit copies)   NYPL (B)   Y (B)

9740. Poems . . .

Boston and New York   Houghton, Mifflin and Company   The Riverside Press, Cambridge ⟨1901⟩

Vellum binding.

Reprint. Presumably prepared for copyright renewal only.

Deposited Aug. 9, 1901.

LC

9741. HEROINES OF FICTION . . .

HARPER & BROTHERS PUBLISHERS   NEW YORK AND LONDON   1901

2 Vols.

1: ⟨i⟩-⟨viii⟩, 1-⟨239⟩. Frontispiece and 40 plates inserted. 8¼" x 5⅜".
2: ⟨i⟩-⟨viii⟩, 1-⟨274⟩; blank, p. ⟨275⟩; advertisement, p. ⟨276⟩. Frontispiece and 27 plates inserted.

1: ⟨-⟩⁴, A-I, K-P⁸.
2: ⟨-⟩⁴, A-I, K-R⁸, S².

T cloth: sage. White laid paper end papers. Top edges gilt.

On copyright page: *October, 1901* Advertised for Oct. 25, PW Oct. 19, 1901. Deposited Oct. 26, 1901. H copy presented to C. E. Norton by Howells Oct. 28, 1901. Listed PW Nov. 2, 1901. The London (Harper) edition listed Ath Feb. 1, 1902.

H   NYPL

9742. Italian Journeys . . .

London   William Heinemann   1901

A revision of the 1872 edition. "A Confidence," pp. v-vi.

Also see entry Nos. 9551, 9560, 9743.

Issued in a trade edition; and, a de luxe edition limited to 50 copies printed on Japanese vellum.

Advertised for Oct. 26, Bkr Oct. 1901. Noted for *today* PC Oct. 26, 1901. Vellum copy received by BMU Nov. 5, 1901. Listed PC Nov. 9, 1901; Bkr Dec. 1901.

H (vellum)   NYPL (trade)

9743. Italian Journeys . . .

. . . MDCCCCI

A revision of the 1872 edition.

Also see entry Nos. 9551, 9560, 9742.

Limited Edition

Imprint: Cambridge Printed at the Riverside Press MDCCCCI

"A Confidence," pp. ⟨v⟩-vi.

Paper boards sides, cloth shelfback, printed paper label on spine. Limited to three hundred numbered copies.

Trade Edition

Imprint: Boston and New York   Houghton, Mifflin & Company   The Riverside Press, Cambridge   MDCCCCI

"A Confidence," pp. ⟨v⟩-vi.

Cloth.

Limited edition deposited Nov. 12, 1901. Trade edition listed PW Nov. 23, 1901.

BA (trade)   H (both)   LC (limited)   NYPL (limited)

9744. Florence in Art and Literature   Course X: Booklovers Reading Club . . . ⟨Edited⟩ by William Dean Howells and Russell Sturgis

⟨Philadelphia: The Booklovers Library, 1901⟩

Printed paper wrapper.

"Supplementary Books Recommended for This Course by William Dean Howells," pp. 113-114.

Deposited Dec. 13, 1901.

H   LC

9745. The Indicator   A Hesperian Leaflet . . .

Published by John Scott & Co., Three Rivers Elm, North Bend, Hamilton County, Ohio . . . ⟨1901⟩

Printed paper wrapper. Cover-title.

"Hot," pp. 26-28.

CAW

9746. Speeches at the Lotos Club Arranged by John Elderkin   Chester S. Lord   Horatio N. Fraser

New York   Privately Printed   MCMI

"At the Dinner to Samuel L. Clemens (Mark Twain), November 10, 1900," pp. 394-396.

For comment see entry No. 3469.

9747. THE KENTONS   A NOVEL ...

NEW YORK AND LONDON   HARPER & BROTHERS PUBLISHERS   1902

⟨i-iv⟩, ⟨1⟩-317; blank leaf. 7³⁄₁₆″ x 4¾″.

⟨-⟩², ⟨1⟩-20⁸.

Two states (printings?) noted:

1: Pp. ⟨319-320⟩ blank.

2: Pp. ⟨319-320⟩ imprinted with advertisements.

V cloth: red. White laid paper end papers.

Note: Sheets of both states also occur in maroon T cloth, possibly prepared for the Tabard Inn Library; see BAL, Vol. 1, pp. xxxii-xxxiii. Two states of the variant binding have been noted; no sequence has been determined and the designations are for identification only:

A: With the author's name on the front cover.

B: Without the author's name on the front cover.

On copyright page: *Published April, 1902* Noted for the *18th inst.* PW April 12, 1902. Deposited April 18, 1902. H copy (1st state) presented by Howells to C. E. Norton April 19, 1902. Listed PW April 26, 1902. A copy of the second state received by H April 29, 1902. The London (Harper) edition listed Ath May 17, 1902.

H (1st; 2nd; variant)   NYPL (2nd)   Y (1st)

9748. THE FLIGHT OF PONY BAKER   A BOY'S TOWN STORY ...

NEW YORK AND LONDON   HARPER & BROTHERS PUBLISHERS   1902

Title-page in black and red.

⟨i-ii⟩, ⟨i⟩-⟨vi⟩, ⟨1⟩-⟨223⟩. Frontispiece and 7 plates inserted. 7¼″ scant x 4⅞″.

⟨-⟩⁴, ⟨1⟩-14⁸.

V cloth: red. White laid paper end papers. Lettered in silver; pictorial binding. Also occurs

in maroon T cloth, lettered in gold, typographic stamping only; presumably prepared for the Tabard Inn Library; see BAL, Vol. I, pp. xxxii-xxxiii. *Note:* There is in AAS a curious example of unknown status: Rose-red S cloth, wholly unstamped save for the spine which is lettered in gold: FLIGHT / OF / PONY / BAKER / ⟨rule⟩ / HOWELLS.

On copyright page: *Published September, 1902.* Deposited Sept. 26, 1902. Listed PW Oct. 4, 1902. BA copy received Oct. 7, 1902. The London (Harper) edition listed Ath Dec. 13, 1902.

H   JB (variant)   LC   Y

9749. LITERATURE AND LIFE   STUDIES ...

HARPER & BROTHERS PUBLISHERS   NEW YORK AND LONDON   1902

⟨i-ii⟩, ⟨i⟩-⟨x⟩, 1-⟨323⟩. Frontispiece and 31 plates inserted. 8¼″ x 5⁷⁄₁₆″.

⟨-⟩⁶, ⟨1⟩-20⁸, 21².

T cloth: sage. White laid paper end papers. Top edges gilt.

On copyright page: *Published October, 1902.* Noted for the *14th inst.* PW Oct. 11, 1902. Deposited Oct. 14, 1902. BPL copy received Oct. 20, 1902; BA copy Oct. 21, 1902. Listed PW Oct. 25, 1902. The London (Harper) edition listed Ath Nov. 15, 1902. See entry No. 9812.

H   NYPL

9750. A Foregone Conclusion ...

Boston and New York   Houghton, Mifflin and Company   The Riverside Press, Cambridge   ⟨1902⟩

Reprint. Presumably prepared for copyright renewal only.

Deposited Nov. 17, 1902. For first edition see entry No. 9568.

LC

9751. The Hesperian Tree   An Annual of the Ohio Valley   1903   Edited by John James Piatt ...

Columbus, Ohio   S. F. Harriman   1903

Reprint save for:

"Success—A Parable," p. ⟨50⟩.

"Awaiting His Exequatur," pp. 425-429.

For comment see entry No. 3013.

9752. QUESTIONABLE SHAPES ...

NEW YORK AND LONDON HARPER & BROTHERS PUBLISHERS 1903

⟨i-vi⟩, ⟨1⟩-219; blank, p. ⟨220⟩; 4 pp. advertisements; blank leaf. Frontispiece and 3 plates inserted. 7¼″ scant x 4¾″.

⟨-⟩⁴, ⟨1⟩-14⁸.

V cloth: red. Spine stamped: QUESTIONABLE / SHAPES / ⟨rule⟩ / HOWELLS / HARPERS White laid paper end papers. *Note:* Also issued in maroon T cloth, presumably for the Tabard Inn Library; see BAL, Vol. 1, pp. xxxii-xxxiii. The presumed Tabard Inn format is stamped on the spine: ⟨rule⟩ / Question- / able / Shapes / ⟨acorn⟩ / HOWELLS / ⟨rule⟩

On copyright page: *Published May, 1903* Advertised for *May 19,* PW May 16, 1903. Deposited May 19, 1903. A copy in H presented by Howells to C. E. Norton May 20, 1903; another H copy received May 21, 1903. Listed PW June 6, 1903. The London (Harper) edition listed Ath June 20, 1903.

H JB (variant) NYPL

9753. LETTERS HOME ...

NEW YORK AND LONDON HARPER & BROTHERS PUBLISHERS 1903

⟨i-iv⟩, 1-299. 7³⁄₁₆″ full x 4¾″ full.

⟨1², 2-19⁸, 20⁴, 21²⟩.

V cloth: red. White laid paper end papers. *Note:* Two states of the binding have been noted; the sequence, if any, has not been determined and the designations are for identification only:

A: HOWELLS on spine measures 1″ scant wide, ³⁄₃₂″ tall.

B: HOWELLS on spine measures 1″ wide, ⅛″ tall.

On copyright page: *Published September, 1903.* Noted for *early in September* PW Aug. 22, 1903. Noted as *just ready* PW Sept. 12, 1903. Deposited Sept. 18, 1903. BPL (binding B) received Sept. 22, 1903. Listed under Harper's fall publications, PW Sept. 26, 1903. Copy presented to C. E. Norton by Howells (in H; binding A) Oct. 1, 1903. Listed PW Oct. 3, 1903. The London (Harper) edition listed Ath Oct. 31, 1903.

BPL (B) H (A) NYPL (A) Y (A,B)

9754. Mark Twain's Birthday Report of the Celebration of the Sixty-Seventh Thereof at the Metropolitan Club, New York November 28th 1902

⟨New York, Privately Printed, 1903⟩

Speech, pp. 2-4.

For comment see entry No. 761.

9755. Charles Dudley Warner by Mrs. James T. Fields ...

New York McClure, Phillips & Co. MCMIV

Tribute to Warner, pp. 199-208.

On copyright page: *Published, March, 1904,* N H copy received March 26, 1904. Listed PW April 2, 1904.

H NYPL

9756. Clarence King Memoirs The Helmet of Mambrino

Published for the King Memorial Committee of the Century Association by G. P. Putnam's Sons New York and London 1904

"Meetings with Clarence King," pp. 135-156.

For comment see entry No. 30.

9757. The Parlor Car ...

Boston and New York Houghton, Mifflin & Co. ⟨1904⟩

Reprint. Probably prepared for copyright renewal only.

Deposited Oct. 3, 1904.

LC

9758. THE SON OF ROYAL LANGBRITH A NOVEL ...

NEW YORK AND LONDON HARPER & BROTHERS PUBLISHERS 1904

Title-page in black and red.

⟨i-vi⟩, 1-⟨369⟩. 8³⁄₁₆″ x 5⅜″.

⟨1⁴, 2-24⁸⟩. Signature marks 2, 3, 4, 5, on pp. 17, 33, 49, 65, respectively.

S cloth: blue. White laid paper end papers. Top edges gilt.

On copyright page: *Published October, 1904.* Deposited Oct. 6, 1904. Noted for the *6th inst.* PW Oct. 1, 1904. BPL copy received Oct. 10, 1904; BA copy Oct. 11, 1904. Noted as *just ready* PW Oct. 15, 1904. Listed PW Oct. 15, 1904. The London (Harper) edition advertised as though published Ath Nov. 26, 1904; listed Ath Nov. 26, 1904; Bkr Dec. 1904.

BPL H

9759. Out of the Question . . .

Boston and New York: Houghton, Mifflin and Company. The Riverside Press, Cambridge. ⟨1905⟩

Reprint. Presumably prepared for copyright renewal only.

Deposited Dec. 31, 1904.

LC

9760. MISS BELLARD'S INSPIRATION A NOVEL . . .

NEW YORK AND LONDON   HARPER & BROTHERS PUBLISHERS   1905

⟨i-x⟩, 1-⟨224⟩, 3 blank leaves. *Note:* First and final leaves used as pastedowns. 7⅜″ x 5″ scant.

⟨1⟩-15⁸.

V cloth: green. Stamped in gold and colors. Leaves ⟨1⟩₁ and 15₈ used as pastedowns. *Note:* Also noted in a variant (remainder?) binding of gray-black V cloth stamped in orange, green and white; variant in H.

On copyright page: *Published June, 1905.* Advertised as *new* and noted as *just ready* PW May 13, 1905. Noted as *will publish shortly* PW June 3, 1905. Deposited June 8, 1905. A copy at H received June 15, 1905. Listed PW June 17, 1905. The London (Harper) edition advertised as though published Ath June 24, 1905. Listed Ath July 1, 1905.

H   NYPL

9761. A Counterfeit Presentment . . .

Boston and New York   Houghton, Mifflin and Company   The Riverside Press, Cambridge ⟨1905⟩

Reprint. Presumably prepared for copyright renewal only.

Deposited Sept. 14, 1905.

LC

9762. LONDON FILMS . . .

HARPER & BROTHERS PUBLISHERS   NEW YORK AND LONDON   1905

⟨i-x⟩, 1-⟨241⟩, 2 blank leaves. Frontispiece and 23 plates inserted. 8¼″ x 5⁷⁄₁₆″.

⟨1⟩-16⁸.

T cloth: sage. Top edges gilt.

On copyright page: *Published October, 1905.* Deposited Oct. 12, 1905. NYPL copy received Oct. 12, 1905. Noted as *just published* PW Oct. 14, 1905. A copy in H presented by Howells to

C. E. Norton Oct. 15, 1905. Listed PW Oct. 21, 1905. The London (Harper) edition advertised as *immediately* Ath Oct. 14, 1905; as though published Ath Oct. 28, 1905; listed Ath Nov. 11, 1905. Also see entry No. 9813.

H   NYPL

9763. Autobiography. Life of Vittorio Alfieri. With an Essay by William D. Howells.

Boston: Houghton, Mifflin and Company. The Riverside Press, Cambridge. ⟨1905⟩

Reprint. Presumably prepared for copyright renewal only.

Deposited Oct. 21, 1905. See entry No. 9580.

LC

9764. Autobiography. Lives of Lord Herbert of Cherbury and Thomas Ellwood. With Essays by William D. Howells.

Boston: Houghton, Mifflin and Company. The Riverside Press, Cambridge. ⟨1905⟩

Reprint. Presumably prepared for copyright renewal only.

Deposited Oct. 21, 1905. See entry No. 9579.

LC

9765. Autobiography. Memoirs of Edward Gibbon, Esq. Translated from the Original French, by John Black. With an Essay by William D. Howells.

Boston: Houghton, Mifflin and Company. The Riverside Press, Cambridge. ⟨1905⟩

Reprint. Presumably prepared for copyright renewal only.

Deposited Oct. 21, 1905. See entry No. 9582.

LC

9766. Autobiography. Memoirs of Frederica Sophia Wilhelmina, Princess Royal of Prussia, Margravine of Baireuth, Sister of Frederick the Great. With an Essay by William D. Howells . . .

Boston: Houghton, Mifflin and Company. The Riverside Press, Cambridge. ⟨1905⟩

2 Vols. Reprint. Presumably prepared for copyright renewal only.

Deposited Oct. 21, 1905. See entry No. 9578.

LC

9767. Autobiography. Memoirs of Carlo Goldoni. Translated from the Original French, by John Black. With an Essay by William D. Howells.

Boston: Houghton, Mifflin and Company. The Riverside Press, Cambridge. ⟨1905⟩

Reprint. Presumably prepared for copyright renewal only.

Deposited Oct. 26, 1905. See entry No. 9581.

LC

9768. Mark Twain's Seventieth Birthday Record of a Dinner Given in His Honor ...

Harper & Brothers, Publishers New York and London ⟨1905; *i.e.*, 1906⟩

Unpaged. Contains a "Sonnet ⟨of 28 lines⟩ to Mark Twain" and remarks.

For comment see entry No. 770A.

9769. Their Husbands' Wives

1906

Two editions have been seen.

First Edition

Harper's Novelettes Their Husbands' Wives Edited by William Dean Howells and Henry Mills Alden

Harper & Brothers Publishers New York and London 1906

On copyright page: *Published March, 1906.*

Does not contain Howells's introduction.

Sig. ⟨1⟩ is a normal 8vo containing no cancels or inserts.

Binding: S cloth: green. Stamped in silver and gold.

Copies thus deposited for copyright March 8, 1906.

Second Edition

Their Husbands' Wives Harper's Novelettes Edited by William Dean Howells and Henry Mills Alden

Harper & Brothers Publishers New York and London 1906

On copyright page: *Published March, 1906.*

Contains a two-page introduction by Howells, pp. ⟨v-vi⟩.

Sig. ⟨1⟩ altered by the excision of leaf 2. On the stub of the excised leaf is pasted a four-page insertion comprising the title-leaf and an introduction by Howells.

Binding: Two bindings have been reported on the extended second edition; the order of presentation is all but certain:

A: S cloth: green. Stamped in gold and silver.

B: T cloth: red. Stamped in gold only. *Reported, not seen.* Seen by BAL on known reprints.

Deposited March 8, 1906. Noted as *just ready* PW March 10, 1906. Published March 15, 1906 (publisher's records). Listed PW March 24, 1906. The London (Harper) edition listed Ath June 2, 1906.

H (2nd, binding A) LC (1st, binding A; being a deposit copy) NYPL (2nd, binding A) Y (2nd, binding A)

9770. Under the Sunset Harper's Novelettes Edited by William Dean Howells and Henry Mills Alden

Harper & Brothers Publishers New York and London 1906

"Introduction," pp. ⟨v⟩-vii.

On copyright page: *Published May, 1906.* Deposited May 11, 1906. Noted for *today* PW May 12, 1906. BA copy received May 15, 1906. Listed PW May 19, 1906.

BA H NYPL

9771. Autobiography. Memoirs of Jean François Marmontel. With an Essay by William D. Howells ...

Boston and New York Houghton, Mifflin and Company The Riverside Press, Cambridge ⟨1906⟩

2 Vols.

Reprint. Presumably prepared for copyright renewal only.

Deposited July 13, 1906. See entry No. 9583.

LC

9772. Different Girls Harper's Novelettes Edited by William Dean Howells and Henry Mills Alden

Harper & Brothers Publishers New York and London 1906

"Introduction," pp. ⟨v⟩-vii.

"Editha," pp. ⟨131⟩-158.

Deposited Aug. 17, 1906. Listed PW Feb. 23, 1907.

BPL H NYPL Y

9773. Quaint Courtships Harper's Novelettes Edited by William Dean Howells and Henry Mills Alden

Harper & Brothers Publishers London and New York 1906

"Introduction," pp. ⟨v⟩-vi.

"Braybridge's Offer," pp. ⟨204⟩-232.

For comment see entry No. 6381.

Daisy Miller by Henry James ...

Harper & Brothers New York and London ⟨1906; *i.e.,* after Feb. 28, 1916⟩

See entry No. 9845.

9774. CERTAIN DELIGHTFUL ENGLISH TOWNS WITH GLIMPSES OF THE PLEASANT COUNTRY BETWEEN ...

HARPER & BROTHERS PUBLISHERS NEW YORK AND LONDON 1906

Trade Edition

⟨i-ii⟩, ⟨i⟩-⟨viii⟩, 1-⟨290⟩; 2 blank leaves. Frontispiece and 47 plates inserted. 8¼" x 5⁷⁄₁₆".

⟨1⟩-19⁸.

T cloth: sage. Top edges gilt. Stamped in gold and red.

Traveller's Edition

⟨i-ii⟩, ⟨i⟩-⟨viii⟩, 1-⟨290⟩; 2 blank leaves. Frontispiece and 47 plates inserted. 7" full x 4¹⁵⁄₁₆".

⟨1⟩-19⁸.

Flexible green morocco-grained skiver. Stamped in gold. Mottled green and white end papers. Edges stained pale yellow. Flyleaves.

Note: Copies of the trade edition have been seen in a variant binding (remainder?): Red V cloth, stamped in black, top edges plain.

On copyright page: *Published October, 1906.* Noted as *in preparation* PW Aug. 11, 1906. Noted for *next week* PW Oct. 20, 1906. Deposited (trade edition) Oct. 26, 1906. NYPL copy (trade edition) received Oct. 27, 1906. A copy in H (trade edition) received Oct. 29, 1906; another presented by Howells to C. E. Norton Nov. 2, 1906. Listed PW (trade edition) Nov. 3, 1906. The London (Harper) edition advertised as though published Ath March 9, 1907; listed Ath March 16, 1907.

H (trade; variant; *Traveller's*) NYPL (trade)

9775. The Heart of Childhood Harper's Novelettes Edited by William Dean Howells and Henry Mills Alden

Harper & Brothers Publishers New York and London 1906

"Introduction," pp. ⟨iii⟩-iv.

"The Amigo," pp. ⟨143⟩-152.

Note: As published the book was bound in green S cloth stamped in gold and silver. Copies were deposited, but not so published, bound in green S cloth with crudely printed paper label on spine; cloth unstamped.

Deposited Dec. 1, 1906. Listed PW Feb. 23, 1907.

H NYPL Y

9776. ... Henry Mills Alden's 70th Birthday Souvenir of Its Celebration ...

⟨New York⟩ ... 1906 ... Harper & Brothers

"To a Great Editor," p. 1812.

For comment see entry No. 6613.

9777. THE MULBERRIES IN PAY'S GARDEN ...

JOHN SCOTT & CO., THREE RIVERS ELM, NORTH BEND, O. THE WESTERN LITERARY PRESS. CINCINNATI. ⟨1906⟩

⟨i-ii⟩, ⟨1⟩-27; advertisements, pp. ⟨28-30⟩. Frontispiece inserted. Laid paper. 7" x 4⅝".

⟨1-4⁴⟩.

V cloth: red.

Issued in *The Swallow-Flight Series.*

Contents:

"The Mulberries in Pay's Garden"; previously in entry No. 9730.

"The Mulberries"; reprinted from *Poems,* 1873.

Listed PW June 1, 1907.

H Y

9778. Southern Lights and Shadows Harper's Novelettes Edited by William Dean Howells and Henry Mills Alden

Harper & Brothers Publishers New York and London 1907

"Introduction," pp. ⟨v⟩-vi.

Deposited Feb. 28, 1907.

H NYPL Y

9779. THROUGH THE EYE OF THE NEEDLE A ROMANCE ...

HARPER & BROTHERS PUBLISHERS NEW YORK AND LONDON 1907

⟨i-iv⟩, ⟨i⟩-⟨xiv⟩, ⟨1⟩-⟨233⟩; blank, pp. ⟨234-238⟩. First and last leaves used as pastedowns. 8⅛" x 5⁵⁄₁₆".

⟨-⟩, ⟨1⟩-15⁸.

V cloth: green. Leaves ⟨-⟩₁ and 15₈ used as pastedowns. Top edges gilt.

On copyright page: *Published April, 1907.* Noted for *this month* PW April 6, 1907. Deposited April 18, 1907. BA copy received April 23, 1907; H copy April 25, 1907. Listed PW April 27, 1907. The London (Harper) edition listed Ath May 18, 1907.

H NYPL

9780. The Life and Works of Paul Laurence Dunbar ... by Lida Keck Wiggins and an Introduction by William Dean Howells ...

... Naperville, Ill. ... ⟨1907⟩

Reprint. For fuller description see BAL, Vol. 2, p. 505.

The "Introduction" by Howells is reprinted from Dunbar's *Lyrics of Lowly Life ...* , 1896 (BAL No. 4918).

W

9781. Shapes That Haunt the Dusk Harper's Novelettes Edited by William Dean Howells and Henry Mills Alden

Harper & Brothers Publishers New York and London 1907

"Introduction," pp. ⟨v⟩-vii.

Deposited June 14, 1907. Listed PW Dec. 21, 1907.

H NYPL Y

9782. Minor Dramas ...

Edinburgh David Douglas, Castle Street 1907 ...

2 Vols.

Reprint save for:

"A Letter to the Publisher," Vol. 1, pp. v-xii.

"A Masterpiece of Diplomacy," Vol. 2, pp. 220-269.

"Her Opinion of His Story," Vol. 2, pp. 398-426.

Listed Ath July 20, 1907; Bkr Aug. 1907.

H

9783. BETWEEN THE DARK AND THE DAYLIGHT ROMANCES ...

HARPER & BROTHERS PUBLISHERS NEW YORK AND LONDON 1907

⟨i-x⟩, ⟨1⟩-⟨185⟩. Frontispiece and 5 plates inserted. 8³⁄₁₆" x 5⅜".

⟨-⟩², ⟨1⟩-6, ⟨7⟩-8, ⟨9⟩-12⁸.

V cloth: green. Stamped in gold and blind. Top edges gilt. *Note:* Also noted in a presumed remainder binding: Red V cloth, stamped in black and blind, top edges plain.

On copyright page: *Published October, 1907.* Noted for Oct. 24, 1907, PW Oct. 19, 1907. Deposited Oct. 24, 1907. A copy in H presented by Howells to C. E. Norton Oct. 29, 1907; another H copy received Nov. 1, 1907. Listed PW Nov. 9, 1907. The London (Harper) edition advertised as *shortly* Ath Oct. 5, 1912; listed Ath Oct. 26, 1912.

BPL (variant) H NYPL

9784. Venetian Life ...

1907

Issued in two formats:

New Holiday Edition

Imprint: Boston and New York Houghton, Mifflin & Company MDCCCVII

Boards, cloth shelfback.

"The Author to the Reader," pp. ⟨xiii⟩-xxii.

"Venice Revisited," pp. ⟨406⟩-423.

Autograph Edition

Imprint: Cambridge: Printed at the Riverside Press: MDCCCVII

2 Vols. Boards, cloth shelfback; printed label (leather; and, paper noted) on spine.

550 numbered copies signed by author, illustrator and publisher.

"The Author to the Reader," Vol. 1, pp. ⟨ix⟩-xviii. "Venice Revisited," Vol. 2, pp. ⟨168⟩-185.

Deposited (*Autograph Edition*) Nov. 1, 1907. Both formats published Nov. 9, 1907 (publisher's records). *Published today*—PW Nov. 9, 1907. BA copy (*New Holiday Edition*) received Nov. 13, 1907. Listed PW (both formats) Nov. 16, 1907. The London (Constable) edition advertised for *next week* Ath Nov. 30; Dec. 7, 1907; listed Ath Dec. 14, 1907. Reissued not before 1908 with the imprint of Houghton Mifflin Company ⟨1907⟩. For other editions see entry Nos. 9546, 9547, 9550, 9562, 9664.

BA (both) BPL (Autograph Edition) H (both) NYPL (both)

9785. ADDRESS AT THE CELEBRATION OF THE ONE HUNDREDTH ANNIVERSARY OF THE BIRTH OF HENRY WADSWORTH LONGFELLOW SANDERS THEATRE, FEB. 27, 1907 ... [REPRINTED FROM PROCEEDINGS OF THE CAMBRIDGE HISTORICAL SOCIETY, II]

‹Cambridge: Cambridge Historical Society, 1907›

Cover-title.

‹59›-72, blank leaf. Laid paper. 9⁹⁄₁₆″ x 6½″. P. ‹59› blank.

‹-›⁸. Signature mark 5 on p. 65.

Printed buff paper wrapper.

Offprint from *The Cambridge Historical Society Publications II Proceedings October 23, 1906–October 22, 1907*, Cambridge, 1907.

H

9786. Life at High Tide   Harper's Novelettes Edited by William Dean Howells and Henry Mills Alden

Harper & Brothers Publishers   New York and London   1907

Issued 1908?

Deposited (reprints) Dec. 24, 1908. Listed PW June 5, 1909.

NYPL

9787. FENNEL AND RUE   A NOVEL ...

HARPER & BROTHERS PUBLISHERS   NEW YORK AND LONDON   1908

‹i-vi›, 1-‹130›. Frontispiece and three plates inserted. 8¼″ x 5⅜″.

‹1›⁴, 2-9⁸.

V cloth: green. Top edges gilt.

On copyright page: *Published March, 1908.* Noted as *in press* PW Feb. 8, 1908. Noted for the *12th inst.* PW March 7, 1908. Deposited March 13, 1908. BPL copy received March 16, 1908; BA copy March 17, 1908. Listed PW March 21, 1908. The London (Harper) edition advertised as *shortly* Ath March 28, 1908; listed Ath April 4, 1908.

H   NYPL

9788. The Undiscovered Country ...

Boston and New York. Houghton Mifflin Company. The Riverside Press   Cambridge. ‹1908›

Reprint. Presumably prepared for copyright renewal only.

Deposited June 22, 1908. For first printing see entry No. 9589.

LC

9789. Christmas Every Day   A Story Told a Child ...

New York and London   Harper & Brothers Publishers   1908

Reprinted from *Christmas Every Day and Other Stories ... , 1893.*

On copyright page: *Published October, 1908.* Deposited Oct. 15, 1908.

B   LC   Y

9790. The Whole Family   A Novel by Twelve Authors ...

New York and London   Harper & Brothers Publishers   MCMVIII

"The Father," pp. 3-29.

On copyright page: *Published October, 1908.* Deposited Oct. 15, 1908. Listed PW Oct. 24, 1908.

Note: Usually occurs in blue T cloth, stamped in gold. A variant (remainder?) binding has been noted: Red T cloth, stamped in black. A copy of the second printing has been noted in the variant binding also.

AAS   BA   H   NYPL   SG (variant)   Y

9791. ROMAN HOLIDAYS AND OTHERS ...

HARPER & BROTHERS PUBLISHERS   NEW YORK AND LONDON   1908

Trade Edition

‹i-viii›, 1-‹303›. Frontispiece and 51 plates inserted. 8⁹⁄₁₆″ scant x 5⅜″. Sheets bulk 1¼″ scant.

‹-›⁴, ‹1›-19⁸.

T cloth: sage. Top edges gilt. Stamped in gold and red.

Traveller's Edition

‹i-viii›, 1-‹303›. Frontispiece and 51 plates inserted. 7″ x 4¹⁵⁄₁₆″. Sheets bulk ⅞″.

‹1⁴, 2-10¹⁶, 11⁸›. *Signed:* ‹-›⁴, ‹1›-19⁸.

Flexible green morocco-grained skiver. Stamped in gold and blind. Mottled green and white end papers. Edges stained green. Flyleaves.

Note: Copies of the trade edition have been seen in a variant (remainder?) binding: Green V cloth, stamped in black, top edges plain. *And:* Copies of the *Traveller's Edition* have been seen in a variant (remainder?) binding: Tan paper boards, printed in black, edges plain.

On copyright page: *Published October, 1908.* Noted for probable fall publication PW July 11, 1908. Noted as *just ready* PW Oct. 10, 1908. Deposited (trade edition) Oct. 22, 1908. NYPL (trade edition) received Oct. 22, 1908. Both formats advertised PW Nov. 28, 1908. Listed PW (trade edition) Dec. 12, 1908. The London (Harper) edition advertised as *immediately* Ath Oct. 10, 1908; listed Ath (trade edition?) Nov. 21, 1908.

Note: Portions of the text were deposited in galley proof; the setting presumed to be that of the original printing in the *New York Sun.* LC has the following portions: *Rome, April 10,* deposited April 23, 1908; *Rome, April 20,* deposited April 30, 1908; *Rome, April 27,* deposited May 9, 1908.

AAS (variant *Traveller's Edition*) BPL (variant *Traveller's Edition*) H (trade; trade variant; *Traveller's Edition*) NYPL (trade) Y (variant *Traveller's Edition*)

9792. In Memory of Edmund Clarence Stedman A Meeting Held at Carnegie Lyceum, New York on the Afternoon of January 13, 1909

⟨New York⟩ The De Vinne Press 1909

Printed paper wrapper.

Letter, Feb. 5, 1909, pp. 32-34.

H copy received April 27, 1909.

H NYPL

9793. THE MOTHER AND THE FATHER DRAMATIC PASSAGES ...

HARPER & BROTHERS PUBLISHERS NEW YORK AND LONDON 1909

⟨i-viii⟩, ⟨1⟩-⟨55⟩. Frontispiece and 3 plates inserted. 8¾₁₆″ x 5¼″.

⟨1-8⁴⟩.

V cloth: green. Stamped in gold and blind. Top edges gilt. A variant (remainder?) binding has been noted: Red V cloth, stamped in black and blind, top edges plain.

On copyright page: *Published May, 1909.* Noted as *at once* PW May 15, 1909. Deposited May 20, 1909. BPL copy received May 22, 1909. Listed PW June 12, 1909.

BA (1st) H (both) NYPL (both)

9794. Boy Life Stories and Readings Selected from the Works of William Dean Howells ... by Percival Chubb ...

Harper & Brothers Publishers New York and London MCMIX

Reprint.

On copyright page: *Published September, 1909.* Deposited Sept. 11, 1909.

H NYPL

9795. SEVEN ENGLISH CITIES ...

HARPER & BROTHERS PUBLISHERS NEW YORK AND LONDON 1909

⟨i-x⟩, ⟨1⟩-⟨201⟩. Frontispiece and 31 plates inserted. 8¾₁₆″ x 5⅜″.

⟨-⟩², ⟨1⟩-13⁸.

T cloth: sage. Stamped in gold and red. Top edges gilt. Also noted in a variant (remainder?) binding: V cloth (both green and tan noted), stamped in black; top edges not gilded.

On copyright page: *Published October, 1909.* Noted for publication *during the month* PW Oct. 16, 1909. NYPL copy (1st) received Oct. 21, 1909; BA copy (1st) Nov. 3, 1909. Listed PW Nov. 6, 1909. The London (Harper) edition listed Ath Nov. 13, 1909.

BA BPL (variant) H (both) NYPL Y

9796. The Swiss Family Robinson ... by David Wyss ... Introduction by W. D. Howells

Harper & Brothers New York and London MCMIX

"Introduction," pp. xi-⟨xiii⟩.

On copyright page: *Published November, 1909.*

Y

9797. ... Doorstep Acquaintance and Other Sketches ...

Boston New York Chicago Houghton Mifflin Company The Riverside Press Cambridge ⟨1909⟩

Printed paper wrapper. At head of title: The Riverside Literature Series Issued as No. 139 of the series.

Reprint.

NYPL

9798. In After Days Thoughts on the Future Life by W. D. Howells ... Thomas Wentworth Higginson ... ⟨and Others⟩

Harper & Brothers Publishers New York and London MCMX

"A Counsel of Consolation," pp. 3-16.

For comment see entry No. 8498.

9799. Mark Twain's Speeches with an Introduction by William Dean Howells

New York and London   Harper & Brothers Publishers   1910

"Introduction," pp. ⟨vii-viii⟩.

For comment see entry No. 3513.

9800. Proceedings of the American Academy of Arts and Letters and of the National Institute of Arts and Letters   Number I: 1909–1910

New York ⟨June 10, 1910⟩

Printed paper wrapper.

"Opening Address . . . ," pp. ⟨5⟩-8.

H   Y

9801. The Children's Plutarch   Tales of the Greeks by F. J. Gould with an Introduction by W. D. Howells . . .

Harper & Brothers Publishers   New York and London   MCMX

"Introduction," pp. vii-⟨x⟩.

On copyright page: *Published July, 1910.* Deposited July 22, 1910.

H   Y

9802. The Children's Plutarch   Tales of the Romans by F. J. Gould with an Introduction by W. D. Howells . . .

Harper & Brothers Publishers   New York and London   MCMX

"Introduction," pp. vii-xi.

Deposited July 22, 1910.

H

9803. MY MARK TWAIN   REMINISCENCES AND CRITICISMS . . .

HARPER & BROTHERS PUBLISHERS   NEW YORK AND LONDON   1910

⟨i-viii⟩, ⟨1⟩-⟨187⟩. Frontispiece portraits of Clemens and of Howells; and, 6 plates; all inserted. *See note below.*

⟨-⟩², ⟨1⟩-12⁸.

T cloth: sage. *See note below.*

Two binding variants noted; the sequence has not been established and the designations are almost purely arbitrary:

A

Photographer's name not present in frontispiece plate of Mark Twain.

Top edges gilt, other edges trimmed. Leaf: 8⅛″ full x 5⅜″.

The copyright deposit copies thus.

B

Photographer's name (Rockwood) at lower left of frontispiece plate of Mark Twain. In this form also noted in reprints.

Top edges gilt, other edges untrimmed. Leaf: 8³⁄₁₆″ x 5⁷⁄₁₆″ scant.

On copyright page: *Published September, 1910.* Deposited (Variant A) Sept. 10, 1910. Noted for *this week* PW Sept. 10, 1910. BA copy (Variant A) received Sept. 13, 1910. Listed PW Sept. 17, 1910. A reprint noted by PW Dec. 24, 1910. The London (Harper) edition advertised as *immediately* Ath Sept. 17, 1910; listed Ath Oct. 1, 1910.

H (A)   NYPL (A, B)   Y (A, B)

9804. IMAGINARY INTERVIEWS . . .

HARPER & BROTHERS PUBLISHERS   NEW YORK AND LONDON   1910

⟨i⟩-⟨viii⟩, 1-⟨359⟩. Frontispiece and 7 plates inserted. 8⅛″ x 5⅜″ scant.

⟨1⟩-23⁸.

T cloth: sage. Top edges gilt. Stamped in gold and red.

Also noted in the following variant (remainder?) bindings. Sequence, if any, not known; the designations are for identification only.

A: Green V cloth; front and spine lettered in black; top edges plain.

B: Green V cloth; stamped in black; spine lettered; front not lettered but decorated with a leafy spray; top edges plain.

On copyright page: *Published October, 1910* Deposited Oct. 15, 1910. BA copy received Oct. 18, 1910; BPL Oct. 20, 1910. Listed PW Oct. 22, 1910. The London (Harper) edition listed Bkr Nov. 11, 1910.

H (all three)   BA (1st)   Y (variant A)

9805. The Cliff-Dwellers   An Account of Their Organization . . .

Chicago   168 Michigan Avenue   MCMX

Printed paper wrapper.

Letter, p. 50.

H   NYPL

9806. History of the Western Reserve by Harriet Taylor Upton H. G. Cutler ... and a Staff of Leading Citizens ...

1910 The Lewis Publishing Company Chicago New York

Probably issued in a variety of bindings.

3 Vols. Continuous pagination.

Letter, p. 577, Vol. 1.

H

9807. My Literary Passions Criticism & Fiction ...

Harper & Brothers Publishers New York and London ‹1895; i.e., ca. 1910›

Pp. 283. Not to be confused with entry No. 9814.

Reprint.

H

My Literary Passions Criticism & Fiction ...

... ‹1910; i.e., 1911›

See entry No. 9814.

9808. PARTING FRIENDS A FARCE ...

HARPER & BROTHERS PUBLISHERS NEW YORK AND LONDON MCMXI

‹1›-57. Frontispiece and 4 plates inserted; all reckoned in the printed pagination. 5³⁄₁₆″ x 3¾″.

‹1›-6⁴.

V cloth: blue.

On copyright page: Published June, 1911 Deposited June 17, 1911. Listed PW June 24, 1911.

Note: According to The United States Catalog ... 1921–1924, the Samuel French, N. Y., edition issued under copyright date 1910; and with the statement Published June, 1911, was in fact issued in 1922.

H NYPL

9809. A Hazard of New Fortunes ...

Harper & Brothers Publishers New York and London ‹1911›

See entries 9641A, 9646.

Reprint save for "Bibliographical," pp. v-‹ix›.

Issued as a volume in The Writings of William Dean Howells, Library Edition.

Note: A set of thirty-two volumes under the designation The Writings of William Dean

Howells, Library Edition, was projected but abandoned after publication of the following six volumes: A Hazard of New Fortunes; The Landlord at Lion's Head; Literary Friends and Acquaintance; Literature and Life; London Films and Certain Delightful English Towns; My Literary Passions ‹and› Criticism & Fiction. These may be identified by an inserted general title-page for the set printed in black and orange; each contains a new introduction; see entries 9809-9814. For an account of the project see "William Dean Howells and His Library Edition," by Robert W. Walts, in Papers of the Bibliographical Society of America, Vol. 52, 4th Quarter, 1958. According to information supplied by the Copyright Office the six volumes were published as a set on July 26, 1911, but not deposited for copyright until Jan. 30, 1913.

Howells prepared introductions for the following: The Coast of Bohemia ‹and› The Story of a Play; Heroines of Fiction; The Shadow of a Dream; The Son of Royal Langbrith; A Traveler from Altruria ‹and› Through the Eye of the Needle. Galley-proofs of these introductions are in H. For first publication of these introductions see entry No. 9874.

H LC Y

9810. The Landlord at Lion's Head A Novel ...

Harper & Brothers Publishers New York and London ‹1911›

Reprint save for "Bibliographical," pp. vii-‹x›.

Issued as a volume in The Writings of William Dean Howells, Library Edition.

See note under entry No. 9809. Also see entry Nos. 9713, 9714.

LC Y

9811. Literary Friends and Acquaintance ...

Harper & Brothers Publishers New York and London ‹1911›

Reprint save for "Bibliographical," pp. ix-‹xi›; and, "Belated Guest," pp. 289-‹305›.

Issued as a volume in The Writings of William Dean Howells, Library Edition.

See note under entry No. 9809. For first edition see entry No. 9736.

H LC Y

9812. Literature and Life Studies ...

Harper & Brothers Publishers New York and London ‹1911›

Reprint save for an extended version of the introductory paper of the 1902 edition here titled "Bibliographical," pp. ix-<xii>.

Issued as a volume in *The Writings of William Dean Howells, Library Edition.*

Two formats noted:

A: Green T cloth. Stamped in gold. Top edges gilt, other edges untrimmed. Leaf: 8¹¹⁄₁₆″ x 5¾″. A deposit copy thus.

B: Gray V cloth. Stamped in black. Top edges plain. All edges trimmed. Leaf: 7¹¹⁄₁₆″ x 5⅛″. Presumably a remainder issue.

See note under entry No. 9809. For first edition see entry No. 9749.

H (A, B)   LC (A)   Y (A)

9813. London Films and Certain Delightful English Towns . . .

Harper & Brothers Publishers   New York and London <1911>

Reprint save for "Bibliographical," pp. ix-<xi>.

Issued as a volume in *The Writings of William Dean Howells, Library Edition.*

Two formats noted:

A: Green T cloth. Stamped in gold. Top edges gilt, other edges untrimmed. Leaf: 8¹¹⁄₁₆″ x 5¾″. A deposit copy thus.

B: Gray V cloth. Stamped in black. Top edges plain. All edges trimmed. Leaf: 7¹¹⁄₁₆″ x 5″. Presumably a remainder issue.

See note under No. 9809. Also see entry No. 9762.

BPL (A)   H (A, B)   LC (A)   NYPL (A)

9814. My Literary Passions   Criticism & Fiction . . .

Harper & Brothers Publishers   New York and London <1910; *i.e.,* 1911>

Reprint save for "Bibliographical," pp. ix-<xii>.

Issued as a volume in *The Writings of William Dean Howells, Library Edition.*

See note under entry No. 9809. Also see entry Nos. 9656, 9694, 9807.

LC Y

9815. Poems by Madison Cawein . . .

New York   The Macmillan Company   1911 . . .

"The Poetry of Madison Cawein," p. xiii-xix.

For comment see entry No. 3025.

9816. The Henry James Year Book Selected and Arranged by Evelyn Garnaut Smalley with an Introduction by Henry James and William Dean Howells

Richard G. Badger   The Gorham Press   Boston <1911>

Cloth over flexible boards, red ribbon marker.

"One of the Public to the Author," pp. <10-11>.

Listed PW Sept. 16, 1911. Deposited Sept. 27, 1911. The London (Dent) edition listed Bkr Nov. 2, 1912.

AAS   H   NYPL

9817. Tom Brown's School-Days by an Old Boy (Thomas Hughes) . . . with an Introduction by W. D. Howells

Harper & Brothers   New York and London MCMXI

"Introduction," pp. ix-<xii>.

On copyright page: *Published October, 1911* Deposited Oct. 16, 1911.

UV

9818. Proceedings of the American Academy of Arts and Letters and of the National Institute of Arts and Letters <in Memory of Samuel L. Clemens, Carnegie Hall, Nov. 30, 1910> No. III: 1910–1911

New York <1911>

Cover-title. Printed self-wrapper.

Opening address, pp. <5>-6; remarks, pp. 11-12, 15, 18, 21, 24, 29.

H   Y

9819. "In This Book Stedman Speaks to His Friends Again"   Life and Letters of Edmund Clarence Stedman by Laura Stedman and George M. Gould . . .

Moffat, Yard & Co., 31 East 17th Street, New York <n.d., 1911?>

4 pp. Issued as an advertisement.

Extract from a review of the book (*Life and Letters of . . . Stedman*), p. <2>.

NYPL

9820. The House of Harper   A Century of Publishing in Franklin Square by J. Henry Harper . . .

Harper & Brothers Publishers   New York and London MCMXII

Material by Howells, pp. 319-327, 522, ⟨637⟩.

For comment see entry No. 791.

9821. ... A Tribute to William Dean Howells Souvenir of a Dinner Given to the Eminent Author in Celebration of His Seventy-Fifth Birthday ...

⟨New York: Harper & Brothers, 1912⟩

Cover-title. At head of title: March 9, 1912 In Two Parts—Part II ⟨of *Harper's Weekly*⟩

Issued as a supplement to *Harper's Weekly.* Paged ⟨27⟩-34.

Speech, pp. 28-29.

BPL

9822. Artemus Ward's Best Stories Edited by Clifton Johnson with an Introduction by W. D. Howells ...

Harper & Brothers Publishers New York and London MCMXII

"Introduction," pp. vii-⟨xvi⟩.

On copyright page: *Published October, 1912;* and, code letters H-M, signifying *printed Aug. 1912.* Deposited Oct. 5, 1912. The London (Harper) edition was *promised* Ath Nov. 9, 1912; listed Bkr Nov. 15, 1912.

H   Y

9823. Francis Davis Millet Memorial Meeting The American Federation of Arts ... Held in the National Museum Washington, D. C. MCMXII

⟨Washington, 1912⟩

Printed wrapper.

Letter, May 5, 1912, pp. 51-52.

CC   H

9824. John Bigelow Memorial Addresses Delivered before the Century Association March 9, 1912 Resolutions Adopted December 19, 1911

New York Printed for the Century Association 1912

Printed paper wrapper; and, boards, leather shelfback and corners.

Letter, March 5, 1912, pp. 37-40.

CC   H   Y

9825. NEW LEAF MILLS A CHRONICLE ...

HARPER & BROTHERS PUBLISHERS NEW YORK AND LONDON MCMXIII

⟨i-vi⟩, 1-⟨154⟩. 8⅛″ scant x 5⅜″.

⟨1⟩-10⁸.

V cloth: green. Top edges gilt.

Three printings noted; the following is sufficient for identification:

1

Dated MCMXIII

Code letters M-M (signifying *printed Dec. 1912*) on copyright page. Bound in green V cloth, stamped in gold and blind, top edges gilt.

2

Same as preceding save for the code letters which in this second printing are F-N, signifying *printed June, 1913.*

3

Misdated MCMXIII

Code letters F-O (signifying *printed June, 1914*) on copyright page. Bound in gray-green V cloth, stamped in black only, top edges plain.

On copyright page: *Published January, 1913;* and code letters M-M, signifying *printed Dec. 1912.* Deposited Feb. 21, 1913. H copy received Feb. 24, 1913; BA Feb. 25, 1913. The London (Harper) edition listed Bkr Feb. 28, 1913.

H (1, 2, 3)

9826. FAMILIAR SPANISH TRAVELS ...

HARPER & BROTHERS PUBLISHERS NEW YORK AND LONDON MCMXIII

⟨i-xiv⟩, 1-⟨327⟩, blank leaf. Frontispiece and 31 plates inserted. 8¼″ scant x 5⅜″.

⟨-⟩⁴, ⟨1⟩-21⁸.

C cloth: green. Top edges gilt.

On copyright page: *Published October, 1913;* and, code letters K-N, signifying *printed Oct. 1913.* Deposited Oct. 18, 1913. NYPL copy received Oct. 25, 1913. The London (Harper) edition described as *in preparation* Bkr Nov. 7, 1913; listed Bkr Nov. 14, 1913.

H NYPL

9827. Gulliver's Travels ... by Jonathan Swift ... with an Introduction by W. D. Howells ...

Harper & Brothers Publishers New York & London MCMXIII

"Introduction," pp. xv-‹xvi›.

On copyright page: *Published October, 1913*; and, code letters K-N, signifying *printed Oct. 1913*. Deposited Oct. 18, 1913.

LC

9828. The Complete Poems of Paul Laurence Dunbar with the Introduction to "Lyrics of Lowly Life" by W. D. Howells

New York   Dodd, Mead and Company   1913

Reprint. For comment see entry No. 4961.

9829. THE SEEN AND UNSEEN AT STRAT-FORD-ON-AVON   A FANTASY . . .

HARPER & BROTHERS PUBLISHERS   NEW YORK AND LONDON   MCMXIV

‹i-x›, 1-‹112›, 3 blank leaves. 8¼″ x 5⁵⁄₁₆″. The first and final leaves used as pastedowns.

‹1›-8⁸. Leaves ‹1›₁ and 8₈ used as pastedowns.

V cloth: grass green. Top edges gilt. Stamped in gold and blind.

Note: The spine imprint noted in two forms; sequence, if any, not determined; the following designations are for identification only.

A: Spine imprint from a face ³⁄₃₂″ scant tall. A deposit copy thus.

B: Spine imprint from a face ¹⁄₁₆″ tall.

Also note: Also noted in a variant (remainder?) binding of pale green V cloth, stamped in black, top edges plain.

On copyright page: *Published May, 1914*; and, code letters D-O, signifying *printed April, 1914*. The BA copy (B binding) received May 9, 1914. Deposited (A binding) May 11, 1914. Listed PW May 16, 1914. NYPL copy (A binding) received May 22, 1914. A copy in H (A binding) received June 1, 1914. The London (Harper) edition noted as *in preparation* Bkr May 29, 1914; as *within the next few days* Ath May 30, 1914; listed Bkr June 5, 1914; noted as *just published* Bkr June 5, 1914.

BA (B binding)   BPL (variant)   H (A binding, B binding, variant)   NYPL (A binding)

9830. Hans Andersen   Fairy Tales and Wonder Stories . . . Introduction by W. D. Howells

Harper & Brothers Publishers   New York and London   MCMXIV

"Introduction," pp. xi-‹xiii›.

On copyright page: *Published October, 1914*; and, code letters K-O, signifying *printed Oct.*

1914. Deposited Oct. 17, 1914. The earliest British listing noted is in Bkr Oct. 1922.

LC

9830A. King Albert's Book   A Tribute to the Belgian King and People from Representative Men and Women throughout the World ‹Edited by Hall Caine›

The Daily Telegraph ‹London› in Conjunction with The Daily Sketch   The Glasgow Herald   and Hodder and Stoughton ‹1914›

Contribution, p. 112. For American edition see entry 9831A.

Published Dec. 16, 1914 (publisher's records). The book "was printed jointly by 31 London firms owing to the large demand; 400,000 copies were ordered before publication."—Publisher's letter to BAL, Dec. 21, 1961. All examined copies carry the imprint and device of Knight's Manufacturing Company, Ltd., The Complete Press, on the reverse of the title-leaf. The *Special Birthday Edition* (so marked on the dust jacket by a sticker) issued with a loosely inserted printed envelope containing portraits of the King and Queen of the Belgians.

H

9831. Anecdotes of the Hour by Famous Men as Told by Winston Churchill . . . Jack London . . . and about 100 Other Notable Men . . .

New York   Hearst's International Library Co.   1914

Anecdote, p. 127.

H

9831A. King Albert's Book   A Tribute to the Belgian King and People from Representative Men and Women throughout the World ‹Edited by Hall Caine›

New York   Hearst's International Library Co. ‹1914; *i.e.,* 1915›

First American edition. See entry No. 9830A.

Contribution, p. 112.

Listed (cloth; and, leather) PW March 20, 1915.

Printed in Great Britain. All examined copies carry the imprint and device of Knight's Manufacturing Company, Ltd., The Complete Press, on the reverse of the title-leaf. See publication and printing note, entry No. 9830A.

H

9832. The Shoes of Happiness and Other Poems
... by Edwin Markham ...

Garden City New York Doubleday, Page
& Company 1915

Brief comment, p. 192.

Listed PW March 27, 1915.

H

9833. Sixty American Opinions on the War

London: T. Fisher Unwin, Ltd. 1 Adelphi
Terrace W. C. ⟨1915⟩

Contribution, pp. 90-91.

On copyright page: *First published in 1915*
Advertised as though published PC May 15, 1915.
Deposited BMU May 25, 1915. Listed PC May
29, 1915. NYPL copy received June 2, 1915.

H NYPL

9834. Proceedings of the American Academy of
Arts and Letters and of the National Institute of Arts and Letters Number VIII: 1915 ...

New York ⟨1915⟩

Cover-title. Self-wrapper.

"Address," p. 7.

H

9835. Walt Whitman, As Man, Poet and Friend
... Being Autograph Pages from Many Pens,
Collected by Charles N. Elliot

Boston: Richard G. Badger The Gorham
Press ⟨1915⟩

Note, p. 117.

For comment see entry No. 6635.

9836. The Book of the Homeless (Le Livre des
Sans-Foyer) Edited by Edith Wharton ...

New York Charles Scribner's Sons MDCCC-
XVI

Boards, cloth shelfback.

"The Little Children," p. 17.

"... in addition to the regular edition, there
have been printed and numbered one hundred
and seventy-five copies de luxe, of larger format.
Numbers 1-50 on French hand-made paper,
containing four facsimiles of manuscripts and
a second set of illustrations in portfolio. Numbers 51-175 on Van Gelder paper."—Colophon.

Deposited Jan. 25, 1916.

H NYPL

9837. THE DAUGHTER OF THE STORAGE
AND OTHER THINGS IN PROSE AND
VERSE ...

HARPER & BROTHERS PUBLISHERS NEW YORK
AND LONDON ⟨1916⟩

⟨i-viii⟩, ⟨1⟩-⟨352⟩. 7⁵⁄₁₆″ x 5″.

⟨-⟩⁴, ⟨1⟩-4, ⟨5⟩-14, ⟨15-16⟩, 17-22⁸.

V cloth: blue. *Note:* Also noted in a variant
(remainder?) binding of tan paper boards,
printed in black.

On copyright page: *Published April, 1916*; and,
code letters D-Q, signifying *printed April, 1916.*
Noted for April 14, 1916, PW April 8, 1916.
BA copy received April 25, 1916. Deposited
April 27, 1916. Listed PW April 29, 1916. The
London (Harper) edition listed Bkr July 1916.

H (cloth; boards) NYPL (cloth)

9838. They of the High Trails ⟨by⟩ Hamlin
Garland ...

Harper & Brothers Publishers New York
and London ⟨1916⟩

"Preface," pp. xi-⟨xvi⟩.

On copyright page: *Published April, 1916*
Listed PW April 29, 1916.

Note: According to the publisher's records this
book was published April 20, 1916. However,
the only copies examined have the code letters
A-R or D-R present on the copyright page, indicating *printed Jan. 1917* and *April, 1917*, respectively. BAL is not convinced that it has located a copy of the earliest printing.

H (Jan. 1917) NYPL (April, 1917)

9839. Buying a Horse ...

Boston and New York Houghton Mifflin
Company The Riverside Press Cambridge
1916

Paper boards, printed paper label on front.

Reprinted from *A Day's Pleasure,* 1881.

BPL copy received Sept. 16, 1916; NYPL Sept. 19,
1916. Deposited Sept. 21, 1916. Listed PW Sept.
23, 1916.

BPL H NYPL Y

9840. THE LEATHERWOOD GOD ...

NEW YORK THE CENTURY CO. 1916

⟨i-viii⟩, ⟨1⟩-236, blank leaf. Frontispiece and
7 plates inserted; the seven plates in the body
of the book are considered in the printed
pagination. 7½″ x 5⅛″.

⟨1-14⁸, 15⁴⟩.

V cloth: orange-red.

On copyright page: *Published, October, 1916*
Noted for the week of Oct. 2, 1916, PW Sept.
23, 1916. Noted for the week of Oct. 23, 1916,
PW Oct. 14, 21, 1916. Advertised as *at all book-
stores* PW Oct. 21, 1916. Deposited Nov. 2, 1916.
Listed PW Nov. 4, 1916.

H NYPL

9841. YEARS OF MY YOUTH . . .

HARPER & BROTHERS PUBLISHERS NEW YORK
AND LONDON ⟨1916⟩

⟨i-x⟩, ⟨1⟩-⟨239⟩, 3 blank leaves. *See note below.* 8⅛″ x 5⁵⁄₁₆″.

⟨1⟩-16⁸. *See note below.*

Note: The first and final leaves (⟨1⟩₁ and 16₈)
used as pastedowns. In at least one copy leaf
16₈ has been excised and leaf 16₇ is used as the
pastedown.

T cloth: green. Top edges gilt.

On copyright page: *Published October, 1916*;
and, code letters F-Q, signifying *printed June,
1916*. Reprinted Oct. 1916; such copies have
code letters K-Q. Deposited Nov. 7, 1916. NYPL
copy received Nov. 7, 1916; BA Nov. 15, 1916.
Listed PW Nov. 25, 1916. The London (Harper)
edition described as *in preparation* Bkr Nov.
1916; listed Bkr Jan. 1917. An *Illustrated Edition* (New York ⟨1917⟩), was deposited for
copyright Nov. 5, 1917; code letters K-R (signifying *printed Oct. 1917*) on copyright page;
BA copy received Nov. 6, 1917; noted as *just
brought out* PW Nov. 10, 1917; listed PW Nov.
24, 1917.

BPL H Y

9842. Bazaar Daily . . .

⟨Boston⟩ December 9 . . . ⟨to⟩ 20, 1916 . . .

"A Daily Paper of the Past," No. 4, Dec. 13,
1916, p. 27.

For comment see entry No. 407.

9843. The Country Printer An Essay . . .

Privately Printed ⟨Norwood, Mass.: The
Plimpton Press, 1896; *i.e.*, 1916⟩

Boards, cloth shelfback.

Reprinted from *Impressions and Experiences*,
1896.

400 copies only.

". . . printed . . . and distributed as a Christmas
souvenir in 1916."—Letter, March 11, 1931, The

Plimpton Press to Clarence S. Brigham; letter
in AAS.

BPL H NYPL

The Daughter of the Storage . . .

Harper & Brothers . . . ⟨1916; *i.e.*, 1918⟩

See entry No. 9855.

9844. TRIBUTES TO CANADA BY
CHARLES W. ELIOT . . . AND W. D.
HOWELLS . . . AUTOGRAPH LETTERS
ADDRESSED TO PROFESSOR W. H.
SCHOFIELD, CHAIRMAN OF THE COM-
MITTEE FOR CANADIAN DAY AT THE
NATIONAL ALLIED BAZAAR HELD IN
BOSTON, DECEMBER NINTH TO
TWENTIETH, NINETEEN HUNDRED
AND SIXTEEN

⟨Boston, 1916?⟩

Single cut sheet folded to make 4 pages. Leaf:
8⁵⁄₁₆″ x 5¹⁵⁄₁₆″. P. ⟨1⟩ as above. Howells's letter,
Dec. 9, 1916, on p. ⟨2⟩. Letter from Eliot, p.
⟨3⟩. P. ⟨4⟩ blank.

H

9845. Henry James

1916–1918

Howells's appreciation of Henry James is a revised version of "Mr. James's Daisy Miller," in
Heroines of Fiction, 1901, Vol. 2, pp. 164-176.
It was prepared after James's death, Feb. 28,
1916. It has been located in the following two
books. No sequence has been established and
the designations are for identification only. The
publishers have been unable to furnish reliable
information regarding publication.

A

Daisy Miller by Henry James, Jr., Illustrated
from Drawings by Harry W. McVickar

Harper & Brothers New York and London
⟨1906; *i.e.*, after Feb. 28, 1916⟩

"Introduction," pp. vii-xv.

Locations: H

B

Daisy Miller An International Episode by
Henry James

Boni and Liveright, Inc. Publishers New
York ⟨n.d., 1918⟩

Imitation leather. *Note:* Many unidentified
printings from the same plates. It is probable
later printings omit *Inc* from the imprint.

"Introduction," pp. i-ix.

Listed PW Dec. 7, 1918.

Locations: H

9846. The Books of Kathleen Norris . . .

〈n.p., n.d., Garden City, New York, Double-day, Page & Co., *ca.* April, 1917〉

Four-page leaflet. The above on p. 〈2〉. Issued as an advertisement.

A paragraph on Kathleen Norris, p. 〈1〉, extracted from NAR Dec. 1914.

WMG

9847. The Second Odd Number　Thirteen Tales by Guy de Maupassant　The Translation by Charles Henry White　An Introduction by William Dean Howells

Harper & Brothers Publishers　New York and London 〈1917〉

"Introduction," pp. 〈vii-xii〉.

On copyright page: Code letters C-R, signifying *printed March, 1917.* Deposited May 5, 1917. Listed PW May 12, 1917.

H

9848. The Story of a Country Town by E. W. Howe with an Appreciation by William Dean Howells

Harper & Brothers Publishers　New York and London 〈1917〉

Extract from a letter, Howells to Howe, p. 〈ii〉.

"An Appreciation," pp. 〈v-vi〉.

On copyright page: *Published September, 1917;* and, code letters I-R, signifying *printed Sept. 1917.* Published Sept. 25, 1917 (publisher's records).

AAS

9849. For France . . . 〈Edited by Charles Hanson Towne〉

Garden City　New York　Doubleday, Page & Company　MCMXVII

Brief statement, p. 11.

Deposited Oct. 18, 1917.

H

9850. A Treasury of War Poetry . . . Edited, with Introduction and Notes, by George Herbert Clarke . . .

Boston and New York　Houghton Mifflin Company　The Riverside Press　Cambridge 1917

"The Passengers of a Retarded Submersible," pp. 136-138.

On copyright page: *Published October 1917*

H　NYPL

9851. The Harper Centennial 1817–1917　A Few of the Greetings and Congratulations

Harper & Brothers Publishers　New York and London 〈1917〉

Letter, New York, 1917, p. 9.

Paper boards. 1250 copies printed.

On copyright page: *Published December, 1917;* and code letters M-R, signifying *printed Dec. 1917.*

H

9852. IMMORTALITY AND SIR OLIVER LODGE . . .

〈New-Church Book Rooms, n.d., *ca.* 1917–1920〉

Caption-title. The above on p. 〈1〉. Imprint at foot of p. 〈4〉.

Single cut sheet folded to make 4 pages. Leaf: 6⁷⁄₁₆″ x 4⅞″. Unpaged. Wove paper watermarked: 〈Warren's Olde Style?〉.

Reprinted from *Harper's Monthly Magazine,* Nov. 1917.

SG

9853. . . . Pride and Prejudice by Jane Austen with an Introduction by William Dean Howells

Charles Scribner's Sons　New York　Chicago　Boston 〈1918〉

At head of title: The Modern Student's Library

"Introduction," pp. v-xxiii.

Deposited April 4, 1918.

H

9854. The Actor-Manager by Leonard Merrick with an Introduction by W. D. Howells

Hodder & Stoughton　London　New York Toronto 〈n.d., 1918〉

"Introduction," pp. v-xiv.

Listed Bkr Nov. 1918. See entry No. 9859 for American edition.

H

9855. The Daughter of the Storage . . .

Harper & Brothers Publishers　New York and London 〈1916; *i.e.,* 1918〉

Reprinted from *The Daughter of the Storage and Other Things* ⟨1916⟩.

On p. ⟨1⟩: *Compliments of David Fireproof Storage Warehouses Chicago Christmas 1918*

On copyright page: Code letters M-S, signifying *printed Dec. 1918.*

There was a printing in 1928 for the Security Storage Company of Washington, D. C., with the code letters F-C (*i.e., printed June, 1928*) on the copyright page.

H (1928)   LC (1928)   UV (1918)

9856. ... Defenders of Democracy ... Edited by the Gift Book Committee of the Militia of Mercy ...

New York: John Lane Company London: John Lane, The Bodley Head MCMXVIII

At head of title: President's Edition

Four-line note, Oct. 14, 1917, p. xiv.

Trade edition as above; cloth, color print pasted to front cover; leaf: 9¹¹⁄₁₆″ x 6¹³⁄₁₆″.

Also a de luxe edition, limited to 1000 copies; printed paper boards, cloth shelfback; leaf: 11″ x 8¼″.

H   NYPL

9857. The Shadow of the Cathedral A Novel by Vincent Blasco Ibañez Translated from the Spanish by Mrs. W. A. Gillespie with a Critical Introduction by W. D. Howells

New York E. P. Dutton & Company 681 Fifth Avenue ⟨1919⟩

"Introduction," pp. v-xiv.

Noted as *ready* PW Jan. 4, 1919. Deposited Jan. 14, 1919. Listed PW Feb. 1, 1919. Earliest London notice noted (Unwin edition) is a listing in PC Feb. 23, 1924.

H

9858. The World War Utterances Concerning Its Issues and Conduct by Members of the American Academy of Arts and Letters ...

Published by the Academy 347 Madison Avenue, New York 1919

"The Incredible Cruelty of the Teutons," pp. 20-21.

For comment see entry No. 2198.

9859. The Actor-Manager by Leonard Merrick with an Introduction by William Dean Howells

New York E. P. Dutton and Company 681 Fifth Avenue ⟨1919⟩

First American edition. See entry No. 9854.

Limited to 1550 copies—p. ⟨vi⟩.

"Introduction," pp. v-xiv.

Boards, cloth shelfback, printed paper labels. According to the publication record present in the fourth printing the first American printing was issued on May 12, 1919. Listed PW June 14, 1919.

BPL   H

9860. Hither and Thither in Germany ...

Harper & Brothers Publishers New York and London ⟨1920⟩

Reprint save for a brief introductory note, "Hither and Thither in Germany," p. ⟨1⟩.

Note: In all examined copies leaf ⟨1⟩₅ excised.

On copyright page: *Published January, 1920*; and, code letters M-T (signifying *printed Dec. 1919*). Deposited Jan. 16, 1920. BPL copy received Jan. 24, 1920. Listed PW Jan. 24, 1920.

BA   H   LC   Y

9861. The Great Modern American Stories An Anthology Compiled and Edited with an Introduction by William Dean Howells

New York Boni and Liveright 1920

"A Reminiscent Introduction," pp. vii-xiv.

Deposited July 3, 1920. BA copy received July 8, 1920. Listed PW July 10, 1920.

BA   H   NYPL   Y

9862. THE VACATION OF THE KELWYNS AN IDYL OF THE MIDDLE EIGHTEEN-SEVENTIES ...

HARPER & BROTHERS PUBLISHERS   NEW YORK AND LONDON ⟨1920⟩

⟨i-vi⟩, 1-⟨257⟩. Portrait frontispiece inserted. 7⅞″ x 5⅝₆″.

⟨1⟩-16⁸, 17⁴.

V cloth: green.

On copyright page: *Published September, 1920*; and, code letters H-U, signifying *printed Aug. 1920.* Note: A reprint has been seen with code letters M-U (Dec. 1920) on the copyright page. Deposited Sept. 25, 1920. BPL copy received Sept. 30, 1920. Listed PW Oct. 9, 1920. The London (Harper) edition was advertised without comment in Ath Oct. 7, 1911; however, the advertisement is extraordinarily premature; no British printing or edition listed in *English*

Catalogue prior to Dec. 1920; the Harper edition listed Bkr Jan. 1921.

H NYPL

9863. ... EIGHTY YEARS AND AFTER ... REPRINTED FROM HARPER'S MAGAZINE, DECEMBER, 1919

PRESENTED WITH THE COMPLIMENTS OF THE PUBLISHERS AT THE MEETING IN COMMEMORATION OF THE EIGHTY-FOURTH ANNIVERSARY OF THE BIRTH OF MR. HOWELLS MCMXXI

Cover-title. At head of title: HARPERS MAGAZINE All the preceding printed in brown

⟨1-8⟩. 9⅜″ x 6⁷⁄₁₆″.

⟨-⟩⁴.

Printed buff paper wrapper.

Distributed at a meeting held March 1, 1921. Republished 1937 by The American Academy of Arts and Letters.

BPL H NYPL

9864. MRS. FARRELL A NOVEL ... WITH AN INTRODUCTION BY MILDRED HOWELLS

HARPER & BROTHERS PUBLISHERS NEW YORK AND LONDON ⟨1921⟩

⟨i-iv⟩, ⟨i⟩-⟨xii⟩, 1-⟨266⟩; 2 pp. advertisements; 2 blank leaves. *See binding note below.* 7⅛″ x 5⁵⁄₁₆″.

⟨-⟩⁸, 1-17⁸.

V cloth: green. *See note below.*

Note: The following binding variants have been seen; sequence, if any, not determined and the designations are for identification only.

A: Leaves ⟨-⟩₁ and 17₈ used as pastedowns. Both deposit copies thus.

B: Leaf ⟨-⟩₁ used as pastedown. Leaf 17₈ excised. True end paper at back.

C: Leaves ⟨-⟩₁ and 17₈ excised True end papers at back and at front.

On copyright page: Code letters G-V, signifying *printed July, 1921.* Deposited Sept. 3, 1921. Listed PW Sept. 3, 1921. The London (Harper) edition listed NA Sept. 24, 1921.

Note: The novel was first published in *Atlantic Monthly,* 1875–1876, under the title *Private Theatricals.* A contemporary Edinburgh printing of the book is rumored but thus far no such printing has been seen. For the source of the rumor see "A Suppressed Novel of Mr. Howells," by *Ricus,* in *The Bookman,* New York, Oct. 1910. Gibson & Arms, p. 73, report an al-

leged publication in German translation, 1878.

H LC NYPL Y

9865. A Thanksgiving ...

⟨The Unbound Anthology, Published by the Poets' Guild, 147 Avenue B, New York, n.d., *ca.* 1922⟩

Single leaf. Printed on recto only.

Reprinted from *Poems,* 1873.

NYPL

9866. ... Glory and Endless Years ... ⟨Music by Mabel W. Daniels⟩

The Arthur P. Schmidt Co., Boston ... New York ... ⟨1923⟩

Sheet music. Cover-title. At head of title: ... Arthur P. Schmidt's Octavo Edition ... Plate number A.P.S. 13006-3.

Otherwise "For One of the Killed," *Poems,* 1873.

Deposited Aug. 27, 1923.

LC

9867. Don Quixote by Miguel de Cervantes Saavedra ⟨Translated by Charles Jervas⟩ Edited by William Dean Howells with an Introduction by Mildred Howells

Publishers Harper & Brothers New York and London MCMXXIII

On copyright page: *First Edition;* and, code letters E-X, signifying *printed May, 1923.*

Deposited Sept. 14, 1923. Listed PW Oct. 6, 1923.

AAS H NYPL

9868. ... Germinal Translated from the French by Havelock Ellis with an Essay by William Dean Howells

Published in New York by Boni and Liveright, 1924

At head of title: Émile Zola

"Émile Zola," pp. v-xviii.

Cloth, printed paper label on spine.

2050 copies only; but note that very few copies (the number is not known) contain the Howells introduction. The reason for this condition is not known. Presumably the Howells essay was used without authorization and the publishers were obliged to remove it from unsold copies.

WMG

9869. Hamlin Garland   A Son of the Middle Border

⟨n.p., n.d., New York, *ca.* 1926⟩

Printed paper wrapper.

"A Son of the Middle Border," pp. 21-23. Reprinted from the *New York Times,* Aug. 30, 1917.

NYPL   Y

9870. LIFE IN LETTERS OF WILLIAM DEAN HOWELLS EDITED BY MILDRED HOWELLS . . .

GARDEN CITY, NEW YORK   DOUBLEDAY, DORAN & COMPANY, INC. 1928

Title-pages in black and red. 2 Vols.

1: ⟨i-ii⟩, ⟨i⟩-⟨xiv⟩, 1-429, 2 blank leaves. Frontispiece and 5 plates inserted. 9⅜" x 6¼".
2: ⟨i⟩-⟨xii⟩, 1-426, 2 blank leaves. Frontispiece and 6 plates inserted.

1: ⟨1⁹, 2-28⁸⟩. Leaf ⟨1⟩₃ inserted.
2: ⟨1⁹, 2-26⁸, 27⁴, 28⁸⟩. Leaf ⟨1⟩₂ inserted.

Gray-blue V cloth sides, maroon V cloth shelf-back. Printed label on spine. Top edges gilt.

Note: The spine label occurs in the following states; sequence, if any, not determined and the designations are for identification only:

A: *Life and / Letters* . . .

B: *Life in / Letters* . . .

On copyright page: *First Edition*   BA copy received Nov. 13, 1928. Listed PW Nov. 17, 1928. Deposited Nov. 19, 1928. The London (Heinemann) edition announced for May 23, 1929 PC May 18, 1929; listed PC June 8, 1929.

H   NYPL

9871. *Entry cancelled.*

9872. Twenty-Seventh Annual Report of the Bibliophile Society 1901–1929

⟨Boston, 1929⟩

Boards, printed paper label on spine.

"The Letters of Howells to ⟨Thomas Wentworth⟩ Higginson," pp. 17-56.

H   NYPL   Y

9873. Maggie together with George's Mother and the Blue Hotel ⟨by⟩ Stephen Crane . . .

Alfred A Knopf   New York   MCMXXXI

"An Appreciation," pp. 135-136. For prior publication see entry No. 9705.

Deposited Sept. 28, 1931.

BPL   H   Y

9873A. The American Theatre As Seen by its Critics 1752–1934 Edited by Montrose J. Moses and John Mason Brown

W. W. Norton & Company, Inc. New York ⟨1934⟩

"Edward Harrigan's Comedies," pp. 132-135.

On copyright page: *First Edition*

H

9873B. Recognition of Robert Frost   Twenty-Fifth Anniversary Edited by Richard Thornton

New York   Henry Holt and Company ⟨1937⟩

"First American Notice," pp. 44-45. Reprinted from *Harper's Monthly Magazine,* Sept. 1915.

H

9874. HOWELLS'S UNPUBLISHED PREFACES EDITED BY GEORGE ARMS

REPRINTED FROM THE NEW ENGLAND QUARTERLY VOLUME XVII, NUMBER 4, DECEMBER, 1944

Cover-title.

⟨579⟩-591. 9³⁄₁₆" x 6". Wove paper watermarked *Warren's Olde Style.*

7 leaves.

Printed green paper wrapper.

First publication of a series of prefaces printed (but not published) *ca.* 1910–1911. For comment see entry No. 9809.

H

9875. The Question of Henry James   A Collection of Critical Essays Edited by F. W. Dupee

New York: Henry Holt and Company ⟨1945⟩

"Mr. Henry James's Later Work," pp. 6-19.

On copyright page: *First Printing*   Listed PW Nov. 17, 1945.

BA   NYPL

9876. William Dean Howells   Representative Selections, with Introduction, Bibliography, and Notes by Clara Marburg Kirk . . . and Rudolf Kirk . . .

American Book Company   New York   Cincinnati   Chicago   Boston   Atlanta   Dallas   San Francisco ⟨1950⟩

On copyright page of the first printing is the publisher's code symbol: *E.P.1*

Reprint save for:

"Henry James, Jr.," pp. 345-355. Reprinted from *Century Magazine*, Nov. 1882.

"The Smiling Aspects of American Life," pp. 356-358. Reprinted from *Harper's Monthly Magazine*, Sept. 1886. In revised form appears in *Criticism and Fiction*, 1891.

"Pernicious Fiction," pp. 359-363. Reprinted from *Harper's Monthly Magazine*, April, 1887. In revised form appears in *Criticism and Fiction*, 1891.

"Breadth and Literature," pp. 364-366. Reprinted from *Harper's Monthly Magazine*, Sept. 1887. In revised form appears in *Criticism and Fiction*, 1891.

"Tolstoy's Creed," pp. 367-368. Reprinted from *Harper's Monthly Magazine*, July, 1887.

"Frank Norris," pp. 384-394. Reprinted from NAR Dec. 1902.

Deposited July 26, 1950.

LC

9877. Selected Writings ... Edited, with an Introduction, by Henry Steele Commager

Random House New York ‹1950›

Reprint. On copyright page: *First Printing*

Deposited Sept. 15, 1950.

LC

9878. Prefaces to Contemporaries (1882–1920) by William Dean Howells ... with an Introduction and Bibliographical Note by George Arms William M. Gibson Frederic C. Marston, Jr.

Gainesville, Florida Scholars' Facsimiles & Reprints 1957

Thirty-four prefaces by Howells here first brought together in a single volume.

B H

9879. HOWELLS AND JAMES: A DOUBLE BILLING NOVEL-WRITING AND NOVEL-READING AN IMPERSONAL EXPLANATION ... EDITED BY WILLIAM M. GIBSON HENRY JAMES AND THE BAZAR LETTERS EDITED BY LEON EDEL AND LYALL H. POWERS

NEW YORK THE NEW YORK PUBLIC LIBRARY 1958

‹1›-55. 10" full x 6^{15}⁄$_{16}$".

‹-›^{28}. Signature mark 2 on p. 13.

Printed laid yellow paper wrapper.

"Reprinted from the *Bulletin* of the New York Public Library January and February 1958 ..." —p. ‹2›.

According to the printer's code, p. ‹2›, 1000 copies printed Oct. 3, 1958.

LC Y

9880. CRITICISM AND FICTION AND OTHER ESSAYS ... EDITED WITH INTRODUCTIONS AND NOTES BY CLARA MARBURG KIRK AND RUDOLF KIRK

NEW YORK UNIVERSITY PRESS 1959

‹iii›-‹xx›, ‹1›-413. Frontispiece. 8^{5}⁄$_{16}$" full x 5^{13}⁄$_{16}$".

‹1-11^{16}, 12^{8}, 13-14^{16}›

V cloth: blue.

Deposited Feb. 27, 1959.

Contains many pieces here first published in book form.

H LC

9881. MARK TWAIN—HOWELLS LETTERS THE CORRESPONDENCE OF SAMUEL L. CLEMENS AND WILLIAM D. HOWELLS 1872–1910 EDITED BY HENRY NASH SMITH AND WILLIAM M. GIBSON WITH THE ASSISTANCE OF FREDERICK ANDERSON

THE BELKNAP PRESS OF HARVARD UNIVERSITY PRESS CAMBRIDGE, MASSACHUSETTS 1960

2 Vols. Title-pages in black and gold.

1: ‹i›-‹xxvi›, ‹1›-454. Illustrations: Inserted frontispiece; 4 inserted leaves printed on both sides; one illustration in text. 9^{1}⁄$_{4}$" scant x 6^{1}⁄$_{8}$". Wove paper watermarked *Warren's Olde Style*. 2: ‹i-viii›, 455-948, blank leaf. Illustrations: 6 inserted leaves printed on 11 sides.

1: ‹1^{8}, 2-15^{16}, 16^{8}›.
2: ‹1^{8}, 2-16^{16}, 17^{4}›.

V cloth: slate-black. Buff paper end papers.

Deposited March 11, 1960.

H

9882. THE COMPLETE PLAYS OF W. D. HOWELLS ‹Edited by› WALTER J. MESERVE ... UNDER THE GENERAL EDITORSHIP OF WILLIAM M. GIBSON AND GEORGE ARMS

NEW YORK UNIVERSITY PRESS 1960

⟨i⟩-⟨xxxvi⟩, 1-649, blank leaf. 10″ x 7³⁄₁₆″.

⟨1-20¹⁶, 21⁸, 22¹⁶⟩.

V cloth: orange-brown. Tan end papers imprinted in black with facsimile of Boston Museum program.

Contains much material by Howells here first published or here first in book form. See entry No. 9621.

Deposited Oct. 3, 1960.

H

9882A. LETTERS OF AN ALTRURIAN TRAVELLER (1893–94) . . . A FACSIMILE REPRODUCTION WITH AN INTRODUCTION BY CLARA M. KIRK AND RUDOLF KIRK

GAINESVILLE, FLORIDA SCHOLARS' FACSIMILES & REPRINTS 1961

⟨i⟩-xii, 13-127. Illustrated. 8½″ x 5⁷⁄₁₆″.

⟨1-8⁸⟩.

V cloth: blue.

Reproduced photographically from the original printing in *The Cosmopolitan* magazine.

"William Dean Howells wrote for *The Cosmopolitan* twenty-three Altrurian essays between November, 1892, and September, 1894. The first twelve, forming a series entitled *A Traveller from Altruria*, were re-issued as a book in 1894; the other eleven essays, called *Letters of an Altrurian Traveller*, have never before been reprinted in full since their first appearance. Two of these Letters remained in *The Cosmopolitan* until the present; several are to be found, with deletions and alterations, in a volume of essays by Howells, *Impressions and Experiences* (1896); portions of others make up Part First of *Through the Eye of the Needle* (1907)."—P. v. See entry No. 9685.

No copyright deposit record found. A copy received by LC Jan. 12 (13?), 1961.

H

9882B. DISCOVERY OF A GENIUS WILLIAM DEAN HOWELLS AND HENRY JAMES COMPILED AND EDITED BY ALBERT MORDELL . . .

TWAYNE PUBLISHERS NEW YORK ⟨1961⟩

⟨1⟩-207. 8¼″ scant x 5⁷⁄₁₆″.

⟨1-5¹⁶, 6⁸, 7¹⁶⟩.

V cloth: maroon.

". . . the first collection of the published articles and book reviews written by William Dean Howells about Henry James's publications. Except for an article—*Daisy Miller,* and a small piece on James in *My Literary Passions,*—reprinted by Howells and for two articles included in other anthologies, these critical estimates have remained buried in the periodicals in which they first appeared."—P. 7.

For a comment on the authorship of two pieces included herein see "William Dean Howells: Two Mistaken Attributions," by George Monteiro, in *The Papers of the Bibliographical Society of America,* Vol. 56, second quarter, 1962, pp. 254-257.

Deposited July 1, 1961.

H

REPRINTS

The following publications contain material by Howells reprinted from earlier books.

[No. 213.] New England Loyal Publication Society. Office, No. 8 Studio Building, Boston. August 9, 1864.

Single sheet. Printed on recto only.

Folk Songs Selected and Edited by John Williamson Palmer . . . a New Edition, Revised and Enlarged.

New York: Charles Scribner and Company. M DCCC LXVII.

Advertised ALG Nov. 1, 1867, as in turkey extra; turkey antique; cloth.

The Sunnyside Book . . .

New York . . . 1871

"Venice," pp. ⟨27⟩-31; previously in *No Love Lost,* 1869. For comment see entry No. 1721.

Illustrated Library of Favorite Song . . . Edited by J. G. Holland . . .

New York . . . ⟨1873⟩

For comment see entry No. 2853.

Sea and Shore . . .

Boston . . . 1874.

For comment see entry No. 4043.

. . . Little Classics. Edited by Rossiter Johnson. Life . . .

Boston . . . 1875.

"A Romance of Real Life," pp. ⟨26⟩-43; reprinted from *Suburban Sketches,* 1871. For comment see entry No. 8576.

Songs of Three Centuries. Edited by John Greenleaf Whittier.

Boston . . . 1876.

For comment see entry No. 2857.

Poems of Places Edited by Henry W. Longfellow . . . Italy. Vol. I.

Boston . . . 1877.

For comment see in list of Oliver Wendell Holmes reprints.

Poems of Places Edited by Henry W. Longfellow . . . Germany. Vol. I.

Boston . . . 1877.

For comment see BAL, Vol. 1, p. 296.

Poetry of America Selections from One Hundred American Poets from 1776 to 1876 . . . by W. J. Linton.

London: George Bell & Sons, York Street, Covent Garden. 1878.

Poems of Places Edited by Henry W. Longfellow . . . Middle States.

Boston . . . 1879.

For comment see BAL, Vol. 1, p. 74.

Home Life in Song with the Poets of To-Day . . .

New York . . . ⟨1879⟩

For comment see entry No. 432.

One Hundred Choice Selections No. 19 . . .

. . . Philadelphia . . . 1881.

For comment see entry No. 3392.

Selections in Verse . . .

Philadelphia . . . 1881.

For comment see BAL, Vol. 1, p. 74.

The Cambridge Book of Poetry and Song . . . by Charlotte Fiske Bates . . .

New York . . . ⟨1882⟩

For comment see entry No. 7887.

Surf and Wave: The Sea As Sung by the Poets. Edited by Anna L. Ward . . .

New York: Thomas Y. Crowell & Co. 13 Astor Place. ⟨1883⟩

Flowers from Glade and Garden Poems Arranged . . . by Susie Barstow Skelding . . .

New York . . . 1884

For comment see BAL, Vol. 2, p. 39.

Flowers for Winter Days . . . Arranged and Illustrated by Susie Barstow Skelding . . .

New York White, Stokes, & Allen 1885

Tied. Unpaged. Color print pasted to front. Deposited Aug. 3, 1885.

March Edited by Oscar Fay Adams . . .

Boston . . . ⟨1886⟩

"Prelude," *Poems of Two Friends*, 1860, appears herein under the title "In March I Sing." For comment see entry No. 60.

Bugle-Echoes . . . Edited by Francis F. Browne

New York . . . MDCCCLXXXVI

For comment see BAL, Vol. 1, p. 75.

Representative Poems of Living Poets . . .

. . . New York 1886

For comment see entry No. 436.

May Edited by Oscar Fay Adams . . .

Boston . . . ⟨1886⟩

For comment see entry No. 63.

June Edited by Oscar Fay Adams . . .

Boston . . . ⟨1886⟩

For comment see entry No. 64.

July Edited by Oscar Fay Adams . . .

Boston . . . ⟨1886⟩

For comment see entry No. 65.

August Edited by Oscar Fay Adams . . .

Boston . . . ⟨1886⟩

For comment see entry No. 66.

Belford's Annual 1886–7. Edited by Thomas W. Handford . . .

Chicago and New York: Belford Clarke & Co. ⟨1886⟩

Boards, printed in imitation of tree calf.

Selections from American Humour. By Mark Twain . . .

Leipzig . . . 1888.

"Love's Young Dream," pp. 147-158, reprinted from *A Chance Acquaintance*, 1873. For comment see entry No. 3646.

. . . Harper's Fifth Reader American Authors

New York . . . 1889

"The Mouse," pp. 433-439; reprinted from

Venetian Life, 1866. For comment see entry No. 7917.

Beiträge von Literaten und Künstlern zum Deutschen Hospital Bazaar ...

⟨New York, 1889⟩

For comment see entry No. 4369.

Half-Hours with the Best Humorous Authors. Selected ... by Charles Morris ... American.

Philadelphia ... 1889.

For comment see entry No. 3813.

Werner's Readings and Recitations. No. 2. Compiled ... by Elsie M. Wilbor.

New York ... 1890.

For comment see BAL, Vol. 1, p. 249.

The Poets' Year ... Edited by Oscar Fay Adams ...

Boston ... ⟨1890⟩

For comment see entry No. 80.

Local and National Poets of America ... Edited ... ⟨by⟩ Thos. W. Herringshaw ...

Chicago ... 1890.

For comment see BAL, Vol. 2, p. 391.

The Speakers' Library ... Edited by Daphne Dale.

1890 ... Chicago Philadelphia.

For comment see entry No. 6324.

No. 31. Standard Recitations by Best Authors ... Compiled ... by Frances P. Sullivan ... March 1891 ...

... N. Y. ... ⟨1891⟩

For comment see BAL, Vol. 2, p. 275.

Out of the Heart Poems ... Selected by John White Chadwick ... and Annie Hathaway Chadwick ...

Troy, N. Y. ... 1891

For comment see BAL, Vol. 2, p. 452.

The Lover's Year-Book of Poetry ... Vol. I. January to June

Boston ... 1891

For comment see entry No. 4015.

Younger American Poets 1830–1890 Edited by Douglas Sladen ...

... London ... 1891

For comment see entry No. 6557.

Younger American Poets 1830–1890 Edited by Douglas Sladen ...

... New York   1891

For comment see entry No. 6558.

Random Rhymes. ⟨Edited by Roland R. Conklin⟩

⟨n.p., Kansas City, Mo., 1893⟩

A Souvenir and a Medley: Seven Poems ... by Stephen Crane ...

... East Aurora, N. Y. Eighteen Hundred and Ninety-Six.

For comment see entry No. 4074.

Through Love to Light A Selection ... by John White Chadwick and Annie Hathaway Chadwick

Boston ... 1896

For comment see entry No. 2633.

Voices of Doubt and Trust Selected by Volney Streamer

New York Brentano's 1897

Deposited Sept. 2, 1897.

Anthology of Living American Poets, 1898. Arranged by Deborah Ege Olds.

Cincinnati. The Editor Publishing Company. 1898.

Songs of Nature Edited by John Burroughs

New York ... MCMI ...

For comment see entry No. 2169.

Modern Eloquence ... ⟨Edited by⟩ Thomas B. Reed ...

... Philadelphia ⟨1900; *i.e.,* 1901⟩

For comment see entry No. 3467.

Mark Twain's Library of Humor   Men and Things ...

... New York ... MCMVI

For comment see entry No. 3666.

Mark Twain's Library of Humor   Women and Things ...

... New York ... MCMVI

"Their First Quarrel," pp. ⟨170⟩-175, reprinted from *Their Wedding Journey,* 1872.

For comment see entry No. 3667.

Mark Twain's Library of Humor The Primrose Way ...

... New York ... MCMVI

"At Niagara," pp. ⟨121⟩-125, reprinted from *Their Wedding Journey*, 1872. For comment see entry No. 3668.

Mark Twain's Library of Humor A Little Nonsense ...

... New York ... MCMVI

"Custom-House Morals," pp. ⟨293-294⟩, reprinted from *Their Wedding Journey*, 1872.

For comment see entry No. 3669.

Fifty-Two New Stories for Boys ... Edited by Alfred H. Miles ...

London: Hutchinson & Co., 34, Paternoster Row. ⟨1906⟩

Not seen. "A Hairbreadth Escape," pp. 303-313, is a reprint of Chapter III, *The Flight of Pony Baker*, 1902. Received at BMU Nov. 23, 1906.

The Meaning of Modern Life ... Edited ... by Charles F. Horne ...

Issued under the Auspices of the National Alumni Union Square New York ⟨1907⟩

Probably issued with varying imprints and in a variety of bindings.

Through Italy with the Poets Compiled by Robert Haven Schauffler ...

New York Moffat, Yard & Company 1908

On copyright page: *Published March, 1908.* Noted as *at once* PW Jan. 11, 1908. Listed PW Feb. 15, 1908.

Poets of Ohio ... Edited by Emerson Venable

Cincinnati ... MDCCCCIX

For fuller entry see BAL, Vol. 2, p. 96.

The Oxford Book of American Essays Chosen by Brander Matthews ...

New York Oxford University Press American Branch: 35 West 32nd Street London, Toronto, Melbourne, and Bombay Humphrey Milford 1914 All Rights Reserved

Deposited Dec. 18, 1914. Listed PW Jan. 2, 1915. Deposited BMU April 22, 1915. Listed Bkr April 30, 1915; PC May 1, 1915.

America in the War by Louis Raemaekers ...

New York ... 1918

For comment see entry No. 810. "The Passengers of a Retarded Submersible," *A Treasury of War Poetry*, 1917, appears herein under the title "The Massacre of the Innocents."

Books by E. W. Howe Sold at Johnson's Book Store Atchison, Kansas

⟨Atchison, Kansas, n.d., *ca.* 1919⟩

4 pp. leaflet.

American Mystical Verse An Anthology Selected by Irene Hunter ...

D. Appleton and Company New York MCMXXV

⟨24th⟩ Annual Report of the Bibliophile Society for 1925

⟨Boston, 1926⟩

Boards, printed paper label on spine. " 'Old Brown,' " pp. 54-55. In spite of the statement "hitherto unpublished," p. 53, the poem had prior publication; see entry No. 9536.

Harper Essays Edited by Henry Seidel Canby ...

New York and London Harper & Brothers Publishers MCMXXVII

Boards, cloth shelfback, printed paper label on front. Deposited Oct. 6, 1927.

Mark Twain ... Notes on His Life and Works Containing a Biographical Sketch by Albert Bigelow Paine Tributes by Famous Authors ...

Harper & Brothers New York and London M DCCCC XXVIII

Paper wrapper, printed paper label.

The St. Nicholas Anthology Edited by Henry Steele Commager ...

Random House New York ⟨1948⟩

Listed PW Nov. 20, 1948.

REFERENCES AND ANA

La Primavera Ode di Wm. D. Howells Console degli Stati Uniti Residente a Venezia Versione dall'Inglese di D. C. Dott. Frattini

⟨n.p., n.d., Padua, 1863⟩

Single cut sheet folded to make 4 pp. Unwatermarked white wove paper. The above on p. ⟨1⟩. Text on pp. ⟨3-4⟩. P. ⟨2⟩ blank. Imprint below text, p. ⟨4⟩: *Tip. Seminario.* Page: 8½" x 5¾".

"I enclose for father a poem of mine, translated and printed at Padua, on occasion of the Zeni-Foratti Nuptials. It is the custom in

Italy, when people get married, to print little copies of verse and circulate among their friends. The abbè ⟨sic⟩ Fratini ⟨sic⟩, a professor in the University of Padua, made this translation, which has been much admired in that ancient city. It was printed at the University office. The original English has never been printed."—Letter, Howells to Anne T. Howells, Venice, Sept. 17, 1863, in *Life in Letters of William Dean Howells,* Vol. 1, p. 76.

The original English text, dated at end *1861,* appears under the title "A Springtime," *Poems,* 1873.

H

The Novice: Or, Mother Church Thwarted. A Tale of the Great Earthquake in 1755. By Jane G. Austin.

Boston: Elliott, Thomes & Talbot, 63 Congress Street ⟨1865⟩

For comment see entry No. 515.

"How I Got in Love," pp. ⟨96⟩-100, credited to *W.D.H.* By William Dean Howells?

Mose Evans: A Simple Statement of the Singular Facts of His Case. By William M. Baker . . .

New York: Published by Hurd and Houghton. Cambridge: The Riverside Press. 1874.

Dedicated to Howells and possibly edited by him. The novel first appeared in *Atlantic Monthly* and was reviewed by Howells in that periodical Aug. 1874.

"As this book was written in moments snatched from that Profession ⟨the clergy⟩ which is the chief business of my life, it has devolved . . . a degree of labor upon you as Editor . . ."—From the dedication.

The present entry is but representative of the many works which underwent Howells's editorial supervision. A full list would run to impressive length and include works by, among others, H. H. Boyesen and Mark Twain.

The Boyhood of Living Authors by William H. Rideing . . .

New York Thomas Y. Crowell & Co. 13 Astor Place ⟨1887⟩

For comment see entry No. 1262.

"William Dean Howells," pp. 74-85; a distorted digest of Howells's "Year in a Log-Cabin," *Youth's Companion,* May 12, 1887.

For book publication of the Howells text see *My Year in a Log Cabin,* 1893.

How They Succeeded Life Stories of Successful Men Told by Themselves By Orison Swett Marden . . .

Lothrop Publishing Company Boston ⟨1901⟩

"How William Dean Howells Worked to Secure a Foothold," an interview with Howells, pp. 171-184; written by Theodore Dreiser although his name does not appear.

The interview, with slight alterations, appears also in *Little Visits with Great Americans . . . ,* edited by Orison Swett Marden, New York, 1903.

Deposited April 25, 1901. Listed PW May 4, 1901.

For a comment on these Marden compilations see "Theodore Dreiser, Success Monger," and, "Dreiser and Success: An Additional Note," both by John F. Huth, Jr., in *The Colophon,* Winter, 1938, Vol. 3, New Series, No. 1; and, Summer, 1938, Vol. 3, New Series, Number 3.

The Magic Book.

1901.

Not found. Entry from CHAL, Vol. 4, p. 665, where a book so titled is given as with a contribution by Howells. BAL theorizes that *The Magic Book* is a highly garbled entry for *The Niagara Book,* 1901.

Literature in the Making by Some of Its Makers Presented by Joyce Kilmer

Harper & Brothers New York and London ⟨1917⟩

"War Stops Literature," pp. 3-⟨15⟩; an interview.

On copyright page: *Published April, 1917;* and, code letters D-R, signifying *printed April, 1917.* Deposited May 5, 1917. Listed PW May 12, 1917.

William Dean Howells A Study of the Achievement of a Literary Artist by Alexander Harvey

New York B. W. Huebsch 1917

Deposited Nov. 26, 1917.

The William Dean Howells Memorial Meeting March 1, 1921 Stuart Gallery of the New York Public Library

⟨n.p., n.d., New York, 1921⟩

Cover-title. Printed paper wrapper.

William Dean Howells A Critical Study by Delmar Gross Cooke

> New York E. P. Dutton & Company 681 Fifth Avenue ⟨1922⟩
>
> "Bibliography," pp. 257-272. Deposited Oct. 30, 1922.

Public Meeting of the American Academy and the National Institute of Arts and Letters in Honor of William Dean Howells . . .

> ⟨New York⟩ American Academy of Arts and Letters 1922
>
> Printed paper wrapper.

William Dean Howells A Study by Oscar W. Firkins

> Cambridge Harvard University Press 1924
>
> Deposited Nov. 24, 1924. Listed PW Dec. 13, 1924.

The Rise of Silas Lapham A Comedy in Four Acts . . . by Lillian Sabine . . .

> . . . 1927 . . . New York Samuel French Publisher 25 West 45th Street . . .
>
> Printed paper wrapper. Deposited Jan. 3, 1928.

Life of Abraham Lincoln by W. D. Howells . . . Corrected by the Hand of Abraham Lincoln in the Summer of 1860 . . .

> Springfield, Illinois Abraham Lincoln Association 1938
>
> Boards, cloth shelfback, printed paper label on front. Facsimile of Lincoln's copy of Howells's life. 1250 copies only.

Five Interviews with William Dean Howells Edited by George Arms . . . and William M. Gibson . . .

> Reprinted from Vol. xxxvii, No. 2, April, 1943, of "Americana," . . .
>
> Printed paper wrapper. Cover-title.

A Bibliography of William Dean Howells by William M. Gibson . . . and George Arms . . .

> New York The New York Public Library 1948
>
> Printed paper wrapper. 500 copies printed.

. . . Howells & Italy

> Duke University Press Durham, North Carolina 1952

At head of title: James L. Woodress, Jr. Deposited July 28, 1952.

Howells and the Age of Realism by Everett Carter

> J. B. Lippincott Company Philadelphia New York ⟨1954⟩
>
> On copyright page: *First Edition* Deposited Oct. 5, 1954.

. . . The Road to Realism The Early Years 1837–1885 of William Dean Howells

> Syracuse University Press ⟨Syracuse, N. Y., 1956⟩
>
> At head of title: Edwin H. Cady Deposited Oct. 15, 1956.

. . . The Realist at War The Mature Years 1885–1920 of William Dean Howells

> Syracuse University Press ⟨Syracuse, N. Y., 1958⟩
>
> At head of title: Edwin H. Cady Deposited Oct. 6, 1958.

. . . In Quest of America A Study of Howells' Early Development As a Novelist

> Upsala ⟨University of Upsala⟩ 1958
>
> Printed paper wrapper. At head of title: Olov W. Fryckstedt Also issued with the imprint: *Harvard University Press Cambridge, Massachusetts, 1958*

William Dean Howells The Development of a Novelist ⟨by⟩ George N. Bennett

> Norman University of Oklahoma Press ⟨1959⟩
>
> Deposited Feb. 17, 1959.

Howells His Life and World by Van Wyck Brooks

> E. P. Dutton & Co., Inc. New York 1959
>
> On copyright page: *First Edition* Deposited Oct. 15, 1959.

The Quiet Rebel William Dean Howells As Social Commentator by Robert L. Hough

> University of Nebraska Press Lincoln 1959
>
> Deposited Nov. 23, 1959.

W. D. Howells, Traveler from Altruria 1889–1894 by Clara Marburg Kirk

> Rutgers University Press New Brunswick New Jersey ⟨1962⟩

JAMES GIBBONS HUNEKER

1 8 5 7 – 1 9 2 1 *

9883. MEZZOTINTS IN MODERN MUSIC
. . .

NEW YORK   CHARLES SCRIBNER'S SONS 1899

⟨i-viii⟩, 1-318, blank leaf. Laid paper. 7⅝″ x 4¹⁵⁄₁₆″.

⟨1-20⁸, 21⁴⟩. *Signed:* ⟨-⟩⁴, 1-20⁸.

Green sateen. Double flyleaves of laid paper. Top edges gilt.

Published March 11, 1899, in a printing of 1030 copies; publisher's records. Deposited March 11, 1899. The London (Reeves) edition listed by Ath Feb. 24, 1900.

AAS BPL NYPL

9884. Anton Seidl A Memoir by His Friends

New York Charles Scribner's Sons MDCCC-XCIX

Tribute, pp. 114-117.

1000 numbered copies only.

Deposited March 30, 1899. ". . . printed from type in February and March, 1899 . . ."—Certificate of issue.

NYPL

9885. The Standard Operaglass Detailed Plots of the Celebrated Operas . . . by Charles Annesley ⟨*i.e.,* Charles and Anna Tittman⟩ with a Prelude by James Huneker

New York Brentano's 1899

"Prelude," pp. 1-8.

Deposited June 5, 1899.

AAS H

9886. CHOPIN THE MAN AND HIS MUSIC . . .

NEW YORK   CHARLES SCRIBNER'S SONS 1900

* *Huneker's birthdate is usually given as 1860. For confirmation of the date 1857 see "Huneker's Hidden Birthdate," by Arnold T. Schwab, in* American Literature, *Nov. 1951.*

⟨i⟩-viii, ⟨1⟩-415; blank, p. ⟨416⟩; 2 pp. advertisements; blank leaf. Laid paper. Frontispiece inserted. 7⅝″ x 5″.

⟨1-26⁸, 27⁶⟩. *Signed:* ⟨-⟩⁴, ⟨1⟩-26⁸, ⟨27⟩²; *16 missigned 11.*

Khaki sateen. White laid paper flyleaves. Double flyleaf at front. Top edges gilt.

Published April 7, 1900, in a printing of 2000 copies, of which 210 copies in sheets were sent to William Reeves, London; publisher's records. Deposited April 7, 1900. Listed PW April 14, 1900. The London (Reeves) edition listed Ath Jan. 12, 1901.

H

9887. Modern Masters of Music Course II: Booklovers Reading Club Books Selected for This Reading Course by Reginald De Koven

⟨Philadelphia: The Booklovers Library, 1901⟩

Printed paper wrapper.

"The Caprices of Musical Taste: A Talk," pp. 81-89.

Deposited Jan. 17, 1902.

AAS LC

9888. MELOMANIACS . . .

NEW YORK   CHARLES SCRIBNER'S SONS 1902

⟨i⟩-⟨x⟩, 1-350; plus: 4 pp. advertisements. Laid paper. 7½″ x 4⅞″.

⟨1-22⁸, 23⁴; plus: 24²⟩. *Signed:* ⟨-⟩⁵, 1-21⁸, 22⁹.

V cloth: red. Flyleaves. Top edges gilt.

On copyright page: *Published, February, 1902* Published Feb. 21, 1902, in a printing of 2000 copies; publisher's records. Deposited Feb. 21, 1902. Listed PW March 1, 1902. The London (Laurie) edition listed Ath Sept. 29, 1906.

BPL

9889. Forty Piano Compositions ⟨by⟩ Frédéric Chopin Edited by James Huneker . . .

Boston: Oliver Ditson Company New York: Chas. H. Ditson & Co. Chicago: Lyon & Healy Philadelphia: J. E. Ditson & Co. ⟨1902⟩

Cloth; and, printed paper wrapper.

"Frédéric Chopin," pp. ⟨ix⟩-xiii.

Deposited Oct. 9, 1902.

NYPL

9890. Forty Songs by Johannes Brahms Edited by James Huneker . . .

Boston: Oliver Ditson Company New York: Chas. H. Ditson & Co. Chicago: Lyon & Healy Philadelphia: J. E. Ditson & Co. [Price: Paper, $1.50; Cloth, $2.50] ⟨1903⟩

Cloth; and, printed paper wrapper, cloth shelf-back.

"Johannes Brahms," pp. ⟨ix⟩-xii.

Edited for *High Voice* (deposited June 25, 1903); and, for *Low Voice* (deposited Sept. 14, 1903).

H   Y

9891. OVERTONES   A BOOK OF TEM-PERAMENTS . . .

NEW YORK   CHARLES SCRIBNER'S SONS   1904

⟨i⟩-⟨viii⟩, 1-335; blank, p. ⟨336⟩; plus: 4 pp. advertisements. Laid paper. Frontispiece inserted. 7 9/16″ x 4 7/8″.

⟨A⟩⁴, B-⟨C⟩, D-I, K-U, X-Y⁸; plus: ⟨Z⟩².

Blue sateen. White laid paper end papers. Top edges gilt. Flyleaves.

Two printings noted:

1

As above.

2

⟨i⟩-⟨viii⟩, 1-335; blank, p. ⟨336⟩; 4 pp. advertisements; 2 blank leaves.

⟨1-22⁸⟩. Signed as above.

Flyleaf at front.

On copyright page: *Published March, 1904.* Published March 17, 1904, in a printing of 2000 copies; publisher's records. *Coming March 12—* PW March 5, 1904. Deposited March 17, 1904. Noted for March 17, 1904, PW March 12, 1904. Listed PW March 26, 1904. The London (Isbister) edition listed Ath June 18, 1904.

AAS (1st)   H (1st)   LC (1st, being a deposit copy) Y (2nd)

9892. ICONOCLASTS   A BOOK OF DRAM-ATISTS . . .

NEW YORK   CHARLES SCRIBNER'S SONS   1905

⟨i⟩-⟨viii⟩, 1-430; 4 pp. advertisements; blank leaf. 7 11/16″ x 4 7/8″. *Laid paper; but see note below.*

⟨1-27⁸, 28⁶⟩.

Note: Printed on lightly calendered laid paper save for leaves ⟨28⟩2-5 which are printed on appreciably heavier uncalendered laid paper. *Cancels?*

Maroon sateen. White laid paper end papers. Top edges gilt. Double flyleaves.

Two printings noted:

1

As above.

Sheets bulk ¾″.

Norwood Press imprint on copyright page.

2

⟨i-ii⟩, ⟨i⟩-⟨viii⟩, 1-430; 4 pp. advertisements; 2 blank leaves. Wove paper. Sheets bulk 1¼″ scant.

⟨1-28⁸⟩.

Norwood Press imprint not present on copyright page.

Issued without flyleaves.

On copyright page: *Published, March, 1905* Noted as *in press* PW Feb. 18, 1905. Advertised for *March* PW March 4, 1905. Published March 25, 1905; publisher's records. Listed PW April 1, 1905. The London (Laurie) edition listed Ath July 1, 1905.

BPL (2nd)   Y (1st, 2nd)

9893. VISIONARIES . . .

NEW YORK   CHARLES SCRIBNER'S SONS   1905

⟨i⟩-⟨viii⟩, 1-342; 2 pp. advertisements; plus: 2 pp. advertisements. Laid paper. 7⅝″ x 4⅞″.

⟨1-22⁸; plus: 23¹⟩.

V cloth: red. White laid paper end papers. Flyleaves. Top edges gilt.

On copyright page: *Published October, 1905.* Advertised for fall publication PW Sept. 30, 1905. Deposited Oct. 13, 1905. Published Oct. 14, 1905, in a printing of 2100 copies, of which 370 were sent in sheets to Laurie (London); publisher's records. Noted for *to-day* PW Oct. 14,

1905. Listed PW Oct. 28, 1905. The London (Laurie) edition noted as *shortly* Ath Oct. 21, 1905; listed Ath Jan. 13, 1906.

H NYPL

9894. A WORD ON THE DRAMATIC OPIN-IONS AND ESSAYS OF G. BERNARD SHAW ...

NEW YORK BRENTANO'S 1906

Cover-title.

ix-xix. Laid paper. 7⁹⁄₁₆″ x 5³⁄₁₆″.

⟨-⟩⁶.

Printed mottled gray-blue paper wrapper.

Prepared for copyright purposes only. For formal publication see next entry.

Deposited Oct. 19, 1906.

LC

9895. Dramatic Opinions and Essays by G. Bernard Shaw Containing As Well a Word on the Dramatic Opinions and Essays of G. Bernard Shaw by James Huneker ...

New York: Brentano's MCMVI

2 Vols. Cloth, printed paper label on spine.

"A Word on the Dramatic Opinions and Essays of G. Bernard Shaw," Vol. 1, pp. ix-xix. For another printing see preceding entry.

On copyright page: *Published October, 1906* Noted for Oct. 31, 1906, PW Oct. 27, 1906. Deposited Oct. 30, 1906. Noted as *just ready* PW Dec. 1, 1906. Listed PW Dec. 8, 1906. The London (Constable) edition listed Ath Feb 9, 1907; announced ⟨sic⟩ Bkr March, 1907.

LC

9896. The Greater Chopin Edited by James Huneker ...

Boston: Oliver Ditson Company New York: Chas. H. Ditson & Co. Chicago: Lyon & Healy Philadelphia: J. E. Ditson & Co. [Price: Paper, $1.50; Cloth, $2.50] ⟨1908⟩

"The Greater Chopin," pp. ⟨ix⟩-xiv.

Cloth; and, printed paper wrapper, cloth shelf-back.

Deposited Nov. 23, 1908. Noted as *just ... out* PW Jan. 9, 1909.

H

9897. EGOISTS A BOOK OF SUPERMEN ...

NEW YORK CHARLES SCRIBNER'S SONS 1909

⟨i-viii⟩, 1-372; 4 pp. advertisements. Frontispiece and 1 two-page facsimile inserted; facsimile of a Flaubert letter in text. 7½″ x 4⅞″.

⟨1-24⁸⟩.

V cloth: blue-green. Top edges gilt.

On copyright page: *Published March, 1909* Noted for *this month* PW March 13, 1909. Deposited March 26, 1909. Noted as *just ... out* PW March 27, 1909. Published March 27, 1909, in a printing of 3150 copies, of which 250 sets of sheets were exported to London for publication by Laurie; publisher's records. BA copy received March 30, 1909. Listed PW April 3, 1909. The London (Laurie) edition listed Bkr June 4, 1909.

H NYPL

9898. Eight Essays on Joaquín Sorolla y Bastida by Aureliano de Beruete ... James Gibbons Huneker ...

The Hispanic Society of America New York 1909

2 Vols.

"Sorolla y Bastida," Vol. 1, pp. 371-402.

BPL

9899. PROMENADES OF AN IMPRESSION-IST ...

NEW YORK CHARLES SCRIBNER'S SONS 1910

⟨i-x⟩, 1-390; plus: Advertisements, pp. 1-4. 7½″ x 4¹⁵⁄₁₆″.

⟨1-25⁸; plus: 26²⟩.

Printed brown paper boards sides, maroon sateen shelfback. Top edges stained brown. *Note:* Two states of the binding have been noted; the sequence, if any, has not been determined; the designations are for identification only:

A: The publisher's spine imprint is stamped from what appears to be a hand-lettered face. The initial *S* is ⅛″ tall.

B: The publisher's spine imprint is stamped from a relatively conventional face. The initial *S* is ⁵⁄₃₂″ tall.

On copyright page: *Published March, 1910* Published March 26, 1910; publisher's records. BPL copy received March 28, 1910. Listed PW April 2, 1910. The London (Laurie) edition listed Bkr July 8, 1910.

BA (B) Y (A, B)

9900. Selected Piano Compositions ⟨by⟩ Johannes Brahms Edited by Rafael Joseffy with a Preface by James Huneker . . .

Boston: Oliver Ditson Company New York: Chas. H. Ditson & Co. Chicago: Lyon & Healy Philadelphia: J. E. Ditson & Co. [Price: Paper, $1.50; Cloth, $2.50] ⟨1910⟩

Cloth; and, printed paper wrapper, cloth shelf-back.

"The Pianoforte Music of Johannes Brahms," pp. ⟨vii⟩-xv.

Deposited Nov. 5, 1910.

NYPL

9901. Forty Songs by Richard Strauss Edited by James Huneker for High Voice . . .

Boston: Oliver Ditson Company New York: Chas. H. Ditson & Co. Chicago: Lyon & Healy Philadelphia: J. E. Ditson & Co. [Price: Paper, $1.50; Cloth, $2.50] ⟨1910⟩

Cloth; and, printed paper wrapper, cloth shelf-back.

"Richard Strauss," pp. ⟨ix⟩-xiii.

Y

9902. FRANZ LISZT . . .

NEW YORK CHARLES SCRIBNER'S SONS 1911

⟨i-x⟩, 1-458; advertisements, pp. ⟨459-463⟩; blank, p. ⟨464⟩; blank leaf. Frontispiece and 15 plates inserted. 7⁹⁄₁₆″ x 4¹³⁄₁₆″.

⟨1-29⁸, 30⁶⟩.

Maroon sateen. Top edges gilt. "It has been stated that the first binding is silk-like cloth with top edges gilt; second binding, red cloth."—Johnson, p. 274; further information wanting.

On copyright page: *Published September, 1911* Published Oct. 7, 1911; publisher's records. BA copy received Oct. 10, 1911. Listed PW Oct. 14, 1911. The London (Chapman & Hall) edition listed Bkr Jan. 26, 1912.

H

9903. Henrik Ibsen by Edmund Gosse with Essays on Ibsen by Edward Dowden and James Huneker

New York Charles Scribner's Sons 1912

The Works of Henrik Ibsen . . . , Vol. 13.

"Henrik Ibsen," pp. 261-292; reprinted from *Egoists,* 1909.

Deposited March 7, 1912.

BA LC

9904. Forty Songs by Peter Ilyitch Tchaïkovsky Edited by James Huneker . . .

Boston: Oliver Ditson Company New York: Chas. H. Ditson & Co. Chicago: Lyon & Healy [Price: Paper, $1.50; Cloth, $2.50] ⟨1912⟩

Cloth; and, printed paper wrapper, cloth shelf-back.

"Peter Ilyitch Tchaïkovsky," pp. ⟨ix⟩-xiii.

Edition for *High Voice* deposited Dec. 7, 1912. Edition for *Low Voice* deposited March 31, 1913.

Note: The first printing (printings?) has the imprint as above; later printings omit the prices.

H NYPL

9905. THE PATHOS OF DISTANCE A BOOK OF A THOUSAND AND ONE MOMENTS . . .

NEW YORK CHARLES SCRIBNER'S SONS 1913

⟨i-ii⟩, ⟨i⟩-viii, ⟨1⟩-394; 6 pp. advertisements; blank leaf. 7⁷⁄₁₆″ x 4⁷⁄₈″.

⟨1-25⁸, 26⁶⟩.

Two printings noted:

1

As above.

The date *1913* in the imprint set from a face in which the *9* and the *3* extend below the line. A surviving copyright deposit copy (rebound) thus.

On the spine the space from the bottom of the box and the top of the initial *S* in *Scribners* is 5⁷⁄₁₆″.

2

⟨i-ii⟩, ⟨i⟩-viii, ⟨1⟩-394, 4 pp. advertisements.

⟨1-25⁸, 26⁴⟩.

The date *1913* in the imprint set from a face in which all the numerals are the same height.

On the spine the space from the bottom of the box and the top of the *S* in *Scribners* is 5⁵⁄₁₆″.

V cloth: blue-green; green. Top edges gilt.

On copyright page: *Published May, 1913* Published May 10, 1913; publisher's records. BPL copy (1st) received May 10, 1913; BA copy (1st) May 13, 1913. Listed PW May 17, 1913. The London (Laurie) edition described as *nearly ready* Bkr June 13, 1913; listed Bkr June 27, 1913.

H (1st) NYPL (2nd) Y (1st, 2nd)

9906. OLD FOGY HIS MUSICAL OPINIONS AND GROTESQUES WITH AN INTRODUCTION AND EDITED BY JAMES HUNEKER

THEODORE PRESSER CO. 1712 CHESTNUT STREET PHILADELPHIA LONDON, WEEKES & CO. ⟨1913⟩

⟨1⟩-195. $6^{15}/_{16}$" x $4^5/_8$". Wove paper watermarked *Regal Antique.*

⟨1-12⁸, 13²⟩.

Printed pale buff boards, T grained. White paper end papers imprinted in orange with a floral decoration. Also occurs with plain white end papers; precise status not determined but possibly a secondary binding.

Deposited May 20, 1913.

Note: The wording of the title-page notwithstanding, the author was Huneker.

AAS H

9907. Joseph Conrad ...

D P & Co ⟨Garden City, N. Y.: Doubleday, Page & Co., n.d., 1914?⟩

Printed paper wrapper. Cover-title.

"Joseph Conrad: A Pen Portrait," p. ⟨1⟩. Also appears in *The Country Life Press Garden City, New York,* Published for the Friends of Doubleday, Page & Company, MCMXIX, pp. 99-100.

H NYPL

9908. NEW COSMOPOLIS A BOOK OF IMAGES ...

NEW YORK CHARLES SCRIBNER'S SONS 1915

⟨i-ii⟩, ⟨i⟩-⟨x⟩, ⟨1⟩-344, 4 pp. advertisements. $7^7/_{16}$" x $4^7/_8$".

⟨1-22⁸, 23⁴⟩.

V cloth: blue-green. Top edges gilt.

On copyright page: *Published March, 1915* Published March 13, 1915; publisher's records. Listed PW March 13, 1915. BPL copy received March 15, 1915. Deposited March 17, 1915. The London (Laurie) edition listed Ath Aug. 21, 1915.

H LC

9909. ... Frédéric Chopin Complete Works for the Pianoforte ... Revised and Fingered by Rafael Joseffy ⟨and, Arthur Friedheim⟩ ...

1915-1918

Caution: The present entry is for the record only and does not pretend to be definitive. See BAL, Vol. 1, pp. xxi-xxii.

16 parts. Noted in printed paper wrapper; cloth; half morocco.

1: ... Book One Waltzes ... with a Biographical Sketch and Prefatory Note by James Huneker

New York: G. Schirmer London: G. Schirmer, Ltd. Boston: The Boston Music Co. Copyright, 1915 ...

"Frédéric-François Chopin," pp. iii-x. Plate number 25502.

Deposited July 19, 1915. *Note:* Also occurs with New York and Boston imprints only.

H NYPL

2: ... Book Two Mazurkas ... with a Prefatory Note by James Huneker

New York: G. Schirmer London: G. Schirmer, Ltd. Boston: The Boston Music Co. Copyright, 1915 ...

"The Mazurkas," pp. iii-vii. Plate number 25503.

Deposited Dec. 27, 1915.

H NYPL

3: *Not located.*

4: ... Book Four Nocturnes ... with a Prefatory Note by James Huneker

New York: G. Schirmer London: G. Schirmer, Ltd. Boston: The Boston Music Co. Copyright, 1915 ...

"The Nocturnes," pp. iii-v. Plate number 25438.

Deposited Aug. 6, 1915.

H NYPL

5: ... Book Five Ballades ... with a Prefatory Note by James Huneker

New York: G. Schirmer London: G. Schirmer, Ltd. Boston: The Boston Music Co. Copyright, 1916 ...

"The Ballades," pp. iii-v. Plate number 25646.

Deposited Feb. 21, 1916.

H NYPL

6: ... Book Six Impromptus ... with a Prefatory Note by James Huneker

New York: G. Schirmer London: G. Schirmer, Ltd. Boston: The Boston Music Co. Copyright, 1915 ...

"The Impromptus," pp. iii-iv. Plate number 25405.

Deposited Aug. 21, 1915.

H NYPL

7: ... Book Seven   Scherzi and Fantasy ... with a Prefatory Note by James Huneker

New York: G. Schirmer   London: G. Schirmer, Ltd.   Boston: The Boston Music Co. Copyright, 1915 ...

"Four Scherzi and Fantasy," pp. iii-v. Plate number 25489.

Deposited Nov. 18, 1915.

H NYPL

8: ... Book Eight   Études ... with a General Prefatory Note by James Huneker ...

New York: G. Schirmer   Boston: The Boston Music Co. Copyright, 1916 ...

"The Etudes," pp. iii-vii. Plate number 25647.

Deposited July 27, 1916.

H NYPL

9: ... Book Nine   Preludes ... with a Prefatory Note by James Huneker

New York: G. Schirmer   London: G. Schirmer, Ltd.   Boston: The Boston Music Co. Copyright, 1915 ...

"The Preludes," pp. iii-vi. Plate number 25454.

Deposited Aug. 13, 1915.

H NYPL

10: ... Book Ten   Rondos ... with a Prefatory Note by James Huneker

New York: G. Schirmer   London: G. Schirmer, Ltd.   Boston: The Boston Music Co. Copyright, 1916 ...

"Three Rondos," p. iii. Plate number 25455.

Deposited Feb. 3, 1916. *Note:* Original copyright date ‹1915?› altered to 1916.

H NYPL

11: *Not located.*

12: ... Book Twelve   Various Compositions ... with a Prefatory Note by James Huneker

New York: G. Schirmer   Boston: The Boston Music Co. Copyright, 1916 ...

"Various Compositions," pp. iii-iv. Plate number 25649.

Deposited Aug. 22, 1916.

NYPL

13: *Not located.*

14: ... Book Fourteen   Concerto in E Minor ... with an Introductory Note by James Huneker

New York: G. Schirmer   Boston: The Boston Music Co. Copyright, 1918 ...

"Piano Concerto in E Minor," pp. iii-iv. Plate number 25650.

Deposited Oct. 29, 1918.

Note: Also occurs with varying title-page, a principal difference being the imprint which is *G. Schirmer (Inc.), New York Copyright, 1918* ... Copy in H.

NYPL

15: ... Book Fifteen   Concerto in F Minor ... with an Introductory Note by James Huneker

G. Schirmer, Inc., New York ... 1918 ...

"Piano Concerto in F Minor," p. ‹1›. Plate number 25651.

Deposited June 27, 1918.

H

16: ... Concert Pieces ...

New York: G. Schirmer   Boston: The Boston Music Co. Copyright, 1918 ...

"Four Concert Pieces," pp. iii-iv. Plate number 25578.

Deposited March 4, 1918.

NYPL

9910. IVORY   APES   AND   PEACOCKS ...

NEW YORK   CHARLES SCRIBNER'S SONS   1915

‹i-ii›, ‹i›-‹x›, 1-328; 4 pp. advertisements. Frontispiece inserted. 7$\frac{7}{16}$" x 4$\frac{7}{8}$".

‹1-21^8, 22^4›.

V cloth: blue-green. Top edges gilt.

On copyright page: *Published September, 1915* Published Sept. 25, 1915, in a printing of 2525 copies, of which 250 sets of sheets were sent to London for publication by Laurie; publisher's records. Deposited Sept. 30, 1915. Listed PW Oct. 2, 1915. BA copy received Oct. 5, 1915. The London (Laurie) edition listed Ath Dec. 4, 1915.

H

9911. THE DEVELOPMENT OF PIANO MUSIC FROM THE DAYS OF THE CLAVICHORD AND HARPSICHORD TO THE PRESENT TIME REPRESENTED IN SIX PROGRAMS BY OSSIP GABRILÓWITSCH ‹with› HISTORICAL AND BIOGRAPHICAL NOTES BY JAMES HUNEKER

NEW YORK   BOSTON   CHICAGO   1915–1916

⟨1⟩-⟨16⟩. 8¼″ x 5½″.

⟨-⟩⁸.

Printed blue-gray paper wrapper.

Note: Apparently prepared for distribution at the several Gabrilowitsch recitals in various cities; and, reprinted as required. No sequence has been established for the following printings noted; the designations are completely arbitrary and are for identification only.

A: Imprint of Reliance Printing Co., p. ⟨16⟩. Lyre decoration on title-page.

B: No imprint on p. ⟨16⟩. Lyre decoration on title-page.

C: Imprint of Reliance Printing Co., p. ⟨16⟩. Pan and pipes vignette on title-page.

LC (B)   NYPL (A)   Y (C)

9912. UNICORNS ...

NEW YORK   CHARLES SCRIBNER'S SONS   1917

⟨i-ii⟩, ⟨i⟩-⟨x⟩, 1-361; blank, p. ⟨362⟩; 4 pp. advertisements; blank leaf. 7½″ x 4⅞″.

⟨1-23⁸, 24⁶⟩.

V cloth: blue-green. Top edges gilt.

On copyright page: *Published September, 1917* Published Sept. 22, 1917, in a printing of 2000 copies; publisher's records. Deposited Sept. 25, 1917. BA copy received Sept. 25, 1917. Listed PW Sept. 29, 1917. The London (Laurie) edition listed Bkr Nov. 1918.

H

9913. For France ...

Garden City   New York   Doubleday, Page & Company   MCMXVII

"A French Poe," pp. 401-407.

For comment see entry No. 485.

9914. Rodin the Man and His Art with Leaves from His Note-Book Compiled by Judith Cladel and Translated by S. K. Star with Introduction by James Huneker ...

New York   The Century Co.   1917

Boards, cloth shelfback.

"August Rodin," pp. vii-xxii.

On copyright page: *Published, October, 1917* Deposited Oct. 30, 1917. The London (Batsford) edition listed Bkr Aug. 1918.

NYPL

9915. THE PHILHARMONIC SOCIETY OF NEW YORK AND ITS SEVENTY-FIFTH ANNIVERSARY A RETROSPECT ...

⟨n.p., n.d., New York, 1917? 1918?⟩

⟨i-iv⟩, ⟨1⟩-130, blank leaf. Frontispiece and 6 plates inserted. 7½″ x 5⅛″.

⟨1², 2-9⁸, 10²⟩.

Note: Examination of a number of copies of this book indicates that the body, pp. ⟨1⟩-128, was printed on unwatermarked wove paper; that the first and the final gatherings (⟨1⟩ and ⟨10⟩) were printed on wove paper watermarked *Flemish Book.* Since ⟨1⟩ and ⟨10⟩ are cut sheets not all examples display the watermark.

T cloth: blue. Top edges gilt. Inserted in some copies is a printed presentation slip: *Compliments of the Philharmonic Society of New York Carnegie Hall, N. Y.*

Listed PW Nov. 16, 1918.

AAS   H   NYPL   Y

9916. ... Romantic Preludes and Studies for Piano ... Collected and Arranged by James Huneker   Revised and Fingered by Arthur Friedheim, James Huneker, and Others

G. Schirmer, Inc., New York ... 1919 ...

At head of title: Schirmer's Library of Musical Classics Vol. 1257

Printed paper wrapper. Plate number 27818.

"Introduction," pp. ⟨iii-v⟩.

Deposited March 9, 1919.

NYPL

9917. THE STEINWAY COLLECTION OF PAINTINGS BY AMERICAN ARTISTS TOGETHER WITH PROSE PORTRAITS OF THE GREAT COMPOSERS ...

PUBLISHED BY STEINWAY & SONS   MCMXIX

⟨1-56⟩. Laid paper watermarked *Arches.* 12⅞″ x 9¹¹⁄₁₆″. A color-plate tipped to each of the following pages: ⟨10, 14, 18, 22, 26, 30, 34, 38, 42, 46, 50, 54⟩.

⟨1-7⁴⟩.

Brown Japan paper boards sides, white imitation vellum shelfback. White end papers of book stock.

"... limited to Five Thousand copies of which this is No. ...."—Certificate of issue tipped to p. ⟨1⟩.

Deposited June 12, 1919. Listed PW Dec. 20, 1919.

AAS   H

9918. The Poems and Prose Poems of Charles Baudelaire ⟨Translated by F. P. Sturm⟩ with an Introductory Preface by James Huneker

New York Brentano's 1919

Boards, printed paper labels.

"Charles Baudelaire," pp. ix-lvii. A slightly revised version of "The Baudelaire Legend," in *Egoists,* 1909.

Deposited June 13, 1919. Listed PW July 14, 1919.

AAS Y

9919. BEDOUINS ...

NEW YORK CHARLES SCRIBNER'S SONS 1920

⟨i-ii⟩, ⟨i⟩-⟨x⟩, ⟨1⟩-271; blank, p. ⟨272⟩; 4 pp. advertisements. Frontispiece and 5 plates inserted. 7½" x 4⅞".

⟨1-18⁸⟩.

V cloth: blue-green.

On copyright page: *Published February, 1920* Published Feb. 27, 1920; publisher's records. Listed PW March 6, 1920. The London (Laurie) edition listed Ath July 16, 1920.

H NYPL

9920. STEEPLEJACK ...

NEW YORK CHARLES SCRIBNER'S SONS 1920

2 Vols.

1: ⟨i-ii⟩, ⟨i⟩-⟨x⟩, ⟨1⟩-320. Laid paper. Frontispiece and 10 plates inserted. 8⅛" x 6".
2: ⟨i⟩-⟨viii⟩, ⟨1⟩-327. Frontispiece and 13 plates inserted.

1: ⟨1⁶, 2-21⁸⟩.
2: ⟨1-21⁸⟩.

V cloth: blue.

On copyright page: *Published September, 1920* Published Sept. 10, 1920, in a printing of 2000 copies, of which 190 in sheets and 50 copies in binding, were shipped to Laurie (London); publisher's records. Listed PW Sept. 11, 1920. Deposited Sept. 14, 1920. BPL copy received Sept. 14, 1920. The London (Laurie) edition listed Ath Jan. 14, 1921.

H

9921. PAINTED VEILS ...

BONI AND LIVERIGHT PUBLISHERS NEW YORK ⟨1920⟩

⟨i-xiv⟩, ⟨11⟩-⟨298⟩, blank leaf. 9⁹⁄₁₆" x 6³⁄₁₆". Printed on laid paper watermarked *Blandford Book U.S.A.*

⟨1-19⁸⟩.

Blue paper boards sides, linen-weave finish, imitation white vellum shelfback. Goldstamped black leather label on spine. Blue paper, linen-weave finish, end papers.

1200 numbered copies signed by the author.

Note: A type facsimile forgery exists; printed on unwatermarked laid paper. The blue paper used for end papers and sides is not finished with the linen weave embossing. Definite information is wanting but the forgery is believed to have been done by a New York bookseller almost immediately after publication of the genuine.

Listed PW Jan. 8, 1921. Deposited June 14, 1921.

H LC Y (both genuine and forgery)

9922. VARIATIONS ...

NEW YORK CHARLES SCRIBNER'S SONS 1921

⟨i⟩-viii, 1-279. 7½" x 5".

⟨1-18⁸⟩.

V cloth: greenish-black.

On copyright page: *Published November, 1921* Published Nov. 18, 1921, in a printing of 3000 copies; publisher's records. NYPL copy received Nov. 25, 1921. Deposited Nov. 28, 1921. BA copy received Nov. 29, 1921. Listed PW Dec. 3, 1921. The London (Laurie) edition listed NA May 13, 1922; Bkr June, 1922.

BA NYPL Y

9923. LETTERS OF JAMES GIBBONS HUNEKER COLLECTED AND EDITED BY JOSEPHINE HUNEKER

NEW YORK CHARLES SCRIBNER'S SONS 1922

Trade Edition

⟨i⟩-xvi, ⟨1⟩-324; plus: 4 pp. advertisements. Portrait frontispiece inserted. 8¹³⁄₁₆" x 6¹⁄₁₆".

⟨1-17⁸, 18¹⁰, 19-21⁸; plus: 22²⟩.

T cloth: green.

Limited Edition

Title-page in black and green.

⟨i-iv⟩, ⟨i⟩-⟨xviii⟩, ⟨1⟩-324; blank leaf. 9¹⁄₁₆" x 6". Laid paper watermarked *Alexandra.* Note: The certificate of issue (see below) printed on *Alexandra Brilliant.* Frontispiece and 4 plates inserted; 1 folded facsimile inserted.

⟨1², 2-22⁸, 23⁴⟩.

The certificate of issue is printed on ⟨1⟩₂ᵥ.

Limited to 260 numbered copies signed by the editor.

Tan laid paper boards sides, maroon buckram shelfback, printed paper label on spine. White laid paper end papers. Extra label tipped in at back.

On copyright page: *Published October, 1922* Published Oct. 6, 1922; publisher's records. Deposited (trade) Oct. 9, 1922. Trade copies received by BPL Oct. 11, 1922; BA and H Oct. 17, 1922. Listed (trade) PW Oct. 21, 1922. The London (Laurie) edition listed NA March 10, 1923; Bkr April, 1923.

H (trade)   Y (limited)

9924. INTIMATE LETTERS OF JAMES GIBBONS HUNEKER COLLECTED AND EDITED BY JOSEPHINE HUNEKER

ISSUED FOR SUBSCRIBERS ONLY BY BONI AND LIVERIGHT ‹NEW YORK› 1924

‹1›-322, blank leaf. Laid paper watermarked with publisher's device. Frontispiece and 6 plates inserted. 8⅞″ x 5⅞″.

‹1-19⁸, 20¹⁰›. *Note:* In all examined copies, including the copyright deposit copies, leaf ‹20›9 is a cancel.

Laid brown paper boards sides, red-brown buckram shelfback. Printed paper label on spine.

Limited to 2050 numbered copies.

Listed PW Nov. 29, 1924. Deposited Jan. 20, 1925.

H NYPL

9925. A LETTER FROM JAMES GIBBONS HUNEKER TO JOSEPH CONRAD

‹London: The First Edition Club, 1926›

Cover-title. The above printed in black, red, gray-green.

‹1-7›. 7⅞″ scant x 5⅝″. Laid paper watermarked *Etruria Italy.*

‹-›⁴.

Printed self-wrapper.

220 copies only.

Issued as one of a group of eleven pamphlets under the general title *Twenty Letters to Joseph Conrad,* London, 1926.

H LC Y

9926. Essays ... Selected with an Introduction by H. L. Mencken

New York   Charles Scribner's Sons   1929

Reprint.

Listed PW Oct. 26, 1929. BA copy received Oct. 28, 1929. Deposited Oct. 29, 1929. The London (Laurie) edition listed PC Aug. 30, 1930; noted as *shortly* PC Sept. 6, 1930.

BA   H   LC   Y

9927. AN EARLY ESTIMATE OF SADA-KICHI HARTMANN BY JAMES G. HUNE-KER (MUSICAL AMERICA, 1897) ...

‹n.p., n.d., possibly Guido Bruno, New York, ca. 1930›

Caption-title. The above at head of the first of two single leaves, printed on recto only, 8⁹⁄₁₆″ x 5⁹⁄₁₆″.

This curious publication may be some sort of a hoax. *Musical America,* from which the text allegedly was taken, was not established until 1898. The text has not been located elsewhere. Perhaps reprinted from *The Musical Courier?*

Copy received by NYPL Feb. 19, 1936.

NYPL

9928. Concert Life in New York 1902–1923 by Richard Aldrich

G. P. Putnam's Sons   New York   ‹1941›

Reviews by Huneker pp. 567-597.

"During the season of 1918–1919 Richard Aldrich served in the United States Army. His position ‹as reviewer on *The New York Times*› was occupied by James Gibbons Huneker."—P. 567.

Deposited Dec. 8, 1941.

LC   Y

REPRINTS, REFERENCES AND ANA

Nassau: Island of New Providence, Bahamas.

New York ‹1877?›

Contains "An Isle of June," by Huneker. *Not seen.* Further information wanting. Entry from Johnson. Possibly a ghost.

The Print-Collector's Bulletin   An Illustrated Catalogue of Painter-Etchings for Sale by Frederick Keppel & Co. 4 East 39th Street, New York

‹New York: Frederick Keppel & Co., Oct. 20, 1908›

Printed paper wrapper. Cover-title.

"Henry Wolf," p. 25. First published in the *New York Sun,* Dec. 1, 1907.

Writing of Today: Models of Journalistic Prose Selected and Discussed by J. W. Cunliffe . . . and Gerhard R. Lomer . . .

New York   The Century Co.   1915

Reprint. On copyright page *Published, August, 1915*

Loan Exhibition of Paintings, Watercolors, Drawings Etchings & Sculpture by Arthur B. Davies

Macbeth Galleries   450 Fifth Avenue, New York   1918

Boards, cloth shelfback, printed paper label on spine.

"In Praise of Unicorns," pp. ⟨5⟩-9, reprinted from *Unicorns,* 1917.

James Gibbons Huneker by Benjamin DeCasseres

New York   Joseph Lawren Publisher ⟨1925⟩

Boards, printed paper label on front. Bibliography, pp. ⟨41⟩-62. Deposited Aug. 19, 1926.

The American Theatre as Seen by its Critics 1752–1934 Edited by Montrose J. Moses and John Mason Brown

W. W. Norton & Company, Inc. New York ⟨1934⟩

Reprint. On copyright page: *First Edition*

JOSEPH HOLT INGRAHAM

1809-1860

NOTE

Most of Ingraham's novels were flimsy productions. BAL has been unable to locate all of them in original state and consequently certain of the entries, *none specified herein,* are based on examination of two, occasionally more, incomplete copies. The presence of a location in this list, unlike all other BAL locations, does not necessarily indicate that the institutions or individuals cited do in fact have complete copies of the books described.

Ingraham produced so rapidly and so prolifically that it is extremely doubtful a correct chronology can be established. Some indication of the problem is suggested by the following extracts:

"For a period after the publication of these ⟨earlier⟩ books Ingraham wrote so rapidly that it is no longer possible to trace all of his works."—DAB

"In the afternoon, Ingraham the novelist called. A young, dark man, with soft voice. He says he has written eighty novels, and of these twenty during the last year; till it has grown to be merely mechanical with him. These novels are published in the newspapers. They pay him something more than three thousand dollars a year."—H. W. Longfellow's journal, entry for March 6, 1846, as given in *Life of Henry Wadsworth Longfellow* ... , by Samuel Longfellow, Boston & New York, 1891, Vol. 2, p. 35.

In this list BAL has relied heavily on the deposit dates of the title-pages in the establishment of chronology; but the statement "title-page deposited for copyright" must not be taken too literally. Frequently the "title-pages" were not formal title-pages at all but merely caption-titles clipped from periodicals. Such token "title-pages" were acceptable under the then existing copyright requirements. Hence, the deposit date of a "title-page" may be misleading and have small relation to the true date of publication. Many "title-page" deposits, a preliminary step in securing copyright, were not followed by publication.

Further uncertainty is introduced by the following comment extracted from Ingraham's "Advertisement" in *The Prince of the House of David,* 1859: "... several cheap works, written by persons unknown ... also translations from French authors, have been unblushingly published as ⟨mine⟩ ... by unprincipled men, while many of ⟨my⟩ ... books have been injuriously altered in both text and title." If Ingraham ever compiled a list of such falsely attributed, or mis-titled works, it is unknown to BAL. BAL conjectures that a case in point is *Fanny; or, the Hunchback and the Roué* which was issued under the cover-title *Fanny H———; or, the Hunchback and the Roué,* which titillating alteration we assume was perpetrated to suggest that the purchaser was buying a copy of John Cleland's notorious novel.

Many of the posthumous publications are revisions (by Ingraham's son, Col. Prentiss Ingraham) of the earlier novels issued under radically altered titles. Commenting on one of these Johannsen, Vol. 2, p. 153, quite correctly says: "The foundation is the same, but there has been so much revision that parts are almost unrecognizable. Even the names of most of the characters have been changed."

Those posthumous revisions which BAL has been able to recognize are identified. There remain, however, a few (also listed) which BAL has been unable to identify with any of the earlier separately published novels. Some, perhaps, are first separate printings of texts taken from periodicals but the cautious user of this list will view with suspicion all of the posthumous publications.

BAL is by no means certain it has located, and described, or noted, all of Ingraham's separate productions. A list of unlocated titles is given at the end of the list.

9929. THE SOUTH-WEST. BY A YANKEE
. . .

NEW-YORK: HARPER & BROTHERS, CLIFF-ST. 1835.

2 Vols.

1: ⟨i⟩-⟨xii⟩, ⟨13⟩-264, 263-276, blank leaf. 7⅜" x 4½".
2: ⟨v⟩-⟨xii⟩, ⟨9⟩-294, blank leaf.

1: ⟨A⟩-I, K-U, X-Z⁶, Aa².
2: ⟨A⟩⁴, B-I, K-U, X-Z, Aa-Bb⁶.

Coarse-grained CM cloth: tan. P cloth: purple; tan. S cloth (moiréd): tan. Printed paper label on spine. Flyleaves.

Reviewed by κ Dec. 1835. Listed AMM Jan. 1836. Deposited Feb. 6, 1836.

NYHS NYSL UV Y

9930. LAFITTE: THE PIRATE OF THE GULF. BY THE AUTHOR OF "THE SOUTH WEST." . . .

NEW-YORK: PUBLISHED BY HARPER & BROTHERS, NO. 82 CLIFF-STREET. MDCCCXXXVI.

2 Vols. See next entry for revised edition.

1: ⟨1⟩-213, blank leaf. P. 203 mispaged 303. 7⅜″ x 4⁷⁄₁₆″.
2: ⟨1⟩-216.

1: ⟨1⟩-18⁶.
2: ⟨1⟩-18⁶.

AR cloth: black; blue. T-like cloth, brown, embossed with ferns. T-like cloth, green, purple, embossed with florets. Flyleaves.

Six-line errata notice, Vol. 2, p. 212.

Note: Folio *75,* Vol. 2, in all examined copies lacks the numeral 5.

Also note: The running head, Vol. 2, p. 101, occurs in two states of undetermined sequence:

A: L AFITTE

B: LAFITTE

κ Dec. 1841, p. 567, quotes from one who asserts that the novel was "mainly written by another person, a . . . graduate of Cambridge University, from whom ⟨Ingraham⟩ . . . borrowed it in *ms.*" When the *ms* was returned, the alleged author found that "nearly the whole ⟨of *Lafitte*⟩ was taken bodily from the *ms.*" κ "opens" its columns to a reply from Ingraham; no such reply noted but κ ("Editor's Table") Jan.-Feb., 1842, reports that the charge was denied by Ingraham.

Copy in Y inscribed by early owner July 19, 1836. ". . . in press . . . will be published before the close of the month, simultaneously in London and New York."—κ July, 1836. "It is . . . to be dramatized by Miss Medina"—κ July, 1836. Deposited Aug. 11, 1836. Reviewed κ Aug. 1836.

London Publication

Under the title *The Pirate of the Gulf; or, Lafitte,* issued in London by A. K. Newman. Advertised in LG April 8, 1837. Advertised by Newman as *this day published* Ath April 15, 1837. Listed and reviewed LG April 22, 1837. De-

scribed as *just published* BMLA June, 1837. Reviewed Ath Aug. 5, 1837, where it is described as "a reprint of an American Novel." Received by BMu Nov. 30, 1837. BAL has found no evidence to support the possibility of simultaneous publication in New York and London.

An undated reprint was issued *ca.* 1850, by De-Witt & Davenport, New York.

H NYPL UV Y

9931. Lafitte: The Pirate of the Gulf. By the Author of "The South West." . . . Second Edition . . .

New York: Published by Harper & Brothers, No. 82 Cliff Street. 1836.

2 Vols. Cloth, printed paper label on spine.

"Preface to the Second Edition," Vol. 1, p. ⟨9⟩; dated at end *September, 1836.* For first edition see preceding entry.

". . . carefully revised . . ."—P. ⟨9⟩.

AAS UP Y

9932. The Portland Sketch Book. Edited by Mrs. Ann S. Stephens.

Portland: Colman & Chisholm. Arthur Shirley, Printer. 1836.

"The Village Prize," pp. ⟨126⟩-134.

BA

9933. The Token and Atlantic Souvenir A Christmas and New Year's Present Edited by S. G. Goodrich.

Boston. Published by Charles Bowen. MDCCCXXXVII.

"The Prophecy of Uiquera," pp. ⟨315⟩-331.

For comment see entry No. 7580.

9934. BURTON; OR, THE SIEGES. A ROMANCE. BY THE AUTHOR OF "THE SOUTHWEST" AND "LAFITTE." . . .

NEW-YORK: HARPER & BROTHERS, 82 CLIFF-STREET. 1838.

2 Vols.

Two printings noted. The following sequence is presumed correct:

A

1: ⟨i⟩-⟨xii⟩, ⟨13⟩-261, blank leaf. Pp. ⟨ii-iii⟩ paged 2, 21. 7⁷⁄₁₆″ x 4⁷⁄₁₆″.
2: ⟨1⟩-277; blank, p. ⟨278⟩; advertisements, pp. ⟨1⟩-8, 19-24.
1: ⟨A⟩-I, K-U, X-Y⁶.
2: ⟨A⟩-I, K-U, X-Z⁶, ⟨-⟩⁸.

B

1: ⟨v⟩-⟨xii⟩, ⟨13⟩-261, blank leaf.
2: ⟨1⟩-277; blank, p. ⟨278⟩; *Valuable Works* . . . , pp. ⟨1⟩-2; plus: pp. 3-8, 19-24.

1: ⟨A⟩⁴, B-I, K-U, X-Y⁶. 4 pp. advertisements, dated *May, 1838,* inserted at front.
2: ⟨A⟩-I, K-U, X-Z⁶, ⟨-⟩²; plus: ⟨*⟩⁶.

Purple muslin. Rose T-like cloth with a pattern (in white) of coral-like branches. Green vaguely T-like muslin embossed with a floral pattern. Green P-like cloth embossed with a pattern of coral-like branches. Green linen. Tan paper boards sides, purple A cloth shelfback. Flyleaves. A copy of Vol. 1 has been noted with a flyleaf at front, two flyleaves at back. Printed paper label on spine.

Title-page deposited June 11, 1838; copies of the book not deposited until Sept. 6, 1839⟨*sic*⟩. BA copy (Printing A) received June 26, 1838. UV copy (Printing A) inscribed by early owner July 2, 1838. Reviewed K July, 1838: "The first edition was gone in a week, and a second large one hurried to press before the author had an opportunity to correct a few errors." Y copy (Printing B) inscribed by Ingraham Sept. 14, 1838. Distributed in London by Wiley & Putnam; see note below. Published in London under the title *Quebec and New York;* see entry No. 9942.

London Publication

Distributed in London by Wiley & Putnam. The writer of a letter from New York, LG July 14, 1838, commenting on the book, states that he "understands" that Murray, London, will issue it. No Murray edition found in the 1838 records. Reviewed LG Aug. 18–Oct. 6, 1838. Advertised as *this day published* Ath Aug. 18, 1838. Listed Ath Sept. 1, 1838; LG Sept. 1, 1838; PC Sept. 1, 1838; BMLA Sept. 1838. See entry No. 9942.

AAS (A)   H (B)   NYPL (A,B)   UV (A)   Y (B)

9935. The Gift: A Christmas and New Year's Present for 1839. Edited by Miss Leslie.

Philadelphia: E. L. Carey & A. Hart. ⟨1838⟩

"Mrs. Nicholas Muggs; or, the Hoax," pp. 110-144.

For comment see entry No. 991.

9936. The Token and Atlantic Souvenir, a Christmas and New Year's Present. Edited by S. G. Goodrich.

Boston: Otis, Broaders, and Company. M DCCC XXXIX.

"The Sacred Fire," pp. ⟨242⟩-280.

Title-page deposited Aug. 10, 1838. Reviewed by K Sept. 1838.

CH

9937. CAPTAIN KYD; OR, THE WIZARD OF THE SEA. A ROMANCE. BY THE AUTHOR OF "THE SOUTHWEST," . . .

NEW-YORK: HARPER & BROTHERS, 82 CLIFF-STREET. 1839.

2 Vols.

1: ⟨1⟩-237, blank leaf. 7⁵⁄₁₆″ x 4½″.
2: ⟨1⟩-229; blank, p. ⟨230⟩; advertisements, pp. ⟨1⟩-10.

1: ⟨A⟩-I, K-U⁶.
2: ⟨A⟩-I K-T, ⟨U⟩⁶.

Issued in a variety of cloths. The following have been noted; the designations are for identification only and the order of presentation is wholly arbitrary. *Note:* A copy has been seen in paper boards, printed paper label; BAL is convinced that the binding is not original but of recent fabrication.

A: H cloth: blue.

B: Muslin: black.

C: Muslin: black. Embossed with a leafy pattern.

D: Muslin: blue, brown. Embossed with an S-like grain underlay on which an embossed floral pattern.

E: P cloth: rose.

F: P-like cloth: purple. Embossed with a curve maze pattern.

G: Polished muslin: purple. Embossed with a branch pattern.

H: S-like cloth: purple. Embossed with a grill pattern.

I: T-like cloth: blue, rose. Embossed with a floral pattern.

J: T-like cloth: blue. Embossed with a leafy pattern.

Printed paper label on spine. Inserted at front of Vol. 1 is a four-page publisher's catalog dated Jan. 1839.

Noted by K March, 1839: ". . . its sale . . . equals the anticipation of the publishers." Under the title *Captain Kyd; or, the Pirate of Hell Gate,* a version was issued in 1877, by Norman L. Munro, N. Y., as Vol. 3, No. 62, of the *New York Boys' Library;* deposited Dec. 26, 1877. Under the title *Captain Kyd, the King of the Black Flag; or, the Witch of Death Castle,* a version was issued in 1880 as No. 109 in *Beadle's Dime Library.*

London Publication

Distributed in London by Wiley & Putnam. Advertised as *just ready* Ath March 23, 1839. Advertised as *just published* PC April 1, 1839. Listed PC April 1, 1839; Ath April 13, 1839.

Under the title *Kyd the Buccanier, or the Wizard of the Sea* (title based on contemporary notices) advertised by A. K. Newman as *this day* BMLA June 10, 1839. Listed LG and Ath July 20, 1839.

Issued by T. L. Holt as Nos. 33-35 in *The Novel Newspaper,* under the title *Captain Kyd; or, the Wizard of the Sea. A Romance.* Date of publication not known but almost certainly not first publication in London.

B   H   NYPL   UV   Y

9938. Kyd the Buccanier, or the Wizard of the Sea.

London: A. K. Newman, 1839.

Not seen. 3 Vols. Reprint.

See publication notes under entry No. 9937.

9939. THE AMERICAN LOUNGER; OR, TALES, SKETCHES, AND LEGENDS GATHERED IN SUNDRY JOURNEYINGS. BY THE AUTHOR OF "LAFITTE," &c.

PHILADELPHIA: LEA & BLANCHARD, SUCCESSORS TO CAREY & CO. 1839.

⟨i-x⟩, ⟨15⟩-273. 7⅜″ x 4⅜″.

⟨-⟩², ⟨1⟩², 2-22⁶, 23⁴, ⟨24⟩¹.

Purple muslin embossed with a floral pattern. Printed paper label on spine. Flyleaves.

Deposited June 25, 1839. What appears to be this book listed under sub-title, NYR Jan. 1840.

H   NYHS   NYPL

9940. Captain Kyd; or, the Wizard of the Sea. A Romance. By the Author of "The Southwest," ...

London: Published by T. L. Holt, 266, Strand. 1839.

The Novel Newspaper series.

Probably issued in printed paper wrapper. See publication notes under entry No. 9937.

UP   Y

9941. The Pirate: Or, Lafitte of the Gulf of Mexico. By the Author of "Captain Kyd." ...

London: Printed and Published by T. L. Holt, 266, Strand. 1839.

Reprint of *Lafitte* ... , 1836. *The Novel Newspaper* series.

Printed paper wrapper?

Y

9942. Quebec and New York; or, the Three Beauties. An Historical Romance of 1775. By the Author of the Pirate of the Gulf, &c ...

London: A. K. Newman and Co. 1839.

3 Vols. Reprint of *Burton* ... , 1838.

Boards, cloth shelfback, printed paper label on spine.

Advertised and listed PC Oct. 1, 1838. Advertised BMLA Nov. 10, 1838. Listed LG Nov. 17, 1838. Received by BMU Nov. 29, 1838.

NYPL

9943. THE QUADROONE: OR, ST. MICHAEL'S DAY. BY THE AUTHOR OF "THE PIRATE OF THE GULF," ...

LONDON: RICHARD BENTLEY, NEW BURLINGTON STREET, 1840.

3 Vols. *Note:* Each title-page varies slightly from the others in punctuation. For first American edition see under 1841.

1: ⟨i-viii⟩, ⟨1⟩-282. 7⁷⁄₁₆″ x 4⁹⁄₁₆″.
2: ⟨i-iv⟩, ⟨1⟩-294.
3: ⟨i-iv⟩, ⟨1⟩-288.

1: ⟨A⟩⁴, B-I, K-M¹², N⁹. So signed.
2: ⟨A⟩², B-I, K-N¹², O³. So signed.
3: ⟨A⟩², B-I, K-N¹². So signed.

Warning: Pagination and signature collation tentative.

Probably issued in paper boards, printed paper label on spine.

Note: In Vol. 2, p. 30, the following superfluous line appears as the fourth line from the bottom: *over his head since he came to the government* All copies thus? Misplaced line?

Advertised Ath as *just ready* June 20, 27, 1840. Advertised as *just ready* PC July 1, 1840. Advertised as *new* LG July 4, 1840. Advertised Ath July 4, 1840, as *immediately.* Advertised Ath July 11, 1840, as *now ready.* Listed Ath July 11, 1840. Reviewed LG July 11, 1840. Listed LG July 11, 1840. Advertised LG July 11, 1840 as *now ready.* Listed PC July 15, 1840. Reviewed

Ath July 18, 1840. κ Sept. 1840 noted: *issued in London by Bentley.*

HML

9944. American Melodies . . . Compiled by George P. Morris . . .

New-York: Published by Linen and Fennell, No. 229 Broadway. 1841.

"The Raritan," pp. 130-131.

For comment see entry No. 997.

9945. T'Is Merry to Hear at Evening Time A Canadian Song Words Taken from Professor Ingraham's Novel, Burton or the Sieges . . . ⟨Music⟩ by C. H. Weber . . .

Philadelphia, George Willig 171 Chesnut St. ⟨1841⟩

Sheet music. Cover-title. Reprinted from *Burton . . .* , 1838, Vol. 1, pp. 158-159.

Deposited Jan. 21, 1841.

LC

9946. THE QUADROONE; OR, ST. MICHAEL'S DAY. BY THE AUTHOR OF "LAFITTE," . . .

NEW-YORK: HARPER & BROTHERS, 82 CLIFF-STREET. 1841.

2 Vols. First American edition. For an earlier printing see under 1840.

1: ⟨i⟩-⟨xii⟩, ⟨13⟩-244. 7½″ x 4½″.
2: ⟨1⟩-218; advertisements, pp. ⟨i-iv⟩, 1-2; plus: 3-18.

1: ⟨A⟩-⟨E⟩, F-I, K-U⁶, X².
2: ⟨A⟩-I, K-S⁶, T⁴; plus ⟨-⟩⁸.

Issued in a variety of cloths. The following have been noted; the designations are for identification only and the order of presentation is wholly arbitrary.

A: H cloth: brown-purple; purple.

B: S-like cloth: blue; green. Embossed with a lozenge grill.

C: S-like cloth: purple. Damasked with a maze-like pattern.

D: S-like cloth: purple. Embossed with a wavy wood-grain pattern.

E: TZ cloth: purple. Damasked with a maze-like pattern.

Flyleaves. Printed paper label on spine.

Listed NYR April, 1841. Reviewed κ April, 1841.

H NYHS NYPL UV

9947. THE DANCING FEATHER, OR THE AMATEUR FREEBOOTERS. A ROMANCE OF NEW YORK . . .

BOSTON: PUBLISHED BY GEORGE ROBERTS, AT OFFICE NOS. 3 & 5 STATE STREET. 1842. PRICE 12 1-2 CENTS SINGLE COPY; $8 PER 100; 10 COPIES FOR $1.00.

Cover-title.

⟨1⟩-32. 11⅝″ x 8″.

⟨-⟩¹⁶.

Printed pink paper wrapper.

Richter's "Detached Thoughts," p. 30 (below Ingraham's text) to p. 32.

Noted as *for sale, Daily Evening Transcript,* Boston, May 4, 1842. See next entry for a second edition and publication comments.

H UP

9948. . . . The Dancing Feather, or the Amateur Freebooters. A Romance of New York . . . ⟨Second Edition⟩

Boston. Published by George Roberts, at Office Nos. 3 & 5 State Street. 1842. Price 12 1-2 Cents Single Copy; $8 per 100; 10 Copies for $1.00. [Only One Printed Sheet.]

Cover-title. Printed self-wrapper. Pp. ⟨1⟩-31; advertisements, p. ⟨32⟩. 12⅜″ x 9″. *See preceding entry.*

At head of title: Boston Notion-Extra.

A truncated version of the first edition with certain passages omitted from chapters 9-10. Does not contain Richter's "Detached Thoughts."

Note: Certain errors present which are common to both editions. Other errors were introduced when the plates were altered for the second edition; or, perhaps, when repairs were made to the plates. The following are representative of the errors found only in the second edition:

First Edition	Second Edition
p. 14, column 1, last 2 lines:	p. 16, column 1, last 2 lines:
. . . cel- / lar?' /	. . . cel- / rla? /
p. 29, column 1, line 9 from bottom:	P. 31, column 1, line 23:
. . . sons . . .	. . . songs . . .

" . . . originally published in the *Boston Notion* ⟨1841–1842⟩ and afterwards went through four editions of 5,000 copies each, in pamphlet form . . . it is now quite out of print. The recent publication by the author of a sequel ⟨*Morris Græme,* 1843⟩ . . . has rendered it necessary to put another edition . . . immediately to press. The publisher . . . will publish on . . .

August 9 the fifth edition ...."—*Boston Notion*, Aug. 5, 1843. The fifth edition ‹*i.e., printing*› referred to was issued as *Boston Notion, Extra Series*, under date of *August, 1843*; copies in B, CU, UP. The publisher's reference to "four editions" suggests the possibility that BAL has located but three of five printings; but information is wanting. However, it may be that the third and fourth printings were dated 1843 and are so readily identifiable as reprints.

Reprinted, together with the sequel *Morris Græme*, and published 1850 by W. F. Burgess, New York. The Burgess printing reissued not before 1857 by Dick & Fitzgerald, New York, n.d.

BPL   Y

9949. EDWARD AUSTIN: OR, THE HUNTING FLASK. A TALE OF THE FOREST AND TOWN ...

BOSTON: PFBLISHED‹*sic*› BY F. GLEASON, 1 1-2 TREMONT ROW. 1842.

‹3›-66. 9⁵⁄₁₆″ x 6″.

‹1›-4⁸.

Printed paper wrapper?

Unsold copies were issued in 1845 with printed wrapper so dated and with (on the wrapper) an 1844 copyright notice; copies in CU, H, LC.

AAS   B   CU   H   LC   UC   UP   UV

9950. The Polish Maiden's Farewell ... Words by Professor Ingraham ... Music Arranged by Miss Frances P. Wood.

Philadelphia   A. Fiot, 196 Chesnut St. ....
1842 ...

Sheet music. The above at head of p. ‹1›.

EM

9951. THE GIPSY OF THE HIGHLANDS OR, THE JEW AND THE HEIR. BEING THE ADVENTURES OF DUNCAN POWELL AND PAUL TATNALL ...

BOSTON: PUBLISHED BY REDDING & CO., NO. 8 STATE STREET. 1843.

Cover-title.

‹1›-31. 11⁷⁄₁₆″ x 8⅛″.

‹-›¹⁶. *Signed:* ‹1›-4⁴.

Printed self-wrapper.

Title-page deposited March 20, 1843. Listed NAR July, 1843.

AAS   B   BA   H   LC   UP   UV

9952. JEMMY DAILY: OR, THE LITTLE NEWS VENDER. A TALE OF YOUTHFUL STRUGGLES, AND THE TRIUMPH OF TRUTH AND VIRTUE OVER VICE AND FALSEHOOD ...

BOSTON: BRAINARD & CO. 1843.

‹3›-54. 9³⁄₁₆″ x 5¹¹⁄₁₆″.

‹1›-3⁸, 4².

Printed off-white paper wrapper; also, probably issued in printed green paper wrapper.

Title-page deposited June 23, 1843. Listed NAR Jan. 1844.

AAS   B   BA   H   LC   UP

9953. Lame Davy's Son: with the Birth, Education, and Career of Foraging Peter. A Tale of Boston Aristocracy. The "Odd Fellow," or the Secret Association; a Tale Portraying the Principles, Character, and Usefulness of the Order of Odd Fellows. Dedicated to the Association of "Odd Fellows" in the United States. Two Nouvellettes ...

Boston: George Roberts, 5 State Street ... ‹1843›

Cover-title. ‹1›-32. 11⅝″ x 7¹⁵⁄₁₆″. Printed paper wrapper.

A twilight book (*see* BAL, *Vol. 1, p. xxi*); sheets of *The Boston Notion*, Vol. 1, Nos. 9-10, March, 1843, issued in printed paper wrapper as above. See *The Odd Fellow* ... , 1846.

Listed NAR July, 1843.

AAS   B   UP

9954. MORRIS GRÆME: OR, THE CRUISE OF THE SEA-SLIPPER. A SEQUEL TO THE DANCING FEATHER. A TALE OF THE LAND AND THE SEA ...

BOSTON. PUBLISHED BY E. P. WILLIAMS, NO. 22 CONGRESS-STREET; AND FOR SALE AT ALL THE LITERARY DEPOTS THROUGHOUT THE UNION. 1843.

Note: In some copies the period following FEATHER is not present.

‹1›-32. 11½″ x 8⅜″.

‹-›¹⁶.

Printed yellow paper wrapper; also, printed faun paper wrapper.

Wrapper noted in two states; sequence, if any, not determined and the order of presentation is arbitrary. Printed simultaneously from multiple setting?

A: Inner front wrapper blank. Yellow paper.

B: Inner front wrapper imprinted with *A View of Oak Hall, Rebuilt* ... Faun paper.

Advertised as though published *Boston Advertiser*, Aug. 2, 1843. Deposited Sept. 4, 1843. Listed NAR Oct. 1843.

AAS (B) B H (A) NYHS NYPL (A) UP UV (A)

Reprints Noted

Morris Græme. Or, the Cruise of the Sea-Slipper. By Professor Ingraham. [Entered ... 1843, by E. P. Williams ...

Caption-title. The above at head of p. ⟨3⟩. Noted in printed paper wrapper dated 1845. Pp. ⟨3⟩-50. Here noted since when stripped of wrapper it may be mistaken for an 1843 publication.

AAS B CU H UP Y

Morris Græme; or, the Cruise of the Sea-Slipper ...

⟨Entered ... 1843, by E. P. Williams ...⟩

Pp. ⟨49⟩-92. Not issued as a separate but as the concluding portion of *The Dancing Feather* ..., New York & Cincinnati, 1849, with separate title-page, p. ⟨49⟩, as given.

A copy of the complete work is in SRL.

Reprinted without date by Dick & Fitzgerald, N. Y., not before 1857.

9955. FANNY H_____. OR, THE HUNCHBACK AND THE ROUÉ ...

BOSTON. PUBLISHED BY EDWARD P. WILLIAMS, NO. 22 CONGRESS-STREET: G. W. REDDING & CO., 8 STATE-STREET. NEW-YORK: BURGESS & STRINGER AND MOSES Y. BEACH. PHILADELPHIA: ZEIBER ⟨sic⟩ & CO. FOR SALE AT ALL PERIODICAL DEPOTS. 1843 ...

Cover-title.

⟨1⟩-32. 11⁵⁄₁₆ x 8³⁄₁₆″.

⟨1-2⁸⟩.

Two states noted; the order presented is presumed correct:

A: P. 32 mispaged 23.

B: P. 32 so paged.

Printed yellow paper wrapper.

Deposited Sept. 4, 1843.

NYPL (B) UV (A) Y (B)

9956. MARK MANLY: OR, THE SKIPPER'S LAD. A TALE OF BOSTON IN THE OLDEN TIME ...

BOSTON. PUBLISHED BY E. P. WILLIAMS, 22 CONGRESS-STREET: AND FOR SALE AT ALL PERIODICAL DEPOTS. 1843 ...

Cover-title.

⟨1⟩-45, blank leaf. 8⁹⁄₁₆″ x 5⁹⁄₁₆″.

⟨1-3⁸⟩.

Printed yellow paper wrapper.

Deposited Sept. 4, 1843. Listed NAR Oct. 1843.

Y

9957. FRANK RIVERS: OR, THE DANGERS OF THE TOWN. A STORY OF TEMPTATION, TRIAL AND CRIME ...

BOSTON. PUBLISHED BY E. P. WILLIAMS, 22 CONGRESS-STREET: AND FOR SALE AT ALL PERIODICAL DEPOTS. 1843 ...

Cover-title.

⟨1⟩-32. 11½″ x 8⅛″.

⟨1-2⁸⟩.

Printed buff paper wrapper.

Deposited Sept. 22, 1843. Noted by K Nov. 1843 as Ingraham's "last infliction upon the public." Listed NAR Jan. 1844, pp. 32. Noted as on sale by *Boston Evening Transcript*, Sept. 23, 1843. Reprinted and reissued by DeWitt & Davenport, New York ⟨1853⟩; by R. M. DeWitt, New York, n.d., not before *ca.* 1860; not before 1880 by M. J. Ivers & Co., New York.

Note: An 1844 printing, pp. 47, has been reported; not seen.

LC

9958. THE YOUNG GENIUS; OR, TRIALS AND TRIUMPHS ...

BOSTON: PUBLISHED BY E. P. WILLIAMS, 22 CONGRESS-STREET. MOSES Y. BEACH, NEW-YORK. FOR SALE AT ALL PERIODICAL DEPOTS. 1843.

Cover-title.

⟨1⟩-36. 10¹¹⁄₁₆″ x 7″.

⟨1-2⁸, 3²⟩.

Printed pink paper wrapper.

Noted as *for sale, Boston Evening Transcript*, Nov. 24, 1843. Listed NAR Jan. 1844.

Y

9959. HOWARD: OR, THE MYSTERIOUS DISAPPEARANCE. A ROMANCE OF THE TRIPOLITAN WAR . . .

BOSTON. PUBLISHED BY EDWARD P. WILLIAMS, NO. 22 CONGRESS-STREET: AND FOR SALE AT ALL PERIODICALDEPOTS⟨sic⟩. 1843 . . .

Cover-title.

⟨1⟩-31. 11¾″ x 8⅜″.

⟨1-4⁴⟩.

Printed yellow paper wrapper.

UV

9960. BLACK RALPH: OR, THE HELMS-MAN OF HURLGATE. A TALE . . .

BOSTON. PUBLISHED BY EDWARD P. WILLIAMS, 22 CONGRESS STREET. FOR SALE AT ALL PERIODI-CAL DEPOTS. 1844.

⟨1⟩-35. 8¹⁵⁄₁₆″ full x 5¾″.

⟨1-2⁸, 3²⟩.

Printed yellow paper wrapper.

Advertised in *Boston Daily Advertiser*, Feb. 15, 1844. Listed WPLNL March, 1844.

AAS   H   UP   UV

9961. THEODORE; OR, THE 'CHILD OF THE SEA.' BEING A SEQUEL TO THE NOVEL OF "LAFITTE, THE PIRATE OF THE GULF." . . .

BOSTON: PUBLISHED BY EDWARD P. WILLIAMS, 22 CONGRESS-STREET, AND FOR SALE AT ALL BOOKSTORES. 1844.

⟨1⟩-36. 10½″ x 6¹³⁄₁₆″.

⟨1-2⁸, 3²⟩.

Printed blue-gray paper wrapper.

Title deposited Feb. 21, 1844. Advertised in *Boston Daily Advertiser*, March 6, 1844. Under the title *Theodore, the Child of the Sea; or, the Adopted Son of Lafitte* . . . , reissued ⟨1853⟩ by DeWitt & Davenport, New York; and, by Rob-ert M. DeWitt, New York, n. d., not before 1860. A version by Prentiss Ingraham, under the title *Lafitte's Lieutenant, or Theodore the Child of the Sea*, was issued *ca.* 1884 as *Beadle's Dime Library*, No. 316.

AAS

9962. RODOLPHE IN BOSTON! A TALE . . .

BOSTON: PUBLISHED BY E. P. WILLIAMS, NO. 22 CONGRESS-STREET, AND FOR SALE AT ALL PERI-ODICAL DEPOTS. 1844.

⟨1⟩-48. 8⅝″ x 5¾″.

⟨1-3⁸⟩.

Printed yellow paper wrapper.

Title-page deposited April 6, 1844. Advertised *Boston Daily Advertiser*, April 6, 1844.

AAS   B   BPL   UP   Y

9963. BIDDY WOODHULL; OR, THE PRETTY HAYMAKER. A TALE . . .

BOSTON: PUBLISHED BY E. P. WILLIAMS, NO. 22 CONGRESS-STREET, AND FOR SALE AT ALL PERI-ODICAL DEPOTS. 1844.

⟨1⟩-44, 2 blank leaves. 8⅞″ x 5⅝″.

⟨1-3⁸⟩.

Printed paper wrapper?

Listed WPLNL April, 1844. Reissued with added material (by Ingraham?) as *Biddy Woodhull: Or, the Beautiful Haymaker* . . . , New York: H. Long & Brother; copyright notice dated: . . . *One Thousand Eight Hundred and Fifty ⟨Four?⟩* . . . The date has been altered in the plate; complete transcription therefore cannot be given.

AAS   B   P

9964. THE CORSAIR OF CASCO BAY OR THE PILOT'S DAUGHTER . . .

GARDINER—MAINE. PUBLISHED BY G. M. ATWOOD. 1844.

⟨3⟩-58. 9¹⁄₁₆″ x 5¾″.

⟨1-7⁴⟩.

Printed green paper wrapper. The only ex-amined wrapper has the following imprint on front: *Boston: Hotchkiss & Co., 13, Court Street . . . 1844.* It is probable that the front of wrapper varied for each of the several presumed distributors.

Deposited May 10, 1844. Advertised in *Boston Daily Advertiser*, May 11, 1844.

AAS   BPL   CU   H   UP   Y

9965. ELLEN HART: OR, THE FORGER'S DAUGHTER . . .

BOSTON, PUBLISHED AT THE 'YANKEE' OFFICE, NO. 22 CONGRESS STREET; AND FOR SALE AT ALL PERIODICAL DEPOTS. 1844.

Cover-title.

⟨1⟩-46; ⟨1 leaf of advertisements?⟩. 8¹¹⁄₁₆″ x 5¾″.

⟨1-3⁸⟩. Leaf ⟨3⟩₈ lacking in only examined copy.

Printed yellow paper wrapper.

Title deposited April 6, 1844. Advertised *Boston Daily Advertiser,* June 8, 1844.

Note: A book titled *Ellen Hart; or, the Little Servant Girl* was listed NAR July, 1839, as a publication of the American Sunday-School Union. Not located and presumed not to be Ingraham's novel of similar name.

AAS

9966. THE MISERIES OF NEW YORK. OR THE BURGLAR AND COUNSELLOR . . .

> BOSTON, PUBLISHED AT THE 'YANKEE' OFFICE, NO. 22 CONGRESS STREET, AND FOR SALE AT ALL PERIODICAL DEPOTS. 1844. ENTERED . . . 1843 . . .

Cover-title.

⟨1⟩-48. 8¾″ x 5⅞″.

⟨1-3⁸⟩.

Printed paper wrapper; peach; and, yellow, noted.

Advertised *Boston Daily Advertiser* July 24, 1844. Deposited July 25, 1844.

LC   Y

9967. STEEL BELT . . .

> BOSTON . . . 1844 . . .

Cover-title.

⟨1⟩-48. 8⅝″ x 5¾″. Illustrated.

⟨1-3⁸⟩.

Two states of the wrapper noted. The sequence, if any, has not been determined and the designations are for identification only. Perhaps the wrappers were printed simultaneously from multiple settings. The following is sufficient for identification:

Wrapper A

Tan and pink papers noted. Front: STEEL BELT; / OR THE / THREE MASTED GOLETA. / A Tale / OF BOSTON BAY. / ⟨etc., etc.⟩/BOSTON. / PUBLISHED AT THE "YANKEE" OFFICE, No. 22 CONGRESS ST. / FOR SALE AT ALL PERIODICAL DLPOTS⟨sic⟩. / ⟨rule⟩ / 1844. / ⟨rule⟩ / Entered ⟨etc., etc.⟩

Wrapper B

Pale mauve paper noted. Front: STEEL BELT: / OR, THE / THREE MASTED GOLETA! / A Tale / OF BOSTON BAY. / ⟨etc., etc.⟩ / BOSTON, / PUBLISHED AT THE 'YANKEE' OFFICE, NO. 22 CONGRESS STREET, AND / FOR SALE AT ALL PERIODICAL DEPOTS. / ⟨rule⟩ / 1844. / ⟨rule⟩ / Entered ⟨etc., etc.⟩

Title deposited July 25, 1844.

H (A)   NYHS (A)   NYPL (A)   Y (B)

9968. ARNOLD: OR THE BRITISH SPY! A TALE OF TREASON AND TREACHERY . . .

> BOSTON: PUBLISHED AT THE 'YANKEE' OFFICE, 22 CONGRESS-STREET. AND FOR SALE AT ALL PERIODICAL DEPOTS. 1844.

⟨1⟩-39. 8⅝″ x 5¹¹⁄₁₆″.

⟨1-2⁸, 3⁴⟩.

Printed peach paper wrapper.

Also contains "The Bold Insurgent. A Tale of the Year 1768." For another printing of this tale see *The Young Artist, and the Bold Insurgent,* 1846.

Advertised *Boston Daily Advertiser,* Aug. 9, 1844.

B   BPL   NYPL   Y

9969. THE MIDSHIPMAN, OR THE CORVETTE AND BRIGANTINE. A TALE OF SEA AND LAND . . .

> BOSTON: F. GLEASON, PUBLISHER, 1 1-2 TREMONT ROW. 1844.

⟨1⟩-64. 9⁷⁄₁₆″ x 5¹⁵⁄₁₆″.

⟨1⟩-4⁸.

Printed green paper wrapper.

Title-page deposited Aug. 12, 1844. Advertised *Boston Daily Advertiser,* Aug. 17, 1844.

AAS   CU   LC   UV

9970. LA BONITA CIGARERA. ⟨Cover-title⟩ 1844.

Two forms of the wrapper have been noted. The sequence, if any, has not been determined and the order of presentation is arbitrary. That both were printed simultaneously from multiple settings is a possibility that should not be overlooked. The wrapper serves as title-page. Pink and yellow papers noted.

A

LA BONITA CIGARERA; OR THE BEAUTIFUL CIGAR VENDER. A TALE OF NEW YORK . . .

> BOSTON. PUBLISHED AT THE "YANKEE" OFFICE, NO. 22 CONGRESS ST. FOR SALE AT ALL PERIODICAL DEPOTS. 1844. ENTERED . . . 1844 . . .

B

LA BONITA CIGARERA: OR, THE BEAUTIFUL CIGAR-VENDER! A TALE OF NEW YORK . . .

> BOSTON, PUBLISHED AT THE 'YANKEE' OFFICE, 22 CONGRESS ST. FOR SALE AT ALL PERIODICAL DEPOTS. 1844.

Sheets

⟨1⟩-48. 9″ x 5⅞″.

⟨1-3⁸⟩.

The heading, p. ⟨1⟩, has been noted in two forms. The sequence has not been determined and the designations are for identification only.

Heading A

THE BEAUTIFUL CIGAR VENDER. / ⟨*wavy rule*⟩ / WRITTEN BY PROFESSOR INGRAHAM. / ⟨*wavy rule*⟩ / ⟨*vignette*⟩

Heading B

THE BEAUTIFUL CIGAR-VENDER. / ⟨*tapered rule*⟩ / BY PROFESSOR INGRAHAM. / ⟨*tapered rule*⟩ / ⟨*vignette*⟩

Other Variations

The following typographic and other textual variations have been noted. Logic suggests the following.

First	*Revised*

P. 30

Footnote not present. Footnote present.

P. 41

Paged 14. Paged 41.

P. 43, last line, column 1

Exclamation point inverted. Exclamation point not inverted.

Note: Intermediates occur exhibiting features of the first and revised printings.

Also note: All examined copies have the error BEAUTIFTL *for* BEAUTIFUL in the running head, p. 23.

Title-page deposited Oct. 1, 1844. Advertised in *Boston Daily Advertiser*, Oct. 7, 1844.

B NYPL (Wrapper B) UP UV Y (Wrapper A)

9971. THE SPANISH GALLEON, OR THE PIRATE OF THE MEDITERRANEAN. A ROMANCE OF THE CORSAIR KIDD ...

BOSTON: F. GLEASON, PUBLISHER, 1 1-2 TREMONT ROW. 1844.

⟨1⟩-64. 8⁹⁄₁₆″ x 5⁹⁄₁₆″.

⟨1⟩-4⁸.

Printed tan paper wrapper.

Title deposited Oct. 11, 1844. Advertised in *Boston Daily Advertiser*, Oct. 17, 1844. Listed WPLNL Nov. 1844.

AAS B BA NYPL UV Y

9972. ESTELLE: OR, THE CONSPIRATOR OF THE ISLE. A TALE OF THE WEST INDIAN SEAS ...

BOSTON, PUBLISHED AT THE 'YANKEE' OFFICE, NO. 22 CONGRESS STREET, AND FOR SALE AT ALL PERIODICAL DEPOTS. 1844 ...

Cover-title.

⟨1⟩-46, blank leaf. 8⁹⁄₁₆″ x 5⁹⁄₁₆″.

⟨1-3⁸⟩.

Printed yellow paper wrapper.

Advertised in *Boston Daily Advertiser*, Oct. 30, 1844.

Y

9973. THE SILVER BOTTLE

PART 1

THE SILVER BOTTLE: OR, THE ADVENTURES OF "LITTLE MARLBORO'" IN SEARCH OF HIS FATHER ...

BOSTON. PUBLISHED AT THE "YANKEE" OFFICE, NO. 22 CONGRESS ST. FOR SALE AT ALL PERIODICAL DEPOTS. 1844 ...

Cover-title. *Issued without title-page.*

⟨1⟩-45; note, p. ⟨46⟩: [*Here ends the narrative ... The second part ... will be ready ... in a few days ...*]; blank leaf. 8½″ full x 6¹⁄₁₆″.

⟨1-3⁸⟩.

Printed paper wrapper; both green and yellow noted.

No record of copyright found.

PART 2

Two printings of *Part Two* noted. The sequence has not been established and the designations are for identification only.

Printing A

THE SILVER BOTTLE. OR, THE ADVENTURES OF 'LITTLE MARLBORO' IN SEARCH OF HIS FATHER. SECOND AND LAST PART ...

⟨Boston: The "Yankee" Office, 1844⟩

Issued with title-page.

⟨1⟩-48.

⟨1-3⁸⟩.

Printed paper wrapper; noted in yellow.

Title-page: THE SILVER BOTTLE. / ⟨*etc., etc.*⟩

Copyright notice on front of wrapper in name of *H. L. Williams.*

Printing B

THE SILVER BOTTLE; OR, THE ADVEN-
TURES OF 'LITTLE MARLBORO" IN
SEARCH OF HIS FATHER. SECOND AND
LAST PART ...

⟨Boston: The "Yankee" Office, 1844⟩

Issued with title-page.

⟨1⟩-48.

⟨1-3⁸⟩.

Printed paper wrapper; noted in yellow.

Title-page: THE / SILVER BOTTLE; / ⟨etc., etc.⟩

Copyright notice on front of wrapper in name
of *G. H. Williams.*

Title-page for Part 2 deposited by G. H. Williams, Nov. 1, 1844.

AAS (Part 1; Part 2, Printing A) B (Part 1; Part
2, Printing A) Y (Part 1; Part 2, Printing B)

9974. HERMAN DE RUYTER: OR, THE
MYSTERY UNVEILED. A SEQUEL TO
THE BEAUTIFUL CIGAR VENDER. A
TALE OF THE METROPOLIS ...

BOSTON, PUBLISHED AT THE 'YANKEE' OFFICE,
22 CONGRESS ST. FOR SALE AT ALL PERIODICAL
DEPOTS. 1844.

Cover-title.

⟨1⟩-47. Frontispiece. 8⅝" scant x 5⅝".

⟨1-3⁸⟩.

Printed yellow paper wrapper.

Title deposited Dec. 10, 1844.

NYPL UP Y

9975. THE DIARY OF A HACKNEY COACH-
MAN ...

⟨Boston: Published at the Yankee Office,
1844⟩

⟨3⟩-42. 9¼" x 5¹³⁄₁₆".

⟨1-2⁸, 3⁴⟩.

Printed paper wrapper; cream; and, faun noted.

Also contains "Donald Fay," pp. 36-42.

Advertised *Boston Daily Advertiser*, Dec. 11,
1844.

NYPL UV Y

9976. SANTA CLAUS. OR, THE MERRY
KING OF CHRISTMAS. A TALE FOR
THE HOLIDAYS ...

BOSTON; PUBLISHED BY H. L. WILLIAMS, 22
CONGRESS STREET 1844.

⟨3⟩-34. Frontispiece. 8⅜" x 5¼".

⟨1-4⁴⟩(?).

Printed paper wrapper?

Two states (probably printings) of unknown sequence noted:

A(B?): Copyright notice in the name of *H. L.
Williams.*

B(A?): Copyright notice in name of *G. H. Williams.*

Title-page deposited by H. L. Williams Dec. 10,
1844. Advertised (by Redding & Co., Boston)
in *Boston Daily Advertiser*, Dec. 23, 1844.

B (A) NYHS (B) NYPL (B)

9977. CAROLINE ARCHER; OR, THE
MILINER'S ⟨sic⟩ APPRENTICE. A STORY
THAT HATH MORE TRUTH THAN
FICTION IN IT ...

BOSTON. PUBLISHED BY EDWARD P. WILLIAMS,
22 CONGRESS STREET. FOR SALE AT ALL PERIODI-
CAL DEPOTS. ⟨1844; date taken from wrapper⟩

⟨1⟩-38, blank leaf. 8¹⁵⁄₁₆" x 5⅝".

⟨1⁸, 2⁴, 3⁸⟩.

Printed green paper wrapper.

Also contains "The Pretty Feet," pp. 22-38.

AAS Y

9978. ELEANOR SHERWOOD, THE BEAU-
TIFUL TEMPTRESS! ...

⟨Boston: The Yankee Office, 1844⟩

Note: Entry on the basis of a single incomplete copy. The above at head of first page of
text. Collation tentative.

⟨1⟩-56. P. 49 mispaged 19. 8½" x 5¾".

⟨1-3⁸, 4⁴⟩.

Printed paper wrapper?

Y

Rafael

Boston ... 1844⟨i.e., 1845⟩

See entry No. 9984.

9979. THE CLIPPER-YACHT; OR, MO-
LOCH, THE MONEY-LENDER! A TALE
OF LONDON, AND THE THAMES ...

... 1845 ... BOSTON: PUBLISHED BY H. L. WIL-
LIAMS, AT THE 'YANKEE' OFFICE, 22 CONGRESS-
STREET.

⟨3⟩-54; advertisement for Oak Hall, pp. ⟨55-56⟩; blank, p. ⟨57⟩; publisher's advertisement, p. ⟨58⟩. 8⅝" x 5¾" full.

⟨1-3⁸, 4⁴⟩.

Two states of the wrapper noted. The sequence, if any, has not been determined and the designations are for identification only. Perhaps the wrappers were printed simultaneously from multiple settings. The following is sufficient for identification:

Wrapper A

Green paper. Front: THE / CLIPPER YACHT: / ⟨*etc., etc.*⟩

Wrapper B

Green paper. Front: THE CLIPPER-YACHT; / ⟨*etc., etc.*⟩

Title deposited Jan. 22, 1845.

AAS B NYPL (Wrapper A) UV (Wrapper A) Y (Wrapper B)

9980. MARIE: OR, THE FUGITIVE ...

BOSTON ... ⟨1845⟩

Two printings noted. The sequence has not been determined and the designations are for identification only.

Printing A

MARIE: OR, THE FUGITIVE! A ROMANCE OF MOUNT BENEDICT ...

BOSTON: PUBLISHED AT THE 'YANKEE' OFFICE, 22 CONGRESS ST. ⟨1845⟩

⟨1⟩-48. 9⁹⁄₁₆" x 6¼".

⟨1-4⁶⟩.

Printing B

MARIE; OR, THE FUGITIVE. A ROMANCE OF MOUNT BENEDICT ...

⟨Boston. Published at the 'Yankee' Office, 22 Congress-St. For Sale at All Periodical Depots. 1845.⟩

Imprint taken from wrapper.

Noted in the following wrappers. Sequence, if any, not determined and the designations are for identification only. Possibly simultaneously printed from multiple settings. The following is sufficient for identification:

Wrapper A

Pale buff paper.

Front of wrapper: MARIE: / OR, / THE FUGITIVE! / A ROMANCE OF / MOUNT BENEDICT. / ⟨*etc., etc.*⟩

Wrapper B

Pale green paper.

Front of wrapper: ⟨*Copyright notice*⟩ / MARIE: / OR, / THE FUGITIVE! / A Romance of Mount Benedict! / ⟨*etc., etc.*⟩

Wrapper C

Tan paper.

Front of wrapper: MARIE; / OR, / THE FUGITIVE. / A ROMANCE OF MOUNT BENEDICT. / ⟨*etc., etc.*⟩

Title deposited Jan. 22, 1845.

AAS (Printing B, Wrapper A) B (Printing A, Wrapper C) CU (Printing A, Wrapper A) EM (Printing A, Wrapper A) UP (Printing A) UV (Printing A) Y (Printing B, Wrapper B)

9981. FREEMANTLE: OR, THE PRIVATEERSMAN! A NAUTICAL ROMANCE OF THE LAST WAR ...

BOSTON: PUBLISHED BY GEORGE W. REDDING & CO., NO. 8 STATE STREET. ⟨1845⟩

⟨3⟩-46, 2 blank leaves. 8¾" x 5⅝".

⟨1-3⁸⟩.

Printed paper wrapper?

Two states (printings?) noted. The sequence has not been determined and the designations are purely arbitrary:

A: On title-page a double rule above author's name and a double rule above the imprint.

B: On title-page a double rule above imprint; no double rule above author's name.

Title-page deposited Feb. 15, 1845.

H (B) NYPL (A) UP (B) UV (A)

9982. SCARLET FEATHER, OR THE YOUNG CHIEF OF THE ABENAQUIES. A ROMANCE OF THE WILDERNESS OF MAINE ...

BOSTON: PUBLISHED BY F. GLEASON, 1 1-2 TREMONT ROW. 1845 ...

⟨3⟩-66. 9⅜" x 5¹⁵⁄₁₆". *Note:* Folios 45, 58, 64, not present in some copies.

⟨1-2⟩, 3-4⁸.

Two states of the wrapper noted. The sequence has not been determined and the order of presentation here is purely arbitrary; the designations are for identification only. White and tan papers noted.

A

Front: No quotation mark preceding the title *Edward Austin* in list of Ingraham's works.

Outer back: Gleason's / PUBLISHING HALL, / No. 1 1-2 Tremont Row ⟨dots⟩ BOSTON. / ⟨etc., etc.⟩

B

Front: The title *Edward Austin* appears in single quotation marks thus: 'Edward Austin'.

Outer back: GLEASON'S / PUBLISHING HALL, / No. 1 1-2 TREMONT ROW, / ⟨etc., etc.⟩

Title-page deposited March 3, 1845.

AAS (B) BA CU (A) NYPL (A,B) UP (A) UV (A) Y

9983. FORRESTAL: OR THE LIGHT OF THE REEF. A ROMANCE OF THE BLUE WAERS⟨sic⟩ ...

BOSTON: H. L. WILLIAMS, (YANKEE OFFICE,) 22 CONGRESS STREET. FOR SALE AT ALL BOOKSTORES. 1845.

⟨1⟩-140. 7⅝" x 4⅞".

⟨1⟩-11⁶, 12⁴.

Two states (printings?) noted. The order is presumed correct:

A

On title-page: WAERS *for* WATERS

Inset, gathering 9, incorrectly signed 9.

B

On title-page: WATERS *not* WAERS

Inset, gathering 9, correctly signed 9*.

Possibly issued in printed paper wrapper but noted only either unbound; or, in purple P-like cloth. This latter occurs in two states of unknown sequence; the designations are for identification only:

A: Front unlettered.

B: Front lettered in gold: FORRESTAL.

Title-page deposited March 4, 1845. Reprinted and reissued, New York, 1850, together with *Mary Wilbur* (entry No. 10005).

CWB (Sheets B, Binding B) UP (Sheets A, unbound) UV (Sheets, B, Binding A)

9984. RAFAEL

1845

The wrapper (which serves as title) noted in two states. Simultaneously printed from multiple settings? The sequence has not been determined and the order of presentation is arbitrary. Author's name in heading, p. ⟨1⟩.

A(B?)

RAFAEL

BOSTON; PUBLISHED BY H. L. WILLIAMS, (YANKEE OFFICE) 22 CONGRESS-STREET. FOR SALE AT ALL PERIODICAL DEPOTS. 1844. ⟨i.e., 1845⟩

B(A?)

RAFAEL

BOSTON; PUBLISHED BY H. L. WILLIAMS, AT THE 'YANKEE' OFFICE, 22 CONGRESS-STREET. 1845.

Note: The wrappers are of pale tan paper; and, cream-white paper.

Note: Other variations in the wrapper are present; the above is sufficient for ready identification.

⟨1⟩-47. 9¼" x 6³⁄₁₆". Illustrated.

⟨1-3⁸⟩.

The date *1844* (on wrapper A) is erroneous. The title-page for the work was deposited March 4, 1845. Further, wrapper A lists on the outer back at least four of Ingraham's novels which were issued in 1845.

AAS (B) H LC (B) N (A) NYPL UP (B) UV (A) Y (B)

9985. THE KNIGHTS OF SEVEN LANDS ...

BOSTON: PUBLISHED BY F. GLEASON, 1 1-2 TREMONT ROW. 1845.

See next entry.

⟨3⟩-64, blank leaf. 9⅜" scant x 5¾" full.

⟨1⟩-4⁸.

Printed white paper wrapper. *Two states of the wrapper noted.* The sequence, if any, has not been determined and the designations are for identification only. Perhaps the wrappers were printed simultaneously from multiple settings. The following is sufficient for identification:

A

On front: Ingraham credited with authorship of three titles.

On outer back: Publishing Hall, / No. 1 1-2 Tremont Row, / ⟨etc., etc.⟩

B

On front: Ingraham credited with authorship of four titles.

On outer back: Publishing Hall, / No. 1 1-2 Tremont Row ⟨dots⟩ Boston. / ⟨etc., etc.⟩

Contains *seven* sketches; "Sir Henry Percie, the English Knight," which appears herein, does not appear in the following entry.

AAS B (B) BPL (A) CU UP (A) UV (A) Y

9986. THE SEVEN KNIGHTS; OR TALES OF MANY LANDS. BEING CERTAIN ROMANCEROS OF CHIVALRY ...

BOSTON: H. L. WILLIAMS, 22 CONGRESS STREET. ⟨1845⟩

Note: Contains the same text as the preceding entry save for "Sir Henry Percie, the English Knight," which does not appear herein but does appear in the preceding entry. *Publication sequence for this and for the preceding entry has not been established.*

⟨1⟩-43. 9$\frac{5}{16}$" x 6$\frac{1}{16}$".

⟨1⁶, 2-3⁸⟩.

Printed cream-white paper wrapper. *Three states of the wrapper noted; the order of presentation is presumed correct but positive evidence is lacking:*

A

On the front of wrapper: THE ⟨roman⟩ / SEVEN KNIGHIS. ⟨note misspelling; set in an ornate face⟩ / ⟨etc., etc.⟩

B

On the front of wrapper: THE ⟨roman⟩ / SEVEN KNIGHTS. ⟨note correct spelling; set in an ornate face⟩ / ⟨etc., etc.⟩

Note: Common to both of the above: The word PUBLISHED (in the imprint) is set with an inverted *R* instead of a *B*.

C

On the front of wrapper: THE ⟨roman⟩ / SEVEN KNIGHTS. ⟨roman⟩ / ⟨etc., etc.⟩

Title deposited March 12, 1845.

AAS B CU NYPL SG (C) UP (B) UV Y (A)

9987. MONTEZUMA, THE SERF, OR THE REVOLT OF THE MEXITILI⟨:⟩ A TALE OF THE LAST DAYS OF THE AZTEC DYNASTY. BY THE AUTHOR OF 'LAFITTE,' ... VOL. I. ⟨II.⟩

BOSTON: PUBLISHED BY H. L. WILLIAMS. 1845.

Issued in five paper parts. Title-page for Vol. 1 in *Part 1;* title-page for Vol. 2 in *Part 3.*

Part 1

⟨1⟩-64. 8$\frac{7}{8}$" x 5$\frac{11}{16}$".

⟨1⁴, 2-4⁸, 5⁴⟩. *Signed:* ⟨1⟩-8⁴.

Part 2

65-108.

⟨1⁶, 2-3⁸⟩. *Signed:* 9-13⁴, 14².

Part 3

109-122; blank leaf (excised in some copies); ⟨1⟩-32. P. ⟨1⟩ is the title-page for Vol. 2.

⟨1-3⁸⟩. Leaf ⟨1⟩8 excised in some copies. *Signed:* ⟨-⟩², ⟨15⟩⁴, 16², ⟨1⟩-4⁴.

Part 4

33-80.

⟨1-3⁸⟩. *Signed:* 5-10⁴.

Part 5

81-116.

Three printings of Part 5 *have been noted;* this suggests that one or more of the preceding parts may also have been reprinted but BAL has been unable to find any evidence to support the possibility. The following appears to be a correct statement of sequence:

1

⟨1-3⁶⟩. *Signed:* 11-14⁴, 15².

2(3?)

⟨1², 2⁴, 3¹²⟩. *Signed:* 11-14⁴, 15².

3(2?)

⟨1-2⁸, 3²⟩. *Signed:* 11-14⁴, 15².

Printed green paper wrappers. The wrappers for *Parts 1-3* carry the statement: ... IN FOUR PARTS; *Parts 4-5* carry the statement: ... IN FIVE PARTS.

Note: The parts, stripped of the wrappers, were bound as a single volume, printed paper wrapper, and issued by Burgess, Stringer, & Co., 222 Broadway, New York.

Title-page deposited April 7, 1845. Noted as *passing through the press* K Dec. 1845. Reprinted from the original plates, not before 1858, and reissued by Dick & Fitzgerald, N. Y., under the title *Montezuma; or, the Serf Chief.*

B LC UP UV Y

9988. WILL TERRIL: OR, THE ADVENTURES OF A YOUNG GENTLEMAN BORN IN A CELLAR ...

BOSTON. PUBLISHED AT THE 'YANKEE OFFICE,' 22 CONGRESS STREET FOR SALE AT ALL BOOKSTORES. 1845.

⟨1⟩-48. 9$\frac{1}{4}$" x 6".

⟨1-3⁸⟩.

Printed pale green paper wrapper.

Title-page deposited April 5, 1845. Listed BJl May 17, 1845.

AAS H

9989. NORMAN; OR, THE PRIVATEERS-MAN'S BRIDE. A SEQUEL TO "FREE-MANTLE." ...

BOSTON: PUBLISHED AT THE 'YANKEE' OFFICE, 22 CONGRESS ST. FOR SALE AT ALL BOOK-STORES. 1845.

Cover-title.

⟨1⟩-48. 9⁵⁄₁₆″ x 6⅛″.

⟨1-3⁸⟩.

Printed green paper wrapper.

Title-page deposited June 3, 1845.

AAS H LC UP UV Y

9990. ... NEAL NELSON; OR, THE SEIGE ⟨sic⟩ OF BOSTON. A TALE OF THE REVOLUTION ...

BOSTON: HENRY L. WILLIAMS. 1845.

At head of title: Copyright notice, misdated 1855, in two lines.

Cover-title.

⟨1⟩-48. 9¼″ x 6″. Illustrated.

⟨1-3⁸⟩.

Printed yellow paper wrapper.

Title-page deposited July 12, 1845.

AAS H UV Y

9991. A ROMANCE OF THE SUNNY SOUTH. OR FEATHERS FROM A TRAVELLER'S WING ...

BOSTON. PUBLISHED BY H. L. WILLIAMS, 22 CONGRESS-ST. 1845.

Cover-title: The Southern Belle

⟨1⟩-35. 9¼″ x 6″. Illustrated.

⟨1-3⁶⟩. Note: Each gathering is in the following abnormal state which suggests correction of improper imposition by the binder: 1 and 6 conjugate; 2 and 3 conjugate; 4 and 5 singletons.

Note: It is possible that copies exist with scrambled text but no such copy has been reported.

Two states of p. 33 noted; the following sequence is presumed correct:

A: The folio is at the left.

B: The folio is correctly placed at the right.

Printed pale buff paper wrapper.

Title-page deposited Sept. 25, 1845.

AAS (B) Y (A)

9992. PAUL DEVERELL, OR TWO JUDGMENTS FOR ONE CRIME: A TALE OF THE PRESENT DAY. ⟨Part One⟩ ...

BOSTON: PUBLISHED BY H. L. WILLIAMS. 1845.

For Part 2 see next entry.

⟨1⟩-36. 2 plates inserted. 8⅜″ x 5⅝″.

Signed: ⟨1⟩-4⁴, 5².

Printed pale buff paper wrapper.

Title-page entered April 5, 1845. Listed WPLNL Sept. 1845.

NYPL

9993. ... PART II. PAUL DEVERELL: OR, TWO JUDGMENTS FOR ONE CRIME ...

BOSTON; PUBLISHED BY H. L. WILLIAMS, AT THE 'YANKEE' OFFICE, 22 CONGRESS-STREET. 1845.

Cover-title. At head of title: IN TWO PARTS, PRICE 12 1-2 CENTS EACH.

For Part 1 see preceding entry.

37-72. 2 plates inserted. 8⅜″ x 5⅝″. Note: Pagination tentative.

Signed: ⟨-⟩², 6-9⁴.

Printed green paper wrapper.

Reprinted, both parts in a single volume: Pp. ⟨1⟩-72; 4 full-page plates, each an integral part of its gathering, none reckoned in the printed pagination; ⟨1-2⁸, 3-4⁴, 5-6⁸⟩. A second printing collates: ⟨1-5⁸⟩. Copies of the first printing in AAS, B, UP; second printing in Y. Reissued not before 1858 by Dick & Fitzgerald, No. 18 Ann Street, New York, n.d.; copy in CU.

NYPL

9994. PAUL PERRIL, THE MERCHANT'S SON: OR THE ADVENTURES OF A NEW-ENGLAND BOY LAUNCHED UPON LIFE ... PART FIRST.

BOSTON: WILLIAMS & BROTHERS, 22, CONGRESS-STREET. ⟨n.d., 1845?⟩

For Part Second see entry No. 10018.

Issued thus? As a separate? See note below.

⟨1⟩-104. 9⅜″ x 6³⁄₁₆″.

⟨1-6⁸, 7⁴⟩.

Printed paper wrapper?

Title deposited Nov. 25, 1845.

Note: Quite probably issued as a separate as described above. However, the only copies located are bound together with Part Second in printed paper wrapper dated 1847.

Note: All copies examined have the reading END OE PART FIRST, p. 104.

AAS   B   LC   UV   Y

9995. THE ADVENTURES OF WILL WIZARD! CORPORAL OF THE SACCARAPA VOLUNTEERS ...

> BOSTON; PUBLISHED BY H. L. WILLIAMS, AT THE 'YANKEE' OFFICE, 22 CONGRESS-STREET. 1845.

‹1›-32. 9⅛" scant x 6".

‹1-2⁸›.

Printed pale buff paper wrapper.

AAS   UP

9996. ALICE MAY, AND BRUISING BILL ...

> BOSTON: GLEASON'S PUBLISHING HALL, 1 1-2 TREMONT ROW. 1845.

See next entry for another printing of "Alice May."

‹3›-50. 9³⁄₁₆" x 5⅞".

‹1›-3⁸. *Note:* Signature mark 3 not present in some copies.

Printed white paper wrapper.

H   NYPL   UP   UV   Y

9997. ALICE MAY; OR, THE LOST OF MOUNT AUBURN ...

> BOSTON: HENRY L. WILLIAMS, 22 CONGRESS-STREET, 1845.

Title and imprint postulated. Presumably issued in printed paper wrapper, with front of wrapper serving as title-page.

‹3›-29. 8¾" x 5⅝".

‹-›¹⁴.

Note: Reprint? Published previously in the preceding entry? Or, perhaps, issued prior to the preceding? Not from the same setting as the preceding.

Also note: On the back of the wrapper of Ingraham's *The Mast-Ship* ... , 1845, the following title appears in a list of Ingraham's books published by Henry L. Williams, Boston: *Alice May; or, the Lost of Mount Auburn.* The printing described above is presumed to be the publication thus listed.

UV

9998. BERTRAND, OR, THE STORY OF MARIE DE HEYWODE. BEING A SEQUEL TO MARIE, THE FUGITIVE ...

> BOSTON; PUBLISHED BY H. L. WILLIAMS, AT THE 'YANKEE' OFFICE, 22 CONGRESS-STREET. 1845.

‹1›-40. 9⅜" x 6⅛". Illustrated.

‹1-2⁸, 3⁴›.

Printed cream-white paper wrapper.

AAS   B   NYPL   Y

9999. CHARLES BLACKFORD ...

1845

The following printings of this novel have been noted. The sequence has not been determined and the designations are arbitrary.

SINGLE COLUMN PRINTING

CHARLES BLACKFORD. OR, THE ADVENTURES OF A STUDENT IN SEARCH OF A PROFESSION ...

> BOSTON. PUBLISHED AT THE 'YANKEE OFFICE,' 22 CONGRESS STREET. FOR SALE AT ALL BOOK-STORES. 1845.

‹1›-48. 9¾" x 6⅛".

Two printings in this format noted. The sequence is probable:

Single Column, Printing A

‹1-3⁸›.

Single Column, Printing B

‹1-4⁶›. In this printing the period is not present after the word STREET in the imprint.

The following features are common to both printings:

No copyright notice.

P. 13, running head: RLACKFORD *for* BLACKFORD

P. 30, running head: RLACKFORD *for* BLACKFORD

P. 33, running head: BLACKFOKD *for* BLACKFORD

P. 41, running head: CHARLAS *for* CHARLES

P. 46, line 2 from bottom of page: immedieatly *for* immediately

Issued in printed paper wrapper. *Three states of the wrapper noted.* Sequence, if any, has not been determined and the designations are for identification only. Perhaps the wrappers were simultaneously printed from multiple settings. The following is sufficient for identification:

Wrapper A

Blue-green paper. Front: CHARLES BLACKFORD: / Or, The Adventures of a Student. / *‹vignette captioned:›* CHARLES BLACKFORD RESCUING MISS GORDON. / *‹rule›* / *‹etc., etc.›*

Wrapper B

Blue-green paper. Front: CHARLES BLACKFORD: / Or, The Adventures of a Student. / *‹vignette*

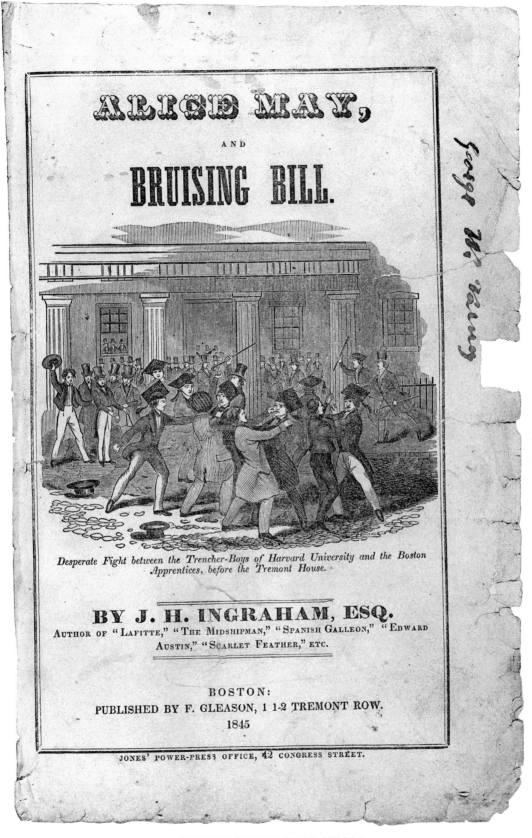

ALICE MAY,

AND

BRUISING BILL.

Desperate Fight between the Trencher-Boys of Harvard University and the Boston Apprentices, before the Tremont House.

BY J. H. INGRAHAM, ESQ.

AUTHOR OF "LAFITTE," "THE MIDSHIPMAN," "SPANISH GALLEON," "EDWARD AUSTIN," "SCARLET FEATHER," ETC.

BOSTON:
PUBLISHED BY F. GLEASON, 1 1-2 TREMONT ROW,
1845

JONES' POWER-PRESS OFFICE, 42 CONGRESS STREET.

George W. King

captioned:⟩ CHARLES BLACKFORD RESCUING MISS GORDON. / ⟨*double rule*⟩ / ⟨*etc., etc.*⟩

Wrapper C

Buff paper. Front: CHARLES BLACKFORD: / OR, THE ADVENTURES OF A STUDENT! / BY J. H. INGRAHAM, ESQ. / ⟨*etc., etc.*⟩

AAS (Printing A, Wrapper B) B (Printing A, unbound; Printing B, Wrapper C) H (Printing B, Wrapper C) LC (Printing B, unbound) UP (Printing A, unbound) UV (Printing A, unbound) Y (Printing A, Wrapper A)

TWO COLUMN PRINTING

CHARLES BLACKFORD, OR THE ADVENTURES OF A STUDENT IN SEARCH OF A PROFESSION, SHOWING HOW MUCH IT COSTS TO BECOME A GENTLEMAN. A ROMANCE OF NEW-ENGLAND. BY THE AUTHOR OF 'LAFITTE," ...

⟨Boston: G. W. Redding, 8 State Street, n.d., 1845?⟩

Caption-title. The above on p. ⟨1⟩. Imprint on p. 32.

⟨1⟩-32. 9⅝" x 6⅛".

⟨1-4⁴⟩ (?).

Printed paper wrapper?

Note: A printing was issued *ca.* 1890 by Cameron & Ferguson, Glasgow and London, n.d.; printed paper wrapper.

H   Y

10000. THE CRUISER OF THE MIST ...

NEW-YORK: BURGESS, STRINGER AND COMPANY. 1845.

⟨1⟩-52. 9⅝" x 5⅞".

⟨1⟩-3⁸, ⟨4⟩². Also signed: ⟨1⟩-2⁸, 3², 3⁸ ⟨*sic*⟩.

Printed tan laid paper wrapper. Inserted at the back of some copies is a publisher's catalog, pp. ⟨3⟩-10.

AAS   NYPL   UP   UV   Y

10001. FLEMING FIELD; OR THE YOUNG ARTISAN. A TALE OF THE DAYS OF THE STAMP ACT ...

NEW-YORK: BURGESS, STRINGER AND COMPANY. 222 BROADWAY, CORNER OF ANN-STREET. 1845.

⟨1⟩-96; plus: publisher's catalog, pp. ⟨1⟩-⟨16⟩. Illustrated. 10" scant x 5¹⁵⁄₁₆".

⟨1⟩-5, 5⟨*sic*⟩⁸; plus: ⟨7⟩⁸.

Printed pale tan paper wrapper. *Note:* Front

of wrapper hand-colored. Wrapper imprint dated 1846.

AAS   LC   UP   UV   Y

10002. GRACE WELDON, OR FREDERICA, THE BONNET-GIRL: A TALE OF BOSTON AND ITS BAY ...

BOSTON: PUBLISHED BY H. L. WILLIAMS. 1845.

Three printings noted; the following sequence is suggested:

A

⟨1⟩-108. 8¾" x 5⁹⁄₁₆".

⟨1-2¹², 3⁶, 4-5¹²⟩. *Signed:* ⟨1⟩-13⁴, 14².

B

⟨1⟩-108, 4 pp. advertisements. 10¼" x 6⁹⁄₁₆".

⟨1-7⁸⟩. *Signed:* ⟨1⟩-14⁴.

C

⟨1⟩-108. 8⁹⁄₁₆" x 5¹⁄₁₆".

⟨1-4¹², 5⁶⟩. *Signed:* ⟨1⟩-8, ⟨9⟩, 10-13⁴, 14².

Printed buff paper wrapper noted on Printing B.

Reissued not before 1849 by W. F. Burgess, 22 Ann Street, New York, n.d.. Reissued *ca.* 1865 by Dick & Fitzgerald, New York, n.d..

AAS (A)   LC (B)   UV (C)   Y (B)

10003. HARRY HAREFOOT ...

BOSTON ... 1845.

Cover-title. *Two states of wrapper noted.* The sequence, if any, has not been determined and the designations are for identification only. Printed simultaneously from multiple settings?

A

Tan-orange paper.

HARRY HAREFOOT; OR, THE THREE TEMPTATIONS. A STORY OF CITY SCENES. SHOWING THE ALLUREMENTS TO VICE, WITH THE INCENTIVES TO VIRTUE, WHICH A METROPOLIS OFFERS TO ALL YOUNG ADVENTURERS, AND HOW THE ONE MAY BE ATTAINED AND THE OTHER AVOIDED. BY PROFESSOR J. H. INGRAHAM.

BOSTON; PUBLISHED BY H. L. WILLIAMS, AT THE 'YANKEE' OFFICE FOR SALE AT ALL PERIODICAL DEPOTS. 1845.

B

Cream-white paper.

HARRY HAREFOOT; OR, THE THREE TEMPTATIONS. A STORY OF CITY SCENES. BY PROFESSOR INGRAHAM.

> BOSTON: PUBLISHED AT THE 'YANKEE' OFFICE, 22 CONGRESS ST. FOR SALE AT ALL BOOK-STORES. 1845.

<1>-61, blank leaf. 8⅞₁₆″ x 5⁹₁₆″.

<1-4⁸>.

Two states of sheets noted. The order is presumed correct:

A: P. 49 mispaged 94.

B: P. 49 correctly paged.

AAS (Sheets B) B (Sheets A, Wrapper B) NYPL (Sheets A, Wrapper A) UP (Sheets B) UV (Sheets B) Y (Sheets B)

10004. HENRY HOWARD; OR, TWO NOES MAKE ONE YES ...

> BOSTON: HENRY L. WILLIAMS. 1845.

<1>-32. 9⅛″ x 6¼″.

<1-2⁸>.

Also contains "Trout-Fishing: Or, Who Is the Captain," pp. <15>-32.

Printed paper wrapper. *Two states of the wrapper noted.* The sequence, if any, has not been determined and the designations are for identification only. Perhaps the wrappers were printed simultaneously from multiple settings. The following is sufficient for identification:

A

Blue-green paper.

Imprint: BOSTON <3-like flourish> / PUBLISHED BY H. L. WILLIAMS, (Yankee Office) 22 CONGRESS-STREET. / FOR SALE AT ALL PERIODICAL DEPOTS. / 1845.

B

Green paper.

Imprint: BOSTON; / PUBLISHED BY H. L. WILLIAMS, AT THE 'YANKEE' OFFICE, / 22 CONGRESS-STREET. / 1845.

LC (A) UP (B) Y (A)

10005. MARY WILBUR: OR, THE DEACON AND THE WIDOW'S DAUGHTER ...

> BOSTON, PUBLISHED AT THE 'YANKEE' OFFICE, 22 CONGRESS ST. FOR SALE AT ALL PERIODICAL DEPOTS. <1845>

<3>-50. 8¹¹₁₆″ x 5⁷₁₆″.

<1-3⁸>.

Printed yellow paper wrapper.

B CU DU UV

10006. THE MAST-SHIP: OR, THE BOMBARDMENT OF FALMOUTH ...

> BOSTON; HENRY L. WILLIAMS, 22 CONGRESS-STREET. 1845.

<3>-50. 9³₁₆″ x 6¼″.

<1-3⁸>.

Printed pale green paper wrapper.

B UV Y

10007. THE WING OF THE WIND. A NOUVELETTE OF THE SEA ...

> NEW-YORK: BURGESS, STRINGER AND COMPANY. 222 BROADWAY, CORNER OF ANN-STREET. 1845.

<1>-96. 9⅞″ x 5¹⁵₁₆″. Illustrated.

<1>-6⁸.

Printed paper wrapper; tan; and, off-white noted.

AAS LC UMn UP UV Y

10008. *Entry cancelled.*

10009. The May Flower, for M DCCC XLVI. Edited by Robert Hamilton.

> Boston: Published by Saxton & Kelt. 1846.

"Edward Ogilvie or the Foraging Party. A Tale of the Last War," pp. <39>-52.

For comment see entry No. 8089.

10010. ARTHUR DENWOOD: OR THE MAIDEN OF THE INN. A TALE OF THE WAR OF 1812 ...

> BOSTON: H. L. WILLIAMS, YANKEE OFFICE, 22 CONGRESS STREET. NEW YORK: BURGESS, STRINGER & CO., 222 BROADWAY; W. H. GRAHAM, TRIBUNE BUILDINGS. 1846.

Note: Pagination and signature collation postulated.

<3>-95; <leaf of advertisements?>. Illustrated. 9⅛″ x 6³₁₆″.

<1>-6⁸.

Printed paper wrapper?

Title-page deposited Feb. 19, 1846.

Y

10011. . . . THE LADY OF THE GULF. A RO-
MANCE OF THE CITY AND THE SEAS
. . .

BOSTON: PUBLISHED BY H. L. WILLIAMS, 22
CONGRESS STREET; AND 2 ANN STREET, NEW YORK.
1846.

At head of title: PRICE TWENTY-FIVE CENTS.

⟨1⟩-95. 10″ x 6⅛″.

⟨1-6⁸⟩. *Signed:* ⟨1⟩-12⁴.

Two states (printings?) noted. The sequence
presented is probable:

A: P. ⟨96⟩ blank.

B: P. ⟨96⟩ imprinted with an advertisement
for *Genevieve.*

Printed tan paper wrapper.

Title-page deposited March 28, 1846. Reprinted
and reissued, anonymously, New York: Burgess
& Garrett, 22 Ann Steret ⟨*sic*⟩, n.d., *ca.* 1850.

AAS (A)   B (B)   Y (A)

10012. LEISLER: OR THE REBEL AND THE
KING'S MAN. A TALE OF THE REBEL-
LION OF 1689 . . .

BOSTON. HENRY L. WILLIAMS, 22 CONGRESS-
STREET, AND NO. 2 ANN-STREET, NEW YORK. 1846.

⟨3⟩-90. Illustrated. 9¹³⁄₁₆″ x 6³⁄₁₆″.

⟨1-5⁸, 6⁴⟩.

Printed tan paper wrapper.

Title-page deposited April 28, 1846.

AAS   B   LC   UV

10013. RAMERO: OR, THE PRINCE AND
THE PRISONER! A ROMANCE OF THE
MORO ⟨*sic*⟩ CASTLE! . . .

BOSTON. HENRY L. WILLIAMS, 22 CONGRESS-
STREET. AND 1 3-4 ANN STREET, NEW YORK. 1846.

⟨3⟩-114; plus: advertisements, p. ⟨115⟩. 9¾″ x
6³⁄₁₆″.

⟨1-7⁸, plus: 8¹⟩.

Printed paper wrapper?

Title-page deposited May 21, 1846.

B

10014. WINWOOD: OR, THE FUGITIVE
OF THE SEAS . . .

PUBLISHED BY H. L. WILLIAMS, 1 3-4 ANN STREET,
NEW YORK, AND 22 CONGRESS STREET, BOSTON.
J. A. PENTON, LOUISVILLE, KY. 1846.

⟨3⟩-93; advertisements, pp. ⟨94-97⟩. 9¼″ x
6¹⁄₁₆″.

⟨1⟩-6⁸.

Printed pale green paper wrapper.

Title-page deposited Aug. 17, 1846.

LC   SRL   Y

10015. BONFIELD: OR, THE OUTLAW OF
THE BERMUDAS. A NAUTICAL NOVEL
. . .

PUBLISHED BY H. L. WILLIAMS, 24 ANN STREET,
NEW YORK, AND 22 CONGRESS STREET, BOSTON.
J. A. PENTON, LOUISVILLE, KY. 1846.

⟨3⟩-98. 9⁷⁄₁₆″ x 6⁵⁄₁₆″.

⟨1-5⁸, 6-7⁴⟩. *Signed:* ⟨1⟩-⟨3⟩, 4-6⁸.

Printed off-white paper wrapper.

Title-page deposited Sept. 29, 1846.

B   LC   NYPL   UV   Y

10016. The Snow Flake: A Gift for Innocence
and Beauty. Edited by T. S. Arthur. MD-
CCCXLVI.

E. Ferrett & Co. New York and Philadelphia.
1846.

Leather.

"The Pet Squirrel: Or, a Ruse of Love," pp.
⟨163⟩-186.

Reviewed NYM Oct. 31, 1845. Listed WPLNL Dec.
1845.

H

10017. THE SILVER SHIP OF MEXICO. A
TALE OF THE SPANISH MAIN . . .

PUBLISHED BY H. L. WILLIAMS, 24 ANN STREET,
NEW YORK, AND 22 CONGRESS STREET, BOSTON.
1846

⟨3⟩-98. 10⁷⁄₁₆″ x 6¹⁵⁄₁₆″.

⟨1⟩-5⁸, 6-7⁴.

Printed off-white paper wrapper.

Also contains, pp. ⟨74⟩-98, "Arnold Allen: A
Romance of the Old Tower at Concord"; by
Ingraham?

Title-page deposited Nov. 21, 1846. Listed LW
March 27, 1847. Reprinted as *The Penny Library of Famous Books,* No. 63, London, n.d.,
1897.

LC   Y

10018. PAUL PERRIL, THE MERCHANT'S SON: OR THE ADVENTURES OF A NEW-ENGLAND BOY LAUNCHED UPON LIFE ... PART SECOND.

BOSTON: WILLIAMS & BROTHERS, 22 CONGRESS STREET. ⟨n.d., 1846?⟩

For *Part First* see entry No. 9994.

Issued thus? As a separate? See note below.

⟨1⟩-96. Illustrated. 9⅜″ x 6³⁄₁₆″.

⟨1-4⁸, 5-8⁴⟩.

Printed paper wrapper?

Title deposited Nov. 23, 1846.

Note: Quite probably issued as a separate as described above. However, the only copies located are bound together with *Part First* in printed paper wrapper dated 1847.

AAS B LC UV Y

10019. BERKELEY: OR, THE LOST AND REDEEMED. A NOVEL ...

BOSTON. HENRY L. WILLIAMS, 22 CONGRESS-STREET. 1846.

Note: Pagination and signature collation postulated.

⟨1⟩-80. 8⅞″ x 5¹³⁄₁₆″.

⟨1-5⁸⟩.

Printed paper wrapper?

Y

10020. MATE BURKE; OR, THE FOUNDLINGS OF THE SEA ...

NEW YORK: BURGESS, STRINGER AND COMPANY, 222 BROADWAY. 1846.

⟨1⟩-93; blank, p. ⟨94⟩; advertisement, p. ⟨95⟩; blank, p. ⟨96⟩. 9⅞″ x 5¹⁵⁄₁₆″.

⟨1⟩-6⁸.

Printed ecru paper wrapper.

AAS B BA Y

10021. THE MYSTERIOUS STATE-ROOM; A TALE OF THE MISSISSIPPI ...

BOSTON: GLEASON'S PUBLISHING HALL, 1 1-2 TREMONT ROW. 1846.

⟨3⟩-50. 9″ x 5¾″ scant. Illustrated.

⟨1-2⟩, 3⁸.

Printed blue paper wrapper.

AAS LC Y

10022. THE ODD FELLOW, OR, THE SECRET ASSOCIATION, AND FORAGING PETER ...

BOSTON: UNITED STATES PUBLISHING COMPANY. 1846. ENTERED ... 1844 ...

⟨3⟩-18, 35-82. 9¼″ x 5⅞″. Note regarding mispagination on p. 82.

⟨1⟩-4⁸.

Printed paper wrapper; pale yellow and off-white papers noted.

For prior publication of the material herein see *Lame Davy's Son* ... ⟨1843⟩.

AAS LC NYPL UV Y

10023. PIERCE FENNING, OR, THE LUGGER'S CHASE. A ROMANCE ...

BOSTON. HENRY L. WILLIAMS, 22 CONGRESS-STREET, AND NO. 2 ANN-STREET, NEW YORK. 1846.

Note: Pagination and signature collation postulated.

⟨3⟩-95; advertisements(?), pp. ⟨96-98⟩. Illustrated. 9⅛″ x 5½″.

⟨1-2⟩, 3-⟨4⟩, 5-⟨6⟩⁸.

Printed paper wrapper?

Y

10024. THE RINGDOVE; OR, THE PRIVATEER AND THE CUTTER ...

BOSTON: H. L. WILLIAMS, 1846.

Not located.

Entry from Wright, p. 307, on the basis of information derived from "various sources, including advertisements." Mr. Wright informs BAL that since publication of his work he has found further evidence indicating that the novel was issued in 1846.

A copy of a printing issued by Robert M. De-Witt, New York, under copyright date 1869, is in Y.

10025. THE SLAVE KING
1846

Vol. 1

THE SLAVE KING; OR THE TRIUMPH OF LIBERTY ...

ENTERED ... 1846 ... H. L. WILLIAMS ... ⟨BOSTON⟩

⟨3⟩-90. 8⁹⁄₁₆″ x 5⅞″. Illustrated.

⟨1-3⟩, 4, ⟨5⟩⁸, ⟨6⟩⁴.

Printed paper wrapper?

Vol. 2

VOLUME II. THE SLAVE KING; OR THE TRIUMPH OF LIBERTY . . .

⟨BOSTON: H. L. WILLIAMS⟩ 1846.

⟨3⟩-82. Illustrated.

⟨1⟩-5⁸.

Printed paper wrapper?

Part 2 listed LW March 27, 1847.

AAS UMn Y

10026. THE SPECTRE STEAMER, AND OTHER TALES . . .

BOSTON: UNITED STATES PUBLISHING COMPANY. 1846.

⟨5⟩-100. 10³⁄₁₆″ x 6¹³⁄₁₆″.

⟨1⟩-6⁸.

Printed paper wrapper; off-white and pale tan noted. Advertisement for *The Flag of Our Union,* printed on a single leaf of pink paper, inserted at back.

AAS B H LC UMn UV

10027. THE YOUNG ARTIST, AND THE BOLD INSURGENT . . .

BOSTON: UNITED STATES PUBLISHING COMPANY. 1846.

⟨3⟩-58. 9⅛″ x 5¹⁵⁄₁₆″.

⟨1⟩-3⁸, 4⁴.

Printed blue paper wrapper.

For an earlier printing of "The Bold Insurgent" see *Arnold . . . ,* 1844.

AAS CU UP UV Y

10028. THE SURF SKIFF: OR, THE HERO-INE OF THE KENNEBEC . . .

PUBLISHED BY WILLIAMS BROTHERS, 24 ANN STREET, NEW YORK; AND 22 CONGRESS STREET, BOSTON. 1847.

⟨3⟩-98. 10″ x 6½″.

⟨1⟩-6⁸.

Printed off-white paper wrapper.

Title-page deposited Feb. 27, 1847.

Also contains "Captain Velasco . . . ," pp. ⟨86⟩-98.

H LC NYPL Y

10029. THE TRUCE: OR ON AND OFF SOUNDINGS. A TALE OF THE COAST OF MAINE . . .

PUBLISHED BY WILLIAMS BROTHERS, 24 ANN STREET, NEW YORK; AND 22 CONGRESS STREET, BOSTON. 1847.

⟨1⟩-103. 9¾″ x 6¼″.

⟨1⟩-4, ⟨5⟩-68⁸, ⟨7⟩⁴.

Printed green paper wrapper.

Title-page deposited March 15, 1847.

AAS LC Y

10030. BLANCHE TALBOT: OR, THE MAIDEN'S HAND. A ROMANCE OF THE WAR OF 1812 . . .

PUBLISHED BY WILLIAMS BROTHERS, 24 ANN STREET, NEW YORK; AND 22 CONGRESS STREET, BOSTON. 1847.

⟨3⟩-122. 9¾″ x 6⁷⁄₁₆″.

⟨1⟩-3⁸, 4⁴, ⟨5-8⟩⁸.

Printed cream-white paper wrapper.

Also contains "Henry Temple: Or, a Father's Crime," pp. ⟨73⟩-122.

Title-page deposited April 19, 1847.

LC UV Y

10031. THE BRIGANTINE: OR, GUI-TIERRO AND THE CASTILIAN. A TALE BOTH OF BOSTON AND CUBA. BY IN-GRAHAM.

PUBLISHED BY WILLIAMS BROTHERS, 24 ANN STREET, NEW YORK; AND 22 CONGRESS STREET, BOSTON. 1847

⟨1⟩-96. 9⁵⁄₁₆″ x 6¼″.

⟨1-6⁸⟩.

Printed paper wrapper?

Also contains "The Old Beau; or, the New Valet," pp. 86-96.

Title-page deposited March 15, 1847. Listed LW June 5, 1847. Advertised NYM June 5, 1847, as a May publication.

AAS B Y

10032. EDWARD MANNING: OR, THE BRIDE AND THE MAIDEN . . .

PUBLISHED BY WILLIAMS BROTHERS, 24 ANN STREET, NEW YORK, AND 6 WATER STREET, BOS-TON. J. A. PENTON, LOUISVILLE, KY. 1847.

⟨1⟩-120. 9¼″ x 6¹⁄₁₆″.

⟨1⟩-7⁸, 8⁴.

Printed pale green paper wrapper.

Advertised NYM July 3, 1847, for the week ending July 1, 1847. Listed LW July 10, 1847.

AAS LC P UV Y

10033. BEATRICE, THE GOLDSMITH'S DAUGHTER. A STORY OF THE REIGN OF THE LAST CHARLES ...

PUBLISHED BY WILLIAMS BROTHERS, 24 ANN STREET, NEW YORK, AND 6 WATER STREET, BOSTON. 1847.

Note: Two states of the title-page have been seen. The order of presentation is presumed correct:

A: ... A STORY OF THE REIGN ...

B: ... ⟨A ST⟩ORY OF THE REIGN ...

⟨1⟩-93, blank leaf. $9^{11}/_{16}''$ x $6^{5}/_{16}''$.

⟨1-6⁸⟩.

Printed paper wrapper. *Note:* Two states of the wrapper have been seen; sequence, if any, not determined. Printed simultaneously from multiple settings? The designations are for identification only.

A

White paper.

Front: PRICE 25 CENTS. / BEATRICE, / THE GOLDSMITH'S DAUGHTER. / A STORY OF THE REIGN OF THE LAST CHARLES. / ⟨vignette⟩ / ⟨etc., etc.⟩

B

Cream-white paper.

Front: BEATRICE, / THE GOLDSMITH'S DAUGHTER. / ⟨vignette⟩ / ⟨etc., etc.⟩

Also contains "Duncan Campbell," pp. 80-93.

Title-page deposited June 7, 1847. Advertised for week ending Aug. 28th, NYM Aug. 28, 1847. Listed LW Aug. 28, 1847.

AAS (State B sheets, Wrapper A) LC (State B sheets, Wrapper B) NYPL (State B sheets) Y (State A sheets)

10034. RINGOLD GRIFFITT: OR, THE RAFTSMAN OF THE SUSQUEHANNAH. A TALE OF PENNSYLVANIA ...

BOSTON: PUBLISHED BY F. GLEASON, AT THE FLAG OF OUR UNION OFFICE, CORNER OF COURT AND TREMONT STREETS. 1847.

⟨5⟩-100. $10^{3}/_{16}''$ x $6^{5}/_{8}''$.

⟨1⟩-6⁸.

Printed pinkish-white paper wrapper.

Title-page deposited Oct. 20, 1847.

AAS LC Y

10035. THE FREE-TRADER: OR, THE CRUISER OF NARRAGANSETT BAY ...

NEW-YORK: PUBLISHED BY WILLIAMS BROTHERS. 24 ANN-STREET. 1847.

⟨1⟩-96. $10^{3}/_{8}''$ x 7" scant.

⟨1-2⟩, 3-4, ⟨5-6⟩⁸.

Printed cream-white paper wrapper.

Title-page deposited Nov. 1, 1847.

UV Y

10036. THE TEXAN RANGER; OR THE MAID OF MATAMORAS ...

WILLIAMS BROTHERS, PUBLISHERS, 24 ANN STREET, NEW YORK. 1847.

⟨1⟩-96. $9^{3}/_{8}''$ scant x $5^{15}/_{16}''$.

⟨1-6⁸⟩.

Printed paper wrapper?

Also contains "Alice Brandon: Or, the Sewing Girl," pp. 89-96.

Precise publication information wanting. No record of copyright deposit found for the period Sept. 1846–May, 1848.

AAS UT

10037. The Treason of Arnold. A Tale of West Point. During the American Revolution. By the Author of "Lafitte," ...

Jonesville, (Templeton) Mass. Published by James M. Barnes. 1847.

Reprint of *Arnold; or, the British Spy*, Boston, 1844.

Printed paper wrapper: Yellow, and, green, printed in orange; and, cream-white paper printed in black.

AAS NYPL UV Y

10038. WILDASH; OR, THE CRUISER OF THE CAPES. A NAUTICAL ROMANCE ...

WILLIAMS BROTHERS, PUBLISHERS. 24 ANN STREET, NEW YORK. 1847.

⟨1⟩-96; plus: 8 pp. advertisements. $9^{3}/_{4}''$ x $6^{5}/_{8}''$.

⟨1-2⟩, 3-4, ⟨5-6⟩⁸; plus: ⟨7⟩⁴.

Printed off-white paper wrapper.

Also contains "The Fire-Screen . . . ," pp. 77-86; and, "The Embroidery-Worker . . . ," pp. 86-96.

AAS   B   LC   Y

10039. JENNETTE ALISON: OR THE YOUNG STRAWBERRY GIRL. A TALE OF THE SEA AND THE SHORE . . .

BOSTON: PUBLISHED BY F. GLEASON, AT THE FLAG OF OUR UNION OFFICE, CORNER OF COURT AND TREMONT STREETS. 1848

⟨5⟩-100. 10" x 6⅝".

⟨1⟩-6⁸.

Printed pinkish-white paper wrapper.

Title-page deposited Nov. 8, 1847.

P   UP   UV   Y

10040. Report upon a Proposed System of Public Education, for the City of Nashville, Respectfully Addressed to Its Citizens . . .

Nashville: W. F. Bang & Co., Printers. 1848.

Printed paper wrapper.

"Address," pp. ⟨5⟩-27. Letter, June 9, 1848, p. ⟨4⟩.

H

10041. The Beautiful Cigar Vender, and Its Sequel, Herman de Ruyter. Tales of City Life, Founded on Facts . . .

New York. Williams Brothers, Morning Star Office, No. 102 Nassau Street. 1849.

Printed paper wrapper?

Reprint of La Bonita Cigarera . . . , 1844; and, Herman de Ruyter, 1844.

Also contains an anonymous tale, "The Suicide," pp. ⟨94⟩-96. By Ingraham?

UMn   Y

10042. NOBODY'S SON; OR, THE LIFE AND ADVENTURES OF PERCIVAL MAYBERRY. WRITTEN BY HIMSELF . . .

PHILADELPHIA: A. HART, LATE CAREY & HART. 126 CHESTNUT STREET. 1851.

Pseudonymous. Pagination and signature collation in doubt.

⟨11⟩-225; blank leaf?. 7⁹⁄₁₆" x 4⁹⁄₁₆".

⟨1⟩¹, 2-19⁶.

Printed paper wrapper?

LC

10043. MAN: A SERMON, PREACHED IN ST. JOHN'S CHURCH, ABERDEEN, MISS., JANUARY, 1852 . . .

NEW YORK: MᶜSPEDON & BAKER, PRINTERS, 25 PINE STREET. 1852.

⟨1⟩-23. 8⁹⁄₁₆" x 5⅝".

⟨1⟩⁸, 2⁴.

Printed glazed white paper wrapper.

BPL

10044. Josephene; or, the Maid of the Gulf. By the Author of 'The Pirate Chief," . . .

New-York: Garrett & Co., Publishers, No. 18 Ann-Street. ⟨n.d., 1853?⟩

On title-page: Josephene; on wrapper: Josephine.

Printed paper wrapper. Reprint of The Lady of the Gulf, 1846.

Reprinted and reissued by Dick & Fitzgerald, New York, n.d., not before 1859.

B   UV

10045. The Life and Adventures of Percival Mayberry. An Autobiography . . .

Philadelphia: T. B. Peterson, No. 102 Chestnut Street. ⟨1854⟩

Printed paper wrapper. Pseudonymous.

Reprint of Nobody's Son . . . , 1851.

Deposited Aug. 24, 1854. Published since September 1—NLG Sept. 15, 1854. Reprinted and reissued with the publisher's later address: 306 Chestnut Street.

LC   UP   UV

10046. PAMPHLETS FOR THE PEOPLE. IN ILLUSTRATION OF THE CLAIMS OF THE CHURCH AND METHODISM. BY A PRESBYTER OF MISSISSIPPI.

PHILADELPHIA: PUBLISHED BY H. HOOKER, COR. OF CHESTNUT AND EIGHTH STS. 1854.

⟨1⟩-4, 7-119, blank leaf. 7⁹⁄₁₆" x 4½".

⟨1⟩-10⁶.

Probably issued in printed blue paper wrapper.

Note: The Third Edition, Philadelphia, 1857, was issued under the author's name and contains revisions. The unlocated Second Edition may contain the revisions.

LCP (1st)   Y (3rd)

10047. THE ARROW OF GOLD: OR, THE SHELL GATHERER. A STORY THAT UNFOLDS ITS OWN MYSTERIES AND MORAL. BY THE AUTHOR OF "SECRETS OF THE CELLS."

NEW YORK: PUBLISHED BY SAMUEL FRENCH, 121 NASSAU STREET. ⟨n.d., 1854–1857⟩

⟨5⟩-100. 9″ scant x 6⅛″.

⟨1⟩-6⁸.

Printed paper wrapper?

"The Arrow of Gold," pp. ⟨7⟩-80; material by authors other than Ingraham, pp. ⟨81⟩-100.

Reprinted and reissued by *The Flag of Our Union & Ballou's Dollar Monthly,* 1862, under the author's name. Copy in AAS.

AAS

10048. THE PRINCE OF THE HOUSE OF DAVID; OR THREE YEARS IN THE HOLY CITY. BEING A SERIES OF THE LETTERS OF ADINA, A JEWESS OF ALEXANDRIA, SOJOURNING IN JERUSALEM IN THE DAYS OF HEROD ... EDITED BY THE REV. PROFESSOR J. H. INGRAHAM ...

NEW-YORK: PUDNEY & RUSSELL, PUBLISHERS, NO. 79 JOHN-STREET. 1855.

⟨i-iv⟩, ⟨i⟩-⟨xx⟩, ⟨1⟩-456. Frontispiece, vignette title-page, and 3 plates inserted. P. 3 paged at left. 7⁷⁄₁₆″ x 5″.

⟨-⟩, 1-19¹². In all examined copies inset for Sig. 3 signed 3, not 3*.

The binding has been noted in two states; sequence, if any, not determined; the designations are for identification only.

A: A cloth: red. TZ cloth; gray-blue; green. Cream-white coated paper end papers. Flyleaves. On the spine: Two cross-like ornaments stamped in blind.

B: A cloth: red. TZ cloth: brown. Cream-white coated paper end papers. Flyleaves. On the spine: Two ovoid stylized chrysanthemums stamped in blind.

Title-page deposited Oct. 6, 1855. Listed APC Nov. 24, 1855. Listed PC Dec. 17, 1855. See under 1856, 1859 for other editions.

British Publication

Hall, Virtue
Listed Bkr March, 1859; PC March 15, 1859. Reissued by Virtue Bros. & Company, 1863.

Strahan
Listed PC June 1, 1869.

Routledge
Listed PC Sept. 1, 1869. Other listings: PC Sept. 1, 1874.

Ward, Lock, & Tyler
Listed Ath Aug. 1, 1874; PC Aug. 17, 1874. Reissued 1875 in the *Home Treasury Library.*

Weldon & Co.
Not before 1875.

Warne
Listed PC March 16, 1878; Bkr April, 1878.

Blackwood
Listed PC June 2, 1879.

Scott
Listed PC Aug. 1, 1883.

Nicholson
Listed PC Dec. 18, 1883.

Hodder & Stoughton
Listed PC Oct. 15, 1886.

CWB (Binding B)   LC (Binding B; not a deposit copy)   Y (Binding A)

10049. RIVINGSTONE; OR, THE YOUNG RANGER HUSSAR. A ROMANCE OF THE REVOLUTION ...

NEW YORK: DE WITT & DAVENPORT, 160 & 162 NASSAU ST. 1855.

⟨5⟩-100. 10⅛″ x 6⁵⁄₁₆″.

⟨1⟩-6⁸.

Printed yellow paper wrapper.

At pp. ⟨67⟩-100: "The Young Sculptor," by a Mrs. Ellis.

Listed CRN April 26, 1856. Reissued under the title *Rivingstone; or, the Young Ranger of the Revolution,* Robert M. De Witt, N. Y., n.d., not before *ca.* 1860.

UV

10050. The Prince of the House of David; or Three Years in the Holy City ... Twentieth Thousand, Revised and Corrected ...

New York: Pudney & Russell, Publishers, No. 79 John-Street. Dayton & Burdick, General Agents 1856.

For first edition see under 1855.

Text ends on p. 454.

Contains a 10-line preliminary "Advertisement" by Ingraham not present in the first edition.

Earliest revised printing located; possibly preceded by an earlier. See under 1859 for another edition.

H

10051. ... The Dancing Star: Or, the Smuggler of the Chesapeake. A Story of the Coast and Sea ...

Boston: Office of the Flag of Our Union, Ballou's Pictorial, and Ballou's Dollar Monthly. No. 22 Winter Street. ⟨1857⟩

Cover-title. At head of title: Eight Illustrations. Complete. Price, 16 Cents ...

Pp. ⟨321⟩-384. Illustrated. 12⅝″ x 9⅜″.

A twilight book (see BAL, Vol. 1, p. xxi); sheets of *The Weekly Novelette*, Vol. 1, Nos. 21-24, Aug. 8–29, 1857, issued in printed blue paper wrapper.

Advertised in *The Weekly Novelette*, Oct. 17, 1857, as *just issued*. Another printing, but with some rearrangement of the plates, issued in 1859, paged ⟨3⟩-48.

H

10052. The Prince of the House of David ... Carefully Revised and Corrected ...

New-York: Pudney & Russell, Publishers, No. 79 John-Street. 1859.

For first edition see under 1855. Also see under 1856 for another edition.

"Preface to the New Issue," dated at end *September, 1858*, pp. ⟨ix⟩-xii. The preliminary "Advertisement" extended to seventeen lines.

Also issued with the imprint: *New York: Pudney & Russell Publishers. H. Dayton General Agent, 107 Nassau Street. 1859.*

Listed PC April 1, 1859. Copy in H inscribed by early owner April 16, 1859.

AAS H NYPL UP

10053. THE PILLAR OF FIRE; OR, ISRAEL IN BONDAGE ...

NEW-YORK: PUDNEY & RUSSELL, PUBLISHERS, 79 JOHN-STREET. 1859.

Also issued with the following imprints; sequence, if any, not determined:

B

NEW-YORK: PUDNEY & RUSSELL, PUBLISHERS, 79 JOHN-STREET. SHELDON & CO., 115 NASSAU-STREET. 1859.

C

NEW-YORK: PUDNEY & RUSSELL, PUBLISHERS, 79 JOHN-STREET. H. DAYTON, 107 NASSAU-STREET. 1859.

D

NEW-YORK: PUDNEY & RUSSELL, PUBLISHERS, 79 JOHN-STREET. BLAKEMAN & MASON, 310 BROADWAY. 1859. *Noted only as a cancel.*

⟨1⟩-600. Frontispiece inserted. 7⅝″ x 4¹⁵⁄₁₆″.

⟨1⟩-22, ⟨23⟩-25¹².

BD cloth: black; blue; brown; purple-brown. T cloth: blue. TZ cloth: purple. Bevelled covers. Yellow end papers. Flyleaves.

Advertised BM March 15, 1859, for April 11, 1859. Title-page deposited March 17, 1859. Listed BM April 15, 1859. H copy inscribed by early owner April 16, 1859.

Note: Reprinted and reissued by G. G. Evans, Philadelphia. According to an advertisement in APC Nov. 19, 1859, Evans had "purchased the Stereotype Plates, Copyrights, etc., of ... *The Prince of the House of David ... The Pillar of Fire ...*" Advertised as *now ready* BM Feb. 1, 1860, and with the statement *new and revised;* examination shows no revisions.

A Note on British Publication

Virtue Brothers
Listed Ath Oct. 7, 1865; PC Oct. 17, 1865; Bkr Oct. 31, 1865.

Strahan
Listed PC July 1, 1869.

Routledge
Listed PC Oct. 16, 1869; Ath Nov. 6, 1869. A "new edition" listed PC Sept. 16, 1874. Another listed PC March 1, 1879.

Ward, Lock, & Tyler
Listed PC Oct. 1, 1874. Reissued, 1875, in *Home Treasury Library.* Another printing listed PC Dec. 31, 1878.

Warne
Listed PC March 16, 1878.

Blackwood
Listed PC June 2, 1879.

Nisbet
Listed PC July 15, 1887.

Gall & Inglis
Listed PC Sept. 16, 1893.

NYPL UV Y

10054. THE THRONE OF DAVID; FROM THE CONSECRATION OF THE SHEPHERD OF BETHLEHEM, TO THE REBELLION OF PRINCE ABSALOM ...

PHILADELPHIA: G. G. EVANS, PUBLISHER, NO. 439 CHESTNUT STREET, 1860.

Also issued with the imprint: PHILADELPHIA: G. G. EVANS, PUBLISHER, NO. 439 CHESTNUT STREET, 1860. NEW YORK: D. W. EVANS & CO., NO. 677 BROADWAY.

⟨1⟩-603. Frontispiece and 4 plates inserted. $7\frac{1}{4}$" x $4\frac{13}{16}$".

⟨1⟩-37⁸, 38⁶.

BD cloth: greenish slate; purplish slate; purplish brown. Yellow end papers. Flyleaves.

Advertised as *in press* BM Feb. 1, 1860. Noted for *early this month* BM April 16, 1860. Listed BM May 15, 1860. Listed PC June 15, 1860. Deposited July 30, 1860.

A Note on British Publication

Virtue
Issued in 1862 according to *The English Catalogue of Books*. An 1866 printing listed Ath Sept. 22, 1866; Bkr Sept. 29, 1866; PC Oct. 1, 1866.

Strahan
Listed PC July 1, 1869.

Routledge
Listed PC Nov. 15, 1869. A "new edition" listed Bkr Oct. 1874. Another printing listed PC March 1, 1879.

Ward, Lock & Tyler
Listed PC Oct. 16, 1874. Reissued 1875 in the *Home Treasury Library*. Again listed PC Dec. 31, 1878.

Warne
Listed PC March 16, 1878.

Blackwood
Listed PC June 2, 1879.

AAS NYPL UP

10055. THE SUNNY SOUTH; OR, THE SOUTHERNER AT HOME, EMBRACING FIVE YEARS' EXPERIENCE OF A NORTHERN GOVERNESS IN THE LAND OF THE SUGAR AND THE COTTON. EDITED BY PROFESSOR J. H. INGRAHAM . . .

PHILADELPHIA: G. G. EVANS, PUBLISHER, NO. 439 CHESTNUT STREET. 1860.

⟨1⟩-526; advertisements, pp. ⟨1⟩-18. $7\frac{5}{16}$" x $4\frac{15}{16}$".

⟨1⟩-33⁸, plus: ⟨34⟩⁸.

Two states (printings?) noted:

1: P. 7 of the terminal advertisements is an advertisement for *The Prince of the House of David.*

2: P. 7 of the terminal advertisements is an advertisement for *Kit Carson* and other books.

BD cloth: blue; brown; green; red. Yellow end papers. Flyleaves.

Deposited July 30, 1860. Listed PC Oct. 16, 1860.

AAS (2nd) BA (1st) LC (1st, being a deposit copy) NYHS (1st)

10056. The Beautiful Cigar Girl or, the Mysteries of Broadway . . .

New York: Robert M. De Witt, Publisher. 13 Frankfort Street. ⟨n.d., not before *ca.* 1860⟩

Reprint of *La Bonita Cigarera . . .* , 1844. Printed paper wrapper.

Reprinted and reissued by De Witt, 33 Rose Street, N. Y., n.d., not before *ca.* 1870. Reissued by M. J. Ivers & Co., 86 Nassau Street, N. Y., n.d., *ca.* 1885

NYPL

10057. . . . The Lady Imogen: Or, the Wreck and the Chase. A Tale of Block Island and the Sound . . .

Boston: Office of the Flag of Our Union, the Welcome Guest, and Ballou's Dollar Monthly. No. 22 1-2 Winter Street. ⟨1861⟩

Cover-title. At head of title: Twelve Illustrations. No. 52. Complete. Price, 16 Cents . . .

Pp. ⟨353⟩-416. Illustrated. 12" x 9".

A twilight book (see BAL, Vol. 1, p. xxi); sheets of *The Weekly Novelette*, Vol. 8, Nos. 23-26, Feb. 16, 23, March 2, 9, 1861, issued in printed buff paper wrapper.

Advertised in *The Weekly Novelette*, March 16, 1861, as "now on hand . . . in bound form."

AAS

10058. MORTIMER; OR, THE BANKRUPT'S HEIRESS. A HOME ROMANCE . . .

NEW YORK: FREDERIC A. BRADY, PUBLISHER. NO. 22 ANN STREET. ⟨1865⟩

⟨1⟩-87; advertisement, p. ⟨88⟩. $9\frac{1}{8}$" x $5\frac{13}{16}$". Illustrated.

⟨1-5⁸, 6⁴⟩.

Printed paper wrapper?

UP

10059. The Rebel Coaster; or, the Escape from the Press-Gang. A Thrilling Story of the Revolution. By the Author of "The Beautiful Cigar Girl," ...

New York: Robert M. De Witt, Publisher 13 Frankfort Street ... 1867 ...

Probably issued in printed paper wrapper.

A version of *Pierce Fenning* ... , 1846.

Reprinted not before 1870 with the publisher's later address in the imprint: *33 Rose Street;* copies in H, NYPL.

UP

10060. The Eagle Crest: or, the Duke's Heir ...

New-York: Robert M. De Witt, Publisher, No. 13 Frankfort Street ... 1868 ...

Printed paper wrapper. *De Witt's Ten Cent Romances,* No. 30.

A version of *The Silver Bottle* ... , 1844.

Title-page deposited Dec. 9, 1868. On the inner front of the wrapper No. 31 of the series is advertised for Dec. 4, 1868.

NYPL

10061. WILDBIRD: OR, THE THREE CHANCES ...

NEW YORK: ROBERT M. DE WITT, PUBLISHER, NO. 13 FRANKFORT STREET ... 1869 ...

⟨5⟩-100. Illustrated. 6¼" x 4¹/₁₆".

⟨1-3¹⁶⟩.

Printed yellow-orange paper wrapper.

De Witt's Ten Cent Romances, No. 33.

On the inner front of the wrapper *The Island of Gold* is advertised for Jan. 30, 1869. Reprinted and reissued not before 1870 with the publisher's later address: 33 Rose Street, N. Y.

By Ingraham? An unrecognized version of an earlier Ingraham novel?

Y

10062. THE RED WING; OR, BELMONT, THE BUCCANEER OF THE BAY ...

NEW-YORK: ROBERT M. DE WITT, PUBLISHER, NO. 13 FRANKFORT STREET ... 1869 ...

Not located. Title and imprint postulated. Entry on the basis of a reprint issued with the publisher's address (1870 and later) 33 Rose Street.

Almost certainly uniform with the sequel, *The Avenging Brother,* 1869.

Title-page deposited April 9, 1869.

A copy of the reprint was in the collection of the late Frank C. Willson, in Oct. 1959.

By Ingraham? An unrecognized version of an earlier Ingraham novel?

10063. THE AVENGING BROTHER; OR, THE TWO MAIDENS ...

NEW YORK: ROBERT M. DE WITT, PUBLISHER, NO. 13 FRANKFORT STREET ... 1869 ...

⟨5⟩-100. Illustrated. 6¼" x 4¹/₁₆".

⟨1-3¹⁶⟩.

Printed wrapper of orange-coated on white paper.

De Witt's Ten Cent Romances, No. 37. A sequel to *The Red Wing,* 1869, *q.v.*

No. 38 of the series advertised on the inner front of the wrapper for March 31, 1869. Title deposited May 8, 1869.

Also contains, here reprinted, *Arnold; or, the British Spy.*

By Ingraham? An unrecognized version of an earlier Ingraham novel?

G

10064. Moloch, the Money-Lender, or, the Beautiful Jewess ...

New York: Robert M. De Witt, Publisher, No. 13 Frankfort Street ... 1869 ...

Printed paper wrapper. *De Witt's Ten Cent Romances,* No. 38.

Reprint. See *The Clipper-Yacht* ... , 1845.

NYPL

10065. The Fair Joceline; or, the Jailer's Daughter ...

New York: Robert M. De Witt, Publisher, No. 13 Frankfort Street ... 1869 ...

Printed paper wrapper. *De Witt's Ten Cent Romances,* No. 40.

A truncated version of *Ramero* ... , 1846.

Inner front of the wrapper advertises No. 41 of the series for June 12, 1869.

LC

10066. ... The Rose of the Rio Grande ...

Glasgow & London: Cameron & Ferguson. ⟨n.d., after July 1, 1869⟩

Anonymous. Printed paper wrapper. At head of title: The Climax of Cheapness!! ...

A partial reprint of *The Texan Ranger* . . . , 1847. Also contains three other stories, pp. 48-64; authorship unknown. See next entry.

NYPL

10067. . . . The Fair Maiden's Rescue; or, the Mexican Bravo. A Sequel to "The Rose of the Rio Grande." . . .

Glasgow and London: Cameron & Ferguson. ⟨n.d., after July 1, 1869⟩

Anonymous. Printed paper wrapper. At head of title: The Climax of Cheapness!! . . .

A partial reprint of *The Texan Ranger* . . . ,' 1847. Also contains "The Young Mustanger," pp. 32-64; authorship unknown. See preceding entry.

NYPL

10068. THE PIRATE CHIEF; OR, THE CUT-TER OF THE OCEAN. BY THE AUTHOR OF "THE MAID OF THE GULF," . . .

NEW YORK: DICK & FITZGERALD, NO. 18 ANN STREET. ⟨n.d., *ca.* 1860-18—⟩

Not seen. Entry from Wright (Vol. 2); and, a photographic copy of the title-page of the only located copy in HEH.

99 pages.

Printed paper wrapper.

Note: Dick & Fitzgerald were at the above address from 1857 until well into the 20th century.

Query: Is the above by Ingraham? Reprinted and republished by Norman L. Munro, New York, 1877, as Vol. 2, No. 34, of *The Best Boys' Stories by the Greatest Authors . . . The New York Boys' Library.*

10069. Annie Temple; or, the Bankrupt's Heiress. A Home Romance . . .

New York: Frank Starr & Co., Publishers, 41 Platt Street. ⟨1870⟩

Printed paper wrapper. *Frank Starr's Fifteen Cent Illustrated Novels,* No. 5.

Reprint of *Mortimer* . . . ⟨1865⟩.

Reissued by Beadle & Adams, 98 William Street, New York ⟨1870; *i.e.,* 1876⟩.

LC

10070. The Texan Ranger; or, The Rose of the Rio Grande . . .

New-York: Robert M. De Witt, Publisher, No. 13 Frankfort St. . . . 1870 . . .

Printed paper wrapper. *De Witt's Ten Cent Romances,* No. 53.

A truncated version of *The Texan Ranger,* 1847.

Advertised for Feb. 11, 1870, in Ingraham's *Ringdove,* 1869. A reprint issued with the publisher's later address: 33 Rose Street, N. Y.

NYPL

10071. The Mexican Bravo or, the Fair Maiden's Rescue. A Sequel to "The Texan Ranger." . . .

New-York: Robert M. De Witt, Publisher, No. 13 Frankfort St. . . . 1870 . . .

Printed paper wrapper. *De Witt's Ten Cent Romances,* No. 54.

A truncated version of *The Texan Ranger* . . . , 1847.

Title-page deposited Jan. 25, 1870.

NYPL

10072. Jeannette Wetmore; or the Burglar and the Counsellor . . .

New-York: Robert M. De Witt, Publisher, No. 33 Rose Street . . . 1870 . . .

Printed paper wrapper. *De Witt's Ten Cent Romances,* No. 60.

Reprint of *The Miseries of New York* . . . , 1844.

NYPL

10073. The Red Arrow: Or, Winwood, the Fugitive . . .

New-York: Robert M. De Witt, Publisher, No. 33 Rose Street . . . 1870 . . .

Printed paper wrapper. *De Witt's Ten Cent Romances,* No. 75.

A truncated version of *Winwood,* 1846.

NYPL

10074. The Ocean Bloodhound; or, the Convict-Brother . . .

New-York: Robert M. De Witt, Publisher, No. 33 Rose Street . . . 1870 . . .

Printed paper wrapper. *De Witt's Ten Cent Romances,* No. 76.

A truncated version of *Winwood,* 1846.

NYPL

10075. Nick's Mate. Or, On and Off Soundings. A Tale of the Coast of Maine . . .

New York: Robert M. De Witt, Publisher, No. 33 Rose Street . . . 1871 . . .

Printed paper wrapper. *De Witt's Ten Cent Romances*, No. 87.

A version of *The Truce* . . . , 1847.

NYPL

10076. . . . Josephine: Or, the Lady of the Gulf . . .

. . . 1877 . . . Norman L. Munro, Publisher, No. 74 Beekman St. New York . . .

Caption-title. Printed self-wrapper.

At head of title: The New York Boys' Library

Vol. 2, No. 37, of the series.

A version of *The Lady of the Gulf*, 1846.

Deposited Nov. 15, 1877.

LC

10077. . . . The Yankee Privateer . . .

. . . 1877 . . . Norman L. Munro, Publisher, No. 74 Beekman St., New York . . .

Caption-title. Printed self-wrapper.

At head of title: . . . The New York Boys' Library

Vol. 2, No. 48, of the series.

Deposited (as above) Dec. 6, 1877.

By Ingraham? An unrecognized revision of an earlier Ingraham novel?

There was also a printing, almost surely a reprint, issued by Dick & Fitzgerald, New York, n.d.

LC

10078. . . . The Pirate Schooner . . .

. . . 1877 . . . Norman L. Munro, Publisher, No. 74 Beekman St., New York . . .

Caption-title. Printed self-wrapper.

At head of title: . . . The New York Boys' Library

Vol. 3, No. 57, of the series.

Deposited Dec. 18, 1877.

Reprint of *The Dancing Feather*, 1842.

LC

10079. . . . The Pirates of America . . .

. . . 1877 . . . Norman L. Munro, Publisher, No. 74 Beekman St., New York . . .

Caption-title. Printed self-wrapper.

At head of title: . . . The New York Boys' Library

Vol. 3, No. 59, of the series.

Non-fiction. A fairly detailed history of piracy during the 17th century with particular emphasis on the pirate Morgan. By Ingraham?

Deposited Dec. 26, 1877.

LC

10080. . . . Captain Kyd; or, the Pirate of Hell Gate . . .

. . . 1877 . . . Norman L. Munro, Publisher, No. 74 Beekman St., New York . . .

Caption-title. Printed self-wrapper.

At head of title: . . . The New York Boys' Library

Vol. 3, No. 62, of the series.

A truncated version of *Captain Kyd* . . . , 1839.

Deposited Dec. 26, 1877.

LC

10081. . . . Three-Fingered Jack. By the Author of "Captain Kyd." . . .

. . . 1877 . . . Norman L. Munro, Publisher, No. 74 Beekman St., New York . . .

Caption-title. Printed self-wrapper.

At head of title: . . . The New York Boys' Library

Vol. 3, No. 64, of the series.

Deposited Jan. 5, 1878.

By Ingraham? An unrecognized version of an earlier Ingraham novel?

LC

10082. . . . The Pirates of the Shoals . . .

. . . 1877 . . . Norman L. Munro, Publisher, No. 74 Beekman St., New York . . .

Caption-title. Printed self-wrapper.

At head of title: . . . The New York Boys' Library

Vol. 4, No. 73, of the series.

Deposited Jan. 16, 1878.

By Ingraham? An unrecognized version of an earlier Ingraham novel?

LC

10083. Not "A Fool's Errand." Life and Experience of a Northern Governess in the Sunny South . . .

New-York: Copyright, 1880, by G. W. Carleton & Co., Publishers. London: S. Low, Son & Co. MDCCCLXXX.

Reprint (the final lines of the original deleted) of *The Sunny South,* 1860.

Listed PW March 5, 1881.

Note: In some copies the following front matter has been excised: "Editorial Letter to . . ." George G. Evans; and, the "Preface."

B   H   NYPL

10084. . . . The Sea Slipper; or, the Amateur Freebooters . . .

⟨New York: Beadle's New York Dime Library, 1880⟩

Cover-title. At head of title: Beadle's New York Dime Library . . . 1880 . . .

Vol. 9, No. 113 of the series.

Printed self-wrapper.

An abridgement of *The Dancing Feather* . . . , 1842; and, *Morris Græme* . . . , 1843.

LC

10085. . . . The Burglar Captain; or, the Fallen Star. A Romance of Mystery and Crime in New York Forty Years Ago . . .

⟨New York: Beadle's New York Dime Library, 1881⟩

Cover-title. At head of title: Beadle's New York Dime Library . . . 1881 . . .

Vol. 10, No. 118, of the series.

Printed self-wrapper.

A version of *La Bonita Cigarera,* 1844.

LC

10086. . . . Lafitte's Lieutenant; or, Theodore, the Child of the Sea . . .

⟨New York: Beadle's New York Dime Library, 1884⟩

Not seen. Entry on the basis of Johannsen.

Cover-title. At head of title: Beadle's New York Dime Library . . . 1884 . . .

No. 316 of the series.

A version of *Theodore* . . . , 1844.

10087. . . . The Flying Fish; or, Running the Blockade of Boston Harbor . . .

⟨New York: The Camp-Fire Library, 1887⟩

Caption-title. Printed self-wrapper.

Vol. 1, No. 1, of the series.

A version of *Mark Manly,* 1843.

NYPL

10088. . . . The Patriot Cruiser; or, Mystery of the Three-Masted Schooner . . .

⟨New York: The Camp-Fire Library, 1887⟩

Caption-title. Printed self-wrapper.

Vol. 1, No. 4, of the series.

A version of *Steel Belt* . . . , 1844.

NYPL

10089. . . . Sons of Liberty; or, the Cruise for the Powder Ship . . .

⟨New York: The Camp-Fire Library, 1887⟩

Caption-title. Printed self-wrapper.

Vol. 1, No. 8, of the series.

Deposited Nov. 12, 1887.

Reprint of *Neal Nelson,* 1845.

LC

10090. . . . A Yankee Blue-Jacket; or, the Cruise of the Ringdove . . .

⟨New York: The Camp-Fire Library, 1888⟩

Caption-title. Printed self-wrapper.

Vol. 2, No. 46, of the series.

Reprint of *The Ringdove,* 1846.

NYPL

10091. . . . The Kennebec Cruiser; or, Chased by the Coast Blockaders . . .

⟨New York: The Camp-Fire Library, 1888⟩

Caption-title. Printed self-wrapper.

Vol. 3, No. 65, of the series.

A version of *Arthur Denwood,* 1846.

NYPL

10092. . . . The Hunted Sloop; or, On and Off Soundings . . .

⟨New York: The Camp-Fire Library, 1889⟩

Caption-title. Printed self-wrapper.

Vol. 3, No. 69, of the series.

Reprint of *Nick's Mate,* 1871.

NYPL

10093. ... The Hunted Slaver; or, Wrecked in Port ...

⟨New York: The Camp-Fire Library, 1889⟩

Caption-title. Printed self-wrapper.

Vol. 4, No. 84, of the series.

Reprint of *The Red Arrow,* 1870.

NYPL

10094. Kate's Experiences. A Southern Story ...

New York ... 1880 ... G. W. Dillingham, Publisher, Successor to G. W. Carleton & Co. MDCCCXCI.

Printed paper wrapper.

Reprint of *Not "A Fool's Errand."* ... , 1880.

DU   UP

UNLOCATED BOOKS

The following books remain unlocated. The source of each title is given. See note at the head of this list regarding the deposit of title-pages. The order of presentation is alphabetical.

The Beautiful Unknown; or, Massey Fink

Listed by Wright as an unlocated title. Advertised by Redding & Company, Boston, in *Boston Daily Advertiser,* Nov. 10, 1844.

The Bloody Butcher

K Aug. 1845, reported that Ingraham was "engaged" in writing a book of this title.

The East Indian; or, the Privateersman's Mate

Listed by Wright as an unlocated title. Possibly a tentative title for *Norman; or, the Privateersman's Bride,* 1845.

Edward Betham; or, What is True Respectability

Mentioned by Ingraham in the opening chapter of his *Charles Blackford,* 1845.

A Romance of Palenque

Noted by USDR Nov. 1841, as "shortly ... ready for press."

St. Paul, the Roman Citizen

"Just before his untimely death Ingraham had been negotiating in the North for the publication of a new work to be entitled *St. Paul, the Roman Citizen.*"—DAB

Secrets of the Cells

Ingraham's *Arrow of Gold,* New York, n.d., ca. 1854–1857, has the following statement on the title-page: *By the Author of Secrets of the Cells.*

The Serf

Listed by Wright as an unlocated title. Possibly a tentative title for *Montezuma, the Serf* ... , 1845.

The Two Apprentices

In the opening lines of *Charles Blackford,* 1845, Ingraham states that he wrote a tale called *The Two Apprentices,* also stating that he "recently contributed" it to *The Philadelphia Saturday Courier.*

Not to be confused with *The Two Apprentices* ... , a tract issued in Newburyport, Mass., 1813; nor, *The Two Apprentices* ... , New York, 1835, which is "a reprint of one of the publications of the London Religious Tract Society," with revisions by an American editor.

White Wing; or, el Pirata of Rigolets

Listed by Wright as an unlocated title issued prior to 1851. Sabin (note under entry No. 34776) describes a printing issued by R. M. De Witt, New York, 1868.

Xariffa; or, the Triumph of Liberty

Listed by Wright as an unlocated title issued prior to 1851. Listed in Roorbach, 1820–1852. Title-page deposited Nov. 2, 1846. Possibly a tentative title for *The Slave King* ... , 1846.

NOTE

Roorbach lists the following titles as by Ingraham:

The Flying Cloud; a Romance of New York Bay.

New York: Stringer & Townsend, 1854.

Roorbach's entry is erroneous and quite probably based on Stringer & Townsend's advertisement in NLG Oct. 2, 1854 where the title, miscredited to Ingraham, is described as *just ready.* A similar statement appears editorially in NLG Oct. 16, 1854. No evidence found of Ingraham's authorship. Wright (entry No.

2671) credits the title to Greenliffe Warren. In the terminal advertisements of Ingraham's *Grace Weldon ...*, *Printing B*, 1845, Warren is credited with authorship of *The Flying Cloud*. In 1871 R. M. De Witt, New York, issued the story with authorship credited to Ingraham, as *De Witt's Ten Cent Romances*, No. 93. Reissued under the title *The Steel Mask; or, Mystery of the Flying Cloud*, New York, 1888, as Vol. 3, No. 56, of *The Camp-Fire Library*.

Olph; or, the Pirate of the Shoals

New York: Garrett, *ca.* 1852–1855.

Entry from Roorbach. Wright (entry No. 2672) credits authorship to Greenliffe Warren. Under the title *Olph; or, the Wreckers of the Isle* ⟨sic⟩ *of Shoals,* advertised in Ingraham's *Grace Weldon ...* , *Printing B*, 1845, with authorship credited to Greenliffe Warren.

ANA

Wacousta; or, the Prophecy: A Tale of the Canadas ... by the Author of "Écarté." ...

London: T. Cadell, Strand; and, W. Blackwood, Edinburgh. 1832.

3 Vols. An edition in two volumes was issued in Philadelphia, 1833.

Sometimes misattributed to Ingraham. The author was John Richardson (1797–1863).

West Point; or a Tale of Treason, an Historical Drama, in Three Acts. Dramatised from Ingraham's *Romance of American History*, by Joseph Breck, Esq. With a Prologue by John. H. Hewitt, Esq. Epilogue by R. Horace Pratt, Esq.

Baltimore: Printed by Bull & Tuttle. 1840.

Printed paper wrapper? Presumably dramatized from the text as published in a periodical prior to publication in Ingraham's *Arnold: Or, the British Spy*, 1844.

"Note. The dramatist of *West Point* claims but little originality in this composition. His chief merit consists in adapting a well written tale to dramatic representation. This note is only added to counteract the personal malevolence of one or two contemptible individuals, whose insignificance is hardly worthy of even this attention."—P. ⟨2⟩.

Mary Grey; or, the Faithful Nurse. By the Author of "Ellen Hart."

Philadelphia: American Sunday-School Union ... ⟨1849⟩

Presumably not by Ingraham. See entry No. 9965.

... *The Prince of the House of David* ... by the Rev. Prof. J. H. Ingraham ...

New-York: Pudney & Russell, Publishers, 79 John-Street. 1856. H. Dayton, General Agent, 79 John-St., N. Y.

At head of title: ⟨hand⟩ Please preserve this till called for. ⟨hand⟩

24 pp. Printed paper wrapper. At head of front of wrapper: ... 10,000 Sold, and Only 3 Months Published. Issued as part of a sales promotion. Contains a version (by Ingraham?) of the introduction to *The Prince of the House of David*, synopses of chapters, personal and other testimonials.

A later edition (... *12,000 sold* ... at head of front of wrapper) contains a brief, non-committal, comment by H. W. Longfellow, not present in the earlier edition.

Both the above in B.

Ada, the Betrayed; or, the Child of Destiny ...

New-York: Robert M. De Witt, Publisher, No. 33 Rose Street ... 1870 ...

Not seen. Entry on the basis of Johannsen. Printed paper wrapper. *De Witt's Ten Cent Romances,* No. 61.

Not by Ingraham; see Johannsen, Vol. 2, p. 250.

... *Captain Kyd, the King of the Black Flag; or, the Witch of Death Castle.* By Colonel Prentiss Ingraham ...

⟨New York: Beadle's New York Dime Library, 1880⟩

Cover-title. At head of title: Beadle's New York Dime Library ... 1880 ... Printed self-wrapper. Vol. 9, No. 109, of the series. A version of Joseph Holt Ingraham's *Captain Kyd* ... , 1839. See next entry.

... *Black Plume, the Devil of the Sea; or, the Sorceress of Hell Gate* ... by Colonel Prentiss Ingraham ...

⟨New York: Beadle's New York Dime Library, 1881⟩

Cover-title. At head of title: Beadle's New York Dime Library ... 1881 ... Printed self-wrapper. Vol. 9, No. 116, of the series. A version of the final part of Joseph Holt Ingraham's *Captain Kyd* ... , 1839. See preceding entry.

The Flying Cloud. A Romance of New York Bay ...

New York: Robert M. De Witt, Publisher, No. 33 Rose Street . . . 1871 . . .

Printed paper wrapper. *De Witt's Ten Cent Romances,* No. 93.

Not by Ingraham. See NOTE above.

. . . The Steel Mask; or, Mystery of the Flying Cloud . . .

‹New York: The Camp-Fire Library, 1888›

Reprint of the preceding. Cover-title. Printed self-wrapper. Issued as Vol. 3, No. 56 of the series.

REPRINTS

The Prairie Guide: Or, the Rose of the Rio Grande. A Tale of the Mexican War. By Newton M. Curtis . . .

New York: Williams Brothers, Morning Star Office, No. 102, Nassau Street. ‹1847; *i.e.,* not before 1848›

Printed paper wrapper. Reprints Ingraham's *The Texan Ranger* . . . , 1847.

The Chameleon; or, the Mysterious Cruiser! By an Old Salt . . .

New York: Smith, Adams & Smith, Office of "The Island City." 1848.

Printed paper wrapper. Cover-title: *The Mysterious Cruiser; or, the Chameleon.* Front wrapper dated 1849. Reprints Ingraham's *Arnold; or, the British Spy,* 1844.

Illuminated Quadruple Sheet. The Constellation.

New York, 1859. George Roberts, Editor & Publisher . . .

Caption-title. An 8-page 'newspaper' measuring 4' 1½" x 2' 11". Contains Ingraham's "The Pretty Feet," reprinted from *Caroline Archer* ‹1844›; and, *Arnold; or the British Spy,* 1844.

Initials, Pseudonyms, and Anonyms for Volume IV

Additional Verse, to the Star-Spangled Banner. *By Oliver Wendell Holmes. See entry No. 8806.*

Affecting Ballad of the Oysterman. *See entry No. 8720.*

Army Hymn, *O Lord of Hosts! Almighty King* ...   By Oliver Wendell Holmes

Author of *A Winter in the West.* By Charles Fenno Hoffma

——*Captain Kyd.* By Joseph Holt Ingraham

——*Lafitte.* By Joseph Holt Ingraham

——*Oliver Cromwell.* By Henry William Herbert

——*Passion-Flowers.* By Julia Ward Howe

——*Percy's Masque.* By James A. Hillhouse

——*The Secrets of the Cells.* An unlocated work; presumably by Joseph Holt Ingraham.

——*The Beautiful Cigar Girl.* By Joseph Holt Ingraham

——*The Brothers.* By Henry William Herbert

——*The Maid of the Gulf.* See entry No. 10044

——*The Pirate Chief.* By Joseph Holt Ingraham

——*The Pirate of the Gulf.* By Joseph Holt Ingraham

——*The Scourge of the Ocean.* See entry No. 8126

——*The South West.* By Joseph Holt Ingraham

——*The Southwest.* By Joseph Holt Ingraham

Author's Private Copy ... Hang out our banners on the stately tower ... *By Oliver Wendell Holmes*

Autocrat of the Breakfast-Table. *By Oliver Wendell Holmes*

Ballad of the Oyster-Man, The. *See entry No. 8720*

Bonaparte, Aug. 15th, 1769.—Humboldt, Sept. 14th, 1769 ... *By Oliver Wendell Holmes*

Bread-Winners, The. *By John Hay*

Brothers, The. A Tale of the Fronde. *By Henry William Herbert*

Brothers of the Association of the Alumni ... *See entries 8827, 8853*

Brothers, Sisters and Friends: My first, pleasant duty is to give expression to the cordial delight ... *See entry No. 8977*

Carrier's Address to the Patrons of the Daily Illinois State Journal. January 1, 1861. *See entry No. 7728*

Cuisine Creole, La, a Collection of Culinary Recipes ... *By Lafcadio Hearn*

Curtain, The, rose; in thunders long and loud ...   *Opening line of Oliver Wendell Holmes's The Heart's Own Secret; see entry No. 8770*

Dorothy Q. A Family Portrait. *See entry No. 9170*

Editor of Valerie, The. *See entry No. 8126*

1861. A New Year's Poem, to the Patrons of the Missouri Democrat. Jan. 1, 1861. *See entry No. 7729*

Emerson, (Phila., 1889). *By Oliver Wendell Holmes*

Fair Maiden's Rescue, The. *By Joseph Holt Ingraham*

Family Record, A, Woodstock, Connecticut, July 4th, 1877. *By Oliver Wendell Holmes*

Fanshawe, a Tale. *By Nathaniel Hawthorne*

Forester, Frank. *Pseud. for Henry William Herbert*

Francis Parkman (He rests from toil ...) *By Oliver Wendell Holmes*

Frank Forester. *Pseud. for Henry William Herbert*

Getting a Wrong Start. *By Emerson Hough*

Golyer. *By John Hay.* See entry No. 7736.

H., O. W. *Oliver Wendell Holmes*

H., W. D. *William Dean Howells*

Harmonics. *See entry No. 9372.*

Harvard. "Christo et Ecclesiae." . . . "Veritas." . . . *By Oliver Wendell Holmes*

Heart's Own Secret, The. *By Oliver Wendell Holmes*

I thank you, Mr. President, you've kindly broke the ice . . . *By Oliver Wendell Holmes*

Illustrations of the Athenæum Gallery of Paintings . . . M DCCC XXX. *See entry No. 8716*

In cultivating the general intelligence . . . ⟨an address⟩. *See entry No. 8837*

In Memory of Fitz-Greene Halleck. Read at the Dedication of His Monument, in Guilford, Connecticut, July 8, 1869. *By Oliver Wendell Holmes*

Ladies and Gentlemen: The pleasant duty of bidding a hearty welcome to the clergy—to the wives and daughters of the clergy . . . ⟨an address⟩. *See entry No. 8946*

Lady of Ohio, A. *See entry No. 9540*

Lecture.—1863. [Private Copy.] . . . *By Oliver Wendell Holmes*

Lecture. 1865. [Private Copy.] . . . *By Oliver Wendell Holmes*

Lord, Thou hast led us as of old . . . *See entry No. 8993*

Love and Oysters. *See entry No. 8720*

Mayberry, Percival. *See entry No. 10042*

Nearing the Snow-Line. *By Oliver Wendell Holmes*

New England's Master-Key. *By Oliver Wendell Holmes*

New-Yorker, A. *Pseud. for Charles Fenno Hoffman*

Nonsense of It, The. *By Thomas Wentworth Higginson*

O.W.H. *Oliver Wendell Holmes*

Ocean, The. *By Nathaniel Hawthorne*

Old King Cole, and the Ballad of the Oyster-Man. *See entry No. 8720*

Old Noll; or, the Days of the Ironsides. *See entry No. 8156*

Oliver Cromwell: An Historical Romance. Edited by Horace Smith. *By Henry William Herbert*

One Who Knows. *See The Spider and the Fly in list of Henry William Herbert reprints*

Parley, Peter. *See entry No. 7582*

Parting Song, The. *By Oliver Wendell Holmes*

Passion-Flowers. *By Julia Ward Howe*

Percival Mayberry. *See entry No. 10042*

Percy's Masque: A Drama, in Five Acts. *By James A. Hillhouse*

Peter Parley. *See entry No. 7582*

Poems of Two Friends. *By William Dean Howells and John James Piatt*

Poet, The, at the Breakfast-Table. *By Oliver Wendell Holmes*

Presbyter of Mississippi, A. *Pseud. for Joseph Holt Ingraham*

Proudly beneath her glittering dome . . . *By Oliver Wendell Holmes. See entry No. 9015*

Review of de Lamartine's Jocelyn. *By Julia Ward Howe? See in Howe list, under* References and Ana.

Rose of the Rio Grande, The. *See entry No. 10066*

Sachem's Wood: A Short Poem. *By James A. Hillhouse*

Scintilla, A ⟨and⟩, The Task. *See entry No. 8752*

Sister Years, The. *By Nathaniel Hawthorne*

Song of '29, A. *See entry No. 8760*

. . . Songs for Christmas Festival, 1857. *By Thomas Wentworth Higginson*

Stockholder, A, Who Don't Mean to Be Done. *See entry No. 8110*

Tall Young Oyster Man, and the Young Mutineer. *See entry No. 8720*

... These hallowed precincts, long to memory dear ... *See entry No. 8925*

Thou gracious power, whose mercy lends ... *See entry No. 8867*

Time's Portraiture, 1838. *By Nathaniel Hawthorne*

Titcomb, Timothy. *Pseud. for Josiah Gilbert Holland*

Titcomb's Letters to Young People. *By Josiah Gilbert Holland*

To the Young Men of Worcester County ... *By Thomas Wentworth Higginson. See entry No. 8214.*

Triple Health to Friendship ... , A. *By Oliver Wendell Holmes*

Turner Sargent ... 1877. *By Oliver Wendell Holmes*

Twice had the mellowing sun of autumn crowned ... *See entry No. 8997*

Visit, A, to the Celestial City. *See entry No. 7655A.*

W.D.H. *William Dean Howells*

Welcome, A, to Dr. Benjamin Apthorp Gould. *By Oliver Wendell Holmes*

Worcester Free Church. Songs for the Christmas Festival, 1857. *By Thomas Wentworth Higginson*

Yankee, A. *Pseud. for Joseph Holt Ingraham*